Common Symbols and Notation (continued)

P_E	price of common stock
P_i	price of security i
P_{pfd}	price of preferred stock
P_{rep}	stock price with share repurchase
P_T	pre-merger share price of target
P_t	stock price at the end of year t, price on date t
$Pr(\cdot)$	probability of
$P\%$	fraction of the firm financed with preferred stock
PV	present value
PV_t	present value on date t
r	interest rate, discount rate or projected cost of capital
r_n	interest rate or discount rate for an n-year term, interest rate or discount rate for a cash flow that arrives in period n
r_E, r_D	equity and debt costs of capital
r_f	risk-free interest rate
r_{FOC}	foreign currency risk-free interest rate
r_L	cost of capital for an insured loss
r_{pfd}	preferred stock cost of capital
$\tilde{r}_t$	floating interest rate on date t
r_U	unlevered cost of capital
r_{wacc}	weighted average cost of capital
r_{HOC}^*	home currency cost of capital
r_{HOC}^*	home currency risk-free interest rate
r_{FOC}^*	foreign currency cost of capital
$\bar{R}$	average return
R_P	return on portfolio P
R_t	realized or total return of a security from date t-1 to t
S	spot exchange rate, value of all synergies
$SD(R)$	standard deviation of return R
$SD(R_i)$	standard deviation (volatility) of the return of security i
T	pre-merger total value of target
T_c	marginal corporate tax rate
U	market value of unlevered equity
UCC	undepreciated capital cost
V^L	value of firm with leverage
V_O^L	initial levered value
V_t	enterprise value on date t
V^u	value of the unlevered firm
$Var(R)$	variance of return R
$Var(Ri)$	variance of the return of security i
w_i	fraction of the portfolio invested in security i (its relative *weight* in the portfolio)
x	number of new shares issued by acquirer to pay for target
y	yield to maturity
YTC	yield to call on a callable bond
YTM	yield to maturity on a bond
YTM_n	yield to maturity on a bond with n periods to maturity
β_i	beta of a security i with respect to market portfolio
β_L	beta of an insured loss

FUNDAMENTALS OF CORPORATE FINANCE

CANADIAN EDITION

JONATHAN **BERK**
STANFORD UNIVERSITY

PETER **DEMARZO**
STANFORD UNIVERSITY

JARRAD **HARFORD**
UNIVERSITY OF WASHINGTON

DAVID **STANGELAND**
UNIVERSITY OF MANITOBA

CONTRIBUTOR:
JERROD FALK
UNIVERSITY OF MANITOBA

FUNDAMENTALS OF CORPORATE FINANCE

CANADIAN EDITION

PEARSON

Toronto

Vice-President, Editorial Director: Gary Bennett
Editor-in-Chief: Nicole Lukach
Acquisitions Editor: Claudine O'Donnell
Senior Marketing Manager: Leigh-Anne Graham
Supervising Developmental Editor: Maurice Esses
Developmental Editor: Toni Chahley
Project Managers: Sarah Lukaweski, Rachel Thompson
Manufacturing Coordinator: Susan Johnson
Production Editor: Vasundhara Sawhney, Cenveo Publisher Services
Proofreader: Audrey Dorsch
Compositor: Cenveo Publisher Services
Photo and Permissions Researcher: Rosie Gowsell
Art Director: Julia Hall
Cover and Interior Designer: Anthony Leung
Cover Image: Shutterstock Images

Credits and acknowledgments for material borrowed from other sources and reproduced, with permission, in this textbook appear on the appropriate page within the text (or on page C1).

10 9 8 7 6 5 4 3 2 1 [CKV]

Library and Archives Canada Cataloguing in Publication

Fundamentals of corporate finance / Jonathan Berk ... [et al.].
    Canadian ed.

Includes index.
ISBN 978-0-321-49406-1

    1. Corporations—Finance—Textbooks. I. Berk, Jonathan B., 1962- II. Title.

HG4026.F845 2011   658.15   C2011-905835-9

ISBN 978-0-321-49406-1

To my family, friends, colleagues and God for all the love, support and encouragement, and to Canada for all the freedoms we can enjoy, especially free enterprise.

—David Stangeland

To my family for their patience, love, and support.

—Jerrod Falk

Brief Contents

Detailed Contents

Chapter on the Web

This Online Chapter is on MyFinanceLab at
www.myfinancelab.com

Chapter 25W   Corporate Governance

About the Authors

Jonathan Berk, Peter DeMarzo, and Jarrad Harford

Jonathan Berk is the A.P. Giannini Professor of Finance at the Stanford Graduate School of Business and is a Research Associate at the National Bureau of Economic Research. Prior to Stanford he taught at the Haas School of Business at the University of California–Berkeley, where the introductory Corporate Finance course was among his assignments. Before earning his PhD from Yale University, he worked as an associate at Goldman Sachs, where his education in finance really began. Professor Berk is an Associate Editor of the *Journal of Finance*. His research has won a number of awards including the TIAA-CREF Paul A. Samuelson Award, the Smith Breeden Prize, Best Paper of the Year in The Review of Financial Studies, and the FAME Research Prize. His paper, "A Critique of Size-Related Anomalies," was recently selected as one of the two best papers ever published in *The Review of Financial Studies*. In recognition of his influence on the practice of finance, he has received the Bernstein-Fabozzi/Jacobs Levy Award, the Graham and Dodd Award of Excellence, and the Roger F. Murray Prize. Born in Johannesburg, South Africa, Professor Berk is married, has two daughters, and is an avid skier and biker.

Peter DeMarzo is the Mizuho Financial Group Professor of Finance at the Stanford Graduate School of Business and is a Research Associate at the National Bureau of Economic Research. He received his PhD in economics from Stanford University. Currently, Professor DeMarzo teaches the "turbo" core finance course for first-year MBA students. Prior to Stanford, he taught at the Haas School of Business and the Kellogg Graduate School of Management, and he was a National Fellow at the Hoover Institution. Professor DeMarzo received the Sloan Teaching Excellence Award at Stanford and the Earl F. Cheit Outstanding Teaching Award at University of California–Berkeley. Professor DeMarzo has served as an Associate Editor for *The Review of Financial Studies, Financial Management,* and the *B.E. Journals in Economic Analysis and Policy*, as well as the Vice President of the Western Finance Association. Professor DeMarzo has received numerous awards for his research including the Western Finance Association Corporate Finance Award and the Barclays Global Investors/Michael Brennan Best Paper Award from *The Review of Financial Studies*. Professor DeMarzo was born in Whitestone, New York, is married and has three sons. He and his family enjoy hiking, biking, and skiing.

Jarrad Harford is the Marion B. Ingersoll Professor of Finance at the University of Washington. Prior to Washington, Professor Harford taught at the Lundquist College of Business at the University of Oregon. He received his PhD in Finance with a minor in Organizations and Markets from the University of Rochester. Professor Harford has taught the core undergraduate finance course, Business Finance, for eleven years, as well as an elective in Mergers and Acquisitions, and "Finance for Non-financial Executives" in the executive education program. He has won numerous awards for his teaching, including the Interfraternity Council Excellence in Teaching Award (2007 and 2008), ISMBA Excellence in Teaching Award (2006), and the Wells Fargo Faculty Award for Undergraduate Teaching (2005). He is also the Faculty Director of the UW Business School Undergraduate Honors Program. Professor Harford serves as an Associate Editor for *The Journal of Financial Economics, Journal of Financial and Quantitative Analysis,* and *Journal of Corporate Finance.* Professor Harford was born in State College, Pennsylvania, is married, and has two sons. He and his family enjoy traveling, hiking, and skiing.

Jerrod Falk and David Stangeland

David Stangeland, PhD, BComm (Distinction), CMA, did his undergraduate and graduate university education at the University of Alberta in Edmonton. In 1991 he moved to Winnipeg where he joined the Accounting & Finance Department at the I. H. Asper School of Business at the University of Manitoba. Dr. Stangeland is a Professor of Finance, was Head of the Department of Accounting & Finance for nine years, and is now the Associate Dean of the I. H. Asper School of Business responsible for general administration, the Career Development Centre, and the following programs: Undergraduate, MBA, Co-op, and International Exchange.

Professor Stangeland teaches finance courses at the University of Manitoba and in the Canadian Executive MBA program at the Warsaw School of Economics in Poland. His teaching spans undergraduate, MBA, and PhD courses in corporate finance, investment banking, and international finance.

Professor Stangeland's research interests are in the areas of corporate governance, corporate control, and corporate finance. His work is well cited and has been published in several journals including the *Journal of Financial and Quantitative Analysis,* the *Journal of Banking & Finance,* the *Journal of Corporate Finance, Financial Management,* the *Stanford Journal of Law, Business & Finance*, and numerous others.

Dr. Stangeland served on the Board of Directors of CMA Canada and he chaired CMA Canada's Pension Committee. He is a member of the Pension Committee for the University of Manitoba Pension Plans, a member of the Investment committee for the Teachers Retirement Allowance Fund, and serves on the Independent Review Committee for a mutual fund company. Professor Stangeland is a two-time recipient of the CMA Canada Academic Merit Award for Teaching and Research, a four-time winner of the University of Manitoba Teaching Services Award, and a recipient of the Associates Award for Research.

Professor Stangeland was born and raised in Edmonton, Alberta, where he learned to appreciate the outdoors including running, cycling, hiking, and skiing, and in the winter, travelling to warmer climates.

Jerrod Falk deserves special thanks as a major contributor to the First Canadian Edition. Jerrod graduated with his Bachelor of Commerce (Honours) degree at the University of Manitoba in 1992 and went on to complete his Certified Management Accountant designation (and was the Gold Medal winner) in 1997. His career in corporate finance has spanned both business and government organizations in various roles including corporate controller. Since 2000, Jerrod has been an instructor at the University of Manitoba and is a recipient of multiple teaching awards. In addition to his teaching, Jerrod is a valued member of the Asper School of Business Executive Education team. He also consults with CMA Canada on their CMA-CPFA dual designation program and has been very active in the processes for the development of the CMA Entrance and Case Examinations. Jerrod's work on the chapter revisions was invaluable, and we are honoured to have him as part of the team in the production of the First Canadian Edition.

Study Aids with a Practical Focus

To be successful, students need to master the core concepts and learn to identify and solve problems that today's practitioners face.

▸ The **Valuation Principle** is presented as the foundation of all financial decision making: The central idea is that a firm should take projects or make investments that increase the value of the firm. The tools of finance determine the impact of a project or investment on the firm's value by comparing the costs and benefits in equivalent terms. The Valuation Principle is first introduced in Chapter 3, revisited in the part openers, and integrated throughout the text.

▸ **Guided Problem Solutions (GPS)** are Examples that accompany every important concept using a consistent problem-solving methodology that breaks the solution process into three steps: Plan, Execute, and Evaluate. This approach aids student comprehension, enhances their ability to model the solution process when tackling problems on their own, and demonstrates the importance of interpreting the mathematical solution.

▸ **Personal Finance GPS** Examples showcase the use of financial analysis in everyday life by setting problems in scenarios such as purchasing a new car or house, and saving for retirement.

▸ **Common Mistake** boxes alert students to frequently made mistakes stemming from misunderstanding core concepts and calculations, as well as those made in the field.

▸ Using Excel boxes describe Excel techniques and include screenshots to serve as a guide for students using this technology.

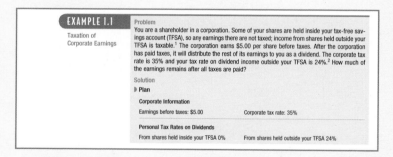

EXAMPLE 1.1
Taxation of Corporate Earnings

Problem

You are a shareholder in a corporation. Some of your shares are held inside your tax-free savings account (TFSA), so any earnings there are not taxed; income from shares held outside your TFSA is taxable.[1] The corporation earns $5.00 per share before taxes. After the corporation has paid taxes, it will distribute the rest of its earnings to you as a dividend. The corporate tax rate is 35% and your tax rate on dividend income outside your TFSA is 24%.[2] How much of the earnings remains after all taxes are paid?

Solution

▸ **Plan**

Corporate Information

Earnings before taxes: $5.00	Corporate tax rate: 35%

Personal Tax Rates on Dividends

From shares held inside your TFSA 0%	From shares held outside your TFSA 24%

Common Mistake   Mismatched Ratios

When considering valuation (and other) ratios, be sure that the items you are comparing both represent amounts related to the entire firm or that both represent amounts related solely to equity holders. For example, a firm's share price and market capitalization are values associated with the firm's equity. Thus, it makes sense to compare them to the firm's earnings per share or net income, which are amounts to equity holders after interest has been paid to debt holders. We must be careful, however, if we compare a firm's market capitalization to its revenues, operating income, or EBITDA. These amounts are related to the whole firm, and both debt and equity holders have a claim to them. Therefore, it is better to compare revenues, operating income, or EBITDA to the enterprise value of the firm, which includes both debt and equity.

INTERVIEW WITH Fatoumata Diané,
CIBC World Markets

McGill University, 2010

"We frequently use
comparable
companies' analysis
as a valuation tool."

As an investment banking analyst for CIBC World Markets in Montreal, Quebec, Fatoumata Diané works with a team of analysts offering advisory services for large clients looking to undertake a variety of transactions, including mergers and acquisitions, and debt and equity financing deals. Financial analysis is instrumental in helping her clients make decisions.

Fatoumata, who received a Bachelor of Commerce (Honours) degree in 2010 from McGill University, frequently makes use of the knowledge she gained from her finance courses. "My education has provided me with a solid base in financial statements analysis, which quickly came in handy on the job. I am responsible for doing the financial analysis that is instrumental in helping client companies in their decision making process. We frequently use comparable companies' analysis as a valuation tool."

The first step in valuing a company is assessing past performance and determining its current financial position using information contained in the publicly available financial statements. "I start by using information in the most recent financial statements to compute the enterprise value of the set of companies we are looking at. I do not limit my analysis to the summary statements. I read through notes, disclosures and management's discussion and analysis to check if significant one-time charges occurred."

Analyzing financial statements gives Fatoumata insight into a company's current financial position and its performance over time. "It is essential to develop a comprehensive understanding of the relationship between each financial statement, how they work and interact with one another, and where you can see the impact of transactions that flow through the business."

INTERVIEW WITH
Dan MacDonald

*D*an MacDonald is president and CEO of InNOVAcorp. Based in Halifax, InNOVAcorp is an early-stage venture capital firm, focusing on high-potential venture-grade companies in the areas of information technology, life sciences, and clean technology.

QUESTION: *How did you get to be where you are today in terms of your professional career?*

ANSWER: I have gotten to where I am today by being honest and having high integrity. I have been on a journey of learning as much as I can about the businesses that I have been in. I have changed careers four times: from engineering to marketing to general management and now into investments and mergers and acquisitions. I have been able to do that because I have learned as much as I possibly can about the businesses and business models I have been in.

QUESTION: *Why does a company choose to acquire other companies?*

ANSWER: Companies acquire other companies to grow. The goal may be to gain a particular market share jump—for example, to move from being a tier three player to being tier two or tier one. Another goal is to gain instant access to an installed base of customers. A third goal might be to get a particular piece of strategic technology. In the pharmaceutical industry, one of the most famous acquisitions was Pfizer's acquisition of Warner Lambert, which allowed Pfizer to acquire a blockbuster drug named Lipitor. Companies really decide whether to build or buy, be it technology, a market base, or market share. Public companies are expected to deliver growth at a rate of 10+% per year. Sometimes that is impossible to do organically. Acquisitions make that growth possible.

QUESTION: *Why do mergers and acquisitions fail?*

must make it clear to all those people involved that there are particular pieces of the acquired culture that they want to remain, to encourage, and to flourish.

QUESTION: *Are there any common flaws in the negotiations component of an acquisition?*

ANSWER: Flaws usually occur when defining expectations. If one public company acquires another, that is easier because the financial information and data are already public. When acquiring a private company, much less data is available. Often there are things that the acquiring company really never gets to know truly until a year or more after the acquisition, such as the state of quality of the product, the state of satisfaction of the customers, or the satisfaction of the employees.

QUESTION: *Can you comment on the value creation process in an acquisition?*

ANSWER: Value can be added when you find what you really need as a company. This is a little counterintuitive. If you are a company with a very well-known corporate brand, you should not be buying companies to strengthen your brand. You should be buying very specific special technologies or products that you can bring into your portfolio to leverage your brand. If you are a company trying to break into a new market segment where you do not have brand awareness, it might make sense to buy a brand that is already in that market area.

QUESTION: *What do you look out for in an acquisition?*

ANSWER: I have been personally involved in about a dozen acquisitions. Whether I am buying or selling a company, I try to make sure that everyone agrees on the key value and focus on that.

Google's IPO

On April 29, 2004, Google, Inc. announced plans to go public. Breaking with tradition, Google startled Wall Street by declaring its intention to rely heavily on the auction IPO mechanism for distributing its shares. Google had been profitable since 2001, so according to Google executives, access to capital was not the only motive for going public. The company also wanted to provide employees and private equity investors with liquidity.

One of the major attractions of the auction mechanism was the possibility of allocating shares to more individual investors. Google also hoped to set an accurate offer price by letting market bidders set the IPO price. After the internet stock market boom, there were many lawsuits related to the way underwriters allocated shares. Google hoped to avoid the allocation scandals by letting the auction allocate shares.

Investors who wanted to bid opened a brokerage account with one of the deal's underwriters and then placed their bids with the brokerage house. Google and its underwriters identified the highest bid that allowed the company to sell all of the shares being offered. They also had the flexibility to choose to offer shares at a lower price.

On August 18, 2004, Google sold 19.6 million shares at $85 per share. The $1.67 billion raised was easily the largest auction IPO ever. Google stock (ticker symbol: GOOG) opened trading on the NASDAQ market the next day at $100 per share. Although the Google IPO sometimes stumbled along the way, it represents the most significant example of the use of the auction mechanism as an alternative to the traditional IPO mechanism.

Sources: Kevin Delaney and Robin Sidel, "Google IPO Aims to Change the Rules," *Wall Street Journal*, April 30, 2004, p. C1; Ruth Simon and Elizabeth Weinstein, "Investors Eagerly Anticipate Google's IPO," *Wall Street Journal*, April 30, 2004, p. C1; Gregory Zuckerman, "Google Shares Prove Big Winners—for a Day," *Wall Street Journal*, August 20, 2004, p. C1.

Applications That Reflect Real Practice

Fundamentals of Corporate Finance features actual companies and practitioners in the field.

▶ **Chapter-Opening Interviews** with recent university graduates now working in the business world underscore the relevance of the finance concepts to students who are encountering them for the first time.

▶ **Practitioner Interviews** from notable professionals are featured in many chapters.

▶ **General Interest boxes** highlight timely material from financial publications that shed light on business problems and real-company practices.

Teaching Students to Think Finance

With consistency in presentation and an innovative set of learning aids, *Fundamentals of Corporate Finance* simultaneously meets the needs of both finance majors and non-finance business majors. This textbook truly shows every student how to "think finance."

Simplified Presentation of Mathematics

Because one of the hardest parts of learning finance is mastering the jargon, math, and non-standardized notation, Fundamentals of Corporate Finance systematically uses:

▶ **Notation Boxes.** Each chapter begins with a Notation box that defines the variables and the acronyms used in the chapter and serves as a 'legend' for students' reference.

▶ **Numbered and Labelled Equations.** The first time a full equation is given in notation form it is numbered. Key equations are titled and revisited in the summary and in end papers.

▶ **Financial Calculator** instructions, including a box in Chapter 4 on solving for future and present values, and appendices to Chapters 4, 6, and 14 with keystrokes for HP-10BII and TI BAII Plus Professional, highlight this problem-solving tool.

▶ **Spreadsheet Tables.** Select tables are available on the textbook Web site as Excel files, enabling students to change inputs and manipulate the underlying calculations.

▶ **Using Excel** boxes describe Excel techniques and include screenshots to serve as a guide for students using this technology.

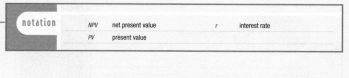

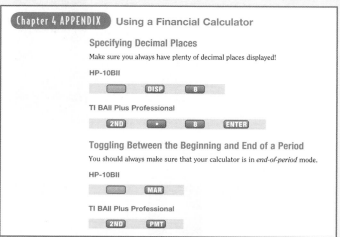

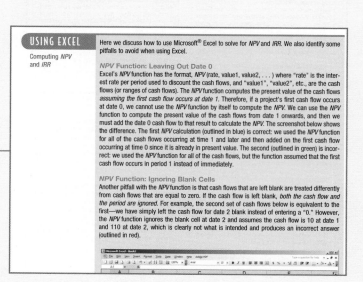

Practice Finance to Learn Finance

Working problems is the proven way to cement and demonstrate an understanding of finance.

MyFinanceLab

Here is what you should know after reading this chapter. MyFinanceLab will help you identify what you know, and where to go when you need to practice.

Key Points and Equations	Terms	Online Practice Opportunities
1.1 Why Study Finance?		
▶ Finance and financial decisions are everywhere in our daily lives.		
▶ Many financial decisions are simple, but others are complex. All are tied together by the Valuation Principle—the foundation for financial decision making—which you will learn in this book.		
1.2 The Three Types of Firms	business income trust, p. 9	MyFinanceLab
▶ There are three types of firms in Canada: sole proprietorships, partnerships, and corporations.	corporation, p. 6	Study Plan 1.2
▶ Firms with unlimited personal liability include sole proprietorships and partnerships (for general partners).	dividend payments, p. 7 energy trust, p. 9 equity, p. 7	
▶ Firms with limited liability include limited partnerships (for limited partners but not for general partners) and corporations.	equity holder, p. 7 flow-through entity, p. 9 general partnership, p. 6	
▶ A corporation is a legally defined artificial being (a judicial person or legal entity) that has many of the legal powers people have. It can enter into	income trust, p. 9 limited liability, p. 6 limited liability partnership, p. 6 limited partnership, p. 6	

▶ **Concept Check questions** at the end of each section enable students to test their understanding and target areas in which they need further review.

▶ **End-of-chapter problems written personally by Jonathan Berk, Peter DeMarzo, Jarrad Harford, David Stangeland, and Jerrod Falk** offer instructors the opportunity to assign first-rate materials to students for homework and practice with the confidence that the problems are consistent with the chapter content. Both the problems and solutions, which were also written by the authors, have been class-tested and accuracy checked to ensure quality.

End-of-Chapter Materials Reinforce Learning

Testing understanding of central concepts is crucial to learning finance.

▶ **MyFinanceLab Chapter Summary** presents the key points and conclusions from each chapter, provides a list of key terms with page numbers, and indicates online practice opportunities.

▶ **Data Cases** present in-depth scenarios in a business setting with questions designed to guide students' analysis. Many questions involve the use of Internet resources.

▶ **Integrative Cases** occur at the end of most parts and present a capstone extended problem for each part with a scenario and data for students to analyze based on that subset of chapters.

Data Case

This is your second interview with a prestigious brokerage firm for a job as an equity analyst. You survived the morning interviews with the department manager and the vice-president of equity. Everything has gone so well that they want to test your ability as an analyst. You are seated in a room with a computer and a list with the names of two companies—Caterpillar, Inc. (ticker symbol: CAT) and Microsoft (ticker symbol: MSFT). You have 90 minutes to complete the following tasks:

1. Download the annual income statements, balance sheets, and cash flow statements for the last four fiscal years from MarketWatch (www.marketwatch.com). Enter each company's ticker symbol and then go to "Financials." Export the statements to Microsoft Excel.

2. Find historical stock prices for each firm from Yahoo! Finance (http://finance.yahoo.com). Enter your ticker symbol, click on "Historical Prices" in the left column, and enter the proper date range to cover the last day of the month corresponding to the date of each financial statement. Use the closing stock prices (not the adjusted close). To calculate the firms' market capitalization at each date, we multiply the number of shares outstanding (see "Basic Weighted Shares Outstanding" on the income statement) by the firm's historic stock

Preface

When we told our friends and colleagues that we had decided to write an MBA corporate finance textbook, most of them had the same response: *Why now*? After the successful publication of our MBA textbook, the question became, *"How soon can you write an undergraduate version?"* Our sincere hope is that *Fundamentals of Corporate Finance* will shape the way students learn corporate finance for years to come.

We spent two years writing a book that stays true to the successful philosophy of the MBA book but, most importantly, is accessible to an undergraduate non-finance major. We know that countless undergraduate students have felt that corporate finance is challenging. It is tempting to make the subject more accessible by de-emphasizing the core principles and instead concentrating on the results. In our over 40 years of combined teaching experience, we have found that this approach actually makes the subject matter less accessible. The core concepts in finance are clear and intuitive. What makes the subject challenging is that it is often difficult for a novice to distinguish between these core ideas and other intuitively appealing approaches that, if used in financial decision making, will lead to incorrect decisions. Therefore, our primary motivation is to equip students with a solid grounding in the core financial concepts and tools needed to make good decisions. Such grounding will serve these students well, whether this is their only course in finance, or it is the foundation of their major.

The field of finance has undergone significant change in the last 30 years. Yet much of the empirical evidence in financial economics amassed over this time period supports the existing theory and strengthens the importance of understanding and applying corporate financial principles. Many of the problems of the recent financial crises arose because of practitioners' poor decision making when they did not understand, or chose to ignore, the core concepts that underlie finance and the pedagogy in this book. With the increasing focus on finance in the news, today's undergraduate students arrive in the classroom with a greater interest in finance than many of their predecessors. The challenge is to use that natural interest and motivation to overcome their fear of the subject and communicate these time-tested core principles. Again, we take what has worked in the classroom and apply it to the text: By providing examples involving familiar companies such as Starbucks, Air Canada, and Apple, making consistent use of real-world data, and demonstrating personal finance applications of core concepts, we strive to keep even non-finance majors engaged.

Our commitment to setting a new standard for undergraduate corporate finance textbooks extends beyond the printed page. We invite you to turn to page xxxvi to learn about MyFinanceLab, the technology breakthrough with the potential to fundamentally change the way your students learn.

Core Concepts

Fundamentals of Corporate Finance provides thorough coverage of core finance topics to provide students with a comprehensive—but manageable—introduction to the topic.

Valuation as the Unifying Framework

In our experience, students learn best when the material in a course is presented as one unified whole rather than a series of separate ideas. As such, this book presents corporate finance as an application of a subset of simple, powerful ideas. The first is that valuation drives decision making—the firm should take projects for which the value of the benefits exceeds the value of the costs. The second is that in a competitive market, market prices (rather than individual preferences) determine values. The combination of these two ideas is what we call the *Valuation Principle*, and from it we establish all of the key ideas in corporate finance, including the NPV rule, security pricing, the relation between risk and return, and the tradeoffs associated with capital structure and payout policies.

We use the Valuation Principle as a compass; it keeps financial decision makers on the right track. We introduce it in Chapter 3 along with its direct application, Net Present Value. Each part opener relates the topics in that part to the Valuation Principle running theme.

Emphasis on Application

Applying the Valuation Principle provides skills to make the types of comparisons—among loan options, investments, and projects—that will turn students into knowledgeable, confident financial consumers and managers. When students see how to apply finance to their personal lives and future careers, they grasp that finance is more than abstract, mathematically based concepts. Who better than a peer to reinforce this message? Each chapter opens with a profile of a recent university graduate putting the tools of finance to work each day in their business career (whether they work in finance or other areas of a business).

Reinforcement of the Basic Tools

Mastering the tools for discounting cash flows is central to students' success in the introductory course. As always, mastery comes with practice and by approaching complex topics in manageable units. To this end, we focus on time value of money basics in Part 2. Chapter 3 briefly introduces the time value of money for single-period investments as a critical component of the Valuation Principle. Chapter 4 then focuses on the time value of money for cash flows lasting several periods. Finally, Chapter 5 demonstrates how interest rates are quoted and determined. We present a methodical approach to the cash flows in each problem within this framework:

- Introduce timelines in Chapter 4 and stress the importance of creating timelines for every problem that involves cash flows.
- Include a timeline as the critical first step in each example involving cash flows.
- Incorporate financial calculator keystrokes and Excel techniques into the presentation.

Focus on Capital Budgeting

The capital budgeting decision is one of the most important decisions in corporate finance. We emphasize it early in the textbook, by introducing the NPV rule in Chapter 3 to weigh the costs and benefits of a decision. Building on this coverage of the NPV rule, Chapter 7 evaluates this and other investment decision rules. In Chapter 8 on capital budgeting, we examine the valuation of projects within a firm and provide a clear and systematic presentation of the difference between earnings and free cash flow. This early introduction to capital budgeting allows us to present the idea of the cost of capital conceptually, which then motivates the risk and return coverage. In Chapter 12, we calculate and use the firm's overall cost of capital with the WACC method.

New Ideas

Fundamentals of Corporate Finance carefully balances the latest advancements in research and practice with thorough coverage of core finance topics. Innovations that distinguish this textbook include the following:

- ▶ Chapter 9 on stock valuation values a firm's equity by considering its future dividends, free cash flows, or how its value compares to that of similar, publicly traded companies.
- ▶ Chapter 16 on payout policy examines the role of asymmetric information between managers and investors and how payout decisions may signal this information.
- ▶ Chapter 17 distinguishes between sustainable and value-increasing growth with a focus on determining whether "growth" will increase or decrease the value of the firm.

The Tools Your Students Need to Succeed

Pages xxvi–xxix detail the features we crafted to enhance students' ability to master the core concepts. Two areas stand out.

Problem-Solving Methodology

Guided Problem Solutions (GPS) of worked examples appear along side every important concept. Finance is about much more than the numerical solution: To be successful, students must understand the underlying intuition and interpret the mathematical solution. To foster this mindset, after the problem statement a three-step solution process—Plan, Execute, Evaluate—aids students' comprehension and models the process they should follow when tackling problems and cases on their own. We also identify the seminal errors our students have made over the years in Common Mistake boxes within each chapter.

Applied Approach

References to well-known companies, such as Apple, Air Canada, and Starbucks, add color and interest to each chapter. We even include two case-based chapters (13 and 14) that profile RealNetworks and Hertz. Chapter conclusions offer bottom-line advice on the key take-away points for financial managers. Interviews with notable professionals such as John Connors, former Microsoft CFO, support this practical perspective. We take the interviews beyond the boardroom and into the trenches with profiles of recent college graduates using the concepts in their professional lives in every chapter opener.

An applied approach also involves presenting the tools on which practitioners rely. Excel boxes and chapter-ending appendices teach students Excel techniques, while designated Spreadsheet Tables available online enable students to enter their own inputs and formulas.

New to the First Canadian Edition

A Canadian text should reflect Canadian realities and show how they fit in the bigger world picture. For instance, the institutional environment in Canada is different. While Canadian banks came out of the financial crisis with great admiration for their performance relative to banks around the world, Canada's success at corporate law enforcement (laws relating to competition, insider trading, options backdating, and other aspects of corporate governance) is sometimes criticized relative to other developed countries. The Canadian tax system also differs from the US and other countries. It would be a pity if students were only exposed to the US tax system and missed the realities of capital cost allowance, capital gains taxes, tax free savings accounts, and registered retirement savings plan accounts – all of which are very important for Canadian investors. We feel it is important for students to understand the Canadian system but to also be able to understand that other systems exist too. Other countries' institutional systems may be better or worse than what exists in Canada. We believe it is especially important to point out where other systems seem better than what exists in Canada because our students will go on to be business and political leaders and may be the instruments to push for change in Canada that will make us stronger.

David Stangeland and Jerrod Falk are also proud Canadians and we celebrate the great success stories that have emerged in Canadian business. We also recognize some stories of failure and rebirth that have taken place. As such, we feature Canadian businesses in the text when they make suitable examples. A side benefit for students of this is that they can learn about some Canadian corporate history and become more familiar with the firms that may eventually be their employers. We do not exclude non-Canadian businesses. For example, when we want to look at the dominance of the corporate form in terms of business revenue in the world, there is only one largest company, Wal-Mart, so it has its place in the text. Again, though, when appropriate, we bring in Canadian corporations and their relative position for comparative purposes. Many firms not headquartered in Canada are so familiar and important to Canadians it would be foolish to exclude them when they make good examples. Apple and Starbucks are two of such firms.

An additional advantage of a Canadian text is that because Canada is a smaller player on the world scene than the US, Canadians must think more internationally. Thus, the Canadian edition has more of an international focus than the original US edition.

Table of Contents Overview

Fundamentals of Corporate Finance offers coverage of the major topical areas for introductory-level undergraduate courses. Our focus is on financial decision making related to the corporation's choice of which investments to make or how to raise the capital required to fund an investment. We designed the book with the need for flexibility and with consideration of time pressures throughout the semester in mind.

Part 1: Introduction

Ch. 1: Corporate Finance and the
        Financial Manager

Ch. 2: Introduction to Financial
        Statement Analysis

> Includes Canadian business-forms, taxes, and market information. Also an enhanced discussion of stakeholder view compared to shareholder wealth maximization view.

> Introduces CCA with depreciation discussion and includes reference to SEDAR for Canadian public company filings. Includes discussion of the impact of the Sarbanes-Oxley Act, specifically how changes resulted in Canada that are different than in the U.S.

Part 2: Interest Rates and Valuing Cash Flows

Ch. 3: The Valuation Principle: The Foundation of Financial Decision Making
Ch. 4: NPV and the Time Value of Money
Ch. 5: Interest Rates
Ch. 6: Bonds

Enhanced discussion of arbitrage with reference to the economic forces of supply and demand.

Comprehensive time value coverage including growing annuities and perpetuities and why they are relevant.

Part 3: Valuation and the Firm

Ch. 7: Investment Decision Rules
Ch. 8: Fundamentals of Capital Budgeting
Ch. 9: Valuing Stocks

Enhanced discussion of interest rate conversions. Canadian mortgages included.

Part 4: Risk and Return

Ch. 10: Risk and Return in Capital Markets
Ch. 11: Systematic Risk and the Equity Risk Premium
Ch. 12: Determining the Cost of Capital

Integrates a hypothetical project of RIM as an example throughout the chapter. Full CCA coverage is included.

Builds on capital budgeting by valuing the claim to a firm's free cash flows. Also addresses market efficiency and behavioural finance.

Part 5: Long-Term Financing

Ch. 13: Raising Equity Capital
Ch. 14: Debt Financing

Calculates and uses the firm's overall costs of capital and the WACC method.

Part 6: Capital Structure and Payout Policy

Ch. 15: Capital Structure
Ch. 16: Payout Policy

Understand private and public equity and debt financing, covenants, and repayment options.

These chapters start with perfect markets and then show how market imperfections, such as agency costs and asymmetric information, can influence financial policy.

Part 7: Financial Planning and Forecasting

Ch. 17: Financial Modeling and Pro Forma analysis
Ch. 18: Working Capital Management
Ch. 19: Short-Term Financial Planning

Forecasting and managing cash needs on a short-term basis are discussed.

Part 8: Special Topics

Ch. 20: Option Applications and Corporate Finance

Both payoffs and profits of options are discussed. Option valuation and the application to corporate finance is included.

Ch. 21: Risk Management
Ch. 22: International Corporate Finance
Ch. 23: Leasing
Ch. 24: Mergers and Acquisitions

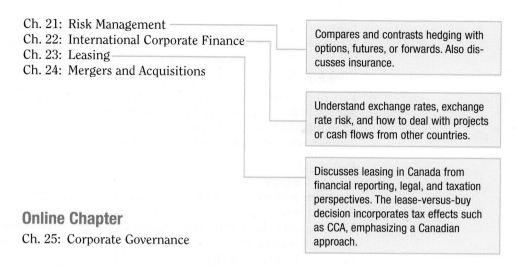

Compares and contrasts hedging with options, futures, or forwards. Also discusses insurance.

Understand exchange rates, exchange rate risk, and how to deal with projects or cash flows from other countries.

Discusses leasing in Canada from financial reporting, legal, and taxation perspectives. The lease-versus-buy decision incorporates tax effects such as CCA, emphasizing a Canadian approach.

Online Chapter

Ch. 25: Corporate Governance

Parts 1 and 2 lay the foundation for our study of corporate finance. In **Chapter 1**, we introduce the corporation and related business forms. We then examine the role of financial managers and outside investors in decision making for the firm. **Chapter 2** reviews basic corporate accounting principles and the financial statements on which the financial manager relies.

Part 2 presents the basic tools that are the cornerstones of corporate finance. **Chapter 3** introduces the Valuation Principle, which underlies all of finance and links all of the ideas throughout this book. **Chapter 4** on the time value of money analyzes cash flow streams lasting several periods. We explain how to value a series of future cash flows and derive shortcuts for computing the present value of annuities and perpetuities. We focus on how interest rates are quoted and determined in **Chapter 5**, with an emphasis on how to use market interest rates to determine the appropriate discount rate for a set of cash flows. In **Chapter 6**, we demonstrate an application of the time value of money tools using interest rates: valuing the bonds issued by corporations and governments.

Part 3 addresses the most important decision financial managers face: the choice of which investments the corporation should make, driving the value of the firm. **Chapter 7** presents the investment decision rules that guide a financial manager's decision making. In **Chapter 8** on capital budgeting, we outline estimating a project's incremental cash flows, which then become the inputs to the NPV decision rule. Capital budgeting decisions determine value creation in the firm, so **Chapter 9** turns to valuing the ownership claim in the firm—its stock. After valuing a firm's equity with various methods, we discuss market efficiency and its implications for financial managers.

Part 4 looks at the critical concept of risk and return. We explain how to measure and compare risks across investment opportunities to determine the cost of capital for each investment opportunity. **Chapter 10** introduces the key insight that investors only demand a risk premium for non-diversifiable risk. In **Chapter 11**, we quantify this idea, leading to the Capital Asset Pricing Model (CAPM). In **Chapter 12**, we apply what we've learned to estimate a company's overall weighted average cost of capital.

Part 5 shows how the firm raises the funds it needs to undertake its investments. We explain the mechanics of raising equity in **Chapter 13** and debt markets in **Chapter 14** (where we also continue the institutional overview of bond markets that began in Chapter 6). **Part 6** on capital structure builds on this foundation by examining the impact of financing choices on the value of the firm. **Chapter 15** on capital structure opens by intuitively establishing the Modigliani and Miller result and then turns to the impact of important market imperfections. Payout policy is the focus of **Chapter 16**.

Part 7 turns to the details of running the financial side of a corporation on both a long-term and day-to-day basis. **Chapter 17** develops the tools to forecast the cash flows and long-term financing needs of a firm. In **Chapter 18** we discuss how firms manage their working capital requirements, while **Chapter 19** explains how firms finance their short-term cash needs.

Part 8 addresses select special topics in corporate finance. **Chapter 20** introduces options; **Chapter 21** then focuses on the corporation's use of options, futures, forwards, insurance and other methods to manage risk. **Chapter 22** examines the issues a firm faces when making a foreign investment, including exchange rate risk, and addresses the valuation of foreign projects. **Chapter 23** introduces an alternative to long-term debt financing, leasing. By presenting leasing as a financing alternative, we apply the Law of One Price to determine that the benefits of leasing must derive from the tax differences, incentive effects, or other market imperfections. The Law of One Price continues to provide a unifying framework as we consider the topics of Mergers and Acquisitions in **Chapter 24** and Corporate Governance in **Chapter 25**.

A Complete Instructor and Student Support Package

MyFinanceLab

The moment you know.

Educators know it. Students know it. It's that inspired moment when something that was difficult to understand suddenly makes perfect sense. Our MyLab products have been designed and refined with a single purpose in mind—to help educators create that moment of understanding with their students.

MyFinanceLab delivers **proven results** in helping individual students succeed. It provides **engaging experiences** that personalize, stimulate, and measure learning for each student. And, it comes from a **trusted partner** with educational expertise and an eye on the future.

MyFinanceLab can be used by itself or linked to any learning management system. To learn more about how **MyFinanceLab** combines proven learning applications with powerful assessment, visit www.myfinancelab.com.

MyFinanceLab—the moment you know.

Videos

Video clips available in MyFinanceLab profile firms through interviews and analysis. The videos focus on core topical areas such as capital budgeting and feature well-known companies.

Technology Specialists. Pearson's Technology Specialists work with faculty and campus course designers to ensure that Pearson technology products, assessment tools, and online course materials are tailored to meet your specific needs. This highly qualified team is dedicated to helping schools take full advantage of a wide range of educational resources, by assisting in the integration of a variety of instructional materials and media formats. Your local Pearson Education sales representative can provide you with more details on this service program.

CourseSmart for Instructors. CourseSmart goes beyond traditional expectations-providing instant, online access to the textbooks and course materials you need at a lower cost for students. And even as students save money, you can save time and hassle with a digital eTextbook that allows you to search for the most relevant content at the very moment you need it. Whether it's evaluating textbooks or creating lecture notes to help students with difficult concepts, CourseSmart can make life a little easier. See how when you visit www.coursesmart.com/instructors.

CourseSmart for Students. CourseSmart goes beyond traditional expectations-providing instant, online access to the textbooks and course materials you need at an average savings of 60%. With instant access from any computer and the ability to search your text, you'll find the content you need quickly, no matter where you are. And with online tools like highlighting and note-taking, you can save time and study efficiently. See all the benefits at www.coursesmart.com/students.

Pearson eText. Pearson eText gives students access to the text whenever and wherever they have access to the Internet. eText pages look exactly like the printed text, offering powerful new functionality for students and instructors. Users can create notes, highlight text in different colours, create bookmarks, zoom, click hyperlinked words and phrases to view definitions, and view in single-page or two-page view. Pearson eText allows for quick navigation to key parts of the eText using a table of contents and provides full-text search. The eText may also offer links to associated media files, enabling users to access videos, animations, or other activities as they read the text.

The **Instructor's Resource CD-ROM [0321548728]** includes the following instructor supplements:

- The **Solutions Manual** provides students with detailed, accuracy-verified solutions to the problems in the book. The solutions, like the problems, were written by the authors themselves. Each solution has been scrutinized for accuracy and quality and is presented in the same Guided Problem Solution framework introduced in the text. Spreadsheet solutions in Excel®, which allow the student to see the effect of changes in the input variables on the outcome, are also available to instructors for designated problems on the Instructor's Resource CD-ROM. The Solutions Manual also includes solutions to the Data Cases and Integrative Cases, as well as answers to the Review Questions and Critical Thinking Questions in the textbook.

- The **PowerPoint Presentation**, authored by Anas Aboulamer at Concordia University, is available in lecture form and includes art and tables from the book and additional examples. The PowerPoint materials, including all tables and figure files, examples, key terms, and spreadsheet tables from the text are also available in a separate **Image Bank** for professors to build into their personal PowerPoint presentations.

- The **Test Bank**, authored by Ron Mackinnon at the University of British Columbia, provides a wealth of accuracy-verified testing material. Each chapter offers a wide variety of true/false, short answer, and multiple-choice questions. Questions are verified by difficulty level and skill type, and correlated to the chapter topics. very question in the Test Bank is also available in **TestGen®** software for both Windows® and Macintosh® computers. This easy-to-use testing software is a valuable test preparation tool that allows professors to view, edit, and add questions.

- The **Instructor's Manual** was written by Bill Fletcher at St. Mary's University, and contains chapter outlines and overviews, lecture launchers, further questions for class discussion, and the answers to the practitioner interview questions found in the book. The **Instructor's Manual** is included on the Instructor's Resource CD-ROM and is also be available for download as Microsoft® Word files or as Adobe® PDF files from the Instructor Resource Center.

Study on the Go.

Featured at the end of each chapter, you will find a unique barcode providing access to Study on the Go, an unprecedented mobile integration between text and online content. Students link to Pearson's unique Study on the Go content directly from their smartphones, allowing them to study whenever and wherever they wish! Go to one of the sites below to see how you can download an app to your smartphone for free. Once the app is installed, your phone will scan the code and link to a website containing Pearson's Study on the Go content, including the popular study tools Glossary Flashcards, Audio Summaries, and Quizzes, which can be accessed anytime.

ScanLife
http://getscanlife.com/

NeoReader
http://get.neoreader.com/

QuickMark
http://www.quickmark.com.tw/

Acknowledgments

Given the scope of this project, identifying the many people who made it happen is a tall order. This textbook was the product of the expertise and hard work of many talented colleagues. We are especially gratified with the work of those who developed the array of print supplements that accompany the book: Ron Mackinnon for the Test Bank; Bill Fletcher, for the Instructor's Manual; Anas Aboulamer, for the PowerPoint lecture notes; and our MyFinanceLab content development author, Therese Trainor. We're also deeply appreciative of Dennis Ng's work conducting the lively interviews with recent graduates that open each chapter.

At Pearson Education Canada, we would like to thank

- ▶ Vice President, Editorial Director, Gary Bennett
- ▶ Editor-in-Chief, Nicole Lukach
- ▶ Acquisitions Editor, Claudine O'Donnell
- ▶ Senior Marketing Manager, Leigh-Anne Graham
- ▶ Developmental Editor, Toni Chahley
- ▶ Project Managers, Sarah Lukaweski, Rachel Thompson
- ▶ Production Editor, Vasundhara Sawhney
- ▶ Designer, Anthony Leung
- ▶ Proofreader, Audrey Dorsch

We are indebted to our colleagues for the time and expertise invested as manuscript reviewers. The sound guidance from these trusted advisors throughout the writing process was truly invaluable. We strived to incorporate every contributor's input and are truly grateful for each comment and suggestion. The book has benefited enormously from this input.

Reviewers for the First Canadian Edition

Trevor Chamberlain, *McMaster University*
Bin Cheng, *University of Ontario Institute of Technology*
Kirk Collins, *St. Francis Xavier University*
Bill Fletcher, *St. Mary's University*
Yi Feng, *Ryerson University*
Merlyn Foo, *Athabasca Univerisity*
Larbi Hammabi, *McGill University*
Robert Ironside, *Kwantlen University*
Raad Jassim, *McGill University*
Garth Jensen, *Laurentian University*
Lew Johnson, *Queen's University*

Keith Christian Jensen, *Vancouver Island University*
Vic Kariappa, *Carleton University*
Dave Kennedy, *Lethbridge College*
Kai Li, *University of British Columbia*
Audrey Lowry, *Grant MacEwan*
Andras Marosi, *University of Alberta*
Eloisa Perez, *Grant MacEwan*
Ian Rakita, *Concordia University*
Shishir Singh, *University of Manitoba*
Jun Yang, *Acadia University*

PART 1

Introduction

Valuation Principle Connection. What is corporate finance? No matter what your role in a corporation, an understanding of why and how financial decisions are made is essential. The focus of this book is how to make optimal corporate financial decisions. In this part of the book, we lay the foundation for our study of corporate finance. In Chapter 1, we begin by introducing the corporation and related business forms. We then examine the role of financial managers and outside investors in decision making for the firm. To make optimal decisions, a decision maker needs information. Therefore, in Chapter 2 we review and analyze an important source of information for corporate decision making—the firm's accounting statements. These chapters will introduce us to the role and objective of the financial manager and some of the information the financial manager uses in applying the Valuation Principle to make optimal decisions. In the next section of the book, we will introduce and begin applying the Valuation Principle.

Chapter 1
Corporate Finance and the Financial Manager

Chapter 2
Introduction to Financial Statement Analysis

1

Corporate Finance and the Financial Manager

▶ Grasp the importance of financial information in both your personal and business lives

▶ Understand the important features of the three main types of firms and see why the advantages of the corporate form have led it to dominate economic activity

▶ Explain the goal of the financial manager and the reasoning behind that goal, as well as understand the three main types of decisions a financial manager makes

▶ Know how a corporation is managed and controlled, the financial manager's place in it, and some of the ethical issues financial managers face

▶ Understand the importance of financial markets, such as stock markets, to a corporation and the financial manager's role as liaison to those markets

▶ Recognize the role that financial institutions play in the financial cycle of the economy

INTERVIEW WITH Amy Kwan,
Certified Management Accountants of Ontario

Amy Kwan, who received a Bachelor of Science (Honours) degree in kinesiology and health science from York University in 2006 before completing her Master of Management and Professional Accounting degree at the University of Toronto in 2009, was already finding her finance courses useful prior to graduation. "While pursuing my master's, I worked at a public accounting firm. My accounting and finance knowledge was immediately put to work, as I was assisting with the audit of financial statements of both public and private companies. No matter what the size of the company, understanding the basics of capital structure, the role of financial markets, and financial instruments, was essential for the job."

Amy currently works as a manager for program content development at Certified Management Accountants of Ontario, where she applies her finance knowledge on a daily basis. "I continually find myself using the skills that I attained though courses such as business finance and financial management. Whether it is making decisions to manage resources for capital and non-capital expenditures, capital budgeting, building a business case for a new program, or analyzing how to maximize return on investment for new and existing programs, I always find myself resorting to the fundamentals learned in the classroom."

Amy encourages students not to be intimidated by the rigour of finance courses. "No matter where I have worked, I have found that the foundational tools learned in the classroom are almost always applied and put to use in the practical world. These tools have been a pivotal aid in solving business problems of all sizes and complexities."

Corporations have existed in Canada since before Canada was a nation. One of the oldest and most recognized corporations in Canada is the Hudson's Bay Company (HBC). HBC was given its charter in 1670 and still continues its operation today. In 1970, the head office of HBC moved from London, England, to Winnipeg; it is now in Toronto. Ownership and control of the HBC has changed location over the years too, from England, where it was originally, to Canada and then to the United States. Corporations are arguably the most important business organizations in Canada and around the world because of their dominance in terms of products produced, revenues and profits generated, and people employed.

This book focuses on how people in corporations make financial decisions. Although the subject of this book is *corporate* finance, much of what we discuss applies to the financial decisions made within any organization, including not-for-profit entities such as charities and universities. In this chapter, we introduce the corporation and alternative business organizational forms common in Canada. We also highlight the financial manager's critical role inside any business enterprise. What products to launch, how to pay to develop those products, what profits to keep, and how to return profits to investors—all of these decisions and many more fall within corporate finance. The financial manager makes these decisions with the goal of maximizing the value of the business, which is determined in the financial markets. In this chapter and throughout the book, we will expand on this goal, provide you with the tools to make financial management decisions, and show you how the financial markets provide funds to a corporation and produce market prices that are key inputs to any financial manager's investment analysis.

Why Study Finance?

Finance and financial thinking are everywhere in our daily lives. Consider your decision to go to university. You surely weighed alternatives, such as starting a full-time job immediately, and then decided that university provided you with the greatest net benefit. More and more, individuals are taking charge of their personal finances with decisions such as these:

- ▶ When to start saving and how much to save for retirement.
- ▶ Whether a car loan or lease is more advantageous.
- ▶ Whether a particular stock is a good investment.
- ▶ How to evaluate the terms for a home mortgage.

Our career paths have become less predictable and more dynamic. In previous generations, it was common to work for one employer your entire career. Today, that would be highly unusual. Most of us will instead change jobs, and possibly even careers, many times. With each new opportunity, we must weigh all the costs and benefits, financial and otherwise.

Some financial decisions, such as whether to pay $2.00 for your morning espresso, are simple, but most are more complex. In your business career, whether you are in finance or another field, you may face such questions as these:

- ▶ Should your firm launch a new product?
- ▶ Should a marketing plan be undertaken?
- ▶ Which supplier should your firm choose?
- ▶ Should your firm upgrade its information systems?
- ▶ Is a new staff training initiative worth its cost?
- ▶ Should your firm produce a part of the product or outsource production?
- ▶ Should your firm issue new stock or borrow money instead?
- ▶ How can you raise money for your start-up firm?

In this book, you will learn how all of these decisions in your personal life and inside a business are tied together by one powerful concept, the Valuation Principle. It shows how to make the costs and benefits of a decision comparable so that we can weigh them properly. Learning to apply the Valuation Principle will give you the skills to make the types of comparisons—among loan options, investments, and projects—that will turn you into a knowledgeable, confident consumer and manager. Finally, in each chapter you will hear from a former student—someone who opened a book like this one not that long ago—who talks about his or her job and the critical role finance plays in it.

Whether you plan to major in finance or simply take this one course, you will find the fundamental financial knowledge gained here to be essential in your personal and business lives.

The Three Types of Firms

We begin by introducing the three major types of firms: sole proprietorships, partnerships, and corporations. We explain each organizational form in turn, but our primary focus is on the most important form—the corporation. Although the number of proprietorships and partnerships in the Canadian economy is greater than the number of corporations, corporations tend to be much larger and are the most significant business organizations in Canada, as demonstrated by their dominance in terms of business income generated (see Figure 1.1). In addition to describing what a corporation is, we also provide an overview of why corporations are so successful.

Sole Proprietorships

sole proprietorship
A business owned and run by one person.

A **sole proprietorship** is a business owned and run by one person. Sole proprietorships are usually very small with few, if any, employees. Although they are the most common type of business unit in the economy, sole proprietorships are relatively small in terms of revenues and profits produced and people employed.

We now consider the key features of a sole proprietorship.

1. Sole proprietorships have the advantage of being straightforward to set up. Consequently, many new businesses use this organizational form.

2. The principal limitation of a sole proprietorship is that there is no separation between the firm and the owner—the firm can have only one owner who runs the business, and the business income is taxed as personal income of the owner. If there are other investors, they cannot hold an ownership stake in the firm; this limits the ability of the owner to raise additional money for the business.

3. The owner has unlimited personal liability for any of the firm's debts. That is, if the firm defaults on any debt payment, the lender can (and will) require the owner to repay the loan from personal assets. An owner who cannot afford to repay a loan for which he or she is personably liable must declare personal bankruptcy.

4. The life of a sole proprietorship is limited to the life of the owner. It is also difficult to transfer ownership of a sole proprietorship.

For most growing businesses, the disadvantages of a sole proprietorship outweigh the advantages. As soon as the firm reaches the point at which it can borrow without the owner agreeing to be personally liable, the owner typically converts the business into another form. Conversion also has other benefits that we will consider as we discuss the other forms below.

Partnerships

Partnerships can be organized as general partnerships or limited partnerships. The common feature of all partnerships is that income from the partnership is taxed at the personal level. The income is split among partners according to their ownership in the partnership.

FIGURE 1.1

2009 Canadian Business Net Income Before Tax: Corporate vs. Non-Corporate (Statistics Canada)

Comparing incorporated firms to unincorporated firms, even though there are many more unincorporated businesses, 60% of business income is generated by corporations.

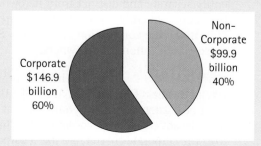

Corporate $146.9 billion 60%

Non-Corporate $99.9 billion 40%

general partnership
A business owned and run by more than one owner.

A **general partnership** is a partnership owned and run by more than one owner—each called a general partner. Key features include the following:

1. *All general partners have unlimited liability.* That is, a lender can require *any* partner to repay *all* the firm's outstanding debts. Similarly, in a legal judgment against the partnership, each partner is fully liable; thus, partners must be chosen carefully, as any single partner's actions can affect the exposure of all the partners.

2. The partnership ends in the event of the death or withdrawal of any single partner. Partners can avoid liquidation if the partnership agreement provides for alternatives such as a buyout of a deceased or withdrawn partner.

Some old and established businesses around the world remain as general partnerships or sole proprietorships. Often these firms are the types of businesses in which the owners' personal reputations are the basis for the businesses. For example, law firms and accounting firms in some countries are organized as general partnerships. For such enterprises, the partners' personal liability increases the confidence of the firm's clients that the partners will strive to maintain the firm's reputation.

limited partnership
A partnership with two kinds of owners, general partners and limited partners.

limited liability Liability that is limited to the limited partner's investment.

limited liability partnership (LLP)
A form of partnership used in Canada for law and accounting firms that provides partial limitation of a partner's liability.

A **limited partnership** is a partnership with two kinds of owners, general partners and limited partners. In this case, the general partners have the same rights and privileges as partners in any general partnership—they are personally liable for the firm's obligations. Limited partners, however, have **limited liability**—that is, their liability is limited to their investment. Their private property cannot be seized to pay off the firm's outstanding debts. Furthermore, the death or withdrawal of a limited partner does not dissolve the partnership, and a limited partner's interest is transferable. However, a limited partner has no management authority and cannot legally be involved in the managerial decision making for the business.

In Canada a special type of partnership called a **limited liability partnership (LLP)** can be used in the legal and accounting professions. An LLP is similar to a general partnership in that the partners can be active in the management of the firm, and they do have a degree of unlimited liability. The limitation on a partner's liability is only in cases related to actions of negligence of other partners or those supervised by other partners. In all other respects, including a particular partner's own negligence or the negligence of those supervised by the particular partner, that partner has unlimited personal liability. In addition, the assets of the business are potentially at risk of seizure due to the actions of anyone within the partnership. Thus, while a partner's personal assets are protected from the negligent actions of other partners, the investment in the overall partnership may be lost.

Corporations

corporation A legally defined, artificial being, separate from its owners.

A **corporation** is a legally defined, artificial being (a legal entity), separate from its owners. As such, it has many of the legal powers that people have. It can enter into contracts, acquire assets, incur obligations, and receive similar protection against the seizure of its property as that received by an individual. Because a corporation is a legal entity separate and distinct from its owners, it is solely responsible for its own obligations. Consequently, the owners of a corporation (its shareholders) are not liable for any obligations the corporation enters into. Similarly, the corporation is not liable for any personal obligations of its owners.

Formation of a Corporation. In most provinces, corporations are defined under the provincial Business Corporations Act or the Canada Business Corporations Act. Corporations must be legally formed, which means that the articles of incorporation must be filed with the relevant registrar of corporations. The articles of incorporation, sometimes referred to as the corporate charter, are like a corporate constitution that sets out the terms of the corporation's ownership and existence. Setting up a corporation is therefore considerably more costly than setting up a sole proprietorship. Most firms hire lawyers to create the formal articles of incorporation and a set of bylaws.

Ownership of a Corporation. There is no limit on the number of owners a corporation can have. Because most corporations have many owners, each owner owns only a fraction of the corporation. The entire ownership stake of a corporation is divided into shares known as **stock**. The collection of all the outstanding shares of a corporation is known as the **equity** of the corporation. An owner of a share of stock in the corporation is known as a **shareholder, stockholder**, or **equity holder**. Shareholders are entitled to **dividend payments**, that is, payments made at the discretion of the corporation's board of directors to the equity holders. Shareholders usually receive voting rights and dividend rights that are proportional to the amount of stock they own. For example, a shareholder who owns 30% of the firm's shares will be entitled to 30% of the votes at an annual meeting and 30% of the total dividend payment. In Canada, many corporations have a dominant shareholder (controlling in excess of 25% of the equity); in the United States, more corporations are considered widely held (with the largest shareholder holding less than 5% of the equity). About 19% of Canadian corporations listed on the Toronto Stock Exchange (TSX) have multiple classes of stock such that some classes may have more voting rights than others even though they have the same rights to dividends.

A unique feature of a corporation is that there is no limitation on who can own its stock. That is, an owner of a corporation need not have any special expertise or qualification. This feature allows free trade in the shares of the corporation and provides one of the most important advantages of organizing a firm as a corporation rather than as sole proprietorship or partnership. Corporations can raise substantial amounts of capital because they can sell ownership shares to anonymous outside investors.

As shown in Figure 1.1, the availability of outside funding has enabled corporations to dominate the economy compared to unincorporated businesses. Let's take the world's largest corporation ranked by sales in the 2010 Fortune Global 500 survey, Wal-Mart Stores Inc., headquartered in Bentonville, Arkansas. For the fiscal year ending January 31, 2010, Wal-Mart's annual report indicated revenue was about $408 billion, and the total value of the company's shares (the wealth in the company the owners collectively owned) was almost $200 billion. It employed over 2.1 million people. Let's put these numbers into perspective. According to the World Bank, a country with $408 billion in gross domestic product (GDP) in 2009 would rank just behind Poland and just ahead of Sweden as the 22nd richest country (out of more than 200). Poland has over 38 million people, about 18 times as many people as employees at Wal-Mart. Indeed, if the number of employees was used as the "population" of Wal-Mart, Wal-Mart would rank as the 142nd largest country, just behind Namibia. To put Wal-Mart's numbers in a Canadian perspective, in 2010 the *Globe and Mail* ranked the Royal Bank of Canada as Canada's most profitable firm. The Royal Bank of Canada had revenues of about $38 billion—quite impressive in its own right. However, this is less than one-tenth of Wal-Mart's revenues. As shown in Table 1.1, the sum of the revenues of Canada's top 10 most profitable firms is about $189 billion—again very impressive, but less than half of that of Wal-Mart.

stock The ownership or equity of a corporation divided into shares.

equity The collection of all the outstanding shares of a corporation.

shareholder (also stockholder or equity holder) An owner of a share of stock or equity in a corporation.

dividend payments Payments made at the discretion of the corporation to its equity holders.

Tax Implications for Corporate Entities

An important difference between the types of corporate organizational forms is the way they are taxed. Because a corporation is a separate legal entity, a corporation's profits are subject to taxation separate from its owners' tax obligations. In effect, shareholders of a corporation pay taxes twice. First, the corporation pays tax on its profits, and then when the remaining profits are distributed to the shareholders as dividends, the shareholders pay their own personal income tax on this income. This system is sometimes referred to as double taxation.

TABLE 1.1 Canada's Top 10 Corporations Ranked by Profit	**Rank (by Profitability*)**	**Company Name**	**Total Revenue**
	1	Royal Bank of Canada	$38.14 billion
	2	Bank of Nova Scotia	$25.06 billion
	3	Toronto-Dominion Bank	$25.42 billion
	4	Research In Motion	$14.98 billion
	5	EnCana Corp.	$11.30 billion
	6	Canadian National Railway	$7.64 billion
	7	Teck Resources	$8.68 billion
	8	Bank of Montreal	$16.07 billion
	9	Great-West Life Assurance	$24.15 billion
	10	BCE Inc.	$17.77 billion
		Sum	$189.22 billion

*Note, firms are ranked by profitability but revenues are shown (to be consistent with the Wal-Mart discussion). Thus revenue rankings are not in the same order as profit ranks. The profit numbers and revenue numbers were taken for the fiscal year closest to December 31, 2009, and range between October 2009 and February 2010.

Source: Rankings of Canada's top 1000 public companies by profit
Globe and Mail Update
Published Friday, June 18, 2010, 8:41 a.m. EDT
Last updated Thursday, Sep. 23, 2010, 11:01 a.m. EDT

EXAMPLE 1.1

Taxation of Corporate Earnings

Problem

You are a shareholder in a corporation. Some of your shares are held inside your tax-free savings account (TFSA), so any earnings there are not taxed; income from shares held outside your TFSA is taxable.[1] The corporation earns $5.00 per share before taxes. After the corporation has paid taxes, it will distribute the rest of its earnings to you as a dividend. The corporate tax rate is 35% and your tax rate on dividend income outside your TFSA is 24%.[2] How much of the earnings remains after all taxes are paid?

Solution

▶ **Plan**

Corporate Information

Earnings before taxes: $5.00   Corporate tax rate: 35%

Personal Tax Rates on Dividends

From shares held inside your TFSA 0%   From shares held outside your TFSA 24%

---

[1]Income earned within a registered retirement savings account (RRSP) is not taxed, but when money is withdrawn from an RRSP it is fully taxable. Other tax-sheltered investments include a registered education savings plan (RESP), a registered retirement income fund (RRIF), and a pension plan.

[2]The tax on dividend income from a Canadian corporation is determined by Canada Revenue Agency's requirement to gross up the dividend amount by 41%, apply your tax rate to the grossed up amount, and then receive a dividend tax credit of 16.4354% of the actual dividend. According to Ernst & Young, in the 2010 tax year, this resulted in combined federal and provincial tax rates on dividends that ranged from 15.88% in Alberta to 33.58% in Nova Scotia and were around 24% in many of the other provinces.

We first need to calculate the corporation's earnings after taxes by subtracting the taxes paid from the pre-tax earnings of $5.00. The taxes paid will be 35% (the corporate tax rate) of $5.00. Since all of the after-tax earnings per share will be paid to you as a dividend, you will pay taxes of 0% on the dividend for the shares inside your TFSA and 24% on the dividend for the shares outside your TFSA. The amount left over is what remains after all taxes are paid.

▶ **Execute**

$5.00 per share × 0.35 = $1.75 in taxes at the corporate level, leaving $5.00 − $1.75 = $3.25 in after-tax earnings per share to distribute as a dividend.

For each share within your TFSA, you will pay no tax at the personal level for the dividend, leaving you with the full $3.25 dividend. For each dividend from the shares outside your TFSA, you will pay $3.25 × 0.24 = $0.78 in taxes on that dividend, leaving you with $2.47 from the original $5.00 after all taxes.

▶ **Evaluate**

Each of your shares within your TFSA allows you to keep $3.25 of the original $5.00 in earnings; only the corporate tax of $1.75 is paid, and your total effective tax rate is just the corporate tax rate of 35%.

Each of your shares outside your TFSA allows you to keep $2.47 of the original $5.00 in earnings; the remaining $1.75 + $0.78 = $2.53 is paid as taxes. Thus, your total effective tax rate is 2.53/5 = 50.6%.

flow-through entity A business in which all income produced flows to the investors and virtually no earnings are retained within the business.

income trust A trust that holds income-producing assets directly or holds all the debt and equity securities of an income-producing corporation within the trust.

business income trust An income trust that holds all the debt and equity securities of a corporation (the underlying business).

unit holders The owners of an income trust.

energy trust An income trust that holds resource properties directly or holds all the debt and equity securities of a resource corporation within the trust.

real estate investment trust (REIT) An income trust that holds real estate properties directly or holds all the debt and equity securities of a corporation that owns real estate properties.

The corporate organizational structure is the only organizational structure subject to double taxation. However, the Canada Revenue Agency allows an exemption from double taxation for certain **flow-through entities** where all income produced by the business flows to the investors and virtually no earnings are retained within the business. These entities are called **income trusts** and come in three forms. A **business income trust** holds all the debt and equity securities of a corporation (the underlying business) in trust for the trust's owners, called the **unit holders**. An **energy trust** either holds resource properties directly or holds all the debt and equity securities of a resource corporation within the trust. A **real estate investment trust (REIT)** either holds real estate properties directly or holds all the debt and equity securities of a corporation that owns real estate properties. For income trusts formed before November 2006, there is no tax at the business level until 2011. REITs will continue to have no tax at the business level beyond 2011, but the other forms of income trusts will not. When income from a flow-through entity is received at the personal level, it is taxed as regular income unless received within a tax-sheltered investment (such as a TFSA or RRSP).

EXAMPLE 1.2

Taxation of a Real Estate Investment Trust (REIT)

Problem

Rework Example 1.1 assuming the corporation in that example was actually a real estate investment trust and flowed through all earnings to trust unit owners. Again, assume you hold some of the trust units within your TFSA so they are not subject to personal taxes. For the trust units held outside your TFSA, suppose you pay tax at a rate of 46% (equal to the tax rate on regular income).

Solution

▶ Plan

REIT Information

Earnings before taxes: $5.00   Tax at the business level: 0%

Personal Tax Rates on Regular Income

From units held inside your TFSA 0%   From units held outside your TFSA 46%.

Since there is no tax at the business level, the entire $5.00 of earnings is passed through to the unit holders. The $5.00 received is taxed as ordinary income at the personal level. However, for the units held within your TFSA, you will pay no tax. For the units held outside your TFSA, you will pay tax at a rate of 46% on the REIT distribution. The amount left over is what remains after all taxes are paid.

▶ Execute

$5.00 per unit is distributed to each unit holder.

For each unit within your TFSA, you will pay no tax at the personal level, leaving you the full $5.00 amount. For each distribution from the units outside your TFSA, you will pay $5.00 × 0.46 = $2.30 in taxes on that distribution, leaving you with $2.70 from the original $5.00 after all taxes.

▶ Evaluate

Each of your shares within your TFSA allows you to keep the full $5.00 in earnings, so your total effective tax rate is 0%.

Each of your shares outside your TFSA allows you to keep $2.70 of the original $5.00 in earnings; the remaining $2.30 is paid as taxes. Thus, your total effective tax rate is 46% (the rate of tax you pay on regular income).

As we have discussed, there are three main types of firms: sole proprietorships, partnerships (general and limited), and corporations. In addition, a business or particular assets may be held within an income trust for tax purposes. Table 1.2 compares and contrasts the main characteristics of each.

Concept Check

1. What are the advantages and disadvantages of organizing a business as a corporation?

2. What is a limited liability partnership (LLP)? How does it differ from a limited partnership?

3. What is an income trust? Which type of trust will still get preferential tax treatment after 2011?

Corporate Taxation Around the World

In most countries, there is some relief from double taxation. Thirty countries make up the Organisation for Economic Co-operation and Development (OECD), and of these countries, only Ireland and Switzerland offer no relief from double taxation. In Canada, the dividend tax credit gives some relief by effectively giving a lower tax rate on dividend income than on other sources of income. In the 2010 tax year, for most provinces dividend income was taxed at a rate of about 21% less than ordinary income; for example, in Ontario the effective personal tax rates (combined provincial and federal) were 26.57% for dividends and 46.41% for regular income for individuals in the top tax bracket. A few countries, including Australia, Finland, Mexico, New Zealand, and Norway, offer complete relief by effectively not taxing dividend income.

	Number of Owners	Liability for Firm's Debts	Owners Manage the Firm	Ownership Change Dissolves the Firm	Taxation
TABLE 1.2 Characteristics of Different Types of Firms					
Sole proprietorship	One	Yes	Yes	Yes	Personal
General partnership	Unlimited	Yes	Yes	Yes	Personal
Limited partnership	At least one general partner, no limit on number of limited partners	General partners: yes Limited partners: no	General partners: yes Limited partners: no	General partners: yes Limited partners: no	Personal
Corporation	Unlimited	No	No (but they may legally)	No	Business and personal
Income trust (or investment trust)	Unlimited	No	No	No	Personal

1.3 The Financial Manager

As of October 15, 2010, Apple, Inc. had more than 909 *million* shares of stock held by 29,405 owners.[3] Because a corporation has many owners, each of whom can freely trade his or her stock, often it is not feasible for the owners of a corporation to have direct control of the firm. The financial manager has responsibility for making the financial decisions of the business for the stockholders. Within the corporation, the financial manager has three main tasks:

1. Make investment decisions.
2. Make financing decisions.
3. Manage short-term cash needs.

We will discuss each of these in turn, along with the financial manager's overarching goal.

Making Investment Decisions

The financial manager's most important job is to make the firm's investment decisions. The financial manager must weigh the costs and benefits of each investment or project and decide which of them qualify as good uses of the money stockholders have invested in the firm. These investment decisions fundamentally shape what the firm does and whether it will add value for its owners. For example, it may seem hard to imagine now, but there was a time when Apple's financial managers were evaluating whether to invest in the development of the first iPod. They had to weigh the substantial development and production costs against uncertain future sales. Their

---

[3]Apple, Inc., 10-K Form for fiscal year ended September 25, 2010.

analysis indicated that it was a good investment, and the rest is history. In this book, we will develop all the tools necessary to make these investment decisions.

Making Financing Decisions

Once the financial manager has decided which investments to make, he or she also decides how to pay for them. Large investments may require the corporation to raise additional money. The financial manager must decide whether to raise more money from new and existing owners by selling more shares of stock (equity) or to borrow the money instead (debt). In this book, we will discuss the characteristics of each source of money and how to decide which one to use in the context of the corporation's overall mix of debt and equity.

Managing Short-Term Cash Needs

The financial manager must ensure that the firm has enough cash on hand to meet its obligations from day to day. This job, also commonly known as managing working capital,[4] may seem straightforward, but in a young or growing company, it can mean the difference between success and failure. Even companies with great products require a lot of money to develop and bring those products to market. Consider the costs to Apple of launching the iPhone, which included developing the technology and creating a huge marketing campaign, or the costs to Boeing of producing the 787—billions of dollars were spent before the first 787 left the ground. A company typically burns through a significant amount of cash before the sales of the product generate income. The financial manager's job is to make sure that access to cash does not hinder the firm's success.

The Goal of the Financial Manager

shareholder wealth maximization The overriding corporate objective that seeks to maximize the financial benefit to all persons holding stock in the corporation by maximizing the current value of the company's share price.

The financial manager makes all these decisions within the context of the overriding goal of a firm's management—**shareholder wealth maximization**. The stockholders have invested in the corporation, putting their money at risk to become the owners of the corporation. Thus, the firm's management is a caretaker of the money stockholders have invested and makes decisions in their interests. Many corporations have thousands of owners (shareholders). These shareholders vary from large institutions to small first-time investors, from retirees living off their investments to young employees just starting to save for retirement. Each owner is likely to have different interests and priorities. Whose interests and priorities determine the goals of the firm? You might be surprised to learn that the interests of shareholders are aligned for many, if not most, important decisions. Regardless of their own personal financial position and stage in life, all shareholders will agree that they are better off if the value of their investment in the corporation is maximized. For example, suppose the decision concerns whether to develop a new product that will be a profitable investment for the corporation. All shareholders will probably agree that developing this product is a good idea. Returning to our iPod example, by late 2010, Apple shares were worth about 36 times as much as they were in October 2001, when the first iPod was introduced. All Apple shareholders

---

[4]Working capital refers to things such as cash on hand, inventories, raw materials, loans to suppliers, and payments from customers—the grease that keeps the wheels of production moving. We will discuss working capital in more detail in the next chapter and devote all of Chapter 18 to working capital management.

at the time of the development of the first iPod are clearly much better off because of it, whether they have since sold their shares of Apple to pay for retirement or are still watching those shares appreciate in their retirement accounts.

Even when all the owners of a corporation agree on the goals of the corporation, these goals must be implemented. In the next section, we discuss the financial manager's place in the corporation and how owners exert control over the corporation.

Concept Check

4. What are the main types of decisions that a financial manager makes?
5. What is the goal of the financial manager?

1.4 The Financial Manager's Place in the Corporation

We've established that the stockholders own the corporation but rely on the firm's managers to actively manage the corporation. The *board of directors* and the management team headed by the *chief executive officer* have direct control of the corporation. In this section, we explain how the responsibilities for the corporation are divided between these two entities and describe conflicts that arise between stockholders and the management team.

The Corporate Management Team

board of directors
A group of people elected by shareholders who have the ultimate decision-making authority in the corporation.

The shareholders of a corporation exercise their control by electing a **board of directors**, a group of people who have the ultimate decision-making authority in the corporation. In most corporations, each share of stock gives a shareholder one vote in the election of the board of directors, so investors with more shares have more influence. When one or two shareholders own a very large proportion of the outstanding stock, these shareholders might either be on the board of directors themselves, or they may have the right to appoint a number of directors.

The board of directors makes rules on how the corporation should be run (including how the top managers in the corporation are compensated), sets policy, and monitors the performance of the company. The board of directors delegates most decisions that involve the day-to-day running of the corporation to its management.

chief executive officer (CEO) The person charged with running the corporation by instituting the rules and policies set by the board of directors.

The **chief executive officer (CEO)** is charged with running the corporation by implementing the rules and policies set by the board of directors. The size of the rest of the management team varies from corporation to corporation. In some corporations, the separation of powers between the board of directors and CEO is not always distinct. In fact, the CEO can also be the chair of the board of directors. The most senior financial manager is the chief financial officer (CFO), who often reports directly to the CEO. Figure 1.2 presents part of a typical organizational chart for a corporation, highlighting the positions a financial manager may take.

Ethics and Incentives in Corporations

A corporation is run by a management team, separate from its owners. How can the owners of a corporation ensure that the management team will implement their goals?

Principal-Agent Problem. Many people claim that because of the separation of ownership and control in a corporation, managers have little incentive to work in the interests of the shareholders when this means working against their own self-interest. As a manager, wouldn't it be more fun to relax all day and freely eat in the company's gourmet

FIGURE 1.2   The Financial Functions Within a Corporation

The board of directors, representing the stockholders, controls the corporation and hires the top management team. A financial manager might hold any of the green-shaded positions, including that of chief financial officer (CFO). The controller oversees accounting and tax functions. The treasurer oversees more traditional finance functions, such as capital budgeting (making investment decisions), risk management (managing the firm's exposure to movements in the financial markets), and credit management (managing the terms and policies of any credit the firm extends to its suppliers and customers).

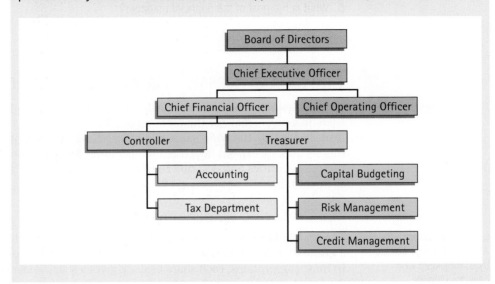

shirking Neglecting the responsibilities of managing the business.

perquisites Benefits provided free of charge to the managers of a corporation.

principal-agent problem When managers, despite being hired as the agents of shareholders, put their own self-interest ahead of the interests of the shareholders (the principals).

dining room? Unfortunately for shareholders, they benefit little by managers' **shirking** or consuming **perquisites**, which of course benefits managers considerably. Economists call this the **principal-agent problem**—when managers, despite being hired as the agents of shareholders, put their own self-interest ahead of the interests of those shareholders (also called the principals). Managers face the ethical dilemma of whether to do what is in their own best interests or adhere to their responsibility to put the interests of shareholders first. This problem is commonly addressed in practice by minimizing the number of decisions managers make that require putting their self-interest in conflict with the interests of the shareholders. For example, managers' compensation contracts are designed to ensure that most decisions in the shareholders' interests are also in the managers' interests; shareholders often tie the compensation of top managers to the corporation's profits or perhaps to its stock price. There is, however, a limitation to this strategy. By tying compensation too closely to performance, the shareholders might be asking managers to take on more risk than they are comfortable taking. As a result, the managers may not make decisions that the shareholders want them to, or finding talented managers willing to accept the job may be difficult. For example, biotech firms take big risks on drugs that fight cancer, AIDS, and other widespread diseases. The market for a successful drug is huge, but the risk of failure is high. Investors who put only some of their money in biotech may be comfortable with this risk, but a manager who has all of his or her compensation tied to the success of such a drug might opt to develop a less risky drug that has a smaller market.

Further potential for conflicts of interest and ethical considerations arise when some stakeholders in the corporation benefit from and others lose because of a decision.

stakeholder satisfaction
A corporate objective
that seeks to meet
the interests of all
stakeholders of the
corporation.

Shareholders and managers are two stakeholders in the corporation, but others include the regular employees, customers, suppliers, and the communities in which the company operates. Managers may decide to take the interests of other stakeholders into account in their decisions, such as keeping a loss-generating factory open because it is the main provider of jobs in a small town, paying above local market wages to factory workers in a developing country, or operating a plant at a higher environmental standard than local law mandates. In Japan and some European countries, this **stakeholder satisfaction** view seems to be more highly regarded than the shareholder wealth maximization view.

In many cases, though, these actions that benefit other stakeholders may also benefit the firm's shareholders by creating a more dedicated workforce, generating positive publicity with customers, enhancing the firm's reputation or brand, or other indirect effects. Thus, for the most part, stakeholder satisfaction is consistent with shareholder wealth maximization. In other instances, when these decisions benefit other stakeholders at shareholders' expense, they represent a form of corporate charity. Indeed, many if not most corporations explicitly donate (on behalf of their shareholders) to local and global causes. Shareholders often approve of such actions, even though they are costly. Whether such donations increase the reputation and goodwill of the firm and thus increase shareholder wealth or cost more than the benefits and so reduce shareholder wealth is an open question. While it is the manager's job to make decisions that maximize shareholder value, shareholders—who own the firm—also want the firm's actions to reflect their moral and ethical values and enhance the long-term reputation of the corporation. Of course, shareholders may not have identical preferences in these matters, leading to potential sources of conflict.

The CEO's Performance. Another way shareholders can encourage managers to work in the interests of shareholders is to discipline them if they do not. If shareholders are unhappy with a CEO's performance, they could, in principle, pressure the board to oust the CEO. Disney's Michael Eisner, Hewlett Packard's Carly Fiorina, and Home Depot's Robert Nardelli were all forced to resign by their boards. Despite these high-profile examples, directors and top executives are rarely replaced through a grassroots shareholder uprising. Instead, dissatisfied investors often choose to sell their shares. Of course, somebody must be willing to buy the shares from the dissatisfied shareholders. If enough shareholders are dissatisfied, the only way to entice investors to buy (or hold) the shares is to offer them a low price. Similarly, investors who see a well-managed corporation will want to purchase shares, which drives the stock price up. Thus, the stock price of the corporation is a barometer for corporate leaders that continuously gives them feedback on the shareholders' opinion of their performance.

When the stock performs poorly, the board of directors might react by replacing the CEO. In some corporations, however, the senior executives might be entrenched because boards of directors do not have the independence or motivation to replace them. Often the reluctance to fire results when the board is composed of people who are close friends of the CEO and lack objectivity. In corporations in which the CEO is entrenched and doing a poor job, the expectation of continued poor performance will cause the stock price to be low. Low stock prices create a profit opportunity. In a **hostile takeover**, an individual or organization—sometimes known as a corporate raider—can purchase a large fraction of the company's stock and in doing so get enough votes to replace the board of directors and the CEO. With a new, superior management team, the stock is a much more attractive investment, which would probably result in a price rise and a profit for the corporate raider and the other shareholders. Although the words "hostile" and "raider" have negative connotations, corporate raiders themselves provide an important service to shareholders. The mere threat of being removed as a result of a hostile takeover is often enough to discipline bad managers and motivate boards of

hostile takeover A
situation in which an
individual or organization,
sometimes referred to
as a corporate raider,
purchases a large fraction
of a target corporation's
stock and in doing so gets
enough votes to replace
the target's board of
directors and its CEO.

stock market (also stock exchange or bourse) An organized market on which the shares of many corporations are traded.

directors to make difficult decisions. Consequently, the fact that a corporation's shares can be publicly traded creates a "market for corporate control" that encourages managers and boards of directors to act in the interests of their shareholders. If there is a dominant shareholder or a shareholder that owns a class of shares with multiple votes, it may be impossible for the market for corporate control to work as desired, because not enough shares can be purchased on the market to accumulate enough votes to change control. Shareholder rights activists point out this problem for many Canadian firms that have multiple voting classes or a dominant shareholder tied to management, so as investors we might want to reconsider investing in such firms.

Concept Check

6. How do shareholders control a corporation?

7. What types of jobs would a financial manager have in a corporation?

8. What ethical issues could confront a financial manager?

1.5 The Stock Market

In Section 1.3, we established the goal of the financial manager, shareholder wealth maximization: to maximize the wealth of the owners, the stockholders. The value of the owners' investments in the corporation is determined by the price of a share of the corporation's stock. Corporations can be private or public. A private corporation has a limited number of owners and there is no organized market for its shares, making it hard to determine the market price of its shares at any point in time. A public corporation has many owners and its shares trade on an organized market, called a **stock market** (or **stock exchange** or **bourse**). These markets provide *liquidity* for a company's shares and determine the market price for those shares. An investment is said to be **liquid** if it can easily be turned into cash by selling it immediately at a price at which it could be contemporaneously bought. An investor in a public company values the ability to turn his investment into cash easily and quickly by simply selling his shares on one of these markets. In this section, we provide an overview of the functioning of the major stock markets. The analysis and trading by participants in these markets provide an evaluation of financial managers' decisions that not only determine the stock price, but also provide feedback to the managers on their decisions.

liquid In reference to an investment, one that can easily be turned into cash because it can be sold immediately at a competitive market price.

primary market The market where new shares of stock are issued by a corporation and sold to investors.

secondary market Markets, such as the TSX, NYSE, or NASDAQ, where shares of a corporation are traded between investors without the involvement of the corporation.

The Largest Stock Markets

The largest stock market in the world is the New York Stock Exchange (NYSE). Billions of dollars of stock are exchanged every day on the NYSE. Rounding out the five largest markets in the world are the Tokyo Stock Exchange, the NASDAQ (US), the NYSE Euronext (Europe), and the London Stock Exchange. Based on 2009 year-end domestic market capitilization, the Toronto Stock Exchange (TSX Group) was the eighth largest exchange in the world. Figure 1.3 ranks the world's 20 largest stock exchanges by domestic market capitalization and value of trades for 2009.

All of these markets are *secondary markets*. The term **primary market** refers to a corporation issuing new shares of stock and selling them to investors. After this initial transaction between the corporation and investors, the shares continue to trade in a **secondary market** between investors without the involvement of the corporation. For example, if you wish to buy 100 shares of the Starbucks Coffee Company, you could place an order on the NASDAQ, where Starbucks trades under the ticker symbol SBUX. You would buy your shares from someone who already held shares of Starbucks, not from Starbucks itself.

FIGURE 1.3

Worldwide Stock Markets Ranked by Two Common Measures.

The 20 largest stock markets in the world ranked on (a) the total value of all domestic corporations on the market as of the end of 2009 and on (b) the total value of the volume of shares traded during the year 2009.

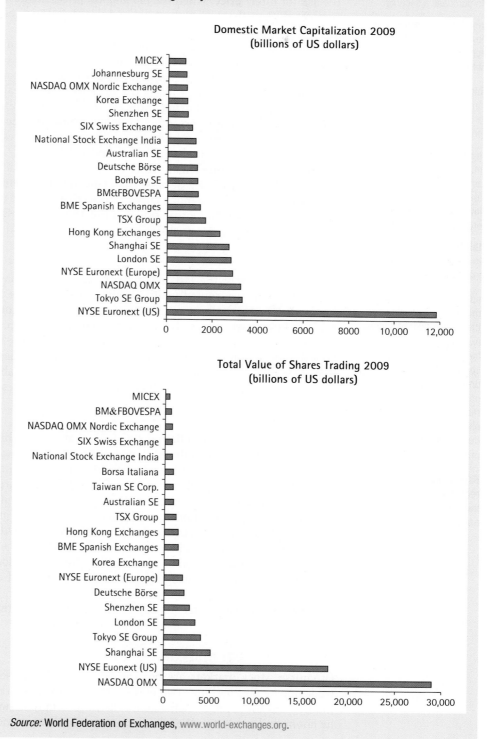

Source: World Federation of Exchanges, www.world-exchanges.org.

TSX

bid price The highest price in a market for which someone is willing to purchase a security.

ask (or **offer**) **price** The lowest price in a market for which someone is willing to sell a security.

bid-ask spread The amount by which the ask price exceeds the bid price.

transaction cost In most markets, an expense such as a broker commission and the bid-ask spread investors must pay in order to trade securities.

thinly traded In reference to a security, one that is infrequently traded.

specialists or market makers Individuals on the trading floor of a stock exchange who match buyers with sellers. These specialists are given preferential access to orders but must also stand ready to buy or sell shares on their own account at their posted bid and ask prices.

listing standards The requirements a company must meet to be traded on an exchange.

The TSX is an electronic exchange. Investors (individuals and institutions) can post orders onto the TSX trading system from anywhere. The highest price being quoted to buy a stock is called the **bid price**. The lowest price being quoted to sell a stock is called the **ask** (or **offer**) **price**. When the bid and ask prices are at the same price, the trade is completed, then the next highest bid and next lowest ask become the quoted bid and ask prices respectively.

Posted ask prices exceed the posted bid prices. This difference between the ask price and bid price is called the **bid-ask spread**. If you enter the market wanting to buy a stock, you can post your order, but until your order matches the ask price (the amount for which someone will sell the stock to you), no trade will take place. Because customers end up always buying at the ask (the higher price) and selling at the bid (the lower price), the bid-ask spread is an implicit **transaction cost** investors have to pay in order to trade. Companies that are more interesting to investors are frequently traded and many investors put in orders to buy and sell the stock. In these cases, the bid-ask spread is generally quite small. Other companies that attract fewer investors' interest are said to be **thinly traded**. Because not many investors want to trade these stocks, the bid-ask spreads tend to be much larger. Stocks that trade on the TSX tend to have lower bid-ask spreads than those that trade on the TSX Venture Exchange (an exchange for relatively small-company stocks).

NYSE

The NYSE is one of the last major stock exchanges to have an active trading floor to which orders are routed for the trading of shares. The NYSE also has **specialists** (or **market makers**) who are given preferential access to orders but must also stand ready to buy or sell shares at their posted bid and ask prices. Recently, the NYSE has combined electronic trading with the trading on the floor. It is likely that the role of floor trading and the importance of the specialist will decline as the need for a specialist to make a market in a company's stock is replaced by the ability of investors to access an electronic exchange and post their own bid and ask prices directly.

Listing Standards

Each exchange has its own **listing standards** that outline the requirements a company must meet to be traded on the exchange. These standards usually require that the company have enough shares outstanding for shareholders to have a liquid market and to be of interest to a broad set of investors. The NYSE's standards are more stringent than the TSX's standards, which are more stringent than the standards for listing on the TSX Venture Exchange. Traditionally, there has been a certain pride in being listed on the NYSE, and many Canadian companies list on the NYSE in addition to the TSX as a signal of their higher quality. Exchanges around the world compete actively over listings of companies, and the decision of where to list often comes down to which exchange the company's board believes will give its stockholders the best execution and liquidity for their trades. For example, the TSX is popular for energy-related companies while the NASDAQ is popular for technology-related companies (although many companies in many different industries trade on all these exchanges).

Other Financial Markets

Of course, stock markets are not the only financial markets. There are markets to trade practically anything. Two of the largest financial markets in the world, the bond market and the foreign exchange market, are simply networks of dealers connected by phone and computer. We will discuss each of these in more detail in later chapters (bonds in Chapters 6 and 14 and foreign exchange in Chapter 22). Commodities like oil, wheat, and canola are traded on commodity markets. *Derivative securities,* which are complicated financial products used to hedge risks, are traded in locations such as the Chicago Board Options Exchange and the Montreal Exchange (discussed in Chapters 20 and 21).

Concept Check

9. What advantage does a stock market provide to corporate investors?
10. What is the importance of a stock market to a financial manager?

 ## 1.6 Financial Institutions

The spread of the financial crisis from subprime mortgages in the United States to stock markets to traditional banks and businesses drew everyone's attention to *financial institutions* and their role in the economy. In general, **financial institutions** are entities that provide financial services, such as taking deposits, managing investments, brokering financial transactions, or making loans. In this section, we describe the key types of financial institutions and their function.

financial institutions
Entities that provide financial services, such as taking deposits, managing investments, brokering financial transactions, or making loans.

The Financial Cycle

Keeping straight the names and roles of the different types of financial institutions can be challenging. It is helpful to keep in mind the basic financial cycle, depicted in Figure 1.4,

FIGURE 1.4

The Financial Cycle

This figure depicts the basic financial cycle, which matches funds from savers to companies that have projects requiring funds and then returns the profits from those projects back to the savers.

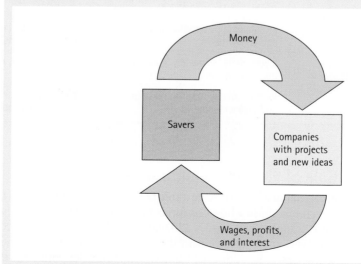

as context. In the financial cycle, (1) people invest and save their money, (2) that money, through loans and stock, flows to companies that use it to fund growth through new products, generating profits and wages, and (3) the money then flows back to the savers and investors. All financial institutions play a role at some point in this cycle of connecting money with ideas and returning the profits back to the investors.

Types of Financial Institutions

Table 1.3 summarizes the major categories of financial institutions, provides examples of representative firms, and details the institutions' sources and uses of funds.

One major financial institution not listed in the table is an investment bank, because it is involved in many different aspects of the financial cycle. Investment banks operate as the "grease for the wheels" of the financial system, brokering many of the transactions that take place between institutions and between companies and institutions. Finally, financial conglomerates, sometimes referred to as financial services firms, combine more than one type of institution. Examples include the largest Canadian banks, which operate in commercial banking, insurance, mutual funds, investment banking, and other areas.

TABLE 1.3   Financial Institutions and Their Role in the Financial Cycle

Institution	Money Source	Money Use
Banks and Credit Unions *CIBC, Royal Bank*	Deposits (Savings)	Loans to people and businesses
Insurance Companies *Great West Life, Manulife Financial*	Premiums and investment earnings	Invests mostly in bonds and some stocks, using the investment income to pay claims
Mutual Funds *AGF Investments, CI Investments*	People's investments (savings)	Buys stocks, bonds, and other financial instruments on behalf of its investors
Pension Funds *Ontario Teachers Pension Plan, Caisse de dépôt et placement du Québec*	Retirement savings contributed through the workplace	Similar to mutual funds, except with the purpose of providing retirement income
Hedge Funds *Bridgewater, Soros Fund*	Investments by wealthy individuals and endowments	Invests in any kind of investment with an attempt to maximize returns for relatively low risk
Venture Capital Funds *Covington Capital, GrowthWorks*	Investments by wealthy individuals and endowments	Invests in start-up, entrepreneurial firms
Private Equity Funds *KKR, Onex*	Investments by wealthy individuals and endowments	Purchases whole companies by using a small amount of equity and borrowing the rest.

Role of Financial Institutions

Financial institutions have a role beyond moving funds from those who have extra funds (savers) to those who need funds (borrowers and firms): they also move funds through time. Suppose you need a $20,000 car loan. You need $20,000 now but do not have it. However, you will have it in the future, as you earn a salary. The financial institution, in this case a bank or credit union, helps transfer your future salary into funds today by issuing you a loan.

Financial institutions also help spread out risk bearing. Insurance companies essentially pool premiums together from policyholders and pay the claims of those who have an accident, fire, or medical need, or who die. This process spreads the financial risk of these events out across a large pool of policyholders and the investors in the insurance company. Similarly, mutual funds and pension funds take your savings and spread them out among the stocks and bonds of many different companies, limiting your risk exposure to any one company.

While you may have seen coverage of the stock markets and discussion of financial institutions on the news, it is unlikely that you have had any exposure to the finance function within the firm. In this chapter, we provided a sense of what corporate finance is all about, what a financial manager does, and the importance of stock markets and financial institutions. In the coming chapters, you will learn how to make financial management decisions and how to use financial market information. We will develop the tools of financial analysis and a clear understanding of when to apply them and why they work.

Concept Check

11. What is the basic financial cycle?

12. What are the three main roles financial institutions play?

MyFinanceLab   Here is what you should know after reading this chapter. MyFinanceLab will help you identify what you know, and where to go when you need to practice.

Key Points	Terms	Online Practice Opportunities
1.1 Why Study Finance? ▶ Finance and financial decisions are everywhere in our daily lives. ▶ Many financial decisions are simple, but others are complex. All are tied together by the Valuation Principle—the foundation for financial decision making—which you will learn in this book.		
1.2 The Three Types of Firms ▶ There are three types of firms in Canada: sole proprietorships, partnerships, and corporations. ▶ Firms with unlimited personal liability include sole proprietorships and partnerships (for general partners). ▶ Firms with limited liability include limited partnerships (for limited partners but not for general partners) and corporations. ▶ A corporation is a legally defined artificial being (a judicial person or legal entity) that has many of the legal powers people have. It can enter into	business income trust, p. 9 corporation, p. 6 dividend payments, p. 7 energy trust, p. 9 equity, p. 7 equity holder, p. 7 flow-through entity, p. 9 general partnership, p. 6 income trust, p. 9 limited liability, p. 6 limited liability partnership, p. 6 limited partnership, p. 6	MyFinanceLab Study Plan 1.2

contracts, acquire assets, and incur obligations, and it enjoys protection against the seizure of its property.

▶ The shareholders in a corporation effectively must pay tax twice. The corporation pays tax once and then investors must pay personal tax on any funds that are distributed. A flow-through entity such as a real estate investment trust does not pay tax at the business level.

▶ The ownership of a corporation is divided into shares of stock collectively known as equity. Investors in these shares are called shareholders, stockholders, or equity holders.

real estate investment
trust (REIT), p. 9
shareholder, p. 7
sole proprietorship, p. 5
stock, p. 7
unit holders, p. 9

1.3 The Financial Manager

▶ The financial manager makes investing, financing, and cash flow management decisions.

▶ The goal of the financial manager is to maximize the wealth of the shareholders (maximize the stock price).

shareholder wealth
maximization, p. 12

MyFinanceLab
Study Plan 1.3

1.4 The Financial Manager's Place in the Corporation

▶ The ownership and control of a corporation are separate. Shareholders exercise their control indirectly through the board of directors.

board of directors, p. 13
chief executive officer
(CEO), p. 13
hostile takeover, p. 15
perquisites, p. 14
principal-agent
problem, p. 14
shirking, p. 14
stakeholder
satisfaction, p. 15

MyFinanceLab
Study Plan 1.4

1.5 The Stock Market

▶ The shares of public corporations are traded on stock markets. The shares of private corporations do not trade on a stock market.

▶ When a firm sells shares to investors, that is a primary market. The stock markets, such as the TSX and NYSE, are secondary markets where investors trade shares among each other.

ask price, p. 18
bid-ask spread, p. 18
bid price, p. 18
bourse, p. 16
liquid, p. 16
listing standards, p. 18
market makers, p. 18
primary market, p. 16
secondary market, p. 16
specialists, p. 18
stock exchange, p. 16
stock market, p. 16
thinly traded, p. 18
transaction cost, p. 18

MyFinanceLab
Study Plan 1.5

1.6 Financial Institutions

▶ In the basic financial cycle, money flows from savers and investors to companies and entrepreneurs with ideas, and then back to the savers and investors in the form of profits and interest.

▶ Financial institutions all play some role in this cycle.

▶ Financial institutions also help move money through time (e.g., loans against future wages) and spread risk across large investor bases.

financial institutions, p. 19

MyFinanceLab Study Plan 1.6

Problems

All problems in this chapter are available in MyFinanceLab.

The Three Types of Firms

1. What is the most important difference between a corporation and *all* other organization forms?

2. What does the phrase *limited liability* mean in a corporate context?

3. Which organizational forms give their owners limited liability?

4. What are the main advantages and disadvantages of organizing a firm as a corporation?

5. Explain the difference between a real estate corporation and a real estate investment trust (REIT).

 6. You are a shareholder in a corporation. The corporation earns $2.00 per share before taxes. Once it has paid taxes, it will distribute the rest of its earnings to you as a dividend. The corporate tax rate is 34%, the personal tax rate on dividend income is 18%, and the personal tax rate on ordinary income is 40%. How much is left for you after all taxes are paid?

 7. Repeat Problem 6 except assume the corporation is now a real estate investment trust (REIT) and you own units in the trust.

The Financial Manager

8. What is the most important type of decision that the financial manager makes?

9. Why do all shareholders agree on the same goal for the financial manager?

The Financial Manager's Place in the Corporation

10. Corporate managers work for the owners of the corporation. Consequently, corporate managers should make decisions that are in the interests of the owners, rather than in their own interests. What strategies are available to shareholders to help ensure that managers are motivated to act this way?

11. Think back to the last time you ate at an expensive restaurant where you paid the bill. Now think about the last time you ate at a similar restaurant, but your parents paid the bill. Did you order more food (or more expensive food) when your parents paid? Explain how this relates to the principal-agent problem in corporations.

12. Suppose you are considering renting an apartment. You, the renter, can be viewed as an agent, while the company that owns the apartment can be viewed as the principal. What principal-agent conflicts do you anticipate? Suppose, instead, that you work for the apartment company. What features would you put into the lease agreement that would give the renter incentives to take good care of the apartment?

13. You are the CEO of a company and are considering entering into an agreement to have your company buy another company. You think the price might be too high, but you will be the CEO of the combined, much larger company. You know that when the company gets bigger, your pay and prestige will increase. What is the nature of the principal-agent problem here, and how is it related to ethical considerations?

14. Suppose your local supermarket manager decides that, to increase profit, milk held in the store's storage room will no longer be refrigerated. Milk on the display shelf will still be refrigerated. What stakeholders might this affect? Will the impact of this decision be positive or negative for the stakeholders? Will it be positive or negative for the shareholders? Explain.

The Stock Market

15. What is the difference between a public and a private corporation?

16. What is the difference between a primary and a secondary market?

17. Explain why the bid-ask spread is a transaction cost.

18. The following quote on Yahoo! stock appeared on September 6, 2011 on Yahoo! Finance:

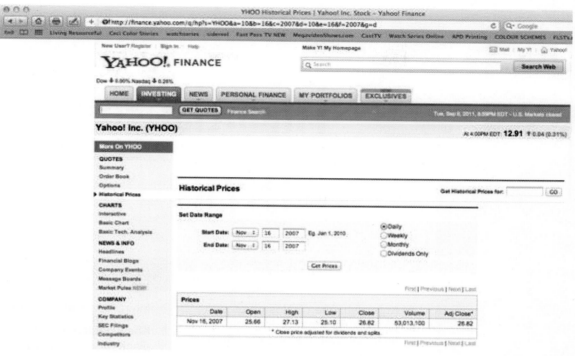

Source: Yahoo! Finance.

If you wanted to buy Yahoo!, what price would you pay? How much would you receive if you wanted to sell Yahoo!?

Introduction to Financial Statement Analysis

- Know why the disclosure of financial information through financial statements is critical to investors

- Understand the function of the balance sheet

- Use the balance sheet to analyze a firm

- Understand how the income statement is used

- Analyze a firm through its income statement, including using the DuPont Identity

- Interpret a statement of cash flows

- Know what management's discussion and analysis and the statement of shareholders' equity are

- Understand the main purpose and aspects of the Sarbanes-Oxley reforms following Enron and other financial scandals

INTERVIEW WITH Fatoumata Diané, CIBC World Markets

McGill University, 2010

"We frequently use comparable companies' analysis as a valuation tool."

As an investment banking analyst for CIBC World Markets in Montreal, Quebec, Fatoumata Diané works with a team of analysts offering advisory services for large clients looking to undertake a variety of transactions, including mergers and acquisitions, and debt and equity financing deals. Financial analysis is instrumental in helping her clients make decisions.

Fatoumata, who received a Bachelor of Commerce (Honours) degree in 2010 from McGill University, frequently makes use of the knowledge she gained from her finance courses. "My education has provided me with a solid base in financial statements analysis, which quickly came in handy on the job. I am responsible for doing the financial analysis that is instrumental in helping client companies in their decision making process. We frequently use comparable companies' analysis as a valuation tool."

The first step in valuing a company is assessing past performance and determining its current financial position using information contained in the publicly available financial statements. "I start by using information in the most recent financial statements to compute the enterprise value of the set of companies we are looking at. I do not limit my analysis to the summary statements. I read through notes, disclosures and management's discussion and analysis to check if significant one-time charges occurred."

Analyzing financial statements gives Fatoumata insight into a company's current financial position and its performance over time. "It is essential to develop a comprehensive understanding of the relationship between each financial statement, how they work and interact with one another, and where you can see the impact of transactions that flow through the business."

As we discussed in Chapter 1, anyone with money to invest is a potential investor who can own shares in a corporation. As a result, corporations are often widely held, with investors ranging from individuals who hold one share to large financial institutions that own millions of shares. For example, in 2010, International Business Machines Corporation (ticker symbol: IBM) had over 1.3 billion shares outstanding held by over 546,000 shareholders. Although the corporate organizational structure greatly facilitates the firm's access to investment capital, it also means that stock ownership is most investors' sole tie to the company. How, then, do investors learn enough about a company to know whether or not they should invest in it? One way firms evaluate their performance and communicate this information to investors is through their *financial statements*. Financial statements also enable financial managers to assess the success of their own firm and compare it to competitors.

Firms regularly issue financial statements to communicate financial information to the investment community. A detailed description of the preparation and analysis of these statements is sufficiently complicated that to do it justice would require an entire book. In this chapter, we briefly review the subject, emphasizing only the material that investors and corporate financial managers need in order to make the corporate finance decisions we discuss in the text.

We review the four main types of financial statements, present examples of these statements for a firm, and discuss where an investor or manager might find various types of information about the company. We also discuss some of the financial ratios used to assess a firm's performance and value. We close the chapter with a look at highly publicized financial reporting abuses at Enron.

Firms' Disclosure of Financial Information

financial statements
Accounting reports issued by a firm quarterly and/or annually present past performance information and a snapshot of the firm's assets and financing of those assets.

annual report The yearly summary of business sent by public companies to their shareholders that accompanies or includes the financial statement.

Financial statements are accounting reports issued by a firm periodically (usually quarterly and annually) that present past performance information and a snapshot of the firm's assets and the financing of those assets. Canadian public companies are required to file these reports (called interim financial statements and **annual reports**) with their provincial securities commissions. This process is centralized nationally through the System for Electronic Document Analysis and Retrieval (SEDAR). At www.sedar.com, Canadian company filings can be easily accessed. U.S. public companies are required to file their financial statements with the U.S. Securities and Exchange Commission (SEC) on a quarterly basis on form 10-Q and annually on form 10-K.[1] Companies in Canada and the United States must also send an annual report with their financial statements to their shareholders each year. Often, private companies also prepare financial statements, but they usually do not have to disclose these reports to the public. Financial statements are important tools with which investors, financial analysts, and other interested outside parties (such as creditors) obtain information about a corporation. They are also useful for managers within the firm as a source of information for the corporate financial decisions we discussed in the previous chapter. In this section, we examine the guidelines for preparing financial statements and introduce the different types of financial statements.

International Financial Reporting Standards

Generally Accepted Accounting Principles (GAAP) differ among countries. As a result, companies face tremendous accounting complexities when they operate internationally. Investors also face difficulty interpreting financial statements of foreign companies, which discourages them from investing abroad. As companies and capital markets become more global, however, interest in harmonization of accounting standards across countries has increased.

The most important harmonization project began in 1973 when representatives of 10 countries (including Canada) established the International Accounting Standards Committee. This effort led to the creation of the International Accounting Standards Board (IASB) in 2001, with headquarters in London. Now the IASB has issued a set of International Financial Reporting Standards (IFRS).

The IFRS are taking root throughout the world. The European Union (EU) approved an accounting regulation in 2002 requiring all publicly traded EU companies

to follow IFRS in their consolidated financial statements starting in 2005. Canadian publicly accountable enterprises (referred to as public companies from this point on) must follow IFRS in their financial statements beginning January 1, 2011. Many other countries have adopted IFRS for all listed companies, including Australia and several countries in Latin America and Africa. In fact, all major stock exchanges around the world accept IFRS except the United States and Japan, which maintain their local GAAP.

Convergence to IFRS in the United States is likely in the near future. In 2008, the SEC eliminated the requirement for foreign firms listing in U.S. markets to reconcile IFRS to U.S. GAAP. This is important for Canadian firms, as they will no longer have to do this reconciliation if their filings correspond to IFRS. In 2010, the SEC further affirmed its support of a single standard, with IFRS the preferred method. The SEC will study and revisit the issue in 2011; U.S. companies may start to report according to IFRS as soon as 2015 or 2016.

---

[1]The Securities and Exchange Commission was established by Congress in 1934 to regulate securities (e.g., stocks and bonds) issued to the public and the financial markets (exchanges) on which those securities trade.

Preparation of Financial Statements

Reports about a company's performance must be understandable and accurate. **GAAP** provide a conceptual framework including assumptions and qualitative characteristics that help standardize the format companies use when they prepare their reports. This standardization also makes it easier to compare the financial results of different firms.

Investors also need some assurance that the financial statements are prepared accurately. Corporations are required to hire a neutral third party, known as an **auditor**, to check the annual financial statements, ensure they are prepared according to GAAP, and provide evidence to support the reliability of the information.

Types of Financial Statements

Every public company is required to produce four financial statements: the *balance sheet,* the *statement of comprehensive income* (which includes the *income statement*), the *statement of cash flows,* and the *statement of changes in equity*. These financial statements provide investors and creditors with an overview of the firm's financial performance. In the sections that follow, we take a close look at the content of these financial statements.

Concept Check

1. What is the role of an auditor?

2. What are the four financial statements that all public companies must produce?

2.2 The Balance Sheet

The **balance sheet,** or statement of financial position,[2] lists the firm's *assets* and *liabilities,* providing a snapshot of the firm's financial position at a given point in time. Table 2.1 shows the balance sheet for a fictitious company, Global Corporation. Notice that the balance sheet is divided into two parts ("sides") with the assets on the left side and the liabilities on the right side:

1. The **assets** list the firm's cash, inventory, property, plant and equipment, and any other investments the company has made.

2. The **liabilities** show the firm's obligations to its creditors.

3. Also shown with liabilities on the right side of the balance sheet is the *shareholders' equity.* **Shareholders' equity,** the difference between the firm's assets and liabilities, is an accounting measure of the firm's net worth. For Global, the shareholders' equity has two parts: (1) *common stock,* the amount that shareholders have directly invested in the firm through purchasing stock from the company; and (2) *retained earnings,* which are profits made by the firm but retained within the firm and reinvested in assets or held as cash. We will take a more detailed look at retained earnings in our discussion of the statement of cash flows later in this chapter.

The assets on the left side show how the firm uses its capital (its investments), and the information on the right side summarizes the sources of capital, or how the firm

Generally Accepted Accounting Principles (GAAP) A common set of rules and a standard format for companies to use when they prepare their financial reports.

auditor A neutral third party, which corporations are required to hire, that checks a firm's annual financial statements to ensure they are prepared according to GAAP and provide evidence to support the reliability of the information.

balance sheet A list of a firm's assets and liabilities that provides a snapshot of the firm's financial position at a given point in time.

assets The cash, inventory, property, plant and equipment, and other investments a company has made.

liabilities A firm's obligations to its creditors.

shareholders' equity An accounting measure of a firm's net worth that represents the difference between the firm's assets and its liabilities.

---

[2]In IFRS, the balance sheet is referred to as the *statement of financial position.*

Assets	2011	2010	Liabilities and Shareholders' Equity	2011	2010
Current Assets			Current Liabilities		
Cash	23.2	20.5	Accounts payable	29.2	26.5
Accounts receivable	18.5	13.2	Notes payable/short-term debt	5.5	3.2
Inventories	15.3	14.3			
Total current assets	57.0	48.0	Total current liabilities	34.7	29.7
Long-Term Assets			Long-Term Liabilities		
Net property, plant, and equipment	113.1	80.9	Long-term debt	113.2	78.0
Total long-term assets	113.1	80.9	Total long-term liabilities	113.2	78.0
			Total Liabilities	**147.9**	**107.7**
			Shareholders' Equity		
			Common stock	8.0	8.0
			Retained earnings	14.2	13.2
			Total Shareholders' Equity	**22.2**	**21.2**
Total Assets	**170.1**	**128.9**	**Total Liabilities and Shareholders' Equity**	**170.1**	**128.9**

TABLE 2.1

Global Corporation Balance Sheet for 2011 and 2010

raises the money it needs. Because of the way shareholders' equity is calculated, the left and right sides must balance:

The Balance Sheet Identity

$$\text{Assets} = \text{Liabilities} + \text{Shareholders, Equity} \qquad (2.1)$$

In Table 2.1, total assets for 2011 ($170.1 million) are equal to total liabilities ($147.9 million) plus shareholders' equity ($22.2 million).

We now examine the firm's assets, liabilities, and shareholders' equity in more detail. Finally, we evaluate the firm's financial standing by analyzing the information contained in the balance sheet.

Assets

In Table 2.1, Global's assets are divided into *current* and *long-term assets*. We discuss each in turn.

current assets Cash or assets that could be converted into cash within one year.

Current Assets. **Current assets** are either cash or assets that could be converted into cash within one year. This category includes the following:

marketable securities Short-term, low-risk investments that can be easily sold and converted to cash.

1. Cash and other **marketable securities**, which are short-term, low-risk investments that can be easily sold and converted to cash (such as money market investments, like government debt, that mature within a year)

accounts receivable Amounts owed to a firm by customers who have purchased goods or services on credit.

2. **Accounts receivable**, which are amounts owed to the firm by customers who have purchased goods or services on credit

inventories A firm's raw materials as well as its work in progress and finished goods.

3. **Inventories**, which are composed of raw materials as well as work in progress and finished goods

4. Other current assets, which is a catch-all category that includes items such as prepaid expenses (expenses that have been paid in advance, such as rent or insurance)

long-term assets Assets that produce tangible benefits for more than one year.

Long-Term Assets. Assets such as real estate or machinery that produce tangible benefits for more than one year are called **long-term assets**. If Global spends $2 million on new equipment, this $2 million will be included with net property, plant, and equipment under long-term assets on the balance sheet. Because equipment tends to wear out or become obsolete over time, Global will reduce the value recorded for this equipment through a yearly deduction called **depreciation** according to a depreciation schedule that

depreciation A yearly deduction a firm makes from the value of its fixed assets (other than land) over time, according to a depreciation schedule that depends on an asset's life span.

depends on an asset's life span. Depreciation is not an actual cash expense that the firm pays; it is a way of recognizing that buildings and equipment wear out and thus become less valuable the older they get. The **book value** of an asset is equal to its acquisition cost less accumulated depreciation. The figures for net property, plant, and equipment show the total book value of these assets.

Other long-term assets can include such items as property not used in business operations, start-up costs in connection with a new business, trademarks and patents, property held for sale, and goodwill. The sum of all the firm's assets is the total assets at the bottom of the left side of the balance sheet in Table 2.1.

Liabilities

We now examine the liabilities shown on the right side of the balance sheet, which are divided into *current* and *long-term liabilities*.

Current Liabilities. Liabilities that will be satisfied within one year are known as **current liabilities**. They include the following:

1. **Accounts payable**, the amounts owed to suppliers for products or services purchased with credit

2. **Notes payable** and **short-term debt**, loans that must be repaid in the next year. Any repayment of long-term debt that will occur within the next year would also be listed here as current maturities of long-term debt.

3. Accrual items, such as salary or taxes, that are owed but have not yet been paid, and deferred or unearned revenue, which is revenue that has been received for products that have not yet been delivered

The difference between current assets and current liabilities is the firm's **net working capital**, the capital available in the short term to run the business:

$$\text{Net Working Capital} = \text{Current Assets} - \text{Current Liabilities} \qquad (2.2)$$

For example, in 2011, Global's net working capital totaled $22.3 million ($57.0 million in current assets—$34.7 million in current liabilities). Firms with low (or negative) net working capital may face a shortage of funds. In such cases, the liabilities due in the short term exceed the company's cash and expected payments on receivables.

Long-Term Liabilities. Long-term liabilities are liabilities that extend beyond one year. When a firm needs to raise funds to purchase an asset or make an investment, it may borrow those funds through a long-term loan. That loan would appear on the balance sheet as **long-term debt**, which is any loan or debt obligation with a maturity of more than a year.

Shareholders' Equity

The sum of the current liabilities and long-term liabilities is total liabilities. The difference between the firm's assets and liabilities is the *shareholders' equity*; it is also called the **book value of equity**. As we stated earlier, it represents the net worth of the firm from an accounting perspective.

Ideally, the balance sheet would provide us with an accurate assessment of the true value of the firm's equity. Unfortunately, this is unlikely to be the case. First, many of the assets listed on the balance sheet are valued based on their historical cost rather than their true value today. For example, an office building is listed on the balance sheet according to its historical cost less its accumulated depreciation. But the actual value of the office building today may be very different than this amount; in fact, it may be much

book value The acquisition cost of an asset less its accumulated depreciation.

current liabilities Liabilities that will be satisfied within one year.

accounts payable The amounts owed to creditors for products or services purchased with credit.

notes payable, short-term debt Loans that must be repaid in the next year.

net working capital The difference between a firm's current assets and current liabilities that represents the capital available in the short term to run the business.

long-term debt Any loan or debt obligation with a maturity of more than a year.

book value of equity The difference between the book value of a firm's assets and its liabilities; also called shareholders' equity, it represents the net worth of a firm from an accounting perspective.

more than the amount the firm paid for it years ago. The same is true for other property, plant, and equipment: the true value today of an asset may be very different from, and even exceed, its book value. A second, and probably more important, problem is that *many of the firm's valuable assets are not captured on the balance sheet.* Consider, for example, the expertise of the firm's employees, the firm's reputation in the marketplace, the relationships with customers and suppliers, and the quality of the management team. All these assets add to the value of the firm but do not appear on the balance sheet.

For these reasons, the book value of equity is an inaccurate assessment of the actual value of the firm's equity. Thus, it is not surprising that the book value of equity will often differ substantially from the amount investors are willing to pay for the equity. The total market value of a firm's equity equals the market price per share times the number of shares, referred to as the company's **market capitalization**. The market value of a stock does not depend on the historical cost of the firm's assets; instead, it depends on what investors expect those assets to produce in the future. To see the difference, think about what happens when a company like Bombardier unveils a new plane. If investors have favourable expectations about future cash flows from selling those planes, the stock price will increase immediately, elevating Bombardier's market value. However, the revenue from selling the planes will be reflected in Bombardier's financial statements only when the company actually sells them.

market capitalization
The total market value of equity; equals the market price per share times the number of shares.

EXAMPLE 2.1

Market Versus Book Value

Problem
If Global has 3.6 million shares outstanding, and these shares are trading for a price of $10.00 per share, what is Global's market capitalization? How does the market capitalization compare to Global's book value of equity?

Solution

▶ **Plan**
Market capitalization is equal to price per share times shares outstanding. We can find Global's book value of equity at the bottom of the right side of its balance sheet.

▶ **Execute**
Global's market capitalization is 3.6 million shares × 10.00/share = $36 million. This market capitalization is significantly higher than Global's book value of equity of $22.2 million.

▶ **Evaluate**
Global must have sources of value that do not appear on the balance sheet. These include potential opportunities for growth, the quality of the management team, relationships with suppliers and customers, etc.

Finally, we note that the book value of equity can be negative (liabilities exceed assets) and that a negative book value of equity is not necessarily an indication of poor performance. Successful firms are often able to borrow in excess of the book value of their assets because creditors recognize that the market value of the assets is far higher. For example, in June 2005, Amazon.com had total liabilities of $2.6 billion and a book value of equity of –$64 million. At the same time, the market value of its equity was over $15 billion. Clearly, investors recognized that Amazon's assets were worth far more than the book value reported on the balance sheet. By 2010, several years of strong growth had brought its book value of equity to over $5 billion and its market value of equity to more than $50 billion!

Concept Check

3. What is depreciation designed to capture?

4. The book value of a company's assets usually does not equal the market value of those assets. What are some reasons for this difference?

Balance Sheet Analysis

liquidation value The value of a firm after its assets are sold and liabilities paid.

What can we learn from analyzing a firm's balance sheet? Although the book value of a firm's equity is not a good estimate of its true value as an ongoing firm, it is sometimes used as an estimate of the **liquidation value** of the firm, the value that would be left after its assets were sold and liabilities paid. We can also learn a great deal of useful information from a firm's balance sheet that goes beyond the book value of the firm's equity. We now discuss analyzing the balance sheet to assess the firm's value, its leverage, and its short-term cash needs.

Market-to-Book Ratio

market-to-book ratio (price-to-book [P/B] ratio) The ratio of a firm's market (equity) capitalization to the book value of its shareholders' equity.

In Example 2.1, we compared the market and book values of Global's equity. A common way to make this comparison is to compute the **market-to-book ratio** (also called the **price-to-book [P/B] ratio**), which is the ratio of a firm's market capitalization to the book value of shareholders' equity:

$$\text{Market-to-Book Ratio} = \frac{\text{Market Value of Equity}}{\text{Book Value of Equity}} \tag{2.3}$$

It is one of many financial ratios used to evaluate a firm. The market-to-book ratio for most successful firms substantially exceeds 1, indicating that the value of the firm's assets when put to use exceeds their historical cost (or liquidation value). The ratio will vary across firms due to differences in fundamental firm characteristics as well as the value added by management. Thus, this ratio is one way a company's stock price provides feedback to its managers on the market's assessment of their decisions.

value stocks Firms with low market-to-book ratios.

growth stocks Firms with high market-to-book ratios.

In mid 2006, Ford Motor Company (ticker symbol: F) had a market-to-book ratio of 0.89, a reflection of investors' assessment that many of Ford's plants and other assets were unlikely to be profitable and were worth less than their book value. In the following years, Ford had such large losses that its book value of equity fell below zero and the market-to-book ratio fell to −35.57 by late 2010. In 2010, the average market-to-book ratio for large U.S. firms was close to 4.0. Analysts often classify firms with low market-to-book ratios as **value stocks**, and those with high market-to-book ratios as **growth stocks**. Negative market-to-book ratios (like Ford's in 2010) are not considered meaningful, because we normally associate a higher ratio with a better assessment of a firm's future performance. With a negative market-to-book ratio, a higher ratio (close to zero) can occur when the market value of a firm is close to zero or when the book value of equity is far below zero. A near-zero market-to-book value is consistent with expectations that the firm will probably not survive. In contrast, a firm with a book value of equity far below zero may be a turnaround prospect and its future may be quite bright. The implication of a negative market-to-book value ratio is simply not clear.

Debt-Equity Ratio

leverage A measure of the extent to which a firm relies on debt as a source of financing.

debt-equity ratio The ratio of a firm's total amount of short- and long-term debt (including current maturities) to the value of its equity, which may be calculated based on market or book values.

Another important piece of information that we can learn from a firm's balance sheet is the firm's **leverage**, or the extent to which it relies on debt as a source of financing. The **debt-equity ratio** is a common ratio used to assess a firm's leverage that we calculate by dividing the total amount of short- and long-term debt (including current maturities) by the total shareholders' equity:

$$\text{Debt-Equity Ratio} = \frac{\text{Total Debt}}{\text{Total Equity}} \tag{2.4}$$

We can calculate this ratio using either book or market values for equity and debt. From Table 2.1, note Global's debt in 2011 includes notes payable ($5.5 million) and long-term debt ($113.2 million), for a total of $118.7 million. Therefore, using the book value of equity, its *book* debt-equity ratio is 118.7/22.2 = 5.3. Note the large increase from 2010, when the book debt-equity ratio was only (3.2 + 78)/21.2 = 3.8.

Because of the difficulty interpreting the book value of equity, the book debt-equity ratio is not especially useful. It is more informative to compare the firm's debt to the market value of its equity. Global's debt-equity ratio in 2010, using the market value of equity (from Example 2.1), is 118.7/36 = 3.3, which means Global's debt is a bit more than triple the market value of its equity.[3] As we will see later in the text, a firm's *market* debt-equity ratio has important consequences for the risk and return of its stock.

Enterprise Value

enterprise value The total market value of a firm's equity and debt, less the value of its cash and marketable securities. It measures the value of the firm's underlying business.

A firm's market capitalization measures the market value of the firm's equity, or the value that remains after the firm has paid its debts. But what is the value of the business itself? The **enterprise value** of a firm assesses the value of the underlying business assets, unencumbered by debt and separate from any cash and marketable securities. We compute it as follows:

$$\text{Enterprise Value} = \text{Market Value of Equity} + \text{Debt} - \text{Cash} \qquad (2.5)$$

For example, given its market capitalization from Example 2.1, Global's enterprise value in 2011 is 36 + 118.7 − 23.2 = $131.5 million. We can interpret the enterprise value as the cost to take over the business. That is, it would cost 36 + 118.7 = $154.7 million to buy all of Global's equity and pay off its debts. Because we would acquire Global's $23.2 million in cash, the net cost is only 154.7 − 23.2 = $131.5 million.

EXAMPLE 2.2

Computing Enterprise Value

Problem

On December 31, 2009, Maple Leaf Foods Inc. (ticker symbol: MFI) had a share price of $11.67, 136.8 million shares outstanding, a market-to-book ratio of 1.34, a book debt-equity ratio of 0.88, and cash of $29 million. What was Maple Leaf's market capitalization? What was its enterprise value?

Solution

▶ Plan

Share Price	$11.67
Shares Outstanding	136.8 mllion
Market-to-Book	1.34
Cash	$29 million
Debt-to-Equity (Book)	0.88

We will solve the problem using Equation 2.5: Enterprise Value = Market Value of Equity + Debt − Cash. We can compute the market capitalization by multiplying the share price by the shares outstanding. We are given the amount of cash. We are not given the debt directly, but we are given the book debt-equity ratio. If we knew the book value of equity, we could use the ratio to infer the value of the debt. Since we can compute the market value of equity (market capitalization) and we have the market-to-book ratio, we can compute the book value of equity, so that is the last piece of information we will need.

---

[3]In this calculation, we have compared the market value of equity to the book value of debt. Strictly speaking, it would be best to use the market value of debt. But because the market value of debt is generally not very different from its book value, this distinction is often ignored in practice.

> ▶ **Execute**
> Maple Leaf had a market capitalization of $11.67 × 136.8 million shares = $1.596 billion. Since Maple Leaf's market-to-book = 1.34 = $1.596 billion /book equity, then book equity = $1.596 billion /1.34 = $1.19 billion. Given that the book equity is $1.19 billion and a book debt-equity ratio of 0.88, the total value of Maple Leaf's debt is $1.19 billion × 0.88 = $1.048 billion.
>
> ▶ **Evaluate**
> Thus, Maple Leaf's enterprise value was $1.596 + $1.048 − 0.029 = $2.615 billion.

Other Balance Sheet Information

current ratio The ratio of current assets to current liabilities.

quick ratio ("acid-test" ratio) The ratio of current assets other than inventory to current liabilities.

Creditors often compare a firm's current assets and current liabilities to assess whether the firm has sufficient working capital to meet its short-term needs. This comparison is sometimes summarized in the firm's **current ratio**, the ratio of current assets to current liabilities, or its **quick ratio ("acid-test" ratio),** the ratio of current assets other than inventory to current liabilities. A higher current or quick ratio implies less risk of the firm experiencing a cash shortfall in the near future:

$$\text{Current Ratio} = \frac{\text{Current Assets}}{\text{Current Liabilities}} \qquad (2.6)$$

$$\text{Quick Ratio} = \frac{\text{Current Assets} - \text{Inventory}}{\text{Current Liabilities}} \qquad (2.7)$$

Analysts also use the information on the balance sheet to watch for trends that could provide information regarding the firm's future performance. For example, an unusual increase in inventory could be an indicator that the firm is having difficulty selling its products. The market-to-book ratio is an indicator of potential growth and of managers' ability to generate value from the firm's assets above their historical cost. We can assess a firm's financial health by looking at trends in leverage through analysis of its debt-equity ratio and equity multiplier. Increasing ratios may indicate a problem in meeting borrowing obligations in the future, adding to the risk of the firm. Deteriorating current and quick ratios might indicate similar problems with respect to paying short-term obligations as they come due, such as amounts owing to suppliers of goods and services.

5. What does a high debt-equity ratio tell you?

6. What is a firm's enterprise value?

2.4 The Income Statement

income statement A list of a firm's revenues and expenses over a period of time.

net income or earnings The last or "bottom" line of a firm's income statement that is a measure of the firm's income over a period of time.

When you want someone to get to the point, you might ask them for the "bottom line." This expression comes from the *income statement*. The **income statement** lists the firm's revenues and expenses over a period of time. The last or "bottom" line of the income statement shows the firm's **net income**, which is a measure of its profitability during the period. The income statement is sometimes called a *profit and loss*, or *"P&L,"* statement, and the net income is also referred to as the firm's **earnings**. In this section, we examine the components of the income statement in detail and introduce ratios we can use to analyze this data.

Table 2.2 shows Global's income statement for 2011 and 2010.

TABLE 2.2	GLOBAL CORPORATION Income Statement Year ended December 31 (in $ millions)		
Global Corporation		**2011**	**2010**
	Net sales	186.7	176.1
	Cost of sales	−153.4	−147.3
	Gross Profit	33.3	28.8
	Selling, general, and administrative expenses	−13.5	−13
	Research and development	−8.2	−7.6
	Depreciation and amortization	−1.2	−1.1
	Operating Income	10.4	7.1
	Other income	—	—
	Earnings Before Interest and Taxes (EBIT)	10.4	7.1
	Interest income (expense)	−7.7	−4.6
	Pretax Income	2.7	2.5
	Taxes	−0.7	−0.6
	Net Income	2.0	1.9
	Earnings per share:	$0.56	$0.53
	Diluted earnings per share:	$0.53	$0.50

Earnings Calculations

Whereas the balance sheet shows the firm's assets and liabilities at a given point in time, the income statement shows the flow of revenues and expenses generated by those assets and liabilities between two dates. We examine each category on Global's statement.

gross profit The third line of an income statement that represents the difference between a firm's sales revenues and its costs.

Gross Profit. The first two lines of the income statement list the revenues from sales of products and the costs incurred to make and sell the products. Note that in accounting terms *revenues* and *net sales* are often used interchangeably. Net sales is simply gross sales minus any returns, discounts, and allowances. We will simply use the term *sales* from here on. The third line is **gross profit**, the difference between sales revenues and the costs.

Operating Expenses. The next group of items is operating expenses. These are expenses from the ordinary course of running the business that are not directly related to producing the goods or services being sold. They include administrative expenses and overhead, salaries, marketing costs, and research and development expenses. The third type of operating expense, depreciation and amortization (a charge that captures the change in value of acquired assets), is not an actual cash expense but represents an estimate of the costs that arise from wear and tear or obsolescence of the firm's assets.[4] The firm's gross profit net of operating expenses is called **operating income**.

operating income A firm's gross profit less its operating expenses.

Earnings Before Interest and Taxes. We next include other sources of income or expenses that arise from activities that are not the central part of a company's business. Cash flows from the firm's financial investments are one example of other income that

---

[4]Depreciation and amortization are not deductible for tax purposes. Instead, the Canada Revenue Agency (CRA) uses capital cost allowance (CCA) for tax purposes. CCA rates vary depending on the asset type (or class) and cover tangible and intangible assets (e.g., patents).

would be listed here. After we have adjusted for other sources of income or expenses, we have the firm's earnings before interest and taxes, or **EBIT**.

EBIT A firm's earnings before interest and taxes are deducted.

Pretax and Net Income. From EBIT, we deduct the interest paid on outstanding debt to compute Global's pre-tax income, and then we deduct corporate taxes to determine the firm's net income.

Net income represents the total earnings of the firm's equity holders. It is often reported on a per-share basis as the firm's **earnings per share (EPS)**, which we compute by dividing net income by the total number of shares outstanding:

earnings per share (EPS) A firm's net income divided by the total number of shares outstanding.

$$\text{EPS} = \frac{\text{Net Income}}{\text{Shares Outstanding}} = \frac{\$2.0 \text{ million}}{3.6 \text{ million shares}} = 0.56 \text{ per share} \quad (2.8)$$

Although Global has only 3.6 million shares outstanding as of the end of 2011, the number of shares outstanding may grow if Global has made commitments that would cause it to issue more shares. Consider these two examples:

stock options Right to buy a certain number of shares of stock by a specific date at a specific price.

1. Suppose Global compensates its employees or executives with **stock options** that give the holder the right to buy a certain number of shares by a specific date at a specific price. If employees "exercise" these options, the company issues new stock and the number of shares outstanding will grow.

convertible bonds Corporate bonds with a provision that gives the bondholder an option to convert each bond owned into a fixed number of shares of common stock.

2. The number of shares may also grow if the firm issues **convertible bonds**, a form of debt that can be converted to shares of common stock.

In the cases of stock options and convertible bonds, because there will be more total shares to divide the same earnings, this growth in the number of shares is referred to as **dilution**. Firms disclose the potential for dilution from options they have awarded by reporting **diluted EPS**, which shows the earnings per share the company would have if the stock options were exercised. For example, if Global has awarded options for 200,000 shares of stock to its key executives, its diluted EPS is $2.0 million/3.8 million shares = $0.53.

dilution An increase in the total number of shares that will divide a fixed amount of earnings.

diluted EPS A firm's disclosure of its potential for dilution from options it has awarded.

Concept Check

7. What do a firm's earnings measure?
8. What is meant by dilution?

2.5 Income Statement Analysis

The income statement provides very useful information regarding the profitability of a firm's business and how it relates to the value of the firm's shares. We now discuss several ratios that are often used to evaluate a firm's performance and value.

Profitability Ratios

We introduce three profitability ratios: *gross margin, operating margin,* and *net profit margin.*

gross margin The ratio of gross profit to revenues (sales), it reflects the ability of the company to sell a product for more than the sum of the direct costs of making it.

Gross Margin. The **gross margin** of a firm is the ratio of gross profit to revenues (sales):

$$\text{Gross Margin } = \frac{\text{Gross Profit}}{\text{Sales}} \quad (2.9)$$

The gross margin simply reflects the ability of the company to sell a product for more than the sum of the direct costs of making it. All of the firm's other expenses of doing business (those not directly related to producing the goods sold) must be covered by this margin.

In 2011, Global's gross profit was $33.3 million and its sales were $186.7 million, for a gross margin of 33.3/186.7 = 17.84%.

Operating Margin. Because operating income reflects all of the expenses of doing business, another important profitability ratio is the **operating margin**, the ratio of operating income to revenues:

$$\text{Operating Margin} = \frac{\text{Operating Income}}{\text{Total Sales}} \quad (2.10)$$

operating margin The ratio of operating income to revenues, it reveals how much a company has earned from each dollar of sales before interest and taxes are deducted.

The operating margin reveals how much a company earns before interest and taxes from each dollar of sales. Global's operating margin in 2011 was 10.4/186.7 = 5.57%, an increase from its 2010 operating margin of 7.1/176.1 = 4.03%. By comparing operating margins across firms within an industry, we can assess the relative efficiency of firms' operations. For example, in 2009, Air Canada (ticker symbol: AC.B) had an operating margin of –3.2% (i.e., it lost 3 cents for each dollar in revenues). However, competitor Westjet (ticker symbol: WJA) had an operating margin of 9.2%.

Differences in operating margins can also result from differences in strategy. For example, in 2010, Canadian Tire Corporation (ticker symbol: CTC) had an operating margin of 5.52% while Lululemon Athletica Inc. had an operating margin of 19.1%. In this case, Canadian Tire's lower operating margin is not a result of its inefficiency but is part of its strategy of offering lower prices to sell common products in high volume. Indeed, Canadian Tire's sales were more than 19 times higher than those of Lululemon.

net profit margin The ratio of net income to revenues, it shows the fraction of each dollar in revenues that is available to equity holders after the firm pays its expenses, plus interest and taxes.

Net Profit Margin. A firm's **net profit margin** is the ratio of net income to revenues:

$$\text{Net Profit Margin} = \frac{\text{Net Income}}{\text{Total Sales}} \quad (2.11)$$

The net profit margin shows the fraction of each dollar in revenues that is available to equity holders after the firm pays its expenses, plus interest and taxes. Global's net profit margin in 2011 was 2.0/186.7 = 1.07%. Differences in net profit margins can be due to differences in efficiency, but they can also result from differences in leverage (the firm's reliance on debt financing), which determines the amount of interest payments.

Asset Efficiency

A financial manager can use the combined information in the firm's income statement and balance sheet to gauge how efficiently his or her firm is using its assets. A first broad measure of efficiency is asset turnover, the ratio of sales to total assets:

$$\text{Asset Turnover} = \frac{\text{Sales}}{\text{Total Assets}} \quad (2.12)$$

Low values of asset turnover indicate that the firm is not generating much revenue (sales) per dollar of assets. In 2011, Global's $170.1 million in assets generated $186.7 million in sales, for an asset turnover ratio of 1.1. Since total assets includes assets, such as cash, that are not directly involved in generating sales, Global's manager might also look at Global's fixed asset turnover, which is equal to sales divided by fixed assets:

$$\text{Fixed Asset Turnover} = \frac{\text{Sales}}{\text{Fixed Assets}} \quad (2.13)$$

Global's fixed assets in 2011 were $113.1 million worth of property, plant, and equipment, yielding a fixed asset turnover of 1.7 (= $186.7/$113.1). Low asset turnover ratios indicate that the firm is generating relatively few sales given the amount of assets it employs.

accounts receivable days (average collection period or days sales outstanding) An expression of a firm's accounts receivable in terms of the number of days' worth of sales that the accounts receivable represents.

accounts payable days An expression of a firm's accounts payable in terms of the number of days' worth of cost of goods sold that the accounts payable represents.

inventory days An expression of a firm's inventory in terms of the number of days' worth of cost of goods sold that the inventory represents.

inventory turnover ratio Sales divided by either the latest cost of inventory or the average inventory over the year, it shows how efficiently companies turn their inventory into sales.

EBITDA A computation of a firm's earnings before interest, taxes, depreciation, and amortization are deducted.

interest coverage ratio or times interest earned (TIE) ratio An assessment by lenders of a firm's leverage, it is equal to a measure of earnings divided by interest.

Working Capital Ratios

Global's managers might be further interested in how efficiently they are managing their net working capital. We can express the firm's accounts receivable in terms of the number of days' worth of sales that it represents, called the **accounts receivable days, average collection period**, or **days sales outstanding**:[5]

$$\text{Accounts Receivable Days} = \frac{\text{Accounts Receivable}}{\text{Average Daily Sales}} \qquad (2.14)$$

Given average daily sales of \$186.7 million/365 = \$0.51 million in 2011, Global's receivables of \$18.5 million represent 18.5/0.51 = 36 days' worth of sales. In other words, Global takes a little over one month to collect payment from its customers, on average. In 2006, Global's accounts receivable represented only 27 days' worth of sales. Although the number of receivable days can fluctuate seasonally, a significant unexplained increase could be a cause for concern (perhaps indicating the firm is doing a poor job collecting from its customers or is trying to boost sales by offering generous credit terms). Similar ratios exist for accounts payable and inventory. Those ratios are called **accounts payable days** (accounts payable divided by average daily cost of goods sold) and **inventory days** (inventory divided by average daily cost of goods sold).

We can also compute how efficiently firms use inventory. The **inventory turnover ratio** is equal to cost of goods sold divided by the average inventory over the year:

$$\text{Inventory Turnover} = \frac{\text{Cost of Goods Sold}}{\text{Average Inventory}} \qquad (2.15)$$

A normal level for this ratio, similar to the others in this section, can vary substantially for different industries, although a higher level (more dollars of sales per dollar of inventory) is generally better.

EBITDA

Financial analysts often compute a firm's earnings before interest, taxes, depreciation, and amortization, or **EBITDA**. Because depreciation and amortization are not cash expenses for the firm, EBITDA reflects the cash a firm has earned from its operations. Global's EBITDA in 2011 was 10.4 + 1.2 = \$11.6 million.

Leverage Ratios

Lenders often assess a firm's leverage by computing an **interest coverage ratio**, also known as a **times interest earned (TIE) ratio**, which, as its name suggests, is equal to a measure of earnings divided by interest. Financial managers watch these ratios carefully because they assess how easily the firm will be able to cover its interest payments. There is no one accepted measure of earnings for these ratios; it is common to consider operating income, EBIT, or EBITDA as a multiple of the firm's interest expenses. When this ratio is high, it indicates that the firm is earning much more than is necessary to meet its required interest payments.

---

[5]Accounts receivable days can also be calculated based on the average accounts receivable at the end of the current and prior years. This is generally an acceptable approach whenever a ratio compares an income statement figure to a balance sheet figure. Since the income statement figure is measured over a period of time, taking the simple average of the balance sheet figure can approximate its amount over the same period of time.

Investment Returns

return on equity (ROE) The ratio of a firm's net income to the book value of its equity.

Analysts and financial managers often evaluate the firm's return on investment by comparing its income to its investment using ratios such as the firm's **return on equity (ROE)**[6]:

$$\text{Return on Equity} = \frac{\text{Net Income}}{\text{Book Value of Equity}} \tag{2.16}$$

Global's ROE in 2011 was 2.0/22.2 = 9.0%. The ROE provides a measure of the return that the firm has earned on its past investments. A high ROE may indicate the firm is able to find investment opportunities that are very profitable. Of course, one weakness of this measure is the difficulty in interpreting the book value of equity.

return on assets (ROA) The ratio of net income to the total book value of the firm's assets.

Another common measure is the **return on assets (ROA)**, which is net income divided by the total assets. A firm must earn both a positive ROE and ROA to grow.

The DuPont Identity

DuPont Identity Expresses return on equity as the product of profit margin, asset turnover, and a measure of leverage.

Global's financial manager will need to know that its ROE is 9%, but that financial manager would also need to understand the drivers of his or her firm's ROE. High margins, efficient use of assets, or even simply high leverage could all lead to a higher ROE. By delving deeper into the sources of ROE, the financial manager can gain a clear sense of the firm's financial picture. One common tool for doing so is the **DuPont Identity**, named for the company that popularized it, which expresses return on equity as the product of profit margin, asset turnover, and a measure of leverage.

To understand the DuPont Identity, we start with ROE and decompose it in steps into the drivers identified in the identity. First, we simply multiply ROE by (sales/sales), which is just 1, and rearrange terms:

$$\text{ROE} = \left(\frac{\text{Net Income}}{\text{Total Equity}}\right)\left(\frac{\text{Sales}}{\text{Sales}}\right) = \left(\frac{\text{Net Income}}{\text{Sales}}\right)\left(\frac{\text{Sales}}{\text{Total Equity}}\right) \tag{2.17}$$

This expression says that ROE can be thought of as net income per dollar of sales (profit margin) times the amount of sales per dollar of equity. For example, Global's ROE comes from its profit margin of 1.1% multiplied by its sales per dollar of equity of (186.7/22.2 = 8.41): 1.1% × 8.41 = 9%.[7] While this can be a useful insight into ROE, we can take the decomposition further by multiplying Equation 2.17 by assets/assets, which again is just 1, and rearranging the terms:

$$\text{ROE} = \left(\frac{\text{Net Income}}{\text{Sales}}\right)\left(\frac{\text{Sales}}{\text{Total Equity}}\right)\left(\frac{\text{Total Assets}}{\text{Total Assets}}\right)$$

$$= \left(\frac{\text{Net Income}}{\text{Sales}}\right)\left(\frac{\text{Sales}}{\text{Total Assets}}\right)\left(\frac{\text{Total Assets}}{\text{Total Equity}}\right) \tag{2.18}$$

equity multiplier A measure of leverage equal to total assets divided by total equity.

This final expression says that ROE is equal to net income per dollar of sales (profit margin) times sales per dollar of assets (asset turnover) times assets per dollar of equity (a measure of leverage called the **equity multiplier**). Equation 2.18 is the DuPont Identity, expressing return on equity as the product of profit margin, asset turnover, and the equity multiplier. Turning to Global, its equity multiplier is 7.7 (= 170.1/22.2).

---

[6]As indicated earlier, because net income is measured over the year, the ROE can also be calculated based on the average book value of equity at the end of the current and prior years.

[7]Due to rounding to two decimal places in the financial statements and our calculations, the calculations for Global will not exactly match the ROE we computed.

A financial manager at Global looking for ways to increase ROE could turn to the DuPont Identity to assess the drivers behind its current ROE. With a profit margin of 1.1%, asset turnover of 1.1, and an equity multiplier of 7.7, we have

$$ROE = 9\% = (1.1\%)(1.1)(7.7)$$

This decomposition of ROE shows that leverage is already high (confirmed by the fact that the book debt-equity ratio shows that Global's debt is more than five times its equity). However, Global is operating with only 1% profit margins and relatively low asset turnover. Thus, Global's manager could pursue lowering costs to increase profit margin and utilizing the firm's existing assets more efficiently.[8]

EXAMPLE 2.3

DuPont Analysis

Problem

The following table contains information about Canadian Tire (ticker symbol: CTC.A) and Lululemon Athletica (ticker symbol: LLL). Compute their respective ROEs and then determine how much Canadian Tire would need to increase its profit margin in order to match Lululemon's ROE.

	Profit Margin	Asset Turnover	Equity Multiplier
Canadian Tire	3.9%	0.99	2.38
Lululemon	12.9%	1.47	1.32

Solution

▶ **Plan and Organize**

The table contains all the relevant information to use the DuPont Identity to compute the ROE. We can compute the ROE of each company by multiplying together its profit margin, asset turnover, and equity multiplier. In order to determine how much Canadian Tire would need to increase its margin to match Lululemon's ROE, we can set Canadian Tire's ROE equal to Lululemon's, keep its turnover and equity multiplier fixed, and solve for the profit margin.

▶ **Execute**

Using the DuPont Identity, we have:

$$ROE_{CTC.A} = 3.9\% \times 0.99 \times 2.38 = 9.2\%$$
$$ROE_{LLL} = 12.9\% \times 1.47 \times 1.32 = 25.0\%$$

Now, using Lululemon's ROE but Canadian Tire's asset turnover and equity multiplier, we can solve for the margin that Canadian Tire needs to achieve Lululemon's ROE:

$$25.0\% = \text{Margin} \times 0.99 \times 2.38$$

$$\text{Margin} = \frac{25.0\%}{2.36} = 10.6\%$$

▶ **Evaluate**

Canadian Tire would have to increase its profit margin from 3.9% to 10.6% in order to match Lululemon's ROE. It would be able to achieve Lululemon's ROE even with a lower margin than Lululemon (10.6% vs. 12.9%) and lower turnover (0.99 vs. 1.47) because of its higher leverage.

---

[8]Although the DuPont Identity gives the impression that you can increase ROE just by increasing leverage, it is not quite that simple. An increase in leverage will increase your interest expense, decreasing your profit margin.

Valuation Ratios

price-earnings ratio (P/E) The ratio of the market value of equity to the firm's earnings, or its share price to its earnings per share.

Analysts and investors use a number of ratios to gauge the market value of the firm. The most important is the firm's **price-earnings ratio (P/E)**:

$$\text{P/E Ratio} = \frac{\text{Market Capitalization}}{\text{Net Income}} = \frac{\text{Share Price}}{\text{Earnings per Share}} \qquad (2.19)$$

That is, the P/E ratio is the ratio of the value of equity to the firm's earnings, either on a total basis or on a per-share basis. For example, Global's P/E ratio in 2011 was $36/2.0 = 10/0.56 = 18$. The P/E ratio is a simple measure that is used to assess whether a stock is over- or under-valued, based on the idea that the value of a stock should be proportional to the level of earnings it can generate for its shareholders. P/E ratios can vary widely across industries and tend to be higher for industries with high growth rates. One way to capture the idea that a higher P/E ratio can be justified by a higher growth rate is to compare it to the company's expected earnings growth rate. For example, if Global's expected growth rate is 18%, then it would have a P/E to Growth, or **PEG ratio**, of 1. Some investors consider PEG ratios of 1 or below as indicating the stock is fairly priced but would question whether the company is potentially overvalued if the PEG is higher than 1. P/E ratios also vary widely across time and tend to be low when the economy is headed for a downturn but high when an economy starts rebounding.

PEG ratio The ratio of a firm's P/E to its expected earnings growth rate.

The P/E ratio considers the value of the firm's equity and so depends on its leverage. Recall that the amount of assets controlled by the equity holders can be increased through the use of leverage. To assess the market value of the underlying business, it is common to consider valuation ratios based on the firm's enterprise value. Typical ratios include the ratio of enterprise value to revenue, or enterprise value to operating income or EBITDA. These ratios compare the value of the business to its sales, operating profits, or cash flow. Similar to the P/E ratio, these ratios are used to make intra-industry comparisons of how firms are priced in the market.

Common Mistake   Mismatched Ratios

When considering valuation (and other) ratios, be sure that the items you are comparing both represent amounts related to the entire firm or that both represent amounts related solely to equity holders. For example, a firm's share price and market capitalization are values associated with the firm's equity. Thus, it makes sense to compare them to the firm's earnings per share or net income, which are amounts to equity holders after interest has been paid to debt holders. We must be careful, however, if we compare a firm's market capitalization to its revenues, operating income, or EBITDA. These amounts are related to the whole firm, and both debt and equity holders have a claim to them. Therefore, it is better to compare revenues, operating income, or EBITDA to the enterprise value of the firm, which includes both debt and equity.

The P/E ratio is not useful when the firm's earnings are negative. In this case, it is common to look at the firm's enterprise value relative to sales. The risk in doing so, however, is that earnings might be negative because the firm's underlying business model is fundamentally flawed, as was the case for many internet firms in the late 1990s.

EXAMPLE 2.4

Computing
Profitability and
Valuation Ratios

Problem

Consider the following data from December 31, 2009, for Canadian Pacific Railway (ticker symbol: CP) and Canadian National Railway (ticker symbol: CNR):

	Canadian Pacific Railway Limited (CP) ($ millions)	Canadian National Railway Company (CNR) ($ millions)
Sales	4303	7367
Operating Income	900	2406
Net Income	612	1854
Market Capitalization	9569	25,604
Cash	679	352
Debt	4495	6461

Compare CP's and CN's operating margin, net profit margin, P/E ratio, and the ratio of enterprise value to operating income and sales.

Solution

▶ **Plan**

The table contains all of the raw data, but we need to compute the ratios using the inputs in the table.

Operating Margin = Operating Income / Sales
Net Profit Margin = Net Income / Sales
P/E ratio = Price / Earnings
Enterprise value to operating income = Enterprise Value / Operating Income
Enterprise value to sales = Enterprise Value / Sales

▶ **Execute**

CP had an operating margin of 900/4303 = 20.9%, a net profit margin of 612/4303 = 14.2%, and a P/E ratio of 9569/612 = 15.6. Its enterprise value was 9569 + 4495 − 679 = $13,385 million, which has a ratio of 13,385/900 = 14.9 to operating income and 13,385/4303 = 3.1 to sales.

    CN had an operating margin of 2406/7367 = 32.7%, a net profit margin of 1854/7367 = 25.2%, and a P/E ratio of 25,604/1854 = 13.8. Its enterprise value was 25,604 + 6461 − 352 = $31,713 million, which has a ratio of 31,713/2406 = 13.2 to operating income and 31,713/7367 = 4.3 to sales.

▶ **Evaluate**

Note that despite their large difference in size, CP's and CN's P/E and enterprise value to operating income ratios were similar, with CP's results slightly higher in both cases. CN's profitability was somewhat higher than CP's, however, explaining the difference in the ratio of enterprise value to sales.

Table 2.3 summarizes income statement ratios and provides typical values of those ratios during an economic expansion, as well as what happened to them during the financial crisis and ensuing recession.

9. How can a financial manager use the DuPont Identity to assess the firm's ROE?

10. How do you use the price-earnings (P/E) ratio to gauge the market value of a firm?

| TABLE 2.3 | Income Statement Ratios | | | | | |

Ratio	Formula	Manufacturing	Retail	Service	S&P 500	Financial Crisis and Recession
Profitability Ratios						
Gross margin	$\dfrac{\text{Gross Profit}}{\text{Sales}}$	34.3%	30.8%	50.4%	38.4%	—
Operating margin	$\dfrac{\text{Operating Income}}{\text{Sales}}$	8.4%	7.4%	8.7%	19.7%	↓
Net Profit margin	$\dfrac{\text{Net Income}}{\text{Sales}}$	2.0%	2.3%	2.1%	8.7%	↓↓
Leverage Ratio						
Interest coverage ratio (TIE)	$\dfrac{\text{Operating Income}}{\text{Interest Expense}}$	4.78	7.16	3.58	12.13	↓
Investment Return Ratios						
Return on equity	$\dfrac{\text{Net Income}}{\text{Book Value of Equity}}$	7.9%	10.6%	7.9%	15.8%	↓
Return on assets	$\dfrac{\text{Net Income}}{\text{Total Assets}}$	1.6%	4.3%	1.1%	5.4%	↓↓
Valuation Ratio						
Price-to-earnings ratio	$\dfrac{\text{Share Price}}{\text{Earnings per Share}}$	10.0	15.2	9.3	18.0	↓
Efficiency and Working Capital Ratios						
Accounts receivable days	$\dfrac{\text{Accounts Receivable}}{\text{Average Daily Sales}}$	56.8	6.7	62.5	57.5	—
Fixed asset turnover	$\dfrac{\text{Sales}}{\text{Fixed Assets}}$	5.6	6.3	11.8	5.2	—
Total asset turnover	$\dfrac{\text{Sales}}{\text{Total Assets}}$	0.9	1.8	0.8	0.7	—
Inventory turnover	$\dfrac{\text{Cost of Goods Sold}}{\text{Inventory}}$	4.2	6.5	21.5	6.2	—

Notes: A "—" in the recession column indicates that any changes in the ratio during the recession were too small to be economically significant or were not broadly felt across sectors. Two arrows indicate a larger move than a single arrow.

Because many firms had losses (negative earnings) during the recession, the P/E ratio was not meaningful and was not calculated. For those that maintained positive earnings, the ratio fell.

Source: Standard and Poors' Compustat.

 2.6 ## The Statement of Cash Flows

The income statement provides a measure of the firm's profit over a given time period. However, it does not indicate the amount of *cash* the firm has earned. There are two reasons that net income does not correspond to cash earned. First, there are non-cash entries on the income statement, such as depreciation and amortization. Second, certain uses, such as the purchase of a building or expenditures on inventory, and sources of cash, such as the collection of accounts receivable, are not reported on the income

statement of cash flows
An accounting statement that shows how a firm has used the cash it earned during a set period.

statement. The firm's **statement of cash flows** uses the information from the income statement and balance sheet to determine how much cash the firm has generated, and how that cash has been allocated, during a set period. Cash is important because it is needed to pay bills and maintain operations and is the source of any return of investment for investors. Thus, from the perspective of an investor attempting to value the firm or a financial manager concerned about cash flows (vs. earnings), the statement of cash flows provides what may be the most important information of the four financial statements.

The statement of cash flows is divided into three sections: operating activities, investment activities, and financing activities. These sections roughly correspond to the three major jobs of the financial manager.

1. Operating activity starts with net income from the income statement. It then adjusts this number by adding back all non-cash entries related to the firm's operating activities.

2. Investment activity lists the cash used for investment.

3. Financing activity shows the flow of cash between the firm and its investors.

Global's statement of cash flows is shown in Table 2.4. In this section, we take a close look at each component of the statement of cash flows.

Operating Activity

The first section of Global's statement of cash flows adjusts net income by all non-cash items related to operating activity. For instance, depreciation is deducted when computing net income, but it is not an actual cash expense. Thus, we add it back to net income when determining the amount of cash the firm has generated. Similarly, we add back any other non-cash expenses (e.g., future income taxes).

TABLE 2.4	GLOBAL CORPORATION Statement of Cash Flows Year ended December 31 (in $ millions)		
Global Corporation's Statement of Cash Flows for 2011 and 2010		**2011**	**2010**
	Operating activities		
	Net income	2.0	1.9
	Depreciation and amortization	1.2	1.1
	Cash effect of changes in		
	Accounts receivable	−5.3	−0.3
	Accounts payable	2.7	−0.5
	Inventory	−1.0	−1.0
	Cash from operating activities	**−0.4**	**1.2**
	Investment activities		
	Capital expenditures	−33.4	−4.0
	Acquisitions and other investing activity		
	Cash from investing activities	**−33.4**	**−4.0**
	Financing activities		
	Dividends paid	−1.0	−1.0
	Sale or purchase of stock	—	—
	Increase in short-term borrowing	2.3	3.0
	Increase in long-term borrowing	35.2	2.5
	Cash from financing activities	**36.5**	**4.5**
	Change in cash and cash equivalents	**2.7**	**1.7**

Source: Compustat.

Next, we adjust for changes to net working capital that arise from changes to accounts receivable, accounts payable, or inventory. When a firm sells a product, it records the revenue as income even though it may not receive the cash from that sale immediately. Instead, it may grant the customer credit and let the customer pay in the future. The customer's obligation adds to the firm's accounts receivable. We use the following guidelines to adjust for changes in working capital:

1. Accounts receivable: When a sale is recorded as part of net income, but the cash has not yet been received from the customer, we must adjust the cash flows by *deducting* the increases in accounts receivable. These increases represent additional lending by the firm to its customers and it reduces the cash available to the firm.

2. Accounts payable: Similarly, we *add* increases in accounts payable. Accounts payable represents borrowing by the firm from its suppliers. This borrowing increases the cash available to the firm.

3. Inventory: Finally, we *deduct* increases in inventory. Increases in inventory are not recorded as an expense and do not contribute to net income (the cost of the goods are included in net income only when the goods are actually sold). However, the cost of increasing inventory is a cash expense for the firm and must be deducted.

Working capital adjustments address the difference between the time when sales and costs is recorded on the income statement and when the cash actually goes in and out of the firm. For example, in 2011, we subtracted the $5.3 million increase in accounts receivable from net income as part of the operating cash flow calculation. What happened? From Table 2.3, we see that Global had $10.6 million more in sales in 2011 than in 2010. However, from Table 2.1, we also see that Global's accounts receivable increased to $18.5 million in 2011 from $13.2 million in 2010. So, even though Global's sales were up considerably, the company has not yet collected all the cash flow for those sales; instead Global's customers owe the company $5.3 million more at the end of 2011 than they did at the end of 2010. Because the statement of cash flows starts with net income, which includes sales for which Global has not yet been paid, we deduct the additional $5.3 million in sales Global is still owed when computing the actual cash flows it generated.

We must make a similar adjustment for inventory. Global does not record the cost of the inventory until it is sold, when it is in cost of goods sold. However, when the company actually pays for the inventory, cash has flowed out of Global, decreasing operating cash flow. The opposite is true for accounts payable—Global has recorded additional expenses without actually paying for them yet. Those expenses reduce net income but do not represent cash outflows.

Finally, we add depreciation to net income before calculating operating cash flow. Depreciation is an accounting adjustment to book value that is an expense but not a cash outflow. That is, when Global's property, plant, and equipment depreciate by $1.2 million, the loss does not literally cost Global $1.2 million in cash flow. Because this is an expense that reduces net income but is not an actual cash outflow, we must add it back to calculate cash flow. We will talk more about depreciation when we do capital budgeting in Chapter 9. All these adjustments mean that cash flows can be very different from net income. Although Global showed positive net income on the income statement, it actually had a negative $0.4 million cash flow from operating activity, in large part because of the increase in accounts receivable.

Investment Activity

capital expenditures Purchases of new property, plant, and equipment.

The next section of the statement of cash flows shows the cash required for investment activities. Purchases of new property, plant, and equipment are referred to as **capital expenditures**. Recall that capital expenditures do not appear immediately as expenses on the income statement. Instead, the firm depreciates these assets and deducts depreciation expenses over time. To determine the firm's cash flow, we already added back depreciation, because it is not an actual cash expense. Now, we subtract the actual capital expenditure that the firm made. Similarly, we also deduct other assets purchased or investments made by the firm, such as acquisitions. In Table 2.4, we see that in 2011 Global spent $33.4 million in cash on investing activities.

Financing Activity

The last section of the statement of cash flows shows the cash flows from financing activities. Dividends paid to shareholders are a cash outflow. Global paid $1 million to its shareholders as dividends in 2011.

retained earnings The difference between a firm's net income and the amount it spends on dividends.

The difference between a firm's net income and the amount it spends on dividends is referred to as the firm's **retained earnings** for that year:

$$\text{Retained Earnings} = \text{Net Income} - \text{Dividends} \tag{2.20}$$

payout ratio The ratio of a firm's dividends to its net income.

Global retained $2 million − $1 million = $1 million, or 50% of its earnings in 2011. This makes its *payout ratio* for 2011 equal to 50%. A firm's **payout ratio** is the ratio of its dividends to its net income:

$$\text{Payout Ratio} = \frac{\text{Dividends}}{\text{Net Income}} \tag{2.21}$$

Also listed under financing activity is any cash the company received from the sale of its own stock, or cash spent buying (repurchasing) its own stock. Global did not issue or repurchase stock during this period.

The last items to include in this section result from changes to Global's short-term and long-term borrowing. Global raised money by issuing debt, so the increases in short-term and long-term borrowing represent cash inflows. The last line of the statement of cash flows combines the cash flows from these three activities to calculate the overall change in the firm's cash balance over the period of the statement. In this case, Global had cash inflows of $2.7 million. By looking at the statement in Table 2.4 as a whole, we can determine that Global chose to borrow (mainly in the form of long-term debt) to cover the cost of its investment and operating activities. Although the firm's cash balance has increased, Global's negative operating cash flows and relatively high expenditures on investment activities might give investors some reasons for concern. If that pattern continues, Global will need to continue to borrow to remain in business.

EXAMPLE 2.5	
The Impact of Depreciation on Cash Flow	**Problem** Suppose Global had an additional $1 million depreciation expense in 2011. If Global's tax rate on pre-tax income is 26%, what would be the impact of this expense on Global's earnings? How would it impact Global's cash at the end of the year? **Solution** ▶ **Plan** Depreciation is an operating expense, so Global's operating income, EBIT, and pre-tax income would be affected. With a tax rate of 26%, Global's tax bill will decrease by 26 cents for every dollar that pre-tax income is reduced. In order to determine how Global's cash would be

affected, we have to determine the effect of the additional depreciation on cash flows. Recall that depreciation is not an actual cash outflow, even though it is treated as an expense, so the only effect on cash flow is through the reduction in taxes.

▶ **Execute**
Global's operating income, EBIT, and pre-tax income would fall by $1 million because of the $1 million in additional operating expense due to depreciation.

This $1 million decrease in pre-tax income would reduce Global's tax bill by 26% × $1 million = $0.26 million. Therefore, net income would fall by $1 − 0.26 = $0.74 million.

On the statement of cash flows, net income would fall by $0.74 million, but we would add back the additional depreciation of $1 million, because it is not a cash expense. Thus, cash from operating activities would rise by −0.74 + 1 = $0.26 million. Therefore, Global's cash balance at the end of the year would increase by $0.26 million, the amount of the tax savings that resulted from the additional depreciation deduction.

▶ **Evaluate**
The increase in cash balance comes completely from the reduction in taxes. Because Global pays $0.26 million less in taxes even though its cash expenses have not increased, it has $0.26 million more in cash at the end of the year.

Concept Check

11. Why does a firm's net income not correspond to cash earned?

12. What are the components of the statement of cash flows?

2.7 Other Financial Statement Information

The most important elements of a firm's financial statements are the balance sheet, income statement, and the statement of cash flows, which we have already discussed. Several other pieces of information contained in the financial statements warrant brief mention: the *management discussion and analysis,* the *statement of shareholders' equity*, and *notes to the financial statements*.

Management Discussion and Analysis

management discussion and analysis (MD&A) A preface to the financial statements in which a company's management discusses the recent year (or quarter), providing a background on the company and any significant events that may have occurred.

The **management discussion and analysis (MD&A)** is a preface to the financial statements in which the company's management discusses the recent year (or quarter), providing a background on the company and any significant events that may have occurred. Management may also discuss the coming year and outline goals and new projects.

Management must also discuss any important risks that the firm faces or issues that may affect the firm's liquidity or resources. Management is also required to disclose any **off-balance sheet transactions**, which are transactions or arrangements that can have a material impact on the firm's future performance yet do not appear on the balance sheet. For example, if a firm has made guarantees that it will compensate a buyer for losses related to an asset purchased from the firm, these guarantees represent a potential future liability for the firm that must be disclosed as part of the MD&A.

off-balance sheet transactions Transactions or arrangements that can have a material impact on a firm's future performance yet do not appear on the balance sheet.

Statement of Shareholders' Equity

The **statement of shareholders' equity** breaks down the shareholders' equity computed on the balance sheet into the amount that came from issuing new shares versus retained earnings. Because the book value of shareholders' equity is not a useful assessment of value for financial purposes, the information contained in the statement of shareholders' equity is also not particularly revealing, so we do not spend time on the statement here.

Notes to the Financial Statements

In addition to the four financial statements, companies provide extensive notes with additional details on the information provided in the statements. For example, the notes document important accounting assumptions that were used in preparing the statements. They often provide information specific to a firm's subsidiaries or its separate product lines. They show the details of the firm's stock-based compensation plans for employees and the different types of debt the firm has outstanding. Details of acquisitions, spinoffs, leases, taxes, and risk management activities are also given. The information provided in the notes is often very important to a full interpretation of the firm's financial statements.

Concept Check

13. Where do off-balance sheet transactions appear in a firm's financial statements?

14. What information do the notes to financial statements provide?

2.8 Financial Reporting in Practice

The various financial statements we have examined are of critical importance to investors and financial managers alike. Even with safeguards such as GAAP and auditors, financial reporting abuses unfortunately do take place. We now review one of the most infamous recent examples and offer some concluding thoughts to guide financial managers through the complexities of financial statements.

Enron

Enron is the most well-known of the accounting scandals of the early 2000s. Enron started as an operator of natural gas pipelines but evolved into a global trader dealing in a range of products including gas, oil, electricity, and even broadband internet capacity. A series of events unfolded that led Enron to file the largest bankruptcy filing in U.S. history in December 2001. By the end of 2001, the market value of Enron's shares had fallen by over $60 billion.

Interestingly, throughout the 1990s and up to late 2001, Enron was touted as one of the most successful and profitable companies in the United States. *Fortune* magazine rated Enron "The Most Innovative Company in America" for six straight years, from 1995 to 2000. But while many aspects of Enron's business were successful, subsequent investigations suggest that Enron executives had been manipulating Enron's financial statements to mislead investors and artificially inflate the price of Enron's stock and to maintain its credit rating. In 2000, for example, 96% of Enron's reported earnings were the result of accounting manipulation.[9]

---

[9]John R. Kroger, "Enron, Fraud and Securities Reform: An Enron Prosecutor's Perspective," *University of Colorado Law Review,* December, 2005, pp. 57–138.

Although the accounting manipulations that Enron used were quite sophisticated, the essence of most of the deceptive transactions was surprisingly simple. Enron sold assets at inflated prices to other firms (or, in many cases, business entities that Enron's CFO Andrew Fastow had created), together with a promise to buy back those assets at an even higher future price. Thus, Enron was effectively borrowing money, receiving cash today in exchange for a promise to pay more cash in the future. But Enron recorded the incoming cash as revenue and then, in a variety of ways, hid the promises to buy the assets back.[10] In the end, much of Enron's revenue growth and profits in the late 1990s were the result of this type of manipulation.

The Sarbanes-Oxley Act

Sarbanes-Oxley Act (SOX) Legislation passed by the U.S. Congress in 2002, intended to improve the accuracy of financial information given to both boards and shareholders.

The Enron case highlights the importance to investors of accurate and up-to-date financial statements for firms they choose to invest in. In 2002, the U.S. Congress passed the **Sarbanes-Oxley Act (SOX)**, which requires, among other things, that CEOs and CFOs certify the accuracy and appropriateness of their firm's financial statements and increases the penalties against them if the financial statements later prove to be fraudulent. While SOX contains many provisions, the overall intent of the legislation was to improve the accuracy of information given to both boards and to shareholders. SOX attempted to achieve this goal in three ways: (1) by overhauling incentives and independence in the auditing process, (2) by stiffening penalties for providing false information, and (3) by forcing companies to validate their internal financial control processes. Many of the problems at Enron and elsewhere were kept hidden from boards and shareholders until it was too late. In the wake of these scandals, many people felt that the accounting statements of these companies, while often remaining true to the letter of GAAP, did not present an accurate picture of the financial health of a company.

Auditing firms are supposed to ensure that a company's financial statements accurately reflect the financial state of the firm. In reality, most auditors have a long-standing relationship with their audit clients; this extended relationship and the auditors' desire to keep the lucrative auditing fees make auditors less willing to challenge management. More importantly perhaps, most accounting firms have developed large and extremely profitable consulting divisions. Obviously, if an audit team refuses to accommodate a request by a client's management, that client will be less likely to choose the accounting firm's consulting division for its next consulting contract. SOX addressed this concern by putting strict limits on the amount of non-audit fees (consulting or otherwise) that an accounting firm can earn from the same firm that it audits. It also required that audit partners rotate every five years to limit the likelihood that auditing relationships become too cozy over long periods of time. Finally, SOX called on the SEC to force companies to have audit committees that are dominated by outside directors, and required that at least one outside director have a financial background.

SOX also stiffened the criminal penalties for providing false information to shareholders. It required both the CEO and the CFO to personally attest to the accuracy of the financial statements presented to shareholders and to sign a statement to that effect. Penalties for providing false or misleading financial statements were increased under SOX—fines of as much as $5 million and imprisonment of a maximum of 20 years are permitted. Further, CEOs and CFOs must return bonuses or profits from the sale of stock or the exercise of options during any period covered by statements that are later restated.

---

[10]In some cases, these promises were called "price risk management liabilities" and hidden with other trading activities; in other cases they were off-balance sheet transactions that were not fully disclosed.

INTERVIEW WITH
SUE FRIEDEN

Sue Frieden

*S*ue Frieden is Ernst & Young's Global Managing Partner, Quality & Risk Management. A member of the Global Executive board, she is responsible for every aspect of quality and risk management—employees, services, procedures, and clients.

QUESTION: *Do today's financial statements give the investing public what they need?*

ANSWER: Globally, we are seeing an effort to provide more forward-looking information to investors. But fundamental questions remain, such as how fully do investors understand financial statements and how fully do they read them? Research shows that most individual investors don't rely on financial statements much at all. We need to determine how the financial statements can be improved. To do that we will need a dialogue involving investors, regulators, analysts, auditors, stock exchanges, academics, and others to ensure that financial statements are as relevant as they can be.

QUESTION: *Ernst & Young is a global organization. How do accounting standards in the U.S. compare to those elsewhere?*

ANSWER: In January of 2005, 100 countries outside the United States began the process of adopting new accounting standards (International Financial Reporting Standards) that would in large measure be based on principles rather than rules. As global markets become more complex, we all need to be playing by the same set of rules. As a first step we need consistency from country to country. There are definite challenges to overcome in reconciling principle-based and rules-based systems, but we are optimistic that these challenges will inevitably get resolved. At the same time, there are efforts under way to ensure that auditing standards are globally consistent. Ultimately, financial statements prepared under global standards and audited under consistent global auditing standards will better serve investors.

QUESTION: *What role does the audit firm play in our financial markets, and how has that changed since the collapse of Arthur Andersen?*

ANSWER: The accounting profession has seen unprecedented change in the past few years as well. The passage of Sarbanes-Oxley and other changes are helping to restore public trust. We're now engaging on a regular basis with a wider range of stakeholders—companies, boards, policymakers, opinion leaders, investors, and academia. And we've had the chance to step back and ask ourselves why we do what we do as accounting professionals, and why it matters. In terms of the services we offer, much of what we do helps companies comply with regulations, guard against undue risks, and implement sound transactions. Part of the value in what we do is providing the basis to all stakeholders to understand whether companies are playing by the rules—whether it is accounting rules, financial reporting rules, or tax rules. The public may not fully understand precisely what auditors do or how we do it, but they care that we exist because it provides them the confidence they so badly need and want.

QUESTION: *Accounting standards seem to be shifting from historical cost-based methods to methods that rely on current market values of assets. During the financial crisis, however, many financial institutions complained that "mark-to-market" rules exacerbated their financial difficulties. Do you believe accounting professionals should rethink the wisdom of moving to market-based accounting methods?*

ANSWER: Fair value accounting can certainly be improved, particularly in light of the difficulty in applying fair value in illiquid markets, which the financial crisis highlighted, and because of some of the anomalies that fair value accounting can produce. But by and large, fair value accounting provided transparency into reality for investors. It is the most transparent way to reflect the economic reality of prevailing market conditions and provide investors and companies with current financial information on which they can base investment and management decisions. Fair value accounting did not cause the economic crisis; it simply kept a fair scorecard

Finally, Section 404 of SOX requires senior management and the boards of public companies to be comfortable enough with the process through which funds are allocated and controlled, and outcomes monitored throughout the firm, to be willing to attest to their effectiveness and validity. Section 404 has arguably garnered more attention than any other section in SOX because of the potentially enormous burden it places on every firm to validate its entire financial control system. When the SEC estimated the cost of implementing Section 404, its staff economists put the total cost at $1.24 billion. Recent estimates based on surveys by Financial Executives International and the American Electronics Association predict that the actual cost will be between $20 billion and $35 billion.[11] The burden of complying with this provision is greater, as a fraction of revenue, for smaller companies. The surveys cited earlier found that multibillion-dollar companies will pay less than 0.05% of their revenues to comply, whereas small companies with less than $20 million in revenues will pay more than 3% of their revenues to comply.

Following the Sarbanes-Oxley Act in the United States, Canada adopted similar measures that came into effect in 2005. In Canada, the response and implementation of changes were somewhat measured in comparison with those in the United States, partly due to the fact that the same scale of corporate fraud had yet to be experienced in Canada. Additional differences between Canada and the United States also contributed to differences in adoption. For example, Canada does not have a national securities commission, whereas the United States does. Creating uniform change across Canada is problematic, as agreement among 13 different authorities would be needed. Canada also has a much larger percentage of public firms with a controlling shareholder. Implementing SOX requirements such as increasing the proportion of independent directors might be unworkable in Canada, as many controlling shareholders may desire to name board representatives. Finally, Canadian companies tend to have lower market capitalization compared to U.S. firms. As mentioned above, forcing companies to validate their financial control processes in a more formalized way can increase costs significantly, putting a greater burden on smaller firms than on larger ones

The Financial Statements: A Useful Starting Point

In this chapter, we have highlighted the role of the financial statements in informing outside analysts, investors, and the financial managers themselves about the performance, position, and financial condition of the firm. However, especially from the financial manager's perspective, financial statements are only a starting point. For example, we have emphasized the importance of market values over book values. We have also shown that while much can be learned through ratio analysis, these ratios are only markers that point the financial manager toward areas where the firm is doing well or where he or she needs to focus effort for improvement. No single ratio tells the whole story. However, by studying all of the financial statements and considering ratios that assess profitability, leverage, and efficiency, you should be able to develop a clear sense of the health and performance of the firm. Finally, using the case of Enron, we emphasize that the usefulness of the financial statements to investors relies on the ethics of those constructing them. Even in these cases of deception, however, an informed reader of the financial statements could have spotted the warning signs by focusing on the statement of cash flows and carefully reading the notes to the financial statements.

Concept Check

15. Describe the transactions Enron used to increase its reported earnings.

16. What is the Sarbanes-Oxley Act?

---

[11]American Electronics Association, "Sarbanes-Oxley Section 404: The 'Section' of Unintended Consequences and Its Impact on Small Business" (2005).

MyFinanceLab

Here is what you should know after reading this chapter. MyFinanceLab will help you identify what you know, and where to go when you need to practice.

Key Points and Equations	Terms	Online Practice Opportunities
2.1 Firms' Disclosure of Financial Information ▶ Financial statements are accounting reports that a firm issues periodically to describe its past performance. ▶ Investors, financial analysts, managers, and other interested parties, such as creditors, rely on financial statements to obtain reliable information about a corporation. ▶ The main types of financial statements are the balance sheet, the income statement, and the statement of cash flows.	annual report, p. 28 auditor, p. 29 balance sheet, p. 29 financial statements, p. 28 Generally Accepted Accounting Principles (GAAP), p. 29	MyFinanceLab Study Plan 2.1
2.2 The Balance Sheet ▶ The balance sheet shows the current financial position (assets, liabilities, and shareholders' equity) of the firm at a single point in time. ▶ The two sides of the balance sheet must balance: Assets = Liabilities + Shareholders' Equity (2.1) ▶ Shareholders' equity is the book value of the firm's equity. It differs from the market value of the firm's equity, its market capitalization, because of the way assets and liabilities are recorded for accounting purposes.	accounts payable, p. 31 accounts receivable, p. 30 assets, p. 29 book value, p. 31 book value of equity, p. 31 current assets, p. 30 current liabilities, p. 31 depreciation, p. 30 inventories, p. 30 liabilities, p. 29 long-term assets, p. 30 long-term debt, p. 31 marketable securities, p. 30 market capitalization, p. 32 net working capital, p. 31 notes payable, p. 31 shareholders' equity, p. 29 short-term debt, p. 31	MyFinanceLab Study Plan 2.2
2.3 Balance Sheet Analysis ▶ A successful firm's market-to-book ratio typically exceeds 1. ▶ A common ratio used to assess a firm's leverage is: $$\text{Debt-Equity Ratio} = \frac{\text{Total Debt}}{\text{Total Equity}} \quad (2.4)$$ ▶ This ratio is most informative when computed using the market value of equity. It indicates the degree of leverage of the firm. ▶ The enterprise value of a firm is the total value of its underlying business operations: Enterprise Value = Market Capitalization + Debt − Cash (2.5)	current ratio, p. 35 debt-equity ratio, p. 33 enterprise value, p. 34 growth stocks, p. 33 leverage, p. 33 liquidation value, p. 33 market-to-book ratio (price-to-book [P/B] ratio), p. 33 quick ratio ("acid-test" ratio), p. 35 value stocks, p. 33	MyFinanceLab Study Plan 2.3

2.4 The Income Statement

▶ The income statement reports the firm's revenues and expenses, and it computes the firm's bottom line of net income, or earnings.

▶ Net income is often reported on a per-share basis as the firms earnings per share:

Earnings per Share (EPS)

$$= \text{Net Income/Shares Outstanding} \qquad (2.8)$$

▶ We compute diluted EPS by adding to the number of shares outstanding the possible increase in the number of shares from the exercise of stock options the firm has awarded.

convertible bonds, p. 37
diluted EPS, p. 37
dilution, p. 37
earnings per share
  (EPS), p. 37
EBIT, p. 37
gross margin, p. 37
gross profit, p. 36
income statement, p. 35
net income or earnings,
  p. 35
operating income, p. 36
stock options, p. 37

MyFinanceLab
Study Plan 2.4

2.5 Income Statement Analysis

▶ Profitability ratios show the firm's operating or net income as a fraction of sales, and they are an indication of a firm's efficiency and its pricing strategy.

▶ Asset efficiency ratios assess how efficiently the firm is using its assets by showing how many dollars of revenues the firm produces per dollar of assets.

▶ Working capital ratios express the firm's working capital as a number of days of sales (for receivables) or cost of sales (for inventory or payables).

▶ Interest coverage ratios indicate the ratio of the firm's income or cash flows to its interest expenses, and they are a measure of financial strength.

▶ Return on investment ratios, such as ROE or ROA, express the firm's net income as a return on the book value of its equity or total assets.

▶ Valuation ratios compute market capitalization or enterprise value of the firm relative to its earnings or operating income.

▶ The P/E ratio computes the value of a share of stock relative to the firm's EPS. P/E ratios tend to be high for fast-growing firms.

▶ When comparing valuation ratios, it is important to be sure both numerator and denominator match in terms of whether they include debt.

accounts payable days,
  p. 39
accounts receivable days,
  p. 39
average collection
  period, days sales
  outstanding, p. 39
DuPont Identity, p. 40
EBITDA, p. 39
equity multiplier, p. 40
interest coverage
  ratio, p. 39
inventory days, p. 39
inventory turnover
  ratio, p. 41
net profit margin, p. 38
operating margin, p. 38
price-earnings ratio
  (P/E), p. 42
return on assets
  (ROA), p. 40
return on equity
  (ROE), p. 40
times interest earned
  (TIE) ratio, p. 39

MyFinanceLab
Study Plan 2.5

2.6 The Statement of Cash Flows

▶ The statement of cash flows reports the sources and uses of the firm's cash. It shows the adjustments to net income for non-cash expenses and changes to net working capital, as well as the cash used (or provided) from investing and financing activities.

capital expenditures, p. 46
payout ratio, p. 47
retained earnings, p. 47
statement of cash flows,
  p. 45

MyFinanceLab
Study Plan 2.6

2.7 Other Financial Statement Information

▶ The management discussion and analysis section of the financial statement contains management's overview of the firm's performance, as well as disclosure of risks the firm faces, including those from off-balance sheet transactions.

▶ The statement of shareholders' equity breaks down the shareholders' equity computed on the balance sheet into the amount that came from issuing new shares versus retained earnings. It is not particularly useful for financial valuation purposes.

▶ The notes to a firm's financial statements generally contain important details regarding the numbers used in the main statements.

management discussion and analysis (MD&A), p. 48
off-balance sheet transactions, p. 48
statement of shareholders' equity, p. 49

MyFinanceLab
Study Plan 2.7

2.8 Financial Reporting in Practice

▶ Recent accounting scandals have drawn attention to the importance of financial statements. New legislation has increased the penalties for fraud, and tightened the procedures firms must use to assure that statements are accurate.

Sarbanes-Oxley Act (SOX), p. 50

MyFinanceLab
Study Plan 2.8

Review Questions

1. Why do firms disclose financial information?

2. Who reads financial statements? List at least three different categories of people. For each category, provide an example of the type of information they might be interested in and discuss why.

3. What four financial statements can be found in a firm's filing with its provincial securities commission? What checks exist to ensure the accuracy of these statements?

4. What is the purpose of the balance sheet?

5. How can you use the balance sheet to assess the health of the firm?

6. What is the purpose of the income statement?

7. How are the balance sheet and the income statement related?

8. What is the DuPont Identity and how can a financial manager use it?

9. How does the statement of cash flows differ from the income statement?

10. Can a firm with positive net income run out of cash? Explain.

11. What can you learn from management's discussion or the notes to the financial statements?

12. How did accounting fraud contribute to the collapse of Enron?

Problems

All problems in this chapter are available in MyFinanceLab. An asterisk (*) indicates problems with a higher level of difficulty.

Firm's Disclosure of Financial Information

1. What financial statements can be found in a firm's annual report? What checks exist to ensure the accuracy of these statements?

2. Find the most recent financial statements for Starbuck's Corporation (stock symbol: SBUX) using the following sources:
   a. From the company's webpage www.starbucks.com (*Hint:* Search for "investor relations").
   b. From the SEC website www.sec.gov (*Hint:* Search for company filings in the EDGAR database).
   c. From the Yahoo finance website finance.yahoo.com.
   d. From at least one other source (*Hint:* Enter "SBUX 10K" at www.google.com).
   e. Repeat the analysis for Tim Hortons (www.timhortons.com). In addition to the EDGAR site, check www.sedar.com for Canadian filings.

The Balance Sheet

3. Consider the following potential events that might have occurred at Global on December 30, 2011. For each one, indicate which line items in Global's balance sheet would be affected and by how much. Also indicate the change to Global's book value of equity.
   a. Global used $20 million of its available cash to repay $20 million of its long-term debt.
   b. A warehouse fire destroyed $5 million worth of uninsured inventory.
   c. Global used $5 million in cash and $5 million in new long-term debt to purchase a $10 million building.
   d. A large customer owing $3 million for products it already received declared bankruptcy, leaving no possibility that Global would ever receive payment.
   e. Global's engineers discover a new manufacturing process that will cut the cost of its flagship product by over 50%.
   f. A key competitor announces a radical new pricing policy that will drastically undercut Global's prices.

4. What was the change in Global's book value of equity from 2010 to 2011 according to Table 2.1? Does this imply that the market price of Global's shares increased in 2011? Explain.

5. Use Google Finance (www.google.com/finance) to find the balance sheet data for Qualcomm as of September 27, 2009.
   a. How much did Qualcomm have in cash and short-term investments?
   b. What were Qualcomm's total accounts receivable?
   c. What were Qualcomm's total assets?
   d. What were Qualcomm's total liabilities? How much of this was long-term debt?
   e. What was the book value of Qualcomm's equity?

6. Find online the annual 10-K report for Peet's Coffee and Tea (stock symbol: PEET) for 2008 (filed in March 2009). Answer the following questions from its balance sheet:
   a. How much cash did Peet's have at the start of 2008?
   b. What were Peet's total assets?

c. What were Peet's total liabilities? How much debt did Peet's have?

d. What was the book value of Peet's equity?

Balance Sheet Analysis

 7. In June 2007, General Electric (ticker symbol: GE) had a book value of equity of $117 billion, 10.3 billion shares outstanding, and a market price of $38.00 per share. GE also had cash of $16 billion and total debt of $467 billion.

   a. What was GE's market capitalization? What was GE's market-to-book ratio?

   b. What was GE's book debt-equity ratio? What was GE's market debt-equity ratio?

   c. What was GE's enterprise value?

 8. In July 2007, Apple had cash of $7.12 billion, current assets of $18.75 billion, and current liabilities of $6.99 billion. It also had inventories of $0.25 billion.

   a. What was Apple's current ratio?

   b. What was Apple's quick ratio?

   c. In July 2007, Dell had a quick ratio of 1.25 and a current ratio of 1.30. What can you say about the asset liquidity of Apple relative to Dell?

9. In April 2010, the following information was true about Abercrombie and Fitch (ticker symbol: ANF) and The Gap (ticker symbol: GPS), both clothing retailers. Values (except price per share) are in millions of dollars.

	Book Equity	Price per Share	Number of Shares
ANF	1788	46.67	88.17
GPS	4769	25.00	667.42

   a. What is the market-to-book ratio of each company?

   b. What conclusions do you draw from comparing the two ratios?

The Income Statement and Income Statement Analysis

 10. Find online the annual 10-K report for Peet's Coffee and Tea (ticker symbol: PEET) for 2008 (filed in April 2009). Answer the following questions from the income statement:

   a. What were Peet's revenues for 2008? By what percentage did revenues grow from 2005?

   b. What were Peet's operating and net profit margins in 2008? How do they compare with its margins in 2007?

   c. What were Peet's diluted earnings per share in 2008? What number of shares is this EPS based on?

11. Local Co. has sales of $10 million and cost of sales of $6 million. Its selling, general, and administrative expenses are $500,000 and its research and development expense is $1 million. Finally it has annual depreciation charges of $1 million and a tax rate of 35%.

   a. What is Local's gross margin?

   b. What is Local's operating margin?

   c. What is Local's net profit margin?

12. If Local Co., the company in question 11, had an increase in selling expenses of $300,000, how would that affect each of its margins?

13. If Local Co., the company in question 11, had interest expense of $800,000, how would that affect each of its margins?

14. Chutes & Co. has interest expense of $1 million and an operating margin of 10% on total sales of $30 million. What is Chutes' interest coverage ratio?

15. Ladders, Inc. has a net profit margin of 5% on sales of $50 million. It has book value of equity of $40 million and total book liabilities of $30 million. What is Ladders' ROE? ROA?

16. JPJ Corp has sales of $1 million, accounts receivable of $50,000, total assets of $5 million, of which $3 million are fixed assets, inventory of $150,000, and cost of goods sold of $600,000.

    What is JPJ's accounts receivable days? Fixed asset turnover? Total asset turnover? Inventory turnover?

*17. Suppose that in 2011, Global launched an aggressive marketing campaign that boosted sales by 15%. However, its operating margin fell from 5.57% to 4.50%. Suppose that the company had no other income, interest expenses were unchanged, and the corporate tax rate for 2011 is 25%.

    a. What was Global's EBIT in 2011?
    b. What was Global's income in 2011?
    c. If Global's P/E ratio and number of shares outstanding remained unchanged, what was Global's share price in 2011?

18. Suppose a firm's tax rate is 35%.

    a. What effect would a $10 million operating expense have on this year's earnings? What effect would it have on next year's earnings?

    b. What effect would a $10 million capital expense have on this year's earnings if the capital is depreciated at a rate of $2 million per year for five years? What effect would it have on next year's earnings?

19. You are analyzing the leverage of two firms, and you note the following (all values in millions of dollars):

	Debt	Book Equity	Market Equity	Operating Income	Interest Expense
Firm A	500	300	400	100	50
Firm B	80	35	40	8	7

    a. What is the market debt-equity ratio of each firm?
    b. What is the book debt-equity ratio of each firm?
    c. What is the interest coverage ratio of each firm?
    d. Which firm will have more difficulty meeting its debt obligations?

20. For 2010, Wal-Mart and Target had the following information (all values are in millions of dollars):

	Sales (Income Statement)	Cost of Goods Sold (Income Statement)	Accounts Receivable (Balance Sheet)	Inventory (Balance Sheet)
Wal-Mart	408,214	304,657	4144	30,254
Target	65,357	45,583	6966	7179

    a. What is each company's accounts receivable days?
    b. What is each company's inventory turnover?
    c. Which company is managing its accounts receivable and inventory more efficiently?

*21. Quisco Systems has 6.5 billion shares outstanding and a share price of $18.00. Quisco is considering developing a new networking product in house at a cost of $500 million. Alternatively, Quisco can acquire a firm that already has the technology for $900 million worth (at the current price) of Quisco stock. Suppose that absent the expense of the new technology, Quisco will have EPS of $0.80.
   a. Suppose Quisco develops the product in house. What impact would the development cost have on Quisco's EPS? Assume all costs are incurred this year and are treated as a research and development expense, Quisco's tax rate is 35%, and the number of shares outstanding is unchanged.
   b. Suppose Quisco does not develop the product in house but instead acquires the technology. What effect would the acquisition have on Quisco's EPS this year? (Note that acquisition expenses do not appear directly on the income statement. Assume the acquired firm has no revenues or expenses of its own, so the only effect on EPS is due to the change in the number of shares outstanding.)
   c. Which method of acquiring the technology has a smaller impact on earnings? Is this method cheaper? Explain.

22. In January 2009, American Airlines (ticker symbol: AMR) had a market capitalization of $1.7 billion, debt of $11.1 billion, and cash of $4.6 billion. American Airlines had revenues of $23.8 billion. British Airways (ticker symbol: BABWF) had a market capitalization of $2.2 billion, debt of $4.7 billion, cash of $2.6 billion, and revenues of $13.1 billion.
   a. Compare the market capitalization–to-revenue ratio (also called the price-to-sales ratio) for American Airlines and British Airways.
   b. Compare the enterprise value–to-revenue ratio for American Airlines and British Airways.
   c. Which of these comparisons is more meaningful? Explain.

*23. Find online the annual 10-K report for Peet's Coffee and Tea (ticker symbol: PEET) for 2008 (filed in early April 2009).
   a. Compute Peet's net profit margin, total asset turnover, and equity multiplier.
   b. Verify the DuPont Identity for Peet's ROE.
   c. If Peet's managers wanted to increase its ROE by 1 percentage point, how much higher would the company's asset turnover need to be?

24. Repeat the analysis from parts a and b of the previous problem for Starbucks Coffee (ticker symbol: SBUX). Based on the DuPont Identity, what explains the difference between the two firms' ROEs?

25. Consider a retailing firm with a net profit margin of 3.5%, a total asset turnover of 1.8, total assets of $44 million, and a book value of equity of $18 million.
   a. What is the firm's current ROE?
   b. If the firm increased its net profit margin to 4%, what would its ROE be?
   c. If, in addition, the firm increased its revenues by 20% (while maintaining this higher profit margin and without changing its assets or liabilities), what would its ROE be?

The Statement of Cash Flows

26. Find online the annual 10-K report for Peet's Coffee and Tea (ticker symbol: PEET) for 2008 (filed in early 2009). Answer the following questions from its cash flow statement:
   a. How much cash did Peet's generate from operating activities in 2008?
   b. What was Peet's depreciation expense in 2008?
   c. How much cash was invested in new property and equipment (net of any sales) in 2008?
   d. How much did Peet's raise from the sale of shares of its stock (net of any purchases) in 2008?

27. See the cash flow statement here for H.J. Heinz (ticker symbol: HNZ) (all values in thousands of dollars):

Period Ending	29-Oct-08	30-Jul-08	30-Apr-08	30-Jan-08
Net income	276,710	228,964	194,062	218,532
Operating Activities, Cash Flows Provided by or Used in				
Depreciation	69,997	75,733	74,570	73,173
Adjustments to net income	14,359	(13,142)	48,826	(47,993)
Changes In accounts receivables	(38,869)	(53,218)	100,732	(84,711)
Changes in liabilities	82,816	(111,577)	201,725	39,949
Changes in inventories	(195,186)	(114,121)	85,028	57,681
Changes in other operating activities	17,675	(26,574)	12,692	(2097)
Total Cash Flow from Operating Activities	227,502	(13,935)	717,635	254,534
Investing Activities, Cash Flows Provided by or Used in				
Capital expenditures	(82,584)	(41,634)	(100,109)	(69,170)
Investments	(5465)	5465	(93,153)	(48,330)
Other cash flows from investing activities	(108,903)	732	(58,069)	20,652
Total Cash Flows from Investing Activities	(196,952)	(35,437)	(251,331)	(96,848)
Financing Activities, Cash Flows Provided by or Used in				
Dividends paid	(131,483)	(131,333)	(119,452)	(121,404)
Sale purchase of stock	78,774	1210	(76,807)	(79,288)
Net borrowings	515,709	114,766	(283,696)	64,885
Other cash flows from financing activities	(282)	2000	(46,234)	39,763
Total Cash Flows from Financing Activities	462,718	(13,357)	(526,189)	(96,044)
Effect of exchange rate changes	(119,960)	(610)	32,807	6890
Change in Cash and Cash Equivalents	$373,308	(63,339)	(27,078)	$68,532

a. What were Heinz's cumulative earnings over these four quarters? What were its cumulative cash flows from operating activities?
b. What fraction of the cash from operating activities was used for investment over the four quarters?
c. What fraction of the cash from operating activities was used for financing activities over the four quarters?

28. Suppose your firm receives a $5 million order on the last day of the year. You fill the order with $2 million worth of inventory. The customer picks up the entire order the same day and pays $1 million up front in cash; you also issue a bill for the customer to pay the remaining balance of $4 million within 40 days. Suppose your firm's tax rate is 0% (i.e., ignore taxes). Determine the consequences of this transaction for each of the following:
a. Revenues
b. Earnings
c. Receivables
d. Inventory
e. Cash

29. Nokela Industries purchases a $40 million cyclo-converter. It will be depreciated by $10 million per year over four years, starting this year. Suppose Nokela's tax rate is 40%.
    a. What impact will the cost of the purchase have on earnings for each of the next four years?
    b. What impact will the cost of the purchase have on the firm's cash flow for the next four years?

Other Financial Statement Information

30. The balance sheet information for Clorox Co. (ticker symbol: CLX) in 2004–05 is shown here (all values in thousands of dollars):

Balance Sheet:	31-Mar-05	31-Dec-04	30-Sep-04	30-Jun-04
Assets				
Current Assets				
Cash and cash equivalents	293,000	300,000	255,000	232,000
Net receivables	401,000	362,000	385,000	460,000
Inventory	374,000	342,000	437,000	306,000
Other current assets	60,000	43,000	53,000	45,000
Total Current Assets	1,128,000	1,047,000	1,130,000	1,043,000
Long-term investments	128,000	97,000	—	200,000
Property, plant, and equipment	979,000	991,000	995,000	1,052,000
Goodwill	744,000	748,000	736,000	742,000
Other assets	777,000	827,000	911,000	797,000
Total Assets Liabilities	3,756,000	3,710,000	3,772,000	3,834,000
Current Liabilities				
Accounts payable	876,000	1,467,000	922,000	980,000
Short/current long-term debt	410,000	2000	173,000	288,000
Other current liabilities	—	—	—	—
Total Current Liabilities	1,286,000	1,469,000	1,095,000	1,268,000
Long-term debt	2,381,000	2,124,000	474,000	475,000
Other liabilities	435,000	574,000	559,000	551,000
Total Liabilities	4,102,000	4,167,000	2,128,000	2,294,000
Total Shareholder Equity	−346,000	−457,000	1,644,000	1,540,000
Total Liabilities and Shareholder Equity	$3,756,000	$3,710,000	$3,772,000	$3,834,000

    a. What change in the book value of Clorox's equity took place at the end of 2004?
    b. Is Clorox's market-to-book ratio meaningful? Is its book debt-equity ratio meaningful? Explain.
    c. Find Clorox's other financial statements from that time online. What was the cause of the change to Clorox's book value of equity at the end of 2004?
    d. Does Clorox's book value of equity in 2005 imply that the firm is unprofitable? Explain.

Financial Reporting in Practice

31. Find online the annual 10-K report for Peet's Coffee and Tea (ticker symbol: PEET) for 2008 (filed in early 2009).
    a. Which auditing firm certified these financial statements?
    b. Which officers of Peet's certified the financial statements?

Data Case

This is your second interview with a prestigious brokerage firm for a job as an equity analyst. You survived the morning interviews with the department manager and the vice-president of equity. Everything has gone so well that they want to test your ability as an analyst. You are seated in a room with a computer and a list with the names of two companies—Caterpillar, Inc. (ticker symbol: CAT) and Microsoft (ticker symbol: MSFT). You have 90 minutes to complete the following tasks:

1. Download the annual income statements, balance sheets, and cash flow statements for the last four fiscal years from MarketWatch (www.marketwatch.com). Enter each company's ticker symbol and then go to "Financials." Export the statements to Microsoft Excel.

2. Find historical stock prices for each firm from Yahoo! Finance (http://finance.yahoo.com). Enter your ticker symbol, click on "Historical Prices" in the left column, and enter the proper date range to cover the last day of the month corresponding to the date of each financial statement. Use the closing stock prices (not the adjusted close). To calculate the firms' market capitalization at each date, we multiply the number of shares outstanding (see "Basic Weighted Shares Outstanding" on the income statement) by the firm's historic stock price.

3. For each of the four years of statements, compute the following ratios for each firm:

   Valuation Ratios
   Price-earnings ratio (for EPS use diluted EPS total)
   Market-to-book ratio
   Enterprise value–to-EBITDA
   (For debt, include long-term and short-term debt; for cash, include market-able securities.)

   Profitability Ratios
   Operating margin (use operating income after depreciation)
   Net profit margin
   Return on equity

   Financial Strength Ratios
   Current ratio
   Book debt-equity ratio
   Market debt-equity ratio
   Interest coverage ratio (EBIT ÷ interest expense)

4. Obtain industry averages for each firm from Reuters.com (www.reuters.com/finance/stocks). Click on "Stocks," enter the symbol, then click on "Ratios."
   a. Compare each firm's ratios to the available industry ratios for the most recent year. (Ignore the "Company" column as your calculations will be different.)
   b. Analyze the performance of each firm versus the industry and comment on any trends in each individual firm's performance. Identify any strengths or weaknesses you find in each firm.

5. Examine the market-to-book ratios you calculated for each firm. Which, if either, of the two firms can be considered "growth firms" and which, if either, can be considered "value firms"?

6. Compare the valuation ratios across the two firms. How do you interpret the difference between them?

7. Consider the enterprise value of each firm for each of the four years. How have the values of each firm changed over the time period?

Interest Rates and Valuing Cash Flows

PART 2

Valuation Principle Connection. In this part of the text, we introduce the basic tools for making financial decisions. Chapter 3 presents the most important idea in this book, the *Valuation Principle*. The Valuation Principle states that we can use market prices to determine the value of an investment opportunity to the firm. As we progress through our study of corporate finance, we will demonstrate that the Valuation Principle is the one unifying principle that underlies all of finance and links all of the ideas throughout this book.

For a financial manager, evaluating financial decisions involves computing the net present value of a project's future cash flows. We use the Valuation Principle's Law of One Price to derive a central concept in financial economics—the *time value of money*. In Chapter 4, we explain how to value any series of future cash flows and derive a few useful shortcuts for valuing various types of cash flow patterns. Chapter 5 discusses how interest rates are quoted in the market and how to handle interest rates that compound more frequently than once per year. We apply the Valuation Principle to demonstrate that the return required from an investment will depend on the rate of return of investments with maturity and risk similar to the cash flows being valued. This observation leads to the important concept of the *cost of capital* of an investment decision. In Chapter 6, we demonstrate an application of the time value of money tools using interest rates: valuing the bonds issued by corporations and governments.

The Valuation Principle: The Foundation of Financial Decision Making

LEARNING OBJECTIVES

▶ Identify the role of financial managers in decision making

▶ Recognize the role competitive markets play in determining the value of a good

▶ Understand the Valuation Principle and how it can be used to identify decisions that increase the value of the firm

▶ Assess the effect of interest rates on today's value of future cash flows

▶ Use the net present value decision rule to make investment decisions

▶ Understand the Law of One Price

notation

NPV	net present value	*r*	interest rate
PV	present value		

Karrilyn Wilcox, an employee at Marshall & Stevens Valuation Consulting practice in New York City, provides clients with valuation and financial advisory services. Her finance background comes into play regularly. "I need to understand the industry and economy the business operates in, in order to more effectively forecast the business's financial statements, which are the basis of discounted cash flow analysis."

Having graduated from Saint Mary's University in Halifax in 2007 with a Bachelor of Commerce degree, Karrilyn understands well the importance of interest rates and their effect on today's value of future cash flows. "For instance, if we are valuing a business in a different country with high interest rates and sovereign risk, we need to understand the impact this has on the valuation. For one thing, it would be inappropriate to use the same discount rate as another company that operates in the same industry and has the same capital structure and credit rating but operates in a low interest rate environment with little sovereign risk."

Karrilyn credits her finance courses with providing her with the tools to perform her job, and for having set her on an exciting career path. "Without my strong background in finance, I would not be where I am today."

In September 2010, Research In Motion (RIM) decided to directly enter the tablet computer market dominated by Apple's iPad by unveiling the BlackBerry PlayBook. How did RIM's managers decide this was the right decision for the company?

Every decision has future consequences that will affect the value of the firm. These consequences will generally include both benefits and costs. For example, in addition to the upfront cost of developing the Play-Book's hardware and software, RIM will also incur ongoing costs associated with future software development, marketing efforts, and customer support for PlayBook buyers. The benefits to RIM include the revenues from PlayBook sales, but also maintaining revenues from BlackBerry users who might otherwise switch to iPhones after purchasing iPads. This decision will increase RIM's value if these benefits outweigh the costs.

More generally, a decision is good for the firm's investors if it increases the firm's value by providing benefits whose value exceeds the costs. But comparing costs and benefits is often complicated because they occur at different points in time, or are in different currencies, or have different risks associated with them. To make a valid comparison, we must use the tools of finance to express all costs and benefits in common terms. In this chapter, we introduce the central concept of finance, and the unifying theme of this book, the *Valuation Principle*. The Valuation Principle states that we can use current market prices to determine the value today of the different costs and benefits associated with a decision. The Valuation Principle allows us to apply the concept of *net present value (NPV)* to compare the costs and benefits of a project in terms of a common unit—namely, dollars today. We will then be able to evaluate a decision by answering this question: *Does the cash value today of its benefits exceed the cash value today of its costs?* In addition, we will see that the difference between the cash values of the benefits and costs indicates the net amount by which the decision will increase the value of the firm and therefore the wealth of its investors. The Valuation Principle also leads to the important concept of the *Law of One Price*, which will prove to be a key tool in understanding the value of stocks, bonds, and other securities that are traded in the market.

3.1 Managerial Decision Making

A financial manager's job is to make decisions on behalf of the firm's investors. For example, a manager of a manufacturing company has to decide how much to produce. By increasing production, more units can be sold, but the price per unit will probably be lower. Does it make sense to increase production? A manager of another company might expect an increase in demand for her products. Should she raise prices or increase production? If the decision is to increase production and a new facility is required, is it better to rent or purchase the facility? When should managers give their workers a pay increase? These are a few examples of the kinds of choices managers face every day.

Our objective in this book is to explain how to make decisions that increase the value of the firm to its investors. In principle, the idea is simple and intuitive: For good decisions, the benefits exceed the costs. Of course, real-world opportunities are usually complex, and so the costs and benefits are often difficult to quantify. Quantifying them often involves using skills from other management disciplines, as in the following examples:

> *Marketing:* to determine the increase in revenues resulting from an advertising campaign
>
> *Economics:* to determine the increase in demand from lowering the price of a product
>
> *Organizational behaviour:* to determine the effect of changes in management structure on productivity
>
> *Strategy:* to determine a competitor's response to a price increase
>
> *Operations:* to determine production costs after the modernization of a manufacturing plant

For the remainder of this text, we will assume that we can rely on experts in these different areas to provide this information so that the costs and benefits associated with a decision have already been identified. With that task done, the financial manager's job is to compare the costs and benefits and determine the best decision to make for the value of the firm.

Your Personal Financial Decisions

While the focus of this text is on the decisions a financial manager makes in a business setting, you will soon see that concepts and skills you will learn here apply to personal decisions as well. As a normal part of life, we all make decisions that trade off benefits and costs across time. Going to university, purchasing this book, saving for a new car or house down payment, taking out a car loan or home loan, buying shares of stock, and deciding between jobs are just a few examples of such decisions that you have faced or could face in the not-too-distant future. In this chapter, we develop the *Valuation Principle* as the foundation of all financial decision making—whether in a business or in a personal context—and begin to show how it is a unifying theme applicable to all the financial concepts you will learn.

 Concept Check

1. What defines a good decision?

2. What is the financial manager's role in decision making for the firm?

3.2 Cost-Benefit Analysis

As we have already seen, the first step in decision making is to identify the costs and benefits of a decision. The next step is quantifying the costs and benefits. Any decision in which the value of the benefits exceeds the costs will increase the value of the firm. To evaluate the costs and benefits of a decision, we must value the effects in the same terms—cash today. Let's make this concrete with a simple example.

Suppose a jewellery manufacturer has the opportunity to trade 200 ounces of silver for 10 ounces of gold today. An ounce of silver differs in value from an ounce of gold. Consequently, it is incorrect to compare 200 ounces to 10 ounces and conclude that the larger quantity is better. Instead, to compare the costs of the silver and benefit of the gold, we first need to quantify their values in equivalent terms—cash today.

Consider the silver. What is its cash value today? Suppose silver can be bought and sold for a current market price of $25 per ounce. Then the 200 ounces of silver we give up has a cash value of[1]

$$(200 \text{ ounces of silver}) \times (\$25/\text{ounce of silver}) = \$5000$$

If the current market price for gold is $1300 per ounce, then for the 10 ounces of gold we receive a cash value of

$$(10 \text{ ounces of gold}) \times (\$1300/\text{ounce of gold}) = \$13{,}000$$

We have now quantified the decision. The jeweller's opportunity has a benefit of $13,000 and a cost of $5000. The net benefit of the decision is $13,000 − $5000 = $8000 today. The net value of the decision is positive, so by accepting the trade, the jewellery firm will be richer by $8000.

EXAMPLE 3.1

Comparing Costs and Benefits

Problem

Suppose you work as a customer account manager for an importer of frozen seafood. A customer is willing to purchase 300 kilograms of frozen shrimp today for a total price of $1500, including delivery. You can buy frozen shrimp on the wholesale market for $3 per kilogram today, and arrange for delivery at a cost of $100 today. Will taking this opportunity increase the value of the firm?

Solution

▶ **Plan**

To determine whether this opportunity will increase the value of the firm, we need to value the benefits and the costs using market prices. We have market prices for our costs:

Wholesale price of shrimp: $3/kilogram   Delivery cost: $100

We have a customer offering the following market price for 300 kilograms of shrimp delivered: $1500. All that is left is to compare the prices.

▶ **Execute**

The benefit of the transaction is $1500 today. The costs are 300 kilograms × $3/kilogram = $900 today for the shrimp, and $100 today for delivery, for a total cost of $1000 today. If you are certain about these costs and benefits, the right decision is obvious: you should seize this opportunity because the firm will gain $1500 − $1000 = $500.

▶ **Evaluate**

Thus, taking this opportunity contributes $500 to the value of the firm, in the form of cash that can be paid out immediately to the firm's investors.

---

[1]You might worry about commissions or other transactions costs (such as transportation costs) that are incurred when buying or selling silver, in addition to the market price. For now, we will ignore transactions costs and discuss their effect later.

3. How do we determine whether a decision increases the value of the firm?

4. When costs and benefits are in different units or goods, how can we compare them?

3.3 Valuation Principle

In the previous examples, the right decisions for the firms were clear because the costs and benefits were easy to evaluate and compare. They were easy to evaluate because we were able to use current market prices to convert them into equivalent cash values. Once we can express costs and benefits in terms of "cash today," it is a straightforward process to compare them and determine whether the decision will increase the firm's value.

Note that in both examples we used market prices to assess the values of the different commodities involved. What about the firm's other possible uses for those commodities? For example, consider the jewellery manufacturer with the opportunity to trade silver for gold. When evaluating the trade, we did not concern ourselves with whether the jeweller thought that the price was fair or whether the jeweller would actually have a use for the silver or gold. Suppose, for example, that the jeweller thinks the current price of silver is too high. Does this matter—would he value the silver at less than $5000? The answer is no—he can always sell the silver at the current market price and receive $5000 right now, so he would never place a lower value on the silver. Similarly, he also will not pay more than $5000 for the silver. Even if he really needs silver or for some reason thinks the price of silver is too low, he can always buy 200 ounces of silver for $5000 and so would not pay more than that amount. Thus, independent of his own views or preferences, the value of the silver to the jeweller is $5000.

Note that the jeweller can both buy and sell silver at its current market price. His personal preferences or use for the silver and his opinion of the fair price are therefore irrelevant in evaluating the value of this opportunity. This observation highlights an important general principle related to goods trading in a **competitive market**, a market in which a good can be bought *and* sold at the same price. Whenever a good trades in a competitive market, that price determines the value of the good. This point is one of the central and most powerful ideas in finance. It will underlie almost every concept that we develop throughout the text.

competitive market
A market in which a good can be bought *and* sold at the same price.

EXAMPLE 3.2

Competitive Market Prices Determine Value

Problem
You have just won a radio contest and are disappointed to find out that the prize is four tickets to the Celine Dion concert (face value $80 each). Not being a fan of Celine (as you were traumatized by having to watch the movie *Titanic* several times when you were younger), you have no intention of going to the show. However, it turns out that there is a second choice: two tickets to Justin Bieber's sold-out show (face value $50 each). You notice that on eBay, tickets to the Celine Dion show are being bought and sold for $60 apiece and tickets to Justin Bieber's show are being bought and sold at $100 each. What should you do?

Solution

▶ **Plan**
Market prices, not your personal preferences (nor the face value of the tickets), are relevant here:

    4 Celine Dion tickets at $60 apiece

    2 Justin Bieber tickets at $100 apiece

You need to compare the market value of each option and choose the one with the highest market value.

▶ **Execute**

The Celine Dion tickets have a total value of $240 (4 × $60) versus the $200 total value of the Justin Bieber tickets (2 × $100). Instead of taking the tickets to Justin Bieber, you should accept the Celine Dion tickets, sell them on eBay, and use the proceeds as you wish.

▶ **Evaluate**

Even though Celine Dion's music brings back traumatic *Titanic* memories, you should still take the opportunity to get the Celine Dion tickets. As we emphasized earlier, whether this opportunity is attractive depends on its net value using market prices. Because the value of the Celine Dion tickets is $40 more than the value of the Justin Bieber tickets, the opportunity is appealing.

Once we use market prices to evaluate the costs and benefits of a decision in terms of cash today, it is then a simple matter to determine the best decision for the firm. The best decision makes the firm and its investors wealthier, because the value of its benefits exceeds the value of its costs. We call this idea the Valuation Principle:

valuation principle The value of a commodity or an asset to the firm or its investors is determined by its competitive market price.

The Valuation Principle:

The value of a commodity or an asset to the firm or its investors is determined by its competitive market price.

The Valuation Principle provides the basis for decision making throughout this text. In the remainder of this chapter, we first apply it to decisions whose costs and benefits occur at different points in time and develop the main tool of project evaluation, the *net present value rule*. We then consider its consequences for the prices of assets in the market and develop the concept of the *Law of One Price*.

When Competitive Market Prices Are Not Available

Competitive market prices allow us to calculate the value of a decision without worrying about the tastes or opinions of the decision maker. When competitive prices are not available, we can no longer do this. Prices at retail stores, for example, are one-sided: you can buy at the posted price, but you cannot sell the good to the store at that same price. We cannot use these one-sided prices to determine an exact cash value. They determine the maximum value of the good (since it can always be purchased at that price), but an individual may value it for much less depending on his or her preferences for the good.

Let's consider an example. It has long been common for banks to try to entice people to open accounts by offering them something for free in exchange (it used to be a toaster). Suppose a bank is offering new customers a free iPod nano if they open a new chequing account and make two deposits. Assume the retail price of that model of nano was $159. Because there is no competitive market to trade iPods, the value of the nano depends on whether you were going to buy one or not.

If you planned to buy a nano anyway, then the value to you of the nano is $159, the price you would otherwise pay for it. In this case, the value of the bank's offer is $159. But suppose you do not want or need a nano. If you were to get it from the bank and then sell it, the value of taking the deal would be whatever price you could get for the nano. For example, if you could sell the nano for $100 to your friend, then the bank's offer is worth $100 to you. Thus, depending on your desire to own a new nano, the bank's offer is worth somewhere between $100 (you don't want a nano) and $159 (you definitely want one).

EXAMPLE 3.3

Applying the
Valuation Principle

Problem

You are the operations manager at your firm. Due to a pre-existing contract, you have the opportunity to acquire 200 barrels of oil and 3000 pounds of copper for a total of $25,000. The current market price of oil is $90 per barrel and copper is $3.50 per pound. You are not sure that you need all of the oil and copper, so you are wondering if you should take this opportunity. How valuable is it? Would your decision change if you believed the value of oil or copper would plummet over the next month?

Solution

▶ **Plan**

We need to quantify the costs and benefits using market prices. We are comparing $25,000 with

    200 barrels of oil at $90 per barrel
    3000 pounds of copper at $3.50 per pound

▶ **Execute**

Using the competitive market prices we have:

$$(3000 \text{ pounds of copper}) \times (\$3.50/\text{pound today}) = \$10,500 \text{ today}$$

$$(200 \text{ barrels}) \times (\$90/\text{barrel today}) = \$18,000 \text{ today}$$

The value of the opportunity is the value of the oil plus the value of the copper less the cost of the opportunity, or $18,000 + $10,500 − $25,000 = $3500 today. Because the value is positive, we should take it. This value depends only on the *current* market prices for oil and copper. If we do not need all of the oil and copper, we can sell the excess at current market prices. Even if we thought the value of oil or copper was about to plummet, the value of this investment would be unchanged. (We can always exchange them for dollars immediately at the current market prices.)

▶ **Evaluate**

Since we are transacting today, only the current prices in a competitive market matter. Our own use for or opinion about the future prospects of oil or copper does not alter the value of the decision today. This decision is good for the firm, and will increase its value by $3500.

Concept Check

5. How should we determine the value of a good?

6. If crude oil trades in a competitive market, would an oil refiner that has a use for the oil value it differently than another investor would?

3.4 The Time Value of Money and Interest Rates

For most financial decisions, unlike in the examples presented so far, costs and benefits occur at different points in time. For example, typical investment projects incur costs up front and provide benefits in the future. In this section, we show how to account for this time difference when using the Valuation Principle to make a decision.

The Time Value of Money

Consider a firm's investment opportunity with the following cash flows:

Cost: $100,000 today
Benefit: $105,000 in one year

Because both are expressed in dollar terms, are the cost and benefit directly comparable? Calculating the project's net value as $105,000 − $100,000 = $5000 is incorrect because it ignores the *timing* of the costs and benefits. That is, it treats money today as equivalent to money in one year. In general, a dollar today is worth *more* than a dollar in one year. To see why, note that if you have $1 today, you can invest it. For example, if you deposit it in a bank account paying 7% interest, you will have $1.07 at the end of one year. We call the difference in value between money today and money in the future the **time value of money**. We now develop the tools needed to value our $100,000 investment opportunity correctly.

time value of money
The difference in value between money today and money in the future; also, the observation that two cash flows at two different points in time have different values.

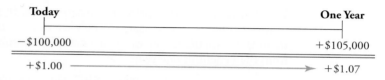

The Interest Rate: Converting Cash Across Time

By depositing money into a savings account, we can convert money today into money in the future with no risk. Similarly, by borrowing money from the bank, we can exchange money in the future for money today. The rate at which we can exchange money today for money in the future is determined by the current interest rate. In the same way that a currency exchange rate allows us to convert money from one currency to another, the interest rate allows us to convert a currency from one point in time to the same currency at another point in time. In essence, an interest rate is an exchange rate across time. It tells us the market price today of money in the future.

Suppose the current annual interest rate is 7%. By investing $1 today, we can convert this $1 into $1.07 in one year. Similarly, by borrowing at this rate, we can exchange $1.07 in one year for $1 today. More generally, we define the **interest rate**, r, for a given period as the interest rate at which one currency can be borrowed or lent over that period. In our example, the interest rate is 7% and we can exchange $1 today for $(1 + 0.7)$ dollars in the future. In general, we can exchange $1 today for $(1 + r)$ dollars in the future, and vice versa. We refer to $(1 + r)$ as the **interest rate factor** for cash flows; it defines how we convert cash flows across time, and has units of "$ in one year/$ today."

interest rate The rate at which one currency can be borrowed or lent over a given period.

interest rate factor One plus the interest rate, the rate of exchange between dollars today and dollars in the future. It has units of "$ in one year/$ today."

As with other market prices, the interest rate ultimately depends on supply and demand. In particular, at the market-determined interest rate, the supply of savings equals the demand for borrowing. Regardless of how it is determined, once we know the interest rate, we can apply the Valuation Principle and use it to evaluate other decisions in which costs and benefits are separated in time.

Value of $100,000 Investment in One Year. Let's reevaluate the investment we considered earlier, this time taking into account the time value of money. If the interest rate is 7%, then we can express the cost of the investment as

$$\text{Cost} = (\$100,000 \text{ today}) \times (1.07 \$ \text{ in one year/}\$ \text{ today})$$

$$= \$107,000 \text{ in one year}$$

future value The value of a cash flow that is moved forward in time.

This $107,000 amount is called a **future value**. For a one period case, the future value is calculated as follows:

$$FV_1 = C_0 \times (1 + r) \tag{3.1}$$

where FV_1 is the future value after one period, C_0 is the amount invested or borrowed now (at time 0), and r is the interest rate.

Think of this $107,000 amount as the opportunity cost of spending $100,000 today: The firm gives up the $107,000 it would have had in one year if it had left the money in the bank. Alternatively, by borrowing the $100,000 from the same bank, the firm would owe $107,000 in one year.

	Today	One Year
Investment	−$100,000	+$105,000
Bank	−$100,000	+$107,000

We have used a market price, the interest rate, to put both the costs and benefits in terms of "dollars in one year," so now we can use the Valuation Principle to compare them and compute the investment's net value by subtracting the cost of the investment from the benefit in one year:

$$\$105,000 - \$107,000 = -\$2000 \text{ in one year}$$

In other words, the firm could earn $2000 more in one year by putting the $100,000 in the bank rather than making this investment. Because the net value is negative, we should reject the investment: if we took it, the firm would be $2000 poorer in one year than if we did not.

Value of $100,000 Investment Today. The previous calculation expressed the value of the costs and benefits in terms of a future value amount: dollars in one year. Alternatively, we can use the interest rate factor to convert to a present value amount: dollars today. Consider the benefit of $105,000 in one year. What is the equivalent amount in terms of dollars today? That is, how much would we need to have in the bank today so that we would end up with $105,000 in the bank in one year? We find this amount by dividing by the interest rate factor:

$$\text{Benefit} = (\$105,000 \text{ in one year}) \div (1.07 \text{ \$ in one year/\$ today})$$

$$= \$98,130.84 \text{ today}$$

present value (PV) The value of a cost or benefit computed in terms of cash today.

This $98,130.84 amount is called a **present value (PV)**. For a one-period case, the present value is calculated as follows:

$$PV_0 = C_1 \div (1 + r) = \frac{C_1}{(1 + r)} = C_1 \times \frac{1}{(1 + r)} \tag{3.2}$$

where PV_0 is the present value now (at time 0), C_1 is the cash flow in one year (at time 1), and r is the interest rate.

This $98,130.84 is also the amount the bank would lend to us today if we promised to repay $105,000 in one year.[2] Thus, it is the competitive market price at which we can "buy" or "sell" $105,000 in one year.

---

[2]We are assuming the bank is willing to lend at the same 7% interest rate, which would be the case if there were no risk associated with the cash flow.

	Today		One Year

Value of Cost Today $-\$100,000$ $+\$105,000$

Value of Benefit Today $+\$\ 98,130.84 \longleftarrow \dfrac{105,000}{1.07} \longleftarrow$

Now we are ready to compute the net value of the investment by subtracting the cost from the benefit:

$$\$98,130.84 - \$100,000 = -\$1869.16 \text{ today}$$

Once again, the negative result indicates that we should reject the investment. Taking the investment would make the firm $1869.16 poorer today because it gave up $100,000 for something worth only $98,130.84.

Present Versus Future Value. This calculation demonstrates that our decision is the same whether we express the value of the investment in terms of the future value amount (dollars in one year) or the present value amount (dollars today): we should reject the investment. Indeed, if we convert from dollars today to dollars in one year,

$$(-\$1869.16 \text{ today}) \times (1.07 \text{ \$ in one year/\$ today}) = -\$2000 \text{ in one year}$$

we see that the two results are equivalent, but expressed as values at different points in time.

discount factor $\frac{1}{(1+r)}$ is the rate of exchange between dollars in the future and dollars today. It has the units of "$ today/$ in one year."

discount rate The appropriate rate to discount a stream of cash flows to determine their value at an earlier time.

Discount Factors and Rates. In the preceding calculation, we can interpret

$$\frac{1}{1+r} = \frac{1}{1.07} = 0.93458$$

as the *price* today of $1 in one year. In other words, for just under 93.5 cents, you can "buy" $1 to be delivered in one year. Note that the value is less than $1—money in the future is worth less today, and so its price reflects a discount. Because it provides the discount at which we can purchase money in the future, the amount $\frac{1}{(1+r)}$ is called the one-year **discount factor**. The interest rate is also referred to as the **discount rate** for an investment.

EXAMPLE 3.4

Comparing Revenues at Different Points in Time

Problem

The launch of Sony's PlayStation 3 was delayed until November 2006, giving Microsoft's Xbox 360 a full year on the market without competition. Imagine that it is November 2005 and you are the marketing manager for the PlayStation. You estimate that if PlayStation 3 were ready to be launched immediately, you could sell $2 billion worth of the console in its first year. However, if your launch is delayed a year, you believe that Microsoft's head start will reduce your first-year sales by 20%. If the interest rate is 8%, what is the cost of a delay of the first year's revenues in terms of dollars in 2005?

Solution

▶ **Plan**

Revenues if released today: $2 billion. Revenue decrease if delayed: 20%. Interest rate: 8%.

We need to compute the revenues if the launch is delayed and compare them to the revenues from launching today. In order to make a fair comparison, however, we need to convert the future revenues of the PlayStation if they are delayed into an equivalent present value of those revenues today.

▶ **Execute**

If the launch is delayed to 2006, revenues will drop by 20% of $2 billion, or $400 million, to $1.6 billion. To compare this amount to revenues of $2 billion if launched in 2005, we must convert it using the interest rate of 8%:

$1.6 billion in 2006 ÷ ($1.08 in 2006/$1 in 2005) = $1.481 billion in 2005

Therefore, the cost of a delay of one year is

$2 billion − $1.481 billion = $0.519 billion ($519 million).

▶ **Evaluate**

Delaying the project for one year was equivalent to giving up $519 million in revenue. In this example, we focused only on the effect on the first year's revenues. However, delaying the launch delays the entire revenue stream by one year, so the total cost would be calculated in the same way by summing the cost of delay for each year of revenues.

We can use the interest rate to determine values in the same way we used competitive market prices. Figure 3.1 illustrates how we use competitive market prices and interest rates to convert between dollars today and other goods, or dollars in the future. Once we quantify all the costs and benefits of an investment in terms of dollars today, we can rely on the Valuation Principle to determine whether the investment will increase the firm's value.

FIGURE 3.1

Converting Between Dollars Today and Gold or Dollars in the Future

We can convert dollars today to different goods or points in time by using the competitive market price or interest rate. Once values are in equivalent terms, we can use the Valuation Principle to make a decision.

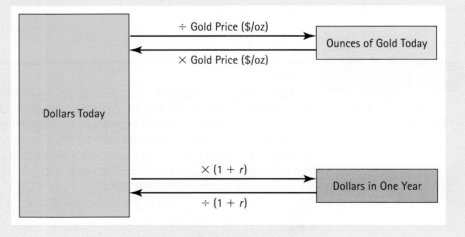

7. How do you compare costs at different points in time?

8. Is the value today of money to be received in one year higher when interest rates are high or when interest rates are low?

3.5 The *NPV* Decision Rule

In Section 3.4, we converted between cash today and cash in the future using the interest rate. As long as we convert costs and benefits to the same point in time, we can use the Valuation Principle to make a decision. In practice, however, most corporations prefer to measure values in terms of their present value—that is, in terms of cash today. In this section, we apply the Valuation Principle to derive the concept of the *net present value* or *NPV*, which we can use to define the "golden rule" of financial decision making, the *NPV decision rule*.

Net Present Value

net present value (NPV)
The difference between the present value of a project's or investment's benefits and the present value of its costs.

When the value of a cost or benefit is computed in terms of cash today, we refer to it as the present value (*PV*). Similarly, we define the **net present value (NPV)** of a project or investment as the difference between the present value of its benefits and the present value of its costs:

Net Present Value

$$NPV = PV(\text{Benefits}) - PV(\text{Costs}) \tag{3.3}$$

Let's consider a simple example. Suppose your firm is offered the following investment opportunity: in exchange for $500 today, you will receive $550 in one year. If the interest rate is 8% per year, then

$$PV(\text{Benefit}) = (\$550 \text{ in one year}) \div (1.08 \text{ \$ in one year/\$ today})$$

$$= \$509.26 \text{ today}$$

This *PV* is the amount you would need to put in the bank today to generate $550 in one year ($509.26 $\times$ 1.08 = $550). In this case, *the present value is the value today of the benefit that is to be received in one year.*

Once the costs and benefits are in present value terms, we can compute the investment's *NPV*:

$$NPV = \$509.26 - \$500 = \$9.26 \text{ today}$$

But what if you don't have the $500 needed to cover the initial cost of the project? Does the project still have the same value? Because we computed the value using competitive market prices, it should not depend on your tastes or the amount of cash you have in the bank. If you don't have the $500, suppose you borrow $509.26 from the bank at the 8% interest rate and then take the project. What are your cash flows in this case?

$$\text{Today: } \$509.26 \text{ (loan)} - \$500 \text{ (invested in the project)} = \$9.26$$

$$\text{In one year: } \$550 \text{ (from project)} - \$509.26 \times 1.08 \text{ (loan balance)} = \$0$$

This transaction leaves you with exactly $9.26 extra cash in your pocket today and no future net obligations. So taking the project is similar to having an extra $9.26 in cash up front. Thus, the *NPV* expresses the value of an investment decision as an amount of cash received today. *As long as the NPV is positive, the decision increases the value of the firm and is a good decision regardless of your current cash needs or preferences regarding when to spend the money.*

The *NPV* Decision Rule

As shown in the last example, the Valuation Principle implies that we should undertake projects with a positive *NPV*. That is, good projects are those for which the present value of the benefits exceeds the present value of the costs. As a result, the value of the firm increases and investors are wealthier. Projects with negative *NPV*s have costs that exceed their benefits. Accepting them is equivalent to losing money today.

NPV decision rule When choosing among investment alternatives, take the alternative with the highest *NPV*. Choosing this alternative is equivalent to receiving its *NPV* in cash today.

We capture this logic in the **NPV decision rule**:

When choosing among investment alternatives, take the alternative with the highest NPV. Choosing this alternative is equivalent to receiving its NPV in cash today.

Because *NPV* is expressed in terms of cash today, using the *NPV* decision rule is a simple way to apply the Valuation Principle. Decisions that increase wealth are superior to those that decrease wealth. We don't need to know anything about the investor's preferences to reach this conclusion. As long as we have correctly captured all of the cash flows of a project, being wealthier increases our options and makes us better off, whatever our preferences are.

We now look at some common ways the *NPV* decision rule is applied in practice.

Accepting or Rejecting a Project. A common financial decision is whether to accept or reject a project. Because rejecting the project generally has *NPV* = 0 (there are no new costs or benefits from not doing the project), the *NPV* decision rule implies that we should

  ▶ accept positive-*NPV* projects, because accepting them is equivalent to receiving their *NPV* in cash today, and

  ▶ reject negative-*NPV* projects, because accepting them would reduce the value of the firm, whereas rejecting them has no cost (*NPV* = 0).

If the *NPV* is exactly zero, then you will neither gain nor lose by accepting the project instead of rejecting it, which also has an *NPV* of zero. It is not a bad project because it does not reduce the firm's value, but it does not add value to the firm either.

EXAMPLE 3.5

The *NPV* Is Equivalent to Cash Today

Problem

After saving $1500 waiting tables, you are about to buy a 50-inch plasma TV. You notice that the store is offering a "one-year same as cash" deal. You can take the TV home today and pay nothing until one year from now, when you will owe the store the $1500 purchase price. If your savings account earns 5% per year, what is the *NPV* of this offer? Show that its *NPV* represents cash in your pocket.

Solution

▶ **Plan**

You are getting something (the TV) worth $1500 today and in exchange will need to pay $1500 in one year. Think of it as getting back the $1500 you thought you would have to spend today to get the TV. We treat it as a positive cash flow.

  Cash flows:

Today	In one year
+$1500	$1500

The discount rate for calculating the present value of the payment in one year is your interest rate of 5%. You need to compare the present value of the cost ($1500 in one year) to the benefit today (a $1500 TV).

▶ **Execute**

$$NPV = +1500 - \frac{1500}{(1.05)} = 1500 - 1428.57 = \$71.43$$

You could take $1428.57 of the $1500 you had saved for the TV and put it in your savings account. With interest, in one year it would grow to $1428.57 × (1.05) = $1500, enough to pay the store. The extra $71.43 is money in your pocket to spend as you like.

▶ **Evaluate**

By taking the delayed payment offer, we have extra net cash flows of $71.43 today. If we put $1428.57 in the bank, it will be just enough to offset our $1500 obligation in the future. Therefore, this offer is equivalent to receiving $71.43 today, without any future net obligations.

Choosing Among Alternatives. Managers also use the *NPV* decision rule to choose among projects. Suppose you own a coffee stand across from the campus and you hire someone to operate it for you. You will be graduating next year and have started to consider selling it. An investor has offered to buy the business from you for $20,000 whenever you are ready. Your interest rate is 10% and you are considering three alternatives:

1. Sell the business now.
2. Operate normally for one more year and then sell the business (requiring you to spend $5000 on supplies and labour now, but earn $10,000 at the end of the year).
3. Be open only in the mornings for one more year and then sell the business (requiring you to spend $3000 on supplies and labour now, but earn $6000 at the end of the year).

The cash flows and *NPVs* are given in Table 3.1.

TABLE 3.1		Now	One Year	NPV
Cash Flows and *NPVs* for Coffee Stand Alternatives	Sell	+$20,000	0	$20,000
	Operate Normally	−$5000	+$10,000 +$20,000	$-5000 + \dfrac{\$30,000}{1.10} = \$22,273$
	Mornings Only	−$3000	+$6000 +$20,000	$-3000 + \dfrac{\$26,000}{1.10} = \$20,636$

Among these three alternatives, you would choose the one with the highest *NPV*: operate normally for one year and then sell.

NPV and Cash Needs

When we compare projects with different patterns of present and future cash flows, we may have preferences regarding when to receive the cash. Some people may need cash today; others may prefer to save for the future. In our coffee stand example, operating normally for one more year and then selling has the highest *NPV*. However, this option does require an initial outlay for supplies (as opposed to selling the coffee stand and receiving $20,000 today). Suppose we would prefer to avoid the negative cash flow today. Would selling the business be a better choice in that case?

As was true for the jeweller in Section 3.2 considering trading silver for gold, the answer is again no. As long as we are able to borrow and lend at the interest rate, operating for one more year is superior, whatever our preferences regarding the timing of the cash flows. To see why, suppose we borrow $25,000 at the rate of 10% (in one year, we will owe $25,000 × [1.10] = $27,500) and operate the stand normally for one more year. Our total cash flows are shown in Table 3.2. Compare these cash flows to those for selling. The combination of borrowing and operating for a year generates the same initial cash flow as selling. Notice, however, that there is a higher final cash flow ($2500 versus $0). Thus, we are better off operating for a year and borrowing $25,000 today than we would be selling immediately.

TABLE 3.2		Cash Flow Today	Cash Flow in One Year
Cash Flows from Combining One More Year of Operating with Borrowing	Operate Normally	−$5000	$30,000
	Borrow	$25,000	−$25,000 × (1.10) = −$27,500
	Total	$20,000	$2500
	Sell Today	$20,000	0

This example illustrates the following general principle:

Regardless of our preferences for cash today versus cash in the future, we should always maximize NPV first. We can then borrow or lend to shift cash flows through time and find our most preferred pattern of cash flows.

Concept Check

9. What is the *NPV* decision rule? How is it related to the Valuation Principle?
10. Why doesn't the *NPV* decision rule depend on the investor's preferences?

3.6 The Law of One Price

Up to this point, we have emphasized the importance of using competitive market prices to compute the *NPV*. But is there always only one such price? What if the same good trades for different prices in different markets? Consider gold. Gold trades in many different markets, with the largest markets in New York and London. Gold can trade easily in many markets because investors are not literally transacting in the gold bars themselves (which are quite heavy!), but are trading ownership rights to gold that is stored securely elsewhere.[3] To value an ounce of gold, we could look up the competitive price in either of these markets. But suppose gold is trading for $1200 per ounce in New York and $1300 per ounce in London. Which price should we use?

In fact, situations such as this one, where the same asset is trading with different prices, should not occur in a competitive market. Let's see why. Recall that these are competitive market prices, at which you can both buy *and* sell. Thus, you can make money in this situation simply by buying gold for $1200 per ounce in New York and then

---

[3]Many countries store their gold reserves five floors under the Federal Reserve Bank of New York building in New York City. If a trade occurs, the physical gold is actually moved, but it is moved only a few feet from one country's compartment to another. Thus, transportation costs are insignificant even to these types of trades. If you plan to visit New York, you can make an advance booking for a tour of the gold vault (see the Federal Reserve Bank of New York website, www.ny.frb.org/aboutthefed/visiting.html).

immediately selling it for $1300 per ounce in London. You will make $1300 − $1200 = $100 per ounce for each ounce you buy and sell. Trading 1 million ounces at these prices, you would make $100 million with no risk or investment! This is a case where that old adage, "Buy low, sell high," can be followed perfectly.

Of course, you will not be the only one making these trades. Everyone who sees these prices will want to trade as many ounces as possible. Within seconds, the market in New York would be flooded with buy orders, and the market in London would be flooded with sell orders. Although a few ounces (traded by the lucky individuals who spotted this opportunity first) might be exchanged at these prices, the price of gold in New York would quickly rise in response to the excess demand, and the price in London would rapidly fall in response to the excess supply. Prices would continue to change until they were equalized somewhere in the middle, such as $1250 per ounce. This example illustrates an *arbitrage opportunity*, the focus of this section.

Arbitrage

arbitrage The practice of buying and selling equivalent goods or portfolios to take advantage of a price difference.

arbitrage opportunity Any situation in which it is possible to make a profit without taking any risk or making any investment.

The practice of buying and selling equivalent goods in different markets to take advantage of a price difference is known as **arbitrage**. More generally, we refer to any situation in which it is possible to make a profit without taking any risk or making any investment as an **arbitrage opportunity**. Because an arbitrage opportunity has positive *NPV*, whenever an arbitrage opportunity appears in financial markets, the Valuation Principle indicates that investors will race to take advantage of it. Those investors who spot the opportunity first and who can trade quickly will have the ability to exploit it. Once they place their trades, prices will respond due to the interaction of supply and demand forces, causing the arbitrage opportunity to evaporate.

Arbitrage opportunities are like money lying in the street; once spotted, they will quickly disappear. Thus, the normal state of affairs in markets should be that no arbitrage opportunities exist.

Law of One Price

In a competitive market, the price of gold at any point in time will be the same in London and New York. The same logic applies more generally whenever equivalent investment opportunities trade in two different competitive markets. If the prices in the two markets differ, investors will profit immediately by buying in the market where the price is cheap and selling in the market where it is expensive. In doing so, supply and

An Old Joke

There is an old joke that many finance professors enjoy telling their students. It goes like this:

A finance professor and a student are walking down a street. The student notices a $100 bill lying on the pavement and leans down to pick it up. The finance professor immediately intervenes and says, "Don't bother; there is no free lunch. If that were a real $100 bill lying there, somebody would already have picked it up!"

This joke makes fun of the principle of no arbitrage in competitive markets. But have you ever *actually* found a

real $100 bill lying on the pavement? Herein lies the real lesson behind the joke.

This joke sums up the point of focusing on markets in which no arbitrage opportunities exist. Free $100 bills lying on the pavement, like arbitrage opportunities, are extremely rare for two reasons: (1) Because $100 is a large amount of money, people are especially careful not to lose it, and (2) in the rare event when someone does inadvertently drop $100, the likelihood of your finding it before someone else does is extremely small.

Law of One Price
In competitive markets, securities or portfolios with the same cash flows must have the same price.

demand forces will equalize the prices. As a result, prices will not differ (at least not for long). This important property is the **Law of One Price**:

> *If equivalent investment opportunities trade simultaneously in different competitive markets, then they must trade for the same price in both markets.*

The Law of One Price will prove to be a powerful tool later in the text when we value securities such as stocks or bonds. We will show that any financial security can be thought of as a claim to future cash flows. The Law of One Price implies that if there is another way to recreate the future cash flows of the financial security, then the price of the financial security and the cost of recreating it must be the same. Recall that earlier we defined the present value of a cash flow to be the cost of recreating it in a competitive market. Thus, we have the following key implication of the Law of One Price for financial securities:

> *The price of a security should equal the present value of the future cash flows obtained from owning that security.*

EXAMPLE 3.6

Pricing a Security Using the Law of One Price

Problem
You are considering purchasing a security, a "bond," that pays $1000 without risk in one year, and has no other cash flows. If the interest rate is 5%, what should its price be?

Solution

▶ **Plan**
The security produces a single cash flow in one year:

The Law of One Price tells you that the value of a security that pays $1000 in one year is the present value of that $1000 cash flow, calculated as the cash flow discounted at the interest rate. The 5% interest rate implies that $1.05 in one year is worth $1 today.

▶ **Execute**
The present value of the $1000 cash flow is:

$$1000 \text{ in one year} \div \frac{1.05 \text{ \$ in one year}}{\text{\$ today}} = \$952.38 \text{ today}$$

Therefore, the price must be $952.38.

▶ **Evaluate**
Because we can receive $1000 in one year for a "price" of $952.38 by simply investing at the interest rate (i.e., $952.38 × 1.05 = $1000), the Law of One Price tells you that the price of the security must equal this "do it yourself" price, which is the present value of its cash flow evaluated using market interest rates. To see why this must be so, consider what would happen if the price were different. If the price were $950, you could borrow $950 at 5% interest and buy the bond. In one year, you would collect the $1000 from the bond and pay off your loan ($950 × 1.05 = $997.50), pocketing the difference. In fact, you would try to do the same thing for as many bonds as possible. But everyone else would also want to take advantage of this arbitrage by buying the bond, and so, due to the excess demand, its price would quickly rise. Similarly, if the price were above $952.38, everyone would sell the bond, invest the proceeds at 5%, and in one year would have more than the $1000 needed to pay the buyer of the security. The selling, and resulting excess supply, would cause the price of the bond to drop until this arbitrage was no longer possible—when it reaches $952.38. This powerful application of the Law of One Price shows that the price you pay for a security's cash flows cannot be different from their present value.

Transactions Costs

In our examples up to this point, we have ignored the costs of buying and selling goods or securities. In most markets, there are additional costs that you will incur when trading assets, called **transactions costs**. As discussed in Chapter 1, when you trade securities in markets such as the TSX, NYSE, and NASDAQ, you must pay two types of transactions costs. First, you must pay your broker a commission on the trade. Second, because you will generally pay a slightly higher price when you buy a security (the ask price) than you will receive when you sell (the bid price) it, you will also pay the bid-ask spread. For example, a share of Research In Motion stock (ticker symbol RIM) might be quoted as follows:

Bid: $49.80   Ask: $49.90

We can interpret these quotes as if the competitive price for RIM were $49.85, but there is a transaction cost of $0.05 per share when buying or selling.

What consequence do these transaction costs have for no-arbitrage prices and the Law of One Price? Earlier we stated that the price of gold in New York and London must be identical in competitive markets. Suppose, however, that total transactions costs of $5 per ounce are associated with buying gold in one market and selling it in the other. Then, if the price of gold is $1326 per ounce in New York and $1330 per ounce in London, the "Buy low, sell high" strategy no longer works:

Cost: $1326 per ounce (buy gold in New York) + $5 (transactions costs)

Benefit: $1330 per ounce (sell gold in London)

NPV: $1330 − $1326 − $5 = −$1 per ounce

Indeed, there is no arbitrage opportunity in this case until the prices diverge by more than $5, the amount of the transactions costs.

In general, we need to modify our previous conclusions about prices and values by appending the phrase "up to transactions costs." In this example, there is only one competitive price for gold—up to a discrepancy of the $5 transactions cost.

Fortunately, for most financial markets, these costs are small. For example, on the TSX, many actively traded stocks have bid-ask spreads of only between 1 and 10 cents per share. Less actively traded shares (such as those on the TSX Venture Exchange), though, do have larger spreads—this can be thought of as a less liquid or less competitive market. As a first approximation, we can ignore these spreads in our analysis. Only in situations in which the *NPV* is small (relative to the transactions costs) will any discrepancy matter. In that case, we will need to carefully account for all transaction costs to decide whether the *NPV* is positive or negative.

To summarize, when there are transactions costs, arbitrage keeps prices of equivalent goods and securities close to each other. Prices can deviate but not by more than the amount of the transactions costs.

---

transactions costs
Expenses such as broker commission and the bid-ask spread investors must pay in most markets in order to trade securities.

In the rest of the text, we will explore the details of implementing the Law of One Price to value securities. Specifically, we will determine the cash flows associated with stocks, bonds, and other securities, and learn how to compute the present value of these cash flows by taking into account their timing and risk.

11. If the Law of One Price were violated, how could investors profit?

12. What implication does the Law of One Price have for the price of a financial security?

MyFinanceLab

Here is what you should know after reading this chapter.
MyFinanceLab will help you identify what you know,
and where to go when you need to practice.

Key Points and Equations	Terms	Online Practice Opportunities
3.1 Managerial Decision Making ▶ To evaluate a decision, we must value the incremental costs and benefits associated with that decision. A good decision is one for which the value of the benefits exceeds the value of the costs.		MyFinanceLab Study Plan 3.1
3.2 Cost-Benefit Analysis ▶ To compare costs and benefits that occur at different points in time, we must put all costs and benefits in common terms. Typically, we convert costs and benefits into cash today.		MyFinanceLab Study Plan 3.2
3.3 Valuation Principle ▶ A competitive market is one in which a good can be bought and sold at the same price. We use prices from competitive markets to determine the cash value of a good. ▶ The Valuation Principle states that the value of a commodity or an asset to the firm or its investors is determined by its competitive market price. The benefits and costs of a decision should be evaluated using those market prices. When the value of the benefits exceeds the value of the costs, the decision will increase the market value of the firm.	competitive market, p. 70 Valuation Principle, p. 71	MyFinanceLab Study Plan 3.3
3.4 The Time Value of Money and Interest Rates ▶ The time value of money is the difference in value between money today and money in the future. ▶ The rate at which we can exchange money today for money in the future by borrowing or investing is the current market interest rate. ▶ The present value (*PV*) of a cash flow is its value in terms of cash today.	discount factor, p. 75 discount rate, p. 75 future value, p. 74 interest rate, p. 73 interest rate factor, p. 73 present value (*PV*), p. 74 time value of money, p. 73	MyFinanceLab Study Plan 3.4
3.5 The *NPV* Decision Rule ▶ The net present value (*NPV*) of a project is *PV*(Benefits) − *PV*(Costs). ▶ A good project is one with a positive net present value. ▶ The *NPV* decision rule states that when choosing from among a set of alternatives, choose the one with the highest *NPV*. The *NPV* of a project is equivalent to the cash value today of the project.	net present value (*NPV*), p. 77 *NPV* decision rule, p. 78	MyFinanceLab Study Plan 3.5

▶ Regardless of our preferences for cash today versus cash in the future, we should always first maximize *NPV*. We can then borrow or lend to shift cash flows through time and find our most preferred pattern of cash flows.

3.6 The Law of One Price

▶ Arbitrage is the process of trading to take advantage of equivalent goods that have different prices in different competitive markets.

▶ The Law of One Price states that if equivalent goods or securities trade simultaneously in different competitive markets, they will trade for the same price in each market. This law is equivalent to saying that no arbitrage opportunities should exist.

▶ The price of a security should equal the present value of the expected future cash flows obtained from owning that security.

arbitrage, p. 81
arbitrage opportunity,
  p. 81
Law of One Price, p. 82
transactions costs, p. 83

MyFinanceLab
  Study Plan 3.6

Review Questions

1. What makes an investment decision a good one?

2. How important are our personal preferences in valuing an investment decision?

3. Why are market prices useful to a financial manager?

4. How does the Valuation Principle help a financial manager make decisions?

5. Can we directly compare dollar amounts received at different points in time?

6. How is the net present value decision rule related to cost-benefit analysis?

7. If there is more than one project to take, how should the financial manager choose among them?

8. What is the relation between arbitrage and the Law of One Price?

Problems

All problems in this chapter are available in MyFinanceLab. An asterisk (*) indicates problems with a higher level of difficulty.

Cost-Benefit Analysis

1. Honda Motor Company is considering offering a $2000 rebate on its minivan, lowering the vehicle's price from $30,000 to $28,000. The marketing group estimates that this rebate will increase sales over the next year from 40,000 to 55,000 vehicles. Suppose Honda's profit margin with the rebate is $6000 per vehicle. If the change in sales is the only consequence of this decision, what are its costs and benefits? Is it a good idea?

2. You are an international shrimp trader. A food producer in the Czech Republic offers to pay you 2 million Czech koruna today in exchange for a year's supply of frozen

shrimp. Your Thai supplier will provide you with the same supply for 3 million Thai baht today. If the current competitive market exchange rates are 25.50 koruna per dollar and 41.25 baht per dollar, what is the value of this deal?

3. Suppose your employer offers you a choice between a $5000 bonus and 100 shares of the company's stock. Whichever one you choose will be awarded today. The stock is currently trading for $63 per share.
   a. Suppose that if you receive the stock bonus, you are free to trade it. Which form of the bonus should you choose? What is its value?
   b. Suppose that if you receive the stock bonus, you are required to hold it for at least one year. What can you say about the value of the stock bonus now? What will your decision depend on?

Valuation Principle

4. Bubba is a shrimp farmer. In an ironic twist, Bubba is allergic to shellfish, so he cannot eat any shrimp. Each day he has a one-tonne supply of shrimp. The market price of shrimp is $10,000 per tonne.
   a. What is the value of a tonne of shrimp to him?
   b. Would this value change if he were not allergic to shrimp? Why or why not?

5. Brett has almond orchards, but he is sick of almonds and prefers to eat walnuts instead. The owner of the walnut orchard next door has offered to swap this year's crop with him in an even exchange. Assume he produces 1000 tonnes of almonds and his neighbour produces 800 tonnes of walnuts. If the market price of almonds is $100 per tonne and the market price of walnuts is $1.10 per tonne:
   a. Should he make the exchange?
   b. Does it matter whether he prefers almonds or walnuts? Why or why not?

The Time Value of Money and Interest Rates

6. You have $100 and a bank is offering 5% interest on deposits. If you deposit the money in the bank, how much will you have in one year?

7. You expect to have $1000 in one year. A bank is offering loans at 6% interest per year. How much can you borrow today?

 8. A friend asks to borrow $55 from you and in return will pay you $58 in one year. If your bank is offering a 6% interest rate on deposits and loans:
   a. How much would you have in one year if you deposited the $55 instead?
   b. How much money could you borrow today if you pay the bank $58 in one year?
   c. Should you lend the money to your friend or deposit it in the bank?

 9. Suppose the interest rate is 4%.
   a. Having $200 today is equivalent to having what amount in one year?
   b. Having $200 in one year is equivalent to having what amount today?
   c. Which would you prefer, $200 today or $200 in one year? Does your answer depend on when you need the money? Why or why not?

The *NPV* Decision Rule

10. Your storage firm has been offered $100,000 in one year to store some goods for one year. Assume your costs are $95,000, payable immediately, and the interest rate is 8%. Should you take the contract?

 11. You run a construction firm. You have just won a contract to build a government office building. Building it will require an investment of $10 million today and $5 million in one year. The government will pay you $20 million in one year upon the building's completion. Suppose the interest rate is 10%.

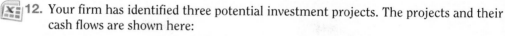

    a. What is the *NPV* of this opportunity?

    b. How can your firm turn this *NPV* into cash today?

12. Your firm has identified three potential investment projects. The projects and their cash flows are shown here:

Project	Cash Flow Today ($)	Cash Flow in One Year ($)
A	−10.00	20.00
B	5.00	5.00
C	20.00	−10.00

Suppose all cash flows are certain and the interest rate is 10%.

    a. What is the *NPV* of each project?

    b. If the firm can choose only one of these projects, which should it choose?

    c. If the firm can choose any two of these projects, which should it choose?

13. Your computer manufacturing firm must purchase 10,000 keyboards from a supplier. One supplier demands a payment of $100,000 today plus $10 per keyboard payable in one year. Another supplier will charge $21 per keyboard, also payable in one year. The interest rate is 6%.

    a. What is the difference in their offers in terms of dollars today? Which offer should your firm take?

    b. Suppose your firm does not want to spend cash today. How can it take the first offer and not spend $100,000 of its own cash today?

The Law of One Price

14. Suppose Bank One offers an interest rate of 5.5% on both savings and loans, and Bank Two offers an interest rate of 6% on both savings and loans.

    a. What arbitrage opportunity is available?

    b. Which bank would experience a surge in the demand for loans? Which bank would receive a surge in deposits?

    c. What would you expect to happen to the interest rates the two banks are offering?

15. If the cost of buying a CD and ripping the tracks to your iPod (including your time) is $25, what is the most Apple could charge on iTunes for a whole 15-track CD?

16. Some companies cross-list their shares, meaning that their stock trades on more than one stock exchange. For example, Research In Motion, the maker of BlackBerry mobile devices, trades on both the TSE and NASDAQ. If its price in Toronto is 100 Canadian dollars per share and anyone can exchange Canadian dollars (CAD) for U.S. dollars (USD) at the rate of 0.95 USD/CAD, what must RIM's price be on NASDAQ?

*17. Use the concept of arbitrage and the fact that interest rates are positive to prove that time travel will never be possible.

4

NPV and the Time Value of Money

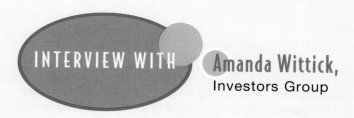

INTERVIEW WITH Amanda Wittick,
Investors Group

University of Manitoba, 2008

"We calculate the *NPV* of the project when making our decision."

Amanda Wittick is a senior business analyst for Investors Group, one of Canada's largest providers of personal financial planning services. She graduated from the University of Manitoba in 2008 with a Bachelor of Commerce degree.

Amanda works out of the company's Winnipeg office, providing liaison support between the IT and business units. "I help define business needs and facilitate the implementation of projects," she says. "While the project manager defines the project needs and assigns resources, I go through the business requirements and identify the potential risks and their impact on the project."

Her job often requires her to apply some of the tools learned in finance class. "When we're looking at implementing a new project, we need to go through a cost-benefit analysis to see if the project is worthwhile. We calculate the *NPV* of the project when making our decision. For example, since many projects we undertake involve the hiring of new employees, when calculating the *PV* of the employees' salaries we make the assumption that these new employees will be around forever, and we use the perpetuity formula taught in finance class. Our finance department will provide us with an appropriate discount rate."

Amanda credits her finance classes with providing her with the necessary background to excel at her occupation. "My studies in finance have provided me with a crucial understanding of the products we offer our clients, without which I would not be capable of effectively performing my job."

As we discussed in Chapter 3, to evaluate a project a financial manager must compare its costs and benefits. In most cases, the cash flows in financial investments involve more than one future period. Thus, the financial manager is faced with the task of trading off a known upfront cost against a series of uncertain future benefits. As we learned, calculating the net present value does just that, such that if the *NPV* of an investment is positive, we should take it.

Calculating the *NPV* requires tools to evaluate cash flows lasting several periods. We develop these tools in this chapter. The first tool is a visual method for representing a series of cash flows: the *timeline*. After constructing a timeline, we establish three important rules for moving cash flows to different points in time. Using these rules, we show how to compute the present and future values of the costs and benefits of a general stream of cash flows, and how to compute the *NPV*. Although we can use these techniques to value any type of asset, certain types of assets have cash flows that follow a regular pattern. We develop shortcuts for *annuities*, *perpetuities*, and other special cases of assets with cash flows that follow regular patterns.

In Chapter 5, we will learn how interest rates are quoted and determined. Once we understand how interest rates are quoted, it will be straightforward to extend the tools of this chapter to cash flows that occur more frequently than once per year.

The Timeline

stream of cash flows
A series of cash flows lasting several periods.

timeline A linear representation of the timing of (potential) cash flows.

We begin our discussion of valuing cash flows lasting several periods with some basic vocabulary and tools. We refer to a series of cash flows lasting several periods as a **stream of cash flows**. We can represent a stream of cash flows on a **timeline**, a linear representation of the timing of the expected cash flows. Timelines are an important first step in organizing and then solving a financial problem. We use them throughout this text.

Constructing a Timeline

To illustrate how to construct a timeline, assume that a friend owes you money. He has agreed to repay the loan by making two payments of $10,000 at the end of each of the next two years. We represent this information on a timeline as follows:

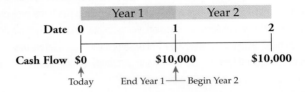

Date 0 represents the present. Date 1 is one year later and represents the end of the first year. The $10,000 cash flow below date 1 is the payment you will receive at the end of the first year. Date 2 is two years from now; it represents the end of the second year. The $10,000 cash flow below date 2 is the payment you will receive at the end of the second year.

Identifying Dates on a Timeline

To track cash flows, we interpret each point on the timeline as a specific date. The space between date 0 and date 1 then represents the time period between these dates—in this case, the first year of the loan. Date 0 is the beginning of the first year, and date 1 is the end of the first year. Similarly, date 1 is the beginning of the second year, and date 2 is the end of the second year. By denoting time in this way, date 1 signifies *both* the end of year 1 and the beginning of year 2, which makes sense since those dates are effectively the same point in time.[1]

Distinguishing Cash Inflows from Outflows

In this example, both cash flows are inflows. In many cases, however, a financial decision will involve both inflows and outflows. To differentiate between the two types of cash flows, we assign a different sign to each: Inflows (cash flows received) are positive cash flows, whereas outflows (cash flows paid out) are negative cash flows.

To illustrate, suppose you have agreed to lend your brother $10,000 today. Your brother has agreed to repay this loan in two installments of $6000 at the end of each of the next two years. The timeline is

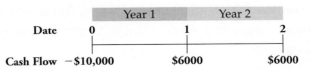

---

[1]That is, there is no real time difference between a cash flow paid at 11:59 P.M. on December 31 and one paid at 12:01 A.M. on January 1, although there may be some other differences such as taxation that we will overlook for now.

Notice that the first cash flow at date 0 (today) is represented as –$10,000 because it is an outflow. The subsequent cash flows of $6000 are positive because they are inflows.

Representing Various Time Periods

So far, we have used timelines to show the cash flows that occur at the end of each year. Actually, timelines can represent cash flows that take place at any point in time. For example, if you pay rent each month, you could use a timeline such as the one in our first example to represent two rental payments, but you would replace the "year" label with "month."

Many of the timelines included in this chapter are very simple. Consequently, you may feel that it is not worth the time or trouble to construct them. As you progress to more difficult problems, however, you will find that timelines identify events in a transaction or investment that are easy to overlook. If you fail to recognize these cash flows, you will make flawed financial decisions. Therefore, approach *every* problem by drawing the timeline as we do in this chapter.

Concept Check

1. What are the key elements of a timeline?
2. How can you distinguish cash inflows from outflows on a timeline?

4.2 Valuing Cash Flows at Different Points in Time

Financial decisions often require comparing or combining cash flows that occur at different points in time. In this section, we introduce three important rules central to financial decision making that allow us to compare or combine values.

Rule 1: Comparing and Combining Values

Our first rule is that it is only possible to compare or combine values at the same point in time. This rule restates a conclusion introduced in Chapter 3: Only cash flows in the same units can be compared or combined. A dollar today and a dollar in one year are not equivalent. Having money now is more valuable than having money in the future; if you have the money today you can earn interest on it.

Common Mistake　　**Summing Cash Flows Across Time**

Once you understand the time value of money, our first rule may seem straightforward. However, it is very common, especially for those who have not studied finance, to violate this rule, simply treating all cash flows as comparable, regardless of when they are received. One example of this is in sports contracts. In 2007, Alex Rodriguez and the New York Yankees were negotiating what was repeatedly referred to as a "$275 million" contract. The $275 million comes from simply adding up all of the payments that he would receive over the ten years of the contract and an additional ten years of deferred payments—treating dollars received in 20 years the same as dollars received today. The same thing occurred when David Beckham signed a "$250 million" contract with the LA Galaxy soccer team.

To compare or combine cash flows that occur at different points in time, you first need to convert the cash flows into the same units by moving them to the same point in time. The next two rules show how to move the cash flows on the timeline.

Rule 2: Compounding

Suppose we have $1000 today, and we wish to determine the equivalent amount in one year's time. As we saw in Chapter 3, if the current market interest rate is $r = 10\%$, we can use the interest rate factor $(1 + r) = 1.10$ as an exchange rate through time—meaning the rate at which we exchange a currency amount today for the same currency but in one year. That is:

$$(\$1000 \text{ today}) \times (1.10 \text{ \$ in one year} / \text{\$ today}) = \$1100 \text{ in one year}$$

In general, if the market interest rate for the year is r, then we multiply by the interest rate factor $(1 + r)$ to move the cash flow from the beginning to the end of the year. We multiply by $(1 + r)$ because at the end of the year you will have $(1 \times \text{your original investment})$ plus interest in the amount of $(r \times \text{your original investment})$. This process of moving forward along the timeline to determine a cash flow's value in the future (its **future value**) is known as **compounding**. *Our second rule stipulates that to calculate a cash flow's future value, you must compound it.*

future value The value of a cash flow that is moved forward in time.

compounding Computing the future value of a cash flow over a long horizon by multiplying by the interest rate factors associated with each intervening period.

We can apply this rule repeatedly. Suppose we want to know how much the $1000 is worth in two years' time. If the interest rate for year 2 is also 10%, then we convert as we just did:

$$(\$1100 \text{ in one year}) \times (1.10 \text{ \$ in two years} / \text{\$ in one year}) = \$1210 \text{ in two years}$$

Let's represent this calculation on a timeline:

```
        0              1              2
        |              |              |
      $1000  ------>  $1100  ------>  $1210
              × 1.10          × 1.10
```

Given a 10% interest rate, all of the cash flows—$1000 at date 0, $1100 at date 1, and $1210 at date 2—are equivalent. They have the same value to us but are expressed in different units (dollars at different points in time). An arrow that points to the right indicates that the value is being moved forward in time—that is, it is being compounded.

In the preceding example, $1210 is the future value of $1000 two years from today. Note that the value grows as we move the cash flow further in the future. In Chapter 3, we defined the time value of money as the difference in value between money today and money in the future. Here, we can say that $1210 in two years is the equivalent amount to $1000 today. The reason money is more valuable to you today is that you have opportunities to invest it. As in this example, by having money sooner, you can invest it (here at a 10% return) so that it will grow to a larger amount of money in the future. Note also that the equivalent amount grows by $100 the first year, but by $110 the second year. In the second year, we earn interest on our original $1000, plus we earn interest on the $100 interest we received in the first year. This effect of earning interest both on the original principal and on the accrued interest, is known as **compound interest**. Figure 4.1 shows how over time the amount of money you earn from interest on interest grows so that it will eventually exceed the amount of money that you earn as interest on your original deposit.

compound interest The combination of earning interest on the original principal and earning interest on accrued interest.

FIGURE 4.1

The Composition of Interest over Time

This bar graph shows how the account balance and the composition of the interest changes over time when an investor starts with an original deposit of $1000, represented by the red area, in an account earning 10% interest over a 20-year period. Note that the turquoise area representing interest on interest grows, and by year 15 has become larger than the interest on the original deposit, shown in green. Over the 20 years of the investment, the interest on interest the investor earned is $3727.50, while the interest earned on the original $1000 principal is $2000. The total compound interest over the 20 years is $5727.50 (the sum of the interest on interest and the interest on principal). Combining the original principal of $1000 with the total compound interest gives the future value after 20 years of $6727.50.

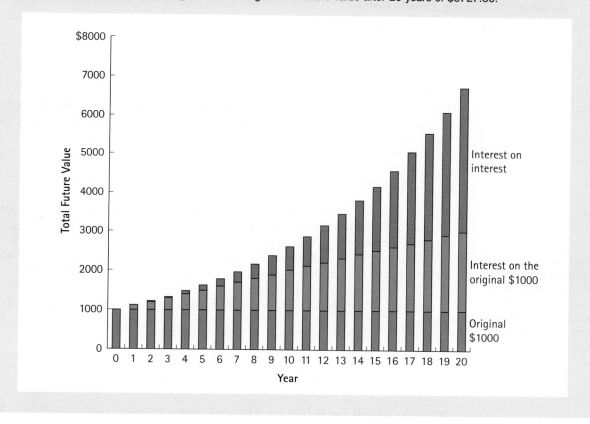

How does the future value change in the third year? Continuing to use the same approach, we compound the cash flow a third time. Assuming the competitive market interest rate is fixed at 10%, we get

$$\$1000 \times (1.10) \times (1.10) \times (1.10) = \$1000 \times (1.10)^3 = \$1331$$

In general, if we have a cash flow now, C_0, to compute its value n periods into the future, we must compound it by the n intervening interest rate factors. If the interest rate r is constant, this calculation yields

Future Value of a Cash Flow

$$FV_n = C_0 \times \underbrace{(1 + r) \times (1 + r) \times \cdots \times (1 + r)}_{n \text{ times}} = C_0 \times (1 + r)^n \qquad (4.1)$$

Rule of 72

Another way to think about the effect of compounding is to consider how long it will take your money to double, given different interest rates. Suppose you want to know how many years it will take for $1 to grow to a future value of $2. You want the number of years, *n*, to solve

$$FV_n = \$1 \times (1 + r)^n = \$2$$

If you solve this formula for different interest rates, you will find the following approximation:

Years to double $\approx 72 \div$ (interest rate in percent)

This simple "Rule of 72" is fairly accurate (i.e., within one year of the exact doubling time) for interest rates higher than 2%. For example, if the interest rate is 9%, the doubling time should be about $72 \div 9 = 8$ years. Indeed, $1.09^8 = 1.99$! So, given a 9% interest rate, your money will approximately double every eight years.

Rule 3: Discounting

The third rule describes how to put a value today on a cash flow that comes in the future. Suppose you would like to compute the value today of $1000 that you anticipate receiving in one year. If the current market interest rate is 10%, you can compute this value by converting units as we did in Chapter 3:

($1000 in one year) $\div$ (1.10 $ in one year / $ today) = $909.09 today

discounting Finding the equivalent value today of a future cash flow by multiplying by a discount factor, or equivalently, dividing by 1 plus the discount rate.

That is, to move the cash flow back along the timeline, we divide it by the interest rate factor $(1 + r)$ where *r* is the interest rate—this is the same as multiplying by the discount factor, $\frac{1}{(1 + r)}$. This process of finding the equivalent value today of a future cash flow is known as **discounting**. *Our third rule stipulates that to calculate the value of a future cash flow at an earlier point in time, we must discount it.*

Suppose that you anticipate receiving the $1000 two years from today rather than in one year. If the interest rate for both years is 10%, you can prepare the following timeline:

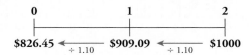

When the interest rate is 10%, all of the cash flows—$826.45 at date 0, $909.09 at date 1, and $1000 at date 2—are equivalent. They represent the same value to us but in different units (different points in time). The arrow points to the left to indicate that the value is being moved backward in time or discounted. Note that the value decreases the further in the future is the original cash flow.

The value of a future cash flow at an earlier point on the timeline is its present value at the earlier point in time. That is, $826.45 is the present value at date 0 of $1000 in two years. Recall from Chapter 3 that the present value is the "do-it-yourself" price to produce a future cash flow. Thus, if we invested $826.45 today for two years at 10% interest, we would have a future value of $1000, using the second rule of valuing cash flows:

Suppose the $1000 were three years away and you wanted to compute the present value. Again, if the interest rate is 10%, we have:

That is, the present value today of a cash flow of $1000 in three years is given by:

$$\$1000 \div (1.10) \div (1.10) \div (1.10) = \$1000 \div (1.10)^3 = \$751.31$$

In general, to compute the present value today (date 0) of a cash flow C_n that comes n periods from now, we must discount it by the n intervening interest rate factors. If the interest rate r is constant, this yields:

Present Value of a Cash Flow

$$PV_0 = C_n \div (1 + r)^n = \frac{C_n}{(1 + r)^n} \tag{4.2}$$

EXAMPLE 4.1

Present Value of a Single Future Cash Flow

Problem

You are considering investing in a Government of Canada bond that will pay $15,000 in ten years. If the competitive market interest rate is fixed at 6% per year, what is the bond worth today?

Solution

▶ **Plan**

First setup your timeline. The cash flows for this bond are represented by the following timeline:

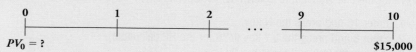

Thus, the bond is worth $15,000 in ten years. To determine the value today, PV_0, we compute the present value using Equation 4.2 with our interest rate of 6%.

▶ **Execute**

$$PV_0 = \frac{15,000}{1.06^{10}} = \$8375.92 \text{ today}$$

Using a financial calculator or Excel (see the appendix for step-by-step instructions):

	N	I/Y	PV	PMT	FV
Given:	10	6		0	15,000
Solve for:			−8375.92		

Excel Formula: $= PV(RATE, NPER, PMT, FV) = PV(0.06, 10, 0, 15000)$

▶ **Evaluate**

The bond is worth much less today than its final payoff because of the time value of money.

Using a Financial Calculator: Solving for Present and Future Values

So far, we have used formulas to compute present values and future values. Both financial calculators and spreadsheets have these formulas pre-programmed to quicken the process. In this box, we focus on financial calculators, but spreadsheets such as Excel have very similar shortcut functions.

Financial calculators have a set of functions that perform the calculations that finance professionals do most often. The functions are all based on the following timeline, which among other things can handle most types of loans:

```
0            1            2          NPER
|------------|------------|----...----|
PV          PMT          PMT        PMT + FV
```

There are a total of five variables: N, PV, PMT, FV, and the interest rate, denoted I/Y. Each function takes four of these variables as inputs and returns the value of the fifth one that ensures that the NPV of the cash flows is zero.

By setting the intermediate payments equal to 0, you could compute present and future values of single cash flows such as we have done above using Equations 4.1 and 4.2. In the examples in Section 4.5, we will calculate cash flows using the PMT button. The best way to learn to use a financial calculator is by practising. We present one example below. We will also show the calculator buttons for any additional examples in this chapter that can be solved with financial calculator functions. Finally, the appendix to this chapter contains step-by-step instructions for using the two most popular financial calculators.

Example

Suppose you plan to invest $20,000 in an account at the Canadian Western Bank paying 8% interest. How much will you have in the account in 15 years? We represent this problem with the following timeline:

```
0                1                2            NPER = 15
|----------------|----------------|----...-------|
PV = -$20,000   PMT = $0         $0            FV = ?
```

To compute the solution, we enter the four variables we know, $N = 15$, $I/Y = 8$, $PV = -20,000$, PMT = 0, and solve for the one we want to determine: FV. Specifically, for the HP-10BII or TI-BAII Plus calculators:

1. Enter 15 and press the N key.
2. Enter 8 and press the I/Y key (I/YR for the HP calculator).
3. Enter −20,000 and press the PV key.
4. Enter 0 and press the PMT key.
5. Press the FV key (for the Texas Instruments calculator, press CPT and then FV).

	N	I/Y	PV	PMT	FV
Given:	15	8	−20,000	0	
Solve for:					63,443

Excel Formula: $=FV(0.08,15,0,-20000)$

The calculator then shows a future value of $63,443.

Note that we entered PV as a negative number (the amount we are putting *into* the bank), and FV is shown as a positive number (the amount we can take *out* of the bank). It is important to use signs correctly to indicate the direction in which the money is flowing when using the calculator functions. You will see more examples of getting the sign of the cash flows correct throughout the chapter.

Excel has the same functions, but it calls "N," "NPER" and "I/Y," "RATE". *Also, it is important to note that you enter an interest rate of 8% as "8" in a financial calculator, but as 0.08 in Excel.*

Applying the Rules of Valuing Cash Flows

The rules of cash flow valuation allow us to compare and combine cash flows that occur at different points in time. Suppose we plan to deposit into our President's Choice Financial bank account $1000 at the end of each of the next three years. If we earn a fixed 10% interest rate on our savings, how much will we have three years from today (just after the last deposit)?

Again, we start with a timeline:

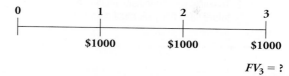

The timeline shows the three deposits we plan to make. We need to compute their value at the end of three years.

We can use the cash flow valuation rules in a number of ways to solve this problem. First, we can take the deposit at date 1 and move it forward to date 2. Because it is then in the same time period as the date 2 deposit, we can combine the two amounts to find out the total in the bank on date 2:

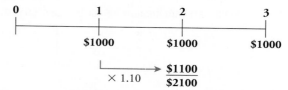

Using the first two rules, we find that our total savings on date 2 will be $2100. Continuing in this fashion, we can solve the problem as follows:

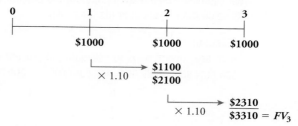

The total amount we will have in the President's Choice Financial bank account at the end of three years is $3310. This amount is the future value of our three $1000 savings deposits.

Another approach to the problem is to compute the future value in year 3 of each cash flow separately. Once all three amounts are in year 3 dollars, we can then combine them.

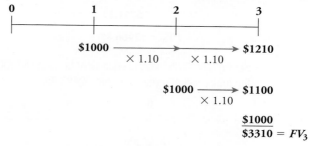

Both calculations give the same future value of $3310. As long as we follow the rules, we get the same result. The order in which we apply the rules does not matter. The calculation we choose depends on which is more convenient for the problem at hand. Table 4.1 summarizes the three rules of valuing cash flows and their associated formulas.

	Rule	Formula
TABLE 4.1 The Three Rules of Valuing Cash Flows	1: Only values at the same point in time can be compared or combined.	None
	2: To calculate a cash flow's future value, we must compound it.	Future value of a cash flow: $FV_n = C_0 \times (1 + r)^n$
	3: To calculate the present value of a future cash flow, we must discount it.	Present value of a cash flow: $PV_0 = C_n \div (1 + r)^n = \dfrac{C_n}{(1 + r)^n}$

EXAMPLE 4.2

Personal Finance
Computing the Future Value

Problem
Let's revisit the savings plan we considered earlier: We plan to save $1000 at the end of each of the next three years. At a fixed 10% interest rate, how much will we have in the President's Choice Financial bank account three years from today?

Solution

▶ **Plan**
We'll start with the timeline for this savings plan:

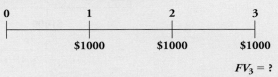

Let's solve this problem in a different way than we did in the text, while still following the rules we established. First we'll compute the present value of the cash flows. Then we'll compute its value three years later (its future value).

▶ **Execute**
There are several ways to calculate the present value of the cash flows. Here, we treat each cash flow separately and then combine the present values.

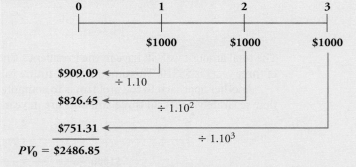

Saving $2486.85 today is equivalent to saving $1000 per year for three years. Now let's compute the future value in year 3 of that $2486.85:

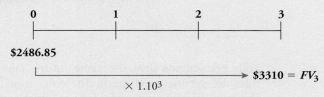

▶ **Evaluate**

This answer of $FV_3 = \$3310$ is precisely the same result we found earlier. As long as we apply the three rules of valuing cash flows, we will always get the correct answer.

Concept Check

3. Can you compare or combine cash flows at different times?

4. What do you need to know to compute a cash flow's present or future value?

4.3 Valuing a Stream of Cash Flows

Most investment opportunities have multiple cash flows that occur at different points in time. In Section 4.2, we learned the rules to value such cash flows. Now we formalize this approach by deriving a general formula for valuing a stream of cash flows.

Consider a stream of cash flows: C_0 at date 0, C_1 at date 1, and so on, up to C_n at date n. We represent this cash flow stream on a timeline as follows:

Using the rules of cash flow valuation, we compute the present value of this cash flow stream in two steps. First, we compute the present value of each individual cash flow. Then, once the cash flows are in common units of dollars today, we can combine them.

For a given interest rate r, we represent this process on the timeline as follows:

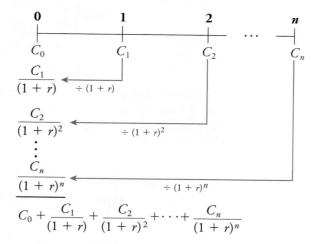

This equation provides the general formula for the present value of a cash flow stream:

$$PV_0 = C_0 + \frac{C_1}{(1 + r)} + \frac{C_2}{(1 + r)^2} + \cdots + \frac{C_n}{(1 + r)^n} \tag{4.3}$$

That is, the present value of the cash flow stream is the sum of the present values of each cash flow. Recall from Chapter 3 that we defined the present value as the dollar amount you would need to invest today to produce the single cash flow in the future. The same idea holds in this context. The present value is the amount you need to invest today to generate the cash flows stream $C_0, C_1, \ldots, C_n$. That is, receiving those cash flows is equivalent to having their present value in the bank today.

EXAMPLE 4.3

Personal Finance
Present Value of
a Stream of Cash
Flows

Problem

You have just graduated and need money to buy a new car. Your rich Uncle Henry will lend you the money so long as you agree to pay him back within four years, and you offer to pay him the rate of interest that he would otherwise get by putting his money in a savings account. Based on your earnings and living expenses, you think you will be able to pay him $5000 in one year, and then $8000 each year for the next three years. If Uncle Henry would otherwise earn 6% per year on his savings, how much can you borrow from him?

Solution

▶ **Plan**

The cash flows you can promise Uncle Henry are as follows:

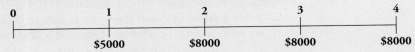

How much money should Uncle Henry be willing to give you today in return for your promise of these payments? He should be willing to give you an amount that is equivalent to these payments in present value terms. This is the amount of money that it would take him to produce these same cash flows. We will (1) solve the problem using Equation 4.3 and then (2) verify our answer by calculating the future value of this amount.

▶ **Execute**

1. We can calculate the PV as follows:

$$PV = \frac{5000}{1.06} + \frac{8000}{1.06^2} + \frac{8000}{1.06^3} + \frac{8000}{1.06^4}$$

$$= 4716.98 + 7119.97 + 6716.95 + 6336.75$$

$$= \$24{,}890.65$$

Now suppose that Uncle Henry gives you the money, and then deposits your payments to him in the bank each year. How much will he have four years from now?

We need to compute the future value of the annual deposits. One way to do so is to compute the bank balance each year:

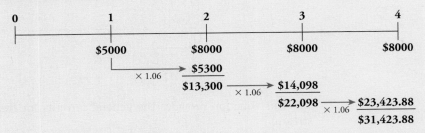

2. To verify our answer, suppose your uncle kept his $24,890.65 in the bank today earning 6% interest. In four years he would have:

$$FV_4 = \$24{,}890.65 \times (1.06)^4 = \$31{,}423.87 \text{ in 4 years}$$

We get the same answer both ways (within a penny, which is because of rounding).

▶ **Evaluate**

Thus, Uncle Henry should be willing to lend you $24,890.65 in exchange for your promised payments. This amount is less than the total you will pay him ($5000 + $8000 + $8000 + $8000 = $29,000) due to the time value of money.

Example 4.3 illustrates that if you want to compute the future value of a stream of cash flows, you can do it directly (the first approach used in Example 4.3), or you can first compute the present value and then move it to the future (the second approach). As always, we use Eq. 4.1 to calculate the future value of any present value. Because we obey the rules of valuing cash flows in both cases, we get the same result.

Concept Check

5. How do you calculate the present value of a cash flow stream?

6. How do you calculate the future value of a cash flow stream?

4.4 The Net Present Value of a Stream of Cash Flows

Now that we have established how to compute present and future values, we are ready to address our central goal: calculating the *NPV* of future cash flows to evaluate an investment decision. The Valuation Principle tells us that the value of a decision is the value of its benefits minus the value of its costs. *NPV* values those benefits and costs in today's dollars. Recall from Chapter 3 that we defined the net present value (*NPV*) of an investment decision as follows:

$$NPV = PV(\text{benefits}) - PV(\text{costs})$$

In this context, the benefits are the cash inflows, and the costs are the cash outflows. We can represent any investment decision on a timeline as a cash flow stream, where the cash outflows (investments) are negative cash flows and the inflows are positive

---

EXAMPLE 4.4

Personal Finance

Net Present Value of an Investment Opportunity

Problem

You have been offered the following investment opportunity: If you invest $1000 today, you will receive $500 at the end of each of the next two years, followed by $550 at the end of the third year. If you could otherwise earn 10% per year on your money, should you undertake the investment opportunity?

Solution

▶ **Plan**

As always, start with a timeline. We denote the upfront investment as a negative cash flow (because it is money you need to spend) and the money you receive as a positive cash flow.

To decide whether you should accept this opportunity, you'll need to compute the *NPV* by computing the present value of the stream.

▶ **Execute**

The *NPV* is:

$$NPV = -1000 + \frac{500}{1.10} + \frac{500}{1.10^2} + \frac{550}{1.10^3} = \$280.99$$

▶ **Evaluate**

Because the *NPV* is positive, the benefits exceed the costs and you should make the investment. Indeed, the *NPV* tells us that taking this opportunity is equivalent to getting an extra $280.99 that you can spend today. To illustrate, suppose you borrow $1000 to invest in the opportunity and an extra $280.99 to spend today. How much would you owe on the $1280.99 loan in three years? At 10% interest, the amount you would owe would be:

$$FV_3 = (\$1000 + \$280.99) \times (1.10)^3 = \$1705 \text{ in three years}$$

At the same time, the investment opportunity generates cash flows. If you put these cash flows into a bank account, how much will you have saved three years from now? The future value of the savings is

$$FV_3 = (\$500 \times 1.10^2) + (\$500 \times 1.10) + \$550 = \$1705 \text{ in three years}$$

As you see, you can use your bank savings to repay the loan. Taking the opportunity therefore allows you to spend $280.99 today at no extra cost.

cash flows. Thus, the *NPV* of an investment opportunity is also the *present value* of the stream of cash flows of the opportunity:

$$NPV = PV(\text{benefits}) - PV(\text{costs}) = PV(\text{benefits} - \text{costs})$$

In principle, we have met the goal we set at the beginning of the chapter: How financial managers should evaluate a project. We have developed the tools to evaluate the cash flows of a project. We have shown how to compute the *NPV* of an investment opportunity that lasts more than one period. In practice, when the number of cash flows exceeds four or five (as it most likely will), the calculations can become tedious. Fortunately, a number of special cases do not require us to discount each cash flow separately. We derive these shortcuts in the next section.

Concept Check

7. What benefit does a firm receive when it accepts a project with a positive *NPV*?

8. How do you calculate the net present value of a cash flow stream?

4.5 Perpetuities, Annuities, and Other Special Cases

The formulas we have developed so far allow us to compute the present or future value of any cash flow stream. In this section, we consider two types of cash flow streams, *perpetuities* and *annuities,* and learn shortcuts for valuing them. These shortcuts are possible because the cash flows follow a regular pattern.

Perpetuities

perpetuity A stream of equal cash flows that occurs at regular intervals and lasts forever.

consol A bond that promises its owner a fixed cash flow every year, forever.

A **perpetuity** is a stream of equal cash flows that occur at regular intervals and last forever. One example is the British government bond called a **consol** (or perpetual bond). Consol bonds promise the owner a fixed cash flow every year, forever.

Here is the timeline for a perpetuity:

Note from the timeline that the first cash flow does not occur immediately; *it arrives at the end of the first period.* This timing is sometimes referred to as payment *in arrears* and is a standard convention in loan payment calculations and elsewhere, so we adopt it throughout this text.

Using the formula for the present value, the present value of a perpetuity with payment C and interest rate r is given by:

$$PV = \frac{C}{(1+r)} + \frac{C}{(1+r)^2} + \frac{C}{(1+r)^3} + \cdots$$

Notice that all of the cash flows (C in the formula) are the same because the cash flow for a perpetuity is constant: thus we do not need a time subscript on each one. Also, because the first cash flow is in one period, there is no cash flow at time 0 ($C_0 = 0$).

To find the value of a perpetuity by discounting one cash flow at a time would take forever—literally! You might wonder how, even with a shortcut, the sum of an infinite number of positive terms could be finite. The answer is that the cash flows in the future are discounted for an ever increasing number of periods, so their contribution to the sum eventually becomes negligible.

To derive the shortcut, we calculate the value of a perpetuity by creating our own perpetuity. The Valuation Principle tells us that the value of a perpetuity must be the same as the cost we incurred to create our own identical perpetuity. To illustrate, suppose you could invest $100 in a bank account paying 5% interest per year forever. At the end of one year, you will have $105 in the bank—your original $100 plus $5 in interest. Suppose you withdraw the $5 interest and reinvest the $100 for a second year. Again, you will have $105 after one year, and you can withdraw $5 and reinvest $100 for another year. By doing this year after year, you can withdraw $5 every year in perpetuity:

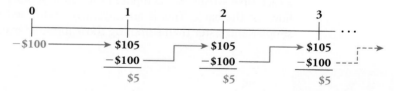

By investing $100 in the bank today, you can, in effect, create a perpetuity paying $5 per year. Recall from Chapter 3 that the Law of One Price tells us that equivalent cash flows must have the same price in every market. Because the bank will "sell" us (allow us to create) the perpetuity for $100, the present value of the $5 per year in perpetuity is this "do-it-yourself" cost of $100.

Now let's generalize this argument. Suppose we invest an amount P in a bank account with an interest rate r. Every year we can withdraw the interest we have earned, $C = r \times P$, leaving the principal, P, in the bank. Because our cost for creating the perpetuity is only the initial investment of principal (P), the value of receiving C in perpetuity is therefore the upfront cost P. Rearranging $C = r \times P$ to solve for P we have $P = C/r$. Therefore

Present Value of a Perpetuity with Constant Cash Flows, C, and Discount Rate, r

$$PV_0 = \frac{C}{r} \tag{4.4}$$

Historical Examples of Perpetuities

Companies sometimes issue bonds that they call perpetuities, but in fact are not really perpetuities. For example, according to *Dow Jones International News* (February 26, 2004), in 2004 Korea First Bank sold $300 million of debt in "the form of a so-called 'perpetual bond' that has no fixed maturity date." Although the bond has no fixed maturity date, Korea First Bank has the right to pay it back after 10 years, in 2014. Korea First Bank also has the right to extend the maturity of the bond for another 30 years after 2014. Thus, although the bond does not have a fixed maturity date, it will eventually mature—in either 10 or 40 years. The bond is not really a perpetuity because it does not pay interest forever.

Perpetual bonds were some of the first bonds ever issued. The oldest perpetuities that are still making interest payments were issued by the *Hoogheemraadschap Lekdijk Bovendams,* a seventeenth-century Dutch water board responsible for upkeep of the local dikes. The oldest bond dates from 1624. Two finance professors at Yale University, William Goetzmann and Geert Rouwenhorst, personally verified that these bonds continue to pay interest. On behalf of Yale, they purchased one of these bonds on July 1, 2003, and collected 26 years of back interest. On its issue date in 1648, this bond originally paid interest in Carolus guilders. Over the next 355 years, the currency of payment changed to Flemish pounds, Dutch guilders, and most recently euros. Currently, the bond pays interest of €11.34 annually.

Although the Dutch bonds are the oldest perpetuities still in existence, the first perpetuities date from much earlier times. For example, *census agreements* and *rentes,* which were forms of perpetuities and annuities, were issued in the twelfth century in Italy, France, and Spain. They were initially designed to circumvent the usury laws of the Catholic Church: Because they did not require the repayment of principal, in the eyes of the church they were not considered loans.

By depositing the amount $\dfrac{C}{r}$ today, we can withdraw interest of $\dfrac{C}{r} \times r = C$ each period in perpetuity. Note, the first cash flow of C is received one period after the deposit is made. Thus it is important to remember that the *PV* calculated is one period before the first cash flow.

Our methodology can be summarized as follows. To determine the present value of a cash flow stream, we computed the "do-it-yourself" cost of creating those same cash flows at the bank. This is an extremely useful and powerful approach—and is much simpler and faster than summing those infinite terms!

EXAMPLE 4.5

Personal Finance
Endowing a
Perpetuity

Problem
You want to endow an annual graduation party at your university. You want the event to be a memorable one, so you budget $30,000 per year forever for the party. If the university earns 8% per year on its investments, and if the first party is in one year's time, how much will you need to donate to endow the party?

Solution

▶ **Plan**
The timeline of the cash flows you want to provide is:

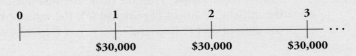

This is a standard perpetuity of $30,000 per year. The funding you would need to give the university in perpetuity is the present value of this cash flow stream.

▶ **Execute**

Use the formula for a perpetuity:

$$PV_0 = C/r = \$30,000/0.08 = \$375,000 \text{ today}$$

▶ **Evaluate**

If you donate $375,000 today, and if the university invests it at 8% per year forever, then the graduates will have $30,000 every year for their graduation party.

Annuities

annuity A stream of equal cash flows arriving at a regular interval over a specified time period.

An **annuity** is a stream of n equal cash flows paid at regular intervals. The difference between an annuity and a perpetuity is that an annuity ends after some fixed number of payments. Most car loans, mortgages, and some bonds are annuities. We represent the cash flows of an annuity on a timeline as follows:

Common Mistake · Discounting One Too Many Times

The perpetuity formula assumes that the first payment occurs at the end of the first period (at date 1). Sometimes perpetuities have cash flows that start later in the future. In this case, we can adapt the perpetuity formula to compute the present value, but we need to do so carefully to avoid a common mistake.

To illustrate, consider the graduation party described in Example 4.6. Rather than starting in one year, suppose that the first party will be held two years from today. How would this delay change the amount of the donation required?

Now the timeline looks like this:

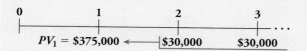

We need to determine the present value of these cash flows, as it tells us the amount of money in the bank needed today to finance the future parties. We cannot apply the perpetuity formula directly, however, because these cash flows are not *exactly* a perpetuity as we defined it. Specifically, the cash flow in the first period is "missing." But consider the situation on date 1—at that point, the first party is one period away and then the cash flows occur regularly. From the perspective of date 1, this *is* a

perpetuity, and we can apply the formula (effectively getting PV_1). From the preceding calculation, we know we need $375,000 on date 1 to have enough to start the parties on date 2. We rewrite the timeline as follows:

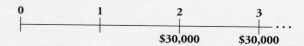

Our goal can now be restated more simply: How much do we need to invest today to have $PV_1 = \$375,000$ in one year? This is a simple present value calculation:

$$PV_0 = \frac{PV_1}{(1 + r)}$$

$$PV_0 = \$375,000/1.08 = \$347,222 \text{ today}$$

A common mistake is to discount the $375,000 twice because the first party is in two periods. Remember— the present value formula for the perpetuity already discounts the cash flows to one period prior to the first cash flow. Keep in mind that this common mistake may be made with perpetuities, annuities, and all of the other special cases discussed in this section. All of these formulas discount the cash flows to one period prior to the first cash flow.

Note that just as with the perpetuity, we adopt the convention that the first payment takes place at date 1, one period from today. The present value of an n-period annuity with payment C and interest rate r is:

$$PV_0 = \frac{C}{(1 + r)} + \frac{C}{(1 + r)^2} + \frac{C}{(1 + r)^3} + \cdots + \frac{C}{(1 + r)^n}$$

Present Value of an Annuity. To find a simpler formula, we use the same approach we followed with the perpetuity: find a way to create your own annuity. To illustrate, suppose you invest $100 in a bank account paying 5% interest. At the end of one year, you will have $105 in the bank—your original $100 plus $5 in interest. Using the same strategy as you did for calculating the value of a perpetuity, suppose you withdraw the $5 interest and reinvest the $100 for a second year. Once again you will have $105 after one year. You can repeat the process, withdrawing $5 and reinvesting $100, every year. For a perpetuity, you left the principal in the bank forever. Alternatively, you might decide after 20 years to close the account and withdraw the principal. In that case, your cash flows will look like this:

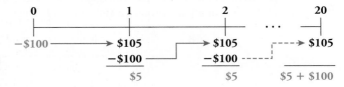

With your initial $100 investment, you have created a 20-year annuity of $5 per year, plus you will receive an extra $100 at the end of 20 years. Again, the Valuation Principle's Law of One Price tells us that because it only took an initial investment of $100 to create the cash flows on the timeline, the present value of these cash flows is $100, or:

$$\$100 = PV(\text{20-year annuity of \$5 per year}) + PV(\$100 \text{ in 20 years})$$

So if we invest $100 now, we can receive $5 per year for 20 years as well as $100 in the 20th year, representing the following cash flows:

Rearranging the equation above shows that the cost of a 20-year annuity of $5 per year is $100 minus the present value of $100 in 20 years.

$$PV(\text{20-year annuity of \$5 per year}) = \$100 - PV(\$100 \text{ in 20 years})$$

$$= \$100 - \frac{\$100}{(1.05)^{20}} = \$100 - \$37.69 = \$62.31$$

0	1	2	20
$-\$100$	$5	$5	$5 + $100

Removing the $100 in 20 years and its present value leaves the following cash flows:

$-\$62.31$	$5	$5	$\cdots$	$5

So the present value of $5 for 20 years is $62.31. Intuitively, the value of the annuity is the initial investment in the bank account minus the present value of the principal that will be left in the account after 20 years.

The $5 we receive every year is the interest on the $100 and can be written as $100(.05) = $5. Rearranging, we have $100 = $5/.05. If we substitute $5/.05 into our formula above, we can represent the *PV* of the annuity as a function of its cash flow ($5), the discount rate (5%), and the number of years (20):

$$PV(\text{20-year annuity of \$5 per year}) = \frac{\$5}{.05} - \frac{\frac{\$5}{.05}}{(1.05)^{20}} = \frac{\$5}{.05}\left(1 - \frac{1}{(1.05)^{20}}\right)*$$

$$= \$5 \times \frac{1}{.05}\left(1 - \frac{1}{(1.05)^{20}}\right)$$

This method is very useful because we will most often want to know the *PV* of the annuity given its cash flow, discount rate, and number of years. We can write this as a general formula for the present value of an annuity of *C* for *n* periods:

Present Value of an *n*-Period Annuity with Constant Cash Flows, *C*,
and Discount Rate, *r*

$$PV_0 = C \times \frac{1}{r}\left(1 - \frac{1}{(1+r)^n}\right) \tag{4.5}$$

Let's revisit the cash flows presented in Example 4.2 ($1000 invested at the end of each of the next three years). Using equation 4.5, we get the following:

$$PV_0 = \$1000 \times \frac{1}{.10}\left(1 - \frac{1}{(1 + .10)^3}\right) = \$2486.85$$

As you can see, this is the same result we obtained when discounting the cash flows individually. Equation 4.5, though, does the calculation in one step instead of having to do calculations for each cash flow as we did in Example 4.2. Using the present value of an annuity formula can save a lot of time when analyzing annuities that have many cash flows.

EXAMPLE 4.6

Personal Finance
Present Value of
a Lottery Prize
Annuity

Problem

While vacationing in the US, you purchased a state lottery ticket and now you are the lucky winner of the $30 million prize. Upon reading the fine print, though, you find that you can take your prize money either as (a) 30 payments of $1 million per year (starting today), or (b) $15 million paid today. If the interest rate is 8%, which option should you take?

Solution

▶ **Plan**

Option (a) provides $30 million in prize money but paid over time. To evaluate it correctly, we must convert it to a present value. Here is the timeline:

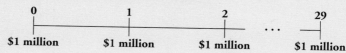

---

*An early derivation of this formula is attributed to the astonomer Edmond Halley in *Of Compound Interest*, published after Halley's death by Henry Sherwin, Sherwin's Mathematical Tables (London: W. and J. Mount, T. Page and Son, 1761).

Because the first payment starts today, the last payment will occur in 29 years (for a total of 30 payments).[2] The $1 million at date 0 is already stated in present value terms, but we need to compute the present value of the remaining payments. Fortunately, this case looks like a 29-year annuity of $1 million per year, so we can use the annuity formula.

▶ **Execute**

We use the annuity formula:

$$PV(\text{29-year annuity of \$1 million}) = \$1 \text{ million} \times \frac{1}{0.08}\left(1 - \frac{1}{1.08^{29}}\right)$$

$$= \$11,158,406.01 \text{ today}$$

Thus, the total present value of the cash flows is $1 million + $11,158,406.01 = $12,158,406.01. In timeline form:

0	1	2	29
$1 million	$1 million	$1 million	$1 million

$11,158,406.01

$12,158,406.01

Option (b), $15 million upfront, is more valuable—even though the total amount of money paid is half that of option (a).

Financial calculators or Excel can handle annuities easily—just enter the cash flow in the annuity as the *PMT:*

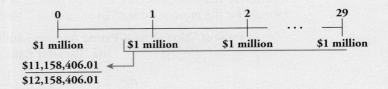

	N	I/Y	PV	PMT	FV
Given:	29	8		1,000,000	0
Solve for:			−11,158,406.01		
Excel Formula: =PV(RATE,NPER,PMT,FV)=PV(0.08,29,1000000,0)					

Both the financial calculator and Excel will give you the *PV* of the 29 payments ($11.16 million) to which you must add the first payment of $1 million just as above.

▶ **Evaluate**

The reason for the difference is the time value of money. If you have the $15 million today, you can use $1 million immediately and invest the remaining $14 million at an 8% interest rate. This strategy will give you $14 million × 8% = $1.12 million per year in perpetuity! Alternatively, you can spend $15 million − $11.16 million = $3.84 million today, and invest the remaining $11.16 million, which will still allow you to withdraw $1 million each year for the next 29 years before your account is depleted.

---

[2]An annuity in which the first payment occurs immediately is sometimes called an *annuity due.* Throughout this text, we always use the term "annuity" to mean one that is paid in arrears (i.e., at the end of each period).

Future Value of an Annuity. Now that we have derived a simple formula for the present value of an annuity, it is easy to find a simple formula for the future value. If we want to know the value n years in the future, we move the present value n periods forward on the timeline.

$$PV_0 = \frac{C}{r}\left(1 - \frac{1}{(1+r)^n}\right)$$

$$FV_n = \frac{C}{r}\left(1 - \frac{1}{(1+r)^n}\right) \times (1 + r)^n$$

As the timeline shows, we compound the present value for n periods at interest rate r:

Future Value of an n-Period Annuity with Constant Cash Flows, C, and Interest Rate, r

$$FV_n = PV_0 \times (1 + r)^n$$

$$= \frac{C}{r}\left(1 - \frac{1}{(1+r)^n}\right) \times (1 + r)^n$$

$$= C \times \frac{1}{r}\left((1 + r)^n - 1\right) \tag{4.6}$$

This formula is useful if we want to know how a savings account will grow over time and the investor deposits the same amount every period. We can reevaluate the cash flows in Example 4.2 ($1000 invested at the end of each of three years) to get their future value using Equation 4.6.

$$FV_3 = \$1000 \times \frac{1}{0.10}\left((1 + 0.10)^3 - 1\right) = \$3310$$

As you can see, this gives the same result, in one step, as the three calculations used in Example 4.2.

EXAMPLE 4.7

Personal Finance
Retirement Savings
Plan Annuity

Problem

Ellen is 35 years old and she has decided it is time to plan seriously for her retirement. At the end of each year until she is 65, she will save $10,000 in a registered retirement savings account (RRSP). If the account earns 10% per year, how much will Ellen have saved at age 65?

Solution

▶ **Plan**

As always, we begin with a timeline. In this case, it is helpful to keep track of both the dates and Ellen's age:

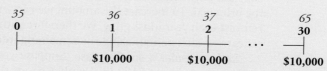

Ellen's savings plan looks like an annuity of $10,000 per year for 30 years. (*Hint:* It is easy to become confused when you just look at age, rather than at both dates and age. A common error is to think there are only $65 - 36 = 29$ payments. Writing down both dates and age avoids this problem.)

To determine the amount Ellen will have in the bank at age 65, we'll need to compute the future value of this annuity.

▶ **Execute**

$$FV = \$10,000 \times \frac{1}{0.10}(1.10^{30} - 1)$$

$$= \$1,644,940.23 \text{ million at age 65}$$

Using a financial calculator or Excel:

	N	I/Y	PV	PMT	FV
Given:	30	10	0	−10,000	
Solve for:					1,644,940
Excel Formula:			$=FV(RATE,NPER,PMT,PV)=FV(0.10,30,-10000,0)$		

▶ **Evaluate**

By investing $10,000 per year for 30 years (a total of $300,000) and earning interest on those investments, the compounding will allow her to retire with about $1.645 million in her RRSP.

Growing Cash Flows

So far, we have considered only cash flow streams that have the same cash flow every period. If, instead, the cash flows are expected to grow at a constant rate in each period, we can also derive a simple formula for the present value of the future stream.

growing perpetuity
A stream of cash flows that occurs at regular intervals and grows at a constant rate forever.

Growing Perpetuity. A **growing perpetuity** is a stream of cash flows that occurs at regular intervals and grows at a constant rate forever. For example, a growing perpetuity with a first payment of $100 that grows at a rate of 3% has the following timeline:

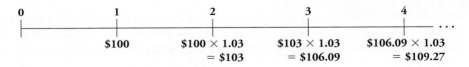

0	1	2	3	4	
	$100	$100 × 1.03 = $103	$103 × 1.03 = $106.09	$106.09 × 1.03 = $109.27	...

To derive the formula for the present value of a growing perpetuity, we follow the same logic used for a regular perpetuity: Compute the amount you would need to deposit today to create the perpetuity yourself. In the case of a regular perpetuity, we created a constant payment forever by withdrawing the interest earned each year and reinvesting the principal. To increase the amount we can withdraw each year, the principal that we reinvest each year must grow. We therefore withdraw less than the full amount of interest earned each period, using the remaining interest to increase our principal.

Let's consider a specific case. Suppose you want to create a perpetuity growing at 2%, so you invest $100 in a bank account that pays 5% interest. At the end of one year, you will have $105 in the bank—your original $100 plus $5 in interest. If you withdraw only $3, you will have $102 to reinvest—2% more than the amount you had initially. This amount will then grow to $102 × 1.05 = $107.10 in the following year, and you can withdraw $3 × 1.02 = $3.06, which will leave you with principal of $107.10 − $3.06 = $104.04. Note that $102 × 1.02 = $104.04. That is, both the amount you withdraw and the principal you reinvest grow by 2% each year. On a timeline, these cash flows look like this:

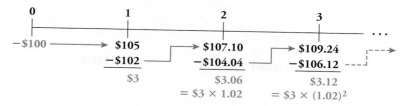

By following this strategy, you have created a growing perpetuity that starts at $3 and grows 2% per year. This growing perpetuity must have a present value equal to the cost of $100.

We can generalize this argument. If we want to increase the amount we withdraw from the bank each year by g, then the principal in the bank will have to grow by the same factor g. That is, instead of reinvesting P in the second year, we should reinvest $P(1 + g) = P + gP$. In order to increase our principal by gP, we need to leave gP of the interest in the account, so of the total interest of rP, we can only withdraw $rP − gP = P(r − g)$. We demonstrate this for the first year of our example:

Initial amount deposited	$100	P
Interest earned	(0.05)($100)	rP
Amount needed to increase principal	(0.02)($100)	gP
Amount withdrawn	(0.05)($100) − (0.02)($100)	$rP − gP$
	= $100(0.05 − 0.02)	= $P(r − g)$

Denoting our withdrawal as C_1, we have $C_1 = P(r − g)$. Solving this equation for P, the initial amount deposited in the bank account, gives the present value of a growing perpetuity with C_1 as the initial cash flow.[3]

Present Value of a Growing Perpetuity with first cash flow, C_1, and growth rate, g

$$PV_0 = \frac{C_1}{r - g}$$

(4.7)

---

[3]Suppose $g \geq r$. Then the cash flows grow even faster than they are discounted; each term in the sum gets larger, rather than smaller. In this case, the sum is infinite! What does an infinite present value mean? Remember that the present value is the "do-it-yourself" cost of creating the cash flows. An infinite present value means that no matter how much money you start with, it is *impossible* to reproduce those cash flows on your own. Growing perpetuities of this sort cannot exist in practice because no one would be willing to offer one at any finite price. A promise to pay an amount that forever grew faster than the interest rate is also unlikely to be kept (or believed by any savvy buyer). The only viable growing perpetuities are those where the growth rate is less than the interest rate, so we assume that $g < r$ for a growing perpetuity.

EXAMPLE 4.8

Personal Finance
Endowing a
Growing Perpetuity

Problem

In Example 4.5, you planned to donate money to your university to fund an annual $30,000 graduation party. Given an interest rate of 8% per year, the required donation was the present value of:

$$PV_0 = \$30,000/0.08 = \$375,000 \text{ today}$$

Before accepting the money, however, the student association has asked that you increase the donation to account for the effect of inflation on the cost of the party in future years. Although $30,000 is adequate for next year's party, the students estimate that the party's cost will rise by 4% per year thereafter. To satisfy their request, how much do you need to donate now?

Solution

▶ **Plan**

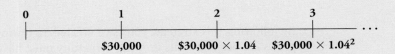

The cost of the party next year is $30,000, and the cost then increases 4% per year forever. From the timeline, we recognize the form of a growing perpetuity and can value it that way.

▶ **Execute**

To finance the growing cost, you need to provide the present value today of:

$$PV_0 = \$30,000/(0.08 - 0.04) = \$750,000 \text{ today}$$

▶ **Evaluate**

You need to double the size of your gift!

Growing Annuity. A **growing annuity** is a stream of n growing cash flows, paid at regular intervals. It is a growing perpetuity that eventually comes to an end. The following timeline shows a growing annuity with initial cash flow C_1, growing at rate g every period until period n:

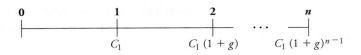

As with growing perpetuities discussed earlier, we adopt the convention that the first payment occurs at date 1. Since the first payment, C_1, occurs at date 1 and the nth payment, C_n, occurs at date n, there are only $n - 1$ periods of growth between these payments.

The present value of an n-period growing annuity with initial cash flow C_1, growth rate g, and interest rate r is given by

Present Value of a Growing Annuity

$$PV = C_1 \times \frac{1}{r - g}\left(1 - \left(\frac{1 + g}{1 + r}\right)^n\right) \tag{4.8}$$

Because the annuity has only a finite number of terms, Eq. 4.8 also works when $g > r^7$. The process of deriving this simple expression for the present value of a growing annuity is the same as for a regular annuity. Interested readers may consult the online appendix for details.

EXAMPLE 4.9

Personal Finance
Retirement Savings
with a Growing
Annuity

Problem

In Example 4.7, Ellen considered saving $10,000 per year for her retirement. Although $10,000 is the most she can save in the first year, she expects her salary to increase each year so that she will be able to increase her savings by 5% per year. With this plan, if she earns 10% per year in her RRSP, what is the present value of her planned savings and how much will Ellen have saved at age 65?

Solution

▶ **Plan**

As always, we begin with a timeline. Again, it is helpful to keep track of both the dates and Ellen's age:

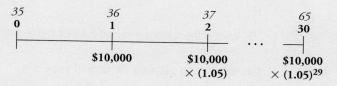

This example involves a 30-year growing annuity, with a growth rate of 5%, and an initial cash flow of $10,000.

▶ **Execute**

The present value of this growing annuity is given by

$$PV = \$10{,}000 \times \frac{1}{0.10 - 0.05}\left(1 - \left(\frac{1.05}{1.10}\right)^{30}\right)$$

$$= \$10{,}000 \times 15.0463$$

$$= \$150{,}463 \text{ today}$$

To determine the amount she will have at age 65, we need to move this amount forward 30 years:

$$FV = \$150{,}463 \times 1.10^{30}$$

$$= \$2.625 \text{ million in 30 years}$$

Unfortunately your financial calculator and Excel do not have pre-programmed functions to handle growing annuities.

▶ **Evaluate**

By investing the growing amounts (starting with $10,000) each year for 30 years, Ellen's proposed savings plan is equivalent to having $150,463 in the bank *today*.

Ellen will have saved $2.625 million at age 65 using the new savings plan. This sum is almost $1 million more than she would have had in her RRSP without the additional annual increases in savings (as shown in Example 4.7).

Finding a simple formula for the future value of a growing annuity is easy, just as we saw for regular annuities. If we want to know the value n years in the future, we move the present value n periods forward on the timeline; that is, we compound the present value for n periods at interest rate r:

Future Value of a Growing Annuity

$$PV_0 = C_1 \times \frac{1}{r - g}\left(1 - \left(\frac{1 + g}{1 + r}\right)^n\right)$$

$$FV_n = PV_0 \times (1 + r)^n = C_1 \times \frac{1}{r - g}\left(1 - \left(\frac{1 + g}{1 + r}\right)^n\right) \times (1 + r)^n \qquad (4.9)$$

$$FV_n = C_1 \times \frac{1}{r - g}\left((1 + r)^n - (1 + g)^n\right)$$

Try using this formula in Example 4.9 to get the future value of Ellen's savings when she is 65.

Concept Check

9. What is the reasoning behind the fact that an infinite stream of cash flows has a finite present value?

10. How do you calculate the present value of a
    a. perpetuity?
    b. annuity?
    c. growing perpetuity?
    d. growing annuity?

 4.6 **Solving for Variables Other Than Present Value or Future Value**

So far, we have calculated the present value or future value of a stream of cash flows. Sometimes, however, we know the present value or future value, but do not know one of the variables that so far we have been given as an input. For example, when you take out a loan, you may know the amount you would like to borrow, but may not know the loan payments that will be required to repay it. Or, if you make a deposit into a bank account, you may want to calculate how long it will take before your balance reaches a certain level. In such situations, we use the present and/or future values as inputs, and solve for the variable we are interested in. We examine several special cases in this section.

Solving for the Cash Flows

Let's consider an example where we know the present value of an investment, but do not know the cash flows. The best example is a loan—you know how much you want to borrow (the present value) and you know the interest rate, but you do not know how much you need to repay each year. Suppose you are opening a business that requires an initial investment of $100,000. Your bank manager has agreed to lend you this money. The terms of the loan state that you will make equal annual payments for the next ten years and will pay an interest rate of 8% with the first payment due one year from today. What is your annual payment?

From the bank's perspective, the timeline looks like this:

The bank will give you $100,000 today in exchange for ten equal payments over the next decade. You need to determine the size of the payment C that the bank will require. For the bank to be willing to lend you $100,000, the loan cash flows must have a present value of $100,000 when evaluated at the bank's interest rate of 8%. That is:

$$100,000 = PV(\text{10-year annuity of } C \text{ per year, evaluated at the loan rate})$$

Using the formula for the present value of an annuity,

$$100,000 = C \times \frac{1}{0.08}\left(1 - \frac{1}{1.08^{10}}\right) = C \times 6.71$$

solving this equation for C gives:

$$C = \frac{100,000}{6.71} = \$14,903$$

You will be required to make ten annual payments of $14,903 in exchange for $100,000 today.

We can also solve this problem with a financial calculator or Excel:

	N	I/Y	PV	PMT	FV
Given:	10	8	100,000		0
Solve for:				−14,903	
Excel Formula: =PMT(RATE,NPER,PV,FV)=PMT(0.08,10,100000,0)					

In general, when solving for a loan payment, think of the amount borrowed (the loan principal) as the present value of the payments. If the payments of the loan are an annuity, we can solve for the payment of the loan by inverting the annuity formula. Writing the equation for the payments formally for a loan with principal P, requiring n periodic payments of C and interest rate r, we have

Loan payment

$$C = \frac{P}{\frac{1}{r}\left(1 - \frac{1}{(1 + r)^n}\right)} \tag{4.10}$$

EXAMPLE 4.10

Computing a Loan Payment

Problem

Your firm plans to buy a warehouse for $100,000. The bank offers you a 30-year loan with equal annual payments and an interest rate of 8% per year. The bank requires that your firm pay 20% of the purchase price as a down payment, so you can borrow only $80,000. What is the annual loan payment?

Solution

▶ **Plan**

We start with the timeline (from the bank's perspective):

Using Eq. 4.10, we can solve for the loan payment, C, given $n = 30$, $r = 8\%$ (0.08) and $P = \$80,000$.

▶ **Execute**

Eq. 4.10 gives the following payment (cash flow):

$$C = \frac{P}{\frac{1}{r}\left(1 - \frac{1}{(1+r)^n}\right)} = \frac{80,000}{\frac{1}{0.08}\left(1 - \frac{1}{(1.08)^{30}}\right)}$$

$$= \$7106.19$$

Using a financial calculator or Excel:

	N	I/Y	PV	PMT	FV
Given:	30	8	−80,000		0
Solve for:				7106.19	
	Excel Formula:	=$PMT(RATE,NPER,PV,FV)=PMT(0.08,30,-80000,0)$			

▶ **Evaluate**

Your firm will need to pay $7106.19 each year to repay the loan. The bank is willing to accept these payments because the *PV* of 30 annual payments of $7106.19 at 8% interest rate per year is exactly equal to the $80,000 it is giving you today.

We can use this same idea to solve for the cash flows when we know the future value rather than the present value. As an example, suppose you have just graduated from college and you decide to be prudent and start saving for a down payment on a house. You would like to have $60,000 saved 10 years from now. If you can earn 7% per year on your savings, how much do you need to save each year to meet your goal?

The timeline for this example is

That is, you plan to save some amount C per year, and then withdraw $60,000 from the bank in ten years. Therefore, we need to find the annuity payment that has a future value of $60,000 in ten years. Use the formula for the future value of an annuity from Eq. 4.6:

$$60,000 = FV(\text{annuity}) = C \times \frac{1}{0.07}(1.07^{10} - 1) = C \times 13.816448$$

Therefore, $C = \frac{60,000}{13.816448} = \$4343.65$. Thus, you need to save $4343.65 per year. If you do, then at a 7% interest rate your savings will grow to $60,000 in 10 years when you are ready to buy a house.

Now let's solve this problem using a financial calculator or Excel:

	N	I/Y	PV	PMT	FV
Given:	10	7	0		60,000
Solve for:				−4343	
	Excel Formula: =PMT(RATE,NPER,PV,FV)=PMT(0.07,10,0,60000)				

Once again, we find that you need to save $4343 for 10 years to accumulate $60,000.

Internal Rate of Return

In some situations, you know the present value and cash flows of an investment opportunity but you do not know the interest rate that equates them. This interest rate is called the **internal rate of return (IRR)**, defined as the interest rate that sets the net present value of the cash flows equal to zero.

For example, suppose that you have an investment opportunity that requires a $1000 investment today and will have a $2000 payoff in six years. This would appear on a timeline as

0   1   2   ...   6

−$1000 $2000

One way to analyze this investment is to ask the question: What interest rate, r, would you need so that the NPV of this investment is zero?

$$NPV = -1000 + \frac{2000}{(1 + r)^6} = 0$$

Rearranging this calculation gives the following:

$$1000 \times (1 + r)^6 = 2000$$

That is, r is the interest rate you would need to earn on your $1000 to have a future value of $2000 in six years. We can solve for r as follows:

$$1 + r = \left(\frac{2000}{1000}\right)^{1/6} = 1.1225$$

Or, $r = 12.25\%$. This rate is the *IRR* of this investment opportunity. Making this investment is like earning 12.25% per year on your money for six years.

When there are just two cash flows, as in the preceding example, it is easy to compute the *IRR*. Consider the general case in which you invest an amount P today, and receive FV in n years:

$$P \times (1 + IRR)^n = FV$$

$$1 + IRR = (FV/P)^{1/n}$$

Now let's consider a more sophisticated example. Suppose your firm needs to purchase a new forklift. The dealer gives you two options: (1) a price for the forklift if you pay cash and (2) the annual payments if you take out a loan from the dealer. To evaluate the loan that the dealer is offering you, you will want to compare the rate on the loan

---

internal rate of return (IRR) The interest rate that sets the net present value of the cash flows equal to zero.

with the rate that your bank is willing to offer you. Given the loan payment that the dealer quotes, how do you compute the interest rate charged by the dealer?

In this case, we need to compute the *IRR* of the dealer's loan. Suppose the cash price of the forklift is $40,000, and the dealer offers financing with no down payment and four annual payments of $15,000. This loan has the following timeline:

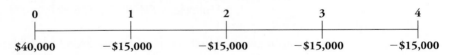

From the timeline, it is clear that the loan is a four-year annuity with a payment of $15,000 per year and a present value of $40,000. Setting the *NPV* of the cash flows equal to zero requires that the present value of the payments equals the purchase price:

$$40,000 = 15,000 \times \frac{1}{r}\left(1 - \frac{1}{(1 + r)^4}\right)$$

The value of r that solves this equation, the *IRR*, is the interest rate charged on the loan. Unfortunately, in this case there is no simple way to solve for the interest rate r.[4] The only way to solve this equation is to guess at values of r until you find the right one.

Start by guessing $r = 10\%$ In this case, the value of the annuity is

$$15,000 \times \frac{1}{0.10}\left(1 - \frac{1}{(1.10)^4}\right) = 47,548$$

The present value of the payments is too large. To lower it, we need to use a higher interest rate. We guess 20% this time:

$$15,000 \times \frac{1}{0.20}\left(1 - \frac{1}{(1.20)^4}\right) = 38,831$$

Now the present value of the payments is too low, so we must pick a rate between 10% and 20%. We continue to guess until we find the right rate. Let's try 18.45%:

$$15,000 \times \frac{1}{0.1845}\left(1 - \frac{1}{(1.1845)^4}\right) = 40,000$$

The interest rate charged by the dealer is 18.45%.

An easier solution than guessing the *IRR* and manually calculating values is to use a spreadsheet or calculator to automate the guessing process. When the cash flows are an annuity, as in this example, we can use a financial calculator or Excel to compute the *IRR*. Both solve (with slightly varying notation) the following equation:

$$NPV = PV + PMT \times \frac{1}{I/Y}\left(1 - \frac{1}{(1 + I/Y)^n}\right) + \frac{FV}{(1 + I/Y)^n} = 0$$

The equation ensures that the *NPV* of investing in the annuity is zero. When the unknown variable is the interest rate, it will solve for the interest rate that sets the *NPV*

---

[4]With five or more periods and general cash flows, there is *no* general formula to solve for r; trial and error and interpolation (by hand or computer) is the *only* way to compute the *IRR*.

USING EXCEL

Computing *NPV*
and *IRR*

Here we discuss how to use Microsoft® Excel to solve for *NPV* and *IRR*. We also identify some pitfalls to avoid when using Excel.

NPV Function: Leaving Out Date 0

Excel's *NPV* function has the format, *NPV* (rate, value1, value2, . . .) where "rate" is the interest rate per period used to discount the cash flows, and "value1", "value2", etc., are the cash flows (or ranges of cash flows). The *NPV* function computes the present value of the cash flows *assuming the first cash flow occurs at date 1.* Therefore, if a project's first cash flow occurs at date 0, we cannot use the *NPV* function by itself to compute the *NPV*. We can use the *NPV* function to compute the present value of the cash flows from date 1 onwards, and then we must add the date 0 cash flow to that result to calculate the *NPV*. The screenshot below shows the difference. The first *NPV* calculation (outlined in blue) is correct: we used the *NPV* function for all of the cash flows occurring at time 1 and later and then added on the first cash flow occurring at time 0 since it is already in present value. The second (outlined in green) is incorrect: we used the *NPV* function for all of the cash flows, but the function assumed that the first cash flow occurs in period 1 instead of immediately.

NPV Function: Ignoring Blank Cells

Another pitfall with the *NPV* function is that cash flows that are left blank are treated differently from cash flows that are equal to zero. If the cash flow is left blank, *both the cash flow and the period are ignored.* For example, the second set of cash flows below is equivalent to the first—we have simply left the cash flow for date 2 blank instead of entering a "0." However, the *NPV* function ignores the blank cell at date 2 and assumes the cash flow is 10 at date 1 and 110 at date 2, which is clearly not what is intended and produces an incorrect answer (outlined in red).

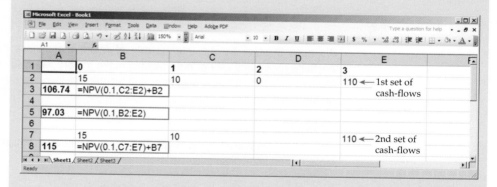

Because of these idiosyncrasies, we avoid using Excel's *NPV* function. It is more reliable to compute the present value of each cash flow separately in Excel, and then sum them to determine the *NPV*.

IRR Function

Excel's *IRR* function has the format *IRR* (values, guess), where "values" is the range containing the cash flows, and "guess" is an optional starting guess where Excel begins its search for an *IRR*. Two things to note about the *IRR* function:

1. The values given to the *IRR* function should include all of the cash flows of the project, including the one at date 0. In this sense, the *IRR* and *NPV* functions in Excel are inconsistent.
2. Like the *NPV* function, the *IRR* ignores the period associated with any blank cells.

equal to zero—that is, the *IRR*. For this case, you could use a financial calculator or Excel, as follows:

	N	I/Y	PV	PMT	FV
Given:	4		40,000	−15,000	0
Solve for:		18.45			

Excel Formula: =RATE(*NPER,PMT,PV,FV*)=RATE(4,−15000,40000,0)

Both the financial calculator and Excel correctly compute an *IRR* of 18.45%.

EXAMPLE 4.11

Personal Finance
Computing the
Internal Rate of
Return with a
Financial Calculator

Problem
Let's return to the lottery prize in Example 4.6. How high a rate of return do you need to earn investing on your own in order to prefer the $15 million payout?

Solution

▶ **Plan**
Recall that the lottery offers you the following deal: take either (a) $15 million lump sum payment immediately, or (b) 30 payments of $1 million per year starting immediately. This second option is an annuity of 29 payments of $1 million plus an initial $1 million payment.

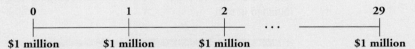

0	1	2		29
$1 million	$1 million	$1 million	⋯	$1 million

We need to solve for the internal rate of return that makes the two offers equivalent. Anything above that rate of return would make the present value of the annuity lower than the $15 million lump sum payment, and anything below that rate of return would make it greater than the $15 million.

▶ **Execute**
First, we set the present value of option (b) equal to option (a), which is already in present value since it is an immediate payment of $15 million:

$$\$15\text{ million} = \$1\text{ million} + \$1\text{ million} \times \frac{1}{r}\left(1 - \frac{1}{(1+r)^{29}}\right)$$

$$\$14\text{ million} = \$1\text{ million} \times \frac{1}{r}\left(1 - \frac{1}{(1+r)^{29}}\right)$$

Using a financial calculator to solve for *r*:

	N	I/Y	PV	PMT	FV
Given:	29		−14,000,000	1,000,000	0
Solve for:		5.72			

Excel Formula: =RATE(*NPER,PMT,PV,FV*)=RATE(29,1000000,−14000000,0)

The *IRR* equating the two options is 5.72%.

▶ **Evaluate**

A rate of 5.72% makes giving up the $15 million payment and taking the 30 installments of $1 million exactly a zero *NPV* action. If you could earn more than 5.72% investing on your own, then you could take the $15 million, invest it and generate 30 installments that are each more than $1 million. If you could not earn at least 5.72% on your investments, you would be unable to replicate the $1 million installments on your own and would be better off taking the installment plan.

Solving for *n* the Number of Periods

In addition to solving for cash flows or the interest rate, we can solve for the amount of time it will take a sum of money to grow to a known value. In this case, the interest rate, present value, and future value are all known. We need to compute how long it will take for the present value to grow to the future value.

Suppose we invest $10,000 in an account paying 10% interest, and we want to know how long it will take for the amount to grow to $20,000.

```
0            1            2            ...          n
|————————————|————————————|————————     ————————————|
-$10,000                                          $20,000
```

We want to determine *n*.

In terms of our formulas, we need to find *n* so that the future value of our investment equals $20,000:

$$FV = \$10{,}000 \times 1.10^n = \$20{,}000 \tag{4.11}$$

One approach is to use trial and error to find *n*, as with the *IRR*. For example, with $n = 7$ years, $FV = \$19{,}487$, so it will take longer than 7 years. With $n = 8$ years, $FV = \$21{,}436$, so it will take between 7 and 8 years.

Alternatively, this problem can be solved on a financial calculator or Excel. In this case, we solve for *n*:

	N	I/Y	PV	PMT	FV
Given:		10	−10,000	0	20,000
Solve for:	7.27				
Excel Formula: =NPER(RATE,*PMT,PV,FV*)=NPER(0.10,0,−10000,20000)

It will take about 7.3 years for our savings to grow to $20,000.

Solving for *n* Using Logarithms

The problem of solving for the number of periods can be solved mathematically as well. Dividing both sides of Eq. 4.11 by $10,000, we have:

$$1.10^n = 20{,}000 / 10{,}000 = 2$$

To solve for an exponent, we take the logarithm of both sides, and use the fact that $\ln(X^y) = y \ln(X)$:

$$n \ln(1.10) = \ln(2)$$
$$n = \ln(2)/\ln(1.10) = 0.6931/0.0953 \approx 7.3 \text{ years}$$

EXAMPLE 4.12

Personal Finance
Solving for the
Number of Periods
in a Savings Plan

Problem
Let's return to your savings for a down payment on a house. Imagine that some time has passed and you have $10,050 saved already, and you can now afford to save $5000 per year at the end of each year. Also, interest rates have increased so that you now earn 7.25% per year on your savings. How long will it take you to get to your goal of $60,000?

Solution

▶ **Plan**
The timeline for this problem is:

0	1	2		n
−$10,050	−$5000	−$5000	⋯	−$5000 +$60,000

We need to find n so that the future value of your current savings plus the future value of your planned additional savings (which is an annuity consisting of n payments) equals your desired amount. There are two contributors to the future value: the initial lump sum of $10,050 that will continue to earn interest, and the annuity contributions of $5000 per year that will earn interest as they are contributed. Thus, we need to find the future value of the lump sum plus the future value of the annuity.

▶ **Execute**
We can solve this problem using a financial calculator or Excel:

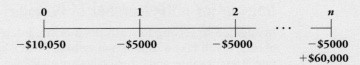

	N	I/Y	PV	PMT	FV
Given:		7.25	−10,050	−5000	60,000
Solve for:	7.00				

Excel Formula: =NPER(RATE,*PMT,PV,FV*)=NPER(0.0725,−5000,−10050,60000)

There is also a mathematical solution. We can calculate the future value of the initial cash flow by using Eq. 4.1 and the future value of the annuity using Eq. 4.6:

$$10,050 \times 1.0725^n + 5000 \times \frac{1}{0.0725} (1.0725^n - 1) = 60,000$$

Rearranging the equation to solve for n,

$$1.0725^n = \frac{60,000 \times 0.0725 + 5000}{10,050 \times 0.0725 + 5000} = 1.632$$

we can then solve for n:

$$n = \frac{\ln(1.632)}{\ln(1.0725)} = 7 \text{ years}$$

▶ **Evaluate**
It will take seven years to save the down payment.

We began this chapter with the goal of developing the tools a financial manager needs to be able to apply the Valuation Principle by computing the net present value of a decision. Starting from the fundamental concept of the time value of money—a dollar today is worth more than a dollar tomorrow—we learned how to calculate the equivalent value of future cash flows today and today's cash flows in the future. We then learned some shortcuts for handling common sets of regular cash flows such as those found in perpetuities and loans. As we have seen, the discount rate is a critical input to any of our present value or future value calculations. Throughout this chapter, we have taken the discount rate as given.

What determines these discount rates? The Valuation Principle shows us that we must rely on market information to assess the value of cash flows across time. In the next chapter, we will learn the drivers of market interest rates as well as how they are quoted. Understanding interest rate quoting conventions will also allow us to extend the tools we developed in this chapter to situations where the interest rate is compounded more frequently than once per year.

Concept Check

11. How do you calculate the cash flow of an annuity?

12. What is the internal rate of return, and how do you calculate it?

13. How do you solve for the number of periods to pay off an annuity?

MyFinanceLab Here is what you should know after reading this chapter. MyFinanceLab will help you identify what you know, and where to go when you need to practice.

Key Points and Equations	Terms	Online Practice Opportunities
4.1 The Timeline ▶ Timelines are a critical first step in organizing the cash flows in a financial problem.	stream of cash flows, p. 88 timeline, p. 88	MyFinanceLab Study Plan 4.1

4.2 Valuing Cash Flows at Different Points in Time
 ▶ There are three rules of valuing cash flows:
   a. Only cash flows that occur at the same point in time can be compared or combined.
   b. To calculate a cash flow's future value, you must compound it.
   c. To calculate a cash flow's present value, you must discount it.
 ▶ The future value in n years of a cash flow C today is:
 	
 $$C = (1 + r)^n \qquad (4.1)$$
 	
 ▶ The present value today of a cash flow C received in n years is:
 	
 $$C \div (1 + r)^n \qquad (4.2)$$
	compounding, p. 92
	 compound interest, p. 92
	 discounting, p. 94
	 future value, p. 92
		MyFinanceLab
		 Study Plan 4.2

4.3 Valuing a Stream of Cash Flows

▶ The present value of a cash flow stream is

MyFinanceLab
Study Plan 4.3

$$PV = C_0 + \frac{C_1}{(1+r)} + \frac{C_2}{(1+r)^2} + \cdots + \frac{C_n}{(1+r)^n} \quad (4.3)$$

4.4 The Net Present Value of a Stream of Cash Flows

▶ The *NPV* of an investment opportunity is $PV(\text{benefits} - \text{costs})$.

MyFinanceLab
Study Plan 4.4

4.5 Perpetuities, Annuities, and Other Special Cases

▶ A perpetuity is a constant cash flow C paid every period, forever. The present value of a perpetuity is

annuity, p. 105
consol, p. 102
growing perpetuity, p. 110
perpetuity, p. 102

MyFinanceLab
Study Plan 4.5

Interactive Annuity
Calculator

$$PV_0 = \frac{C}{r} \quad (4.4)$$

▶ An annuity is a constant cash flow C paid every period for n periods. The present value of an annuity is

$$PV_0 = C \times \frac{1}{r}\left(1 - \frac{1}{(1+r)^n}\right) \quad (4.5)$$

▶ The future value of an annuity at the end of the annuity is

$$FV_n = C \times \frac{1}{r}\left((1+r)^n - 1\right) \quad (4.6)$$

▶ In a growing perpetuity, the cash flows grow at a constant rate g each period. The present value of a growing perpetuity is

$$PV_0 = \frac{C_1}{r - g} \quad (4.7)$$

▶ A growing annuity is a growing series of cash flows, starting with C_1 paid every year for n years. The present value of a growing annuity is

$$PV_0 = C_1 \times \frac{1}{r - g}\left(1 - \left(\frac{1+g}{1+r}\right)^n\right) \quad (4.8)$$

▶ The future value of a growing annuity is

Cash flow in an Annuity (Loan Payment)

$$C_1 \times \frac{1}{r - g}\left((1+r)^n - (1+g)^n\right) \quad (4.9)$$

4.6 Solving for Variables Other Than Present Value or Future Value

▶ The annuity and perpetuity formulas can be used to solve for the annuity payments when either the present value or the future value is known.

▶ The periodic payment on an n-period loan with principal P and interest rate r is:

$$\frac{P}{\frac{1}{r}\left(1 - \frac{1}{(1 + r)^n}\right)} \qquad (4.10)$$

▶ The internal rate of return (*IRR*) of an investment opportunity is the interest rate that sets the *NPV* of the investment opportunity equal to zero.

▶ The annuity formulas can be used to solve for the number of periods it takes to save a fixed amount of money.

internal rate of return (*IRR*), p. 117

MyFinanceLab
Study Plan 4.6

Using Excel:
Computing *NPV*s
and *IRR*

Review Questions

1. Why is a cash flow in the future worth less than the same amount today?

2. What is compound interest?

3. What is the reasoning behind the geometric growth in interest?

4. What is a discount rate?

5. What is the reasoning behind the fact that the present value of a stream of cash flows is just the sum of the present values of each individual cash flow?

6. What must be true about the cash flow stream in order for us to be able to use the shortcut formulas?

7. What is the difference between an annuity and a perpetuity?

8. What is an internal rate of return?

Problems

All problems in this chapter are available in MyFinanceLab. An asterisk (*) indicates problems with a higher level of difficulty.

The Timeline

1. You have just taken out a five-year loan from a bank to buy an engagement ring. The ring costs $5000. You plan to put down $1000 and borrow $4000. You will need to make annual payments of $1000 at the end of each year. Show the timeline of the loan from your perspective. How would the timeline differ if you created it from the bank's perspective?

2. You currently have a one-year-old loan outstanding on your car. You make monthly payments of $300. You have just made a payment. The loan has four years to go (i.e., it had an original term of five years). Show the timeline from your perspective. How would the timeline differ if you created it from the bank's perspective?

Valuing Cash Flows at Different Points in time

3. Calculate the future value of $2000 in
   a. 5 years at an interest rate of 5% per year.
   b. 10 years at an interest rate of 5% per year.
   c. 5 years at an interest rate of 10% per year.
   d. Why is the amount of interest earned in part (a) less than half the amount of interest earned in part (b)?

4. What is the present value of $10,000 received
   a. 12 years from today when the interest rate is 4% per year?
   b. 20 years from today when the interest rate is 8% per year?
   c. 6 years from today when the interest rate is 2% per year?

5. Your brother has offered to give you either $5000 today or $10,000 in 10 years. If the interest rate is 7% per year, which option is preferable?

6. Your cousin is currently 12 years old. She will be going to university in six years. Your aunt and uncle would like to have $100,000 in a savings account to fund her education at that time. If the account promises to pay a fixed interest rate of 4% per year, how much money do they need to put into the account today to ensure that they will have $100,000 in six years?

 7. Your mom is thinking of retiring. Her retirement plan will pay her either $250,000 immediately on retirement or $350,000 five years after the date of her retirement. Which alternative should she choose if the interest rate is
   a. 0% per year?
   b. 8% per year?
   c. 20% per year?

 8. Your grandfather put some money in an account for you on the day you were born. You are now 18 years old and are allowed to withdraw the money for the first time. The account currently has $3996 in it and pays an 8% interest rate.
   a. How much money would be in the account if you left the money there until your twenty-fifth birthday?
   b. What if you left the money until your sixty-fifth birthday?
   c. How much money did your grandfather originally put in the account?

Valuing a Stream of Cash Flows

 9. You have just received a windfall from an investment you made in a friend's business. She will be paying you $10,000 at the end of this year, $20,000 at the end of the following year, and $30,000 at the end of the year after that (three years from today). The interest rate is 3.5% per year.
   a. What is the present value of your windfall?
   b. What is the future value of your windfall in three years (on the date of the last payment)?

10. You have a loan outstanding. It requires making three annual payments of $1000 each at the end of the next three years. Your bank has offered to allow you to skip making the next two payments in lieu of making one large payment at the end of the loan's term

in three years. If the interest rate on the loan is 5%, what final payment will the bank require you to make so that it is indifferent to the two forms of payment?

11. You are wondering whether going to university would be worthwhile. You figure that the total cost of going to university for four years, including lost wages, is $40,000 per year. However, you feel that if you get a university degree, the present value of your lifetime wages from graduation onward will be $300,000 greater than if you did not go to university. If your discount rate is 9%, what is the NPV of going to university?

The Net Present Value of a Stream of Cash Flows

12. You have been offered a unique investment opportunity. If you invest $10,000 today, you will receive $500 one year from now, $1500 two years from now, and $10,000 ten years from now.
   a. What is the NPV of the opportunity if the interest rate is 6% per year? Should you take the opportunity?
   b. What is the NPV of the opportunity if the interest rate is 2% per year? Should you take it now?

13. Renuka Gupta owns her own business and is considering an investment. If she undertakes the investment, it will pay $4000 at the end of each of the next three years. The opportunity requires an initial investment of $1000 plus an additional investment at the end of the second year of $5000. What is the NPV of this opportunity if the interest rate is 2% per year? Should Renuka take it?

Perpetuities, Annuities, and Other Special Cases

14. Your friend majoring in mechanical engineering has invented a money machine. The main drawback of the machine is that it is slow. It takes one year to manufacture $100. However, once built, the machine will last forever and will require no maintenance. The machine can be built immediately, but it will cost $1000 to build. Your friend wants to know if she should invest the money to construct it. If the interest rate is 9.5% per year, what should your friend do?

15. How would your answer to Problem 14 change if the machine takes one year to build (so the $1000 outflow is today but the first $100 inflow occurs two years from today)?

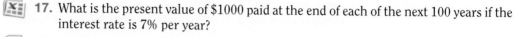

16. The British government has a consol bond outstanding paying £100 per year forever. Assume the current interest rate is 4% per year.
   a. What is the value of the bond immediately after a payment is made?
   b. What is the value of the bond immediately before a payment is made?

17. What is the present value of $1000 paid at the end of each of the next 100 years if the interest rate is 7% per year?

*18. When you purchased your car, you took out a five-year annual-payment loan with an interest rate of 6% per year. The annual payment on the car is $5000. You have just made a payment and have now decided to pay the loan off by repaying the outstanding balance. What is the payoff amount if
   a. you have owned the car for one year (so there are four years left on the loan)?
   b. you have owned the car for four years (so there is one year left on the loan)?

19. Your grandmother has been putting $1000 into a savings account on every birthday since your first (that is, when you turned one). The account pays an interest rate of 3%. How much money will be in the account on your eighteenth birthday immediately after your grandmother makes the deposit on that birthday?

20. Assume that your parents wanted to have $160,000 saved for university by your eighteenth birthday and they started saving on your first birthday. If they saved the same amount each year on your birthday and earned 8% per year on their investments,
    a. how much would they have to save each year to reach their goal?
    b. if they think you will take five years instead of four to graduate and decide to have $200,000 saved just in case, how much more would they have to save each year to reach their new goal?

21. A rich relative has bequeathed you a growing perpetuity. The first payment will occur in a year and will be $1000. Each year after that, you will receive a payment on the anniversary of the last payment that is 8% larger than the last payment. This pattern of payments will go on forever. If the interest rate is 12% per year,
    a. what is today's value of the bequest?
    b. what is the value of the bequest immediately after the first payment is made?

*22. You are thinking of building a new machine that will save you $1000 in the first year. The machine will then begin to wear out so that the savings decline at a rate of 2% per year forever. What is the present value of the savings if the interest rate is 5% per year?

23. You work for a pharmaceutical company that has developed a new drug. The patent on the drug will last 17 years. You expect that the drug's profits will be $2 million in its first year and that this amount will grow at a rate of 5% per year for the next 17 years. Once the patent expires, other pharmaceutical companies will be able to produce the same drug and competition will likely drive profits to zero. What is the present value of the new drug if the interest rate is 10% per year?

24. A rich aunt has promised you $5000 one year from today. In addition, each year after that, she has promised you a payment (on the anniversary of the last payment) that is 5% larger than the last payment. She will continue to show this generosity for 20 years, giving a total of 20 payments. If the interest rate is 5%, what is her promise worth today?

*25. You are running a hot internet company. Analysts predict that its earnings will grow at 30% per year for the next five years. After that, as competition increases, earnings growth is expected to slow to 2% per year and continue at that level forever. Your company has just announced earnings of $1 million. What is the present value of all future earnings if the interest rate is 8%? (Assume all cash flows occur at the end of the year.)

*26. In 2000, when Alex Rodriguez signed his contract to join the Texas Rangers baseball team, he received a lot of attention for his "$252 million" contract (the total of the payments promised was $252 million). Assume the following:

Rodriguez was set to earn $16 million in the first year, $17 million per year in years 2 through 4, $19 million in each of years 5 and 6, $23 million in year 7, and $27 million per year in years 8 through 10. He would also receive his $10 million signing bonus spread equally over the first 5 years ($2 million per year). His deferred payments were to begin in 2011. The deferred payment amounts total $33 million and are $5 million, then $4 million, then 8 amounts of $3 million (ending in 2020). However, the actual payouts will be different. All of the deferred payments will earn 3% per year until they are paid. For example, the $5 million is deferred from 2001 to 2011, or 10 years, meaning that it will actually be $6.7196 million when paid. Assume that the $4 million payment deferred to 2012 is deferred from 2002 (each payment is deferred 10 years).

The contract is a 10-year contract, but each year has a deferred component so that cash flows are paid out over a total of 20 years. The contractual payments, signing bonus, and deferred components are given below. Note that, by contract, the deferred components are not paid in the year they are earned, but instead are paid (plus interest) 10 years later.

2001	2002	2003	2004	2005	2006	2007	2008	2009	2010
$16M	$17M	$17M	$17M	$19M	$19M	$23M	$27M	$27M	$27M
$2M	$2M	$2M	$2M	$2M					
Deferred									
$5M	$4M	$3M	$3M	$3M	$3M	$3M	$3M	$3M	$3M

Assume that an appropriate discount rate for A-Rod to apply to the contract payments is 7% per year.

a. Calculate the true promised payments under this contract, including the deferred payments with interest.

b. Draw a timeline of all of the payments.

c. Calculate the present value of the contract.

d. Compare the present value of the contract to the quoted value of $252 million. What explains the difference?

*27. You are trying to decide how much to save for retirement. Assume you plan to save $5000 per year with the first investment made one year from now. You think you can earn 10% per year on your investments and you plan to retire in 43 years, immediately after making your last $5000 investment.

a. How much will you have in your retirement account on the day you retire?

b. If, instead of investing $5000 per year, you wanted to make one lump-sum investment today for your retirement, how much would that lump sum need to be?

c. If you hope to live for 20 years in retirement, how much can you withdraw every year in retirement (starting one year after retirement) so that you will just exhaust your savings with the twentieth withdrawal (assume your savings will continue to earn 10% in retirement)?

d. If, instead, you decide to withdraw $300,000 per year in retirement (again with the first withdrawal one year after retiring), how many years will it take until you exhaust your savings?

e. Assuming the most you can afford to save is $5000 per year, but you want to retire with $1 million in your investment account, how high a return do you need to earn on your investments?

28. Your brother has offered to give you $1000 in one year, and after that, yearly payments growing at 3% each year and ending in 20 years. If you deposit each of these payments into your TD Bank account, how much will you accumulate 20 years from today if the interest rate is 7% per year?

Solving for Variables Other Than Present Value or Future Value

29. You have decided to buy a perpetuity. The bond makes one payment at the end of every year forever and has an interest rate of 5%. If you initially put $1000 into the bond, what is the payment every year?

30. You are thinking of purchasing a house. The house costs $350,000. You have $50,000 in cash that you can use as a down payment on the house, but you need to borrow

the rest of the purchase price. The bank is offering a 30-year mortgage that requires annual payments and has an interest rate of 7% per year. What will your annual payment be if you sign up for this mortgage?

*31. You are thinking about buying a piece of art that costs $50,000. The art dealer is proposing the following deal: He will lend you the money, and you will repay the loan by making the same payment every two years for the next 20 years (i.e., a total of 10 payments). If the interest rate is 4% per year, how much will you have to pay every two years?

*32. You would like to buy the house and take the mortgage described in Problem 30. You can afford to pay only $23,500 per year. The bank agrees to allow you to pay this amount each year, yet still borrow $300,000. At the end of the mortgage (in 30 years), you must make a balloon payment; that is, you must repay the remaining balance on the mortgage. How much will this balloon payment be?

*33. You are saving for retirement. To live comfortably, you decide you will need to save $2 million by the time you are 65. Today is your twenty-second birthday, and you decide, starting today and continuing on every birthday up to and including your sixty-fifth birthday, that you will put the same amount into a savings account. If the interest rate is 5%, how much must you set aside each year to make sure that you will have $2 million in the account on your sixty-fifth birthday?

*34. You realize that the plan in Problem 33 has a flaw. Because your income will increase over your lifetime, it would be more realistic to save less now and more later. Instead of putting the same amount aside each year, you decide to let the amount that you set aside grow by 7% per year. Under this plan, how much will you put into the account today? (Recall that you are planning to make the first contribution to the account today.)

35. You have an investment opportunity that requires an initial investment of $5000 today and will pay $6000 in one year. What is the *IRR* of this opportunity?

36. You are shopping for a car and read the following advertisement in the newspaper: "Own a new Spitfire! No money down. Four annual payments of just $10,000." You have shopped around and know that you can buy a Spitfire for cash for $32,500. What is the interest rate the dealer is advertising (what is the *IRR* of the loan in the advertisement)? Assume that you must make the annual payments at the end of each year.

37. A local bank is running the following advertisement in the newspaper: "For just $1000 we will pay you $100 forever!" The fine print in the ad says that for a $1000 deposit, the bank will pay $100 every year in perpetuity, starting one year after the deposit is made. What interest rate is the bank advertising (what is the *IRR* of this investment)?

*38. The Laiterie de Coaticook in the Eastern Townships of Quebec produces several types of cheddar cheese. It markets this cheese in 4 varieties: aged 2 months, 9 months, 15 months, and 2 years. At the producer's store, 2 kg of each variety sells for the following prices: $7.95, $9.49, $10.95, and $11.95, respectively. Consider the cheese maker's decision whether to continue to age a particular 2-kg block of cheese. At 2 months, he can either sell the cheese immediately or let it age further. If he sells it now, he will receive $7.95 immediately. If he ages the cheese, he must give up the $7.95 today to receive a higher amount in the future. What is the *IRR* (expressed in percent per month) of the investment of giving up $79.50 today by choosing to store 20 kg of cheese that is currently 2 months old and instead selling 10 kg of this cheese when it has aged 9 months, 6 kg when it has aged 15 months, and the remaining 4 kg when it has aged 2 years?

*39. Your grandmother bought an annuity from Great-West Life Insurance Company for $200,000 when she retired. In exchange for the $200,000, Great-West Life will pay her $25,000 per year until she dies. The interest rate is 5%. How long must she live after the day she retired to come out ahead (that is, to get more in value than what she paid in)?

*40. You are thinking of making an investment in a new plant. The plant will generate revenues of $1 million per year for as long as you maintain it. You expect that the maintenance costs will start at $50,000 per year and will increase 5% per year thereafter. Assume that all revenue and maintenance costs occur at the end of the year. You intend to run the plant as long as it continues to make a positive cash flow (as long as the cash generated by the plant exceeds the maintenance costs). The plant can be built and become operational immediately. If the plant costs $10 million to build, and the interest rate is 6% per year, should you invest in the plant?

*41. You have just turned 22 years old, have just received your bachelor's degree, and have accepted your first job. Now you must decide how much money to put into your registered retirement savings plan (RRSP). The RRSP works as follows: Every dollar in the RRSP earns 7% per year. You will not make withdrawals until you retire on your sixty-fifth birthday. After that point, you can make withdrawals as you see fit. You decide that you will plan to live to 100 and work until you turn 65. You estimate that to live comfortably in retirement, you will need $100,000 per year, starting at the end of the first year of retirement (i.e., when you turn 66) and ending on your one-hundredth birthday. You will contribute the same amount to the RRSP at the end of every year that you work. How much do you need to contribute each year to fund your retirement?

*42. Problem 41 is not very realistic because most people do not contribute a fixed amount to their RRSP each year. Instead, they are more likely to contribute a fixed percentage of their salary. Assume that your starting salary is $45,000 per year and it will grow 3% per year until you retire. Assuming everything else stays the same as in Problem 41, what percentage of your income do you need to contribute to the RRSP every year to fund the same retirement income?

Data Case

Assume today is July 30, 2010. Natasha Kingery is 30 years old and has a bachelor of science degree in computer science. She is currently employed at Open Text Corporation in Ottawa, and earns $38,000 a year that she anticipates will grow at 3% per year. Natasha hopes to retire at age 65 and has just begun to think about the future.

Natasha has $75,000 that she recently inherited from her aunt. She invested this money in 10-year Government of Canada bonds. She is considering whether she should further her education and would use her inheritance to pay for it.

She has investigated a couple of options and is asking for your help as a financial planning intern to determine the financial consequences associated with each option. Natasha has already been accepted to both of these programs, and could start either one soon.

One alternative that Natasha is considering is attaining a certification in network design. This certification would automatically promote her to a new position and give her a raise of $10,000. This salary differential will grow at a rate of 3% per year as long as she keeps working. The certification program requires the completion of 20 web-based courses and a score of 80% or better on an exam at the end of the course work. She has learned that the average amount of time necessary to finish the program is one year. The total cost of the program is $5000, due when she enrolls in the program. Because she will do all the work for the certification on her own time, Natasha does not expect to lose any income during the certification.

Another option is going back to school for an MBA degree. With an MBA degree, Natasha expects to be promoted to a managerial position at Open Text. The managerial position pays $20,000 a year more than her current position. She expects that this salary differential will also grow at a rate of 3% per year for as long as she keeps working. The evening program, which will take three years to complete, costs $25,000 per year, due at the beginning of each of her three years in school. Because she will attend classes in the evening, Natasha doesn't expect to lose any income while she is earning her MBA if she chooses to undertake the MBA.

1. Determine the interest rate she is currently earning on her inheritance by going to the Bank of Canada website (http://www.bankofcanada.ca/en/) and clicking on Interest Rates under the Rates and Statistics tab. Then click on "Canadian Bonds." Once there, click on "10-year lookup." Enter the appropriate date you want, July 30, 2010, and check off the desired bond, "10 year" (daily prices) to obtain the average yield or interest rate that she is earning. Use this interest rate as the discount rate for the remainder of this problem.

2. Create a timeline in Excel for her current situation, as well as the certification program and MBA degree options, using the following assumptions:
   a. Salaries for the year are paid only once, at the end of each year of your timeline.
   b. The salary increase becomes effective immediately upon graduating from the MBA program or being certified. That is, because the increases become effective immediately but salaries are paid at the end of the year, the first salary increase will be paid exactly one year after graduation or certification.

3. Calculate the present value of the salary differential for completing the certification program. Subtract the cost of the program to get the *NPV* of undertaking the certification program.

4. Calculate the present value of the salary differential for completing the MBA degree. Calculate the present value of the cost of the MBA program. Based on your calculations, determine the *NPV* of undertaking the MBA.

5. Based on your answers to Questions 3 and 4, what advice would you give to Natasha? What if the two programs are mutually exclusive? If Natasha undertakes one of the programs, there is no further benefit to undertaking the other program. Would your advice change?

Chapter 4 APPENDIX Using a Financial Calculator

Specifying Decimal Places

Make sure you always have plenty of decimal places displayed!

HP-10BII

TI BAII Plus Professional

Toggling Between the Beginning and End of a Period

You should always make sure that your calculator is in *end-of-period* mode.

HP-10BII

TI BAII Plus Professional

Set the Number of Periods per Year

You will avoid a lot of confusion later if you always set your periods per year "P/Y" to 1:

HP-10BII

TI BAII Plus Professional

General TVM Buttons

HP-10BII

TI BAII Plus Professional

Solving for the Present Value of a Single Future Cash Flow (Example 4.1)

You are considering investing in a Government of Canada bond that will make one payment of $15,000 in 10 years. If the competitive market interest rate is fixed at 6% per year, what is the bond worth today? [Answer: $8375.92]

HP-10BII

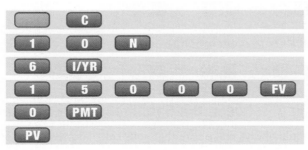

[Orange Shift] [C]	Press [Orange Shift] and then the [C] button to clear all previous entries.
1 0 N	Enter the Number of periods.
6 I/YR	Enter the market annual interest rate.
1 5 0 0 0 FV	Enter the Value you will receive in 10 periods.
0 PMT	Indicate that there are no payments.
PV	Solve for the Present Value.

TI BAII Plus Professional

2ND FV	Press [2ND] and then the [FV] button to clear all previous entries.
3 0 N	Enter the Number of periods.
1 0 I/Y	Enter the market annual interest rate.
1 0 0 0 0 PMT	Enter the payment amount per period.
0 PV	Indicate that there is no initial amount in the retirement account.
CPT FV	Solve for the Future Value.

Solving for the Future Value of an Annuity (Example 4.7)

Ellen is 35 years old, and she has decided it is time to plan seriously for her retirement. At the end of each year until she is 65, she will save $10,000 in a retirement account. If the account earns 10% per year, how much will Ellen have saved at age 65? [Answer: $1,644,940]

HP-10BII

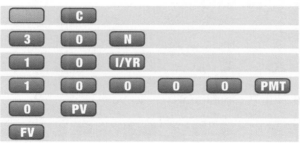

[Orange Shift] [C]	Press [Orange Shift] and then the [C] button to clear all previous entries.
3 0 N	Enter the Number of periods.
1 0 I/YR	Enter the market annual interest rate.
1 0 0 0 0 PMT	Enter the Payment amount per period.
0 PV	Indicate that there is no initial amount in the retirement account.
FV	Solve for the Future Value.

TI BAII Plus Professional

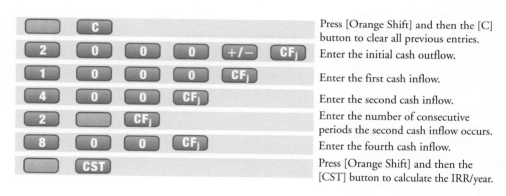

[2ND] [FV]		Press [2ND] and then the [FV] button to clear all previous entries.
[1] [0] [N]		Enter the Number of periods.
[6] [I/Y]		Enter the market annual interest rate.
[1] [5] [0] [0] [0] [FV]		Enter the Value you will receive in 10 periods.
[0] [PMT]		Indicate that there are no payments.
[CPT] [PV]		Solve for the Present Value.

Solving for the Internal Rate of Return

If you have an initial cash outflow of $2000 and one cash inflow per year for the following four years of $1000, $400, $400, and $800, what is the internal rate of return on the project per year? [Answer: 12.12%]

HP-10BII

[ ] [C]	Press [Orange Shift] and then the [C] button to clear all previous entries.
[2] [0] [0] [0] [+/−] [CFⱼ]	Enter the initial cash outflow.
[1] [0] [0] [0] [CFⱼ]	Enter the first cash inflow.
[4] [0] [0] [CFⱼ]	Enter the second cash inflow.
[2] [ ] [CFⱼ]	Enter the number of consecutive periods the second cash inflow occurs.
[8] [0] [0] [CFⱼ]	Enter the fourth cash inflow.
[ ] [CST]	Press [Orange Shift] and then the [CST] button to calculate the IRR/year.

TI BAII Plus Professional

[CF]	Access Cash Flow Worksheet.
[2ND] [CE|C]	Press [2ND] and then the [CE/C] button to clear all previous entries.
[2] [0] [0] [0] [+/−] [ENTER]	Enter the initial cash outflow.
[↓] [1] [0] [0] [0] [ENTER]	Enter the first cash inflow.
[↓]	Leave the frequency of the initial cash inflow at 1 (Default Setting).
[↓] [4] [0] [0] [ENTER]	Enter the second cash inflow.
[↓] [2] [ENTER]	Enter the frequency of the second cash inflow as 2.
[↓] [8] [0] [0] [ENTER]	Enter the fourth cash inflow.
[↓]	Leave the frequency of the fourth cash inflow at 1 (Default Setting).
[IRR] [CPT]	Solve for the IRR.

5

Interest Rates

LEARNING OBJECTIVES

▶ Understand the different ways interest rates are quoted

▶ Use quoted rates to calculate loan payments and balances

▶ Know how inflation, expectations, and risk combine to determine interest rates

▶ See the link between interest rates in the market and a firm's opportunity cost of capital

notation

APR	annual percentage rate	*n*	number of periods
APY	annual percentage yield	*NPV*	net present value
C	cash flow	*PV*	present value
C_n	cash flow that arrives in period *n*	*r*	interest rate or discount rate
EAR	effective annual rate	r_n	interest rate or discount rate for an *n*-year term
FV	future value		
m	compounding frequency of a quoted interest rate		

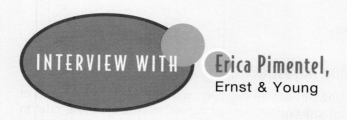

INTERVIEW WITH Erica Pimentel,
Ernst & Young

McGill University, 2008

"A client may provide
me with the purchase
price of a property and
the interest rate on a
loan, but it's up to me
to calculate an amorti-
zation schedule."

Erica Pimentel graduated in 2008 from McGill University with a Bachelor of Commerce degree. As a senior tax staff member at Ernst & Young in Montreal, she provides professional services and tax advice to corporate customers. "My role is focused on preparing tax returns, auditing tax provisions, and providing tax advice related to Canadian tax compliance."

Her work requires her to deal with both Canadian corporations and Canadian subsidiaries of foreign companies, and the knowledge acquired in her finance courses has become an invaluable tool for performing her job. "It's often the case that clients will provide you with a small amount of information, and I need to use the skills I learned in finance class to fully analyze the situation," Erica explains. "For example," she continues, "a client may provide me with the purchase price of a property and the interest rate on a loan, but it's up to me to calculate an amortization schedule."

She deals with calculations involving interest rates in many situations. In particular, she often needs to find a client's total interest costs for tax purposes, as well as use discount rates for *NPV* calculations. "I also make use of concepts like *NPV* and cash flow forecasting to help clients make the decisions that best suit their needs," she says.

In Chapter 4, we explored the mechanics of computing present values and future values given a market interest rate. Recall that an interest rate allows us to convert money at one point in time to another. But how do we determine that interest rate? In this chapter, we consider the factors that affect interest rates and discuss how to determine the appropriate discount rate for a set of cash flows. We begin by looking at the way interest is paid and interest rates are quoted, and we show how to calculate the effective interest paid in one year given different quoting conventions. We then consider some of the main determinants of interest rates—namely, inflation and economic growth. Because interest rates tend to change over time, investors will demand different interest rates for different investment horizons, based on their expectations and the risk involved in longer time horizons.

Interest Rate Quotes and Adjustments

If you spend some time looking through a newspaper, you will find literally dozens of interest rates discussed and advertised, from savings deposit rates to auto loan rates to interest rates being paid on the government's debt. Interest rates are clearly central to the functioning of any financial system. To understand interest rates, it's important to think of interest rates as a price—the price of using money. When you borrow money to buy a car, you are using the bank's money now to get the car and paying the money back over time. The interest rate on your loan is the price you pay to be able to convert your future loan payments into the money needed to buy a car today. Similarly, when you deposit money into a savings account, you are letting the bank use your money until you withdraw it later. The interest the bank pays you on your deposit is the price it pays to have the use of your money (for things like making car loans).

Just like any other price, interest rates are set by market forces, in particular the supply of and demand for funds. When the supply (savings) is high and the demand (borrowing) is low, interest rates are low, other things being equal. Additionally, as we discuss later in the chapter, interest rates are also influenced by expected inflation and risk.

To be able to study and use interest rates, we have to understand how they are quoted. In practice, interest is paid and interest rates are quoted in different ways. For example, in November 2010, ING Direct offered a 5-year guaranteed investment certificate (GIC) with an interest rate of 2.75% per year with annual compounding, while President's Choice Financial offered an interest rate of 2.96% per year, but with the interest compounded on a monthly basis. Interest rates can also change through time and differ depending on the investment horizon. On January 31, 1990, investors earned about 11% on 1-year risk-free (Government of Canada) investments but earned only about 9.3% on 20-year risk-free investments. This is in sharp contrast to February 16, 2010, when investors earned only 0.63% on 1-year risk-free investments but 4.06% on 20-year risk-free investments. Interest rates can also vary due to risk. For example, the Canadian government is able to borrow at a much lower interest rate than Molson Coors Brewing Company.

Because interest rates may be quoted for different time intervals, such as monthly, semi-annual, or annual, it is often necessary to adjust the interest rate to a time period that matches that of our cash flows. We explore these mechanics of interest rates in this section.

The Effective Annual Rate

effective annual rate (EAR) or annual percentage yield (APY) The total amount of interest that will be earned at the end of one year.

Interest rates are sometimes reported as an **effective annual rate (EAR)**, which indicates the total amount of interest that will be earned at the end of one year.[1] We have used this method of quoting the interest rate thus far in this textbook, and in Chapter 4 we used the *EAR* as the discount rate r in our time value of money calculations. For example, with an *EAR* of 5%, a $100 investment grows to

$$\$100 \times (1 + r) = \$100 \times (1.05) = \$105$$

in one year. After two years it will grow as follows:

$$\$100 \times (1 + r)^2 = \$100 \times (1.05)^2 = \$110.25$$

Year:	0		1		2
Cash flow:	$100	× (1.05)	= $105	× (1.05)	= $110.25
	$100	×	(1.05)²	=	$110.25
	$100	×	(1.1025)	=	$110.25

[1]The effective annual rate is also referred to as the *effective annual yield* (*EAY*).

Adjusting the Effective Annual Rate to an Effective Rate Over Different Time Periods

The preceding example shows that earning an effective annual rate of 5% for two years is equivalent to earning 10.25% in total interest over the entire period:

$$\$100 \times (1.05)^2 = \$100 \times 1.1025 = \$110.25$$

In general, by raising the interest rate factor $(1 + r)$ to the appropriate power, we can compute an equivalent effective interest rate for a longer time period.

We can use the same method to find the equivalent effective interest rate for periods shorter than one year. In this case, we raise the interest rate factor $(1 + r)$ to the appropriate fractional power. For example, earning 5% interest in one year is equivalent to receiving

$$(1 + r)^{0.5} = (1.05)^{0.5} = \$1.0247$$

for each $1 invested every six months (0.5 years). That is, a 5% effective annual rate is equivalent to an interest rate of approximately 2.47% earned every six months—this would be an effective six-month rate. We can verify this result by computing the interest we would earn in one year by investing for two six-month periods at this rate:

$$(1 + r)^2 = (1.0247)^2 = \$1.05$$

Year:	**0**		$\frac{1}{2}$		**1**

Cash flow:	$1	× (1.0247)	= $1.0247	× (1.0247)	= $1.05
	$1	×	$(1.0247)^2$	=	$1.05
	$1	×	(1.05)	=	$1.05

In general, we can convert an effective discount rate of r for one period to an equivalent effective discount rate for n periods using the following formula:

$$(1 + \text{Equivalent } n\text{-Period Effective Rate}) = (1 + r)^n \tag{5.1}$$
$$\text{and thus, the Equivalent } n\text{-Period Effective Rate} = (1 + r)^n - 1$$

In this formula, n can be larger than 1 (to compute an effective rate over more than one period) or smaller than 1 (to compute an effective rate over a fraction of a period).

When computing present or future values, you should adjust the discount rate to match the time period of the cash flows.

This adjustment is necessary to apply the perpetuity or annuity formulas to non-annual cash flows, as in the following example.

EXAMPLE 5.1

Personal Finance

Valuing Monthly Cash Flows

Problem

Suppose your bank account pays interest monthly with an effective annual rate of 6%. What amount of interest will you earn each month?

If you have no money in the bank today, how much will you need to save at the end of each month to accumulate $100,000 in 10 years?

Solution

▶ **Plan**

We can use Equation 5.1 to convert the *EAR* to an effective monthly rate, answering the first part of the question. The second part of the question is a future value of an annuity question.

It is asking how big a monthly annuity we would have to deposit to end up with $100,000 in 10 years. However, to do this problem, we need to write the timeline in terms of *monthly* periods, because our cash flows (deposits) will be monthly:

Month: 0   1   2   120

Cash flow: C C C

That is, we can view the savings plan as a monthly annuity with $10 \times 12 = 120$ monthly payments. We have the future value of the annuity ($100,000) and the length of time (120 months), and we will have the monthly interest rate from the first part of the question. We can then use the future value of an annuity formula (Equation 4.6) to solve for the monthly deposit.

▶ **Execute**

From Equation 5.1, a 6% *EAR* is equivalent to earning $(1.06)^{1/12} - 1 = 0.4868\%$ as the effective rate per month. The exponent in this equation is 1/12 because the period is 1/12 of a year (a month).

To determine the amount to save each month to reach the goal of $100,000 in 120 months, we must determine the amount C of the monthly payment that will have a future value of $100,000 in 120 months, given an interest rate of 0.4868% per month. Now that we have all of the inputs in terms of months (monthly payment, effective monthly interest rate, and total number of months), we use the future value of annuity formula from Chapter 4 to solve this problem:

$$FV(\text{annuity}) = C \times \tfrac{1}{r}[(1 + r)^n - 1]$$

We solve for the payment C using the equivalent effective monthly interest rate $r = 0.4868\%$, and $n = 120$ months:

$$C = \frac{FV(\text{annuity})}{\tfrac{1}{r}[(1+r)^n - 1]} = \frac{\$100{,}000}{\tfrac{1}{0.004868}[(1.004868)^{120} - 1]} = \$615.47 \text{ per month}$$

We can also compute this result using a financial calculator:

	N	I/Y	PV	PMT	FV
Given:	120	0.4868	0		100,000
Solve for:				−615.47	

Excel Formula: = PMT(RATE,NPER,PV,FV) = PMT(0.004868,120,0,100000)

▶ **Evaluate**

Thus, if we save $615.47 per month and we earn interest monthly at an effective annual rate of 6%, we will have $100,000 in 10 years. Notice that the timing in the annuity formula must be consistent for all of the inputs. In this case, we had a monthly deposit, so we needed to convert our interest rate to an effective monthly interest rate and then use total number of months (120) instead of years.

annual percentage rate (APR) The amount of simple interest earned in one year without considering the effects of compounding that may occur.

simple interest Interest earned only on the original principal amount without considering compounding of interest or interest earned on accrued interest.

Annual Percentage Rates

The most common way to quote interest rates is in terms of an **annual percentage rate (APR)**, which indicates the amount of **simple interest** earned in one year, that is, the amount of interest earned *without* the effect of compounding even though compounding may occur. Because it does not include the effect of compounding, the *APR* quote is typically less than the actual amount of interest that you will earn. To compute the actual amount that you will earn in one year, you must first convert the *APR* to an effective annual rate.

For example, suppose Scotiabank advertises savings accounts with an interest rate of "6% *APR* with monthly compounding." By convention, this rate quote implies you will earn an effective monthly rate of 6%/12 = 0.5% every month. So an *APR* with monthly compounding is actually a way of indirectly quoting an *effective monthly* interest rate, rather than an effective annual interest rate. Because the interest compounds each month, you will earn

$$\$1 \times (1.005)^{12} = \$1.061678$$

at the end of one year, for an effective annual rate of 6.1678%. The 6.1678% that you earn on your deposit is higher than the quoted 6% *APR* due to compounding; in later months, you earn interest on the interest paid in earlier months. To summarize, an actual rate of 0.5% *per month* can be stated in either of the following ways:

▷ 6% *APR*, compounded monthly

▷ *EAR* of 6.1678%, which indicates the total amount of interest earned *per year*

It is important to remember that because the *APR* does not reflect the true amount you will earn over one year, *the APR itself cannot be used as a discount rate*. Instead, the *APR* is an indirect way of quoting the actual interest earned each compounding period:

$$\text{Implied Effective Interest Rate per Compounding Period} = \frac{APR}{m}$$

(5.2)

(m = number of compounding periods per year, also known as the compounding frequency)

We call this rate an implied effective rate because it shows the actual interest earned over the compounding period and, by convention, it is what is implied from an *APR* quote. In our example of 6% *APR* with monthly compounding, the 0.5% equivalent will be the implied effective rate per month. Once we have computed the implied effective rate per compounding period from Equation 5.2, we can compute the equivalent effective rate for any other time interval using Equation 5.1. The effective annual

---

Common Mistake   **Using the *APR* or *EAR* in the Annuity Formula**

At this point, many students make the mistake of trying to use the *APR* or *EAR* in the annuity formula. The interest rate in the annuity formula must match the frequency of the cash flows. That's why in Example 5.1 we first converted the *EAR* into a monthly rate and then used the annuity formula to compute the monthly loan payments. The common mistake in this case would be to use an *APR* or an *EAR* in the annuity formula to obtain annual cash flows, and then divide those cash flows by 12 to obtain the monthly payments.

This process will produce the wrong answer. To see why, consider the timing of the first deposit in Example 5.1. With a monthly rate and monthly payments, the annuity formula assumes that the first payment will be made one month from now. It then assumes that you will be making 11 more monthly deposits before the end of the first year. Each of those deposits will start earning interest as soon you make it. In contrast, if you use an annual rate and calculate an annual cash flow, the formula assumes that you will make your first deposit one *year* from now, so that you will forgo a whole year of interest before you start earning anything. Thus, you can see that using an annual rate misses the fact that you are making deposits earlier and more often than annually, so you are adding to your interest-earning principal more frequently than once per year.

rate corresponding to an *APR* with m compounding periods per year is given by the following conversion formula:

Converting an *APR* to an *EAR*

$$(1 + EAR) = \left(1 + \frac{APR}{m}\right)^m \text{ and thus the } EAR = \left(1 + \frac{APR}{m}\right)^m - 1 \qquad (5.3)$$

Table 5.1 shows the effective annual rates that correspond to an *APR* of 6% with different compounding intervals. The *EAR* increases with the frequency of compounding because of the ability to earn interest on interest sooner. Investments can compound even more frequently than daily. In principle, the compounding interval could be hourly or every second. As a practical matter, compounding more frequently than daily has a negligible impact on the effective annual rate and is rarely observed.

When working with *APRs*, we must first convert the *APR* to an implied effective discount rate per compounding interval using Equation 5.2. We can then use Equation 5.1 to convert the effective rate per compounding period to an equivalent effective rate per *different* compounding period. If we need to convert our *APR* to an effective rate per year, i.e., an *EAR*, we can use Equation 5.3 (which is a special case of applying both Equations 5.2 and 5.1 simultaneously).

TABLE 5.1	Compounding Interval	Effective Annual Rate
Effective Annual Rates for a 6% *APR* with Different Compounding Periods	Annual	$1 + \left(\frac{0.06}{1}\right)^1 - 1 = 6\%$
	Semi-annual	$1 + \left(\frac{0.06}{2}\right)^2 - 1 = 6.09\%$
	Monthly	$1 + \left(\frac{0.06}{12}\right)^{12} - 1 = 6.1678\%$
	Daily	$1 + \left(\frac{0.06}{365}\right)^{365} - 1 = 6.1831\%$

EXAMPLE 5.2

Converting the *APR* to a Discount Rate

Problem

Your firm is purchasing a new telephone system that will last for four years. You can purchase the system for an upfront cost of $150,000, or you can lease the system from the manufacturer for $4000 paid at the end of each month. The lease price is offered for a 48-month lease with no early termination—you cannot end the lease early. Your firm can borrow at an interest rate of 6% *APR* with monthly compounding. Should you purchase the system outright or pay $4000 per month?

Solution

▶ **Plan**

The cost of leasing the system is a 48-month annuity of $4000 per month:

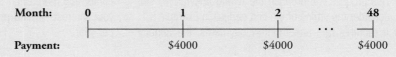

Month:	0	1	2	48
Payment:		$4000	$4000	$4000

We can compute the present value of the lease cash flows using the annuity formula, but first we need to compute the effective discount rate that corresponds to a period length of one month. To do so, we convert the borrowing cost of 6% *APR* with monthly compounding to an implied effective monthly discount rate using Equation 5.2. Once we have a monthly rate, we can use the present value of annuity formula (Equation 4.5) to compute the present value of the monthly payments and compare it to the cost of buying the system.

▶ **Execute**

As Equation 5.2 shows, the 6% *APR* with monthly compounding implies 6%/12 = 0.5% every month. The 12 comes from the fact that there are 12 monthly compounding periods per year. Now that we have the true rate corresponding to the quoted *APR*, we can use that discount rate in the annuity formula (Equation 4.5) to compute the present value of the monthly payments:

$$PV = 4000 \times \frac{1}{0.005}\left(1 - \frac{1}{1.005^{48}}\right) = \$170{,}321.27$$

Using a financial calculator or Excel:

	N	I/Y	PV	PMT	FV
Given:	48	0.5		−4000	0
Solve for:			170,321.27		
Excel Formula: = PV(RATE,NPER,PMT,FV) = PV(0.005,48,−4000,0)					

▶ **Evaluate**

Thus, paying $4000 per month for 48 months is equivalent to paying a present value of $170,321.27 today. This cost is $170,321.27 − $150,000 = $20,321.27 higher than the cost of purchasing the system, so it is better to pay $150,000 for the system rather than lease it.

Concept Check

1. What is the difference between an *EAR* and an *APR* quote?

2. Why can't the *APR* be used as a discount rate?

5.2 Application: Discount Rates and Loans

Now that we have explained how to compute the discount rate from an interest rate quote, let's apply the concept to solve two common financial problems: calculating a loan payment and calculating the remaining balance on a loan.

Computing Loan Payments

amortizing loan A loan on which the borrower makes monthly payments that include interest on the loan plus some part of the loan balance.

Many loans, such as personal and car loans, have monthly payments and are quoted in terms of an *APR* with monthly compounding. These types of loans are **amortizing loans**, which means that each month you pay interest on the loan plus some part of the loan balance. Each monthly payment is the same, and the loan is fully repaid with the final payment. Typical terms for a new car loan might be "6.75% *APR* for 60 months." Most provinces in Canada have harmonized their cost of credit disclosure requirements so that when the compounding interval for the *APR* is not stated explicitly, it is equal to the interval between the payments, or one month in this case.[2] Thus, this quote means that the loan will be repaid with 60 equal monthly payments, computed using a 6.75% *APR* with monthly compounding. Let's look at the cash flows associated with this loan. The bank will give you $30,000 in cash today to use to buy the car. In return, you will give the bank 60 equal payments each month for 60 months, starting 1 month from now. For the bank to be willing to accept this exchange, it must be true that the present value of what you will give the bank, discounted at the loan's interest rate, is equal to the amount of cash the bank is giving you now. Here is the timeline for a $30,000 car loan with these terms:

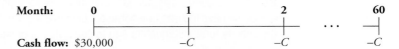

Month:	0	1	2	60
Cash flow:	$30,000	$-C$	$-C$	$-C$

The payment, C, is set so that the present value of the cash flows, evaluated using the loan interest rate, equals the original principal amount of $30,000. In this case, the 6.75% *APR* with monthly compounding corresponds to a one-month discount rate of $6.75\%/12 = 0.5625\%$. It is important that the discount rate match the frequency of the cash flows—here we have a monthly discount rate and a monthly loan payment, so we can proceed. Because the loan payments are an annuity, we can use Equation 4.10 to find C:

$$C = \frac{P}{\frac{1}{r}\left(1 - \frac{1}{(1 + r)^n}\right)} = \frac{30,000}{\frac{1}{0.005625}\left(1 - \frac{1}{(1 + 0.005625)^{60}}\right)} = \$590.50$$

Alternatively, we can solve for the payment C using a financial calculator or a spreadsheet:

	N	I/Y	PV	PMT	FV
Given:	60	0.5625	30,000		0
Solve for:				−590.50	
Excel Formula: = PMT(RATE,NPER,PV,FV) = PMT(0.005625,60,30000,0)					

Your loan payment each month includes interest and repayment of part of the principal, reducing the amount you still owe. Because the loan balance (amount you still owe) is decreasing each month, the interest that accrues on that balance is decreasing. As a result, even though your payment stays the same over the entire 60-month life of the loan, the part of that payment needed to cover interest each month is constantly decreasing and the part left over to reduce the principal further is constantly increasing. We illustrate this effect in panel (a) of Figure 5.1, which shows the proportion of each monthly loan payment that covers interest (red) and the portion left over to reduce the principal (turquoise). As you can see, $168.75 of your first $590.50 payment is needed just to cover interest accrued over the first month ($30,000 × 0.005625 = $168.75). However, this amount steadily decreases so that by the end of the loan, nearly all of your payment is going toward principal.

Panel (b) of Figure 5.1 shows the effect of your payments on the loan balance. When you make your first payment of $590.50, $168.75 covers interest on the loan, leaving $421.75 to reduce the principal to $30,000 − $421.75 = $29,578.25. The next month,

---

[2]An important exception is Canadian mortgages. These are quoted with *APR*s using semi-annual compounding even though payments are usually monthly.

FIGURE 5.1

Amortizing Loan

Panel (a) shows how the interest (red) and principal portions (turquoise) of the monthly payment on the $30,000 car loan change over the life of the loan. Panel (b) illustrates the effect on the outstanding balance (principal) of the loan. Note that as the balance decreases, the amount of the payment needed to cover interest on that balance decreases, allowing more of the payment to be used to reduce the principal.

Panel (a)

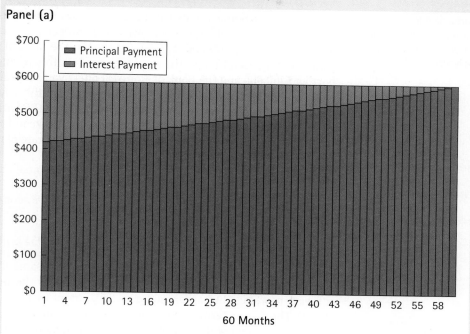

Panel (b)

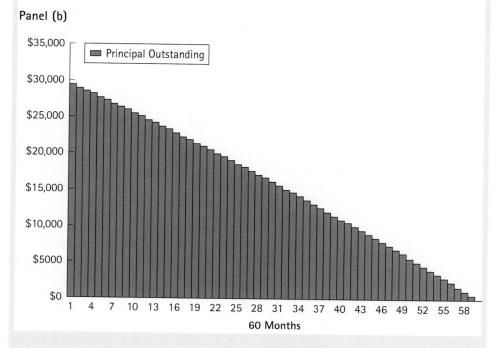

you owe interest only on the $29,578.25 loan balance, which is $166.38, leaving more of your $590.50 payment to reduce the principal further. This effect continues so that each month more of your payment is available to reduce the principal, causing the principal to decrease rapidly toward the end of the loan as you are paying off bigger and bigger amounts of the balance.

Computing Canadian Mortgage Payments

mortgage A loan for which the borrower offers property as security for the lender.

When you buy a home, you usually need to borrow money. This is done using a **mortgage**, which is a loan for which the borrower offers property as security for the lender. Rates for Canadian mortgages are typically quoted in the form of an *APR* with semi-annual compounding even though the mortgage has monthly payments. Suppose you need to borrow $400,000 and the Bank of Montreal offers you a 5-year term for a mortgage with a rate of 7.252% to be amortized over 25 years of monthly payments. To determine your monthly payments, you need to convert the 7.252% *APR* with semi-annual compounding into an equivalent effective rate per month. This requires two steps. First, you can use Equation 5.2 to get the implied effective interest rate per semi-annual period:

$$\frac{7.252\%}{2} = 3.626\% \text{ per semi-annual period}$$

Then you can use Equation 5.1 to convert the effective semi-annual rate to the equivalent effective monthly rate:

$$(1.03626)^{1/6} - 1 = 0.005954 \text{ or } 0.5954\% \text{ per month}$$

You can calculate the monthly payments using the same method as shown above for loan payments. However, you might get confused by the terms of the mortgage. It is a 5-year mortgage but amortized over 25 years of monthly payments. What does this mean? The 5-year term of the mortgage means that the quoted rate is fixed for the 5 years. At the end of the 5 years, you must renegotiate the mortgage at prevailing rates or pay off the outstanding balance. The amortization over 25 years means that your payments are calculated as though the interest rate will stay at the quoted *APR* for the full 25 years and the same 300 monthly payments will be made over this entire time. So using Equation 4.10, we can solve for the monthly mortgage payments, C:

$$C = \frac{P}{\frac{1}{r}\left(1 - \frac{1}{(1+r)^n}\right)} = \frac{400,000}{\frac{1}{0.005954}\left(1 - \frac{1}{(1+0.005954)^{300}}\right)} = \$2,864.17$$

Although the payments are calculated as though 300 monthly payments will be made, they are paid only over the term of the mortgage (5 years, or 60 months). When the term of the mortgage is over, you can either repay the outstanding balance in full or you can refinance it (usually by renewing your mortgage).

Computing the Outstanding Loan Balance

As Figure 5.1 shows, the outstanding balance on an amortizing loan is different each month. The amount you owe at any point in time can be calculated as the present value of your future obligations on the loan. So, the outstanding balance, also called the outstanding principal, is equal to the present value of the remaining future loan payments, again evaluated using the loan interest rate. We calculate the outstanding loan balance by determining the present value of the remaining loan payments using the loan rate as the discount rate.

EXAMPLE 5.3

Personal Finance
Computing the
Outstanding Loan
Balance on a
Canadian Mortgage

Problem

Returning to our previous hypothetical Bank of Montreal mortgage example, we are interested in what your outstanding balance will be at the end of the mortgage's initial five-year term.

Solution

▶ **Plan**

We have already determined that the monthly payments on the mortgage are $2864.17. At the end of the mortgage's 5-year term, there are 20 years of monthly payments remaining (or 240 monthly payments). The remaining balance on the loan is the present value of the remaining 240 months of payments. Thus, we can just use the annuity formula with the monthly rate of 0.5954%, a monthly payment of $2864.17, and 240 months remaining.

▶ **Execute**

$$\text{Balance after five years} = \$2864.17 \times \frac{1}{0.005954}\left(1 - \frac{1}{1.005954^{240}}\right) = \$365{,}321.11$$

Thus, after five years, you owe $365,321.11 on the loan.

Using a financial calculator or Excel:

	N	**I/Y**	**PV**	**PMT**	**FV**
Given:	240	0.5954		−2864.17	0
Solve for:			365,321.11		

Excel Formula: = PV(RATE,NPER,PMT,FV) = PV(0.005954,240,−2864.17,0)

▶ **Evaluate**

At any point in time, including when you first take out the loan, you can calculate the balance of the loan as the present value of your remaining payments. Since your initial principal was $400,000 and your outstanding balance at the end of the mortgage's term is $365,321.11, you paid a total of $34,678.89 toward principal. Since you paid 60 payments of $2864.17 summing to $171,850.20, the amount of your payments that went to interest charges is $171,850.20 − $34,678.89 = $137,171.31.

Concept Check

3. How is the principal repaid in an amortizing loan?

4. Why does the part of your loan payment covering interest change over time?

5.3 The Determinants of Interest Rates

Now that we understand how interest rates are quoted and used in loans, we turn to a broader question: how are interest rates determined? Fundamentally, interest rates are determined by market forces based on the relative supply and demand of funds. This supply and demand is in turn determined by the willingness of individuals, banks, and firms to borrow, save, and lend. Changes in interest rates affect consumer decisions, such as how much you can borrow for a car loan or mortgage. Because they change the present value of future cash flows, changes in interest rates also have a broad impact on capital budgeting decisions within a firm. In this section, we look at some of the factors that may influence interest rates, such as inflation, current economic activity, and expectations of future growth.

Inflation and Real Versus Nominal Rates

Inflation measures how the purchasing power of a given amount of currency declines due to increasing prices. How many times have you heard the expression "A dollar just doesn't buy what it used to"? We've all witnessed the steady upward climb of prices—for example, your morning coffee probably costs a little more today than it did five years ago. Inflation affects how we evaluate the interest rates being quoted by banks and other financial institutions. Those interest rates, and the ones we have used for discounting cash flows in this book, are **nominal interest rates**, which indicate the rate at which your money will grow if invested for a certain period. Of course, if prices in the economy are also increasing due to inflation, the nominal interest rate does not represent the true increase in purchasing power that will result from investing.

nominal interest rates Interest rates quoted by banks and other financial institutions that indicate the rate at which money will grow if invested for a certain period of time.

For example, let's say that a cup of coffee costs $1 this year. If you have $100, you could buy 100 coffees. Instead, if you put that $100 in a bank account earning 5.06% per year, you will have $105.06 at the end of the year. But how much better off will you really be? That depends on how much prices have increased over the same year. If inflation was 3% over the year, then that cup of coffee would cost 3% more, or $1.03 at the end of the year. Thus, you could take your $105.06 and buy $105.06/$1.03 = 102 coffees, so you're really only 2% better off.

real interest rate The rate of growth of purchasing power after adjusting for inflation.

That 2% is your **real interest rate**—the rate of growth of your purchasing power, after adjusting for inflation. Just as in the example, we can calculate the rate of growth of purchasing power as follows:

$$1 + \text{Growth in Purchasing Power} = 1 + \text{real rate} = \frac{1 + \text{nominal rate}}{1 + \text{inflation rate}}$$

$$= \frac{\text{Growth of Money}}{\text{Growth of Prices}} \qquad (5.4)$$

We can rearrange Equation 5.4 to find the following formula for the real interest rate, together with a convenient approximation for the real interest rate when inflation rates are low:

The Real Interest Rate

$$\text{real rate} = \frac{\text{nominal rate} - \text{inflation rate}}{1 + \text{inflation rate}} \approx \text{nominal rate} - \text{inflation rate} \qquad (5.5)$$

That is, the real interest rate is approximately equal to the nominal interest rate less the rate of inflation.[3]

EXAMPLE 5.4

Calculating the Real Interest Rate

Problem

In the year 2000, short-term Canadian government bond rates were about 5.8% and the rate of inflation was about 3%. In 2003, interest rates were about 2.7% and inflation was about 3.1%. What was the real interest rate in 2000 and 2003?

Solution

▶ **Plan**

The bond rates tell us the nominal rates. Given the nominal rates and inflation for each year, we can use Equation 5.5 to calculate the real interest rate.

---

[3]The real interest rate should not be used as a discount rate for future cash flows. It can be used as a discount rate only if the cash flows are not the expected cash flows that will be paid, but are the equivalent cash flows before being adjusted for growth due to inflation. (In that case, we say the cash flows are in real terms.) This approach is error prone, however, so throughout this book we will always forecast cash flows including any growth due to inflation, and discount using nominal interest rates.

▶ **Execute**

Eq. (5.5) says:

$$\text{real rate} = \frac{\text{nominal rate} - \text{inflation rate}}{1 + \text{inflation rate}}$$

Thus, the real interest rate in 2000 was (0.058 − 0.03)/(1.03) = 0.0272 or 2.72% (which is approximately equal to the difference between the nominal rate and inflation: 5.8% − 3% = 2.8%). In 2003, the real interest rate was (0.027 − 0.031)/(1.031) = −0.0039 or −0.39%.

▶ **Evaluate**

Note that the real interest rate was negative in 2003, indicating that interest rates were insufficient to keep up with inflation. As a result, investors in Canadian government bonds were able to buy less at the end of the year than they could have purchased at the start of the year.

Figure 5.2 shows the history of nominal interest rates and inflation rates in Canada since 1962. Note that the nominal interest rate tends to move with inflation. Individuals' willingness to save will depend on the growth in purchasing power they can expect (given by the real interest rate). Thus, when the inflation rate is high, a higher nominal interest rate is needed to induce individuals to save.

Investment and Interest Rate Policy

Interest rates affect not only individuals' propensity to save, but also firms' incentive to raise capital and invest. Consider an opportunity that requires an upfront investment of

FIGURE 5.2

Canadian Interest Rates and Inflation Rates, 1962–2009

Interest rates are average three-month treasury bill rates, and inflation rates are based on year-to-year changes in the Consumer Price Index (CPI) compiled by Statistics Canada.

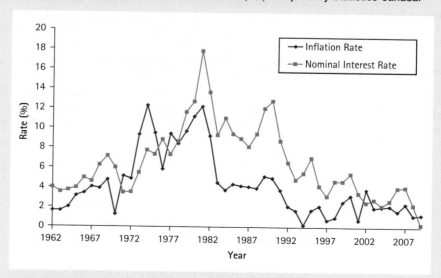

Source: Statistics Canada.

$10 million and generates a cash flow of $3 million per year for four years. If the interest rate is 5%, this investment has an *NPV* of:

$$NPV = -10 + \frac{3}{1.05} + \frac{3}{1.05^2} + \frac{3}{1.05^3} + \frac{3}{1.05^4} = \$0.638 \text{ million}$$

If the interest rate is 9%, the *NPV* falls to

$$NPV = -10 + \frac{3}{1.09} + \frac{3}{1.09^2} + \frac{3}{1.09^3} + \frac{3}{1.09^4} = -\$0.281 \text{ million}$$

and the investment is no longer profitable. The reason, of course, is that we are discounting the positive cash flows (that occur in the future) at a higher rate, which reduces their present value. The cost of $10 million occurs today, however, so its present value is independent of the discount rate.

More generally, when the costs of an investment precede the benefits, an increase in the interest rate will decrease the investment's *NPV*. All else being equal, higher interest rates will therefore tend to shrink the set of positive-*NPV* investments available to firms. The Bank of Canada and central banks in other countries attempt to use this relationship between interest rates and investment incentives when trying to guide the economy. They will often lower interest rates in attempts to stimulate investment if the economy is slowing, and they will raise interest rates to reduce investment if the economy is "overheating" and inflation is on the rise.

The Yield Curve and Discount Rates

term structure The relationship between the investment term and the interest rate.

yield curve A plot of bond yields as a function of the bonds' maturity date.

risk-free interest rate The interest rate at which money can be borrowed or lent without risk over a given period.

The interest rates that banks offer on investments or charge on loans depend on the horizon, or *term,* of the investment or loan. For example, a bank may offer you a higher rate of interest on a two-year locked-in guaranteed investment certificate (GIC) than it will offer for a GIC that is locked in for only one year. The relationship between the investment term and the interest rate is called the **term structure** of interest rates. We can plot this relationship on a graph called the **yield curve**. Figure 5.3 shows the term structure and corresponding yield curve of risk-free Canadian interest rates that were available to investors in January of 2004, 2008, 2009, and 2010. In each case, note that the interest rate depends on the horizon, and that the difference between short-term and long-term interest rates was especially pronounced in 2010. The rates plotted are interest rates for Canadian government debt securities, which are considered to be free of any risk of default (the Canadian government will not default on its loans). Thus, each of these rates is a **risk-free interest rate**, which is the interest rate at which money can be borrowed or lent without risk over a given period.

We can use the term structure to compute the present and future values of a risk-free cash flow over different investment horizons. For example, $100 invested for 1 year at the 1 year interest rate in January 2004 would grow to a future value of

$$\$100 \times 1.025875 = \$102.59$$

at the end of 1 year, and $100 invested for 10 years at the 10-year interest rate in January 2004 would grow to[4]

$$\$100 \times (1.048969)^{10} = \$161.30$$

We can apply the same logic when computing the present value of cash flows with different maturities. A risk-free cash flow received in two years should be discounted at

---

[4]We could also invest for 10 years by investing at the 1 year interest rate for 10 years in a row. However, because we do not know what future interest rates will be when we start our investment, our ultimate payoff would not be risk free.

FIGURE 5.3

Term Structure of Risk-Free Canadian Interest Rates, January 2004, 2008, 2009, and 2010

Term (Years)	Date Jan. 2004	Jan. 2008	Jan. 2009	Jan. 2010
0.25	2.6990	3.8327	0.8310	0.1597
1	2.5875	3.6641	0.8908	0.7381
2	3.0484	3.6220	1.1881	1.5069
3	3.4756	3.6651	1.5043	2.0958
4	3.8278	3.7159	1.7811	2.5152
5	4.1399	3.7588	2.0239	2.8189
6	4.4059	3.7942	2.2449	3.0579
7	4.6099	3.8252	2.4539	3.2665
8	4.7494	3.8545	2.6571	3.4624
9	4.8379	3.8843	2.8571	3.6513
10	4.8969	3.9157	3.0533	3.8315
11	4.9469	3.9485	3.2424	3.9981
12	5.0023	3.9819	3.4191	4.1453
13	5.0696	4.0145	3.5779	4.2682
14	5.1490	4.0444	3.7135	4.3637
15	5.2363	4.0701	3.8218	4.4307
16	5.3252	4.0902	3.9007	4.4701
17	5.4089	4.1041	3.9500	4.4845
18	5.4815	4.1113	3.9713	4.4776
19	5.5385	4.1123	3.9681	4.4540
20	5.5774	4.1078	3.9448	4.4181
21	5.5973	4.0988	3.9065	4.3746
22	5.5993	4.0866	3.8584	4.3272
23	5.5855	4.0724	3.8050	4.2794
24	5.5590	4.0577	3.7507	4.2337
25	5.5232	4.0435	3.6986	4.1920
26	5.4814	4.0308	3.6514	4.1556
27	5.4368	4.0205	3.6107	4.1251
28	5.3922	4.0132	3.5778	4.1010
29	5.3497	4.0092	3.5531	4.0832
30	5.3109	4.0089	3.5368	4.0714

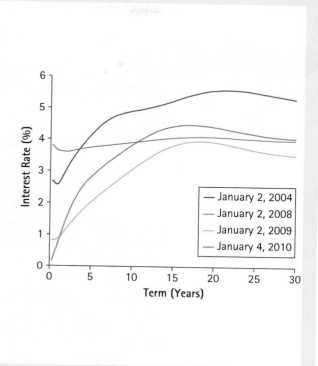

Source: Bank of Canada.

the 2-year interest rate, and a cash flow received in 10 years should be discounted at the 10-year interest rate. In general, a risk-free cash flow of C_n received in n years has the present value

$$PV = \frac{C_n}{(1 + r_n)^n} \qquad (5.6)$$

where r_n is the risk-free interest rate for an n-year term. In other words, when computing a present value, we must match the term of the cash flow with the term of the discount rate.

Combining Equation 5.6 for cash flows in different years leads to the general formula for the present value of a cash flow stream:

Present Value of a Cash Flow Stream Using a Term Structure of Discount Rates

$$PV = \frac{C_1}{1 + r_1} + \frac{C_2}{(1 + r_2)^2} + \cdots + \frac{C_n}{(1 + r_n)^n} \qquad (5.7)$$

Note the difference between Equation 5.7 and Equation 4.3. Here, we use a different discount rate for each cash flow, based on the rate from the yield curve with the same term. When interest rates are very similar across maturities, we say that the yield curve is flat, because it is close to a flat line. When the yield curve is relatively flat, as it was in January 2008, the distinction of using different rates for each cash flow is relatively minor and is often ignored by discounting using a single "average" interest rate r. But when short-term and long-term interest rates vary widely, as they did in January 2010, Equation 5.7 should be used.

Warning: All of our shortcuts for computing present values (annuity and perpetuity formulas, and financial calculators) are based on discounting all of the cash flows *at the same rate*. They *cannot* be used in situations in which cash flows need to be discounted at different rates.

EXAMPLE 5.5

Using the Term Structure to Compute Present Values

Problem
Compute the present value of a risk-free five-year annuity of $1000 per year, given the yield curve data for January 2010 in Figure 5.3.

Solution

▶ **Plan**
The timeline of the cash flows of the annuity is:

We can use the table next to the yield curve to identify the interest rate corresponding to each length of time: 1, 2, 3, 4, and 5 years. With the cash flows and those interest rates, we can compute the *PV*.

▶ **Execute**
From Figure 5.3, we see that the interest rates are 0.7381%, 1.5069%, 2.0958%, 2.5152%, and 2.8189% for terms of 1, 2, 3, 4, and 5 years, respectively.

To compute the present value, we discount each cash flow by the corresponding interest rate:

$$PV = \frac{1000}{1.007381} + \frac{1000}{1.015069^2} + \frac{1000}{1.020958^3} + \frac{1000}{1.025152^4} + \frac{1000}{1.028189^5} = \$4678.52$$

▶ **Evaluate**
The yield curve tells us the market interest rate per year for each different maturity. To correctly calculate the *PV* of cash flows from five different maturities, we need to use the five different interest rates corresponding to those maturities. Note that we cannot use the annuity formula here because the discount rates differ for each cash flow.

Common Mistake   **Using the Annuity Formula When Discount Rates Vary**

When computing the present value of an annuity, a common mistake is to use the annuity formula with a single interest rate even though interest rates vary with the investment horizon. For example, we *cannot* compute the present value of the five-year annuity in Example 5.5 using the five-year interest rate from January 2005:

$$PV \neq \$1000 \times \frac{1}{0.028189}\left(1 - \frac{1}{1.028189^5}\right) = \$4603.48$$

If we want to find the single interest rate that we could use to value the annuity, we must first compute the present value of the annuity using Equation 5.7 and then

solve for its *IRR*. For the annuity in Example 5.5, we use a financial calculator or spreadsheet to find its IRR of 2.2569%. The *IRR* of the annuity is always between the highest and lowest discount rates used to calculate its present value, as is the case in this example.

	N	I/Y	PV	PMT	FV
Given:	5		−4678.52	1000	0
Solve for:		2.2569			

Excel Formula: = RATE(NPER,PMT,PV,FV) = RATE (5,1000,−4678.52,0)

The Yield Curve and the Economy

As Figure 5.3 illustrates, the yield curve changes over time. Sometimes, short-term rates are close to long-term rates (as in 2008), and at other times they may be very different (as in 2010). What accounts for the changing shape of the yield curve?

overnight rate The rate at which banks can borrow cash reserves on an overnight basis from the Bank of Canada.

Interest Rate Determination. The Bank of Canada determines very short-term interest rates through its influence on the **overnight rate**, which is the rate at which banks can borrow cash reserves on an overnight basis. All other interest rates on the yield curve are set in the market and are adjusted until the supply of lending matches the demand for borrowing at each loan term. As we shall see in a moment, expectations of future interest rate changes have a major effect on investors' willingness to lend or borrow for longer terms and, therefore, on the shape of the yield curve.

Suppose short-term interest rates are equal to long-term interest rates. If interest rates are expected to rise in the future, investors would not want to make long-term investments. Instead, they could do better by investing on a short-term basis and then reinvesting after interest rates rose. Thus, if interest rates are expected to rise, long-term interest rates will tend to be higher than short-term rates to attract investors.

Similarly, if interest rates are expected to fall in the future, then borrowers would not wish to borrow at long-term rates that are equal to short-term rates. They would do better by borrowing on a short-term basis and then taking out a new loan after rates fall. So, if interest rates are expected to fall, long-term rates will tend to be lower than short-term rates to attract borrowers.

Yield Curve Shape. These arguments indicate that the shape of the yield curve will be strongly influenced by interest rate expectations. A sharply increasing (*steep*) yield curve, with long-term rates much higher than short-term rates, generally indicates that interest rates are expected to rise in the future. A decreasing (*inverted*) yield curve, with long-term rates lower than short-term rates, generally signals an expected decline in future interest rates. Because interest rates tend to drop in response to a slowdown in the economy, an inverted yield curve is often interpreted as a negative forecast for economic growth. Conversely, the yield curve tends to be steep as the economy comes out of a recession and interest rates are expected to rise.

The normal shape of the yield curve is moderately upward sloping. This would be the case if investors almost always believed that interest rates were going to rise in the future. But that is unlikely, so there have to be other forces at work to cause long-term interest rates normally to be higher than short-term rates. The most commonly cited reason is that, for the most part, investors have a preference for liquidity, and they would probably want to be able to have their investment mature (or to be able to sell it) in a shorter time frame than that covered by the term of a longer-term bond. Thus, long-term investments, such as loaning money to the government by buying a long-term Government of Canada bond, are riskier for most investors than short-term investments (such as buying a Government of Canada bond with 1 year left until maturity). Suppose you would like to liquidate your investment in 1 year. If you invest in a 30-year bond today and lock in the interest rate, you know exactly what you will get if you hold the bond for the entire 30 years. However, in 1 year, given that interest rates may have changed, the price (which equals the present value of the remaining bond payments discounted using the new, currently unknown, interest rate) may be much different than you anticipated. In fact, the present value of the payments you receive from a bond is very sensitive to even small changes in market interest rates and this sensitivity is higher for longer-term bonds. If, instead, you had invested in a 1-year bond, then at the time you liquidate your investment, you know exactly what you will have as the bond matures at that time and pays you its face value with no risk. This increased sensitivity of bond prices for longer-maturity bonds is due to the effect of compounding a change in interest rates over a longer period. To see this effect, consider the following example.

EXAMPLE 5.6

Long-term Versus
Short-term Lending

Problem

Suppose it is January 2011, and you are considering lending $10,000 to the Government of Canada, as a form of investing, and you need to choose between buying a bond that gives you a payment in 5 years or in 30 years. Assume the term structure is flat and both terms have an interest rate of 4%. You intend to liquidate your investment after 1 year and are concerned about the risk associated with the price you will receive when you sell the claim to your loan to the Government of Canada. Consider what will happen if market interest rates on these loans stay the same or either rise or fall by 1% by the time you sell your investment.

Solution

▶ **Plan**

Each of these loans has only one repayment cash flow at the end of the loan. They differ only by the time to repayment. You need to figure out what these locked-in repayments will be and then you can consider what happens, in January 2012, to the present value of these repayments, given the different possible interest rates. That will let you see how risky your own cash flow will be in January 2012 and also how risky your return will be by holding the investment from January 2011 to January 2012.

▶ **Execute**

The 5-year loan locks in a payment of

$$\$10,000 \times (1 + .04)^5 = \$12,166.53 \text{ to be paid in January, 2016.}$$

The 30-year loan locks in a payment of

$$\$10,000 \times (1 + .04)^{30} = \$32,433.98 \text{ to be paid in January, 2041.}$$

Now calculate the present value of these payments as of January 2012, given the possible changes in interest rates. For the loan that matures in 2016, its present value will be

$$PV_{2012} = \frac{\$12,166.53}{(1 + r)^4}$$

and for the loan that matures in 2041, its present value will be

$$PV_{2012} = \frac{\$32,433.98}{(1 + r)^{29}}$$

The following table shows the present values calculated for different interest rates.

Prices in 2012 given new rates	2016 Maturity Loan		2041 Maturity Loan	
	Rate	PV in 2012	Rate	PV in 2012
Rates rise 1%	5%	$10,009.43	5%	$7879.71
Rates constant	4%	$10,400.00	4%	$10,400.00
Rates drop 1%	3%	$10,809.80	3%	$13,763.24

To determine your rate of return by holding your investment from 2011 to 2012 (one year), you can do the following calculation:

$$\frac{2012 \text{ Price} - \$10,000}{\$10,000} = \text{return}$$

The following table shows the returns calculated based on the 2012 prices shown above

Returns from 2011 to 2012 given new rates	2016 Maturity Loan		2041 Maturity Loan	
	New Rate	Return	New Rate	Return
Rates rise 1%	5%	0.0943%	5%	−21.2029%
Rates constant	4%	4.0000%	4%	4.0000%
Rates drop 1%	3%	8.0980%	3%	37.6324%

▶ **Evaluate**

Depending on the new interest rates after 1 year, the value of the 5-year loan ranged from $10,009.43 to $10,809.80, giving a 1-year realized return of from 0.0943% to 8.0980%, but the value of the 30-year loan ranged from only $7879.71 to $13,763.24, giving a 1-year realized return of from −21.2029% to 37.6324%. The small change in market interest rates, compounded over a longer period, resulted in a much larger change in the present value of the loan repayment and the possible return realized by the investor. You can see why investors who have a liquidity preference (a preference for shorter-term investments) view longer-term loans as being riskier than short-term loans.

In addition to specifying the discount rates for risk-free cash flows that occur at different horizons, the yield curve provides information about future interest rate expectations and is also a potential leading indicator of future economic growth. Due to these qualities, the yield curve provides extremely important information for a business manager.

Concept Check

5. What is the difference between a nominal and real interest rate?
6. How are interest rates and the level of investment made by businesses related?

5.4 The Opportunity Cost of Capital

As we have seen in this chapter, the interest rates we observe in the market will vary based on quoting conventions, the term of the investment, and risk. In this chapter, we have developed the tools to account for these differences and gained some insights into how interest rates are determined. This knowledge will provide the foundation for our study of bonds in the next chapter.

In Chapter 3, we argued that the Valuation Principle tells us to use the "market interest rate" to compute present values and evaluate an investment opportunity. But with so many interest rates to choose from, the term "market interest rate" is inherently ambiguous. Therefore, going forward in the textbook, we will base the discount rate that we use to evaluate cash flows on the investor's **opportunity cost of capital** (or more simply, the **cost of capital**), which is *the best available expected return offered in the market on an investment of comparable risk and term to the cash flow being discounted.*

In order to understand the definition of opportunity cost of capital, it helps to think of yourself as a financial manager competing with financial managers at other firms to attract investors' funds (capital). To attract investors to invest in your firm or creditors to lend to your firm, you have to be able to offer them an expected return at least as good as what they could get elsewhere in the market for the same risk and length of investment. Now it is easier to see where the term (opportunity) cost of capital comes from—investors in your firm are giving up the opportunity to invest their funds elsewhere. This is an opportunity cost to them, and to overcome it you must offer them a return equal to or better than their opportunity cost of capital. Even if you already have the funds internally in the firm to invest, the logic still applies. You could either return the funds to your shareholders to invest elsewhere or reinvest the funds in a new project; however, you should reinvest them only if doing so provides a better return than the shareholders' other opportunities.

opportunity cost of capital or **cost of capital** The best available expected return offered in the market on an investment of comparable risk and term to the cash flow being discounted; the return the investor forgoes on an alternative investment of equivalent risk and term when the investor takes on a new investment.

Interest Rates, Discount Rates, and the Cost of Capital

By now, you may have noticed that we are using three terms to refer to rates of return. While many people use these three terms interchangeably, they are distinct. Throughout this book, we will use "interest rate" to mean a quoted rate in the market. A "discount rate" is the appropriate rate for discounting a given cash flow, *matched to the frequency of the cash flow*. Finally, we use "cost of capital" to indicate the rate of return on an investment of similar risk.

The opportunity cost of capital is the return the investor forgoes when the investor takes on a new investment. For a risk-free project, the opportunity cost of capital will typically correspond to the interest rate on Government of Canada securities with a similar term. But the opportunity cost of capital is a much more general concept that can be applied to risky investments as well.

EXAMPLE 5.7

The Opportunity Cost of Capital

Problem

Suppose a friend offers to borrow $100 from you today and in return pay you $110 one year from today. Looking in the market for other options for investing the $100, you find your best alternative option that you view as equally risky as lending it to your friend. That option has an expected return of 8%. What should you do?

Solution

▶ **Plan**

Your decision depends on what the opportunity cost is of lending your money to your friend. If you lend her the $100, then you cannot invest it in the alternative with an 8% expected return. Thus, by making the loan, you are giving up the opportunity to invest for an 8% expected return. You can make your decision by using your 8% opportunity cost of capital to value the $110 in one year.

▶ **Execute**

The value of the $110 in one year is its present value, discounted at 8%:

$$PV = \frac{\$110}{(1.08)^1} = \$101.85$$

The $100 loan is worth $101.85 to you today, so you make the loan.

▶ **Evaluate**

The Valuation Principle tells us that we can determine the value of an investment by using market prices to value the benefits net of the costs. As this example shows, market prices determine what our best alternative opportunities are so that we can decide whether an investment is worth the cost.

Chapter 3 introduced the Valuation Principle as a unifying theme in finance. In this and the preceding chapter, we have developed the fundamental tools a financial manager needs to value cash flows at different points in time. In this last section, we have reiterated the importance of using market information to determine the opportunity cost of capital, which is your discount rate in valuation calculations. In the next chapter, we will study bonds and how they are priced, which provides us with an immediate application of the knowledge we have built so far.

Concept Check

7. What is the opportunity cost of capital?

8. Can you ignore the cost of capital if you already have the funds inside the firm?

MyFinanceLab

Here is what you should know after reading this chapter. MyFinanceLab will help you identify what you know, and where to go when you need to practice.

Key Points and Equations	Terms	Online Practice Opportunities
5.1 Interest Rate Quotes and Adjustments		
▶ Just like any other price, interest rates are set by market forces, in particular the supply and demand of funds.	annual percentage rate (*APR*), p. 140	MyFinanceLab Study Plan 5.1
▶ The effective annual rate (*EAR*) indicates the actual amount of interest earned in one year. The *EAR* can be used as a discount rate for annual cash flows.	effective annual rate (*EAR*), p. 138	
▶ Given an *EAR*, r, the equivalent effective rate for an n-year time interval, where n may be more than one year or less than or equal to one year (a fraction), is: Equivalent n-period Effective Rate $$= (1 + r)^n - 1 \qquad (5.1)$$	simple interest, p. 140	
▶ An annual percentage rate (*APR*) is a common way of quoting interest rates. It indicates the amount of simple interest per year and does not consider the effects of compounding.		
▶ An *APR* quote gives an Implied Effective Interest Rate per $$\text{Compounding Period} = APR/m \qquad (5.2)$$ (m = number of compounding periods per year, also known as the compounding frequency).		
▶ We need to know the compounding frequency of an *APR* to determine the *EAR*: $$1 + EAR = \left(1 + \frac{APR}{m}\right)^m \qquad (5.3)$$		
▶ For a given *APR*, the *EAR* increases with the compounding frequency.		
5.2 Application: Discount Rates and Loans		
▶ Loan rates are typically stated as *APR*s. The outstanding balance of a loan is equal to the present value of the loan cash flows, when evaluated using the actual interest rate per payment interval based on the loan rate.	amortizing loan, p. 143 mortgage, p. 146	MyFinanceLab Study Plan 5.2
▶ In each loan payment on an amortizing loan, you pay interest on the loan plus some part of the loan balance.		

5.3 The Determinants of Interest Rates

▶ Quoted interest rates are nominal interest rates, which indicate the rate of growth of the money invested. The real interest rate indicates the rate of growth of one's purchasing power after adjusting for inflation.

▶ Given a nominal interest rate and an inflation rate, the real interest rate is:

$$\text{Real Rate} = \frac{\text{Nominal Rate} - \text{Inflation Rate}}{1 + \text{Inflation Rate}}$$

$$\approx \text{Real Rate} - \text{Inflation Rate} \qquad (5.5)$$

▶ Nominal interest rates tend to be high when inflation is high and low when inflation is low.

▶ Higher interest rates tend to reduce the attractiveness of typical investment projects. The Bank of Canada raises interest rates to moderate investment and combat inflation and lowers interest rates to stimulate investment and economic growth.

▶ Interest rates differ with the investment horizon according to the term structure of interest rates. The graph plotting interest rates as a function of the horizon is called the yield curve.

▶ Cash flows should be discounted using the discount rate that is appropriate for their horizon. Thus, the *PV* of a cash flow stream is:

$$PV = \frac{C_1}{1 + r_1} + \frac{C_2}{(1 + r_2)^2} + \cdots + \frac{C_n}{(1 + r_n)^n} \qquad (5.7)$$

▶ Annuity and perpetuity formulas cannot be applied when discount rates vary with the horizon.

▶ The shape of the yield curve tends to vary with investors' expectations of future economic growth and interest rates. It tends to be inverted prior to recessions and to be steep coming out of a recession. Because investors have a liquidity preference and thus view long-term loans as riskier, long-term rates are generally higher than short-term rates.

overnight rate, p. 153
nominal interest rates, p. 148
real interest rate, p. 148
risk-free interest rate, p. 150
term structure, p. 150
yield curve, p. 150

MyFinanceLab
Study Plan 5.3

Interactive Yield Curve

5.4 The Opportunity Cost of Capital

▶ An investor's opportunity cost of capital (or simply, the cost of capital) is the best available expected return offered in the market on an investment of comparable risk and term to the cash flow being discounted.

(opportunity) cost of capital, p. 155

MyFinanceLab
Study Plan 5.4

Review Questions

1. Explain how an interest rate is just a price.

2. Why is the *EAR* for 6% *APR*, with semi-annual compounding, higher than 6%?

3. Why is it so important to match the frequency of the interest rate to the frequency of the cash flows?

4. Why aren't the payments for a 15-year mortgage twice the payments for a 30-year mortgage at the same rate?

5. What mistake do you make when you discount real cash flows with nominal discount rates ?

6. How do changes in inflation expectations affect interest rates?

7. Can the nominal interest rate available to an investor be negative? (*Hint:* Consider the interest rate earned from saving cash "under the mattress.") Can the real interest rate be negative?

8. In the early 1980s, inflation was in the double digits and the yield curve sloped sharply downward. What did the yield curve say about investors' expectations about future inflation rates?

9. What do we mean when we refer to the "opportunity cost" of capital?

Problems

All problems in this chapter are available in MyFinanceLab. An asterisk (*) indicates problems with a higher level of difficulty.

Interest Rate Quotes and Adjustments

1. Your bank is offering you an account that will pay 20% interest in total for a two-year deposit. Determine the equivalent discount rate for a period length of
   a. six months.
   b. one year.
   c. one month.

2. Do the relevant calculations so you can indicate which you prefer: a bank account that pays 5% per year (*EAR*) for three years or
   a. an account that pays 2.5% every 6 months for 3 years?
   b. an account that pays 7.5% every 18 months for 3 years?
   c. an account that pays 0.5% per month for 3 years?

3. You have been offered a job with an unusual bonus structure. As long as you stay with the firm, you will get an extra $70,000 every 7 years, starting 7 years from now. What is the present value of this incentive if you plan to work for the company for a total of 42 years and the interest rate is 6% (*EAR*)?

4. You have found three investment choices for a one-year deposit: 10% *APR* compounded monthly, 10% *APR* compounded annually, and 9% *APR* compounded daily. Compute the *EAR* for each investment choice. (Assume that there are 365 days in the year.)

5. Your bank account pays interest with an *EAR* of 5%. What is the *APR* quote for this account based on semi-annual compounding? What is the *APR* with monthly compounding?

 6. Suppose the interest rate is 8% *APR* with monthly compounding. What is the present value of an annuity that pays $100 every six months for five years?

 7. You have been accepted into university. The university guarantees that your tuition will not increase for the four years you attend. The first $10,000 tuition payment is due in six months. After that, the same payment is due every six months until you have made a total of eight payments. The university offers a bank account that allows you to withdraw money every six months and has a fixed *APR* of 4% (semi-annual) guaranteed to remain the same over the next four years. How much money must you deposit today if you intend to make no further deposits and would like to make all the tuition payments from this account, leaving the account empty when the last payment is made?

Application: Discount Rates and Loans

8. You make monthly payments on your car loan. It has a quoted *APR* of 5% (monthly compounding). What percentage of the outstanding principal do you pay in interest each month?

9. Suppose Capital One is advertising a 60-month, 5.99% *APR* motorcycle loan. If you need to borrow $8000 to purchase your dream Harley-Davidson, what will your monthly payment be?

10. Suppose the Bank of Montreal is offering a 30-year mortgage with an *EAR* of 6.80%. If you plan to borrow $150,000, what will your monthly payment be?

11. You have decided to refinance your mortgage. You plan to borrow whatever is outstanding on your current mortgage. The current monthly payment is $2356, and you have made every payment on time. The original term of the mortgage was 30 years, and the mortgage is exactly 4 years and 8 months old. You have just made your monthly payment. The mortgage interest rate is 6.2% (*APR* with semi-annual compounding). How much do you owe on the mortgage today?

12. You have just sold your house for $1,000,000 in cash. Your mortgage was originally a 30-year mortgage with monthly payments and an initial balance of $800,000. The mortgage is currently exactly 18.5 years old, and you have just made a payment. If the interest rate on the mortgage is 7.75% (*APR* with semi-annual compounding), how much cash will you have from the sale once you pay off the mortgage?

13. You have just purchased a home and taken out a $500,000 mortgage. The mortgage has a 30-year term with monthly payments and an *APR* (with semi-annual compounding) of 6.5%.
   a. How much will you pay in interest, and how much will you pay in principal, during the 1st year?

b. How much will you pay in interest, and how much will you pay in principal, during the 20th year (i.e., between 19 and 20 years from now)?

14. You have just purchased a car and taken out a $50,000 loan. The loan has a five-year term with monthly payments and an *APR* of 6%.

    a. How much will you pay in interest, and how much will you pay in principal, during the first month, second month, and first year? (*Hint:* Compute the loan balance after one month, two months, and one year.)

    b. How much will you pay in interest, and how much will you pay in principal, during the fourth year (i.e., between three and four years from now)?

*15. You have some extra cash this month and are considering putting it toward your car loan. Your interest rate is 7%, your loan payments are $600 per month, and you have 36 months left on your loan. If you pay an additional $1000 with your next regular $600 payment (due in one month), how much will it reduce the amount of time left to pay off your loan?

*16. You have an outstanding student loan with required payments of $500 per month for the next four years. The interest rate on the loan is 9% *APR* (monthly). You are considering making an extra payment of $100 today (i.e., you will pay an extra $100 that you are not required to pay). If you are required to continue to make payments of $500 per month until the loan is paid off, what is the amount of your final payment? What effective rate of return (expressed as an *APR* with monthly compounding) have you earned on the $100?

*17. Consider again the situation in Problem 16. Now that you realize your best investment is to prepay your student loan, you decide to prepay as much as you can each month. Looking at your budget, you can afford to pay an extra $250 per month in addition to your required monthly payments of $500, or $750 in total each month. How long will it take you to pay off the loan?

*18. If you decide to take the mortgage described in Problem 10, the Bank of Montreal will offer you the following deal: instead of making the monthly payment you computed in that problem every month, you can make half the payment every two weeks (so that you will make 52/2 = 26 payments per year). How long will it take to pay off the mortgage if the *EAR* remains the same at 6.80%?

*19. Your friend tells you he has a very simple trick for taking one-third off the time it takes to repay your mortgage: use your year-end bonus to make an extra payment on January 1 of each year (that is, pay your monthly payment due on that day twice). If you take out your mortgage on July 1, so that your first monthly payment is due August 1, and you make an extra payment every January 1, how long will it take to pay off the mortgage? Assume that the mortgage has an original term of 30 years and an *APR* (with semi-annual compounding) of 12%.

*20. The mortgage on your house in Winnipeg is 5 years old. It required monthly payments of $1402, had an original term of 30 years, and had an interest rate of 9% (*APR* with semi-annual compounding). In the intervening 5 years, interest rates have fallen, housing prices in the United States have fallen, and you have decided to retire to Florida. You have decided to sell your house in Winnipeg and use your equity for the down payment on a condo in Florida. You will roll over the outstanding balance of your old mortgage into a new mortgage in Florida.

The new mortgage has a 30-year term, requires monthly payments, and has an interest rate of 6.625% (*APR* with monthly compounding which is typical for U.S. mortgages).

   a. What monthly repayments will be required with the new loan?
   b. If you still want to pay off the mortgage in 25 years, what monthly payment should you make on your new mortgage?
   c. Suppose you are willing to continue making monthly payments of $1402. How long will it take you to pay off the new mortgage?
   d. Suppose you are willing to continue making monthly payments of $1402 and want to pay off the new mortgage in 25 years. How much additional cash can you borrow today as part of the new financing?

21. You have credit card debt of $25,000 that has an *APR* (monthly compounding) of 15%. Each month you pay a minimum monthly payment only. You are required to pay only the outstanding interest. You have received an offer in the mail for an otherwise identical credit card with an *APR* of 12%. After considering all your alternatives, you decide to switch cards, roll over the outstanding balance on the old card into the new card, and borrow additional money as well. How much can you borrow today on the new card without changing the minimum monthly payment you will be required to pay?

22. Your firm has taken out a $500,000 loan with 9% *APR* (compounded monthly) for some commercial property. As is common in commercial real estate, the loan *is a* 5-year loan based on a 15-year amortization. This means that your loan payments will *be* calculated as if you will take 15 years to pay off the loan, but you actually must do so in 5 years. To do this, you will make 59 equal payments based on the 15-year amortization schedule and then make a final 60th payment to pay the remaining balance.

   a. What will your monthly payments be?
   b. What will your final payment be?

The Determinants of Interest Rates

23. In 1974, interest rates were 7.782% and the rate of inflation was 12.299% in Canada. What was the real interest rate in 1974? How would the purchasing power of your savings have changed over the year?

24. If the rate of inflation is 5%, what nominal interest rate is necessary for you to earn a 3% real interest rate on your investment?

25. Consider a project that requires an initial investment of $100,000 and will produce a single cash flow of $150,000 in five years.

   a. What is the *NPV* of this project if the five-year interest rate is 5% (*EAR*)?
   b. What is the *NPV* of this project if the five-year interest rate is 10% (*EAR*)?
   c. What is the highest five-year interest rate such that this project is still profitable?

26. What is the shape of the yield curve given in the following term structure? What expectations are investors likely to have about future interest rates?

Term	1 year	2 years	3 years	5 years	7 years	10 years	20 years
Rate (*EAR*, %)	1.99	2.41	2.74	3.32	3.76	4.13	4.93

The Opportunity Cost of Capital

27. You are thinking about investing $5000 in your friend's landscaping business. Even though you know the investment is risky and you can't be sure of the outcome, you expect your investment to be worth $5750 next year. You notice that the rate for one-year treasury bills is 1%. However, you feel that other investments of equal risk to your friend's landscape business offer a 10% expected return for the year. What should you do?

6

Bonds

notation

CPN	coupon payment	*PV*	present value
FV	face value of a bond	r_n	interest rate or discount rate for a cash flow that arrives in period *n*
n	number of periods	YTM_n	yield to maturity on a bond with *n* periods to maturity
P	initial price of a bond		

INTERVIEW WITH Shaun O'Malley,
RBC Dominion Securities

Queen's University, 2007

"Every client has different financial goals and a different tolerance for risk. This requires me to deal with both corporate and government bonds having a wide range of yields and maturities."

Shaun O'Malley is an investment advisor for RBC Dominion Securities. He received a master's degree in political science from Queen's University in 2007 but chose to pursue a career that put his University of British Columbia undergraduate finance classes to use. "I advise clients on appropriate security selection in equities, fixed income, and options. I also provide wealth management services in financial planning, insurance, and will and estate consulting."

Shaun's job requires him to keep a close eye on bond markets and interest rate movements. Interest rates are always changing as economic conditions change, and expectations of the future direction of the economy also change. "We are always revising our yield curve projections, which we use to build appropriate portfolios for our clients," Shaun says.

An important part of his job is matching the needs of clients with the appropriate levels of risk and return available in the market. "Every client has different financial goals and a different tolerance for risk," he continues. "This requires me to deal with both corporate and government bonds having a wide range of yields and maturities. We adjust the duration of our portfolios based on interest rates, yield curve projections, and other market conditions."

In this chapter, we introduce bonds and apply our tools for valuing cash flows to them. Bonds are simply loans. When an investor buys a bond from an issuer, the investor is lending money to the bond issuer. Who are the issuers of bonds? Federal, provincial, and local governments issue bonds to finance long-term projects, and many companies issue bonds as part of their debt financing. The bond markets are very large and very liquid; in May, 2010, the Bank of Canada reported that there were about $900 billion of government bonds outstanding and over $500 billion of corporate bonds outstanding.

Understanding bonds and their pricing is useful for several reasons. First, we can use the prices of risk-free government bonds to determine the risk-free interest rates that produce the yield curve discussed in Chapter 5. As we saw there, the yield curve provides important information for valuing risk-free cash flows and assessing expectations of inflation and economic growth. Second, firms often issue bonds to fund their own investments. The return investors receive on those bonds is one factor determining a firm's cost of capital. Finally, bonds provide an opportunity to begin our study of how securities are priced in a competitive market. Further, the ideas we develop in this chapter will be helpful when we turn to the topic of valuing stocks in Chapter 9.

Pricing bonds gives us an opportunity to apply what we've learned in the last three chapters about valuing cash flows using competitive market prices. As we explained in Chapter 3, the Valuation Principle implies that the price of a security in a competitive market should be the present value of the cash flows an investor will receive from owning it. Thus, we begin the chapter by evaluating the promised cash flows for different types of bonds. If a bond is risk free, so that the promised cash flows will be paid with certainty, we can use the Law of One Price to directly relate the return of a bond and its price. We then discuss how and why bond prices change over time. Once we have a firm understanding of the pricing of bonds in the absence of risk, we add the risk of default, where cash flows are not known with certainty. The risk of default and its implications are important considerations for a financial manager who is considering issuing corporate bonds. (In Chapter 14, we will discuss the details of issuing debt financing and cover some additional corporate bond features.)

Bond Terminology

bond indenture
A statement of the terms of a bond, as well as the amounts and dates of all payments to be made.

maturity date The final repayment date of a bond.

term The time remaining until the final repayment date of a bond.

face value The notional amount of a bond used to compute its interest payments. The face value of the bond is generally due at the bond's maturity. Also called **par value** or principal amount.

coupons The promised interest payments of a bond, paid periodically until the maturity date of the bond.

coupon rate The rate that determines the amount of each coupon payment of a bond. The coupon rate indicates the percentage of the face value paid out as coupons each year.

Recall from Chapter 3 that a bond is a security sold by governments and corporations to raise money from investors today in exchange for a promised future payment. The terms of the bond are described as part of the **bond indenture**, which indicates the amounts and dates of all payments to be made. Payments on the bond are made until a final repayment date called the **maturity date** of the bond. The time remaining until the repayment date is known as the **term** of the bond.

Bonds typically make two types of payments to their holders. The principal or **face value** (also known as **par value**) of a bond is the notional amount we use to compute the interest payments. Typically, the face value is repaid at maturity. It is generally denominated in standard increments such as $1000. A bond with a $1000 face value, for example, is often referred to as a "$1000 bond."

In addition to the face value, some bonds also promise additional payments called **coupons**. The bond indenture typically specifies that the coupons will be paid periodically (e.g., semi-annually) until the maturity date of the bond. Historically, on a payment date the holder of the bond would clip off the next coupon for the next payment and present it for payment. It follows that the interest payments on the bond are called coupon payments. Today, the majority of bonds are registered electronically but the term remains.

The amount of each coupon payment is determined by the **coupon rate** of the bond. This coupon rate is set by the issuer and stated on the bond indenture. By convention, the coupon rate indicates the percent of face value paid out as coupons each year; thus each coupon payment, *CPN,* is:

Coupon Payment

$$CPN = \frac{\text{Coupon Rate} \times \text{Face Value}}{\text{Number of Coupon Payments per Year}} \qquad (6.1)$$

For example, a "$1000 bond with a 10% coupon rate and semi-annual payments" will pay coupon payments of $1000 × 10%/2 = $50 every six months.

Table 6.1 summarizes the bond terminology we have presented thus far.

TABLE 6.1

Review of Bond Terminology

Maturity Date	Final repayment date of the bond. Payments continue until this date.
Term	The time remaining until the final repayment date.
Coupons	The promised interest payments of a bond. Usually they are paid semi-annually, but the frequency is specified in the bond indenture. The amount paid is equal to: $$\frac{\text{Coupon Rate} \times \text{Face Value}}{\text{Number of Coupon Payments per Year}}$$
Principal or Face Value	The notional amount used to compute the interest payment. It is usually repaid on the maturity date.

Concept Check

1. What types of cash flows does a bond buyer receive?

2. How are the periodic coupon payments on a bond determined?

6.2 Zero-Coupon Bonds

zero-coupon bond
A bond with its only payment occurring at maturity.

Treasury bills Zero-coupon bonds, with a maturity of up to one year, issued by a national government such as the Government of Canada or the U.S. government.

Not all bonds have coupon payments. Bonds without coupons are called **zero-coupon bonds**. As these are the simplest type of bond, we will analyze them first. The only cash payment an investor in a zero-coupon bond receives is the face value of the bond on the maturity date. **Treasury bills**, which are bonds issued by a national government (such as the Government of Canada or the U.S. government) are zero-coupon bonds with a maturity of up to one year.

Zero-Coupon Bond Cash Flows

There are only two cash flows if we purchase and hold a zero-coupon bond. First, we pay the bond's current market price at the time we make the purchase. Then, at the maturity date, we receive the bond's face value. For example, suppose that a one-year, risk-free, zero-coupon bond with a $100,000 face value has an initial price of $96,618.36. If you purchased this bond and held it to maturity, you would have the following cash flows:

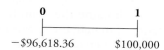

discount A price at which bonds trade that is less than their face value.

pure discount bond
A zero-coupon bond.

Note that although the bond pays no "interest" directly, as an investor you are compensated for the time value of your money by purchasing the bond at a discount to its face value. Recall from Chapter 3 that the present value of a future cash flow is less than the cash flow itself. As a result, prior to its maturity date, the price of a zero-coupon bond is always less than its face value. That is, zero-coupon bonds always trade at a **discount** (a price lower than the face value), so they are also called **pure discount bonds**.

Yield to Maturity of a Zero-Coupon Bond

Now that we understand the cash flows associated with a zero-coupon bond, we can calculate the IRR of buying a bond and holding it until maturity. Recall from Chapter 4 that we can always find the rate of return of an investment opportunity as the discount rate that equates the present value and the future value. With a zero-coupon bond, the present value is the cost of the bond and the future value is the principal amount. So the rate of return on the zero-coupon bond is the discount rate that equates the cost of the bond with the present value of the future cash flow received. We can extend this concept to a coupon bond: the rate of return is the discount rate at which the present value of all future cash flows from the bond equals the price of the bond. The rate of return, or *IRR*, of an investment in a bond is given a special name, the **yield to maturity (*YTM*)** or just the *yield*: *The yield to maturity of a bond is the discount rate that sets the present value of the promised bond payments equal to the current market price of the bond.*

yield to maturity (*YTM*)
The *IRR*, or rate of return, of an investment in a bond that is held to its maturity date. The *YTM* is the discount rate that sets the present value of the promised bond payments equal to the current market price for the bond.

Intuitively, the yield to maturity for a zero-coupon bond is the return you will earn as an investor by buying the bond at its current market price, holding the bond to maturity, and receiving the promised face value payment.

Let's determine the yield to maturity of the one-year zero-coupon bond discussed earlier in this chapter. According to the definition, the yield to maturity of the one-year bond solves the following equation:

$$96{,}618.36 = \frac{100{,}000}{1 + YTM_1}$$

In this case,

$$1 + YTM = \frac{100,000}{96,618.36} = 1.035 \therefore YTM_1 = 0.035 = 3.5\%$$

That is, the yield to maturity for this bond is 3.5%. Because the bond is risk free, investing in this bond and holding it to maturity is like earning 3.5% interest on your initial investment:

$$\$96,618.36 \times 1.035 = \$100,000$$

We can use a similar method to find the yield to maturity for any maturity zero-coupon bond:

$$1 + YTM_1 = \left(\frac{\text{Face Value}}{\text{Price}}\right)^{1/n} \therefore YTM_n = \left(\frac{\text{Face Value}}{\text{Price}}\right)^{1/n} - 1 \qquad (6.2)$$

The yield to maturity (YTM_n) in Equation 6.2 is the effective rate of return per period for holding the bond from today until maturity *n periods in the future*. It is important to note that if n is not in years, then the YTM_n calculated in Equation 6.2 will not be an effective rate per year. For example, if n is 20 semi-annual periods, then YTM_{20} is an effective rate per semi-annual period for a bond held for 20 semi-annual periods or 10 years. This peculiarity of the notation is not so important for zero-coupon bonds, as n is normally in years; it becomes more important further on in this chapter when we learn how to calculate and quote the *YTM* for a coupon-paying bond.

Risk-Free Interest Rates

Above, we calculated the yield to maturity of the one-year risk-free bond as 3.5%. But recall that the Valuation Principle's Law of One Price implies that all one-year risk-free investments must earn this same return of 3.5%. That is, 3.5% must be *the* competitive market risk-free interest rate.

More generally, in the last chapter we discussed the competitive market interest rate r_n available from today until date n for risk-free cash flows. Recall that we used this interest rate as the cost of capital for a risk-free cash flow that occurs on date n. A default-free zero-coupon bond that matures on date n provides a risk-free return over the same period. So the Law of One Price guarantees that the risk-free interest rate equals the yield to maturity on such a bond. Consequently, we will often refer to the yield to maturity of the appropriate maturity, zero-coupon risk-free bond as *the* risk-free interest rate. Some financial professionals also use the term **spot interest rates** to refer to these default-free, zero-coupon yields, because these rates are offered "on the spot" at that point in time.

spot interest rates The current default-free, zero-coupon yields.

In Chapter 5, we introduced the yield curve, which plots the risk-free interest rate for different maturities. These risk-free interest rates correspond to the yields of risk-free zero-coupon bonds. Thus, the yield curve we introduced in Chapter 5 is also referred to as the **zero-coupon yield curve**. Figure 6.1 illustrates the yield curve consistent with the zero-coupon bond prices in Example 6.1.

zero-coupon yield curve A plot of the yields of risk-free zero-coupon bonds as a function of the bonds' maturity date.

In that example, we used the bond's price to compute its yield to maturity. But from the definition of the yield to maturity, we can also use a bond's yield to compute its price. In the case of a zero-coupon bond, the price is simply equal to the present value of the bond's face value, discounted at the bond's yield to maturity.

EXAMPLE 6.1

Yields for Different
Maturities

Problem

Suppose the following zero-coupon bonds are trading at the prices shown below per $100 face value. Determine the corresponding yield to maturity for each bond.

Maturity	1 year	2 years	3 years	4 years
Price	$96.62	$92.45	$87.63	$83.06

Solution

▶ **Plan**

We can use Equation 6.2 to solve for the *YTM* of the bonds. The table gives the prices and number of years to maturity, and the face value is $100 per bond.

▶ **Execute**

Using Equation 6.2, we have

$$YTM_1 = (100/96.62)^{1/1} - 1 = 3.50\%$$

$$YTM_2 = (100/92.45)^{1/2} - 1 = 4.00\%$$

$$YTM_3 = (100/87.63)^{1/3} - 1 = 4.50\%$$

$$YTM_4 = (100/83.06)^{1/4} - 1 = 4.75\%$$

▶ **Evaluate**

Solving for the *YTM* of a zero-coupon bond is the same process we used to solve for the internal rate of return in Chapter 4. Indeed, the *YTM* is the internal rate of return of buying the bond.

FIGURE 6.1

Zero-Coupon Yield Curve Consistent with the Bond Prices in Example 6.1

Recall from Chapter 5 that a yield curve simply plots the yield to maturity of investments of different maturities. This figure shows the yield curve that would be produced by plotting the yields to maturity determined by the bond prices in Example 6.1. Note that as in this figure, the longer maturities generally have higher yields.

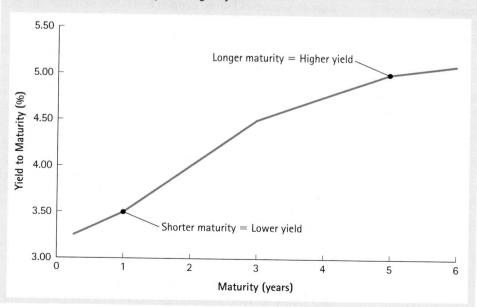

Concept
Check

3. Why would you want to know the yield to maturity of a bond?

4. What is the relationship between a bond's price and its yield to maturity?

EXAMPLE 6.2

Computing the
Price of a Zero-
Coupon Bond

Problem
Given the yield curve shown in Figure 6.1, what is the price of a five-year risk-free zero-coupon bond with a face value of $100?

Solution

▶ **Plan**

We can compute the bond's price as the present value of its face amount, where the discount rate is the bond's yield to maturity. From the yield curve, the yield to maturity for five-year risk-free zero-coupon bonds is 5.0%.

▶ **Execute**

$$P = 100/(1.05)^5 = 78.35$$

▶ **Evaluate**

We can compute the price of a zero-coupon bond simply by computing the present value of the face amount using the bond's yield to maturity. Note that the price of the five-year zero-coupon bond is even lower than the price of the other zero-coupon bonds in Example 6.1, because the face amount is the same but we must wait longer to receive it.

Coupon Bonds

coupon bonds Bonds that pay regular coupon interest payments up to maturity, when the face value is also paid.

Government of Canada bond A bond issued by the Government of Canada.

Like zero-coupon bonds, **coupon bonds** pay investors the face value at maturity. In addition, these bonds make regular coupon interest payments. As of the end of 2010, the Government of Canada had bonds outstanding with maturities from 1 to 34 years into the future. Normally, at issue, the **Government of Canada bonds** are sold with maturities of 2, 5, 10, or 30 years.

Coupon Bond Cash Flows

While an investor's return on a zero-coupon bond comes from buying it at a discount to its principal value, the return on a coupon bond comes from two sources: (1) any difference between the purchase price and the principal value and (2) its periodic coupon payments. Before we can compute the yield to maturity of a coupon bond, we need to know all of its cash flows, including the coupon interest payments and when they are paid. In Example 6.3, we translate a bond description into the bond's cash flows.

Yield to Maturity of a Coupon Bond

Once we have determined the coupon bond's cash flows, given its market price we can determine its yield to maturity. Recall that the yield to maturity for a bond is the *IRR*

EXAMPLE 6.3

The Cash Flows of
a Coupon Bond

Problem

Assume that it is May 15, 2012, and the Government of Canada has just issued bonds with a
May 2017 maturity, $1000 par value, and a 5% coupon rate with semi-annual coupons. The
first coupon payment will be paid on November 15, 2012. What cash flows will you receive if
you hold this bond until maturity?

Solution

▶ **Plan**

The description of the bond should be sufficient to determine all of its cash flows. The phrase
"May 2017 maturity, $1000 par value" tells us that this is a bond with a face value of $1000
and five years to maturity. The phrase "5% coupon rate with semi-annual coupons" tells
us that the bond pays a total of 5% of its face value each year in two equal semi-annual
installments. Finally, we know that the first coupon is paid on November 15, 2012.

▶ **Execute**

The face value of this bond is $1000. Because this bond pays coupons semi-annually, using
Equation 6.1, you determine that you will receive a coupon payment every six months of
$CPN = \$1000 \times 5\%/2 = \$25$. Here is the timeline based on a six-month period, and there
are a total of 10 cash flows:

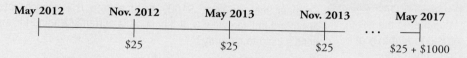

Note that the last payment occurs five years (10 six-month periods) from now and is composed
of both a coupon payment of $25 and the face value payment of $1000.

▶ **Evaluate**

Since a bond is just a package of cash flows, we need to know those cash flows in order to
value the bond. That's why the description of the bond contains all of the information we would
need to construct its cash flow timeline.

of investing in the bond and holding it to maturity. This investment has the cash flows
shown in the timeline below:

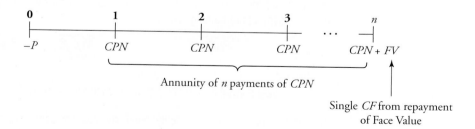

The yield to maturity of the bond is the *single* discount rate, YTM_n, that equates the
present value of the bond's remaining cash flows to its current price. For zero-coupon
bonds, there were only two cash flows, but coupon bonds have many cash flows, complicating the yield to maturity calculation. From the timeline, we see that the coupon

payments represent an annuity, so the yield to maturity is the interest rate YTM_n that solves the following equation:

Yield to Maturity of a Coupon Bond

Annuity Factor using the YTM_n

$$P = CPN \times \underbrace{\frac{1}{YTM_n}\left(1 - \frac{1}{(1 + YTM_n)^n}\right)}_{\text{Present Value of all of the periodic coupon payments}} + \underbrace{\left(\frac{FV}{(1 + YTM_n)^n}\right)}_{\substack{\text{Presnt Value of the} \\ \text{Face Value repayment} \\ \text{using the } YTM_n}} \qquad (6.3)$$

Unfortunately, unlike zero-coupon bonds, there is no simple formula to solve for the yield to maturity directly. Instead, we need to use a financial calculator or a spreadsheet (using Excel's *IRR* function), introduced in Chapter 4.

When we calculate a bond's yield to maturity by solving Equation 6.3, the yield we compute will be an effective rate *per coupon interval*. However, yields are typically quoted as *APRs*, so we multiply by the number of coupons per year, thereby converting the answer into an *APR* quote compounded over the same time as the time period between coupons.

EXAMPLE 6.4

Computing the Yield to Maturity of a Coupon Bond

Problem

Consider the five-year, $1000 bond with a 5% coupon rate and semi-annual coupons described in Example 6.3. If this bond is currently trading for a price of $957.35, what is the bond's yield to maturity?

Solution

▶ **Plan**

We worked out the bond's cash flows in Example 6.3. From the cash flow timeline, we can see that the bond consists of an annuity of 10 payments of $25, paid every six months, and one lump-sum payment of $1000 in five years (10 six-month periods). We can use Equation 6.3 to solve for the yield to maturity. However, we must use six-month intervals consistently throughout the equation.

▶ **Execute**

Because the bond has 10 remaining coupon payments, we compute its YTM_{10} by solving Equation 6.3 for this bond:

$$957.35 = 25 \times \frac{1}{YTM_{10}}\left(1 - \frac{1}{(1 + YTM_{10})^{10}}\right) + \frac{1000}{(1 + YTM_{10})^{10}}$$

We can solve it by using a financial calculator or a spreadsheet. To use a financial calculator, we enter the price we pay as a negative number for the *PV* (it is a cash outflow), the coupon payments as the *PMT*, and the bond's par value as its *FV*. Finally, we enter the number of coupon payments remaining (10) as *N*.

	N	I/Y	PV	PMT	FV
Given:	10		−957.35	25	1000
Solve for:		3.00			
	Excel Formula: = *RATE(NPER,PMT,PV,FV)* = *RATE*(10,25,−957.35,1000)				

Therefore, $YTM_{10} = 3\%$. Because the bond pays coupons semi-annually, YTM_{10} is an effective rate for a six-month period. As coupon-paying bond yields are normally quoted as an *APR* with semi-annual compounding, we must do an interest rate conversion by manipulating Equation 5.2 to get the *APR* with semi-annual compounding. Therefore, we multiply the 3% by 2 (i.e., we multiply by the number of coupon payments per year). Thus, this five-year bond has a quoted yield to maturity, YTM_5 (where 5 is the number of years) equal to a 6% *APR* with semi-annual compounding.

> ▶ **Evaluate**
> As the equation shows, the yield to maturity is the discount rate that equates the present value of the bond's cash flows with its price. Bonds with semi-annual payments normally have their yields to maturity quoted as an *APR* with semi-annual compounding.

We can also use Equation 6.3 to compute a bond's price based on its yield to maturity. We simply discount the cash flows using the yield, as in Example 6.5.

EXAMPLE 6.5

Computing a Bond Price from Its Yield to Maturity

Problem

Consider again the five-year, $1000 bond with a 5% coupon rate and semi-annual coupons in Example 6.4. Suppose interest rates drop and the bond's yield to maturity decreases to 4.50% (expressed as an *APR* with semi-annual compounding). For what price is the bond trading now? What is this bond's yield to maturity expressed as an effective annual rate?

Solution

▶ **Plan**

Given the yield, we can compute the price using Equation 6.3. First, note that a 4.50% APR with semi-annual compounding gives an implied effective semi-annual rate of 2.25% (see Equation 5.2). Also, recall that the cash flows of this bond are an annuity of 10 payments of $25, paid every six months, and one lump-sum cash flow of $1000 (the face value), paid in five years (10 six-month periods). Given the implied effective semi-annual rate of 2.25%, we can convert this into another equivalent effective rate using Equation 5.1. This will allow us to compute the bond's yield to maturity expressed as an effective annual rate.

▶ **Execute**

Using Equation 6.3 and the six-month yield of 2.25%, the bond price must be:

$$P = 25 \times \frac{1}{0.0225}\left(1 - \frac{1}{1.0225^{10}}\right) + \frac{1000}{1.0225^{10}} = \$1022.17$$

To compute the effective annual yield, we first converted the *APR* with semi-annual compounding to the implied effective rate per six-month period by dividing the *APR* by 2 (see Equation 5.2). This gives 2.25% per six months. Then, using Equation 5.1, we convert the effective six-month rate to an equivalent effective annual rate as follows:

$$EAR = (1 + 0.0225)^2 = 0.04550625 = 4.550625\%$$

We can also use a financial calculator to determine the bond price:

	N	I/Y	PV	PMT	FV
Given:	10	2.25		25	1000
Solve for:			−1022.17		
	Excel Formula: = PV(RATE,NPER,PMT,FV) = PV(.0225,10,25,1000)				

▶ **Evaluate**

The bond's price has risen to $1022.17, lowering the return from investing in it from 3% to 2.25% per six-month period. Interest rates have dropped, so the lower return brings the bond's yield into line with the lower competitive rates being offered for bonds of similar risk and maturity elsewhere in the market.

Finding Bond Prices on the Web

Unlike the TSX or NYSE where many stocks are traded, there is no particular physical location where bonds are traded. Instead, they are traded electronically. In the United States, the Financial Industry Regulatory Authority (FINRA) has made an effort to make bond prices more widely available. FINRA's website (www.finra.org/marketdata) allows anyone to search for the most recent trades and quotes for bonds. In Canada, institutional investors use two electronic platforms to trade bonds (in addition to directly trading with each other): Can Deal and CBID. Here we show a screen shot from the CBID website (CanadianFixedIncome.ca) displaying the pricing information for some provincial and corporate bonds on December 17, 2010.

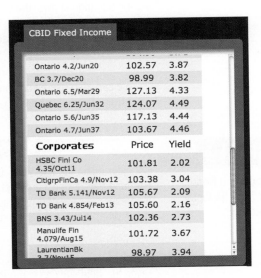

CBID Fixed Income		
Ontario 4.2/Jun20	102.57	3.87
BC 3.7/Dec20	98.99	3.82
Ontario 6.5/Mar29	127.13	4.33
Quebec 6.25/Jun32	124.07	4.49
Ontario 5.6/Jun35	117.13	4.44
Ontario 4.7/Jun37	103.67	4.46
Corporates	Price	Yield
HSBC Finl Co 4.35/Oct11	101.81	2.02
CitigrpFinCa 4.9/Nov12	103.38	3.04
TD Bank 5.141/Nov12	105.67	2.09
TD Bank 4.854/Feb13	105.60	2.16
BNS 3.43/Jul14	102.36	2.73
Manulife Fin 4.079/Aug15	101.72	3.67
LaurentianBk 3.7/Nov15	98.97	3.94

Coupon Bond Price Quotes

Because we can convert any price into a yield, and vice versa, prices and yields are often used interchangeably. For example, the bond in Example 6.5 could be quoted as having a yield of 4.50% or a price of $1022.17 per $1000 face value. Indeed, bond traders generally quote bond yields rather than bond prices. One advantage of quoting the yield to maturity rather than the price is that the yield is independent of the face value of the bond. When prices are quoted in the bond market, they are conventionally quoted per $100 face value. Thus, the bond in Example 6.5 would be quoted as having a price of $102.217 (per $100 face value), which would imply an actual price of $1022.17, given the $1000 face value of the bond.

Concept Check

5. What cash flows does a company pay to investors holding its coupon bonds?
6. What do we need in order to value a coupon bond?

6.4 Why Bond Prices Change

As we mentioned earlier, zero-coupon bonds always trade for a discount—that is, prior to maturity, their price is less than their face value. But as shown in Examples 6.4 and 6.5, coupon bonds may trade at a discount, or at a **premium** (a price greater than their face value). In this section, we identify when a bond will trade at a discount or premium, as well as how the bond's price will change due to the passage of time and fluctuations in interest rates.

premium A price at which coupon bonds trade that is greater than their face value.

par A price at which coupon bonds trade that is equal to their face value.

Most issuers of coupon bonds choose a coupon rate so that the bonds will *initially* trade at, or very close to, **par** (that is, at the bond's face value). For example, the Government of Canada sets the coupon rates on its bonds in this way. After the issue date, the market price of a bond generally changes over time for two reasons. First, as time passes, the bond gets closer to its maturity date. Holding fixed the bond's yield to maturity, the present value of the bond's remaining cash flows changes as the time to maturity decreases. Second, at any point in time, changes in market interest rates affect the bond's yield to maturity and its price (the present value of the remaining cash flows). We explore these two effects in the remainder of this section.

Interest Rate Changes and Bond Prices

If a bond sells at par (at its face value), the only return investors will earn is from the coupons that the bond pays. Therefore, the bond's coupon rate will exactly equal its yield to maturity. As interest rates in the economy fluctuate, the yields that investors demand to invest in bonds will also change. Consider the Government of Canada bond of Examples 6.3 to 6.5, and suppose that the government issued the bond when market interest rates imply a *YTM* of 5%, and thus they set the coupon rate to be 5%. Suppose interest rates then rise so that new bonds have a *YTM* of 9%. These new bonds would have a coupon rate of 9% and sell for $1000. So, for $1000, an investor would get $90 per year until the bond matured. The 5% coupon-rate bond was issued when rates were lower such that its coupon is fixed at 5%, so it offers payments of $50 per year until maturity. Because its cash flows are lower, the 5% coupon-rate bond must have a lower price than the 9% coupon-rate bond.[1] Thus, the price of the 5% bond will fall until the investor is indifferent between buying the 5% bond and buying the 9% bond. Figure 6.2 illustrates the relationship between the bond's price and its yield to maturity.

In our example, the price of the 5% bond will drop to below face value ($1000), so it will be trading at a discount (also called trading *below par*). If the bond trades at a discount, an investor who buys the bond will earn a return both from receiving the coupons and from receiving a face value that exceeds the price paid for the bond. As a result, if a bond trades at a discount, its yield to maturity will exceed its coupon rate.

FIGURE 6.2   Bond's Price vs. Its Yield to Maturity

At a price of $1000, the 5% coupon-rate bond (from Examples 6.3 to 6.5) offers a 5% *YTM*. If rates have risen to 9%, in order for the 5% coupon-rate bond to offer a competitive yield to maturity, its price must fall until its yield to maturity rises to the 9% yield being offered by otherwise similar bonds. In the example depicted here, for a bond with five years left to maturity, its price must fall to $841.75 before investors will be indifferent between buying it and the 9% coupon-rate bond priced at $1000.

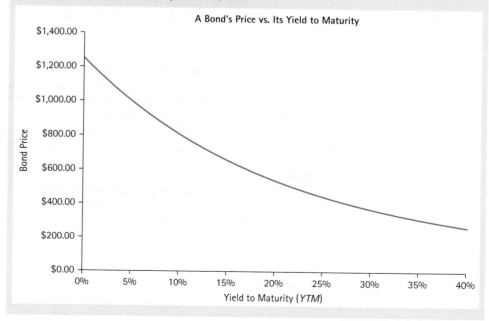

---

[1] Otherwise, if the 5% bond had the same or higher price, there would be an arbitrage opportunity: one could sell the 5% bond and buy the 9% bond, receiving cash today and higher coupons going forward.

A bond that pays a coupon can also trade at a premium to its face value (trading *above par*). Imagine what would have happened in our example if interest rates had gone down to 3% instead of up to 9%. Then, the holder of the existing 5% bond would not part with it for $1000. Instead, its price would have to rise until the yield to maturity from buying it at that price would be 3%. In this case, an investor's return from the coupons is diminished by receiving a face value less than the price paid for the bond. *Thus, a bond trades at a premium whenever its yield to maturity is less than its coupon rate.*[2]

This example illustrates a general phenomenon. A higher yield to maturity means that investors demand a higher return for investing. They apply a higher discount rate for a bond's remaining cash flows, reducing their present value and hence the bond's price. The reverse holds when interest rates fall. Investors then demand a lower yield to maturity, reducing the discount rate applied to the bond's cash flows and raising the price. Therefore, *as interest rates and bond yields rise, bond prices will fall, and vice versa, so that interest rates and bond prices always move in the opposite direction.*

Table 6.2 summarizes the relationship between interest rates and bond prices.

TABLE 6.2	Bond Prices Immediately After a Coupon Payment		
When the Bond Price is . . .	Greater Than the Face Value	Equal to the Face Value	Less than the Face Value
We Say the Bond Trades . . .	"above par" or "at a premium"	"at par"	"below par" or "at a discount"
This Occurs When . . .	coupon rate > yield to maturity	coupon rate = yield to maturity	coupon rate < yield to maturity

---

EXAMPLE 6.6

Determining the Discount or Premium of a Coupon Bond

Problem
Consider three 30-year bonds with annual coupon payments. One bond has a 10% coupon rate, one has a 5% coupon rate, and one has a 3% coupon rate. If the yield to maturity of each bond is 5%, what is the price of each bond per $100 face value? Which bond trades at a premium, which trades at a discount, and which trades at par?

Solution

▶ **Plan**

From the description of the bonds, we can determine their cash flows. Each bond has 30 years to maturity and pays its coupons annually. Therefore, each bond has an annuity of coupon payments, paid annually for 30 years, and then the face value paid as a lump sum in 30 years. They are all priced so that their yield to maturity is 5%, meaning that 5% is the discount rate that equates the present value of the cash flows to the price of the bond. Therefore, we can use Equation 6.3 to compute the price of each bond as the *PV* of its cash flows, discounted at 5%.

▶ **Execute**

For the 10% coupon bond, the annuity cash flows are $10 per year (10% of each $100 face value). Similarly, the annuity cash flows for the 5% and 3% bonds are $5 and $3 per year. We use a $100 face value for all of the bonds.

---

[2] The terms "discount" and "premium" are simply descriptive and are not meant to imply that you should try to buy bonds at a discount and avoid buying bonds at a premium. In a competitive market, the Law of One Price ensures that all similar bonds are priced to earn the same return. That is why buying a bond is a zero *NPV* proposition: the price exactly equals the present value of the bond's cash flows, so you earn a fair return but not an abnormally good (or bad) return.

Using Equation 6.3 and these cash flows, the bond prices are:

$$P(10\% \text{ coupon}) = 10 \times \frac{1}{0.05}\left(1 - \frac{1}{1.05^{30}}\right) + \frac{100}{1.05^{30}} = \$176.86 \text{ (trades at a premium)}$$

$$P(5\% \text{ coupon}) = 5 \times \frac{1}{0.05}\left(1 - \frac{1}{1.05^{30}}\right) + \frac{100}{1.05^{30}} = \$100.00 \text{ (trades at a par)}$$

$$P(3\% \text{ coupon}) = 3 \times \frac{1}{0.05}\left(1 - \frac{1}{1.05^{30}}\right) + \frac{100}{1.05^{30}} = \$69.26 \text{ (trades at a discount)}$$

▶ **Evaluate**
The prices reveal that when the coupon rate of the bond is higher than its yield to maturity, it trades at a premium. When its coupon rate equals its yield to maturity, it trades at par. When its coupon rate is lower than its yield to maturity, it trades at a discount.

Time and Bond Prices

Let's consider the effect of time on the price of a bond. As the next payment from a bond grows nearer, the price of the bond increases to reflect the increasing present value of that cash flow. Take a bond paying semi-annual coupons of $50 and imagine tracking the price of the bond starting on the day after the last coupon payment was made. The price would slowly rise over the following six months as the next $50 coupon payment grows closer and closer. It will peak right before the coupon payment is made, when buying the bond still entitles you to receive the $50 payment immediately. If you buy the bond right after the coupon payment is made, you do not have the right to receive that $50 coupon. The price you are willing to pay for the bond will therefore be $50 less than it was right before the coupon was paid. This pattern—the price slowly rising as a coupon payment nears and then dropping abruptly after the payment is made—continues for the life of the bond. Figure 6.3 illustrates this phenomenon.

EXAMPLE 6.7

The Effect of Time on the Price of a Bond

Problem
Suppose you purchase a 30-year, zero-coupon bond with a yield to maturity of 5%. For a face value of $100, the bond will initially trade for:

$$P(30 \text{ years to maturity}) = \frac{100}{1.05^{30}} = \$23.14$$

If the bond's yield to maturity remains at 5%, what will its price be 5 years later? If you purchased the bond at $23.14 and sold it 5 years later, what would the *IRR* of your investment be?

Solution

▶ **Plan**
If the bond was originally a 30-year bond and 5 years have passed, then it has 25 years left to maturity. If the yield to maturity does not change, then you can compute the price of the bond with 25 years left exactly as we did for 30 years, but using 25 years of discounting instead of 30. Once you have the price in 5 years, you can compute the *IRR* of your investment just as we did in Chapter 4. The *FV* is the price in 5 years, the *PV* is the initial price ($23.14), and the number of years is 5.

▶ **Execute**

$$P(25 \text{ years to maturity}) = \frac{100}{1.05^{25}} = \$29.53$$

If you purchased the bond for $23.14 and then sold it after five years for $29.53, the *IRR* of your investment would be as follows:

$$\left(\frac{29.53}{23.14}\right)^{1/5} - 1 = 5.0\%$$

That is, your return is the same as the yield to maturity of the bond.

▶ **Evaluate**
Note that the bond price is higher, and hence the discount from its face value is smaller, when there is less time to maturity. The discount shrinks because the yield has not changed, but there is less time until the face value will be received. This example illustrates a more general property for bonds. *If a bond's yield to maturity does not change, then the* IRR *of an investment in the bond equals its yield to maturity even if you sell the bond early.*

FIGURE 6.3

The Effect of Time on Bond Prices

The graph illustrates the effects of the passage of time on bond prices when the yield remains constant (in this case, 5%). The price of a zero-coupon bond rises smoothly. The prices of the coupon bonds are indicated by the zigzag lines. Notice that the prices rise between coupon payments but tumble on the coupon date, reflecting the amount of the coupon payment. For each coupon bond, the grey line shows the trend of the bond price just after each coupon is paid.

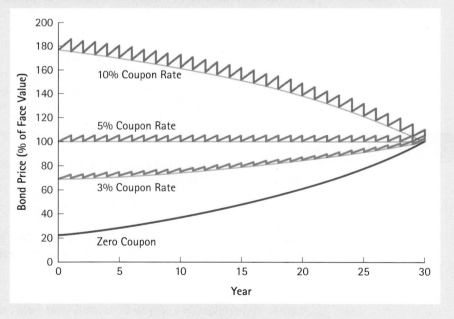

Interest Rate Risk and Bond Prices

While the effect of time on bond prices is predictable, unpredictable changes in interest rates will also affect bond prices. Further, bonds with different characteristics will respond differently to changes in interest rates—some bonds will react more strongly than others. We showed in Chapter 5 that investors view long-term loans to be riskier than short-term loans. Because bonds are just loans, the same is true of short-term versus long-term bonds.

The example illustrates how bonds of different maturity will have different sensitivities to interest rate changes. However, even bonds with the same maturity will differ in interest rate sensitivity if their coupon rates are different. Because they pay higher cash flows up front, bonds with higher coupon rates are less sensitive to interest rate changes than otherwise identical bonds with lower coupon rates.[3] Table 6.3 summarizes this conclusion.

TABLE 6.3

Bond Prices and Interest Rates

Bond Characteristic	Effect on Interest Rate Risk
Longer term to maturity	Increase
Higher coupon payments	Decrease

EXAMPLE 6.8

The Interest Rate Sensitivity of Bonds

Problem

Consider a 10-year coupon bond and a 30-year coupon bond, both with 10% annual coupons. By what percentage will the price of each bond change if its yield to maturity increases from 5% to 6%?

Solution

▶ **Plan**

We need to compute the price of each bond for each yield to maturity and then calculate the percentage change in the prices. For both bonds, the cash flows are $10 per year for $100 in face value and then the $100 face value repaid at maturity. The only difference is the maturity: 10 years and 30 years. With those cash flows, we can use Equation 6.3 to compute the prices.

▶ **Execute**

Yield to Maturity	10-Year, 10% Annual Coupon Bond	30-Year, 10% Annual Coupon Bond
5%	$10 \times \dfrac{1}{0.05}\left(1 - \dfrac{1}{1.05^{10}}\right) + \dfrac{100}{1.05^{10}} = \$138.61$	$10 \times \dfrac{1}{0.05}\left(1 - \dfrac{1}{1.05^{30}}\right) + \dfrac{100}{1.05^{30}} = \$176.86$
6%	$10 \times \dfrac{1}{0.06}\left(1 - \dfrac{1}{1.06^{10}}\right) + \dfrac{100}{1.06^{10}} = \$129.44$	$10 \times \dfrac{1}{0.06}\left(1 - \dfrac{1}{1.06^{30}}\right) + \dfrac{100}{1.06^{30}} = \$155.06$

The price of the 10-year bond changes by $(129.44 - 138.61)/138.61 = -6.6\%$ if its yield to maturity increases from 5% to 6%. For the 30-year bond, the price change is $(155.06 - 176.86)/176.86 = -12.3\%$

▶ **Evaluate**

The 30-year bond is almost twice as sensitive as the 10-year bond to a change in the yield. In fact, if we graph the price and yields of the two bonds, we can see that the line for the 30-year bond, shown in blue, is steeper throughout than the green line for the 10-year bond, reflecting its heightened sensitivity to interest rate changes.

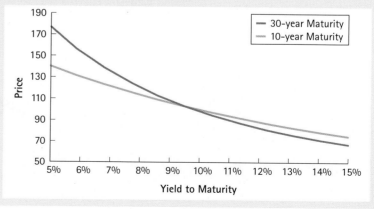

---

[3] Duration is a bond characteristic that combines the effect of a bond's maturity and the size of its coupon payments to give the average maturity of all the bond's cash flows. Longer-duration bonds are more sensitive to interest rate changes. A full discussion of the concept of duration is beyond the scope of this book.

Bond Prices in Practice

In actuality, bond prices are subject to the effects of both the passage of time and changes in interest rates. Bond prices converge to the bond's face value due to the time effect, but simultaneously move up and down due to unpredictable changes in bond yields. Figure 6.4

FIGURE 6.4   Yield to Maturity and Bond Price Fluctuations over Time

The graphs illustrate changes in price and yield for a 30-year zero-coupon bond over its life. Panel (a) illustrates the changes in the bond's yield to maturity (*YTM*) over its life. In Panel (b), the actual bond price is shown in blue. Because the *YTM* does not remain constant over the bond's life, the bond's price fluctuates as it converges to the face value over time. Also shown is the price if the *YTM* remained fixed at 4%, 5%, or 6%. Panel (a) shows that the bond's *YTM* mostly remained between 4% and 6%. The broken lines in Panel (b) show the price of the bond if its *YTM* had remained constant at those levels. Note that in all cases, the bond's price must eventually converge to $100 on its maturity date.

Panel (a) The Bond's Yield to Maturity over Time

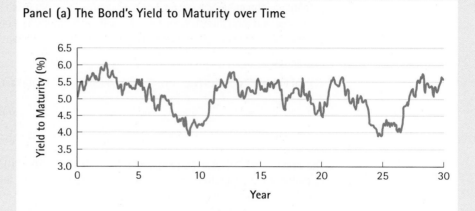

Panel (b) The Bond's Price over Time (Price = $100 on Maturity Date)

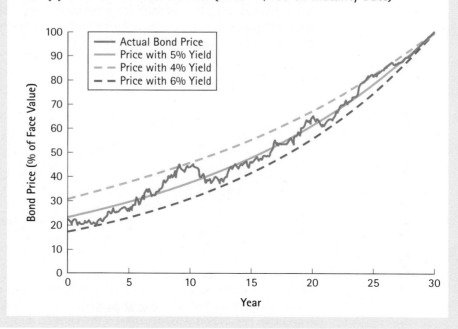

illustrates this behaviour by demonstrating how the price of the 30-year, zero-coupon bond might change over its life. Note that the bond price tends to converge to the face value as the bond approaches the maturity date but also moves higher when its yield falls and lower when its yield rises.

EXAMPLE 6.9

Coupons and
Interest Rate
Sensitivity

Problem

Consider two bonds, each of which pays semi-annual coupons and has five years left until maturity. One has a coupon rate of 5% and the other has a coupon rate of 10%, but both currently have a yield to maturity of 8%. How much will the price of each bond change if its yield to maturity decreases from 8% to 7%?

Solution

▶ Plan

As in Example 6.8, we need to compute the price of each bond at 8% and 7% yield to maturities and then compute the percentage change in price. Each bond has 10 semi-annual coupon payments remaining, along with the repayment of par value at maturity. The cash flows per $100 of face value for the first bond are $2.50 every six months and then $100 at maturity. The cash flows per $100 of face value for the second bond are $5 at six months and then $100 at maturity. Since the cash flows are semi-annual, the yield to maturity is quoted as a semi-annually compounded *APR*, so we convert the yields to match the frequency of the cash flows by dividing by 2. With semi-annual rates of 4% and 3.5%, we can use Equation 6.3 to compute the prices.

▶ Execute

Yield to Maturity	5-Year, 5% Coupon Bond	5-Year, 10% Coupon Bond
8%	$2.50 \times \dfrac{1}{0.04}\left(1 - \dfrac{1}{1.04^{10}}\right) + \dfrac{100}{1.04^{10}} = \$87.83$	$5 \times \dfrac{1}{0.04}\left(1 - \dfrac{1}{1.04^{10}}\right) + \dfrac{100}{1.04^{10}} = \$108.11$
7%	$2.50 \times \dfrac{1}{0.035}\left(1 - \dfrac{1}{1.035^{10}}\right) + \dfrac{100}{1.035^{10}} = \$91.68$	$5 \times \dfrac{1}{0.035}\left(1 - \dfrac{1}{1.035^{10}}\right) + \dfrac{100}{1.035^{10}} = \$112.47$

The 5% coupon bond's price changed from $87.83 to $91.68, or 4.4%, but the 10% coupon bond's price changed from $108.11 to $112.47, or 4.0%. You can calculate the price change very quickly with a financial calculator. Take the 5% coupon bond for example:

	N	I/Y	PV	PMT	FV
Given:	10	4		2.50	100
Solve for:			−87.83		
	Excel Formula: = PV(RATE,NPER,PMT,FV) = PV(.04,10,2.5,100)				

With all of the basic bond information entered, you can simply change the *I/Y* by entering 3.\5 and pressing *I/Y* and then solve for *PV* again. So, with just a few keystrokes, you will have the new price of $91.68.

▶ Evaluate

The bond with the smaller coupon payments is more sensitive to changes in interest rates. Because its coupons are smaller relative to its par value, a larger fraction of its cash flows is received later. As we learned in Example 6.8, later cash flows are affected more greatly by changes in interest rates, so compared to the 10% coupon bond, the effect of the interest change is greater for the cash flows of the 5% bond.

As the fluctuating price in Figure 6.4 demonstrates, prior to maturity the bond is exposed to interest rate risk. If an investor chooses to sell and the bond's yield to maturity has decreased, then the investor will receive a high price and earn a high return. If the yield to maturity has increased, the bond price is low at the time of sale and the investor will earn a low return.

Concept Check

7. Why do interest rates and bond prices move in opposite directions?
8. If a bond's yield to maturity does not change, how does its cash price change between coupon payments?

6.5 Corporate Bonds

In the previous sections, we developed the basics of bond pricing in the context of Government of Canada bonds, which have no risk of default. In this section, our focus is on **corporate bonds**, which are bonds issued by corporations. We will examine the role of default risk in the price and yield to maturity of corporate bonds. As we will see, corporations with higher default risk will need to pay higher coupons to attract buyers to their bonds.

corporate bonds Bonds issued by a corporation.

Credit Risk

Table 6.4 lists the interest rates paid for a five-year bond by a number of different borrowers on December 17, 2010. Why do these interest rates vary so widely? The lowest interest rate is the 2.39% rate paid on Government of Canada bonds. Government of Canada securities are widely regarded to be risk free, because there is virtually no chance the government will fail to pay the interest and default on these bonds. Thus, as we noted in Section 6.1, when we refer to the "risk-free interest rate," we mean the rate on Government of Canada bills or bonds.

The remaining bonds are all corporate bonds. The issuer of a corporate bond may default—that is, it might not pay back the full amount promised in the bond prospectus. For example, a company with financial difficulties may be unable to fully repay the loan. This risk of default, which is known as the **credit risk** of the bond, means that the bond's cash flows are not known with certainty. To compensate for the risk that the firm may default, investors demand a higher interest rate than the rate on Government of

credit risk The risk of default by the issuer of any bond that is not default free; it is an indication that the bond's cash flows are not known with certainty.

TABLE 6.4	Interest Rates on Five-Year Bonds for Various Borrowers, December 17, 2010

Borrower	Interest Rate	Credit Spread
Government of Canada	2.39%	
Bank of Montreal	3.58%	
TD Bank	3.58%	
CIBC	3.60	
Rogers Communications	3.76%	
GE Capital	3.88%	
Shaw Communications	4.14%	
Manitoba Telecom	4.35	

Source: CanadianFixedIncome.ca

Canada bonds.[4] The difference between the interest rate of the loan and the Government of Canada bond rate will depend on investors' assessment of the likelihood that the firm will default. For example, investors place a higher probability of default on Manitoba Telecom than on the Bank of Montreal, forcing Manitoba Telecom to pay a larger credit spread, which is reflected in a higher interest rate.

Corporate Bond Yields

How does the credit risk of default affect bond prices and yields? The cash flows promised by the bond are the most that bondholders can hope to receive. Due to credit risk, the cash flows that a purchaser of a corporate bond actually *expects* to receive may be less than that amount. For example, GM was struggling financially in 2006 and 2007, substantially increasing the chance that it would default on its bonds. Realizing this, in 2007, investors in GM bonds incorporated an increased probability that the bond payments would not be made as promised, and prices of the bonds fell. Because the yield to maturity of GM's bonds is computed by comparing the price to the *promised* cash flows, the yield to maturity in 2007 and 2008 *increased* as the probability of being paid as promised decreased. This example highlights the following general truths:

1. Investors pay less for bonds with credit risk than they would for an otherwise identical default-free bond.

2. Because the yield to maturity for a bond is calculated using the promised cash flows instead of the *expected* cash flows, the yield of bonds with credit risk will be higher than that of otherwise identical default-free bonds.

3. Because the expected return includes the possibility that the bond will pay as promised and the possibility that the bond will pay less due to default, if the bond of a corporation at risk of bankruptcy actually does default, the actual return to an investor in the bond will be lower than the return expected when the bond was purchased.

These three points lead us to an important conclusion: *the yield to maturity of a defaultable bond is not equal to the expected return of investing in the bond.* The promised cash flows used to determine the yield to maturity are always higher than the expected cash flows investors use to calculate the expected return. As a result, the yield to maturity will always be higher than the expected return of investing in the bond. *Moreover, a higher yield to maturity does not necessarily imply that a bond's expected return is higher. In the case of GM, the actual return to bondholders was substantially less than both the promised yield and the expected return when investors bought the bonds in 2007, as GM filed for bankruptcy on June 1, 2009.*

Bond Ratings

The probability of default clearly affects the price you are willing to pay for a corporate bond. How do you assess a firm's likelihood of default? Several companies rate the creditworthiness of bonds and make this information available to investors. By consulting these ratings, investors can assess the creditworthiness of a particular bond issue. The ratings therefore encourage widespread investor participation and relatively liquid markets. The three best-known bond-rating companies in Canada are the Dominion Bond Rating Service (DBRS), a privately held Canadian firm, Standard & Poor's (which acquired the Canadian Bond Rating Service), and Moody's Investors Service. Table 6.5 summarizes the rating classes each company uses. Bonds with the highest rating are judged to be least likely to default.

---

[4] Because trading in corporate bonds is much less liquid than trading in government bonds, part of the increased interest rate is to compensate investors for this lack of liquidity.

TABLE 6.5	Bond Ratings in Canada		

Dominion Bond Rating Service (DBRS)	Moody's	Standard & Poor's	Description (Moody's)
Investment Grade Debt			
AAA	Aaa	AAA	Judged to be of the best quality. They carry the smallest degree of investment risk and are generally referred to as "gilt edged." Interest payments are protected by a large or an exceptionally stable margin and principal is secure. While the various protective elements are likely to change, such changes as can be visualized are most unlikely to impair the fundamentally strong position of such issues.
AA	Aa	AA	Judged to be of high quality by all standards. Together with the Aaa group, they constitute what are generally known as high-grade bonds. They are rated lower than the best bonds, because margins of protection may not be as large as in Aaa securities, or fluctuation of protective elements may be of greater amplitude, or there may be other elements present that make the long-term risk appear somewhat larger than for the Aaa securities.
A	A	A	Possess many favourable investment attributes and are considered as upper-medium-grade obligations. Factors giving security to principal and interest are considered adequate, but elements may be present that suggest a susceptibility to impairment some time in the future.
BBB	Baa	BBB	Are considered as medium-grade obligations (i.e., they are neither highly protected nor poorly secured). Interest payments and principal security appear adequate for the present, but certain protective elements may be lacking or may be characteristically unreliable over any great length of time. Such bonds lack outstanding investment characteristics and, in fact, have speculative characteristics as well.
Speculative Bonds			
BB	Ba	BB	Judged to have speculative elements; their future cannot be considered as well assured. Often the protection of interest and principal payments may be very moderate, and thereby not well safeguarded during both good and bad times over the future. Uncertainty of position characterizes bonds in this class.
B	B	B	Generally lack characteristics of the desirable investment. Assurance of interest and principal payments of maintenance of other terms of the contract over any long period of time may be small.
CCC	Caa	CCC	Are of poor standing. Such issues may be in default, or there may be present elements of danger with respect to principal or interest.
CC	Ca	CC	Are speculative in a high degree. Such issues are often in default or have other marked shortcomings.
C, D	C	C, D	Lowest-rated class of bonds, and issues so rated can be regarded as having extremely poor prospects of ever attaining any real investment standing.

Sources: Moody's, DBRS, TD Waterhouse Canada Inc.

investment-grade bonds Bonds in the top four categories of creditworthiness with a low risk of default.

speculative bonds (junk bonds or **high-yield bonds)** Bonds in one of the bottom five categories of creditworthiness (below investment grade) that have a high risk of default.

Bonds in the top four categories are often referred to as **investment-grade bonds** because of their low default risk. Bonds in the bottom five categories are often called **speculative bonds, junk bonds,** or **high-yield bonds,** because the likelihood of their default is high and so they promise higher yields. The rating depends on the risk of bankruptcy, as well as the bondholders' ability to lay claim to the firm's assets in the event of such a bankruptcy. Thus, debt issues with a low-priority claim in bankruptcy will have a lower rating than issues from the same company that have a high priority in bankruptcy or that are backed by a specific asset, such as a building or a plant.

Corporate and Provincial Yield Curves

Just as we can construct a yield curve from risk-free Government of Canada securities, we can plot a similar yield curve for provincial and corporate bonds. Figure 6.5 shows the yield curve of Bell Canada Enterprises (BCE) debt, which has a low-A DBRS credit rating for senior unsecured corporate debentures. Figure 6.5 also shows yield curves for Province of British Columbia strip bonds and Government of Canada strip bonds. We

---

FIGURE 6.5

Corporate and Provincial Yield Curves for May 25, 2011

This figure shows the yield curve for strip bonds from the Government of Canada, Province of British Columbia, and Bell Canada Enterprises (BCE) on May 25, 2011. Note how the yield to maturity is higher for lower-rated bonds, which have a higher probability of default.

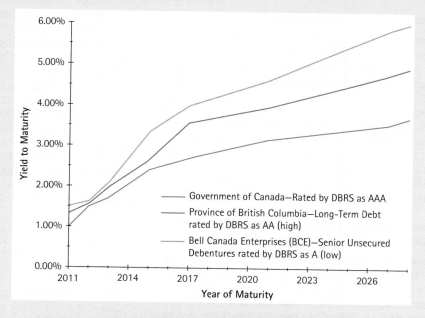

Sources: www.moodys.com, www.dbrs.com, TD Waterhouse Canada Inc.

INTERVIEW WITH
Lisa Black

*L*isa Black is Managing Director at Teachers Insurance and Annuity Association (*TIAA-CREF*), a major financial services company. A Chartered Financial Analyst, she oversees a variety of fixed income funds, including money market, intermediate bond, high-yield, emerging market debt, and inflation-linked bond funds.

QUESTION: *When many people think about the financial markets, they picture the equity markets. How big and how active are the bond markets compared to the equity markets?*

ANSWER: The dollar volume of bonds traded daily is about 10 times that of equity markets. For example, a single $15 billion issue of 10-year U.S. treasury bonds will sell in one day. The market value of the Barclays Capital U.S. Universal Bond Index of dollar-denominated debt as of June 30, 2009, was $13.8 trillion, with the U.S. Aggregate Index (investment-grade debt) accounting for almost 90%. It includes treasuries, agencies, corporate bonds, and mortgage-backed securities. Other major sectors of the Universal Index include corporate high-yield bonds, Eurodollar bonds, emerging markets, and private placements.

QUESTION: *How do the bond markets operate?*

ANSWER: Firms and governments turn to bond markets when they need to borrow money to fund new construction projects, finance acquisitions, and to serve general corporate purposes. On the other side, institutions like TIAA-CREF, endowments, and foundations have funds to invest. Investment bankers serve as intermediaries, matching borrowers with creditors in terms of maturity needs and risk appetite. Because we provide annuities for professors, for example, we invest money for longer periods of time than an insurance company that needs funds to pay claims. In the institutional world, bond funds typically trade in blocks of bonds ranging from $5 million to $50 million at a time.

QUESTION: *What drives changes in the values of government bonds?*

ANSWER: The simple answer is that when interest rates rise, bond prices fall. The key is to dig below that reality to see why interest rates rise and fall. A major factor is investors' expectations for inflation and economic growth. Interest rates generally rise when the expectation is that growth will accelerate, because inflation won't be far behind. During the 2008–09 recession, interest rates dropped as the U.S. Federal Reserve and other central banks around the world injected liquidity into the system. There was also a flight to quality after the bankruptcy of Lehman Brothers. The value of The Reserve Fund (a U.S. money market fund) fell drastically as its holdings of about $785 million of Lehman's short-term debt securities became all but worthless. Worried retail and institutional investors sold their money market funds and purchased U.S. treasury bills and notes to protect their principal. With increased demand, interest rates on risk-free U.S. treasury securities fell sharply. At one point T-bills even had a negative yield.

QUESTION: *What impact did the 2008–09 financial crisis have on the bond market? What changes do you anticipate going forward as a result?*

ANSWER: While the effects of the crisis on equity markets have been widely discussed, the effects on the bond market have been just as profound. Particularly noteworthy is the role governments and central bankers have played—and likely will continue to play—to stabilize financial institutions deemed too big or important to fail. The U.S. Federal Reserve introduced an unprecedented number of stimulus programs to unfreeze credit markets, including programs to guarantee money funds. The challenge will be how and when the various support programs and financial infusions will end and/or be paid back. In addition, the rating agencies' role and ratings methodologies will likely be subject to greater scrutiny, both from regulators and investors.

In the corporate sector, many borrowers—the automotive industries, for example—could not raise debt financing during the crisis. Credit spreads widened dramatically as investors shunned even AAA- and AA-rated credits. Major institutional investors sat on the sidelines for several months, and the corporate bond new issue market was essentially nonexistent. Not until federal governments announced programs to increase liquidity did institutional investors re-enter the market, first buying only the highest credit quality instruments, such as first mortgage bonds issued by utilities and government-guaranteed mortgage-backed securities. Investors then began to move down the credit quality chain, selectively focusing on issuers that could weather an economic downtown.

Discussion Questions

1. In what ways might you as a financial manager make use of the information in interest rate changes and the yield curve?

2. How do you think financial managers will prepare the companies for future credit market crises?

default spread (credit spread) The difference between the risk-free interest rate on Government of Canada bonds and the interest rates on all other loans. The magnitude of the credit spread will depend on investors' assessment of the likelihood that a particular bond issuer will default

refer to the difference between the yields of the various bonds and the Government of Canada yields as the **default spread** or **credit spread**. Credit spreads fluctuate as investors' perceptions regarding the probability of default change. Note that the credit spread is higher for bonds with lower ratings and therefore a greater likelihood of default. The British Columbia bonds have a positive credit spread of between 0.09% and 1.22% (as of May 25, 2011), but BCE has a larger credit spread ranging from 0.13% to 2.31%. The credit spreads are higher for longer terms to maturity. You might wonder why there would be any credit spread for British Columbia, as it seems unimaginable that a province would default on its debt. In fact, the province with the lowest current credit spread, Alberta, is also the only province to have defaulted on its debt; this occurred in 1936.

As we indicated at the beginning of this chapter, the bond market, while less well known than the stock markets, is large and important. Because debt is a substantial part

EXAMPLE 6.10

Credit Spreads and Bond Prices

Problem

Your firm has a credit rating of AA. You notice that the credit spread for five-year maturity debt is 90 basis points (0.90%). Your firm's five-year debt has a coupon rate of 5%. You see that new five-year Government of Canada bonds are being issued at par with a coupon rate of 4.5%. What should the price of your outstanding five-year bonds be?

Solution

▶ **Plan**

If the credit spread is 90 basis points, then the yield to maturity (*YTM*) on your debt should be the *YTM* on similar Government of Canada bonds plus 0.9%. The fact that new five-year Government of Canada bonds are being issued at par with coupons of 4.5% means that with a coupon rate of 4.5%, these bonds are selling for $100 per $100 face value. Thus, their *YTM* is 4.5% and your debt's *YTM* should be 4.5% + 0.9% = 5.4%. The cash flows on your bonds are $5 per year for every $100 face value, paid as $2.50 every six months (for a total of 10 coupon payments). The implied effective six-month rate corresponding to a 5.4% yield (*APR* with semi-annual compounding) is 5.4%/2 = 2.7%. Armed with this information, you can use Equation 6.3 to compute the price of your bonds.

▶ **Execute**

$$2.50 \times \frac{1}{0.027}\left(1 - \frac{1}{1.027^{10}}\right) + \frac{100}{1.027^{10}} = \$98.27$$

▶ **Evaluate**

Your bonds offer a higher coupon (5% vs. 4.5%) than Government of Canada bonds of the same maturity, but sell for a lower price ($98.27 vs. $100). The reason is the credit spread. Your firm's higher probability of default leads investors to demand a higher *YTM* on your debt. To provide a higher *YTM*, the purchase price for the debt must be lower. If your debt paid a 5.4% coupon rate, it would sell at $100, the same as the Government of Canada bonds. But to get that price, you would have to offer coupons that are 90 basis points higher than those on the Government of Canada bonds—exactly enough to offset the credit spread.

The Credit Crisis and Bond Yields

The financial crisis that engulfed the world's economies in 2008 originated as a credit crisis that first emerged in August 2007. At that time, problems in the U.S. mortgage market had led to the bankruptcy of several large mortgage lenders there. The default of these firms, and the downgrading of much of the short-term commercial paper and long-term bonds backed by mortgages these firms had made, caused many investors to reassess the risk of commercial paper, bankers' acceptances, and other bonds in their portfolios.[5] In Canada and around the world, fear spread that debt securities might be exposed to the same problem, as it was not clear whether the debt issuers held claims to U.S. mortgages as part of their assets. As perceptions of risk increased, and investors attempted to move into safer government securities, the prices of corporate debt fell, and so their credit spreads rose relative to riskless debt (such as Government of Canada treasury bills). Figure 6.6 shows how the credit spreads of bankers' acceptances (the highest-rated short-term corporate debt) rose dramatically over this time period. The normal credit spread of less than 0.2% jumped dramatically to over 1.5%. The effect was even more pronounced for commercial paper and long-term corporate debt. In some cases, it became impossible for corporations to borrow new money or to refinance current obligations coming due. This problem with borrowing costs and feasibility made it extremely difficult for firms to raise the capital needed for new investment and, in the case of some firms that were not able to refinance, led to bankruptcy. The net result was a dramatic slowing in economic growth that turned into an economic contraction in most countries around the world. The decline in these credit spreads in early 2009 (facilitated by central banks like the U.S. Federal Reserve and the Bank of Canada keeping their lending rates low and buying corporate debt) was viewed by many people as an important first step in mitigating the ongoing impact of the financial crisis on the rest of the economy.

FIGURE 6.6 — Credit Spreads on Banker's Acceptances Over Time

Canadian three-month bankers' acceptance rates minus three-month Government of Canada treasury bill rates

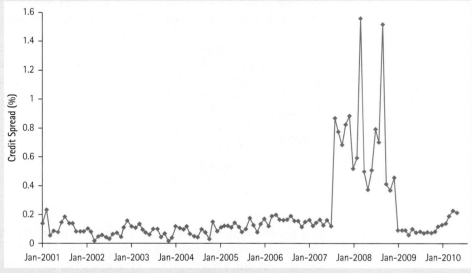

Source: Bank of Canada.

---

[5] Commercial paper is short-term debt usually issued by large firms with high credit ratings. Bankers' acceptances are commercial paper guaranteed by a bank.

of the financing of most corporations, a financial manager needs to understand bonds and how investors price the company's bonds. In this chapter, we have introduced you to the major types of bonds, how bonds repay investors, and how bonds are priced. In Chapter 14, we will discuss the bond markets further, including the process a firm goes through to issue debt.

Concept Check

9. What is a junk bond?

10. How will the yield to maturity of a bond vary with the bond's risk of default?

MyFinanceLab

Here is what you should know after reading this chapter. MyFinanceLab will help you identify what you know, and where to go when you need to practice.

Key Points and Equations	Terms	Online Practice Opportunities
6.1 Bond Terminology ▶ Bonds pay both coupon and principal, or face value, payments to investors. By convention, the coupon rate of a bond is the percent of face value paid out as coupons each year; thus, each coupon payment, *CPN*, is: $$CPN = \frac{\text{Coupon Rate} \times \text{Face Value}}{\text{Number of Coupon Payments per Year}} \quad (6.1)$$	bond indenture, p. 166 coupon rate, p. 166 coupons, p. 166 face value, p. 166 maturity date, p. 166 par value, p. 166 term, p. 166	MyFinanceLab Study Plan 6.1
6.2 Zero-Coupon Bonds ▶ Zero-coupon bonds make no coupon payments, so investors receive only the bond's face value. ▶ The internal rate of return of a bond is called its yield to maturity (or yield). The yield to maturity of a bond is the discount rate that sets the present value of the promised bond payments equal to the current market price of the bond. ▶ The yield to maturity for a zero-coupon bond is given by $$1 + YTM_n = \left(\frac{\text{Face Value}}{\text{Price}}\right)^{1/n} \quad (6.2)$$ ▶ The risk-free interest rate for an investment until date *n* equals the yield to maturity of a risk-free zero-coupon bond that matures on date *n*. A plot of these rates against maturity is called the zero-coupon yield curve.	discount, p. 167 pure discount bond, p. 167 spot interest rates, p. 168 treasury bills, p. 167 yield to maturity (*YTM*), p. 167 zero-coupon bond, p. 167 zero-coupon yield curve, p. 168	MyFinanceLab Study Plan 6.2

6.3 Coupon Bonds

▶ The yield to maturity for a coupon bond (expressed as an effective rate compounded over the same time period as the time between coupon payments) is the discount rate, YTM_n, that equates the present value of the bond's future cash flows with its price:

$$P = CPN \times \frac{1}{YTM_n}\left(1 - \frac{1}{(1 + YTM_n)^n}\right) + \frac{FV}{(1 + YTM_n)^n} \quad (6.3)$$

coupon bonds, p. 170
Government of Canada bonds, p. 170

MyFinanceLab
Study Plan 6.3

6.4 Why Bond Prices Change

▶ A bond will trade at a premium if its coupon rate exceeds its yield to maturity. It will trade at a discount if its coupon rate is less than its yield to maturity. If a bond's coupon rate equals its yield to maturity, it trades at par.
▶ As a bond approaches maturity, the price of the bond approaches its face value.
▶ Bond prices change as interest rates change. When interest rates rise, bond prices fall, and vice versa.
▶ Long-term zero-coupon bonds are more sensitive to changes in interest rates than are short-term zero-coupon bonds.
▶ Bonds with low coupon rates are more sensitive to changes in interest rates than are bonds with similar maturity and high coupon rates.

par, p. 174
premium, p. 174

MyFinanceLab
Study Plan 6.4

Interactive Interest Rate Sensitivity Analysis

6.5 Corporate Bonds

▶ When a bond issuer does not make a bond payment in full, the issuer has defaulted.
▶ The risk that default can occur is called default or credit risk. Government of Canada securities are free of default risk.
▶ The expected return of a corporate bond, which is the firm's debt cost of capital, equals the risk-free rate of interest plus a risk premium. The expected return is less than the bond's yield to maturity, because the yield to maturity of a bond is calculated using the promised cash flows, not the expected cash flows.
▶ Bond ratings summarize the creditworthiness of bonds for investors.
▶ The difference between yields on Government of Canada securities and yields on corporate bonds is called the credit spread or default spread. The credit spread compensates investors for the difference between promised and expected cash flows and for the risk of default.

corporate bonds, p. 182
credit risk, p. 182
default (credit) spread, p. 187
high-yield bonds, p. 185
investment-grade bonds, p. 185
junk bonds, p. 185
speculative bonds, p. 185

MyFinanceLab
Study Plan 6.5

Review Questions

1. How is a bond like a loan?

2. How does an investor receive a return from buying a bond?

3. How is yield to maturity related to the concept of internal rate of return?

4. Does a bond's yield to maturity determine its price, or does the price determine the yield to maturity?

5. Explain why the yield of a bond that trades at a discount exceeds the bond's coupon rate.

6. Explain the relationship between interest rates and bond prices.

7. Why are longer-term bonds more sensitive to changes in interest rates than shorter-term bonds?

8. Explain why the expected return of a corporate bond does not equal its yield to maturity.

Problems

All problems in this chapter are available in MyFinanceLab. An asterisk (*) indicates problems with a higher level of difficulty.

Bond Terminology

1. Consider a 10-year bond with a face value of $1000 that has a coupon rate of 5.5%, with semi-annual payments.
   a. What is the coupon payment for this bond?
   b. Draw the cash flows for the bond on a timeline.

2. Assume that a bond will make payments every six months as shown on the following timeline (using six-month periods):

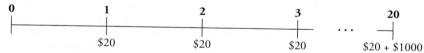

   a. What is the maturity of the bond (in years)?
   b. What is the coupon rate (as a percentage)?
   c. What is the face value?

Zero-Coupon Bonds

3. Your company wants to raise $10 million by issuing 20-year zero-coupon bonds. If the yield to maturity on the bonds will be 6% (*EAR*), what total face value amount of bonds must you issue?

4. The following table summarizes prices of various default-free zero-coupon bonds (expressed as a percentage of the face value):

Maturity (years)	1	2	3	4	5
Price (per $100 face value)	$95.51	$91.05	$86.38	$81.65	$76.51

   a. Compute the yield to maturity for each bond.

   b. Plot the zero-coupon yield curve (for the first five years).

   c. Is the yield curve upward sloping, downward sloping, or flat?

Use the following information for Problems 5 to 7. The current zero-coupon yield curve for risk-free bonds is as follows:

Maturity (years)	1	2	3	4	5
YTM	5%	5.5%	5.75%	5.95%	6.05%

 5. What is the price per $100 face value of a two-year, zero-coupon, risk-free bond?

 6. What is the price per $100 face value of a four-year, zero-coupon, risk-free bond?

 7. What is the risk-free interest rate for a five-year maturity?

Coupon Bonds

8. For each of the following pairs of Government of Canada bonds, identify which will have the higher price as a percentage of the face value.

   a. A three-year zero-coupon bond or a five-year zero-coupon bond

   b. A three-year zero-coupon bond or a three-year 4% coupon bond

   c. A two-year 5% coupon bond or a two-year 6% coupon bond

9. The yield to maturity of a $1000 bond with a 7% coupon rate, semi-annual coupons, and two years to maturity is 7.6% *APR*, compounded semi-annually. What must its price be?

10. Assume the current yield curve shows that the spot rates for six months, one year and one and a half years are 1%, 1.1% and 1.3%, respectively, all quoted as semi-annually compounded *APR*s. What is the price of a $1000 par, 4% coupon bond maturing in one and a half years (the next coupon is exactly six months from now)?

11. Suppose a 10-year, $1000 bond with an 8% coupon rate and semi-annual coupons is trading for a price of $1034.74.

   a. What is the bond's yield to maturity (expressed as an *APR* with semi-annual compounding)?

   b. If the bond's yield to maturity changes to 9% *APR*, what will the bond's price be?

12. Suppose a five-year, $1000 bond with annual coupons has a price of $900 and a yield to maturity of 6%. What is the bond's coupon rate?

Why Bond Prices Change

13. The prices of several bonds with face values of $1000 are summarized in the following table:

Bond	A	B	C	D
Price	$972.50	$1040.75	$1150.00	$1000.00

For each bond, state whether it trades at a discount, at par, or at a premium.

14. You have purchased a 10% coupon bond for $1040. What will happen to the bond's price if market interest rates rise?

15. Suppose a seven-year, $1000 bond with an 8% coupon rate and semi-annual coupons is trading with a yield to maturity of 6.75%.

a. Is this bond currently trading at a discount, at par, or at a premium? Explain.
b. If the yield to maturity of the bond rises to 7.00% (*APR* with semi-annual compounding), what price will the bond trade for?

Suppose that General Motors Acceptance Corporation issued a bond with 10 years until maturity, a face value of $1000, and a coupon rate of 7% (annual payments). The yield to maturity on this bond when it was issued was 6%. Use this information for Problems 16 to 18.

16. What was the price of this bond when it was issued?

17. Assuming the yield to maturity remains constant, what is the price of the bond immediately before it makes its first coupon payment?

18. Assuming the yield to maturity remains constant, what is the price of the bond immediately after it makes its first coupon payment?

19. Your company currently has 6% coupon-rate bonds (coupons are paid semi-annually) with 10 years to maturity and a price of $1000. If you want to issue new 10-year coupon bonds at par, what coupon rate do you need to set?

20. Suppose you purchase a 10-year bond with 6% annual coupons. You hold the bond for four years, and sell it immediately after receiving the fourth coupon. If the bond's yield to maturity was 5% when you purchased and sold the bond,
a. What cash flows will you pay and receive from your investment in the bond per $100 face value?
b. What is the internal rate of return of your investment?

Consider the following bonds for Problems 21 and 22:

Bond	Coupon Rate (annual payments)	Maturity (years)
A	0%	15
B	0%	10
C	4%	15
D	8%	10

21. What is the percentage change in the price of each bond if its yield to maturity falls from 6% to 5%?

22. Which of the bonds A to D is most sensitive to a 1% drop in interest rates from 6% to 5% and why? Which bond is least sensitive? Provide an intuitive explanation for your answer.

23. Suppose you purchase a 30-year, zero-coupon bond with a yield to maturity of 6%. You hold the bond for five years before selling it.
a. If the bond's yield to maturity is 6% when you sell it, what is the internal rate of return of your investment?
b. If the bond's yield to maturity is 7% when you sell it, what is the internal rate of return of your investment?
c. If the bond's yield to maturity is 5% when you sell it, what is the internal rate of return of your investment?
d. Even if a bond has no chance of default, is your investment risk free if you plan to sell it before it matures? Explain.

Corporate Bonds

24. The following table summarizes the yields to maturity on several one-year, zero-coupon securities:

Security	Yield (%)
Treasury	3.1
AAA corporate	3.2
BBB corporate	4.2
B corporate	4.9

a. What is the price (expressed as a percentage of the face value) of a one-year, zero-coupon corporate bond with an AAA rating?
b. What is the credit spread on AAA-rated corporate bonds?
c. What is the credit spread on B-rated corporate bonds?
d. How does the credit spread change with the bond rating? Why?

25. Andrew Industries is contemplating issuing a 30-year bond with a coupon rate of 7% (annual coupon payments) and a face value of $1000. Andrew believes it can get a rating of A from Standard & Poor's. However, due to recent financial difficulties at the company, Standard & Poor's is warning that it may downgrade Andrew Industries bonds to BBB. Yields on A-rated, long-term bonds are currently 6.5%, and yields on BBB-rated bonds are 6.9%.
a. What is the price of the bond if Andrew maintains the A rating for the bond issue?
b. What will the price of the bond be if it is downgraded?

26. HMK Enterprises would like to raise $10 million to invest in capital expenditures. The company plans to issue five-year bonds with a face value of $1000 and a coupon rate of 6.5% (annual payments). The following table summarizes the yield to maturity for five-year (annual-payment) coupon corporate bonds of various ratings:

Rating	AAA	AA	A	BBB	BB
YTM	6.20%	6.30%	6.50%	6.90%	7.50%

a. Assuming the bonds will be rated AA, what will the price of the bonds be?
b. How much of the total principal amount of these bonds must HMK issue to raise $10 million today, assuming the bonds are AA rated? (Because HMK cannot issue a fraction of a bond, assume that all fractions are rounded to the nearest whole number.)
c. What must the rating of the bonds be for them to sell at par?
d. Suppose that when the bonds are issued, the price of each bond is $959.54. What is the likely rating of the bonds? Are they junk bonds?

27. A BBB-rated corporate bond has a yield to maturity of 8.2%. A U.S. treasury security has a yield to maturity of 6.5%. These yields are quoted as *APR*s with semi-annual compounding. Both bonds pay semi-annual coupons at a rate of 7% and have five years to maturity.
a. What is the price (expressed as a percentage of the face value) of the treasury bond?
b. What is the price (expressed as a percentage of the face value) of the BBB-rated corporate bond?
c. What is the credit spread on the BBB bonds?

Data Case

You are an intern with Ford Motor Company in its corporate finance division. The firm is planning to issue $50 million of 12% annual coupon bonds with a 10-year maturity. The firm anticipates an increase in its bond rating. Your boss wants you to determine the gain in the proceeds of the new issue if it is rated above the firm's current bond rating. To prepare this information, you will have to determine Ford's current debt rating and the yield curve for its particular rating.

1. Begin by finding the current U.S. treasury yield curve. At the U.S. treasury website (www.treas.gov), search using the term "yield curve" and select "US Treasury—Daily Treasury Yield Curve." *Beware*: There will probably be two links with the same title. Look at the description below the link and select the one that does *not* say "Real Yield " You want the nominal rates. Copy the table into an Excel file.

2. Find the current yield spreads for the various bond ratings. Unfortunately, the current spreads are available only for a fee, so you will use old ones. Go to BondsOnline (www.bondsonline.com) and click on "Today's Market." Next, click on "US Corporate Bond Spreads." Copy this table to the Excel file into which you copied the U.S. treasury yields.

3. Find the current bond rating for Ford Motor Co. Go to Standard & Poor's Web site (www.standardandpoors.com). Select your country. Look for the "Find a Rating" box under "Ratings" and enter "Ford Motor Co." and select "Ford Motor Co." from the list it returns. At this point you will have to register (free of charge) or enter the username and password provided by your instructor. Use the issuer credit rating for "local long term."

4. Return to Excel and create a timeline with the cash flows and discount rates you will need to value the new bond issue.
   a. To create the required spot rates for Ford's issue, add the appropriate spread to the treasury yield of the same maturity.
   b. The yield curve and spread rates you have found do not cover every year that you will need for the new bonds. Specifically, you do not have yields or spreads for 4-, 6-, 8-, and 9-year maturities. Fill these in by linearly interpolating the given yields and spreads. For example, the 4-year spot rate and spread will be the average of the 3- and 5-year rates. The 6-year rate and spread will be the average of the 5- and 7-year rates. For years 8 and 9, you will have to spread the difference between years 7 and 10 across the 2 years.
   c. To compute the spot rates for Ford's current debt rating, add the yield spread to the treasury rate for each maturity. However, note that the spread is in basis points, which are 1/100th of a percentage point.
   d. Compute the cash flows that would be paid to bondholders each year and add them to the timeline.

5. Use the spot rates to calculate the present value of each cash flow paid to the bondholders.

6. Compute the issue price of the bond and its initial yield to maturity.

7. Repeat steps 4 to 6 based on the assumption that Ford is able to raise its bond rating by one level. Compute the new yield based on the higher rating and the new bond price that would result.

8. Compute the additional cash proceeds that could be raised from the issue if the rating were improved.

Chapter 6 APPENDIX A — Solving for the Yield to Maturity of a Bond Using a Financial Calculator

You are looking to purchase a three-year, $1000 par, 10% annual coupon bond. Payments begin one year from now in November 2008. The price of the bond is $1074.51 per $1000 par value. What is the yield to maturity of the bond? [answer: 7.15%]?

HP-10BII

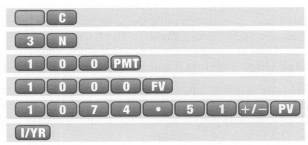

Press [Orange Shift] and then the [C] button to clear all previous entries.

Enter the Number of periods.

Enter the payment amount per period.

Enter the par value of the bond you will receive in year 3.

Enter present value or price of the bond you solved for earlier.

Solves for the yield to maturity.

TI-BAII Plus Professional

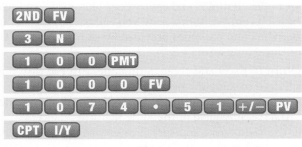

Press [2ND] and then the [FV] button to clear all previous entries.

Enter the Number of periods.

Enter the payment amount per period.

Enter the par value of the bond you will receive in year 3.

Enter present value or price of the bond you solved for earlier.

Solves for the yield to maturity.

Chapter 6 APPENDIX B The Yield Curve and the Law of One Price

Thus far, we have focused on the relationship between the price of an individual bond and its yield to maturity. In this section, we explore the relationship between the prices and yields of different bonds. In Chapter 3, we saw how market forces keep the same asset from having two prices at the same time; we call this the Law of One Price. Using the Law of One Price, we show that, given the spot interest rates, which are the yields of default-free zero-coupon bonds, we can determine the price and yield of any other default-free bond. As a result, the yield curve provides sufficient information to evaluate all such bonds.

Valuing a Coupon Bond with Zero-Coupon Prices

We begin with the observation that it is possible to replicate the cash flows of a coupon bond using zero-coupon bonds. Therefore, we can use the Valuation Principle's Law of One Price to compute the price of a coupon bond from the prices of zero-coupon bonds. For example, we can replicate a three-year, $1000 bond that pays 10% annual coupons using three zero-coupon bonds as follows:

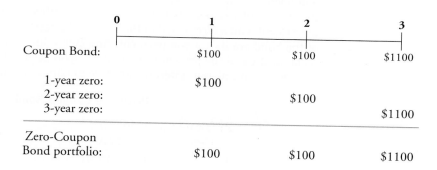

We match each coupon payment to a zero-coupon bond with a face value equal to the coupon payment and a term equal to the time remaining to the coupon date. Similarly, we match the final bond payment (final coupon plus return of face value) in three years to a three-year, zero-coupon bond with a corresponding face value of $1100. Because the coupon bond cash flows are identical to the cash flows of the portfolio of zero-coupon bonds, the Law of One Price states that the price of the portfolio of zero-coupon bonds must be the same as the price of the coupon bond.

To illustrate, assume that current zero-coupon bond yields and prices are as shown in Table 6.6 (they are the same as in Example 6.1).

TABLE 6.6	Yields and Prices (per $100 Face Value) for Zero-Coupon Bonds			
Maturity	**1 Year**	**2 Years**	**3 Years**	**4 Years**
YTM	3.50%	4.00%	4.50%	4.75%
Price	$96.62	$92.45	$87.63	$83.06

Source: www.moodys.com, www.dbrs.com, TD Waterhouse Canada Inc.

We can calculate the cost of the zero-coupon bond portfolio that replicates the three-year coupon bond as follows:

Zero-Coupon Bond	Face Value Required	Cost
1 Year	100	96.62
2 Years	100	92.46
3 Years	1100	$11 \times 87.63 = 963.93$

Total Cost: $1153.00

By the Law of One Price, the three-year coupon bond must trade for a price of $1153. If the price of the coupon bond were higher, you could earn an arbitrage profit by selling the coupon bond and buying the zero-coupon bond portfolio. If the price of the coupon bond were lower, you could earn an arbitrage profit by buying the coupon bond and selling the zero-coupon bonds.

Valuing a Coupon Bond Using Zero-Coupon Yields

To this point, we have used the zero-coupon bond *prices* to derive the price of the coupon bond. Alternatively, we can use the zero-coupon bond *yields*. Recall that the yield to maturity of a zero-coupon bond is the competitive market interest rate for a risk-free investment with a term equal to the term of the zero-coupon bond. Since the cash flows of the bond are its coupon payments and face value repayment, the price of a coupon bond must equal the present value of its coupon payments and face value discounted at the competitive market interest rates (see Equation 5.7 in Chapter 5),

Price of a Coupon Bond

$$P = PV(\text{Bond Cash Flows})$$
$$= \frac{CPN}{1 + YTM_1} + \frac{CPN}{(1 + YTM_2)^2} + \cdots + \frac{CPN + FV}{(1 + YTM_n)^n} \tag{6.4}$$

where *CPN* is the bond coupon payment, YTM_n is the yield to maturity of a *zero-coupon* bond that matures at the same time as the *n*th coupon payment, and *FV* is the face value of the bond. For the three-year, $1000 bond with 10% annual coupons considered earlier, we can use Equation 6.4 to calculate its price using the zero-coupon yields in Table 6.6:

$$P = \frac{100}{1.035} + \frac{100}{1.04^2} + \frac{100 + 1000}{1.045^3} = \$1153$$

This price is identical to the price we computed earlier by replicating the bond. Thus, we can determine the no-arbitrage price of a coupon bond by discounting its cash flows using the zero-coupon yields. In other words, the information in the zero-coupon yield curve is sufficient to price all other risk-free bonds.

Coupon Bond Yields

Given the yields for zero-coupon bonds, we can use Equation 6.4 to price a coupon bond. In Section 6.1, we saw how to compute the yield to maturity of a coupon bond from its price. Combining these results, we can determine the relationship between the yields of zero-coupon bonds and coupon-paying bonds.

Consider again the three-year, $1000 bond with 10% annual coupons. Given the zero-coupon yields in Table 6.6, we calculate a price for this bond of $1153. From Equation 6.3, the yield to maturity of this bond is the rate YTM_3 that satisfies:

$$P = 1153 = \frac{100}{(1 + YTM_3)} + \frac{100}{(1 + YTM_3)^2} + \frac{100 + 1000}{(1 + YTM_3)^3}$$

We can solve for the yield by using a financial calculator:

	N	I/Y	PV	PMT	FV
Given:	3		−1153	100	1000
Solve for:		4.44			

Excel Formula: $= RATE(NPER,PMT,PV,FV) = RATE(3,100,-1153,1000)$

Therefore, the yield to maturity of the bond is 4.44%. We can check this result directly as follows:

$$P = \frac{100}{1.0444} + \frac{100}{1.0444^2} + \frac{100 + 1000}{1.0444^3} = \$1153$$

Because the coupon bond provides cash flows at different points in time, the yield to maturity of a coupon bond is a weighted average of the yields of the zero-coupon bonds of equal and shorter maturities. The weights depend (in a complex way) on the magnitude of the cash flows each period. In this example, the zero-coupon bonds yields were 3.5%, 4.0%, and 4.5%. For this coupon bond, most of the value in the present value calculation comes from the present value of the third cash flow, because it includes the principal, so the yield is closest to the three-year, zero-coupon yield of 4.5%.

Example 6.11 shows that coupon bonds with the same maturity can have different yields depending on their coupon rates. The yield to maturity of a coupon bond is a weighted average of the yields on the zero-coupon bonds. As the coupon increases, earlier cash flows become relatively more important than later cash flows in the calculation of the present value. The shape of the yield curve keys us in on trends with the yield to maturity:

1. If the yield curve is upward sloping (as it is for the yields in Example 6.11), the resulting yield to maturity decreases with the coupon rate of the bond.
2. When the zero-coupon yield curve is downward sloping, the yield to maturity will increase with the coupon rate.
3. With a flat yield curve, all zero-coupon and coupon-paying bonds will have the same yield, independent of their maturities and coupon rates.

Government of Canada Yield Curves

As we have shown in this section, we can use the zero-coupon yield curve to determine the price and yield to maturity of other risk-free bonds. The plot of the yields of coupon bonds of different maturities is called the coupon-paying yield curve. When Canadian bond traders refer to "the yield curve," they are often referring to the coupon-paying Government of Canada bond yield curve. As we show in Example 6.11,

EXAMPLE 6.11

Yields on Bonds
with the Same
Maturity

Problem

Given the following zero-coupon yields, compare the yield to maturity for a three-year, zero-coupon bond; a three-year coupon bond with 4% annual coupons; and a three-year coupon bond with 10% annual coupons. All of these bonds are default free.

Solution

▶ **Plan**

Maturity	1 Year	2 Years	3 Years	4 Years
Zero-coupon *YTM*	3.50%	4.00%	4.50%	4.75%

From the information provided, the yield to maturity of the three-year, zero-coupon bond is 4.50%. Also, because the yields match those in Table 6.6, we already calculated the yield to maturity for the 10% coupon bond as 4.44%. To compute the yield for the 4% coupon bond, we first need to calculate its price, which we can do using Equation 6.4. Since the coupons are 4%, paid annually, they are $40 per year for three years. The $1000 face value will be repaid at that time. Once we have the price, we can use Equation 6.3 to compute the yield to maturity.

▶ **Execute**

Using Equation 6.4, we have:

$$P = \frac{40}{1.035} + \frac{40}{1.04^2} + \frac{40 + 1000}{1.045^3} = \$986.98$$

The price of the bond with a 4% coupon is $986.98. From Equation 6.4:

$$\$986.98 = \frac{40}{(1 + YTM_3)} + \frac{40}{(1 + YTM_3)^2} + \frac{40 + 1000}{(1 + YTM_3)^3}$$

We can calculate the yield to maturity using a financial calculator or spreadsheet:

	N	I/Y	PV	PMT	FV
Given:	3		−986.98	40	1000
Solve for:		4.47			

Excel Formula: = *RATE(NPER,PMT,PV,FV)* = *RATE*(3,40,−986.98,1000)

To summarize, for the three-year bonds considered:

Coupon Rate	0%	4%	10%
YTM_3	4.50%	4.47%	4.44%

▶ **Evaluate**

Note that even though the bonds all have the same maturity, they have different yields. In fact, holding constant the maturity, the yield decreases as the coupon rate increases. We discuss why below.

two coupon-paying bonds with the same maturity may have different yields. By convention, practitioners always plot the yield of the most recently issued bonds, termed the on-the-run bonds. Using similar methods to those employed in this section, we can apply the Law of One Price to determine the zero-coupon bond yields using the coupon-paying yield curve. Thus, either type of yield curve provides enough information to value all other risk-free bonds.

PART 3

Valuation and the Firm

Valuation Principle Connection. One of the most important decisions facing a financial manager is the choice of which investments the corporation should make. These decisions fundamentally drive value in the corporation. We introduced the *NPV* decision rule in Chapter 3 as an application of the Valuation Principle. Now, in Chapter 7, we establish the usefulness of the *NPV* decision rule for making investment decisions. We also discuss alternative rules found in practice and their drawbacks. The process of allocating the firm's capital for investment is known as capital budgeting. In Chapter 8, we outline how to estimate a project's incremental cash flows, which then become the inputs to the *NPV* decision rule. Chapter 8 also provides a practical demonstration of the power of the discounting tools that were introduced in Chapters 4 and 5. Capital budgeting drives value in the firm, so in Chapter 9 we turn to valuing the ownership claim in the firm—its stock. We show how the Valuation Principle leads to several alternative methods for valuing a firm's equity by considering its future dividends, free cash flows, or how its value compares to that of similar publicly traded companies.

Investment Decision Rules

LEARNING OBJECTIVES

▶ Use the *NPV* rule to make investment decisions

▶ Understand alternative decision rules and their drawbacks

▶ Choose between mutually exclusive alternatives

▶ Rank projects when a company's resources are limited so that it cannot take all positive-*NPV* projects

notation

C_n	cash flow that arrives at date n	*NPV*	net present value
I	initial investment or initial capital committed to the project	*PV*	present value
IRR	internal rate of return	r	discount rate

Ryerson University, 2010

"We need to choose the best projects using all of the tools that my education in finance has taught me."

Jeff Blake, a graduate of Ryerson University in 2010, works as a financial analyst for Porter Airlines Inc., a Toronto-based airline specializing in short-haul flights in Canada and the United States. "We are a fast-growing company with a lot of positive-*NPV* projects. Sometimes we cannot do all the projects, so we need to choose the best projects using all of the tools that my education in finance has taught me."

In addition to *NPV*, companies often use other techniques to compare projects. Jeff's finance education comes in handy when evaluating potential investments. "At Porter we use *NPV*, *IRR*, payback period, and equivalent annual cost. All of them need to be considered together." While the *NPV* rule maximizes the value of the firm, sometimes small, quickly growing firms like Porter have shorter-term goals that need to be met. When resources are limited, taking all positive-*NPV* projects is not possible, so Jeff needs to decide which project will rank the highest. "We often take the positive-*NPV* projects that also have quick payback periods."

In addition to the investment decision rules, Jeff notes that other factors have to be considered when selecting which project will be undertaken. "We must take into account our opportunity cost of capital, given the risk of our business. As well, we need to make sure that the project fits with our firm's competitive strengths and overall corporate strategy."

In 2000, Toshiba and Sony began experimenting with new DVD technology, leading to Sony's decision to develop and produce Blu-ray high-definition DVD players and Toshiba's decision to develop and produce the HD-DVD player and format. So began an eight-year format war that ended in February 2008 when Toshiba decided to stop producing HD-DVD players and abandon the format. How did Toshiba and Sony managers arrive at the decision to invest in new DVD formats? How did Toshiba managers conclude that the best decision was to stop producing HD-DVD?

We focus in this chapter on the decision-making tools managers use to evaluate investment decisions. Examples of these decisions include new products, equipment purchases, and marketing campaigns. Earlier, in Chapter 3, we introduced the *NPV* rule. Although the *NPV* investment rule maximizes the value of the firm, some firms nevertheless use other techniques to evaluate investments and decide which projects to pursue. In this chapter, we explain some commonly used techniques—namely, the *payback rule* and the *internal rate of return rule* (*IRR*). In each case, we define the decision rule and compare decisions based on this rule to decisions based on the *NPV* rule. We also illustrate the circumstances in which each of the alternative rules is likely to lead to bad investment decisions. After establishing these rules in the context of a single, stand-alone project, we broaden our perspective to include evaluating multiple opportunities to select the best one. We conclude with a look at project selection when the firm faces limits on capital or managers' time.

7.1 Using the *NPV* Rule

We begin our discussion of investment decision rules by considering a take-it-or-leave-it decision involving a single, stand-alone project. By undertaking this project, the firm does not constrain its ability to take other projects. We initiate our analysis with the familiar *NPV* rule from Chapter 3: *When making an investment decision, take the alternative with the highest NPV. Choosing this alternative is equivalent to receiving its NPV in cash today.* The *NPV* rule is a direct application of the Valuation Principle and, as such, will always lead to the correct decision. In the case of a stand-alone project, the alternatives we are considering are to accept or reject a project. The *NPV* rule then implies that we should compare the project's *NPV* to zero (the *NPV* of rejecting the project and doing nothing). Thus, we should accept the project if its *NPV* is positive.

Organizing the Cash Flows and Computing the *NPV*

Researchers at Saskatchewan Fertilizer Ltd. (SFL) have made a breakthrough. They believe that they can produce a new, environmentally friendly fertilizer at a substantial cost saving over the company's existing line of fertilizer. The fertilizer will require a new plant that can be built immediately at a cost of $81.6 million. Financial managers estimate that the benefits of the new fertilizer will be $28 million per year, starting at the end of the first year and lasting for four years, as shown by the following timeline:

Month: 0   1   2   3   4

Cash flow: −$81.60   +$28   +$28   +$28   +$28

Thus, the cash flows are an immediate $81.6 million outflow followed by an annuity inflow of $28 million per year for four years. Therefore, given a discount rate, *r*, the *NPV* of this project is:

$$NPV = -81.6 + \frac{28}{1+r} + \frac{28}{(1+r)^2} + \frac{28}{(1+r)^3} + \frac{28}{(1+r)^4} \qquad (7.1)$$

We can also use the annuity formula from Chapter 4 to write the *NPV* as:

$$NPV = -81.6 + \frac{28}{r}\left(1 - \frac{1}{(1+r)^4}\right) \qquad (7.2)$$

To apply the *NPV* rule, we need to know the cost of capital. The financial managers responsible for this project estimate a cost of capital of 10% per year. If we replace *r* in Equation 7.1 or 7.2 with the project's cost of capital of 10%, we get an *NPV* of $7.2 million, which is positive. Recall that a net present value tells us the present value of the benefits (positive cash flows) net of the costs (negative cash flows) of the project. By putting everything into present values, the *NPV* puts all the costs and benefits on an equal footing for comparison. In this case, the benefits outweigh the costs by $7.2 million in present value. The *NPV* investment rule indicates that by making the investment, SFL will increase the value of the firm today by $7.2 million, so SFL should undertake this project.

The *NPV* Profile

NPV profile A graph of a project's *NPV* over a range of discount rates.

The *NPV* of the project depends on its appropriate cost of capital. Often, there may be some uncertainty regarding the project's cost of capital. In that case, it is helpful to compute an *NPV* **profile**, which graphs the project's *NPV* over a range of discount rates.

It is easiest to prepare the *NPV* profile using a spreadsheet such as Excel. We simply repeat our calculation of the *NPV* above using a range of different discount rates instead of only 10%. Figure 7.1 presents the *NPV* profile for SFL's project by plotting the *NPV* as a function of the discount rate, r.[1]

Notice that the *NPV* is positive only for discount rates that are less than 14% (the green shaded area in Figure 7.1). Referring to the graph and the accompanying data table, we see that at 14%, the *NPV* is zero. Recall from Chapter 4 that an investment's internal rate of return (*IRR*) is the discount rate that sets the net present value of the cash flows equal to zero. Thus, by constructing the *NPV* profile, we have determined that SFL's project has an *IRR* of 14%. As we showed in Chapter 4, we can also compute the *IRR*, without graphing the *NPV*, by using a financial calculator or a spreadsheet's *IRR* function (see the appendix to Chapter 4 for detailed calculator instructions).

Measuring Sensitivity with *IRR*

In our SFL example, the firm's managers provided the cost of capital. If you are unsure of your cost of capital estimate, it is important to determine how sensitive your analysis is to errors in this estimate. The *IRR* can provide this information. *IRR* measures the return of the project and is the discount rate that equates the *PV* of the project's inflows to the *PV* of the project's outflows (i.e., it is the disount rate that makes *NPV* = 0). For SFL, if the cost of capital estimate is more than the 14% *IRR*, the *NPV* will be negative (see the red shaded area in Figure 7.1). Therefore, as long as our estimate of the cost of

---

FIGURE 7.1   *NPV* of SFL's New Project

The graph in panel (b) shows the *NPV* as a function of the discount rate based on the data in panel (a). The *NPV* is positive, represented by the green-shaded area, only for discount rates that are less than 14%, the internal rate of return (*IRR*). Given the cost of capital of 10%, the project has a positive *NPV* of $7.2 million. The red-shaded area indicates discount rates above 14% *IRR* with negative *NPV*s.

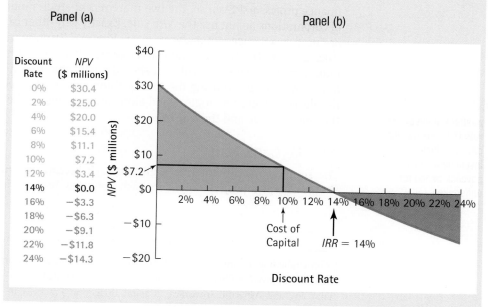

Discount Rate	NPV ($ millions)
0%	$30.4
2%	$25.0
4%	$20.0
6%	$15.4
8%	$11.1
10%	$7.2
12%	$3.4
14%	$0.0
16%	−$3.3
18%	−$6.3
20%	−$9.1
22%	−$11.8
24%	−$14.3

---

[1]In the appendix to this chapter, we show you how to create an *NPV* profile in Excel.

capital of 10% is within 4% of the true cost of capital, our decision to accept the project is correct. In general, what the difference between the cost of capital and the *IRR* tells us is the amount of estimation error in the cost of capital estimate that can exist without altering the original decision.

Alternative Rules Versus the *NPV* Rule

The *NPV* rule indicates that SFL should undertake the investment in fertilizer technology. As we evaluate alternative rules for project selection in the subsequent sections, keep in mind that sometimes other investment rules may give the same answer as the *NPV* rule, but at other times they may disagree. When the rules conflict, always base your decision on the *NPV* rule, which is the most accurate and reliable decision rule.

1. Explain the *NPV* rule for stand-alone projects.

2. How can you interpret the difference between the cost of capital and the *IRR*?

Alternative Decision Rules

Even though the *NPV* rule is the most accurate and reliable rule, in practice a wide variety of rules are applied, often in tandem with the *NPV* rule. In a 2001 study, John Graham and Campbell Harvey[2] found that 74.9% of the firms they surveyed used the *NPV* rule for making investment decisions. In a 1995 study, Vijay Jog and Ashwani Srivastava[3] found less than 50% of Canadian firms used *NPV*, but about 75% used some form of discounted cash flow (DCF) analysis. These results are substantially different from that found in a similar study in 1977 by L. J. Gitman and J. R. Forrester,[4] who found that only 9.8% of firms used the *NPV* rule. Business students in recent years have been listening to their finance professors! Even so, the two more recent studies indicate that over one-quarter of corporations do not use the *NPV* rule. Exactly why other capital budgeting techniques are used in practice is not always clear. Figure 7.2 summarizes the top three decision rules given in the Graham and Harvey survey. Because you may encounter these techniques in the business world, you should know what they are, how they are used, and how they compare to using the *NPV* decision rule. In this section, we examine alternative decision rules for single, stand-alone projects within the firm. The focus here is on the *payback rule* and the *IRR rule*.

The Payback Rule

payback investment rule Only projects that pay back their initial investment within the payback period are undertaken.

The simplest investment rule is the **payback investment rule**, which states that you should accept a project only if its cash flows pay back its initial investment within a

---

[2]John Graham and Campbell Harvey, "The Theory and Practice of Corporate Finance: Evidence from the Field," *Journal of Financial Economics* 60 (2001): 187–243.

[3]Vijay Jog and Ashwani Srivastava, "Capital Budgeting Practices in Corporate Canada," *Financial Practice and Education* 5 (1995): 37–43.

[4]L. J. Gitman and J. R. Forrester, Jr., "A Survey of Capital Budgeting Techniques Used by Major U.S. Firms," *Financial Management* 6 (1977): 66–71.

| **FIGURE 7.2** | The Most Popular Decision Rules Used by CFOs |

The bar graph shows the most popular decision rules used by CFOs in the Graham and Harvey 2001 survey. Many CFOs used more than one method, but no other methods were mentioned by more than half of CFOs.

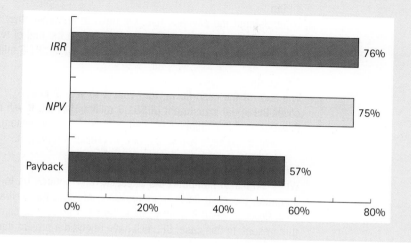

pre-specified period. The rule is based on the notion that an opportunity that pays back its initial investment quickly is a good idea. To apply the payback rule,

payback period The amount of time until the cash flows from a project offset the initial investment. The time it takes to pay back the initial investment.

1. Calculate the amount of time it takes to pay back the initial investment, called the **payback period**.

2. Accept the project if the payback period is less than a prespecified length of time—usually a few years.

3. Reject the project if the payback period is greater than that prespecified length of time.

For example, a firm might adopt any project with a payback period of less than two years.

Relying on the payback rule analysis in Example 7.1, SFL will reject the project. However, as we saw earlier, with a cost of capital of 10%, the *NPV* is $7.2 million. Following the payback rule would be a mistake because SFL will pass up a project worth $7.2 million.

The payback rule is not as reliable as the *NPV* rule because it (1) ignores the time value of money, (2) ignores cash flows after the payback period, and (3) lacks a decision criterion grounded in economics (what is the right number of years to require for a payback period?).[5] Some companies have addressed the first failing by computing the payback period using discounted cash flows (called discounted payback). However, this does not solve the fundamental problem, because the other two failings remain. Despite these failings, Graham and Harvey found that about 57% of the firms they surveyed reported using the payback rule as part of the decision-making process.

---

[5]A version of the payback rule called the discounted payback rule also exists. It uses the same methodology except the future cash flows are all discounted rather than kept at their nominal values. The discounted payback rule still suffers from the second and third problems indicated about the payback rule. The *NPV* rule avoids all these problems and is no more complex than the discounted payback rule; therefore, we recommend using the *NPV* rule.

EXAMPLE 7.1

Using the Payback Rule

Problem

Assume SFL requires all projects to have a payback period of two years or less. Would the firm undertake the fertilizer project under this rule?

Solution

▶ **Plan**

To implement the payback rule, we need to know whether the sum of the inflows from the project will exceed the initial investment before the end of two years. The project has inflows of $28 million per year and an initial investment of $81.6 million.

▶ **Execute**

The sum of the cash flows from year 1 to year 2 is $28 × 2 = $56 million, which will not cover the initial investment of $81.6 million. In fact, it will not be until year 3 that the cash flows exceed the initial investment ($28 × 3 = $84 million). Because the payback period for this project exceeds two years, SFL will reject the project.

▶ **Evaluate**

While simple to compute, the payback rule requires us to use an arbitrary cutoff period in summing the cash flows. Further, also note that the payback rule does not discount future cash flows. Instead it simply sums the cash flows and compares them to a cash outflow in the present. In this case, SFL will have rejected a project that would have increased the value of the firm.

Why do some companies consider the payback rule? The answer probably relates to its simplicity. This rule is typically used for small investment decisions—for example, whether to purchase a new copy machine or to service the old one. In such cases, the cost of making an incorrect decision might not be large enough to justify the time required to calculate the *NPV*. The appeal of the payback rule is that it favours short-term projects. Some firms are unwilling to commit capital to long-term investments. Also, if the required payback period is short (one to two years), then most projects that satisfy the payback rule will have a positive *NPV*. So firms might save effort by first applying the payback rule, and only if the rule rejects the project will they then take the time to compute the project's *NPV*.

The Internal Rate of Return Rule

internal rate of return (*IRR*) investment rule
A decision rule that accepts any investment opportunity where the *IRR* exceeds the opportunity cost of capital and otherwise rejects the opportunity.

Like the *NPV* rule, the **internal rate of return** *(IRR)* **investment rule** is based on the concept that if the return on the investment opportunity you are considering is greater than the return on other alternatives in the market with equivalent risk and maturity (i.e., the project's cost of capital), you should undertake the investment opportunity. We state the rule formally as follows:

> ***IRR Investment Rule:*** *Take any investment opportunity where IRR exceeds the opportunity cost of capital. Turn down any opportunity whose IRR is less than the opportunity cost of capital.*

The *IRR* investment rule will give the correct answer (that is, the same answer as the *NPV* rule) in many—but not all—situations. For instance, it gives the correct answer for SFL's fertilizer opportunity. From Figure 7.1, whenever the cost of capital is in the green area below the *IRR* (14%), the project has a positive *NPV* and you should undertake the investment. Table 7.1 summarizes our analysis of SFL's new project. The *NPV* and *IRR* rules agree, but using the payback rule with a required payback period of two years or less would cause SFL to reject the project.

TABLE 7.1	Summary of *NPV, IRR,* and Payback for SFL's New Project	
NPV at 10%	$7.2 million	Accept ($7.2 million > 0)
Payback period	3 years	Reject (3 years > 2 year required payback)
IRR	14%	Accept (14% > 10% cost of capital)

In general, the *IRR* rule works for a stand-alone project if all of the project's negative cash flows precede its positive cash flows. But in other cases, the *IRR* rule may disagree with the *NPV* rule and thus be incorrect. Let's examine several situations in which the *IRR* fails.

Unconventional Cash Flows. Star hockey player Maurice Lafleur is graduating from university with a degree in finance and is preparing for the NHL draft. Several companies have already approached him with endorsement contracts. Two competing sports drink companies are trying to sign him. QuenchIt offers him a single upfront payment of $1 million to exclusively endorse its sports drink for three years. PowerUp offers $500,000 per year, payable at the end of each of the next three years, to endorse its product exclusively. Which offer is better? One direct way to compare the two contracts is to realize that signing with QuenchIt causes Maurice to forgo the PowerUp contract, or $500,000 per year. Considering the risk of his alternative income sources and available investment opportunities, Maurice estimates his opportunity cost of capital to be 10%. The timeline of Maurice's investment opportunity is:

0	1	2	3
$1,000,000	−$500,000	−$500,000	−$500,000

The *NPV* of Maurice's investment opportunity is:

$$NPV = 1,000,000 - \frac{500,000}{1+r} - \frac{500,000}{(1+r)^2} - \frac{500,000}{(1+r)^3}$$

By setting the *NPV* equal to zero and solving for *r*, we find the *IRR*. We can use either a financial calculator or a spreadsheet to find the *IRR*:

	N	I/Y	PV	PMT	FV
Given:	3		1,000,000	−500,000	0
Solve for:		23.38			

Excel Formula: = RATE(NPER,PMT,PV,FV) = RATE(3,−500000,1000000,0)

The 23.38% *IRR* is larger than the 10% opportunity cost of capital. According to the *IRR* rule, Maurice should sign the deal. But what does the *NPV* rule say?

$$NPV = 1,000,000 - \frac{500,000}{1.1} - \frac{500,000}{1.1^2} - \frac{500,000}{1.1^3} = -\$243,426$$

At a 10% discount rate, the *NPV* is negative, so signing the deal would reduce Maurice's wealth. He should not sign the endorsement deal with QuenchIt; he should sign with PowerUp instead.

To resolve this conflict, we can prepare an *NPV* profile for the QuenchIt contract. Figure 7.3 plots the *NPV* of the investment opportunity for a range of discount rates. It shows that, no matter what the cost of capital is, the *IRR* rule and the *NPV* rule will give

| FIGURE 7.3 | *NPV* of Maurice Lafleur's $1 Million QuenchIt Deal |

When the benefits of an investment occur before the costs, the *NPV* is an increasing function of the discount rate. The *NPV* is positive in the green-shaded areas and negative in the red-shaded areas. Notice that the *NPV* is positive when the cost of capital is above 23.38%, the *IRR*, so the *NPV* and *IRR* rules conflict.

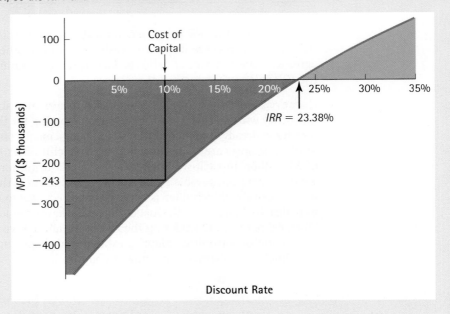

exactly opposite recommendations. That is, the *NPV* is positive only when the opportunity cost of capital is *above* 23.38% (the *IRR*). Maurice should accept the investment only when the opportunity cost of capital is greater than the *IRR*, the opposite of what the *IRR* rule recommends.

Figure 7.3 also illustrates the problem with using the *IRR* rule in this case. For most investment opportunities, expenses occur initially and cash is received later. In this case, Maurice gets cash *up front* from QuenchIt, but the forgone cash flows from PowerUp occurred later. It is as if Maurice borrowed money, and when you borrow money you prefer as *low* a rate as possible. Maurice's optimal rule is to borrow money as long as the rate at which he borrows is *less* than the cost of capital. Thus the *IRR* rule must be reversed for projects with unconventional cash flows (or borrowing-type cash flows).

Even though the conventional *IRR* rule fails to give the correct answer in this case, the *IRR* itself still provides useful information *in conjunction* with the *NPV* rule. As mentioned earlier, the *IRR* provides information on how sensitive the investment decision is to uncertainty in the cost of capital estimate. In this case, the difference between the cost of capital and the *IRR* is large—10% versus 23.38%. Maurice would have had to underestimate the cost of capital by 13.38% to make the *NPV* positive.

Multiple *IRRs*. Maurice has informed QuenchIt that it needs to sweeten the deal before he will accept it. In response, the company has agreed to make an additional payment of $600,000 in 10 years as deferred compensation for the long-term increase in sales that even a short-term endorsement by Maurice would bring. Should he accept or reject the new offer?

We begin with the new timeline:

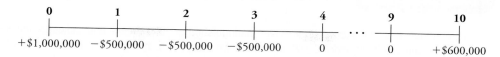

The *NPV* of Maurice's new investment opportunity is:

$$NPV = 1,000,000 - \frac{500,000}{1+r} - \frac{500,000}{(1+r)^2} - \frac{500,000}{(1+r)^3} + \frac{600,000}{(1+r)^{10}}$$

We can find the *IRR* for this investment opportunity by creating an *NPV* profile and noting where it crosses zero. Figure 7.4 plots the *NPV* of the opportunity at different discount rates. In this case, there are two *IRR*s—that is, there are two values of *r* that set the *NPV* equal to zero. You can verify this fact by substituting *IRR*s of 5.79% and 13.80% for *r* into the equation. Because there is more than one *IRR*, we cannot apply the *IRR* rule. It is also worth noting that you should take special care when using a spreadsheet or financial calculator to determine the *IRR*. Recall that both solve for the *IRR* through trial and error. In cases where there is more than one *IRR*, the spreadsheet or calculator will simply produce the first one that it finds, with no mention that there could be others! Thus, it always pays to create the *NPV* profile.

FIGURE 7.4

NPV of Maurice Lafleur's Sports Drink Deal with Additional Deferred Payments

The graph in panel (b) shows the *NPV* of Maurice's deal with additional deferred payment based on the data in panel (a). In this case, there are two *IRR*s, invalidating the *IRR* rule. If the opportunity cost of capital is either below 5.79% or above 13.80%, Maurice should accept the deal because the *NPV* is then positive, as indicated by the green-shaded areas. At any point between the two *IRR*s, the *NPV* is negative (see the red-shaded area).

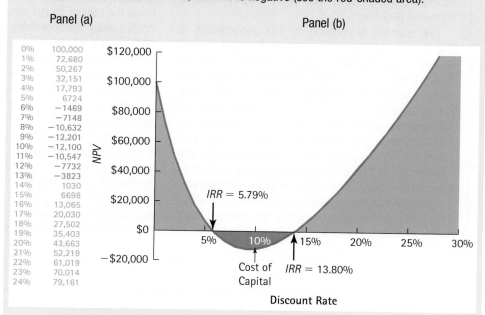

Common Mistake   *IRR* Versus the *IRR* Rule

Throughout this subsection, we have distinguished between the *IRR* itself and the *IRR* rule. While we have pointed out the shortcomings of using the *IRR* rule to make investment decisions, *the IRR itself remains a very useful tool*. The *IRR* measures the average return of the investment and indicates the sensitivity of the *NPV* to estimation error in the cost of capital. Thus, knowing the *IRR* can be very useful, but relying on it to make investment decisions can be hazardous.

For guidance, let's turn to the *NPV* rule. If the cost of capital were *either* below 5.79% or above 13.80%, Maurice should undertake the opportunity. But given his cost of capital of 10%, he should still turn it down. Notice that even though the *IRR* rule fails in this case, the two *IRR*s are still useful as bounds on the cost of capital estimate. If the cost of capital estimate is wrong, and it is actually smaller than 5.79% or larger than 13.80%, the decision not to pursue the project will change because it will have a positive *NPV*.

There is no easy fix for the *IRR* rule when there are multiple *IRR*s. Although the *NPV* is negative between the *IRR*s in this example, the reverse is also possible (see Figure 7.5). In that case, the project would have a positive *NPV* for discount rates between the *IRR*s rather than for discount rates lower or higher than the *IRR*s. Furthermore, there are situations in which more than two *IRR*s exist.[6] It is not uncommon for projects to have

Why Do Rules Other Than the *NPV* Rule Persist?

Professors Graham and Harvey found that a sizable minority of firms (25%) in their study do not use the *NPV* rule at all. In addition, about 50% of firms surveyed used the payback rule. Furthermore, it appears that most firms use both the *NPV* rule and the *IRR* rule. Why do firms use rules other than *NPV* if they can lead to erroneous decisions?

One possible explanation for this phenomenon is that Graham and Harvey's survey results might be misleading. CFOs who were using the *IRR* as a sensitivity measure in conjunction with the *NPV* rule might have checked both the *IRR* box and the *NPV* box on the survey. The question they were asked was, "How frequently does your firm use the following techniques when deciding which projects or acquisitions to pursue?" By computing the *IRR* and using it in conjunction with the *NPV* rule to estimate the sensitivity of their results, they might have felt they were using both techniques. Nevertheless, a significant minority of managers surveyed replied that they used only the *IRR* rule, so this explanation cannot be the whole story.

One common reason that managers give for using the *IRR* rule exclusively is that you do not need to know the opportunity cost of capital to calculate the *IRR*. On a superficial level, this is true: the *IRR* does not depend on the cost of capital. You may not need to know the cost of capital to calculate the *IRR*, but you certainly need to know the cost of capital when you apply the *IRR* rule. Consequently, the opportunity cost is as important to the *IRR* rule as it is to the *NPV* rule.

In our opinion, some firms use the *IRR* rule exclusively because the *IRR* sums up the attractiveness of an investment opportunity in a single number without requiring the person running the numbers to make an assumption about the cost of capital. However, if a CFO wants a brief summary of an investment opportunity but does not want her employee to make a cost of capital assumption, she can also request a plot of the *NPV* as a function of the discount rate. Neither this request nor a request for the *IRR* requires knowing the cost of capital, but the *NPV* profile has the distinct advantage of being much more informative and reliable.

---

[6]In general, there can be as many *IRR*s as the number of times the project's cash flows change signs over time. So, if you are analyzing a project and the signs of the cash flows change more than once, beware that there can be more than one *IRR*.

cash flows that can result in multiple *IRR*s. For instance, in many resource extraction projects (such as mining or oil extraction) there are upfront outflows required to get the project going, followed by inflows as the resource is extracted and sold, but then followed by outflows as the site is cleaned up and the land is restored to its original condition. This pattern of outflows, inflows, outflows may result in more than one *IRR*. In such situations, our only choice is to rely on the *NPV* rule.

Concept Check

3. How do you apply the payback rule?

4. Under what conditions will the *IRR* rule lead to the same decision as the *NPV* rule?

7.3 Choosing Between Projects

Thus far, we have considered only decisions in which the choice is either to accept or to reject a single, stand-alone project. Sometimes, however, a firm must choose just one project from among several possible projects. For example, a manager may be evaluating alternative package designs for a new product. The manager must choose only one of the designs. When choosing any one project excludes us from taking the other projects, we are facing **mutually exclusive projects**.

mutually exclusive projects Projects that compete with one another; by accepting one, you exclude the others.

When projects, such as the package designs, are mutually exclusive, it is not enough to determine which projects have positive *NPV*s. With mutually exclusive projects, the manager's goal is to rank the projects and choose only the best one. In this situation, the *NPV* rule provides a straightforward answer: *pick the project with the highest NPV.*

Because the *IRR* is a measure of the expected return of investing in the project, you might be tempted to extend the *IRR* investment rule to the case of mutually exclusive projects by picking the project with the highest *IRR*. Unfortunately, picking one project over another simply because it has a larger *IRR* can lead to mistakes. Problems arise when the mutually exclusive investments have differences in scale (require different initial investments) and when they have different cash flow patterns. We discuss each of these situations in turn.

Differences in Scale

Would you prefer a 200% return on $1 or a 10% return on $1 million? The former return certainly sounds impressive and gives you great bragging rights, but at the end of the day you make only $2. The latter opportunity may sound much more mundane, but you make $100,000. This comparison illustrates an important shortcoming of *IRR*: because it is a return, you cannot tell how much value has actually been created without knowing the basis for the return—a 10% *IRR* can have very different value implications for an initial investment of $1 million versus an initial investment of $100 million.

If a project has a positive *NPV*, then if we can double its size, its *NPV* will double: by the Valuation Principle, doubling the cash flows of an investment opportunity must make it worth twice as much. However, the *IRR* rule does not have this property—it is unaffected by the scale of the investment opportunity because the *IRR* measures the average return of the investment. Hence, the *IRR* rule cannot be used to compare projects of different scales. Let's illustrate this concept in the context of an example.

EXAMPLE 7.2

NPV and Mutually
Exclusive Projects

Problem

You own a small piece of commercial land near a university. You are considering what to do with it. You have recently received an offer to buy it for $220,000. You are also considering using the land for three possible alternatives: a bar, a coffee shop, and an apparel store. You assume that you would operate your choice indefinitely, eventually leaving the business to your children. You have collected the following information about the uses. What should you do?

	Initial Investment	Cash flow in the First Year	Growth Rate	Cost of Capital
Bar	$400,000	$60,000	3.5%	12%
Coffee shop	$200,000	$40,000	3%	10%
Apparel store	$500,000	$75,000	3%	13%

Solution

▶ **Plan**

Since you can do only one project (you have only one piece of land), these are mutually exclusive projects. To decide which project is most valuable, you need to rank them by *NPV*. Each of these projects (except for selling the land) has cash flows that can be valued as a growing perpetuity, so from Chapter 4, the present value of the inflows is $CF_1/(r - g)$. The *NPV* of each investment will be:

$$\frac{CF_1}{r - g} - \text{Initial Investment}$$

▶ **Execute**

The *NPV*s are:

$$\text{Bar}: \frac{\$60,000}{0.12 - 0.035} - \$400,000 = \$305,882$$

$$\text{Coffee Shop}: \frac{\$40,000}{0.10 - 0.03} - \$200,000 = \$371,429$$

$$\text{Apparel Store}: \frac{\$75,000}{0.13 - 0.03} - \$500,000 = \$250,000$$

So, the ranking is:

Alternative	NPV
Coffee shop	$371,429
Bar	$305,882
Apparel store	$250,000
Sell the land	$220,000

and you should choose the coffee shop.

▶ **Evaluate**

All of the alternatives have positive *NPV*s, but you can take only one of them, so you should choose the one that creates the most value. Even though the coffee shop has the lowest cash flows, its lower start-up cost, coupled with its lower cost of capital (it is less risky), make it the best choice.

Identical Scale. We begin by considering two mutually exclusive projects with the same scale. Marek is evaluating two investment opportunities. If he went into business with his girlfriend, he would need to invest $10,000 and the business would generate incremental cash flows of $6000 per year for three years. Alternatively, he could start a two-computer internet café. The computer setup will cost $10,000 and will generate $5000 for three years. The opportunity cost of capital for both opportunities is 12%, and both will require all his time, so Marek must choose between them. How valuable is each opportunity, and which one should Marek choose?

Let's consider both the *NPV* and *IRR* of each project. The timeline for the investment with Marek's girlfriend is:

0	1	2	3
−10,000	+6000	+6000	+6000

The *NPV* of the investment opportunity when $r = 12\%$ is:

$$NPV = -10,000 + \frac{6000}{1.12} + \frac{6000}{1.12^2} + \frac{6000}{1.12^3} = \$4411$$

We can determine the *IRR* of this investment by using a financial calculator or spreadsheet:

	N	I/Y	PV	PMT	FV
Given:	3		−10,000	6000	0
Solve for:		36.3			
Excel Formula:	= RATE(NPER,PMT,PV,FV)= RATE(3,6000,−10000,0)				

Thus, the *IRR* for Marek's investment in his girlfriend's business is 36.3%. The timeline for his investment in the internet café is:

0	1	2	3
−10,000	+5000	+5000	+5000

The *NPV* of the investment opportunity is:

$$NPV = -10,000 + \frac{5000}{1.12} + \frac{5000}{1.12^2} + \frac{5000}{1.12^3} = \$2009$$

The $2009 *NPV* of the internet café is lower than the $4411 *NPV* for his girlfriend's business, so Marek should join his girlfriend in business. Luckily, it appears that Marek does not need to choose between his chequebook and his relationship!

We could also compare *IRR*s. For the internet café, we would find that the *IRR* is 23.4%. The internet café has a lower *IRR* than the investment in his girlfriend's business. As Figure 7.5 shows, in this case the project with the higher *IRR* has the higher *NPV*.

Change in Scale. What happens if we change the scale of one of the projects? Marek's finance professor points out that, given the space available in the facility, he could just as easily install five times as many computers in the internet café. His setup cost would now be $50,000, and his annual cash flows would be $25,000. What should Marek do now?

FIGURE 7.5   *NPV* of Marek's Investment Opportunities with the Two-Computer Internet Café

The *NPV* of his girlfriend's business is always larger than the *NPV* of the two-computer internet café. The same is true for the *IRR*; the *IRR* of his girlfriend's business is 36.3%, while the *IRR* for the internet café is 23.4%.

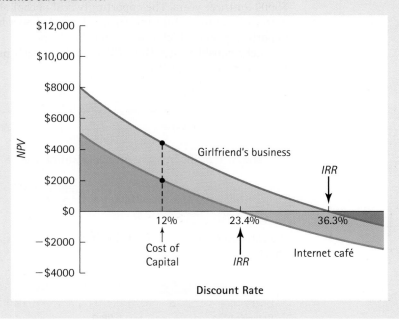

Note that the *IRR* is unaffected by the scale. Because we are scaling all the cash flows up by a factor of 5, a 10-computer internet café has exactly the same *IRR* as a 2-computer internet café, so his girlfriend's business still has a higher *IRR* than the internet café:

	N	I/Y	PV	PMT	FV
Given:	3		−50,000	25,000	0
Solve for:		36.3			
Excel Formula: = *RATE(NPER,PMT,PV,FV)* = *RATE*(3,25000,−50000,0)					

However, the *NPV* of the internet café does grow by the scale. It is five times larger:

$$NPV = -50{,}000 + \frac{25{,}000}{1.12} + \frac{25{,}000}{1.12^2} + \frac{25{,}000}{1.12^3} = \$10{,}046$$

Now Marek should invest in the 10-computer internet café. As Figure 7.6 shows, the *NPV* of the 10-computer internet café exceeds the *NPV* of going into business with his girlfriend whenever the cost of capital is less than 20%. In this case, even though the *IRR* of going into business with his girlfriend exceeds the *IRR* of the internet café, picking the investment opportunity with the higher *IRR* does not result in taking the opportunity with the higher *NPV*.

Percentage Return Versus Dollar Impact on Value. This result might seem coun-terintuitive, and you can imagine Marek having a difficult time explaining to his

| **FIGURE 7.6** | *NPV* of Marek's Investment Opportunities with the 10-Computer Internet Café |

As in Figure 7.5, the *IRR* of his girlfriend's business is 36.3%, while the *IRR* for the internet café is 23.4%. But in this case, the *NPV* of his girlfriend's business is larger than the *NPV* of the 10-computer internet café only for discount rates over 20%.

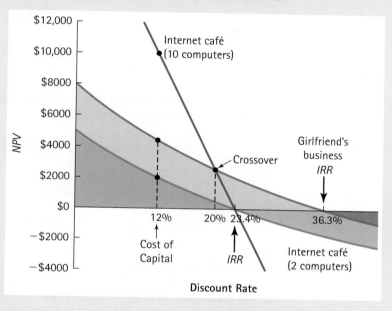

girlfriend why he is choosing a lower return over going into business with her. Why would anyone turn down an investment opportunity with a 36.3% return (*IRR*) in favour of one with only a 23.4% return? The answer is that the latter opportunity, the internet café, makes more money. Recall the comparison at the beginning of this section: a 200% return on $1 versus a 10% return on $1 million. We agreed that ranking the returns was not the same as ranking the value created. The *IRR* is a measure of the average return, which can be valuable information. When you are comparing mutually exclusive projects of different scale, however, you need to know the dollar impact on value—the *NPV*.

| **EXAMPLE 7.3** | **Problem** |

IRR of Incremental Cash Flows and Computing the Crossover Point

Problem

Solve for the crossover point for Marek from Figure 7.6.

Solution

▶ **Plan**

The crossover point is the discount rate that makes the *NPV* of the two alternatives equal. We can find the discount rate by setting the equations for the *NPV* of each project equal to each other and solving for the discount rate. If we take the cash flows of the larger project and subtract the cash flows of the smaller project, we have the incremental cash flows of doing the large project instead of the small project. The crossover point is the *IRR* of these incremental cash flows, and at this *IRR*, the difference in *NPV*s is zero.

▶ **Execute**

Setting the difference equal to 0,

$$NPV = -50,000 + \frac{25,000}{1+r} + \frac{25,000}{(1+r)^2} + \frac{25,000}{(1+r)^3}$$

$$- \left(-10,000 + \frac{6000}{(1+r)} + \frac{6000}{(1+r)^2} + \frac{6000}{(1+r)^3} \right) = 0$$

$$-40,000 + \frac{19,000}{(1+r)} + \frac{19,000}{(1+r)^2} + \frac{19,000}{(1+r)^3} = 0$$

As you can see, solving for the crossover point is just like solving for the *IRR*, so we will need to use a financial calculator or spreadsheet:

	N	I/Y	PV	PMT	FV
Given:	3		−40,000	19,000	0
Solve for:		20.04			
	Excel Formula: = RATE(NPER,PMT,PV,FV) = RATE(3,19000,−40000,0)				

We find that the crossover occurs at a discount rate of 20% (20.04%, to be exact).

▶ **Evaluate**

Just as the *NPV* of a project tells us the value impact of taking the project, so the difference of the *NPV*s of two alternatives tells us the *incremental* impact of choosing one project over another. The crossover point is the *IRR* of the incremental cash flows determined by taking the larger project instead of the smaller project. It is the discount rate at which we would be indifferent about which of the two projects to take, because the incremental value of choosing one over the other would be zero.

We can use the *IRR* of the incremental cash flows as an alternative to comparing the *NPV*s of the large ansd small projects. Effectively, if we apply the *IRR* rule to the incremental cash flows, we are analyzing whether the decision to switch from the small to the large project is correct. If the *IRR* of the incremental cash flows exceeds our hurdle rate (in this case, the cost of capital of 12%), then the decision is correct. Given that the *IRR* of the incremental cash flows is 20%, our *IRR* rule applied to the incremental cash flows agrees with our analysis of comparing the *NPV*s for the small and large projects.

Timing of the Cash Flows

Even when projects have the same scale, the *IRR* may lead you to rank them incorrectly due to differences in the timing of the cash flows. The reason for this is that the *IRR* is expressed as a return, but the dollar value of earning a given return—and therefore the *NPV*—depends on how long the return is earned. Consider a high-*IRR* project with cash flows paid back quickly. It may have a lower *NPV* than a project with a lower *IRR* whose cash flows are paid back over a longer period. This sensitivity to timing is another reason why you cannot use the *IRR* to choose between mutually exclusive investments. To see this in the context of an example, let's return to Marek's internet café.

Marek believes that after starting the internet café, he may be able to sell his stake in the business at the end of the first year for $40,000 (he will continue to stay on and manage the business after he sells). Thus, counting his first-year profit of $25,000, he would earn a total of $65,000 after one year. In that case, the timeline is

```
        0            1
        |            |
     −$50,000    +$65,000
```

INTERVIEW WITH
Dick Grannis

*D*ick Grannis is senior vice president and treasurer of Qualcomm Incorporated, a world leader in digital wireless communications technology and semiconductors. Qualcomm technologies are used in many mobile phones, including some of Research In Motion's BlackBerries and Apple's iPhones. He joined the company in 1991 and oversees its $10 billion cash investment portfolio. He works primarily on investment banking, capital structure, and international finance. Here, he talks about project evaluation within Qualcomm and the discount rates Qualcomm uses for the project's forecasted incremental cash flows.

QUESTION: *Qualcomm has a wide variety of products in different business lines. How does your capital budgeting process for new products work?*

ANSWER: Qualcomm evaluates new projects (such as new products, equipment, technologies, research and development, acquisitions, and strategic investments) by using traditional financial measurements, including DCF models, *IRR* levels, the time needed to reach cumulative positive cash flows, the short-term impact of the investment on our reported net earnings, and tracking the maximum amount of funding the project will require. For strategic investments, we consider the possible value of financial, competitive, technology, and/or market value enhancements to our core businesses—even if those benefits cannot be quantified. Overall, we make capital budgeting decisions based on a combination of objective analyses and our own business judgment.

We do not engage in capital budgeting and analysis if the project represents an immediate and necessary requirement for our business operations. One example is new software or production equipment to start a project that has already received approval.

We are also mindful of the opportunity costs of allocating our internal engineering resources on one project versus another project. We view this as a constantly challenging but worthwhile exercise, because we have many attractive opportunities but limited resources to pursue them.

QUESTION: *How often does Qualcomm evaluate its discount rates and what factors does it consider in setting them? How do you allocate capital across areas and regions and assess the risk of international investments?*

ANSWER: Qualcomm encourages its financial planners to utilize hurdle (or discount) rates that vary according to the risk of the particular project. We expect a rate of return commensurate with the project's risk. Our finance staff considers a wide range of discount rates and chooses one that fits the project's expected risk profile and time horizon. The range can be from 6% to 8% for relatively safe investments in the domestic market to 50% or more for equity investments in foreign markets that may be illiquid and difficult to predict. We reevaluate our hurdle rates at least every year.

We analyze key factors including (1) market adoption risk (whether or not customers will buy the new product or service at the price and volume we expect), (2) technology development risk (whether or not we can develop and patent the new product or service as expected), (3) execution risk (whether we can launch the new product or service cost effectively and on time), and (4) dedicated asset risk (the amount of resources that must be consumed to complete the work).

QUESTION: *How are projects categorized and how are the hurdle rates for new projects determined? What would happen if Qualcomm simply evaluated all new projects against the same hurdle rate?*

ANSWER: We primarily categorize projects by risk level, but we also categorize projects by the expected time horizon. We consider short-term and long-term projects to balance our needs and achieve our objectives. For example, immediate projects and opportunities may demand a great amount of attention, but we also stay focused on long-term projects because they often create greater long-term value for stockholders.

Discussion Questions

Grannis mentions that Qualcomm does not do analysis if the project is required by an already approved project.

1. Should such potential requirements of a project enter into the investment decision process somewhere? If so, where?

If we were to evaluate all new projects against the same hurdle rate, then our business planners would, by default, consistently choose to invest in the highest risk projects, because those projects would appear to have the greatest expected returns in DCF models or *IRR* analyses. That approach would probably not work well for very long.

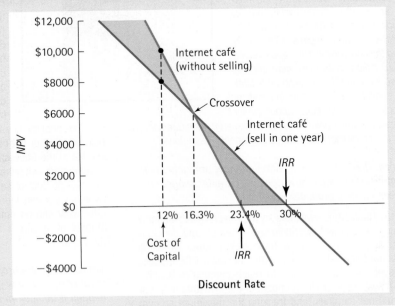

FIGURE 7.7

NPV with and without Selling

The *IRR* from selling after one year (30%) is larger than the *IRR* without selling (23.4%). However, the *NPV* from selling after one year exceeds the *NPV* without selling only for discount rates that are in excess of 16.3% (see the yellow-shaded area vs. the blue-shaded area). Thus, given a cost of capital of 12%, it is better not to sell the internet café after one year, despite the higher *IRR*.

Figure 7.7 plots the *NPV* profile for the café with and without selling it after one year. If Marek sells, *the NPV* profile crosses the horizontal axis at 30%, which is its *IRR*. The *IRR* for the café if he does not sell is still 23.4%. Therefore, if Marek picks the alternative with the higher *IRR*, he will sell. However, since the height of each line indicates the *NPV* of that decision, we can see that his *NPV*, given a 12% cost of capital, is higher if he chooses not to sell. (In fact, the *NPV* is higher as long as the cost of capital is less than 16.3%.) The intuition is as follows: while the 30% *IRR* from selling is high, this return is earned only in the first year. While the 23.4% *IRR* from not selling is not as high, it is still attractive relative to the cost of capital, and it is earned over a longer period. Again, only by comparing the *NPV* can we determine which option is truly more valuable.

The Bottom Line on *IRR*. As these examples make clear, picking the investment opportunity with the largest *IRR* can lead to a mistake. In general, it is dangerous to use the *IRR* in cases where you are choosing between projects, or any time when your decision to accept or reject one project would affect your decision on another project. In such a situation, always rely on *NPV*.

Concept Check

5. What is the most reliable way to choose between mutually exclusive projects?

6. For mutually exclusive projects, explain why picking one project over another because it has a larger *IRR* can lead to mistakes.

7.4 Evaluating Projects with Different Lives

Often, a company will need to choose between two solutions to the same problem. A complication arises when those solutions last for different periods of time. For example, a firm could be considering two vendors for its internal network servers. Each vendor offers the same level of service, but they use different equipment. Vendor A offers a more expensive server with lower per-year operating costs that it guarantees to last for three years. Vendor B offers a less expensive server with higher per-year operating costs that it will guarantee for only two years. The costs are shown in Table 7.2 along with the present value of the costs of each option, discounted at the 10% cost of capital for this project.

Note that all of the cash flows are negative, and so is the present value. This is a choice of an internal server, where the project must be taken and the benefits are diffuse (the company could not function effectively without an internal network). Thus, we are trying to minimize the cost of providing this service for the company. Table 7.2 shows that option A is more expensive on a present value basis (–$12,490 versus –$10,470). However, the comparison is not that simple: option A lasts for three years while option B only lasts for two. The decision comes down to whether it is worth paying $2000 more for option A to get the extra year. One method that is used to evaluate alternatives such as these that have different lives is to compute the **equivalent annual annuity** for each project, which is the level annual cash flow with the same present value as the cash flows of the project. The intuition is that we can think of the cost of each solution as the constant annual cost that gives us the same present value of the lumpy cash flows of buying and operating the server.

equivalent annual annuity The level annual cash flow that has the same present value as the cash flows of a project. Used to evaluate alternative projects with different lives.

TABLE 7.2

Cash Flows ($ Thousands) for Network Server Options

Year	PV at 10%	0	1	2	3
A	−12.49	−10	−1	−1	−1
B	−10.47	−7	−2	−2	

When you have a level cash flow at a constant interval, you are dealing with an annuity, and that is exactly how to approach this problem. We know the present value (–$12.49), the number of years (3), and the discount rate (10%). We need to solve for the cash flow of an equivalent annuity. Recall from Chapter 4 that the formula (Equation 4.8) for solving for the cash flow in an annuity is

$$\text{Cash Flow} = \frac{\text{Present Value}}{\frac{1}{r}\left(1 - \frac{1}{(1+r)^N}\right)} = \frac{-12.49}{\frac{1}{0.10}\left(1 - \frac{1}{(1.10)^3}\right)} = -5.02$$

So, buying and operating server A is equivalent to spending $5020 per year to have a network server. We can repeat the calculation for server B, but for a two-year annuity because server B has only a two-year life (the change in exponent is highlighted):

$$\text{Cash Flow} = \frac{\text{Present Value}}{\frac{1}{r}\left(1 - \frac{1}{(1+r)^N}\right)} = \frac{-10.47}{\frac{1}{0.10}\left(1 - \frac{1}{(1.10)^2}\right)} = -6.03$$

Therefore, we can reinterpret the cost of each alternative as shown in Table 7.3:

TABLE 7.3	Cash Flows ($ Thousands) for Network Server Options, Expressed as Equivalent Annual Annuities				
Year	PV at 10%	0	1	2	3
A	−12.49	0	−5.02	−5.02	−5.02
B	−10.47	0	−6.03	−6.03	

Now we are ready to choose between the two servers. Server A is equivalent to spending $5020 per year and server B is equivalent to spending $6030 per year to have a network server. Seen in this light, server A appears to be the less expensive solution.

Important Considerations When Using the Equivalent Annual Annuity

Although server A appears to be the lowest-cost alternative, there are a number of factors to consider before making our decision.

Required Life. We computed the equivalent annual cost of server A assuming we would use it for three years. But suppose it is likely that we will not need the server in the

---

EXAMPLE 7.4	**Problem**

Computing an Equivalent Annual Annuity

You are about to sign the contract for server A from Table 7.2 when a third vendor approaches you with another option that lasts for four years. The cash flows for server C are given below. Should you choose the new option or stick with server A?

Server C   −14   −1.2   −1.2   −1.2   −1.2

Solution

▶ **Plan**

To compare this new option to server A, we need to put server C on an equal footing by computing its annual cost. We can do this by:

1. Computing its *NPV* at the 10% discount rate we used above.
2. Computing the equivalent four-year annuity with the same present value.

▶ **Execute**

$$PV = -14 - 1.2\left[\frac{1}{0.10} - \frac{1}{0.10(1.10)^4}\right] = -17.80$$

$$\text{Cash Flow} = \frac{PV}{\left[\dfrac{1}{0.10} - \dfrac{1}{0.10(1.10)^4}\right]} = \frac{-17.80}{\left[\dfrac{1}{0.10} - \dfrac{1}{0.10(1.10)^4}\right]} = -5.62$$

Server C's annual cost of 5.62 is greater than the annual cost of server A (5.02), so we should still choose server A.

▶ **Evaluate**

In this case, the additional cost associated with purchasing and maintaining server C is not worth the extra year we get from choosing it. By putting all of these costs into an equivalent annuity, the equivalent annuity tool allows us to see that.

third year. Then we would be paying for something that we would not use. In that case, it may be cheaper to purchase server B, which provides coverage for the years we will need it at a lower total cost.[7]

Replacement Cost. When we compare servers A and B based on their equivalent annual cost, we are assuming that the cost of servers will not change over time. But suppose we believe a dramatic change in technology will reduce the cost of servers by the third year to an annual cost of $2000 per year. Then server B has the advantage that we can upgrade to the new technology sooner. The cost of three years of service from either server in this case can be represented as follows:

Year	PV at 10%	0	1	2	3
A	−12.49	0	−5.02	−5.02	−5.02
B	−11.97	0	−6.03	−6.03	−2.00

Therefore, when cost or performance is expected to change significantly over time, it may be cheaper to purchase server B despite its higher equivalent annual cost because it gives us the option to switch to the new technology sooner.

Concept Check

7. Explain why choosing the option with the highest *NPV* is not always correct when the options have different lives.

8. What issues should you keep in mind when choosing among projects with different lives?

7.5 Choosing Among Projects When Resources Are Limited

In the previous sections, we compared projects that had *identical* resource needs. For example, in Marek's case, we assumed that both the internet café and his girlfriend's business demanded 100% of his time. In this section, we develop an approach for situations in which the choices have differing resource needs.

Evaluating Projects with Different Resource Requirements

In some situations, different investment opportunities demand different amounts of a particular resource. If there is a fixed supply of the resource so that you cannot undertake all possible opportunities, simply picking the highest *NPV* opportunity might not lead to the best decision.

We usually assume that you will be able to finance all positive-*NPV* projects that you have. In reality, managers work within the constraint of a budget that restricts the amount of capital they may invest in a given period. Such a constraint would force a manager to choose among positive-*NPV* projects to maximize the total *NPV* while staying within her budget. For example, assume you are considering the three projects in Table 7.4, and that you have a budget of $200 million. Table 7.4 shows the *NPV* of each project and the initial investment that each project requires. Project A has the highest *NPV* but uses up the entire budget. Projects B and C can *both* be undertaken (together

---

[7]In this scenario, we should also consider any salvage value that server A might have if we sold it after two years.

Project	NPV ($ millions)	Initial Investment ($ millions)	NPV/Initial Investment
A	100	200	0.500
B	75	120	0.625
C	70	80	0.875

TABLE 7.4

Possible Projects for $200 Million Budget

they use the entire budget), and their combined *NPV* exceeds the *NPV* of project A; thus, you should initiate them both. Together, their *NPV* is $145 million compared with just $100 million for project A alone.

Profitability Index. Note that in the last column of Table 7.4 we included the ratio of the project's *NPV* to its initial investment. We can interpret this as telling us that for every dollar invested in project A, we will generate 50 cents in value (over and above the dollar investment).[8] Both projects B and C generate higher *NPV*s per dollar invested than project A, consistent with the fact that, given our budget of $200 million, projects B and C together created a higher *NPV* than just project A.

In this simple example, identifying the optimal combination of projects to undertake is straightforward. In actual situations replete with many projects and resources, finding the optimal combination can be difficult. Practitioners often use the **profitability index** to help identify the optimal combination of projects to undertake in such situations:

profitability index

Measures the *NPV* per unit of resource consumed.

Profitability Index

$$\text{Profitability Index} = \frac{\text{Value Created}}{\text{Resource Consumed}} = \frac{NPV}{\text{Resource Consumed}} \tag{7.3}$$

The profitability index measures the "bang for your buck"—that is, the value created in terms of *NPV* per unit of resource consumed. After computing the profitability index, we can rank projects based on it. Starting with the project with the highest index, we move down the ranking, taking all projects until the resource is consumed. In Table 7.4, the ratio in the last column is the profitability index. Note how the profitability index rule would correctly select projects B and C.

Shortcomings of the Profitability Index. Although the profitability index is simple to compute and use, in some situations it does not give an accurate answer. For example, suppose in Example 7.5 that NetIt has an additional small project with an *NPV* of only $100,000 that requires three engineers. The profitability index in this case is 0.1/3 = 0.03, so this project would appear at the bottom of the ranking. However, notice that 3 of the 190 employees are not being used after the first four projects are selected. As a result, it would make sense to take on this project even though it would be ranked last, because it would exactly use up our constraint.

In general, because the profitability index already includes the cost of capital (in computing the *NPV*), it would be better if the firm could raise additional funding to relieve the constraint. If the constraint is something else (such as engineers or physical capacity), there may be no way to relieve the constraint quickly enough to avoid having to choose among projects. Nonetheless, because all of the projects being ranked are value-increasing positive-*NPV* projects, it is still better to focus on relieving the constraint.

---

[8]Sometimes, practitioners add 1 to this ratio such that the interpretation would be that every dollar invested returned $1.50. Leaving off the additional 1 allows the ratio to be applied to resources other than budgets, as we show in Example 7.5.

EXAMPLE 7.5

Profitability Index
with a Human
Resource Constraint

Problem

Your division at NetIt, a large networking company, has put together a project proposal to develop a new home networking router. The expected *NPV* of the project is $17.7 million, and the project will require 50 software engineers. NetIt has a total of 190 engineers available and is unable to hire additional qualified engineers in the short run. Therefore, the router project must compete with the following other projects for these engineers' attention:

Project	NPV ($ millions)	Engineering Headcount
Router	17.7	50
Project A	22.7	47
Project B	8.1	44
Project C	14.0	40
Project D	11.5	61
Project E	20.6	58
Project F	12.9	32
Total	107.5	332

How should NetIt prioritize these projects?

Solution

▶ **Plan**

The goal is to maximize the total *NPV* that we can create with 190 engineers (at most). We can use Equation 7.3 to determine the profitability index for each project. In this case, since engineers are our limited resource, we will use the engineering headcount in the denominator. Once we have the profitability index for each project, we can sort them based on the index.

▶ **Execute**

Project	NPV ($ millions)	Engineering Headcount (EHC)	Profitability Index (NPV per EHC)	Cumulative EHC Required
Project A	22.7	47	0.483	47
Project F	12.9	32	0.403	79 (47 + 32)
Project E	20.6	58	0.355	137 (79 + 58)
Router	17.7	50	0.354	187 (137 + 50)
Project C	14.0	40	0.350	
Project D	11.5	61	0.189	
Project B	8.1	44	0.184	

We now assign the resource to the projects in descending order according to the profitability index. The final column shows the cumulative use of the resource as each project is taken on until the resource is used up. To maximize *NPV* within the constraint of 190 engineers, NetIt should choose the first four projects on the list.

> ▶ **Evaluate**
>
> By ranking projects in terms of their *NPV* per engineer, we find the most value we can create, given our 190 engineers. There is no other combination of projects that will create more value without using more engineers than we have. This ranking also shows us exactly what the engineering constraint costs us—this resource constraint forces NetIt to forgo three otherwise valuable projects (C, D, and B) with a total *NPV* of $33.6 million.

A more serious problem occurs when multiple resource constraints apply. In this case, the profitability index can break down completely. The only surefire way to find the best combination of projects is to search through all of them. Although this process may sound exceedingly time-consuming, there are more advanced techniques that can tackle this specific kind of problem.[9] By using these techniques on a computer, the solution can usually be obtained almost instantaneously.

Concept Check

9. Explain why picking the project with the highest *NPV* might not be optimal when you evaluate projects with different resource requirements.

10. What does the profitability index tell you?

 ## Putting It All Together

In Table 7.5, we summarize the decision rules outlined in this chapter. As a financial manager, you are likely to run into many different types of investment decision rules in your career. In fact, in the interview in this chapter, the treasurer of Qualcomm mentions five different decision rules his company uses when evaluating investments. We have demonstrated that while alternative decision rules may sometimes (or even often) agree with the *NPV* decision rule, only the *NPV* decision rule is always correct. This is because the *NPV* provides you with a dollar-value measure of the impact of the project on shareholder wealth. Thus, it is the only rule that is directly tied to your goal of maximizing shareholder wealth. Computing the *IRR* can be a useful supplement to the *NPV* because knowing the *IRR* allows you to gauge how sensitive your decision is to errors in your discount rate. Some decision metrics are much simpler to calculate, such as the payback period. However, you should never rely on an alternative rule to make investment decisions.

If you are employed by a firm that uses the *IRR* rule (or another rule) exclusively, our advice is to always calculate the *NPV*. If the two rules agree, you can feel comfortable reporting the *IRR* rule recommendation. If they do not agree, you should investigate—by using the concepts in this chapter—why the *IRR* rule failed. Once you have identified the problem, you can alert your superiors to it and perhaps persuade them to adopt the *NPV* rule.

---

[9]Specifically, there are techniques called integer and linear programming that can be used to find the combination with the highest *NPV* when there are multiple constraints that must be satisfied. These methods are available, for example, in many spreadsheet programs.

TABLE 7.5	Summary of Decision Rules

NPV

Definition	▶ The difference between the present value of an investment's benefits and the present value of its costs
Rule	▶ Take any investment opportunity where the *NPV* is positive; turn down any opportunity where it is negative
Advantages	▶ Corresponds directly to the impact of the project on the firm's value ▶ Direct application of the Valuation Principle
Disadvantages	▶ Relies on an accurate estimate of the discount rate ▶ Can be time-consuming to compute

IRR

Definition	▶ The interest rate that sets the net present value of the cash flows equal to zero; the average return of the investment
Rule	▶ Take any investment opportunity where *IRR* exceeds the opportunity cost of capital; turn down any opportunity whose *IRR* is less than the opportunity cost of capital
Advantages	▶ Related to the *NPV* rule and usually yields the same (correct) decision for conventional projects.
Disadvantages	▶ Hard to compute ▶ Multiple *IRR*s or no *IRR* leads to ambiguity ▶ Special care must be taken to choose among projects. ▶ Rule must be reversed for unconventional (borrowing-type) projects.

Payback Period

Definition	▶ The amount of time it takes to pay back the initial investment
Rule	▶ Accept the project if the payback period is less than a prespecified length of time (usually a few years); otherwise, reject it
Advantages	▶ Simple to compute ▶ Favours liquidity
Disadvantages	▶ No guidance as to correct payback cutoff period ▶ Ignores cash flows after the cutoff completely ▶ Often an incorrect decision will result

Profitability Index

Definition	▶ *NPV*/resource consumed
Rule	▶ Rank projects according to their profitability index based on the constrained resource and move down the list accepting value-creating projects until the resource is exhausted
Advantages	▶ Uses the *NPV* to measure the benefit ▶ Allows projects to be ranked on value created per unit of resource consumed
Disadvantages	▶ Breaks down when there is more than one constraint ▶ Requires careful attention to make sure the constrained resource is completely used

MyFinanceLab

Here is what you should know after reading this chapter. MyFinanceLab will help you identify what you know, and where to go when you need to practice.

Key Points and Equations	Terms	Online Practice Opportunities
7.1 Using the *NPV* Rule ▶ If your objective is to maximize wealth, the *NPV* rule always gives the correct answer. ▶ The difference between the cost of capital and the *IRR* is the maximum amount of estimation error that can exist in the cost of capital estimate without altering the original decision.	*NPV* profile, p. 206	MyFinanceLab Study Plan 7.1 Using Excel: Making an *NPV* Profile
7.2 Alternative Decision Rules ▶ Payback investment rule: Calculate the amount of time it takes to pay back the initial investment (the payback period). If the payback period is less than a prespecified length of time, accept the project. Otherwise, turn it down. ▶ *IRR* investment rule: Take any investment opportunity whose *IRR* exceeds the opportunity cost of capital. Turn down any opportunity whose *IRR* is less than the opportunity cost of capital. ▶ The conventional *IRR* rule may give the wrong answer if used to analyze a project with unconventional cash flows (a borrowing-type project with an upfront inflow). When there are multiple *IRR*s or the *IRR* does not exist, the *IRR* rule cannot be used to make a decision.	internal rate of return (*IRR*) investment rule, p. 210 payback investment rule, p. 208 payback period, p. 209	MyFinanceLab Study Plan 7.2 Interactive *IRR* Analysis
7.3 Choosing Between Projects ▶ When choosing among mutually exclusive investment opportunities, pick the opportunity with the highest *NPV*. Do not use *IRR* to choose among mutually exclusive investment opportunities.	mutually exclusive projects, p. 215	MyFinanceLab Study Plan 7.3
7.4 Evaluating Projects with Different Lives ▶ When choosing among projects with different lives, you need a standard basis of comparison. First compute an annuity with a present value equivalent to the *NPV* of each project. Then the projects can be compared on their cost or value created *per year*.	equivalent annual annuity, p. 223	MyFinanceLab Study Plan 7.4

7.5 Choosing Among Projects When Resources Are Limited

▶ When choosing among projects competing for the same resource, rank the projects by their profitability indices and pick the set of projects with the highest profitability indices that can still be undertaken given the limited resource.

Profitability index, p. 226

MyFinanceLab
Study Plan 7.5

$$\text{Profitability Index} = \frac{\text{Value Created}}{\text{Resource Consumed}}$$

$$= \frac{NPV}{\text{Resource Consumed}} \quad (7.3)$$

Review Questions

1. How is the *NPV* rule related to the goal of maximizing shareholder wealth?

2. What is the intuition behind the payback rule? What are some of its drawbacks?

3. What is the intuition behind the *IRR* rule? What are some of its drawbacks?

4. Under what conditions will the *IRR* rule and the *NPV* rule give the same accept/reject decision?

5. When is it possible to have multiple *IRRs*?

6. Why is it generally a bad idea to use *IRR* to choose between mutually exclusive projects?

7. When should you use the equivalent annual annuity?

8. What is the intuition behind the profitability index?

Problems

All problems in this chapter are available in MyFinanceLab. An asterisk (*) indicates problems with a higher level of difficulty.

Using the *NPV* Rule

 1. Your factory has been offered a contract to produce a part for a new printer. The contract would last for three years, and your cash flows from the contract would be $5 million per year. Your upfront setup costs to be ready to produce the part would be $8 million. Your discount rate for this contact is 8%.
   a. What does the *NPV* rule say you should do?
   b. If you take the contract, what will be the change in the value of your firm?

2. You are considering opening a new plant. The plant will cost $100 million up front and will take one year to build. After that, it is expected to produce profits of $30 million at the end of every year of production. The cash flows are expected to last forever. Calculate the *NPV* of this investment opportunity if your cost of capital is 8%. Should

you make the investment? Calculate the *IRR* and use it to determine the maximum deviation allowable in the cost of capital estimate to leave the decision unchanged.

 3. Bill Clinton reportedly was paid $10 million to write his book *My Way*. The book took three years to write. In the time he spent writing, Clinton could have been paid to make speeches. Given his popularity, assume that he could earn $8 million per year (paid at the end of the year) speaking instead of writing. Assume his cost of capital is 10% per year.

    a. What is the *NPV* of agreeing to write the book (ignoring any royalty payments)?

    b. Assume that, once the book is finished, it is expected to generate royalties of $5 million in the first year (paid at the end of the year), and these royalties are expected to decrease at a rate of 30% per year in perpetuity. What is the *NPV* of the book with the royalty payments?

 *4. FastTrack Bikes, Inc. is thinking of developing a new composite road bike. Development will take 6 years, and the cost is $200,000 per year. Once in production, the bike is expected to make $300,000 per year for 10 years.

    a. Calculate the *NPV* of this investment opportunity. Should the company make the investment?

    b. Calculate the *IRR* and use it to determine the maximum deviation allowable in the cost of capital estimate to leave the decision unchanged.

    c. How long must development last to change the decision?

Assume the cost of capital is 14%.

    d. Calculate the *NPV* of this investment opportunity. Should the company make the investment?

    e. How much must this cost of capital estimate deviate to change the decision?

    f. How long must development last to change the decision?

 5. OpenSeas, Inc. is evaluating the purchase of a new cruise ship. The ship would cost $500 million, but would operate for 20 years. OpenSeas expects annual cash flows from operating the ship to be $70 million and its cost of capital is 12%.

    a. Prepare an *NPV* profile of the purchase.

    b. Identify the *IRR* on the graph.

    c. Should OpenSeas go ahead with the purchase?

    d. How far off could OpenSeas' cost of capital estimate be before your purchase decision would change?

Alternative Decision Rules

    6. You are a real estate agent thinking of placing a sign advertising your services at a local bus stop. The sign will cost $5000 and will be posted for one year. You expect that it will generate additional revenue of $500 per month. What is the payback period?

 7. Does the *IRR* rule agree with the *NPV* rule in Problem 1?

 8. How many *IRR*s are there in part (a) of Problem 3? Does the *IRR* rule give the right answer in this case?

 9. How many *IRR*s are there in part (b) of Problem 3? Does the *IRR* rule work in this case?

 10. Professor Wendy Smith has been offered the following deal: A law firm would like to retain her for an upfront payment of $50,000. In return, for the next year the firm would have access to eight hours of her time every month. Smith's rate is $550 per hour and her opportunity cost of capital is 15% per year. What does the *IRR* rule advise regarding this opportunity? What about the *NPV* rule?

11. Innovation Company is thinking about marketing a new software product. Upfront costs to market and develop the product are $5 million. The product is expected to generate profits of $1 million per year for 10 years. The company will have to provide product support expected to cost $100,000 per year in perpetuity. Assume all profits and expenses occur at the end of the year.

    a. What is the *NPV* of this investment if the cost of capital is 6%? Should the firm undertake the project? Repeat the analysis for discount rates of 2% and 11%.

    b. How many *IRR*s does this investment opportunity have?

    c. What does the *IRR* rule indicate about this investment?

 12. You own a coal mining company and are considering opening a new mine. The mine itself will cost $120 million to open. If this money is spent immediately, the mine will generate $20 million every year for the next 10 years. After that, the coal will run out and the site must be cleaned and maintained at environmental standards. The cleaning and maintenance are expected to cost $2 million per year in perpetuity. What does the *IRR* rule say about whether you should accept this opportunity? If the cost of capital is 8%, what does the *NPV* rule say?

 13. Your firm is considering a project that will cost $4.55 million up front, generate cash flows of $3,500,000 per year for three years, and then have a cleanup and shut-down cost of $6,000,000 in the fourth year.

    a. How many *IRR*s does this project have?

    b. Create an *NPV* profile for this project (plot the *NPV* as a function of the discount rate—see the appendix).

    c. Given a cost of capital of 10%, should this project be accepted? Justify your answer.

14. You have just been offered a contract worth $1 million per year for five years. However, to take the contract, you will need to purchase some new equipment. Your discount rate for this project is 12%. You are still negotiating the purchase price of the equipment. What is the most you can pay for the equipment and still have a positive *NPV*?

 *****15.** You are considering investing in a new gold mine in South Africa. Gold in South Africa is buried very deep, so the mine will require an initial investment of $250 million. Once this investment is made, the mine is expected to produce revenues of $30 million per year for the next 20 years. It will cost $10 million per year to operate the mine. After 20 years, the gold will be depleted. The mine must then be stabilized on an ongoing basis, which will cost $5 million per year in perpetuity. Calculate the *IRR* of this investment. (*Hint:* Plot the *NPV* as a function of the discount rate.)

16. You are considering making a movie. The movie is expected to cost $10 million up front and take a year to make. After that, it is expected to make $5 million in the year it is released and $2 million for the following four years. What is the payback period of this investment? If you require a payback period of two years, will you make the movie? Does the movie have positive *NPV* if the cost of capital is 10%?

Choosing Between Projects

 17. You are choosing between two projects, but can only take one. The cash flows for the projects are given in the following table:

	0	1	2	3	4
A	−$50	25	20	20	15
B	−$100	20	40	50	60

a. What are the *IRR*s of the two projects?

b. If your discount rate is 5%, what are the *NPV*s of the two projects?

c. Why do *IRR* and *NPV* rank the two projects differently?

18. You are deciding between two mutually exclusive investment opportunities. Both require the same initial investment of $10 million. Investment A will generate $2 million per year (starting at the end of the first year) in perpetuity. Investment B will generate $1.5 million at the end of the first year, and its revenues will grow at 2% per year for every year after that.

a. Which investment has the higher *IRR*?

b. Which investment has the higher *NPV* when the cost of capital is 7%?

c. In this case, when does picking the higher *IRR* give the correct answer as to which investment is the best opportunity?

 19. You are considering the following two projects and can only take one. Your cost of capital is 11%.

	0	1	2	3	4
A	−100	25	30	40	50
B	−100	50	40	30	20

a. What is the *NPV* of each project at your cost of capital?

b. What is the *IRR* of each project?

c. At what cost of capital do you become indifferent about which project to choose?

d. What should you do?

 20. You need a particular piece of equipment for your production process. An equipment leasing company has offered to lease you the equipment for $10,000 per year if you sign a guaranteed five-year lease. The company would also maintain the equipment for you as part of the lease. Alternatively, you could buy and maintain the equipment yourself. The cash flows (in thousands) from doing so are listed below (the equipment has an economic life of five years). If your discount rate is 7%, what should you do?

0	1	2	3	4	5
−40	−2	−2	−2	−2	−2

Evaluating Projects with Different Lives

21. Gateway Tours is choosing between two bus models. One is more expensive to purchase and maintain but lasts much longer than the other. Its discount rate is 11%. The company plans to continue with one of the two models for the foreseeable future. Which one should it choose? Based on the costs of each model shown below, which should it choose?

Model	0	1	2	3	4	5 ...	7
Old Reliable	−200	−4	−4	−4	−4	−4 ...	−4
Short and Sweet	−100	−2	−2	−2	−2		

22. Hassle-Free Web is bidding to provide webpage hosting services for Hotel Lisbon. Hotel Lisbon pays its current provider $10,000 per year for hosting its webpage and handling transactions on it, etc. Hassle-Free figures that it will need to purchase equipment worth $15,000 up front and then spend $2000 per year on monitoring, updates, and bandwidth to provide the service for three years. If Hassle-Free's cost of capital is 10%, can it bid less than $10,000 per year to provide the service and still increase its value by doing so?

Choosing Among Projects When Resources Are Limited

23. Fabulous Fabricators needs to decide how to allocate space in its production facility this year. It is considering the following contracts:

	NPV	Use of Facility
A	$2 million	100%
B	$1 million	60%
C	$1.5 million	40%

a. What are the profitability indexes of the projects?

b. What should Fabulous Fabricators do?

24. Kartman Corporation is evaluating four real estate investments. Management plans to buy the properties today and sell them three years from today. The annual discount rate for these investments is 15%. The following table summarizes the initial cost and the sale price in three years for each property:

	Cost Today	Sale Price in Year
Parkside Acres	$500,000	$900,000
Real Property Estates	800,000	1,400,000
Lost Lake Properties	650,000	1,050,000
Overlook	150,000	350,000

Kartman has a total capital budget of $800,000 to invest in properties. Which properties should it choose?

25. Orchid Biotech Company is evaluating several development projects for experimental drugs. Although the cash flows are difficult to forecast, the company has come up with the following estimates of the initial capital requirements and *NPV*s for the projects. Given a wide variety of staffing needs, the company has also estimated the number of research scientists required for each development project (all cost values are given in millions of dollars).

Project Number	Initial Capital	Number of Research Scientists	NPV
I	$10	2	$10.1
II	15	3	19.0
III	15	4	22.0
IV	20	3	25.0
V	30	10	60.2

a. Suppose that Orchid has a total capital budget of $60 million. How should it prioritize these projects?

b. Suppose that Orchid currently has 12 research scientists and does not anticipate being able to hire any more in the near future. How should Orchid prioritize these projects?

● Data Case

On October 6, 2004 Sirius Satellite Radio announced that it had reached an agreement with Howard Stern to broadcast his radio show exclusively on its system. As a result of this announcement, the Sirius stock price increased dramatically. You are currently working as a stock analyst for a large investment firm, and XM Radio, also a satellite radio firm, is one of the firms you track. Your boss wants to be prepared if XM follows Sirius in trying to sign a major personality. Therefore, she wants you to estimate the net cash flows the market had anticipated from the signing of Stern. She advises that you treat the value anticipated by the market as the *NPV* of the signing, then work backward from the *NPV* to determine the annual cash flows necessary to generate that value. The potential deal had been rumoured for some time prior to the announcement. As a result, the stock price for Sirius increased for several days before the announcement. Thus, your boss advises that the best way to capture all of the value is to take the change in stock price from September 28, 2004, through October 7, 2004. You nod your head in agreement, trying to look like you understand how to proceed. You are relatively new to the job and the term "*NPV*" is somewhat familiar to you.

1. To determine the change in stock price over this period, go to Yahoo! Finance (http://finance.yahoo.com) and enter the ticker symbol for Sirius (SIRI). Then click on "Historical Prices" and enter the appropriate dates. Use the adjusted closing prices for the two dates.

2. To determine the change in value, multiply the change in stock price by the number of shares outstanding. The number of shares outstanding around those dates can be found by going to http://finance.google.com and typing "SIRI" into the "Search" window. Next, select the Income Statement link on the left side of the screen, and then select "Annual Data" in the upper right-hand corner. The "Diluted Weighted Average Shares" can be found for the 12/31/2004 income statement on that page.

   Because the change in value represents the "expected" *NPV* of the project, you will have to find the annual net cash flows that would provide this *NPV*. For this analysis, you will need to estimate the cost of capital for the project. We show how to calculate the cost of capital in subsequent chapters; for now, use the New York University (NYU) cost of capital website (http://pages.stern.nyu.edu/~adamodar/New_Home_Page/datafile/wacc.htm). Locate the cost of capital in the far-right column for the "Entertainment Tech" industry.

3. Use the cost of capital from the NYU website and the *NPV* you computed to calculate the constant annual cash flow that provides this *NPV*. Compute cash flows for 5-, 10-, and 15-year horizons.

4. Your boss mentioned that she believes that the Howard Stern signing by Sirius was actually good for XM because it signalled that the industry has valuable growth potential. To see if she appears to be correct, find the percentage stock price reaction to XM Radio (XMSR) over this same period.

Chapter 7 APPENDIX   Using Excel to Make an *NPV* Profile

Constructing an *NPV* profile of a project is a very useful way to really see the project's *IRR*(s) and how the *NPV* of the project changes with the discount rate. Consider SFL's fertilizer project from Section 7.1. In the Excel screen shot below, the cash flows from that project are in black in cells D2 to H2. Cell B5 shows the *NPV*, taking the contents of cell B1 as the discount rate. The formula for doing this is shown just to the left of cell B5. Note that in order to make the *NPV* a dynamic function of whatever discount rate is entered into cell B1, you enter "B1" instead of "10%" where the formula takes this discount rate. For reference, we also compute the *IRR* in cell B3, and the formula for doing so is given just to the left of B3.

With the cash flows set up and the *NPV* entered in cell B5 as a dynamic function of the discount rate, we are ready to use the Data Table function of Excel to calculate the *NPV* for a range of different discount rates. A data table shows us how the outcome of a formula (such as *NPV*) changes when we change one of the cells in the spreadsheet (such as the discount rate). To do this

1. Enter the range of discount rates down a column, as shown below in cells A6 to A30. The placement of these rates is important. They must start in the cell below and to the left of the cell with the *NPV*. (Cell A6 is immediately below and to the left of cell B5.)

2. Highlight the area containing your range of discount rates and the *NPV* cell, as shown in the screen shot (cells A5 to B30).

3. From the Data pull-down menu, select Table.
4. Since our discount rates are in a column, we are using a "Column input cell" instead of a "Row input cell." In the Column input cell box, enter B1 or click on the B1 cell. By doing this, you are telling Excel to recalculate the *NPV* by substituting the numbers running down the column into cell B1, which contains the discount rate.
5. Click OK.

After clicking OK, the cells next to the range of discount rates will fill with the *NPV*s corresponding to each of the discount rates, as shown in the screen shot below. To create an *NPV* profile graphing these *NPV*s as a function of the discount rates,

1. Highlight the discount rates and *NPV*s: cells A6 to B30.
2. Click on the Chart icon or select Chart from the Insert pull-down menu.
3. Choose XY(Scatter) as your Chart type and click on the Chart sub-type shown below in the screen shot.
4. Click Next to customize your chart further or click Finish to display the chart.

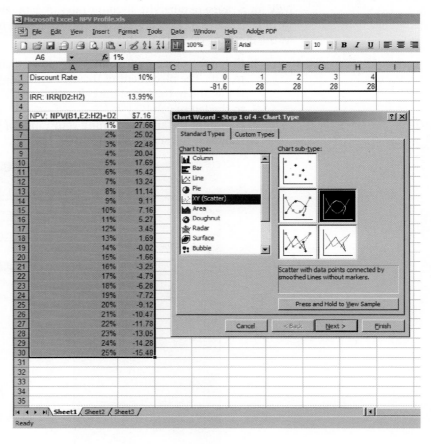

Fundamentals of Capital Budgeting

LEARNING OBJECTIVES

▶ Identify the types of cash flows needed in the capital budgeting process

▶ Forecast incremental earnings in a pro forma earnings statement for a project

▶ Convert forecasted earnings to free cash flows and compute a project's *NPV*

▶ Recognize common pitfalls that arise in identifying a project's incremental free cash flows

▶ Assess the sensitivity of a project's *NPV* to changes in your assumptions

▶ Identify the most common options available to managers in projects and understand why these options can be valuable

notation

CapEx	capital expenditures	*NPV*	net present value
CCA	capital cost allowance	*NWC_t*	net working capital in year *t*
EBIT	earnings before interest and taxes	*PV*	present value
FCF_t	free cash flow in year *t*	*r*	projected cost of capital
IRR	internal rate of return	*UCC*	undepreciated capital cost

Miriam Waldman,
TD Commercial Banking

University of Manitoba, 2006

"What helped me the most from finance classes was going through different scenarios to calculate the risk-adjusted return on capital. This is an important tool in portfolio management."

Miriam Waldman is the manager of commercial services, national real estate group at TD Commercial Banking, where she oversees lending operations to real estate developers. "We do a specific form of financing: real estate credit. We look at real estate projects and analyze several factors including budgets, financial statements, market dynamics, and borrower strengths in order to make decisions on whether to extend credit to a customer."

Miriam graduated in 2006 with a Bachelor of Commerce (Honours) degree from the University of Manitoba with a major in finance. Her finance background serves her well, as the decisions involved in lending to real estate developers require the same tools and analysis used by firms when choosing between investment projects. As Miriam explains: "Say we have a client developing a new neighbourhood. We do a net present value calculation of developing the land and selling it as individual housing lots."

A key part of the *NPV* calculation is deciding what discount rate to use. "To get the correct discount rate, we compare the project with recent projects across Canada, and we also have research groups analyzing the real estate market," Miriam says. "We take these and other factors into account, but in the end, experience will guide us."

Since there is always some uncertainty involved in the outcome of a project, Miriam must also check the sensitivity of the *NPV* to uncertainty in their projections: "What helped me the most from finance classes was going through different scenarios to calculate the risk-adjusted return on capital. This is an important tool in portfolio management."

An important responsibility of corporate financial managers is determining which projects or investments a firm should undertake. Capital budgeting, the focus of this chapter, is the process of analyzing investment opportunities and deciding which ones to accept. In doing so, we are allocating the firm's funds to various projects—we are budgeting its capital. Chapter 7 covered the various methods for evaluating projects and proved that *NPV* will be the most reliable and accurate method for doing so. In retrospect, this may not be surprising, as it is the only rule directly tied to the Valuation Principle. To implement the *NPV* rule, we must compute the *NPV* of our projects and accept only those projects for which the *NPV* is positive. We spoke in the last chapter about Sony and Toshiba each using investment decision rules to pursue competing high definition DVD standards (and eventually for Toshiba, to decide to abandon HD-DVD). To implement the investment decision rules, financial managers from Toshiba, for example, had first to forecast the incremental cash flows associated with the investments and later to forecast the incremental cash flows associated with the decision to stop investing in HD-DVD. The process of forecasting those cash flows, crucial inputs in the investment decision process, is our focus in this chapter. We begin by estimating the project's expected cash flows by forecasting the project's revenues and costs. Using these cash flows, we can compute the project's *NPV*—its contribution to shareholder value. Then, because the cash flow forecasts almost always contain uncertainty, we demonstrate how to compute the sensitivity of the *NPV* to the uncertainty in the forecasts. Finally, we examine the relationship between a project's flexibility and its *NPV*.

The Capital Budgeting Process

capital budget A list of the projects that a company plans to undertake during the next period.

capital budgeting The process of analyzing investment opportunities and deciding which ones to accept.

The first step in analyzing various investment opportunities is compiling a list of potential projects. A **capital budget** lists the projects and investments that a company plans to undertake during future years. To create this list, firms analyze alternative projects and decide which ones to accept through a process called **capital budgeting**. This process begins with forecasts of each project's future consequences for the firm. Some of these consequences will affect the firm's revenues; others will affect its costs. Our ultimate goal is to determine the effect of the decision to accept or reject a project on the firm's cash flows, and evaluate the *NPV* of these cash flows to assess the consequences of the decision for the firm's value. Figure 8.1 depicts the types of cash flows found in a typical project. We will examine each of these as we proceed through our discussion of capital budgeting.

Of course, forecasting these cash flows is frequently challenging. We will often need to rely on different experts within the firm to obtain estimates for many of these cash flows. For example, the marketing department may provide sales forecasts, the operations manager may provide information about production costs, and the firm's engineers may estimate the upfront research and development expenses that are required to launch the project. Another important source of information comes from looking at past projects of the firm, or those of other firms in the same industry. In particular, practitioners often base their assessments of a project's revenues and costs using information on revenues and costs that can be learned from the historical financial statements of the firm or its competitors.

Once we have these estimates, how do we organize them? One common starting point is first to consider the consequences of the project for the firm's earnings. Thus, we will *begin* our analysis in Section 8.2 by determining the **incremental earnings** of a project—that is, the amount by which the firm's earnings are expected to change as a result of the investment decision. The incremental earnings forecast tells us how the decision will affect the firm's reported profits from an accounting perspective. However, as we emphasized in Chapter 2, *earnings are not actual cash flows*. We need to estimate

incremental earnings The amount by which a firm's earnings are expected to change as a result of an investment decision.

FIGURE 8.1	Cash Flows in a Typical Project

The diagram shows some typical cash flows in project analysis and their timing.

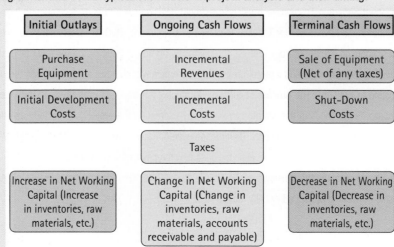

the project's cash flows to determine its *NPV* and decide whether it is a good project for the firm. Therefore, in Section 8.3, we demonstrate how to use the incremental earnings to forecast the actual cash flows of the project. Understanding how to compute the cash flow consequences of an investment based on its earning consequences is important for a number of reasons. First, as a practical matter, financial managers often begin by forecasting earnings. Second, if we are looking at historical data, accounting information is often the only information that is readily available.

Concept Check

1. What is capital budgeting, and what is its goal?
2. Why is computing a project's effect on the firm's earnings insufficient for capital budgeting?

8.2 Forecasting Incremental Earnings

Let's consider a hypothetical capital budgeting decision faced by managers of Research In Motion (ticker symbol: RIM), the maker of the BlackBerry. RIM is considering the development of the BlackBerry Presenter, a personal digital assistant that combines all the standard features of a BlackBerry such as phone and email with the capability to have a high-resolution interface with monitors or data projectors so that users can do professional presentations from their BlackBerry without needing to bring their own laptop or use another computer.

Revenue and Cost Estimates

Forecasting future revenues and costs is challenging. The most successful practitioners collect as much information as possible before tackling this task—they will talk to members of marketing and sales teams as well as company economists to develop an estimate of sales, and they will talk to engineering and production teams to refine their estimate of costs.

There are several factors to consider when estimating a project's revenues and costs, including the following:

1. A new product typically has lower sales initially, as customers gradually become aware of the product. Sales will then accelerate, plateau, and ultimately decline as the product nears obsolescence or increased competition is encountered.

2. The average selling price of a product and its cost of production will generally change over time. Prices and costs tend to rise with the general level of inflation in the economy. The prices of technology products, however, often fall over time as newer, superior technologies emerge and production costs decline.

3. For most industries, competition tends to reduce profit margins over time.

Our focus here is on how to get from these forecasts to incremental earnings and then to cash flows; Chapter 17 discusses forecasting methods in more detail.

All our revenue and cost estimates should be *incremental*, meaning that we account only for additional sales and costs generated by the project. For example, if we are evaluating the purchase of a faster manufacturing machine, we are concerned only with how many additional units of the product we will be able to sell (and at what price) and any additional costs created by the new machine. We do not forecast total sales and costs, because those include our production using the old machine. *Remember, we are evaluating how the project will change the cash flows of the firm. That is why we focus on incremental revenues and costs.*

Let's return to our BlackBerry Presenter example. The target market for BlackBerry Presenter includes business people and academics who travel frequently to make presentations. Based on extensive marketing surveys, the sales forecast for BlackBerry Presenter is 100,000 units per year. Given the pace of technological change, RIM expects the product will have a four-year life. It will be sold through phone companies and wireless providers either individually or as part of a package with a contract for a wireless subscription. The expected wholesale price is $260 per unit.

Developing the new hardware will be relatively inexpensive, as existing technologies can be simply modified and repackaged in the newly designed BlackBerry Presenter. RIM expects total engineering and design costs to amount to $5 million. Once the design is finalized, actual production will be outsourced at a cost (including packaging) of $110 per unit.

In addition to the hardware requirements, RIM must build a new software application to allow fully functional PowerPoint, Keynote, or other presentations to run on the BlackBerry Presenter. This software development project requires coordination with each of the presentation-software companies and is expected to take a dedicated team of 50 software engineers a full year to complete. The cost of a software engineer (including benefits and related costs) is $200,000 per year.

The software and hardware design will be completed at the end of one year. At that time, the BlackBerry Presenter will be ready to ship. RIM expects to spend $2.8 million per year on marketing and support for this product.

Capital Expenditures and Capital Cost Allowance. To verify the compatibility of the BlackBerry Presenter with the various software and hardware combinations, RIM must also build a new lab for testing purposes. This lab will occupy existing facilities but will require $7.5 million of new equipment. Recall from Chapter 2 that while investments in plant, property, and equipment are a cash expense, they are not directly listed as expenses when calculating *earnings*. Instead, the firm deducts a fraction of the cost of these items each year for tax purposes as **capital cost allowance** or **CCA**—the Canada Revenue Agency (CRA) version of depreciation. Different methods can be used to compute depreciation. For financial reporting purposes, *CCA* is usually *not* used. For tax purposes, though, *CCA* is required. It is thus very important when doing capital budgeting to use *CCA*, the method specified by the CRA, because it affects the company's taxable income, the actual amount of tax paid, and the firm's cash flows. To calculate the annual *CCA* deductions, RIM must first determine the **tax year** in which the purchase takes place. We will assume that an asset purchased at date 0 is actually purchased at the beginning of the first tax year relevant to the project. Thus, the first *CCA* deduction affects the taxable income and taxes for date 1 (the end of the first year). To calculate the *CCA* amounts, RIM must determine the **asset class** for the computer equipment and the relevant **CCA rate**, denoted as d, for the asset class. Computer equipment falls under asset class 45 and has a *CCA* rate of $d = 45\%$. CRA has a "**half-year rule**" that is meant to compensate for the fact that sometimes assets are bought at the beginning of the year and other times they are bought at the end of the year. CRA assumes assets qualify for half a year's worth of *CCA* in the first tax year. Thus, when an asset is purchased, one half of its cost, denoted *CapEx*, is added to the **undepreciated capital cost (UCC)** for the **asset pool** (the collection of assets) in the same class. We denote this addition to the *UCC* as UCC_1. Thus $UCC_1 = 0.5 \times CapEx$. For a particular asset, the incremental *CCA* deduction that can be claimed at the end of the tax year is equal to the incremental undepreciated capital cost associated with that asset multiplied by the *CCA* rate, d:

$$CCA_t = UCC_t \times d \qquad (8.1)$$

capital cost allowance (CCA) The Canada Revenue Agency method of depreciation for income tax purposes.

tax year The fiscal year relevant for tax and *CCA* calculations for the Canada Revenue Agency.

asset classes Categories defined by the Canada Revenue Agency to indicate types of depreciable property that will be given the same treatment for *CCA* calculations.

CCA rate The proportion of undepreciated capital cost that can be claimed as *CCA* in a given tax year.

half-year rule A rule stating that, as assets may be purchased at any time throughout a year, it can be assumed that on average an asset is owned for half a year during the first tax year of its ownership. Thus, the CRA allows only half of the *CapEx* to generate *CCA* in the first tax year (the year in which a purchase takes place).

undepreciated capital cost (UCC) The balance, at a point in time, calculated by deducting an asset's current and prior *CCA* amounts from the original cost of the asset (the *CapEx*).

asset pool The sum of all assets in one class.

where CCA_t is the incremental CCA deduction for an asset taken in tax year t; UCC_t is the incremental undepreciated capital cost for an asset in tax year t prior to the asset's CCA deduction in year t; d is the CCA rate that determines the proportion of UCC that can be claimed as a CCA deduction.

After a CCA deduction is claimed, the UCC is reduced for the next year. However, for the second tax year we must also remember to add in the other half of $CapEx$ into the incremental UCC. In general, we can determine the incremental UCC for an asset as follows.

Year t	Incremental UCC used for calculating the CCA for tax year t
$t = 1$	$UCC_1 = 0.5 \times CapEx$
$t \geq 2$	$UCC_t = CapEx \times \left(1 - \frac{d}{2}\right) \times (1 - d)^{t-2}$

(8.2)

We assume the asset is purchased sometime during the first tax year, so the first CCA deduction affects the end-of-year calculation of taxable income. The UCC calculation above is the undepreciated capital cost remaining in year t just before the CCA deduction of year t.

RIM's calculation of the CCA amounts for the first five years of the BlackBerry Presenter project is shown in the spreadsheet in Table 8.1. There will still be a positive UCC balance after the CCA deduction in year 5. This means that RIM can claim CCA deductions in future years too. In fact, because the CCA calculation always deducts a proportion of the UCC, UCC will never fall to zero (as long as the asset is not sold), so CCA *deductions can continue forever.* For now we will ignore the CCA deductions beyond year 5. In Section 8.4, we will address how to properly deal with all the CCA effects.

Deducting CCA from the Table 8.1 spreadsheet completes the forecast for the BlackBerry Presenter's earnings before interest and taxes ($EBIT$) shown in line 7 of the Table 8.2 spreadsheet. Since the capital expenditures do not show up as a cash outflow in the earnings calculation and the non-cash CCA deduction does, we can see why earnings are not an accurate representation of cash flows.

Incremental Revenue and Cost Estimates

Given the revenue and cost estimates, we can forecast the BlackBerry Presenter's incremental earnings, as shown in Table 8.2. After the product is developed in year 0, it will generate sales of 100,000 units $\times$ \$260/unit = \$26 million each year for the

TABLE 8.1

The BlackBerry Presenter's Schedule of *CCA* and *UCC* for the First Five Years

Year	0	1	2	3	4	5
Capital Expenditure, *CCA*, and *UCC* Forecasts ($000s)						
1 *CapEx* (half added into *UCC₁*, half added into *UCC₂*)	7500	–	–	–	–	–
2 *UCC_t*	–	3750	5813	3197	1758	967
3 *CCA_t = UCC_t × d*	–	1688	2616	1439	791	435
4 CCA rate, *d*	45%					

Notes: $UCC_1 = 0.5 \times CapEx$
$UCC_2 = UCC_1 - CCA_1 + (0.5 \times CapEx)$
For the yellow cells, $UCC_t = UCC_{t-1} - CCA_{t-1}$
Since $CCA_5 < UCC_5$, there will be a positive balance remaining for UCC_6

TABLE 8.2   The BlackBerry Presenter's Incremental Earnings Forecast

Year	0	1	2	3	4	5
Incremental Earnings Forecast ($000s)						
1 Sales	–	26,000	26,000	26,000	26,000	–
2 Cost of Goods Sold	–	(11,000)	(11,000)	(11,000)	(11,000)	–
3 Gross Profit	–	15,000	15,000	15,000	15,000	–
4 Selling, General, and Administrative	–	(2800)	(2800)	(2800)	(2800)	–
5 Research and Development	(15,000)	–	–	–	–	–
6 Capital Cost Allowance (*CCA*)	–	(1688)	(2616)	(1439)	(791)	(435)
7 *EBIT*	(15,000)	10,513	9584	10,761	11,409	(435)
8 Income Tax at 40%	6000	(4205)	(3834)	(4305)	(4564)	174
9 Unlevered Net Income	(9000)	6308	5751	6457	6845	(261)

next four years. The cost of producing these units is 100,000 units × $110/unit = $11 million per year. Thus, the BlackBerry Presenter will produce a gross profit of $26 million − $11 million = $15 million per year, as shown in line 3 of the spreadsheet in Table 8.2.[1]

The project's operating expenses include $2.8 million per year in marketing and support costs, which are listed as selling, general, and administrative expenses. In year 0, RIM will spend $5 million on design and engineering, together with 50 × $200,000 = $10 million on software, for a total of $15 million in research and development expenditures.

We can calculate the incremental earnings before interest and taxes by using Equation 8.3:

$$\text{Incremental Earnings Before Interest and Taxes } (EBIT) = \qquad (8.3)$$
$$\text{Incremental Revenue} - \text{Incremental Costs} - CCA$$

marginal corporate tax rate The tax rate a firm will pay on an incremental dollar of pre-tax income.

Taxes. The final expense we must account for is corporate taxes. The correct tax rate to use is the firm's **marginal corporate tax rate**, which is the tax rate it will pay on an *incremental* dollar of pre-tax income. In Table 8.2, we assume the marginal corporate tax rate for the BlackBerry Presenter project is 40% each year. The incremental income tax expense is calculated in line 8 as

$$\text{Income Tax} = EBIT \times \tau_c \qquad (8.4)$$

where τ_c is the firm's marginal corporate tax rate.

In year 1, the BlackBerry Presenter will contribute an additional $10.513 million to RIM's *EBIT*, which will result in an additional $10.513 million × 40% = $4.205 million in corporate tax that RIM will owe. We deduct this amount to determine the BlackBerry Presenter's after-tax contribution to net income.

---

[1] While revenues and costs occur throughout the year, the standard convention, which we adopt here, is to list revenues and costs in the year in which they occur. Thus cash flows that occur at the end of one year will be listed in a different column than those that occur at the start of the next year, even though they may occur only weeks apart. When additional precision is required, cash flows are often estimated on a quarterly or monthly basis.

Taxes and Negative *EBIT*. Notice that in year 0 the BlackBerry Presenter's *EBIT* is negative. Are taxes relevant in this case? Yes. The BlackBerry Presenter will reduce RIM's taxable income in year 0 by $15 million. As long as RIM earns taxable income elsewhere in year 0 against which it can offset the BlackBerry Presenter's losses, RIM will owe $15 million × 40% = $6 million *less* in taxes in year 0 than if it were not undertaking the project. Because the credits come from the research and development expense for the BlackBerry Presenter project, the firm should credit this tax savings to the BlackBerry Presenter project.

EXAMPLE 8.1	**Problem**
Taxing Losses for Projects in Profitable Companies	Kellogg Company plans to launch a new line of high-fibre, zero–trans-fat breakfast pastries. The heavy advertising expenses associated with the new product launch will generate operating losses of $15 million next year for the product. Kellogg expects to earn pre-tax income of $460 million from operations other than the new pastries next year. If Kellogg pays a 40% tax rate on its pre-tax income, what will it owe in taxes next year without the new pastry product? What will it owe with the new product?

Solution

▶ **Plan**

We need Kellogg's pre-tax income with and without the new product losses and its tax rate of 40%. We can then compute the tax without the losses and compare it to the tax with the losses.

▶ **Execute**

Without the new product, Kellogg will owe $460 million × 40% = $184 million in corporate taxes next year. With the new product, Kellogg's pre-tax income next year will be only $460 million − $15 million = $445 million, and it will owe $445 million × 40% = $178 million in tax.

▶ **Evaluate**

Thus, launching the new product reduces Kellogg's taxes next year by $184 million − $178 million = $6 million. Because the losses on the new product reduce Kellogg's taxable income dollar for dollar, it is the same as if the new product had a tax bill of negative $6 million.

unlevered net income
Net income that does not include interest expenses associated with debt.

Unlevered Net Income Calculation. We can express the data in Table 8.2 by combining Equations 8.3 and 8.4 as the following shorthand formula for **unlevered net income**:

$$\text{Incremental Unlevered Net Income} = EBIT \times (1 - \tau_c) =$$
$$(\text{Incremental Revenue} - \text{Incremental Costs} - CCA) \times (1 - \tau_c) \qquad (8.5)$$

Note: The *EBIT* calculated in Table 8.2 used *CCA* instead of accounting depreciation. When you see *EBIT* numbers in financial reports, those numbers are normally based on accounting depreciation. If this is the case, then the *EBIT* in Equation 8.4 must be replaced with ($EBIT$ + Depreciation − CCA).

pro forma statement
A statement that is not based on actual data but rather depicts a firm's financials under a given set of hypothetical assumptions.

Pro Forma Statement. Table 8.2 shows the incremental unlevered net income for our BlackBerry Presenter project. This is often referred to as a **pro forma statement**, because it is not based on actual data but rather depicts the firm's financials under a given set of hypothetical as sumptions. In our RIM example, the firm's forecasts of revenues and costs were assumptions that allowed RIM to forecast incremental earnings in a pro forma statement.

What About Interest Expenses? In Chapter 2, we saw that to compute a firm's net income, we must first deduct interest expenses from *EBIT*. When evaluating a capital budgeting decision, however, we generally *do not include interest expenses*. Any incremental interest expenses will be related to the firm's decision regarding how to finance the project, which is a separate decision. Here, we wish to evaluate the earnings contributions from the project on its own, separate from the financing decision. Ultimately, managers may also look at the additional earnings consequences associated with different methods of financing the project.

Thus, we evaluate a project *as if* the company will not use any debt to finance it (whether or not that is actually the case), and we postpone the consideration of alternative financing choices until Part 5 of this book. Because we calculate the net income assuming no debt (no leverage), we refer to the net income we compute in Table 8.2 using Equation 8.5, the unlevered net income of the project, to indicate that it does not include any interest expenses associated with debt.

3. How are operating expenses and capital expenditures treated differently when calculating incremental earnings?

4. Why do we focus only on incremental revenues and costs, rather than all revenues and costs of the firm?

8.3 Determining Incremental Free Cash Flow

As discussed in Chapter 2, earnings are an accounting measure of the firm's performance. They do not represent real profits: the firm cannot use its earnings to buy goods, pay employees, fund new investments, or pay dividends to shareholders. To do those things, the firm needs cash. Thus, to evaluate a capital budgeting decision, we must determine its consequences for the firm's available cash. The incremental effect of a project on the firm's available cash is the project's incremental **free cash flow.**

free cash flow The incremental effect of a project on a firm's available cash.

Calculating Free Cash Flow from Earnings

As discussed in Chapter 2, there are important differences between earnings and cash flow. Earnings include non-cash charges, such as *CCA* (or depreciation for financial reporting purposes), but do not include the cost of capital investment (the capital expenditures). To determine a project's free cash flow from its incremental earnings, we must adjust for these differences.

Capital Expenditures and Capital Cost Allowance. *CCA* is not a cash expense that the firm pays. Rather, it is a method used for accounting and tax purposes to allocate the original purchase cost of the asset over its life. Because *CCA* is not a cash flow, we do not include it in the cash flow forecast. However, that does not mean we can ignore *CCA*. The *CCA* deduction reduces our taxable earnings and in doing so reduces our taxes. Taxes are cash flows, so because *CCA* affects our cash flows, it still matters. Our approach for handling *CCA* is to add it back to the incremental earnings to recognize the fact that we still have the cash flow associated with it.

For example, a project has incremental gross profit (revenues minus costs) of $1 million and a $200,000 *CCA* deduction. If the firm's tax rate is 40%, then the incremental earnings will be ($1,000,000 − $200,000) × (1 − 0.40) = $480,000. However, the firm will still have $680,000 because the $200,000 *CCA* deduction is not an actual cash outflow. Table 8.3 shows the calculation to get the incremental free cash flow in this case. Blue boxes surround all of the actual cash flows in the column labelled "Correct." A good way to check to make sure the incremental free cash flow is correct is to sum the actual cash flows. In this case, the firm generated $1,000,000 in gross profit (a positive cash flow), paid $320,000 in taxes (a negative cash flow), and was left with

TABLE 8.3

Deducting and Then Adding Back *CCA*

	Correct	Incorrect
Incremental Gross Profit	$1,000,000	$1,000,000
CCA	−$200,000	
EBIT	$800,000	$1,000,000
Tax at 40%	−$320,000	−$400,000
Incremental Earnings	$480,000	$600,000
Add Back *CCA*	$200,000	
Incremental Free Cash Flow	$680,000	$600,000

$1,000,000 − $320,000 = $680,000$, which is the amount shown as the incremental free cash flow. In the last column, labelled "Incorrect," we show what would happen if you just ignored *CCA* altogether. Because *EBIT* would be too high, the taxes would be too high as well, and consequently the incremental free cash flow would be too low. (Note that the difference of $80,000 between the two cases is entirely due to the difference in tax payments.)

EXAMPLE 8.2

Incremental Free Cash Flows

Problem

Let's return to the BlackBerry Presenter example. In Table 8.2, we computed the incremental earnings for the BlackBerry Presenter, but we need the incremental free cash flows to decide whether RIM should proceed with the project.

Solution

▶ **Plan**

The difference between the incremental earnings and incremental free cash flows in the BlackBerry Presenter example will be driven by the equipment purchased for the lab. We need to recognize the $7.5 million cash outflow associated with the purchase in year 0 and add back the *CCA* deductions from years 1 to 5, as they are not actually cash outflows.

▶ **Execute**

Year	0	1	2	3	4	5
Incremental Earnings Forecast						
1 Sales	–	26,000	26,000	26,000	26,000	–
2 Cost of Goods Sold	–	(11,000)	(11,000)	(11,000)	(11,000)	–
3 Gross Profit	–	15,000	15,000	15,000	15,000	–
4 Selling, General, and Administrative	–	(2800)	(2800)	(2800)	(2800)	–
5 Research and Development	(15,000)	–	–	–	–	–
6 Capital Cost Allowance (*CCA*)	–	(1688)	(2616)	(1439)	(791)	(435)
7 *EBIT*	(15,000)	10,513	9584	10761	11,409	(435)
8 Income Tax at 40%	6000	(4205)	(3834)	(4305)	(4564)	174
9 Unlevered Net Income	(9000)	6308	5751	6457	6845	(261)
Free Cash Flow ($000s)						
10 Plus: *CCA*	–	1688	2616	1439	791	435
11 Less: Capital Expenditures	(7500)					
13 Free Cash Flow	(16,500)	7995	8366	7895	7636	174

> ▶ **Evaluate**
> By recognizing the outflow from purchasing the equipment in year 0, we account for the fact that $7.5 million left the firm at that time. By adding back the *CCA* deductions in years 1 to 5, we adjust the incremental earnings to reflect the fact that *CCA* deductions are not cash outflows.

Net Working Capital. Another way that incremental earnings and free cash flows can differ is if there are changes in net working capital. We defined net working capital (*NWC*) in Chapter 2 as the difference between current assets and current liabilities. The main components of net working capital are cash, inventory, receivables, and payables:

$$NWC = \text{Current Assets} - \text{Current Liabilities} =$$
$$\text{Cash} + \text{Inventory} + \text{Receivables} - \text{Payables} \tag{8.6}$$

Most projects will require the firm to invest in *NWC*. Firms may need to maintain a minimum cash balance[2] to meet unexpected expenditures, and inventories of raw materials and finished product to accommodate production uncertainties and demand fluctuations. Also, customers may not pay for the goods they purchase immediately. While sales are immediately counted as part of earnings, the firm does not receive any cash until the customers actually pay. In the interim, the firm includes the amount that customers owe in its receivables. Thus, the firm's receivables measure the total credit that the firm has extended to its customers. In the same way, payables measure the credit the firm has received from its suppliers. The difference between receivables and payables is the net amount of the firm's capital that is consumed as a result of these credit transactions, known as **trade credit**.

trade credit The difference between receivables and payables that is the net amount of a firm's capital consumed as a result of those credit transactions; the credit that a firm extends to its customers.

As discussed in Chapter 2, we do not included short-term financing items such as notes payable or short-term debt, because those represent financing decisions that we keep separate from our investment decisions.

We care about *NWC* because it reflects a short-term investment that ties up cash flow that could be used elsewhere. For example, when a firm holds a lot of unsold inventory or has a lot of outstanding receivables, cash flow is tied up in the form of inventory or in the form of credit extended to customers. It is costly for the firm to tie up that cash flow, because it delays the time until the cash flow is available for reinvestment or distribution to shareholders. Since we know that money has time value, we cannot ignore this delay in our forecasts for the project. Thus, whenever *NWC* increases, reflecting additional investment in working capital, it represents a reduction in cash flow that year.

It is important to note that only changes in *NWC* affect cash flows. For example, consider a three-year project that causes the firm to build up initial inventory by $20,000 and maintain that level of inventory in years 1 and 2, before drawing it down as the project ends and the last product is sold. It is often necessary for the initial increase in inventory to occur prior to the first sale so that the higher level of inventory would be achieved by the end of year 0. The level of the incremental *NWC* in each year, the associated change in *NWC*, and the cash flow implications would be as shown in the table below:

	Year	0	1	2	3
1					
2	Level of Incremental *NWC*	20,000	20,000	20,000	0
3	*Change* in Incremental *NWC*	+20,000	0	0	−20,000
4	Cash Flow from Change in *NWC*	−20,000	0	0	+20,000

---

[2] The cash included in net working capital is cash that is *not* invested to earn a market rate of return. It includes cash held in the firm's chequing account, in a company safe or cash box, in cash registers (for retail stores), and other sites.

Note that the cash flow effect from a change in *NWC* is always equal and opposite in sign to the change in *NWC*. For example, an increase in inventory represents an investment or cash outflow, while a reduction in that inventory frees up that investment of capital and represents a cash inflow. Thus, in capital budgeting we subtract changes in *NWC* to arrive at the cash flows. Also notice that since the level of incremental *NWC* did not change in years 1 and 2, there was no new cash flow effect. Intuitively, as the firm is using up inventory and replenishing it, the net new investment in inventory is zero, so no additional cash outflow is required. Finally, note that over the life of the project, the incremental *NWC* returns to zero so that the changes (in year 0 and in year 3) sum to zero. Accounting principles ensure this by requiring the recapture of working capital over the life of the project.

More generally, we define the change in *NWC* in year *t* as:

$$\text{Change in } NWC \text{ in year } t = NWC_t - NWC_{t-1} \tag{8.7}$$

When a project causes a change in *NWC*, that change must be subtracted from incremental earnings to arrive at incremental free cash flows.

EXAMPLE 8.3

Incorporating Changes in Net Working Capital

Problem

Suppose that the BlackBerry Presenter will have no incremental cash or inventory requirements (products will be shipped directly from the contract manufacturer to customers). However, receivables related to the BlackBerry Presenter are expected to account for 15% of annual sales, and payables are expected to be 15% of the annual cost of goods sold (COGS). Fifteen percent of $26 million in sales is $3.9 million, and 15% of $11 million in COGS is $1.65 million. BlackBerry Presenter's *NWC* requirements are shown in the following table:

	Year	0	1	2	3	4	5
1							
2	Net Working Capital Forecast ($000s)						
3	Cash Requirements	0	0				0
4	Inventory	0	0				0
5	Receivables (15% of Sales)	0	3900	3900	3900	3900	0
6	Payables (15% of COGS)	0	−1650	−1650	−1650	−1650	0
7	**Net Working Capital**	0	2250	2250	2250	2250	0

How does this requirement affect the project's free cash flow?

Solution

▶ **Plan**

Any increases in *NWC* represent an investment that reduces the cash available to the firm and so reduces free cash flow. We can use our forecast of the BlackBerry Presenter's *NWC* requirements to complete our estimate of BlackBerry Presenter's free cash flow. In year 1, *NWC* increases by $2.250 million. This increase represents a cost to the firm. This reduction of free cash flow corresponds to the fact that $3.900 million of the firm's sales in year 1, and $1.625 million of its costs, have not yet been paid.

In years 2 to 4, *NWC* does not change, so no further contributions are needed. In year 5, when the project is shut down, *NWC* falls by $2.250 million as the payments of the last customers are received and the final bills are paid. We add this $2.250 million to free cash flow in year 5.

▶ **Execute (in $000s)**

Year		0	1	2	3	4	5
1	Year	0	1	2	3	4	5
2	Net Working Capital	0	2250	2250	2250	2250	0
3	Change in *NWC*		+2250	0	0	0	−2250
4	Cash Flow Effect		−2250	0	0	0	+2250

The incremental free cash flows would then be:

Year	0	1	2	3	4	5
Incremental Earnings Forecast ($000s)						
1 Sales	–	26,000	26,000	26,000	26,000	–
2 Cost of Goods Sold	–	(11,000)	(11,000)	(11,000)	(11,000)	–
3 Gross Profit	–	15,000	15,000	15,000	15,000	–
4 Selling, General, and Administrative	–	(2800)	(2800)	(2800)	(2800)	–
5 Research and Development	(15,000)	–	–	–	–	–
6 Capital Cost Allowance (*CCA*)	–	(1688)	(2616)	(1439)	(791)	(435)
7 *EBIT*	(15,000)	10,513	9584	10,761	11,409	(435)
8 Income Tax at 40%	6000	(4205)	(3834)	(4305)	(4564)	174
9 Unlevered Net Income	(9000)	6308	5751	6457	6845	(261)
Free Cash Flow ($000s)						
10 Plus: *CCA*	–	1688	2616	1439	791	435
11 Less: Capital Expenditures	(7500)					
12 Less: Increases in *NWC*	–	(2250)	–	–	–	2250
13 Free Cash Flow	(16,500)	5745	8366	7895	7636	2424

▶ **Evaluate**
The free cash flows differ from unlevered net income by reflecting the cash flow effects of capital expenditures on equipment, *CCA*, and changes in *NWC*. Note that in the first two years, free cash flow is lower than unlevered net income, reflecting the upfront investment in equipment and *NWC* required by the project. In later years, free cash flow exceeds unlevered net income because depreciation is not a cash expense. In the last year, the firm ultimately recovers the investment in *NWC*, further boosting the free cash flow.

Calculating Free Cash Flow Directly

As we noted at the outset of this chapter, because practitioners usually begin the capital budgeting process by first forecasting earnings, we have chosen to do the same. However, we can calculate a project's free cash flow directly by using the following formula:

$$\text{Free Cash Flow}$$

$$\text{Free Cash Flow} = \overbrace{(\text{Revenues} - \text{Costs} - CCA) \times (1 - \text{tax rate})}^{\text{Unlevered Net Income}} + CCA - CapEx - \text{Change in } NWC \tag{8.8}$$

Note that we first deduct *CCA* when computing the project's incremental earnings and then add it back (because it is a non-cash expense) when computing free cash flow.

Thus, the only effect of *CCA* is to reduce the firm's taxable income. Indeed, we can rewrite Equation 8.8 as:

$$\text{Free Cash Flow} = (\text{Revenues} - \text{Costs}) \times (1 - \text{tax rate}) - CapEx$$
$$- \text{Change in } NWC + \text{tax rate} \times CCA \qquad (8.9)$$

CCA tax shield The tax savings that results from the ability to deduct depreciation.

The last term in Equation 8.9, tax rate $\times$ *CCA*, is called the **CCA tax shield**, which is the tax savings that results from the ability to deduct *CCA*. As a consequence, *CCA* deductions have a *positive* impact on free cash flow. Returning to our example in Table 8.3, if the firm ignored *CCA*, its taxes were $400,000 instead of $320,000, leaving it with incremental free cash flow of $600,000 instead of $680,000. Notice that the $80,000 difference is exactly equal to the tax rate (40%) multiplied by the *CCA* deduction ($200,000). Every dollar of *CCA* deducted saves the firm 40 cents in taxes, so the $200,000 *CCA* deduction translates into an $80,000 tax savings.

Firms often report a different depreciation expense for accounting purposes and use *CCA* deductions for tax purposes. Because only the tax consequences of *CCA* are relevant for free cash flow, we should use the *CCA* deductions that the firm will use for tax purposes in our forecast.

Calculating the *NPV*

The goal of forecasting the incremental free cash flows is to have the necessary inputs to calculate the project's *NPV*. To compute a project's *NPV*, we must discount its free cash flow at the appropriate cost of capital. As discussed in Chapter 5, the cost of capital for a project is the expected return that investors could earn on their best alternative investment with similar risk and maturity. We will develop the techniques needed to estimate the cost of capital in Part 4 of this text, when we discuss risk and return. For now, we take the cost of capital as given.

We compute the present value of each free cash flow in the future by discounting it at the project's cost of capital. As explained in Chapter 4, using r to represent the cost of capital, the present value of the free cash flow in year t (or FCF_t) is

$$PV(FCF_t) = \frac{FCF_t}{(1+r)^t} = FCF_t \times \underbrace{\frac{1}{(1+r)^t}}_{t\text{-year discount factor}} \qquad (8.10)$$

EXAMPLE 8.4

Calculating the Project's *NPV*

Problem

Assume that RIM's managers believe that the BlackBerry Presenter project has risks similar to those of RIM's existing projects, for which it has a cost of capital of 12%. Compute the *NPV* of the BlackBerry Presenter project.

Solution

▶ **Plan**

From Example 8.3, the incremental free cash flows for the BlackBerry Presenter project are (in $000s):

1	Year	0	1	2	3	4	5
2	Incremental Free Cash Flows	(16,500)	5745	8366	7895	7636	2424

To compute the *NPV*, we sum the present values of all of the cash flows, noting that the year 0 cash outflow is already a present value.

▶ **Execute**

Using Equation 8.10,

$$NPV = -16{,}500 + \frac{5745}{(1.12)^1} + \frac{8366}{(1.12)^2} + \frac{7895}{(1.12)^3} + \frac{7636}{(1.12)^4} + \frac{2424}{(1.12)^5} = 7147$$

▶ **Evaluate**

Based on our estimates, the BlackBerry Presenter's *NPV* is $7.147 million. While the BlackBerry Presenter's upfront cost is $16.5 million, the present value of the additional free cash flow that RIM will receive from the project is $23.647 million. Thus, taking the BlackBerry Presenter project is equivalent to RIM having an extra $7.147 million in the bank today.

Concept Check

5. If depreciation expense is not a cash flow, why do we have to subtract it and add it back? Why not just ignore it?

6. Why does an increase in *NWC* represent a cash outflow?

8.4 Other Effects on Incremental Free Cash Flows

When computing the incremental free cash flows of an investment decision, we should include *all* changes in the firm's free cash flows with the project versus without the project. These include opportunities forgone due to the project and effects of the project on other parts of the firm. In this section, we discuss these other effects, some of the pitfalls and common mistakes to avoid, and finally the complications that can arise when forecasting incremental free cash flows.

Opportunity Costs

Many projects in the company use a resource that it already owns. Because the firm does not need to pay cash to acquire this resource for a new project, it is tempting to assume that the resource is available for free. However, in many cases the resource could provide value for the firm in another opportunity or project. The **opportunity cost** of using a resource is the value it could have provided in its best alternative use.[3] Because this value is lost when the resource is used by another project, we should include the opportunity cost as an incremental cost of the project. For example, your company may be considering building a retail store on some land that it owns. Even though it already owns the land, it is not free to the store project. If it did not put its store on the land, the company could sell the land, for example. This forgone market price for the land is an opportunity cost of the retail store project.

opportunity cost The value a resource could have provided in its best alternative use.

---

[3] In Chapter 5, we defined the opportunity cost of capital as the rate you could earn on an alternative investment with equivalent risk. We similarly define the opportunity cost of using an existing asset in a project as the cash flow generated by the next-best alternative use for the asset.

Common Mistake   The Opportunity Cost of an Idle Asset

A common mistake is to conclude that if an asset is currently idle, its opportunity cost is zero. For example, the firm might have a warehouse that is currently empty or a machine that is not being used. Often, the asset may have been idled in anticipation of taking on the new project, and would have otherwise been put to use by the firm. Even if the firm has no alternative use for the asset, the firm could choose to sell or rent the asset. The value obtained from the asset's alternative use, sale, or rental represents an opportunity cost that must be included as part of the incremental cash flows.

Project Externalities

project externalities
Indirect effects of a project that may increase or decrease the profits of other business activities of a firm.

cannibalization The displacement of the sales of one of a firm's existing products by the sales of the firm's new product.

Project externalities are indirect effects of a project that may increase or decrease the profits of other business activities of the firm. For instance, some purchasers of Apple's iPhone would otherwise have bought Apple's iPod nano. When sales of a new product displace sales of an existing product, the situation is often referred to as **cannibalization**. The lost sales of the existing project are an incremental cost to the company of going forward with the new product.

Sunk Costs

sunk cost Any unrecoverable cost for which a firm is already liable.

A **sunk cost** is any unrecoverable cost for which the firm is already liable. Sunk costs have been or will be paid regardless of whether or not the decision is made to proceed with the project. Therefore, they are not incremental with respect to the current decision and should not be included in its analysis. You may hire a market research firm to do market analysis to determine whether there is demand for a new product you are considering and the analysis may show that there is not enough demand, so you decide not to go forward with the project. Does that mean you do not have to pay the research firm's bill? Of course you still have to pay the bill, emphasizing that the cost was sunk and incurred whether you went forward with the project or not.

A good rule to remember is that *if your decision does not affect a cash flow, then the cash flow should not affect your decision.* If the cash flow is the same regardless of the decision, then it is not relevant to your decision. Following are some common examples of sunk costs you may encounter.

Common Mistake   The Sunk Cost Fallacy

Being influenced by sunk costs is such a widespread mistake that it has a special name: sunk cost fallacy. The most common problem is that people "throw good money after bad." That is, people sometimes continue to invest in a project that has a negative *NPV* because they have already invested a large amount in the project and feel that by not continuing it, the prior investment will be wasted. The sunk cost fallacy is also sometimes called the "Concorde effect," a term that refers to the British and French governments' decision to continue funding the joint development of the Concorde aircraft even after it was clear that sales of the plane would fall far short of those necessary to justify its continued development. The British government viewed the project as a commercial and financial disaster. However, the political implications of halting the project—and thereby publicly admitting that all past expenses on the project would result in nothing—ultimately prevented either government from abandoning the project.

Fixed Overhead Expenses. **Overhead expenses** are associated with activities that are not directly attributable to a single business activity but instead affect many different areas of the corporation. Examples include the cost of maintaining the company's headquarters and the salary of the CEO. These expenses are often allocated to the different business activities for accounting purposes. To the extent that these overhead costs are fixed and will be incurred in any case, they are not incremental to the project and should not be included. Include as incremental expenses only the *additional* overhead expenses that arise because of the decision to take on the project.

Past Research and Development Expenditures. A pharmaceutical company may spend tens of millions of dollars developing a new drug, but if it fails to produce an effect in trials (or worse, has only negative effects), should it proceed? The company cannot get its development costs back, and the amount of those costs should have no bearing on whether to continue developing a failed drug.

When a firm has already devoted significant resources to develop a new product, there may be a tendency to continue investing in the product even if market conditions have changed and the product is unlikely to be viable. The rationale that is sometimes given is that if the product is abandoned, the money that has already been invested will be "wasted." In other cases, a decision is made to abandon a project because it cannot possibly be successful enough to recoup the investment that has already been made. In fact, neither argument is correct: any money that has already been spent is a sunk cost and therefore irrelevant. The decision to continue or abandon should be based only on the incremental costs and benefits of the product going forward.

Adjusting Free Cash Flow

Here, we describe a number of complications that can arise when estimating a project's free cash flow.

Timing of Cash Flows. For simplicity, we have treated the cash flows in our examples as if they occur at annual intervals. In reality, cash flows will be spread throughout the year. While it is common to forecast at the annual level, we can forecast free cash flow on a quarterly or monthly basis when greater accuracy is required. In practice, firms often choose shorter intervals for riskier projects so that they might forecast cash flows at the monthly level for projects that carry considerable risk. For example, cash flows for a new facility in Europe may be forecasted at the quarterly or annual level, but if that same facility were located in a politically unstable country, the forecasts would probably be at the monthly level.

Perpetual *CCA* Tax Shields. The free cash flows we estimated over the five years of the project will miss the value of *CCA* tax shields that occur after the project has ended. If an asset is not sold, it will generate *CCA* expenses and the resulting tax shields every year into perpetuity. Since the *CCA* deducted each year is a proportion of the *UCC*, *UCC* never falls to zero. In Table 8.1 we have the *CCA* deductions for the first five years. You may not see an obvious pattern in the *CCA* deductions, but there is one, and it relates to the way the CRA requires *CCA* to be calculated. Recall that one-half of the *CapEx* is added into the *UCC* initially, and the second half of the *CapEx* is added into the *UCC* in the second year. In effect, one half of the *CapEx* starts having *CCA* applied initially and the other half of the *CapEx* starts having *CCA* applied in the second year. Table 8.4 shows the *CCA* calculated in this way.

Line 7 of the Table 8.4 spreadsheet shows the sum of the *CCA*s calculated from line 2 and line 6. If you compare the *CCA*s in line 7 to those shown in Table 8.1, you will see that they are the same. Why is this useful? Because it will help us calculate the present value of the *CCA* tax shields, including those that continue perpetually.

TABLE 8.4

Breaking Down the CCA into Two Perpetuities

Equivalent CCA calculation using $CCA_t = UCC_t \times d$ and splitting CapEx across two years

Year		0	1	2	3	4	5
Capital Expenditure, CCA, and UCC Forecasts ($000s)							
1	CapEx added to UCC_1	3750					
2	UCC_t	−	3750	2063	1134	624	343
3	$CCA_t = UCC_t \times d$	−	1688	928	510	281	154
4	CapEx added to UCC_2	3750					
5	UCC_t		−	3750	2063	1134	624
6	$CCA_t = UCC_t \times d$		−	1688	928	510	281
7	CCA (line 3) + CCA (line 6)		1688	2616	1439	791	435
8	CCA rate, d	45%					

Notes: For the yellow cells, $UCC_t = UCC_{t-1} - CCA_{t-1}$
Since $CCA_5 < UCC_5$, there will be a positive balance remaining for UCC_6

Recall that each year we can determine the CCA tax shield as $\tau_c \times CCA$. Following the CCA calculations in Table 8.4, Table 8.5 spreadsheet shows the calculations of the CCA tax shields.

The CCA tax shields in line 4 are nothing more than a growing perpetuity with growth rate equal to −45% (thus growth = −d). The first cash flow of this perpetuity occurs in one year, and the cash flow amount is

$$0.5 \times CapEx \times d \times \tau_c$$

The CCA tax shields in line 8 are identical, except they are delayed one additional year. To determine the present value of the total CCA tax shields, we can use the Law of One Price and add the present value of the perpetuity in line 4 to the present value of the perpetuity in line 8. We use the formula for the present value of a growing perpetuity and insert −d for the growth rate.

TABLE 8.5

Breaking Down the CCA Tax Shields into Two Perpetuities

Equivalent CCA, calculation using $CCA_t = UCC_t \times d$ and splitting CapEx across two years

Year		0	1	2	3	4	5	6	...
Capital Expenditure, CCA, and UCC Forecasts ($000s)									
1	CapEx added to UCC_1	3750							
2	UCC_t		3750	2063	1134	624	343	189	...
3	$CCA_t = UCC_t \times d$		1688	928	510	281	154	85	...
4	CCA tax shield = $\tau_c \times CCA$		675	371	204	112	62	34	...
5	CapEx added to UCC_2	3750							
6	UCC_t			3750	2063	1134	624	343	...
7	$CCA_t = UCC_t \times d$			1688	928	510	281	154	...
8	CCA tax shield = $\tau_c \times CCA$			675	371	204	112	62	...
9	Total CCA = CCA (line 3) + CCA (line 7)		1688	2616	1439	791	435	239	...
10	Total CCA tax shield = $\tau_c \times$ Total CCA		675	1046	575	316	174	96	...
11	CCA rate, d	45%							
12	Tax rate, τ_c	40%							

PV of CCA tax shields from line 4: $PV = \dfrac{0.5 \times CapEx \times d \times \tau_c}{r + d}$

PV of CCA tax shields from line 8: $PV = \dfrac{0.5 \times CapEx \times d \times \tau_c}{r + d} \times \dfrac{1}{(1 + r)}$

Summing these two amounts together and simplifying we get the following:

$$PV = \frac{0.5 \times CapEx \times d \times \tau_c}{r + d} \times \frac{(1 + r)}{(1 + r)} + \frac{0.5 \times CapEx \times d \times \tau_c}{r + d} \times \frac{1}{(1 + r)}$$

$$= \frac{0.5 \times CapEx \times d \times \tau_c}{r + d} \times \frac{(2 + r)}{(1 + r)}$$

This results in our formula for the present value the *CCA* tax shield perpetuity:

$$PV_{CCA\ \text{tax shields}} = \frac{CapEx \times d \times \tau_c}{r + d} \times \frac{(1 + \frac{r}{2})}{(1 + r)} \qquad (8.11)$$

If the asset is not sold, then Equation 8.11 gives the present value of all the *CCA* tax shields, including those that continue beyond the end of the project.

If we use Equation 8.11 to get the present value of all the *CCA* tax shields, then we must adjust our calculation of free cash flows so that we do not count any *CCA* tax shields twice. The free cash flows we estimated for the BlackBerry Presenter in Table 8.2 include the *CCA* tax shields for the first five years. To remove the *CCA* tax shields, we can adjust Equations 8.8 and 8.9 by removing all references to *CCA*. Equation 8.12, below, shows the calculation of free cash flows, excluding *CCA* tax shields.

$$FCF_{\text{excluding } CCA \text{ tax shield}} = (\text{Revenues} - \text{Costs}) \times (1 - \tau_c) - CapEx - \Delta NWC \quad (8.12)$$

Equation 8.12 can be used only when we account for the value of *CCA* tax shields separately (as done with Equation 8.11 above or Equation 8.16 below). The Table 8.6 spreadsheet shows the free cash flows and *NPV* recalculated when we separate the *CCA* tax shields in the analysis.

The *PV* of *CCA* tax shields shown in line 17 is calculated as follows:

$$PV_{CCA\ \text{tax shields}} = \frac{7500 \times 0.45 \times 0.40}{0.12 + 0.45} \times \frac{(1 + \frac{0.12}{2})}{(1 + 0.12)} = 2242$$

The *NPV* shown in line 18 of the Table 8.6 spreadsheet is the sum of the present values of the free cash flows (excluding *CCA* tax shields) shown in line 16 and the *PV* of the *CCA* tax shield perpetuity shown in line 17:

$$NPV = -16{,}500 + 4527 + 5835 + 5210 + 4652 + 1277 + 2242 = 7243$$

As you can see, the *NPV* rises from $7.147 million to $7.243 million when we include all the *CCA* tax shield effects. If we were to forget to include the *CCA* tax shields after year 5, then we would underestimate the *NPV* by about $96,000.

Liquidation or Salvage Value. Assets that are no longer needed often have a resale value or some salvage value if the parts are sold for scrap. Some assets may have a negative liquidation value. For example, it may cost money to remove and dispose of the used equipment.

TABLE 8.6	The BlackBerry Presenter's *FCF* and *NPV* with *CCA* Tax Shields Treated Separately					
Year	**0**	**1**	**2**	**3**	**4**	**5**
Incremental Earnings Forecast ($000s)						
1 Sales	–	26,000	26,000	26,000	26,000	–
2 Cost of Goods Sold	–	(11,000)	(11,000)	(11,000)	(11,000)	–
3 Gross Profit	–	15,000	15,000	15,000	15,000	–
4 Selling, General, and Administrative	–	(2800)	(2800)	(2800)	(2800)	–
5 Research and Development	(15,000)	–	–	–	–	–
6 Capital Cost Allowance (*CCA*)		not included, as analyzed separately				
7 *EBIT*	(15,000)	12,200	12,200	12,200	12,200	–
8 Income Tax at 40%	6000	(4880)	(4880)	(4880)	(4880)	–
9 Unlevered Net Income	(9000)	7320	7320	7320	7320	–
Free Cash Flow ($000s)						
10 Plus: *CCA*		not included, as analyzed separately				
11 Less: Net Capital Expenditures	(7500)					
12 Less: Increases in *NWC*	–	(2250)	–	–	–	2250
13 Free Cash Flow_excluding *CCA* tax shields	(16,500)	5070	7320	7320	7320	2250
14 Project Cost of Capital	12%					
15 Discount Factor	1.0000	0.8929	0.7972	0.7118	0.6355	0.5674
16 PV of Free Cash Flow_excluding *CCA* tax shield	(16,500)	4527	5835	5210	4652	1277
17 PV of *CCA* tax Shields (Equation 8.11)	2242					
18 *NPV*	7243					

In the calculation of expected free cash flow for date t, we include the expected liquidation value of any assets that are expected to be sold during year t. In addition, we need to include the expected tax effects from selling the asset. There are two main tax effects. First, there will be a **capital gain tax** if the asset is sold for an amount greater than its original purchase price, denoted by *CapEx*. CRA taxes one-half of the gain at the corporate tax rate:

capital gain tax A tax collected on the profit (the amount by which the sale price exceeds the original purchase price) from assets in the year in which the assets are sold.

$$\text{Capital Gain Tax} = \tfrac{1}{2} \times (\text{Sale Price} - CapEx)\, \tau_c \qquad (8.13)$$

The capital gain tax will be paid in the tax year the asset is sold and will be included in the free cash flow for that year as a negative effect. When we discussed purchasing an asset at date 0, we assumed the tax effect (the *CCA* tax shield) would occur at date 1 because the asset was purchased just after the year 0 end-of-year for tax purposes. To be consistent, we will assume that an asset sale at date t is actually at the beginning of the tax year $t + 1$. Thus, given an asset sale at date t, the capital gain tax should be deducted from the free cash flow for date $t + 1$.[4]

The second tax effect from selling an asset is that the subsequent *CCA* deductions and tax shields will change. The *UCC* for the asset will be reduced by the asset sale in the tax year of the asset sale. The minimum of the Sale Price and the original purchase price, *CapEx*, is subtracted from the *UCC* to get the Post-Sale *UCC*. If the asset is sold at date t, we will continue our assumption that the sale is at the beginning of tax year $t + 1$.

$$\text{Post-Sale } UCC_{t+1} = UCC_{t+1} - \text{minimum of (Sale Price}_t, CapEx) \qquad (8.14)$$

---

[4] Other assumptions can be made about the timing of the asset sale. If the asset sale occurs within tax year t rather than at the beginning of tax year $t + 1$, then the capital gain tax would reduce the free cash flow for date t.

Post-Sale UCC_{t+1} will be used as the basis to determine CCA_{t+1} and subsequent CCA deductions.

The way post-sale CCA deductions are calculated depends on whether Post-Sale UCC_{t+1} for the asset pool is positive or negative, whether or not the firm still owns any assets in that asset pool, and whether or not the firm will be buying additional assets in that pool with value greater than the asset's expected Sale Price. We will assume that other assets remain in the asset pool and Post-Sale UCC_{t+1} for the asset pool remains positive. With this assumption we have what is called a **continuing pool**. We will also assume that in the tax year of the asset sale, future purchases of assets (for other projects) will be less than the asset's expected Sale Price; this is referred to as **negative net additions**.[5]

Continuing Pool, Negative Net Additions: With a continuing pool and negative net additions, adjustments must be made to the post-sale CCA amounts and resulting tax shields. The effect of the asset sale is fully recognized in the tax year of the sale and the UCC is reduced accordingly. Utilizing what we know from deriving Equation 8.11, the present value of the reduction in CCA tax shields can be calculated as follows:

$$PV_{\text{lost CCA tax shields}} = \frac{\min(\text{Sale Price}_t, CapEx) \times d \times \tau_c}{r + d} \times \frac{1}{(1+r)^t} \qquad (8.15)$$

In Equation 8.15, the first reduction in CCA tax shields is in year $t + 1$. The growing perpetuity formula discounts the lost CCA tax shields back to date t; the last term on Equation 8.15 discounts from date t to date 0.

We can combine Equations 8.11 and 8.15 to get the overall present value of expected CCA tax shields under the condition of an expected continuing pool of assets and negative net additions when the asset is sold:

$$PV_{\text{CCA tax shields}} = \frac{CapEx \times d \times \tau_c}{r + d} \times \frac{(1 + \frac{r}{2})}{(1 + r)}$$
$$- \frac{\min(\text{Sale Price}_t, CapEx) \times d \times \tau_c}{r + d} \times \frac{1}{(1+r)^t} \qquad (8.16)[6]$$

Remember to consider all the effects of the asset sale. Given our assumptions about the timing of the asset purchase and sale with respect to the relevant tax years, we consider the sale price, CCA tax shield effects, and capital gain tax as follows. We add the sale price to the free cash flow for year t. We use Equation 8.16 instead of Equation 8.11 in order to calculate the present value of all the expected CCA tax shields. If there is a capital gain, we subtract the capital gain tax (Equation 8.13) from the free cash flow for year $t + 1$.

continuing pool An asset pool in which there exists positive undepreciated capital cost (UCC) for which the company still own assets.

negative net additions A situation in which a continuing asset pool has asset purchases less than asset sales in the same tax year. (The UCC of the pool will decline but still remain positive.)

[5] If purchases of other assets are less than the disposed asset's expected sale price, they are referred to as positive net additions. The formula for calculating the present value of lost CCA tax shields when positive net additions exist is the same as for negative net additions, except that the half-year rule is applied to the calculation. Further complications arise when the asset pool does not continue, giving rise to either terminal loss or recaptured CCA tax effects. These topics are reserved for intermediate-level corporate finance textbooks.

[6] Alternative assumptions about the timing of the asset purchase or sale can be easily accommodated. For instance, if the asset is purchased at the end of tax year 0 rather than the beginning of tax year 1, the first term of Equation 8.16 would have to be multiplied by $(1 + r)$. If the asset is expected to be sold at the end of tax-year t rather than the beginning of tax year $t + 1$, then the last term of Equation 8.16 would be multiplied by $(1 + r)$. Often business reasons (rather than just the tax implications) drive the timing of the asset sale, so it is important to understand how to adjust these formulas.

EXAMPLE 8.5

Adding Salvage Value and *CCA* Effects to the Analysis

Problem

RIM is expected to sell the specialized computer equipment at date 4 (or the beginning of tax year 5), as the lab will be shut down at that point. The expected Sale Price is high, $8 million, because of the expected appreciation of precious minerals used within the computer equipment. It is expected that RIM will still own other computer equipment at that time but will not be making such purchases in excess of $8 million in tax year 5. Redo the *NPV* calculation for the BlackBerry Presenter project, given this new information.

Solution

▶ **Plan**

In order to compute the after-tax cash flow, you will need to incorporate the effects on cash flows of the salvage value, the capital gains tax (using Equation 8.13), and the lost *CCA* tax shields (using Equation 8.16).

▶ **Execute**

Add in the $8 million to the free cash flow for year 4 and replace Equation 8.11 with Equation 8.16 to take into account how *CCA* tax shields will be changed by the asset sale. Since there is a capital gain, calculate the capital gain tax and deduct it from the free cash flow for year 5. The results are shown in the spreadsheet below.

Year		0	1	2	3	4	5
	Incremental Earnings Forecast ($000s)						
1	Sales	–	26,000	26,000	26,000	26,000	–
2	Cost of Goods Sold	–	(11,000)	(11,000)	(11,000)	(11,000)	–
3	Gross Profit	–	15,000	15,000	15,000	15,000	–
4	Selling, General, and Administrative	–	(2800)	(2800)	(2800)	(2800)	–
5	Research and Development	(15,000)	–	–	–	–	–
6	Capital Cost Allowance (*CCA*)		not included, as analyzed separately				
7	*EBIT*	(15,000)	12,200	12,200	12,200	12,200	–
8	Income Tax at 40%	6000	(4880)	(4880)	(4880)	(4880)	–
9	Unlevered Net Income	(9000)	7320	7320	7320	7320	–
	Free Cash Flow ($000s)						
10	Plus: *CCA*		not included, as analyzed separately				
11	Less: Net Capital Expenditures	(7500)	–	–	–	8000	–
12	Less: Increases in *NWC*	–	(2250)	–	–	–	2250
13	Less: Capital Gain Tax	–	–	–	–	–	(100)
14	Free Cash Flow_{excluding *CCA* tax shields}	(16,500)	5070	7320	7320	15320	2150
15	Project Cost of Capital	12%					
16	Discount Factor	1.0000	0.8929	0.7972	0.7118	0.6355	0.5674
17	*PV* of Free Cash Flow_{excluding *CCA* tax shield}	(16,500)	4527	5835	5210	9736	1220
18	*PV* of *CCA* tax Shields (Equation 8.16)	736					
19	*NPV*	10,765*					

Note that the $8 million from the asset sale is the same as a negative capital expenditure. It is reflected in line 11 of the spreadsheet and is added into the free cash flow for year 4. The capital gain tax shown in line 13 is calculated using Equation 8.13 as follows.

$$\text{Capital Gain Tax} = \frac{1}{2} \times (8000 - 7500) \times 0.40 = 100$$

Since the asset is sold at the beginning of tax year 5, the capital gain tax reduces free cash flow for year 5. The present value of *CCA* tax shields, using Equation 8.16, in line 18 is calculated as follows:

$$PV_{CCA\ tax\ shields} = \frac{7500 \times 0.45 \times 0.40}{0.12 + 0.45} \times \frac{(1 + \frac{0.12}{2})}{(1 + 0.12)} - \frac{7500 \times 0.45 \times 0.40}{0.12 + 0.45} \times \frac{1}{(1 + 0.12)^4}$$

The *NPV* (line 19) is the sum of the present values of the free cash flows (excluding *CCA* tax shields) plus the *PV* of *CCA* tax shields calculated with Equation 8.16.

$$NPV = -16,500 + 4527 + 5835 + 5210 + 9736 + 1220 + 736$$

$$= 10,764\ (^*\text{difference is due to rounding})$$

▶ **Evaluate**

You should notice that the *NPV* is much higher than what was calculated in the Table 8.6 spreadsheet. The reason it is higher is because of the large asset sale price. Also note that the *PV* of *CCA* tax shields is lower and there is a capital gain; these are the other effects of the asset sale.

Tax Carryforwards. A firm generally identifies its marginal tax rate by determining the tax bracket that it falls into based on its overall level of pre-tax income. Two additional features of the tax code, called **tax loss carryforwards** and **carrybacks**, allow corporations to take losses during a current year and offset them against gains in nearby years. In Canada, companies can "carry back" losses for 3 years and, for tax years after 2005, companies can "carry forward" losses for 20 years. This tax rule means that a firm can offset losses during 1 year against income for the last 3 years, or save the losses to be offset against income during the next 20 years. When a firm can carry back losses, it receives a refund for back taxes in the current year. Otherwise, the firm must carry forward the loss and use it to offset future taxable income. When a firm has tax loss carry forwards well in excess of its current pre-tax income, then additional income it earns today will simply increase the taxes it owes after it exhausts its carryforwards.

tax loss carryforwards and **carrybacks** Two features of the U.S. tax code that allow corporations to take losses during a current year and offset them against gains in nearby years. Since 1997, companies can "carry back" losses for 2 years and "carry forward" losses for 20 years.

Replacement Decisions

Often the financial manager must decide whether to replace an existing piece of equipment. The new equipment may allow increased production, resulting in incremental revenue, or it may simply be more efficient, lowering costs. The typical incremental effects associated with such a decision are salvage value from the old machine, purchase of the new machine, cost savings and revenue increases, and depreciation effects.

EXAMPLE 8.6

Replacing an Existing Machine

Problem

You are trying to decide whether to replace a machine on your production line. The new machine will cost $1.25 million but will be more efficient than the old machine, reducing costs by $500,000 per year. Your old machine could be sold for $50,000. You expect to sell the new machine for $100,000 after five years. While the company does not intend to add any more assets into the pool in five years, it does have many assets in the pool, so the pool will continue indefinitely. The new machine will not change your working capital needs. The *CCA* rate is 45%. The tax rate is 40% and the firm expects a 12% return on this project.

Solution

▶ **Plan**

Incremental revenues: 0

Incremental costs: −$500,000 (a reduction in costs will appear as a positive number in the costs line of our analysis)

Incremental capital expenditure: $1.25 million − $50,000 = $1.2 million. This is the net change to the asset pool upon replacement.

Cash flow from salvage value: +$100,000

▶ **Execute**

Year	0	1	2	3	4	5
Incremental Earnings Forecast ($000s)						
1 Sales	–	–	–	–	–	–
2 Cost of Goods Sold	–	500,000	500,000	500,000	500,000	500,000
3 Gross Profit	–	500,000	500,000	500,000	500,000	500,000
6 Capital Cost Allowance (*CCA*)		not included, as analyzed separately				
7 *EBIT*	–	500,000	500,000	500,000	500,000	500,000
8 Income Tax at 40%	–	(200,000)	(200,000)	(200,000)	(200,000)	(200,000)
9 Unlevered Net Income	–	300,000	300,000	300,000	300,000	300,000
Free Cash Flow ($000s)						
10 Plus: *CCA*		not included, as analyzed separately				
11 Less: Net Capital Expenditures	(1,200,000)	–	–	–	–	100,000
14 Free Cash Flow$_{\text{excluding } CCA \text{ tax shields}}$	(1,200,000)	300,000	300,000	300,000	300,000	400,000
15 Project Cost of Capital	12%					
16 Discount Factor	1.0000	0.8929	0.7972	0.7118	0.6355	0.5674
17 *PV* of Free Cash Flow$_{\text{excluding } CCA \text{ tax shield}}$	(1,200,000)	267,857	239,158	213,534	190,655	226,971
18 *PV* of *CCA* tax Shields (Equation 8.16)	338,578					
19 *NPV*	276,753					

▶ **Evaluate**

Even though the decision has no impact on revenues, it still matters for cash flows because it reduces costs. Just as important are the tax implications of both selling the old machine and buying the new machine. Notice that the *PV* of the *CCA* tax shields is greater than the *NPV*. Had we not considered these tax implications, the replacement opportunity would not have looked like a good one.

Concept Check

7. Should we include sunk costs in the cash flows of a project? Why or why not?
8. Explain why it is advantageous for a firm to use the most accelerated depreciation schedule possible for tax purposes.

8.5 Analyzing the Project

When evaluating a capital budgeting project, financial managers should make the decision that maximizes *NPV*. As we have discussed, to compute the *NPV* for a project you need to estimate the incremental free cash flows and choose a discount rate. Given these inputs, the *NPV* calculation is relatively straightforward. The most difficult part of capital budgeting is deciding how to estimate the cash flows and cost of capital. These estimates are often subject to significant uncertainty. In this section, we look at methods that assess the importance of this uncertainty and identify the drivers of value in the project.

Sensitivity Analysis

sensitivity analysis
An important capital budgeting tool that shows how the *NPV* varies as a single underlying assumption is changed.

An important capital budgeting tool for assessing the effect of uncertainty in forecasts is sensitivity analysis. **Sensitivity analysis** breaks the *NPV* calculation into its component assumptions and shows how the *NPV* varies as the underlying assumptions change. In this way, sensitivity analysis allows us to explore the effects of errors in our *NPV* estimates for a project. By conducting a sensitivity analysis, we learn which assumptions are the most important; we can then invest further resources and effort to refine these assumptions. Such an analysis also reveals which aspects of a project are most critical when we are actually managing the project.

In fact, we have already performed a type of sensitivity analysis in Chapter 7 when we constructed an *NPV* profile. By graphing the *NPV* of a project as a function of the discount rate, we are assessing the sensitivity of our *NPV* calculation to uncertainty about the correct cost of capital to use as a discount rate. In practice, financial managers explore the sensitivity of their *NPV* calculation to many more factors than just the discount rate.

To illustrate, consider the assumptions underlying the calculation of the BlackBerry Presenter's *NPV* in Example 8.4. There is likely to be significant uncertainty surrounding each revenue and cost assumption. In addition to the base-case assumptions about units sold, sale price, cost of goods sold, *NWC*, and cost of capital, RIM's managers would also identify best and worst case scenarios for each. For example, assume that they identified the best- and worst-case assumptions listed in Table 8.7. Note that these are best- and worst-case scenarios for each parameter rather than representing one worst-case scenario and one best-case scenario.

To determine the importance of this uncertainty, we recalculate the *NPV* of the BlackBerry Presenter project under the best- and worst-case assumptions for each parameter. For example, if the number of units sold is only 70,000 per year, the *NPV* of the project falls to −$1.053 million. We repeat this calculation for each parameter. The result is shown in Figure 8.2, which reveals that the parameter assumptions with the largest effect on *NPV* are the number of units sold and the sale price per unit. As a result, these assumptions deserve the greatest scrutiny during the estimation process. In addition, as the most important drivers of the project's value, these factors deserve close attention when managing the project after it starts.

Break-Even Analysis

break-even The level for which an investment has an *NPV* of zero.

A natural extension of the sensitivity analysis is to ask at what level of each parameter the project would just break even, that is, the level—or **break-even**—for which the investment has an *NPV* of zero. One example that we have already considered is the calculation of the internal rate of return (*IRR*). Recall from Chapter 7 that the difference between the *IRR* of a project and the cost of capital tells you how much error in the cost of capital it would take to change the investment decision. By either graphing the *NPV* profile or using the Excel function *IRR*, we would find that the incremental cash flows of the BlackBerry Presenter given in Example 8.4 imply an *IRR* of 29.3%. Hence, the true cost of capital can be as high as 29.3% and the project will still have a positive *NPV*.

TABLE 8.7	Parameter	Initial Assumption	Worst Case	Best Case
	Units Sold (thousands)	100	70	130
Best- and Worst-Case Assumptions for Each Parameter in the BlackBerry Presenter Project	Sale Price ($/unit)	260	240	280
	Cost of Goods ($/unit)	110	120	100
	NWC ($ thousands)	2250	3050	1450
	Cost of Capital	12%	15%	10%

FIGURE 8.2

BlackBerry's *NPV* Under Best- and Worst-Case Parameter Assumptions

Bars show the change in *NPV* going from the best-case assumption to the worst-case assumption for each parameter. For example, the *NPV* of the project ranges from −$1.053 million if only 70,000 units are sold, to $15.348 million if 130,000 units are sold. Under the initial assumptions, BlackBerry Presenter's *NPV* is $7.147 million.

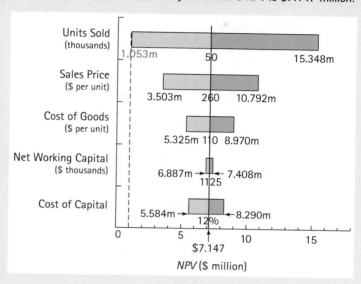

We can determine the uncertainty of other parameters as well. In a **break-even analysis**, for each parameter we calculate the value at which the *NPV* of the project is zero. This would be tedious to do by hand, so in practice it is always done with a spreadsheet. As with the *NPV* profile for the discount rate, we can graph the *NPV* as a function of each of the critical assumptions. In each case, we keep all of the other parameters fixed at their base-case values and vary only the parameter in question. Figure 8.3 does this for the BlackBerry Presenter.

break-even analysis A calculation of the value of each parameter for which the *NPV* of the project is zero.

Accounting Break-Even. We have examined the break-even levels in terms of the project's *NPV*, which is the most useful perspective for decision making. Other accounting notions of break-even are sometimes considered, however. For example, we could compute the *EBIT* **break-even** for sales, which is the level of sales for which the project's *EBIT* is zero.

Recall from Equation 8.3 that the project's *EBIT* is Revenues − Costs − CCA. Costs include cost of goods sold and selling, general, and administrative expense (SG&A), and research and development (R&D). Revenues equal Units Sold Sale Price, and cost of goods sold equals Units Sold × Cost per Unit, so we have *EBIT* = (Units Sold × Sale Price) − (Units Sold × Cost per Unit) − SG&A − R&D − CCA. Setting this equal to zero and solving for units sold:

EBIT break-even The level of a particular parameter for which a project's *EBIT* is zero.

$$\text{Units Sold} \times (\text{Sale Price} - \text{Cost per unit}) - \text{SG\&A} - \text{Depreciation} = 0$$

$$\text{Units Sold} = \frac{\text{SG\&A} + \text{R\&D} + CCA}{\text{Sales Price} - \text{Cost per unit}} = \frac{\$2,800,000 + 0 + 1,688,500}{260 - 110} = 29,923$$

However, this *EBIT* break-even number is misleading. First, it is difficult to derive much use from the year 1 break-even unit sales, as the break-even number

FIGURE 8.3

Break-Even Analysis Graphs

The graphs in panels (a) and (b) relate two of the key parameters to the project's *NPV* to identify the parameters' break-even points. For example, based on the initial assumptions, the BlackBerry Presenter project will break even with a sales level of just under 74,000 units per year. Similarly, holding sales and the other parameters constant at their initial assumed values, the project will break even at a cost of goods sold of just over $149 per unit.

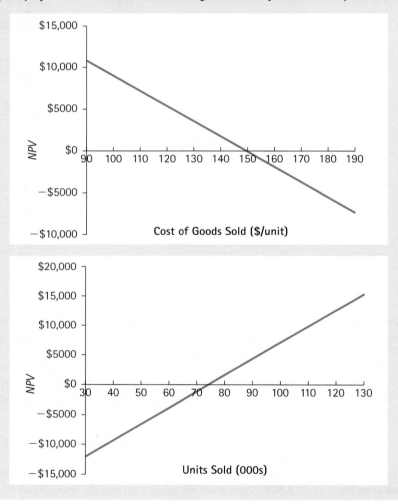

would change each year due to the fact that *CCA* deductions will differ each year. Additionally, while BlackBerry Presenter's *EBIT* break-even level of sales in the first year is only 29,923 units per year, given the large upfront investment and research and development (incurred in year 0) required in the BlackBerry Presenter project, its *NPV*, −$12.011 million, is at that sales level.

scenario analysis
An important capital budgeting tool that shows how the *NPV* varies as a number of the underlying assumptions are changed simultaneously.

Scenario Analysis

In the analysis thus far, we have considered the consequences of varying only one parameter at a time. In reality, certain factors may affect more than one parameter. **Scenario analysis** considers the effect on *NPV* of changing multiple project parameters. For example, lowering the BlackBerry Presenter's price may increase the number of

TABLE 8.8	Strategy	Sale Price ($/unit)	Expected Units Sold (thousands)	NPV ($ thousands)
Scenario Analysis of Alternative Pricing Strategies	Current Strategy	260	100	7147
	Price Reduction	245	110	6874
	Price Increase	275	90	6874

FIGURE 8.4

Price and Volume Combinations for BlackBerry Presenter with Equivalent *NPV*

The graph shows alternative price per unit and annual volume combinations that lead to an *NPV* of $7.147 million. Pricing strategies with combinations above this line will lead to a higher *NPV* and are superior. For example, if RIM managers think they will be able to sell 90,000 units at a price of $300, this strategy would yield a higher *NPV* ($10,974 million).

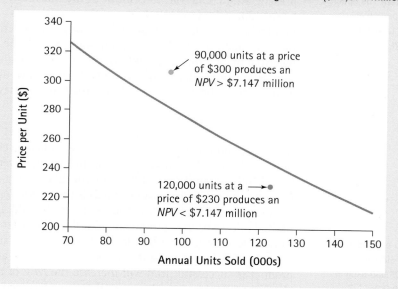

units sold. We can use scenario analysis to evaluate alternative pricing strategies for the BlackBerry Presenter product in Table 8.8. In this case, the current strategy is optimal. Figure 8.4 shows the combinations of price and volume that lead to the same *NPV* of $7.147 million for the BlackBerry Presenter as the current strategy. Only strategies with price and volume combinations above the line will lead to a higher *NPV*.

Concept Check

9. What is sensitivity analysis?
10. How does scenario analysis differ from sensitivity analysis?

8.6 Real Options in Capital Budgeting

real option The right to make a particular business decision, such as a capital investment.

Our approach to capital budgeting thus far has focused on the initial investment decision without explicitly considering future decisions that may need to be made over the life of a project. Rather, we assumed that our forecast of a project's expected future cash flows already incorporated the effect of future decisions that would be made. In truth, most projects contain *real options*. A **real option** is the right, but not the obligation, to make a particular business decision. Because you are not obligated to take the action, you will do so only if it increases the *NPV* of the project. In particular, because real options allow a decision maker to choose the most attractive alternative after new information has been learned, the presence of real options adds value to an investment opportunity. The tools to estimate the actual value created by real options are beyond the scope of this chapter and are provided later in the book. However, we introduce the concept here to give you a sense of the types of real options you may encounter and establish the idea that flexibility (more options) is valuable. Let's look at some of the most common real options in the context of RIM's BlackBerry Presenter project.

Option to Delay

option to delay commitment The option to time a particular investment, which is almost always present.

The **option to delay commitment** (the option to time the investment) is almost always present. RIM could wait to commit to the BlackBerry Presenter project. Waiting could be valuable if RIM expects prices of the components—for example, soon-to-be-released new technology that will make the existing components obsolete—to decrease substantially. In addition, RIM may simply want more time to gather information about the potential market for the BlackBerry Presenter. As with any other capital budgeting decision, RIM would choose to delay only if doing so would increase the *NPV* of the project by more than the cost of capital over the time of delay.

Option to Expand

In the section on sensitivity analysis, we looked at changes in our assumptions about units sold. All of the analysis was performed, however, under the assumption that RIM would fully commit to and roll out the BlackBerry Presenter worldwide. We did not consider the option to expand, which is the option to start with limited production and expand only if the product is successful. RIM could, instead, testmarket the product in limited release before committing to it fully. Doing so would create an **option to expand** worldwide only if the BlackBerry Presenter were successful in limited release. It is possible that, by reducing its upfront commitment and choosing to expand only if the product is successful, RIM will increase the *NPV* of the BlackBerry Presenter product. However, in this particular case, there are large costs of development that would be paid whether RIM sells one or hundreds of thousands of units, so limiting the initial market does not reduce the financial commitment substantially. Thus, in the case of the BlackBerry Presenter, it is unlikely that RIM would choose a limited release with an option to expand.

option to expand The option to start with limited production and expand only if the project is successful.

Option to Abandon

abandonment option An option for an investor to cease making investments in a project. Abandonment options can add value to a project because a firm can drop a project if it turns out to be unsuccessful.

An **abandonment option** is the option to walk away. Abandonment options can add value to a project because a firm can drop a project if it turns out to be unsuccessful. Imagine that a competitor developed new technology that allowed it to introduce a competing product priced at $170. At that price, RIM would produce substantially lower cash flows every year. Would RIM continue to sell the BlackBerry Presenter if it had to do so at a loss? Probably not. RIM has an option to abandon the project. It could stop producing the BlackBerry Presenter and sell the equipment. Depending on how much RIM believes the equipment would sell for if it abandoned the project, the abandonment option could make the BlackBerry Presenter attractive even if there was a substantial risk of a competing product.

Many industries regularly make use of real options. For example, most movie producers build in an option for a sequel if the first movie does well. Pharmaceutical developers such as Merck develop new drugs in stages, allowing the company to abandon development if tests do not go well. All these options point to the same conclusion: *if you can build greater flexibility into your project, you will increase the NPV of the project.* In Chapter 20, we will discuss how to value options so that you can estimate just how much more valuable the project is with greater flexibility.

Concept Check

11. What are real options?

12. Why do real options increase the *NPV* of the project?

MyFinanceLab Here is what you should know after reading this chapter. MyFinanceLab will help you identify what you know, and where to go when you need to practice.

Key Points and Equations	Terms	Online Practice Opportunities
8.1 The Capital Budgeting Process ▶ Capital budgeting is the process of analyzing investment opportunities and deciding which ones to accept. A capital budget is a list of all projects that a company plans to undertake during the next period. ▶ We use the *NPV* rule to evaluate capital budgeting decisions, making decisions that maximize *NPV*. When deciding to accept or reject a project, we accept projects with a positive *NPV*.	capital budget, p. 242 capital budgeting, p. 242 incremental earnings, p. 242	MyFinanceLab Study Plan 8.1
8.2 Forecasting Incremental Earnings ▶ The incremental earnings of a project comprise the amount by which the project is expected to change the firm's earnings. ▶ Incremental earnings should include all incremental revenues and costs associated with the project. $$\text{Incremental Earnings} = (\text{Incremental Revenues} - \text{Incremental Cost} - \text{Depreciation}) \times (1 - \text{Tax Rate}) \quad (8.3)$$ ▶ Interest and other financing-related expenses are excluded to determine the project's unlevered net income.	asset classes, p. 244 asset pool, p. 244 capital cost allowance (CCA), p. 244 CCA rate, p. 244 half-year rule, p. 244 marginal corporate tax rate, p. 246 pro forma statement, p. 247 tax year, p. 244 undepreciated capital cost (UCC), p. 244 unlevered net income, p. 247	MyFinanceLab Study Plan 8.2
8.3 Determining Incremental Free Cash Flow ▶ We compute free cash flow from incremental earnings by eliminating all non-cash expenses and including all capital investment. ▶ Depreciation is not a cash expense, so it is added back.	CCA tax shield, p. 253 free cash flow, p. 248 trade credit, p. 250	MyFinanceLab Study Plan 8.3

▶ Actual capital expenditures are deducted.

▶ Increases in *NWC* are deducted and decreases are added. *NWC* is defined as

$$\text{Cash} + \text{Inventory} + \text{Receivables} - \text{Payables} \quad (8.6)$$

▶ The basic calculation for free cash flow is

$$\text{Free Cash Flow} = \overbrace{(\text{Revenues} - \text{Costs} - CCA)}^{\text{Unlevered Net Income}} \\ \times (1 - \text{tax rate}) + CCA \quad (8.8) \\ - CapEx - \text{Change in } NWC$$

8.4 Other Effects on Incremental Free Cash Flows

▶ An opportunity cost is the cost of using an existing asset.

▶ Project externalities are cash flows that occur when a project affects other areas of the company's business.

▶ A sunk cost is an unrecoverable cost that has already been incurred.

▶ Depreciation expenses affect free cash flow only through the depreciation tax shield. The firm should use the most accelerated depreciation schedule possible.

▶ The discount rate for a project is its cost of capital: the expected return of securities with comparable risk and horizon.

▶ When you sell an asset, the portion of the proceeds above its book value is taxed:

$$\text{After-Tax Cash Flow from Asset Sale} = \text{Sale Price} - (\text{Tax Rate} \times \text{Capital Gain})$$

cannibalization, p. 255
capital gain tax, p. 259
continuing pool, p. 260
negative net additions, p. 260
opportunity cost, p. 254
overhead expenses, p. 256
project externalities, p. 255
sunk cost, p. 255
tax loss carryforwards and carrybacks, p. 262

MyFinanceLab
Study Plan 8.4

BlackBerry
Presenter Example
Spreadsheet

8.5 Analyzing the Project

▶ Sensitivity analysis breaks the *NPV* calculation down into its component assumptions, showing how the *NPV* varies as the values of the underlying assumptions change.

▶ Break-even analysis computes the level of a parameter that makes the project's *NPV* equal zero.

▶ Scenario analysis considers the effect of changing multiple parameters simultaneously.

break-even, p. 264
break-even analysis, p. 265
EBIT break-even, p. 265
scenario analysis, p. 266
sensitivity analysis, p. 264

MyFinanceLab
Study Plan 8.5

Interactive
Sensitivity
Analysis, Using
Excel: Performing
Sensitivity Analysis

8.6 Real Options in Capital Budgeting

▶ Real options are options to make a business decision, often after gathering more information. The presence of real options in a project increases the project's *NPV*.

abandonment option, p. 268
option to expand, p. 268
option to delay commitment, p. 268
real option, p. 267

MyFinanceLab
Study Plan 8.6

Review Questions

1. What are pro forma incremental earnings?

2. What is the difference between pro forma incremental earnings and pro forma free cash flow?

3. Why do we convert from incremental earnings to free cash flow when performing capital budgeting?

4. What is the role of NWC in projects?

5. How does NWC affect the cash flows of a project?

6. Why is it important to adjust project sales and costs for externalities?

7. How is sensitivity analysis performed and what is its purpose?

Problems

All problems in this chapter are available in MyFinanceLab. An asterisk (*) indicates problems with a higher level of difficulty.

The Capital Budgeting Process

1. Daily Enterprises is purchasing a $10 million machine. It will cost $50,000 to transport and install the machine. The machine has a depreciable life of five years and will have no salvage value. Assume that CCA deductions are the same as depreciation expenses. If Daily uses straight-line depreciation, what are the depreciation expenses associated with this machine?

2. The machine in Problem 1 will generate incremental revenues of $4 million per year along with incremental costs of $1.2 million per year. If Daily's marginal tax rate is 35%, what are the incremental earnings associated with the new machine?

3. You are upgrading to better production equipment for your firm's only product. The new equipment will allow you to make more of your product in the same amount of time. Thus, you forecast that total sales will increase next year by 20% over the current amount of 100,000 units. If your sales price is $20 per unit, what are the incremental revenues next year from the upgrade?

4. Pisa Pizza, a seller of frozen pizza, is considering introducing a healthier version of its pizza that will be low in cholesterol and contain no trans-fats. The firm expects that sales of the new pizza will be $20 million per year. While many of these sales will be to new customers, Pisa Pizza estimates that 40% will come from customers who switch to the new, healthier pizza instead of buying the original version.
   a. Assume customers will spend the same amount on either version. What level of incremental sales is associated with introducing the new pizza?
   b. Suppose that 50% of the customers who would switch from Pisa Pizza's original pizza to its healthier pizza will switch to another brand if Pisa Pizza does not introduce a healthier pizza. What level of incremental sales is associated with introducing the new pizza in this case?

5. Kokomochi is considering the launch of an advertising campaign for its latest dessert product, the Mini Mochi Munch. Kokomochi plans to spend $5 million on TV, radio, and print advertising this year for the campaign. The ads are expected to boost sales of the Mini Mochi Munch by $9 million this year and by $7 million next year. In addition, the company expects that new consumers who try the Mini Mochi Munch will be more likely to try Kokomochi's other products. As a result, sales of other products are expected to rise by $2 million each year.

Kokomochi's gross profit margin for the Mini Mochi Munch is 35%, and its gross profit margin averages 25% for all other products. The company's marginal corporate tax rate is 35% both this year and next year. What are the incremental earnings associated with the advertising campaign?

6. Hyperion, Inc. currently sells its latest high-speed colour printer, the Hyper 500, for $350. It plans to lower the price to $300 next year. Its cost of goods sold for the Hyper 500 is $200 per unit, and this year's sales are expected to be 20,000 units.
   a. Suppose that if Hyperion drops the price to $300 immediately, it can increase this year's sales by 25% to 25,000 units. What would be the incremental impact on this year's *EBIT* of such a price drop?
   b. Suppose that for each printer sold, Hyperion expects additional sales of $75 per year on ink cartridges for the next three years, and Hyperion has a gross profit margin of 70% on ink cartridges. What is the incremental impact on *EBIT* for the next three years of a price drop this year?

Determining Incremental Free Cash Flow

7. You are forecasting incremental free cash flows for Daily Enterprises. Based on the information in Problems 1 and 2, what are the incremental free cash flows associated with the new machine?

8. Royal Mount Games would like to invest in a division to develop software for video games. To evaluate this decision, the firm first attempts to project the working capital needs for this operation. Its chief financial officer has developed the following estimates (in millions of dollars):

1	Year	1	2	3	4	5
2	Cash	6	12	15	15	15
3	Accounts Receivable	21	22	24	24	24
4	Inventory	5	7	10	12	13
5	Accounts Payable	18	22	24	25	30

Assuming that Royal Mount Games currently does not have any working capital invested in this division, calculate the cash flows associated with changes in working capital for the first five years of this investment.

9. Anola Inc.'s projected receivables are 15% of sales and its payables are 15% of cost of goods sold (*COGS*). Forecast the required investment in *NWC* for Anola Inc. assuming that sales and *COGS* will be:

1	Year	0	1	2	3	4
2	Sales		23,500	26,438	23,794	8566
3	*COGS*		9500	10,688	9619	3483

10. Etobicoke Enterprises is deciding whether to expand its production facilities. Although long-term cash flows are difficult to estimate, management has projected the following cash flows for the first two years (in millions of dollars):

1	Year	1	2
2	Revenues	125	160
3	Operating Expenses (other than depreciation)	40	60
4	CCA	25	36
5	Increase in Net Working Capital	2	8
6	Capital Expenditures	30	40
7	Marginal Corporate Tax Rate	35%	35%

a. What are the incremental earnings for this project for years 1 and 2?

b. What are the free cash flows for this project for the first two years?

11. Atlantic Telecom reported net income of $250 million for the most recent fiscal year. The firm had *CCA* deductions of $100 million (assume reported depreciation was equal to this *CCA*), capital expenditures of $200 million, and no interest expenses. *NWC* increased by $10 million. Calculate the free cash flow for Atlantic Telecom for the most recent fiscal year.

12. Recall the BlackBerry Presenter example from this chapter. Suppose the BlackBerry Presenters will be housed in warehouse space that the company could have otherwise rented out for $200,000 per year during years 1 to 4. How does this opportunity cost affect Presenter's incremental earnings?

*13. One year ago, your company purchased a machine used in manufacturing for $110,000. You have learned that a new machine is available that offers many advantages, and you can purchase it for $150,000 today. The *CCA* rate applicable to both machines is 40%; neither machine will have any long-term salvage value. You expect that the new machine will produce earnings before interest, taxes, depreciation, and amortization (*EBITDA*) of $40,000 per year for the next 10 years. The current machine is expected to produce *EBITDA* of $20,000 per year. All other expenses of the two machines are identical. The market value today of the current machine is $50,000. Your company's tax rate is 45%, and the opportunity cost of capital for this type of equipment is 10%. Should your company replace its year-old machine?

*14. Big Rock Brewery currently rents a bottling machine for $50,000 per year, including all maintenance expenses. The company is considering purchasing a machine instead and is comparing two options:

a. Purchase the machine it is currently renting for $150,000. This machine will require $20,000 per year in ongoing maintenance expenses.

b. Purchase a new, more advanced machine for $250,000. This machine will require $15,000 per year in ongoing maintenance expenses and will lower bottling costs by $10,000 per year. Also, $35,000 will be spent up front in training the new operators of the machine.

Suppose the appropriate discount rate is 8% per year and the machine is purchased today. Maintenance and bottling costs are paid at the end of each year, as is the rental of the machine. Assume also that the machines are subject to a *CCA* rate of 25% and will have negligible salvage value in ten year's time (the end of each machine's life). The marginal corporate tax rate is 35%. Should Big Rock Brewery continue to rent, purchase its current machine, or purchase the advanced machine?

Other Effects on Incremental Free Cash Flows

15. Home Builder Supply, a retailer in the home improvement industry, currently operates seven retail outlets in the Maritimes. Management is contemplating building an eighth retail store across town from its most successful retail outlet. The company already owns the land for this store, which currently has an abandoned warehouse located on it. Last month, the marketing department spent $10,000 on market research to determine the extent of customer demand for the new store. Now Home Builder Supply must decide whether to build and open the new store.

Which of the following should be included as part of the incremental earnings for the proposed new retail store?

a. The original purchase price of the land where the store will be located.

b. The cost of demolishing the abandoned warehouse and clearing the lot.

c. The loss of sales in the existing retail outlet if customers who previously drove from Dartmouth to Halifax to shop at the existing outlet become customers of the new store instead.

d. The $10,000 in market research spent to evaluate customer demand.

e. Construction costs for the new store.

f. The value of the land if sold.

g. Interest expense on the debt borrowed to pay the construction costs.

16. Spherical Manufacturing recently spent $15 million to purchase some equipment used in the manufacture of disk drives. This equipment has a *CCA* rate of 25%, and Spherical's marginal corporate tax rate is 35%.

a. What are the annual *CCA* deductions associated with this equipment for the first five years?

b. What are the annual *CCA* tax shields for the first five years?

c. What is the present value of the first five *CCA* tax shields if the appropriate discount rate is 10% per year?

d. What is the present value of all the *CCA* tax shields, assuming the equipment is never sold and the appropriate discount rate is 10% per year?

e. How might your answer to part (d) change if Spherical anticipates that its marginal corporate tax rate will increase substantially over the next five years?

17. You are a manager at Northern Fibre, which is considering expanding its operations in synthetic fibre manufacturing. Your boss comes into your office, drops a consultant's report on your desk, and complains, "We owe these consultants $1 million for this report, and I am not sure their analysis makes sense. Before we spend the $25 million on new equipment needed for this project, look it over and give me your opinion." You open the report and find the following estimates (in thousands of dollars):

1	Year	1	2	...	9	10
2	Sales Revenue	30,000	30,000		30,000	30,000
3	Costs of Goods Sold	18,000	18,000		18,000	18,000
4	Gross Profit	12,000	12,000		12,000	12,000
5	General, Sales, and Administrative Expenses	2000	2000		2000	2000
6	Depreciation	2500	2500		2500	2500
7	**Net Operating Income**	7500	7500		7500	7500
8	Income Tax	2625	2625		2625	2625
9	**Net Income**	4875	4875		4875	4875

All of the estimates in the report seem correct. You note that the consultants used straight-line depreciation for the new equipment that will be purchased today (year 0), which is what the accounting department recommended. CRA allows a *CCA* rate of 30% on the equipment for tax purposes. The report concludes that because the project will increase earnings by $4.875 million per year for 10 years, the project is worth $48.75 million. You think back to your glory days in finance class and realize there is more work to be done!

First, you note that the consultants have not factored in the fact that the project will require $10 million in working capital up front (year 0), which will be fully recovered in year 10. Next, you see they have attributed $2 million of selling, general, and administrative expenses to the project, but you know that $1 million of this amount is overhead that will be incurred even if the project is not accepted. Finally, you know that accounting earnings are not the right thing to focus on!

a. Given the available information, what are the free cash flows in years 0 through 10 that should be used to evaluate the proposed project?

b. If the cost of capital for this project is 14%, what is your estimate of the value of the new project?

Analyzing the Projects

 18. Buhler Industries is a farm implement manufacturer. Management is currently evaluating a proposal to build a plant that will manufacture lightweight tractors. Buhler plans to use a cost of capital of 12% to evaluate this project. Based on extensive research, it has prepared the following incremental free cash flow projections (in millions of dollars):

	Year 0	Years 1–9	Year 10
Revenues		100.0	100.0
− Manufacturing expenses (other than depreciation)		−35.0	−35.0
− Marketing expenses		−10.0	−10.0
− CCA		?	?
= EBIT		?	?
− Taxes (35%)		?	?
= Unlevered net income		?	?
+ CCA		?	?
− Increases in net working capital		−5.0	−5.0
− Capital expenditures	−150.0		
+ Continuation value			+12.0
= Free cash flow	−150.0	?	?

The relevant *CCA* rate for capital expenditures is 10%. Assume assets are never sold.

a. For this base-case scenario, what is the *NPV* of the plant to manufacture lightweight tractors?

b. Based on input from the marketing department, Buhler is uncertain about its revenue forecast. In particular, management would like to examine the sensitivity of the *NPV* to the revenue assumptions. What is the *NPV* of this project if revenues are 10% higher than forecast? What is the *NPV* if revenues are 10% lower than forecast?

c. Rather than assuming that cash flows for this project are constant, management would like to explore the sensitivity of its analysis to possible growth in revenues and operating expenses. Specifically, management would like to assume that revenues, manufacturing expenses, and marketing expenses are as given in the table for year 1 and grow by 2% per year every year starting in year 2. Management also plans to assume that the initial capital expenditures (and therefore *CCA*), additions to working capital, and continuation value remain as initially specified in the table. What is the *NPV* of this project under these alternative assumptions? How does the *NPV* change if the revenues and operating expenses grow by 5% per year rather than by 2%?

d. To examine the sensitivity of this project to the discount rate, management would like to compute the *NPV* for different discount rates. Create a graph, with the discount rate on the *x*-axis and the *NPV* on the *y*-axis, for discount rates ranging from 5% to 30%. For what ranges of discount rates does the project have a positive *NPV*?

*19. Buckingham Packaging is considering expanding its production capacity by purchasing a new machine, the XC-750. The cost of the XC-750 is $2.75 million. Unfortunately, installing this machine will take several months and will partially disrupt production. The firm has just completed a $50,000 feasibility study to analyze the decision to buy the XC-750, resulting in the following estimates:

▶ *Marketing:* Once the XC-750 is operational next year, the extra capacity is expected to generate $10 million per year in additional sales, which will continue for the 10-year life of the machine.

▶ *Operations:* The disruption caused by the installation will decrease sales by $5 million this year. As with Buckingham's existing products, the cost of goods for the products produced by the XC-750 is expected to be 70% of their sale price. The increased production will also require increased inventory on hand of $1 million during the life of the project, including year 0.

▶ *Human Resources:* The expansion will require additional sales and administrative personnel at a cost of $2 million per year.

▶ *Accounting:* The XC-750 has a *CCA* rate of 30%, and no salvage value is expected. The firm expects receivables from the new sales to be 15% of revenues and payables to be 10% of the cost of goods sold. Buckingham's marginal corporate tax rate is 35%.

a. Determine the incremental earnings (using *CCA*) from the purchase of the XC-750.
b. Determine the free cash flow from the purchase of the XC-750.
c. If the appropriate cost of capital for the expansion is 10%, compute the *NPV* of the purchase (incluing all *CCA* tax shield effects).
d. While the expected new sales will be $10 million per year from the expansion, estimates range from $8 million to $12 million. What is the *NPV* in the worst case? In the best case?
e. What is the break-even level of new sales from the expansion? What is the break-even level for the cost of goods sold?
f. Buckingham could instead purchase the XC-900, which offers even greater capacity. The cost of the XC-900 is $4 million. The extra capacity would not be useful in the first two years of operation, but would allow for additional sales in years 3 to 10. What level of additional sales (above the $10 million expected for the XC-750) per year in those years would justify purchasing the larger machine?

Real Options in Capital Budgeting

20. Why is it that real options must have positive value?

21. What kind of real option does the XC-900 machine (see Problem 19) provide to Buckingham?

22. If Buckingham (see Problem 19) knows that it can sell the XC-750 to another firm for $2 million in two years, what kind of real option would that provide?

Data Case

You have just been hired by Dell Computers in its capital budgeting division. Your first assignment is to determine the net cash flows and *NPV* of a proposed new type of portable computer system that is similar in size to a BlackBerry handheld device but has the operating power of a high-end desktop system.

Development of the new system will initially require an investment equal to 10% of net property, plant, and equipment (PPE) for the fiscal year ended February 1, 2008. The project will then require an additional investment equal to 10% of the initial investment after the first year of the project, a 5% of initial investment after the second year, and 1% of initial investment after the third, fourth, and fifth years. The product is expected to have a life of five years. First-year revenues for the new product are expected to be 3% of total revenue for Dell's fiscal year ended Feb. 1, 2008. The new product's revenues are expected to grow at 15% for the second year, then 10% for the third, and 5% annually for the final two years of the expected life of the project. Your job is to determine the rest of the cash flows associated with this project. Your boss has indicated that the operating costs and *NWC* requirements are similar to those of the rest of the company's products and that depreciation is straight-line for capital budgeting purposes (so *CCA* is not applicable here). Since your boss hasn't been much help, here are some tips to guide your analysis:

1. Obtain Dell's financial statements. (If you really worked for Dell, you would already have this data, but at least here you won't get fired if your analysis is off target.) Download the annual income statements, balance sheets, and cash flow statements for the last four fiscal years from the MarketWatch website (www. marketwatch. com). Enter Dell's ticker symbol (DELL) and then go to "Financials." Export the statements to Excel by right-clicking while the cursor is in each statement.

2. You are now ready to determine the free cash flow. Compute the free cash flow for each year using Equation 8.8 in this chapter (replacing *CCA* with Depreciation for the U.S. company):

$$\text{Free Cash Flow} = \overbrace{(\text{Revenues} - \text{Costs} - \text{Depreciation}) \times (1 - \text{tax rate})}^{\text{Unlevered Net Income}} \quad (8.17)$$
$$+ \text{Depreciation} - CapEx - \text{Change in } NWC$$

Set up the timeline and computation of the free cash flow in separate, contiguous columns for each year of the project life. Be sure to make outflows negative and inflows positive.

a. Assume that the project's profitability will be similar to Dell's existing projects in 2007, and estimate each year by using the 2007 *EBITDA*/Sales profit margin.

b. Determine the annual depreciation by assuming Dell depreciates these assets by the straight-line method over a 10-year life.

c. Determine Dell's tax rate by using the income tax rate in 2007.

d. Calculate the *NWC* required each year by assuming that the level of *NWC* will be a constant percentage of the project's sales. Use Dell's 2007 *NWC*/Sales to estimate the required percentage. (Use only accounts receivable, accounts payable, and inventory to measure working capital. Other components of current assets and liabilities—for example, Dell's cash holdings—are harder to interpret and not necessarily reflective of the project's required *NWC*.)

e. To determine the free cash flow, calculate the *additional* capital investment and the *change* in NWC each year.

3. Determine the *IRR* of the project and the *NPV* of the project at a cost of capital of 12% using the Excel functions. For the calculation of *NPV*, include cash flows 1 through 5 in the *NPV* function and then subtract the initial cost (i.e., = $NPV(\text{rate}, CF_1 : CF_5) + CF_0$). For *IRR*, include cash flows 0 through 5 in the cash flow range.

Chapter 8 APPENDIX A　Using Excel for Capital Budgeting

In this appendix, we illustrate how to build a pro forma statement and perform a sensitivity analysis in Excel.

Building a Pro Forma Statement

The key to frustration-free capital budgeting is to base your analysis on a spreadsheet containing a flexible model of the project's pro forma free cash flows.

List Assumptions

Start by creating a box in the spreadsheet with all of your assumptions, shown here shaded in grey:

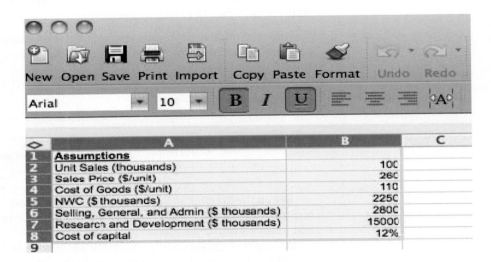

Although this step will take you a little more time up front, it has two advantages. First, you are forced to present all of your major assumptions clearly, so you can see the drivers of your analysis. Second, setting them apart this way makes it far easier to change your assumptions later and quickly see the impact on the incremental free cash flows.

Base Cell Formulas on Assumptions

Once you have listed all of your assumptions, it is time to build the pro forma statement by referring back to the cells containing your assumptions. Here, we will show how to build the first year's pro forma cash flows. For example, rather than entering $26,000 into the Sales line of year 1, you will enter the formula shown in the screen shot.

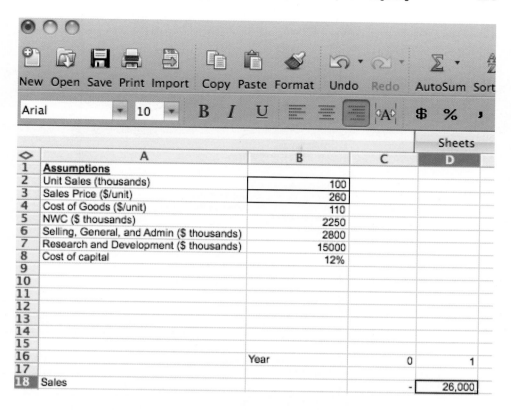

This formula is simply the cell-referenced version of our calculation from the initial BlackBerry Presenter information earlier in this chapter: Unit Sold × Price per Unit = 100 × $260 = $26,000. As you can see from the screen shot, we have referred back to our assumptions box for each of these inputs (units sold and price per unit). Look at the formula bar at the top of the screen shot to see the cell references. Later, if we want to change the assumption for price per unit, we can change it in our assumptions box and it will automatically change the calculation for Sales in year 1.

To complete the pro forma statement for year 1, we continue down the column. Each time we need to draw on an assumed number, we refer back to our assumptions box. For calculations such as Gross Profit, we simply refer to the cells in the column: summing Sales and the negative Cost of Goods Sold. Formulas used in column D to calculate year 1 amounts are displayed in column E.

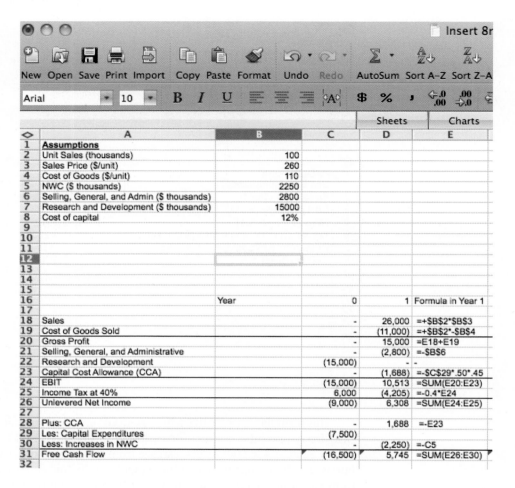

	A	B	C	D	E
1	**Assumptions**				
2	Unit Sales (thousands)	100			
3	Sales Price ($/unit)	260			
4	Cost of Goods ($/unit)	110			
5	NWC ($ thousands)	2250			
6	Selling, General, and Admin ($ thousands)	2800			
7	Research and Development ($ thousands)	15000			
8	Cost of capital	12%			
9					
10					
11					
12					
13					
14					
15					
16		Year	0	1	Formula in Year 1
17					
18	Sales		-	26,000	=+$B$2*$B$3
19	Cost of Goods Sold		-	(11,000)	=+$B$2*-$B$4
20	Gross Profit		-	15,000	=E18+E19
21	Selling, General, and Administrative		-	(2,800)	=-$B$6
22	Research and Development	(15,000)		-	-
23	Capital Cost Allowance (CCA)		-	(1,688)	=-$C$29*.50*.45
24	EBIT	(15,000)		10,513	=SUM(E20:E23)
25	Income Tax at 40%	6,000		(4,205)	=-0.4*E24
26	Unlevered Net Income	(9,000)		6,308	=SUM(E24:E25)
27					
28	Plus: CCA		-	1,688	=-E23
29	Les: Capital Expenditures	(7,500)			
30	Less: Increases in NWC		-	(2,250)	=-C5
31	Free Cash Flow	(16,500)		5,745	=SUM(E26:E30)
32					

As you can imagine, building a pro forma statement like this greatly eases our analysis of the effects of changes in our assumptions. In the next section, we will show how to use a spreadsheet similar to the one we just constructed to perform sensitivity analysis.

Performing Sensitivity Analysis

Rather than recalculating the BlackBerry Presenter's *NPV* for each possible number of units sold, we can use Excel's Data Table tool. In Chapter 7, we used the Data Table tool to construct an *NPV* profile. Recall that a data table shows us how the outcome of a formula (such as the *NPV* of the BlackBerry Presenter) changes when we change one of the cells in the spreadsheet (such as the number of units sold). Previously, we showed how to build a pro forma statement of the BlackBerry Presenter using Excel that would make it easy to change our assumptions later. That is exactly what we do in sensitivity analysis: change our assumptions and see how the *NPV* changes. This screen shot shows a completed Excel pro forma statement of the incremental free cash flows of the BlackBerry Presenter project. It also shows the *NPV* calculation and a data table (outlined in red) for our assumption on Units Sold:

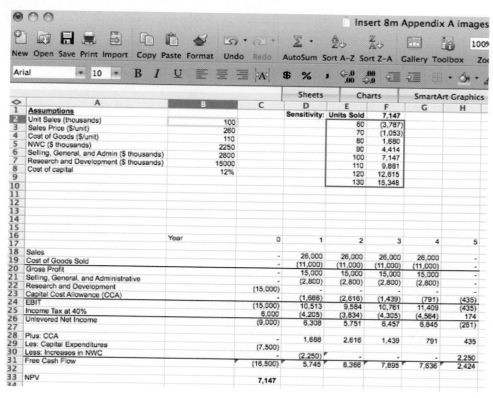

To set up the data table, we first create a cell that simply repeats the *NPV*. In this case, cell F1 is set to equal cell C33 to create a new *NPV* column. Next, we create the column that will contain the different assumptions of Units Sold. This column must be directly to the left of the *NPV* cell (F1). We fill in the different values we want to incorporate into the *NPV* calculation directly below the Units Sold heading. Finally, we highlight the Units Sold and *NPV* columns (at this point, the *NPV* column is blank with the exception of the first row in our table), and select Table from the Data menu.

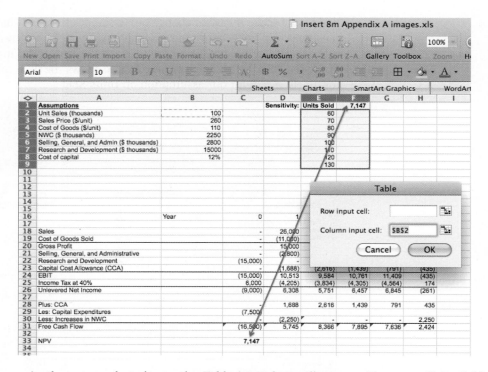

As the screen shot shows, the Table input box will appear. Since our Units Sold assumptions are in a column, we enter, into the column input cell (not the row input cell), the cell in our spreadsheet containing the base-case Units Sold assumption (B2). Once we do this and hit Enter, Excel will create the sensitivity table shown in the first screen shot. We could now create an *NPV* profile based on the differing quantities of units sold.

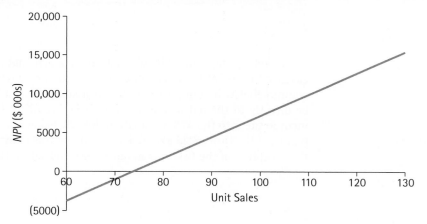

9 Valuing Stocks

▌ Describe the basics of common stock, preferred stock, and stock quotes

▌ Value a stock as the present value of its expected future dividends

▌ Understand the tradeoff between dividends and growth in stock valuation

▌ Appreciate the limitations of valuing a stock based on expected dividends

▌ Value a stock as the present value of either the company's total payout or its free cash flows

▌ Value a stock by applying common multiples based on the values of comparable firms

▌ Understand how information is incorporated into stock prices through competition in efficient markets

▌ Describe some behavioural biases that influence the way individual investors trade

notation

Div_t	dividends paid in year t	n	terminal date or forecast horizon
$EBIT$	earnings before interest and taxes	P_t	stock price at the end of year t
$EBITDA$	earnings before interest, taxes, depreciation, and amortization	PV	present value
EPS_t	earnings per share on date t	r_E	equity cost of capital
FCF_t	free cash flow on date t	r_{wacc}	weighted average cost of capital
g	expected dividend growth rate	V_t	enterprise value on date t
g_{FCF}	expected free cash flow growth rate		

INTERVIEW WITH Christopher Ellis-Ferrara

AllianceBernstein

Williams College, 2007

"The dividend discount model allows us to express our views of a company's forward earnings prospects in the valuation."

Christopher Ellis-Ferrara is a business analyst covering U.S. real estate investment trusts (REITs) for the Bernstein Value Equities research department of AllianceBernstein in New York City. He received his degree in economics and geosciences at Williams College, Williamstown, Massachusetts, in 2007. "My primary responsibility is to conduct in-depth fundamental research on the real estate industry, including tracking and forecasting supply and demand for various markets and property types," says Chris. "Senior analysts incorporate my research into their company analyses. I also assist the chief investment officer of my product in portfolio analytics and management."

In addition to an array of other valuation tools, AllianceBernstein uses the dividend discount model (DDM) to help identify undervalued stocks for clients. "One attraction of the DDM is that it allows us to express our views of a company's forward earnings prospects in the valuation," says Chris. "This is a characteristic absent in other common tools." Chris acknowledges that forecasting future earnings and dividends is an inherently challenging task—but essential for an accurate valuation. "Relative to other companies, however, REIT earnings and dividends are generally more predictable."

No single valuation model is perfect, so AllianceBernstein uses several to arrive at intrinsic value. "In addition to the DDM, some of the models and metrics we use for real estate companies include price-to-net asset value (NAV), earnings and cash flow multiples, enterprise value to *EBITDA*, and discounted cash flow analysis. Once we have conviction that the market price of a stock is less than its intrinsic value and that it does not alter the acceptable risk in our portfolio, we will invest."

The recent stock market volatility has heightened the opportunity to earn higher returns. "Now more than ever, we strive to stay disciplined in our investment process and identify pricing anomalies that volatility inevitably generates. To take advantage of these anomalies, we have improved our nimbleness to respond quickly. We also spend more time on balance sheet analysis, because the credit crisis severely impaired access to capital for real estate companies."

At 5 p. m. on March 17, 2010, footwear and apparel maker Nike, Inc. announced that its quarterly revenue growth would be higher than expected and that revenue and profit growth for the following year would be strong as well. The next day, Nike's stock price increased by more than 5% on the New York Stock Exchange (NYSE) to $74.66, with almost 11 million shares being traded—more than four times its average daily volume.

How might an investor decide whether to buy or sell a stock such as Nike at this price? Why would the stock suddenly be worth 5% more after the announcement of this news? What actions can Nike's managers take to increase the stock price?

To answer these questions, we turn to the Valuation Principle. It indicates that the price of a security should equal the present value of the expected cash flows an investor will receive from owning it. In this chapter, we apply this idea to stocks. Thus, to value a stock, we need to know the expected cash flows an investor will receive and the appropriate cost of capital with which to discount those cash flows. Both of these quantities can be challenging to estimate, and we will discuss many of the details needed to do so throughout the remainder of this text. In this chapter, we begin our study of stock valuation by identifying the relevant cash flows and developing the main tools that practitioners use to evaluate them.

Our analysis opens with a consideration of the dividends and capital gains received by investors who hold the stock for different periods, from which we develop the *dividend-discount model* of stock valuation. Next, we apply the tools described in Chapter 7 to value stocks based on the free cash flows generated by the firm. Having developed these stock valuation methods based on discounted cash flows, we then relate them to the practice of using valuation multiples based on those of comparable firms. We conclude the chapter by discussing the role of competition in the information contained in stock prices and its implications for investors and corporate managers.

9.1   Stock Basics

As discussed in Chapter 1, the ownership of a corporation is divided into shares of stock. A public corporation has many owners, and its shares trade on a stock market that provides liquidity for a company's shares and determines the market price for those shares. In this section, we explain what a stock market quote is and introduce the two types of stocks, *common* and *preferred*.

Stock Market Reporting: Stock Quotes

common stock A share of ownership in the corporation, which confers rights to any common dividends as well as rights to vote on election of directors, mergers, or other major events.

ticker symbol A unique abbreviation assigned to each publicly traded company.

Figure 9.1 shows a stock quote with basic information about Nike's stock from the Google Finance web (www.google.com/finance) for May 11, 2010.[1] Nike's **common stock**, which means a share of ownership in the corporation, gives its owner rights to any common dividends, as well as rights to vote on the election of directors, mergers, and other major events. The website notes that the company is a public corporation (its shares are widely held and traded in a market) and that its shares trade on the NYSE under the *ticker symbol* NKE. A **ticker symbol** (or stock symbol) is a unique abbreviation assigned to a publicly traded company, used when its trades are reported on the ticker (a real-time electronic display of trading activity). Shares on the NYSE have ticker symbols consisting of three or fewer characters, while shares on the NASDAQ generally have four or more characters in their ticker symbols. In Canada, many companies' shares trade on the Toronto Stock Exchange (TSX). For example, Bell Canada Enterprises Inc., Canada's largest communications company, trades on the TSX under the ticker symbol BCE.

During the time period February through early March 2010, Nike paid one quarterly dividend to its common shareholders, on March 4. The dividends are marked by a "D" and the amount of the dividend is shown. In this case, the dividend was 27 cents per share. Thus, if you owned 1000 shares of NKE, you would have received $0.27 \times 1000 = 270 when Nike paid that dividend. The chart also clearly shows the jump in the price of NKE shares in March 2010 that we discussed in the introduction to this chapter.

Finally, the website displays some basic information about the performance of NKE stock. Notice the price of the last trade of NKE shares in the market ($76.43), the price that shares started at when the market opened that day ($75.80), the range of low to high prices reached so far during trading that day ($75.76 and $77.07), and the volume of trading for the day (3.43 million shares). The total value of all of the equity of NKE is its market capitalization, equal to the price per share multiplied by the number of shares outstanding: on May 11, 2010, it was 76.43×485.7 million $= 37.12 billion. Over the past 52 weeks, NKE achieved a high price of $78.55 and a low price of $48.76 and had average daily volume of shares traded of 2.79 million shares. Also, note some basic information about the company: the price-earnings ratio (P/E) and earnings

---

[1]There are many places on the internet to get free stock information, such as the websites of the TMX Group (tmx.com), the NYSE (nyse.com), and the NASDAQ (nasdaq.com).

FIGURE 9.1

Stock Price Quote for Nike (NKE)

This screenshot from the Google Finance website shows the basic stock price information and price history charting for the common stock of Nike. The historical price chart covers the period February through early May 2010. The price of $76.43 is for May 11, 2010.

Source: Google Finance.

per share (*EPS*), both of which we discussed in Chapter 2. The website also notes that NKE's *beta* is 0.87.[2]

Although the current price of NKE is $76.43, the stock's price has varied over time. In preceding chapters, we learned how financial managers make decisions that affect the value of their company.

Common Stock

We now examine the rights of common stockholders, including their voice in the running of the corporation. All rights accruing to the shareholders are in proportion to the number of shares they hold.

straight voting Voting for directors during which shareholders must vote for each director separately, with each shareholder having as many votes as shares held.

cumulative voting Voting for directors during which each shareholder is allocated votes equal to the number of open spots multiplied by his or her number of shares.

Shareholder Voting. To illustrate the shareholder voting process, consider an election of 10 directors at a company with only 2 shareholders: Donna and Jonathan. Donna has 600 shares and Jonathan has 400, but they have very different views on how the company should be run. If the company has **straight voting**, each shareholder has as many votes for each director as shares held. That is, for each director, Donna will have 600 votes and Jonathan 400, so Jonathan will lose every vote and have no representation on the board. If the company has **cumulative voting**, each shareholder's total vote allocation for all directors is equal to the number of open spots multiplied by his or her number of shares. With 10 directors up for election, Jonathan is allocated a total of 10 times 400 votes (4000 votes) and Donna is allocated 10 times 600 votes (6000 votes), to use across the 10 director spots.

---

[2]*Beta* is a measure of risk that we will discuss in Chapter 11.

Jonathan could allocate all his votes to 4 directors, ensuring that he has 4 directors representing his views on the board. Donna would do the same for 6 directors, ensuring her representation. With cumulative voting, even shareholders with minority blocks (less than 50%) have a chance at representation on the board.

This example is based on the concept of one share, one vote. Some companies have different types of common stock, called *Classes*, which carry different voting rights. This is typical in companies that are family run, or where the founder is still active. For example, Nike has Class A and Class B stock. Phil Knight, Nike's founder, owns almost all the Class A stock, which carries the rights to elect 9 of the company's 12 directors. Google also has Class A and Class B stock. Class A stock has been sold to the public, while Google's founders and managers hold all the Class B stock, each share of which carries 10 times the voting power of a share of Class A stock.

Shareholder Rights. Each year, companies hold an **annual meeting** at which managers and directors answer questions from shareholders, and shareholders vote on the election of directors and other proposals. All shareholders have the right to attend the annual meeting and cast their votes directly. In practice, though, most either allow the board to vote for them or direct that their shares be voted for them via **proxy**, or explicit instructions on how they should be voted. Typically matters at the annual meeting are uncontested, but occasionally a dissident shareholder group will propose an alternative slate of directors or oppose a management proposal. In that case, each side will actively solicit the proxies of all the shareholders so they may win the vote in a **proxy contest**.

As an ownership claim, common stock carries the right to share in the profits of the corporation through dividend payments. Recall from Chapter 1 that dividends are periodic payments, usually in the form of cash, which firms make to shareholders as a partial return on their investment in the corporation. The board of directors decides the timing and amount of each dividend. Shareholders are paid dividends in proportion to the amount of shares they own. If the company is liquidated through bankruptcy and there are assets left over after satisfying the claims of the bondholders, shareholders divide the remaining assets proportionally based on each shareholder's number of shares.

Preferred Stock

Some companies have an additional issue of stock called **preferred stock**, which has preference over common shares in the distribution of dividends or liquidation. While the directors can at their discretion choose not to pay the preferred dividend, they may not pay a dividend to common stockholders unless they pay the promised dividend to preferred shareholders first. For example, Nike has preferred shares that pay a $0.10 dividend per share each year. The firm must pay this dividend before common shareholders can receive a dividend.

Cumulative Versus Non-Cumulative Preferred Stock. There are two types of preferred stock: *cumulative* and *non-cumulative*. With **cumulative preferred stock**, any unpaid dividends are carried forward. For example, if DuPont fails to pay its preferred dividend for several years, its obligation to its cumulative preferred shareholders accumulates, and it cannot pay any dividends to common shareholders until it has paid all the unpaid preferred dividends. With **non-cumulative preferred stock**, missed dividends do not accumulate, and the firm can pay current dividend payments first to preferred and then to common stock shareholders. Many Canadian banks (e.g., Canadian Imperial Bank of Commerce [CIBC]) have non-cumulative preferred stock outstanding. Some companies provide preferred stockholders with additional features such as the right to elect a director to the board if the firm is substantially in arrears on preferred dividends.

Preferred Stock: Equity or Debt? You may have wondered how to think about preferred stock—is it equity or is it debt? Economically, it is like a perpetual bond. It has a promised cash flow to holders, and there are consequences if these cash flows are not paid.

---

annual meeting Meeting held once per year at which shareholders vote on directors and other proposals, as well as ask managers questions.

proxy A written authorization for someone else to vote your shares.

proxy contest A contest between two or more groups competing to collect proxies to prevail in the matter up for shareholder vote (such as election of directors).

preferred stock Stock with preference over common shares in payment of dividends and in liquidation.

cumulative preferred stock Preferred stock for which all missed preferred dividends must be paid before any common dividends may be paid.

non-cumulative preferred stock Preferred stock for which missed preferred dividends do not accumulate. Only the current dividend is owed before common dividends may be paid.

However, preferred shareholders cannot force the firm into bankruptcy. Preferred shareholders stand in line in front of common shareholders for annual dividends but behind regular bondholders, whose interest payments come first. If the firm is bankrupt, the same priority is followed in settling claims: bondholders, preferred shareholders, and then common shareholders. Finally, as long as the firm is meeting its preferred dividend obligations, the preferred shareholders have none of the control rights of owners, such as voting on directors or other important matters. However, despite all these similarities to debt, preferred shares are, for all tax and legal purposes, treated as equity.

Concept Check

1. What is a share of stock and what are dividends?

2. What are some key differences between preferred and common stock?

The Dividend-Discount Model

The Valuation Principle implies that to value any security, we must determine the expected cash flows that an investor will receive from owning it. We begin our analysis of stock valuation by considering the cash flows for an investor with a one-year investment horizon. We will show how the stock's price and the investor's return from the investment are related. We then consider the perspective of investors with long investment horizons. Finally, we will reach our goal of establishing the first stock valuation method: the *dividend-discount model*.

A One-Year Investor

There are two potential sources of cash flows from owning a stock:

> **1.** The firm might pay out cash to its shareholders in the form of a dividend.
>
> **2.** The investor might generate cash by selling the shares at some future date.

The total amount received in dividends and from selling the stock will depend on the investor's investment horizon. Let's begin by considering the perspective of a one-year investor.

When an investor buys a stock, she will pay the current market price for a share, P_0. While she continues to hold the stock, she will be entitled to any dividends the stock pays. Let Div_1 be the total dividends paid per share during the year. At the end of the year, the investor will sell her share at the new market price. Let P_1 be the price the investor expects to sell her share for at the end of the year. Assuming for simplicity that all dividends are paid at the end of the year, we have the following timeline for this investment:

Of course, the future dividend payment and stock price in this timeline are not known with certainty. Rather, these values are based on the investor's expectations at the time the stock is purchased. Given these expectations, the investor will be willing to pay a price today up to the point that the benefits equal the costs—that is, up to the point at which the current price equals the present value of the expected future dividend and sale price.

Because these cash flows are risky, we cannot discount them using the risk-free interest rate, but instead must use the cost of capital for the firm's equity. We have previously

equity cost of capital The expected rate of return available in the market on other investments that have risk equivalent to that associated with the firm's shares.

defined the cost of capital of any investment to be the expected return that investors could earn on their best alternative investment with similar risk and maturity. Thus we must discount the equity cash flows based on the **equity cost of capital**, r_E, for the stock, which is the expected return of other investments available in the market with risk equivalent to that of the firm's shares. Doing so leads to the following equation for the stock price:

$$P_0 = \frac{Div_1 + P_1}{1 + r_E} \tag{9.1}$$

If the current stock price were less than this amount, the cost would be less than the *PV* of the benefits, so investors would to rush in and buy it, driving up the stock's price. If the stock price exceeded this amount, selling it would be attractive and the stock price would quickly fall.

Dividend Yields, Capital Gains, and Total Returns

A critical part of Equation 9.1 for determining the stock price is the firm's equity cost of capital, r_E. At the beginning of this section, we pointed out that an investor's return from holding a stock comes from dividends and cash generated from selling the stock. We can rewrite Equation 9.1 to show these two return components. If we multiply by $(1 + r_E)$, divide by P_0, and subtract 1 from both sides, we have

Total Return

$$r_E = \frac{Div_1 + P_1}{P_0} - 1 = \underbrace{\frac{Div_1}{P_0}}_{\text{Dividend Yield}} + \underbrace{\frac{P_1 - P_0}{P_0}}_{\text{Capital Gain Rate}} \tag{9.2}$$

dividend yield The expected annual dividend of a stock divided by its current price; the percentage return an investor expects to earn from the dividend paid by the stock.

capital gain The amount by which the selling price of an asset exceeds its initial purchase price.

capital gain rate An expression of capital gain as a percentage of the initial price of the asset.

total return The sum of a stock's dividend yield and its capital gain rate.

The first term on the right side of Equation 9.2 is the stock's **dividend yield**, which is the expected annual dividend of the stock divided by its current price. The dividend yield is the percentage return the investor expects to earn from the dividend paid by the stock. The second term on the right side of Equation 9.2 reflects the **capital gain** the investor will earn on the stock, which is the difference between the expected sale price and the original purchase price for the stock, $P_1 - P_0$. We divide the capital gain by the current stock price to express the capital gain as a percentage return, called the **capital gain rate**.

The sum of the dividend yield and the capital gain rate is called the **total return** of the stock. The total return is the expected return that the investor will earn for a one-year investment in the stock. Equation 9.2 states that the stock's total return should equal the equity cost of capital. In other words, *the expected total return of the stock should equal the expected return of other investments with equivalent risk that are available in the market.*

This result is exactly what we would expect: the firm must pay its shareholders a return commensurate with the return they can earn elsewhere while taking the same risk. If the stock offered a higher return than other securities with the same risk, investors would sell those other investments and buy the stock instead. This activity would then drive up the stock's current price, lowering its dividend yield and capital gain rate until Equation 9.2 holds true. If the stock offered a lower expected return, investors would sell the stock and drive down its price until Equation 9.2 was again satisfied.

A Multi-Year Investor

We now extend the reasoning we developed for the one-year investor's return to a multi-year investor. Equation 9.1 depends on the expected stock price in one year, P_1. But suppose we planned to hold the stock for two years. Then we would receive

EXAMPLE 9.1

Stock Prices and
Returns

Problem

Suppose you expect Shoppers Drug Mart to pay an annual dividend of $0.56 per share in the coming year and to trade for $45.50 per share at the end of the year. If investments with risk equivalent to that of Shoppers' stock have an expected return of 6.80%, what is the most you would pay today for Shoppers' stock? What dividend yield and capital gain rate would you expect at this price?

Solution

▶ **Plan**

We can use Equation 9.1 to solve for the beginning price we would pay now (P_0), given our expectations about dividends ($Div_1 = 0.56$) and future price ($P_1 = 45.50) and the return we need to expect to earn to be willing to invest ($r_E = 6.8\%$). We can then use Equation 9.2 to calculate the dividend yield and capital gain.

▶ **Execute**

Using Equation 9.1, we have

$$P_0 = \frac{Div_1 + P_1}{1 + r_E} = \frac{0.56 + 45.50}{1.0680} = \$43.13$$

Referring to Equation 9.2, we see that at this price, Shoppers' dividend yield is $Div_1/P_0 = 0.56/43.13 = 1.30\%$. The expected capital gain is $\$45.50 - \$43.13 = \$2.37$ per share, for a capital gain rate of $2.37/43.13 = 5.50\%$.

▶ **Evaluate**

At a price of $43.13, Shoppers' expected total return is $1.30\% + 5.50\% = 6.80\%$, which is equal to its equity cost of capital (the return being paid by investments with equivalent risk to Shoppers'). This amount is the most we would be willing to pay for Shoppers' stock. If we paid more, our expected return would be less than 6.8% and we would rather invest elsewhere.

dividends in both year one and year two before selling the stock, as shown in the following timeline:

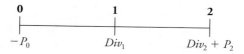

Setting the stock price equal to the present value of the future cash flows in this case implies the following:[3]

$$P_0 = \frac{Div_1}{1 + r_E} + \frac{Div_2 + P_2}{(1 + r_E)^2} \tag{9.3}$$

Equations 9.1 and 9.3 are different: as two-year investors, we care about the dividend and stock price in year two, but these terms do not appear in Equation 9.1. Does this difference imply that a two-year investor will value the stock differently than a one-year investor?

---

[3]In using the same equity cost of capital for both periods, we are assuming that the equity cost of capital does not depend on the term of the cash flows; that is, r_E is not different for year two (or any other year). Otherwise, we would need to adjust for the term structure of the equity cost of capital (as we did with the yield curve for risk-free cash flows in Chapter 5). This step would complicate the analysis but would not change its results.

The answer to this question is no. A one-year investor does not care about the dividend and stock price in year two directly. She will care about them indirectly, however, because they will affect the price for which she can sell the stock at the end of year one. For example, suppose the investor sells the stock to another one-year investor with the same expectations. The new investor will expect to receive the dividend and stock price at the end of year two, so he will be willing to pay

$$P_1 = \frac{Div_2 + P_2}{1 + r_E}$$

for the stock. Substituting this expression for P_1 into Equation 9.1, we get the same result as in Equation 9.3:

$$P_0 = \frac{Div_1 + P_1}{1 + r_E} = \frac{Div_1}{1 + r_E} + \frac{1}{1 + r_E} \overbrace{\left(\frac{Div_2 + P_2}{1 + r_E}\right)}^{P_1}$$

$$= \frac{Div_1}{1 + r_E} + \frac{Div_2 + P_2}{(1 + r_E)^2}$$

Thus the formula for the stock price for a two-year investor is the same as that for a sequence of two one-year investors.

Dividend-Discount Model Equation

dividend-discount model
A model that values shares of a firm according to the present value of the future dividends the firm will pay.

We can continue this process for any number of years by replacing the final stock price with the value that the next holder of the stock would be willing to pay. Doing so leads to the general **dividend-discount model** for the stock price, where the horizon n is arbitrary:

Dividend-Discount Model

$$P_0 = \frac{Div_1}{1 + r_E} + \frac{Div_2}{(1 + r_E)^2} + \cdots + \frac{Div_n}{(1 + r_E)^n} + \frac{P_n}{(1 + r_E)^n} \qquad (9.4)$$

Equation 9.4 applies to a single n-year investor, who will collect dividends for n years and then sell the stock, or to a series of investors who hold the stock for shorter periods and then resell it. Note that Equation 9.4 holds for any horizon n. As a consequence, all investors (with the same expectations) will attach the same value to the stock, independent of their investment horizons. How long they intend to hold the stock and whether they collect their return in the form of dividends or capital gains is irrelevant. For the special case in which the firm eventually pays dividends and is never acquired or liquidated, it is possible to hold the shares forever. In this scenario, rather than having a stopping point where we sell the shares, we rewrite Equation 9.4 to show that the dividends go on into the future:

$$P_0 = \frac{Div_1}{1 + r_E} + \frac{Div_2}{(1 + r_E)^2} + \frac{Div_3}{(1 + r_E)^3} + \cdots \qquad (9.5)$$

That is, *the price of the stock is equal to the present value of all of the expected future dividends it will pay.*

3. How do you calculate the total return of a stock?

4. What discount rate do you use to discount the future cash flows of a stock?

9.3 Estimating Dividends in the Dividend-Discount Model

Equation 9.5 expresses the value of a stock in terms of the expected future dividends the firm will pay. Of course, estimating these dividends—especially for the distant future—is difficult. A commonly used approximation is to assume that in the long run, dividends will grow at a constant rate. In this section, we consider the implications of this assumption for stock prices and explore the tradeoff between dividends and growth.

Constant Dividend Growth

The simplest forecast for the firm's future dividends states that they will grow at a constant rate, g, forever. That case yields the following timeline for the cash flows for an investor who buys the stock today and holds it:

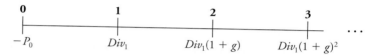

Because the expected dividends are a constant growth perpetuity, we can use Equation 4.9 to calculate their present value. We then obtain the following simple formula for the stock price:[4]

constant dividend growth model A model for valuing a stock by viewing its dividends as a constant growth perpetuity.

Constant Dividend Growth Model

$$P_0 = \frac{Div_1}{r_E - g} \tag{9.6}$$

According to the **constant dividend growth model**, the value of the firm depends on the dividend level next year, divided by the equity cost of capital adjusted by the growth rate.

EXAMPLE 9.2

Valuing a Firm with Constant Dividend Growth

Problem

Hydro One is a regulated utility company that provides transmission and distribution of electricity in Ontario. Suppose Hydro plans to pay $2.30 per share in dividends in the coming year. If its equity cost of capital is 7% and dividends are expected to grow by 2% per year in the future, estimate the value of Hydro's stock.

Solution

▶ **Plan**

Because the dividends are expected to grow perpetually at a constant rate, we can use Eq. 9.6 to value Hydro. The next dividend (Div_1) is expected to be $2.30, the growth rate ($g$) is 2%, and the equity cost of capital (r_E) is 7%.

▶ **Execute**

$$P_0 = \frac{Div_1}{r_E - g} = \frac{\$2.30}{0.07 - 0.02} = \$46.00$$

---

[4]As discussed in Chapter 4, this formula requires that $g < r_E$. Otherwise, the present value of the growing perpetuity is infinite. The implication here is that it is impossible for a stock's dividends to grow at a rate $g > r_E$ forever. If the growth rate does exceed r_E, the situation must be temporary, and the constant growth model cannot be applied in such a case.

> ▶ **Evaluate**
> You would be willing to pay 20 times this year's dividend of $2.30 to own Hydro One stock because you are buying a claim to this year's dividend *and* to an infinite growing series of future dividends.
>   For another interpretation of Equation 9.6, note that we can rearrange it as follows:
>
> $$r_E = \frac{Div_1}{P_0} + g \tag{9.7}$$

Comparing Equation 9.7 with Equation 9.2, we see that g equals the expected capital gain rate. In other words, with constant expected dividend growth, the expected growth rate of the share price matches the growth rate of the dividends.

Dividends Versus Investment and Growth

In Equation 9.6, the firm's share price increases with the current dividend level, Div_1, and the expected growth rate, g. To maximize its share price, a firm would like to increase both these quantities. Often, however, the firm faces a tradeoff: increasing growth may require investment, and money spent on investment cannot be used to pay dividends. The constant dividend growth model provides insight into this tradeoff.

A Simple Model of Growth. What determines the rate of growth of a firm's dividends? If we define a firm's **dividend payout rate** as the fraction of its earnings that the firm pays as dividends each year, then we can write the firm's dividend per share at date t as follows:

dividend payout rate The fraction of a firm's earnings that the firm pays out as dividends each year.

$$Div_t = \underbrace{\frac{Earnings_t}{Share\ Outstanding_t}}_{EPS_t} \times Dividend\ Payout\ Rate_t \tag{9.8}$$

That is, the dividend each year is equal to the firm's earnings per share (*EPS*) multiplied by its dividend payout rate. The firm can, therefore, increase its dividend in three ways:

1. It can increase its earnings (net income).
2. It can increase its dividend payout rate.
3. It can decrease its number of shares outstanding.

Suppose for now that the firm does not issue new shares (or buy back its existing shares), so that the number of shares outstanding remains fixed. We can then explore the tradeoff between options 1 and 2.

A firm can do one of two things with its earnings: It can pay them out to investors, or it can retain and reinvest them. By investing cash today, a firm can increase its future dividends. For simplicity, let's assume that if no investment is made, the firm does not grow, so the current level of earnings generated by the firm remains constant. If all increases in future earnings result exclusively from new investment made with retained earnings, then

$$Change\ in\ Earnings = New\ Investment \times Return\ on\ New\ Investment \tag{9.9}$$

retention rate The fraction of a firm's current earnings that the firm retains.

New investment equals the firm's earnings multiplied by its **retention rate**, or the fraction of current earnings that the firm retains:

$$New\ Investment = Earnings \times Retention\ Rate \tag{9.10}$$

Substituting Equation 9.10 into Equation 9.9 and dividing by earnings gives an expression for the growth rate of earnings:

$$\text{Earnings Growth Rate} = \frac{\text{Change in Earnings}}{\text{Earnings}}$$

$$= \text{Retention Rate} \times \text{Return on New Investment} \quad (9.11)$$

If the firm chooses to keep its dividend payout rate constant, then the growth in its dividends will equal the growth in its earnings:

$$g = \text{Retention Rate} \times \text{Return on New Investment} \quad (9.12)$$

Profitable Growth. Equation 9.12 shows that a firm can increase its growth rate by retaining more of its earnings. However, if the firm retains more earnings, it will be able to pay out less of those earnings; according to Equation 9.8, the firm will then have to reduce its dividend. If a firm wants to increase its share price, should it cut its dividend and invest more, or should it cut its investments and increase its dividend? Not surprisingly, the answer to this question will depend on the profitability of the firm's investments. Let's consider an example.

In Example 9.3, cutting the firm's dividend in favour of growth raised the firm's stock price. This is not always the case, however, as Example 9.4 demonstrates.

EXAMPLE 9.3

Cutting Dividends for Profitable Growth

Problem

The Forzani Group expects to have earnings per share of $6 in the coming year. Rather than reinvest these earnings and grow, the firm plans to pay out all of its earnings as a dividend. With these expectations of no growth, Forzani's current share price is $60.

Suppose Forzani could cut its dividend payout rate to 75% for the foreseeable future and use the retained earnings to open new stores. The return on its investment in these stores is expected to be 12%. If we assume that the risk of these new investments is the same as the risk of its existing investments, then the firm's equity cost of capital is unchanged. What effect would this new policy have on Forzani's stock price?

Solution

▶ **Plan**

To figure out the effect of this policy on Forzani's stock price, we need to know several things. First, we need to compute its equity cost of capital. Next, we must determine Forzani's dividend and growth rate under the new policy.

Because we know that Forzani currently has a growth rate of 0 ($g = 0$), a dividend of $6, and a price of $60, we can use Equation 9.7 to estimate r_E. Next, the new dividend will simply be 75% of the old dividend of $6. Finally, given a retention rate of 25% and a return on new investment of 12%, we can use Equation 9.12 to compute the new growth rate (g). Finally, armed with the new dividend, Forzani's equity cost of capital, and its new growth rate, we can use Equation 9.6 to compute the price of Forzani's shares if it institutes the new policy.

▶ **Execute**

Using Equation 9.7 to estimate r_E, we have

$$r_E = \frac{Div_1}{P_0} + g = 10\% + 0\% = 10\%$$

In other words, to justify Forzani's stock price under its current policy, the expected return of other stocks in the market with equivalent risk must be 10%.

Next, we consider the consequences of the new policy. If Forzani reduces its dividend payout rate to 75%, then from Equation 9.8 its dividend this coming year will fall to $Div_1 = EPS_1 \times 75\% = \$6 \times 75\% = \$4.50$.

At the same time, because the firm will now retain 25% of its earnings to invest in new stores, from Equation 9.12 its growth rate will increase to

$$g = \text{Retention Rate} \times \text{Return on New Investment} = 25\% \times 12\% = 3\%$$

Assuming Forzani can continue to grow at this rate, we can compute its share price under the new policy using the constant dividend growth model of Equation 9.6:

$$P_0 = \frac{Div_1}{r_E - g} = \frac{\$4.50}{0.10 - 0.03} = \$64.29$$

▶ **Evaluate**

Forzani's share price should rise from $60 to $64.29 if the company cuts its dividend in order to increase its investment and growth, implying that the investment has a positive *NPV*. By using its earnings to invest in projects that offer a rate of return (12%) greater than its equity cost of capital (10%), Forzani has created value for its shareholders.

EXAMPLE 9.4

Unprofitable Growth

Problem

Suppose the Forzani Group decides to cut its dividend payout rate to 75% to invest in new stores, as in Example 9.3. But now suppose that the return on these new investments is 8%, rather than 12%. Given its expected earnings per share this year of $6 and its equity cost of capital of 10% (we again assume that the risk of the new investments is the same as that of its existing investments), what will happen to Forzani's current share price in this case?

Solution

▶ **Plan**

We will follow the steps in Example 9.3, except that in this case, we assume a return on new investments of 8% when computing the new growth rate (*g*) instead of 12% as in Example 9.3.

▶ **Execute**

Just as in Example 9.3, Forzani's dividend will fall to $6 × 75% = $4.50. Its growth rate under the new policy, given the lower return on new investment, will now be $g = 25\% \times 8\% = 2\%$. The new share price is therefore

$$P_0 = \frac{Div_1}{r_E - g} = \frac{\$4.50}{0.10 - 0.02} = \$56.25$$

▶ **Evaluate**

Even though Forzani will grow under the new policy, the new investments have a negative *NPV*. The company's share price will fall if it cuts its dividend to make new investments with a return of only 8%. By reinvesting its earnings at a rate (8%) that is lower than its equity cost of capital (10%), Forzani has reduced shareholder value.

Comparing Example 9.3 with Example 9.4, we see that the effect of cutting the firm's dividend to grow crucially depends on the value of the new investments the firm plans to make. In Example 9.3, the return on new investment of 12% exceeds the firm's equity cost of capital of 10%, so the investment is a good one. In Example 9.4, however, the return on new investment is only 8%, so the new investment's return is below the firm's cost of capital. In that case, the new investment is not worthwhile even though it will lead to earnings growth. In this example, we can check that cutting the firm's dividend to increase investment will create value and raise the stock price if, and only if, the new investments generate a greater return than their cost of capital. In the next chapter, we will consider more generally how to identify projects that create value and thus increase stock price.

Changing Growth Rates

Successful young firms often have very high initial earnings growth rates. During this period of high growth, firms often retain 100% of their earnings to exploit profitable investment opportunities. As they mature, their growth slows to rates more typical of established companies. At that point, their earnings exceed their investment needs and they begin to pay dividends.

We cannot use the constant dividend growth model to value the stock of such a firm for two reasons:

1. These firms often pay *no* dividends when they are young.
2. Their growth rate continues to change over time until they mature.

However, we can use the general form of the dividend-discount model to value such a firm by applying the constant growth model to calculate the future share price of the stock P_n once the firm matures and its expected growth rate stabilizes:

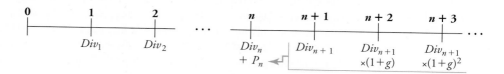

Specifically, if the firm is expected to grow at a long-term rate g after year $n + 1$, then from the constant dividend growth model,

$$P_n = \frac{Div_{n+1}}{r_E - g} \tag{9.13}$$

We can then use this estimate of P_n as a final cash flow in the dividend-discount model. Intuitively, we value the stock as the present value of the dividends we will receive plus the present value of the price we expect to be able to sell the stock for in the future. For example, consider a company with expected dividends of $2.00, $2.50, and $3.00 in each of the next three years. After that point, its dividends are expected to grow at a constant rate of 5%. If its equity cost of capital is 12%, we can find the current price. Using Equation 9.13, we can compute the price in year three:

$$P_n = \frac{Div_{n+1}}{r_E - g} = \left(\frac{\$3.00(1.05)}{0.12 - 0.05} \right) = 45.00$$

Now, using Equation 9.4, we can calculate the current price as the *PV* of the first three years' dividends and then the price at the end of year three:

$$P_0 = \frac{\$2.00}{1.12} + \frac{\$2.50}{(1.12)^2} + \frac{\$3.00}{(1.12)^3} + \frac{\$45.00}{(1.12)^3} = \$37.94$$

Common Mistake   **The First Dividend**

The most common mistake in handling growing dividends is to use the current period's dividend in the numerator of the growing perpetuity formula. In the example just discussed in the text, the dividends reached $3 in year three, and then grew by 5% per year thereafter. A common mistake is to calculate the growing stream of dividends as, $\frac{3.00}{.12 - .05}$ forgetting that next year's dividend (the numerator) has already grown by 5%! As we show in the example, the correct calculation is $\frac{3.00 \times (1.05)}{.12 - .05} = \$45$. Also, remember to avoid the common mistake from Chapter 4: the growing perpetuity formula gives the value in year n for dividends starting in year $n + 1$. In the example above, the formula gives the value in year three of the growing dividend stream starting in year four. That is why we discount the $45 back only three years.

This example also reinforces an important point: the constant growth dividend model (Equation 9.13) is just a special case of the general dividend-discount formula (Equation 9.4). We can always value all the stream of dividends using Equation 9.4. However, if we assume constant growth, we can apply the growing perpetuity shortcut to all or part of the dividend stream, depending on whether the constant growth starts now or at some point in the future.

EXAMPLE 9.5

Valuing a Firm
with Two Different
Growth Rates

Problem

Small Fry, Inc. has just invented a potato chip that looks and tastes like a french fry. Given the phenomenal market response to this product, Small Fry is reinvesting all of its earnings to expand its operations. Earnings were $2 per share this past year and are expected to grow at a rate of 20% per year until the end of year four. At that point, other companies are likely to bring out competing products. Analysts project that at the end of year four, Small Fry will cut its investment and begin paying 60% of its earnings as dividends. Its growth will also slow to a long-run rate of 4%. If Small Fry's equity cost of capital is 8%, what is the value of a share today?

Solution

▶ **Plan**

We can use Small Fry's projected earnings growth rate and payout rate to forecast its future earnings and dividends. After year four, Small Fry's dividends will grow at a constant 4%, so we can use the constant dividend growth model (Equation 9.13) to value all dividends after that point. Finally, we can pull everything together with the dividend-discount model (Equation 9.4).

▶ **Execute**

The following spreadsheet projects Small Fry's earnings and dividends:

1	Year	0	1	2	3	4	5	6
2	Earnings							
3	*EPS* Growth Rate (versus prior year)		20%	20%	20%	20%	4%	4%
4	*EPS*	$2.00	$2.40	$2.88	$3.46	$4.15	$4.31	$4.49
5	Dividends							
6	Dividend Payout Rate		0%	0%	0%	60%	60%	60%
7	Div		$ —	$ —	$ —	$2.49	$2.59	$2.69

Starting from $2.00 in year zero, *EPS* grows by 20% per year until year four, after which growth slows to 4%. Small Fry's dividend payout rate is zero until year four, when competition reduces its investment opportunities and its payout rate rises to 60%. Multiplying *EPS* by the dividend payout ratio, we project Small Fry's future dividends in line 4.

After year four, Small Fry's dividends will grow at the expected long-run rate of 4% per year. Thus we can use the constant dividend growth model to project Small Fry's share price at the end of year three. Given its equity cost of capital of 8%,

$$P_3 = \frac{Div_4}{r_E - g} = \frac{\$2.49}{0.08 - 0.04} = \$62.25$$

We then apply the dividend-discount model (Equation 9.4) with this terminal value:

$$P_0 = \frac{Div_1}{1 + r_E} + \frac{Div_2}{(1 + r_E)^2} + \frac{Div_3}{(1 + r_E)^3} + \frac{P_3}{(1 + r_E)^3} = \frac{\$62.25}{(1.08)^3} = \$49.42$$

▶ **Evaluate**

The dividend-discount model is flexible enough to handle any forecasted pattern of dividends. Here the dividends were zero for several years and then settled into a constant growth rate, allowing us to use the constant growth rate model as a shortcut.

Table 9.1 summarizes the dividend-discount model, including how to apply the shortcut for constant growth.

Value Drivers and the Dividend-Discount Model

Now that we have fully developed the dividend-discount model, it is worth assessing how well it does in capturing the intuitive drivers of stock value. When we think about how valuable a company is, we usually focus on how profitable it is now and how that profitability will grow or decline in the future, along with the risk of investing in the company. Where are these measures captured in the dividend-discount model? Profitability determines the company's ability to pay dividends, so implicitly in the forecasted dividend stream, we are forecasting the company's profitability. As for the risk, that is captured in the equity cost of capital we use to discount those forecasted dividends. Riskier investments require higher expected returns, which enter the dividend-discount model as higher equity cost of capital.

TABLE 9.1	The Dividend-Discount Model

General Formula	$P_0 = \dfrac{Div_1}{1 + r_E} + \dfrac{Div_2}{(1 + r_E)^2} + \cdots + \dfrac{Div_n}{(1 + r_E)^n} + \dfrac{P_n}{(1 + r_E)^n}$
If dividend growth is constant	$P_0 = \dfrac{Div_1}{r_E - g}$
If early growth is variable followed by constant growth	$P_0 = \dfrac{Div_1}{1 + r_E} + \dfrac{Div_2}{(1 + r_E)^2} + \cdots + \dfrac{Div_n}{(1 + r_E)^n} + \left(\dfrac{1}{(1 + r_E)^n}\right)\dfrac{Div_n(1 + g)}{r_E - g}$

5. What are three ways that a firm can increase the amount of its future dividends per share?
6. Under what circumstances can a firm increase its share price by cutting its dividend and investing more?

 9.4 # Limitations of the Dividend-Discount Model

The dividend-discount model values a stock based on a forecast of the future dividends paid to shareholders. But unlike a Government of Canada bond, whose cash flows are known with virtual certainty, a tremendous amount of uncertainty is associated with any forecast of a firm's future dividends.

Let's reconsider the example of Nike (ticker symbol: NKE). In 2010, NKE paid annual dividends of $1.08 (by paying four quarterly dividends of 27 cents each). With an equity cost of capital of 10% and expected dividend growth of 8.5%, the constant dividend growth model implies a share price for NKE of

$$P_0 = \frac{Div_1}{r_E - g} = \frac{\$1.08(1 + 0.085)}{0.10 - 0.085} = \$78.12$$

which is reasonably close to the $76.43 share price that the stock had at the time. With a 9% dividend growth rate, however, this estimate would rise to almost $118 per share; with a 6% dividend growth rate, the estimate falls to almost $29 per share. As we see in Figure 9.2, even small changes in the assumed dividend growth rate can lead to large changes in the estimated stock price.

FIGURE 9.2

NKE Stock Prices for Different Expected Growth Rates

Stock prices are based on the constant dividend growth model. We assume a dividend next year of $1.08 and an equity cost of capital of 10%. The expected dividend growth rate varies from 0% to 9%. Note how even a small change in the expected growth rate produces a large change in the stock price, especially at higher growth rates.

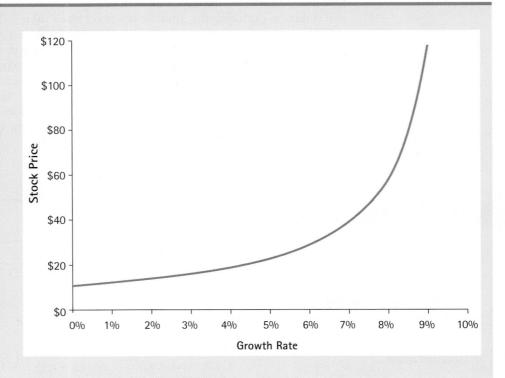

Furthermore, it is difficult to know which estimate of the dividend growth rate is more reasonable. NKE more than doubled its dividend between 2005 and 2010, but its earnings growth rate then moderated. Consequently, this rate of increase is not sustainable. From Equation 9.8, forecasting dividends requires forecasting the firm's earnings, dividend payout rate, and future share count. Future earnings, however, will depend on interest expenses (which, in turn, depend on how much the firm borrows), and the firm's share count and dividend payout rate will depend on whether NKE uses a portion of its earnings to repurchase shares. Because borrowing and repurchase decisions are at management's discretion, they can be more difficult to forecast reliably than other, more fundamental aspects of the firm's cash flows.[5]

Non-Dividend-Paying Stocks

Many companies do not pay cash dividends—Research In Motion, Air Canada, Apple, Starbucks, and Google are just a few examples. How then do we value those stocks? In the next section, we discuss a small modification to the dividend-discount model to capture total payouts to shareholders, whether the payouts are dividends or not. We will then discuss other valuation approaches that do not rely on payouts. Those approaches will be more meaningful once we have covered how financial managers create value within the firm through decisions about which projects to approve. So, in the next two chapters, we will cover investment decision rules and project evaluation.

Concept Check

7. What are the main limitations of the dividend-discount model?

8. What pieces of information are needed to forecast dividends?

9.5 Share Repurchases and the Total Payout Model

share repurchase A firm's use of cash to buy back its own stock.

total payout model A method that values shares of a firm by discounting the firm's total payouts to equity holders (i.e., all the cash distributed as dividends and stock repurchases) and then dividing by the current number of shares outstanding.

In our discussion of the dividend-discount model, we implicitly assumed that any cash paid out by the firm to shareholders takes the form of a dividend. In recent years, an increasing number of firms have replaced dividend payouts with *share repurchases*. In a **share repurchase**, the firm uses excess cash to buy back its own stock. Share repurchases have two consequences for the dividend-discount model. First, the more cash the firm uses to repurchase shares, the less cash it has available to pay dividends. Second, by repurchasing shares, the firm decreases its share count, which increases its earning and dividends on a per-share basis.

In the dividend-discount model, we valued a share from the perspective of a single shareholder, discounting the dividends the shareholder will receive:

$$P_0 = PV(\text{Future Dividends per Share}) \tag{9.14}$$

An alternative method that may be more reliable when a firm repurchases shares is the **total payout model**, which values *all* of the firm's equity, rather than a single share. To use this model, we discount the total payouts that the firm makes to shareholders, which is the total amount spent on both dividends *and* share repurchases

---

[5]We discuss management's decision to borrow funds or repurchase shares in Part 6 of the text.

(net of new share issuance).[6] This gives the total value of the firm's equity. We then divide by the current number of shares outstanding to determine the share price:

Total Payout Model

$$P_0 = \frac{PV(\text{Future Total Dividends and Repurchases})}{\text{Shares Outstanding}_0}$$ (9.15)

We can apply the same simplifications that we obtained by assuming constant growth in Section 9.2 to the total payout method. The only change is that *we discount total dividends and share repurchases and use the growth rate of earnings (rather than earnings per share) when forecasting the growth of the firm's total payouts.* When the firm uses share repurchases, this method can be more reliable and easier to apply than the dividend-discount model.

EXAMPLE 9.6

Valuation with
Share Repurchases

Problem

Suppose Buhler Industries has 217 million shares outstanding and expects earnings at the end of this year of $860 million. Buhler plans to pay out 50% of its earnings in total, paying 30% as a dividend and using 20% to repurchase shares. If Buhler's earnings are expected to grow by 7.5% per year and these payout rates remain constant, determine Buhler's share price assuming an equity cost of capital of 10%.

Solution

▶ **Plan**

Based on the equity cost of capital of 10% and an expected earnings growth rate of 7.5%, we can compute the present value of Buhler's future payouts as a constant growth perpetuity. The only input missing here is Buhler's total payouts this year, which we can calculate as 50% of its earnings. The present value of all of Buhler's future payouts is the value of its total equity. To obtain the price of a share, we divide the total value by the number of shares outstanding (217 million).

▶ **Execute**

Buhler will have total payouts this year of 50% × $860 million = $430 million. Using the constant growth perpetuity formula, we have

$$PV(\text{Future Total Dividends and Repurchases}) = \frac{\$430 \text{ million}}{0.10 - 0.075} = \$17.2 \text{ billion}$$

This present value represents the total value of Buhler's equity (i.e., its market capitalization). To compute the share price, we divide by the current number of shares outstanding:

$$P_0 = \frac{\$17.2 \text{ billion}}{217 \text{ million shares}} = \$79.26 \text{ per share}$$

▶ **Evaluate**

Using the total payout method, we did not need to know the firm's split between dividends and share repurchases. To compare this method with the dividend-discount model, note that Buhler will pay a dividend of 30% × $860 million/(217 million shares) = $1.19 per share, for

---

[6]You can think of the total payouts as the amount you would receive if you owned 100% of the firm's shares: You would receive all of the dividends, plus the proceeds from selling shares back to the firm in the share repurchase.

a dividend yield of $1.19/79.26 = 1.50\%$. From Equation 9.7, Buhler's expected *EPS*, dividend, and share price growth rate is $g = r_E - Div_1/P_0 = 8.50\%$. This growth rate exceeds the 7.50% growth rate of earnings because Buhler's share count will decline over time owing to its share repurchases.[7]

9.6 The Discounted Free Cash Flow Model

discounted free cash flow model A method for estimating a firm's enterprise value by discounting its future free cash flow.

In the total payout model, we first value the firm's equity, rather than just a single share. The **discounted free cash flow model** goes one step further and begins by determining the total value of the firm to all investors—both equity holders *and* debt holders. That is, we begin by estimating the firm's enterprise value, which we defined in Chapter 2 as follows:[8]

$$\text{Enterprise Value} = \text{Market Value of Equity} + \text{Debt} - \text{Cash} \qquad (9.16)$$

Because the enterprise value is the value of the firm's underlying business, unencumbered by debt and separate from any cash or marketable securities, it is also the value of the underlying business to all investors. We can interpret the enterprise value as the net cost of acquiring the firm's equity, taking its cash, and paying off all debt; in essence, it is equivalent to owning the unlevered business. The advantage of the discounted free cash flow model is that it allows us to value a firm without explicitly forecasting its dividends, share repurchases, or use of debt.

Valuing the Enterprise.   How can we estimate a firm's enterprise value? To estimate the value of the firm's equity, we compute the present value of the firm's total payouts to equity holders. Likewise, to estimate a firm's enterprise value, we compute the present value of the *free cash flow* (*FCF*) that the firm has available to pay all investors, both debt and equity holders. We saw how to compute the free cash flow for a project in Chapter 8; we now perform the same calculation for the entire firm:

$$\text{Free Cash Flow} = EBIT \times (1 - \text{tax rate}) + \text{Depreciation}$$
$$- \text{Capital Expenditures} - \text{Increases in Net Working Capital} \quad (9.17)$$

Note: As in Chapter 8, if capital cost allowance (*CCA*) replaces depreciation for tax purposes, then *CCA* would be used in the calculation of *EBIT* and would replace depreciation in Equation 9.17.

Free cash flow measures the cash generated by the firm before any payments to debt or equity holders are considered. Thus, just as we determine the value of a project by calculating the *NPV* of the project's free cash flow, so we estimate a firm's current enterprise value, V_0, by computing the present value of the firm's free cash flow:

Discounted Free Cash Flow Model

$$V_0 = PV(\text{Future Free Cash Flow of Firm}) \qquad (9.18)$$

---

[7]We can check that an 8.5% *EPS* growth rate is consistent with 7.5% earnings growth and Buhler's repurchase plans as follows: Given an expected share price of $79.26 \times 1.085 = \$86.00$ next year, Buhler will repurchase 20% × \$860 million ÷ (\$86.00 per share) = 2 million shares next year. With the decline in the number of shares from 217 million to 215 million, *EPS* grows by a factor of $1.075 \times (217/215) = 1.085$ or 8.5%.

[8]To be precise, when we say "cash," we are referring to the firm's cash in excess of its working capital needs, which is the amount of cash it has invested at a competitive market interest rate.

Given the enterprise value, we can estimate the share price by using Equation 9.16 to solve for the value of equity and then divide by the total number of shares outstanding:

$$P_0 = \frac{V_0 + \text{Cash}_0 - \text{Debt}_0}{\text{Shares Outstanding}_0} \tag{9.19}$$

In the dividend-discount model, the firm's cash and debt are included indirectly through the effect of interest income and expenses on earnings. By contrast, in the discounted free cash flow model, we ignore interest income and expenses because free cash flow is based on *EBIT* (earnings *before* interest and taxes), but we then adjust for cash and debt directly (in Equation 9.19).

Implementing the Model. A key difference between the discounted free cash flow model and the earlier models we have considered is the discount rate. In previous calculations, we used the firm's equity cost of capital, r_E, because we were discounting the cash flows to equity holders. Here, we are discounting the free cash flow that will be paid to both debt and equity holders. Thus we should use the firm's **weighted average cost of capital (WACC)**, denoted by r_{wacc}; it is the cost of capital that reflects the risk of the overall business, which is the combined risk of the firm's equity *and* debt. We interpret r_{wacc} as the expected return the firm must pay to investors to compensate them for the risk of holding the firm's debt and equity together. If the firm has no debt, then $r_{wacc} = r_E$. We will develop methods to calculate the WACC explicitly in Part 4 of this text.[9]

Given the firm's WACC, we implement the discounted free cash flow model in much the same way as we did the dividend-discount model. That is, we forecast the firm's free cash flow up to some horizon, together with a terminal (continuation) value of the enterprise:

> **weighted average cost of capital (WACC)** The cost of capital that reflects the risk of the overall business, which is the combined risk of the firm's equity and debt.

$$V_0 = \frac{FCF_1}{1 + r_{wacc}} + \frac{FCF_2}{(1 + r_{wacc})^2} + \cdots + \frac{FCF_n}{(1 + r_{wacc})^n} + \frac{V_n}{(1 + r_{wacc})^n} \tag{9.20}$$

Often, we estimate the terminal value by assuming a constant long-run growth rate, g_{FCF}, for free cash flows beyond year n, so that

$$V_n = \frac{FCF_{n+1}}{r_{wacc} - g_{FCF}} = \left(\frac{1 + g_{FCF}}{r_{wacc} - g_{FCF}} \right) \times FCF_n \tag{9.21}$$

The long-run growth rate g_{FCF} is typically based on the expected long-run growth rate of the firm's revenues.

EXAMPLE 9.7

Valuing Nike Stock Using Free Cash Flow

Problem

Nike (ticker symbol: NKE) had sales of $19.2 billion in 2009. Suppose you expect its sales to grow at a rate of 10% in 2010, but then slow by 1% per year to the long-run growth rate that is characteristic of the apparel industry—5%—by 2015. Based on Nike's past profitability and investment needs, you expect *EBIT* to be 10% of sales, increases in net working capital requirements to be 10% of any increase in sales, and capital expenditures to equal depreciation expenses. If Nike has $2.3 billion in cash, $32 million in debt, 486 million shares

---

[9]We can also interpret the firm's weighted average cost of capital as the average cost of capital associated with all of the firm's projects. In that sense, the WACC is the expected return associated with the average risk of the firm's investments.

outstanding, a tax rate of 24%, and a WACC of 10%, what is your estimate of the value of Nike's stock in early 2010?

Solution

▶ **Plan**

We can estimate Nike's future free cash flow by constructing a pro forma statement as we did for Research In Motion in Chapter 8. The only difference is that the pro forma statement is for the whole company, rather than just one project. Further, we need to calculate a terminal (or continuation) value for Nike at the end of our explicit projections. Because we expect Nike's free cash flow to grow at a constant rate after 2015, we can use Equation 9.21 to compute a terminal enterprise value. The present value of the free cash flows during the years 2010 to 2015 and the terminal value will be the total enterprise value for Nike. Using that value, we can subtract the debt, add the cash, and divide by the number of shares outstanding to compute the price per share (Equation 9.19).

▶ **Execute**

The spreadsheet below presents a simplified pro forma statement for Nike based on the information we have:

1	Year	2009	2010	2011	2012	2013	2014	2015
2	FCF Forecast ($ million)							
3	Sales	19,200.0	21,120.0	23,020.8	24,862.5	26,602.8	28,199.0	29,609.0
4	Growth Versus Prior Year		10.0%	9.0%	8.0%	7.0%	6.0%	5.0%
5	EBIT (10% of sales)		2112.0	2302.1	2486.2	2660.3	2819.9	2960.9
6	Less: Income Tax (24%)		506.9	552.5	596.7	638.5	676.8	710.6
7	Plus: Depreciation		—	—	—	—	—	—
8	Less: Capital Expenditures		—	—	—	—	—	—
9	Less: Increase in NWC (10% Δ Sales)		192.0	190.1	184.2	174.0	159.6	141.0
10	Free Cash Flow		1413.1	1559.5	1705.3	1847.8	1983.5	2109.3

Because capital expenditures are expected to equal depreciation, lines 7 and 8 in the spreadsheet cancel out. We can set them both to zero rather than explicitly forecast them.

Given our assumption of constant 5% growth in free cash flows after 2015 and a WACC of 10%, we can use Equation 9.21 to compute a terminal enterprise value:

$$V_{2015} = \left(\frac{1 + g_{FCF}}{r_{wacc} - g_{FCF}}\right) \times FCF_{2015} = \left(\frac{1.05}{0.10 - 0.05}\right) \times 2109.3 = \$44,295 \text{ million}$$

From Eq. 9.20, Nike's current enterprise value is the present value of its free cash flows plus the firm's terminal value:

$$V_0 = \frac{1413.1}{1.10} + \frac{1559.5}{1.10^2} + \frac{1705.3}{1.10^3} + \frac{1847.8}{1.10^4} + \frac{1983.5}{1.10^5}$$

$$+ \frac{2109.3}{1.10^6} + \frac{44,295.0}{1.10^6} = \$32,542.4 \text{ million}$$

We can now estimate the value of a share of Nike's stock using Equation 9.19:

$$P_0 = \frac{\$32{,}542.4 + \$2300 - \$32}{486} = \$71.63$$

▶ **Evaluate**

The total value of all the claims, both debt and equity, on the firm must equal the total present value of all cash flows generated by the firm, in addition to any cash it currently has. The total present value of all cash flows to be generated by Nike is $32,542 million, and it has $2300 million in cash. Subtracting the value of the debt claims ($32 million) leaves us with the total value of the equity claims, and dividing by the number of shares produces the value per share.

Connection to Capital Budgeting. There is an important connection between the discounted free cash flow model and the *NPV* rule for capital budgeting that we developed in Chapter 7. Because the firm's free cash flow is equal to the sum of the free cash flows from the firm's current and future investments, we can interpret the firm's enterprise value as the total *NPV* that the firm will earn from continuing its existing projects and initiating new ones. Hence, the *NPV* of any individual project represents its contribution to the firm's enterprise value. To maximize the firm's share price, we should accept those projects that have a positive *NPV*.

Recall also from Chapter 7 that many forecasts and estimates were necessary to estimate the free cash flows of a project. The same is true for the firm: we must forecast its future sales, operating expenses, taxes, capital requirements, and other factors to obtain its free cash flow. On the one hand, estimating free cash flow in this way gives us flexibility to incorporate many specific details about the future prospects of the firm. On the other hand, some uncertainty inevitably surrounds each assumption. Given this fact, it is important to conduct a sensitivity analysis, as described in Chapter 7, to translate this uncertainty into a range of potential values for the stock.

EXAMPLE 9.8

Sensitivity Analysis
for Stock Valuation

Problem

In Example 9.7, Nike's *EBIT* was assumed to be 10% of sales. If Nike can reduce its operating expenses and raise its *EBIT* to 11% of sales, how would the estimate of the stock's value change?

Solution

▶ **Plan**

In this scenario, *EBIT* will increase by 1% of sales compared with 10% in Example 9.7. From there, we can use the tax rate (24%) to compute the effect on the free cash flow for each year. Once we have the new free cash flows, we repeat the approach in Example 9.7 to arrive at a new stock price.

▶ **Execute**

In year 1, *EBIT* will be 1% × $21,120.0 million = $211.2 million higher. After taxes, this increase will raise the firm's free cash flow in year 1 by (1 − 0.24) × $211.2 million = $160.5 million, to $1573.6 million. Doing the same calculation for each year, we get the following revised *FCF* estimates:

Year	2010	2011	2012	2013	2014	2015
FCF	1573.6	1734.5	1894.3	2050.0	2197.8	2334.3

We can now re-estimate the stock price as in Example 9.7. The terminal value is $V_{2015} = [1.05/(0.10 - 0.05)] \times 2334.3 = \$49,020.3$ million, so

$$V_0 = \frac{1573.6}{1.10} + \frac{1734.5}{1.10^2} + \frac{1894.3}{1.10^3} + \frac{2050.0}{1.10^4} + \frac{2197.8}{1.10^5}$$
$$+ \frac{2334.3}{1.10^6} + \frac{49,020.3}{1.10^6} = \$36,040.4 \text{ million}$$

The new estimate for the value of the stock is $P_0 = (36,040.4 + 2300 - 32)/486 = \$78.82$ per share, a difference of about 10% compared with the result found in Example 9.7.

▶ **Evaluate**

Nike's stock price is fairly sensitive to changes in the assumptions about its profitability. A 1% permanent change in its margins affects the firm's stock price by 10%.

Figure 9.3 summarizes the different valuation methods we have discussed so far. The value of the stock is determined by the present value of its future dividends. We can estimate the total market capitalization of the firm's equity from the present value of the firm's total payouts, which includes dividends and share repurchases. Finally, the present value of the firm's free cash flow, which is the amount of cash the firm has available to make payments to equity or debt holders, determines the firm's enterprise value.

FIGURE 9.3

A Comparison of Discounted Cash Flow Models of Stock Valuation

By computing the present value of the firm's dividends, total payouts, or free cash flows, we can estimate the value of the stock, the total value of the firm's equity, or the firm's enterprise value. The final column details what adjustment is necessary to obtain the stock price

Present Value of...	Determines the...	To Get Stock Price Estimate...
Dividend Payments	Stock Price	No adjustment necessary
Total Payouts (All dividends and repurchases)	Equity Value	Divide by shares oustanding
Free Cash Flow (Cash available to pay all security holders)	Enterprise Value	Subtract what does not belong to equity holders (debt and perferred stock), add back cash and marketable securities, and divide by shares outstanding

Concept Check

9. What is the relation between capital budgeting and the discounted free cash flow model?

10. Why do we ignore interest payments on the firm's debt in the discounted free cash flow model?

9.7 Valuation Based on Comparable Firms

So far, we have valued a firm or its stock by considering the expected future cash flows it will provide to its owner. The Valuation Principle then tells us that its value is the present value of its future cash flows, because the present value is the amount we would need to invest elsewhere in the market to replicate the cash flows with the same risk.

Another application of the Law of One Price is the method of comparables. In the **method of comparables** (or "comps"), rather than value the firm's cash flows directly, we estimate the value of the firm based on the value of other, comparable firms or investments that we expect will generate very similar cash flows in the future. For example, consider the case of a new firm that is *identical* to an existing publicly traded company. Recall that from competitive market prices, the Valuation Principle implies that two securities with identical cash flows must have the same price. Thus, if firms will generate identical cash flows, we can use the market value of the existing company to determine the value of the new firm.

Of course, identical companies do not really exist. Even two firms in the same industry selling the same types of products, while similar in many respects, are likely to be of a different size or scale. For example, Hewlett-Packard and Dell both sell personal computers directly to consumers using the internet. In 2009, Hewlett-Packard had sales of $115 billion, whereas Dell had sales of approximately $53 billion. In this section, we consider ways to adjust for scale differences to use comparables to value firms with similar businesses and then discuss the strengths and weaknesses of this approach.

method of comparables An estimate of the value of a firm based on the value of other, comparable firms or other investments that are expected to generate very similar cash flows in the future.

Valuation Multiples

We can adjust for differences in scale between firms by expressing their value in terms of a **valuation multiple**, which is a ratio of the value to some measure of the firm's scale. As an analogy, consider valuing an office building. A natural measure to consider would be the price per square foot for other buildings recently sold in the area. Multiplying the size of the office building under consideration by the average price per square foot would typically provide a reasonable estimate of the building's value. We can apply this same idea to stocks, replacing square footage with some more appropriate measure of the firm's scale.

valuation multiple A ratio of a firm's value to some measure of the firm's scale or cash flow.

The Price-Earnings Ratio. The most common valuation multiple is the price-earnings (P/E) ratio, which we introduced in Chapter 2. The P/E ratio is so common that it is almost always part of the basic statistics computed for a stock (as shown in Figure 9.1, the screenshot from the Google Finance website for NKE). A firm's P/E ratio is equal to the share price divided by its earnings per share. The reasoning behind its use is that, when you buy a stock, you are in a sense buying the rights to the firm's future earnings. If differences in the scale of firms' earnings are likely to persist, you should be willing to pay proportionally more for a stock with higher current earnings. Using this idea, we can estimate the value of a firm's share by multiplying its current earnings per share by the average P/E ratio of comparable firms.

We can compute a firm's P/E ratio by using either **trailing earnings** (earnings over the prior 12 months) or **forward earnings** (expected earnings over the coming 12 months), with the resulting ratios being called the **trailing P/E** or the **forward P/E**, respectively. For valuation purposes, the forward P/E is generally preferred, as we are most concerned about future earnings.

trailing earnings A firm's earnings over the prior 12 months.

forward earnings A firm's anticipated earnings over the coming 12 months.

trailing P/E A firm's P/E ratio calculated using its trailing earnings.

forward P/E A firm's P/E ratio calculated using its forward earnings.

To understand how P/E ratios relate to other valuation techniques we have discussed, consider the dividend-discount model introduced earlier in the chapter.[10] For example, in the case of constant dividend growth, dividing through Equation 9.6 we had

$$P_0 = \frac{Div_1}{r_E - g}$$

Dividing through by EPS_1, we find that

$$\text{Forward P/E} = \frac{P_0}{EPS_1} = \frac{Div_1/EPS_1}{r_E - g} = \frac{\text{Dividend Payout Rate}}{r_E - g} \qquad (9.22)$$

Earlier, we showed that Nike's current price is consistent with an equity cost of capital of 10% and an expected dividend growth rate of 8.5%. From the Nike quote, we can also see that Nike has earnings per share (EPS) of \$3.51 and a dividend of \$0.27 per quarter, or \$1.08 per year. If these were forward earnings, then we could compute the forward P/E as:

$$\text{Forward P/E} = \frac{1.08/3.51}{0.10 - 0.085} = 20.51, \text{ which is not far off its reported P/E of 21.78.}$$

Equation 9.22 suggests that firms and industries that have high growth rates, and that generate cash well in excess of their investment needs so that they can maintain high payout rates, should have high P/E multiples. In the Nike example, we showed that at an expected growth rate of 8.5%, it would have a P/E ratio of 20.51. If our growth expectations were lower, its P/E would drop. Holding current earnings, dividends, and equity cost of capital constant, but decreasing the growth rate to 5%, we would have:

$$\text{Forward P/E} = \frac{1.08/3.51}{0.10 - 0.05} = 6.15$$

This result is much lower than its current P/E of 21.78, making it clear that simply comparing P/E ratios without taking into account growth prospects can be highly misleading. Figure 9.4 shows the relationship between expected earnings growth and P/E ratios.

EXAMPLE 9.9
Growth Prospects and the Price–Earnings Ratio

Problem

Amazon.com and Sears are both retailers. In 2010, Amazon stock had a price of \$138.71 and a forward earnings per share of \$2.61. Sears had a price of \$20.87 and forward earnings per share of \$1.87. Calculate their forward P/E ratios and explain the difference.

Solution

▶ **Plan**

We can calculate their P/E ratios by dividing each company's price per share by its forward earnings per share. The difference is most likely due to different growth expectations.

▶ **Execute**

The forward P/E for Amazon = \$138.71/\$2.61 = 53. The forward P/E for Sears = \$20.87/\$1.87 = 11.16. Amazon's P/E ratio is higher because investors expect its earnings to grow more than those of Sears.

▶ **Evaluate**

Although both companies are retailers, they have very different growth prospects, as reflected in their P/E ratios. Investors in Amazon.com are willing to pay 53 times this year's expected earnings because they are also buying the present value of high future earnings created by expected growth.

---

[10]We use the dividend discount model rather than discounted cash flows because price and earnings are variables associated exclusively with equity.

FIGURE 9.4

Relating the P/E Ratio to Expected Future Growth

The graph shows the expected growth in earnings under two growth scenarios for Nike: 8.5% and 5%. Current earnings per share is $3.51. Higher growth increases the *PV* of the earnings stream, which means that the price increases. The result is that the higher price divided by current earnings yields a higher P/E ratio. We found that a growth rate of 8.5% implied a P/E ratio of 20.51 while a growth rate of 5% implied a P/E ratio of 6.15. The graph shows how higher expected growth translates into a higher P/E.

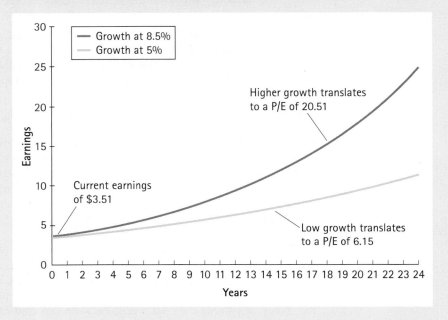

Enterprise Value Multiples. The P/E ratio has the same limitations as the dividend-discount model—because it related exclusively to equity, it ignores the effect of debt. Consequently, it is also common practice to use valuation multiples based on the firm's enterprise value. By representing the total value of the firm's underlying business rather than just the value of equity, the enterprise value allows us to compare firms with different amounts of leverage.

Because the enterprise value represents the entire value of the firm before the firm pays its debt, to form an appropriate multiple, we divide it by a measure of earnings or cash flows before interest payments are made. Common multiples to consider are enterprise value to *EBIT*, *EBITDA* (earnings before interest, taxes, depreciation, and amortization), and free cash flow. However, because capital expenditures can vary substantially from period to period (e.g., a firm may need to add capacity and build a new plant one year, but then may not need to expand further for many years), most practitioners rely on enterprise value to *EBITDA* multiples. From Equation 9.21, if expected free cash flow growth is constant, then

$$\frac{V_0}{EBITDA_1} = \frac{\dfrac{FCF_1}{r_{wacc} - g_{FCF}}}{EDITDA_1} = \frac{FCF_1/EBITDA_1}{r_{wacc} - g_{FCF}} \tag{9.23}$$

As with the P/E multiple, this valuation multiple is higher for firms with high growth rates and low capital requirements (which means that free cash flow is high in proportion to *EBITDA*).

EXAMPLE 9.10

Valuation Using the
Enterprise Value
Multiple

Problem

Westcoast Port, Inc. is an ocean transport company with *EBITDA* of $50 million, cash of
$20 million, debt of $100 million, and 10 million shares outstanding. The ocean transport industry as a whole has an average enterprise-value-to-*EBITDA* (*EV/EBITDA*) ratio of 8.5. What is one
estimate of Westcoast's enterprise value? What is a corresponding estimate of its stock price?

Solution

▶ **Plan**

To estimate Westcoast's enterprise value, we multiply its *EBITDA* by the average *EV/EBITDA*
ratio of its industry. From there, we can subtract Westcoast's debt and add its cash to calculate its equity value. Finally, we can divide by the number of shares outstanding to arrive at
its stock price.

▶ **Execute**

Westcoast's enterprise value estimate is $50 million × 8.5 = $425 million.
Next, subtract the debt from its enterprise value and add in its cash:

$425 million − $100 million + $20 million = $345 million, which is an estimate of the equity value.

Its stock price estimate is equal to its equity value estimate divided by the number of shares
outstanding:

$345 million/10 million = $34.50.

▶ **Evaluate**

If we assume that Westcoast should be valued similarly to the rest of the industry, then
$425 million is a reasonable estimate of its enterprise value and $34.50 is a reasonable estimate
of its stock price. However, we are relying on the assumption that Westcoast's expected free cash
flow growth is similar to the industry average. If that assumption is wrong, so is our valuation.

Other Multiples. Many other valuation multiples are possible. Looking at the enterprise
value as a multiple of sales can be useful if it is reasonable to assume that the firm will
maintain a similar margin in the future. For firms with substantial tangible assets, the
ratio of price to book value of equity per share is sometimes used as a valuation multiple.
Some multiples are specific to an industry. In the cable TV industry, for example, it is
natural to consider enterprise value per subscriber.

Limitations of Multiples

If comparables were identical to those of the firms being valued, the firms' multiples
would match precisely. Of course, firms are not identical, so the usefulness of a valuation multiple will inevitably depend on the nature of the differences between firms and
the sensitivity of the multiples to these differences.

Table 9.2 lists several valuation multiples, as of May 2010, for firms in the footwear
industry that could be used as comparables for Nike. Also shown in the table is the average for each multiple, together with the range around the average (in percentage terms).
The bottom rows showing the range make it clear that the footwear industry has a lot of
dispersion for all of the multiples (for example, Deckers has a price-to-book [P/B] ratio
of 3.59, while Rocky Shoes & Boots has a P/B ratio of only 0.56). While the P/E multiple
shows the smallest variation, even with it we cannot expect to obtain a precise estimate
of a firm's value.

The differences in these multiples most likely reflect differences in expected future
growth rates, risk (and therefore costs of capital), and, in the case of Puma, differences
in the accounting conventions used in Germany, where Puma is based, and in the

TABLE 9.2		Stock Prices and Multiples for the Footwear Industry (excluding Nike), May 2010				
Name	Market Capitalization ($ million)	Enterprise Value ($ million)	P/E	Price/Book	Enterprise Value/Sales	Enterprise Value/*EBITDA*
Adidas AG	8950	8554	21.90	2.34	0.82	11.08
Puma AG	3680	2984	17.91	2.92	1.21	11.48
Deckers Outdoor Corp.	1760	1400	14.63	3.59	1.68	6.94
Skechers U.S.A.	1730	1420	17.11	2.20	0.89	8.37
Wolverine World Wide	1460	1380	18.72	3.08	1.22	9.28
Volcom, Inc.	531	455	21.21	2.37	1.62	12.64
Weyco Group	281	252	20.24	1.74	1.11	10.75
LaCrosse Footwear	118	99	15.14	1.95	0.67	6.54
R.G. Barry Corp.	114	79	11.11	1.96	0.63	4.64
Rocky Shoes & Boots	45	89	25.96	0.56	0.38	5.45
		Average	18.39	2.27	1.02	8.72
		Maximum	+41%	+58%	+64%	+45%
		Minimum	−40%	−75%	−63%	−47%

United States, where other firms to which it is being compared are based. As with Puma, differences in accounting conventions are especially problematic for Canadian firms. This is due to the lack of many comparable companies (that match based on industry and size) in Canada; the comparables are often chosen from the United States, where the accounting rules sometimes differ in important ways. Investors in the market understand that these differences exist, so the stocks are priced accordingly. When valuing a firm using multiples, however, there is no clear guidance about how to adjust for these differences other than by narrowing the set of comparables used and being very careful in interpreting the accounting information given.

Another limitation of comparables is that they provide only information regarding the value of the firm *relative to* the other firms in the comparison set. Using multiples will not help us determine whether an entire industry is overvalued, for example. This issue became especially important during the internet boom of the late 1990s. Because many of these firms did not have positive cash flows or earnings, new multiples were created to value them (e.g., price to "page views"). While these multiples could justify the value of these firms in relation to one another, it was much more difficult to justify the stock prices of many of these firms using a realistic estimate of cash flows and the discounted free cash flow approach.

Comparison with Discounted Cash Flow Methods

The use of a valuation multiple based on comparables is best viewed as a shortcut to the discounted cash flow methods of valuation. Rather than separately estimate the firm's cost of capital and future earnings or free cash flows, we rely on the market's assessment of the value of other firms with similar future prospects. In addition to its simplicity, the multiples approach has the advantage of being based on actual stock prices of real firms, rather than on what may be unrealistic forecasts of future cash flows.

The most important shortcoming of the comparables approach is that it does not take into account the important differences among firms. For example, the approach ignores the fact that some firms have exceptionally talented managers, others have developed more efficient manufacturing processes, and still others might hold a patent on a new technology. Discounted cash flows methods have an advantage in this respect, in that they allow us to incorporate specific information about the firm's cost of capital or future growth. Thus, because the true driver of value for any firm is its ability to generate cash flows for its investors, using the discounted cash flow methods has the potential to be more accurate than using a valuation multiple.

Stock Valuation Techniques: The Final Word

In the end, no single technique provides a final answer regarding a stock's true value. Indeed, all approaches inevitably require assumptions or forecasts that are too uncertain to provide a definitive assessment of the firm's value. Most real-world practitioners use a combination of these approaches and gain confidence in the outcome if the results are consistent across a variety of methods.

Figure 9.5 compares the ranges of values for Nike stock using the different valuation methods discussed in this chapter. The firm's stock price of $76.43 on May 11, 2010, was within the range estimated by some methods, but higher than the range suggested by some multiples. Hence, based on this evidence alone, we would not conclude that the stock is obviously under- or overpriced.

We now return to the questions posed at the beginning of this chapter. First, how would an investor decide whether to buy or sell Nike stock? She would value the stock

---

FIGURE 9.5   Range of Valuations for Nike Stock Using Various Valuation Methods

Valuations from multiples are based on the low, high, and average values of the comparable firms from Table 9.2 (see Problems 12 and 13 at the end of this chapter). The constant dividend growth model is based on a 10% equity cost of capital and dividend growth rates of 6% to 9%, as discussed at the beginning of Section 9.3. The discounted free cash flow model is based on Example 9.7 with the same range of parameters as in Problem 8 at the end of this chapter. Midpoints are based on average multiples or base-case assumptions. Red and blue regions show the variation between the lowest-multiple/worst-case scenario and the highest-multiple/best-case scenario. Nike's actual share price of $76.43 is indicated by the grey line.

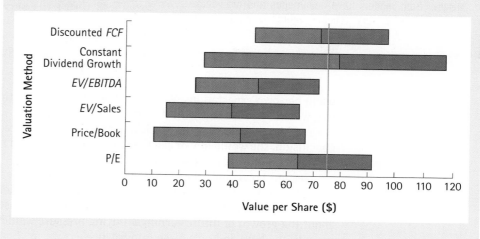

INTERVIEW WITH

Marilyn Fedak

Marilyn G. Fedak is the vice chair, investment services, and was formerly head of global value equities at AllianceBernstein, a publicly traded global asset management firm with approximately $450 billion in assets.

QUESTION: *What valuation methods do you use to identify buying opportunities for value stocks?*

ANSWER: We use both a dividend-discount model (DDM) and a proprietary quantitative return model called the Global Edge Model (GEM). For our non-U.S. portfolios, we use the GEM model; in the United States, we use a combination of GEM and the DDM.

At its most basic level, the DDM provides a way to evaluate how much we need to pay today for a company's future earnings and cash flow.* All things being equal, we are looking to buy as much earnings power as cheaply as we can. It is a very reliable methodology *if* you have the right forecasts for companies' future earnings. Our GEM model encompasses a variety of valuation measures, such as P/E and price-to-book ratios and selected success factors—for example, ROE and price momentum.

In both the U.S. and non-U.S. portfolios, we use these valuation tools to rank companies from the most undervalued to the most expensive. We focus on the stocks that rank the highest. Our decision-making bodies, the investment policy groups, meet with analysts to quality-control the forecasts for the highest-ranked group of stocks. Once the forecasts are approved, we add risk tools to construct optimal portfolios.

QUESTION: *Are there drawbacks to these models?*

ANSWER: Both models have advantages and drawbacks. The DDM is a very reliable valuation methodology.

However, its focus on forecasts of cash flow or earnings over some future period requires a large, highly skilled body of research analysts. And, it is oriented to the long term, so the timing of purchases and sales can be too early.

The GEM is very useful for efficiently evaluating investments within large universes. However, it is very oriented to current profitability and valuation metrics—not the future. As such, judgment has to be applied to determine if a company is likely to sustain similar characteristics going forward.

QUESTION: *Did the precipitous decline in stock prices in late 2008 and early 2009 cause you to retool your valuation methodology?*

ANSWER: In 2006, we began studying the interaction of the DDM and the GEM, and determined that combining the two models gives us superior results to a single methodology when evaluating U.S. securities. The DDM focuses on forecasts of a company's future, whereas the quant [quantitative] return model captures a company's history and current status. This new methodology was very helpful to us in 2008, when the GEM signalled caution for certain sectors that looked inexpensive based on the DDM.

We have also broadened our research to incorporate more external inputs and have assigned a higher probability to unlikely events, such as the recent government intervention in the financial and auto industries. On the risk side, we have added a refinancing risk tool and are tracking short interest in various equities.

*Because of historical usage, many practitioners use the term "dividend-discount model" to refer to the entire class of cash flow discount models.

using her own expectations. We showed one set of expectations about dividend growth that would be consistent with the price. If her expectations were substantially different, she might conclude that the stock was over- or underpriced at $76.43. Based on that conclusion, she would buy or sell the stock, and time would reveal whether her expectations were better than those of the markets.

Second, how could Nike stock suddenly be worth 5% more after Nike's announcement? As investors digested the news and updated their expectations, they would have determined that the previous day's closing price was too low based on the new information about the growth of future earnings. Buying pressure would then drive the stock price up until the buys and sells came into balance.

Third, what should Nike's managers do to raise the stock price further? The only way to raise the stock price is to make value-increasing decisions. As shown in Chapters 7 and 8, through capital budgeting analysis, managers can identify projects that have a positive *NPV*. The present value of the incremental future free cash flows from such projects is greater than the present value of the costs. By increasing that present value through good investment decisions, Nike's managers can increase the stock price.

We have concluded that Nike's stock is not obviously under- or overpriced. But consider what would happen if this were not the case: what if these valuation techniques produced valuations markedly different from prices the stock is trading at in the market? In the next section, we tackle this question.

Concept Check

11. What are some common valuation multiples?

12. What implicit assumptions are made when valuing a firm using multiples based on comparable firms?

 ## Information, Competition, and Stock Prices

As shown in Figure 9.6, the models described in this chapter link the firm's expected future cash flows, its cost of capital (determined by its risk), and the value of its shares. But what conclusions should we draw if the actual market price of a stock does not appear to be consistent with our estimate of its value? Is it more likely that the stock is mispriced or that we are mistaken about its risk and future cash flows?

Information in Stock Prices

Suppose you are a new junior analyst assigned to research Nike's stock and assess its value. You scrutinize the company's recent financial statements, look at the trends in the industry, and forecast the firm's future earnings, dividends, and free cash flows. After you carefully crunch the numbers, you estimate the stock's value to be $85 per share. On your way to present your analysis to your boss, you run into a slightly more experienced colleague in the elevator. It turns out that your colleague has been researching the same stock. But according to her analysis, the value of Nike stock is only $65 per share. What would you do?

FIGURE 9.6

The Valuation Triad

Valuation models determine the relationship among the firm's future cash flows, its cost of capital, and the value of its shares. The stock's expected cash flows and cost of capital can be used to assess its market price (share value). Conversely, the market price can be used to assess the firm's future cash flows or cost of capital.

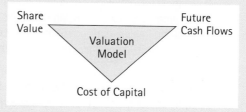

Although you could just assume your colleague is wrong, most of us would reconsider our own analysis. The fact that someone else who has carefully studied the same stock has come to a very different conclusion is powerful evidence that we might be mistaken. In the face of this information from our colleague, we would probably adjust our assessment of the stock's value downward. Of course, our colleague might also revise her opinion upward based on our assessment. After sharing our analyses, we would probably end up with a consensus estimate somewhere between $65 and $85 per share.

This type of encounter happens millions of times every day in the stock market. When a buyer seeks to buy a stock, the willingness of other parties to sell the same stock suggests that they value the stock differently. This information should lead both buyers and sellers to revise their valuations. Ultimately, investors trade until they reach a consensus regarding the value (market price) of the stock. In this way, stock markets aggregate the information and views of many different investors.

Thus, if your valuation model suggests a stock is worth $30 per share when it is trading for $20 per share in the market, the discrepancy is equivalent to knowing that thousands of investors—many of them professionals who have access to the best information about the stock available—disagree with your assessment. This knowledge should make you reconsider your original analysis. You would need a very compelling reason to trust your own estimate in the face of such contrary opinions.

What conclusion can we draw from this discussion? Recall Figure 9.6, in which a valuation model links the firm's future cash flows, its cost of capital, and its share price. In other words, given accurate information about any two of these variables, a valuation model allows us to make inferences about the third variable. Thus the way we use a valuation model will depend on the quality of our information: the model will tell us the most about the variable for which our prior information is the least reliable.

The market price of a publicly traded firm should already provide very accurate information, aggregated from a multitude of investors, regarding the true value of its shares. In most situations, a valuation model is best applied to tell us something about the firm's future cash flows or cost of capital, based on its current stock price. Only in the relatively rare case in which we have some superior information that other investors lack regarding the firm's cash flows and cost of capital would it make sense to second-guess the stock price.

EXAMPLE 9.11

Using the Information in Market Prices

Problem
Suppose Tecnorth Industries will have free cash flows next year of $40 million. Its weighted average cost of capital is 11%, and you expect its free cash flows to grow at a rate of approximately 4% per year, though you are somewhat unsure of the precise growth rate. Tecnorth has 10 million shares outstanding, no debt, and $20 million in cash. If Tecnorth's stock is currently trading at $55.33 per share, how would you update your beliefs about its dividend growth rate?

Solution

▶ Plan
If we apply the growing perpetuity formula for the growing *FCF* based on a 4% growth rate, we can estimate a stock price using Equations 9.18 and 9.19. If the market price is higher than our estimate, it implies that the market expects higher growth in *FCF* than 4%. Conversely, if the market price is lower than our estimate, the market expects *FCF* growth to be less than 4%.

▶ Execute
Applying the growing perpetuity formula, we have $PV(FCF) = 40/(0.11 - 0.04) = \$571.43$ million.
Applying Equation 9.18, the price per share would be ($571.43 million − 0 + $20 million)/10 million

shares = $59.14 per share. The market price of $55.33, however, implies that most investors expect *FCF* to grow at a somewhat slower rate.

▶ **Evaluate**

Given the $55.33 market price for the stock, we should lower our expectations for the *FCF* growth rate from 4% unless we have very strong reasons to trust our own estimate.

Competition and Efficient Markets

The idea that market prices reflect the information of many investors is a natural consequence of investor competition. If information were available that indicated that buying a stock had a positive *NPV*, investors with that information would choose to buy the stock; their attempts to purchase it would then drive up the stock's price. By a similar logic, investors with information that selling a stock had a positive *NPV* would sell it, and so the stock's price would fall.

The idea that competition among investors works to eliminate *all* positive-*NPV* trading opportunities is referred to as the **efficient markets hypothesis**. It implies that securities will be fairly priced, based on their future cash flows, given all information that is available to investors. Figure 9.7 indicates three forms of market efficiency— weak, semistrong, and strong.

What happens if new information about a stock arrives? The answer depends on the degree of competition, that is, on the number of investors who have access to this new information. Consider two important cases.

efficient markets hypothesis The idea that competition among investors works to eliminate all positive-*NPV* trading opportunities. It implies that securities will be fairly priced, based on their future cash flows, given all information that is available to investors.

Public, Easily Interpretable Information. Information that is available to all investors includes information in news reports, financial statements, corporate press releases, or other public data sources. If investors can readily ascertain the effects of this information on the firm's future cash flows, then all investors can determine how this information will change the firm's value.

In this situation, we expect competition between investors to be fierce and the stock price to react nearly instantaneously to such news. A few lucky investors might be able to trade a small quantity of shares before the price has fully adjusted. Most investors, however, would find that the stock price already reflected the new information before they were able to trade on it. In other words, the efficient markets hypothesis holds very well with respect to this type of information.

EXAMPLE 9.12

Stock Price Reactions to Public Information

Problem

Myox Labs announces that it is pulling one of its leading drugs from the market, owing to the potential side effects associated with the drug. As a result, its future expected free cash flow will decline by $85 million per year for the next 10 years. Myox has 50 million shares outstanding, no debt, and an equity cost of capital of 8%. If this news came as a complete surprise to investors, what should happen to Myox's stock price upon the announcement?

Solution

▶ **Plan**

In this case, we can use the discounted free cash flow method. With no debt, $r_{wacc} = r_E = 8\%$. The effect on the Myox's enterprise value will be the loss of a 10-year annuity of $85 million. We can compute the effect today as the present value of that annuity.

▶ **Execute**

Using the annuity formula, the decline in expected free cash flow will reduce Myox's enterprise value by

$$\$85 \text{ million} \times \frac{1}{0.08}\left(1 - \frac{1}{1.08^{10}}\right) = \$570.36 \text{ million}$$

Thus the stock price should fall by 570.36/50 = $11.41 per share.

▶ **Evaluate**

Because this news is public and its effect on the firm's expected free cash flow is clear, we would expect the stock price to drop by $11.41 per share nearly instantaneously.

FIGURE 9.7

Forms of Market Efficiency

The type of market efficiency we describe here, where all publicly available information is incorporated very quickly into stock prices, is often called semistrong-form market efficiency. The term "semistrong" indicates that it is not as complete as strong-form market efficiency, where prices immediately incorporate all information, including private information known, for example, only to managers. Finally, the term "weak-form market efficiency" means that only the history of past prices is already reflected in the stock price. It helps to think of the different forms of market efficiency as meaning that prices incorporate a steadily increasing set of information, and that each of these forms encompasses all the lower forms. For example, since the history of past prices is public information, semistrong-form efficiency encompasses weak-form. The diagram illustrates the idea. In the diagram, the information sets of weak-form, semistrong-form, and strong-form efficiency are represented by the blue, green, and yellow circles, respectively.

Not all market participants believe that the stock market is semistrong-form efficient. Technical analysts, who look for patterns in stock prices, do not believe the market is even weak-form efficient. Mutual fund managers and fundamental analysts, such as those who work for brokerages and make stock recommendations, believe that mispricing can be uncovered by careful analysis of company fundamentals. There is evidence that traders with inside information about an upcoming merger or earnings announcements can make abnormal returns by trading (illegally) on that information, so the market is clearly not strong-form efficient.

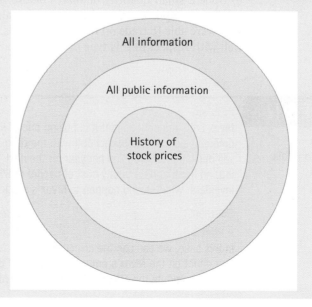

Private or Difficult-to-Interpret Information. Of course, some information is not publicly available. For example, an analyst might spend considerable time and effort gathering information from a firm's employees, competitors, suppliers, or customers that is relevant to the firm's future cash flows. This information is not available to other investors who have not devoted a similar effort to gathering it.

Even when information is publicly available, it may be difficult to interpret. Non-experts in the field may find it difficult to evaluate research reports on new technologies, for example. It may take a great deal of legal and accounting expertise and effort to understand the full consequences of a highly complicated business transaction. Certain consulting experts may have greater insight into consumer tastes and the likelihood of a product's acceptance. In these cases, while the fundamental information may be public, the *interpretation* of how that information will affect the firm's future cash flows is itself private information.

As an example, imagine that Snowy Pharmaceuticals has just announced the development of a new drug for which the company is seeking approval from Health Canada. If the drug is approved and subsequently launched in the Canadian market, the future profits from the new drug will increase Snowy's market value by $750 million, or $15 per share, given its 50 million shares outstanding. Assume that the development of this drug comes as a surprise to investors, and that the average likelihood of Health Canada approval is 10%. In that case, because many investors probably know that the chance of Health Canada approval is 10%, competition should lead to an immediate jump in Snowy's stock price of 10% × $15 = $1.50 per share. Over time, however, analysts and experts in the field will probably make their own assessments of the probable efficacy of the drug. If they conclude that the drug looks more promising than average, they will begin to trade on their private information and buy the stock, and the firm's price will tend to drift higher over time. If the experts conclude that the drug looks less promising than average, however, they will tend to sell the stock, and the firm's price will drift lower over time. Of course, at the time of the announcement, uninformed investors do not know which way it will go. Examples of possible price paths are shown in Figure 9.8.

When private information is in the hands of only a relatively small number of investors, these investors may be able to profit by trading on their information.[11] In this case, the efficient markets hypothesis will not hold in the strict sense. However, as these informed traders begin to trade, their actions will tend to move prices, so over time prices will begin to reflect their information as well.

If the profit opportunities from having this type of information are large, other individuals will attempt to gain the expertise and devote the resources needed to acquire it. As more individuals become better informed, competition to exploit this information will increase. Thus, in the long run, we should expect that the degree of "inefficiency" in the market will be limited by the costs of obtaining the information.

Lessons for Investors and Corporate Managers

The effect of competition based on information about stock prices has important consequences for both investors and corporate managers.

---

[11]Even with private information, informed investors may find it difficult to profit from that information, because they must find others who are willing to trade with them; that is, the market for the stock must be sufficiently *liquid*. A liquid market requires that other investors in the market have alternative motives to trade (e.g., selling shares of a stock to purchase a house) and so be willing to trade even when facing the risk that other traders may be better informed.

| FIGURE 9.8 | Possible Stock Price Paths for Snowy Pharmaceuticals |

Snowy's stock price jumps on the announcement based on the average likelihood of Health Canada approval. The stock price then drifts up (green path) or down (orange path) as informed traders trade on their more accurate assessment of the drug's likelihood of approval and hence entry into the Canadian market. At the time of the announcement, uninformed investors do not know which way the stock will go.

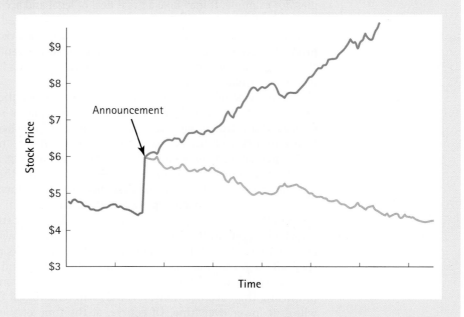

Consequences for Investors. Investors should be able to identify positive-*NPV* trading opportunities in securities markets, as in other markets, only if some barrier or restriction to free competition exists. An investor's competitive advantage may take several forms. For instance, the investor may have expertise or access to information that is known to only a few people. Alternatively, the investor may have lower trading costs than other market participants and so can exploit opportunities that others would find unprofitable. In all cases, the source of the positive-*NPV* trading opportunity must be something that is difficult to replicate; otherwise, any gains would be competed away in short order.

While the fact that positive-*NPV* trading opportunities are hard to come by may be disappointing, there is some good news as well. If stocks are fairly priced according to our valuation models, then investors who buy stocks can expect to receive future cash flows that fairly compensate them for the risk of their investment. In such cases, the average investor can invest with confidence, even if he is not fully informed.

Implications for Corporate Managers. If stocks are fairly valued according to the models we have described, then the value of a firm is determined by the cash flows that it can pay to its investors. This result has several key implications for corporate managers:

▶ *Focus on* NPV *and free cash flow.* A manager seeking to boost the price of her firm's stock should make investments that increase the present value of the firm's free cash flow. Thus the capital budgeting methods outlined in Chapter 7 are fully consistent with the objective of maximizing the firm's share price.

▶ *Avoid accounting illusions.* Many managers make the mistake of focusing on accounting earnings as opposed to free cash flows. According to the efficient markets hypothesis, the accounting consequences of a decision do not directly affect the value of the firm and should not drive decision making.

▶ *Use financial transactions to support investment.* With efficient markets, a firm can sell its shares at a fair price to new investors. As a consequence, the firm should not be constrained from raising capital to fund positive-*NPV* investment opportunities.

The Efficient Markets Hypothesis Versus No Arbitrage

There is an important distinction between the efficient markets hypothesis and the notion of a normal market that we introduced in Chapter 3. An arbitrage opportunity is a situation in which two securities (or portfolios) with *identical* cash flows have different prices. Because anyone can earn a sure profit in this situation by buying the low-priced security and selling the high-priced one, we expect investors to immediately exploit and eliminate these opportunities. Thus, arbitrage opportunities will not be found.

The efficient markets hypothesis states that the best estimate of the value of a share of stock is its market price. That is, investors' own estimates of value are not as accurate as the market price. But that does not mean that the market price always correctly estimates the value of a share of stock. There is a difference between the best estimate and being correct. Thus, there is no reason to expect the market price to always assess value accurately; rather, the price is best viewed as an approximation. However, because the price is the best estimate, the efficient market hypothesis implies that you cannot tell which prices overestimate and which underestimate the true value of a stock.

The question of equivalent risk is one that we will ponder in Part 4 of this text. In the following chapters, we will develop an understanding of the historical tradeoff between risk and return, learn how to measure the relevant risk of a security, and develop a way to estimate a security's expected return given its risk.

Concept Check

13. State the efficient markets hypothesis.

14. What are the implications of the efficient markets hypothesis for corporate managers?

9.9 Individual Biases and Trading

Efficient markets imply that positive-*NPV* trading opportunities will be hard to come by, especially for most individual investors, who are unlikely to have superior information. Yet investors are people and as such are subject to a range of the behavioural biases that affect their investing behaviour. Here we discuss a few of those biases and how they can harm investors.

Excessive Trading and Overconfidence

Trading is expensive; you must pay commissions on top of the difference between the bid and ask, or the spread. Given how hard it should be to identify over- and undervalued stocks, you might then expect individual investors to take a conservative approach to trading. However, in an influential study of the trading behaviour of individual investors that held accounts at a discount brokerage, researchers Brad Barber and Terrance

FIGURE 9.9

Individual Investor Returns Versus Portfolio Turnover

The graph shows the average annual return (net of commissions and trading costs) for individual investors at a large discount brokerage from 1991 to 1997. Investors are grouped into quintiles based on their average annual turnover. While the least-active investors had slightly (but not significantly) better performance than the S&P 500, performance declined with the rate of turnover.

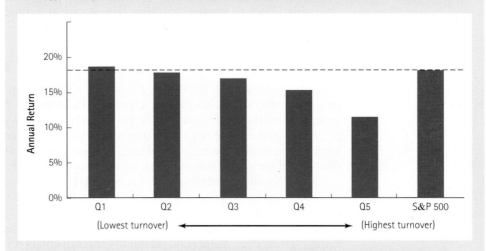

Source: B. Barber and T. Odean, "Trading Is Hazardous to Your Wealth: The Common Stock Investment Performance of Individual Investors," *Journal of Finance* 55 (2000): 773–806.

Odean found that individual investors tend to trade very actively, with average turnover almost 50% above the overall rates during the time period of their study.[12]

What might explain this trading behaviour? Psychologists have known since the 1960s that uninformed individuals tend to overestimate the precision of their knowledge. For example, many sports fans sitting in the stands confidently second guess the coaching decisions on the field, truly believing that they can do a better job. In finance we call investors' presumption of their ability to beat the market by overtrading the **overconfidence hypothesis**. Barber and Odean hypothesized that this kind of behaviour also characterizes individual investment decision making: like sports fans, individual investors believe they can pick winners and losers when, in fact, they cannot; this overconfidence leads them to trade too much.

An implication of this overconfidence hypothesis is that, assuming they have no true ability, investors who trade more will not earn higher returns. Instead, their performance will be worse once we take into account the costs of trading (due to both commissions and bid-ask spreads). Figure 9.9 documents precisely this result, showing that much investor trading appears not to be based on rational assessments of performance.

overconfidence hypothesis The tendency of individual investors to trade too much, based on the mistaken belief that they can pick winners and losers better than investment professionals.

disposition effect The tendency to hold on to stocks that have lost value and sell stocks that have risen in value since the time of purchase.

Hanging on to Losers and the Disposition Effect

Investors tend to hold on to stocks that have lost value and sell stocks that have risen in value since the time of purchase. We call this tendency to keep losers and sell winners the **disposition effect**. Researchers Hersh Shefrin and Meir Statman,

---

[12]B. Barber and T. Odean, "Trading Is Hazardous to Your Wealth: The Common Stock Investment Performance of Individual Investors," *Journal of Finance* 55 (2000): 773–806.

building on the work of psychologists Daniel Kahneman and Amos Tversky, suggest that this effect arises due to investor's increased willingness to take on risk in the face of possible losses.[13] It may also reflect a reluctance to admit a mistake by taking the loss.

Researchers have verified the disposition effect in many studies. For example, in a study of all trades in the Taiwanese stock market from 1995 to 1999, investors in aggregate were twice as likely to realize gains as they were to realize losses. Also, nearly 85% of individual investors were subject to this bias.[14] On the other hand, mutual funds and foreign investors did not exhibit the same tendency, and other studies have shown that more sophisticated investors appear to be less susceptible to the disposition effect.[15]

This behavioural tendency to sell winners and hang on to losers is costly from a tax perspective. Because capital gains are taxed only when the asset is sold, it is optimal for tax purposes to postpone taxable gains by continuing to hold profitable investments; delaying the tax payment reduces its present value. On the other hand, investors should capture tax losses by selling their losing investments, especially near the year's end, in order to accelerate the tax write-off.

Of course, keeping losers and selling winners might make sense if investors forecast that the losing stocks would ultimately "bounce back" and outperform the winners going forward. While investors may in fact have this belief, it does not appear to be justified—if anything, the losing stocks that investors continue to hold tend to underperform the winners they sell. According to one study, losers underperformed winners by 3.4% over the year after the winners were sold.[16]

Investor Attention, Mood, and Experience

Individual investors generally are not full-time traders. As a result, they have limited time and attention to spend on their investment decisions and may be influenced by attention-grabbing news stories or other events. Studies show that individuals are more likely to buy stocks that have recently been in the news, engaged in advertising, experienced exceptionally high trading volume, or had extreme (either positive or negative) returns.[17]

Investment behaviour also seems to be affected by investors' moods. For example, sunshine generally has a positive effect on mood, and studies have found that stock returns tend to be higher when it is a sunny day at the location of the stock exchange. In New York City, the annualized market return on perfectly sunny days is approximately

[13]H. Shefrin and M. Statman, "The Disposition to Sell Winners Too Early and Ride Losers Too Long: Theory and Evidence," *Journal of Finance* 40 (1985): 777–790, and D. Kahneman and A. Tversky, "Prospect Theory: An Analysis of Decision Under Risk," *Econometrica* 47 (1979): 263–291.

[14]B. Barber, Y.T. Lee, Y.J. Liu, and T. Odean, "Is the Aggregate Investor Reluctant to Realize Losses? Evidence from Taiwan," *European Financial Management* 13 (2007): 423–447.

[15]R. Dhar and N. Zhu, "Up Close and Personal: Investor Sophistication and the Disposition Effect," *Management Science* 52 (2006): 726–740.

[16]T. Odean, "Are Investors Reluctant to Realize Their Losses?" *Journal of Finance* 53 (1998): 1775–98.

[17]See G. Grullon, G. Kanatas, and J. Weston, "Advertising, Breadth of Ownership, and Liquidity," *Review of Financial Studies* 17 (2004): 439–461; M. Seasholes and G. Wu, "Predictable Behavior, Profits, and Attention," *Journal of Empirical Finance* 14 (2007): 590–610; B. Barber and T. Odean, "All That Glitters: The Effect of Attention and News on the Buying Behavior of Individual and Institutional Investors," *Review of Financial Studies* 21 (2008): 785–818.

24.8% per year versus 8.7% per year on perfectly cloudy days.[18] Further evidence of the link between investor mood and stock returns comes from the effect of major sports events on returns. One recent study estimates that a loss in the World Cup elimination stage lowers the next day's stock returns in the losing country by about 0.50%, presumably due to investors' poor moods.[19]

Finally, investors appear to put too much weight on their own experience rather than considering all the historical evidence. As a result, people who grow up and live during a time of high stock returns are more likely to invest in stocks than people who grow up and live during a time of low stock returns.[20]

Why would investors continue to make such mistakes? Even if they started with such misconceptions, wouldn't they be able to learn over time the cost of these errors? The challenge is that stock returns are extremely volatile, and this volatility masks the small differences in returns from different trading strategies. We will start the next chapter with a review of the historical evidence on average stock returns and their volatility. There you will see how variable returns are and how there have been long stretches of good returns, as in the 1990s, but also stretches when the total return was negative, as in the 2000s.

Concept Check

15. What are several systematic behavioural biases that individual investors fall prey to?

16. Why would excessive trading lead to lower realized return?

MyFinanceLab

Here is what you should know after reading this chapter. MyFinanceLab will help you identify what you know, and where to go when you need to practice.

Key Points and Equations	Terms	Online Practice Opportunities
9.1 Stock Basics		
▸ Ownership in a corporation is divided into shares of stock. These shares carry rights to share in the profits of the firm through future dividend payments.	annual meeting, p. 288 common stock, p. 286 cumulative preferred stock, p. 288 cumulative voting, p. 287 non-cumulative preferred stock, p. 288 preferred stock, p. 288 proxy, p. 288 proxy contest, p. 288 straight voting, p. 287 ticker symbol, p. 286	MyFinanceLab Study Plan 9.1

---

[18]Based on data from 1982 to 1997; see D. Hirshleifer and T. Shumway, "Good Day Sunshine: Stock Returns and the Weather," *Journal of Finance* 58 (2003): 1009–1032.

[19]A. Edmans, D. Garcia, and O. Norli, "Sports Sentiment and Stock Returns," *Journal of Finance* 62 (2007): 1967–1998.

[20]U. Malmendier and S. Nagel, "Depression Babies: Do Macroeconomic Experiences Affect Risk-Taking?," NBER working paper no. 14813.

9.2 The Dividend-Discount Model

▶ The Valuation Principle states that the value of a stock is equal to the present value of the dividends and future sale price the investor will receive. Because these cash flows are risky, they must be discounted at the equity cost of capital, which is the expected return of other securities available in the market with risk equivalent to that of the firm's equity.

▶ The total return of a stock is equal to the dividend yield plus the capital gain rate. The expected total return of a stock should equal its equity cost of capital:

$$r_E = \frac{Div_1 + P_1}{P_0} - 1 = \underbrace{\frac{Div_1}{P_0}}_{\text{Dividend Yield}} + \underbrace{\frac{P_1 - P_0}{P_0}}_{\text{Capital Gain Rate}} \quad (9.2)$$

▶ When investors have the same beliefs, the dividend-discount model states that, for any horizon n, the stock price satisfies the following equation:

$$P_0 = \frac{Div_1}{1 + r_E} + \frac{Div_2}{(1 + r_E)^2} + \cdots + \frac{Div_n}{(1 + r_E)^n} + \frac{P_n}{(1 + r_E)^n} \quad (9.4)$$

▶ If the stock eventually pays dividends and is never acquired, the dividend-discount model implies that the stock price equals the present value of all future dividends.

capital gain, p. 290
capital gain rate, p. 290
dividend-discount model, p. 292
dividend yield, p. 290
equity cost of capital, p. 290
total return, p. 290

MyFinanceLab
Study Plan 9.2

Using Excel:
Building a Dividend-Discount Model

9.3 Estimating Dividends in the Dividend-Discount Model

▶ The constant dividend growth model assumes that dividends grow at a constant expected rate, g. In that case, g is also the expected capital gain rate, and

$$P_0 = \frac{Div_1}{r_E - g} \quad (9.6)$$

▶ Future dividends depend on earnings, shares outstanding, and the dividend payout rate:

$$Div_t = \underbrace{\frac{Earnings_t}{\text{Share Outstanding}_t}}_{EPS_t} \times \text{Dividend Payout Rate}_t \quad (9.8)$$

▶ If the dividend payout rate and the number of shares outstanding are constant, and if earnings change only as a result of new investment from retained earnings, then the growth rate of the firm's earnings, dividends, and share price is calculated as follows:

$$g = \text{Retention Rate} \times \text{Return on New Investment} \quad (9.12)$$

constant dividend growth model, p. 293
dividend payout rate, p. 294
retention rate, p. 294

MyFinanceLab
Study Plan 9.3

▶ Cutting the firm's dividend to increase investment will raise the stock price if, and only if, the new investments have a positive *NPV*.

▶ If the firm has a long-term growth rate of g after the period $n + 1$, then we can apply the dividend-discount model and use the constant dividend growth formula to estimate the terminal stock value P_n.

9.4 Limitations of the Dividend-Discount Model

▶ The dividend-discount model is sensitive to the dividend growth rate, which is difficult to estimate accurately.

▶ Some companies do not pay cash dividends, making the model inappropriate for valuation in such cases.

MyFinanceLab
Study Plan 9.4

9.5 Share Repurchases and the Total Payout Model

▶ If the firm undertakes share repurchases, it is more reliable to use the total payout model to value the firm. In this model, the value of equity equals the present value of future total dividends and repurchases. To determine the stock price, we divide the equity value by the initial number of shares outstanding of the firm:

$$P_0 = \frac{PV(\text{Future Total Dividends and Repurchases})}{\text{Shares Outstanding}_0} \quad (9.15)$$

discounted free cash flow model, p. 303
share repurchase, p. 301
total payout model, p. 301
weighted average cost of capital (WACC), p. 304

MyFinanceLab
Study Plan 9.5

Interactive
Discounted Cash
Flow Valuation

9.6 The Discounted Free Cash Flow Model

▶ The growth rate of the firm's total payout is governed by the growth rate of earnings, not earnings per share.

▶ When a firm has leverage, it is more reliable to use the discounted free cash flow model. In this model, the enterprise value of the firm equals the present value of the firm's future free cash flow:

$$V_0 = PV(\text{Future Free Cash Flow of Firm}) \quad (9.18)$$

▶ We discount cash flows using the weighted average cost of capital, which is the expected return the firm must pay to investors to compensate them for the risk of holding the firm's debt and equity together.

▶ We can estimate a terminal enterprise value by assuming free cash flow grows at a constant rate (typically equal to the rate of long-run revenue growth).

MyFinanceLab
Study Plan 9.6

▶ We determine the stock price by subtracting debt and adding cash to the enterprise value, and then dividing by the initial number of shares outstanding of the firm:

$$P_0 = \frac{V_0 + \text{Cash}_0 - \text{Debt}_0}{\text{Shares Outstanding}_0} \qquad (9.19)$$

9.7 Valuation Based on Comparable Firms

▶ We can also value stocks by using valuation multiples based on comparable firms. Multiples commonly used for this purpose include the P/E ratio and the ratio of enterprise value to *EBITDA*. When we use multiples, we assume that comparable firms have the same risk and future growth as the firm being valued.

▶ No valuation model provides a definitive value for the stock. It is best to use several methods to identify a reasonable range for the value.

forward earnings, p. 308
forward P/E, p. 308
method of comparables,
  p. 308
trailing earnings, p. 308
trailing P/E, p. 308
valuation multiple, p. 308

MyFinanceLab
Study Plan 9.7

9.8 Information, Competition, and Stock Prices

▶ Stock prices aggregate the information of many investors. Therefore, if our valuation disagrees with the stock's market price, it is most likely an indication that our assumptions about the firm's cash flows are wrong.

▶ Competition between investors tends to eliminate positive-*NPV* trading opportunities. Competition will be strongest when information is public and easy to interpret. Privately informed traders may be able to profit from their information, which is reflected in prices only gradually.

▶ The efficient markets hypothesis states that competition eliminates all positive-*NPV* trades, which is equivalent to stating that securities with equivalent risk have the same expected returns.

▶ In an efficient market, investors will not find positive-*NPV* trading opportunities without some source of competitive advantage. By contrast, the average investor will earn a fair return on his or her investment.

▶ In an efficient market, to raise the stock price, corporate managers should focus on maximizing the present value of the free cash flow from the firm's investments, rather than accounting consequences or financial policy.

efficient markets
  hypothesis, p. 317

MyFinanceLab
Study Plan 9.8

9.9 Individual Biases and Trading

▶ Individual investors display many biases including overconfidence, disposition effect, limited attention, and mood affects.

▶ In an efficient market, these biases can lead to trading losses through excessive trading, or biases in valuations

disposition effect, p. 322
overconfidence
  hypothesis, p. 322

Review Questions

1. What rights come with a share of stock?

2. Which two components make up the total return to an investor in a share of stock?

3. What does the dividend-discount model say about valuing shares of stock?

4. What is the relationship between the NPV of reinvesting cash flows and the change in the price of the stock?

5. How can the dividend-discount model be used with changing growth rates in future dividends?

6. What are some drawbacks of the dividend-discount model?

7. What are share repurchases, and how can they be incorporated into the valuation of a stock?

8. What are the advantages of valuing a stock based on discounted free cash flows?

9. Explain the connection between the *FCF* valuation model and capital budgeting.

10. What is the reasoning behind valuation by multiples and what are the major assumptions?

11. What are the limitations of valuation by multiples?

12. What is an efficient market?

13. How do interactions in a market lead to information being incorporated into stock prices?

14. Why does market efficiency lead a manager to focus on NPV and free cash flow?

15. Why don't investors always trade rationally?

16. What are some of the major behavioural trading biases?

Problems

All problems in this chapter are available in MyFinanceLab. An asterisk (*) indicates problems with a higher level of difficulty.

Stock Basics

1. If you own 15,000 shares of stock of Kenneth Cole Productions and it pays a dividend of $0.18 per share, then what is the total dividend you will receive?

2. You own 20% of the stock of a company with 10 directors on its board. How much representation can you get on the board if the company has cumulative voting? How much representation can you ensure if the company has straight voting?

3. Anzio Inc. has two classes of shares. Class B has 10 times the voting rights of Class A. If you own 10% of the Class A shares and 20% of the Class B shares, what percentage of the total voting rights do you hold?

The Dividend-Discount Model

4. Assume Evco, Inc. has a current stock price of $50 and will pay a $2 dividend in one year; its equity cost of capital is 15%. What price must you expect Evco stock to sell for immediately after the firm pays the dividend in one year to justify its current price?

5. Anle Corporation has a current stock price of $20 and is expected to pay a dividend of $1 in one year. Its expected stock price right after paying that dividend is $22.
   a. What is Anle's equity cost of capital?
   b. How much of Anle's equity cost of capital is expected to be satisfied by dividend yield and how much by capital gain?

6. Achi Corp has preferred stock with an annual dividend of $3. If the required return on Achi's preferred stock is 8%, what is its price? (*Hint:* For a preferred stock, the dividend growth rate is zero.)

7. Ovit, Inc. has preferred stock with a price of $20 and a dividend of $1.50 per year. What is its dividend yield?

8. Suppose Acap Corporation will pay a dividend of $2.80 per share at the end of this year and a dividend of $3.00 per share next year. You expect Acap's stock price to be $52.00 in two years. Assume that Acap's equity cost of capital is 10%.
   a. What price would you be willing to pay for a share of Acap stock today if you planned to hold the stock for two years?
   b. Suppose instead you plan to hold the stock for one year. For what price would you expect to be able to sell a share of Acap stock in one year?
   c. Given your answer to part (b), what price would you be willing to pay for a share of Acap stock today if you planned to hold the stock for one year? How does this price compare to your answer in part (a)?

9. Krell Industries has a share price of $22.00 today. If Krell is expected to pay a dividend of $0.88 this year and its stock price is expected to grow to $23.54 at the end of the year, what is Krell's dividend yield and equity cost of capital?

Estimating Dividends in the Dividend-Discount Model

10. NoGrowth Corporation currently pays a dividend of $0.50 per quarter, and it will continue to pay this dividend forever. What is the price per share of NoGrowth stock if the firm's equity cost of capital is 15%?

11. Summit Systems will pay a dividend of $1.50 this year. If you expect Summit's dividend to grow by 6% per year, what is its price per share if the firm's equity cost of capital is 11%?

12. Dorpac Corporation has a dividend yield of 1.5%. Its equity cost of capital is 8%, and its dividends are expected to grow at a constant rate.
   a. What is the expected growth rate of Dorpac's dividends?
   b. What is the expected growth rate of Dorpac's share price?

13. Laurel Enterprises expects earnings next year of $4 per share and has a 70% retention rate, which it plans to keep constant. Its equity cost of capital is 10%, which is also its expected return on new investment. If its earnings are expected to grow forever at a rate of 4% per year, what do you estimate the firm's current stock price to be?

*14. DFB, Inc. expects earnings this year of $5 per share, and it plans to pay a $3 dividend to shareholders. DFB will retain $2 per share of its earnings to reinvest in new projects that have an expected return of 15% per year. Suppose DFB will maintain the same dividend payout rate, retention rate, and return on new investments in the future and will not change its number of outstanding shares.
   a. What growth rate of earnings would you forecast for DFB?
   b. If DFB's equity cost of capital is 12%, what price would you estimate for DFB stock?
   c. Suppose instead that DFB paid a dividend of $4 per share this year and retained only $1 per share in earnings. If DFB maintains this higher payout rate in the future, what stock price would you estimate for the firm now? Should DFB raise its dividend?

15. Cooperton Mining just announced it will cut its dividend from $4 to $2.50 per share and use the extra funds to expand. Prior to the announcement, Cooperton's dividends were expected to grow at a 3% rate, and its share price was $50. With the planned expansion, Cooperton's dividends are expected to grow at a 5% rate. What share price would you expect after the announcement? (Assume that the new expansion does not change Cooperton's risk.) Is the expansion a positive-*NPV* investment?

16. Gillette Corporation will pay an annual dividend of $0.65 one year from now. Analysts expect this dividend to grow at 12% per year thereafter until the fifth year. Thereafter, growth will level off at 2% per year. According to the dividend-discount model, what is the value of a share of Gillette stock if the firm's equity cost of capital is 8%?

17. Colgate-Palmolive Company has just paid an annual dividend of $0.96. Analysts are predicting an 11% per year growth rate in earnings over the next five years. After that, Colgate's earnings are expected to grow at the current industry average of 5.2% per year. If Colgate's equity cost of capital is 8.5% per year and its dividend payout ratio remains constant, for what price does the dividend-discount model predict Colgate stock should sell?

*18. Halliford Corporation expects to have earnings this coming year of $3 per share. Halliford plans to retain all of its earnings for the next two years. Then, for the subsequent two years, the firm will retain 50% of its earnings. It will retain 20% of its earnings from that point onward. Each year, retained earnings will be invested in new projects with an expected return of 25% per year. Any earnings that are not retained will be paid out as dividends. Assume Halliford's share count remains constant and all earnings growth comes from the investment of retained earnings. If Halliford's equity cost of capital is 10%, what price would you estimate for Halliford stock?

The Total Payout and Free Cash Flow Valuation Models

19. Zoom Enterprises expects that one year from now it will pay a total dividend of $5 million and repurchase $5 million worth of shares. It plans to spend $10 million on dividends and repurchases every year after that forever, although it may not always be an even split between dividends and repurchases. If Zoom's cost of equity capital is 13% and it has 5 million shares outstanding, what is its share price today?

20. AFW Industries has 200 million shares outstanding and expects earnings at the end of this year of $700 million. AFW plans to pay out 60% of its earnings in total, paying 40% as a dividend and using 20% to repurchase shares. If AFW's earnings are

expected to grow by 8% per year and these payout rates remain constant, determine AFW's share price assuming an equity cost of capital of 12%.

21. Suppose Cisco Systems pays no dividends but spent $5 billion on share repurchases last year. If Cisco's equity cost of capital is 12%, and if the amount spent on repurchases is expected to grow by 8% per year, estimate Cisco's market capitalization. If Cisco has 6 billion shares outstanding, to what stock price does this correspond?

*22. Stelco Steel plans to pay a dividend of $3 this year. The company has an expected earnings growth rate of 4% per year and an equity cost of capital of 10%.
   a. Assuming that Stelco's dividend payout rate and expected growth rate remain constant, and that the firm does not issue or repurchase shares, estimate Stelco's share price.
   b. Suppose Stelco decides to pay a dividend of $1 this year and to use the remaining $2 per share to repurchase shares. If Stelco's total payout rate remains constant, estimate Stelco's share price.
   c. If Stelco maintains the dividend and total payout rate given in part (b), at what rates are Stelco's dividends and earnings per share expected to grow?

23. This year, *FCF*, Inc. has earnings before interest and taxes of $10 million, depreciation expense of $1 million, and capital expenditures of $1.5 million, and has increased its net working capital by $500,000. If its tax rate is 35%, what is its free cash flow?

24. Victoria Enterprises expects free cash flows next year of $1 million. Its depreciation and capital expenditures will both be $300,000, and it expects its capital expenditures to always equal its depreciation. Its working capital will increase by $50,000 over the next year. The year-over-year increase in its net working capital will increase by 4% in perpetuity, and its *FCF*s are also expected to increase at 4% per year in perpetuity. If its tax rate is 40% and its WACC is 10%, what is its enterprise value?

25. The present value of JECK Co.'s expected free cash flows is $100 million. If JECK has $30 million in debt, $6 million in cash, and 2 million shares outstanding, what is its share price?

26. Portage Bay Enterprises has no debt and is expected to have free cash flow of $10 million next year. It is then expected to grow at a rate of 3% per year forever. If Portage Bay's equity cost of capital is 11% and it has 5 million shares outstanding, what should the price of Portage Bay's stock be?

27. Heavy Metal Corporation is expected to generate the following free cash flows over the next five years:

Year	1	2	3	4	5
FCF ($ million)	53	68	78	75	82

Thereafter, the free cash flows are expected to grow at the industry average of 4% per year. Use the discounted free cash flow model and a weighted average cost of capital of 14% to estimate the following:
   a. The enterprise value of Heavy Metal
   b. Heavy Metal's share price if the company has no excess cash, debt of $300 million, and 40 million shares outstanding

28. Covan, Inc. is expected to have the following free cash flows:

Year	1	2	3	4	
FCF	10	12	13	14	grow by 4% per year

    a. Covan has 8 million shares outstanding and it has no debt. If its cost of capital is 12%, what should its stock price be?

    b. Covan reinvests all its *FCF*. If you plan to sell Covan at the beginning of year two, what should you expect its price to be?

    c. Assume you bought Covan stock at the beginning of year one. What is your return expected to be from holding Covan stock until year two?

X **29.** Sora Industries has 60 million outstanding shares, $120 million in debt, $40 million in cash, and the following projected free cash flow for the next four years:

1	Year	0	1	2	3	4
2	Earnings and *FCF* Forecast ($ million)					
3	Sales	433.0	468.0	516.0	547.0	574.3
4	*Growth Versus Prior Year*		8.1%	10.3%	6.0%	5.0%
5	Cost of Goods Sold		−313.6	−345.7	−366.5	−384.8
6	Gross Profit		154.4	170.3	180.5	189.5
7	Selling, General, and Administrative		−93.6	−103.2	−109.4	−114.9
8	Depreciation		−7.0	−7.5	−9.0	−9.5
9	*EBIT*		53.8	59.6	62.1	65.2
10	Less: Income Tax at a 40%		−21.5	−23.8	−24.8	−26.1
11	Plus: Depreciation		7.0	7.5	9.0	9.5
12	Less: Capital Expenditures		−7.7	−10.0	−9.9	−10.4
13	Less: Increase in *NWC*		−6.3	−8.6	−5.6	−4.9
14	Free Cash Flow		25.3	24.6	30.8	33.3

    a. Suppose Sora's revenues and free cash flow are expected to grow at a 5% rate beyond year four. If Sora's weighted average cost of capital is 10%, what is the value of Sora's stock based on this information?

    b. Sora's cost of goods sold was assumed to be 67% of sales. If its cost of goods sold is actually 70% of sales, how would the estimate of the stock's value change?

    c. Return to the assumptions of part (a) and suppose Sora can maintain its cost of goods sold at 67% of sales. However, the firm reduces its selling, general, and administrative expenses from 20% of sales to 16% of sales. What stock price would you estimate now? (Assume no other expenses, except taxes, are affected.)

    *d. Sora's net working capital needs were estimated to be 18% of sales (their current level in year zero). If Sora can reduce this requirement to 12% of sales starting in year one, but all other assumptions remain as in part (a), what stock price do you estimate for Sora? (*Hint*: This change will have the largest effect on Sora's free cash flow in year one.)

X **30.** Consider the valuation of Nike given in Example 9.7.

    a. Suppose you believe Nike's initial revenue growth rate will be between 7% and 11% (with growth slowing linearly to 5% by year 2015). What range of prices for Nike stock is consistent with these forecasts?

    b. Suppose you believe Nike's initial revenue *EBIT* margin will be between 9% and 11% of sales. What range of prices for Nike stock is consistent with these forecasts?

c.   Suppose you believe Nike's weighted average cost of capital is between 9.5% and 12%. What range of prices for Nike stock is consistent with these forecasts?

d.   What range of stock prices is consistent if you vary the estimates as in parts (a), (b), and (c) simultaneously?

Valuation Based on Comparable Firms

31. You notice that Dell Computers has a stock price of $27.85 and *EPS* of $1.26. Its competitor Hewlett-Packard has *EPS* of $2.47. What is one estimate of the value of a share of Hewlett-Packard stock?

32. CSH has *EBITDA* of $5 million. You feel that an appropriate *EV/EBITDA* ratio for CSH is 9. CSH has $10 million in debt, $2 million in cash, and 800,000 shares outstanding. What is your estimate of CSH's stock price?

33. After researching the competitors of EJH Enterprises, you determine that most comparable firms have the following valuation ratios:

	Comp 1	Comp 2	Comp 3	Comp 4
EV/EBITDA	12	11	12.5	10
P/E	19	18	20	17

EJH Enterprises has *EPS* of $2, *EBITDA* of $300 million, $30 million in cash, $40 million in debt, and 100 million shares outstanding. What range of prices is consistent with both sets of multiples?

34. Suppose that in May 2010, Nike had *EPS* of $3.51 and a book value of equity of $18.92 per share.

a.   Using the average P/E multiple in Table 9.2, estimate Nike's share price.

b.   What range of share prices do you estimate based on the highest and lowest P/E multiples in Table 9.2?

c.   Using the average price to book value multiple in Table 9.2, estimate Nike's share price.

d.   What range of share prices do you estimate based on the highest and lowest price to book value multiples in Table 9.2?

35. Suppose that in May 2010, Nike had sales of $19,176 million, *EBITDA* of $2809 million, excess cash of $3500 million, $437 million of debt, and 485.7 million shares outstanding.

a.   Using the average enterprise value to sales multiple in Table 9.2, estimate Nike's share price.

b.   What range of share prices do you estimate based on the highest and lowest enterprise value to sales multiples in Table 9.2?

c.   Using the average enterprise value to *EBITDA* multiple in Table 9.2, estimate Nike's share price.

d.   What range of share prices do you estimate based on the highest and lowest enterprise value to *EBITDA* multiples in Table 9.2?

*36. Suppose Rocky Shoes and Boots has earnings per share of $2.30 and *EBITDA* of $30.7 million. The firm also has 5.4 million shares outstanding and debt of $125 million (net of cash). You believe Deckers Outdoor Corporation is comparable to Rocky Shoes and Boots in terms of its underlying business, but Deckers has no debt. If Deckers has a P/E of 13.3 and an enterprise value to *EBITDA* multiple of 7.4, estimate the value of Rocky Shoes and Boots stock using both multiples. Which estimate is likely to be more accurate?

Information, Competition, and Stock Prices

37. Summit Systems (see Problem 11) has an equity cost of capital of 11% and will pay a dividend of $1.50 in one year, and its dividends had been expected to grow by 6% per year. You read in the paper that Summit Systems has revised its growth prospects and now expects its dividends to grow at a rate of 3% per year forever.
    a. What is the new value of a share of Summit Systems stock based on this information?
    b. If you tried to sell your Summit Systems stock after reading this news, what price would you be likely to get? Why?

38. Assume that Coca-Cola Company has a share price of $43. The firm will pay a dividend of $1.24 in one year, and you expect Coca-Cola to raise this dividend by approximately 7% per year in perpetuity.
    a. If Coca-Cola's equity cost of capital is 8%, what share price would you expect based on your estimate of the dividend growth rate?
    b. Given Coca-Cola's share price, what would you conclude about your assessment of Coca-Cola's future dividend growth?

39. Roybus, Inc., a manufacturer of flash memory, just reported that its main production facility in Taiwan was destroyed in a fire. Although the plant was fully insured, the loss of production will decrease Roybus's free cash flow by $180 million at the end of this year and by $60 million at the end of next year.
    a. If Roybus has 35 million shares outstanding and a weighted average cost of capital of 13%, what change in Roybus's stock price would you expect upon this announcement? (Assume the value of Roybus's debt is not affected by the event.)
    b. Would you expect to be able to sell Roybus's stock on hearing this announcement and make a profit? Explain.

*40. Apnex, Inc. is a biotechnology firm that is about to announce the results of its clinical trials of a potential new cancer drug. If the trials are successful, Apnex stock will be worth $70 per share. If the trials are unsuccessful, Apnex stock will be worth $18 per share. Suppose that the morning before the announcement is scheduled, Apnex shares are trading for $55 per share.
    a. Based on the current share price, what sort of expectations do investors seem to have about the success of the trials?
    b. Suppose hedge fund manager Paul Kliner has hired several prominent research scientists to examine the public data on the drug and make their own assessment of the drug's promise. Would Kliner's fund be likely to profit by trading the stock in the hours prior to the announcement?
    c. Which factors would limit the ability of Kliner's fund to profit on its information?

41. You have a $100,000 portfolio made up of 15 stocks. You trade each stock five times this year and each time you trade, you pay about $30 in commissions and spread. You have no special knowledge, so you earn only the average market return of 12% on your investments. How much lower will your total return be because of your trades?

42. Assume the annual return for the lowest turnover portfolio is 18% and the annual return for the highest turnover portfolio is 12%. If you invest $100,000 and have the highest turnover, how much lower will the value of your portfolio be at the end of 10 years than if you had had the lowest turnover?

Data Case

As a new junior analyst for a large brokerage firm, you are anxious to demonstrate the skills you learned in college and prove that you are worth your attractive salary. Your first assignment is to analyze the stock of General Electric Corporation. Your boss recommends determining prices based on both the dividend-discount model and the discounted free cash flow valuation method. GE has a cost of equity of 10.5% and an after-tax weighted average cost of capital of 7.5%. The expected return on its new investments is 12%. You are a little concerned about your boss's recommendation, because your finance professor has told you that these two valuation methods can result in widely differing estimates when applied to real data. You are really hoping that the two methods will reach similar prices. Good luck with that!

1. Go to the Yahoo! Finance website (http://finance.yahoo.com) and enter the ticker symbol for General Electric (GE). From the main page for GE, gather the following information and enter it onto a spreadsheet:
   a. The current stock price (last trade) at the top of the page.
   b. The current dividend amount, which is in the bottom-right cell in the same box as the stock price.

2. Click on "Key Statistics" at the left side of the page. From the Key Statistics page, gather the following information and enter it on the same spreadsheet:
   a. The number of shares of stock outstanding.
   b. The payout ratio.

3. Click on "Analyst Estimates" at the left side of the page. On the Analyst Estimates page, find the expected growth rate for the next five years and enter it onto your spreadsheet. It will be near the very bottom of the page.

4. Click on "Income Statement" near the bottom of the menu on the left. Copy and paste the entire three years' worth of income statements into a new worksheet in your existing Excel file. Repeat this process for both the balance sheet and the cash flow statement for General Electric. Keep all of the different statements in the same Excel worksheet.

5. To determine the stock value based on the dividend-discount model
   a. Create a timeline in Excel for five years.
   b. Use the dividend obtained from Yahoo! Finance as the current dividend to forecast the next five annual dividends based on the five-year growth rate.
   c. Determine the long-term growth rate based on GE's payout ratio (which is 1 minus the retention ratio) using Equation 9.12.
   d. Use the long-term growth rate to determine the stock price for year five using Equation 9.13.
   e. Determine the current stock price using the approach from Example 9.5.

6. To determine the stock value based on the discounted free cash flow method
   a. Forecast the free cash flows using the historic data from the financial statements downloaded from Yahoo! Finance to compute the three-year average of the following ratios:
      i. EBIT/sales
      ii. Tax rate (income tax expense/income before tax)
      iii. Property plant and equipment/sales
      iv. Depreciation/property plant and equipment
      v. Net working capital/sales
   b. Create a timeline for the next seven years.

    c. Forecast future sales based on the most recent year's total revenue growing at the five-year growth rate from Yahoo! Finance for the first five years and then at the long-term growth rate for years six and seven.

    d. Use the average ratios computed in part (a) to forecast *EBIT*; property, plant and equipment; depreciation; and net working capital for the next seven years.

    e. Forecast the free cash flow for the next seven years using Equation 9.17.

    f. Determine the horizon enterprise value for year five using Equation 9.21.

    g. Determine the enterprise value of the firm as the present value of the free cash flows.

    h. Determine the stock price using Equation 9.19.

7. Compare the stock prices produced by the two methods to the actual stock price. What recommendations can you make as to whether clients should buy or sell General Electric's stock based on your price estimates?

8. Explain why the estimates from the two valuation methods differ. Specifically address the assumptions implicit in the models themselves, as well as the assumptions you made in preparing your analysis. Why do these estimates differ from the actual stock price of GE?

PART 3 Integrative Case

This case draws on material from Chapters 7 to 9.

Nanovo, Inc. is a manufacturer of low-cost micro batteries for use in a wide variety of compact electronic devices such as children's toys, wireless transmitters, and sensors. The growth in the use of these devices has steadily increased, leading to an ever-greater demand for Nanovo's products. Nanovo has responded to this increase in demand by expanding its production capacity, more than doubling the firm's size over the last decade. Despite this growth, however, Nanovo does not have sufficient capacity to meet the current demand for its ultra–long-life, low-voltage batteries. You have been asked to evaluate two proposals to expand one of Nanovo's existing plants and make a recommendation.

Proposal 1

The current plant has a capacity of 25,000 cases per month. The first proposal is for a major expansion that would double the plant's current capacity to 50,000 cases per month. After talking with the firm's design engineers, sales managers, and plant operators, you have prepared the following estimates:

▌ Expanding the plant will require the purchase of $3.6 million in new equipment, and entail upfront design and engineering expenses of $3.9 million. These costs will be paid immediately when the expansion begins.

▌ Installing the new equipment and redesigning the plant to accommodate the higher capacity will require shutting down the plant for nine months. During that time, the plant's production will cease. After the expansion is finished, the plant will operate at double its original capacity.

▌ Marketing and selling the additional volume will lead to $1 million per year in additional sales, marketing, and administrative costs. These costs will begin in the first year (even while the plant is under construction and shut down).

Proposal 2

The engineers have also put forth a second proposal for a minor expansion that will increase the firm's capacity by only 50%, to 37,500 cases per month. While the capacity is smaller, such an expansion would be cheaper and less disruptive:

▌ The smaller expansion will require only $2.4 million in new equipment, and $1.5 million in design and engineering expenses.

▶ The existing plant will need to be shut down for only four months.

▶ Sales, marketing, and administrative costs will increase by only $500,000.

Nanovo believes that with or without any expansion, the technology used at the plant will be obsolete after six years and will have no salvage value, and the plant itself will need to be completely overhauled at that time. You also have the following additional general information:

▶ With or without either proposed expansion, Nanovo will be able to sell all it can produce at an average wholesale price of $80 per case. This price is not expected to change during the next six years.

▶ Nanovo has a gross profit margin of 55% on these batteries.

▶ Nanovo's average net working capital at the end of each year will equal 15% of its annual revenue.

▶ Nanovo pays a 40% corporate tax rate.

▶ While all design and engineering costs are immediately deductible as operating expenses, all capital expenditures will be straight-line depreciated for tax purposes over the subsequent six years.

Management believes the risk of the expansion is similar to the risk of Nanovo's existing projects, and because Nanovo is all equity financed, the risk of the expansion is also similar to the risk of Nanovo's stock. You have the following additional information about the stock:

▶ Nanovo has no debt and has 2 million shares outstanding. The firm's current share price is $75 per share.

▶ Analysts are expecting Nanovo to pay a $3 dividend at the end of this year, and to raise its dividend at an average rate of 8% per year in the future.

Based on this information, you have been tasked with preparing expansion recommendations for Nanovo (the use of Excel is optional but recommended).

Case Questions

1. Determine the annual incremental free cash flow associated with each expansion plan relative to the status quo (no expansion).

2. Compute the *IRR* and payback period of each expansion plan. Which plan has a higher *IRR*? Which has a shorter payback period?

3. Estimate Nanovo's equity cost of capital. Use it to determine the *NPV* associated with each expansion plan. Which plan has a higher *NPV*?

4. Should Nanovo expand the plant? If so, which plan should Nanovo adopt? Explain.

5. Suppose Nanovo decides to do the major expansion. If investors are not expecting this expansion, and if they agree with the forecasts above, how will the stock price change when the expansion is announced?

6. Suppose Nanovo announces the major expansion and the stock price reacts as in question 5. Nanovo then issues new shares at this price to cover the upfront free cash flow required to launch the expansion, and thereafter pays out as dividends the total amount it expected to pay prior to the expansion, plus the additional free cash flow associated with the expansion. What dividend per share will Nanovo pay over the next eight years? What is the fair price today for Nanovo's stock given these dividends?

PART 4

Risk and Return

Valuation Principle Connection. To apply the Valuation Principle, we must be able to discount the future costs and benefits of a decision. To do so, we need a discount rate that should reflect the risk, or uncertainty, surrounding those future costs and benefits. Our objective in this part of the book is to explain how to measure and compare risks across investment opportunities and use that knowledge to determine a discount rate, or cost of capital, for each investment opportunity. Chapter 10 introduces the key insight that investors demand a risk premium only for risk they cannot remove themselves without cost by diversifying their portfolios. Hence, only non-diversifiable risk will matter when comparing investment opportunities. In Chapter 11, we quantify this idea, leading to the Capital Asset Pricing Model (CAPM), the central model of financial economics that quantifies what an equivalent risk is and in doing so provides the relationship between risk and return. In Chapter 12, we apply what we've learned to estimate a company's overall cost of capital.

Chapter 10
Risk and Return in Capital Markets

Chapter 11
Systematic Risk and the Equity Risk Premium

Chapter 12
Determining the Cost of Capital

Risk and Return in Capital Markets

LEARNING OBJECTIVES

▶ Identify which types of securities have historically had the highest returns and which have been the most volatile

▶ Compute the average return and volatility of returns from a set of historical asset prices

▶ Understand the tradeoff between risk and return for large portfolios versus individual stocks

▶ Describe the difference between common and independent risk

▶ Explain how diversified portfolios remove independent risk, leaving common risk as the only risk requiring a risk premium

notation

Div_t	dividend paid on date t	$\overline{R}$	average return
P_t	price on date t	$SD(R)$	standard deviation of return R
R_t	realized or total return of a security from date $t-1$ to t	$Var(R)$	variance of return R

INTERVIEW WITH Manmeet Bhatia,
OceanRock Investments

Manmeet Bhatia is the vice president and portfolio manager of OceanRock Investments, part of Qtrade Financial Group. "I started out working with this fund management company, became portfolio manager as we started a separately managed account program, and launched individual, high net worth and institutional management for Canadian clients," he says. "Qtrade does several things," he continues. "We handle wealth management of Canadian investors, with approximately 5 billion dollars of assets under our administration. We have an online brokerage, a mutual fund company, an insurance division, a high net worth wealth management division, and a portfolio management company."

A graduate of the University of Manitoba, Manmeet is keenly aware of the different risk and return options available to him as he manages his clients' assets. Clients have different financial goals in mind, with some looking for higher returns but willing to take on extra risk in order to achieve them. "Whether our clients have invested in our mutual funds or in a high net worth investment program, we believe in achieving their desired goals with as little volatility as possible," Manmeet explains. "We seek to minimize volatility for a given return."

To minimize volatility, Manmeet applies the concepts from his finance classes, making sure his clients' portfolios are adequately diversified. "We try to provide as smooth a ride as possible and we do that via downside risk protection via diversification." He also offers advice to students wishing to pursue careers in portfolio management: "I think the portfolio management business is definitely a satisfying and interesting career, which can also be lucrative. As a service provider, a key element is understanding the customer, whether it be an institutional client or an individual client. In addition, computer skills are essential. Working with Excel spreadsheets is highly valuable and I think any institution is going to take great consideration of someone with experience on that side."

Over the six-year period of 2004 through 2009, investors in Barrick Gold Corporation earned

an average return of 8.3% per year. Within this period there was considerable variation, with the annual return ranging from −7.7% in 2009 to over 17% in 2006. Over the same period, investors in TransCanada Corp. earned an average return of 5.2%. However, these investors lost 18.5% in 2008, and gained 22.6% in 2005. WestJet Airlines average return was −1.6% over the six years but the range was from a low of −41.9% in 2008 to a high of 50.3% in 2007. Finally, investors in three-month Government of Canada treasury bills earned an average return of 2.7% during the period, with a high of 4.3% in 2007 and a low of 0.4% in 2009. Clearly, these four investments offered returns that were very different in terms of their average level and their variability. What accounts for these differences?

In this chapter, our goal is to develop an understanding of how risk relates to return. In the last three chapters, we established that value in projects, and hence in the firm, is determined by the present value of free cash flows. Up until now, we have focused on how to forecast and discount those cash flows. In this chapter and the two that follow, we turn our attention to the discount rate. As we have emphasized, the discount rate should be our cost of capital, and our cost of capital is determined by the risk of the project. But how exactly do we measure risk, and how does a particular level of risk imply a specific cost of capital?

We will see how holding many assets together affects our risk exposure. In the next chapter, we will build on this foundation to develop a theory that explains how to determine the cost of capital for any investment opportunity. Finally, in Chapter 12, we will apply what we've learned about the relationship between risk and return to the cost of capital for a company as a whole.

We begin our investigation of the relationship between risk and return by looking at historical data for publicly traded securities. We will see, for example, that while stocks are riskier investments than bonds, stocks have also earned higher average annual returns. We interpret the higher average return on stocks versus bonds as compensation to investors for the greater risk they are taking. But we will also find that not all risk needs to be compensated. By holding a portfolio of many different investments, investors can eliminate risks that are specific to individual securities. Only risks that cannot be eliminated by holding a large portfolio determine the risk premium investors will require.

10.1 A First Look at Risk and Return

Suppose your great-grandparents had invested only $100 on your behalf at the beginning of 1956, and they instructed their broker to reinvest any dividends or interest earned in the account until the beginning of 2010. How would that $100 have grown if it were invested in one of the following investments?

1. S&P/TSX Composite Index: A portfolio, constructed by Standard & Poor's (S&P), of the largest, most liquid stocks and income trust units traded on the Toronto Stock Exchange (TSX). As of the December 2010, the index comprised 234 firms with market capitalizations averaging about $6.46 billion and ranging from about $32 million to over $75 billion.

2. Standard & Poor's 500 (S&P 500) Index: A portfolio, constructed by Standard & Poor's, comprising 90 U.S. stocks up to 1957 and 500 U.S. stocks after that. The firms represented are leaders in their respective industries and are among the largest firms, in terms of market capitalization (share price times the number of shares in the hands of the shareholders), traded on U.S. markets.

3. Long-term Government of Canada bonds: These bonds have maturities of approximately 30 years.

4. Government of Canada treasury bills: Short-term (with a maturity of up to one year), zero-coupon debt, issued by the Government of Canada to provide financing for the government.

Figure 10.1 shows the result, through the end of 2009, of investing $100 at the beginning of 1956 for each of these four different investment portfolios. The results are striking—had your grandparents invested $100 in the S&P/TSX portfolio, the investment would have been worth over $12,570 at the beginning of 2010! On the other hand, if they had invested in treasury bills, the investment would have been worth only $2563.

For comparison, consider how prices have changed during the same period relative to the consumer price index (CPI), the bottom line in Figure 10.1. Over most of the period from 1956 to 2009, smaller stocks (represented by the S&P/TSX Composite Index) experienced the highest long-term return, followed by the large stocks (as found in the U.S. S&P 500). With the recent downturns of the U.S. markets, the appreciation of the Canadian dollar, and declining interest rates, the Government of Canada long-term

FIGURE 10.1

Value of $100 Invested at the Beginning of 1956 in the S&P/TSX Composite Index, the S&P 500, Long-Term Government of Canada Bonds, and Canadian Treasury Bills

Note that the investments that performed the best in the long run also had the greatest fluctuations from year to year. The change in the consumer price index (CPI) is shown as a reference point.

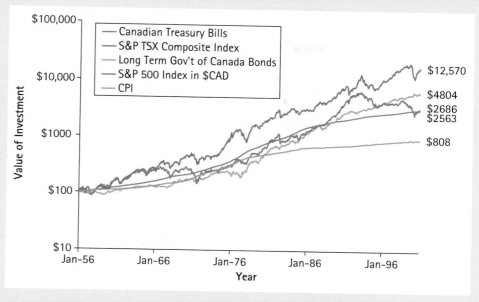

Source: Statistics Canada, Bank of Canada, and Chicago Center for Research in Security Prices.

bonds actually outperformed the S&P 500 over the last part of the period. Treasury bills have the smallest fluctuations in value, but their growth over the period was also the least. All of the investments grew faster than inflation (as measured by the CPI).

There is a second pattern evident in Figure 10.1. While the S&P/TSX Composite Index performed the best in the long run, its value also experienced the largest fluctuations. For example, if your parents had invested $2000 in the S&P/TSX Composite Index in August 1987, for your university education, the investment would have grown to about $10,077 by the end of 2009. In contrast, had your parents invested in long-term Government of Canada bonds, the $2000 investment would have grown to almost $16,381 by the end of 2009, because it would have avoided the major drops caused by the market crash of October 1987, and the downturns in 1998 and 2008. Over the entire time frame from 1956 to 2008, there were some months when the S&P/TSX Composite Index dropped by as much as 22.5% and rose by as much as 16.5% (in one month); its average return was about 0.85% per month. Compare this to Canadian treasury bills that, at their worst, returned about 0% in a month but, at their best, returned about 1.9% in a month; their average return was about 0.5% per month.

Investors are averse to fluctuations in the value of their investments, so riskier investments have higher expected returns. But even more importantly, when times are bad, investors do not like to have their problems further compounded by experiencing losses on their investments. In fact, even if your grandparents had actually put the $100 into the S&P/TSX Composite Index in 1956, it is unlikely you would have received the proceeds. More likely, in the depths of various recessions, your grandparents would have turned to their investments to supplement their income. Recent recessions occurred in the early 1980s and early 1990s. A the same time, the S&P/TSX Composite Index dropped over 30% between 1980 and 1982, and dropped over 20% in the first 10 months of 1990. So, to make matters worse, at the time your grandparents would need to draw on their investments, the value of the investments had dropped significantly.

During the financial crisis of 2008, many people faced similar difficulties. The S&P/TSX dropped over 37% in the final seven months of 2008. Many investors who had all their retirement money invested in stocks saw close to half their retirement income evaporate in a matter of months. Over the previous years, these individuals enjoyed large gains in their retirement portfolios. However, these high returns came at a cost—the risk of large losses in a downturn. Many investors faced a double whammy: an increased risk of being unemployed (as firms started laying off employees) precisely when the value of their savings eroded.

We have established the general principle that investors do not like risk and therefore demand a risk premium to bear it. Our goal in this chapter is to further understand that because investors can eliminate some risk by holding large portfolios of stocks, not all risk is entitled to a risk premium. To show this, we must first develop tools that will allow us to measure risk and return.

Concept Check

1. Historically, which types of investments have had the highest average returns and which have been the most volatile from year to year?

2. Why do investors demand a higher return when investing in riskier securities?

10.2 Historical Risks and Returns of Stocks

In this section, we explain how to compute average returns and a measure of risk, or volatility, using historical stock market data. The distribution of past returns can be useful in estimating the possible future returns for investors. We start by first explaining how to compute historical returns.

Computing Historical Returns

realized return The total return on an investment that occurs over a particular time period.

We begin with *realized returns* for an individual investment and a portfolio. The **realized return** is the total return that occurs over a particular time period.

Individual Investment Realized Return. Suppose you invested $10 in a stock a month ago. Today, it paid a dividend of $0.50 and you then sold it for $11. What was your return? Your return came from two sources: the dividend and the change in price. You earned $0.50 on your $10 investment through the dividend, for a return of $0.50/$10 = 5%, and you earned $1 from the increase in price, for a return of $1/$11 or 10%. Your total return was 15%:

$$\text{Return} = \frac{\$0.50}{\$10} + \frac{(\$11 - \$10)}{\$10} = 5\% + 10\% = 15\%$$

In general, assume you buy a stock on date t for the price on that date, P_t. If the stock pays a dividend, Div_{t+1}, on date $t + 1$, and you sell the stock at that time for price P_{t+1}, then the timeline of your cash flows for the stock looks like this:

$$
\begin{array}{ccc}
t & & t+1 \\
\vdash & \longrightarrow & \vdash \\
-P_t & & +D_{t+1} \\
& & +P_{t+1}
\end{array}
$$

The realized return from your investment in the stock from t to $t + 1$ is:

$$R_{t+1} = \frac{Div_{t+1} + P_{t+1} - P_t}{P_t} = \frac{Div_{t+1}}{P_t} + \frac{P_{t+1} - P_t}{P_t}$$ (10.1)

$$= \text{Dividend Yield} + \text{Capital Gain Yield}$$

Your realized return for the period from t to $t + 1$ is the total of the dividend yield and the capital gain (as a percentage of the initial price); as discussed in Chapter 9, it is also called the total return. For each dollar invested at date t, you will have $1 + R_{t+1}$ at date $t + 1$. We can compute the total return for any security in the same way, by replacing the dividend payments with any cash flows paid by the security (e.g., with a bond, coupon payments would replace dividends).

EXAMPLE 10.1
Realized Return

Problem

Barrick Gold Corp. stock (ticker symbol: ABX). paid a dividend of $0.2042 on June 16, 2008. (Note: Barrick pays dividends in U.S. dollars [USD], so we have converted to Canadian dollars [CAD] using the exchange rate for the dividend date.) Suppose you bought Barrick stock for $41.78 on January 1, 2008, and sold it immediately after the dividend was paid for $40.30. What was your realized return from holding the stock?

Solution

▶ **Plan**

We can use Equation 10.1 to calculate the realized return. Knowing the purchase price ($41.78), the selling price ($40.30), and the dividend ($0.2042), we are ready to proceed.

▶ **Execute**

Using Equation 10.1, the return from January 1, 2008, until June 16, 2008, is equal to:

$$R_{t+1} = \frac{Div_{t+1} + P_{t+1} - P_t}{P_t} = \frac{0.2042 + 40.30 - 41.78}{41.78} = -0.0305, \text{ or } -3.05\%$$

This -3.05% can be broken down into the dividend yield and the capital gain yield:

$$\text{Div Yield} = \frac{Div_{t+1}}{P_t} = \frac{0.2042}{\$41.78} = 0.0049, \text{ or } 0.49\%$$

$$\text{Capital Gain Yield} = \frac{P_{t+1} - P_t}{P_t} = \frac{(40.30 - 41.78)}{41.78} = -0.0354, \text{ or } -3.54\%$$

▶ **Evaluate**

These returns include both the capital gain (or in this case, a capital loss) and the return generated from receiving dividends. Both dividends and capital gains contribute to the total realized return—ignoring either one would give a very misleading impression of Barrick's performance.

If you hold the stock beyond the date of the first dividend, then to compute your return we must specify how you invest any dividends you receive in the interim. To focus on the returns of a single security, we assume that *all dividends are immediately reinvested and used to purchase additional shares of the same stock or security*. In this case, we can use Equation 10.1 to compute a stock's return between dividend payments and then compound the returns from each dividend interval to compute the return over a longer horizon. If a stock pays dividends at the end of each quarter, with realized returns $R_1, \ldots, R_4$ each quarter, then we show the four quarterly returns for this stock as:

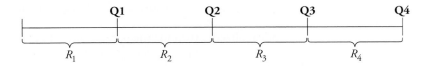

Its annual realized return, R_{annual}, is:

$$1 + R_{annual} = (1 + R_1)(1 + R_2)(1 + R_3)(1 + R_4) \tag{10.2}$$

EXAMPLE 10.2

Compounding
Realized Returns

Problem

Suppose you purchased Barrick Gold Corp. stock (ticker symbol: ABX) on January 1, 2008, and held it for one year, selling on January 1, 2008. What was your realized return?

Solution

▶ **Plan**

We need to analyze the cash flows from holding ABX stock for each quarter. In order to obtain the cash flows, we must look up ABX stock price data at the start and end of both years, as well as at any dividend dates (see Chapter 9 and the textbook's website for online sources of stock price and dividend data). From the data, we can construct the following table to fill out our cash flow timeline:

Date	Price ($)	Dividend ($)*
12/31/07	41.78	
06/16/08	40.30	0.2042
12/15/08	40.64	0.2470
12/31/08	44.85	

*Dividends were declared in USD and were converted to CAD at the exchange rate for the dates given.

Sources: Barrick Gold Corp for Prices and Dividends, Bank of Canada for CAD/USD Exchange Rate

Next, compute the return between each set of dates using Equation 10.1. Then determine each annual return in a way similar to that shown in Equation 10.2 by compounding the returns for all of the periods in that year.

▶ **Execute**

In Example 10.1, we already computed the realized return for January 1, 2008, to June 16, 2008, as −3.05%. We continue as in that example, using Equation 10.1 for each period until we have a series of realized returns. For example, from June 16, 2008, to December 15, 2008, the realized return is:

$$R_{t+1} = \frac{Div_{t+1} + P_{t+1} - P_t}{P_t} = \frac{0.2470 + (40.64 - 40.30)}{40.30} = 0.0146, \text{ or } 1.46\%$$

We then determine the one-year return by compounding.

Note that to use the method in Equation 10.2, we must have an investment to compound, so just as in Chapter 4, when we compounded interest, we add 1 as if we are computing the outcome of investing $1. The first return is -3.05%, giving us $1 + (-0.0305)$, or 0.9695. The same is true when the return is negative: the second return is 1.46%, giving us $1 + 0.0146$, or 1.0146. To compute our final compound return, we simply subtract the initial $1, leaving only the return:

$$1 + R_{annual} = (1 + R_1)(1 + R_2)(1 + R_3)$$
$$1 + R_{annual} = (0.9695)(1.0146)(1.1036) = 1.0855$$
$$R_{annual} = 1.0855 - 1 = 0.0855 \quad \text{or} \quad 8.55\%$$

The table below includes the realized return in each period.

Date	Price ($)	Dividend ($)*	Return
12/31/07	41.78		
06/16/08	40.30	0.2042	−3.05%
12/15/08	40.64	0.2470	1.46%
12/31/08	44.85		10.36%
Annual Return over 2008:			8.55%

▶ **Evaluate**

By repeating these steps, we have successfully computed the realized annual returns for an investor holding ABX stock over this one-year period. From this exercise, we can see that returns are risky. ABX fluctuated up and down over the year, but ended significantly up (8.55%) at the end.

It is unlikely that anyone investing in Barrick on January 1, 2008, expected to receive exactly the realized return we calculated in Example 10.2. In any given year, we observe only one actual realized return from all of the possible returns that could have been realized. However, we can observe realized returns over many years. The realized returns for the S&P/TSX Composite Index are shown in Table 10.1, which for comparison purposes also lists the returns for Barrick Gold Corp. and for three-month treasury bills.

Once we have calculated the realized annual returns, we can compare them to see which investments performed better in a given year. From Table 10.1, we can see that Barrick stock outperformed the S&P/TSX Composite Index in 2001, 2007, and 2008. In 2002, treasury bills performed better than both Barrick stock and the S&P/TSX Composite Index.

Over any particular period, we observe realized returns for different types of securities. By counting the number of times the realized return falls within a particular range, we can start to graph the distribution of possible returns. Let's illustrate this process with the data in Figure 10.1.

In Figure 10.2, we plot the monthly returns for each investment in Figure 10.1 in a histogram. In this histogram, the height of each bar represents the number of months that the returns were in each range indicated on the x-axis. Notice how much more variable stock returns are compared with Canada treasury bills.

TABLE 10.1	Year End	S&P TSX Composite Index Return*	Barrick Gold Corp. Return*	3-Month T-Bill Return
	2000	7.51%	−3.14%	5.56%
Realized Return	2001	−12.57%	4.87%	4.09%
for the S&P/TSX	2002	−12.44%	−3.47%	2.53%
Composite Index,	2003	26.72%	22.15%	2.91%
Barrick Gold Corp.,	2004	14.48%	−0.03%	2.23%
and Treasury Bills,	2005	24.13%	12.77%	2.65%
2000–2009	2006	17.26%	11.15%	4.01%
	2007	9.83%	17.61%	4.28%
	2008	−33.00%	8.55%	2.73%
	2009	35.05%	−6.67%	0.41%
	Average	7.70%	6.38%	3.14%
	Variance	0.0444	0.0094	0.0002
	Standard Deviation	0.2107	0.0969	0.0141

Sources: Statistics Canada, Bank of Canada, Barrick Gold Corp.

Average Annual Returns

Out of the distribution of possible returns for each security depicted in Figure 10.2, we want to know the most likely return, represented by the average. The **average annual return** of an investment during some historical period is simply the average of the realized returns for each year. That is, if R_t is the realized return of a security in each year t, then the average annual return for years 1 through T is:

Average Annual Return of a Security

(10.3)

$$\overline{R} = \frac{1}{T}(R_1 + R_2 + \cdots + R_T)$$

If we assume that the distribution of possible returns is the same over time, the average return provides an estimate of the return we should expect in any given year—the expected return. This idea is not unique to returns. For example, a Tim Hortons manager cannot know exactly how many customers will come in today, but by looking at the average number of customers who have come in historically, the manager can form an expectation to use in staffing and stocking.

Using the S&P/TSX Composite realized returns from Table 10.1, the average return for the S&P/TSX Composite for the years 2000 to 2009 is

$$\frac{1}{10}(7.51\% - 12.57\% - 12.44\% + 26.72\% \cdots + 35.05\%) = 7.70\%$$

The average Canada treasury bill return during the same period was 3.14%. Therefore, during this period investors earned 3.86% (7.70% − 3.14%) more on average holding the S&P/TSX Composite Index than investing in Canada treasury bills. This average is computed over just five years of data. Naturally, our estimate of the true average of the distribution is more precise the more data we use. We display the average returns for different investments from 1950 to 2009 in Figure 10.3.

FIGURE 10.2

The Distribution of Monthly Returns for Canadian Treasury Bills, Long-Term Government of Canada Bonds, U.S. Stocks (S&P 500) Expressed in Canadian Dollars (CAD), and Canadian Stocks (S&P/TSX Composite Index), 1956–2009

The height of each bar represents the number of years that the monthly returns were in each 1% range. Note the greater variability of stock returns (especially smaller Canadian stocks) compared to the returns of Government of Canada bonds or treasury bills.

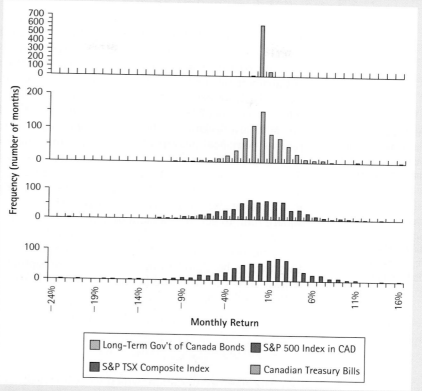

FIGURE 10.3

Average Annual Returns in Canada for S&P/TSX Composite Index, S&P 500 in CAD, Long-Term Government of Canada Bonds, and Three-Month Canadian Treasury Bills, 1950–2009

Each bar represents an investment's average return.

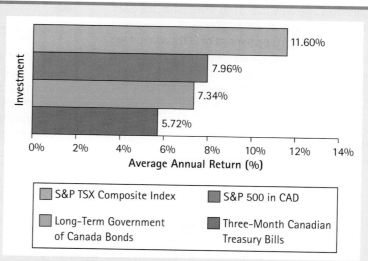

The Variance and Volatility of Returns

Looking at Figure 10.2, we can see that the variability of the returns is very different for each investment. The distribution of Canadian stocks' returns (S&P/TSX Composite Index) is the most widely dispersed. The large company stocks that comprise the S&P 500 have returns that vary less than Canadian stocks, but much more than Government of Canada bonds or treasury bills. While we can see these differences in variability in Figure 10.3, we need a way to formally quantify them. To determine the variability of returns, we calculate the *standard deviation* of the distribution of realized returns. The **standard deviation** is the square root of the *variance* of the distribution of realized returns. **Variance** measures the variability in returns by taking the differences of the returns from the average return and squaring those differences. We have to square the difference of each return from the average because, by definition, the unsquared differences from an average must sum to zero. Because we square the returns, the variance is in units of "$\%^2$" or percentage-squared. That is not very useful to us, so we take the square root, to get the standard deviation, in units of %.

standard deviation
A common method used to measure the risk of a probability distribution— the square root of the variance.

variance A method to measure the variability of returns—the expected squared deviation of returns from the mean.

While that sounds a bit abstract, standard deviation simply indicates the tendency of the historical returns to be different from their average and how far from the average they tend to be. Standard deviation therefore captures our intuition of risk: how often will we miss the mark and how far off will we be? Formally, we calculate the variance with the following equation:[1]

Variance Estimate Using Realized Returns

$$Var(R) = \frac{1}{T - 1}\left((R_1 - \overline{R})^2 + (R_2 - \overline{R})^2 + \cdots + (R_T - \overline{R})^2\right) \qquad (10.4)$$

The standard deviation, which we will call the volatility, is the square root of the variance:[2]

$$SD(R) = \sqrt{Var(R)} \qquad (10.5)$$

Arithmetic Average Returns Versus Compound Annual Returns

In Figure 10.1, we saw that $100 invested in the S&P/TSX Composite Index at the beginning of 1956 would have grown to $12,570 by the end of 2009. What if we wanted to know the average compound annual return for that investment? That's the same as asking what return, earned each year for 54 years, would have caused our $100 to grow to $12,570. We know that the formula for future value tells us that

$$FV = PV(1 + R)^n$$

Thus,

$$\$12,570 = \$100(1 + R)^{54}$$

Solving for R, we get 9.36%.

However, using the same data, we find the average annual return for the S&P/TSX Composite Index for this period was 10.24%. How can the two answers be different?

The difference is due to the fact that returns are volatile. To see the effect of volatility, suppose an investment has

---

[1] You may wonder why we divide by $T - 1$ rather than T here. It is because we are not computing deviations from the true expected return; instead, we are computing deviations from the estimated average return R. Because the average return is derived from the same data, we lose a degree of freedom (in essence, we have used up one of the data points), so that when computing the variance there are really only $T - 1$ additional data points on which to base it.

[2] If the returns used in Equation 10.4 are not annual returns, it is conventional to convert the variance to annual terms by multiplying the number of returns per year. Thus, when using monthly returns, we multiply the variance by 12, and equivalently the standard deviation by $\sqrt{12}$.

annual returns of $+20\%$ one year and -20% the next. The average annual return is:

$$\frac{20\% + (-20\%)}{2} = 0\%$$

But the value of $1 invested after two years is:

$$\$1 \times (1 + 0.20) \times (1 - 0.20) = \$0.96$$

This tells us that an investor would have lost money. Why? Because the 20% gain happens on a $1 investment for a total of 20 cents, whereas the 20% loss happens on a larger investment of $1.20. The loss is 20% of $1.20, or 24 cents.

In this case, the compound annual return is:

$$0.96 = 1(1 + R)^2$$

so solving for R:

$$R = (0.96)^{1/2} - 1 = -2\%$$

We calculated the 10.24% average for the S&P/TSX Composite Index as a simple arithmetic average of the realized returns, while we calculated 9.36% as the average annual compound return that corresponds to the total gain on our $100 investment (called the *geometric* average).

Which is a better description of an investment's return? The compound annual return is a better description of the long-term *historical performance* of an investment. It describes the average annual compound return for that particular history of returns. The ranking of the long-term performance of different investments coincides with the ranking of their compound annual returns. Thus, the compound annual return is the return that is most often used for comparison purposes. For example, mutual funds generally report their compound annual returns over the last 5 or 10 years.

On the other hand, the arithmetic average return should be used when trying to estimate an investment's *expected* return over a *future* horizon based on its past performance. If we view past annual returns as independent realizations of actual returns from the same set of possible returns, then we know from statistics that the arithmetic average provides the best estimate of the true mean. If the investment above is equally likely to have annual returns of $+20\%$ and -20% in the future, then the payoff from a $1 investment after two years will be:

25% of the time: $\$1 \times (1.20) \times (1.20) = \$1.44$

50% of the time: $\$1 \times (1.20) \times (0.80)$
$$= (0.80) \times (1.20) = \$0.96$$

25% of the time: $\$1 \times (0.80) \times (0.80) = \$0.64$

The expected payoff is $25\%(1.44) + 50\%(0.96) + 25\%(0.64) = \$1$, which is consistent with the arithmetic average return of 0%.

EXAMPLE 10.3
Computing Historical Volatility

Problem

Using the data from Table 10.1, what is the standard deviation of the S&P/TSX Composite Index returns for the years 2000 to 2009?

Solution

▶ **Plan**

With the 10 returns, compute the average return using Equation 10.3, because it is an input to the variance equation. Next, compute the variance using Equation 10.4 and then take its square root to determine the standard deviation.

2000	2001	2002	2003	2004	2005	2006	2007	2008	2009
7.51%	−12.57%	−12.44%	26.72%	14.48%	24.13%	17.26%	9.83%	−33.00%	35.05%

▶ **Execute**

In the previous section, we already computed the average annual return of the S&P/TSX Composite Index during this period as 7.70%, so we have all of the necessary inputs for the variance calculation:

Applying Equation 10.4, we have:

$$Var(R) = \frac{1}{T-1}\left((R_1 - \bar{R})^2 + (R_2 - \bar{R})^2 + \cdots + (R_T - \bar{R})^2\right)$$

$$= \frac{1}{10-1}\left((0.0751 - 0.0770)^2 + (-0.1257 - 0.0770)^2\right.$$
$$\left. + \cdots + (0.3505 - 0.0770)^2\right)$$

$$= 0.0444$$

Alternatively, we can break the calculation of this equation out as follows:

	2000	2001	2002	2003	2004	2005	2006	2007	2008	2009
Return	0.0751	−0.1257	−0.1244	0.2672	0.1448	0.2413	0.1726	0.0983	−0.3300	0.3505
Average	0.0770	0.0770	0.0770	0.0770	0.0770	0.0770	0.0770	0.0770	0.0770	0.0770
Difference	−0.0019	−0.2027	−0.2013	0.1903	0.0678	0.1643	0.0956	0.0213	−0.4070	0.2735
Squared	0.0000	0.0411	0.0405	0.0362	0.0046	0.0270	0.0091	0.0005	0.1656	0.0748

Summing the squared differences in the last row, we get 0.3995.

Finally, dividing by $(10 - 1 = 9)$ gives us $0.3995/9 = 0.0444$. The standard deviation is therefore

$$SD(R) = \sqrt{Var(R)} = \sqrt{0.0444} = 0.2107 \text{ or } 21.07\%$$

▶ **Evaluate**

Our best estimate of the expected return for the S&P/TSX Composite Index is its average return, 7.70%, but it is risky, with a standard deviation of 21.07%.

Common Mistake   **Mistakes When Computing Standard Deviation**

Example 10.3 highlights two missteps often made in computing standard deviations.

1. Remember to divide by *one less* than the number of returns you have ($T - 1$, *not T*).

2. Don't forget to take the square root of the variance to obtain the standard deviation. You are not done when you calculate the variance—you have one more step to go.

We began our review of statistics with the goal of being able to quantify the difference in the variability of the distributions that we observed over long periods of time, such as those shown in Figure 10.2. We can now do so by computing the standard deviation of the annual returns on the investments from 1950 to 2009. These results are shown in Figure 10.4.

Comparing the standard deviations in Figure 10.4, we see that, as expected, Canadian stocks had the most variable historical returns, followed by those of larger U.S. companies. The returns of long-term Government of Canada bonds and treasury bills are much less variable than those of stocks, with treasury bills being the least volatile investment category.

USING EXCEL

Computing the
Standard Deviation
of Historical
Returns

1. Enter or import the historical returns into Excel.

2. Next, highlight the cell where you want to produce the standard deviation, and select Function from the Insert pull-down menu.

3. Select the "STDEV" function, highlight the returns for which you want to compute the average, and click OK.

4. *Make sure that you use the STDEV function and* not *the STDEVP function.* STDEV calculates the sample standard deviation as in Equations 10.4 and 10.5, by dividing by $T - 1$. STDEVP assumes that you know with certainty the true mean and calculates the standard deviation by dividing by T. See footnote 1 for more discussion of this important distinction.

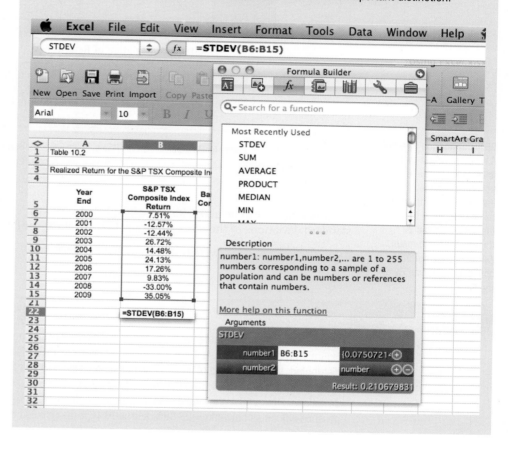

The Normal Distribution

normal distribution A symmetric probability distribution that is completely characterized by its average and standard deviation. Ninety-five percent of all possible outcomes fall within two standard deviations above and below the average.

The standard deviations that we compute in Figure 10.4 are useful for more than just ranking the investments from most to least risky. The standard deviation also plays an important role in describing a **normal distribution**, shown in Figure 10.5, which is a symmetric probability distribution that is completely characterized by its average and standard deviation. Importantly, about two-thirds of all possible outcomes fall within one standard deviation above or below the average, and about 95% of all possible outcomes fall within two standard deviations above and below the average. Figure 10.5 shows these outcomes for small company stocks.

FIGURE 10.4

Volatility (Standard Deviation) of S&P/TSX Composite Index, S&P 500 in CAD, Long-Term Government of Canada Bonds, and Government of Canada Treasury Bills, 1950–2009

Each bar represents the standard deviation of the investment's returns.

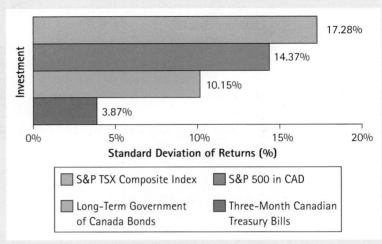

95% confidence interval
A range of values that is likely to include an unknown parameter. If independent samples are taken repeatedly from the same population, then the true parameter will lie outside the 95% confidence interval 5% of the time.

Because we can be about 95% confident that next year's return will be within two standard deviations of the average, we say that the **95% confidence interval** runs from:

$$\text{Average} \pm (2 \times \text{standard deviation})$$

$$\overline{R} \pm (2 \times SD(R)) \tag{10.6}$$

FIGURE 10.5

Normal Distribution

The height of the line reflects the likelihood of each return occurring. Using the data from Figure 10.3 and Figure 10.4, if the returns of the S&P/TSX Composite Index are normally distributed, then two-thirds of all possible outcomes should lie within one standard deviation of the average return of 11.60% (given in Figure 10.3), and 95% should lie within two standard deviations. Figure 10.4 shows the standard deviation to be 17.28%, so that puts 95% of possible outcomes between −22.96% and +46.16% (the shaded area of the distribution).

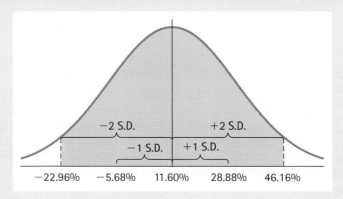

EXAMPLE 10.4
Confidence
Intervals

Problem

In Example 10.3, we found the average return for the S&P/TSX Composite Index from 2000 to 2009 to be 7.70% with a standard deviation of 21.07%. What is a 95% confidence interval for 2010's return?

Solution

▶ **Plan**

We can use Equation 10.6 to compute the confidence interval.

▶ **Execute**

Using Equation 10.6, we have:

$$\text{Average} \pm 2 \times \text{standard deviation} = 7.70\% - 2 \times 21.07\% \text{ to } 7.70\% + 2 \times 21.07\%$$
$$= -34.44\% \text{ to } 49.84\%$$

▶ **Evaluate**

Even though the average return from 2000 to 2009 was 7.70%, the S&P/TSX Composite Index was volatile, so if we want to be 95% confident of 2010's return, the best we can say is that it will lie between −34.44% and +49.84%.

Table 10.2 summarizes the central concepts and equations that we developed in this section. Calculating historical averages and volatilities indicates how investments performed in the past and might perform in the future. Of course, using the past to predict the future is fraught with uncertainty. In the next section, we discuss that uncertainty.

Concept Check

3. For what purpose do we use the average and standard deviation of historical stock returns?

4. How does the standard deviation of historical returns affect our confidence in predicting the next period's return?

TABLE 10.2
Summary of Tools
for Working with
Historical Returns

Concept	Definition	Formula
Realized Returns	Total return earned over a particular period of time	$R_{t+1} = \dfrac{Div_{t+1} + P_{t+1} - P_t}{P_t}$
Average Annual Return	Average of realized returns for each year	$\bar{R} = \dfrac{1}{T}(R_1 + R_2 + \cdots + R_T)$
Variance of Returns	A measure of the variability of returns	$Var(R) = \dfrac{1}{T-1}\big((R_1 - \bar{R})^2 + (R_2 - \bar{R})^2 + \cdots + (R_T - \bar{R})^2\big)$
Standard Deviation or Volatility of Returns	The square root of the variance (which puts it in the same units as the average—namely "%")	$SD(R) = \sqrt{Var(R)}$
95% Confidence Interval	The range of returns within which we are 95% confident that next period's return will lie	$\bar{R} \pm 2 \times SD(R)$

10.3   The Historical Tradeoff Between Risk and Return

Would you intentionally choose to accept additional risk without additional reward? In other words, are you willing to pursue riskier investments if they do not have the potential to generate higher returns? The answer to both of these questions is most likely no. In this section, we will examine the historical tradeoff between risk (as measured by price volatility) and reward (as measured by returns) to see if historically investors behaved as you would.

The Returns of Large Portfolios

In Figures 10.3 and 10.4, we showed the historical average returns and volatilities for a number of different types of investments. In Figure 10.6, we plot the average return versus the volatility of each type of investment from those tables. Note that the investments with higher volatility, measured here with standard deviation, have rewarded investors with higher average returns. Figure 10.6 is consistent with our view that investors are risk averse. Riskier investments must offer investors higher average returns to compensate them for the risk they are taking.

The Returns of Individual Stocks

Figure 10.6 suggests the following simple model of the risk premium: investments with higher volatility should have a higher risk premium and therefore higher returns. Indeed, looking at Figure 10.6, it is tempting to draw a line through the portfolios and conclude that all investments should lie on or near this line—that is, expected return should rise proportionally with volatility. This conclusion appears to be approximately true for the large portfolios we have looked at so far. Is it correct? Does it apply to individual stocks?

FIGURE 10.6

The Historical Tradeoff Between Risk and Return in Large Portfolios, 1926–2005

Note the general increasing relationship between historical volatility (standard deviation) and average return for these large portfolios. For comparison purposes, Canadian treasury bills, long-term Government of Canada bonds, the S&P 500 in CAD, and the TSX/S&P Composite Index are included.

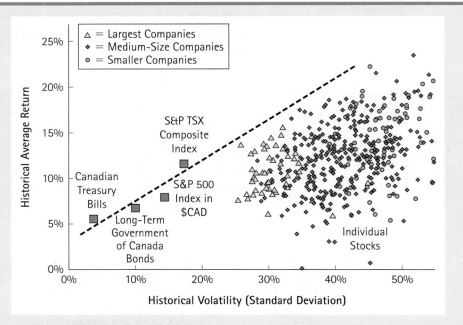

Source: Global Financial Data.

Actually, the answer to both questions is no. There is no clear relationship between volatility and returns for individual stocks. Although it will take more work to establish the relationship between risk and return for individual stocks, the following is true:

1. There is a relationship between size and risk—on average, larger stocks have lower volatility than smaller stocks.

2. Even the largest stocks are typically more volatile than a portfolio of large stocks, such as the S&P 500. The same can be said for stocks of smaller companies in comparison with a portfolio of these companies, such as the S&P/TSX Composite Index.

3. All individual stocks have lower returns and/or higher risk than the portfolios in Figure 10.6. The individual stocks in Figure 10.6 all lie below the line.

Thus, while volatility (standard deviation) seems to be a reasonable measure of risk when evaluating a large portfolio, the volatility of an individual security doesn't explain the size of its average return. What are we to make of this? Why wouldn't investors demand a higher return from stocks with a higher volatility? And how is it that portfolios such as the S&P/TSX Composite Index or the S&P 500 Index are so much less risky than almost all of the 500 stocks individually? To answer these questions, we need to think more carefully about how to measure risk for an investor.

5. What is the relationship between risk and return for large portfolios? How are individual stocks different?

6. Do portfolios or the stocks in the portfolios tend to have the lower volatility?

Common Versus Independent Risk

In this section, we explain why the risk of an individual security differs from the risk of a portfolio composed of similar securities. We begin with an example from the insurance industry to understand how the portfolio of insurance products performs for the insurance company offering them.

Theft Versus Earthquake Insurance: An Example

Consider two types of home insurance an insurance company might offer: theft insurance and earthquake insurance. Let us assume, for the purpose of illustration, that the risk of each of these two hazards is similar for a given home in the San Francisco area—each year there is about a 1% chance the home will be robbed and also a 1% chance that the home will be damaged by an earthquake. In this case, the chance the insurance company will pay a claim for a single home is the same for the two types of insurance policies. Suppose an insurance company writes 100,000 policies of each type for homeowners in San Francisco. We know the risks of the individual policies are similar, but are the risks of the portfolios of 100,000 policies similar?

First consider theft insurance. Because the chance of a theft for any given home is 1%, we would expect about 1% of the 100,000 homes to be robbed. Thus, the number of theft claims will be about 1000 per year. The actual number of claims may be a bit higher or lower each year, but not much. In this case, if the insurance company holds reserves sufficient to cover 1200 claims, it will almost certainly have enough to cover its obligations on its theft insurance policies.

Now consider earthquake insurance. There is a 99% chance that an earthquake will not occur. All the homes are in the same city, so if an earthquake does occur, all homes are likely to be affected and the insurance company can expect 100,000 claims. As a result, the insurance company can expect either 0 claims or 100,000 claims. Because it may have 100,000 claims, it will have to hold reserves of cash (or other investments) sufficient to cover claims on all 100,000 policies it wrote in order to meet its obligations if an earthquake occurs.

Thus, earthquake and theft insurance lead to portfolios with very different risk characteristics. For earthquake insurance, the percentage of claims is very risky—it will most likely be 0, but there is a 1% chance that the insurance company will have to pay claims on *all* the policies it wrote. So the risk of the portfolio of earthquake insurance policies is no different from the risk of any single policy. On the other hand, we've seen that for theft insurance the number of claims in a given year is quite predictable. Year in and year out, it will be very close to 1% of the total number of policies, or 1000 claims. The portfolio of theft insurance policies has almost no risk! That is, the insurance company's payouts are quite stable and predictable over time.

Types of Risk

common risk Risk that is linked across outcomes.

independent risk Risk that bears no relation to other risks. If risks are independent, then knowing the outcome of one provides no information about the other.

diversification The averaging of independent risks in a large portfolio.

Why are the portfolios of insurance policies so different when the individual policies themselves are quite similar? Intuitively, the key difference between them is that an earthquake affects all houses simultaneously, and so the risk is linked across homes, meaning either all homes are damaged or all homes are not damaged. We call risk that is linked in this way **common risk**. In contrast, we have assumed that thefts in different houses are not related to each other—whether one house is burglarized has no effect on another house's chance of being burglarized. **Independent risk**, such as the risk of theft, is not linked across homes. When risks are independent, some individual homeowners are unlucky, others are lucky, but overall the number of claims is similar. The averaging out of risks in a large portfolio is called **diversification**.[3] Table 10.3 summarizes our discussion of common and independent risk.

The principle of diversification is used routinely in the insurance industry. In addition to theft insurance, many other forms of insurance (life, health, auto) rely on the fact that the number of claims is relatively predictable in a large portfolio. Even in the case of earthquake insurance, insurers can achieve some diversification by selling policies in different geographical regions, or by combining different types of policies. Diversification is used to reduce risk in many other settings. For example, many systems are designed with redundancy to decrease the risk of a disruption. Firms often add redundancy to critical parts of the manufacturing process: NASA puts more than one antenna on its space probes, and automobiles contain spare tires.

TABLE 10.3	Type of Risk	Definition	Example	Risk Diversified in Large Portfolio?
Summary of Types of Risk	Common Risk	Risks that are linked across outcomes	Risk of earthquake	No
	Independent Risk	Risks that bear no relation to each other	Risk of theft	Yes

[3] Harry Markowitz was the first to formalize the benefits from diversification. See Markowitz, H.M., "Portfolio Selection," *Journal of Finance* 7(1) (1952): 77–91.

In many settings, the risks lie somewhere in between the common risks and independent risks. For example, you may have applied to more than one school. Your chances of being accepted (or rejected) at any one school are not perfectly linked across schools, because schools have different admissions criteria and are looking for different types of students. However, your risk of rejection is not completely independent, either; all schools look at your high school grades, so the schools' decisions will be related.

EXAMPLE 10.5

Diversification

Problem

You are playing a very simple gambling game with your friend: a $1 bet based on a coin flip. That is, you each bet $1 and flip a coin: heads you win your friend's $1, tails you lose and your friend takes your dollar. How is your risk different if you play this game 100 times in a row versus just betting $100 (instead of $1) on a single coin flip?

Solution

▶ **Plan**

The risk of losing one coin flip is independent of the risk of losing the next one: each time you have a 50% chance of losing, and one coin flip does not affect any other coin flip. We can compute the expected outcome of any flip as a weighted average by weighting your possible winnings (+$1) by 50% and your possible losses (−$1) by 50%. We can then compute the probability of losing all $100 under either scenario.

▶ **Execute**

If you play the game 100 times, you should lose 50% of the time and win 50% of the time, so your expected outcome is $50 \times (+\$1) + 50 \times (-\$1) = \$0$. You should break even. But even if you don't win exactly half of the time, the probability that you would lose all 100 coin flips (and thus lose $100) is exceedingly small (in fact, it is 0.50^{100}, which is far less than even 0.0001%). If it happens, you should take a very careful look at the coin!

If instead you make a single $100 bet on the outcome of one coin flip, you have a 50% chance of winning $100 and a 50% chance of losing $100, so your expected outcome will be the same: break-even. However, there is a 50% chance you will lose $100, so your risk is far greater than it would be for 100 one-dollar bets.

▶ **Evaluate**

In each case, you put $100 at risk, but by spreading out that risk across 100 different bets rather than placing a single $100 bet, you have diversified much of your risk away.

Concept Check

7. What is the difference between common and independent risk?

8. How does diversification help with independent risk?

10.5 Diversification in Stock Portfolios

As the insurance example indicates, the degree of risk related to a portfolio depends on whether the individual risks within it are common or independent. Independent risks are diversified in a large portfolio, whereas common risks are not. Our goal is to understand the relationship between risk and return in the capital markets, so let's consider the implication of this distinction for the risk of stock portfolios.

Unsystematic Versus Systematic Risk

Over any given time period, the risk of holding a stock is that the dividends plus the final stock price will be higher or lower than expected, which makes the realized return risky. What causes dividends or stock prices, and therefore returns, to be higher or lower than we expect? Usually, stock prices and dividends fluctuate due to two types of news:

1. *Company- or industry-specific news:* This is good or bad news about a company (or industry) itself. For example, a firm might announce that it has been success-ful in gaining market share within its industry. Or, the home-building industry may be damaged by a real estate slowdown.

2. *Market-wide news:* This is news that affects the economy as a whole and therefore affects all stocks. For instance, the Bank of Canada might announce that it will lower interest rates in an attempt to boost the economy.

Fluctuations of a stock's return that are due to company or industry-specific news are independent risks. Similar to theft at different homes, these are unrelated across stocks. This type of risk is also referred to as **unsystematic risk**.

On the other hand, fluctuations of a stock's return that are due to market-wide news represent common risk. As with earthquakes, all stocks are affected simultaneously. This type of risk is also called **systematic risk**.

unsystematic risk
Fluctuations of a stock's return that are due to company- or industry-specific news and are independent risks unrelated across stocks.

systematic risk
Fluctuations of a stock's return that are due to market-wide news representing common risk.

When we combine many stocks in a large portfolio, the unsystematic risks for each stock will average out and be eliminated by diversification. Good news will affect some stocks and bad news will affect others, but the amount of good or bad news overall will be relatively constant. The systematic risk, however, will affect all firms—and therefore the entire portfolio—and will not be eliminated by diversification.

Let's consider a hypothetical example. Suppose type S firms are affected *only* by the systematic risk of the strength of the economy, which has a 50–50 chance of being either strong or weak. If the economy is strong, type S stocks will earn a return of 40%, and if the economy is weak, their return will be −20%. Because the risk these firms face (the strength of the economy) is systematic risk, holding a large portfolio of type S stocks will not diver-sify the risk. When the economy is strong, the portfolio will have the same return of 40% as each type S firm. When the economy is weak, the portfolio will also have a return of −20%.

Now consider type U firms, which are affected only by unsystematic risks. Their returns are equally likely to be 35% or −25%, based on factors specific to each firm's local market. Because these risks are firm-specific, if we hold a portfolio of many type U stocks, the risk is diversified. About half of the firms will have returns of 35%, and half will have returns of −25%. The return of the portfolio will be the average return of 50% (0.35) + 50% (−0.25) = 0.05, or 5%, no matter whether the economy is strong or weak.

Figure 10.7 illustrates how volatility, measured by standard deviation, declines with the size of the portfolio for type S and U firms. Type S firms have only systematic risk. Similar to earthquake insurance, the volatility of the portfolio does not change as we increase the number of firms. Type U firms have only unsystematic risk. As with theft insurance, the risk is diversified as the number of firms increases, and volatility declines. As is evident from Figure 10.8, with a large number of firms, type U firms' risk is, essen-tially, completely eliminated.

Of course, actual firms are not similar to type S or U firms. Firms are affected by both systematic, market-wide risks, as well as unsystematic risks. Figure 10.7 also shows how the volatility changes with the number of stocks in a portfolio of typical firms. *When firms carry both types of risk, only the unsystematic risk will be eliminated by diversification when we combine many firms into a portfolio. The volatility will there-fore decline until only the systematic risk, which affects all firms, remains.*

FIGURE 10.7

Volatility of Portfolios of Type S and U Stocks

Because type S firms have only systematic risk, the volatility of the portfolio does not change. Type U firms have only unsystematic risk, which is diversified and eliminated as the number of firms in the portfolio grows. Typical stocks carry a mix of both types of risk, so that the risk of the portfolio declines as unsystematic risk is diversified, but systematic risk remains.

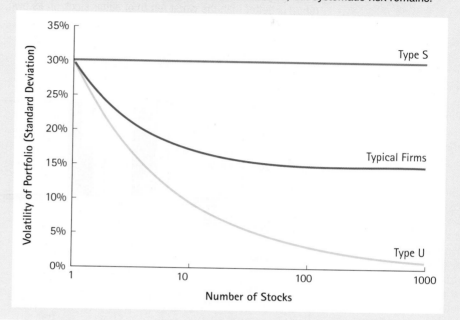

This example explains one of the puzzles from Section 10.3. There we saw that the S&P/TSX Composite Index and the S&P 500 had much lower volatility than any of the individual stocks. Now we can see why—the individual stocks each contain unsystematic risk, which is eliminated when we combine them into a large portfolio. Thus, the portfolio can have lower volatility than each of the stocks within it. Figure 10.8 illustrates this fact. The dotted lines show the extremes of the range of returns of a portfolio of Nike and Starbucks. The returns of each of the two stocks in the portfolio cross at least one of these extremes. Thus, the volatility of the portfolio is lower than the volatility of both of the stocks in the portfolio.

Diversifiable Risk and the Risk Premium

What if you hold only one or two stocks—wouldn't you be exposed to unsystematic risk and demand a premium for it? If the market compensated you with an additional risk premium for choosing to bear diversifiable risk, then other investors could buy the same stocks and earn the additional premium, while putting them in a portfolio so that they could diversify and eliminate the unsystematic risk. By doing so, investors could earn an additional premium without taking additional risk!

This opportunity to earn something for nothing is an arbitrage opportunity as we discussed in Chapter 3, and so it is something investors would find very attractive. As more

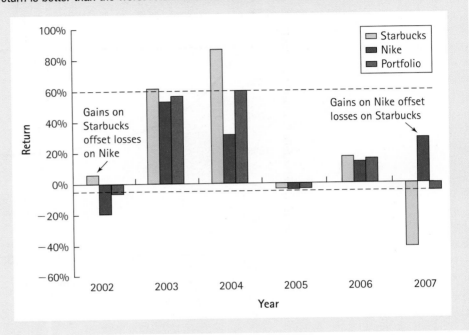

FIGURE 10.8

The Effect of Diversification on Portfolio Volatility

While Nike and Starbucks are each very volatile, some of their movements offset each other. If they are in a portfolio together, as represented by the yellow bars, the total movement of the portfolio is muted relative to the movement of either of the individual stocks. The dotted lines show the highest and lowest return of the portfolio—note that the portfolio's worst return is better than the worst return of either stock on its own.

and more investors take advantage of this situation and purchase shares that pay a risk premium for diversifiable, unsystematic risk, the current share price of those firms would rise, lowering their expected return—recall that the current share price P_t is the denominator when computing the stock's return as in Equation 10.1. This trading would stop only when the risk premium for diversifiable risk dropped to zero. Competition among investors ensures that no additional return can be earned for diversifiable risk. The result:

The risk premium of a stock is not affected by its diversifiable, unsystematic risk.

The argument above is essentially an application of the Valuation Principle's Law of One Price. Imagine a large portfolio of type U firms, which have no systematic risk. As depicted in Figure 10.7, a large portfolio of type U firms eliminates all unsystematic risk, leaving no additional risk. Since that portfolio has no risk, it cannot earn a risk premium and instead must earn the risk-free interest rate. This line of reasoning suggests the following more general principle:

The risk premium for diversifiable risk is zero. Thus, investors are not compensated for holding unsystematic risk.

The Importance of Systematic Risk

Because investors can eliminate unsystematic risk "for free" by diversifying their portfolios, they will not require (nor deserve) a reward or risk premium for bearing it. On the other hand, diversification does not reduce systematic risk: even when holding a large portfolio, an investor will be exposed to risks that affect the entire economy and therefore affect all securities. We can reduce the systematic risk of a portfolio by selling stocks and investing in risk-free bonds, but at the cost of giving up the higher expected return of stocks. Because unsystematic risk can be eliminated for free by diversifying, whereas systematic risk can be eliminated only by sacrificing expected returns, it is a security's systematic risk that determines the risk premium investors require to hold it. This fact, summarized in Table 10.4, leads to the second key principle:

> *The risk premium of a security is determined by its systematic risk and does not depend on its diversifiable risk.*

TABLE 10.4

The Expected Return of Type S and Type U Firms, Assuming the Risk-Free Rate Is 5%

	S Firm	U Firm
Volatility (standard deviation)	30%	30%
Risk-Free Rate	5%	5%
Risk Premium	5%	0%
Expected Return	10%	5%

This principle implies that a stock's volatility, which is a measure of total risk (that is, systematic risk + unsystematic risk), is not useful in determining the risk premium that investors will earn. For example, consider again type S and U firms. As shown in Figure 10.7, the volatility (standard deviation) of a single type S or U firm is 30%. However, as Table 10.4 shows, although they have the same volatility, type S firms have an expected return of 10% and type U firms have an expected return of 5%.

The difference in expected returns is due to the difference in the kind of risk each firm bears. Type U firms have only unsystematic risk, which does not require a risk premium, and so the expected return of 5% for type U firms equals the risk-free interest rate. Type S firms have only systematic risk. Because investors will require compensation for this risk, the expected return of 10% for type S firms provides investors with a 5% risk premium above the risk-free interest rate. Table 10.5 summarizes the main points about systematic and unsystematic risk.

Common Mistake   A Fallacy of Long-Run Diversification

We have seen that investors can greatly reduce risk by dividing their investment dollars over many different investments, eliminating the diversifiable risk in their portfolios. It is sometimes argued that the same logic applies over time: by investing for many years, we can also diversify the risk we face during any particular year. Thus, young investors should choose risky portfolios because they have more time to make up their losses. Is this correct? In the long run, does risk still matter?

It is true that if returns each year are independent, the volatility of the average annual return does decline with the number of years that we invest. But, as long-term investors, we don't care about the volatility of our

TABLE 10.5

Systematic Risk Versus Unsystematic Risk

	Diversifiable?	Requires a Risk Premium?
Systematic Risk	No	Yes
Unsystematic Risk	Yes	No

average return; instead we care about the volatility of our cumulative return over the period. This volatility grows with the investment horizon, as illustrated in the following example.

In 1956, the S&P/TSX Index increased in value by about 11%. We see from Figure 10.1 that if that $100 were invested in 1956, it would have grown to about $12,570 by the end of 2009. But suppose instead that mining and transportation strikes had caused stocks to drop by 44.6% in 1956. Then the initial $100 invested would be worth only $100 × (1 − 44.6%) = $55.60 at the start of 1957. If returns from then on were unchanged, the investment would be worth half as much in 2009, or $6285.

Thus, if future returns are not affected by today's return, then an increase or decline in the value of our portfolio today will translate into the same percentage increase or decrease in the value of our portfolio in the future, and so there is no diversification over time. The only way the length of the time horizon can reduce

risk is if a below-average return this year implies that returns are more likely to be above average in the future (and vice versa). If this were true, past low returns can be used to predict future high returns in the stock market.

For short horizons of a few years, there is no evidence of this predictability in the stock market. For longer horizons, there is some evidence of this historically, but it is not clear how reliable this evidence is (there are not enough decades of accurate stock market data available) or whether the pattern will continue. But even if there is long-run reversal in stock returns, a buy-and-hold diversification strategy is still not optimal: if past returns can be used to predict future returns, it is optimal to invest more in stocks when returns are predicted to be high, and less when they are predicted to be low. Note that this strategy is very different from the diversification we achieve by holding many stocks, where we cannot predict which stocks will have good or bad unsystematic shocks.

We now have an explanation for the second puzzle from Section 10.3. While volatility or standard deviation might be a reasonable measure of risk for a large portfolio, it is not appropriate for an individual security.

Thus, there is no relationship between volatility and average returns for individual securities.

Consequently, to estimate a security's expected return, we need to find a measure of a security's systematic risk.

We began this chapter by showing in Figure 10.1 that your grandparents' and parents' investment in the S&P/TSX Composite Index would have lost a lot of money in periods such as the recessions of the early 1980s and early 1990s. Thus, risk-averse investors will demand a premium to invest in securities that will do poorly in bad times. This idea coincides with the notion of systematic risk we have defined in this chapter. Economy-wide risk, the risk of recessions and booms, is systematic risk that cannot be diversified. Therefore, an asset that moves with the economy contains systematic risk and so requires a risk premium. In the next chapter, we will discuss how to measure an investment's systematic risk and then use that measure to compute its expected return. We can then apply that return expected by investors as our cost of capital.

9. Why is the risk of a portfolio usually less than the average risk of the stocks in the portfolio?

10. Is systematic or unsystematic risk priced? Why?

MyFinanceLab

Here is what you should know after reading this chapter. MyFinanceLab will help you identify what you know, and where to go when you need to practice.

Key Points and Equations	Terms	Online Practice Opportunities
10.1 A First Look at Risk and Return ▶ While in hindsight some investments have had very high returns, they have also had the most volatility over time.		MyFinanceLab Study Plan 10.1
10.2 Historical Risks and Returns of Stocks ▶ The realized return from investing in a stock from time t to $t + 1$ is: $$R_{t+1} = \frac{Div_{t+1} + P_{t+1} - P_t}{P_t} = \frac{Div_{t+1}}{P_t} + \frac{P_{t+1} - P_t}{P_t}$$ $$= \text{Dividend Yield} + \text{Capital Gain Yield} \quad (10.1)$$ ▶ We can calculate the average annual return and variance of realized returns: $$\overline{R} = \frac{1}{T}(R_1 + R_2 + \cdots + R_T) \quad (10.3)$$ $$Var(R) = \frac{1}{T-1}\big((R_1 - \overline{R})^2 + (R_2 - \overline{R})^2 + \cdots + (R_T - \overline{R})^2\big) \quad (10.4)$$ ▶ The square root of the estimated variance is the standard deviation, an estimate of the volatility of returns. ▶ Based on historical data, small stocks have had higher volatility and higher average returns than large stocks, which have higher volatility and higher average returns than bonds. ▶ About 95% of possible outcomes lie within two standard deviations above or below the average outcome.	95% confidence interval, p. 354 average annual return, p. 348 normal distribution, p. 353 realized return, p. 344 standard deviation, p. 350 variance, p. 350	MyFinanceLab Study Plan 10.2 Using Excel: Standard Deviation of Historical Returns
10.3 The Historical Tradeoff Between Risk and Return ▶ There is no clear relationship between the volatility (standard deviation) and return of individual stocks. ▶ Larger stocks tend to have lower overall volatility, but even the largest stocks are typically more risky than a portfolio of large stocks. ▶ All stocks seem to have higher risk and lower returns than would be predicted based on extrapolation of data for large portfolios.		MyFinanceLab Study Plan 10.3

10.4 **Common Versus Independent Risk**		
▸ Common risk is risk that is perfectly linked across investments. ▸ Independent risks are unrelated across investments. ▸ Diversification is the averaging of risks in a large portfolio.	common risk, p. 358 diversification, p. 358 independent risk, p. 358	MyFinanceLab Study Plan 10.4
10.5 **Diversification in Stock Portfolios**		
▸ The total risk of a security represents both unsystematic risk and systematic risk. ▸ Variation in a stock's return due to company- or industry-specific news is called unsystematic risk. ▸ Systematic risk is risk due to market-wide news that affects all stocks simultaneously. ▸ Diversification eliminates unsystematic risk but does not eliminate systematic risk. ▸ Because investors can eliminate unsystematic risk, they do not require a risk premium for it. ▸ Because investors cannot eliminate systematic risk, they must be compensated for it. So, the risk premium for a stock depends on the amount of its systematic risk rather than its total risk.	systematic risk, p. 360 unsystematic risk, p. 360	MyFinanceLab Study Plan 10.5 Interactive Risk and Portfolio Diversification Analysis

Review Questions

1. What does the historical relationship between volatility and return tell us about investors' attitude toward risk?

2. What are the components of a stock's realized return?

3. What is the reasoning behind using the average annual return as a measure of expected return?

4. How does standard deviation relate to the general concept of risk?

5. How does the relationship between the average return and the historical volatility of individual stocks differ from the relationship between the average return and the historical volatility of large, well diversified, portfolios?

6. What is meant by diversification, and how does it relate to common versus independent risk?

7. Which of the following risks of a stock are likely to be unsystematic, diversifiable risks and which are likely to be systematic risks? Which risks will affect the risk premium that investors will demand?
   a. The risk that the founder and CEO retires.
   b. The risk that oil prices rise, increasing production costs.
   c. The risk that a product design is faulty and the product must be recalled.

    d. The risk that the economy slows, reducing demand for the firm's products.

    e. The risk that your best employees will be hired away.

    f. The risk that the new product you expect your R&D division to produce will not materialize.

8. What is the difference between systematic and unsystematic risk?

9. There are three companies working on a new approach to customer-tracking software. You work for a software company that thinks this could be a good addition to its software line. If you invest in one of them versus all three of them,
   a. Is your systematic risk likely to be very different?
   b. Is your unsystematic risk likely to be very different?

10. If you randomly select 10 stocks for a portfolio and 20 other stocks for a different portfolio, which portfolio is likely to have the lower standard deviation? Why?

11. Why doesn't the risk premium of a stock depend on its diversifiable risk?

12. Your spouse works for Southwest Airlines and you work for a grocery store. Is your company or your spouse's company likely to be more exposed to systematic risk?

Problems

All problems in this chapter are available in MyFinanceLab.

Historical Risks and Returns of Stocks

1. You bought a stock one year ago for $50 per share and sold it today for $55 per share. It paid a $1 per share dividend today.
   a. What was your realized return?
   b. How much of the return came from dividend yield and how much came from capital gain?

2. Repeat Problem 1 assuming instead that the stock fell $5 to $45.
   a. Is your capital gain different? Why or why not?
   b. Is your dividend yield different? Why or why not?

3. You have just purchased a share of stock for $20. The company is expected to pay a dividend of $0.50 per share in exactly one year. If you want to earn a 10% return on your investment, what price do you need if you expect to sell the share immediately after it pays the dividend?

4. The table below contains prices and dividends for a stock. All prices are ex-dividend. If you bought the stock on January 1 and sold it on December 31, what is your realized return?

	Price	Div
Jan 1	10.00	
Mar 31	11.00	0.20
June 30	10.50	0.20
Sep 30	11.10	0.20
Dec 31	11.00	0.20

5. Ten annual returns are listed below.

$$-19.9\% \quad 16.6\% \quad 18.0\% \quad -50.0\% \quad 43.3\% \quad 1.2\% \quad -16.5\% \quad 45.6\% \quad 45.2\% \quad -3.0\%$$

   a. What is the arithmetic average return over the 10-year period?
   b. What is the geometric average return over the 10-year period?
   c. If you invested $100 at the beginning of the period, how much would you have at
      the end?

 6. Using the data in the table below, calculate the return for investing in Boeing stock
   from January 1 to December 31.

Stock and Dividend Data for Boeing

Date	Price	Dividend
Jan 1	33.88	
Feb 5	30.67	0.17
May 14	29.49	0.17
Aug 13	32.38	0.17
Nov 12	39.07	0.17
Dec 31	41.99	

7. What was your dividend yield from investing in Boeing in Problem 6? What was your
   capital gain?

8. Consider the following five monthly returns:

$$0.05 \quad -0.02 \quad 0.04 \quad 0.08 \quad -0.01$$

   a. Calculate the arithmetic average return over this period and express your answer
      as a percentage per month.
   b. Calculate the geometric average monthly return over this period.
   c Calculate the monthly variance over this period.
   d. Calculate the monthly standard deviation over this period.

9. Explain the difference between the arithmetic average return you calculated in
   Problem 8a and the geometric average return you calculated in Problem 8b. Are
   both numbers useful? If so, explain why.

10. The last four years of returns for a stock are as follows:

1	2	3	4
−4%	+28%	+12%	+4%

   a. What is the average annual return?
   b. What is the variance of the stock's returns?
   c. What is the standard deviation of the stock's returns?

11. Calculate the 95% confidence intervals for the S&P/TSX Composite Index, the S&P
    500 in CAD, and long-term Government of Canada bonds included in Figures 10.3
    and 10.4.

12. You are choosing between the three investments from Problem 11, and you want
    to be 95% certain that you do not lose more than 18% on your investment. Which
    investments should you choose?

13. You observe a portfolio for five years and determine that its average return is 12% and the standard deviation of its returns is 20%. Can you be 95% confident that this portfolio will not lose more than 40% of its value next year?

Common Versus Independent Risk

14. Consider two local banks. Bank A has 100 loans outstanding, each for $1 million, that it expects will be repaid today. Each loan has a 5% probability of default, in which case the bank is not repaid anything. The chance of default is independent across all the loans. Bank B has only one loan of $100 million outstanding, which it also expects will be repaid today. It also has a 5% probability of not being repaid. Explain the difference between the type of risk each bank faces. Which bank faces less risk? Why?

15. You are a risk-averse investor who is considering investing in one of two economies. The expected return and volatility of all stocks in both economies is the same. In the first economy, all stocks move together—in good times all prices rise together and in bad times they all fall together. In the second economy, stock returns are independent—one stock increasing in price has no effect on the prices of other stocks. Which economy would you choose to invest in? Explain.

11

Systematic Risk and the Equity Risk Premium

notation

β_i	beta of security i with respect to the market portfolio	P_i	price per share of security i
$Corr(R_i, R_j)$	correlation between the returns of security i and security j	r_f	risk-free interest rate
$E[R_i]$	expected return of security i	R_P	return of portfolio P
$E[R_{Mkt}]$	expected return of the market portfolio	$SD(R_i)$	standard deviation (volatility) of the return of security i
MV_i	total market value (market capitalization) of security i	$Var(R_i)$	variance of the return of security i
N_i	number of shares outstanding of security i	w_i	fraction of the portfolio invested in security i (its relative *weight* in the portfolio)

INTERVIEW WITH Alexander Morgan,
Pantheon Ventures

Boston University, 2005

Alexander "Xan" Morgan is an investment associate for Pantheon Ventures, a global private equity firm with more than $23 billion in assets under management. A 2005 graduate of Boston University with finance and entrepreneurship concentrations, he is based in the firm's San Francisco office where he analyzes investments in North American private equity funds. Xan credits his finance education and the experience of applying concepts to case studies with preparing him for this position. "Regardless of how simple case study concepts seemed, I now find that they are intertwined in my everyday work," he says. "Studying portfolio construction provided a broad knowledge base that enables me to perform my job better. Whether I'm analyzing a single investment's performance or focusing on the potential growth of a particular sector, I must always consider whether the fund will fit within our current portfolio."

Diversification is critical to building portfolios and mitigating risk. "If you fail to properly diversify your portfolio, you become far more susceptible to overall market/sector cycles," Xan explains. "In 2000–01, for example, investors with undiversified portfolios of mostly internet-related investments saw the value of their portfolios sharply decline when the entire sector crashed."

Xan considers the different types of associated risk when evaluating investments. "You cannot eliminate systematic risk through diversification," he says. "During the recent subprime mortgage crisis and resulting economic slowdown, even well-diversified funds were negatively affected to some extent by the systemic shock." Unlike systematic risk, unsystematic risk—specific to a single security—can be partially mitigated through portfolio diversification. "If one investment in a portfolio of 50 investments underperforms, it probably will not significantly affect your performance. A well-diversified portfolio can absorb the loss through the stability of other investments."

Investing in a well-diversified "market index" portfolio is a way to minimize unsystematic risk and reduce sector-specific systematic risk. "If you invest across a wide variety of sectors, poor performance from one investment (unsystematic risk) will not have a large impact on your portfolio. Also, if an entire sector faces a downturn (more systematic-type risk), investments in other sectors may still perform well enough to offset your losses."

In Chapter 10, we started our exploration of the tradeoff between risk and return. We found that for large portfolios, while investors should expect to experience higher returns for higher risk, the same does not hold true for individual stocks. Stocks have both unsystematic, diversifiable risk and systematic, undiversifiable risk; only the systematic risk is rewarded with higher expected returns. With no reward for bearing unsystematic risk, rational investors should choose to diversify.

Put yourself in the role of a financial manager at a company such as Research In Motion. One part of your job would be to calculate Research In Motion's cost of equity capital so that its managers know what return its equity investors require. Recall that in Chapter 5 we defined the cost of capital as the best available expected return offered in the market on an investment of comparable risk and term. Since only systematic risk contributes to expected returns, we need to measure the systematic risk of Research In Motion and map it into an expected return for Research In Motion. To do so, we need to think about Research In Motion's stock the way our investors would—as part of a portfolio. As a result, we begin where we left off in the last chapter: with portfolios. After learning how to calculate the risk and expected return of a portfolio, we will focus on the biggest portfolio of them all: the portfolio of *all* risky securities. This portfolio has no diversifiable risk left and can be used as a baseline for measuring systematic risk. From there, we will develop a simple, powerful model that relates the systematic risk of an investment to its expected return. In other words, the model says that the return we should expect on any investment is equal to the risk-free rate of return plus a risk premium proportional to the amount of systematic risk in the investment.

The Expected Return of a Portfolio

In the last chapter, we learned the important role that portfolios play in reducing unsystematic risk. As financial managers, we have to be mindful that investors hold our company's stock as part of a larger portfolio. Thus, it is important to understand how portfolios work and the implications for the return our investors expect on the stock of our company and the projects we undertake in that company.

Portfolio Weights

We begin by calculating the return and expected return of a portfolio. For example, consider a portfolio with 2000 shares of WestJet worth $20 per share ($40,000 total), and 1000 shares of Barrick worth $60 per share ($60,000 total). The total value of the portfolio is $100,000, so WestJet is 40% of the portfolio and Barrick is 60% of the portfolio. More generally, we can describe a portfolio by its **portfolio weights**, which are the fractions of the total investment in the portfolio held in each individual investment in the portfolio:

portfolio weight
The fraction of the total investment in a portfolio held in each individual investment in the portfolio.

$$w_i = \frac{\text{Value of investment } i}{\text{Total value of portfolio}} \qquad (11.1)$$

These portfolio weights add up to 100% (that is, $w_1 + w_2 + \cdots + w_n = 100\%$), so that they represent the way we have divided our money between the different individual investments in the portfolio. We can confirm the portfolio weights for our portfolio of WestJet and Barrick:

$$w_{WestJet} = \frac{2000 \times \$20}{100,000} = 40\% \quad \text{and} \quad w_{Barrick} = \frac{1000 \times \$60}{100,000} = 60\%$$

Portfolio Returns

Once you know the portfolio weight, you can calculate the return on the portfolio. For example, take the portfolio of WestJet and Barrick. If WestJet earns a 10% return and Barrick earns a 15% return, then 40% of the portfolio earns 10% and 60% of the portfolio earns 15%, so the portfolio as a whole earns: $(0.40)(10\%) + (0.60)(15\%) = 13\%$.

return on a portfolio
The weighted average of the returns on the investments in a portfolio, where the weights correspond to the portfolio weights.

The **return on a portfolio** is the weighted average of the returns on the investments in the portfolio, where the weights correspond to portfolio weights.

Formally, suppose $w_1, \ldots, w_n$ are the portfolio weights of the n investments in a portfolio and these investments have returns $R_1, \ldots, R_n$, then the formula for the return on the portfolio is:

$$R_P = w_1 R_1 + w_2 R_2 + \cdots + w_n R_n \qquad (11.2)$$

EXAMPLE 11.1

Calculating Portfolio Returns

Problem

Suppose you invest $100,000 and buy 2000 shares of WestJet at $20 per share ($40,000) and 1000 shares of Barrick at $60 per share ($60,000). If WestJet's stock goes up to $24 per share and Barrick stock falls to $57 per share and neither paid dividends, what is the new value of the portfolio? What return did the portfolio earn? Show that Equation 11.2 is true by calculating the individual returns of the stocks and multiplying them by their weights in the portfolio. If you don't buy or sell any shares after the price change, what are the new portfolio weights?

Solution

▶ **Plan**

Your portfolio: 2000 shares of WestJet: $20 → $24 ($4 capital gain)

1000 shares of Barrick: $60 → $57 ($3 capital loss)

A. To calculate the return on your portfolio, compute its value using the new prices and compare it to the original $100,000 investment.

B. To confirm that Equation 11.2 is true, compute the return on each stock individually using Equation 10.1 from Chapter 10, multiply those returns by their original weights in the portfolio, and compare your answer to the return you just calculated for the portfolio as a whole.

▶ **Execute**

The new value of your WestJet stock is $2000 \times \$24 = \$48,000$, and the new value of your Barrick stock is $1000 \times \$57 = \$57,000$. So, the new value of your portfolio is $\$48,000 + 57,000 = \$105,000$, for a gain of $5000, or a 5% return on your initial $100,000 investment.

Since neither stock paid any dividends, we calculate their returns simply as the capital gain or loss divided by the purchase price. The return on WestJet stock was $4/$20 = 20%, and the return on Barrick stock was $-$3/$60 = -5\%$.

The initial portfolio weights were $40,000/$100,000 = 40% for WestJet and $60,000/$100,000 = 60% for Barrick, so we can also compute the return of the portfolio from Equation 11.2 as:

$$R_P = w_{WestJet}R_{WestJet} + w_{Barrick}R_{Barrick} = 0.40(20\%) + 0.60(-5\%) = 5\%$$

After the price change, the new portfolio weights are equal to the value of your investment in each stock divided by the new portfolio value:

$$w_{WestJet} = \frac{2000 \times \$24}{105,000} = 45.71\% \quad \text{and} \quad w_{Barrick} = \frac{1000 \times \$57}{105,000} = 54.29\%$$

As a check on your work, always make sure that your portfolio weights sum to 100%!

▶ **Evaluate**

The $3000 loss on your investment in Barrick was offset by the $8000 gain in your investment in WestJet, for a total gain of $5000, or 5%. The same result comes from giving a 40% weight to the 20% return on WestJet and a 60% weight to the –5% loss on Barrick—you have a total net return of 5%.

After a year, the portfolio weight on WestJet has increased and the weight on Barrick has decreased. Note that without trading, the portfolio weights will increase for the stock(s) in the portfolio whose returns are above the overall portfolio return.

The charts below show the initial and ending weights on WestJet (shown in yellow) and Barrick (shown in red).

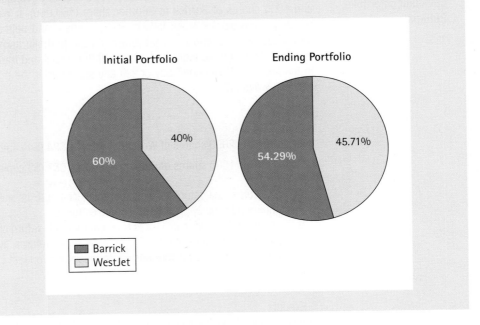

Expected Portfolio Return

expected return of a portfolio The weighted average of expected returns of the investments in a portfolio, where the weights correspond to the portfolio weights.

As we showed in Chapter 10, you can use the historical average return of a security as its expected return. With these expected returns, you can compute the **expected return of a portfolio**, which is simply the weighted average of the expected returns of the investments within it, using the portfolio weights:

$$E[R_P] = w_1 E[R_1] + w_2 E[R_2] + \cdots + w_n E[R_n] \qquad (11.3)$$

We started by stating that you can describe a portfolio by its weights. These weights are used in computing both a portfolio's return and its expected return. Table 11.1 summarizes these concepts.

TABLE 11.1	Term	Concept	Equation
Summary of Portfolio Concepts	Portfolio Weight	The relative investment in your portfolio	$w_i = \dfrac{\text{Value of investment } i}{\text{Total value of portfolio}}$
	Portfolio Return	The total return earned on your portfolio, accounting for the returns of all of the securities in the portfolio and their weights	$R_P = w_1 R_1 + w_2 R_2 + \cdots + w_n R_n$
	Portfolio Expected Return	The return you can expect to earn on your portfolio, given the expected returns of the securities in that portfolio and the relative amount you have invested in each	$E[R_P] = w_1 E[R_1] + w_2 E[R_2] + \cdots + w_n E[R_n]$

EXAMPLE 11.2

Portfolio Expected Return

Problem

Suppose you invest $10,000 in Forzani Group Ltd. (ticker symbol: FGL) stock, and $30,000 in TransCanada Corp. (ticker symbol: TRP) stock. You expect a return of 10% for Forzani, and 16% for TransCanada. What is the expected return for your portfolio?

Solution

▶ **Plan**

You have a total of $40,000 invested:

$10,000/$40,000 = 25% in Forzani: $E[R_{FGL}] = 10\%$

$30,000/$40,000 = 75% in TransCanada: $E[R_{TRP}] = 16\%$

Using Equation 11.3, compute the expected return on your whole portfolio by weighting the expected returns of the stocks in your portfolio by their portfolio weights.

▶ **Execute**

The expected return on your portfolio is:

$$E[R_P] = w_{FGL}E[R_{FGL}] + w_{TRP}E[R_{TRP}]$$

$$E[R_P] = 0.25 \times 10\% + 0.75 \times 16\% = 14.5\%$$

▶ **Evaluate**

The importance of each stock for the expected return of the overall portfolio is determined by the relative amount of money you have invested in it. Most (75%) of your money is invested in TransCanada, so the overall expected return of the portfolio is much closer to TransCanada's expected return than it is to Forzani's.

Concept Check

1. What do the weights in a portfolio tell us?
2. How is the expected return of a portfolio related to the expected returns of the stocks in the portfolio?

11.2 The Volatility of a Portfolio

Investors in a company such as Research In Motion care not only about the return, but also about the risk of their portfolios. Understanding how Research In Motion's investors think about risk requires us to understand how to calculate the risk of a portfolio. As explained in Chapter 10, when we combine stocks in a portfolio, some of their risk is eliminated through diversification. The amount of risk that will remain depends on the degree to which the stocks share common risk. The **volatility of a portfolio** is the total risk, measured as standard deviation, of the portfolio. In this section, we describe the tools to quantify the degree to which two stocks share risk and to determine the volatility of a portfolio.

volatility of a portfolio
The total risk, measured as standard deviation, of a portfolio.

Diversifying Risks

Let's begin with a simple example of how risk changes when stocks are combined in a portfolio. Table 11.2 shows returns for three hypothetical stocks, along with their average returns and volatilities. Note that while the three stocks have the same volatility and average return, the pattern of returns differs. In years when the airline stocks performed well, the oil stock tended to do poorly (see 2005 to 2006), and when the airlines did poorly, the oil stock tended to do well (see 2009 to 2010).

TABLE 11.2		Stock Returns			Portfolio Returns	
					(1)	(2)
Returns for Three Stocks, and Portfolios of Pairs of Stocks	Year	North Jet	South Jet	Alberta Oil	Half N.J. and Half S.J.	Half S.J. and Half A.O.
	2005	21%	9%	−2%	15.0%	3.5%
	2006	30%	21%	−5%	25.5%	8.0%
	2007	7%	7%	9%	7.0%	8.0%
	2008	−5%	−2%	21%	−3.5%	9.5%
	2009	−2%	−5%	30%	−3.5%	12.5%
	2010	9%	30%	7%	19.5%	18.5%
	Avg. Return	10.0%	10.0%	10.0%	10.0%	10.0%
	Volatility	13.4%	13.4%	13.4%	12.1%	5.1%

Table 11.2 also shows the returns for two portfolios of the stocks. The first portfolio is an equal investment in the two airlines, North Jet and South Jet. The second portfolio is an equal investment in South Jet and Alberta Oil. The bottom two rows display the average return and volatility for each stock and portfolio of stocks. Note that the 10% average return of both portfolios is equal to the 10% average return of the stocks, consistent with Equation 11.3. However, as Figure 11.1 illustrates, their volatilities (standard deviations)—12.1% for portfolio 1 and 5.1% for portfolio 2—are very different from the 13.4% volatility for the individual stocks *and* from each other.

This example demonstrates two important things that we learned in the last chapter. First, *by combining stocks into a portfolio, we reduce risk through diversification.* Because the stocks do not move identically, some of the risk is averaged out in a portfolio. As a result, both portfolios have lower risk than the individual stocks.

Second, *the amount of risk that is eliminated in a portfolio depends on the degree to which the stocks face common risks and move together.* Because the two airline stocks tend to perform well or poorly at the same time, the portfolio of airline stocks has a volatility that is only slightly lower than the volatility of the individual stocks. The airline and oil stocks, on the other hand, do not move together. Indeed, they tend to move in opposite directions. As a result, more risk is cancelled out, making that portfolio much less risky.

Measuring Stocks' Comovement: Correlation

Figure 11.1 emphasizes the fact that to find the risk of a portfolio, we need to know more than just the risk of the component stocks: we need to know the degree to which the stocks' returns move together. The stocks' *correlation* is such a measure, ranging from −1 to +1.[1]

---

[1]Correlation is scaled covariance and is defined as:

$$Corr(R_i, R_j) = \frac{Cov(R_i, R_j)}{SD(R_i)\, SD(R_j)}$$

FIGURE 11.1

Volatility of Airline and Oil Portfolios

The figures graph the portfolio returns from Table 11.2. In panel (a), we see that the airline stocks move in synch with each other, so that a portfolio made up of the two airline stocks does not achieve much diversification. In panel (b), because the airline and oil stocks often move in opposite directions, a portfolio of South Jet and Alberta Oil achieves greater diversification and lower portfolio volatility. Because both stocks have an average return of 10%, so does the portfolio, but it achieves that return with much less volatility than either of the stocks.

Panel (a): Portfolio split equally between South Jet and North Jet

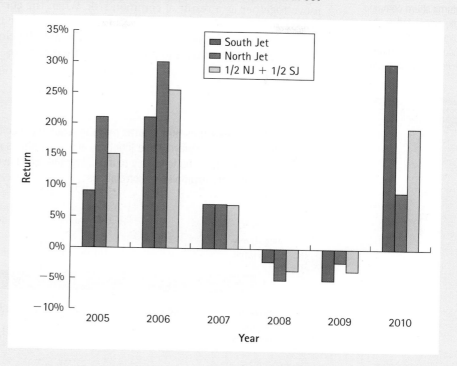

Panel (b): Portfolio split equally between South Jet and Alberta Oil

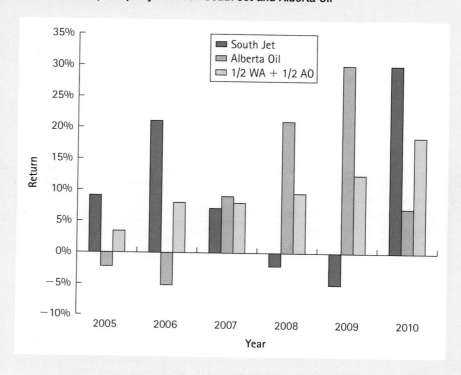

correlation A measure of the degree to which returns share common risk, calculated as the covariance of the returns divided by the standard deviation of each return.

As Figure 11.2 shows, **correlation** is a barometer of the degree to which the returns share common risk. The closer the correlation is to +1, the more the returns tend to move together as a result of common risk. When the correlation equals 0, the returns are *uncorrelated*; that is, they have no tendency to move together or in opposite directions. Independent risks are uncorrelated. Finally, the closer the correlation is to −1, the more the returns tend to move in opposite directions.

FIGURE 11.2

Correlation

The correlation measures how returns move in relation to each other. The correlation is between +1 (returns always move together) and −1 (returns always move oppositely). Independent risks have no tendency to move together and have zero correlation. See Table 11.3 for more examples of correlations.

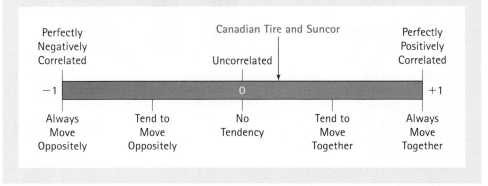

When will stock returns be highly correlated with each other? Stock returns will tend to move together if they are affected similarly by economic events. Thus, stocks in the same industry tend to have more highly correlated returns than stocks in different industries. This tendency is illustrated in Table 11.3, which shows the volatility (standard deviation) of individual stock returns and the correlation between them for several common stocks. The blue-shaded boxes along the diagonal show the correlation of a stock with itself—which has to be 1 (a stock is perfectly correlated

TABLE 11.3

Estimated Annual Volatilities and Correlations for Selected Stocks (Based on Monthly Returns, 2005–2009)

STANDARD DEVIATION	BCE 23%	Canadian Tire 23%	Forzani 40%	Research In Motion 55%	Shoppers Drug Mart 16%	Suncor 38%	WestJet 45%
BCE	1.00	0.27	0.27	0.26	0.12	0.17	0.38
Canadian Tire	0.27	1.00	0.35	0.30	0.02	0.29	0.13
Forzani	0.27	0.35	1.00	0.51	0.02	0.36	0.03
Research In Motion	0.26	0.30	0.51	1.00	0.26	0.28	0.18
Shoppers Drug Mart	0.12	0.02	0.02	0.26	1.00	0.27	0.13
Suncor	0.17	0.29	0.36	0.28	0.27	1.00	0.08
WestJet	0.38	0.13	0.03	0.18	0.13	0.08	1.00

Source: Canadian Financial Markets Research Center (CFMRC).

with itself). The table can be read across the rows or down the columns. Each correlation is repeated twice. For example, reading across the Research In Motion row, the correlation between Research In Motion and Forzani (orange box) is 0.51, which you could also find by reading across the Forzani row for the correlation between Forzani and Research In Motion. These two companies have the highest correlation in the table, 0.51. Forzani (a sporting goods retailer) belongs to the consumer discretionary industry group, whereas Research In Motion (famous for its BlackBerry product line) is in the information technology group. It would seem to make sense that consumers would spend more (or less) during the same economic circumstances for both of these companies' products. All of the correlations are positive, showing the general tendency of stocks to move together. The lowest correlation is shown in the green boxes for Forzani and Shoppers Drug Mart, which is 0.02, implying that there is little relationship between the consumer discretionary and consumer staples industries. Figure 11.3 shows scatter plots for the returns of Forzani and Research In Motion, and Forzani and Shoppers Drug Mart. While there is a clear relationship between the returns of Forzani and Research In Motion, the plot for Forzani and Shoppers Drug Mart looks like an unrelated cloud of returns.

USING EXCEL

Calculating
the Correlation
Between Two Sets
of Returns

The correlations presented in Table 11.3 were all calculated by comparing the returns of two stocks. Here we describe how you can use Excel to calculate these correlations.

1. Enter or import the historical returns for the two stocks into Excel.

2. Next, from the pull-down menus, choose **Tools > Data Analysis > Correlation**.

3. For the "Input Range" box, highlight the two columns of returns, as shown in the screen capture below.

4. Click OK.

5. The answer will appear in a new worksheet as the correlation between "column 1" and "column 2."

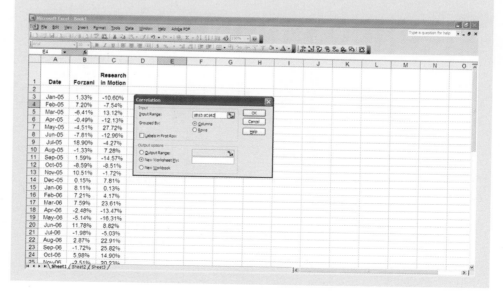

FIGURE 11.3

Scatter Plots of Returns

Plots of pairs of monthly returns for Forzani and Research In Motion, and Forzani and Shoppers Drug Mart. Notice the positive relationship between Forzani and Research In Motion, which move up and down together, versus the lack of a relationship between Forzani and Shoppers Drug Mart.

Source: Canadian Financial Markets Research Center (CFMRC).

Panel (a) Monthly Returns for Forzani and Research In Motion

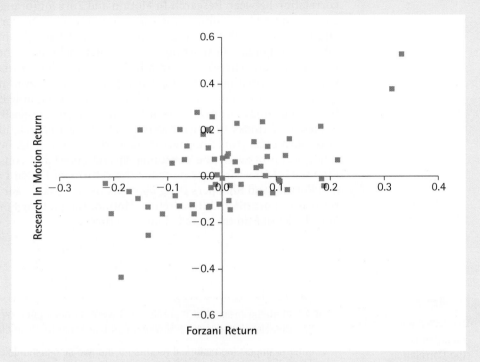

Panel (b) Monthly Returns for Forzani and Shoppers Drug Mart

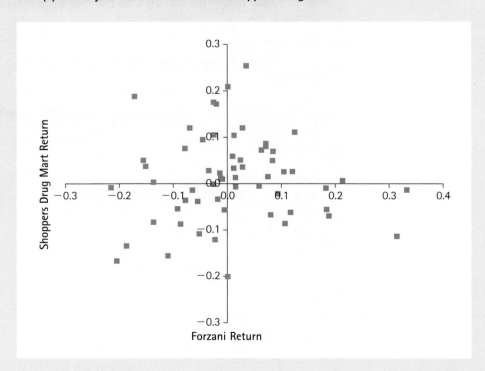

Computing a Portfolio's Variance and Standard Deviation

We now have the tools to formally compute portfolio variance. The formula for the variance of a two-stock portfolio is:

$$Var(R_P) = \overbrace{w_1^2 SD(R_1)^2}^{\substack{\text{Accounting} \\ \text{for the risk} \\ \text{of stock 1}}} + \overbrace{w_2^2 SD(R_2)^2}^{\substack{\text{Accounting} \\ \text{for the risk} \\ \text{of stock 2}}} + \overbrace{2w_1 w_2 Corr(R_1, R_2)SD(R_1)SD(R_2)}^{\substack{\text{Adjustment for how} \\ \text{much the two stocks move together}}} \quad (11.4)$$

The three parts of Equation 11.4 each account for an important determinant of the overall variance of the portfolio: the risk of stock 1, the risk of stock 2, and an adjustment for how much the two stocks move together (their correlation, given as $Corr(R_1, R_2)$).[2] The equation demonstrates that with a positive amount invested in each stock, the more the stocks move together and the higher their correlation, the more volatile the portfolio will be. The portfolio will have the greatest variance if the stocks have a perfect positive correlation of $+1$. In fact, when combining stocks into a portfolio, unless the stocks all have a perfect positive correlation of $+1$ with each other, the risk of the portfolio will be lower than the weighted average volatility of the individual stocks (as shown in Figure 11.1). Contrast this fact with a portfolio's expected return. *The expected return of a portfolio is equal to the weighted average expected return of its stocks, but the volatility of a portfolio is less than the weighted average volatility. As a result, it's clear that we can eliminate some volatility by diversifying.* Equation 11.4 formalizes the concept of diversification introduced in the last chapter. In Example 11.3, we use Equation 11.4 to compute the volatility of a portfolio.

EXAMPLE 11.3

Computing the Volatility of a Two-Stock Portfolio

Problem

Using the data from Table 11.3, what is the volatility (standard deviation) of a portfolio with equal amounts invested in Forzani (ticker symbol: FGL) and Suncor (ticker symbol: SU) stock? What is the standard deviation of a portfolio with equal amounts invested in Forzani and WestJet (ticker symbol: WJA)?

Solution

▶ **Plan**

	Weight	Volatility	Correlation with Forzani
Forzani	0.50	0.40	1
Suncor	0.50	0.38	0.36
Forzani	0.50	0.40	1
WestJet	0.50	0.45	0.03

A. With the portfolio weights, volatility, and correlations of the stocks in the two portfolios, we have all the information we need to use Equation 11.4 to compute the variance of each portfolio.

---

[2]For three stocks, the formula is

$$Var(R_P) = w_1^2 SD(R_1)^2 + w_2^2 SD(R_2)^2 + w_3^2 SD(R_3)^2 + 2w_1 w_2 Corr(R_1, R_2)SD(R_1)SD(R_2)$$
$$+ 2w_2 w_3 Corr(R_2, R_3)SD(R_2)SD(R_3) + 2w_1 w_3 Corr(R_1, R_3)SD(R_1)SD(R_3)$$

and for n stocks, it is

$$\sum_{i=1}^{n}\sum_{j=1}^{n} w_i w_j\, Corr(R_i, R_j)SD(R_i)SD(R_j)$$

B. After computing the portfolio's variance, we can take the square root to get the portfolio's standard deviation.

▶ **Execute**

For Forzani and Suncor, from Equation 11.4 the portfolio's variance is:

$$Var(R_P) = w_{FGL}^2 SD(R_{FGL})^2 + w_{SU}^2 SD(R_{SU})^2$$
$$+ 2w_{FGL}w_{SU} Corr(R_{FGL}, R_{SU})SD(R_{FGL})SD(R_{SU})$$
$$= (0.50)^2(0.40)^2 + (0.50)^2 (0.38)^2 + 2(0.50)(0.50)(0.36)(0.40)(0.38)$$
$$= 0.1035$$

The standard deviation is therefore
$$SD(R_P) = \sqrt{Var(R_P)} = \sqrt{0.1035} = 0.3217, \text{ or } 32.17\%$$

For the portfolio of Forzani and WestJet:

$$Var(R_P) = w_{FGL}^2 SD(R_{FGL})^2 + w_{WJA}^2 SD(R_{WJA})^2$$
$$+ 2w_{FGL}w_{WJA} Corr(R_{FGL}, R_{WJA})SD(R_{FGL})SD(R_{WJA})$$
$$= (0.50)^2(0.40)^2 + (0.50)^2 (0.45)^2 + 2(0.50)(0.50)(0.03)(0.23)(0.45)$$
$$= 0.0922$$

The standard deviation in this case is:
$$SD(R_P) = \sqrt{Var(R_P)} = \sqrt{0.0933} = 0.3036 \text{ or } 30.36\%$$

▶ **Evaluate**

The weights, standard deviations, and correlation of the two stocks are needed to compute the variance and then the standard deviation of the portfolio. Here, we computed the standard deviation of the portfolio of Forzani and Suncor to be 32.2% and of Forzani and WestJet to be 30.6%. Note that the both portfolios are less volatile than either of the individual stocks. The portfolio of Forzani and WestJet is also less volatile than the portfolio of Forzani and Suncor. Even though WestJet is more volatile than Suncor, its much lower correlation with Forzani leads to greater diversification benefits in the portfolio.

The Volatility of a Large Portfolio

We can gain additional benefits of diversification by holding more than two stocks in our portfolio. As we add more stocks to our portfolio, the diversifiable firm-specific risk for each stock matters less and less. Only risk that is common to all of the stocks in the portfolio continues to matter.

NOBEL PRIZE   **Harry Markowitz**

The techniques that allow an investor to find the portfolio with the highest expected return for any level of standard deviation (or volatility) were developed in an article, "Portfolio Selection," published in the *Journal of Finance* in 1952 by Harry Markowitz. Markowitz's approach has become one of the main methods of portfolio optimization used on Wall Street. In recognition of his contribution, Markowitz was the co-winner of the Nobel Prize for Economics in 1990.

equally weighted portfolio A portfolio in which the same dollar amount is invested in each stock.

In Figure 11.4, we graph the volatility for an *equally weighted portfolio* with different numbers of stocks. In an **equally weighted portfolio**, the same amount of money is invested in each stock. Note that the volatility declines as the number of stocks in the portfolio grows. In fact, nearly half the volatility of the individual stocks is eliminated in a large portfolio by diversification. The benefit of diversification is most dramatic initially—the decrease in volatility going from one to two stocks is much larger than the decrease going from 100 to 101 stocks. Even for a very large portfolio, however, we cannot eliminate all of the risk—the systematic risk remains.

FIGURE 11.4

Volatility of an Equally Weighted Portfolio Versus the Number of Stocks

The graph in panel (b) is based on the data in panel (a). Note that the volatility declines as we increase the number of stocks in the portfolio. Yet even in a very large portfolio, systematic (market) risk remains. Also note that the volatility declines at a decreasing rate (the effect of going from one to two stocks, an 8 percentage point decrease in volatility, is bigger than the effect of going from four to five stocks, a 1.1 percentage point decrease). The graph is formed based on the assumption that each stock has a volatility of 40% and a correlation with other stocks of 0.28. Both are average for large stocks.

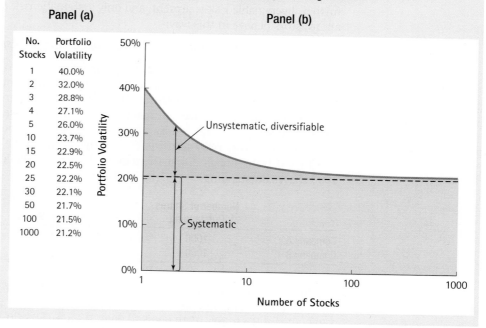

No. Stocks	Portfolio Volatility
1	40.0%
2	32.0%
3	28.8%
4	27.1%
5	26.0%
10	23.7%
15	22.9%
20	22.5%
25	22.2%
30	22.1%
50	21.7%
100	21.5%
1000	21.2%

Concept Check

3. What determines how much risk will be eliminated by combining stocks in a portfolio?
4. When do stocks have more or less correlation?

11.3 Measuring Systematic Risk

Our goal is to understand the impact of risk on the firm's investors. By understanding how they view risk, we can quantify the relationship between risk and required return to produce a discount rate for our present value calculations. In Chapter 10, we established that the only risk that is related to return is systematic risk, but standard deviation measures *total* risk, including the unsystematic part. We need a way to measure just the systematic risk of an investment opportunity. The previous section contains two important insights that we will now build on to determine the sensitivity of individual stocks to risk. To recap,

1. *The amount of a stock's risk that is removed by diversification depends on its correlation with other stocks in the portfolio.* For example, we showed in Example 11.3 that much less of Forzani's risk is diversified away in a portfolio with Suncor than in a portfolio with WestJet.

2. *If you build a large enough portfolio, you can remove all unsystematic risk by diversification, but you will still be left with systematic risk.* Figure 11.4 shows that as the number of stocks in your portfolio grows, the unsystematic positive and negative events affecting only a few stocks will cancel out, leaving systematic events as the only source of risk for the portfolio.

Role of the Market Portfolio

As we explained in the last chapter, investors should diversify their portfolios in order to reduce their risk. If investors choose their portfolios optimally, they will do so until no further diversifiable risk is present, and only systematic risk remains. Let's assume that all investors behave in this way:

Suppose all investors hold portfolios that contain only systematic risk.

If that is the case, then consider the portfolio we obtain by combining the portfolios of every investor. Because each investor's portfolio contains only systematic risk, the same is true for this "aggregate" portfolio. So, the aggregate portfolio held by all investors is a fully diversified, optimal portfolio. Moreover, we can identify this portfolio: because all securities are held by someone, the aggregate portfolio contains all shares outstanding of every risky security. We call this portfolio the **market portfolio**.

market portfolio The portfolio of all risky investments, held in proportion to their value.

To illustrate, imagine that there are only two companies in the world, each with 1000 shares outstanding:

	Number of Shares Outstanding	Price per Share	Market Capitalization
Company A	1000	$40	$40,000
Company B	1000	$10	$10,000

In this simple setting, the market portfolio consists of 1000 shares of each stock and has a total value of $50,000. Stock A's portfolio weight is therefore 80% ($40,000/$50,000) and B's is 20% ($10,000/$50,000). Because all of the shares of A and all of the shares of B must be held by someone, the sum of all investors' portfolios must equal this market portfolio. Note from this example that the portfolio weight of each stock is proportional to the total market value of its outstanding shares, which is called its **market capitalization**:

market capitalization The total market value of equity; equals the market price per share times the number of shares.

$$\text{Market Capitalization} = (\text{Number of Shares Outstanding}) \times (\text{Price per Share}) \qquad (11.5)$$

More generally, the market portfolio will consist of all risky securities in the market, with portfolio weights proportional to their market capitalization. Thus, for example, if Research In Motion's market capitalization were equal to 3% of the total market value of all securities, then it would have a 3% weight in the market portfolio. Because stocks are held in proportion to their market capitalization (value), we say that the market portfolio is a **value-weighted portfolio**.

value-weighted portfolio A portfolio in which each security is held in proportion to its market capitalization.

Because the market portfolio contains only systematic risk, we can use it to measure the amount of systematic risk of other securities in the market. In particular, any risk that is correlated with the market portfolio must be systematic risk. Therefore, by looking at the sensitivity of a stock's return to the overall market, we can calculate the amount of systematic risk the stock has.

Stock Market Indexes as the Market Portfolio

market proxy A portfolio whose return is believed to closely track the true market portfolio.

market index The market value of a broad-based portfolio of securities.

While the market portfolio is easy to identify, actually constructing it is a different matter. Because it should contain all risky securities, we need to include all stocks, bonds, real estate, commodities, and so on, both in Canada and around the word. Clearly, it would be impractical if not impossible to collect and update returns on all risky assets everywhere. In practice, we use a **market proxy**—a portfolio whose return should track the underlying, unobservable market portfolio. The most common proxy portfolios are *market indexes*, which are broadly used to represent the performance of the stock market. A **market index** reports the value of a particular portfolio of securities.

S&P/TSX Composite Index.   The most familiar index in Canada is the S&P/TSX Composite Index. The weights of the components of the index are determined by the market capitalization of the companies in it. Even though the index includes 234 (as of December 2010) of the over 5000 public firms in Canada, because the index includes the largest stocks, it represents about 95% of Canada's equity market capitalization.

S&P/TSX 60 Index.   Another popular index is the S&P/TSX 60. The weights of the 60 companies' stocks are determined partially by their industry sectors that make up the broader composite index. The companies that make up the S&P/TSX 60 Index are large and very liquid. Because of the market capitalization and liquidity of the stocks, investors and portfolio managers consider the S&P/TSX 60 Index easier to replicate than the S&P/TSX Composite Index.

Dow Jones Industrial Average.   Most Canadian media also report on the U.S. stock market. The most widely quoted stock index in the United States is the Dow Jones Industrial Average, or DJIA. This index consists of a portfolio of 30 large, industrial stocks. While these stocks are chosen to be representative of different sectors of the economy, they clearly do not represent the entire market. Despite being non-representative of the entire market, the DJIA remains widely cited because it is one of the oldest stock market indexes (it was first published in 1884).

S&P 500.   A better representation of the entire U.S. stock market is the S&P 500, a value-weighted portfolio of 500 of the largest U.S. stocks.[3] The S&P 500 was the first widely publicized value-weighted index (S&P began publishing its index in 1923), and it is a standard benchmark for professional investors. This index is the most commonly cited index when evaluating the overall performance of the U.S. stock market. It is also the standard portfolio used to represent "the market" in practice. Even though the S&P 500 includes only 500 of the over 7000 individual U.S. stocks, because the S&P 500 includes the largest stocks, it represents more than 70% of the U.S. stock market in terms of market capitalization.

---

[3]There is no precise formula for determining which stocks will be included in the S&P 500. Standard & Poor's periodically replaces stocks in the index (on average about seven or eight stocks per year). While size is one criterion, Standard & Poor's also tries to maintain appropriate representation of different segments of the economy and chooses firms that are leaders in their industries.

> ## Index Funds
>
> One easy way investors can buy (an approximation of) the market portfolio is to invest in an index fund, which in turn invests in stocks and other securities with the goal of matching the performance of a particular market index. Many mutual fund companies offer index funds. For example, BlackRock Asset Management Canada Limited has several funds called iShares that trade on the TSX. Other subsidiaries of BlackRock Inc. have funds that trade on exchanges around the world. For Canadian investors, iShares are available that replicate the Canadian indexes and the different industry sectors for Canada. Also traded on the TSX are iShares that replicate the S&P 500 and other international stock indices.
>
> The Vanguard Group, which specializes in index funds, was the second-largest mutual fund company in 2006. Vanguard was founded in 1975 by John Bogle, who advocates the benefits of index funds for individual investors. Comparing index funds to the strategy of trying to pick hot stocks, Bogle reportedly said: "What's the point of looking for the needle in the haystack? Why not own the haystack?"
>
> In August of 1976, Vanguard created its well-known S&P 500 Index Fund, which tries to match the performance of the S&P 500 index as closely as possible. As of May 2010, this fund had just under $100 billion in assets. Vanguard's Total Stock Market Index Fund is designed to track the performance of the MSCI US Broad Market index, an index that measures the performance of all U.S. stocks with available price data.

Market Risk and Beta

Now that we have established that the market portfolio is a good basis for measuring systematic risk, we can use the relationship between an individual stock's returns and the market portfolio's returns to measure the amount of systematic risk present in that stock. The reasoning is that if a stock's returns are highly sensitive to the market portfolio's returns, then that stock is highly sensitive to systematic risk. That is, events that are systematic and affect the whole market also are strongly reflected in its returns. If a stock's returns do not depend on the market's returns, then it has little systematic risk—when systematic events happen, they are not strongly reflected in its returns. So stocks whose returns are volatile *and* are highly correlated with the market's returns are the riskiest in the sense that they have the most systematic risk.

Specifically, we can measure a stock's systematic risk by estimating the stock's sensitivity to the market portfolio, which we refer to as its **beta(β)**:

beta (β) The expected percent change in the excess return of a security for a 1% change in the excess return of the market (or other benchmark) portfolio.

> *A stock's beta (β) is the percentage change in its excess return that we expect for each 1% change in the market's excess return.*

There are many data sources that provide estimates of beta based on historical data. Typically, these data sources estimate betas using two to five years of weekly or monthly returns, and use the S&P/TSX Composite Index as the market portfolio for Canadian stocks or the S&P 500 as the market portfolio for U.S. stocks. Table 11.4 shows estimates of betas for a number of large stocks and their industries. You can find the betas of other companies by going to the Google Finance website, finance.google.ca, or the Yahoo! Canada Finance website, ca.finance.yahoo.com (on the Yahoo! website, click on "Key Statistics").

As we explain below, the beta of the overall market portfolio is 1, so you can think of a beta of 1 as representing average exposure to systematic risk. However, as Table 11.4 demonstrates, many industries and companies have betas much higher or lower than 1. The differences in betas by industry are related to the sensitivity of each industry's profits to the general health of the economy. For example, Research In Motion and other technology stocks have high betas (near or above 1.5), because demand for their products usually varies with the business cycle (cyclical stocks):

TABLE 11.4

Average Betas for Stocks by Industry (Based on Monthly Data from 2005 to 2009)

Industry	Industry Beta	Company Ticker Symbol	Company Name	Company Beta
Energy	1.4	CNQ	Canadian Natural Resources Limited	1.88
		HSE	Husky Energy Inc.	1.20
Materials	1.2	AEM	Agnico-Eagle Mines Ltd.	1.28
		POT	Potash Corp./Saskatchewan Inc.	1.10
Industrials	0.8	CP	Canadian Pacific Railway	0.77
		STN	Stantec Inc.	1.04
		WJA	WestJet Airlines Ltd.	0.45
Consumer Discretionary	0.6	CTC	Canadian Tire Corporation	0.40
		FGL	Forzani Group Ltd.	1.26
		RET.A	Reitmans (Canada) Limited	0.74
		THI	Tim Hortons Inc.	0.20
Consumer Staples	0.3	L	Loblaw Companies Limited	0.31
		MFI	Maple Leaf Foods Inc.	0.13
		SC	Shoppers Drug Mart Corporation	0.42
Health Care	0.4	SXC	SXC Health Solutions, Corp.	0.49
Financials	0.8	GWO	Great-West Lifeco Inc.	0.88
		MFC	Manulife Financial Corporation	1.26
		TD	The Toronto-Dominion Bank	0.71
Information Technology	1.2	RIM	Research In Motion Limited	1.47
Telecommunications Services	0.5	BCE	BCE Inc.	0.41
		T	TELUS Corporation	0.44
Utilities	0.4	EMA	Emera Inc.	0.15
		FTS	Fortis Inc.	0.16

Source: Canadian Financial Markets Research Center (CFMRC).

companies tend to expand and upgrade their information technology infrastructure when times are good, but cut back on these expenditures when the economy slows. Thus, systematic events have a greater-than-average impact on these firms, and their exposure to systematic risk is greater than average. On the other hand, the demand for personal and household products such as shampoo has very little relationship to

Common Mistake   Mixing Standard Deviation and Beta

Volatility (standard deviation) and beta are measured in different units (standard deviation is measured in % and beta is unitless). So even though total risk (volatility) is equal to the sum of systematic risk (measured by beta) and firm-specific risk, our measure of volatility does not have to be a bigger number than our measure for beta. To illustrate, consider Shoppers Drug Mart Corporation. It has total risk (volatility), measured as standard deviation, of 16%, or 0.16 (see Table 11.3), but Table 11.4 shows that it

has systematic risk, measured as a beta, of 0.42, which is greater than 0.16. Volatility (standard deviation) is measured in percentage terms, but beta is not, so 0.16 does not have to be greater than 0.42. For the same reason, it is possible for Canadian Tire Corporation to have a higher standard deviation than Shoppers Drug Mart (23%), but a lower beta (0.40). Figure 11.5 illustrates one possible breakdown of total risk for Canadian Tire Corporation and Shoppers Drug Mart Corporation that would be consistent with these data.

FIGURE 11.5

Systematic Versus Firm-Specific Risk in Canadian Tire and Shoppers Drug Mart

Beta, measuring systematic risk, and standard deviation, measuring total risk, are in different units. Even though Canadian Tire's total risk (standard deviation) is 0.23 (23%), its beta, measuring only systematic risk, is 0.40. In this case, the beta of 0.40 corresponds to a breakdown in total risk as depicted in the figure. Formally, the portion of Canadian Tire's total risk that is in common with the market is calculated by multiplying the correlation between Canadian Tire and the market by the standard deviation (total risk) of Canadian Tire. We can do a similar breakdown of Shoppers Drug Mart's risk. Note that Shoppers Drug Mart has more total, but less systematic, risk than Canadian Tire.

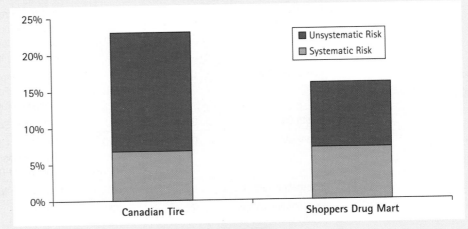

Source: Canadian Financial Markets Research Center (CFMRC).

the state of the economy (stocks of companies providing these types of products are often called defensive stocks). Firms producing or retailing these consumer staples, such as Loblaw Companies Limited, tend to have low betas (below 0.5). Note also that even within an industry, each company's specific strategy and focus can lead to different exposures to systematic events, so there is variation in beta even within industries (see, for example, Reitmans [Canada] Limited, a retailer of women's apparel, and the Forzani Group Ltd., a retailer of sporting goods).

EXAMPLE 11.4

Total Risk Versus Systematic Risk

Problem

Suppose that in the coming year, your expected annual return for the Forzani Group is 12% and for BCE is 7%. What is the expected return and risk (standard deviation) of your portfolio if you hold only Forzani? If you split your money evenly between Forzani and BCE, what is your expected return and risk of your portfolio?

Solution

▶ **Plan**

From Table 11.3, we can get the standard deviations of Forzani and BCE stock, along with their correlation:

$$SD(R_{FGL}) = 0.40, \; SD(R_{BCE}) = 0.23, \; Corr(R_{FGL}, R_{BCE}) = 0.27$$

With this information and the information from the problem, we can compute the expected return of the portfolio using Equation 11.3 and its variance using Equation 11.4:

▶ **Execute**

For the all-Forzani portfolio, we have 100% of our money in Forzani stock, so the expected return and standard deviation of our portfolio is simply the expected return and standard deviation of that stock:

$$E[R_{FGL}] = 0.12, \ SD(R_{FGL}) = 0.40$$

However, if we invest 50% of our money in Forzani and 50% in BCE, the expected return is:

$$E[R_P] = w_{FGL}E[R_{FGL}] + w_{BCE}E[R_{BCE}] = 0.5(0.12) + 0.5(0.07) = 0.095$$

and the standard deviation is:

$$Var(R_P) = w_{FGL}^2 SD(R_{FGL})^2 + w_{BCE}^2 SD(R_{BCE})^2$$
$$+ 2w_{FGL}w_{BCE}Corr(R_{FGL}, R_{BCE})SD(R_{FGL})SD(R_{BCE})$$
$$= (0.50)^2(0.40)^2 + (0.50)^2 (0.23)^2 + 2(0.50)(0.50)(0.27)(0.40)(0.23)$$
$$= 0.0124$$

The standard deviation is therefore:

$$SD(R_P) = \sqrt{Var(R_P)} = \sqrt{0.0124} = 0.1114, \ \text{or} \ 11.14\%$$

▶ **Evaluate**

For a very small reduction in expected return, we gain a large reduction in risk. This is the advantage of portfolios—by selecting stocks with low correlation but similar expected returns, we achieve our target expected return at the lowest possible risk.

Estimating Beta from Historical Returns

A security's beta is the expected percentage change in the return of the security for a 1% change in the return of the market portfolio. That is, beta represents the amount by which risks that affect the overall market are amplified or dampened in a given stock or investment. As demonstrated in Table 11.4, securities whose returns tend to move one for one with the market on average have a beta of 1. Securities that tend to move more than the market have higher betas, while those that move less than the market have lower betas.

Let's look at Research In Motion's stock as an example. Figure 11.6 shows the monthly returns for Research In Motion and the monthly returns for the S&P/TSX Composite Index from the beginning of 2005 to 2009. Note the overall tendency for Research In Motion to have a high return when the market is up and a low return when the market is down. Indeed, Research In Motion tends to move in the same direction as the market, but Research in Motion's movements are larger. The pattern suggests that Research In Motion's beta is greater than 1.

We can see Research In Motion's sensitivity to the market even more clearly by plotting Research In Motion's return as a function of the S&P/TSX Composite Index return, as shown in Figure 11.7. Each point in this figure represents the returns of Research In Motion and the S&P/TSX Composite Index for one of the months in Figure 11.6. For example, in December 2005, Research In Motion's return was 5.5% and the S&P/TSX Composite Index's was 2.1%.

As the scatter plot makes clear, Research In Motion's returns have a positive correlation with the market: Research In Motion tends to be up when the market is up, and vice versa. In practice, we use linear regression to estimate the relationship between Research In Motion's returns and the market's return. The output of the linear regression

FIGURE 11.6

Monthly Excess Returns for Research In Motion Stock and for the S&P/TSX Composite Index, 2005–2009

Note that Research In Motion's returns tend to move in the same direction but farther than those of the S&P/TSX Composite Index.

Source: Canadian Financial Markets Research Center (CFMRC).

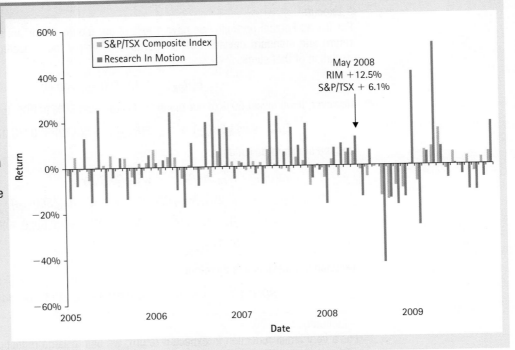

FIGURE 11.7

Scatter Plot of Monthly Returns for Research In Motion Versus the S&P/TSX Composite Index, 2005–2009

Beta corresponds to the slope of the best-fitting line. Beta measures the expected change in Research In Motion's return per 1% change in the market's return. Deviations from the line of best fit, such as in February 2009, correspond to diversifiable, unsystematic risk.

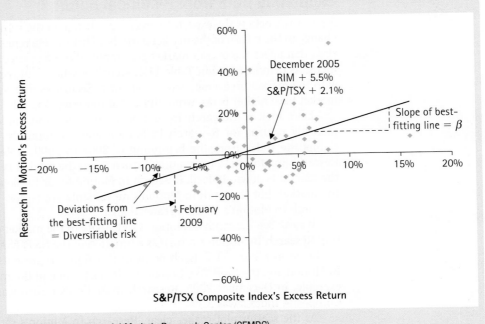

Source: Canadian Financial Markets Research Center (CFMRC).

USING EXCEL

Calculating a
Stock's Beta

1. Enter or import the historical returns for the stock and the S&P/TSX Composite Index into Excel.

2. Next, from the pull-down menus choose **Tools > Data Analysis > Regression**.

3. For the "Input Y Range" box, **highlight the stock's returns**.

4. For the "Input X Range" box, **highlight the S&P/TSX Composite Index's returns**, as shown in the screen capture.

5. Click OK.

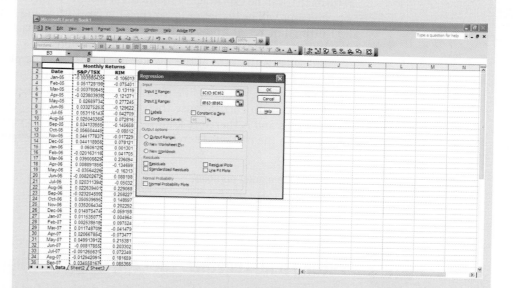

6. The output will appear in a separate sheet. The stock's beta is the coefficient on "X Variable 1." In this case, the beta is 1.466, shown in the screen capture.

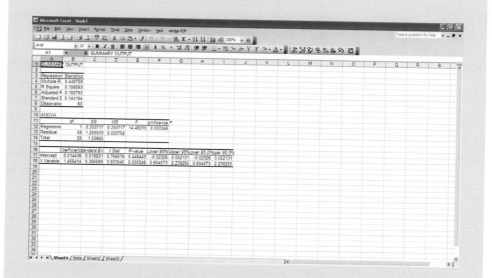

analysis is the best-fitting line (or line of best fit) that represents the historical relationship between the stock and the market. The slope of this line is our estimate of its beta. That slope tells us how much, on average, the stock's return changes for a 1% change in the market's return.[4]

For example, in Figure 11.7 the line of best fit shows that a 5% change in the market's return corresponds to about a 7.5% change in Research In Motion's return. That is, Research In Motion's return moves about 1.5 times (7.5/5) the overall market's movement, and so Research In Motion's beta is about 1.5.

To fully understand this result, recall that beta measures the systematic market risk of a security. The line of best fit in Figure 11.7 captures the components of a security's returns that can be explained by market-risk factors. In any individual month, the security's returns will be higher or lower than the best-fitting line. Such deviations from the best-fitting line result from risk that is not related to the market as a whole. This risk is diversifiable risk that averages out in a large portfolio.

But what is the beta of the market portfolio? Imagine plotting the returns of the S&P/TSX Composite Index against themselves. You would have a line with a slope of 1 and no deviations from that line. Thus, the beta of the market portfolio is 1. What about a risk-free investment? Because the risk-free return is the return earned on Canadian treasury bills and is therefore known in advance, it has no volatility and hence no correlation with the market. Therefore, the beta of the risk-free investment is 0.

Concept Check

5. What is the market portfolio?

6. What does beta (β) tell us?

11.4 Putting It All Together: The Capital Asset Pricing Model

One of our goals in this chapter is to compute the cost of equity capital for Research In Motion, which is the best available expected return offered in the market on an investment of comparable risk and term. Thus, in order to compute the cost of capital, we need to know the relationship between Research In Motion's risk and its expected return. Over the last three sections, we have laid the foundation for a practical way of measuring this relationship. In this section, we put all the pieces together to build a model for determining the expected return of any investment.

The CAPM Equation Relating Risk to Expected Return

As we have learned, only common, systematic risk determines expected returns—firm-specific risk is diversifiable and does not warrant extra return. In the introduction to this chapter, we stated that, intuitively, the expected return on any investment should come from two components:

1. A baseline risk-free rate of return that we would demand to compensate for inflation and the time value of money, even if there were no risk of losing our money.

---

[4]Formally, the beta of an investment is defined as:

$$\beta_i = \frac{\overbrace{SD(R_i) \times Corr(R_i, R_{Mkt})}^{\text{Volatility of } i \text{ that is Common with the Market}}}{SD(R_{Mkt})} = \frac{Cov(R_i, R_{Mkt})}{Var(R_{Mkt})}$$

2. A risk premium that varies with the amount of systematic risk in the investment.

$$\text{Expected Return} = \text{Risk-Free Rate} + \text{Risk Premium for Systematic Risk}$$

We devoted the last section to measuring systematic risk. Beta is our measure of the amount of systematic risk in an investment:

$$\text{Expected Return for Investment} = \text{Risk-Free Rate} + \beta_i \times \text{Risk Premium per Unit of Systematic Risk (per unit of } \beta).$$

market risk premium (equity risk premium) The historical average excess returns on the market portfolio.

But what is the risk premium per unit of systematic risk? Well, we know that the market portfolio, by definition, has exactly one unit of systematic risk (it has a beta of 1). So, a natural estimate of the risk premium per unit of systematic risk is the historical average excess return on the market portfolio, also known as the **market** or **equity risk premium**. Historically, the average excess return of the S&P/TSX Composite Index over the return on Government of Canada bonds (the risk-free rate) has been 4% to 6%, depending on the period of measurement (we'll discuss this more in the next chapter). With this last piece of the puzzle, we can write down the equation for the expected return of an investment:

Capital Asset Pricing Model (CAPM) An equilibrium model of the relationship between risk and return that characterizes a security's expected return based on its beta with the market portfolio.

$$\text{Capital Asset Pricing Model}$$
$$E[R_i] = r_f + \underbrace{\beta_i(E[R_{Mkt}] - r_f)}_{\text{Risk Premium for Security } i} \tag{11.6}$$

This equation for the expected return of any investment is the **Capital Asset Pricing Model (CAPM)**. In words, the CAPM simply says that the return we should expect on any investment is equal to the risk-free rate of return plus a risk premium proportional to the amount of systematic risk in the investment. Specifically, the risk premium of an investment is equal to the market risk premium ($E[R_{Mkt}] - r_f$) multiplied by the amount of systematic (market) risk present in the investment, measured by its beta with the market (β_i). Because investors will not invest in this security unless they can expect at least the return given in Equation 11.6, we also call this return the investment's **required return**.

required return The expected return of an investment that is necessary to compensate for the risk of undertaking the investment.

Why Not Estimate Expected Returns Directly?

If we have to use historical data to estimate beta and determine a security's expected return (or an investment's cost of capital), why not just use the security's historical average return as an estimate for its expected return instead? This method would certainly be simpler and more direct.

The answer is that it is extremely difficult to infer the average return of individual stocks from historical data. Because stock returns are so volatile, with even 100 years of data we would have little confidence in our estimate of the true average. (Imagine drawing 100 numbers from a swimming pool full of widely ranging numbers and being asked to guess the average of all of the numbers in the pool). Worse, few stocks have existed for 100 years, and those that have probably bear little resemblance today to what they were like 100 years ago. If we use less than 10 years of data, we would have very little confidence in our estimate at all. In fact, if the volatility of the stock's return is 20%, it turns out that we would need 1600 years of data to be 95% confident that our estimate of its true average return was within $+/-1\%$ of being correct!

On the other hand, the linear regression technique allows us to infer beta from historical data reasonably accurately with just a few years of data. Thus, in theory at least, using beta and the CAPM can provide much more accurate estimates of expected returns for stocks than we could obtain from their historical average return.

The CAPM is the main method used by most major corporations to determine the equity cost of capital. In a survey of CFOs, Graham and Harvey found that over 70% rely on the CAPM, and Bruner, Eades, Harris, and Higgins report that 85% of a sample of large firms rely on it.[5] It has become the most important model of the relationship between risk and return, and for his contributions to the theory, William Sharpe was awarded the Nobel Prize for Economics in 1990.

EXAMPLE 11.5	
Computing the Expected Return for a Stock	**Problem**
	Suppose the risk-free return is 3% and you measure the market risk premium to be 6%. Research In Motion has a beta of 1.5. According to the CAPM, what is its expected return?
	Solution
	▶ **Plan**
	We can use Equation 11.6 to compute the expected return according to the CAPM. For that equation, we will need the market risk premium, the risk-free return, and the stock's beta. We have all of these inputs, so we are ready to go.
	▶ **Execute**
	Using Equation 11.6:

$$E[R_{RIM}] = r_f + \beta_{RIM}(E[R_{Mkt}] - r_f) = 3\% + 1.5(6\%)$$
$$= 12\%$$

▶ **Evaluate**

Because of Research In Motion's beta of 1.5, investors will require a risk premium of 9% over the risk-free rate for investments in its stock to compensate for the systematic risk of Research In Motion stock. This leads to a total expected return of 12%.

The Security Market Line

Figure 11.8 graphs the relationships between expected return and both total risk and systematic risk (beta) for the stocks in Table 11.4. Recall from Chapter 10 that there is no clear relationship between a stock's standard deviation (total risk) and its expected return, as shown in panel (a). However, the CAPM equation (Equation 11.6) implies that there is a linear relationship between a stock's beta and its expected return. This line is graphed in panel (b) as the line through the risk-free investment (with a beta of 0) and the market (with a beta of 1); it is called the **security market line (SML)**. We see that the relationship between risk and return for individual securities is evident only when we measure market risk as in panel (b), rather than total risk as in panel (a).

security market line (SML) The pricing implication of the CAPM, specifying a linear relationship between the risk premium of a security and its beta with the market portfolio.

The security market line in Figure 11.8 raises the subject of negative beta stocks. While the vast majority of stocks have a positive beta, it is possible to have returns that co-vary negatively with the market. Firms that provide goods or services that are in greater demand in economic contractions than in booms fit this description.

---

[5]J. Graham and C. Harvey, "The Theory and Practice of Corporate Finance: Evidence from the Field," *Journal of Financial Economics* 60 (2001): 187–243; and F. Bruner, K. Eades, R. Harris, and R. Higgins, "Best Practices in Estimating the Cost of Capital: Survey and Synthesis," *Financial Practice and Education* 8 (1998): 13–28.

FIGURE 11.8

Expected Return, Volatility, and Beta

Panel (a) Expected Return and Total Risk (Standard Deviation)
The graph compares the standard deviation and expected returns of the stocks in Table 11.4. There is no relationship between total risk and expected return. Some of the stocks are identified. It is clear that we could not predict Research In Motion's expected return using its total risk (volatility).

Panel (b) Expected Return and Beta
The security market line shows the expected return for each security in Table 11.4 as a function of its beta with the market. According to the CAPM, all stocks and portfolios (including the market portfolio) should lie on the security market line. Thus, Research In Motion's expected return can be determined by its beta, which measures its systematic risk.

Source: Canadian Financial Markets Research Center (CFMRC).

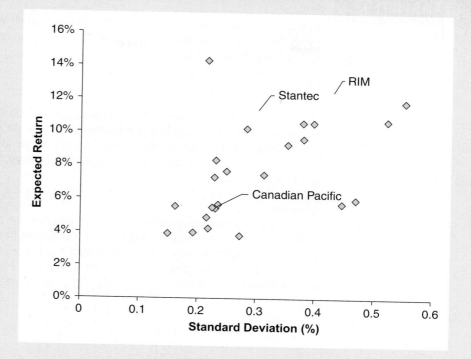

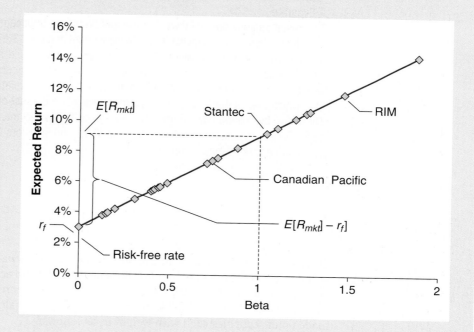

EXAMPLE 11.6

A Negative Beta
Stock

Problem

Suppose the stock of George Weston Limited (ticker symbol: WN) has a negative beta of −0.15. How does its required return compare to the risk-free rate, according to the CAPM? Does your result make sense?

Solution

▶ **Plan**

We can use the CAPM equation, Equation 11.6, to compute the expected return of this negative beta stock just as we would with a positive beta stock. We don't have the risk-free rate or the market risk premium, but the problem doesn't ask us for the exact expected return, just whether or not it will be more or less than the risk-free rate. Using Equation 11.6, we can answer that question.

▶ **Execute**

Because the expected return of the market is higher than the risk-free rate, Equation 11.6 implies that the expected return of WN will be *below* the risk-free rate. As long as the market risk premium is positive (as long as people demand a higher return for investing in the market than for a risk-free investment), then the second term in Equation 11.6 will have to be negative if the beta is negative. For example, if the risk-free rate is 3% and the market risk premium is 6%,

$$E[R_{WN}] = 3\% - 0.15(6\%) = 2.1\%$$

(See Figure 11.8: the SML drops below r_f for $\beta < 0$.)

▶ **Evaluate**

This result seems odd—why would investors be willing to accept a 2.1% expected return on this stock when they can invest in a safe investment and earn 3%? The answer is that a savvy investor will not hold WN alone; instead, the investor will hold it in combination with other securities as part of a well-diversified portfolio. These other securities will tend to rise and fall with the market. But because WN has a negative beta, its correlation with the market is negative, which means that WN tends to perform well when the rest of the market is doing poorly. Therefore, by holding WN, an investor can reduce the overall market risk of the portfolio. In a sense, WN is "recession insurance" for a portfolio, and investors will pay for this insurance by accepting a lower expected return.

The CAPM and Portfolios

Because the security market line applies to all securities, we can apply it to portfolios as well. For example, the market portfolio is on the SML, and according to the CAPM, other portfolios (such as mutual funds) are also on the SML. Therefore, the expected return of a portfolio should correspond to the portfolio's beta. We calculate the beta of a portfolio made up of securities each with weight w_i as follows:

$$\beta_P = w_1\beta_1 + w_2\beta_2 + \cdots + w_n\beta_n \tag{11.7}$$

That is, *the beta of a portfolio is the weighted average beta of the securities in the portfolio.*

EXAMPLE 11.7

The Expected
Return of a
Portfolio

Problem

Suppose the Forzani Group Limited (ticker symbol: FGL) has a beta of 1.26, whereas the beta of BCE Inc. (ticker symbol: BCE) is 0.41. If the risk-free interest rate is 3%, and the market risk premium is 6%, what is the expected return of an equally weighted portfolio of Forzani and BCE, according to the CAPM?

Solution

▶ **Plan**

We have the following information:

$$r_f = 3\% \qquad E[R_{Mkt}] - r_f = 6\%$$

FGL	$\beta_{FGL} = 1.26$	$w_{FGL} = 0.50$
BCE	$\beta_{BCE} = 0.41$	$w_{BCE} = 0.50$

We can compute the expected return of the portfolio in two ways. First, we can use the CAPM (Equation 11.6) to compute the expected return of each stock and then compute the expected return for the portfolio using Equation 11.3.

Or, we could compute the beta of the portfolio using Equation 11.7 and then use the CAPM (Equation 11.6) to find the portfolio's expected return.

▶ **Execute**

Using the first approach, we compute the expected return for FGL and BCE:

$$E[R_{FGL}] = r_f + \beta_{FGL}(E[R_{Mkt}] - r_f) \qquad E[R_{BCE}] = r_f + \beta_{BCE}(E[R_{Mkt}] - r_f)$$
$$E[R_{FGL}] = 3\% + 1.26(6\%) = 10.56\% \qquad E[R_{BCE}] = 3\% + 0.41(6\%) = 5.46\%$$

Then the expected return of the equally weighted portfolio P is:

$$E[R_P] = 0.5(10.56\%) + 0.5(5.46\%) = 8.01\%$$

Alternatively, we can compute the beta of the portfolio using Equation 10.7:

$$\beta_P = w_{FGL}\beta_{FGL} + w_{BCE}\beta_{BCE}$$
$$\beta_P = (0.5)(1.26) + (0.5)(0.41) = 0.835$$

We can then find the portfolio's expected return from the CAPM:

$$E[R_P] = r_f + \beta_P(E[R_{Mkt}] - r_f)$$
$$E[R_P] = 3\% + 0.835(6\%) = 8.01\%$$

▶ **Evaluate**

The CAPM is an effective tool for analyzing securities and portfolios of those securities. You can compute the expected return of each security using its beta and then compute the weighted average of those expected returns to determine the portfolio expected return. Or, you can compute the weighted average of the securities' betas to get the portfolio beta and then compute the expected return of the portfolio using the CAPM. Either way, you will get the same answer.

Summary of the Capital Asset Pricing Model

The CAPM is a powerful tool that is widely used to estimate the expected return on stocks and on investments within companies. The model and its use are summarized below:

▶ Investors require a risk premium proportional to the amount of *systematic* risk they are bearing.

▶ We can measure the systematic risk of an investment by its beta, which is the sensitivity of the investment's return to the market's return. For each 1% change in the market portfolio's return, the investment's return is expected to change by beta percent due to risks that it has in common with the market.

▶ The most common way to estimate a stock's beta is to regress its historical returns on the market's historical returns. The stock's beta is the slope of the line that best explains the relationship between the market's return and the stock's return.

▶ The CAPM says that we can compute the expected, or required, return for any investment using the following equation:

$$E[R_i] = r_f + \beta_i(E[R_{Mkt}] - r_f)$$

which when graphed is called the *security market line*.

The Big Picture

The CAPM marks the culmination of our examination of how investors in capital markets trade off risk and return. It provides a powerful and widely used tool to quantify the return that should accompany a particular amount of systematic risk. We have already reached our goal (in Example 11.5) of estimating the cost of equity capital for Research In Motion. While our finding that equity investors in Research In Motion should reasonably expect (and therefore require) a return of 12% on their investments is an important

---

NOBEL PRIZE **William Sharpe**

The CAPM was proposed as a model of risk and return by William Sharpe in a 1964 paper, and in related papers by Jack Treynor (1961), John Lintner (1965), and Jan Mossin (1966).[*]

Below is an excerpt from a 1998 interview with William Sharpe:

Portfolio Theory focused on the actions of a single investor with an optimal portfolio. I said what if everyone was optimizing? They've all got their copies of Markowitz and they're doing what he says. Then some people decide they want to hold more IBM, but there aren't enough shares to satisfy demand. So they put price pressure on IBM and up it goes, at which point they have to change their estimates of risk and return, because now they're paying more for the stock. That process of upward and downward pressure on prices continues until prices reach an equilibrium and everyone collectively wants to hold what's available. At that point, what can you say about the relationship between risk and return? The answer is that expected return is proportionate to beta relative to the market portfolio.

The CAPM was and is a theory of equilibrium. Why should anyone expect to earn more by investing in one security as opposed to another? You need to

be compensated for doing badly when times are bad. The security that is going to do badly just when you need money when times are bad is a security you have to hate, and there had better be some redeeming virtue or else who will hold it? That redeeming virtue has to be that in normal times you expect to do better. The key insight of the Capital Asset Pricing Model is that higher expected returns go with the greater risk of doing badly in bad times. Beta is a measure of that. Securities or asset classes with high betas tend to do worse in bad times than those with low betas.

Source: Jonathan Burton, "Revisiting the Capital Asset Pricing Model," *Dow Jones Asset Manager* (May/June 1998): 20–28.

---

[*]W.F. Sharpe, "Capital Asset Prices: A Theory of Market Equilibrium Under Conditions of Risk," *Journal of Finance* 19 (September 1964): 425–442.

Jack Treynor, "Toward a Theory of the Market Value of Risky Assets," unpublished manuscript (1961).

J. Lintner, "The Valuation of Risk Assets and the Selection of Risky Investments in Stock Portfolios and Capital Budgets," *Review of Economics and Statistics* 47 (February 1965): 13–37.

J. Mossin, "Equilibrium in a Capital Asset Market," *Econometrica* 34 (4) (1966): 768–783.

piece of information to Research In Motion's managers, it is not the whole picture. While some firms have only equity investors, most have bond investors as well. In the next chapter we will apply what we have learned here and in Chapters 6 and 9 on bonds and stocks to develop the overall cost of capital for a company. The Valuation Principle tells us to use this cost of capital to discount the future expected cash flows of the firm to arrive at the value of the firm. Thus, the cost of capital is an essential input to the financial manager's job of analyzing investment opportunities, so knowing this overall cost of capital is critical to the company's success at creating value for its investors.

Concept Check

7. What does the CAPM say about the required return of a security?

8. What is the security market line?

MyFinanceLab

Here is what you should know after reading this chapter. MyFinanceLab will help you identify what you know, and where to go when you need to practice.

Key Points and Equations	Terms	Online Practice Opportunities
11.1 The Expected Return of a Portfolio ▶ The portfolio weight is the initial fraction w_i of an investor's money invested in each asset. Portfolio weights add up to 1: $$w_i = \frac{\text{Value of investment } i}{\text{Total value of portfolio}} \quad (11.1)$$ ▶ The expected return of a portfolio is the weighted average of the expected returns of the investments within it, using the portfolio weights: $$E[R_P] = w_1 E[R_1] + w_2 E[R_2] \\ + \cdots + w_n E[R_n] \quad (11.3)$$	expected return of a portfolio, p. 374 portfolio weights, p. 372 return on a portfolio, p. 372	MyFinanceLab Study Plan 11.1
11.2 The Volatility of a Portfolio ▶ To find the risk of a portfolio, we need to know the degree to which stock returns move together. Correlation measures the co-movement of returns. The correlation is always between -1 and $+1$. It represents the fraction of the volatility due to risk that is common to the securities. ▶ The variance of a portfolio depends on the correlation of the stocks. For a portfolio with two stocks, the portfolio variance is: $$Var(R_P) \\ = w_1^2 SD(R_1)^2 + w_2^2 SD(R_2)^2 \\ + 2w_1 w_2 Corr(R_1, R_2)SD(R_1)SD(R_2) \quad (11.4)$$	correlation, p. 378 equally weighted portfolio, p. 383 volatility of a portfolio, p. 375	MyFinanceLab Study Plan 11.2 Using Excel: Correlation Between Two Sets of Returns

▶ As we lower the correlation between the two stocks in a portfolio, we lower the portfolio variance.

▶ Diversification eliminates independent, firm-specific risks, and the volatility of a large portfolio results from the common systematic risk between the stocks in the portfolio.

11.3 Measuring Systematic Risk

▶ The market portfolio in theory is a value-weighted index of all risky investments. In practice, we often use a stock market index such as the S&P 500 to represent the market.

▶ A stock's beta is the percentage change in its return that we expect for each 1% change in the market's return.

▶ To estimate beta, we often use historical returns. Most data sources use five years of monthly returns to estimate beta.

▶ Beta also corresponds to the slope of the best-fitting line in the plot of a security's excess returns versus the market's excess returns. We use linear regression to find the best-fitting line.

▶ The beta of a portfolio is the weighted-average beta of the securities in the portfolio.

beta (β), p. 386
market capitalization, p. 384
market index, p. 385
market portfolio, p. 384
market proxy, p. 385
value-weighted portfolio, p. 384

MyFinanceLab
Study Plan 11.3

Interactive Beta
Calculation,
Using Excel:
Calculating a
Stock's Beta

11.4 Putting It All Together: The Capital Asset Pricing Model

▶ According to the CAPM, the risk premium of any security is equal to the market risk premium multiplied by the beta of the security. This relationship is called the security market line (SML), and it determines the expected or required return for an investment:

$$E[R_i] = r_f + \underbrace{\beta_i(E[R_{Mkt}] - r_f)}_{\text{Risk Premium for Security } i} \qquad (11.6)$$

Capital Asset Pricing
Model (CAPM), p. 393
market or equity risk
premium, p. 393
required return, p. 393
security market line
(SML), p. 394

MyFinanceLab
Study Plan 11.5

Appendix: Alternative Models of Systematic Risk

Arbitrage Pricing Theory
(APT), p. 408
Fama-French-Carhart
factor specification
(FFC), p. 409
multi-factor model, p. 408
risk factors, p. 408

Review Questions

1. What information do you need to compute the expected return of a portfolio?

2. What does correlation tell us?

3. Why isn't the total risk of a portfolio simply equal to the weighted average of the risks of the securities in the portfolio?

4. What does beta measure? How do we use beta?

5. What, intuitively, does the CAPM say drives expected return?

6. What relationship is described by the security market line?

Problems

All problems in this chapter are available in MyFinanceLab. An asterisk (*) indicates problems with a higher level of difficulty.

The Expected Return of a Portfolio

1. You buy 100 shares of Tidepool Co. for $40 each and 200 shares of Madfish, Inc. for $15 each. What are the weights in your portfolio?

2. Fairmont Enterprises has an expected return of 15% and Laval News has an expected return of 20%. If you put 70% of your portfolio in Laval and 30% in Fairmont, what is the expected return of your portfolio?

3. You are considering how to invest part of your retirement savings. You have decided to put $200,000 into three stocks: 50% of the money into GoldFinger (currently $25/share), 25% of the money into Moosehead (currently $80/share), and the remainder into Venture Associates (currently $2/share). Suppose that GoldFinger stock goes up to $30/share, Moosehead stock drops to $60/share, and Venture Associates stock rises to $3 per share.
   a. What is the new value of the portfolio?
   b. What return did the portfolio earn?
   c. If you don't buy or sell shares after the price change, what are your new portfolio weights?

4. You have $70,000. You put 20% of your money into a stock with an expected return of 12%, $30,000 into a stock with an expected return of 15%, and the rest into a stock with an expected return of 20%. What is the expected return of your portfolio?

5. There are two ways to calculate the expected return of a portfolio: either calculate the expected return using the value and dividend stream of the portfolio as a whole, or calculate the weighted average of the expected returns of the individual stocks that make up the portfolio. Which return is higher?

The Volatility of a Portfolio

6. If the returns of two stocks have a correlation of 1, what does this imply about the relative movements in the stock prices?

 7. Download the data for Table 11.3 from MyFinanceLab.

Date	BCE	Canadian Tire	Forzani	Research In Motion	Shoppers Drug Mart	Suncor Energy	WestJet
Jan–05	1.83%	−1.85%	1.33%	−10.60%	5.18%	−6.72%	18.02%
Feb–05	−2.10%	14.92%	7.20%	−7.54%	3.98%	20.78%	−22.05%
Mar–05	5.47%	4.91%	−6.41%	13.12%	−0.74%	1.59%	41.89%
Apr–05	0.23%	17.40%	−0.49%	−12.13%	−2.87%	−4.52%	−5.43%
May–05	−4.47%	−4.70%	−4.51%	27.72%	4.72%	6.14%	−7.16%
Jun–05	1.66%	−0.37%	−7.81%	−12.96%	3.78%	17.77%	−0.66%
Jul–05	1.90%	−1.97%	18.90%	−4.27%	−3.53%	3.41%	−4.03%
Aug–05	4.97%	0.98%	−1.33%	7.28%	1.10%	17.36%	−15.27%
Sep–05	3.77%	2.05%	1.59%	−14.57%	−0.39%	0.13%	4.43%
Oct–05	−8.19%	3.48%	−8.59%	−8.51%	−4.39%	−10.01%	−10.18%
Nov–05	−5.30%	6.18%	10.51%	−1.72%	1.24%	4.92%	17.96%
Dec–05	1.77%	11.54%	0.15%	7.81%	10.41%	10.33%	−0.16%
Jan–06	−1.15%	5.30%	8.11%	0.13%	−3.39%	24.22%	2.85%
Feb–06	0.22%	−0.94%	7.21%	4.17%	4.29%	−6.70%	−16.57%
Mar–06	3.12%	9.64%	7.59%	23.61%	0.72%	5.62%	3.04%
Apr–06	−2.03%	−1.94%	−2.48%	−13.47%	−0.11%	6.78%	7.47%
May–06	−3.08%	−5.17%	−5.14%	−16.31%	−5.45%	−6.72%	−1.72%
Jun–06	0.04%	−4.92%	11.78%	8.82%	−3.14%	1.49%	−4.28%
Jul–06	−2.08%	−12.77%	−1.98%	−5.03%	8.53%	1.00%	−4.74%
Aug–06	6.62%	1.57%	2.87%	22.91%	5.98%	−6.42%	−6.42%
Sep–06	11.29%	3.86%	−1.72%	25.82%	−1.72%	−6.10%	2.87%
Oct–06	4.58%	−3.10%	5.98%	14.90%	−0.31%	6.97%	23.38%
Nov–06	−11.51%	0.00%	−2.51%	20.23%	8.73%	5.11%	8.63%
Dec–06	13.25%	−1.92%	12.11%	−5.92%	1.27%	1.96%	11.21%
Jan–07	−2.07%	−5.88%	−0.89%	0.50%	0.46%	−4.97%	0.07%
Feb–07	−0.26%	−4.17%	1.21%	9.75%	1.63%	−4.89%	−3.47%
Mar–07	7.40%	−9.24%	1.56%	−4.15%	0.61%	6.03%	6.43%
Apr–07	14.74%	9.20%	9.42%	−7.35%	−1.13%	1.19%	7.66%
May–07	5.47%	3.30%	18.34%	21.54%	−0.51%	4.63%	−7.96%
Jun–07	3.08%	2.87%	−7.71%	20.33%	−1.82%	2.79%	2.56%
Jul–07	−0.27%	−7.77%	−6.90%	7.23%	5.96%	0.91%	−0.64%
Aug–07	0.47%	−4.44%	−3.41%	18.17%	1.38%	−2.07%	0.51%
Sep–07	−0.51%	−0.65%	1.00%	8.54%	2.91%	−0.21%	10.36%
Oct–07	3.46%	9.78%	−15.09%	20.15%	1.82%	9.63%	15.71%
Nov–07	−4.90%	−7.11%	−21.50%	−3.05%	−0.47%	−7.30%	0.50%
Dec–07	1.90%	−3.49%	18.47%	−1.23%	−2.83%	12.80%	12.26%

(Continued)

Date	BCE	Canadian Tire	Forzani	Research In Motion	Shoppers Drug Mart	Suncor Energy	WestJet
Jan–08	−11.64%	−1.75%	−10.96%	−16.27%	−7.83%	−12.63%	−18.29%
Feb–08	2.14%	−4.67%	8.43%	8.47%	2.46%	7.99%	8.80%
Mar–08	−1.58%	1.86%	8.52%	12.82%	3.46%	−2.56%	−7.24%
Apr–08	5.40%	1.39%	2.49%	6.19%	2.50%	14.47%	−8.45%
May–08	−4.63%	−6.81%	−2.47%	12.24%	5.22%	17.82%	−7.06%
Jun–08	1.74%	−8.52%	−13.64%	−13.32%	0.12%	−11.60%	−20.38%
Jul–08	9.41%	−9.15%	−9.17%	5.68%	−2.74%	−5.37%	17.25%
Aug–08	3.26%	1.36%	2.88%	2.33%	1.77%	7.94%	1.22%
Sep–08	−7.43%	−13.90%	−18.65%	−43.57%	−6.77%	−25.32%	−21.43%
Oct–08	−5.96%	−5.87%	−20.41%	−16.16%	−8.39%	−35.78%	−11.00%
Nov–08	−28.93%	−10.80%	−2.23%	−13.13%	−6.08%	−3.15%	−12.26%
Dec–08	2.35%	2.33%	−17.14%	−6.62%	9.36%	−14.96%	42.90%
Jan–09	−0.16%	9.36%	31.52%	37.67%	−5.74%	−0.97%	−1.07%
Feb–09	−0.88%	8.97%	−13.64%	−25.50%	−4.21%	12.45%	−1.93%
Mar–09	2.19%	2.49%	21.42%	6.96%	0.29%	6.39%	−6.77%
Apr–09	2.16%	12.85%	33.32%	52.51%	−0.72%	7.79%	−1.44%
May–09	−2.23%	−3.17%	6.39%	3.65%	3.60%	27.40%	2.31%
Jun–09	−2.06%	0.84%	3.57%	−3.64%	12.62%	−8.14%	−14.07%
Jul–09	3.07%	2.42%	0.10%	−0.91%	−10.08%	−1.41%	0.97%
Aug–09	8.75%	5.26%	10.74%	−2.25%	−4.34%	−3.89%	17.86%
Sep–09	−0.69%	−2.81%	−15.52%	−9.66%	2.48%	10.93%	−9.25%
Oct–09	−1.89%	0.67%	−5.44%	−12.34%	−1.96%	−3.70%	−1.62%
Nov–09	7.76%	−3.43%	−1.18%	−3.63%	0.54%	7.17%	8.44%
Dec–09	5.22%	−0.80%	12.52%	16.10%	5.52%	−2.73%	4.40%

a. Compute the correlation of monthly returns between BCE and Forzani.
b. Compute the monthly standard deviation of BCE and Forzani.
c. Compute the monthly variance and standard deviation of a portfolio of 30% BCE stock and 70% Forzani stock.

8. Stock A and B have the following returns:

	Stock A	Stock B
1	0.10	0.06
2	0.07	0.02
3	0.15	0.05
4	−0.05	0.01
5	0.08	−0.02

a. What are the expected returns of the two stocks?
b. What are the standard deviations of the two stocks?
c. If their correlation is 0.46, what is the expected return and standard deviation of a portfolio of 40% stock A and 60% stock B?

9. Using the data in the following table, estimate the average return and volatility for each stock.

	Realized Returns	
Year	Stock A	Stock B
1998	−10%	21%
1999	20%	30%
2000	5%	7%
2001	−5%	−3%
2002	2%	−8%
2003	9%	25%

10. Using your estimates from Problem 9 and the fact that the correlation of A and B is 0.48, calculate the volatility (standard deviation) of a portfolio that is 70% invested in stock A and 30% invested in stock B.

11. The following spreadsheet contains monthly returns for Cola Co. and Gas Co. for 2010. Using these data, estimate the average monthly return and volatility for each stock.

Date	Cola Co	Gas Co
Jan	−10.84%	−6.00%
Feb	2.36%	1.28%
Mar	6.60%	−1.86%
Apr	2.01%	−1.90%
May	18.36%	7.40%
Jun	−1.22%	−0.26%
Jul	2.25%	8.36%
Aug	−6.89%	−2.46%
Sep	−6.04%	−2.00%
Oct	13.61%	0.00%
Nov	3.51%	4.68%
Dec	0.54%	2.22%

12. Using the spreadsheet from Problem 11 and the fact that Cola Co. and Gas Co. have a correlation of 0.6083, calculate the volatility (standard deviation) of a portfolio that is 55% invested in Cola Co. stock and 45% invested in Gas Co. stock. Calculate the volatility by
   a. using Equation 11.4, and
   b. calculating the monthly returns of the portfolio and computing its volatility directly.
   c. How do your results compare?

13. Suppose Johnson & Johnson and the Walgreen Company have the expected returns and volatilities shown below, with a correlation of 22%.

	E[R]	SD[R]
Johnson & Johnson	7%	16%
Walgreen Company	10%	20%

For a portfolio that is equally invested in Johnson & Johnson's and Walgreen's stock, calculate the following:

    a. The expected return.

    b. The volatility (standard deviation).

14. You have a portfolio with a standard deviation of 30% and an expected return of 18%. You are considering adding one of the two stocks in the table below. If after adding the stock you will have 20% of your money in the new stock and 80% of your money in your existing portfolio, which one should you add?

	Expected Return	Standard Deviation	Correlation with Your Portfolio's Returns
Stock A	15%	25%	0.2
Stock B	15%	20%	0.6

15. Your client has $100,000 invested in stock A. She would like to build a two-stock portfolio by investing another $100,000 in either stock B or C. She wants a portfolio with an expected return of at least 14% and as low a risk as possible, but the standard deviation must be no more than 40%. What do you advise her to do, and what will be the portfolio expected return and standard deviation?

	Exp Return	Std Dev	Correlation with A
A	15%	50%	1
B	13%	40%	0.2
C	13%	40%	0.3

Measuring Systematic Risk

16. Suppose all possible investment opportunities in the world are limited to the five stocks listed in the table below. What are the market portfolio weights?

Stock	Price/Share ($)	Number of Shares Outstanding (millions)
A	10	10
B	20	12
C	8	3
D	50	1
E	45	20

17. Given $100,000 to invest, construct a value-weighted portfolio of the four stocks listed below.

Stock	Price/Share ($)	Number of Shares Outstanding (millions)
Golden Seas	13	1.00
Jacobs and Jacobs	22	1.25
MAG	43	30
PDJB	5	10

18. If one stock in a value-weighted portfolio goes up in price and all other stock prices remain the same, what trades are necessary to keep the portfolio value weighted?

19. You hear on the news that the S&P/TSX Composite Index was down 2% today relative to the risk-free rate (the market's excess return was –2%). You are thinking about your portfolio and your investments in Research In Motion and WestJet.
    a. If Research In Motion's beta is 1.5, what is your best guess as to Research In Motion's excess return today?
    b. If WestJet's beta is 0.5, what is your best guess as to WestJet's excess return today?

 20. Go to Chapter Resources on MyFinanceLab and use the data in the spreadsheet provided to estimate the beta of Nike stock using linear regression.

 21. The Chapter Resources section of MyFinanceLab has data on Microsoft and the S&P 500 from 1987 to 2006.
    a. Estimate Microsoft's beta using linear regression over the periods 1987–1991, 1992–1996, 1997–2001, and 2002–2006.
    b. Compare the four estimated betas. What do you conclude about how Microsoft's exposure to systematic risk has changed over time? What do you think explains the change?

Putting It All Together: The Capital Asset Pricing Model

22. Suppose the risk-free return is 4% and the market portfolio has an expected return of 10% and a standard deviation of 16%. Suppose Loblaw Companies Limited stock has a beta of 0.32. What is its expected return?

23. What is the sign of the risk premium of a negative-beta stock? Explain. (Assume the risk premium of the market portfolio is positive.)

24. EJH has a beta of 1.2, CSH has a beta of 0.6, and KMS has a beta of 1.0. If you put 25% of your money in EJH, 25% in CSH, and 50% in KMS, what is the beta of your portfolio?

25. Suppose Intel stock has a beta of 1.6, whereas Boeing stock has a beta of 1. If the risk-free interest rate is 4% and the expected return of the market portfolio is 10%, according to the CAPM,
    a. what is the expected return of Intel stock?
    b. what is the expected return of Boeing stock?
    c. what is the beta of a portfolio that consists of 60% Intel stock and 40% Boeing stock?
    d. what is the expected return of a portfolio that consists of 60% Intel stock and 40% Boeing stock? (Solve this in two ways.)

*26. You are thinking of buying a stock priced at $100 per share. Assume that the risk-free rate is about 4.5% and the market risk premium is 6%. If you think the stock will rise to $117 per share by the end of the year, at which time it will pay a $1 dividend, what beta would it need to have for this expectation to be consistent with the CAPM?

*27. You are analyzing a stock that has a beta of 1.2. The risk-free rate is 5% and you estimate the market risk premium to be 6%. If you expect the stock to have a return of 11% over the next year, should you buy it? Why or why not?

28. You have risen through the ranks of a coffee company, from the lowly green-apron barista to the coveted black apron, and all the way to CFO. A quick internet check shows you that your company's beta is 0.6. The risk free rate is 5% and you believe the market risk premium to be 5.5%. What is your best estimate of investors' expected return on your company's stock (its cost of equity capital)?

29. At the beginning of 2007, Apple's beta was 1.4 and the risk-free rate was about 4.5%. Apple's price was $84.84. Apple's price at the end of 2007 was $198.08. If you estimate the market risk premium to have been 6%, did Apple's managers exceed their investors' required return as given by the CAPM?

30. You want to invest $50,000 in a portfolio with a beta of no more than 1.4 and an expected return of 12.4%. Bay Corp has a beta of 1.2 and an expected return of 11.2%; City Corp has a beta of 1.8 and an expected return of 14.8%. The risk-free rate is 4%. You can invest in Bay Corp, City Corp, and the risk-free asset. How much will you invest in each?

| Chapter 11 APPENDIX | Alternative Models of Systematic Risk

While the CAPM is the most widely used model for estimating the cost of capital in practice, recently some practitioners have tried to improve on the CAPM.

Problems with the CAPM in Practice

Researchers have found that using only the S&P 500, or some other simple proxy for the true market portfolio, has led to consistent pricing errors from the CAPM. That is, some stocks and portfolios of stocks earn consistently higher or lower returns than the CAPM would predict. For example, researchers have found that small stocks, stocks with high ratios of book to market value of equity, and stocks that have recently performed very well have consistently earned higher returns than the CAPM would predict using a simple stock market proxy for the market portfolio.

Multi-Factor Models

risk factors Different components of systematic risk (used in a multi-factor model).

multi-factor model A model that uses more than one portfolio to capture systematic risk. Each portfolio can be thought of as either the risk factor itself or a portfolio of stocks correlated with an unobservable risk factor.

Arbitrage Pricing Theory (APT) One of the earliest multi-factor models, relying on the absence of arbitrage to price securities.

These findings have led researchers to add new portfolios to the CAPM pricing equation in an attempt to construct a better proxy for the true market portfolio that captures the components of systematic risk that just using a market proxy such as the S&P 500 alone misses. Although we might not be able to identify a perfect proxy for the true market portfolio, the market portfolio can be constructed from other portfolios. This observation implies that as long as the market portfolio can be constructed from a collection of portfolios, the collection itself can be used to measure risk. *Thus, it is not actually necessary to identify the market portfolio itself.* All that is required is to identify a collection of portfolios from which it can be constructed.

We can use a collection of portfolios to capture the components of systematic risk, referred to as **risk factors**. A model with more than one portfolio to capture risk is known as a **multi-factor model**. Each portfolio can be thought of as either the risk factor itself or a portfolio of stocks correlated with an unobservable risk factor. This particular form of the multi-factor model was originally developed by Professor Stephen Ross, but Professor Robert Merton developed an alternative multi-factor model earlier.[6] The model is also referred to as the **Arbitrage Pricing Theory (APT)**.

Fama-French-Carhart Factor Specification

Practitioners have added portfolios specifically to address the CAPM pricing errors. The first portfolio is one that is constructed by buying small firms and selling large firms. This portfolio is widely known as the small-minus-big (SMB) portfolio. The second portfolio buys firms with a high book-to-market ratio and sells firms with a low book-to-market ratio, and we call it the high-minus-low (HML) portfolio. Finally, the third portfolio buys stocks that have recently done extremely well and sells those that have done extremely poorly. Since this portfolio addresses the problem that this extremely good and bad performance continues in the short run, it is called the prior one-year momentum (PR1YR) portfolio.

---

[6]See Stephen A. Ross, "The Arbitrage Theory of Capital Asset Pricing," *Journal of Economic Theory* 3 (December 1976): 343–62; and Robert C. Merton "An Intertemporal Capital Asset Pricing Model," *Econometrica* 41(1973): 867–887.

The collection of these four portfolios—the stock market (Mkt), SMB, HML, and PR1YR—is the most popular collection of portfolios used as an alternative model to the CAPM and is one example of a multi-factor model. The average monthly returns of these portfolios are shown in Table 11.5.

TABLE 11.5

FFC Portfolio Average
Monthly Returns
(1926–2005)

Average Monthly Return (%)	
Mkt − r_f	0.64
SMB	0.17
HML	0.53
PR1YR	0.76

Source: Professor Kenneth French's personal website.

Fama-French-Carhart factor specification (FFC)
A multi-factor model of risk and return in which the factor portfolios are the market, small-minus-big, high-minus-low, and PR1YR portfolios identified by Fama, French, and Carhart.

Using this collection, the expected return of security i is given by Equation 11.8:

$$E[R_i] = r_f + \beta_i^{Mkt}(E[R_{Mkt}] - r_f) + \beta_i^{SMB}E[R_{SMB}] + \beta_i^{HML}E[R_{HML}]$$
$$+ \beta_i^{PR1YR}E[R_{PR1YR}] \tag{11.8}$$

where β_i^{Mkt}, β_i^{SMB}, β_i^{HML} and β_i^{PR1YR} are the factor betas of stock i and measure the sensitivity of the stock to each portfolio. Because the collection of portfolios (Mkt, SMB, HML, and PR1YR) were identified by Professors Eugene Fama, Kenneth French, and Mark Carhart, we refer to this collection of portfolios as the **Fama-French-Carhart factor specification (FFC)**.

EXAMPLE 11.8

Using the FFC
Factor Specification
to Calculate the
Cost of Capital

Problem

You are currently considering making an investment in a project in the food and beverages industry. You determine the project has the same riskiness as investing in Coca-Cola. You use data over the past five years to estimate the factor betas of Coca-Cola (ticker symbol: KO). Specifically, you regress the monthly excess return (the realized return in each month minus the risk-free rate) of Coca-Cola's stock on the return of each of the four-factor portfolios. You determine that the factor betas for KO are as follows:

$$\beta_{KO}^{Mkt} = 0.158$$
$$\beta_{KO}^{SMB} = 0.302$$
$$\beta_{KO}^{HML} = 0.497$$
$$\beta_{KO}^{PR1YR} = -0.276$$

The current risk-free monthly rate is 5%/12 = 0.42%. Determine the cost of capital by using the FFC factor specification.

Solution

▶ **Plan**
First, gather the information you have. Combining the information in the problem with the data in Table 11.5, you have:

	Average Monthly Return (%)	KO's β with Factor
Mkt − r_f	0.64	0.158
SMB	0.17	0.302
HML	0.53	0.497
PR1YR	0.76	−0.276

Using the information you have collected along with the monthly risk-free rate of 0.42%, you can use Equation 11.8 to calculate the monthly expected return for investing in Coca-Cola. From there, you can multiply by 12 to get the annual expected return, represented as an annual percentage rate.

▶ Execute

Using Equation 11.8, the monthly expected return of investing in Coca-Cola is:

$$E[R_{KO}] = r_f + \beta_{KO}^{Mkt}(E[R_{Mkt}] - r_f) + \beta_{KO}^{SMB}E[R_{SMB}] + \beta_{KO}^{HML}E[R_{HML}] + \beta_{KO}^{PR1\ YR}E[R_{PR1\ YR}]$$

$$= 0.42 + 0.158 \times 0.64 + 0.302 \times 0.17 + 0.497 \times 0.53 - 0.276 \times 0.76$$

$$= 0.626\%$$

The annual expected return is $0.626 \times 12 = 7.5\%$.

▶ Evaluate

By gathering all of the inputs and applying the FFC specification in the same way we would apply the CAPM, we can calculate this alternative estimate of the cost of capital for Coca-Cola. According to this approach, we would conclude that the annual cost of capital of the investment opportunity is about 7.5%.

12 Determining the Cost of Capital

▶ Understand the drivers of the firm's overall cost of capital

▶ Measure the costs of debt, preferred stock, and common stock

▶ Compute a firm's overall, or weighted average, cost of capital

▶ Apply the weighted average cost of capital to value projects

▶ Adjust the cost of capital for the risk associated with the project

▶ Account for the direct costs of raising external capital

notation

$D\%$	fraction of the firm financed with debt	P_{pfd}	price of preferred stock
Div_1	dividend due in one year	r_D	required return (cost of capital) for debt
Div_{pfd}	dividend on preferred stock	r_E	required return (cost of capital) of levered equity
$E\%$	fraction of the firm financed with equity	r_{pfd}	required return (cost of capital) for preferred stock
FCF_t	incremental free cash flow in year t	r_U	required return (cost of capital) of unlevered equity
g	expected growth rate for dividends	r_{wacc}	weighted average cost of capital
$P\%$	fraction of the firm financed with preferred stock	T_c	marginal corporate tax rate
P_E	price of common stock	V_0^L	initial levered value

INTERVIEW WITH Elizabeth Anton,
RBC

University of Western Ontario, 2010

Elizabeth Anton, who received her Master of Business Administration degree from the University of Western Ontario in 2010, is an associate at RBC in the investment banking group. She started out with an undergraduate degree in engineering, but her passion for mathematics led her to work in real estate development, where she became interested in financing projects. Her role at RBC is to advise clients on valuation and on raising capital. "We help companies raise both debt and equity capital, and advise them on their own value, as well as provide valuation of potential takeover targets."

Raising external capital is costly, and thus it is important for companies to have a good idea of the exact costs involved in raising debt and equity, as this will have a large impact on whether acquiring another company is worthwhile. "When we help a company raise debt or equity towards the purchase of another company, we analyze the financial statements," Elizabeth explains. "We need to find out how the market will value the targeted company by comparing it to other similar companies and calculating a multiple of their *EBITDA*," she continues. "If the firm intends to go ahead with the purchase of the target, we need to find out the costs of both debt and equity capital. We do this by looking at recent deals in the market, while keeping in mind our client's unique capital structure and how much debt [it is] able to manage from a cash flow perspective."

Elizabeth's finance courses gave her the preparation necessary to serve her clients: "Everything I learned in finance is being used on a daily basis."

In Chapter 11, we learned how to determine a firm's equity cost of capital. In reality, most firms are financed with a combination of equity, debt, and other securities such as preferred stock. As a result, financial managers must determine their firm's overall cost of capital based on all sources of financing. This overall cost of capital is a critical input into the capital budgeting process. The Valuation Principle tells us that the value of a project is the present value of its benefits net of the present value of its costs. In capital budgeting, we implement this important concept with net present value (*NPV*). To calculate a project's *NPV*, we need a cost of capital to use as a discount rate.

In this chapter, we will learn how to calculate and use the firm's overall cost of capital, which is typically referred to as its weighted average cost of capital (WACC). We will see that the WACC is a weighted average of the costs of capital from each of the firm's different financing sources. After we have learned how to estimate the WACC, we will apply it in capital budgeting. As part of that discussion, we will learn the conditions under which we can use the firm's overall cost of capital as a discount rate, and identify those situations in which we will instead need to determine a cost of capital specific to a project or division of the firm.

A First Look at the Weighted Average Cost of Capital

Most firms draw on some combination of equity, debt, and other securities to raise the funds they need for investment. In this section, we examine the role of financing sources in determining the firm's overall cost of capital. We begin by stepping back to assess these financing sources in the context of the firm's balance sheet.

The Firm's Capital Structure

capital A firm's sources of financing—debt, equity, and other securities that it has outstanding.

A firm's sources of financing, which usually consist of debt and equity, represent its **capital**. The typical firm raises funds to invest by selling shares to shareholders (its equity) and borrowing from lenders (its debt). Recall the most basic form of the balance sheet, as represented in Figure 12.1. The left side of the balance sheet lists the firm's assets, and the right side describes the firm's capital.

capital structure The relative proportions of debt, equity, and other securities that a firm has outstanding.

The relative proportions of debt, equity, and other securities that a firm has outstanding constitute its **capital structure**. When corporations raise funds from outside investors, they must choose which type of security to issue. The most common choices are financing through equity alone and financing through a combination of debt and equity. Figure 12.2 shows the capital structures of Research In Motion and Canadian Natural Resources. Capital structures vary widely across firms. In Chapter 15, we will discuss how a firm sets its capital structure.

Opportunity Cost and the Overall Cost of Capital

Financial managers take into account each component of the firm's capital structure when determining the firm's overall cost of capital. Throughout the discussion that follows, keep in mind the reasoning behind the term "cost of capital." When investors buy the stock or bonds of a company, they forgo the opportunity to invest that money elsewhere. The expected return from those alternative investments constitutes an opportunity cost to them. Thus, to attract their investments as capital to the firm, the firm must offer potential investors an expected return equal to that they could expect to earn elsewhere for assuming the same level of risk. Providing this return is the cost a company bears in exchange for obtaining capital from investors.

weighted average cost of capital (WACC) The average of a firm's equity and debt costs of capital, weighted by the fractions of the firm's value that correspond to equity and debt, respectively.

Weighted Averages and the Overall Cost of Capital

Intuitively, the firm's overall cost of capital should be a blend of the costs of the different sources of capital. In fact, we calculate the firm's overall cost of capital as a weighted average of its equity and debt costs of capital, known as the firm's **weighted average cost of capital (WACC)**.

FIGURE 12.1 A Basic Balance Sheet

This figure provides a very basic balance sheet for reference. As discussed in Chapter 2, the two sides of the balance sheet must equal each other: Assets = Liabilities + Equity. The right side represents the way the assets are financed. In this chapter, we will focus on the required returns for the different forms of financing found on the right side of the balance sheet.

Assets	Liabilities and Equity
Current Assets	Debt
Long-Term Assets	Preferred Stock
	Equity

FIGURE 12.2

Two Capital Structures

This figure shows the capital structures of two real firms. Research In Motion (RIM) is financed 100% with common equity, shown in blue, while Canadian Natural Resources (CNQ) is financed 82% with common equity and 18% with debt, shaded in yellow.

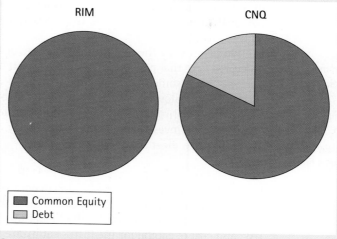

Source: Bloomberg Professional Services.

But what should the weights be? Imagine you owned all of the stock and all of the debt of the firm. If that was all you had in your portfolio, the return on your portfolio would be the total return of the firm. As we showed in Chapter 11, a portfolio return is the weighted average of the returns of the securities in the portfolio. In this case, the return on your portfolio—the total return of the firm—is a weighted average of the return you earn holding all the stock of the firm and the return you earn holding all of the debt. Since you hold all of each, your portfolio weights are just the relative amount of debt and equity issued by the firm. Thus, the weights we use in the WACC are the proportions of debt and equity used in the firm's capital structure. For example, if the firm is financed 30% by debt and 70% by equity, then the weights used in its WACC would be 30% on the debt cost of capital and 70% on the equity cost of capital.

This example suggests that you can determine the weights by looking at the right side of the firm's balance sheet. That assumption is correct, with one important modification: you must use the *market values* of the debt and equity to determine the proportions, not the accounting-based *book values* listed on the balance sheet. Recall from Chapter 2 that book values reflect historical costs, but market values are forward-looking, based on what the assets are expected to produce in the future. Holders of the firm's financial claims—equity and, if the firm has it, debt—assess the firm based on the market value of its assets, not the book value.

market-value balance sheet A balance sheet that is similar to an accounting balance sheet but in which all values are current market values rather than historical costs.

In fact, it is useful to think about the **market-value balance sheet**, where the assets, debt, and equity are all listed in terms of their market values, instead of their book values. Of course, the market-value balance sheet must still balance:

$$\text{Market Value of Equity} + \text{Market Value of Debt} = \text{Market Value of Assets} \quad (12.1)$$

Equation 12.1 states that the total market value of all the claims (equity and debt) issued by the firm must be equal to the total market value of all its assets. This equality drives home the point that the equity and debt issued by the firm derive their value from the underlying assets they claim. The risk, and hence the required return, of the debt and equity of the firm are determined by the risk of the firm's assets. This point will be useful as we derive the firm's WACC.

Weighted Average Cost of Capital Calculations

In this section, we will explore the reasoning behind the use of market-value weights, as well as the link between the risk of the assets and the risk of the debt and equity claims on those assets.

unlevered A firm that does not have debt outstanding.

We begin with the straightforward case of the firm that does not issue debt—the **unlevered** firm that pays out all of the free cash flows generated by its assets to its equity holders. When some of a firm's financing comes from debt, we say the firm is **levered**. Just as a lever allows you to lift a heavy object by exerting relatively little force, so borrowing money through debt allows equity holders to control highly valued assets with relatively little investment of their own money. We refer to the relative amount of debt on the balance sheet as the firm's **leverage**.

levered A firm that has debt outstanding.

leverage The relative amount of debt on a firm's balance sheet.

The Weighted Average Cost of Capital: Unlevered Firm. If a firm is unlevered—so it has no debt—all of the free cash flows generated by its assets are ultimately paid out to its equity holders. Because the free cash flows to the equity holders are the same as the free cash flows from the assets, the Valuation Principle tells us that the market value, risk, and cost of capital for the firm's equity are equal to the corresponding amounts for its assets. Given this relationship, we can estimate the firm's equity cost of capital using the Capital Asset Pricing Model (CAPM). The resulting estimate is the cost of capital for the firm as a whole. For example, Research In Motion does not issue debt, so the cost of capital for Research In Motion's assets is the same as the firms' costs of equity.

The Weighted Average Cost of Capital: Levered Firm. But what if the firm has debt? How should we incorporate the cost of this debt to determine the cost of capital for the firm's assets as a whole? The market-value balance sheet provides the answer. We can interpret the equality in Equation 12.1 in terms of a portfolio: by holding a portfolio of the firm's equity and debt, we can get the same cash flows as if we held the assets directly. Because the return of a portfolio is equal to the weighted average of the returns of the securities in it, this equality implies the following relationship between the required returns (costs) of equity, debt, and assets:

Weighted Average Cost of Capital (Pre-tax)

$$r_{wacc} \equiv \left(\begin{array}{c} \text{Fraction of Firm Value} \\ \text{Financed by Equity} \end{array} \right) \left(\begin{array}{c} \text{Equity} \\ \text{Cost of Capital} \end{array} \right)$$

$$+ \left(\begin{array}{c} \text{Fraction of Firm Value} \\ \text{Financed by Debt} \end{array} \right) \left(\begin{array}{c} \text{Debt} \\ \text{Cost of Capital} \end{array} \right) \qquad (12.2)$$

$$= \left(\begin{array}{c} \text{Asset} \\ \text{Cost of Capital} \end{array} \right)$$

We now have the justification for our reasoning that the overall cost of capital for a firm should be a weighted average of its equity and debt costs of capital. Equation 12.2 shows that we can calculate the cost of capital of the firm's assets by computing the weighted average of the firm's equity and debt cost of capital. In the next section, we explore how to estimate the firm's costs of equity and debt capital.

EXAMPLE 12.1

Calculating the
Weights in the WACC

Problem

Suppose Great Lakes Corp. has debt with a book (face) value of $10 million, trading at 95% of face value. It also has book equity of $10 million, and 1 million shares of common stock trading at $30 per share. What weights should Great Lakes use in calculating its WACC?

Solution

▶ **Plan**

Equation 12.2 tells us that the weights are the fractions of Great Lakes financed with debt and financed with equity. Furthermore, these weights should be based on market values, because the cost of capital is based on investors' current assessment of the value of the firm, not their assessment of accounting-based book values. As a consequence, we can ignore the book values of debt and equity.

▶ **Execute**

Ten million dollars in debt trading at 95% of face value is $9.5 million in market value. One million shares of stock at $30 per share is $30 million in market value. So, the total market value of the firm is $39.5 million. The weights are

$$9.5 \div 39.5 = 24.1\% \text{ for debt and } 30 \div 39.5 = 75.9\% \text{ for equity.}$$

▶ **Evaluate**

When calculating its overall cost of capital, Great Lakes will use a weighted average of the cost of its debt capital and the cost of its equity capital, giving a weight of 24.1% to its cost of debt and a weight of 75.9% to its cost of equity.

Concept
Check

1. Why does a firm's capital have a cost?

2. Why do we use market-value weights in the weighted average cost of capital?

12.2 The Firm's Costs of Debt and Equity Capital

Section 12.1 made it clear that to measure the firm's overall cost of capital, we need to start by determining the cost of each type of capital a firm might use. We now turn to how a company measures the costs of its debt, preferred stock, and common stock. We will use Bell Canada Enterprises (BCE), Canada's largest communications company, as an example.

Cost of Debt Capital

We will start at the top of the right side of the balance sheet with the cost of the firm's debt. A firm's cost of debt is the interest rate it would have to pay to refinance its existing debt, such as through new bond issues. This rate differs from the coupon rate on the firm's existing debt, which reflects the interest rate the firm had to offer at the time the debt was issued.

Yield to Maturity and the Cost of Debt. Existing debt trades in the marketplace, so its price fluctuates to reflect both changes in the overall credit environment and changes in the risk specifically associated with the firm. As we learned in Chapter 6, the market price of the firm's existing debt implies a yield to maturity, which is the return that current purchasers of the debt would earn if they held the debt to maturity and received all of the payments as promised. So, we can use the yield to maturity to estimate the firm's current cost of debt: it is the yield that investors demand to hold the firm's debt (new or existing).[1]

Suppose BCE has debt due in 2017 with a coupon rate of 5.0% priced at $1047.50 per $1000 face value. Because the market price of the debt is above its face value, investors in debt earn a yield that is lower than the 5.0% coupon rate. In fact, using Equation 6.3 in Chapter 6, we can calculate that this price implies a yield to maturity of 4.10%, which is BCE's current cost of debt. In reality, you would not need to actually compute the yield to maturity yourself, because prices and their implied yields to maturity are always quoted together in the bond market.[2]

Taxes and the Cost of Debt. In the case of debt, the return paid to the debt holders is not the same as the cost to the firm. How could this be? The difference arises because interest paid on debt is a tax-deductible expense. When a firm uses debt financing, the cost of the interest it must pay is offset to some extent by the tax savings from the tax deduction.

For example, suppose a firm with a 35% tax rate borrows $100,000 at 10% interest per year. Then its net cost at the end of the year is calculated as follows:

		Year-End
Interest expense	$r_D \times \$100,000 =$	10,000
Tax savings	$- \text{Tax Rate} \times r_D \times \$100,000 =$	−3500
Effective after-tax interest expense	$r_D \times (1 - \text{Tax Rate}) \times \$100,000 =$	$6500

Common Mistake — Using the Coupon Rate as the Cost of Debt

A common mistake in estimating a company's overall cost of capital is to use the coupon rate on its existing debt as its debt cost of capital. The company's cost of capital is forward-looking and based on current conditions. By contrast, the coupon rate on existing debt is historical and set under potentially very different conditions. A better estimate of the firm's debt cost of capital is the yield to maturity of its existing debt, which is the promised return its lenders currently demand.

Consider the effects of the collapse of the U.S. real estate market on companies that build homes, such as KB Homes. KB has bonds that were originally issued in 2004 and are due in 2014; these bonds have a coupon rate of 5.75%. When the markets turned downward, KB's performance suffered, and the risk that it might not be able to meet all of its debt obligations increased. By mid-2010, those 5.75% coupon bonds were rated BB (below investment grade) and trading at a yield to maturity of about 8.6%. Therefore, to be willing to take a creditor position in KB, investors demanded a yield to maturity of 8.6%. Taking into account the probability of default and the expected loss in default, the BB-rated bonds have an average expected loss of 1.3%. The true expected return was closer to 7.3% (8.6% promised minus 1.3% expected loss).

So, which is a better estimate of the cost of debt capital for KB in 2010—the 5.75% coupon or the 8.6% yield to maturity? It would be a mistake for KB to use 5.75% as its cost of debt capital. The 5.75% rate, which was set under different circumstances, is not a relevant measure of KB's debt holders' required return in 2010, so it should not enter into the WACC calculation. Because of the default risk, the 7.3% we calculated would be a much better estimate of KB's cost of debt capital.

---

[1] In fact, the yield to maturity is the *most* the firm will pay, because there is some risk the firm may not repay its debt.

[2] Chapter 6 demonstrated how to find current prices and yields to maturity for corporate bonds. Websites such as those of CanadaFixedIncome.ca (www.canadianfixedincome.ca) and the Financial Industry Regulatory Authority (FINRA) (www.finra.org/marketdata) provide current information on corporate and government debt securities.

effective cost of debt
A firm's net cost of interest on its debt after accounting for the interest tax deduction.

The **effective cost of debt**—the firm's net cost of interest on the debt after taxes—is only $6500/$100,000 = 6.50\%$ of the loan amount, rather than the full 10% interest, because the tax deductibility of interest lowers the effective cost of debt financing for the firm. More generally, with tax-deductible interest and denoting the corporate tax rate as T_C, the effective after-tax borrowing rate is

$$r_D(1 - T_C) \tag{12.3}$$

EXAMPLE 12.2

Effective Cost of Debt

Problem

By using the yield to maturity on BCE's debt, we found that its pre-tax cost of debt is 4.10%. If BCE's tax rate is 20%, what is its effective cost of debt?

Solution

▶ **Plan**

We can use Equation 12.3 to calculate BCE's effective cost of debt: $r_D(1 - T_C)$.

$$r_D = 4.10\% \text{ (pre-tax cost of debt)}$$

$$T_C = 20\% \text{ (corporate tax rate)}$$

▶ **Execute**

BCE's effective cost of debt is $0.0410(1 - 0.20) = 0.0328 = 3.28\%$.

▶ **Evaluate**

For every $1000 it borrows, BCE pays its bondholders $0.0410(\$1000) = \$41.00$ in interest every year. Because it can deduct that $41.00 in interest from its income, every dollar in interest saves BCE 20 cents in taxes, so the interest tax deduction reduces the firm's tax payment to the government by $0.20(\$41.00) = \$8.20$. Thus BCE's net cost of debt is the $41.00 it pays minus the $8.20 in reduced tax payments, which is $32.80 per $1000, or 3.28%.

We have used corporate bonds as an example in estimating the cost of debt. Many smaller companies do not have access to the bond market and use bank debt instead. In their case, they typically have a good sense of their cost of debt from discussions with their banker about interest rates on new loans.

Cost of Preferred Stock Capital

Firms may also raise capital by issuing preferred stock. Typically, holders of the preferred stock are promised a fixed dividend, which must be paid "in preference to" (i.e., before) any dividends can be paid to common stockholders.

If the preferred dividend is known and fixed, we can estimate the preferred stock's cost of capital using Equation 9.7 in Chapter 9,

$$r_E = \frac{Div_1}{P_0} + g$$

where the growth rate $g = 0$. Thus,

$$\text{Cost of Preferred Stock Capital} = \frac{\text{Preferred Dividend}}{\text{Preferred Stock Price}} = \frac{Div_{pfd}}{P_{pfd}} \tag{12.4}$$

For example, BCE's preferred stock has a price of $23.48 and an annual dividend of $1.135. Its cost of preferred stock, therefore, is 1.135/23.48 = 4.83%.[3]

Cost of Common Stock Capital

As we learned in Chapter 11, a company cannot directly observe its cost of common stock (equity), but must instead estimate it. We now present and compare the two major methods for doing so.

Capital Asset Pricing Model. The most common approach is to use the CAPM as presented in Chapter 11. That approach is summarized below:

1. Estimate the firm's beta of equity, typically by regressing 60 months of the company's returns against 60 months of returns for a market proxy, such as the S&P/ TSX Composite Index.

2. Determine the risk-free rate, typically by using the yield on Government of Canada treasury bills or bonds.

3. Estimate the market risk premium, typically by comparing historical returns on a market proxy to contemporaneous risk-free rates.

4. Apply the CAPM:

Cost of Equity = Risk-Free Rate + Equity Beta × Market Risk Premium

For example, suppose the equity beta of BCE is 0.53 and the yield on 10-year Government of Canada bonds is 3.5%, and you estimate the market risk premium to be 6%. BCE's cost of equity is 3.5% + 0.53 × 6% = 6.68%.

Constant Dividend Growth Model. Another way to estimate a company's cost of equity comes from the Constant Dividend Growth Model (CDGM) introduced in Chapter 9. Equation 9.7 from Chapter 9 shows that

$$\text{Cost of Equity} = \frac{\text{Dividend (in one year)}}{\text{Current Price}} + \text{Dividend Growth Rate} = \frac{Div_1}{P_E} + g \quad (12.5)$$

Thus, to estimate the cost of equity, we need the current price of the stock, the expected dividend in one year, and an estimate of the dividend growth rate. The current price of the stock is easy to obtain online. We may even have a reasonable estimate of next year's dividend. However, as we discussed in Chapter 9, estimating the future dividend growth rate can be very difficult. For example, BCE's dividend was $1.20 per share per year from 2000 to 2004 and then increased to $1.32 in 2005 until 2007, when it increased again to $1.46. Further increases in the following years occurred, and by early 2011, the dividends were $1.83 per year. Perhaps it is reasonable to assume that future dividends would be $1.83 per year, but what about the dividend's long-term growth rate? The historical growth rate has been uneven.

Rather than looking backward at historical growth, one common approach is to use estimates produced by stock analysts, as these estimates are forward-looking. As discussed in Chapter 9, if BCE keeps its dividend payout rate constant, then the long-run growth in dividends will equal the long-run growth in earnings. In early 2011, the average forecast for BCE's long-run earnings growth rate was 3.2%. Thus,

---

[3] BCE has multiple classes of preferred shares. These calculations were based on information regarding BCE's Class R preferred shares. The implied rate of BCE's Class T preferred shares, for example, is 4.87%, which is very close to our calculations for R.

	Capital Asset Pricing Model	**Constant Dividend Growth Model**
TABLE 12.1		
Estimating the Cost of Equity		
Inputs	Equity beta	Current stock price
	Risk-free rate	Expected dividend next year
	Market risk premium	Future dividend growth rate
Major Assumptions	Estimated beta is correct	Dividend estimate is correct
	Market risk premium is accurate	Growth rate matches market expectations
	CAPM is the correct model	Future dividend growth is constant

with an expected dividend in one year of $1.83, a price of $35.90, and long-run dividend growth of 3.2%, the CDGM estimates BCE's cost of equity as follows (using Equation 12.5) as:

$$\text{Cost of Equity} = \frac{Div_1}{P_E} + g = \frac{\$1.83}{\$35.90} + 0.032 = 0.083, \text{ or } 8.3\%$$

We should not be surprised that the two estimates of BCE's cost of equity (6.68% and 8.3%) do not match, because each was based on different assumptions. Further, even given an estimate of future growth of dividends, Equation 12.5 makes an assumption that future dividend growth will continue at a constant rate. This assumption is unlikely to be valid for most firms. Looking again at BCE, its dividend was constant for five years and then increased multiple times (at varying rates) over the next five years. Also note that many young, growing firms do not pay a dividend and have no plans to do so in the near future.

We could use any model relating a firm's stock price to its future cash flows to estimate its cost of equity—the CDGM is just one of the possible models. For example, we could use the discounted free cash flow model from Chapter 9 to solve for the firm's cost of equity.

CAPM and CDGM Comparison. Because of the difficulties with the CDGM, the CAPM is the most popular approach for estimating the cost of equity. Table 12.1 above compares the two approaches.

EXAMPLE 12.3

Estimating the Cost of Equity

Problem

Assume the equity beta for Magna International is 0.90. The yield on 10-year Government of Canada bonds is 3.5%, and you estimate the market risk premium to be 6%. Further, suppose Magna issues an annual dividend of $1.50. Its current stock price is $50, and you expect dividends to increase at a constant rate of 4% per year. Estimate Magna's cost of equity in two ways.

Solution

▶ **Plan**

The two ways to estimate Magna's cost of equity are to use the CAPM and the CDGM.

1. The CAPM requires the risk-free rate, an estimate of the equity's beta, and an estimate of the market risk premium. We can use the yield on 10-year Government of Canada bonds as the risk-free rate.

2. The CDGM requires the current stock price, the expected dividend next year, and an estimate of the constant future growth rate for the dividend:

Risk-free rate: 3.5%   Current price: $50
Equity beta: 0.90   Expected dividend: $1.50
Market risk premium: 6%   Estimated future dividend growth rate: 4%

We can use the CAPM from Chapter 11 to estimate the cost of equity using the CAPM approach and Equation 12.5 to estimate it using the CDGM approach.

▶ **Execute**

1. The CAPM says that

$$\text{Cost of Equity} = \text{Risk-Free Rate} + \text{Equity Beta} \times \text{Market Risk Premium}$$

For Magna, this implies that its cost of equity is $3.5\% + 0.90 \times 6\% = 8.9\%$.

2. The CDGM says

$$\text{Cost of Equity} = \frac{\text{Dividend (in one year)}}{\text{Current Price}} + \text{Dividend Growth Rate} = \frac{\$1.50}{\$50} + 4\% = 7\%$$

▶ **Evaluate**

According to the CAPM, the cost of equity capital is 8.9%; the CDGM produces a result of 7%. Because of the different assumptions we make when using each method, the two methods do not have to produce the same answer—in fact, it would be highly unlikely that they would. When the two approaches produce different answers, we must examine the assumptions we made for each approach and decide which set of assumptions is more realistic.

We can also see what assumption about future dividend growth would be necessary to make the answers converge. By rearranging the CDGM and using the cost of equity we estimated from the CAPM, we have

$$\text{Dividend Growth Rate} = \text{Cost of Equity} - \frac{\text{Dividend (in one year)}}{\text{Current Price}} = 8.9\% - 3\% = 5.9\%$$

Thus, if we believe that Magna's dividends will grow at a rate of 5.9% per year, the two approaches would produce the same cost of equity estimate.

Concept Check

3. How can you measure a firm's cost of debt ?
4. What are the major tradeoffs in using the CAPM versus the CDGM to estimate the cost of equity?

12.3 A Second Look at the Weighted Average Cost of Capital

Now that we have estimated the costs of BCE's different sources of capital, we are ready to calculate the firm's overall WACC. The weights are the percentage of firm value financed by equity, preferred stock, and debt. We can represent these as $E\%$, $P\%$, and $D\%$, respectively, and note that they must sum to 100% (i.e., we must account for all the sources of financing).

WACC Equation

Formally, denoting the cost of equity, preferred stock, and debt capital as r_E, r_{pfd}, and r_D, respectively, and the corporate tax rate as T_C, the WACC is as follows:

Weighted Average Cost of Capital

$$r_{wacc} = r_E E\% + r_{pfd}P\% + r_D(1 - T_C)D\% \tag{12.6}$$

For a company that does not have preferred stock, the WACC condenses to

$$r_{wacc} = r_E E\% + r_D(1 - T_C)D\% \tag{12.7}$$

For example, in early 2011, the market values of BCE's common stock, preferred stock, and debt were $25,334 million, $2770 million, and $11,038 million, respectively. Its total value was, therefore, $25,334 million + $2770 million + $11,038 million = $39,142 million. Given the costs of common stock, preferred stock, and debt we have already computed, BCE's WACC in early 2011 was

$$r_{WACC} = r_E E\% + r_{pfd}P\% + (1 - T_C)r_D D\%$$

$$r_{WACC} = 6.68\%\left(\frac{25,334}{39,142}\right) + 4.83\%\left(\frac{2770}{39,142}\right) + (1 - 0.20)4.10\%\left(\frac{11,038}{39,142}\right)$$

$$r_{WACC} = 5.59\%$$

EXAMPLE 12.4

Computing the WACC

Problem

The expected return on Target's equity is 11.5%, and the firm has a yield to maturity on its debt of 6%. Debt accounts for 18% and equity for 82% of Target's total market value. If its tax rate is 35%, what is this firm's WACC?

Solution

▶ **Plan**

We can compute the WACC using Equation 12.7. To do so, we need to know the costs of equity and debt, their proportions in Target's capital structure, and the firm's tax rate. We have all that information, so we are ready to proceed.

▶ **Execute**

$$r_{wacc} = r_E E\% + r_D(1 - T_C)D\% = (0.115)(0.82) + (0.06)(1 - 0.35)(0.18) = 0.101, \quad \text{or} \quad 10.1\%$$

▶ **Evaluate**

Even though we cannot observe the expected return of Target's investments directly, we can use the expected return on its equity and debt and the WACC formula to estimate it, adjusting for the tax advantage of debt. Target needs to earn at least a 10.1% return on its investment in current and new stores to satisfy both its debt and equity holders.

Weighted Average Cost of Capital in Practice

The WACC is driven by the risk of a company's line of business and, because of the tax effect of interest, its leverage. As a result, WACCs vary widely across industries and companies. Figure 12.3 presents the WACC for several real companies to provide a sense of the degree to which the cost of capital can vary. Some lines of business are clearly riskier than others. For example, selling food products, as Maple Leaf Foods does, is a fairly low-risk proposition, but selling smartphones and related software (as Research In Motion does) is much riskier.

FIGURE 12.3

WACCs for Real Companies

The cost of equity is computed using the company's equity beta, a risk-free rate of 3.47%, and a market risk premium of 10.08%. The cost of debt is presented on an after-tax basis. The weights of equity and debt are based on market values. The WACC is computed by multiplying the cost of equity by the weight of equity, multiplying the cost of debt by the weight of debt, and summing the two results. WACC results are shown in the accompanying bar graph. "N/A" means that the cost of debt is not applicable and refers to companies that have no debt.

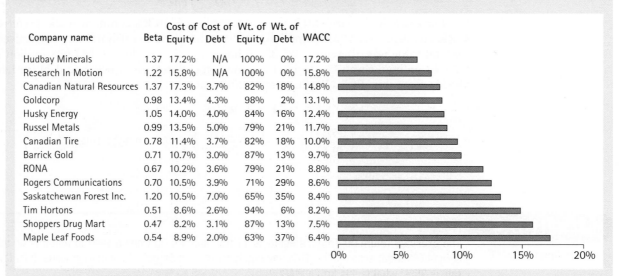

Company name	Beta	Cost of Equity	Cost of Debt	Wt. of Equity	Wt. of Debt	WACC
Hudbay Minerals	1.37	17.2%	N/A	100%	0%	17.2%
Research In Motion	1.22	15.8%	N/A	100%	0%	15.8%
Canadian Natural Resources	1.37	17.3%	3.7%	82%	18%	14.8%
Goldcorp	0.98	13.4%	4.3%	98%	2%	13.1%
Husky Energy	1.05	14.0%	4.0%	84%	16%	12.4%
Russel Metals	0.99	13.5%	5.0%	79%	21%	11.7%
Canadian Tire	0.78	11.4%	3.7%	82%	18%	10.0%
Barrick Gold	0.71	10.7%	3.0%	87%	13%	9.7%
RONA	0.67	10.2%	3.6%	79%	21%	8.8%
Rogers Communications	0.70	10.5%	3.9%	71%	29%	8.6%
Saskatchewan Forest Inc.	1.20	10.5%	7.0%	65%	35%	8.4%
Tim Hortons	0.51	8.6%	2.6%	94%	6%	8.2%
Shoppers Drug Mart	0.47	8.2%	3.1%	87%	13%	7.5%
Maple Leaf Foods	0.54	8.9%	2.0%	63%	37%	6.4%

Source: Bloomberg Professional Services. Note: assumptions with respect to beta estimates may be somewhat different from those presented in the textbook.

Methods in Practice

We now turn to some issues that arise for financial managers when they are estimating the WACC in practice.

Net Debt. When calculating the weights for the WACC, it is increasingly common practice to make an adjustment to the debt. Many practitioners now use **net debt**, the total debt outstanding minus any cash balances:

$$\text{Net Debt} = \text{Debt} - \text{Cash and Risk-Free Securities} \qquad (12.8)$$

net debt Total debt outstanding minus any cash balances.

Why subtract a company's cash from its debt? The assets on a firm's balance sheet include any holdings of cash or risk-free securities. If a firm holds $1 in cash and has $1 of risk-free debt, then the interest earned on the cash will equal the interest paid on the debt. The cash flows from each source cancel each other, just as if the firm held no cash and no debt. In fact, we can view cash as being equivalent to negative debt. Significant excess cash on a firm's balance sheet can complicate the assessment of the risk (and hence the cost of capital) of the assets the firm actually uses in the course of business. Thus, when trying to evaluate a firm's business assets separately from any cash holdings, practitioners often measure the leverage of the firm in terms of its net debt and measure the market value of a firm's business assets using its enterprise value. Recall from Chapter 2 the definition of the enterprise value as the market value of its equity plus its net debt.

Using this approach, the weights in the WACC would then be

$$\left(\frac{\text{Market Value of Equity}}{\text{Enterprise Value}}\right) \text{ and } \left(\frac{\text{Net Debt}}{\text{Enterprise Value}}\right)$$

For firms with substantial excess cash reserves, this adjustment could be important. For firms with relatively low levels of cash, it will not have a large effect on the overall WACC estimate.

The Risk-Free Interest Rate. Estimating the equity cost of capital using the CAPM requires the risk-free interest rate. The risk-free interest rate is generally determined using the yields of Government of Canada debt securities, which are free from default risk. But which horizon should we choose? The CAPM states that we should use the risk-free interest corresponding to the investment horizon of the firm's investors. When surveyed, the vast majority of large firms and financial analysts report using the yields of long-term (10- to 30-year) bonds to determine the risk-free rate.[4]

The Market Risk Premium. Using the CAPM also requires an estimate of the market risk premium. As mentioned in Chapter 10, one way to estimate the market risk premium is to look at historical data. Because we are interested in the *future* market risk premium, we face a tradeoff in terms of the amount of data we use. As noted in Chapter 10, it takes many years of data to produce even moderately accurate estimates of expected returns—yet data that are very old may have little relevance for investors' expectations of the market risk premium today.

Table 12.2 reports excess returns of the S&P/TSX Composite Index versus three-month Canadian treasury bills and long-term Government of Canada bonds. Since 1950, the S&P/TSX Composite Index has produced an average return of almost 6% above the rate for three-month Canadian treasury bills. In the U.S. markets, a comparison of the S&P 500 Index and short-term U.S. Treasury bills from 1926 until 2009 shows an excess return of 7.1%. An interesting change can be seen when comparing the same two U.S. measures over a more recent period of time. Excess returns of the S&P 500 over short-term U.S. Treasury bills from 1959 to 2009 are only 4.7%. The evidence indicates that the market risk premium has declined over time.

How can we explain this decline? One reason may be that as more investors have begun to participate in the stock market and the costs of constructing a diversified portfolio have declined, investors have tended to hold less risky portfolios. As a result, the return they require as compensation for taking on that risk has diminished. In addition, the overall volatility of the market has declined over time. Some researchers believe

TABLE 12.2   Historical Excess Returns of the S&P/TSX Composite Index Compared with Three-Month Canadian Treasury Bills and Long-Term Government of Canada Bonds

Risk-Free Security	Period	S&P/TSX Composite Excess Return
Three-month Canadian treasury bills	1950–2009	5.88%
Long-term Government of Canada bonds	1950–2009	4.26%

---

[4] See Robert Bruner, et al., "Best Practices in Estimating the Cost of Capital: Survey and Synthesis," *Financial Practice and Education* 8 (1998): 13–28.

that the future expected returns for the market are likely to be even lower than these historical numbers, in a range of 3% to 5% over treasury bills.[5] Consequently, many financial managers currently use market risk premiums closer to 5%, rather than 7%.

Concept Check

5. Why do different companies have different WACCs?

6. What are the tradeoffs in estimating the market risk premium?

12.4 Using the WACC to Value a Project

A project's cost of capital depends on its risk. When the market risk of the project is similar to the average market risk of the firm's investments, then its cost of capital is equivalent to the cost of capital for a portfolio of all the firm's securities. In other words, the project's cost of capital is equal to the firm's WACC. As shown in Equation 12.6, the WACC incorporates the benefit of the interest tax deduction by using the firm's *after-tax* cost of capital for debt.

Because the WACC incorporates the tax savings from debt, we can compute the value of an investment including the benefit of the interest tax deduction given the firm's leverage policy, sometimes called the investment's **levered value**. To do so, we discount the firm's future incremental free cash flow using the WACC, a process we refer to as the **WACC method**. Specifically, if FCF_t is the expected incremental free cash flow of an investment at the end of year t, then the Valuation Principle tells us that the investment's levered value, V_0^L, is

levered value The value of an investment, including the benefit of the interest tax deduction, given the firm's leverage policy.

WACC method Discounting future incremental free cash flows using the firm's WACC. This method produces the levered value of a project.

$$V_0^L = \frac{FCF_1}{1 + r_{wacc}} + \frac{FCF_2}{(1 + r_{wacc})^2} + \frac{FCF_3}{(1 + r_{wacc})^3} + \cdots \qquad (12.9)$$

The reasoning behind the WACC method is that the firm's WACC represents the average return the firm must pay to its investors (both debt and equity holders) on an after-tax basis. Thus, to have a positive *NPV*, a project with the same risk as the average risk for the firm's projects should generate an expected return of at least the firm's WACC.

EXAMPLE 12.5

The WACC Method

Problem

Suppose Big Rock Brewery is considering introducing a new ultra-light beer with zero calories to be called BigZero. The firm believes that the beer's flavour and appeal to calorie-conscious drinkers will make it a success. The cost of bringing the beer to market is $200 million, but Big Rock expects first-year incremental free cash flows from BigZero to be $100 million and to grow at 3% per year thereafter. If Big Rock's WACC is 5.7%, should it go ahead with the project?

Solution

▶ **Plan**

We can use the WACC method shown in Equation 12.9 to value BigZero and then subtract the upfront cost of $200 million. We will need Big Rock's WACC, which is 5.7%.

---

[5] See Ivo Welch, "The Equity Premium Consensus Forecast Revisited," Cowles Foundation Discussion Paper 1325 (2001); and John Graham and Campbell Harvey, "The Long-Run Equity Risk Premium," SSRN working paper (2005).

▶ **Execute**

The cash flows for BigZero are a growing perpetuity. Applying the growing perpetuity formula with the WACC method, we have

$$V_0^L = FCF_0 + \frac{FCF_1}{r_{wacc} - g} = -200 + \frac{\$100 \text{ million}}{0.057 - 0.03} = \$3503.7 \text{ million } (\$3.5 \text{ billion})$$

▶ **Evaluate**

The BigZero project has a positive *NPV* because it is expected to generate a return on the $200 million far in excess of Big Rock's WACC of 5.7%. As discussed in Chapter 3, taking positive-*NPV* projects adds value to the firm. Here, we can see that the value is created by exceeding the required return of the firm's investors.

Key Assumptions

While it is common practice to use the WACC as the discount rate in capital budgeting, it is important to be aware of the underlying assumptions. We examine the critical assumptions here and then explore these assumptions further in the context of an application.

Assumption 1: Average Risk. We assume initially that the market risk of the project is equivalent to the average market risk of the firm's investments. In that case, we assess the project's cost of capital based on the risk of the firm.

debt-equity ratio A ratio of the market value of debt to the market value of equity.

Assumption 2: Constant Debt-Equity Ratio. We assume that the firm adjusts its leverage continuously to maintain a constant ratio of the market value of debt to the market value of equity—a relationship referred to as the **debt-equity ratio**. This policy determines the amount of debt the firm will take on when it accepts a new project. It also implies that the risk of the firm's equity and debt, and therefore its WACC, will not fluctuate owing to leverage changes.

Assumption 3: Limited Leverage Effects. We assume initially that the main effect of leverage on valuation follows from the interest tax deduction. We assume that any other factors (such as possible financial distress) are not significant at the level of debt chosen. We discuss these other factors in detail in Chapter 15.

Assumptions in Practice. These assumptions are reasonable for many projects and firms. The first assumption is likely to fit typical projects of firms with investments concentrated in a single industry. In that case, the market risk of both the project and the firm will primarily depend on the sensitivity of the industry to the overall economy. The second assumption, while unlikely to hold exactly, reflects the fact that firms tend to increase their levels of debt as they grow larger; some may even have an explicit target for their debt-equity ratio.[6] Finally, for firms without very high levels of debt, the interest tax deduction is likely to be the most important factor affecting the capital budgeting decision. Hence, the third assumption is a reasonable starting point to begin our analysis.

Of course, while these three assumptions may be a reasonable approximation in many situations, there are certainly projects and firms for which they do not apply.

---

[6] We discuss the tradeoff between debt and equity and the concept of a target debt-equity ratio in Chapter 15.

In the following section, we apply the WACC method under all three assumptions. Next, we relax the first assumption, which states that the project has average risk. (We will relax the other two assumptions in later chapters.)

WACC Method Application: Extending the Life of Facilities at BCE

Let's apply the WACC method to value a project. Suppose BCE is considering an investment that would extend the life of one of its facilities for four years. The project would require upfront costs of $6.67 million plus a $24 million investment in equipment. Assume that the equipment will be obsolete in four years and will be depreciated for tax purposes via the straight-line method over that period.[7] During the next four years, however, BCE expects annual sales of $60 million per year from this facility. Cost of sales and operating expenses are expected to total $25 million and $9 million, respectively, per year. Finally, BCE expects no net working capital requirements for the project, and it pays a corporate tax rate of 35%.

Using this information, the spreadsheet in Table 12.3 forecasts the project's expected free cash flow. The market risk of the project of extending the life of the facility is the same as that for BCE's overall business. As a consequence, we can use BCE's WACC to compute the NPV of the project.

We can determine the value of the project, including the present value of the interest tax deduction from the debt, by calculating the present value of its future free cash flows, V_0^L using the WACC method and BCE's WACC of 5.59%, which we computed in Section 12.3:

$$V_0^L = \frac{19}{1.0559} + \frac{19}{1.0559^2} + \frac{19}{1.0559^3} + \frac{19}{1.0559^4} = \$66.46 \text{ million}$$

Because the upfront cost of extending the facility's life is only $28.34 million, this project is a good idea. Taking the project results in an NPV of $66.46 million – $28.34 million = $38.12 million for the firm.

TABLE 12.3		1	Year	0	1	2	3	4
Expected Free Cash Flow from BCE's Facility Project		2	Incremental Earnings Forecast ($ million)					
		3	Sales	—	60.00	60.00	60.00	60.00
		4	Cost of Sales	—	−25.00	−25.00	−25.00	−25.00
		5	Gross Profit	—	35.00	35.00	35.00	35.00
		6	Operating Expenses	−6.67	−9.00	−9.00	−9.00	−9.00
		7	Depreciation	—	−6.00	−6.00	−6.00	−6.00
		8	EBIT	−6.67	20.00	20.00	20.00	20.00
		9	Income Tax at 35%	2.33	−7.00	−7.00	−7.00	−7.00
		10	Unlevered Net Income	−4.43	13.00	13.00	13.00	13.00
		11	Incremental Free Cash Flow ($ million)					
		12	Plus: Depreciation	—	6.00	6.00	6.00	6.00
		13	Less: Capital Expenditures	−24.00	—	—	—	—
		14	Less: Increases in NWC	—	—	—	—	—
		15	Incremental Free Cash Flow	−28.34	19.00	19.00	19.00	19.00

---

[7]Straight-line method of depreciation is used for simplification purposes. Assets would normally be depreciated for tax purposes using rates and methods prescribed by Canada Revenue Agency.

Summary of the WACC Method

To summarize, the key steps in the WACC valuation method are as follows:

1. Determine the incremental free cash flow of the investment.
2. Compute the weighted average cost of capital using Equation 12.6.
3. Compute the value of the investment, including the tax benefit of leverage, by discounting the incremental free cash flow of the investment using the WACC.

In many firms, the corporate treasurer performs the second step, calculating the firm's WACC. This rate can then be used throughout the firm as the company-wide cost of capital for new investments *that are of comparable risk to the rest of the firm and that will not alter the firm's debt-equity ratio.* Employing the WACC method in this way is very simple and straightforward. As a result, this method is the most commonly used in practice for capital budgeting purposes.

Concept Check

7. What are the main assumptions you make when you use the WACC method?
8. What inputs do you need to be ready to apply the WACC method?

12.5 Project-Based Costs of Capital

Up to this point, we have assumed that both the risk and the leverage of the project under consideration matched those characteristics for the firm as a whole. This assumption allowed us, in turn, to assume that the cost of capital for a project matched the firm's cost of capital.

In reality, specific projects often differ from the average investment made by the firm. Consider General Electric Company (GE), a large firm with many divisions that operate in completely different lines of business. Projects in GE's health care division are likely to have different market risk than projects in its air transportation equipment division or at NBC Universal. Projects may also vary in terms of the amount of leverage they will support—for example, acquisitions of real estate or capital equipment are often highly levered, while investments in intellectual property are not. We will study the effect of leverage on the cost of capital when we cover the leverage decision in Chapter 15. In this section, we show how to calculate the cost of capital for the project's cash flows when a project's risk differs from the firm's overall risk.

Cost of Capital for a New Acquisition

We begin by explaining how to calculate the cost of capital of a project with market risk that is different from the risk for the rest of the firm. Suppose BCE wants to enter the forest products business. To do so, it is considering acquiring Saskatchewan Forest Inc. (SFI), a company that is focused on timber, paper, and other forest products. SFI faces different market risks than BCE does in its communications business. What cost of capital should BCE use to value a possible acquisition of SFI?

Because the risks are different, BCE's WACC would be inappropriate for valuing SFI. Instead, BCE should calculate and use SFI's WACC when assessing the acquisition. In Figure 12.3, we find the following information for SFI:

	Beta	Cost of Equity	Cost of Cost of Debt	% Equity	% Debt	WACC
Saskatchewan Forest Inc.	1.20	10.5%	7.0%	65%	35%	8.4%

Assuming that BCE will find it appropriate to continue to finance SFI with the same mix of debt and equity after it buys SFI,[8] we can use SFI's WACC as the cost of capital for acquiring it. Thus, BCE would use a cost of capital of 8.4% to value SFI for purchase.

Divisional Costs of Capital

Now assume BCE makes a different decision: it decides to create a forest products division internally, rather than buying SFI. What should the cost of capital for the new division be? If BCE plans to finance the division with the same proportion of debt as is used by SFI, then BCE would use SFI's WACC as the WACC for its new division. Because SFI's WACC is the right cost of capital given the risks of forest products and 35% debt financing, it has to be the right cost of capital for an internally created forest products division that is financed 35% with debt.

In reality, firms with more than one division rarely use a single company-wide WACC to evaluate projects. More typically, they perform analyses similar to BCE's analysis of SFI. Multidivisional firms benchmark their own divisions on the basis of companies that compete with their division and are focused in that single line of business. By performing the same analysis as we did in Figure 12.3, the multidivisional firm can estimate the WACCs of its divisions' competitors—adjusting for different financing if necessary—to estimate the cost of capital for each division.

EXAMPLE 12.6

A Project in a New Line of Business

Problem

You are working for Forzani Group Limited, evaluating the possibility of selling smartphones and related software. Forzani's WACC is 8.8%. Smartphones and related software would be a new line of business for Forzani, however, so the systematic risk of this business would probably differ from the systematic risk of Forzani's current business As a result, the assets of this new business should have a different cost of capital. You need to find the cost of capital for the smartphone business. Assuming that the risk-free rate is 3.5% and the market risk premium is 6%, how would you estimate the cost of capital for this type of investment?

Solution

▶ **Plan**

The first step is to identify a company operating in Forzani's targeted line of business. Research In Motion (RIM) is a well-known marketer of smartphones and related software. In fact, that is all RIM does. Thus the cost of capital for RIM would be a good estimate of the cost of capital for Forzani's proposed smartphone business. Many websites are available that provide betas for traded stocks, including the Google Finance website, www.google.com/finance. Suppose you visit that site and find that the beta of RIM stock is 1.44. With this beta, the risk-free rate, and the market risk premium, you can use the CAPM to estimate the cost of equity for RIM. Fortunately for us, RIM has no debt, so its cost of equity is the same as its cost of capital for its assets.

▶ **Execute**

Using the CAPM, we have

RIM's Cost of Equity = Risk-Free Rate + RIM's Equity Beta × Market Risk Premium

= 3.5% + 1.44 × 6% = 12.1%

Because RIM has no debt, its WACC is equivalent to its cost of equity.

---

[8] We consider what to do if BCE wants to change SFI's financing mix in Chapter 15.

▶ **Evaluate**

The correct cost of capital for evaluating a smartphone investment opportunity is 12.1%. If we had used the 8.8% cost of capital that is associated with Forzani's *existing* business, we would have mistakenly used too low a cost of capital. That could lead us to go ahead with the investment, even though it truly had a negative *NPV*.

Concept Check

9. When evaluating a project in a new line of business, which assumptions about the WACC method are most likely to be violated?

10. How can you estimate the WACC to be used in a new line of business?

12.6 When Raising External Capital Is Costly

So far, we have assumed that there are no important factors, other than taxes, to consider in seeking capital. Among other things, this implies that we can raise external capital without any extra costs associated with the capital-raising transaction. As a consequence, we have no reason to treat a project financed with new external funds any differently than a project financed with internal funds (retained earnings).

In reality, issuing new equity or bonds carries a number of costs. These costs include the costs of filing and registering with a provincial regulator (e.g., the Ontario Securities Commission) and the fees charged by investment bankers to place the securities. We will discuss the process for issuing equity and bonds in detail in the next two chapters. Here, we mention it briefly in the context of the cost of capital.

Because of these issuing costs, a project that can be financed from internal funds will be less costly overall than the same project if it were financed with external funds. One approach would be to adjust the costs of equity and debt capital in the WACC to incorporate the issuing costs. A better and far more direct route is to simply treat the issuing costs as what they are—cash outflows that are necessary to the project. We can then incorporate this additional cost as a negative cash flow in the *NPV* analysis.

EXAMPLE 12.7

Evaluating an Acquisition with Costly External Financing

Problem

You are analyzing BCE's potential acquisition of Saskatchewan Forest Inc. (SFI). BCE plans to offer $9 billion as the purchase price for SFI and will need to issue additional debt and equity to finance such a large acquisition. You estimate that the issuance costs will be $350 million and will be paid as soon as the transaction closes. You also estimate that the incremental free cash flows from the acquisition will be $0.6 billion in the first year and will grow at 3% per year thereafter. What is the *NPV* of the proposed acquisition?

Solution

▶ **Plan**

We know from Section 12.5 that the correct cost of capital for this acquisition is SFI's WACC. We can value the incremental free cash flows as a growing perpetuity:

$$PV = FCF_1/(r - g)$$

where

$$FCF_1 = \$0.6 \text{ billion}$$

$$r = \text{SFI's WACC} = 0.088$$

$$g = 0.03$$

The *NPV* of the transaction, including the costly external financing, is the present value of this growing perpetuity net of both the purchase cost and the transaction costs of using external financing.

▶ **Execute**

Noting that $350 million is $0.35 billion,

$$NPV = -\$9 - \$0.35 + \frac{\$0.6}{0.088 - 0.03} = \$0.995 \text{ billion or } \$995 \text{ million}$$

▶ **Evaluate**

It is not necessary to try to adjust SFI's WACC for the issuance costs of debt and equity. Instead, we can subtract the issuance costs from the *NPV* of the acquisition to confirm that the acquisition remains a positive-*NPV* project even if it must be financed externally.

In this chapter, we learned what a firm's cost of capital is, where it comes from, and how it is used in capital budgeting. The role of capital budgeting is to identify positive-*NPV* projects that allow a firm to cover the costs of its various types of capital. Now we turn to another aspect of capital financing—where the firm gets that capital. In the next three chapters, we explore how a firm raises equity and debt capital and how it decides the proportion of each to have in its capital structure.

Concept
Check

11. What types of additional costs does a firm incur when accessing external capital?

12. What is the best way to incorporate these additional costs into capital budgeting?

MyFinance**Lab**   Here is what you should know after reading this chapter. MyFinanceLab will help you identify what you know, and where to go when you need to practice.

Key Points and Equations	Terms	Online Practice Opportunities
12.1 A First Look at the Weighted Average Cost of Capital ▶ A firm's debt and equity represent its capital. The relative proportions of debt, equity, and other securities that a firm has outstanding constitute its capital structure. ▶ Investors of each type of capital have a required return. Providing this return is the cost a company bears to obtain capital from investors.	capital, p. 414 capital structure, p. 414 leverage, p. 416 levered, p. 416 market-value balance sheet, p. 415 unlevered, p. 416 weighted average cost of capital (WACC), p. 414	MyFinanceLab Study Plan 12.1

- We calculate the firm's overall cost of capital as a weighted average of its equity and debt costs of capital, referred to as the firm's weighted average cost of capital.
- The weights in the WACC must be based on the market values of each of the firm's debt and equity, not the book values.

12.2 The Firm's Costs of Debt and Equity Capital

- To estimate the cost of capital for a company as a whole, we usually start by estimating the cost of each of the company's sources of capital.
- The cost of debt is the interest a firm would need to pay on *new* debt. It will generally differ from the coupon rate on existing debt, but can be estimated from the yield to maturity on existing debt.
- The cost of preferred stock is straightforward to estimate because of its constant and known dividend:

$$\text{Cost of Preferred Stock Capital} = \frac{Div_{pfd}}{P_{pfd}} \quad (12.4)$$

- The Capital Asset Pricing Model (CAPM) is the most common approach for estimating the cost of equity capital. To apply the CAPM, we need an estimate of the firm's equity beta, the market risk premium, and the risk-free rate:

$$\text{Cost of Equity} = \text{Risk-Free Rate} + \text{Equity Beta} \times \text{Market Risk Premium}$$

- Another approach to estimating the cost of equity is to use the Constant Dividend Growth Model (CDGM). To apply this model, we need the current stock price, the expected future dividend, and an estimate of the dividend's constant growth rate:

$$\text{Cost of Equity} = \frac{Div_1}{P_E} + g \quad (12.5)$$

effective cost of debt, p. 419

MyFinanceLab
Study Plan 12.2

12.3 A Second Look at the Weighted Average Cost of Capital

- The WACC equation is

$$r_{wacc} = r_E E\% + r_{pfd}P\% + r_D(1 - T_C)D\% \quad (12.6)$$

- For a company that does not have preferred stock, the WACC equation condenses to

$$r_{wacc} = r_E E\% + r_D(1 - T_C)D\% \quad (12.7)$$

net debt, p. 424

MyFinanceLab
Study Plan 12.53

▶ The WACC is driven by the risk of a company's line of business and, because of the tax effect of interest, its leverage. As a result, WACCs vary widely across industries and companies.

12.4 Using the WACC to Value a Project	debt-equity ratio, p. 427	MyFinanceLab Study Plan 12.4
▶ Assuming that a project has average risk for the firm, that the firm will maintain its current leverage ratio, and that a firm's leverage affects its value only through taxes, the WACC can be used to value the cash flows from a new project.	levered value, p. 426 WACC method, p. 426	Spreadsheet Table 12.3
12.5 Project-Based Costs of Capital		
▶ If the project's risk differs from the average risk for the firm, the WACC will not be the appropriate discount rate for the project. Instead, you must estimate the WACC from the WACC of other firms operating in the same line of business as the new project.		MyFinanceLab Study Plan 12.5
12.6 When Raising External Capital Is Costly		
▶ The WACC is calculated without accounting for the direct costs of raising external financing. Rather than adjusting the WACC, the correct way to account for these costs is to subtract their present value from the *NPV* of the project.		MyFinanceLab Study Plan 12.6

Review Questions

1. What does the WACC measure?

2. Why are market-based weights important?

3. Why is the coupon rate of existing debt irrelevant for finding the cost of debt capital?

4. Why is it easier to determine the costs of preferred stock and of debt than it is to determine the cost of common equity?

5. Describe the steps involved in the CAPM approach to estimating the cost of equity.

6. Why would the CDGM and CAPM produce different estimates of the cost of equity capital?

7. Under what assumptions can the WACC be used to value a project?

8. What are some possible problems that might be associated with the assumptions used in applying the WACC method?

9. How should you value a project in a line of business with risk that is different from the average risk of your firm's projects?

10. What is the right way to adjust for the costs of raising external financing?

Problems

All problems in this chapter are available in MyFinanceLab.

A First Look at the Weighted Average Cost of Capital

1. MV Corporation has debt with market value of $100 million, common equity with a book value of $100 million, and preferred stock worth $20 million outstanding. Its common equity trades at $50 per share, and the firm has 6 million shares outstanding. What weights should MV Corporation use in its WACC?

2. Andyco, Inc., has the following balance sheet and an equity market-to-book ratio of 1.5. Assuming the market value of debt equals its book value, what weights should it use for its WACC calculation?

Assets	Liabilities and Equity	
1000	Debt	400
	Equity	600

3. Book Co. has 1 million shares of common equity with a par (book) value of $1 and retained earnings of $30 million, and its shares have a market value of $50 per share. It also has debt with a par value of $20 million that is trading at 101% of par.
   a. What is the market value of its equity?
   b. What is the market value of its debt?
   c. What weights should it use in computing its WACC?

4. Consider a simple firm that has the following market-value balance sheet:

Assets	Liabilities and Equity	
1000	Debt	400
	Equity	600

Next year, there are two possible values for its assets, each equally likely: $1200 and $960. Its debt will be due with 5% interest. Because all of the cash flows from the assets must go to either the debt or the equity, if you hold a portfolio of the debt and equity in the same proportions as the firm's capital structure, your portfolio should earn exactly the expected return on the firm's assets. Show that a portfolio invested 40% in the firm's debt and 60% in its equity will have the same expected return as the assets of the firm. That is, show that the firm's pre-tax WACC is the same as the expected return on its assets.

The Firm's Costs of Debt and Equity Capital

5. Avicorp has a $10 million debt issue outstanding, with a 6% coupon rate. The debt has semi-annual coupons, the next coupon is due in six months, and the debt matures in five years. It is currently priced at 95% of par value.
   a. What is Avicorp's pre-tax cost of debt?
   b. If Avicorp faces a 40% tax rate, what is its after-tax cost of debt?

6. Laurel, Inc., has debt outstanding with a coupon rate of 6% and a yield to maturity of 7%. Its tax rate is 35%. What is Laurel's effective (after-tax) cost of debt?

7. Dewyco has preferred stock trading at $50 per share. The next preferred dividend of $4 is due in one year. What is Dewyco's cost of capital for preferred stock?

8. Steady Company's stock has a beta of 0.20. If the risk-free rate is 6% and the market risk premium is 7%, what is an estimate of Steady Company's cost of equity?

9. Wild Swings, Inc.'s stock has a beta of 2.5. Given the information in Problem 8, what is an estimate of Wild Swings' cost of equity?

10. HighGrowth Company has a stock price of $20. The firm will pay a dividend next year of $1, and its dividend is expected to grow at a rate of 4% per year thereafter. What is your estimate of HighGrowth's cost of equity capital?

11. Slow 'n Steady, Inc., has a stock price of $30, will pay a dividend next year of $3, and has expected dividend growth of 1% per year. What is your estimate of Slow 'n Steady's cost of equity capital?

12. Mackenzie Company has a price of $36 and will issue a dividend of $2 next year. It has a beta of 1.2, the risk-free rate is 5.5%, and the market risk premium is estimated to be 5%.
    a. Estimate the equity cost of capital for Mackenzie.
    b. Under the CGDM, at what rate do you need to expect Mackenzie's dividends to grow to get the same equity cost of capital as in part (a)?

A Second Look at the Weighted Average Cost of Capital

13. CoffeeCarts has a cost of equity of 15%, has an effective cost of debt of 4%, and is financed 70% with equity and 30% with debt. What is this firm's WACC?

14. Pfd Company has debt with a yield to maturity of 7%, a cost of equity of 13%, and a cost of preferred stock of 9%. The market values of its debt, preferred stock, and equity are $10 million, $3 million, and $15 million, respectively, and its tax rate is 40%. What is this firm's WACC?

15. Growth Company's current share price is $20 and is expected to pay a $1 dividend per share next year. After that, the firm's dividends are expected to grow at a rate of 4% per year.
    a. What is an estimate of Growth Company's cost of equity?
    b. Growth Company also has preferred stock outstanding that pays a $2 per share fixed dividend. If this stock is currently priced at $28, what is Growth Company's cost of preferred stock?
    c. Growth Company has existing debt issued three years ago with a coupon rate of 6%. The firm just issued new debt at par with a coupon rate of 6.5%. What is Growth Company's pre-tax cost of debt?
    d. Growth Company has 5 million common shares outstanding and 1 million preferred shares outstanding, and its equity has a total book value of $50 million. Its liabilities have a market value of $20 million. If Growth Company's common and preferred shares are priced at $20 and $28, respectively, what is the market value of Growth Company's assets?
    e. Growth Company faces a 35% tax rate. Given the information in parts (a) to (d), and your answers to those problems, what is Growth Company's WACC?

Using the WACC to Value a Project

16. A retail coffee company is planning to open 100 new coffee outlets that are expected to generate, in total, $15 million in free cash flows per year, with a growth rate of 3% in perpetuity. If the coffee company's WACC is 10%, what is the *NPV* of this expansion?

17. RiverRocks, Inc., is considering a project with the following projected free cash flows:

0	1	2	3	4
−50	10	20	20	15

The firm believes that, given the risk of this project, the WACC method is the appropriate approach to valuing the project. RiverRocks' WACC is 12%. Should it take on this project? Why or why not?

Project-Based Costs of Capital

18. RiverRocks (see Problem 17), whose WACC is 12%, is considering an acquisition of Raft Adventures (whose WACC is 15%). What is the appropriate discount rate for RiverRocks to use to evaluate the acquisition? Why?

19. RiverRocks' purchase of Raft Adventures (see Problem 18) will cost $100 million but will generate cash flows that start at $15 million in one year and then grow at 4% per year forever. What is the *NPV* of the acquisition?

20. CoffeeStop primarily sells coffee. It recently introduced a premium coffee-flavoured liquor. Suppose the firm faces a tax rate of 35% and collects the following information:

	Beta	% Equity	% Debt
CoffeeStop	0.61	96%	4%
Brown-Forman Liquors	0.26	89%	11%

If the company plans to finance 11% of the new liquor-focused division with debt and the rest with equity, what WACC should it use for its liquor division? Assume a cost of debt of 4.8%, a risk-free rate of 4.5%, and a risk-free rate of 4.5%, an equity beta of 0.26, and a market risk premium of 5.5%.

21. Your company has two divisions: one division sells software and the other division sells computers through a direct sales channel, primarily taking orders over the internet. You have decided that Dell Computer is very similar to your computer division, in terms of both risk and financing. You go online and find the following information: Dell's beta is 1.21, the risk-free rate is 4.5%, its market value of equity is $67 billion, and it has $700 million worth of debt with a yield to maturity of 6%. Your tax rate is 35%, and you use a market risk premium of 5% in your WACC estimates.

a. What is an estimate of the WACC for your computer sales division?

b. If your overall company WACC is 12% and the computer sales division represents 40% of the value of your firm, what is an estimate of the WACC for your software division?

When Raising External Capital Is Costly

22. RiverRocks realizes that it will have to raise the financing for the acquisition of Raft Adventures (described in Problem 19) by issuing new debt and equity. RiverRocks estimates that the direct issuing costs will amount to $7 million. How should it account for these costs in evaluating the project? Should RiverRocks go ahead with the project?

● **Data Case**

You work in Walt Disney Company's corporate finance and treasury department and have just been assigned to the team estimating Disney's WACC. You must estimate this WACC in preparation for a team meeting later today. You quickly realize that the information you need is readily available online.

1. Go to the Yahoo! Finance website, http://finance.yahoo.com. Under "Market Summary," you will find the yield to maturity for 10-year treasury bonds listed as "10 Yr Bond(%)." Collect this number as your risk-free rate.

2. In the box next to the "Get Quotes" button, type Walt Disney's ticker symbol (DIS) and press enter. Once you see the basic information for Disney, find and click on "Key Statistics" on the left side of the screen. From the key statistics, collect the information for Disney's market capitalization (its market value of equity), enterprise value (market-value equity + net debt), cash, and beta.

3. To get Disney's cost of debt and the market value of its long-term debt, you will need the price and yield to maturity on the firm's existing long-term bonds. Go to the Financial Industry Regulatory Authority's website, www.finra.org, click on "Investors" and then, under "Market Data," click on "Bonds." Under "Quick Bond Search," click on "Corporate" and type Disney's ticker symbol. A list of Disney's outstanding bond issues will appear. Assume that Disney's policy is to use the yield to maturity on non-callable 10-year obligations as its cost of debt. Find the non-callable bond issue that is as close to 10 years from maturity as possible. (*Hint:* You will see a column titled "Callable"; make sure the issue you choose has "No" in this column.) You may have to choose a bond issued by one if its subsidiaries, such as ABC. Find the yield to maturity for your chosen bond issue (it is in the column titled "Yield") and enter that yield as your pre-tax cost of debt into your spreadsheet. Next, copy and paste the data in the entire table into Excel.

4. You now have the price for each bond issue, but you need to know the size of the issue. From the current webpage, go to the row of the bond you choose and click the Issuer Name in the first column (this will either be Walt Disney Company or ABC or another subsidiary). This brings up a webpage with all of the information about the bond issue. Scroll down until you find "Amount Outstanding" on the right side. Noting that this amount is quoted in thousands of dollars (e.g., $60,000 means $60 million = $60,000,000), record the issue amount in the appropriate row of your spreadsheet. Repeat this step for all of the bond issues.

5. The price for each bond issue in your spreadsheet is reported as a percentage of the bond's par value. For example, 104.50 means that the bond issue is trading at 104.5% of its par value. You can calculate the market value of each bond issue by multiplying the amount outstanding by (Price 100). Do so for each issue and then calculate the total of all the bond issues. This is the market value of Disney's debt.

6. Compute the weights for Disney's equity and debt based on the market value of equity and Disney's market value of debt, computed in step 5.

7. Calculate Disney's cost of equity capital using the CAPM, the risk-free rate you collected in step 1, and a market risk premium of 5%.

8. Assuming that Disney has a tax rate of 35%, calculate its effective cost of debt capital.

9. Calculate Disney's WACC.

10. Calculate Disney's net debt by subtracting its cash (collected in step 2) from its debt. Recalculate the weights for the WACC using the market value of equity, net debt, and enterprise value. Recalculate Disney's WACC using the weights based on the net debt. How much does it change?

11. How confident are you of your estimate? Which implicit assumptions did you make during your data collection efforts?

PART 4 Integrative Case

If the data sets on the websites indicated for this case become unavailable in the future, the data sets will be posted on the textbook's website.

This case draws on material from Chapters 10 to 12.

You work for HydroTech, a large manufacturer of high-pressure industrial water pumps. The firm specializes in natural disaster services, ranging from pumps that draw water from lakes, ponds, and streams in drought-stricken areas to pumps that remove high water volumes in flooded areas. You report directly to the CFO. Your boss has asked you to calculate HydroTech's WACC in preparation for an executive retreat. Too bad you're not invited, as water pumps and skiing are on the agenda in Whistler, BC. At least you have an analyst on hand to gather the following required information:

1. The risk-free rate of interest, in this case, the yield of the 10-year government bond, which is 3%.

2. Specific information for HydroTech:
   a. Market capitalization (its market value of equity), $100 million
   b. CAPM beta, 1.2
   c. Total book value of debt outstanding, $50 million
   d. Cash, $10 million

3. The cost of debt (using the quoted yields on HydroTech's outstanding bond issues), which is 5%.

   With this information in hand, you are now prepared to undertake the analysis.

Case Questions

1. Calculate HydroTech's net debt.

2. Compute HydroTech's equity and (net) debt weights based on the market value of equity and the book value of net debt.

3. Calculate the cost of equity capital using the CAPM, assuming a market risk premium of 5%.

4. Using a tax rate of 35%, calculate HydroTech's effective cost of debt capital.

5. Calculate HydroTech's WACC.

6. When is it appropriate to use this WACC to evaluate a new project?

PART 5

Long-Term Financing

Valuation Principle Connection. How should a firm raise the funds it needs to undertake its investments? In this part of the book, we explain the mechanics of raising equity and issuing debt. Chapter 13 describes the process a company goes through when it raises equity capital. In Chapter 14, we review firms' use of debt markets to raise capital. Later, in the capital structure section of the text, we will discuss the financial manager's choice between these two major categories of financing. A firm's ability to raise capital depends on the value the market applies to its securities. The Valuation Principle tells us that the price of any securities issued by the firm will be the present value of the cash flows accruing to them. Thus, while we discuss the process for raising capital in the following two chapters, it is important to remember that the price investors are willing to pay for a firm's securities depends on the financial manager making investment decisions that maximize the value of the firm.

Chapter 13
Raising Equity Capital

Chapter 14
Debt Financing

Raising Equity Capital

LEARNING OBJECTIVES

▶ Contrast the different ways to raise equity capital for a private company

▶ Understand the process of taking a company public

▶ Gain insight into puzzles associated with initial public offerings

▶ Explain how to raise additional equity capital once the company is public

INTERVIEW WITH Zeke Purves-Smith,
McMillan LLP

Dalhousie, 2006

"My job is to help private and public companies draft agreements for issuing securities."

Zeke Purves-Smith is a corporate and energy lawyer for McMillan LLP. A graduate of Dalhousie University's MBA/LLB program in 2006, Zeke applies his law and business education to help companies meet legal reporting requirements. "As a corporate lawyer, my job is to help private and public companies draft agreements for issuing securities."

Firms looking to raise capital must consider a number of factors when making their decision. First, they must choose whether to raise debt or equity, each of which has certain costs and benefits. If the firm decides to use equity financing, it must then decide whether to look for private sources of funding or access the public markets. Again, the firm must weigh the costs and benefits of each strategy before settling on the best option. One major cost of going public is that the firm will have to publicly report all of its financial information on a regular basis, and this is where Zeke comes in. "Everything must adhere to securities commission filing requirements. The nature of the agreement will depend on the characteristics of the issuer and the purchasers," he says. "For instance," he continues, "when handling a stock issuance, I work closely with financial advisers, who, with the company, will determine the share price. Once this has been determined, I have to fit those terms into securities commission rules, and I have to rely heavily on my finance knowledge."

As we pointed out in Chapter 1, most Canadian businesses are small sole proprietorships and partnerships. That said, these firms as a whole generated only about 40% of 2009 total Canadian business income before tax. Sole proprietorships are not allowed to access outside equity capital, so these businesses have relatively little capacity for growth. Sole proprietors are also forced to hold a large fraction of their wealth in a single asset—the company—and therefore are likely to be undiversified. By incorporating, businesses can gain access to capital and founders can reduce the risk of their portfolios by selling some of their equity and diversifying. Consequently, even though corporations make up the minority of Canadian businesses, they account for 60% of business income before tax in the Canadian economy. The situation is similar in most developed countries. For example, in the United States, over 80% of businesses are either sole proprietorships or partnerships, but nearly 85% of sales are generated by businesses organized as corporations.

In this chapter, we discuss how companies raise equity capital. To illustrate this concept, we follow the case of an actual company, RealNetworks, Inc. (ticker symbol: RNWK). RealNetworks is a leading creator of digital media services and software. Customers use RealNetworks products to find, play, purchase, and manage digital music, videos, and games. RealNetworks was founded in 1993 and incorporated in 1994. Using the example of RealNetworks, we first discuss the alternative ways new companies can raise capital and then examine the impact of these funding alternatives on current and new investors.

13.1 Equity Financing for Private Companies

The initial capital that is required to start a business is usually provided by the entrepreneur and his or her immediate family. Few families, however, have the resources to finance a growing business, so growth almost always requires outside capital. In this section, we examine the sources that can provide this capital to a private company and the effect of the infusion of outside capital on the control of the company.

Sources of Funding

private equity investor
An investor that owns shares of a non-publicly traded company.

When a private company decides to raise outside equity capital, it can seek funding from several potential sources: *angel investors, venture capital firms, institutional investors, sovereign wealth funds,* and *corporate investors.* Any of these investors may be referred to as **private equity investors** if they invest in the stock of a private company (a company with non-publicly traded equity).

angel investors
Individual investors who buy equity in small private firms (often start-up firms).

Angel Investors.   Individual investors who buy equity in small private firms (often start-ups) are called **angel investors**. For many start-ups, often the first round of outside private equity financing is obtained from angels. These investors are frequently friends or acquaintances of the entrepreneur. Because their capital investment is often large relative to the amount of capital already in place at the firm, they typically receive a sizeable equity share in the business in return for their funds. As a result, these investors may have substantial influence in the business decisions of the firm. Angels may also bring expertise to the firm that the entrepreneur lacks.

In most cases, firms need more capital than what a few angels can provide. Finding angels is difficult—often it is a function of how well connected the entrepreneur is in the local community. Most entrepreneurs, especially those launching their first start-up company, have few relationships with people who have substantial capital to invest. At some point, many firms that require equity capital for growth must turn to the *venture capital* industry.

venture capital firm
A limited partnership that specializes in raising money to invest in the private equity of young firms.

Venture Capital Firms.   A **venture capital firm** is a limited partnership that specializes in raising money to invest in the private equity of young firms. Table 13.1 lists the largest venture capital funds raised in Canada between 2002 and 2010.

TABLE 13.1		
The Largest Venture Capital Funds Raised (Over $100 million) in Canada, 2002–10	**Venture Capital Fund**	**Amount Raised ($ millions)**
	Celtic House Venture Partners Fund III	280
	Ventures West 8	250
	MDS Life Sciences Technology Fund	211
	Summerhill Ventures I LP	175
	BlackBerry Partners Fund	151
	Jefferson Partners Fund IV LP	150
	Celtic House Venture Partners Fund II	135
	Skypoint Telecom Fund II	130
	J.L. Albright IV Venture Fund	121
	MMV Financial	112
	iNovia Investment Fund II LP	112
	EdgeStone Capital Venture Fund II LP	108
	CTI Life Sciences Fund	100

Source: Canada's Venture Capital & Private Equity Association Industry Statistics from McKinsey & Company and Thomson Financial Canada.

venture capitalists The general partners who work for and run a venture capital firm.

Typically, institutional investors, such as pension funds, are the limited partners in the venture capital firm. The general partners are known as **venture capitalists** and they work for and run the venture capital firm. Venture capital firms offer limited partners a number of advantages over investing directly in start-ups themselves as angel investors. Because these firms invest in many start-ups, limited partners are more diversified than if they invested on their own. They also benefit from the expertise of the general partners. However, these advantages come at a cost. General partners usually charge substantial fees, taken mainly as a percentage of the positive returns they generate. Most firms charge 20% of any positive returns they make, but the successful firms may charge more than 30%. They also generally charge an annual management fee of about 2% of the fund's committed capital.

Venture capital firms can provide substantial capital for young companies. As you can see in Figure 13.1, in 2008 and 2009, the two years hardest hit by the financial crisis, over 900 financing deals were provided by venture capital firms in Canada, and over $2 billion was raised by venture capitalists. As impressive as this is, though, it pales compared to the years 2000 and 2001, when over 2300 financing deals were provided and over $7.4 billion was raised by venture capitalists.

Paul Gompers and Josh Lerner[1] report that venture capitalists typically control about one-third of the seats on a start-up's board of directors and often represent the single largest voting block on the board. Although entrepreneurs generally view this control as a necessary cost of obtaining venture capital, it can actually be an important benefit of accepting venture financing. Venture capitalists use their control to protect their investments, so they may therefore perform a key nurturing and monitoring role for the firm.

FIGURE 13.1

Venture Capital Funding in Canada, 1995–2009

The bar graph shows the amount of new venture capital funds raised by venture capital firms, and the line graph shows the number of financing deals these venture capital firms completed.

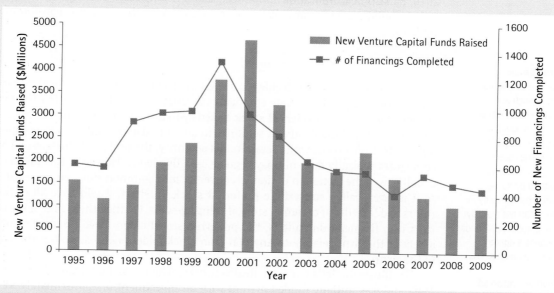

Sources: Canadian Venture Capital Association, Macdonald and Associates Ltd., McKinsey & Company, Thomson Reuters Canada, Industry Canada.

---

[1]Paul A. Gompers and Josh Lerner, *The Venture Capital Cycle* (Cambridge, MA: MIT Press, 1999).

Institutional Investors. Institutional investors such as pension funds, insurance companies, endowments, and foundations manage large quantities of money. They are major investors in many different types of assets, so, not surprisingly, they are also active investors in private companies. Institutional investors may invest directly in private firms, or they may invest indirectly by becoming limited partners in venture capital firms. Institutional interest in private equity has grown dramatically in recent years. For example, McKinsey & Company reported that in Canada institutional investors accounted for 25% (or $20 billion) of private equity funds under management in 2009.

sovereign wealth funds (SWFs) Pools of money controlled by a government, usually raised from royalty or resource revenue or from taxes collected.

Sovereign Wealth Funds. **Sovereign wealth funds (SWFs)** are pools of money controlled by a government, usually raised from royalty or resource revenue or from taxes collected. SWFs have been in existence for many years. For example, the Kuwait Investment Board was founded in 1953 and is now called the Kuwait Reserve for Future Generations. The Alberta Heritage Savings Trust Fund, founded in 1976, is another example. In 2007, SWFs became increasingly newsworthy as they invested in troubled financial institutions. SWFs also play an active role in the private equity market and are the largest limited partners in global private equity markets. According to the SWF Institute (www.swfinstitute.org), as of November 2010, the largest SWF was the Abu Dhabi Investment Authority, with assets of $627 billion. In 2010, the top 10 SWFs in terms of assets came from Abu Dhabi, Norway, Saudi Arabia, China (three funds), Hong Kong, Singapore, Kuwait, and Russia.

corporate investor, corporate partner, strategic partner, strategic investor A corporation that invests in private companies.

Corporate Investors. Many established corporations purchase equity in younger, private companies. A corporation that invests in private companies is referred to by many different names, including **corporate investor, corporate partner, strategic partner, and strategic investor**. Most of the other types of investors in private firms that we have considered so far are primarily interested in the financial return that they will earn on their investments. Corporate investors, by contrast, might invest for corporate strategic objectives in addition to the desire for investment returns. For example, on November 3, 2010, Panasonic Corporation announced that it had invested $30 million in Tesla Motors to help build a multi-year collaboration to accelerate the market expansion of electric vehicles.

Securities and Valuation

preferred stock Stock issued by mature companies such as banks that usually has a preferential dividend and seniority in any liquidation, and sometimes special voting rights. Preferred stock issued by young companies has seniority in any liquidation but typically does not pay cash dividends and contains a right to convert to common stock.

When a company founder decides to sell equity to outside investors for the first time, it is common practice for private companies to issue preferred stock rather than common stock to raise capital. **Preferred stock** issued by mature companies such as banks usually has a preferential dividend and seniority in any liquidation, and sometimes special voting rights. Conversely, while retaining its seniority, the preferred stock issued by young companies typically does not pay regular cash dividends. However, this preferred stock usually gives the owner an option to convert it into common stock on some future date, so it is often called **convertible preferred stock**. In short, it will have all of the future rights and benefits of common stock if things go well. On the other hand, if the company runs into financial difficulties, the preferred stockholders have a senior claim on the assets of the firm relative to any common stockholders (who are often the employees of the firm).

convertible preferred stock A preferred stock that gives the owner an option to convert it into common stock on some future date.

To illustrate, let's consider RealNetworks, which was founded by Robert Glaser in 1993 and was initially funded by him with an investment of approximately $1 million. As of April 1995, Glaser's $1 million initial investment in RealNetworks represented 13,713,439 shares of Series A preferred stock, implying an initial purchase price of about $0.07 per share. RealNetworks needed more capital, and management decided to raise this money by selling equity in the form of convertible preferred stock.

The company's first round of outside equity funding was Series B preferred stock. RealNetworks sold 2,686,567 shares of Series B preferred stock at $0.67 per share in April 1995.[2] It is important to understand that RealNetworks remained a private company after this transaction. Simply selling equity to outside investors does not cause a company to become public. Companies may remain private, meaning their shares are not listed on an exchange and they are not required to file their financial statements with a securities commission (such as the provincial securities commissions in Canada or the Securities and Exchange Commission [SEC] in the United States), as long as the number of shareholders remains small. Later in this chapter, we discuss the process of offering shares to the general public and thereby transitioning to public status. After this funding round, the distribution of ownership was as follows:

	Number of Shares	Price per Share ($)	Total Value ($ millions)	Percentage Ownership
Series A	13,713,439	0.67	9.2	83.6%
Series B	2,686,567	0.67	1.8	16.4%
	16,400,006		11.0	100.0%

pre-money valuation The value of a firm's prior shares outstanding at the price in the funding round.

post-money valuation The value of the whole firm (old plus new shares) at the price at which the new equity is sold.

The Series B preferred shares were new shares of stock being sold by RealNetworks. At the price the new shares were sold for, Glaser's shares were worth $9.2 million and represented 83.6% of the outstanding shares. It is important to note that the increase in the value of Glaser's shares was very uncertain when he founded the company. The value of the prior shares outstanding at the price in the funding round ($9.2 million in this example) is called the **pre-money valuation**. The value of the whole firm (old plus new shares) at the funding round price ($11.0 million) is known as the **post-money valuation**.

EXAMPLE 13.1

Funding and Ownership

Problem

You founded your own firm two years ago. You initially contributed $100,000 of your money and in return received 1.5 million shares of stock. Since then, you have sold an additional 500,000 shares to angel investors. You are now considering raising even more capital from a venture capitalist (VC). This VC would invest $6 million and would receive 3 million newly issued shares. What is the post-money valuation? Assuming that this is the VC's first investment in your company, what percentage of the firm will she end up owning? What percentage will you own? What is the value of your shares?

▶ **Plan**

After this funding round, there will be a total of 5 million shares outstanding:

Your shares	1,500,000
Angel investors' shares	500,000
Newly issued shares	3,000,000
Total	5,000,000

---

[2]The number of shares of RealNetworks preferred stock given here for this and subsequent funding comes from the IPO prospectus (available on EDGAR at www.sec.gov/edgar/searchedgar/webusers.htm). For simplicity, we have ignored warrants to purchase additional shares that were also issued and a small amount of employee common stock that existed.

The VC would be paying $6,000,000/3,000,000 = $2 per share. The post-money valuation will be the total number of shares multiplied by the price paid by the VC. The percentage of the firm owned by the VC is the number of her shares divided by the total number of shares. Your percentage will be the number of your shares divided by the total number of shares, and the value of your shares will be the number of shares you own multiplied by the price the VC paid.

▶ **Execute**

There are 5 million shares and the VC paid $2 per share. Therefore, the post-money valuation would be 5,000,000 × $2 = $10 million.

Because she is buying 3 million shares, and there will be 5 million total shares outstanding after the funding round, the VC will end up owning 3,000,000/5,000,000 = 60% of the firm.

You will own 1,500,000/5,000,000 = 30% of the firm, and the post-money valuation of your shares is 1,500,000 × $2 = $3,000,000.

▶ **Evaluate**

Funding your firm with new equity capital, whether it is from an angel or a venture capitalist, involves a tradeoff—you must give up part of the ownership of the firm in return for the money you need to grow. If you can negotiate a higher price per share, the percentage of your firm that you will have to give up for a specified amount of capital will be smaller.

Over the next few years, RealNetworks raised three more rounds of outside equity in addition to the Series B funding round:

Series	Date	Number of Shares	Share Price ($)	Capital Raised ($ million)
B	Apr 1995	2,686,567	0.67	1.8
C	Oct 1995	2,904,305	1.96	5.7
D	Nov 1996	2,381,010	7.53	17.9
E	July 1997	3,338,374	8.99	30.0

In each case, investors bought preferred stock in the private company. The profile of these investors was very similar to that of typical investors in private firms that we described earlier. Angel investors purchased the Series B stock. The investors in Series C and D stock were primarily venture capital funds. Microsoft purchased the Series E stock as a corporate investor.

Exiting an Investment in a Private Company

exit strategy A strategy detailing how investors in private companies will eventually realize the return from their investment.

Like any relationship, the one between a firm and its investors is subject to change as needs and resources develop. An important consideration for investors in private companies is their **exit strategy**—how they will eventually realize the return from their investment. Investors exit in two main ways: through an acquisition or through an initial public offering (IPO). Often, large corporations purchase successful start-up companies. In such a case, the acquiring company purchases the outstanding stock of the private company, allowing all investors to cash out. In 2008–09, roughly 96% of venture capital exits occurred through mergers or acquisitions (this compares to about 71% that exited through mergers or acquisitions in 2006–07).[3]

---

[3]Thomson Reuters Canada, *Canada's Venture Capital Industry in 2009.*

Over time, the value of a share of RealNetworks' stock and the size of its funding rounds increased. Because investors in Series E were willing to pay $8.99 for a share of preferred stock with equivalent rights in July 1997, the post-money valuation of existing preferred stock was $8.99 per share. RealNetworks was still a private company, however, so investors could not liquidate their investment by selling their stock in the public stock markets. In the next section, we discuss the process a firm goes through to sell shares to the public and have its shares traded on a public market.

Concept Check

1. What are the main sources of funding for private companies to raise outside equity capital?

2. What is a venture capital firm?

13.2 Taking Your Firm Public: The Initial Public Offering

initial public offering (IPO) The process of selling stock to the public for the first time.

The process of selling stock to the public for the first time is called an **initial public offering (IPO)**. In this section, we look at the mechanics of IPOs in two cases—the traditional set-up and recent innovations.

Advantages and Disadvantages of Going Public

Going public provides companies with greater liquidity and better access to capital. By going public, companies give their private equity investors the ability to diversify. In addition, public companies typically have access to much larger amounts of capital through the public markets, both in the IPO and in subsequent offerings. For example, during the first half of 2010, the 10 largest new equity issues (IPOs) in the world each raised $1.5 billion or more, as shown in Table 13.2. In the latter half of 2010, the IPO of the Agricultural Bank of China became the world's largest IPO ever, as over $22 billion was raised. In RealNetworks' case, its last round of private equity funding raised about $30 million in July 1997. The firm raised $43 million when it went public in its IPO in

TABLE 13.2	Issuer Name	Domicile Country	Issuer Business Description	Capital Raised (US $ billions)
Top 10 Global IPOs by Capital Raised in the First Half of 2010	Dai-ichi Life Insurance Co. Ltd.	Japan	Life insurance provider	11.1
	Samsung Life Insurance Co. Ltd.	South Korea	Investment and insurance company	4.4
	Powszechny Zaklad Ubezpieczen SA-PZU SA	Poland	Insurance company	2.7
	Huatai Securities Co. Ltd.	China	Provider of securities brokerage services	2.3
	United Co Rusal Ltd.	Russian Fed	World's largest producer of aluminium	2.2
	Essar Energy plc	India	Electric power generation and oil and gas exploration company	1.9
	Amadeus IT Holding SA	Spain	Travel transaction processor and provider of advanced technology solution	1.9
	China First Heavy Industries	China	Metal casting company	1.7
	Korea Life Insurance Co. Ltd.	South Korea	Life insurance services provider	1.6
	China XD Electric Co. Ltd.	China	Electrical equipment manufacturer	1.5

Sources: Dealogic, Thomson Financial, Ernst & Young, Global IPO trends 2010.

November of the same year; less than two years later, it raised an additional $267 million by selling more stock to the public. As a public company, RealNetworks was able to raise substantially more money.

The major advantage of undertaking an IPO is also one of the major disadvantages of an IPO: when investors sell their stake and thereby diversify their holdings, the equity holders of the corporation become more widely dispersed. This undermines investors' ability to monitor the company's management and thus represents a loss of control. Furthermore, once a company goes public, it must satisfy all of the requirements of public companies. Several high-profile corporate scandals during the early part of the 21st century prompted tougher regulations designed to address corporate abuses. Organizations such as the SEC in the United States, the provincial securities commissions in Canada, the securities exchanges (including the TSX, New York Stock Exchange, and NASDAQ), the U.S. Congress (through the Sarbanes-Oxley Act of 2002), and the Parliament of Canada adopted new standards that focused on more thorough financial disclosure, greater accountability, and more stringent requirements for the board of directors. In general, these standards were designed to provide better protection for investors. However, compliance with the new standards is costly and time-consuming for public companies.

Primary and Secondary IPO Offerings

underwriter An investment banking firm that manages a security issuance and designs its structure.

After deciding to go public, managers of the company work with an **underwriter**, an investment banking firm that manages the security issuance and designs its structure. In this case, the underwriter is managing the company's offering of securities to the public. Choices for the offering's structure include the type of shares to be sold and the mechanism the underwriter will use to sell the stock.

primary offering New shares available in a public offering that raise new capital.

At an IPO, a firm offers a large block of shares for sale to the public for the first time. The shares that are sold in the IPO may either be new shares that raise new capital, known as a **primary offering**, or existing shares that are sold by current shareholders (as part of their exit strategy), known as a **secondary offering**.

secondary offering An equity offering of shares sold by existing shareholders (as part of their exit strategy).

The traditional IPO process follows a standardized form. We will explore the steps that underwriters go though during an IPO.

Underwriters and the Syndicate. Many IPOs, especially the larger offerings, are managed by a group of underwriters. The **lead underwriter** is the primary investment banking firm responsible for managing the security issuance. The lead underwriter provides most of the advice on the sale and arranges for a group of other underwriters, called the **syndicate**, to help market and sell the issue. Table 13.3 shows the lead underwriters that were responsible for the largest value of IPOs globally during 2009. The dominance of U.S. underwriters in the global market has diminished since the financial crisis. In addition, the surge of underwriting of Chinese firms, especially in 2010, has shifted the geography of where underwriting activity occurs. Table 13.4 shows the major underwriters of equity products (including IPOs) in Canada for the first three quarters of 2010.

lead underwriter The primary investment banking firm responsible for managing a security issuance.

syndicate A group of underwriters who jointly underwrite and distribute a security issuance.

Underwriters market the IPO and help the company with all the necessary filings. More importantly, as we discuss below, underwriters actively participate in determining the offer price. In many cases, the underwriter will also commit to making a market in the stock by matching buyers and sellers after the issue, thereby guaranteeing that the stock will be liquid.

registration statement A legal document that provides financial and other information about a company to investors prior to a security issuance.

Regulatory Filings. The relevant securities commissions (each provincial securities commission in Canada and the SEC in the United States) require that companies file certain legal documents that provide financial and other information about the company to investors, prior to an IPO. In the United States, this step is the preparation of the **registration statement**. Company managers work closely with the underwriters to

TABLE 13.3

Top 10 International IPO Underwriters for 2009

Manager	2009 Proceeds ($ billions)	Market Share (%)	Number of Issues
China International Capital Corp. Ltd.	$11.32	9.9	7
Goldman Sachs	$10.25	9.0	33
Morgan Stanley	$8.96	7.8	42
UBS	$7.61	6.7	21
Credit Suisse	$6.95	6.1	31
Bank of Amerca Merrill Lynch	$6.91	6.0	36
JPMorgan	$6.41	5.6	32
CITIC Securities	$6.30	5.5	12
Citigroup	$3.59	3.1	23
Deutsche Bank	$2.97	2.6	18
Top 10 Totals	$71.26	62.4	132
Industry Totals	$114.28	100.0	573

Source: Wall Street Journal.

preliminary prospectus (red herring) Part of the registration statement prepared by a company prior to an IPO that is circulated to investors before the stock is offered.

prepare this registration statement and submit it to the securities commission. Part of the registration statement, called the **preliminary prospectus** or **red herring**, circulates to investors before the stock is offered. In Canada, this first step is the preparation of the preliminary prospectus; there is no separate registration statement. The reason a preliminary prospectus is also called a red herring is because of the red writing on the prospectus indicating that the prospectus is not yet final, the information may not be complete, and the securities may not be sold until a receipt for the

TABLE 13.4

Top 20 Equity-Related Underwriters in Canada for the First Three Quarters of 2010

2010 Rank	Bookrunner	Proceeds ($ milions)	Market Share (%)	Number of Deals
1	GMP Capital Corp.	2746.1	11.9	37
2	BMO Capital Markets	2514.6	10.9	34
3	CIBC World Markets	2205.1	9.6	30
4	RBC Capital Markets	2043.0	8.9	30
5	TD Securities Inc.	1966.3	8.6	27
6	Canaccord Genuity	1704.8	7.4	64
7	Morgan Stanley	1012.3	4.4	4
8	Macquarie Group	900.8	3.9	17
9	ABG Sundal Collier	772.6	3.4	1
10	Scotia Capital Inc.	745.4	3.2	14
11	National Bank Financial Inc.	744.2	3.2	26
12	Cormark Securities Inc.	600.7	2.6	32
13	Credit Suisse	528.8	2.3	5
14	Wellington West Capital Inc.	441.0	1.9	22
15	Dundee Securities Corporation	427.8	1.9	28
16	FirstEnergy Capital Corp.	421.4	1.8	10
17	UBS	362.4	1.6	4
18	Raymond James Financial Inc.	355.8	1.6	14
19	Citigroup	231.4	1.0	1
20	Haywood Securities Ltd.	195.7	0.9	7
	Top 20 Totals	20,920.2	91.0	
	Industry Totals	23,005.9	100.0	382

Source: Thomson Reuters Canada, Canada Equity Capital Markets Review Managing Underwriters: First Nine Months 2010.

final prospectus is obtained from the relevant securities regulators. (Interestingly, the term "red herring" originates from the sport of fox hunting, where traditionally a red herring was used to distract the dogs and throw them off the scent of their prey.)

The securities regulators review the preliminary prospectus to make sure that the company has disclosed all of the information necessary for investors to decide whether to purchase the stock. Once the company has satisfied the regulators' disclosure requirements, the regulators approve the stock for sale to the general public. In Canada, the Ontario Securities Commission usually takes the lead in reviewing and approving the preliminary prospectus, and the other provincial securities commissions usually follow Ontario's decision. The company prepares the **final prospectus** containing all the details of the IPO, including the number of shares offered and the offer price.[4]

To illustrate this process, let's return to RealNetworks. Figure 13.2 shows the cover page for the final prospectus for RealNetworks' IPO. This cover page includes the name of the company, the list of lead underwriters, and summary information about the pricing of the deal. This was a primary offering of 3 million shares.

final prospectus Part of the final registration statement prepared by a company prior to an IPO that contains all the details of the offering, including the number of shares offered and the offer price.

road show The time, during an IPO, when a company's senior management and its lead underwriters travel to promote the company and explain their rationale for an offer price to institutional investors such as mutual funds and pension funds.

Valuation. Before the offer price is set, the underwriters work closely with the company to come up with a price range that they believe provides a reasonable valuation for the firm using the techniques described in Chapter 9. As we pointed out in that chapter, there are two ways to value a company: estimate the future cash flows and compute the present value, or estimate the value by examining comparable companies. Most underwriters use both techniques. However, when these techniques give substantially different answers, underwriters often rely on comparables based on recent IPOs.

Once an initial price range is established, the underwriters try to determine what the market thinks of the valuation. They begin by arranging a **road show**, in which senior management and the lead underwriters travel around the country (and sometimes around the world) promoting the company and explaining their rationale for the offer price to the underwriters' largest customers—mainly institutional investors such as mutual funds and pension funds.

EXAMPLE 13.2

Valuing an IPO
Using Comparables

Problem

Wagner, Inc. is a private company that designs, manufactures, and distributes branded consumer products. During its most recent fiscal year, Wagner had revenues of $325 million and earnings of $15 million. Wagner has filed a registration statement with the SEC for its IPO. Before the stock is offered, Wagner's investment bankers would like to estimate the value of the company using comparable companies. The investment bankers have assembled the following information based on data for other companies in the same industry that have recently gone public. In each case, the ratios are based on the IPO price.

Company	Price-Earnings	Price-Revenues
Ray Products Corp.	18.8×	1.2×
Byce-Frasier Inc.	19.5×	0.9×
Fashion Industries Group	24.1×	0.8×
Recreation International	22.4×	0.7×
Average	21.2×	0.9×

---

[4]Canadian prospectuses may be found at SEDAR, the website for Canadian Securities Administrators: www.sedar.com. For U.S. registration statements, you can check EDGAR, the SEC website providing registration information to investors: www.sec.gov/edgar/searchedgar/webusers.htm.

After the IPO, Wagner will have 20 million shares outstanding. Estimate the IPO price for Wagner using the price-earnings (P/E) ratio and the price-revenues ratio.

Solution

▶ **Plan**

If the IPO price of Wagner is based on a P/E ratio that is similar to those for recent IPOs, then this ratio will equal the average of recent deals. Thus, to compute the IPO price based on the P/E ratio, we will first take the average P/E ratio from the comparison group and multiply it by Wagner's total earnings. This will give us a total value of equity for Wagner. To get the per-share IPO price, we need to divide the total equity value by the number of shares outstanding after the IPO (20 million). The approach will be the same for the price-revenues ratio.

▶ **Execute**

The average P/E ratio for recent deals is 21.2. Given earnings of $15 million, the total market value of Wagner's stock will be $15 million $\times$ 21.2 = $318 million. With 20 million shares outstanding, the price per share should be $318 million/20 million = $15.90.

Similarly, if Wagner's IPO price implies a price-revenues ratio equal to the recent average of 0.9, then using its revenues of $325 million, the total market value of Wagner will be $325 million $\times$ 0.9 = $292.5 million, or $14.63 per share ($292.5/20).

▶ **Evaluate**

As we found in Chapter 9, using multiples for valuation always produces a range of estimates—you should not expect to get the same value from different ratios. Based on these estimates, the underwriters will probably establish an initial price range for Wagner stock of $13 to $17 per share to take on the road show.

book building A process used by underwriters for coming up with an offer price based on customers' expressions of interest.

At the end of the road show, customers inform the underwriters of their interest by telling the underwriters how many shares they may want to purchase. Although these commitments are nonbinding, the underwriters' customers value their long-term relationships with the underwriters, so they rarely go back on their word. The underwriters then add up the total demand and adjust the price until it is unlikely that the issue will fail. This process for coming up with the offer price based on customers' expressions of interest is called **book building**.

firm commitment An agreement between an underwriter and an issuing firm in which the underwriter guarantees that it will sell all of the stock at the offer price.

Pricing the Deal and Managing Risk. In the most common arrangement, an underwriter and an issuing firm agree to a **firm commitment** IPO, in which the underwriter guarantees that it will sell all of the stock at the offer price. The underwriter purchases the entire issue (at a slightly lower price than the offer price) and then resells it at the offer price. If the entire issue does not sell out, the underwriter is on the hook: the remaining shares must be sold at a lower price and the underwriter must take the loss. The most notorious loss in the industry happened when the British government privatized British Petroleum. In a highly unusual deal, the company was taken public gradually. The British government sold its final stake in British Petroleum at the time of the October 1987 stock market crash. The offer price was set just before the crash, but the offering occurred after the crash.[5] At the end of the first day's trading, the underwriters were facing a loss of $1.29 billion. The price then fell even further, until the Kuwaiti Investment Office stepped in and started purchasing a large stake in the company.

---

[5]This deal was exceptional in that the offer price was determined more than a week before the issue date. Typically, the underwriter usually sets the final offer price within a day of the IPO date.

FIGURE 13.2

The Cover Page of RealNetworks' IPO Prospectus

The cover page includes the name of the company, a list of lead underwriters, and summary information about the pricing of the offering.

3,000,000 Shares

RealNetworks, Inc.
(formerly "Progressive Networks, Inc.")

Common Stock
(par value $.001 per share)

All of the 3,000,000 shares of Common Stock offered hereby are being sold by RealNetworks, Inc. Prior to the offering, there has been no public market for the Common Stock. For factors considered in determining the initial public offering price, see "Underwriting".

The Common Stock offered hereby involves a high degree of risk. See "Risk Factors" beginning on page 6.

The Common Stock has been approved for quotation on the Nasdaq National Market under the symbol "RNWK," subject to notice of issuance.

THESE SECURITIES HAVE NOT BEEN APPROVED OR DISAPPROVED BY THE SECURITIES AND EXCHANGE COMMISSION OR ANY STATE SECURITIES COMMISSION NOR HAS THE SECURITIES AND EXCHANGE COMMISSION OR ANY STATE SECURITIES COMMISSION PASSED UPON THE ACCURACY OR ADEQUACY OF THIS PROSPECTUS. ANY REPRESENTATION TO THE CONTRARY IS A CRIMINAL OFFENSE.

	Initial Public Offering Price(1)	Underwriting Discount(2)	Proceeds to Company(3)
Per Share	$12.50	$0.875	$11.625
Total(4)	$37,500,000	$2,625,000	$34,875,000

(1) In connection with the offering, the Underwriters have reserved up to 300,000 shares of Common Stock for sale at the initial public offering price to employees and friends of the Company.

(2) The Company has agreed to indemnify the Underwriters against certain liabilities, including liabilities under the Securities Act of 1933, as amended. See "Underwriting".

(3) Before deducting estimated expenses of $950,000 payable by the Company.

(4) The Company has granted the Underwriters an option for 30 days to purchase up to an additional 450,000 shares at the initial public offering price per share, less the underwriting discount, solely to cover over-allotments. If such option is exercised in full, the total initial public offering price, underwriting discount and proceeds to Company will be $43,125,000, $3,018,750 and $40,106,250, respectively. See "Underwriting".

The shares offered hereby are offered severally by the Underwriters, as specified herein, subject to receipt and acceptance by them and subject to their right to reject any order in whole or in part. It is expected that certificates for the shares will be ready for delivery in New York, New York on or about November 26, 1997, against payment therefor in immediately available funds.

Goldman, Sachs & Co.
BancAmerica Robertson Stephens
NationsBanc Montgomery Securities, Inc.

The date of this Prospectus is November 21, 1997.

Source: Courtesy of RealNetworks, Inc.

spread The fee a company pays to its underwriters that is a percentage of the issue price of a share of stock.

In the RealNetworks' IPO, the final offer price was $12.50 per share.[6] The company agreed to pay the underwriters a fee, called a **spread**, which is a percentage of the issue price of a share of stock, in this case $0.875 per share—exactly 7% of the issue price. Because this was a firm commitment deal, the underwriters bought the stock from RealNetworks for $12.50 − $0.875 = $11.625 per share and then resold it to their customers for $12.50 per share.

Recall that when an underwriter provides a firm commitment, it is potentially exposing itself to the risk that the investment banking firm might have to sell the shares at less than the offer price and take a loss. However, according to Tim Loughran and Jay Ritter, between 1990 and 1998, just 9% of U.S. IPOs experienced a fall in share price on the first day.[7] For another 16% of firms, the price at the end of the first day was the same as the offer price. Therefore, the vast majority of IPOs experienced a price increase on the first day of trading, indicating that the initial offer price was generally lower than the price that stock market investors were willing to pay.

over-allotment allocation (greenshoe provision) In an IPO, an option that allows the underwriter to issue more stock, usually amounting to 15% of the original offer size, at the IPO offer price.

Underwriters appear to use the information they acquire during the book-building stage to intentionally underprice the IPO, thereby reducing their exposure to losses. Furthermore, once the issue price (or offer price) is set, underwriters may invoke another mechanism that allows them to sell extra shares of more successful offerings—the **over-allotment allocation**, or **greenshoe provision**.[8] This option allows the underwriter to issue more stock, amounting to 15% of the original offer size, at the IPO offer price. Look at note 4 on the front page of the RealNetworks prospectus in Figure 13.2. This footnote is a greenshoe provision.

lockup A restriction that prevents existing shareholders from selling their shares for some period (usually 180 days) after an IPO.

Once the IPO process is complete, the company's shares trade publicly on an exchange. The lead underwriter usually makes a market in the stock by matching buyers and sellers and assigns an analyst to cover it. By doing so, the underwriter increases the liquidity of the stock in the secondary market. This service is of value to both the issuing company and the underwriter's customers. A liquid market ensures that investors who purchased shares via the IPO are able to trade those shares easily. If the stock is actively traded, the issuer will have continued access to the equity markets in the event that the company decides to issue more shares in a new offering. In most cases, the existing shareholders are subject to a **lockup**, a restriction that prevents them from selling their shares for some period (usually 180 days) after the IPO. Once the lockup period expires, they are free to sell their shares.

Other IPO Types

Now that we have established the traditional method for IPOs, we will discuss three other ways shares may be sold during an IPO.

best efforts For smaller initial public offerings (IPOs), a situation in which the underwriter does not guarantee that the stock will be sold, but instead tries to sell the stock for the best possible price.

Best-Efforts Basis. For smaller IPOs, the underwriter commonly accepts the deal on a **best-efforts** basis. In this case, the underwriter does not guarantee that the stock will be sold, but instead tries to sell the stock for the best possible price. Often such deals have an all-or-none clause: either all of the shares are sold in the IPO, or the deal is called off.

---

[6]Stock prices for RealNetworks throughout this chapter have not been adjusted for two subsequent stock splits.

[7]Tim Loughran and Jay Ritter,"Why Don't Issuers Get Upset About Leaving Money on the Table in IPOs?," *Review of Financial Studies* 15 (2) (2002): 413–443.

[8]The name derives from the Green Shoe Company, the first issuer to have an over-allotment option in its IPO.

TABLE 13.5	Price	Shares Sought at This Price (in thousands)	Total Shares Sought at or Above This Price (in thousands)
Bids Received to Purchase Shares in a Hypothetical Auction IPO	$16.50	3200	11,800
	$17.00	2900	8600
	$17.50	2700	5700
	$18.00	1925	3000
	$18.50	850	1075
	$19.00	150	225
	$19.50	75	75

auction IPO An online method for selling new issues directly to the public that lets the market determine the price through bids from potential investors.

Auction IPO.   In recent years, the investment banking firm of W.R. Hambrecht and Company has attempted to change the IPO process by selling new issues directly to the public using an online **auction IPO** mechanism called OpenIPO. Rather than setting the price itself in the traditional way, Hambrecht lets the market determine the price of the stock by auctioning off the company.[9] Investors place bids over a set period of time. An auction IPO then sets the highest price such that the number of bids at or above that price equals the number of offered shares. All winning bidders pay this price, even if their bids were higher. The first OpenIPO was the $11.55 million IPO for Ravenswood Winery, completed in 1999.

It's easier to understand how an auction IPO works by considering an example. Your firm is planning an auction IPO for 3 million shares. Potential buyers submit bids at various prices and their bids are then aggregated. Table 13.5 summarizes those bids. The column "Shares Sought at This Price" shows the total number of shares from investors' bids at each price. The last column contains the total number of shares bid at *or above* each price. Because investors are willing to buy at prices lower than the amount they bid, this total represents the number of shares that can be sold at each price. For example, while investors were only willing to buy a total of 75,000 shares at a price of $19.50, at a price of $19.00 a total of 225,000 (150,000 + 75,000) can be sold.

EXAMPLE 13.3

Auction IPO Pricing

Problem
Fleming Educational Software, Inc. is selling 500,000 shares of stock in an auction IPO. At the end of the bidding period, Fleming's investment bank has received the following bids:

Price ($)	Number of Shares Bid
8.00	25,000
7.75	100,000
7.50	75,000
7.25	150,000
7.00	150,000
6.75	275,000
6.50	125,000

What will the offer price of the shares be?

Solution
▶ **Plan**
First, we must compute the total number of shares demanded at or above any given price. Then, we pick the highest price that will allow us to sell the full issue (500,000 shares).

---

[9]You can find details about Hambrecht's auction IPO process at the following website, www.wrhambrecht.com/ind/auctions/openipo/.

▶ **Execute**

Converting the table of bids into a table of cumulative demand produces, we have:

Price ($)	Cumulative Demand
8.00	25,000
7.75	125,000
7.50	200,000
7.25	350,000
7.00	500,000
6.75	775,000
6.50	900,000

For example, the company has received bids for a total of 125,000 shares at $7.75 per share or higher (25,000 + 100,000 = 125,000).

Fleming is offering a total of 500,000 shares. The winning auction price would be $7 per share, because investors have placed orders for a total of 500,000 shares at a price of $7 or higher. All investors who placed bids of at least this price will be able to buy the stock for $7 per share, even if their initial bid was higher.

In this example, the cumulative demand at the winning price exactly equals the supply. If the total demand at this price were greater than the supply, all auction participants who bid prices higher than the winning price would receive their full bid (at the winning price). Shares would be awarded on a pro rata basis to bidders who bid exactly the winning price.

▶ **Evaluate**

Although the auction IPO does not provide the certainty of the firm commitment, it has the advantage of using the market to determine the offer price. It also reduces the underwriter's role and, consequently, fees.

You are interested in selling a total of 3 million shares at the highest price possible. This suggests that you should look in the left column of Table 13.5 to find the highest price at which the total demand is at least 3 million shares. In this case, the highest price at which we can sell 3 million shares is $18. Figure 13.3 shows this graphically.

Although the auction IPO mechanism seems to represent an attractive alternative to traditional IPO procedures, it has not been widely adopted either in Canada, the United States, or abroad. Between 1999 and 2010, Hambrecht completed only 19 auction IPOs (the last two were in 2007). This represents less than 1% of the number of IPOs brought to market during that time period. However, in 2004, Google went public using the auction mechanism (see the box describing Google's IPO), which generated temporarily renewed interest in this alternative. In May 2007, Interactive Brokers Group raised $1.2 billion in its IPO using a Hambrecht OpenIPO auction.

Because no offer price is set in an auction IPO, book building is not as important in that venue as it is in traditional IPOs. In a recent paper, Professors Ravi Jagannathan and Ann Sherman examine why auctions have failed to become a popular IPO method and why they have been plagued by inaccurate pricing and poor performance following the issue. They suggest that because auctions do not use the book-building process, which aids in collecting large investors' valuations of the stock, investors are discouraged from participating in auctions.[10] Table 13.6 summarizes the methods a firm can use for an initial public offering of its stock.

---

[10]Ravi Jagannathan and Ann Sherman, "Why Do IPO Auctions Fail?," NBER working paper 12151, March 2006.

FIGURE 13.3

Aggregating the Shares Sought in the Hypothetical Auction IPO

The figure graphs the last column in Table 13.5, which indicates the total number of shares that can be sold at each price. In this case, investors are willing to buy a total of 3 million shares at or above a price of $18. So, you would set your IPO price at $18 to give you the highest price at which you could place 3 million shares.

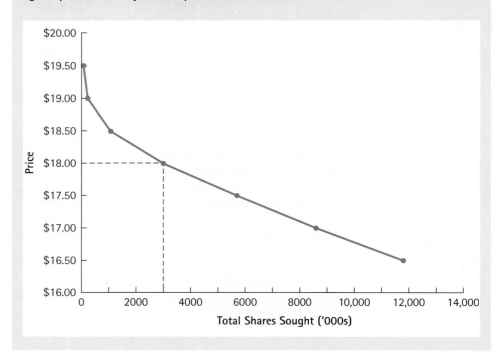

Google's IPO

On April 29, 2004, Google, Inc. announced plans to go public. Breaking with tradition, Google startled Wall Street by declaring its intention to rely heavily on the auction IPO mechanism for distributing its shares. Google had been profitable since 2001, so according to Google executives, access to capital was not the only motive for going public. The company also wanted to provide employees and private equity investors with liquidity.

One of the major attractions of the auction mechanism was the possibility of allocating shares to more individual investors. Google also hoped to set an accurate offer price by letting market bidders set the IPO price. After the internet stock market boom, there were many lawsuits related to the way underwriters allocated shares. Google hoped to avoid the allocation scandals by letting the auction allocate shares.

Investors who wanted to bid opened a brokerage account with one of the deal's underwriters and then placed their bids with the brokerage house. Google and its underwriters identified the highest bid that allowed the company to sell all of the shares being offered. They also had the flexibility to choose to offer shares at a lower price.

On August 18, 2004, Google sold 19.6 million shares at $85 per share. The $1.67 billion raised was easily the largest auction IPO ever. Google stock (ticker symbol: GOOG) opened trading on the NASDAQ market the next day at $100 per share. Although the Google IPO sometimes stumbled along the way, it represents the most significant example of the use of the auction mechanism as an alternative to the traditional IPO mechanism.

Sources: Kevin Delaney and Robin Sidel, "Google IPO Aims to Change the Rules," *Wall Street Journal*, April 30, 2004, p. C1; Ruth Simon and Elizabeth Weinstein, "Investors Eagerly Anticipate Google's IPO," *Wall Street Journal,* April 30, 2004, p. C1; Gregory Zuckerman, "Google Shares Prove Big Winners—for a Day," *Wall Street Journal*, August 20, 2004, p. C1.

TABLE 13.6	**Firm Commitment**	**Best Efforts**	**Auction IPO**
Summary of IPO Methods	Underwriter purchases the entire issue at an agreed price and sells it to investors at a higher price.	Underwriter makes its "best effort" to sell the issue to investors at an agreed price.	Firm or underwriter solicits bids (price and quantity) from investors, and chooses the highest price at which there is sufficient demand to sell the entire issue.

3. What services does the underwriter provide in a traditional IPO?

4. Explain the mechanics of an auction IPO.

13.3 IPO Puzzles

Four characteristics of IPOs puzzle financial economists, and all are relevant to the financial manager:

1. On average, IPOs appear to be underpriced: the price at the end of trading on the first day is often substantially higher than the IPO price.

2. The number of IPOs is highly cyclical. When times are good, the market is flooded with IPOs; when times are bad, the number of IPOs dries up.

3. The transaction costs of the IPO are very high, and it is unclear why firms willingly incur such high costs.

4. The long-run performance of a newly public company (three to five years from the date of issue) is poor. That is, on average, a three- to five-year buy-and-hold strategy appears to be a bad investment.

We will now examine each of these puzzles that financial economists seek to understand.

Underpriced IPOs

Generally, underwriters set the issue price of an IPO so that the average first-day return is positive. For RealNetworks, the underwriters offered the stock at an IPO price of $12.50 per share on November 21, 1997. RealNetworks stock opened trading on the NASDAQ market at a price of $19.375 per share, and it closed at the end of its first trading day at $17.875. So at the end of the first day of trading, its shares were priced $5.375 higher than the IPO price. Such performance is not atypical. On average, between 1960 and 2003, the price in the U.S. aftermarket was 18.3% higher than the IPO price at the end of the first day of trading.[11] As is evident in Figure 13.4, the one-day average return for IPOs has historically been very large around the world. Note that although underpricing is a persistent and global phenomenon, it is generally smaller in more developed capital markets.

Who benefits from the offer price being set below the market price at the end of the first day of trading (underpricing)? We have already explained how the underwriters benefit by controlling their risk—it is much easier to sell the firm's shares if the price is set low. Of course, investors who are able to buy stock from underwriters at the IPO price also gain from the first-day underpricing. Who bears the cost? The pre-IPO shareholders of the issuing firms do. In effect, these owners are selling stock in their firm for less than they could get in the aftermarket.

---

[11]See Tim Loughran, Jay R. Ritter, and Kristian Rydqvist, "Initial Public Offerings: International Insights," *Pacific-Basin Finance Journal* 2 (2004): 165–199.

FIGURE 13.4

International Comparison of First-Day IPO Returns

The bars show the average initial returns from the offer price to the first closing market price. For China, the bar shows the average initial return on A share IPOs, available only to residents of China. The date in parentheses indicates the sample period for each country.

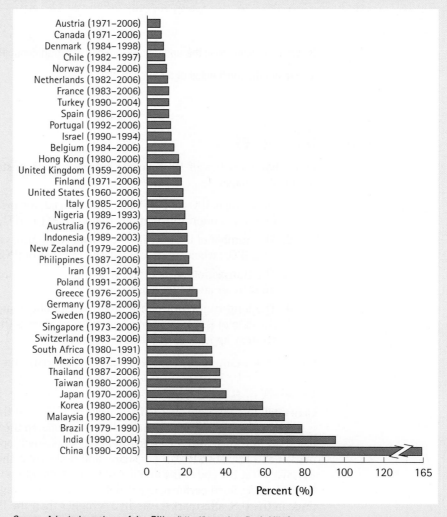

Source: Adapted courtesy of Jay Ritter (http://bear.cba.ufl.edu/ritter).

"Hot" and "Cold" IPO Markets

Figure 13.5 shows the number of U.S. IPOs by year from 1980 to 2009. As the figure makes clear, the dollar volume of IPOs has grown significantly, reaching a peak in 1996. An even more important feature of the data is that the trends related to the number of issues are cyclical. Sometimes, as in 1996, the volume of IPOs is unprecedented by historical standards, yet within a year or two the volume of IPOs may decrease significantly. This cyclicality by itself is not particularly surprising. We would expect there to be a greater need for capital in times with more growth opportunities than in times with fewer growth opportunities. What is surprising is the magnitude of the swings. For

FIGURE 13.5

Cyclicality of Initial Public Offerings in the United States (1980–2009)

The graph shows the number of IPOs by year. The number of IPOs reached a peak in 1996, demonstrating that trends related to the number of issues are highly cyclical.

Source: Adapted courtesy of Jay R. Ritter (http://bear. cba.ufl.edu/ritter).

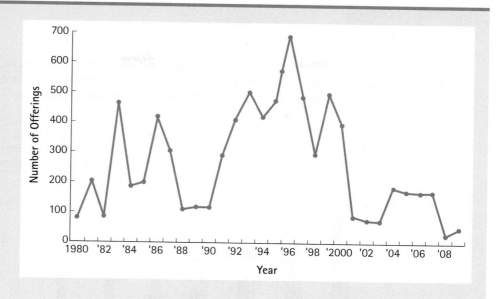

example, it is difficult to explain the almost seven-fold increase in IPOs from the early to mid-1990s, and the nearly 75% drop from 2000 to 2001. It appears that the number of IPOs is not solely driven by the demand for capital. Sometimes firms and investors seem to favour IPOs; at other times firms appear to rely on alternative sources of capital.

2008–09: A Very Cold IPO Market

The drop in IPO issues during the 2008 financial crisis was both global and dramatic. Comparing the fourth quarter of 2007 (a record quarter for IPO issues) with the fourth quarter of 2008, dollar volume dropped a stunning 97% from $102 billion to just $3 billion. Things got even worse in the first quarter of 2009, when just $1.4 billion was raised. The market for IPOs essentially dried up altogether. What accounted for this dramatic decline?

During the 2008 financial crisis, IPO markets were not the only equity issue markets that saw a collapse in volume. Seasoned equity offering and leveraged buyout markets also collapsed. The extreme market uncertainty that existed at the time created a "flight to quality." Investors, wary of taking risk, sought to move their capital into risk-free investments like U.S. Treasury securities. The result was a crash in existing equity prices and a greatly reduced supply of new capital to risky asset classes.

High Cost of Issuing an IPO

In the United States, a typical spread—that is, the discount below the issue price at which the underwriter purchases the shares from the issuing firm—is about 7% of the issue price. For an issue size of $50 million, this amounts to $3.5 million. This fee covers the cost to the underwriter of managing the syndicate and helping the company prepare for the IPO, as well as providing it with a return on the capital employed to purchase and market the issue. By most standards, however, this fee is large, especially considering the additional cost to the firm associated with underpricing. Internationally, spreads are

FIGURE 13.6

Relative Costs of Issuing Securities

This figure shows the total direct costs (all underwriting, legal, and auditing costs) of issuing securities as a percentage of the amount of money raised. The figure reports results for IPOs, seasoned equity offerings (subsequent equity offerings), convertible bonds, and standard bonds for issues of different sizes from 1990 to 1994.

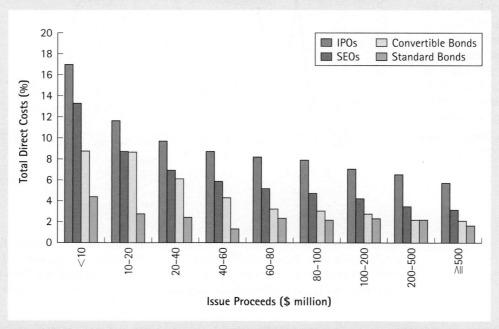

Source: Adapted from I. Lee, S. Lochhead, J. Ritter, and Q. Zhao, "The Costs of Raising Capital," *Journal of Financial Research* 19 (1) (1996): 59–74.

generally about half this amount. As Figure 13.6 shows, compared with other security issues, the total cost of issuing stock for the first time is substantially larger than the costs for other securities.

Even more puzzling is the seeming lack of sensitivity of fees to issue size. Although a large issue requires some additional effort, one would not expect the increased effort to be rewarded as lucratively. For example, Hsuan-Chi Chen and Jay Ritter found that almost all issues ranging in size from $20 million to $80 million paid underwriting fees of about 7% (in addition to other direct costs).[12] It is difficult to understand how a $20 million issue can be profitably done for "only" $1.4 million, while an $80 million issue requires paying fees of $5.6 million. Maher Kooli and Jean-Marc Suret found that the fees for Canadian IPOs are less than those for *similar-sized* IPOs in the United States. For a $50 million IPO, the Canadian spread is only about 6%, compared to 7% in the United States. However, most Canadian IPOs are much smaller than U.S. IPOs. The average Canadian IPO is only about one-fifteenth as large as the average U.S. IPO. For very small IPOs, there is sensitivity of fees to issue size. The total fee, as a percentage of the IPO size, is substantially higher than for large IPOs. As a result, Kooli and Suret

---

[12]Hsuan-Chi Chen and Jay R. Ritter, "The Seven Percent Solution," *Journal of Finance* 55 (3) (2000): 1105–1131.

also found that when the total fee as a percentage of the IPO size is calculated for every IPO, the average percentage spread across all IPOs in Canada is higher than the average percentage spread across all IPOs in the United States.[13]

Poor Post-IPO Long-Run Stock Performance

We know that the shares of IPOs generally perform very well immediately following the public offering. It's perhaps surprising, then, that Jay Ritter found that newly listed firms subsequently appear to perform relatively poorly over the three to five years following their IPOs.[14] Vijay Jog and A. Srivastava found similar results in Canada. Between 1972 and 1993, IPOs underperformed the TSE 300 market index by 17.9%.[15] This creates a puzzle as to why investors are willing to pay as much as they do for the shares when they begin trading after the IPO.

As we will see in the next section, underperformance is not unique to an initial public issuance of equity; it is associated with subsequent issuances as well. Recently, researchers have begun to explore the possibility that underperformance might not result from the issue of equity itself, but rather from the conditions that motivated the equity issuance in the first place. We will explain this idea in more detail in the next section after we explain how a public company issues additional equity.

Concept Check

5. List and discuss four characteristics about IPOs that are puzzling.
6. For each of the characteristics, identify its relevance to financial managers.

13.4 Raising Additional Capital: The Seasoned Equity Offering

seasoned equity offering (SEO) A public company's return to the equity markets with an offer of new shares for sale.

A firm's need for outside capital rarely ends at the IPO. Usually, profitable growth opportunities occur throughout the life of the firm, and in some cases it is not feasible to finance these opportunities out of retained earnings. Thus, a public company more often than not returns to the equity markets and offers new shares for sale in a type of offering called a **seasoned equity offering (SEO)**.

SEO Process

When issuing stock using an SEO, a firm follows many of the same steps as for an IPO. The main difference is that a market price for the stock already exists, so the price-setting process is not necessary.

primary shares New shares issued by a company in an equity offering.

secondary shares Shares sold by existing shareholders in an equity offering.

RealNetworks has conducted several SEOs since its IPO in 1997. On June 17, 1999, the firm offered 4 million shares in an SEO at a price of $58 per share. Of these shares, 3,525,000 were **primary shares**—new shares issued by the company. The remaining 475,000 shares were **secondary shares**—shares sold by existing shareholders, including the company's founder, Robert Glaser, who sold 310,000 of his shares. Most of the rest of RealNetworks' SEOs occurred between 1999 and 2004 and included secondary shares sold by existing shareholders rather than directly by RealNetworks.

---

[13]Maher Kooli and Jean-Marc Suret, "How Cost-Effective are Canadian IPO Markets?," *Canadian Investment Review* (Winter) (2003): 20–28.

[14]Jay R. Ritter, "The Long-Run Performance of Initial Public Offerings," *Journal of Finance* 46 (1) (1991): 3–27.

[15]Vijay Jog and Ashwani Srivastava, "Underpricing of Canadian Initial Public Offerings 1971–1992—an Update," *FINECO* (1994): 81–89.

FIGURE 13.7

Tombstone Advertisement for a RealNetworks SEO

This tombstone appeared in the *Wall Street Journal* and advertised the underwriters' participation in this RealNetworks SEO.

Source: Courtesy RealNetworks, Inc.

4,600,000 Shares

RealNetworks, Inc.

Common Stock

——

Price $58 Per Share

——

Upon request, a copy of the Prospectus describing these securities and the business of the Company may be obtained within any State from any Underwriter who may legally distribute it within such State. The securities are offered only by means of the Prospectus, and this announcement is neither an offer to sell nor a solicitation of an offer to buy.

Goldman, Sachs & Co.

BancBoston Robertson Stephens

Donaldson, Lufkin & Jenrette

Lehman Brothers

Thomas Weisel Partners LLC

Bear, Stearns & Co. Inc.	**Credit Suisse First Boston**	**Ragen MacKenzie** Incorporated
Warburg Dillon Read LLC	**Wasserstein Perella Securities, Inc.**	
Friedman Billings Ramsey	**Pacific Crest Securities Inc.**	

July 7, 1999

---

tombstone Newspaper advertisement in which underwriters advertise a security issuance.

cash offer A type of seasoned equity offering (SEO) in which a firm offers the new shares to investors at large.

rights offer A type of seasoned equity offering (SEO) in which a firm offers the new shares only to existing shareholders.

Historically, underwriters would advertise the sale of stock (both IPOs and SEOs) by taking out newspaper advertisements called **tombstones**. Through these ads, investors would know who to call to buy stock. Today, investors become informed about the impending sale of stock by the news media, via a road show, or through the book-building process, so these tombstones are purely ceremonial. Figure 13.7 shows the tombstone advertisement for one RealNetworks SEO.

Two types of SEOs exist: a cash offer and a rights offer. In a **cash offer**, the firm offers the new shares to investors at large. In a **rights offer**, the firm offers the new shares only to existing shareholders. In Canada and the United States, most offers are cash offers, but the same is not true elsewhere. For example, in the United Kingdom, most seasoned offerings of new shares are rights offers.

Rights offers protect existing shareholders from underpricing. To illustrate, suppose a company holds $100 in cash as its sole asset and has 50 shares outstanding. Each share is worth $2. The company announces a cash offer for 50 shares at $1 per share.

Once this offer is complete, the company will have $150 in cash and 100 shares outstanding. The price per share is now $1.50 to reflect the fact that the new shares were sold at a discount. The new shareholders therefore receive a $0.50 per share windfall at the expense of the old shareholders.

The old shareholders would be protected if, instead of a cash offer, the company did a rights offer. In this case, rather than offer the new shares for general sale, every shareholder would have the right to purchase an additional share for $1 per share. If all shareholders chose to exercise their rights, then after the sale the value of the company would be the same as with a cash offer: it would be worth $150 with 100 shares outstanding and a price of $1.50 per share. In this case, however, the $0.50 windfall accrues to existing shareholders, which exactly offsets the drop in the stock price. Thus, if a firm's management is concerned that its equity may be underpriced in the market, by using a rights offer the firm can continue to issue equity without imposing a loss on its current shareholders.

EXAMPLE 13.4

Raising Money with
Rights Offers

Problem

You are the CFO of a company that has a market capitalization of $1 billion. The firm has 100 million shares outstanding, so the shares are trading at $10 per share. You need to raise $200 million and have announced a rights issue. Each existing shareholder is sent one right for every share he or she owns. You have not decided how many rights you will require to purchase a share of new stock. You will require either four rights to purchase one share at a price of $8 per share, or five rights to purchase two new shares at a price of $5 per share. Which approach will raise more money?

Solution

▶ **Plan**

In order to know how much money will be raised, we need to compute how many total shares would be purchased if all shareholders exercise their rights. Then we can multiply it by the price per share to calculate the total amount of capital raised.

▶ **Execute**

There are 100 million shares, each with one right attached. In the first case, four rights will be needed to purchase a new share, so 100 million/4 = 25 million new shares will be purchased. At a price of $8 per share, that would raise $8 × 25 million = $200 million.

In the second case, for every five rights, two new shares can be purchased, so there will be 2 × (100 million/5) = 40 million new shares. At a price of $5 per share, that would also raise $200 million. If all shareholders exercise their rights, both approaches will raise the same amount of money.

▶ **Evaluate**

In both cases, the value of the firm after the issue is $1.2 billion. In the first case, there are 125 million shares outstanding after the issue, so the price per share after the issue is $1.2 billion/125 million = $9.60. This price exceeds the issue price of $8, so the shareholders will exercise their rights. Because exercising will yield a profit of ($9.60 − $8.00)/4 = $0.40 per right), the total value per share to each shareholder is $9.60 + 0.40 = $10.0. In the second case, the number of shares outstanding will grow to 140 million, resulting in a post-issue stock price of $1.2 billion/140 million shares = $8.57 per share (also higher than the issue price). Again, the shareholders will exercise their rights, and receive a total value per share of $8.57 + 2($8.57 − $5.00)/5 = $10.0. Thus, in both cases the same amount of money is raised and shareholders are equally well off.

SEO Price Reaction

Researchers have found that, on average, the market greets the news of an SEO with a price decline. Often, the value lost due to the price decline can be a significant fraction of the new money raised. Figure 13.8 shows the typical stock price reaction when an SEO is announced. To see why the market price of the stock drops when an SEO is announced, consider the following situation: Suppose a used-car dealer tells you he is willing to sell you a nice-looking sports car for $5000 less than its typical price. Rather than feel lucky, perhaps your first thought is that there must be something wrong with the car—it is probably a "lemon." Buyers will be skeptical of a seller's motivation for selling, because the seller has private information about the quality of the car. Thus, his *desire to sell* reveals the car is probably of low quality. Buyers are therefore reluctant to buy except at heavily discounted prices. Owners of high-quality cars are reluctant to sell because they know buyers will think they are selling a lemon and offer only a low price. Consequently, the quality and prices of cars sold in the used-car market are both low. This lemons principle—that when quality is hard to judge, the average quality of goods being offered for sale will be low—is referred to as **adverse selection**.

> **adverse selection**
> The idea, reflecting the lemons principle, that when quality is hard to judge, the average quality of goods being offered for sale will be low.

The lemons problem is very real for financial managers contemplating selling new equity. Because managers concerned about protecting their existing shareholders will tend to sell only at a price that correctly values or overvalues the firm, investors infer from the decision to sell that the company is likely to be overvalued. As a result, the price drops with the announcement of the SEO.

FIGURE 13.8

Price Reaction to an SEO Announcement

The figure shows the typical stock price reaction to the announcement of an SEO. The days are relative to the announcement day, so that day 0 is the announcement day. Notice that the stock price is typically increasing prior to the announcement—managers do not like to issue stock when its price has been dropping. Also note that the stock drops by about 1.5% when the SEO is announced and remains relatively flat afterward. The data include all SEOs from 2004 to 2007.

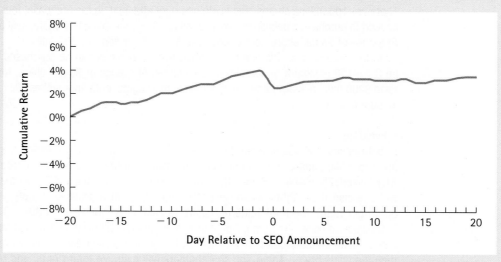

Source: ©2011 CRSP®, Center for Research in Security Prices. Booth School of Business, The University of Chicago. Used with permission. All rights reserved. www.crsp.chicagobooth.edu.

As with IPOs, there are several puzzles surrounding SEOs. First, by offering a rights issue a company can mitigate the problem leading to the price decline (because it is offering the shares directly to its existing shareholders, the firm will not benefit its shareholders by issuing shares that are overvalued). It is not clear, at least in Canada and the United States, why companies do not initiate more rights issues. Second, as with IPOs, evidence suggests that companies underperform following a seasoned offering. This underperformance appears to suggest that the stock price decrease is not large enough, because underperformance implies that the price following the issue was too high.

SEO Costs

Although not as costly as IPOs, seasoned offerings are still expensive, as Figure 13.6 shows. In addition to the price drop when the SEO is announced, the firm must pay direct costs too. Underwriting fees amount to 5% of the proceeds of the issue and, as with IPOs, the variation across issues of different sizes is relatively small. Furthermore, rights offers have lower costs than cash offers.[16] Given the other advantages of a rights offer, it is a puzzle why the majority of offers in Canada and the United States are cash offers. The one advantage of a cash offer is that the underwriter takes on a larger role and, therefore, can credibly attest to the issue's quality.

Concept Check

7. What is the difference between a cash offer and a rights offer for an SEO?

8. What is the typical stock price reaction to an SEO?

MyFinanceLab

Here is what you should know after reading this chapter. MyFinanceLab will help you identify what you know, and where to go when you need to practice.

Key Points	Terms	Online Practice Opportunities
13.1 Equity Financing for Private Companies ▶ Private companies can raise outside equity capital from angel investors, venture capital firms, institutional investors, sovereign wealth funds or corporate investors. ▶ When a company founder sells stock to an outsider to raise capital, the founder's ownership share and control over the company are reduced. ▶ Equity investors in private companies plan to sell their stock eventually through one of two main exit strategies: an acquisition or a public offering.	angel investors, p. 444 convertible preferred stock, p. 446 corporate investor, corporate partner, strategic partner, strategic investor, p. 446 exit strategy, p. 448 post-money valuation, p. 447 preferred stock, p. 446	MyFinanceLab Study Plan 13.1

---

[16]In the United Kingdom, Myron Slovin, Marie Sushka, and Kam Wah Lai found that the average fee for a cash offer is 6.1% versus 4.6% for an underwritten rights offer ("Alternative Flotation Methods, Adverse Selection, and Ownership Structure: Evidence from Seasoned Equity Issuance in the U.K.," *Journal of Financial Economics* 57 [2] [2000]).

pre-money valuation,
  p. 447
private equity investors,
  p. 444
sovereign wealth funds
  (SWFs), p. 446
venture capital firm, p. 444
venture capitalist, p. 445

13.2 Taking Your Firm Public: The Initial Public Offering

▶ An initial public offering (IPO) is the first time a company sells its stock to the public.

▶ The main advantages of going public are greater liquidity and better access to capital. Disadvantages include regulatory and financial reporting requirements, and the undermining of the investors' ability to monitor the company's management.

▶ During an IPO, the shares sold may represent either a primary offering (if the shares are being sold to raise new capital) or a secondary offering (if the shares are sold by earlier investors).

▶ An underwriter is an investment bank that manages the IPO process and helps the company sell its stock.

▶ The lead underwriter is responsible for managing the IPO.

▶ The lead underwriter forms a group of underwriters, called the syndicate, to help sell the stock.

▶ The securities regulators require that a company file a preliminary prospectus (in Canada) or a registration statement (in the United States) prior to an IPO. The preliminary prospectus (which is part of the registration statement in the United States) circulates to investors before the stock is offered. After the deal is completed, the company files a final prospectus and the shares can be sold to the public.

▶ Underwriters value a company before an IPO, using valuation techniques and by book building.

▶ Stock may be sold during an IPO on a best-efforts basis, as a firm commitment IPO, or using an auction IPO. The firm commitment process is the most common practice for large firms in Canada and the United States.

auction IPO, p. 456
best efforts p. 455
book building, p. 453
final prospectus, p. 452
firm commitment, p. 453
initial public offering
  (IPO), p. 449
lead underwriter, p. 450
lockup, p. 455
over-allotment allocation
  (greenshoe provision),
  p. 455
preliminary prospectus
  (red herring), p. 451
primary offering, p. 450
registration statement,
  p. 450
road show, p. 452
secondary offering, p. 450
spread, p. 455
syndicate, p. 450
underwriter, p. 450

MyFinanceLab
Study Plan 13.2

13.3 IPO Puzzles

▶ IPOs are underpriced on average.
▶ New issues are highly cyclical.
▶ The transaction costs of an IPO are very high.
▶ Long-run performance (three to five years) after an IPO is poor on average.

MyFinanceLab Study Plan 13.3

13.4 Raising Additional Capital: The Seasoned Equity Offering

▶ A seasoned equity offering (SEO) is the sale of stock by a company that is already publicly traded.
▶ Two kinds of SEOs exist: a cash offer (when new shares are sold to investors at large) and a rights offer (when new shares are offered only to existing shareholders).
▶ The stock price reaction to an SEO is negative on average.

adverse selection, p. 465
cash offer, p. 464
primary shares, p. 463
rights offer, p. 464
seasoned equity offering (SEO), p. 463
secondary shares, p. 463
tombstone, p. 464

MyFinanceLab Study Plan 13.4

Review Questions

1. What are some of the alternative sources from which private companies can raise equity capital?

2. What are the advantages and the disadvantages to a private company of raising money from a corporate investor?

3. What are the main advantages and disadvantages of going public?

4. What are the main differences between a firm commitment IPO and an auction IPO?

5. Do underwriters face the most risk from a best-efforts IPO, a firm commitment IPO, or an auction IPO?

6. How is the price set in an auction IPO?

7. Why should a financial manager be concerned about underpricing?

8. IPOs are very cyclical. In some years, there are large numbers of IPOs; in other years, there are very few. Why is this cyclicality a puzzle?

9. What are the advantages of a rights offer?

10. What are the advantages to a company of selling stock in an SEO using a cash offer?

11. Why does the stock price typically decrease when a firm announces an SEO?

Problems

All problems in this chapter are available in MyFinanceLab. An asterisk (*) indicates problems with a higher level of difficulty.

Equity Financing for Private Companies

1. You have started a company and are in luck—a venture capitalist has offered to invest. You own 100% of the company with 5 million shares. The VC offers $1 million for 800,000 new shares.
    a. What is the implied price per share?
    b. What is the post-money valuation?
    c. What fraction of the firm will you own after the investment?

2. Starware Software was founded last year to develop software for gaming applications. The founder initially invested $800,000 and received 8 million shares of stock. Starware now needs to raise a second round of capital, and it has identified a venture capitalist who is interested in investing. This venture capitalist will invest $1 million and wants to own 20% of the company after the investment is completed.
    a. How many shares must the venture capitalist receive to end up with 20% of the company? What is the implied price per share of this funding round?
    b. What will the value of the whole firm be after this investment (the post-money valuation)?

3. Your start-up company needs capital. Right now, you own 100% of the firm with 10 million shares. You have received two offers from venture capitalists. The first offers to invest $3 million for 1 million new shares. The second offers $2 million for 500,000 new shares.
    a. What is the first offer's post-money valuation of the firm?
    b. What is the second offer's post-money valuation of the firm?
    c. What is the difference in the percentage dilution caused by each offer?

 4. Three years ago, you founded your own company. You invested $100,000 of your money and received 5 million shares of Series A preferred stock. Your company has since been through three additional rounds of financing.

Round	Price ($)	Number of Shares
Series B	0.50	1,000,000
Series C	2.00	500,000
Series D	4.00	500,000

    a. What is the pre-money valuation for the Series D funding round?
    b. What is the post-money valuation for the Series D funding round?

 5. Based on the information in Problem 4 (and that each share of all series of preferred stock is convertible into one share of common stock), what fractions of the firm do the Series B, C, and D investors each own in the your firm?

 6. Assuming that you own only the Series A preferred stock in Problem 4 (and that each share of all series of preferred stock is convertible into one share of common stock), what percentage of the firm do you own after the last funding round?

Taking Your Firm Public: The Initial Public Offering

7. Roundtree Software is going public using an auction IPO. The firm has received the following bids:

Price ($)	Number of Shares
14.00	100,000
13.80	200,000
13.60	500,000
13.40	1,000,000
13.20	1,200,000
13.00	800,000
12.80	400,000

Assuming Roundtree would like to sell 1.8 million shares in its IPO, what will be the winning auction offer price?

8. If Roundtree (see Problem 7) decides to issue an extra 500,000 shares (for a total of 2.3 million shares), how much total money will it raise?

 9. Three years ago, you founded Outdoor Recreation, Inc., a retailer specializing in the sale of equipment and clothing for recreational activities such as camping, skiing, and hiking. So far, your company has gone through three funding rounds:

Round	Date	Investor	Shares	Share Price ($)
Series A	Feb. 2009	You	500,000	1.00
Series B	Aug. 2010	Angels	1,000,000	2.00
Series C	Sept. 2011	Venture capital	2,000,000	3.50

It is now 2012, and you need to raise additional capital to expand your business. You have decided to take your firm public through an IPO. You would like to issue an additional 6.5 million new shares through this IPO. Assuming that your firm successfully completes its IPO, you forecast that 2012 net income will be $7.5 million.
   a. Your investment banker advises you that the prices of other recent IPOs have been set such that the P/E ratios based on 2012 forecasted earnings average 20.0. Assuming that your IPO is set at a price that implies a similar multiple, what will your IPO price per share be?
   b. What percentage of the firm will you own after the IPO?

10. Your investment bankers price your IPO at $15 per share for 10 million shares. If the price at the end of the first day of trading is $17 per share,
   a. what was the percentage return on the first day of trading?
   b. how much money did the firm miss out on due to underpricing?

11. Margoles Publishing recently completed its IPO. The stock was offered at a price of $14 per share. On the first day of trading, the stock closed at $19 per share.
   a. What was the initial return on Margoles?
   b. Who benefited from this underpricing? Who lost, and why?

12. If Margoles Publishing (see Problem 11) paid an underwriting spread of 7% for its IPO and sold 10 million shares, what was the total cost (exclusive of underpricing) to the company of going public?

13. Chen Brothers, Inc. sold 4 million shares in its IPO, at a price of $18.50 per share. Management negotiated a fee (the underwriting spread) of 7% on this transaction. What was the dollar cost of this fee?

14. Your firm is selling 3 million shares in an IPO. You are targeting an offer price of $17.25 per share. Your underwriters have proposed a spread of 7%, but you would like to lower it to 5%. However, you are concerned that if you do so, they will argue for a lower offer price. Given the potential savings from a lower spread, how much lower can the offer price go before you would have preferred to pay 7% to get $17.25 per share?

Use the following information for Problems 15 through 17: The firm you founded currently has 12 million shares, of which you own 7 million. You are considering an IPO in which you would sell 2 million shares for $20 each.

15. If all of the shares sold are primary shares, how much will the firm raise? What will your percentage ownership of the firm be after the IPO?

16. If all of the shares sold are from your holdings, how much will the firm raise? What will your percentage ownership of the firm be after the IPO?

17. What is the maximum number of secondary shares you could sell and still retain more than 50% ownership of the firm? How much would the firm raise in that case?

Raising Additional Capital: The Seasoned Equity Offering

18. On January 20, Metropolitan, Inc. sold 8 million shares of stock in an SEO. The market price of Metropolitan at the time was $42.50 per share. Of the 8 million shares sold, 5 million shares were primary shares being sold by the company, and the remaining 3 million shares were being sold by the venture capital investors. Assume the underwriter charges 5% of the gross proceeds as an underwriting fee.
   a. How much money did Metropolitan raise?
   b. How much money did the venture capitalists receive?
   c. If the stock price dropped 3% on announcement of the SEO and the new shares were sold at that price, how much money would Metropolitan receive?

*19. Foster Enterprises' stock is trading for $50 per share and there are currently 10 million shares outstanding. It would like to raise $100 million. Assume its underwriter charges 5% of gross proceeds.
   a. How many shares must it sell?
   b. If it expects the stock price to drop by 2% upon announcement of the SEO, how many shares should it plan to sell?
   c. If all of the shares are primary shares and are sold to new investors, what percentage reduction in ownership will all of the existing shareholders experience?

20. MacKenzie Corporation currently has 10 million shares of stock outstanding at a price of $40 per share. The company would like to raise money and has announced a rights issue. Every existing shareholder will be sent one right per share of stock that he or she owns. The company plans to require 10 rights to purchase one share at a price of $40 per share. How much money will it raise if all rights are exercised?

Debt Financing

LEARNING OBJECTIVES

▶ Identify different types of debt financing available to a firm

▶ Understand limits within bond contracts that protect the interests of bondholders

▶ Describe the various options available to firms for the early repayment of debt

notation

YTC	yield to call on a callable bond	PV	present value
YTM	yield to maturity on a bond		

INTERVIEW WITH Damian Creber,
RBC Capital Markets

University of Toronto, 2010

"I work with the company and the rating agencies to find the optimal structure of debt, and determine whether the debt is secured."

Damian Creber is an investment banking analyst with RBC Capital Markets. A graduate of the University of Toronto in 2010, he works in the leveraged financing group, helping clients with acquisitions. "My role is to work with the acquirer, to help them with the valuation of the target, and in particular to help them structure and syndicate the debt used in the transaction."

Firms looking to use debt financing have many different options available to them. "For example, we had a recent client who wanted to do an all cash deal, with no equity. They needed to raise a large amount of debt, in this case preferring long-term debt rather than bank debt," Damian explains. "Possible options are to use revolving credit, or a bridge loan that would eventually become bonds."

Choosing the most suitable loan depends on the firm's current situation, what it will do with the loan proceeds, and how it plans to repay the loan. "I work with the company and the rating agencies to find the optimal structure of debt, and determine whether the debt is secured," Damian says. For him, the key is to strike the right balance between the costs and benefits of taking on additional debt: "I need to minimize their cost of capital while maximizing their flexibility."

In Chapter 13, we discussed the process a firm uses to raise equity capital, starting with angel investors for a young private firm and continuing through to seasoned equity offerings for an established public firm. We noted that each round of new equity financing dilutes the founder's ownership of the firm. An alternative financing source is to borrow the money—debt financing. In fact, debt is the most important source of financing; about $550 billion of Canadian corporate bonds were outstanding at the end of 2009. While debt financing does not dilute the ownership of the firm, the disadvantage is that loans must be repaid. That is, the firm is legally obligated to make interest and principal payments on its debt. If it fails to do so, it is in default and can be forced into bankruptcy. We discuss the relative advantages and disadvantages of debt versus equity financing in Chapter 15. Here, we focus on the process for financing part of the firm with debt and on the features of corporate debt. Corporations are not the only entities that use debt financing. Governments and quasi-government entities (such as Crown corporations) are also major users of debt markets to raise capital. At the end of 2009, the federal, provincial, and municipal governments had a total of $844 billion worth of bonds outstanding. This $844 billion was broken down as follows: $339 billion for the federal government, $440 billion for the provincial governments, and $45 billion for municipalities. Hence, while this chapter is directly applicable to corporations, much of it is also relevant to organizations other than corporations.

In mid-2005, Ford Motor Company decided to put one of its subsidiaries, Hertz Corporation, up for competitive bid. On September 13, 2005, the *Wall Street Journal* reported that a group of private investors led by Clayton, Dubilier & Rice (CDR), a private equity firm, had reached a deal with Ford to purchase Hertz's outstanding equity for $5.6 billion. In addition, Hertz had $9.1 billion in existing debt that it needed to refinance as part of the deal. CDR planned to finance the transaction in part by raising over $11 billion in new debt. We will examine the details of this transaction throughout this chapter to illustrate debt financing.

When companies raise capital by issuing debt, they have several potential sources from which to seek funds. To complete the Hertz purchase, the group led by CDR relied on at least four different kinds of debt:

domestic- and foreign-denominated high-yield bonds, bank loans, and *asset-backed securities*. In addition, each debt issue has its own specific terms determined at the time of issue. Building on the discussion of bond valuation in Chapter 6, we begin our exploration of debt financing by explaining the process of issuing debt and the types of debt available to companies. We continue by discussing restrictions on company actions in the debt agreement. Finally, we discuss some of the more advanced features of bonds, such as the call provision.

14.1 Corporate Debt

Corporate debt can be private debt, which is negotiated directly with a bank or a small group of investors, or public debt, which trades in a public market. As we will see, the Hertz example described in the introduction included both.

Private Debt

The first debt financing many young firms undertake is a bank loan. However, even very large, established firms use bank loans as part of their debt financing. Bank loans are an example of **private debt**, debt that is not publicly traded. The private debt market is larger than the public debt market. Private debt has the advantage that it avoids the cost and delay of registration with a securities commission such as the Ontario Securities Commission (OSC) in Ontario or the Securities and Exchange Commission (SEC) in the United States. The disadvantage is that because private debt is not publicly traded, it is illiquid, meaning that it is hard for a holder of the firm's private debt to sell it in a timely manner.

> **private debt** Debt that is not publicly traded.

Debt Financing at Hertz: Bank Loans

As part of the transaction with CDR, Hertz took out more than $2 billion in bank loans. Hertz negotiated a $1.7 billion syndicated term loan with a seven-year term. Deutsche Bank AG negotiated the loan and then sold portions of it to other banks—mostly smaller regional banks that had excess cash but lacked the resources to negotiate a loan of this magnitude alone. In addition to the term loan, Hertz negotiated an asset-backed revolving line of credit (for five years and $1.6 billion), which it could use as needed. Hertz's initial draw on the line of credit was $400 million.

> **term loan** A bank loan that lasts for a specific term.
>
> **syndicated bank loan** A single loan that is funded by a group of banks rather than just a single bank.
>
> **revolving line of credit** A credit commitment for a specific time period, typically two to three years, which a company can use as needed.
>
> **asset-backed line of credit** A type of credit commitment in which the borrower secures a line of credit by pledging an asset as collateral.

There are several segments of the private debt market: *bank loans* (*term loans* and *lines of credit*) and *private placements*.

Bank Loans. A **term loan** is a bank loan that lasts for a specific term. When a single loan is funded by a group of banks rather than just a single bank, it is called a **syndicated bank loan**. Usually, one member of the syndicate (the lead bank) negotiates the terms of the bank loan. Many companies establish a **revolving line of credit**, a credit commitment for a specific time period up to some limit, typically two to three years, which a company can use as needed. A company may be able to get a larger line of credit or a lower interest rate if it secures the line of credit by pledging an asset as collateral. Such a line of credit is referred to as an **asset-backed line of credit**.

Private Placements.   Recall from Chapter 6 that corporate bonds are securities issued by corporations. They account for a significant amount of invested capital. At the end of 2009, Canadian corporate bonds accounted for over 31% of all bonds outstanding

private placement
A bond issue that does not trade on a public market but rather is sold to a small group of investors.

in Canada. Bonds can be issued publicly or placed privately. A **private placement** is a bond issue that does not trade on a public market but rather is sold to a small group of investors. Because a private placement does not need to be registered with the securities commission, it is less costly to issue, and often a simple promissory note is sufficient. Privately placed debt also need not conform to the same standards as public debt; as a consequence, it can be tailored to the particular situation.

Debt Financing at Hertz: Private Placements

Hertz privately placed an additional $4.2 billion of U.S. asset-backed securities and $2.1 billion of international asset-backed securities. In this case, the assets backing the debt were the fleet of rental cars Hertz owned; hence, this debt was termed "fleet debt."

Hertz had an additional $2.7 billion bond issue that it issued under U.S. SEC Rule 144A.* As part of the offering, it agreed to publicly register the bonds within 390 days. Because the debt was marketed and sold with the understanding that it would become public debt, we classified that issue as public debt.

---

*In 1990, the U.S. SEC issued Rule 144A, which significantly increased the liquidity of certain privately placed debt. Private debt issued under this rule can be traded by large financial institutions among themselves. The rule was motivated by a desire to increase the access of foreign corporations to U.S. debt markets. Bonds that are issued under this rule are nominally private debt, but because they are tradable between financial institutions, they are only slightly less liquid than public debt. Many firms issue debt under Rule 144A with the explicit promise to publicly register the debt within a certain time frame. The advantage of this approach to debt financing is that companies can raise the capital quickly and then spend the time it takes to comply with all of the filing requirements.

Public Debt

indenture A formal contract between a bond issuer and a trust company that specifies the firm's obligations to the bondholders

The Prospectus. A public bond issue is similar to a stock issue. A prospectus or offering memorandum must be produced that describes the details of the offering. Figure 14.1 shows the front page of the Hertz offering memorandum. In addition, the prospectus for a public offering must include an **indenture**, a formal contract that specifies the firm's obligations to the bondholders. This contract is actually written between the bond issuer and a trust company that represents the bondholders and makes sure that the terms of the indenture are enforced. In the case of default, the trust company represents the bondholders' interests. In Chapter 6 we discussed several aspects of the public bond markets for debt. In particular we discussed default risk, bond ratings and the role of ratings agencies. Here we expand our discussion to include the different types of public corporate debt and the markets in which they are offered.

While corporate bonds almost always pay coupons semi-annually, a few corporations (for instance, Coca-Cola) have issued zero-coupon bonds. Corporate bonds have historically been issued with a wide range of maturities. Most corporate bonds have maturities of 30 years or less, although in the past there have even been perpetual bonds (that never mature). In July 1993, for example, Walt Disney Company issued $150 million in bonds with a maturity of 100 years; these bonds soon became known as the "Sleeping Beauty" bonds. Air Canada had several issues of perpetual bonds; however, these defaulted when the company went bankrupt in 2003.

original issue discount (OID) bond A coupon bond issued at a discount.

The face value or principal amount of the bond is denominated in standard increments, usually $1000. The face value does not always correspond to the actual money raised because of underwriting fees and the possibility that the bond might not actually sell for its face value when it is offered for sale initially. If a coupon bond is issued at a discount, it is called an **original issue discount (OID) bond**.

FIGURE 14.1

Front Cover of the Offering Memorandum for the Hertz Junk Bond Issue

Source: Courtesy of Hertz Corporation.

OFFERING MEMORANDUM   CONFIDENTIAL

CCMG Acquisition Corporation
to be merged with and into The Hertz Corporation
$1,800,000,000 8.875% Senior Notes due 2014
$600,000,000 10.5% Senior Subordinated Notes due 2016
€225,000,000 7.875% Senior Notes due 2014

The Company is offering $1,800,000,000 aggregate principal amount of its 8.875% Senior Notes due 2014 (the "Senior Dollar Notes"), $600,000,000 aggregate principal amount of its 10.5% Senior Subordinated Notes due 2016 (the "Senior Subordinated Notes" and, together with the Senior Dollar Notes, the "Dollar Notes"), and €225,000,000 aggregate principal amount of its 7.875% Senior Notes due 2014 (the "Senior Euro Notes"). The Senior Dollar Notes and the Senior Euro Notes are collectively referred to as the "Senior Notes," and the Dollar Notes and the Senior Euro Notes are collectively referred to as the "Notes."

The Senior Notes will mature on January 1, 2014 and the Senior Subordinated Notes will mature on January 1, 2016. Interest on the Notes will accrue from December 21, 2005. We will pay interest on the Notes on January 1 and July 1 of each year, commencing July 1, 2006.

We have the option to redeem all or a portion of the Senior Notes and the Senior Subordinated Notes at any time (1) before January 1, 2010 and January 1, 2011, respectively, at a redemption price equal to 100% of their principal amount plus the applicable make-whole premium set forth in this offering memorandum and (2) on or after January 1, 2010 and January 1, 2011, respectively, at the redemption prices set forth in this offering memorandum. In addition, on or before January 1, 2009, we may, on one or more occasions, apply funds equal to the proceeds from one or more equity offerings to redeem up to 35% of each series of Notes at the redemption prices set forth in this offering memorandum. If we undergo a change of control or sell certain of our assets, we may be required to offer to purchase Notes from holders.

The Senior Notes will be senior unsecured obligations and will rank equally with all of our senior unsecured indebtedness. The Senior Subordinated Notes will be unsecured obligations and subordinated in right of payment to all of our existing and future senior indebtedness. Each of our domestic subsidiaries that guarantees specified bank indebtedness will guarantee the Senior Notes with guarantees that will rank equally with all of the senior unsecured indebtedness of such subsidiaries and the Senior Subordinated Notes with guarantees that will be unsecured and subordinated in right of payment to all existing and future senior indebtedness of such subsidiaries.

We have agreed to make an offer to exchange the Notes for registered, publicly tradable notes that have substantially identical terms as the Notes. The Dollar Notes are expected to be eligible for trading in the Private Offering, Resale and Trading Automated Linkages (PORTAL℠) market. This offering memorandum includes additional information on the terms of the Notes, including redemption and repurchase prices, covenants and transfer restrictions.

Investing in the Notes involves a high degree of risk. See "Risk Factors" beginning on page 23.

We have not registered the Notes under the federal securities laws of the United States or the securities laws of any other jurisdiction. The Initial Purchasers named below are offering the Notes only to qualified institutional buyers under Rule 144A and to persons outside the United States under Regulation S. See "Notice to Investors" for additional information about eligible offerees and transfer restrictions.

Price for each series of Notes: 100%

We expect that (i) delivery of the Dollar Notes will be made to investors in book-entry form through the facilities of The Depository Trust Company on or about December 21, 2005 and (ii) delivery of the Senior Euro Notes will be made to investors in book-entry form through the facilities of the Euroclear System and Clearstream Banking, S.A. on or about December 21, 2005.

Joint Book-Running Managers

Deutsche Bank Securities   **Lehman Brothers**

Merrill Lynch & Co.   **Goldman, Sachs & Co.**   **JPMorgan**

Co-Lead Managers

BNP PARIBAS   **RBS Greenwich Capital**   **Calyon**

The date of this offering memorandum is December 15, 2005.

TABLE 14.1

Types of Corporate Debt

Secured	Unsecured
Mortgage bonds (secured with real property)	Notes (original maturity less than 10 years)
Asset-backed bonds (secured with any asset)	Debentures

unsecured debt A type of corporate debt that, in the event of a bankruptcy, gives bondholders a claim to only the assets of the firm that are not already pledged as collateral on other debt.

notes A type of unsecured corporate debt with maturities shorter than 10 years.

debentures A type of unsecured corporate debt with maturities of 10 years or longer.

secured debt A type of corporate loan or debt security in which specific assets are pledged as a firm's collateral that bondholders have a direct claim to in the event of a bankruptcy.

mortgage bonds A type of secured corporate debt in which real property is pledged as collateral.

asset-backed bonds A type of secured corporate debt in which specific assets are pledged as collateral.

seniority A bondholder's priority, in the event of a default, in claiming assets not already securing other debt.

subordinated debenture A debenture issue that has a lower-priority claim to the firm's assets than other outstanding debt.

Secured and Unsecured Corporate Debt. Four types of corporate debt are typically issued: *notes, debentures, mortgage bonds,* and *asset-backed bonds* (see Table 14.1). These types of debt fall into two categories: *unsecured* and *secured debt*. With **unsecured debt**, in the event of a bankruptcy bondholders have a claim to only the assets of the firm that are not already pledged as collateral on other debt. **Notes** are a type of unsecured debt, typically with maturities of less than 10 years, and **debentures** are a type of unsecured debt with maturities of 10 years or longer. With **secured debt**, specific assets are pledged as collateral that bondholders have a direct claim to in the event of a bankruptcy. **Mortgage bonds** are secured by real property, but **asset-backed bonds** can be secured by any kind of asset. Although the word "bond" is commonly used to mean any kind of debt security, technically a corporate bond must be secured.

Seniority. Debentures and notes are unsecured. Because more than one debenture might be outstanding, the bondholder's priority in claiming assets in the event of default, known as the bond's **seniority**, is important. As a result, most debenture issues contain clauses restricting the company from issuing new debt with priority equal to or higher than that of existing debt.

When a firm conducts a subsequent debenture issue that has lower priority than its outstanding debt, the new debt is known as a **subordinated debenture**. In the event of default, the assets not pledged as collateral for outstanding bonds cannot be used to pay off the holders of subordinated debentures until all more senior debt has been paid off. In Hertz's case, one **tranche** of the junk bond issue is a note that is subordinated to the other two tranches. In the event of bankruptcy, this note has a lower-priority claim on the firm's assets. Because holders of this tranche are likely to receive less in the event Hertz defaults, the yield on this debt is higher than that of the other tranches—10.5% compared with 8.875% for the first tranche.

International Bond Markets. The second tranche of Hertz's junk bond issue is a note that is denominated in euros rather than Hertz's home currency, the U.S. dollar. This is one type of an international bond. International bonds are classified into four broadly defined categories.

1. **Domestic bonds** are bonds issued by a local entity and traded in a local market, but purchased by foreigners. They are denominated in the local currency of the country in which they are issued.

2. **Foreign bonds** are bonds issued by a foreign company in a local market and are intended for local investors. They are also denominated in the local currency. Foreign bonds in Canada are known as Maple bonds; in the United States, foreign bonds are known as Yankee bonds. In other countries, foreign bonds also have special names; for example, in Japan they are called Samurai bonds; in the United Kingdom, they are known as Bulldogs.

Debt Financing at Hertz: Public Debt

As part of the transaction's financing, Hertz planned to issue $2.7 billion worth of unsecured debt—in this case, high-yield notes known as junk bonds. Recall from Chapter 6 that bonds rated below investment grade are called junk bonds. Further, remember that companies such as Standard & Poor's and Moody's rate the creditworthiness of bonds and make this information available to investors (see Table 6.6 for the specific ratings). The high-yield issue for the Hertz transaction was divided into three kinds of debt, or **tranches**, different classes of securities that make up a single bond issue and are paid from the same cash flow source (see Table 14.2), all of which made semi-annual coupon payments and were issued at par. The largest tranche was a $1.8 billion face-value note maturing in eight years. It paid a coupon of 8.875%, which at the time represented a 4.45% spread over Treasuries.

TABLE 14.2

Hertz's December 2005 Junk Bond Issues

	Tranche 1: Senior Dollar-Denominated Note	Tranche 2: Senior Euro-Denominated Note	Tranche 3: Senior Subordinated Dollar-Denominated Note
Face value	$1.8 billion	€225 million	$600 million
Maturity	December 1, 2014	December 1, 2014	December 1, 2016
Coupon	8.875%	7.875%	10.5%
Issue price	Par	Par	Par
Yield	8.875%	7.875%	10.5%
Rating			
Standard and Poor's	B	B	B
Moody's	B1	B1	B3
Fitch	BB—	BB—	BB+

tranches Different classes of securities that make up a single bond issuance.

domestic bonds Bonds issued by a local entity, denominated in the local currency and traded in a local market, but purchased by foreigners.

foreign bonds Bonds issued by a foreign company in a local market and intended for local investors. They are also denominated in the local currency.

Eurobonds International bonds that are not denominated in the local currency of the country in which they are issued.

global bonds Bonds that are offered for sale in several different markets simultaneously.

3. **Eurobonds** are international bonds that are not denominated in the local currency of the country in which they are issued. Consequently, there is no connection between the physical location of the market on which they trade and the location of the issuing entity. Eurobonds can be denominated in any number of currencies that might or might not be connected to the location of the issuer. The trading of these bonds is not subject to any particular nation's regulations.

4. **Global bonds** combine the features of domestic, foreign, and Eurobonds, and are offered for sale in several different markets simultaneously. Unlike Eurobonds, global bonds can be offered for sale in the same currency as the country of issuance. The Hertz junk bond issue is an example of a global bond issue: it was simultaneously offered for sale in the United States and Europe.

A bond that makes its payments in a foreign currency contains the risk of holding that currency and, therefore, is priced on the basis of the yields of similar bonds in that currency. Hence, the euro-denominated note of the Hertz junk bond issue has a different yield than the dollar-denominated note, even though both bonds have the same seniority and maturity. While they have the same default risk, they differ in their exchange rate risk—the risk that the foreign currency will depreciate in value relative to the local currency. (For further discussion of exchange rate risk, see Chapter 22.)

Table 14.3 summarizes Hertz's debt after the leveraged buyout transaction. About $2.7 billion of the $11.1 billion total was public debt and the rest was private debt consisting of a term loan, a revolving line of credit, and fleet debt. Both the fleet debt and the line of credit were backed by specific assets of the firm.

TABLE 14.3

Summary of New Debt Issued as Part of the Hertz Leveraged Buyout

Type of Debt	Amount ($ millions)
Public Debt	
Senior dollar-denominated	1800.0
Senior Euro-denominated (€225 million)	268.9
Subordinated dollar-denominated	600.0
Private Debt	
Term loan	1707.0
Asset-backed revolving line of credit	400.0
Asset-backed "fleet debt"*	6348.0
Total	**$11,123.9**

* The collateral of this debt was Hertz's fleet of rental cars.

1. List the four types of corporate public debt that are typically issued.

2. What are the four categories of international bonds?

14.2 Bond Covenants

covenants Restrictive
clauses in a bond contract
that limit the issuer from
taking actions that may
undercut its ability to
repay the bonds.

Now that we have established the main types of debt, we are prepared to take a closer look at the bond contract provisions. **Covenants** are restrictive clauses in a bond contract that limit the issuer from taking actions that may undercut its ability to repay the bonds. Why are such covenants necessary? After all, why would managers voluntarily take actions that increase the firm's default risk? Remember—managers work for the equity holders, and sometimes there are actions managers can take that benefit the equity holders at the expense of debt holders. Covenants are there to protect debt holders in such cases.

Types of Covenants

Once bonds are issued, equity holders have an incentive to increase dividends at the expense of debt holders. Think of an extreme case in which a company issues a bond and then immediately liquidates its assets, pays out the proceeds (including those from the bond issue) in the form of a dividend to equity holders, and declares bankruptcy. In this case, the equity holders receive the value of the firm's assets plus the proceeds from the bond, while bondholders are left with nothing. Consequently, bond agreements often contain covenants that restrict the ability of management to pay dividends. Other covenants may restrict how much more debt the firm can issue, or they may specify that the firm must maintain a minimum amount of working capital. If the firm fails to live up to any covenant, the bond goes into technical default and the bondholder can demand immediate repayment or force the company to renegotiate the terms of the bond. Table 14.4 summarizes typical

TABLE 14.4	**Type of Action Restricted**	**Typical Restrictions**
Typical Bond Covenants	Issuance of new debt	New debt must be subordinate to existing debt.
		No new debt may be issued unless the firm maintains specific leverage or interest coverage ratios.
	Dividends and share repurchases	Payouts can be made only from earnings generated after the bond issue.
		Payouts can be made only if earnings exceed some threshold.
	Mergers and acquisitions	Mergers are allowed only if the combined firm has a minimum ratio of net tangible assets to debt.
	Asset disposition	The maximum amount of assets that can be sold and/or the minimum amount of assets that must be maintained is set.
		Restrictions are placed on making loans or any other provision of credit.
	Maintenance Required	
	Accounting measures	Minimum retained earnings, working capital, and/or net assets are set.
		Maximum leverage ratios are set.

Source: Adapted from the American Bar Association's Commentaries on Debentures

bond covenants. All of the covenants are designed to limit the company's (the borrower's) ability to increase the risk of the bond. For example, without restrictions on the issuance of new debt, the company could issue new debt with seniority equal to or greater than that of the existing bonds, thus increasing the risk that the firm will not repay the existing bonds.

Advantages of Covenants

You might expect that equity holders would try to include as few covenants as possible in a bond agreement. In fact, this is not necessarily the case. The stronger the covenants in the bond contract, the less likely the firm will be to default on the bond, and thus the lower the interest rate will be that investors will require to buy the bond. That is, by including more covenants, firms can reduce their costs of borrowing. The reduction in the firm's borrowing costs can more than outweigh the cost of the loss of flexibility associated with covenants.

Application: Hertz's Covenants

Covenants in the Hertz junk bond issue limited Hertz's ability to incur more debt, make dividend payments, redeem stock, make investments, transfer or sell assets, and merge or consolidate. They also included a requirement that Hertz offer to repurchase the bonds at 101% of face value if the corporation experiences a change in control.

Concept Check

3. What happens if an issuer fails to live up to a bond covenant?

4. Why can bond covenants reduce a firm's borrowing costs?

14.3 Repayment Provisions

A firm repays its bonds by making coupon and principal payments as specified in the bond contract. However, this is not the only way a firm can repay bonds. For example, the firm can repurchase a fraction of the outstanding bonds in the market, or it can make a tender offer for the entire issue, as Hertz did on its existing bonds. In this section, we explain the three main bonds features affecting the repayment of the bond: *call provisions, sinking funds,* and *convertible provisions.*

Call Provisions

callable bonds Bonds containing a call provision that allows the issuer to repurchase the bonds at a predetermined price.
call date The date in the call provision on or after which the bond issuer has the right to retire the bond.
call price A price, specified at the issuance of a bond, for which the issuer can redeem the bond.

Firms can repay bonds by exercising a *call* provision. **Callable bonds** allow the issuer of the bond to repurchase the bonds at a predetermined price. A call feature also allows the issuer the right (but not the obligation) to retire all outstanding bonds on (or after) a specific date known as the **call date**, for the **call price** that is specified at the issuance of the bond. The call price is expressed as a percentage of the bond's face value and is generally set at or above the face value. The difference (in percent) between the call price and the par value is the call premium. For example, a bond might have a call price of 105%, implying a call premium of 5%.

Hertz's Callable Bonds. Hertz's junk bonds are examples of callable bonds. Table 14.5 lists the call features in each tranche. In Hertz's case, the call dates of the two senior tranches are at the end of the fourth year. For the duration of 2010, the first tranche has a call price of 104.438% of the bond's face value. In the following years, the call price is

	Tranche 1: Senior Dollar-Denominated Note	Tranche 2: Senior Euro-Denominated Note	Tranche 3: Senior Subordinated Dollar-Denominated Note
Call Features	Up to 35% of the outstanding principal callable at 108.875% in the first three years. After four years, fully callable at • 104.438% in 2010. • 102.219% in 2011. Par thereafter.	Up to 35% of the outstanding principal callable at 107.875% in the first three years. After four years, fully callable at • 103.938% in 2010. • 101.969% in 2011. Par thereafter.	Up to 35% of the outstanding principal callable at 110.5% in the first three years. After five years, fully callable at • 105.25% in 2011. • 103.50% in 2012. • 101.75% in 2013.

TABLE 14.5

Call Features of Hertz's Bonds

gradually reduced until, in 2012, the bond becomes callable at par (100% of face value). The euro-denominated bond has similar terms at slightly different call prices. The subordinated tranche's call date is a year later and has a different call-price structure.

The Hertz bonds are also partially callable in the first three years. Hertz has the option to retire up to 35% of the outstanding principal at the call prices listed in Table 14.5, as long as the funds needed to repurchase the bonds are derived from the proceeds of an equity issuance.

Call Provisions and Bond Prices. When would a financial manager choose to exercise the firm's right to call the bond? A firm can always retire one of its bonds early by repurchasing the bond in the open market. If the call provision offers a cheaper way to retire the bond, however, the firm will forgo the option of purchasing the bond in the open market and call the bond instead. Thus, when the market price of the bond exceeds the call price, the firm will call the bond.

We know from Chapter 6 that bond prices rise when market interest rates fall. If market interest rates have decreased since the bond was issued and are now less than the bond's coupon rate, the bond will be trading at a premium. If the firm has the option to call the bond at less than the premium, it could do so and refinance its debt at the new, lower market interest rates.

Given the flexibility a call provision provides to a financial manager, you might expect all bonds to be callable. However, that is not the case; to see why, we must consider how the investor views the call provision. The financial manager will choose to call the bonds only when the coupon rate the investor is receiving exceeds the market interest rate. By calling the bond, the firm is forcing the investor to relinquish the bond at a price below the value it would have were it to remain outstanding. Naturally, investors view this possibility negatively and pay less for callable bonds than for otherwise identical non-callable bonds. That means that a firm raising capital by issuing callable bonds instead of non-callable bonds will have to either pay a higher coupon rate or accept lower proceeds. A firm will choose to issue callable bonds despite their higher yield if it finds the option to refinance the debt in the future particularly valuable.

Yield to Call. A financial manager needs to understand how investors are evaluating the firm's callable bonds. For callable bonds, the **yield to call (YTC)**, the annual yield of a callable bond calculated under the assumption that the bond is called on the earliest call date, is most often quoted. In Chapter 6, we learned how investors evaluate a firm's bonds by computing their yield to maturity. The yield to maturity is always calculated on the assumption that the bond will remain outstanding until maturity and make all of its

yield to call (YTC) The yield of a callable bond calculated under the assumption that the bond will be called on the earliest call date.

TABLE 14.6	Bond Coupons Relative to Market Yields	Bond Price	Likelihood of Call	Yield to Worst
Bond Calls and Yields	Coupons are higher	At a premium	High	Yield to call
	Coupons are lower	At a discount	Low	Yield to maturity

promised payments. In the case of a callable bond, that assumption is not realistic. Thus, the yield to maturity of a callable bond is the interest rate the bondholder receives if the bond is not called and repaid in full. When the bond's coupon rate is above the yield for similar securities, the yield to call is less than the yield to maturity. However, when the bond's coupon rate is below the yield for similar securities, the bond is unlikely to be called (the firm would not call a bond when it is paying a below-market interest rate). In that case, calling would actually be good for the bondholders, and the yield to call would be above the yield to maturity. To keep all this straight, most bond traders quote **yield to worst**, which is the lower of the yield to call or yield to maturity. Table 14.6 summarizes the yield to call and yield to worst.

yield to worst Quoted by bond traders, the lower of the yield to call or yield to maturity.

EXAMPLE 14.1

Calculating the Yield to Call

Problem

Bell Canada Enterprises (BCE) has just issued a callable (at par) five-year, 8% coupon bond with annual coupon payments. The bond can be called at par in one year or any time thereafter on a coupon payment date. It has a price of $103 per $100 face value, implying a yield to maturity of 7.26%. What is the bond's yield to call?

Solution

▶ **Plan**

The timeline of the promised payments for this bond (if it is not called) is:

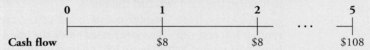

If BCE calls the bond at the first available opportunity, it will call the bond at year 1. At that time, it will have to pay the coupon payment for year 1 ($8 per $100 of face value) and the face value ($100). The timeline of the payments if the bond is called at the first available opportunity (at year 1) is:

Period	0	1
Cash flow		$108

To solve for the yield to call, we use these cash flows and proceed as shown in Chapter 6, setting the price equal to the discounted cash flows and solving for the discount rate.

▶ **Execute**

For the yield to call, setting the present value of these payments equal to the current price gives:

$$103 = \frac{108}{(1 + YTC)}$$

Solving for the yield to call gives:

$$YTC = \frac{108}{103} - 1 = 4.85\%$$

We can use a financial calculator to derive the same result:

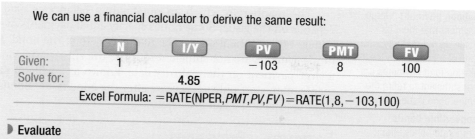

	N	I/Y	PV	PMT	FV
Given:	1		−103	8	100
Solve for:		4.85			

Excel Formula: =RATE(NPER,*PMT,PV,FV*)=RATE(1,8,−103,100)

▶ **Evaluate**

The yield to maturity is higher than the yield to call because the yield to maturity assumes that you will continue receiving your coupon payments for five years, even though interest rates have dropped below 8%. Under the yield to call assumptions, since you are repaid the face value sooner, you are deprived of the extra four years of coupon payments, resulting in a lower total return.

The Canada Call or Make-Whole Call Provision

Canada call or **make-whole call** A callable bond with the call price set equal to the present value of the bond's remaining payments, calculated with a rate adjusted for prevailing interest rates in the economy.

Rather than a standard call provision as just described, many companies have adopted the **"Canada call"** or **"make-whole call"** provision instead. This call provision sets the call price as the present value of the remaining coupons, which is calculated using a rate that adjusts with changes in prevailing interest rates in the economy. Thus, if interest rates fall, the call price rises, and the incentive to call the bond in order to refinance at lower rates is eliminated due to the higher call price that would need to be paid. Gady Jacoby and David Stangeland describe how, in 1993, 41% of Canadian corporate bonds had the standard call provision, while only 23% had the Canada call provision; by 1999, however, only 8% of Canadian corporate bonds had the standard call provision while 47% had the Canada call provision. Why do corporations bother with the Canada call provision instead of just leaving the bonds as non-callable? Perhaps management would like to retire a bond issue for reasons other than a drop in interest rates. For example, if a change in capital structure is desired (see Chapter 15) or if a bond covenant becomes troublesome, then management may prefer retiring the bond issue. It may be less costly to call the bond rather than repurchase it on the open market through a tender offer. This benefit may outweigh the fact that, under a Canada call provision, the call price is greater than the present value of the remaining coupons.[1]

Sinking Funds

sinking fund A method for repaying a bond in which a company makes regular payments into a fund administered by a trustee over the life of the bond. These payments are then used to repurchase bonds, usually at par.

Some bonds are repaid through a **sinking fund**, a provision that allows the company to make regular payments into a fund administered by a trustee over the life of the bond, instead of repaying the entire principal balance on the maturity date. These payments are then used to repurchase bonds, usually at par. In this way, the company can reduce the amount of outstanding debt without affecting the cash flows of the remaining bonds.

Sinking fund provisions usually specify a minimum rate at which the issuer must contribute to the fund. In some cases, the issuer has the option to accelerate these payments. Because the sinking fund allows the issuer to repurchase the bonds at par, the option to accelerate the payments is another form of a call provision. As with all call provisions, this option is not free—including this provision lowers the price the company would get for the bonds initially.

---

[1]See Gady Jacoby and David Stangeland's article "The Make-Whole, Doomsday, and Canada Call Provisions," *Northern Finance Association Conference Proceedings,* September, 2004.

balloon payment A large payment that must be made on the maturity date of a bond when the sinking fund payments are not sufficient to retire the entire bond issue.

The manner in which an outstanding balance is paid off using a sinking fund depends on the issue. Some issues specify equal payments over the life of the bond, ultimately retiring the issue on the maturity date of the bond. In other cases, the sinking fund payments are not sufficient to retire the entire issue, and the company must make a large payment on the maturity date, known as a **balloon payment**. Sinking fund payments often start only a few years after the bond issue. Bonds can be issued with both a sinking fund and a call provision.

Convertible Provisions

Another way to retire bonds is by converting them into equity. **Convertible bonds** are corporate bonds with a provision that gives the bondholder an option to convert each bond owned into a fixed number of shares of common stock at a ratio called the **conversion ratio**. The provision usually gives bondholders the right to convert the bond into stock at any time up to the maturity date for the bond.[2] The conversion ratio is usually stated per $1000 of face value.

convertible bonds Corporate bonds with a provision that gives the bondholder an option to convert each bond owned into a fixed number of shares of common stock.

conversion ratio The ratio used to convert a convertible bond into a fixed number of shares, usually stated per $1000 face value.

conversion price The face value of a convertible bond divided by the number of shares received if the bond is converted.

Convertible Bond Pricing. Consider a convertible bond with a $1000 face value and a conversion ratio of 20. If you converted the bond into stock on its maturity date, you would receive 20 shares. If you did not convert, you would receive $1000. Hence, by converting the bond you essentially "paid" $1000 for 20 shares, implying a price per share of $1000 ÷ 20 shares = $50 per share. This implied price per share equal to the face value of the bond divided by the number of shares received in conversion is called the **conversion price**. If the price of the stock exceeds $50, you would choose to convert; otherwise, you would take the cash. Thus, as shown in Figure 14.2, the value of the bond on its maturity date is the maximum of its face value ($1000) and the value of 20 shares of stock.

FIGURE 14.2

Convertible Bond Value

At maturity, the value of a convertible bond is the maximum of the value of a $1000 straight bond (a non-convertible, non-callable bond) and 20 shares of stock, and it will be converted if the stock is above the conversion price. Prior to maturity, the value of the convertible bond will depend on the likelihood of conversion and will be above that of a straight bond or 20 shares of stock.

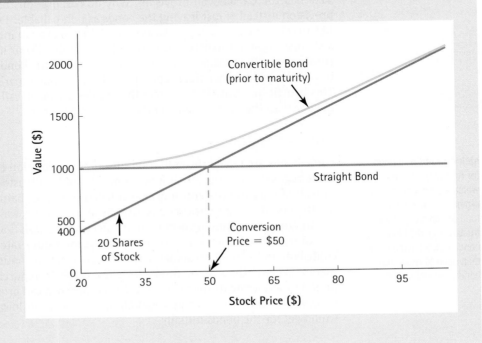

---

[2]Some convertible bonds do not allow conversion for a specified amount of time after the issue date.

Often companies issue convertible bonds that also have a standard call feature. With these bonds, if the issuer calls them, the holder can choose to convert rather than let the bonds be called. When the bonds are called, the holder faces exactly the same decision as he or she would face on the maturity date of the bonds: he or she will choose to convert if the stock price exceeds the conversion price and otherwise will let the bonds be called. Thus, by calling the bonds, a company can force bondholders to make their decision to convert earlier than they would otherwise have preferred.

straight bond
A non-callable, non-convertible bond (also called a plain-vanilla bond).

The option (which is not an obligation) to convert the bonds into equity is worth something to a bondholder. Thus, prior to the bond maturity date, a convertible bond is worth more than an otherwise identical **straight bond**, a non-callable, non-convertible bond (also called a plain-vanilla bond). Consequently, if both bonds are issued at par, the straight bond must offer a higher interest rate. Similarly, the option to receive the bond's face value means the convertible bond is also worth more than 20 shares of stock. This relationship is illustrated in Figure 14.2, where the convertible bond's value prior to maturity (the yellow curve) exceeds the value of both the straight bond (red line) and the stock (blue line). The company's management (on behalf of its existing shareholders) must weigh the benefit of the lower interest rate on the convertible bond against the cost of giving those bondholders the option to buy new shares of stock at a fixed price.

Convertible Bonds and Stock Prices. Note that the likelihood of eventually converting a convertible bond depends on the current stock price. When the stock price is low, conversion is unlikely, and the value of the convertible bond is close to that of a straight bond. When the stock price is much higher than the conversion price, conversion is very likely, and the convertible bond's price is close to the price of the converted shares. Finally, when the stock price is in the middle range, near the conversion price, there is the greatest uncertainty about whether it will be optimal to convert or not. In this case, the bondholder's option to decide later whether to convert is most valuable, and the value of the convertible bond exceeds the value of straight debt or equity by the greatest amount.

Combining Features. Companies have flexibility in setting the features of the bonds they issue. As we mentioned above, companies will often add a call provision to convertible bonds or bonds with sinking funds. Another example of flexibility is to add convertibility to subordinated bonds. Subordinated bonds typically have a higher yield because of their riskier position relative to senior bonds. But if the subordinated bond contains a convertibility feature that the senior bonds do not have, the yield on the subordinated bond could be lower than that of the senior bonds. In Chapter 13, we studied RealNetworks' equity financing. In 2003, RealNetworks issued $100 million in subordinated convertible debt, as described in Table 14.7. The debt also contained a provision allowing the company to call the debt at par any time after July 1, 2008.

TABLE 14.7	Convertible Subordinated Notes	
RealNetworks' 2003 Convertible Debt Issue	Issued Under U.S. SEC Rule 144A	
	Aggregate principal amount	$100 million
	Proceeds net of offering costs	$97.0 million
	Coupon	0%
	Conversion ratio	107.5650 shares per $1000 principal amount
	Call date	July 1, 2008
	Call price	100%
	Maturity	July 1, 2010

leveraged buyout (LBO)
The purchase by a group
of private investors of
all the equity of a public
corporation, primarily
through debt financing.

Leveraged Buyouts. Recall from Chapter 13 our discussion of how private companies become public companies. The deal in which CDR bought Hertz is an example of the opposite transition—a public company becoming private, in this case through a *leveraged buyout*. In a **leveraged buyout (LBO),** a group of private investors purchases all the equity of a public corporation and finances the purchase primarily with debt.[3] With a total value of $15.2 billion,[4] the LBO of Hertz was the second-largest transaction of its kind at the time of its announcement. This left Hertz with a substantial amount of debt on its balance sheet. As with most LBOs, Hertz's long-term plan was to reduce its leverage through continued profitability. In November 2006, Hertz went public again by selling new stock through an IPO. As of 2010, Hertz was still able to meet its debt obligations and had started to reduce the debt burden from the transaction. In Chapter 15, we will examine the tradeoffs a financial manager faces in deciding how much of a company to finance with debt and how much to finance with equity.

Concept Check

5. Do bonds with a standard call feature have a higher or lower yield than otherwise identical bonds without a call feature? Why?

6. Will a drop in interest rates make it advantageous for a company to call a bond with a Canada call feature?

7. What is a sinking fund?

8. Why does a convertible bond have a lower yield than an otherwise identical bond without the option to convert?

MyFinanceLab

Here is what you should know after reading this chapter. MyFinanceLab will help you identify what you know, and where to go when you need to practice.

Key Points	Terms	Online Practice Opportunities
14.1 Corporate Debt ▶ Companies can raise debt using different sources. Typical kinds of debt are public debt, which trades in a public market, and private debt, which is negotiated directly with a bank or a small group of investors. The securities that companies issue when raising debt are called corporate bonds.	asset-backed bonds, p. 479 asset-backed line of credit, p. 476 debentures, p. 479 domestic bonds, p. 479 Eurobonds, p. 479 foreign bonds, p. 479 global bonds, p. 479 indenture, p. 477	MyFinanceLab Study Plan 14.1

---

[3] At the time of the deal, Hertz was a wholly owned subsidiary of Ford Motor Company, which itself is a public company. Prior to Ford's acquisition of Hertz's outstanding shares in 2001, Hertz was publicly traded.

[4] The total value includes $14.7 billion for Hertz, and $0.5 billion in fees and expenses. In addition to $11.1 billion in new debt, the transaction was financed using $1.8 billion of Hertz's own cash and securities (including a $1.2 billion obligation from Ford, which was forgiven as part of the payment to Ford). The remaining $2.3 billion in private equity was contributed by Clayton, Dubilier & Rice, The Carlyle Group, and Merrill Lynch Global Private Equity.

▶ Private debt can be in the form of term loans or private placements. A term loan is a bank loan that lasts for a specific term. A private placement is a bond issue that is sold to a small group of investors.

▶ For public offerings, the bond agreement takes the form of an indenture, a formal contract between the bond issuer and a trust company. The indenture lays out the terms of the bond issue.

▶ Four types of corporate bonds are typically issued: notes, debentures, mortgage bonds, and asset-backed bonds. Notes and debentures are unsecured. Mortgage bonds and asset-backed bonds are secured.

▶ Corporate bonds differ in their level of seniority. In case of bankruptcy, senior debt is paid in full before subordinated debt is paid.

▶ International bonds are classified into four broadly defined categories: domestic bonds purchased by foreign investors; foreign bonds that are issued in a local market by a foreign entity; Eurobonds that are not denominated in the local currency of the country in which they are issued; and global bonds that trade in several markets simultaneously.

mortgage bonds, p. 479
notes, p. 479
original issue discount (OID) bond, p. 477
private debt, p. 476
private placement, p. 477
revolving line of credit, p. 476
secured debt, p. 479
seniority, p. 479
subordinated debenture, p. 479
syndicated bank loan, p. 476
term loan, p. 476
tranches, p. 479
unsecured debt, p. 479

14.2 Bond Covenants

▶ Covenants are restrictive clauses in the bond contract that help investors by limiting the issuer's ability to take actions that will increase its default risk and reduce the value of the bonds.

covenants, p. 481

MyFinanceLab
Study Plan 14.2

14.3 Repayment Provisions

▶ A call provision gives the issuer of the bond the right (but not the obligation) to retire the bond after a specific date (but before maturity).

▶ A callable bond will generally trade at a lower price than an otherwise equivalent non-callable bond.

▶ The yield to call is the yield of a callable bond, assuming that the bond is called at the earliest opportunity.

▶ With a Canada call or make-whole call, the call price is the present value of the bond's remaining payments calculated with a rate adjusted for prevailing interest rates in the economy.

balloon payment, p. 486
call date, p. 482
call price, p. 482
callable bonds, p. 482
Canada call or make-whole call, p. 485
conversion price, p. 486
conversion ratio, p. 486
convertible bonds, p. 486
leveraged buyout (LBO), p. 488
sinking fund, p. 485
straight bond, p. 487
yield to call (*YTC*), p. 483
yield to worst, p. 483

MyFinanceLab
Study Plan 14.3

▶ Another way in which a bond is repaid before maturity is by periodically repurchasing part of the debt through a sinking fund.

▶ Some corporate bonds, known as convertible bonds, have a provision that allows the holder to convert them into equity.

▶ Convertible debt carries a lower interest rate than other comparable non-convertible debt.

Review Questions

1. What are the different types of corporate debt and how do they differ?

2. Explain some of the differences between a public debt offering and a private debt offering.

3. Explain the difference between a secured corporate bond and an unsecured corporate bond.

4. Why do bonds with lower seniority have higher yields than equivalent bonds with higher seniority?

5. What is the difference between a foreign bond and a Eurobond?

6. Why would companies voluntarily choose to put restrictive covenants into a new bond issue?

7. Why would a call feature be valuable to a company issuing bonds?

8. What is the effect of including a standard call feature on the price a company can receive for its bonds?

9. When will the yield to maturity be higher than the yield to call for a bond with a standard call feature?

10. Why might a company's management want to issue a bond with the Canada call provision?

11. How does a sinking fund provision affect the cash flows associated with a bond issue from the company's perspective? From a single bondholder's perspective?

12. Why is the yield on a convertible bond lower than the yield on an otherwise identical bond without a conversion feature?

Problems

All problems in this chapter are available in MyFinanceLab.

Corporate Debt

1. You are finalizing a bank loan for $200,000 for your small business, and the closing fees payable to the bank are 2% of the loan. After paying the fees, what will be the net amount of funds from the loan available to your business?

2. Your firm is issuing $100 million in straight bonds at par with a coupon rate of 6% and paying total fees of 3%. What is the net amount of funds that the debt issue will provide for your firm?

Repayment Provisions

 3. General Electric has just issued a callable (at par) 10-year, 6% coupon bond with annual coupon payments. The bond can be called at par in one year or any time thereafter on a coupon payment date. It has a price of $102.
   a. What is the bond's yield to maturity?
   b. What is its yield to call?
   c. What is its yield to worst?

 4. Boeing Corporation has just issued a callable (at par) three-year, 5% coupon bond with semi-annual coupon payments. The bond can be called at par in two years or any time thereafter on a coupon payment date. It has a price of $99.
   a. What is the bond's yield to maturity?
   b. What is its yield to call?
   c. What is its yield to worst?

5. You own a bond with a face value of $10,000 and a conversion ratio of 450. What is the conversion price?

6. A $1000 face value convertible bond has a conversion ratio of 40 and is about to mature. Ignoring any transaction costs, what price must the stock surpass in order for you to convert?

7. You are the CFO of RealNetworks on July 1, 2008. The company's stock price is $9.70 and its convertible debt (as shown in Table 14.7) is now callable.
   a. What is the value of the shares the bondholders would receive per $1000 bond if they convert?
   b. What is the value per $1000 bond they would receive under the call?
   c. If you call the bonds, will the bondholders convert into shares or accept the call price?

Chapter 14 APPENDIX   Using a Financial Calculator to Calculate Yield to Call

Calculate the yield to call of the bond from Example 14.1. In the example, the bond is called at year 1; however, this can be generalized and solved for periods longer than one year.

HP-10BII

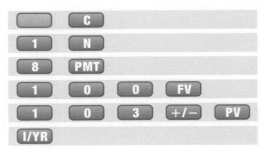

Press [Orange Shift] and then the [C] button to clear all previous entries.

Enter the Number of periods.

Enter the Payment amount per period.

Enter the price you would receive when it is called.

Enter the present value or price of the bond.

Solve for yield to call.

TI-BAII Plus Professional

Press [2nd] and then the [FV] button to clear all previous entries.

Enter the Number of periods.

Enter the Payment amount per period.

Enter the price you would receive when it is called.

Enter the present value or price of the bond.

Solve for yield to call.

If the bond were called after two years, you would simply use 2 instead of 1 for the number of periods.

PART 5 Integrative Case

This case draws on material from Chapters 13 and 14.

On May 8, 1984, Hannah Eisenstat graduated from McGill University. She set to work opening a coffee shop in Montreal called HannaH and found a perfect location in a new development. Using a $50,000 inheritance to finance the venture, together with her own sweat equity, she started the business on August 1, 1984, as a sole proprietorship.

The shop was profitable in the first year. Hannah found, however, that the quality of her coffee was not as high has she had initially envisioned. She discussed this issue with one of her regular customers, Natasha Gagnon. On the spot, Natasha offered to help finance the purchase of a roasting machine. By roasting the beans herself, Hannah could produce higher-quality coffee, as well as expand the business by offering beans for sale.

Expansion. After looking carefully at the financials, Hannah determined that she would need an investment of $75,000 from Natasha to undertake this expansion. In exchange for this investment, Hannah offered her a 40% share in the business. Natasha accepted the offer and the business was incorporated with two owners. The equity consisted of 1,000,000 shares in total, with Natasha owning 400,000 shares and Hannah owning 600,000 shares.

By the end of the second year, the business was doing extremely well. Revenue from the sale of beans soon began to rival beverage sales. In response to this success, Hannah and Natasha decided to expand to five stores over the next two years. Rather than using equity financing, they decided to seek bank financing. Each new store required an investment of $100,000. Opening the stores took longer than planned, but by the end of 1999, there were five HannaH's in Montreal employing 30 people. As planned, this expansion was financed solely with debt that was ultimately consolidated into a $500,000 term loan due in 2004.

Venture Capital. In early 2000, the two owners decided to take a weekend retreat and reevaluate their initial business plan. Perhaps the biggest surprise was the popularity of beans; almost 80% of revenue was attributable to bean sales alone. Furthermore, a buyer from a local supermarket chain had approached HannaH with a proposal to sell the beans in the chain's stores. However, HannaH was currently at its capacity limits—it could barely roast enough coffee for its five stores. More importantly, to enhance the coffee quality further, Hannah proposed that they buy beans directly from coffee farmers in Costa Rica, where she would be able to monitor quality closely. However, the supermarket proposal would require a significant increase in the production of roasted beans. By the end of the retreat, Hannah and Natasha had decided to change the focus of the business from retail beverage and bean sales to wholesale roasted coffee beans. Rather than build new stores, they decided to invest in a state-of-the-art roasting facility.

In the next few weeks, Hannah approached Ricard Partners, a local venture capital firm. On the strength of the commitment from the supermarket chain to carry the coffee, Ricard agreed to invest $3 million to finance the construction of a high-capacity roasting facility in exchange for a 50% share of the company. To accomplish this, 1,000,000 new shares in HannaH were issued to Ricard.

Further Expansion. Hannah's intuition was correct—the quality of the coffee increased significantly. Within eight years, the company had grown to almost 200 employees, and its strong reputation allowed it to sell its coffee for a 50% premium over other brands. To finance the expansion, Ricard made two more equity investments: it paid $4 million for 1,200,000 shares in 2003 and $8 million for 1,500,000 shares in 2006. Further, the term loan was renewed for another five years when it came due in 2004, and in 2007 an additional 400,000 shares were issued to employees as part of their compensation.

IPO. At the beginning of 2008, the board of directors decided to expand the distribution of the coffee throughout Canada and the United States and finance this expansion using the proceeds of an IPO. The plan was to initially raise $20 million in new capital at the IPO and then, within a year or two, raise an additional $20 million in an SEO. Ricard planned on selling 10% of its stake in HannaH at the IPO and subsequently liquidating the rest of its investment by the end of 2009. The IPO was successfully undertaken in August 2008. All told, the company sold 2,000,000 shares for $12 per share at the IPO, including 10% of Ricard's stake (no other existing shareholder sold any shares at the IPO).

SEO. A year later, in August 2009, the company did a cash offer SEO, selling an additional 4,000,000 shares for $20 per share, which included 400,000 shares from each original owner, Hannah and Natasha, and 2,000,000 of Ricard's shares. Thus, of the shares sold, 2,800,000 shares were existing shares and the rest were new shares. Some of the proceeds were used to repay the term loan that matured at the same time as the SEO, and the remaining proceeds were used to finance the continued national expansion. Ricard had been selling additional shares in the secondary market over the prior year, so that issue represented the liquidation of Ricard's final stake—after the sale, Ricard no longer owned shares in HannaH. During this time, an additional 50,000 shares were issued to employees as part of their compensation.

LBO. By 2010, the fortunes of the company had changed. Although HannaH coffee still had a strong brand name and sales continued to grow, the company was experiencing significant growing pains. Hannah herself was no longer directly involved in operations. Soon after the SEO, a new CEO, Luke Ignion, was hired to take over the day-to-day running of the company, but he proved to be a poor fit. By late 2010, the company's share price had dropped to $5 per share. Hannah was distressed to see the value of her remaining stake drop to this level, so she decided to take advantage of what she saw as a buying opportunity. Together with six other key employees, she undertook an LBO of HannaH. At the time of the LBO, the firm had 8,000,000 shares outstanding, because an additional 20,000 shares had been given to key employees. Hannah and the other key employees had already started purchasing shares, so by the time of the LBO announcement, Hannah owned 500,000 shares and the other key employees together owned an additional 100,000 shares. The group issued a tender offer to repurchase the remaining 7,400,000 shares for $7.50 per share. To finance the repurchase, the group combined an additional equity investment of $7,000,000, bank debt, and a private placement of a $30 million semi-annual, 10-year coupon bond. The debt was convertible and callable (at par) in 5 years. It had a conversion ratio of 50, a face value of $1000, and coupon rate of 5%.

Case Questions

1. Natasha is an example of what kind of an investor?

2. At each funding stage prior to the IPO (i.e., 1985, 2000, 2003, and 2006) calculate the pre-money and post-money valuation of the *equity* of the company.

3. What fraction of the IPO was a primary offering, and what fraction was a secondary offering?

4. Immediately following the IPO the shares traded at $14.50.
   a. At this price, what was the value of the whole company? Expressed as a percentage, by how much was the deal underpriced?
   b. In dollars, how much did this underpricing cost existing shareholders?
   c. Assuming that none of the owners purchased additional shares at the IPO, what fraction of the equity did Hannah own, and what was it worth immediately following the IPO?
   d. What was the company's debt-equity ratio—the ratio of the book value of debt outstanding to the market value of equity—immediately following the IPO?

5. Address the following questions related to the SEO:
   a. What fraction of the SEO was a primary offering, and what fraction was a secondary offering?
   b. Assuming that the underwriters charged a 5% fee, what were the proceeds that resulted from Hannah's sale of her stock? How much money did the company raise that would be available to fund future investment and repay the term loan?

6. Immediately following the SEO, the stock price remained at $20 per share.
   a. Once the term loan was repaid, what was the value of the whole company?
   b. What fraction of the equity did Hannah own?

7. Assume the LBO was successful.
   a. How much bank debt was required?
   b. What was the debt-equity ratio immediately following the LBO?

8. A year after the LBO, just after the second payment was made, the convertible debt traded for a price of $950.
   a. What was its yield to maturity?
   b. What was the yield to call?

9. Assume that, in the five years following the LBO, Hannah was able to turn the company around. Over the course of this period, all the bank debt was repaid and the company went public again. The price per share was now $60. Predict what the holders of the convertible debt would do. What would their investment be worth?

PART 6

Capital Structure and Payout Policy

Valuation Principle Connection. One of the fundamental questions of corporate finance is how a firm should choose its capital structure, which is the total amount of debt, equity, and other securities that a firm has outstanding. Does the choice of capital structure affect the value of the firm? Applying the Valuation Principle in perfect capital markets, we show that as long as the cash flows generated by the firm's assets are unchanged, then the value of the firm, which is the total value of its outstanding securities, does not depend on its capital structure. Thus, if capital structure has a role in determining the firm's value, it must come from market imperfections. Chapter 15 is devoted to exploring those imperfections. At the conclusion of the chapter, you will have a strong foundation for considering the tradeoffs that arise in financing decisions.

In Chapter 16, we turn to payout policy—the firm's decisions relating to how much, when, and by what method capital is returned to its equity holders. Again, we start from a setting of perfect markets and apply the Valuation Principle. We show that unless these decisions alter the future cash flows the firm generates, they do not affect the total value that the shareholders receive. The chapter also examines market imperfections such as taxes and how they affect payout policy.

Chapter 15
Capital Structure

Chapter 16
Payout Policy

15 Capital Structure

Learning Objectives

- Examine how capital structures vary across industries and companies

- Understand why investment decisions, rather than financing decisions, fundamentally determine the value and cost of capital of the firm

- Describe how leverage increases the risk of the firm's equity

- Demonstrate how debt can affect the firm's value through taxes and bankruptcy costs

- Show how the optimal mix of debt and equity trades off the costs (including financial distress costs) and benefits (including the tax advantage) of debt

- Analyze how debt can alter the incentives managers have for choosing different projects and can be used as a signal to investors

- Weigh the many costs and benefits to debt that a manager must balance when deciding how to finance the firm's investments

notation

D	market value of debt	r_f	risk-free interest rate
E	market value of levered equity	r_U	expected return (cost of capital) of unlevered equity
EPS	earnings per share	r_{wacc}	weighted average cost of capital
NPV	net present value	T_c	marginal corporate tax rate
PV	present value	U	market value of unlevered equity
r_D	expected return (cost of capital) of debt	V^L	value of the firm with leverage
r_E	expected return (cost of capital) of levered equity	V^U	value of the unlevered firm

The Honors College,
Michigan State University,
2004

"In the hotel industry, we typically finance our property acquisitions with mortgage loans representing 50% to 60% of the asset's value."

"My responsibilities as a director in the corporate finance group of Strategic Hotels & Resorts (SHR) are varied, from internal forecasting and corporate modelling to capital sourcing and balance sheet structuring," says Eric Hassberger, who graduated from the Honors College at Michigan State University in 2004. His understanding of debt financing strategies is important at SHR, a public company that owns and manages 17 upscale hotels with more than 8000 rooms throughout the United States, Mexico, and Europe. "In the hotel industry, we typically finance our property acquisitions with mortgage loans representing 50% to 60% of the asset's value."

The interest rate a lender charges SHR depends on several factors: the loan-to-value and coverage ratios of the asset being financed, the implied credit risk of the borrower, market supply and demand, and underlying interest rates. "Today interest rates in general are historically very low, but spreads being underwritten are high compared to 2005 and 2006," says Eric. "This is a result of the capital market disruption we experienced throughout 2009. As the market recovers and lenders enter or reenter the market, capital supply and competition for good lending opportunities will increase. As long as underlying bank borrowing rates remain low, interest rates should also drop."

In addition to mortgage debt on individual hotel properties, SHR has used unsecured corporate debt, convertible bonds (which convert to equity at a predetermined price upon maturity), and preferred equity. The company monitors its debt ratios carefully. During the boom years from late 2005 through early 2007, hotel industry leverage rose as property values increased and lending standards decreased. With the 2008–2009 recession, hotel companies began decreasing their debt load to reduce the risk of default. "At SHR we look not only at our overall debt ratios but also at our fixed versus floating rate debt exposure," Eric explains. "We are working to lower our total debt-to-equity ratio by paying down corporate debt and deleveraging some assets. When we issue new debt or extend maturities, we stagger maturities to avoid overloading maturities in any one year, which could make it more difficult to refinance if the market is poor."

When a firm needs to raise new funds to undertake its investments, it must decide which type of financing security it will issue to investors. What considerations should guide this decision, and how does this decision affect the value of the firm?

Consider the case of RealNetworks from Chapter 13 issuing new equity in a seasoned equity offering to fund its expansion, or Hertz from Chapter 14 substantially increasing its leverage through its leveraged buyout. More recently, in the summer of 2007, Home Depot dramatically changed its capital structure by reducing its equity by $22 billion and increasing its debt by $12 billion. What led managers at RealNetworks to rely on equity for its expansion and Hertz and Home Depot to choose to increase their debt instead? How might such capital structure decisions affect the value of these firms?

In this chapter, we first explore these questions in a setting of *perfect capital markets*, in which all securities are fairly priced, there are no taxes or transaction costs, and the total cash flows of the firm's projects are not affected by how the firm finances them. Although in reality capital markets are not perfect, this setting provides an important benchmark.

We devote the remainder of the chapter to exploring how violations of our perfect capital markets assumptions affect our conclusions. We further explore how the tax advantage of debt that we briefly discussed in

Chapter 12 makes debt a potentially attractive financing source. We then discuss the costs of financial distress and bankruptcy that firms with debt face. This discussion leads us to the insight that managers choose debt by balancing the tax advantages against the distress costs of debt. After discussing other influences on capital structure, including agency problems and differences in information between managers and investors, we conclude with some recommendations for a financial manager making capital structure decisions.

15.1   Capital Structure Choices

Recall that the relative proportions of debt, equity, and other securities that a firm has outstanding constitute its *capital structure*. When they raise funds from outside investors, corporations must choose which type of security to issue and what type of capital structure to have. The most common choices are financing through equity alone and financing through a combination of debt and equity. How do firms arrive at their capital structures, and what factors should a financial manager consider when choosing among financing alternatives?

First and foremost, various financing choices will promise different future amounts to each security holder in exchange for the cash that is raised today. But beyond that, the firm may also need to consider whether the securities it issues will receive a fair price in the market, have tax consequences, entail transactions costs, or even change its future investment opportunities. A firm's capital structure is also affected by decisions on whether to accumulate cash, pay off debt or pay dividends, or conduct share repurchases. Before exploring the theory underpinning this analysis, we place these financing decisions in the context of actual firm practices.

Capital Structure Choices Across Industries

debt-to-value ratio
The fraction of a firm's total value that corresponds to debt.

Figure 15.1 shows the average debt-to-value ratios across industries for Canadian stocks. A firm's **debt-to-value ratio**, $D/(E + D)$, is the fraction of the firm's total value that corresponds to debt. Notice that the debt levels financial managers choose differ across industries. For example, telecom equipment companies such as Research In Motion are far less levered (have less debt relative to their equity) than are banks such as CIBC.

Capital Structure Choices Within Industries

The differences in capital structures across industries are striking. However, even within industries, two competing firms may make different choices about their debt-to-value ratios. For example, Air Canada and WestJet, both members of the air transport industry, have very different capital structures, as depicted in panels (a) and (b) of Figure 15.2. Air Canada has more debt than equity, as shown in panel (a), and WestJet has much less debt, as shown in panel (b). Even though Air Canada and WestJet are direct competitors, they have very different assets and histories.

Air Canada (formerly Trans-Canada Air Lines) was legislated into existence in 1936 as a subsidiary of the government-owned Canadian National Railway. In 1965, Trans-Canada Air Lines changed its name to Air Canada. Through government regulation, Air Canada enjoyed a favourable position in the industry in terms of landing rights and international routes. In the early 1980s, Air Canada borrowed heavily to update its fleet of aircraft, but in the late 1980s, the government deregulated the airline industry, thus allowing for increased competition. Air Canada was privatized through an initial public offering in 1988. In 1997, Air Canada became a founding member in the Star Alliance, a group of international airlines that cooperated in routes, ticketing, and other services. In 1999, Air Canada was the target of a takeover attempt by Onex Corporation and American

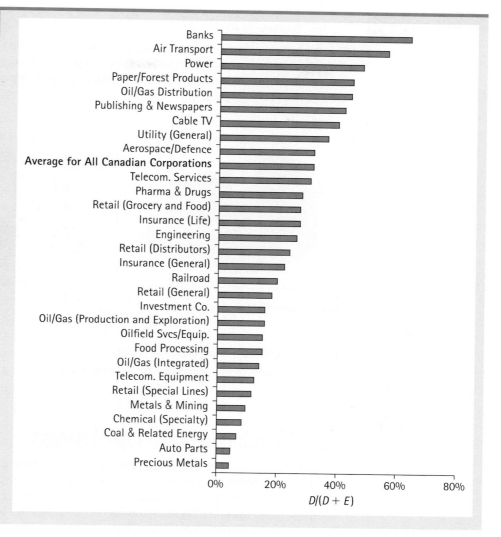

FIGURE 15.1

Debt to Value Ratios, $D/(D + E)$, for the 30 Largest Canadian Industries as of January 2011

Debt levels are determined by book values, and equity by market values. The average debt financing for all Canadian publicly traded companies was about 32%

Sources: Reuters/Forester Reprints.

Airlines that would have merged Air Canada and Canadian Airlines International. In response to the hostile takeover, Air Canada borrowed heavily and took over Canadian Airlines itself. Air Canada's high debt level and the downturn in the industry following the September 11, 2001, terrorist attacks in New York City were two factors that led Air Canada to declare bankruptcy in 2003. After its restructuring in 2004, Air Canada was still left with significant debt. The financial and economic crisis of 2008 pushed Air Canada back into negative net income, and its debt problems resurfaced.

WestJet was founded in 1996 by Clive Beddoe and his partners and began operations as a discount airline. Management grew the airline slowly and carefully, used one type of aircraft, the Boeing 737, and kept a much more conservative route structure and financial structure. Only in recent years has WestJet increased its international flights and joined alliances with other airlines.

In this chapter, we will learn why these differences in assets and business plans would naturally lead to the different capital structures we observe today. In the next section, we start by developing the critical theoretical foundation of any capital structure analysis. Then we move on to important real-world factors that managers must trade off when considering capital structure decisions.

FIGURE 15.2

Capital Structures of Air Canada and WestJet Airlines

The pie charts in panels (a) and (b) show the split between debt and equity in two competing firms, Air Canada and WestJet Airlines. Both are part of the air transport industry, which has an average debt-to-value ratio of 56%. Even within an industry, two companies can choose a different mix of debt and equity.

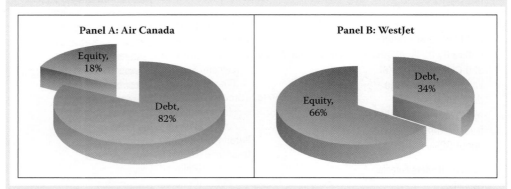

Sources: Capital IQ, Bloomberg.

Concept Check

1. What constitutes a firm's capital structure?

2. What are some factors a manager must consider when making a financing decision?

15.2 Capital Structure in Perfect Capital Markets

When a firm issues debt, equity, or other securities to fund a new investment, its decision has many potential consequences. By far the most important question for a financial manager is whether different choices will affect the value of the firm and thus the amount of capital it can raise. We begin by considering this question in a simple environment— a perfect capital market. A **perfect capital market** has these characteristics:

perfect capital market
A set of conditions in which investors and firms can trade the same set of securities at competitive market prices; in such a market, there are no tax consequences or transactions costs, and the firm's financing decisions do not change the cash flows that its investments generate.

1. *Securities are fairly priced.* Investors and firms can trade the same set of securities at competitive market prices equal to the present value of their future cash flows.

2. *No tax consequences or transactions costs.* There are no tax consequences, transaction costs, or other issuance costs associated with financing decisions or security trading.

3. *Investment cash flows are independent of financing choices.* A firm's financing decisions do not change the cash flows its investments generate, nor do those decisions reveal new information about those cash flows.

The assumption of perfect capital markets may seem narrow and unrealistic. We will see, however, that by starting with them we will gain important insight into the true benefits and costs of leverage.

Application: Financing a New Business

Let's begin with an example of a possible financing decision in a perfect capital market. Imagine you have one year left in university and you want to earn some extra money before graduation. You have been offered the opportunity to run the coffee shop in the lobby of a nearby office building. The owner of the building is willing to grant you this right on a one-year basis prior to a major remodelling of the building.

Your research indicates that you will need to make an upfront investment of $24,000 to start the business. After covering your operating costs, including paying yourself a nice wage, you expect to generate a cash flow of $34,500 at the end of the year. The current risk-free interest rate is 5%. You believe, however, that your profits will be somewhat risky and sensitive to the overall market (which will affect the level of activity in the building and demand for your business), so a 10% risk premium is appropriate, for a total discount rate of 15% (5% + 10%). You therefore calculate the NPV of this investment in the coffee shop as follows:

$$NPV = -\$24,000 + \frac{\$34,500}{1.15} = -\$24,000 + \$30,000$$

$$= \$6000$$

Thus, the investment has a positive NPV.

Even though the investment looks attractive, you still need to raise the money for the upfront investment. How should you raise the funds, and what is the amount you will be able to raise?

Equity Financing. First, you consider raising money solely by selling equity in the business to your friends and family. Given the cash flow estimates, how much would they be willing to pay for those shares? Recall that the value of a security equals the present value of its future cash flows. In this case, equity holders in your firm will expect to receive the payoff of $34,500 at the end of the year, with the same risk as the cash flows generated by the coffee shop. Therefore, your firm's equity cost of capital will be 15% and the value of its equity today will be as follows:

$$PV(\text{equity cash flows}) = \frac{\$34,500}{1.15} = \$30,000$$

unlevered equity Equity in a firm with no debt.

Recall that the absence of debt means the absence of financial leverage. Equity in a firm with no debt is therefore called **unlevered equity**. Because the present value of the equity cash flows is $30,000, you can raise $30,000 by selling all the unlevered equity in your firm. Doing so allows you to keep the NPV of $6000 as profit after paying the investment cost of $24,000. In other words, the project's NPV represents the value to the initial owner of the firm (in this case, you, the entrepreneur) that the project creates.

levered equity Equity in a firm with outstanding debt.

Levered Financing. As an alternative, you also consider borrowing some of the money you will need to invest. Suppose the business's cash flow is certain to be at least $16,000. Then you can borrow $15,000 at the current risk-free interest rate of 5%. You will be able to pay the debt of $15,000 × 1.05 = $15,750 at the end of the year without any risk of defaulting.

How much can you raise selling equity in your business now? Equity in a firm that also has outstanding debt is called **levered equity**. After the debt is repaid, equity holders can expect to receive $34,500 − 15,750 = $18,750. What discount rate should we use to value levered equity? What expected return will investors demand?

It's tempting to use the same 15% equity cost of capital as before. In that case, by selling levered equity, you could raise $18,750/1.15 = $16,304. If this result were correct, then using leverage would allow you to raise a total amount, including the debt, of $15,000 + 16,304 = $31,304, or $1304 more than in the case without leverage.

Thus, it would seem that simply financing a project with leverage can make it more valuable. *But if this sounds too good to be true, it is.* Our analysis assumed that your firm's equity cost of capital remained unchanged at 15% after adding leverage. But as we will see shortly, that will not be the case—leverage will increase the risk of the firm's equity and raise its equity cost of capital. To see why, and to understand what will actually happen, we turn to the hallmark work of researchers Franco Modigliani and Merton Miller.

Leverage and Firm Value

In an important paper, researchers Modigliani and Miller (or simply "M&M") considered whether leverage would increase the total value of the firm. Their answer to this question surprised researchers and practitioners at the time.[1] M&M argued that with perfect capital markets, the total value of a firm should *not* depend on its capital structure. Their reasoning: your firm's total cash flows—those paid to both debt and equity holders—still equal the cash flows of the coffee shop, with the same expected value of $34,500 and the same total risk as before, as shown in Figure 15.3.

FIGURE 15.3

Unlevered Versus Levered Cash Flows with Perfect Capital Markets

When the firm has no debt, as shown in panel (a) the cash flows paid to equity holders correspond to the free cash flows the firm's assets generate. When the firm has the debt shown in panel (b) these cash flows are divided between debt and equity holders. However, with perfect capital markets, the total amount paid to all investors still corresponds to the free cash flows the firm's assets generate. Therefore, the value of the unlevered firm, V^U, must equal the total value of the levered firm, V^L, which is the combined value of its debt D and levered equity E.

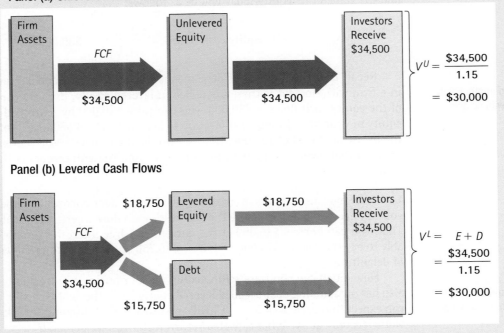

Panel (a) Unlevered Cash Flows

Panel (b) Levered Cash Flows

---

[1]Franco Modigliani and Merton Miller, "The Cost of Capital, Corporation Finance and the Theory of Investment," *American Economic Review* 48 (3) (1958): 261–297.

Because the total cash flows of the debt and equity equal the cash flows of the unlevered firm, the Valuation Principle tells us that their market values must be the same. Specifically, we calculated earlier that the value of the unlevered firm, V^U, is:

$$V^U = \$34,500/1.15 = \$30,000$$

Thus, the total value of the levered firm, V^L, which is the combined value of its debt, D, and levered equity, E, must be the same:

$$V^L = D + E = \$30,000$$

Therefore, if the initial market value of the debt is $D = \$15,000$ (the amount borrowed), the initial market value of the levered equity must be $E = \$30,000 - \$15,000 = \$15,000$.

Thus, M&M argued that leverage merely changes the allocation of cash flows between debt and equity without altering the total cash flows of the firm in a perfect capital market. As a result, they concluded the following:

M&M Proposition I: In a perfect capital market, the total value of a firm is equal to the market value of the free cash flows generated by its assets and is not affected by its choice of capital structure.

We can write this result in an equation as follows:

$$V^L = E + D = V^U \tag{15.1}$$

This equation states that the total value of the firm is the same with or without leverage.

Note in our example that because the cash flows of levered equity are smaller than those of unlevered equity, levered equity will sell for a lower price than unlevered equity ($15,000 versus $30,000). However, the fact that the equity is less valuable with leverage does not mean that you are worse off. You will still raise a total of $30,000 by issuing both debt and levered equity, just as you did with unlevered equity alone, and still keep as profit the $6000 difference between the $30,000 you raise and your $24,000 cost. As a consequence, you will be indifferent about which of these two options to choose for the firm's capital structure.

The Effect of Leverage on Risk and Return

Modigliani and Miller's conclusion went against the common view that even with perfect capital markets, leverage would affect a firm's value. In particular, it was thought that the value of the levered equity should exceed $15,000, because the present value of its expected cash flow at a 15% discount rate is $18,750/1.15 = $16,304, as we calculated earlier. The reason this is *not* correct is that leverage increases the risk of the equity of a firm. Therefore, it is inappropriate to discount the cash flows of levered equity at the same discount rate of 15% that we used for unlevered equity.

Let's take a closer look at the effect of leverage on the firm's equity cost of capital. If equity holders are willing to pay only $15,000 for the levered equity, then given its expected payoff of $18,750, their expected return is as follows:

Expected return of levered equity = $18,750/$15,000 − 1 = 25%

Although this return may seem like a good deal for investors, remember that the coffee shop cash flows are uncertain. Table 15.1 shows the different levels of demand and free cash flows that the coffee shop may generate, and compares the security payoffs

TABLE 15.1	Coffee Shop		Security Cash Flows			Security Returns		
	Demand	Free Cash Flows	Unlevered Equity	Debt	Levered Equity	Unlevered Equity	Debt	Levered Equity
Returns to Equity in Different Scenarios with and without Leverage	Weak	$27,000	$27,000	$15,750	$11,250	−10%	5%	−25%
	Expected	$34,500	$34,500	$15,750	$18,750	15%	5%	25%
	Strong	$42,000	$42,000	$15,750	$26,250	40%	5%	75%

and returns with unlevered equity to the case in which you borrow $15,000 and raise an additional $15,000 using levered equity. Note that the returns are very different with and without leverage. With no debt, the returns of unlevered equity range from −10% to 40%, with an expected return of 15%. With leverage, the debt holders receive a risk-free return of 5%, whereas the returns of levered equity are much more volatile, ranging from −25% to 75%. To compensate for this higher risk, levered equity holders receive a higher expected return of 25%.

We further illustrate the effect of leverage on returns in Figure 15.4. By adding leverage, the returns of the unlevered firm are effectively "split" between low-risk debt and much higher-risk levered equity. Note that the returns of levered equity fall twice as fast as those of unlevered equity if the coffee shops cash flows decline. This doubling of the risk justifies a doubling of the risk premium, which is 15% − 5% = 10% for unlevered equity and 25% − 5% = 20% for levered equity. As this example shows, *leverage increases the risk of equity even when there is no risk that the firm will default.*

EXAMPLE 15.1

The Risk and Return of Levered Equity

Problem

Suppose you borrow only $6000 when financing your coffee shop. According to M&M, what should the value of the equity be? What is the expected return?

Solution

▶ **Plan**

The value of the firm's total cash flows does not change: it is still $30,000. Thus, if you borrow $6000, your firm's equity will be worth $24,000. To determine the equity's expected return, we will compute the cash flows to equity under the two scenarios. The cash flows to equity are the cash flows of the firm net of the cash flows to debt (repayment of principal plus interest).

▶ **Execute**

The firm will owe debt holders $6000 × 1.05 = $6300 in one year. Thus, the expected payoff to equity holders is $34,500 − $6300 = $28,200, for a return of $28,200/$24,000 − 1 = 17.5%.

▶ **Evaluate**

While the total value of the firm is unchanged, the firm's equity in this case is more risky than it would be without debt, but less risky than if the firm borrowed $15,000. To illustrate, note that if demand is weak, the equity holders will receive $27,000 − $6300 = $20,700, for a return of $20,700/$24,000 − 1 = −13.75%. Compare this return to −10% without leverage and −25% if the firm borrowed $15,000. As a result, the expected return of the levered equity is higher in this case than for unlevered equity (17.5% versus 15%), but not as high as in the previous example (17.5% versus 25%).

FIGURE 15.4 Unlevered Versus Levered Returns with Perfect Capital Markets

Leverage splits the firm's return between low-risk debt and high-risk levered equity compared with the equity of an unlevered firm. In this example, the returns of levered equity are twice as sensitive to the firm's cash flows as the returns of unlevered equity are. This doubling of risk implies a doubling of the risk premium from 10% to 20%.

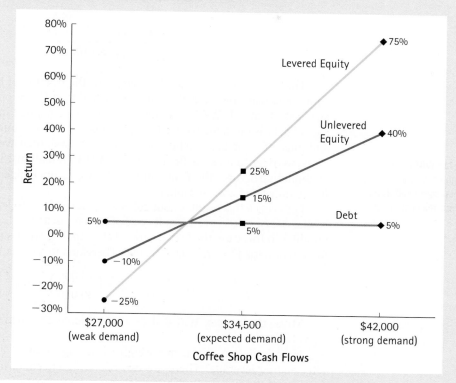

Homemade Leverage

homemade leverage
Leverage that investors use in their own portfolios to adjust the leverage choice a firm has made.

M&M showed that the firm's value is not affected by its choice of capital structure. But suppose investors would prefer an alternative capital structure to the one the firm has chosen. M&M demonstrated that in this case, investors can borrow or lend on their own and achieve the same result. For example, an investor who would like more leverage than the firm has chosen can borrow and thus add leverage to his or her own portfolio. Adding leverage in this way will lower the out-of-pocket cost of the security, but increase the risk of the portfolio. When investors use leverage in their own portfolios to adjust the leverage choice the firm has made, we say that they are using **homemade leverage**. As long as investors can borrow or lend at the same interest rate as the firm, which is true in perfect capital markets, homemade leverage is a perfect substitute for the firm's use of leverage. Thus, because different choices of capital structure offer no benefit to investors in perfect capital markets, those choices do not affect the value of the firm.

Leverage and the Cost of Capital

We can use the insight of M&M to understand the effect of leverage on the firm's cost of capital. Recall from Figure 15.3 and Equation 15.1 that if we look at a portfolio of the equity and debt of a levered firm together, that portfolio has the same value and cash flows as the unlevered firm. Therefore, the expected return of the portfolio should equal the expected return of the unlevered firm. Recall from Chapter 11 that the expected return of the portfolio of equity and debt is simply the weighted average of the expected returns of each security. Thus, with r_E representing the expected return of the levered equity, r_D the expected return of the debt, and r_U the expected return of the unlevered equity, we have the following:

Weighted Average Cost of Capital (Pre-Tax)

$$\underbrace{r_E \frac{E}{E + D} + r_D \frac{D}{E + D}}_{\text{pre-tax WACC}} = r_U \qquad (15.2)$$

pre-tax WACC The weighted average cost of capital computed using the pre-tax cost of debt.

The amounts $\frac{E}{E + D}$ and $\frac{D}{E + D}$ represent the fraction of the firm's value financed by equity and debt, respectively. Thus, the left side of Equation 15.2 is the weighted average cost of capital (WACC) of the firm, which we defined in Chapter 12. Note that the cost of debt is not adjusted for taxes, because we are assuming "perfect capital markets" and thus ignoring taxes. When we compute the weighted average cost of capital without taxes, we refer to it as the firm's **pre-tax WACC**. Equation 15.2 states that for any choice of capital structure, the firm's pre-tax WACC is unchanged and remains equal to the firm's unlevered cost of capital.

Let's check this result for our coffee shop example. With leverage, the firm's debt cost of capital was $r_D = 5\%$, and its equity cost of capital rose to $r_E = 25\%$. What about the portfolio weights? In this case, the firm borrowed $D = 15{,}000$, and issued equity worth $E = 15{,}000$, for a total value $V^L = E + D = 30{,}000$. Therefore, its pre-tax WACC is as follows:

$$r_E \frac{E}{E + D} + r_D \frac{D}{E + D} = 25\% \left(\frac{15{,}000}{30{,}000} \right) + 5\% \left(\frac{15{,}000}{30{,}000} \right) = 15\%$$

Thus, the pre-tax WACC does indeed equal the firm's unlevered cost of capital, $r_U = 15\%$.

How is it that the firm's weighted average cost of capital stays the same even after adding leverage? There are two offsetting effects of leverage: we finance a larger fraction of the firm with debt, which has a lower cost of capital, but at the same time adding leverage raises the firm's equity cost of capital. Because the firm's total risk has not changed (it has just been split between these two securities), these two effects should exactly cancel out and leave the firm's WACC unchanged. In fact, we can use Equation 15.2 to determine the precise impact of leverage on the firm's equity cost of capital. Solving the equation for r_E, we have

M&M Proposition II: The Cost of Capital of Levered Equity

$$r_E = r_U + \frac{D}{E}(r_U - r_D) \qquad (15.3)$$

Or, in words:

M&M Proposition II: The cost of capital of levered equity is equal to the cost of capital of unlevered equity plus a premium that is proportional to the debt-equity ratio (measured using market values).

Let's check M&M Proposition II for the coffee shop example. In this case:

$$r_E = r_U + \frac{D}{E}(r_U - r_D) = 15\% + \frac{15{,}000}{15{,}000}(15\% - 5\%) = 25\%$$

This result matches the expected return for levered equity we calculated in Table 15.1.

FIGURE 15.5

WACC and Leverage with Perfect Capital Markets

Panel (a) represents the data in panel (b) for the coffee shop example. As the fraction of the firm financed with debt increases, both the equity and the debt become riskier, and their cost of capital rises. Yet, because more weight is put on the lower-cost debt, the weighted average cost of capital remains constant.

Panel (a) Equity, Debt, and WACC for Different Amounts of Leverage

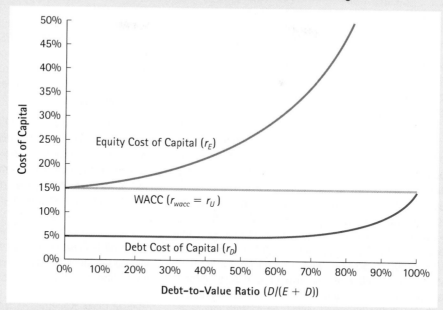

Panel (b) WACC Data for Alternative Capital Structures

E	D	r_E	r_D	$r_E \dfrac{E}{E+D} + r_D \dfrac{D}{E+D}$	$= r_{wacc}$
30,000	0	15.0%	5.0%	15.0% × 1.0 + 5.0% × 0.0	= 15%
24,000	6000	17.5%	5.0%	17.5% × 0.8 + 5.0% × 0.2	= 15%
15,000	15,000	25.0%	5.0%	25.0% × 0.5 + 5.0% × 0.5	= 15%
3000	27,000	75.0%	8.3%	75.0% × 0.1 + 8.3% × 0.9	= 15%

Figure 15.5 illustrates the effect of increasing the amount of leverage in a firm's capital structure on its equity cost of capital, its debt cost of capital, and its WACC. In the figure, the firm's leverage is measured in terms of its debt-to-value ratio, $D/(E + D)$. With no debt, the WACC is equal to the unlevered equity cost of capital. As the firm borrows at the low cost of capital for debt, its equity cost of capital rises, according to Equation 15.3. The net effect is that the firm's WACC is unchanged. Of course, as the amount of debt increases, the debt becomes riskier, because there is a chance the firm will default; as a result, the debt cost of capital also rises. With close to 100% debt, the debt would be almost as risky as the assets themselves (similar to unlevered equity). But even though the debt and equity costs of capital both rise when leverage is high, because more of the firm is financed with debt (which has lower cost), the WACC remains constant.

M&M and the Real World

Our conclusions so far may seem striking at first: in perfect capital markets, leverage does not affect either the cost of capital or firm value, and so the firm's choice of capital structure would be irrelevant! However, capital markets are not perfect in the real world. What then are we to make of M&M's results?

Common Mistake — Capital Structure Fallacies

Here, we take a critical look at two incorrect arguments that are sometimes cited in favour of leverage.

Leverage and Earnings per Share

Fallacy 1: Leverage can increase a firm's expected earnings per share; by doing so, leverage should also increase the firm's stock price.

Consider the coffee shop example. In the all-equity case, if you issued 1000 shares, they would each be worth $30 and the expected earnings per share (*EPS*) would be $34,500/1000 = $34.50. *EPS* would vary from $27 per share to $42 per share in the case of weak or strong demand. In the case with debt, as shown in Table 15.1, you only need to raise $15,000 in equity and so could issue only 500 shares, each worth $30. In this case, your expected *EPS* will be $18,750/500 = $37.50, with a range from $22.50 to $52.50. Thus, although the expected *EPS* is greater with leverage, the variation in *EPS* is also much greater, as shown in the blue and yellow bars. With leverage, *EPS* falls to $22.50 when cash flows are low, which

is much further than *EPS* would have dropped without leverage ($27). Although *EPS* increases on average, this increase is necessary to compensate shareholders for the additional risk they are taking. As a result, the entrepreneur's share price does not increase as a result of issuing debt.

Equity Issuances and Dilution

Fallacy 2: Issuing equity will *dilute* existing shareholders' ownership, so debt financing should be used instead. *Dilution* means that if the firm issues new shares, the cash flows generated by the firm must be divided among a larger number of shares, thereby reducing the value of each individual share.

This line of reasoning ignores the fact that the cash raised by issuing new shares will increase the firm's assets. Consider Google's September 2005 seasoned equity offering of 14,159,265 Class A shares at $295 apiece. Google priced the shares to match the market price of Class A shares on NASDAQ at the time of the offer. The amount raised was then $4,176,983,175, so the total value of Google increased to $60,560,157,355, which, when divided by the new total number of shares (205,288,669), still results in a price of $295 per share.

In general, as long as the firm sells the new shares of equity *at a fair price*, there will be no gain or loss to shareholders associated with the equity issue itself. The money taken in by the firm as a result of the share issue exactly offsets the dilution of the shares. *Any gain or loss associated with the transaction will result from the NPV of the investments the firm makes with the funds raised.*

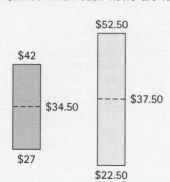

EXAMPLE 15.2

Computing the Equity Cost of Capital

Problem

Suppose you borrow only $6000 when financing your coffee shop. According to M&M Proposition II, what will your firm's equity cost of capital be?

Solution

▶ **Plan**

Because your firm's assets have a market value of $30,000, according to M&M Proposition I, the equity will have a market value of $24,000 = $30,000 − $6000. We can use Equation 15.3 to compute the cost of equity. We know the unlevered cost of equity is $r_U = 15\%$. We also know that r_D is 5%.

▶ **Execute**

$$r_E = 15\% + \frac{6000}{24{,}000}(15\% - 5\%) = 17.5\%$$

▶ **Evaluate**

This result matches the expected return calculated in Example 15.1, where we also assumed debt of $6000. The equity cost of capital should be the expected return of the equity holders.

As an analogy, consider Galileo's law of falling bodies. Galileo overturned the conventional wisdom by showing that without friction, free-falling bodies will fall at the same rate, independent of their mass. If you test this law, you will likely find that it does not hold exactly. The reason, of course, is that unless we are in a vacuum, air friction tends to slow some objects more than others.

M&M's results are similar. In practice, we will find that capital structure can have an effect on a firm's value. Galileo's law of falling bodies reveals that we must look to air friction, rather than any underlying property of gravity, to explain differences in the speeds of falling objects. M&M's propositions reveal that any effects of capital structure must similarly be due to frictions that exist in capital markets. We explore the important sources of these frictions, and their consequences, in the remainder of this chapter.

Nobel Prize   Franco Modigliani and Merton Miller

Franco Modigliani and Merton Miller, the authors of the Modigliani & Miller propositions, have each won the Nobel Prize in Economics for their work in financial economics, including their capital structure propositions. Modigliani won the Nobel Prize in 1985 for his work on personal savings and for his capital structure theorems with Miller. Miller earned his prize in 1990 for his analysis of portfolio theory and capital structure.

In an interview, Miller once described the M&M propositions this way:

> People often ask, "Can you summarize your theory quickly?" Well, I say, you understand the M&M theorem if you know why this is a joke: The pizza delivery man comes to Yogi Berra after the game and says, "Yogi, how do you want this pizza cut, into quarters or eighths?" And Yogi says, "Cut it in eight pieces. I'm feeling hungry tonight."
>
> Everyone recognizes that's a joke because obviously the number and shape of the pieces

don't affect the size of the pizza. And similarly, the stocks, bonds, warrants, etc., issued don't affect the aggregate value of the firm. They just slice up the underlying earnings in different ways.*

Modigliani and Miller each won the Nobel Prize in large part for their observation that the value of a firm should be unaffected by its capital structure in perfect capital markets. Whereas the intuition underlying the M&M propositions may be as simple as slicing pizza, their implications for corporate finance are far-reaching. The propositions imply that the true role of a firm's financial policy is to deal with (and potentially exploit) financial market imperfections such as taxes and transaction costs. M&M's work began a long line of research into these market imperfections, which we will look at in the rest of the chapter.

*Source: Peter J. Tanous, *Investment Gurus* (New York: Institute of Finance, 1997)

Concept Check

3. How does leverage affect the risk and cost of equity for the firm?

4. In a perfect capital market, can you alter the firm's value or WACC by relying more on debt capital?

15.3 Debt and Taxes

So far, we have used the perfect capital markets setting to focus on the fundamental point that the firm's choice of projects and investments is the primary determinant of its value and risk, and hence its overall cost of capital. But in the real world, markets are imperfect, and these imperfections can create a role for the firm's capital structure. In this section, we focus on one important market friction—corporate taxes—and show how the firm's choice of capital structure can affect the taxes that it must pay and therefore its value to investors.

The Interest Tax Deduction and Firm Value

As we discussed in Chapter 12, corporations can deduct interest expenses from their taxable income. The deduction reduces the taxes they pay and thereby increases the amount available to pay investors. In doing so, the interest tax deduction increases the value of the corporation.

To illustrate, let's consider the impact of interest expenses on the taxes paid by Loblaw Companies Limited, a grocery store chain. In 2010, Loblaw had earnings before interest and taxes of $1.269 billion, and interest expenses of $273 million. Given a corporate tax rate of 30%, we can compare Loblaw's actual net income with what it would have been without debt, as shown in Table 15.2.

As we can see from Table 15.2, Loblaw's net income in 2010 was lower with leverage than it would have been without leverage. Thus, Loblaw's debt obligations reduced the value of its equity. But more importantly, the *total* amount available to *all* investors was higher with leverage, as can be seen in the last row of the table. With leverage, Loblaw was able to pay out $970.2 million in total to its investors, versus only $888.3 million without leverage, representing an increase of $81.9 million.

It might seem odd that a firm can be better off with leverage even though its earnings are lower. But recall from Section 15.1 that the value of a firm is the total amount it can raise from all investors, not just equity holders who receive the earnings. Thus, if the firm can pay out more in total with leverage, it will be able to raise more total capital initially.

Where does the additional $81.9 million come from? Looking at Table 15.2, we can see that this gain is equal to the reduction in taxes with leverage: $380.7 million − $298.8 million = $81.9 million. Because Loblaw does not owe taxes on the $273 million of pre-tax earnings it used to make interest payments, this $273 million is *shielded* from the corporate tax, providing the tax savings of 30% × $273 million = $81.9 million.

TABLE 15.2		With Leverage (Actual)	Without Leverage
Loblaw's Income with and without Leverage and the Effect on Payouts Available to Investors, 2010 ($ millions)	EBIT	$1269.00	$1269.00
	Interest expense	$273.00	$0.00
	Income before tax	$996.00	$1269.00
	Taxes 30%	$298.80	$380.70
	Net income	$697.20	$888.30
	Interest paid to debtholders	$273.00	$0.00
	Income available to equity holders	$697.20	$888.30
	Total available to all investors	$970.20	$888.30

interest tax shield The reduction in taxes paid due to the tax deductibility of interest payments.

In general, the gain to investors from the tax deductibility of interest payments is referred to as the **interest tax shield**. The interest tax shield is the additional amount a firm can pay to investors by saving the taxes it would have paid if it did not have leverage. We can calculate the amount of the interest tax shield each year as follows:

$$\text{Interest Tax Shield} = \text{Corporate Tax Rate} \times \text{Interest Payments} \qquad (15.4)$$

EXAMPLE 15.3

Computing the Interest Tax Shield

Problem

Shown below is the income statement for Delta Farm Buildings (DFB). Given its marginal corporate tax rate of 35%, what is the amount of the interest tax shield for DFB in years 2011 through 2014?

1	DFB Income Statement ($ million)	2011	2012	2013	2014
2	Total sales	$3369	$3706	$4077	$4432
3	Cost of sales	−2359	−2584	−2867	−3116
4	Selling, general, and administrative expense	−226	−248	−276	−299
5	Depreciation	−22	−25	−27	−29
6	Operating income	762	849	907	988
7	Other income	7	8	10	12
9	*EBIT*	769	857	917	1000
10	Interest expense	−50	−80	−100	−100
11	Income before tax	719	777	817	900
12	Taxes (35%)	−252	−272	−286	−315
13	Net income	$467	$505	$531	$585

Solution

▶ **Plan**

From Equation 15.4, the interest tax shield is the tax rate of 35% multiplied by the interest payments in each year.

▶ **Execute**

1	($ million)	2011	2012	2013	2014
2	Interest expense	50	80	100	100
3	Interest tax shield (35% × interest expense)	17.5	28	35	35

▶ **Evaluate**

By using debt, DFB is able to reduce its taxable income and therefore decrease its total tax payments by $115.5 million over the four-year period. Thus, the total amount of cash flows available to all investors (debt holders and equity holders) is $115.5 million higher over the four-year period.

Value of the Interest Tax Shield

When a firm uses debt, the interest tax shield provides a corporate tax benefit each year. To determine the benefit of leverage for the value of the firm, we must compute the present value of the stream of future interest tax shields the firm will receive.

As we saw in the previous example, each year a firm makes interest payments, the cash flows it pays to investors will be higher than they would be without leverage by the amount of the interest tax shield:

$$\begin{pmatrix} \text{Cash Flows to Investors} \\ \text{with Leverage} \end{pmatrix} = \begin{pmatrix} \text{Cash Flows to Investors} \\ \text{without Leverage} \end{pmatrix} + (\text{Interest Tax Shield})$$

Figure 15.6 illustrates this relationship. Notice how each dollar of pre-tax cash flows is divided. The firm uses some fraction to pay taxes, and it pays the rest to investors. By increasing the amount paid to debt holders through interest payments, the amount of the pre-tax cash flows that must be paid as taxes decreases. The gain in total cash flows to investors is the interest tax shield.[2]

Because the cash flows of the levered firm are equal to the sum of the cash flows from the unlevered firm plus the interest tax shield, according to the Valuation Principle the same must be true for the present values of these cash flows. Thus, letting V^L and V^U represent the value of the firm with and without leverage, respectively, we have the following change to M&M Proposition I in the presence of taxes:

$$V^L = V^U + PV(\text{Interest Tax Shield}) \tag{15.5}$$

The total value of the levered firm exceeds the value of the firm without leverage due to the present value of the tax savings from debt.

FIGURE 15.6   The Cash Flows of the Unlevered and Levered Firm

By increasing the cash flows paid to debt holders through interest payments, a firm reduces the amount paid in taxes. The increase in total cash flows paid to investors is the interest tax shield. (The figure assumes a 40% marginal corporate tax rate.)

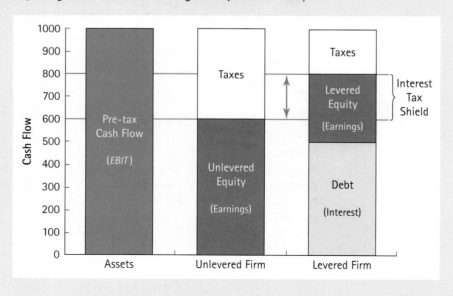

---

[2]If investors are taxed on interest income at a higher rate than they are on capital gains, this personal tax *disadvantage* of debt will partly offset the corporate tax advantage of debt.

Clearly, there is an important tax advantage to the use of debt financing. But how large is this tax benefit? To compute the increase in the firm's total value associated with the interest tax shield, we need to forecast how a firm's debt—and therefore its interest payments—will vary over time. Given a forecast of future interest payments, we can determine the interest tax shield and compute its present value by discounting it at a rate that corresponds to its risk.

EXAMPLE 15.4

Valuing the Interest Tax Shield

Problem

Suppose DFB from Example 15.3 borrows $2 billion by issuing 10-year bonds. DFB's cost of debt is 6%, so it will need to pay $120 million in interest each year for the next 10 years, and then repay the principal of $2 billion in year 10. DFB's marginal tax rate will remain 35% throughout this period. By how much does the interest tax shield increase the value of DFB?

Solution

▶ **Plan**

In this case, the interest tax shield lasts for 10 years, so we can value it as a 10-year annuity. Because the tax savings are as risky as the debt that creates them, we can discount them at DFB's cost of debt: 6%.

▶ **Execute**

The interest tax shield each year is 35% × $120 million = $42 million. Valued as a 10-year annuity at 6%, the interest tax shield is valued as follows:

$$PV(\text{Interest Tax Shield}) = \$42 \text{ milllion} \times \frac{1}{6\%}\left(1 - \frac{1}{1.06^{10}}\right)$$
$$= \$309 \text{ milllion}$$

Because only interest is tax deductible, the final repayment of principal in year 10 is not deductible, so it does not contribute to the interest tax shield.

▶ **Evaluate**

We know that in perfect capital markets, financing transactions have an *NPV* of zero—the interest and principal repayment have a present value of exactly the amount of the bonds: $2 billion. However, the interest tax deductibility makes this a positive-*NPV* transaction for the firm. Because the government effectively subsidizes the payment of interest, issuing these bonds has an *NPV* of $309 million.

The Interest Tax Shield with Permanent Debt

Many factors can affect the future tax savings from interest. Typically, the level of future interest payments varies due to the following:

▶ Changes the firm makes in the amount of debt outstanding

▶ Changes in the interest rate on that debt

▶ Changes in the firm's marginal tax rate

▶ The risk that the firm may default and fail to make an interest payment

Rather than attempting to account for all possibilities here, we will consider the special case in which the firm issues debt and plans to keep the dollar amount of debt constant forever.

For example, the firm might issue a perpetual consol bond, making only interest payments but never repaying the principal. More realistically, suppose the firm issues short-term debt such as a five-year coupon bond. When the principal is due, the firm raises the money needed to pay it by issuing new debt. In this way, the firm never pays off the principal but simply refinances it whenever it comes due. In this situation, the debt is effectively permanent.

Many large firms have a policy of maintaining a certain amount of debt on their balance sheets. As old bonds and loans mature, they take out new loans and issue new bonds. Note that we are considering the value of the interest tax shield with a *fixed* dollar amount of outstanding debt, rather than an amount that changes with the size of the firm.

As we learned in Chapter 6, if the debt is fairly priced, the Valuation Principle implies that the market value of the debt today must equal the present value of the future interest payments:[3]

$$\text{Market Value of Debt} = D = PV(\text{Future Interest Payments}) \qquad (15.6)$$

If the firm's marginal tax rate (T_c) is constant, then we have the following general formula:

Value of the Interest Tax Shield of Permanent Debt

$$
\begin{aligned}
PV(\text{Interest Tax Shield}) &= PV(T_c \times \text{Future Interest Payments}) \\
&= T_c \times PV(\text{Future Interest Payments}) \qquad (15.7) \\
&= T_c \times D
\end{aligned}
$$

This formula shows the magnitude of the interest tax shield. Given a 35% corporate tax rate, it implies that for every $1 in new permanent debt that the firm issues, the value of the firm increases by $0.35.

Leverage and the WACC with Taxes

There is another way we can incorporate the benefit of the firm's future interest tax shield. Recall from Chapter 12 that we defined the WACC with taxes as:

Weighted Average Cost of Capital with Taxes

$$r_{wacc} = r_E \frac{E}{E+D} + r_D(1-T_C)\frac{D}{E+D} \qquad (15.8)$$

In Equation 15.8, we incorporate the benefit of the interest tax shield by adjusting the cost of debt to the firm. If the firm pays interest rate r_D on its debt, then because it receives a tax shield of $T_C \times r_D$, the effective after-tax cost of debt is reduced to $r_D(1-T_C)$. Comparing Equation 15.8 with Equation 15.2 for the pre-tax WACC, we can see that corporate taxes lower the effective cost of debt financing, which translates into a reduction in the WACC. In fact, Equation 15.8 implies the following:

$$r_{wacc} = \underbrace{r_E \frac{E}{E+D} + r_D\frac{D}{E+D}}_{\text{Pre-tax WACC}} - \underbrace{r_D T_C \frac{D}{E+D}}_{\substack{\text{Reduction Due to} \\ \text{Interest Tax Shield}}} \qquad (15.9)$$

Thus, the reduction in the WACC increases with the amount of debt financing. The higher the firm's leverage, the more the firm exploits the tax advantage of debt and the lower its WACC. Figure 15.7 illustrates this decline in the WACC with leverage. The figure also shows the pre-tax WACC, as shown in Figure 15.5.

---

[3]Equation 15.6 is valid even if interest rates fluctuate and the debt is risky, as long as any new debt is also fairly priced. It requires only that the firm never repay the principal on the debt (it either refinances or defaults on the principal).

FIGURE 15.7   The WACC with and without Corporate Taxes

We compute the WACC as a function of leverage using Equation 15.9. Whereas the pre-tax WACC remains constant, with taxes the WACC declines as the firm increases its reliance on debt financing and the benefit of the interest tax deduction grows. The figure assumes a marginal corporate income tax rate of 35%.

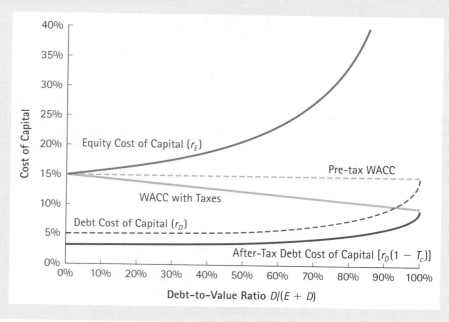

Debt and Taxes: The Bottom Line

In this section, we have seen that the deductibility of interest expenses for corporate taxes creates an advantage for debt financing. We can calculate the value of this benefit to the firm in two ways. First, we can forecast the firm's future interest tax shields and determine their present value. This approach is especially simple when the amount of debt is fixed permanently, in which case the value of the tax shield is equal to $T_C \times D$.

A second way to calculate the benefit of the interest tax shield is to incorporate it into the firm's cost of capital by using the WACC. Unlike the pre-tax WACC, the WACC with taxes declines with leverage because of the interest tax shield. If we use this lower discount rate to compute the present value of the firm's or an investment's free cash flow, the present value will be higher by an amount that reflects the benefit of the future interest tax shields. This approach is simplest to apply when the firm adjusts its debt to keep the fraction of debt financing (its debt-to-value ratio) constant over time.

To summarize, we can include the interest tax shield when assessing the value of a firm or an investment by *either* of these methods:

1. Discounting its free cash flow using the pre-tax WACC, and adding the present value of expected future interest tax shield

2. Discounting its free cash flow using the WACC (with taxes)

Using either of these methods, we will find the value of the firm will increase with leverage. Thus, unlike the setting with perfect capital markets, capital structure matters. But now we face a new puzzle: given the tax benefit, why don't firms use debt financing almost exclusively?

5. How does the interest tax deduction affect firm value?

6. How does the firm's WACC change with leverage?

15.4 The Costs of Bankruptcy and Financial Distress

The previous section presents us with an interesting question: if increasing debt increases the value of the firm, why not shift to nearly 100% debt? One part of the answer comes from bankruptcy costs. With more debt, there is a greater chance that the firm will be unable to make its required interest payments and will default on its debt obligations. A firm that has trouble meeting its debt obligations is in **financial distress**. Bankruptcy is a long and complicated process that imposes both direct and indirect costs on the firm and its investors that the assumption of perfect capital markets ignores.

financial distress The situation that arises when a firm has difficulty meeting its debt obligations.

Direct Costs of Bankruptcy

Each country has a bankruptcy code that details the process for dealing with a firm in default of its debt obligations (see the appendix to this chapter). The bankruptcy code is designed to provide an orderly process for settling a firm's debts. However, the process is still complex, time-consuming, and costly. When a corporation becomes financially distressed, outside professionals, such as legal and accounting experts, consultants, appraisers, auctioneers, and others with experience selling distressed assets, are generally hired. Investment bankers may also assist with a potential financial restructuring.

In addition to the money spent by the firm, the creditors may incur costs during the bankruptcy process. In the case of reorganization, creditors must often wait several years for a reorganization plan to be approved and to receive payment. To ensure that their rights and interests are respected, and to assist in valuing their claims in a proposed reorganization, creditors may seek separate legal representation and professional advice.

Studies typically report that the average direct costs of bankruptcy are approximately 3% to 4% of the pre-bankruptcy market value of total assets. The costs are likely to be higher for firms with more complicated business operations and for firms with larger numbers of creditors, because reaching agreement among many creditors regarding the final disposition of the firm's assets may be more difficult. Because many aspects of the bankruptcy process are independent of the size of the firm, the costs are typically higher, in percentage terms, for smaller firms.

Bankruptcy Can Be Expensive

Outside experts that specialize in aiding distressed firms are costly. At the time Enron entered bankruptcy, it reportedly spent a record $30 million per month on legal and accounting fees, and the total cost ultimately exceeded $750 million. WorldCom paid its advisors $657 million as part of its reorganization to become MCI. Between January 2009 and June 2010, it is estimated that Nortel paid over $290 million in bankruptcy professional fees, or over $16 million per month.*

Whether paid by the firm or its creditors, these direct costs of bankruptcy reduce the value of the assets that the firm's investors will ultimately receive. In the case of Enron, reorganization costs may approach 10% of the value of the assets.

*Source: Diane A. Urquhart, Consolidated and Updated Report—Bankruptcies and Employee Claims—Nortel Case, January 4, 2010

Indirect Costs of Financial Distress

Aside from the direct legal and administrative costs of bankruptcy, many other *indirect* costs are associated with financial distress (whether or not the firm has formally filed for bankruptcy). Whereas these costs are difficult to measure accurately, they are often much larger than the direct costs of bankruptcy.

Indirect bankruptcy costs often occur because the firm may renege on both implicit and explicit commitments and contracts when in financial distress. For example, a bankrupt software manufacturer need not fulfill an obligation to support one of its products. Knowing this, customers who rely on such support might choose to buy software from companies that have a low chance of bankruptcy; that is, companies with lower leverage. Importantly, many of these indirect costs may be incurred even if the firm is not yet in financial distress, but simply faces a significant possibility of bankruptcy in the future. Consider the following examples:

Loss of Customers. Because bankruptcy may enable firms to walk away from future commitments to their customers, those customers may be unwilling to purchase products whose value depends on future support or service from the firm.

Loss of Suppliers. Suppliers may be unwilling to provide a firm with inventory if they fear they will not be paid. For example, Swiss Air was forced to shut down in 2001 because financial concerns caused its suppliers to refuse to fuel its planes.

Cost to Employees. One important cost that often receives a great deal of press coverage is the cost of financial distress to employees. Most firms offer their employees explicit long-term employment contracts, or an implicit promise regarding job security. However, during bankruptcy these contracts and commitments are often ignored, and significant numbers of employees may be laid off. In anticipation of this, employees will be less willing to work for firms with significant bankruptcy risk and so will demand a higher compensation to do so. Thus, hiring and retaining key employees may be costly for a firm with high leverage: Nortel implemented a retention and bonus program costing over $92 million to retain key employees while it was in bankruptcy in 2010.

Fire Sales of Assets. A company in distress may be forced to sell assets quickly to raise cash, possibly accepting a lower price than the assets are actually worth to the firm. This cost is likely to be large when creditors are more pessimistic than management regarding the value of the assets, so creditors will try to force liquidation even at low prices.

In total, the indirect costs of financial distress may be substantial. A study of highly levered firms by Gregor Andrade and Steven Kaplan estimated a potential loss due to financial distress of 10% to 20% of firm value. Importantly, many of these indirect costs may be incurred even if the firm is not yet in financial distress, but simply faces a significant possibility that it may occur in the future.

Concept Check

7. What are the direct costs of bankruptcy?

8. Why are the indirect costs of financial distress likely to be more important than the direct costs of bankruptcy?

15.5 Optimal Capital Structure: The Tradeoff Theory

We can now combine our knowledge of the benefits of leverage from the interest tax shield with the costs of financial distress to determine the amount of debt that a firm should issue to maximize its value. The analysis presented in this section is called the *tradeoff theory* because it weighs the benefits of debt that result from shielding cash flows from taxes against the costs of financial distress associated with leverage. This theory is also sometimes referred to as the *static tradeoff theory*

tradeoff theory The theory that the total value of a levered firm equals the value of the firm without leverage plus the present value of the tax savings from debt, less the present value of financial distress costs.

According to the **tradeoff theory**, the total value of a levered firm equals the value of the firm without leverage plus the present value of the tax savings from debt, less the present value of financial distress costs, as follows:

$$V^L = V^U + PV(\text{Interest Tax Shield}) - PV(\text{Financial Distress Costs}) \qquad (15.10)$$

Equation 15.10 shows that leverage has costs as well as benefits. Firms have an incentive to increase leverage to exploit the tax benefits of debt. But with too much debt, they are more likely to risk default and incur financial distress costs.

Differences Across Firms

Whereas we have seen in Section 15.3 how to calculate the benefits of the interest tax shield, calculating the precise present value of financial distress costs is very difficult if not impossible. Two key qualitative factors determine the present value of financial distress costs: (1) the probability of financial distress and (2) the magnitude of the direct and indirect costs related to financial distress that the firm will incur.

What determines each of these factors? The magnitude of the financial distress costs will depend on the relative importance of the sources of these costs and is likely to vary by industry. For example, telecom equipment firms are likely to incur high costs associated with financial distress, due to the potential for loss of customers and key personnel, as well as a lack of tangible assets that can be easily liquidated. In contrast, power companies are likely to have low costs of financial distress, as much of their value derives from tangible assets (land, buildings, power lines) that can be sold if necessary. Not surprisingly, by reviewing Figure 15.1 we can see that these two industries have very different leverage policies: telecom equipment firms have very low debt, whereas power companies tend to be highly levered. Similarly, in Figure 15.2 we saw that Air Canada has a lot of debt whereas WestJet has substantially less. Part of this is historical and part is a difference in assets. Both companies have similarities in some assets, like airplanes, but Air Canada also owns the rights to international routes, and these rights could potentially be sold to meet the demands of creditors.

The probability of financial distress depends on the likelihood that a firm will be unable to meet its debt commitments and therefore default. This probability increases with the amount of a firm's liabilities (relative to its assets). It also increases with the volatility of a firm's cash flows and asset values. Thus, firms with steady, reliable cash flows, such as power companies, are able to use high levels of debt and still have a very low probability of default. Firms whose value and cash flows are very volatile (for example, telecom firms) must have much lower levels of debt to avoid a significant risk of default.

Optimal Leverage

Figure 15.8 shows how the value of a levered firm, V^L varies with the level of permanent debt, D, according to Equation 15.10. With no debt, the value of the firm is V^U. For low levels of debt, the risk of default remains low, and the main effect of an increase in leverage is an increase in the interest tax shield, which has present value $T_C D$, as shown in Equation 15.7. If there were no costs of financial distress, the value would continue to increase at this rate until the interest on the debt exceeds the firm's earnings before interest and taxes (*EBIT*), and the tax shield is exhausted.

The costs of financial distress reduce the value of the levered firm, V^L. The amount of the reduction increases with the probability of default, which in turn increases with the level of the debt, D. The tradeoff theory states that firms should increase their leverage until it reaches the level D^* for which V_L is maximized. At this point, the tax savings that result from increasing leverage are just offset by the increased probability of incurring the costs of financial distress.

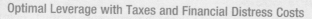

FIGURE 15.8   Optimal Leverage with Taxes and Financial Distress Costs

As the level of debt increases, the tax benefits of debt increase until the interest expense exceeds the firm's *EBIT*. However, the probability of default, and hence the present value of financial distress costs, also increases. The optimal level of debt, D^*, occurs when these effects balance out and the value of the levered firm is maximized. D^* will be lower for firms with higher costs of financial distress.

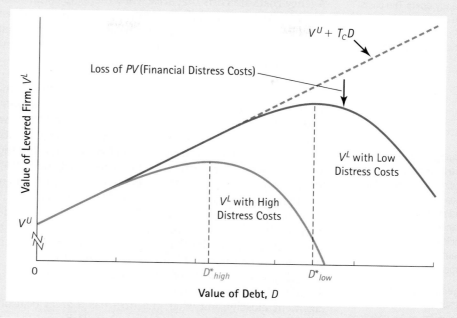

Figure 15.8 also illustrates the optimal debt choices for two types of firms. The optimal debt choice for a firm with low costs of financial distress is indicated by D^*_{low} and the optimal debt choice for a firm with high costs of financial distress is indicated by D^*_{high}. Not surprisingly, with higher costs of financial distress, it is optimal for the firm to choose lower leverage.

The tradeoff theory helps to resolve two important facts about leverage:

1. The presence of financial distress costs can explain why firms choose debt levels that are too low to fully exploit the interest tax shield.

2. Differences in the magnitude of financial distress costs and the volatility of cash flows can explain the differences in the use of leverage across industries.

 Concept Check

9. According to the tradeoff theory, how should a financial manager determine the right capital structure for a firm?

10. Why would managers in one industry choose different capital structures than those in another industry?

15.6 Additional Consequences of Leverage: Agency Costs and Information

Taxes and financial distress costs are not the only capital market imperfections that arise in practice. In this section, we continue to relax the assumption of perfect capital markets to see other ways in which capital structure can affect firm value. We begin by discussing how leverage alters managers' incentives and changes their investment decisions. We then address the complexities of stakeholders in the firm having different information.

Agency Costs

agency costs The costs that arise when there are conflicts of interest between stakeholders.

Agency costs are costs that arise when there are conflicts of interest between stakeholders. In Chapter 1, we briefly mentioned the principal-agent problem that arises when managers put their own interests ahead of shareholders' interest. Here, we discuss how debt can mitigate this problem. However, it may also distort equity holders' preferences for the types of projects the firm pursues.

Managerial Entrenchment. Although managers often do own shares of the firm, in most large corporations they own only a very small fraction of the outstanding shares. Shareholders, through the board of directors, have the power to fire managers. In practice, they rarely do so unless the firm's performance is exceptionally poor.

management entrenchment A situation arising as a result of the separation of ownership and control, in which managers may make decisions that benefit themselves at investors' expense.

This separation of ownership and control creates the possibility of **management entrenchment**; facing little threat of being fired and replaced, managers are free to run the firm in their own best interests. As a result, managers may make decisions that benefit themselves at investors' expense. Managers may reduce their effort (shirk), spend excessively on perquisites such as corporate jets, or undertake wasteful projects that increase the size of the firm (and their paycheques) at the expense of shareholder value, often called "empire building." If these decisions have negative *NPV* for the firm, they are a form of agency cost—the **agency costs of equity**.

agency costs of equity Costs that occur when managers make decisions that benefit themselves at the expense of shareholder value.

These agency costs of equity are most likely to arise when equity ownership is highly diluted (so that no individual shareholder has an incentive to monitor management closely) and when the firm has a great deal of free cash flow available for managers to spend on wasteful projects. Debt can therefore help in two ways. First, by borrowing rather than raising funds by issuing shares, ownership of the firm may remain more concentrated, improving the monitoring of management. Second, by forcing the firm to pay out cash to meet interest and principal payments, debt reduces the free cash flow available at management's discretion. For managers to engage in wasteful investment, they must have the cash to invest. Only when cash is tight will managers be motivated to run the firm as efficiently as possible. Thus, leverage can provide incentives for managers to run the firm efficiently and effectively and thus reduce the agency costs of equity. These benefits provide an additional incentive to use debt rather than equity financing.

Airlines Use Financial Distress to Their Advantage

The need to generate cash flows sufficient to make interest payments may also tie managers' hands and commit them to pursue sound business strategies with greater vigour than they would without the threat of financial distress. For example, in 2004 when Air Canada was in bankruptcy and attempting to reorganize, the firm was able to win wage concessions from all its unions by explaining such concessions were necessary for Air Canada to receive new financing so it could come out of bankruptcy and avoid liquidation. (A similar situation enabled Delta Airlines to persuade its pilots to accept a 33% wage cut in November 2004.) Without the threat of financial distress and possible liquidation (which would have meant all jobs would have been lost), these airlines might not have reached agreements with their unions as quickly or achieved the same wage concessions.

A firm with greater leverage may also become a fiercer competitor and act more aggressively in protecting its markets, because it cannot risk the possibility of bankruptcy. This commitment to aggressive behaviour can scare off potential rivals. (However, this argument can also work in reverse, as a firm weakened by too much leverage might become so financially fragile that it crumbles in the face of competition, allowing other firms to erode its markets.)

Equity–Debt Holder Conflicts. When a firm has leverage, a conflict of interest exists if investment decisions have different consequences for the value of equity and the value of debt. Such a conflict is most likely to occur when the risk of financial distress is high. In some circumstances, managers may take actions that benefit shareholders but harm the firm's creditors and lower the total value of the firm. This is an **agency cost of debt**.

agency cost of debt
A cost that occurs when managers may take actions that benefit shareholders but harm the firm's creditors and lower the total value of the firm.

To illustrate, put yourself in the place of the shareholders of a company in distress that is likely to default on its debt. You could continue as normal, in which case you will very likely lose the value of your shares and hand control of the firm to the bondholders. Alternatively, you could do the following:

1. Roll the dice and take on a risky project that could save the firm, even though its expected outcome is so poor that you normally would not take it on
2. Conserve funds rather than invest in new, promising projects
3. Cash out by distributing as much of the firm's capital as possible to the shareholders before the bondholders take over

excessive risk-taking
A situation that occurs when a company is near distress and shareholders have an incentive to invest in risky negative-*NPV* projects that will destroy value for debt holders and the firm overall.

Why would you roll the dice? Even if the project fails, you are no worse off because you were headed for default anyway. If it succeeds, then you avoid default and retain ownership of the firm. This incentive leads to **excessive risk-taking**, a situation that occurs when a company is near distress and shareholders have an incentive to invest in risky negative-*NPV* projects that will destroy value for debt holders and the firm overall. Anticipating this behaviour, security holders will pay less for the firm initially. This cost is likely to be highest for firms that can easily increase the risk of their investments.

under-investment problem A situation in which shareholders choose not to invest in a positive-*NPV* project because the firm is in financial distress and the value of undertaking the investment opportunity will accrue to bondholders rather than to shareholders.

On the other hand, when default is very likely, a firm may pass up a good project before default, because some or most of the benefit will go to bondholders (by reducing the risk or extent of default). For example, if a firm can invest $100 in a project that will increase the value of its debt by $30 and the value of its equity by $90, then the project has a positive *NPV* of $30 + $90 − $100 = $20. Equity holders will not want to fund it, as their gain ($90) is less than the project's cost of $100. In this case, there is an **under-investment problem**: shareholders choose not to invest in a positive-*NPV* project because the firm is in financial distress and the value of undertaking the investment opportunity will accrue to bondholders rather than themselves. This failure to invest is costly for debt holders and for the overall value of the firm, because it is giving up the *NPV* of the missed opportunities. The cost is highest for firms that are likely to have profitable future growth opportunities requiring large investments.

Financial Distress and Rolling the Dice, *Literally*

Shortly after launching FedEx, founder Frederick Smith was desperate for cash and on the verge of shuttering the company's operations. The problem was massive fixed costs (airplanes, sorting facilities, delivery personnel, etc.) and low initial volume (only 186 packages *total* for its first night of operation). So, Smith went to Las Vegas and played blackjack. He used his winnings (about $27,000) to meet the payroll, and the rest is history.

Source: "Frederick W. Smith: No Overnight Success," *Business Week*, September 20, 2004

The ultimate form of under-investment is cashing out. Knowing that they are likely to lose the firm to the bondholders, shareholders have an incentive to withdraw as much capital from the firm as possible before it enters bankruptcy and transfers to the debt holders. An extreme example of this would be to sell all the assets of the firm and distribute the proceeds to shareholders as a special dividend. The firm would then enter bankruptcy as a worthless shell. As we discussed in Chapter 14, bondholders can anticipate this problem and often require restrictions on the size of dividends and source of funds for those dividends.

Our discussion suggests that we can create a more complete tradeoff model of capital structure by incorporating the possible agency costs and benefits of debt in addition to tax benefits and financial distress costs. This tradeoff model representing optimal leverage is illustrated in Figure 15.9. When debt is too low, adding leverage increases the value of the firm by providing tax benefits and reducing the agency costs of equity by motivating managers to run the firm more efficiently (and avoid wasteful investment). But if debt is too high, the firm will incur financial distress costs and suffer from the agency costs of debt through excessive risk taking and under-investment. The optimal level of debt, D^*, is the point that maximizes firm value by balancing these positive and negative consequences of leverage.

Debt and Information

asymmetric information
The varying information that different parties have, for example, when managers have superior information to that of outside investors regarding the firm's future cash flows.

Our final market imperfection is related to the role of information. Throughout this chapter, we have assumed that managers, stockholders, and creditors have the same information. We have also assumed that securities are fairly priced: the firm's shares and debt are priced according to their true underlying value. These assumptions may not always be accurate in practice. Due to **asymmetric information**, managers' information about the firm and its future cash flows is likely to be superior to that of outside investors. This asymmetric information may motivate managers to alter a firm's capital structure.

FIGURE 15.9   Optimal Leverage with Taxes, Financial Distress, and Agency Costs

As the level of debt increases, the value of the firm increases from the interest tax shield ($T_C D$) as well as improvements in managerial incentives that reduce the agency costs of equity. If leverage is too high, however, the present value of financial distress costs and the agency costs of debt dominate and reduce firm value. The optimal level of debt, D^*, balances these benefits and costs of leverage.

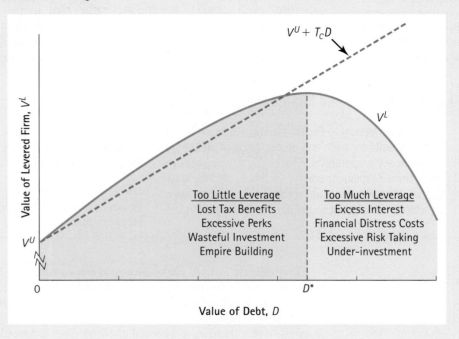

Leverage as a Credible Signal. To convince the stock market that it has great projects, a firm may commit to large future debt payments. If the projects are great, then the firm will have no trouble making the debt payments. But if the firm is making false claims and then does not grow, it will have trouble paying its creditors and will experience financial distress. This distress will be costly for the firm and also for its managers, who will probably lose their jobs. Thus, the managers can use leverage as a way to convince investors that they, the managers, have information that the firm will grow, even if they cannot provide verifiable details about the sources of growth. Investors will interpret the additional leverage as a credible signal of the managers' confidence. The use of leverage as a way to signal good information to investors is known as the **signalling theory of debt**.

signalling theory of debt The use of leverage as a way to signal good information to investors.

Market Timing. When they have better information than outside investors regarding the value of the firm, managers may attempt to engage in **market timing** by selling new shares when they believe the stock is overvalued, and relying on debt and retained earnings (and possibly repurchasing shares) if they believe the stock is undervalued. Managers who successfully time the market in this way benefit long-term shareholders by trading the firm's shares whenever they are mispriced. The firm's capital structure would change as the managers issued new equity (decreasing the leverage) or new debt (increasing the leverage) while attempting to time the market. As a result, the firm's capital structure may deviate above or below the optimal level described by the tradeoff theory, depending on management's view of the share price relative to its true value.

market timing
The selling of new shares by managers because they believe the stock is overvalued, and managers' reliance on debt and retained earnings (and possibly repurchasing of shares) if they believe the stock is undervalued.

Adverse Selection and the Pecking Order Hypothesis. Suppose managers do try to issue equity when it is overpriced relative to its true value. Knowing this, how would investors react? Recall from Chapter 13 the adverse selection, or "lemon," effect in seasoned equity offerings. Fearful that they are being sold a "lemon," investors will discount the price they are willing to pay for the stock.

The adverse selection problem has implications for capital structure. Managers do not want to sell equity if they have to discount it to find buyers. Therefore, managers may seek alternative forms of financing. Debt issues may also suffer from adverse selection. Because the value of low-risk debt is not very sensitive to managers' private information about the firm (but is instead determined mainly by interest rates), the discount needed to attract buyers will be smaller for debt than for equity. Of course, a firm can avoid underpricing altogether by financing investment using its cash (retained earnings) when possible. The **pecking order hypothesis** states what managers will do to avoid this "lemons cost":

pecking order hypothesis The idea that managers will have a preference to fund investment using retained earnings, followed by debt, and will choose to issue equity only as a last resort.

Managers will have a preference to fund investment using retained earnings, followed by debt, and will choose to issue equity only as a last resort.

This hypothesis has implications for firms' capital structure. When firms are profitable and generate sufficient cash to fund their investments, they will not issue debt or equity, but rather rely on retained earnings. Thus, highly profitable firms will have little debt in their capital structure. Only firms that need to raise external capital will have significant debt financing. According to the pecking order hypothesis, firms should almost never issue equity. In reality, it is likely that multiple forces will shape the firm's capital structure, and firms will issue equity when the agency costs or financial distress costs of debt are too great.

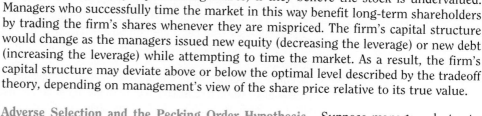

11. How can too much debt lead to excessive risk-taking?

12. What is the pecking order hypothesis?

Concept Check

EXAMPLE 15.5

The Pecking Order of Financing Alternatives

Problem

Axon Industries needs to raise $9.5 million for a new investment project. If the firm issues one-year debt, it may have to pay an interest rate of 8%, although Axon's managers believe that 6% would be a fair rate, given the level of risk. However, if the firm issues equity, the managers believe the equity may be underpriced by 5%. What is the cost to current shareholders of financing the project out of retained earnings, debt, and equity?

Solution

▶ **Plan**

We can evaluate the financing alternatives by comparing what the firm would have to pay to get the financing versus what its managers believe it should pay if the market had the same information they do.

▶ **Execute**

If the firm spends $9.5 million out of retained earnings, rather than paying that money out to shareholders as a dividend, the cost of financing the project is $9.5 million.

Using one-year debt costs the firm $9.5 × (1.08) = $10.26 million in one year, which has a present value based on management's view of the firm's risk of $10.26 ÷ (1.06) = $9.68 million.

If equity is underpriced by 5%, then to raise $9.5 million the firm will need to issue shares that are actually worth $10 million. (For example, if the firm's shares are each worth $50, but it sells them for 0.95 × $50 = $47.50 per share, it will need to sell $9.5 million ÷ $47.50/share = 200,000 shares. These shares have a true value of 200,000 shares × $50/share = $10 million.) Thus, the cost of financing the project with equity will be $10 million.

▶ **Evaluate**

Comparing the three options, retained earnings are the cheapest source of funds, followed by debt, and finally by equity. The ranking reflects the effect of differences in information between managers and investors that result in a lemons problem when they issue new securities, and particularly when they issue new equity.

Capital Structure: Putting It All Together

In this chapter, we have examined a number of factors that might influence a firm's choice of capital structure. What is the bottom line for a financial manager devising the optimal capital structure for a firm? The optimal capital structure depends on market imperfections such as taxes, financial distress costs, agency costs, and asymmetric information, as follows:

1. *Make use of the interest tax shield if your firm has consistent taxable income.* The interest tax shield allows firms to repay investors and avoid the corporate tax.

2. *Balance the tax benefits of debt against the costs of financial distress when determining how much of the firm's income to shield from taxes with leverage.* Whereas the risk of default is not itself a problem, financial distress may lead to other consequences that reduce the value of the firm.

3. *Consider more debt for external financing when agency costs of equity are significant.* When free cash flows are high, too little leverage may encourage wasteful spending and shirking. Beware, though, of too much debt, which can motivate managers and equity holders to take excessive risks or under-invest in a firm and thus cause the agency costs of debt.

4. *Increase leverage to signal managers' confidence in the firm's ability to meet its debt obligations.* Investors understand that bankruptcy is costly for managers.

5. *Be mindful that investors are aware that you have an incentive to issue securities that you know are overpriced.* Thus, when an issue is announced, investors will lower their valuation of that security. This effect is most pronounced for equity issues, because the value of equity is most sensitive to the manager's private information.

6. *Rely first on retained earnings, then debt, and finally equity.* This pecking order of financing alternatives will be most important when managers are likely to have a great deal of private information regarding the value of the firm.

7. *Do not change the firm's capital structure unless it departs significantly from the optimal level.* Actively changing a firm's capital structure (e.g., by selling or repurchasing shares or bonds) entails transactions costs. Most changes to a firm's debt-equity ratio are likely to occur passively, as the market value of the firm's equity fluctuates with changes in the firm's stock price.

MyFinanceLab

Here is what you should know after reading this chapter. MyFinanceLab will help you identify what you know, and where to go when you need to practice.

Key Points and Equations	Terms	Online Practice Opportunities
15.1 Capital Structure Choices	debt-to-value ratio, p. 499	MyFinanceLab Study Plan 15.1
▶ The collection of securities that a firm issues to raise capital from investors is called the firm's capital structure. Equity and debt are the securities most commonly used by firms.		
▶ Various financing choices will promise different future amounts to each security holder in exchange for the cash that is raised today.		
▶ Managers also need to consider whether the securities that the firm issues will receive a fair price in the market, have tax consequences, entail transactions costs, or even change its future investment opportunities.		
15.2 Capital Structure in Perfect Capital Markets	homemade leverage, p. 506 levered equity, p. 502 perfect capital market, p. 501 pre-tax WACC, p. 507 unlevered equity, p. 502	MyFinanceLab Study Plan 15.2 Interactive Leverage Effect Analysis
▶ When equity is used without debt, the firm is said to be unlevered. Otherwise, the amount of debt determines the firm's leverage.		
▶ The owner of a firm should choose the capital structure that maximizes the total value of the securities issued.		
▶ According to M&M Proposition II, the cost of capital for levered equity is: $$r_E = r_U + \frac{D}{E}(r_U - r_D) \qquad (15.3)$$		

▶ Debt is less risky than equity and so has a lower cost of capital. Leverage increases the risk of equity, however, raising the equity cost of capital. The benefit of debt's lower cost of capital is offset by the higher equity cost of capital, leaving a firm's weighted average cost of capital (WACC) unchanged with perfect capital markets.

▶ According to M&M Proposition I, with perfect capital markets the value of a firm is independent of its capital structure. With perfect capital markets, homemade leverage is a perfect substitute for firm leverage.

15.3 Debt and Taxes

▶ Because interest expense is tax deductible, leverage increases the total amount of income available to all investors. The gain to investors from the tax deductibility of interest payments is called the interest tax shield.

$$\text{Interest Tax Shield} = \text{Corporate Tax Rate} \\ \times \text{Interest Payments} \quad (15.4)$$

▶ When we consider corporate taxes, the total value of a levered firm equals the value of an unlevered firm plus the present value of the interest tax shield.

$$V^L = V^U + PV(\text{Interest Tax Shield}) \quad (15.5)$$

▶ When securities are fairly priced, the original shareholders of a firm capture the full benefit of the interest tax shield from an increase in leverage.

▶ When we introduce corporate taxes, the weighted average cost of capital is:

$$r_{wacc} = r_E \frac{E}{E + D} + r_D(1 - T_C)\frac{D}{E + D} \quad (15.8)$$

▶ Absent other market imperfections, the WACC declines with a firm's leverage, because interest expense is tax deductible.

▶ To capture the effect of the interest tax deduction on firm value, you can either compute the *PV* of the future tax shields or use the WACC with taxes to discount the firm's free cash flows, but not both!

interest tax shield, p. 512

MyFinanceLab Study Plan 15.3

15.4 The Costs of Bankruptcy and Financial Distress		
▶ Bankruptcy is a costly process that imposes both direct and indirect costs on a firm and its investors.	financial distress, p. 517	MyFinanceLab Study Plan 15.4
▶ Some direct costs are fees paid to lawyers and bankruptcy experts.		
▶ Some indirect costs are loss of customers, suppliers, or employees, or being forced to sell assets at a deep discount to raise money.		
15.5 Optimal Capital Structure: The Tradeoff Theory		
▶ According to the tradeoff theory, the total value of a levered firm equals the value of the firm without leverage plus the present value of the tax savings from debt minus the present value of financial distress costs:	tradeoff theory, p. 519	MyFinanceLab Study Plan 15.5
$$V^L = V^U + PV(\text{Interest Tax Shield}) \\ - PV(\text{Financial Distress Costs}) \quad (15.10)$$		
▶ The optimal leverage is the level of debt that maximizes V^L.		
15.6 Additional Consequences of Leverage: Agency Costs and Information		
▶ Leverage can reduce the agency costs of equity by improving the incentives for managers to run a firm more efficiently and effectively. However, when a firm enters financial distress, agency cost of debt may occur, as leverage can create incentives to forgo good projects or to take excessive risk.	agency costs, p. 521 agency cost of debt, p. 522 agency costs of equity, p. 521 asymmetric information, p. 523 excessive risk-taking, p. 522 management entrenchment, p. 521 market timing, p. 524 pecking order hypothesis, p. 524 signalling theory of debt, p. 524 under-investment problem, p. 522	MyFinanceLab Study Plan 15.6
▶ When managers have better information than investors, it is asymmetric information. Given asymmetric information, managers may use leverage as a credible signal to investors of the firm's ability to generate future free cash flow.		
▶ Managers who perceive that the firm's equity is underpriced will have a preference to fund investment using retained earnings, or debt, rather than equity. This is called the pecking order hypothesis.		

Review Questions

1. Absent tax effects, why can't we change the cost of capital of the firm by using more debt financing and less equity financing?

2. Explain what is wrong with the following argument: "If a firm issues debt that is risk free because there is no possibility of default, the risk of the firm's equity does not change. Therefore, risk-free debt allows the firm to get the benefit of a low cost of capital of debt without raising its cost of capital of equity."

3. What are the channels through which financing choices can affect firm value?

4. How do taxes affect the choice of debt versus equity?

5. What is meant by "indirect costs of financial distress"?

6. Which type of firm is more likely to experience a loss of customers in the event of financial distress:
   a. Campbell Soup Company or Intuit, Inc. (a maker of accounting software)?
   b. Allstate Corporation (an insurance company) or Reebok International (a footwear and clothing firm)?

7. According to the tradeoff theory, how is capital structure determined?

8. For each pair below, which type of asset is more likely to be liquidated for close to its full market value in the event of financial distress:
   a. An office building or a brand name?
   b. Product inventory or raw materials?
   c. Patent rights or engineering "know-how"?

9. Which of the following industries have low optimal debt levels according to the tradeoff theory? Which have high optimal levels of debt?
   a. Tobacco firms
   b. Accounting firms
   c. Established restaurant chains
   d. Lumber companies
   e. Cell phone manufacturers

10. How can leverage alter the incentives of managers?

Problems

All problems in this chapter are available in MyFinanceLab.

Capital Structure in Perfect Capital Markets

For problems in this section, assume there are no taxes or distress costs.

1. Consider a project with free cash flows in one year of $130,000 or $180,000, with each outcome being equally likely. The initial investment required for the project is $100,000, and the project's cost of capital is 20%. The risk-free interest rate is 10%.
   a. What is the *NPV* of this project?
   b. Suppose that to raise the funds for the initial investment, the project is sold to investors as an all-equity firm. The equity holders will receive the cash flows of the project in one year. How much money can be raised in this way—that is, what is the initial market value of the unlevered equity?

c. Suppose the initial $100,000 is instead raised by borrowing at the risk-free inter-est rate. What are the cash flows of the levered equity, and what is its initial value according to M&M?

2. You are an entrepreneur starting a biotechnology firm. If your research is success-ful, the technology can be sold for $30 million. If your research is unsuccessful, it will be worth nothing. To fund your research, you need to raise $2 million. Investors are willing to provide you with $2 million in initial capital in exchange for 50% of the unlevered equity in the firm.
    a. What is the total market value of the firm without leverage?
    b. Suppose you borrow $1 million. According to M&M, what fraction of the firm's equity will you need to sell to raise the additional $1 million you need?
    c. What is the value of your share of the firm's equity in cases (a) and (b)?

3. Acort Industries owns assets that will have an 80% probability of having a market value of $50 million in one year. There is a 20% chance that the assets will be worth only $20 million. The current risk-free rate is 5%, and Acort's assets have a cost of capital of 10%.
    a. If Acort is unlevered, what is the current market value of its equity?
    b. Suppose instead that Acort has debt with a face value of $20 million due in one year. According to M&M, what is the value of Acort's equity in this case?
    c. What is the expected return of Acort's equity without leverage? What is the ex-pected return of Acort's equity with leverage?
    d. What is the lowest possible realized return of Acort's equity with and without leverage?

4. Suppose there are no taxes. Firm ABC has no debt, and firm XYZ has debt of $5000 on which it pays interest of 10% each year. Both companies have identical projects that generate a free cash flow (FCF) of $800 or $1000 each year. After paying any interest on debt, both companies use all remaining free cash flows to pay dividends each year.

	ABC			XYZ	
FCF	Debt Payments	Equity Dividends		Debt Payments	Equity Dividends
$800					
$1000					

    a. In the table above, fill in the payments debt and equity holders of each firm will receive, given each of the two possible levels of free cash flows.
    b. Suppose you hold 10% of the equity of ABC. What is another portfolio you could hold that would provide the same cash flows?
    c. Suppose you hold 10% of the equity of XYZ. If you can borrow at 10%, what is an alternative strategy that would provide the same cash flows?

5. Hardmon Enterprises is currently an all-equity firm with an expected return of 12%. It is considering borrowing money to buy back some of its existing shares, thus in-creasing its leverage.
    a. Suppose Hardmon borrows to the point that its debt-equity ratio is 0.50. With this amount of debt, the debt cost of capital is 6%. What will the expected return of equity be after this transaction?
    b. Suppose instead Hardmon borrows to the point that its debt-equity ratio is 1.50. With this amount of debt, Hardmon's debt will be much riskier. As a result, the debt cost of capital will be 8%. What will the expected return of equity be in this case?

    c. A senior manager argues that it is in the best interest of the shareholders to choose the capital structure that leads to the highest expected return for the stock. How would you respond to this argument?

6. Microsoft has no debt and a WACC of 9.2%. The average debt-to-value ratio for the software industry is 13%. What would its cost of equity be if it took on the average amount of debt for its industry at a cost of debt of 6%?

Debt and Taxes

7. Pelamed Pharmaceuticals had *EBIT* of $325 million in 2006, interest expenses of $125 million, and a corporate tax rate of 40%.
    a. What was Pelamed's 2006 net income?
    b. What was the total of Pelamed's 2006 net income and interest payments?
    c. If Pelamed had no interest expenses, what would its 2006 net income have been? How does it compare to your answer in part (b)?
    d. What was the amount of Pelamed's interest tax shield in 2006?

8. Grommit Engineering expects to have net income next year of $20.75 million and free cash flow of $22.15 million. Grommit's marginal corporate tax rate is 35%.
    a. If Grommit increases leverage so that its interest expense rises by $1 million, how will its net income change?
    b. For the same increase in interest expense, how will free cash flow change?

9. Assume that Microsoft has a total market value of $300 billion and a marginal tax rate of 35%. If it permanently changes its leverage from no debt by taking on new debt in the amount of 13% of its current market value, what is the present value of the tax shield it will create?

10. Suppose the corporate tax rate is 40%. Consider a firm that earns $1000 before interest and taxes each year with no risk. The firm's capital expenditures equal its depreciation expenses each year, and it will have no changes to its net working capital. The risk-free interest rate is 5%.
    a. Suppose the firm has no debt and pays out its net income as a dividend each year. What is the value of the firm's equity?
    b. Suppose instead the firm makes interest payments of $500 per year. What is the value of equity? What is the value of debt?
    c. What is the difference between the total value of the firm with leverage and without leverage?
    d. To what percentage of the value of the debt is the difference in part (c) equal?

11. Your firm currently has $100 million in debt outstanding with a 10% interest rate. The terms of the loan require the firm to repay $25 million of the balance each year. Suppose that the marginal corporate tax rate is 40%, and that the interest tax shields have the same risk as the loan. What is the present value of the interest tax shields from this debt?

12. Arnell Industries has $10 million in permanent debt outstanding. The firm will pay interest only on this debt. Arnell's marginal tax rate is expected to be 35% for the foreseeable future.
    a. Suppose Arnell pays interest of 6% per year on its debt. What is its annual interest tax shield?
    b. What is the present value of the interest tax shield, assuming its risk is the same as the loan?
    c. Suppose instead that the interest rate on the debt is 5%. What is the present value of the interest tax shield in this case?

13. Rogot Instruments makes fine violins and cellos. It has $1 million in debt outstanding and equity valued at $2 million, and pays corporate income tax at rate 35%. Its cost of equity is 12% and its cost of debt is 7%.
    a. What is Rogot's pre-tax WACC?
    b. What is Rogot's (effective after-tax) WACC?

14. Rumolt Motors has 30 million shares outstanding with a price of $15 per share. In addition, Rumolt has issued bonds with a total current market value of $150 million. Suppose Rumolt's equity cost of capital is 10%, and its debt cost of capital is 5%.
    a. What is Rumolt's pre-tax WACC?
    b. If Rumolt's corporate tax rate is 35%, what is its after-tax WACC?

15. Summit Builders has a market debt-equity ratio of 0.65 and a corporate tax rate of 40%, and pays 7% interest on its debt. By what amount does the interest tax shield from its debt lower Summit's WACC?

16. Milton Industries expects free cash flows of $5 million each year. Milton's corporate tax rate is 35%, and its unlevered cost of capital is 15%. The firm also has outstanding debt of $19.05 million and expects to maintain this level of debt permanently.
    a. What is the value of Milton Industries without leverage?
    b. What is the value of Milton Industries with leverage?

17. NatNah, a builder of acoustic accessories, has no debt and an equity cost of capital of 15%. Suppose NatNah decides to increase its leverage and maintain a market debt-to-value ratio of 0.5. Suppose its debt cost of capital is 9% and its corporate tax rate is 35%. If NatNah's pre-tax WACC remains constant, what will its (effective after-tax) WACC be with the increase in leverage?

18. Kurz Manufacturing is currently an all-equity firm with 20 million shares outstanding and a stock price of $7.50 per share. Although investors currently expect Kurz to remain an all-equity firm, Kurz plans to announce that it will borrow $50 million and use the funds to repurchase shares. Kurz will pay interest only on this debt, and it has no further plans to increase or decrease the amount of debt. Kurz is subject to a 40% corporate tax rate.
    a. What is the market value of Kurz's existing assets before the announcement?
    b. What is the market value of Kurz's assets (including any tax shields) just after the debt is issued but before the shares are repurchased?
    c. What is Kurz's share price just before the share repurchase? How many shares will Kurz repurchase?
    d. What are Kurz's market value balance sheet and share price after the share repurchase?

19. Kohwe Corporation plans to issue equity to raise $50 million to finance a new investment. After making the investment, Kohwe expects to earn free cash flows of $10 million each year. Kohwe currently has 5 million shares outstanding, and it has no other assets or opportunities. Suppose the appropriate discount rate for Kohwe's future free cash flows is 8%, and the only capital market imperfections are corporate taxes and financial distress costs.
    a. What is the NPV of Kohwe's investment?
    b. What is Kohwe's share price today?

20. Suppose Kohwe borrows the $50 million instead. The firm will pay interest only on this loan each year and will maintain an outstanding balance of $50 million on the loan. Suppose that Kohwe's corporate tax rate is 40%, and expected free cash flows are still $10 million each year. What is Kohwe's share price today if the investment is financed with debt?

21. Now suppose that with leverage, Kohwe's expected free cash flows will decline to $9 million per year due to reduced sales and other financial distress costs. Assume that the appropriate discount rate for Kohwe's future free cash flows is still 8%. What is Kohwe's share price today, given the financial distress costs of leverage?

Optimal Capital Structure: The Tradeoff Theory

22. Hawar International is a shipping firm with a current share price of $5.50 and 10 million shares outstanding. Suppose that Hawar announces plans to lower its corporate taxes by borrowing $20 million and repurchasing shares, that Hawar pays a corporate tax rate of 30%, and that shareholders expect the change in debt to be permanent.
    a. If the only imperfection is corporate taxes, what will the share price be after this announcement?
    b. Suppose the only imperfections are corporate taxes and financial distress costs. If the share price rises to $5.75 after this announcement, what is the *PV* of financial distress costs Hawar will incur as the result of this new debt?

23. Marpor Industries has no debt and expects to generate free cash flows of $16 million each year. Marpor believes that if it permanently increases its level of debt to $40 million, the risk of financial distress may cause it to lose some customers and receive less favourable terms from its suppliers. As a result, Marpor's expected free cash flows with debt will be only $15 million per year. Suppose Marpor's tax rate is 35%, the risk-free rate is 5%, the expected return of the market is 15%, and the beta of Marpor's free cash flows is 1.10 (with or without leverage).
    a. Estimate Marpor's value without leverage.
    b. Estimate Marpor's value with the new leverage.

Additional Consequences of Leverage: Agency Costs and Information

24. Dynron Corporation's primary business is natural gas transportation using its vast gas pipeline network. Dynron's assets currently have a market value of $150 million. The firm is exploring the possibility of raising $50 million by selling part of its pipeline network and investing the $50 million in a fibre-optic network to generate revenues by selling high-speed network bandwidth. Whereas this new investment is expected to increase profits, it will also substantially increase Dynron's risk. If Dynron is levered, would this investment be more or less attractive to equity holders than if Dynron had no debt?

25. Consider a firm whose only asset is a plot of vacant land and whose only liability is debt of $15 million due in one year. If left vacant, the land will be worth $10 million in one year. Alternatively, the firm can develop the land for an upfront cost of $20 million. The developed land will be worth $35 million in one year. Suppose the risk-free interest rate is 10%, all cash flows are risk free, and there are no taxes.
    a. If the firm chooses not to develop the land, what is the value of the firm's equity today? What is the value of the debt today?
    b. What is the *NPV* of developing the land?
    c. Suppose the firm raises $20 million from equity holders to develop the land. If the firm develops the land, what is the value of the firm's equity today? What is the value of the firm's debt today?
    d. Given your answer to part (c), would equity holders be willing to provide the $20 million needed to develop the land?

26. Zymase is a biotechnology start-up firm. Researchers at Zymase must choose one of three different research strategies. The payoffs (after taxes) and their likelihood for each strategy are shown below. The risk of each project is diversifiable.

Strategy	Probability (%)	Payoff ($ millions)
A	100	75
B	50	140
	50	0
C	10	300
	90	40

a. Which project has the highest expected payoff?

b. Suppose Zymase has debt of $40 million due at the time of the project's payoff. Which strategy has the highest expected payoff for equity holders?

c. Suppose Zymase has debt of $110 million due at the time of the strategy's payoff. Which strategy has the highest expected payoff for equity holders?

d. If management chooses the strategy that maximizes the payoff to equity holders, what is the expected agency cost to the firm from having $40 million in debt due? What is the expected agency cost to the firm from having $110 million in debt due?

27. You own a firm, and you want to raise $30 million to fund an expansion. Currently, you own 100% of the firm's equity, and the firm has no debt. To raise the $30 million solely through equity, you will need to sell two-thirds of the firm. However, you would prefer to maintain at least a 50% equity stake in the firm to retain control.

a. If you borrow $20 million, what fraction of the equity will you need to sell to raise the remaining $10 million? (Assume perfect capital markets.)

b. What is the smallest amount you can borrow to raise the $30 million without giving up control? (Assume perfect capital markets.)

28. Empire Industries forecasts net income this coming year as shown below (in thousands of dollars):

EBIT	$1000
Interest expense	$0
Income before tax	$1000
Taxes	−$350
Net income	$650

Approximately $200,000 of Empire's earnings will be needed to make new, positive-*NPV* investments. Unfortunately, Empire's managers are expected to waste 10% of its net income on needless perks, pet projects, and other expenditures that do not contribute to the firm. All remaining income will be distributed to shareholders.

a. What are the two benefits of debt financing for Empire?

b. By how much would each $1 of interest expense reduce Empire's distributions to shareholders?

c. What is the increase in the *total* funds Empire will pay to investors for each $1 of interest expense?

29. Info Systems Technology (IST) manufactures microprocessor chips for use in appliances and other applications. IST has no debt and 100 million shares outstanding. The correct price for these shares is either $14.50 or $12.50 per share. Investors view both possibilities as equally likely, so the shares currently trade for $13.50.

    IST must raise $500 million to build a new production facility. Because the firm would suffer a large loss of both customers and engineering talent in the event of financial distress, managers believe that if IST borrows the $500 million, the present value of financial distress costs will exceed any tax benefits by $20 million. At the same time, because investors believe that managers know the correct share price, IST faces a lemons problem if it attempts to raise the $500 million by issuing equity.

    a. Suppose that if IST issues equity, the share price will remain $13.50. To maximize the long-term share price of the firm once its true value is known, would managers choose to issue equity or borrow the $500 million if:
       i. they know the correct value of the shares is $12.50?
       ii. they know the correct value of the shares is $14.50?

    b. Given your answer to part (a), what should investors conclude if IST issues equity? What will happen to the share price?

    c. Given your answer to part (a), what should investors conclude if IST issues debt? What will happen to the share price in that case?

    d. How would your answers change if there were no distress costs, but only the tax benefits of leverage?

Chapter 15 APPENDIX   The Bankruptcy Code

When a firm fails to make a required payment to debt holders, it is in default. Debt holders can then take legal action against the firm to collect payment by seizing the firm's assets. Because most firms have multiple creditors, coordination is required to guarantee that each creditor will be treated fairly. Moreover, because the assets of the firm might be more valuable if kept together, creditors seizing assets in a piecemeal fashion might destroy much of the remaining value of the firm.

Canadian bankruptcy law was created to organize this process so that creditors are treated fairly and the value of the assets is not needlessly destroyed. There are two relevant acts for financially distressed firms in Canada: the Bankruptcy and Insolvency Act (BIA) and the Companies' Creditors Arrangement Act (CCAA).

The BIA applies to businesses and individuals. Usually smaller companies use the BIA and liquidation is often the result. Under the BIA, a firm may put forth a proposal that can either be accepted or rejected by its creditors. To be accepted, each class of creditor must vote and pass the proposal, and the court must also give its approval. A creditor class is said to pass the proposal if at least a majority of the creditors in number and two-thirds in value agree to the proposal. If a proposal does not pass, a trustee is appointed to oversee the liquidation of the firm's assets through an auction. The proceeds from the liquidation are used to pay the firm's creditors, and the firm ceases to exist.

The CCAA applies to firms that owe $5 million or more to creditors. It allows a company to pre-empt going into formal bankruptcy under the BIA and, instead, propose a formal plan of arrangement (or reorganization). Once the company has applied to the court for protection against its creditors—a stay, under the CCAA—all pending collection attempts are automatically suspended, and the firm's existing management is given the opportunity to propose a reorganization plan. While developing the plan, management continues to operate the business under the watch of a monitor (often the company's auditor). The plan of arrangement specifies the treatment of each creditor of the firm. In addition to cash payment, creditors may receive new debt or equity securities of the firm. The value of cash and securities is generally less than the amount each creditor is owed, but more than the creditors would receive if the firm were shut down immediately and be liquidated. The creditors must vote to accept the plan, and it must be approved by the court.[4] If an acceptable plan is not put forth, the company loses its protection under the CCAA and the stay is lifted. The company is not automatically forced to enter into bankruptcy but will likely do so under the BIA, either voluntarily or by petition of its creditors. At this point, liquidation is the likely eventual outcome.

U.S. firms can file for bankruptcy protection under the provisions of the 1978 Bankruptcy Reform Act. In the United States, the main bankruptcy laws for corporations fall under two chapters. Chapter 7 is for liquidation of firms. Chapter 11 is for reorganization and is similar to the CCAA in Canada. A notable difference between the CCAA and Chapter 11 is that, under Chapter 11, the bankruptcy court can impose a plan (in a process commonly known as a "cram down") even if not all creditor classes approve it.

---

[4]Specifically, management holds the exclusive right to propose a plan of arrangement during the initial stay (which is 30 days), and the stay may be extended indefinitely by the court. Thereafter, any interested party may propose a plan. Creditors who will receive full payment or have their claims fully reinstated under the plan are deemed unimpaired and do not vote on the plan of arrangement. All impaired creditors are grouped according to the nature of their claims. If the plan is approved by creditors holding two-thirds of the claim amount in each group and a majority in the number of the claims in each group, the court may sanction the plan. If a class of creditors or the court does not approve the plan of arrangement, the stay is lifted.

16 Payout Policy

LEARNING OBJECTIVES

- Identify the different ways in which corporations can make distributions to shareholders

- Understand why the way in which they distribute cash flow does not affect value absent market imperfections

- Indicate how taxes can create an advantage for share repurchases versus dividends

- Explain how increased payouts can reduce principal-agent problems but potentially reduce financial flexibility

- Describe alternative non-cash methods for payouts

notation

P_{cum}	cum-dividend stock price	P_{rep}	stock price with share repurchase
P_{ex}	ex-dividend stock price	PV	present value

University of Manitoba, 1997

University of Western Ontario, 2001

Paul Asmundson is a senior member of the investment banking department at one of Canada's leading full-service investment dealers. He has a strong finance background gained while earning a Bachelor of Commerce (Honours) degree from the University of Manitoba and a Master of Business Administration degree from the Richard Ivey School of Business at the University of Western Ontario. Paul has chosen a career in which he is using his finance knowledge every day. "I provide investment banking coverage to a broad range of companies and advise them on a variety of issues, including mergers and acquisitions, raising equity and debt capital, and other corporate finance topics such as capital structure and dividend policy."

When Paul advises clients on dividend policy, he considers a variety of factors, including firm-specific factors, as well as market-related factors. As he explains: "In considering the company-specific factors, there are a number of questions that management must ask themselves. What is the free cash flow profile of the business, and what is the potential volatility based on different operating assumptions? What are the alternative uses of capital and the potential returns generated by those alternative uses? These are among the many questions that the company will need to consider."

"We also need to consider how the market will view the dividend policy," he continues. "What level of dividends are other comparable companies paying? Will the market ascribe value to a dividend from the company, which depends on the investing style of existing and potential shareholders? Or would investors rather see the cash reinvested in the business to produce future returns? These, and many other factors, need to be taken into account."

> "Will the market ascribe value to a dividend from the company, which depends on the investing style of existing and potential shareholders? Or would investors rather see the cash reinvested in the business to produce future returns?"

When a firm's investments generate free cash flow, the firm must decide how to use that cash. If the firm has new positive-*NPV* investment opportunities, it can reinvest the cash and increase the value of the firm. Many young, rapidly growing firms reinvest 100% of their cash flows in this way. But mature, profitable firms often find that they generate more cash than they need to fund all of their attractive investment opportunities. When a firm has excess cash, it can hold those funds as part of its cash reserves or pay the cash out to shareholders. If the firm decides to follow the latter approach, it has two choices: it can pay a dividend or it can repurchase shares from current owners. These decisions represent the firm's payout policy.

For many years, Microsoft Corporation chose to distribute cash to investors primarily by repurchasing its own stock. During the five fiscal years ending June 2004, for example, Microsoft spent an average of $5.4 billion per year on share repurchases. Microsoft began paying dividends to investors in 2003, with what CFO John Connors called "a starter dividend" of $0.08 per share. Then, on July 20, 2004, Microsoft stunned financial markets by announcing plans to pay the largest single cash dividend payment in history, a one-time dividend of $32 billion, or $3 per share, to all shareholders of record on November 17, 2004. In addition to this dividend, Microsoft announced plans to repurchase up to $30 billion worth of its stock over the next four years and pay regular quarterly dividends at an annual rate of $0.32 per share. What considerations led financial managers at Microsoft to make this payout? What are the implications of such actions for shareholders and the value of the firm?

In this chapter, we show that, as with capital structure, a firm's payout policy is shaped by market imperfections such as taxes, agency costs, transaction costs, and asymmetric information between managers and investors. We look at why some firms prefer to pay dividends, while others pay no dividends at all and rely exclusively on share repurchases. In addition, we explore why some firms retain cash and build up large reserves, while others tend to pay out their excess cash.

16.1 Distributions to Shareholders

Figure 16.1 illustrates the alternative uses of free cash flow.[1] A firm that chooses to retain free cash flow will invest in new projects or increase cash reserves. The firm pays out free cash flow through distributions to shareholders by repurchasing shares or paying dividends. The way a firm chooses between these alternatives is referred to as its **payout policy**. We begin our discussion of a firm's payout policy by considering the choice between paying dividends and repurchasing shares. In this section, we examine the details of these methods of paying cash to shareholders.

payout policy The way a firm chooses between the alternative ways to pay cash out to shareholders.

Dividends

A public company's board of directors determines the amount of the firm's dividend. The board sets the amount per share that will be paid and decides when the payment will occur. The date on which the board authorizes the dividend is the **declaration date**. After the board declares the dividend, the firm is legally obligated to make the payment.

declaration date The date on which a public company's board of directors authorizes the payment of a dividend.

FIGURE 16.1

Uses of Free Cash Flow

A firm can retain its free cash flow, either investing or accumulating it, or pay out its free cash flow through a dividend or share repurchase. The choice between these options is determined by the firm's payout policy.

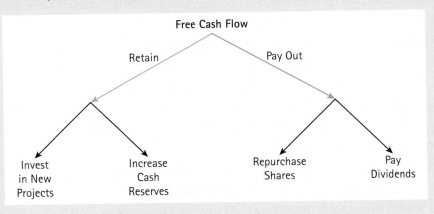

[1]Strictly speaking, Figure 16.1 is for an all-equity firm. For a levered firm, we would begin with the firm's free cash flows to equity, which is free cash flows less after-tax payments to debt holders.

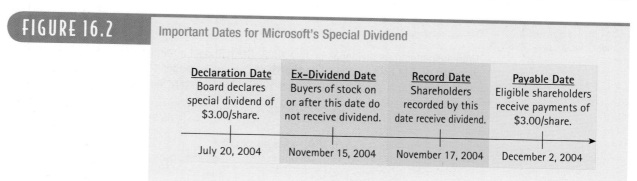

FIGURE 16.2 Important Dates for Microsoft's Special Dividend

Declaration Date	Ex-Dividend Date	Record Date	Payable Date
Board declares special dividend of $3.00/share.	Buyers of stock on or after this date do not receive dividend.	Shareholders recorded by this date receive dividend.	Eligible shareholders receive payments of $3.00/share.
July 20, 2004	November 15, 2004	November 17, 2004	December 2, 2004

record date The specific date set by a public company's board of directors on which a shareholder must be on record as owning the shares in order to qualify to be paid the upcoming dividend.

ex-dividend date A date, two days prior to a dividend's record date, on or after which anyone buying the stock will not be eligible for the dividend.

payable date (distribution date) A date, generally within a month after the record date, on which a firm mails dividend cheques to its registered stockholders.

special dividend A one-time dividend payment a firm makes that is usually much larger than a regular dividend.

return of capital The payment by a firm of dividends from sources such as paid-in capital or the liquidation of assets instead of from current earnings (or accumulated retained earnings).

liquidating dividend A return of capital to shareholders from a business operation that is being terminated.

The firm will pay the dividend to all shareholders of record on a specific date set by the board called the **record date**. Because it takes three business days for shares to be registered, only shareholders who purchase the stock at least three days prior to the record date receive the dividend. As a result, the date two business days prior to the record date is known as the **ex-dividend date**. Anyone who purchases the stock on or after the ex-dividend date will not receive the dividend. Finally, on the **payable date** (or **distribution date**), which is generally within a month after the record date, the firm mails dividend cheques to the registered shareholders. Figure 16.2 shows these dates for Microsoft's $3 dividend.

Microsoft declared the dividend on July 20, 2004, payable on December 2 to all shareholders of record on November 17. Because the record date was November 17, the ex-dividend date was two days earlier, or November 15, 2004.

Special Dividend. Most companies that pay dividends pay them at regular quarterly intervals. Companies usually do not adjust the amount of their dividends, and the amount of the dividend varies little from quarter to quarter. Occasionally, a firm may pay a one-time **special dividend** that is usually much larger than a regular dividend, like Microsoft's $3 dividend in 2004. Figure 16.3 shows the dividends paid by General Motors (GM) from 1983 to 2008. In addition to regular dividends, GM paid special dividends in December 1997 and again in May 1999 (associated with spinoffs of subsidiaries, discussed further in Section 16.6).

While GM raised its dividends throughout the 1980s, it cut its dividends during the recession in the early 1990s. GM raised its dividends again in the late 1990s but was forced to cut its dividends again in early 2006 and suspend them altogether in July 2008 in response to financial difficulties.

Accounting Implications. Dividends are a cash outflow for the firm. From an accounting perspective, dividends generally reduce the firm's current (or accumulated) retained earnings. In some cases, dividends are attributed to other accounting sources, such as paid-in capital or the liquidation of assets. In this case, the dividend is known as a **return of capital** or a **liquidating dividend**. Although the source of the funds makes little difference to a firm or to investors directly, there is a difference in tax treatment: a return of capital is taxed as a capital gain rather than as a dividend for the investor.

FIGURE 16.3

Dividend History for GM Stock, 1983–2008

Until suspending its dividends in July 2008, GM had paid a regular dividend each quarter since 1983. GM paid additional special dividends in December 1997 and May 1999, and had a 2-for-1 stock split in March 1989. GM ultimately filed for bankruptcy in June of 2009.

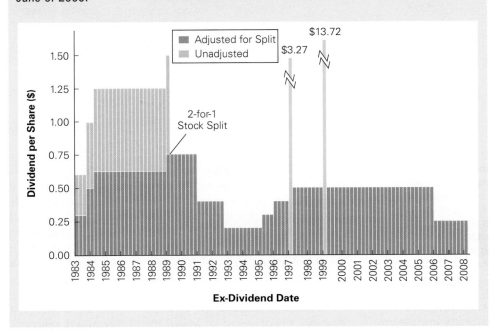

Share Repurchases

An alternative way to pay cash to investors is through a share repurchase or buyback. In this kind of transaction, the firm uses cash to buy shares of its own outstanding stock. These shares are generally held in the corporate treasury, and they can be resold if the company needs to raise money in the future. We now examine three possible transaction types for a share repurchase.

open market repurchase
The repurchasing by a firm of its own shares by buying them on the open market over time.

Open Market Repurchase. With an **open market repurchase**, the most common way that firms repurchase shares, a firm announces its intention to buy its own shares on the open market and then proceeds to do so over time, just as any other investor. The firm may take a year or more to buy the shares, and it is not obligated to repurchase the full amount it originally stated. Also, the firm must not buy its shares in a way that might appear to manipulate the price. For example, both the Toronto Stock Exchange (TSX) and the U.S. Securities and Exchange Commission (SEC) guidelines recommend that the firm not purchase more than 25% of the average daily trading volume in its shares on a single day, nor make purchases at the market open or within 30 minutes of the close of trade.[2]

---

[2]SEC Rule 10b-18, introduced in 1983, defines guidelines for open market share repurchases in the United States. *The TSX Company Manual*, Part VI, Section 629 defines the guidelines for such repurchases in Canada.

While open market share repurchases represent about 95% of all repurchase transactions,[3] other methods are available to a firm that wants to buy back its stock. These methods are used when a firm wishes to repurchase a substantial portion of its shares, often as part of a recapitalization.

Tender Offer. A firm can repurchase shares through a **tender offer** in which it offers to buy shares at a prespecified price during a short time period, generally within 20 days. The price is usually set at a substantial premium (10%–20% is typical) to the current market price. The offer often depends on shareholders tendering a sufficient number of shares. If shareholders do not tender enough shares, the firm may cancel the offer and no buyback occurs.

A related method is the **Dutch auction** share repurchase, in which the firm lists different prices at which it is prepared to buy shares, and shareholders in turn indicate how many shares they are willing to sell at each price. The firm then pays the lowest price at which it can buy back its desired number of shares.

Targeted Repurchase. A firm may also purchase shares directly from a major shareholder in a **targeted repurchase**. In this case, the purchase price is negotiated directly with the seller. A targeted repurchase may occur if a major shareholder desires to sell a large number of shares but the market for the shares is not sufficiently liquid to sustain such a large sale without severely affecting the price. Under these circumstances, the shareholder may be willing to sell shares back to the firm at a discount to the current market price. Alternatively, targeted repurchases may be used if a major shareholder is threatening to take over the firm and remove its management. In a repurchasing tactic known as **greenmail**, the firm may decide to eliminate the threat by buying out the shareholder—often at a large premium over the current market price.

> **tender offer** A public announcement by a firm of an offer to all existing security holders to buy back a specified amount of outstanding securities at a prespecified price over a short time period, generally 20 days.
>
> **Dutch auction** A share repurchase method in which shareholders indicate how many shares they are willing to sell at different prices. The firm then pays the lowest price at which it can buy back its desired number of shares.
>
> **targeted repurchase** The repurchasing of shares by a firm directly from a specific shareholder; the purchase price is negotiated directly with the seller.
>
> **greenmail** A firm's avoidance of a threat of takeover and removal of its management by a major shareholder by buying out the shareholder, often at a large premium over the current market price.

Concept Check

1. How is a stock's ex-dividend date determined, and what is its significance?
2. What is an open-market share repurchase?

16.2 Dividends Versus Share Repurchases in a Perfect Capital Market

If a corporation decides to pay cash to shareholders, it can do so through either dividend payments or share repurchases. How do firms choose between these alternatives? In this section, we show that in the perfect capital markets setting of Modigliani and Miller, the method of payment does not matter.

Consider the case of Genron Corporation, a hypothetical firm. Genron has $20 million in excess cash and no debt. The firm expects to generate additional free cash flows of $48 million per year in subsequent years. If Genron's unlevered cost of capital is 12%, then the enterprise value of its ongoing operations is as follows:

$$\text{Enterprise Value} = PV(\text{Future } FCF) = \frac{\$48 \text{ million}}{12\%} = \$400 \text{ million}$$

Including the cash, Genron's total market value is $420 million.

---

[3]G. Grullon and D. Ikenberry, "What Do We Know About Stock Repurchases?," *Journal of Applied Corporate Finance* 13 (1) (2000): 31–51.

Genron's board is meeting to decide how to pay out its $20 million in excess cash to shareholders. The board is considering three options:

1. Use the $20 million to pay a $2 cash dividend for each of Genron's 10 million outstanding shares.
2. Repurchase shares instead of paying a dividend.
3. Raise additional cash to pay an even larger dividend today and in the future.

Will the amount of the current dividend affect Genron's share price? Which policy would shareholders prefer?

To provide a baseline for our discussion of payout policy, we will analyze the consequences of each of these three alternative policies in the next section and compare them in a setting of perfect capital markets. We will also explore how market imperfections such as taxes and transaction costs affect payout policy.

Alternative Policy 1: Pay a Dividend with Excess Cash

Suppose the board opts for the first alternative and uses all excess cash to pay a dividend. With 10 million shares outstanding, Genron will be able to pay a $2 dividend immediately. Because the firm expects to generate future free cash flows of $48 million per year, it anticipates paying a dividend of $4.80 per share each year thereafter. The board declares the dividend and sets the record date as December 14, so that the ex-dividend date is December 12. To determine the impact of this decision, let's compute Genron's share price just before and after the stock goes ex-dividend.

Recall from Chapter 9 and the Valuation Principle that the fair price for the shares is the present value of the expected dividends, given Genron's equity cost of capital. Because Genron has no debt, its equity cost of capital equals its unlevered cost of capital of 12%. Just before the ex-dividend date, the stock is said to trade **cum-dividend** ("with the dividend") because anyone who buys the stock will be entitled to the dividend. In this case,

cum-dividend
A modifier indicating that the stock is trading before the ex-dividend date, entitling anyone who buys the stock to the dividend.

$$P_{cum} = \text{Current Dividend} + PV(\text{Future Dividends}) = 2 + \frac{4.80}{0.12} = 2 + 40 = \$42$$

After the stock goes ex-dividend, new buyers will not receive the current dividend. At this point, the share price will reflect only the dividends in subsequent years:

$$P_{ex} = PV(\text{Future Dividends}) = \frac{4.80}{0.12} = \$40$$

The share price will drop on the ex-dividend date, December 12, from $42 to $40. The amount of the price drop is equal to the amount of the current dividend, $2. We can also determine this change in the share price using the market value balance sheet:

	December 11 (Cum-Dividend)	December 12 (Ex-Dividend)
Cash	$20,000,000	$0
Other assets	$400,000,000	$400,000,000
Total market value of assets	$420,000,000	$400,000,000
Shares	10,000,000	10,000,000
Share price	$42	$40

As the market value balance sheet shows, the share price falls when a dividend is paid, because the reduction in cash decreases the market value of the firm's assets. Although the stock price falls, holders of Genron stock do not incur a loss overall. Before the dividend, their stock was worth $42. After the dividend, their stock is worth $40 and they hold $2 in cash from the dividend, for a total value of $42. Our analysis of both the stock price and the market value balance sheet leads to the following conclusion:

In a perfect capital market, when a dividend is paid, the share price drops by the amount of the dividend when the stock begins to trade ex-dividend.

Alternative Policy 2: Share Repurchase (No Dividend)

Suppose that Genron does not pay a dividend this year, but instead uses the $20 million to repurchase its shares on the open market. How will the repurchase affect the share price?

With an initial share price of $42, Genron will repurchase $20 million ÷ $42 per share = 0.476 million shares, leaving only 10 million − 0.476 million = 9,523,810 shares outstanding. Once again, we can use Genron's market value balance sheet to analyze this transaction:

	December 11 (Before Repurchase)	December 12 (Ex-Dividend)
Cash	$20,000,000	$0
Other assets	$400,000,000	$400,000,000
Total market value of assets	$420,000,000	$400,000,000
Shares	10,000,000	9,523,810
Share price	$42	$42

In this case, the market value of Genron's assets falls when the company pays out cash, but the number of shares outstanding also falls from 10 million to 9.524 million. The two changes offset each other, so the share price remains the same, at $42.

Genron's Future Dividends. We can also see why the share price does not fall after the share repurchase by considering the effect on Genron's future dividends. In future years, Genron expects to have $48 million in free cash flow, which can be used to pay a dividend of $48 million ÷ 9.524 million shares = $5.04 per share each year. Thus, with a share repurchase, Genron's share price today is as follows:

$$P_{rep} = \frac{5.04}{0.12} = \$42$$

In other words, by not paying a dividend today and repurchasing shares instead, Genron is able to raise its dividends *per share* in the future. The increase in future dividends compensates shareholders for the dividend they give up today. This example illustrates the following general conclusion about share repurchases:

In perfect capital markets, an open market share repurchase has no effect on the stock price, and the stock price is the same as the cum-dividend price if a dividend were paid instead.

Investor Preferences. Would an investor prefer that Genron issue a dividend or repurchase its stock? Both policies lead to the same *initial* share price of $42. But is there a difference in shareholder value *after* the transaction? Consider an investor who currently holds 2000 shares of Genron stock. Assuming the investor does not trade the stock, the investor's holdings after a dividend or share repurchase are as follows:

Dividend	Repurchase
$40 × 2000 = $80,000 stock	$42 × 2000 = $84,000 stock
$2 × 2000 = $4000 cash	

In either case, the value of the investor's portfolio is $84,000 immediately after the transaction. The only difference is the distribution between cash and stock holdings. Thus, it might seem the investor would prefer one approach or the other depending on whether she needs the cash.

But if Genron repurchases shares and the investor wants cash, she can raise cash by selling shares. For example, she can sell 95 shares to raise 95 × $42 per share = $3990 in cash. She will then hold 1905 shares, or 1905 × $42 = $80,010 in stock. Thus, in the case of a share repurchase, by selling shares an investor can create a *homemade dividend.*

Similarly, if Genron pays a dividend and the investor does not want the cash, she can use the $4000 proceeds of the dividend to purchase 100 additional shares at the ex-dividend share price of $40 per share. As a result, she will hold 2100 shares, worth 2100 × $40 = $84,000. In fact, many firms allow investors to register for a dividend reinvestment program, or *DRIP*, that automatically reinvests any dividends into new shares of the stock.

We summarize these two cases below:

Dividend + Buy 100 Shares	Repurchase + Sell 95 Shares
$40 × 2100 = $84,000 stock	$42 × 1905 = $80,010 stock
	$42 × 95 = $3990 cash

By selling shares or reinvesting dividends, the investor can create any combination of cash and stock desired. As a result, the investor is indifferent between the various payout methods the firm might employ:

> *In perfect capital markets, investors are indifferent between the firm distributing funds via dividends versus share repurchases. By reinvesting dividends or selling shares, investors can replicate either payout method on their own.*

Alternative Policy 3: High Dividend (Equity Issue)

Let's look at a third possibility for Genron. Suppose the board wishes to pay an even larger dividend than $2 per share right now. Is that possible and, if so, will the higher dividend make shareholders better off?

Genron plans to pay $48 million in dividends starting next year. Suppose the firm wants to start paying that amount today. Because it has only $20 million in cash today, Genron needs an additional $28 million to pay the larger dividend now. It could raise cash by scaling back its investments. But if the investments have positive NPV, reducing them would lower the firm's value. An alternative way to raise more cash is to borrow money or sell new shares. Let's consider an equity issue. Given a current share price of $42, Genron could raise $28 million by selling $28 million ÷ $42 per share = 0.67 million shares. Because this equity issue will increase Genron's total number of shares outstanding to 10.67 million, the amount of the dividend per share each year will be as follows:

$$\frac{\$48 \text{ million}}{10.67 \text{ million shares}} = \$4.50 \text{ per share}$$

Under this new policy, Genron's cum-dividend share price is:

$$P_{cum} = 4.50 + \frac{4.50}{0.12} = 4.50 + 37.50 = \$42$$

As in the previous examples, the initial share value is unchanged by this policy, and increasing the dividend has no benefit to shareholders.

EXAMPLE 16.1

Homemade Dividends

Problem

Suppose Genron does not adopt the third alternative policy and instead pays a $2 dividend per share today. Show how an investor holding 2000 shares could create a homemade dividend of $4.50 per share × 2000 shares = $9000 per year on her own.

Solution

▶ **Plan**

If Genron pays a $2 dividend, the investor receives $4000 in cash and holds the rest in stock. She can raise $5000 in additional cash by selling 125 shares at $40 per share just after the dividend is paid.

▶ **Execute**

The investor creates her $9000 this year by collecting the $4000 dividend and then selling 125 shares at $40 per share. In future years, Genron will pay a dividend of $4.80 per share. Because she will own 2000 − 125 = 1875 shares, the investor will receive dividends of 1875 × $4.80 = $9000 per year from then on.

▶ **Evaluate**

Again, the policy that the firm chooses is irrelevant—the investor can transact in the market to create a homemade dividend policy that suits her preferences.

Modigliani and Miller and Dividend Policy Irrelevance

In our analysis, we considered three possible dividend policies for the firm: (1) pay out all cash as a dividend, (2) pay no dividend and use the cash instead to repurchase shares, or (3) issue equity to finance a larger dividend. These policies are illustrated in Table 16.1.

TABLE 16.1			Dividend Paid ($ per share)			
		Initial Share Price	Year 0	Year 1	Year 2	...
Genron's Dividends per Share Each Year Under the Three Alternative Policies	Policy 1	$42.00	2.00	4.80	4.80	...
	Policy 2	$42.00	0	5.04	5.04	...
	Policy 3	$42.00	4.50	4.50	4.50	...

Table 16.1 shows an important tradeoff: If Genron pays a higher *current* dividend per share, it will pay lower *future* dividends per share. For example, if the firm raises the current dividend by issuing equity, it will have more shares and therefore smaller free cash flows per share to pay dividends in the future. If the firm lowers the current dividend and repurchases its shares, it will have fewer shares in the future, so it will be able to pay a higher dividend per share. The net effect of this tradeoff is to leave the total present value of all future dividends, and hence the current share price, unchanged at $42.

The logic of this section matches that in our discussion of capital structure in Chapter 15. There, we explained that in perfect capital markets, buying and selling equity and debt are zero-*NPV* transactions that do not affect firm value. Moreover, any choice of leverage by a firm could be replicated by investors using homemade leverage. As a result, the firm's choice of capital structure is irrelevant. Here, we have established the same principle for a firm's choice of a dividend. Regardless of the amount of cash the firm has on hand, it can pay a smaller dividend (and use the remaining cash to repurchase shares) or a larger dividend (by selling equity to raise cash). Because buying or selling shares is a zero-*NPV* transaction, such transactions have no effect on the initial share price. Furthermore, shareholders can create a homemade dividend of any size by buying or selling shares themselves.

M&M Dividend Irrelevance proposition The proposition that, in perfect capital markets, holding fixed the investment policy of a firm, the firm's choice of dividend policy is irrelevant and does not affect the initial share price.

Modigliani and Miller developed this idea in another influential paper published in 1961.[4] As with their result on capital structure, it went against the conventional wisdom that dividend policy could change a firm's value and make its shareholders better off even absent market imperfections. We state here their important proposition:

M&M Dividend Irrelevance proposition: *In perfect capital markets, holding fixed the investment policy of a firm, the firm's choice of dividend policy is irrelevant and does not affect the initial share price.*

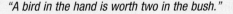

Common Mistake   **The Bird in the Hand Fallacy**

"A bird in the hand is worth two in the bush."

The bird in the hand hypothesis states that firms choosing to pay higher current dividends will enjoy higher stock prices because shareholders prefer current dividends to future ones (with the same present value). According to this view, alternative policy 3 above would lead to the highest share price for Genron.

This view is a misconception. Modigliani and Miller showed that with perfect capital markets, shareholders can generate an equivalent homemade dividend at any time by selling shares. Thus, the dividend choice of the firm should not matter.

---

[4]See M. Modigliani and M. Miller, "Dividend Policy, Growth, and the Valuation of Shares," *Journal of Business* 34 (4) (1961): 411–433. See also J.B. Williams, *The Theory of Investment Value* (Cambridge, MA: Harvard University Press, 1938).

Dividend Policy with Perfect Capital Markets

The examples in this section illustrate the idea that by using share repurchases or equity issues a firm can easily alter its dividend payments. Because these transactions do not alter the value of the firm, neither does dividend policy.

This result may at first seem to contradict the idea that the price of a share should equal the present value of its future dividends. As our examples have shown, however, a firm's choice of dividend today affects the dividends it can afford to pay in the future in an offsetting fashion. Thus, although dividends *do* determine share prices, a firm's choice of dividend policy does not.

As Modigliani and Miller made clear, the value of a firm ultimately derives from its underlying free cash flows. A firm's free cash flows determine the level of payouts that it can make to its investors. In a perfect capital market, whether these payouts are made through dividends or share repurchases does not matter. Of course, in reality capital markets are not perfect. As with capital structure, it is the imperfections in capital markets that should determine the firm's payout policy. The main imperfection we will discuss is taxes: repurchases and dividends have different tax implications and investors also face different tax rates. In addition, when managers have information investors do not, payout policy decisions can help signal that information. We start with taxes.

Concept Check

3. Explain the misconception that when a firm repurchases its own shares, the price rises due to the decrease in the supply of shares outstanding.

4. In a perfect capital market, how important is the firm's decision to pay dividends versus repurchase shares?

16.3 The Tax Disadvantage of Dividends

As with capital structure, taxes are an important market imperfection that influence a firm's decision to pay dividends or repurchase shares.

Taxes on Dividends and Capital Gains

Shareholders typically must pay taxes on the dividends they receive. They must also pay capital gains taxes when they sell their shares. Historically, the taxes applied to dividend income have been higher than taxes applied to capital gains income. The actual difference in tax rates on dividend income and capital gains income has changed over the years in both Canada and the United States. (Since 2003, they have been equal in the United States, but the law specifying these rates was set to expire in 2012.) Table 16.2 shows the marginal tax rates in Canada on personal income for a taxpayer in the top tax bracket in 2010. In many provinces and territories, the tax rates on capital gains income are quite close to the tax rates on dividend income. However, taxes on capital gains income are deferred until the stock is sold; thus the present value of the taxes on capital gains is usually substantially less than the taxes on dividends (that must be paid in the year of the dividend payment).

Do taxes affect investors' preferences for dividends versus share repurchases? When a firm pays a dividend, shareholders are taxed according to the dividend tax rate. If the firm repurchases shares instead, and shareholders sell shares to create a homemade dividend, the homemade dividend will be taxed according to the capital gains tax rate. If dividends are taxed at a higher rate than capital gains, shareholders will prefer share repurchases to dividends. Recent changes to the tax code in the United States have equalized the tax rates on dividends and capital gains. It is probably

TABLE 16.2		Province	Marginal Rate on Regular Income	Marginal Rate on Capital Gains Income	Marginal Rate on Dividend Income
2010 Canadian Personal Income Tax Rates for a Taxpayer in the Top Tax Bracket		B.C.	43.70%	21.85%	21.45%
		Alberta	39.00%	19.50%	15.88%
		Sask.	44.00%	22.00%	21.64%
		Manitoba	46.40%	23.20%	25.10%
		Ontario	46.41%	23.20%	26.57%
		Quebec	48.22%	24.11%	30.68%
		N.B.	43.30%	21.65%	19.47%
		N.S.	50.00%	25.00%	33.58%
		P.E.I.	47.37%	23.69%	25.70%
		Nfld.	43.39%	21.70%	21.76%
		N.W.T.	43.05%	21.53%	19.81%
		Yukon	42.40%	21.20%	18.80%
		Nunavut	40.50%	20.25%	23.64%

Sources: Canada Revenue Agency, Ernst & Young 2010 personal tax calculator.

not coincidental that Microsoft started paying dividends shortly after these changes. Nonetheless, because long-term investors can defer the capital gains tax until they sell, *there is still a tax advantage for share repurchases over dividends.*

Not all countries tax dividends at a higher rate than capital gains. Figure 16.4 shows the dividend and capital gains tax rates for different countries. In Chile, for example, capital gains are taxed at a 45% rate, while dividends are taxed at 35%. A similar tax preference for dividends exists in Australia, Denmark, Finland, and Brazil.

Optimal Dividend Policy with Taxes

When the tax rate on dividends exceeds the tax rate on capital gains, shareholders will pay lower taxes if a firm uses share repurchases for all payouts rather than dividends. This tax savings will increase the value of a firm that uses share repurchases rather than dividends. We can also express the tax savings in terms of a firm's equity cost of capital. Firms that use dividends will have to pay a higher pre-tax return (and thus a higher equity cost of capital) to offer their investors the same after-tax return as firms that use share repurchases. As a result, the optimal dividend policy when the dividend tax rate exceeds the capital gain tax rate is to *pay no dividends at all.*

FIGURE 16.4

Dividend and Capital Gains Tax Rates Around the World

The capital gains tax rate (blue bar) and dividend tax rate (orange bar) for different countries are shown. A missing bar indicates that the distribution is exempt from taxation in that country. Whereas most countries tax dividends at rates greater than or equal to the rate for capital gains, thus providing a tax preference for share repurchases, some countries, such as Chile, tax capital gains at a higher rate. Several countries, including Singapore, Mexico, India, and Hong Kong, do not tax either.

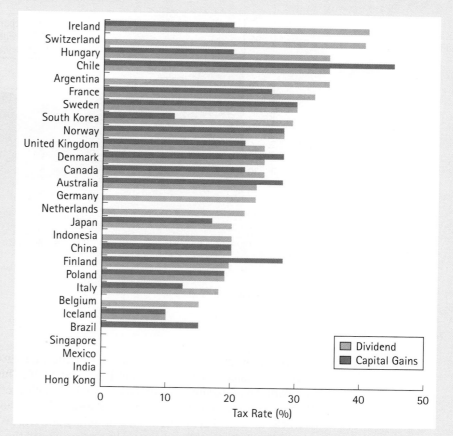

Source: OECD 2007, www.oecd.org; capital gains rates based on marginal rate for an investor with $100,000 in income exceeding any initial exemption.

Dividends in Practice. While firms do still pay dividends, substantial evidence shows that many firms have recognized their tax disadvantage. For example, prior to 1980, most U.S. firms used dividends exclusively to distribute cash to shareholders (see Figure 16.5). But by 2006, only about 25% of U.S. firms relied on dividends. At the same time, 30% of all U.S. firms (and more than half of firms making payouts to shareholders) used share repurchases exclusively or in combination with dividends.

We see a more dramatic trend if we consider the relative magnitudes of both forms of corporate payouts. Figure 16.6 shows the relative importance of share repurchases as a proportion of total payouts to shareholders of U.S. firms. Although dividends accounted for more than 80% of corporate payouts until the early 1980s, the importance

FIGURE 16.5

The Rise of Repurchases

This figure shows the percentage of U.S. firms each year that made payouts to shareholders. The shaded regions show the firms that used dividends exclusively (yellow), repurchases exclusively (blue), or both (green). Note the trend away from the use of dividends over time, with firms that made payouts showing a greater reliance on share repurchases, together with a sharp decrease in the percentage of firms making payouts of any kind.

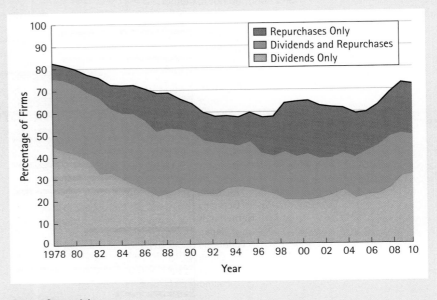

Source: Compustat.

of share repurchases grew dramatically in the mid-1980s. Repurchase activity slows during recessions (see 1990–91, 2001–02, and 2009). This fact highlights the flexibility companies have to adjust repurchase payouts as their profits fluctuate. At the same time, there is a strong expectation that companies will maintain dividend payouts unless they are near distress. Partly due to this flexibility and the tax advantages, by the end of the 1990s distributions through repurchasing surpassed those through dividends.

While the data shown in Figures 16.5 and 16.6 are for U.S. companies, a similar pattern is found for Canadian firms. Luke Schmidt, in his 2006 master's thesis at the University of Saskatchewan, found that in 1995 the dollar amount of dividends was more than four times the dollar amount of share repurchases by Canadian corporations. The dollar amount of dividends fluctuated and rose slightly over time; however, the dollar amount of repurchases grew substantially and eclipsed dividends by 2004.[5]

While this evidence is indicative of the growing importance of share repurchases as a part of firms' payout policies, it also shows that dividends remain a key form of payouts to shareholders. The fact that firms continue to issue dividends despite their tax disadvantage is often referred to as the **dividend puzzle**.[6] Table 16.3 summarizes

dividend puzzle A firm's continuing issuance of dividends despite their tax disadvantage.

---

[5]See L. Schmidt, "Credibility of Corporate Announcements and Market Reaction: Evidence from Canadian Share Repurchase Programs," master's thesis, University of Saskatchewan, 2006.

[6]See F. Black, "The Dividend Puzzle," *Journal of Portfolio Management* 2 (1976): 5–8.

FIGURE 16.6

The Changing Composition of Shareholder Payouts

This figure shows the value of share repurchases as a percentage of total payouts to shareholders (dividends and repurchases). Although initially small, the total dollar amount of share repurchases has grown faster than dividends, so that by the late 1990s share repurchases surpassed dividends to become the largest form of corporate payouts for U.S. industrial firms.

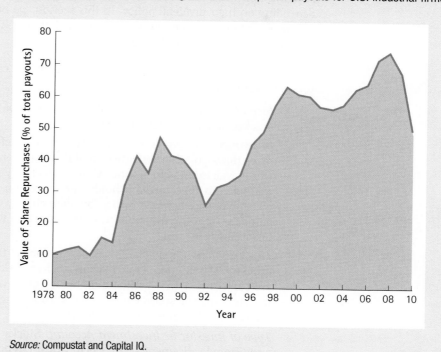

Source: Compustat and Capital IQ.

dividends versus repurchases, highlighting the differences between the two ways to distribute cash to shareholders. In the next section, we consider some factors that may mitigate this tax disadvantage. In Section 16.5, we examine alternative motivations for using dividends based on differences in information between managers and investors.

TABLE 16.3

Summary of Dividends Versus Repurchases

	Dividends	Share Repurchases
How cash is distributed to shareholders	Cash payment made on a per-share basis to all shareholders	Shares repurchased
Participation	Involuntary (everyone with a share receives a dividend)	Voluntary (shareholders choose whether to sell their shares)
Taxation for ordinary investors	Taxed less than regular income (see Table 16.2, as relative rates vary by province or territory)	Taxed as capital gains, which are taxed less than regular income (see Table 16.2, as relative rates vary by province or territory)
Effect on share price	Share price drops by the amount of the dividend	Share price is unaffected as long as shares are repurchased at a fair (market) price

Tax Differences Across Investors

Even though many investors have a tax preference for share repurchases rather than dividends, the strength of that preference depends on the difference between the dividend tax rate and the capital gains tax rate that they face. Tax rates vary by income, by jurisdiction, and by whether the stock is held in a retirement account or tax-free savings account. Because of these differences, firms may attract different groups of investors, depending on their dividend policy. In this section, we highlight the differences in the tax treatment of dividends across investors and discuss how that leads different groups of investors to prefer different payout policies.

Dividend Tax Rate Factors. Tax rates on dividends and capital gains differ across investors for a variety of reasons:

> *Income Level.* Investors with different levels of income fall into different tax brackets and face different tax rates.
>
> *Investment Horizon.* Long-term investors can defer the payment of capital gains taxes (lowering their effective capital gains tax rate even further). An investor who never intends to sell her shares effectively pays no capital gains tax. For example, an investor who holds her shares for a long time period and then plans to donate her shares to a Canadian charity will not have to pay any capital gains tax, and the full amount of the donation will be eligible for a charitable tax credit.
>
> *Tax Jurisdiction.* Canadian investors are subject to provincial taxes that differ by province. U.S. investors in Canadian stocks and Canadian investors in U.S. stocks are subject to a 15% withholding tax for dividends they receive. Other foreign investors may be subject to a higher withholding tax on dividends they receive. There is no similar withholding for capital gains.
>
> *Type of Investor or Investment Account.* Stocks held by individual investors in a registered retirement savings plan (RRSP), registered retirement income fund (RRIF), or tax-free savings account (TFSA) are not subject to taxes on dividends or capital gains.[7] Similarly, stocks held through pension funds or nonprofit endowment funds are not subject to dividend or capital gains taxes. Corporations that hold stocks are able to exclude 100% of dividends they receive from corporate taxes, but are unable to exclude capital gains.

As a result of their different tax rates, these investors have varying preferences regarding dividends:

1. Long-term investors are more heavily taxed on dividends, so they would prefer share repurchases to dividend payments.

2. One-year investors (in some provinces), pension funds, and other non-taxed investors have no tax preference for share repurchases over dividends; they would prefer a payout policy that most closely matches their cash needs. For example, a non-taxed investor who desires current income would prefer high dividends so as to avoid the brokerage fees and other transaction costs of selling the stock.

3. Corporations enjoy a tax *advantage* associated with dividends due to the 100% exclusion allowance. For this reason, a corporation that chooses to invest its cash will prefer to hold stocks with high-dividend yields.

---

[7]While taxes may be owed when the money is withdrawn from the retirement account, these taxes do not depend on whether the money came from dividends or capital gains.

TABLE 16.4	Investor Group	Dividend Policy Preference	Proportion of Investors
Differing Dividend Policy Preferences Across Investor Groups	Individual investors	Tax disadvantage for dividends Prefer share repurchase	~53%
	Institutions, pension funds, retirement accounts	No tax preference Prefer dividend policy that matches income needs	~46%
	Corporations	Tax advantage for dividends	~1%

Source: Proportions based on Federal Reserve Flow of Funds Accounts, 2007.

clientele effects The effects of the tax preferences of a firm's investor clientele on the firm's dividend policy.

Clientele Effects. Table 16.4 summarizes the different preferences across investor groups. These differences in tax preferences create **clientele effects**, in which the dividend policy of a firm is optimized for the tax preference of its investor clientele.

Individual investors (particularly those in the highest tax brackets who tend to make investments) likely have a preference for stocks that have capital gains instead of dividends. These investors are more likely to be long-term investors; thus, capital gains have an advantage over dividends for two reasons. First, capital gains taxes can be deferred compared with taxes on dividends that must be paid immediately. Second, no action needs to be taken to reinvest capital gains, whereas with dividends there may be transaction costs associated with using the cash from dividends to purchase additional shares of stock.

Tax-free investors have no particular preference for stocks with capital gains or dividends unless there are specific cash-flow needs that a payment policy matches. For most pension funds that must pay regular payments to their pensioners, there may be a preference for dividend-paying stock, because the cash flows from dividends help reduce transaction costs that would otherwise be paid if the pension fund sold shares to generate the same cash flows.

Evidence supports the existence of tax clienteles. For example, Franklin Allen and Roni Michaely[8] report that, in 1996, individual investors held 54% of all stocks by market value, yet received only 35% of all dividends paid, indicating that individuals tend to hold stocks with low-dividend yields. Of course, the fact that high-tax investors receive any dividends at all implies that the clienteles are not perfect—dividend taxes are not the only determinants of investors' portfolios.

5. Under what conditions will investors have a tax preference for share repurchases rather than dividends?

6. What is the dividend puzzle?

16.4 Payout Versus Retention of Cash

We have thus far considered only one aspect of a firm's payout policy (shown in Figure 16.1): the choice between paying dividends and repurchasing shares. But how should a firm decide the amount it should pay out to shareholders and the amount it should retain?

---

[8]Franklin Allen and Roni Michaely, "Payout Policy," in *Handbook of the Economics of Finance: Corporate Finance*, vol. 1A, G.M. Constantinides, M. Harris, and R.M. Stulz, eds. (Amsterdam, The Netherlands: Elsevier, 2003).

To answer this question, we must first consider what the firm will do with cash that it retains. It can invest the cash in new projects or in financial instruments. In the next section, we will examine these options in the context of perfect capital markets.

Retaining Cash with Perfect Capital Markets

Once a firm has taken all positive-*NPV* projects, it is left with the question of whether to retain any remaining cash or distribute it to shareholders. If the firm retains the cash, it can hold the cash in the bank or use it to purchase financial assets. The firm can then pay the money to shareholders at a future time or invest it when positive-*NPV* investment opportunities become available.

What are the advantages and disadvantages of retaining cash and investing in financial securities? In perfect capital markets, buying and selling securities is a zero-*NPV* transaction, so it should not affect the firm's value. On their own, shareholders can make any investment a firm makes if the firm pays out the cash. Thus, it should not be surprising that, with perfect capital markets, the retention versus payout decision—just like the dividend versus share repurchase decision—is irrelevant.

EXAMPLE 16.2

Payout Decisions in a Perfect Capital Market

Problem

Yellowknife Mining has $100,000 in excess cash. Yellowknife is considering investing the cash in one-year treasury bills paying 6% interest, and then using the cash to pay a dividend next year. Alternatively, the firm can pay a dividend immediately, and shareholders can invest the cash on their own. In a perfect capital market, which option would shareholders prefer?

Solution

▶ **Plan**

We need to compare what shareholders would receive from an immediate dividend ($100,000) to the present value of what they would receive in one year if Yellowknife invested the cash.

▶ **Execute**

If Yellowknife retains the cash, at the end of one year the company would be able to pay a dividend of $100,000 × (1.06) = $106,000. Note that this payoff is the same as if shareholders had invested the $100,000 in treasury bills themselves. In other words, the present value of this future dividend is exactly $106,000 ÷ (1.06) = $100,000, which is the same as the $100,000 shareholders would receive from an immediate dividend. Thus, shareholders are indifferent about whether the firm pays the dividend immediately or retains the cash.

▶ **Evaluate**

Because Yellowknife is not doing anything that the investors could not have done on their own, it does not create any value by retaining the cash and investing it for the shareholders versus simply paying it to them immediately. As we showed with Genron in Example 16.1, if Yellowknife retains the cash, but investors prefer to have the income today, they could sell $100,000 worth of shares.

M&M Payout Irrelevance proposition The proposition that, in perfect capital markets, if a firm invests excess cash flows in financial securities, the firm's choice of payout versus retention is irrelevant and does not affect the initial value of the firm.

As Example 16.2 illustrates, there is no difference for shareholders if the firm pays the cash immediately or retains the cash and pays it out at a future date. This example provides yet another illustration of Modigliani and Miller's fundamental insight regarding financial policy irrelevance in perfect capital markets:

> **M&M Payout Irrelevance proposition:** *In perfect capital markets, if a firm invests excess cash flows in financial securities, the firm's choice of payout versus retention is irrelevant and does not affect the initial value of the firm.*

Retaining Cash with Imperfect Capital Markets

Based on M&M's payout irrelevance proposition, it is clear that the decision of whether to retain cash depends on market imperfections, which we now address.

Taxes and Cash Retention. The Yellowknife example assumed perfect capital markets and so ignored the effect of taxes. How would our result change with taxes?

EXAMPLE 16.3

Retaining Cash with Corporate Taxes

Problem

Recall Yellowknife Mining from Example 16.2. Suppose Yellowknife must pay corporate taxes at a 35% rate on the interest it will earn from the one-year treasury bills paying 6% interest. Would pension fund investors (who do not pay taxes on their investment income) prefer that Yellowknife use its excess cash to pay the $100,000 dividend immediately or retain the cash for one year?

Solution

▶ **Plan**

As in Example 16.2, the comparison is between what shareholders could generate on their own and what shareholders will receive if Yellowknife retains and invests the funds for them. The key question then is this: What is the difference between the after-tax return that Yellowknife can earn and distribute to shareholders versus the pension fund's tax-free return on investing the $100,000?

▶ **Execute**

Because the pension fund investors do not pay taxes on investment income, the results from Example 16.2 still hold: they would get $100,000, invest it, and earn 6% to receive a total of $106,000 in one year.

If Yellowknife retains the cash for one year, it will earn the following after-tax return on the treasury bills:

$$6\% \times (1 - 0.35) = 3.90\%$$

Thus, at the end of the year Yellowknife will pay a dividend of $100,000 \times (1.039) = $103,900.

▶ **Evaluate**

This amount is less than the $106,000 the investors would have earned if they had invested the $100,000 in treasury bills themselves. Because Yellowknife must pay corporate taxes on the interest it earns, there is a tax disadvantage to retaining cash. Pension fund investors will therefore prefer that Yellowknife pays the dividend now.

As Example 16.3 shows, corporate taxes make it costly for a firm to retain excess cash. This effect is the very same effect we identified in Chapter 15 with regard to leverage: when a firm pays interest, it receives a tax deduction for that interest, whereas when a firm receives interest, it owes taxes on the interest. Cash can be thought of as equivalent to *negative* leverage, so the tax advantage of leverage implies a tax disadvantage to holding cash.

Investor Tax Adjustments. The decision to pay out versus retain cash may also affect the taxes paid by shareholders. Although pension and retirement fund investments are tax exempt, individual investors must pay taxes on interest, dividends, and capital gains if their investments are held outside RRSPs, RRIFs or TFSAs. How do investor taxes affect the tax disadvantage of retaining cash?

Because the dividend tax will be paid whether the firm pays the cash immediately or retains the cash and pays the interest over time, the dividend tax rate does not affect the cost of retaining cash. However, when a firm retains cash, it must pay corporate tax on the interest it earns. In addition, the investor will owe capital gains tax on the increased value of the firm. In essence, the interest on retained cash is taxed twice. If the firm paid the cash to its shareholders instead, they could invest it and be taxed only once on the interest that they earn. The cost of retaining cash therefore depends on the combined effect of the corporate and capital gains taxes, compared to the single tax on interest income. Under most tax regimes there remains a substantial tax *disadvantage* for the firm to retaining excess cash even after adjusting for investor taxes.

Issuance and Distress Costs. If there is a tax disadvantage to retaining cash, why do some firms accumulate large cash balances? Generally, they retain cash balances to cover potential future cash shortfalls. For example, if there is a reasonable likelihood that future earnings will be insufficient to fund future positive-*NPV* investment opportunities, a firm may start accumulating cash to make up the difference. This motivation is especially relevant for firms that may need to fund large-scale research and development projects or large acquisitions.

The advantage of holding cash to cover future potential cash needs is that this strategy allows a firm to avoid the transaction costs of raising new capital (through new debt or equity issues). As we discussed in Chapters 13 and 14, the direct costs of issuance range from 1% to 3% for debt issues and from 3.5% to 7% for equity issues. There can also be substantial indirect costs of raising capital due to the agency and adverse selection (lemons) costs discussed in Chapter 15. A firm must therefore balance the tax costs of holding cash with the potential benefits of not having to raise external funds in the future. Firms with very volatile earnings may also build up cash reserves to enable them to weather temporary periods of operating losses. By holding sufficient cash, these firms can avoid financial distress and its associated costs.

Agency Costs of Retaining Cash. There is no benefit to shareholders when a firm holds cash above and beyond its future investment or liquidity needs. In fact, in addition to the tax cost, there are likely to be agency costs of equity associated with having too much cash in the firm. As discussed in Chapter 15, when firms have excessive cash, managers may use the funds inefficiently by continuing money-losing pet projects, paying excessive executive perquisites (perks), being less diligent in their managing of the firm (shirking), or overpaying for acquisitions. Leverage is one way to reduce a firm's excess cash; dividends and share repurchases perform a similar role by taking cash out of the firm.

Thus, paying out excess cash through dividends or share repurchases can boost the stock price by reducing managers' ability and temptation to waste resources. For example, on April 23, 2004, Value Line announced it would use its accumulated cash to pay a special dividend of $17.50 per share. Value Line's stock increased by roughly $10 on the announcement of its special dividend, very likely due to the perceived tax benefits and reduced agency costs that would result from the transaction.

EXAMPLE 16.4

Cutting Negative-*NPV* Growth

Problem

TarSand Oil is an all-equity firm with 100 million shares outstanding. TarSand has $150 million in cash and expects future free cash flows of $65 million per year. Management plans to use the cash to expand the firm's operations, which will in turn increase future free cash flows to $72.8 million per year. If the cost of capital of TarSand's investments is 10%, how would a decision to use the cash for a share repurchase rather than the expansion change the share price?

Solution

▶ **Plan**

We can use the perpetuity formula to value TarSand under the two scenarios. The repurchase will take place at market prices, so the repurchase itself will have no effect on TarSand's share price. The main question is whether spending $150 million now (instead of repurchasing) to increase cash flows by $7.8 million per year is a positive-*NPV* project.

▶ **Execute**

Investment option:

Using the perpetuity formula, if TarSand invests the $150 million to expand, its market value will be $72.8 million ÷ 10% = $728 million, or $7.28 per share with 100 million shares outstanding.

Repurchase option:

If TarSand does not expand, the value of its future free cash flows will be $65 million ÷ 10% = $650 million. Adding the $150 million in cash it currently has, TarSand's market value is $800 million, or $8.00 per share.

    If TarSand repurchases shares, there will be no change to the share price: the company will repurchase $150 million ÷ $8.00 per share = 18.75 million shares, so it will have assets worth $650 million with 81.25 million shares outstanding, for a share price of $650 million ÷ 81.25 million shares = $8.00 per share.

    In this case, cutting investment and growth to fund a share repurchase increases the share price by $0.72 per share ($8.00 − $7.28).

▶ **Evaluate**

The share price is higher with the repurchase because the alternative of expansion has a negative *NPV:* it costs $150 million but increases future free cash flows by only $7.8 million per year forever, for an *NPV* of:

$$-\$150 \text{ million} + \$7.8 \text{ million}/10\% = -\$72 \text{ million, or } -\$0.72 \text{ per share}$$

Thus, by avoiding the expansion, the repurchase keeps the shares from suffering the $0.72 loss.

TABLE 16.5	Company	Cash ($ billions)	Market Capitalization (%)
	Toyota	41.7	37.5
Selected Firms with Large Cash Balances	Cisco	39.1	29.5
	China Mobile	39.0	19.1
	Microsoft	37.2	16.4
	Google	30.1	19.4
	Apple	23.2	9.8
	Oracle	18.5	15.1
	Intel	18.3	15.1
	Johnson & Johnson	18.0	12.0
	Pfizer	17.3	14.4

Source: Yahoo! Finance.

Ultimately, firms should choose to retain cash for the same reasons they would use low leverage—to preserve financial slack for future growth opportunities and to avoid financial distress costs. These needs must be balanced against the tax disadvantage of holding cash and the agency cost of wasteful investment. It is not surprising, then, that high-tech and biotechnology firms, which typically choose to use little debt, also tend to retain and accumulate large amounts of cash. Table 16.5 contains a list of selected firms with large cash balances.

As with capital structure decisions, however, even though a firm's board of directors sets its payout policy, managers whose incentives may differ from those of shareholders may heavily influence that policy. Managers may prefer to retain and maintain control over the firm's cash rather than pay it out. The retained cash can be used to fund investments that are costly for shareholders but have benefits for managers (e.g., pet projects and excessive salaries), or it can simply be held as a means to reduce leverage and the risk of financial distress that could threaten managers' job security. According to the managerial entrenchment theory of payout policy, managers pay out cash only when pressured to do so by the firm's investors.

Concept Check

7. Is there an advantage for a firm to retain its cash instead of paying it out to shareholders in perfect capital markets?

8. How do corporate taxes affect the decision of a firm to retain excess cash?

16.5 Signalling with Payout Policy

One market imperfection that we have not yet considered is asymmetric information. When managers have better information than investors regarding the future prospects of the firm, managers' payout decisions may signal this information. In this section, we look at managers' motivations when setting a firm's payout policy, and we evaluate what these decisions may communicate to investors.

Dividend Smoothing

Firms can change dividends at any time, but in practice they vary the sizes of their dividends relatively infrequently. For example, General Motors (GM) has changed the amount of its regular dividend only eight times over a 20-year period. Yet during that same period, GM's earnings varied widely, as shown in Figure 16.7.

FIGURE 16.7

GM's Earnings and Dividends per Share, 1985–2008

Compared with GM's earnings, its dividend payments have remained relatively stable. (Data adjusted for splits; earnings exclude extraordinary items.)

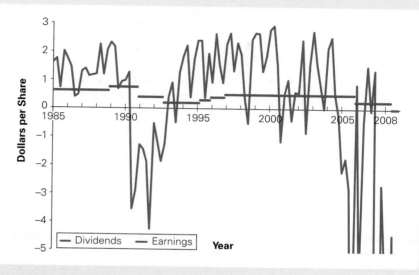

Sources: Compustat and Capital IQ.

dividend smoothing
The practice of maintaining relatively constant dividends.

The pattern seen with GM is typical of most firms that pay dividends. Firms adjust dividends relatively infrequently, and dividends are much less volatile than earnings. This practice of maintaining relatively constant dividends is called **dividend smoothing**. Firms also increase dividends much more frequently than they cut them. For example, from 1971 to 2001, only 5.4% of dividend changes were decreases.[9] In a classic survey of corporate executives, John Lintner suggested that these observations resulted from (1) management's belief that investors prefer stable dividends with sustained growth, and (2) management's desire to maintain a long-term target level of dividends as a fraction of earnings.[10] Thus, firms raise their dividends only when they perceive a long-term sustainable increase in the expected level of future earnings, and cut them only as a last resort. While this is perhaps a good description of how firms *do* set their dividends, as we have shown in this chapter there is no clear reason why firms *should* smooth their dividends. One explanation is that it contributes to signalling with dividends, as discussed in the next section.

[9]Franklin Allen and Roni Michaely, "Payout Policy," in *Handbook of the Economics of Finance: Corporate Finance*, vol. 1A, G.M. Constantinides, M. Harris, and R.M. Stulz, eds. (Amsterdam, The Netherlands: Elsevier, 2003).

[10]J. Lintner, "Distribution of Incomes of Corporations Among Dividends, Retained Earnings and Taxes," *American Economic Review* 46 (1956): 97–113.

How can firms keep dividends smooth as earnings vary? As we have already discussed, firms can maintain almost any level of dividend in the short run by adjusting the number of shares they repurchase or issue and the amount of cash they retain. However, due to the tax and transaction costs of funding a dividend with new equity issues, managers do not wish to commit to a dividend that the firm cannot afford to pay out of regular earnings. For this reason, firms generally set dividends at a level they expect to be able to maintain based on the firm's earnings prospects.

Dividend Signalling

If firms smooth dividends, the firm's dividend choice will contain information regarding management's expectations of future earnings.

1. When a firm increases its dividend, it sends a positive signal to investors that management expects to be able to afford the higher dividend for the foreseeable future.

2. When managers cut the dividend, it may signal that they have given up hope that earnings will rebound in the near term and so need to reduce the dividend to save cash.

dividend signalling hypothesis The idea that dividend changes reflect managers' views about a firm's future earnings prospects.

The idea that dividend changes reflect managers' views about a firm's future earnings prospects is called the **dividend signalling hypothesis**.

While an increase of a firm's dividend may signal management's optimism regarding its future cash flows, it might also signal a lack of investment opportunities. For example, Microsoft's move to initiate dividends in 2003 was largely seen as a result of its declining growth prospects as opposed to a signal about its increased future profitability.[11] Conversely, a firm might cut its dividend to exploit new positive-*NPV* investment opportunities. In this case, the dividend decrease might lead to a positive—rather than negative—stock price reaction (see the box below about Royal & SunAlliance's dividend cut). In general, we must interpret dividends as a signal in the context of the type of new information managers are likely to have.

Royal & SunAlliance's Dividend Cut

In some quarters, Julian Hance must have seemed like a heretic. On November 8, 2001, the finance director of Royal & SunAlliance, a U.K.-based insurance group with £12.6 billion ($20.2 billion) in annual revenue, did the unthinkable—he announced that he would cut the firm's dividend.

Many observers gasped at the decision. Surely, they argued, cutting the dividend was a sign of weakness. Didn't companies cut their dividend only when profits were falling?

Quite the contrary, countered Hance. With insurance premiums rising around the world, particularly following the World Trade Center tragedy, Royal & SunAlliance believed that its industry offered excellent growth opportunities.

"The outlook for business in 2002 and beyond makes a compelling case for reinvesting capital in the business rather than returning it to shareholders," explains Hance.

The stock market agreed with him, sending Royal & SunAlliance's shares up 5% following its dividend news. "Cutting the dividend is a positive move," observed Matthew Wright, an insurance analyst at Credit Lyonnais. "It shows the company expects future profitability to be good."

Source: Justin Wood, http://CFOEurope.com, December 2001.

---

[11]See "An End to Growth?," *The Economist* (July 22, 2004): 61.

INTERVIEW WITH
John Connors

John Connors was senior vice-president and chief financial officer of Microsoft. He retired in 2005 and is now a partner at Ignition Partners, a Seattle venture capital firm.

QUESTION: *Microsoft declared a dividend for the first time in 2003. What goes into the decision of a company to initiate a dividend?*

ANSWER: Microsoft was in a unique position. The company had never paid a dividend and was facing shareholder pressure to do something with its $60 billion cash buildup. The company considered five key questions in developing its distribution strategy:

1. Can the company sustain payment of a cash dividend in perpetuity and increase the dividend over time? Microsoft was confident it could meet that commitment and raise the dividend in the future.

2. Is a cash dividend a better return to stockholders than a stock buyback program? These are capital structure decisions: Do we want to reduce our shares outstanding? Is our stock attractively priced for a buyback, or do we want to distribute the cash as a dividend? Microsoft had plenty of capacity to issue a dividend *and* continue a buyback program.

3. What is the tax effect of a cash dividend versus a buyback to the corporation and to shareholders? From a tax perspective, to shareholders it was largely a neutral decision in Microsoft's case.

4. What is the psychological impact on investors, and how does it fit the story of the stock for investors? This is a more qualitative factor. A regular ongoing dividend put Microsoft on a path to becoming an attractive investment for income investors.

5. What are the public relations implications of a dividend program? Investors don't look to Microsoft to hold cash but to be a leader in software development and provide equity growth. So they viewed the dividend program favourably.

QUESTION: *How does a company decide whether to increase its dividend, have a special dividend, or repurchase its stock to return capital to investors?*

ANSWER: The decision to increase the dividend is a function of cash flow projections. Are you confident that you have adequate cash flow to sustain this and future increases? Once you increase the dividend, investors expect future increases as well. Some companies establish explicit criteria for dividend increases. In my experience as a CFO, the analytic framework involves a set of relative comparables. What are the dividend payouts and dividend yields of the market in general and of your peer group, and where are we relative to them? We talk to significant investors and consider what is best for increasing shareholder value long-term.

A special dividend is a very efficient form of cash distribution that generally involves a nonrecurring situation, such as the sale of a business division or a cash award from a legal situation. Also, companies without a comprehensive distribution strategy use special dividends to reduce large cash accumulations. For Microsoft, the 2004 special dividend and announcement of the stock dividend and stock buyback program resolved the issue of what to do with all the cash and clarified our direction going forward.

QUESTION: *What other factors go into dividend decisions?*

ANSWER: Powerful finance and accounting tools help us to make better and broader business decisions. But these decisions involve as much psychology and market thinking as math. You have to consider non-quantifiable factors such as the psychology of investors. Not long ago, everyone wanted growth stocks; no one wanted dividend-paying stocks. Now dividend stocks are in vogue. You must also take into account your industry and what the competition is doing. In many tech companies, employee ownership in the form of options programs represents a fairly significant percentage of fully diluted shares. Dividend distributions reduce the value of options.*

At the end of the day, you want to be sure that your cash distribution strategy helps your overall story with investors.

Discussion Questions

1. How does Connors's comment about investor preferences for growth versus dividend-paying stocks fit within the framework of the dividend signalling discussion?

2. Does such a preference argument fit the efficient markets hypothesis discussed in Chapter 9?

---

*We discuss options in Chapter 20. The key point here is that employee stock options increase in value when the stock price goes up, but as we learned in this chapter, a dividend reduces the stock price on the ex-dividend day.

Signalling and Share Repurchases

Share repurchases, similar to dividends, may also signal managers' information to the market. However, several important differences distinguish share repurchases and dividends:

1. Managers are much less committed to share repurchases than to dividend payments. As we noted earlier, when firms announce authorization for an open market share repurchase, they generally announce the maximum amount they plan to spend on repurchases. The actual amount spent, however, may be far less. Also, it may take several years to complete the share repurchase.

2. Firms do not smooth their repurchase activity from year to year, as they do with dividends. Thus, announcing a share repurchase today does not necessarily represent a long-term commitment to repurchase shares. In this regard, share repurchases may be less of a signal than dividends are about future earnings of a firm.

3. The cost of a share repurchase depends on the market price of the stock. If managers believe the stock is currently overvalued, a share repurchase will be costly to the firm. That is, buying the stock at its current (overvalued) price is a negative-*NPV* investment. By contrast, repurchasing shares when managers perceive the stock to be undervalued is a positive-*NPV* investment. Managers will clearly be more likely to repurchase shares if they believe the stock to be undervalued.

Thus, share repurchases may signal that managers believe the firm to be undervalued (or at least not severely overvalued). Share repurchases are a credible signal that the shares are underpriced, because if they are overpriced a share repurchase is costly for current shareholders (and particularly for long-term investors who do not sell during the share repurchase). If investors believe that managers have better information regarding the firm's prospects and act on behalf of current shareholders, then investors will react favourably to share repurchase announcements.

In a 2004 survey, 87% of CFOs agreed that firms should repurchase shares when their stock price is a good value relative to its true value,[12] implicitly indicating that most CFOs believe that they should act in the interests of the long-term shareholders. Thus, if investors believe that managers have better information regarding the firm's prospects than they do, then investors should react favourably to share repurchase announcements. Indeed they do: the average market price reaction to the announcement of an open market share repurchase program is about 3% (with the size of the reaction increasing with the portion of shares outstanding sought).[13]

Concept Check

9. What possible signals does a firm give when it cuts its dividend?

10. Would managers be more likely to repurchase shares if they believe the stock is under- or overvalued?

[12]A. Brav, J. Graham, C. Harvey, and R. Michaely, "Payout Policy in the 21st Century," *Journal of Financial Economics* 77 (3) (2005): 483–527.

[13]See D. Ikenberry, J. Lakonishok, and T. Vermaelen, "Market Underreaction to Open Market Share Repurchases," *Journal of Financial Economics* 39 (2) (1995): 181–208.

16.6 Stock Dividends, Splits, and Spinoffs

In this chapter, we have focused on a firm's decision to pay cash to its shareholders. But a firm can pay another type of dividend that does not involve cash: a stock dividend. In this case, each shareholder who owns the stock before it goes ex-dividend receives additional shares of stock of the firm itself (a stock split) or of a subsidiary (a spinoff). Here, we briefly review these two types of transactions.

Stock Dividends and Splits

stock dividend (stock split) The issuing by a company of a dividend in shares of stock rather than cash to its shareholders.

In a **stock dividend**, or **stock split**, the company issues additional shares rather than cash to its shareholders. If a company declares a 10% stock dividend, each shareholder will receive 1 new share of stock for every 10 shares already owned. Stock dividends of 50% or higher are generally referred to as stock splits. For example, with a 50% stock dividend, each shareholder will receive 1 new share for every 2 shares owned. Because a holder of 2 shares will end up holding 3 shares, this transaction is also called a 3:2 ("3-for-2") stock split. Similarly, a 100% stock dividend is equivalent to a 2:1 stock split.

With a stock dividend, a firm does not pay out any cash to shareholders. As a result, the total market value of the firm's assets and liabilities, and therefore of its equity, is unchanged. The only thing that is different is the number of shares outstanding. The stock price will therefore fall, because the same total equity value is now divided over a larger number of shares.

Berkshire Hathaway's A and B Shares

Many managers split their stock to keep the price affordable for small investors, making it easier for them to buy and sell the stock. Warren Buffett, chairman and chief executive of Berkshire Hathaway, disagrees. As he commented in Berkshire's 1983 annual report, "We are often asked why Berkshire does not split its stock . . . we want [shareholders] who think of themselves as business owners with the intention of staying a long time. And, we want those who keep their eyes focused on business results, not market prices." In its 40-year history, Berkshire Hathaway has never split its stock.

As a result of Berkshire Hathaway's strong performance and the lack of stock splits, the stock price climbed. By 1996, it exceeded $30,000 per share. Because this price was much too expensive for some small investors, several financial intermediaries created unit investment trusts whose only investment was Berkshire shares. (Unit investment trusts are similar to mutual funds, but their investment portfolio is fixed.) Investors could buy smaller interests in these trusts, effectively owning Berkshire stock with a much lower initial investment.

In response, Buffett announced in February 1996 the creation of a second class of Berkshire Hathaway stock, the Class B shares. Each owner of the original shares (now called Class A shares) was offered the opportunity to convert each A share into 30 B shares. "We're giving shareholders a do-it-yourself split, if they care to do it," Buffett said. Through the B shares, investors could own Berkshire stock with a smaller investment, and they would not have to pay the extra transaction costs required to buy stock through the unit trusts.

Meanwhile the value of the A shares has continued to do well. After reaching a peak of $148,000 in late 2007 and dropping to below $75,000 in March 2009 (at the bottom of the financial crisis), the price of one share of Berkshire Hathaway Class A shares was more than $128,000 per share in March of 2011.*

---

*We should note that Buffett's logic for not splitting the stock is a bit puzzling. It is unclear why allowing the stock price to rise to a very high level would attract the kind of investors Buffett wanted. If indeed this was the motivation for Buffett's policies, he could have obtained the desired results much earlier by simply doing a reverse stock split.

Unlike cash dividends, stock dividends are not taxed. Thus, from both the firm's and shareholders' perspectives, there is no real consequence to a stock dividend. The number of shares is proportionally increased and the price per share is proportionally reduced so that there is no change in value.

Stock Splits and Share Price. Why, then, do companies pay stock dividends or split their stock? The typical motivation for a stock split is to keep the share price in a range thought to be attractive to small investors. Stocks generally trade in lots of 100 shares, and in any case do not trade in units of less than 1 share. As a result, if the share price rises significantly, it might be difficult for small investors to afford 1 share, let alone 100. Making the stock more attractive to small investors can increase the demand for and the liquidity of the stock, which may in turn boost the stock price. On average, announcements of stock splits are associated with a 2% increase in the stock price.[14]

Most firms use splits to keep their share prices from exceeding $100. From 1990 to 2000, Cisco Systems split its stock nine times, so that 1 share purchased at the IPO split into 288 shares. Had it not split, Cisco's share price at the time of its last split in March 2000 would have been $288 \times \$72.19$, or $20,790.72.

Firms also do not want their stock prices to fall too low. First, a stock price that is very low raises transaction costs for investors. For example, one tick (the minimum spread between the bid and ask price) is $0.01 (for the NYSE and NASDAQ exchanges and for TSX stocks with stock prices greater than $0.50). In percentage terms, the tick size is larger for stocks with a low price than for stocks with a high price. Also, many exchanges require stocks to maintain a minimum price to remain listed on an exchange. (For example, the NYSE and NASDAQ require listed firms to maintain a price of at least $1 per share. The TSX has no such requirement.)

If the price of the stock falls too low, a company can engage in a reverse split and reduce the number of shares outstanding. For example, in a 1 for 10 reverse split, every 10 shares of stock are replaced with a single share. As a result, the share price increases tenfold. Reverse splits became necessary for many dot-coms after the dot-com bust in 2000.

Through a combination of splits and reverse splits, firms on major exchanges (like the NYSE and TSX) can keep their share prices in any range they desire. Almost all firms on major exchanges have stock prices below $100 per share, with most firms' prices being between $5 and $60 per share. In January 2010, the average price for shares traded on the TSX was about $11.62 per share. For exchanges like the TSX Venture Exchange, it is more common for firms to have lower stock prices, including many with prices below $1 per share. In January 2010, the average price for shares traded on the TSX Venture Exchange was about $0.46 per share.

Spinoffs

spinoff The situation in which a firm sells a subsidiary by distributing the subsidiary's shares as a non-cash special dividend.

Rather than pay a dividend using cash or shares of its own stock, a firm can also distribute shares of a subsidiary in a transaction referred to as a **spinoff**, where non-cash special dividends are used to spin off assets or a subsidiary as a separate company. For example, after selling 10% of Northern Electric stock in an IPO in 1973, and further reductions in ownership over the years, Bell Canada Enterprises (BCE) announced it would spin off its 35% ownership of Nortel in May 2000. The

---

[14]S. Nayak and N. Prabhala, "Disentangling the Dividend Information in Splits: A Decomposition Using Conditional Event-Study Methods," *Review of Financial Studies* 14 (4) (2001): 1083–1116.

spinoff was accomplished through a special dividend in which each BCE shareholder received 1.570386 shares of Nortel per share of BCE owned. After receiving the Nortel shares, BCE shareholders could trade them separately from the shares of the parent firm.

Alternatively, BCE could have sold the shares of Nortel and distributed the cash to shareholders as a cash dividend. The transaction BCE chose offers two advantages over that strategy: (1) it avoids the transaction costs associated with such a sale, and (2) the special dividend is not taxed as a cash distribution. Instead, BCE shareholders who received Nortel shares are liable for capital gains tax only at the time they sell the Nortel shares.

Concept Check

11. What is the difference between a stock dividend and a stock split?

12. What are some advantages of a spinoff as opposed to selling the division and distributing the cash?

16.7 Advice for the Financial Manager

Payout policy decisions are related to the capital structure decisions we discussed in Chapter 15. The amount of debt the firm has determines how much cash flow is pre-committed to debt holders as interest payments and how much will be left for possible distribution to shareholders or reinvestment in the firm. Further, distributing capital to shareholders reduces the equity left in the firm, increasing leverage. When setting the amount of the payout to shareholders, the financial manager needs to carefully weigh the future investment plans of the firm. If the manager expects to make large investment expenditures in the near future, then it does not make sense to make a large distribution to shareholders only to quickly return to the markets for new capital financing (either through debt or additional equity as discussed in Chapters 13 and 14). Overall, as a financial manager you should consider the following when making payout policy decisions:

1. For a given payout amount, try to maximize the after-tax payout to the shareholders. Repurchases and dividends are often taxed differently, and one can have an advantage over the other.

2. Repurchases and special dividends are useful for making large, infrequent distributions to shareholders. Neither implies any expectation of repeated payouts.

3. Starting and increasing a regular dividend is seen by shareholders as an implicit commitment to maintain this level of regular payout indefinitely. Set only regular dividend levels that you are confident the firm can maintain.

4. Because regular dividends are seen as an implicit commitment, they send a stronger signal of financial strength to shareholders than do infrequent distributions such as repurchases. However, this signal comes with a cost, because regular payouts reduce a firm's financial flexibility.

5. Be mindful of future investment plans. There are transaction costs associated with both distributions and raising new capital, so it is expensive to make a large distribution and then raise capital to fund a project. It would be better to make a smaller distribution and fund the project internally.

MyFinanceLab

Here is what you should know after reading this chapter. MyFinanceLab will help you identify what you know, and where to go when you need to practice.

Key Points	Terms	Online Practice Opportunities
16.1 Distributions to Shareholders ▶ When a firm wants to distribute cash to its shareholders, it can pay a cash dividend or it can repurchase shares. ▶ Most companies pay regular, quarterly dividends. Sometimes firms announce one-time, special dividends. ▶ Firms repurchase shares using an open market repurchase, a tender offer, a Dutch auction repurchase, or a targeted repurchase. ▶ On the declaration date, firms announce that they will pay dividends to all shareholders of record on the record date. The ex-dividend date is the first day on which the stock trades without the right to an upcoming dividend; it is usually two trading days prior to the record date. Dividend cheques are mailed on the payment date.	declaration date, p. 540 Dutch auction, p. 543 ex-dividend date, p. 541 greenmail, p. 543 liquidating dividend, p. 541 open market repurchase, p. 542 payable date (distribution date), p. 541 payout policy, p. 540 record date, p. 541 return of capital, p. 541 special dividend, p. 541 targeted repurchase, p. 543 tender offer, p. 543	MyFinanceLab Study Plan 16.1
16.2 Dividends Versus Share Repurchases in a Perfect Capital Market ▶ In perfect capital markets, the stock price falls by the amount of the dividend when a dividend is paid. An open market share repurchase has no effect on the stock price, and the stock price is the same as the cum-dividend price if a dividend were paid instead. ▶ The Modigliani & Miller dividend irrelevance proposition states that, in perfect capital markets, holding fixed the investment policy of a firm, the firm's choice of dividend policy is irrelevant and does not affect the initial share price. ▶ In reality, capital markets are not perfect, and market imperfections affect firm dividend policy.	cum-dividend, p. 544 M&M Dividend Irrelevance proposition, p. 548	MyFinanceLab Study Plan 16.2
16.3 The Tax Disadvantage of Dividends ▶ Taxes are an important market friction that affects dividend policy. ▶ Considering taxes as the only market imperfection, when the tax rate on dividends exceeds the tax rate on capital gains, the optimal dividend policy is for firms to pay no dividends. Firms should use share repurchases for all payouts.	clientele effects, p. 555 dividend puzzle, p. 552	MyFinanceLab Study Plan 16.3

▶ The tax impact of a dividend varies across investors for several reasons, including income level, investment horizon, tax jurisdiction, and type of investment account.

▶ Different investor taxes create clientele effects, with the result that the dividend policy of a firm is made to suit the tax preference of its investor clientele.

16.4 Payout Versus Retention of Cash

▶ The Modigliani & Miller payout policy irrelevance proposition says that, in perfect capital markets, if a firm invests excess cash flows in financial securities, the firm's choice of payout versus retention is irrelevant and does not affect the initial share price.

▶ Corporate taxes make it costly for a firm to retain excess cash. Even after adjusting for investor taxes, retaining excess cash is a substantial tax disadvantage for a firm.

▶ Even though there is a tax disadvantage to retaining cash, some firms accumulate cash balances. Cash balances help firms minimize the transaction costs of raising new capital when they have future potential cash needs. However, there is no benefit to shareholders from firms holding cash in excess of future investment needs.

▶ In addition to the tax disadvantage of holding cash, agency costs may arise, as managers may be tempted to shirk or to spend excess cash on inefficient investments and perks. Without pressure from shareholders, managers may choose to hoard cash to spend in this way or as a means of reducing a firm's leverage and increasing their job security.

▶ Dividends and share repurchases help minimize the principal-agent problems of shirking and wasteful spending when a firm has excess cash.

M&M Payout Irrelevance proposition, p. 557

MyFinanceLab Study Plan 16.4

16.5 Signalling with Payout Policy

▶ Firms typically maintain relatively constant dividends. This practice is called dividend smoothing.

▶ The idea that dividend changes reflect managers' views about a firm's future earnings prospects is called the dividend signalling hypothesis.

▶ Managers usually increase dividends only when they are confident the firm will be able to afford higher dividends for the foreseeable future.

dividend signalling hypothesis, p. 562
dividend smoothing, p. 561

MyFinanceLab Study Plan 16.5

▶ When managers cut the dividend, it may signal that they have lost hope that earnings will improve.

▶ Share repurchases may be used to signal positive information, as repurchases are more attractive if management believes the stock is undervalued at its current price.

16.6 Signalling with Payout Policy

▶ In a stock dividend or a stock split, a company distributes additional shares rather than cash to shareholders.

▶ With a stock dividend, shareholders receive either additional shares of stock of the firm itself (a stock split) or shares of a subsidiary (a spinoff). The stock price generally falls proportionally with the size of the split.

spinoff, p. 565
stock dividend (stock split), p. 566

MyFinanceLab
Study Plan 16.6

Review Questions

1. What are the ways in which a corporation can distribute cash to its shareholders?

2. Describe the different mechanisms available to a firm for the repurchase of shares.

3. Without taxes or any other imperfections, why doesn't it matter how the firm distributes cash?

4. What kind of payout preference do tax codes typically create?

5. What are the advantages and disadvantages of retaining excess cash?

6. How can dividends and repurchases be used to signal managers' information about their firms' prospects?

7. Explain under which conditions an increase in the dividend payment can be interpreted as a signal of good news or bad news.

8. Why is an announcement of a share repurchase considered a positive signal?

9. Why do managers split their firms' stock?

Problems

All problems in this chapter are available in MyFinanceLab. An asterisk (*) indicates problems with a higher level of difficulty.

Distributions to Shareholders

1. ABC Corporation announced that it would pay a dividend to all shareholders of record as of Monday, April 3, 2006. It takes three business days after a purchase for the new owners of a share of stock to be registered.

   a. What was the date of the ex-dividend day?

   b. When was the last day an investor could have purchased ABC stock and still received the dividend payment?

2. RFC Corp. has announced a $1 dividend. If RFC's last price cum-dividend is $50, what should its first ex-dividend price be (assuming perfect capital markets)?

3. ECB Co. has 1 million shares outstanding selling at $20 per share. It plans to repurchase 100,000 shares at the market price. What will its market capitalization be after the repurchase? What will its stock price be?

4. KMS corporation has assets of $500 million, $50 million of which are cash. It has debt of $200 million. If KMS repurchases $20 million of its stock,

   a. what changes will occur on its balance sheet?

   b. what will its new leverage ratio be?

5. Suppose that KMS in Problem 4 decides to initiate a dividend instead, but it wants the present value of payout to be the same $20 million. If its cost of equity capital is 10%, to what amount per year in perpetuity should it commit?

Dividends Versus Share Repurchases in a Perfect Capital Market

6. EJH Company has a market capitalization of $1 billion and 20 million shares outstanding. It plans to distribute $100 million through an open market repurchase. Assuming perfect capital markets,

   a. what will the price per share of EJH be right before the repurchase?

   b. how many shares will be repurchased?

   c. what will the price per share of EJH be right after the repurchase?

7. Natsam Corporation has $250 million of excess cash. The firm has no debt and 500 million shares outstanding with a current market price of $15 per share. Natsam's board has decided to pay out this cash as a one-time dividend.

   a. What is the ex-dividend price of a share in a perfect capital market?

   b. If the board instead decided to use the cash to do a one-time share repurchase, in a perfect capital market, what is the price of the shares once the repurchase is complete?

   c. In a perfect capital market, which policy in part (a) or (b) makes investors in the firm better off?

8. Suppose the board of Natsam Corporation decided to do the share repurchase in Problem 7(b), but you as an investor would have preferred to receive a dividend payment. How can you leave yourself in the same position as if the board had elected to make the dividend payment instead?

The Tax Disadvantage of Dividends

9. The HNH Corporation will pay a constant dividend of $2 per share, per year, in perpetuity. Assume all investors pay a 20% tax on dividends and that there is no capital gains tax. The cost of capital for investing in HNH stock is 12%.

   a. What is the price of a share of HNH stock?

   b. Assume that management makes a surprise announcement that HNH will no longer pay dividends but will use the cash to repurchase stock instead. What is the price of a share of HNH stock now?

10. You purchased CSH stock for $40 and it is now selling for $50. The company has announced that it plans a $10 special dividend.
    a. Assuming 2008 tax rates, if you sell the stock or wait and receive the dividend, will you have different after-tax income?
    b. If the capital gains tax rate is 20% and the dividend tax rate is 40%, what is the difference between the two options in part (a)?

Payout Versus Retention of Cash

 11. Assume perfect capital markets. Kay Industries currently has $100 million invested in short-term treasury bills paying 7%, and it pays out the interest payments on these securities as a dividend. The board is considering selling the treasury bills and paying out the proceeds as a one-time dividend payment.
    a. If the board went ahead with this plan, what would happen to the value of Kay stock upon the announcement of a change in policy?
    b. What would happen to the value of Kay stock on the ex-dividend date of the one-time dividend?
    c. Given these price reactions, will this decision benefit investors?

 12. Redo Problem 11, but assume that Kay must pay a corporate tax rate of 35%, and that investors pay no taxes.

 13. Redo Problem 11, but assume that investors pay a 15% tax on dividends but no capital gains taxes, and that Kay does not pay corporate taxes.

Signalling with Payout Policy

Use the following information to answer Problems 14 through 18:

AMC Corporation currently has an enterprise value of $400 million and $100 million in excess cash. The firm has 10 million shares outstanding and no debt. Suppose AMC uses its excess cash to repurchase shares. After the share repurchase, news will come out that will change AMC's enterprise value to either $600 million or $200 million.

 14. What is AMC's share price prior to the share repurchase?

 15. What would AMC's share price be after the repurchase if its enterprise value goes up? What would AMC's share price be after the repurchase if its enterprise value declines?

 *16. Suppose AMC waits until after the news comes out to do the share repurchase. What would AMC's share price be after the repurchase if its enterprise value goes up? What would AMC's share price be after the repurchase if its enterprise value declines?

 17. Suppose AMC management expects good news to come out. Based on your answers to Problems 15 and 16, if management wants to maximize AMC's ultimate share price, will they undertake the repurchase before or after the news comes out? When would management undertake the repurchase if they expect bad news to come out?

 *18. Given your answers to Problem 17, what effect would you expect an announcement of a share repurchase to have on the stock price? Why?

Stock Dividends, Splits, and Spinoffs

19. FCF Co. has 20,000 shares outstanding and a total market value of $1 million, $300,000 of which is debt and the other $700,000 is equity. It is planning a 10% stock dividend.

a. What is the stock price before the dividend, and what will it be after the dividend?

b. If an investor owns 1000 shares before the dividend, what will the total value of her investment in FCF be before and after the dividend?

 20. Suppose the stock of Host Hotels & Resorts is currently trading for $20 per share.

a. If Host issues a 20% stock dividend, what would its new share price be?

b. If Host does a 3:2 stock split, what would its new share price be?

21. If Berkshire Hathaway's A shares are trading at $120,000, what split ratio would it need to bring its stock price down to $50?

22. After the market close on May 11, 2001, Adaptec, Inc., distributed a dividend of shares of the stock of its software division, Roxio, Inc. Each Adaptec shareholder received a 0.1646 share of Roxio stock per share of Adaptec stock owned. At the time, Adaptec stock was trading at a price of $10.55 per share (cum-dividend), and Roxio's share price was $14.23 per share. In a perfect market, what would Adaptec's ex-dividend share price be after this transaction?

Data Case

In your role as a consultant at a wealth management firm, you have been assigned a very powerful client who holds one million shares of Amazon.com purchased on February 28, 2006. In researching Amazon, you discovered that the company is holding a large amount of cash, which was surprising because the firm has only relatively recently begun operating at a profit. The client is considering approaching Amazon's board of directors with a plan for half of the cash the firm has accumulated, but can't decide whether a share repurchase or a special dividend would be better. You have been asked to determine which initiative would generate the greater amount of money after taxes, assuming that with a share repurchase your client would keep the same proportion of ownership. Because both dividends and capital gains are taxed at the same rate (15%), your client has assumed that there is no difference between the repurchase and the dividend. To confirm, you need to "run the numbers" for each scenario.

1. Go to the NASDAQ homepage (www.nasdaq.com), enter the symbol for Amazon (AMZN), and click on "Summary Quotes."

   a. Record the current price and the number of shares outstanding.

   b. Click on "Financials" and then select "Balance Sheets." Copy and paste the balance sheet information into Excel.

2. Using one-half of the most recent "Cash and Cash Equivalents" reported on the balance sheet (in thousands of dollars), compute the following:

   a. The number of shares that would be repurchased given the current market price.

   b. The dividend per share that could be paid given the total number of shares outstanding.

3. Go to the Yahoo! Finance website (http://finance.yahoo.com) to obtain the price at which your client purchased the stock on February 28, 2006.

   a. Enter the symbol for Amazon and click on "Get Quotes."

   b. Click on "Historical Prices," enter the date your client purchased the stock as the start date and the end date, and click on "Get Prices." Record the adjusted closing price.

4. Compute the total cash that would be received by your client with the repurchase and the dividend both before taxes and after taxes (see the tax rates in Table 16.2).

5. The calculation in Step 4 reflects your client's immediate cash flow and tax liability, but it does not consider the final payoff for the client after any shares not sold in a repurchase are liquidated. To incorporate this feature, you first decide to see what happens if the client sells all remaining shares of stock immediately after the dividend or the repurchase. Assume that the stock price will fall by the amount of the dividend if a dividend is paid. What are the client's total after-tax cash flows (considering both the payout and the capital gain) under the repurchase of the dividend in this case?

6. Under which program would your client be better off before taxes? Which program would be better after taxes, assuming the remaining shares are sold immediately after the dividend is paid?

PART 6 Integrative Case

This case draws on material from Chapters 15 to 16.

Maria Suarez returned to her office after spending the afternoon meeting with her firm's investment bankers. Suarez was CFO of Midco Industries, a mid-sized manufacturing firm, and she was taking a hard look at its capital structure and payout policy. Suarez felt that Midco was underlevered and potentially not taking full advantage of the tax benefits of debt. Further complicating matters, Midco's institutional investors had been clamouring for either a repurchase or a special dividend.

One possibility floated by Suarez's investment bankers was a "leveraged recap," in which Midco would issue debt and use the proceeds to repurchase shares. Midco Industries has 20 million shares outstanding with a market price of $15 per share and no debt. The firm has had consistently stable earnings and pays a 35% tax rate. Midco's investment bankers proposed that the firm borrow $100 million on a permanent basis through a leveraged recap in which it would use the borrowed funds to repurchase outstanding shares.

As Suarez sat down at her desk, she stared at her notepad. She had written down several questions that she would need to answer before making her decision.

Case Questions

1. What are the tax consequences of the recap?

2. Based only on the tax effects and the Valuation Principle, what will the total value of the firm be after the recap?
   a. How much of the new value will be equity?
   b. How much will be debt?

3. At what price should Midco be able to repurchase its shares?

4. Who benefits from the recap? Who loses?

5. What other costs or benefits of the additional leverage should Midco's managers consider?

6. If Midco's managers decide to issue the debt and distribute the tax shield as a special dividend instead of repurchasing shares, what will the dividend per share be?

PART 7

Financial Planning and Forecasting

Valuation Principle Connection. In Part 7, we turn to the details of running the financial side of a corporation and focus on forecasting and short-term financial management. We begin in Chapter 17 by developing the tools to forecast the cash flows and long-term financing needs of a firm. We then turn our attention to the important decisions a financial manager makes about the short-term financing and investments of the firm. In Chapter 18, we discuss how firms manage their working capital requirements, including accounts receivable, accounts payable, and inventory. In Chapter 19, we explain how firms finance their short-term cash needs.

In a perfect capital market, the Valuation Principle—in particular, the Law of One Price—and the Modigliani and Miller propositions imply that how a firm chooses to manage its short-term financial needs does not affect the value of the firm. In reality, short-term financial policy does matter because of the existence of market frictions. In this part of the book, we identify these frictions and explain how firms set their short-term financial policies.

577

17

Financial Modelling and Pro Forma Analysis

INTERVIEW WITH Dennis Ng,
PhD Student, University of Manitoba

Dennis Ng is a PhD student in finance at the University of Manitoba's I.H. Asper School of Business. His responsibilities include both teaching and research, preparing him for a future career in the academic world. "There is an important relationship between the world of academia and the world of business," Dennis says. "It goes both ways. Academics might study the best practices of certain businesses or generate case studies, and when the cases or results are published, this helps spread the information throughout the business world. It may also be the case that academics come up with new ideas that help businesses improve their methods. The connection between theory and practice tends to be enhanced by the fact that business schools often look for candidates with business experience when hiring new faculty."

After completing his undergraduate studies at the University of Winnipeg, Dennis continued to Queen's University, where he completed his master's degree in economics in 2004. "Many of the concepts used in financial modelling and pro forma analysis have their origins in the academic literature and have been studied extensively by academics," he says. "The effect of a possible expansion on firm value, for instance, relies on the valuation principal introduced by Modigliani and Miller's pioneering academic papers from the 1960s," he continues. "These concepts have been studied and refined by many academics over many years, and have helped inform the decision-making process for countless businesses over that time."

Another aspect of a career in academia is passing on to university students the knowledge gained from the latest research. "Of course, there is the teaching component as well," Dennis explains. "The concepts taught in finance courses give undergraduates the basic skills that they will use in their future careers in the business world; we hear this from our alumni all the time!"

Most decisions a financial manager makes have long-term consequences. For example, in the late 1990s, Airbus managers decided to bet the future of the company on the market for mega-jets, giving the green light to development of the 555-seat A380. Shortly thereafter, Boeing managers bet that airlines would favour improvements in fuel efficiency and gave the go-ahead to the all-composite, technologically advanced 787. The outcomes of these decisions are still playing out today. In this chapter, we will learn how to build a financial model to analyze the consequences of our financial decisions well into the future. In particular, we will use these models to forecast when the firm will need to secure additional external funding and to determine how the decision will affect the value of the firm.

We will start by explaining the goals of forecasting through financial modelling and pro forma analysis, and how this analysis relates to the overall goal of maximizing firm value. Then, we will move to a basic forecasting technique based on projections of the firm's future sales. Next, we will develop an improved approach to forecasting that produces a more realistic financial model of the firm. Finally, we will use our financial model to value the firm under the new business plan and discuss value-increasing versus value-decreasing growth. In doing so, we will see the connection between the role of forecasting, *NPV* analysis, and the Valuation Principle that underlies all of finance.

17.1 Goals of Long-Term Financial Planning

The goal of the financial manager is to maximize the value of the stockholders' stake in the firm. One tool to help with this goal is long-term financial planning and modelling. In the following sections, we will develop specific methods to forecast the financial statements and cash flows for the firm as a whole. For context, in this section we discuss the objectives of long-term planning.

Identify Important Linkages

As you will see in Sections 17.2 and 17.3, when you build a model of the future course of the firm, by necessity you will uncover important linkages between variables—for example, sales, costs, capital investment, and financing. A well-designed spreadsheet model will allow you to examine how a change in your cost structure will affect your future free cash flows, financing needs, and so on. Some links may be obvious, but others are much more difficult to determine without building a forecast of the entire firm's financial statements years into the future. For example, technological improvements leading to reduced costs could allow the firm to reduce prices and sell more product. However, increased production will require more equipment and facilities, and the associated capital expenditures will require financing and create additional depreciation tax shields. None of these links would be easy to see without a careful forecasting model. This is an important outcome of long-term planning, because it allows the financial manager to understand the business and, through that understanding, to increase its value.

Analyze the Impact of Potential Business Plans

Perhaps your firm is planning a big expansion or considering changes in how it manages its inventory. By building a long-term model of your firm's financials, you can examine exactly how such business plans will affect the firm's free cash flows and hence value. In Chapter 8, we developed the tools of capital budgeting, with the goal of deciding whether to invest in a new project. To consider a fundamental change in the firm's business plan, the financial manager models the firm as a whole, rather than just a single project. In Section 17.3, we will analyze the impact of a firm-wide expansion plan, including necessary capital investment, debt financing, changes in free cash flows, and changes in value.

Plan for Future Funding Needs

Building a model for long-term forecasting reveals points in the future at which the firm will need additional external financing—for example, when its retained earnings will not be enough to fund planned capital investment. Identifying the firm's funding needs in advance gives financial managers enough time to plan for them and line up the source of financing that is most advantageous for the firm. In a perfect capital market, this would be unnecessary—you would be able to secure financing instantaneously for any positive-*NPV* project, and the source of financing would have no effect on the firm's value. However, in reality market frictions mean that you need time to issue debt or new equity and, as we learned in Chapter 15, that financing decisions affect firm value. Thus, identifying and planning for these financing decisions far in advance is a valuable exercise.

 Concept Check

1. How does long-term financial planning fit into the goal of the financial manager?
2. What are the three main things that the financial manager can accomplish by building a long-term financial model of the firm?

17.2 Forecasting Financial Statements: The Percent of Sales Method

We will illustrate our discussion of forecasting financial statements via an application: the firm KXS Designs. KXS Designs is a boutique women's fashion house, specializing in affordable fashionable separates, that has its own production facility. KXS Designs is a growing firm, and its financial managers predict that it will need external financing to fuel its growth. In order to predict when KXS will need this financing and the amount the managers will need to secure, we need to prepare a financial model in Excel for KXS that will allow us to produce pro forma income statements and balance sheets. After developing a technique for forecasting, we will turn to the steps involved in preparing the pro forma income statement and balance sheet.

percent of sales method
A forecasting method that assumes that as sales grow, many income statement and balance sheet items will grow, remaining the same percentage of sales.

Percent of Sales Method

A common starting point for forecasting is the *percent of sales method*. The **percent of sales method** assumes that, as sales grow, many income statement and balance sheet items will grow, maintaining the same percentage of sales. For example, Table 17.1

TABLE 17.1

KXS Designs 2011 Income Statement and Balance Sheet

Year	2011	% of Sales
2 Income Statement ($000s)		
3 Sales	74,889	100%
4 Costs Except Depreciation	−58,413	78%
5 EBITDA	16,476	22%
6 Depreciation	−5492	7.333%
7 EBIT	10,984	15%
8 Interest Expense (net)	−306	NM*
9 Pre-tax Income	10,678	14%
10 Income Tax (35%)	−3737	NM
11 Net Income	6941	9%

*NM indicates that representing the item as a percentage of sales is not meaningful.

Year	2011	% of Sales
2 Balance Sheet ($000s)		
3 Assets		
4 Cash and Equivalents	11,982	16%
5 Accounts Receivable	14,229	19%
6 Inventories	14,978	20%
7 Total Current Assets	41,189	55%
8 Property, Plant, and Equipment	49,427	66%
9 Total Assets	90,616	121%
10 Liabilities and Stockholders' Equity		
11 Accounts Payable	11,982	16%
12 Debt	4500	NM
13 Total Liabilities	16,482	NM
14 Stockholders' Equity	74,134	NM
15 Total Liabilities and Equity	90,616	121%

shows that KXS 's costs excluding depreciation were 78% of sales in 2011. There were sales of $74,889. If KXS forecasts that sales will grow by 18% in 2012, then:

- sales will grow to $74,889 \times 1.18 = $88,369.
- costs excluding depreciation will remain at 78% of sales, so costs will be $88,369 \times 0.78 = $68,928 in 2012.[1]

We are essentially assuming that KXS will maintain its profit margins as its sales revenues grow. We proceed by making similar assumptions about working capital items on the balance sheet, such as cash, accounts receivable, inventory, and accounts payable. The far-right column of Table 17.1 shows what percentage of sales each of these items was in 2011. We can use those percentages to forecast part of the balance sheet in 2012. For example, if sales grow to $88,369 as we predict, then our inventory will need to grow to $88,369 \times 0.20 = $17,674 to support those sales.

Some of the items are marked "NM" for "Not Meaningful" in the percentage of sales column. For example, our assets and accounts payables might reasonably be expected to grow in line with sales, but our long-term debt and equity will not naturally grow in line with sales. Instead, the change in equity and debt will reflect choices we make about dividends and net new financing.

Pro Forma Income Statement

Table 17.2 shows KXS's pro forma income statement for 2012, along with how each line was determined. KXS is forecasting 18% growth in sales from 2011 to 2012. In addition to the sales forecast, we require three other details to prepare the pro forma income statement: costs excluding depreciation in 2011 as a percentage of sales, depreciation as a percentage of sales, and the tax rate. KXS's info from Table 17.1 is as follows:

- Costs excluding depreciation were 78% of sales.
- Depreciation was 7% of sales in 2011.
- KXS pays a 35% tax rate.

TABLE 17.2   KXS Designs Pro Forma Income Statement for 2012

1 Year	2011	2012	Calculation
2 Income Statement ($000s)			
3 Sales	74,889	88,369	74,889 × 1.18
4 Costs Except Depreciation	−58,413	−68,928	78% of Sales
5 EBITDA	16,476	19,441	Lines 3 + 4
6 Depreciation	−5492	−6480	7.333% of Sales
7 EBIT	10,984	12,961	Lines 5 + 6
8 Interest Expense (net)	−306	−306	Remains the same
9 Pre-tax Income	10,678	12,655	Lines 7 + 8
10 Income Tax (35%)	−3737	−4429	35% of Line 9
11 Net Income	6941	8226	Lines 9 + 10

---

[1]For ease of exposition, we will base our forecast on a single year, 2011. Companies often take into account averages and trends over several years in forecasting for the future.

The one final assumption we need to make is about our interest expense.[2] We assume for now that it will remain the same as in 2011 because we will determine if our debt needs will change as part of the forecasting process.

Based on our pro forma balance sheet, we are forecasting an increase in net income of $8226 − $6941 = $1285, which represents an 18.5% increase over 2011 net income.[3] We now turn to forecasting the balance sheet to determine whether we will need any new financing in 2012 to pay for our growth. The net income we forecast in Table 17.2 will be one of the inputs to the pro forma balance sheet. The part of that net income not distributed as dividends will add to stockholders' equity on the balance sheet.

EXAMPLE 17.1

Percent of Sales

Problem

KXS has just revised its sales forecast downward. If KXS expects sales to grow by only 10% next year, what are its costs, except for depreciation, projected to be?

Solution

▶ **Plan**

Forecasted 2012 sales will now be $74,889 × (1.10) = $82,378. With this figure in hand and the information from Table 17.1, we can use the percent of sales method to calculate KXS's forecasted costs.

▶ **Execute**

From Table 17.1, we see that costs are 78% of sales. With forecasted sales of $82,378, that leads to forecasted costs except depreciation of $82,378 × (0.78) = $64,255.

Pro Forma Balance Sheet

Forecasting the balance sheet using the percent of sales method requires a few iterating steps. In any balance sheet analysis, we know that assets and liabilities + equity must be equal. The assets and liabilities + equity sides of the pro forma balance sheet will not balance, however, until we make assumptions about how our equity and debt will grow with sales. We see this point in Table 17.3, where we have taken a first stab at the pro forma balance sheet (we will explain the details of the calculation below). Our assets are projected to be $8396 more than our liabilities and equity. The imbalance indicates that we will need $8396 in *net new financing* to fund our growth. **Net new financing** is the amount of additional external financing we will need to secure to pay for the planned increase in assets. It can be computed as follows:

net new financing The amount of additional external financing a firm needs to secure to pay for the planned increase in assets.

Net New Financing = Projected Assets − Projected Liabilities and Equity

Let's take a closer look at how we arrived at the $8396 figure. Because we are using the percent of sales method, we assume that assets increase in line with sales. Thus, total assets have increased by 18%, the same as sales. The liabilities side of the balance sheet is more complicated. The amount of dividends a company pays will affect the retained

---

[2] The interest expense should be interest paid on debt, net of interest earned on any invested cash—just as interest paid is tax deductible, interest earned is taxable—so KXS's tax shield comes from its net interest expense. In order to focus on forecasting, we will assume that all cash held by KXS is a necessary part of its working capital needed for transactions. Thus, we assume that KXS holds all of its cash in a non–interest-bearing account. In Chapter 18, we will discuss alternative ways to invest cash.

[3] This is higher than the sales growth of 18% because we assumed that interest expenses would not increase.

TABLE 17.3	First-Pass Pro Forma Balance Sheet for 2012			
1	Year	2011	2012	Calculation
2	Balance Sheet ($000s)			
3	Assets			
4	Cash and Cash Equivalents	11,982	14,139	16% of Sales
5	Accounts Receivable	14,229	16,790	19% of Sales
6	Inventories	14,978	17,674	20% of Sales
7	Total Current Assets	41,189	48,603	Lines 4 + 5 + 6
8	Property, Plant, and Equipment	49,427	58,324	66% of Sales
9	Total Assets	90,616	106,927	Lines 7 + 8
10	Liabilities			
11	Accounts Payable	11,982	14,139	16% of Sales
12	Debt	4500	4500	Remains the same
13	Total Liabilities	16,482	18,639	Lines 11 + 12
14	Stockholders' Equity	74,134	79,892	74,134 + 70% of 8226
15	Total Liabilities and Equity	90,616	98,531	Lines 13 + 14
16	Net New Financing		8396	Line 9 − Line 15

earnings it has to finance growth. Further, any increases in debt or equity reflect capital structure decisions and require managers to actively raise capital, as discussed in Chapters 13 and 14. The bottom line is that we cannot simply assume that debt and equity increase in line with sales.

In KXS's case, it has a policy of paying out 30% of its net income as dividends. Thus, $2468 of its forecasted $8226 net income will be distributed to stockholders as dividends:

$$
\begin{array}{ll}
\text{2012 Net Income} & \$8226 \\
-\text{ 2012 Dividends (30\% of NI)} & -\ \$2468 \\
\hline
=\text{ 2012 Retained Earnings} & =\ \$5758
\end{array}
$$

The $5758 in retained earnings (the remaining 70% of net income after dividends are paid) adds to stockholders' equity on the balance sheet. As a result, in Table 17.3 stockholders' equity is forecast to increase from $74,134 to $79,892.

$$
\begin{array}{ll}
\text{2011 Stockholders' Equity} & \$74,134 \\
+\text{ 2012 Retained Earnings} & +\ \$5758 \\
\hline
=\text{ 2012 Stockholders' Equity} & =\ \$79,892
\end{array}
$$

We also assume that accounts payable will grow along with sales, remaining at 16% of sales as they were in 2011, so they are forecast to grow to $14,139. However, our initial assumption is that debt will remain the same, so our forecasted growth in liabilities and equity falls short of our forecasted growth in assets by $8396.

Common Mistake   **Confusing Stockholders' Equity with Retained Earnings**

It is easy to confuse new retained earnings, total retained earnings, and stockholders' equity. As in the example above, new retained earnings are the amount of net income left over after paying dividends. These new retained earnings are then added to the *total* accumulated retained earnings from the life of the firm. Total retained earnings makes up one part of stockholders' equity, which also includes the value of the stock at its original issue price and any paid-in capital.

The Plug: Net New Financing

How do we address this $8396 difference between assets and liabilities? The projected difference between KXS's assets and liabilities in the pro forma balance sheet indicates that KXS will need to obtain new financing from its investors. The net new financing of $8396 in this case is sometimes referred to as **the plug**—the amount we have to add to (plug into) the liabilities and equity side of the pro forma balance sheet to make it balance.

the plug The amount of net new financing that needs to be added to the liabilities and equity side of the pro forma balance sheet to make it balance.

While KXS definitely has to secure $8396 in new financing, it could come from new debt or new equity. We discussed the issues involved in the equity versus debt decision in Chapter 15. It is a complex decision weighing many factors. Rather than complicating our analysis here, we assume that KXS's financial managers have evaluated these factors and decided that the best way to finance the growth is through additional debt. Table 17.4 shows our second-pass pro forma balance sheet, including the $8396 in additional debt financing that brings the sheet into balance.

We should note that the decision to take on additional debt in 2012 makes our initial assumption that our interest expense would remain constant in 2012 potentially incorrect. If KXS takes on the debt before the end of the year, then there will be a partial-year interest expense from the debt. Thus, any increase in interest expense would result in a reduction to net income and retained earnings. The balance sheet would still not quite balance and we would need a bit more financing than first calculated. We would need to adjust the pro forma income statement and iterate with the pro forma balance sheet to get the exact amount of new debt needed. However, we have achieved our primary objective: to identify a future funding need and determine approximately how much we will need and how we will fund it. This will give KXS's managers enough time to begin the debt-issuance process with its bankers. We also note that debt has more than doubled, which justifies our original decision not to assume that it will increase in proportion to sales.

Choosing a Forecast Target

Forecasting by assuming fixed ratios of sales is very common. Another approach is to forecast by targeting specific ratios that the company either wants or needs to maintain. For example, debt covenants (such as those discussed in Chapter 15) often require a company to maintain certain levels of liquidity or minimum interest coverage. The firm does this by specifying a minimum current ratio (current assets/current liabilities)

TABLE 17.4   Second-Pass Pro Forma Balance Sheet for KXS

	Year	2011	2012	Calculation
1				
2	Balance Sheet ($000s)			
3	Assets			
4	Cash and Cash Equivalents	11,982	14,139	16% of Sales
5	Accounts Receivable	14,229	16,790	19% of Sales
6	Inventories	14,978	17,674	20% of Sales
7	Total Current Assets	41,189	48,603	Lines 4 + 5 + 6
8	Property, Plant, and Equipment	49,427	58,324	66% of Sales
9	Total Assets	90,616	106,927	Lines 7 + 8
10	Liabilities			
11	Accounts Payable	11,982	14,139	16% of Sales
12	Debt	4500	**12,896**	4500 + 8396
13	Total Liabilities	16,482	27,035	Lines 11 + 12
14	Stockholders' Equity	74,134	79,892	74,134 + 70% of 8226
15	Total Liabilities and Equity	90,616	106,927	Lines 13 + 14

EXAMPLE 17.2

Net New Financing

Problem

If instead of paying out 30% of earnings as dividends KXS decides not to pay any dividend and instead retains all of its 2011 earnings, how would its net new financing change?

Solution

▶ **Plan**

KXS currently pays out 30% of its net income as dividends, so rather than retaining only $5758, it will retain the entire $8226. This will increase stockholders' equity, reducing the net new financing.

▶ **Execute**

The additional retained earnings are $8226 − $5758 = $2468. In comparison with the amount in Table 17.3, stockholders' equity will be $79,892 + $2468 = $82,360, and total liabilities and equity will also be $2468 higher, rising to $100,999. Net new financing, the imbalance between KXS's assets and liabilities and equity, will decrease to $8396 − $2468 = $5928.

1	Year	2011	2012
2	Balance Sheet ($000s)		
3	Liabilities		
4	Accounts Payable	11,982	14,139
5	Debt	4500	4500
6	Total Liabilities	16,482	18,639
7	Stockholders' Equity	74,134	82,360
8	Total Liabilities and Equity	90,616	100,999
9	Net New Financing		5928

▶ **Evaluate**

When a company is growing faster than it can finance internally, any distributions to shareholders will cause it to seek greater additional financing. It is important not to confuse the need for external financing with poor performance. Most growing firms need additional financing to fuel that growth, as their expenditures for growth naturally precede their income from that growth. We will revisit the issue of growth and firm value in Section 17.5.

of 1.5, or a minimum cash flow-to-interest ratio of 1.2. The company would then incorporate these target ratios into its forecasts to ensure it will be in compliance with its loan covenants.

The need to consider other target ratios is an example of a larger issue in forecasting—that the firm's investment, payout, and financing decisions are linked together and cannot be treated separately. As we saw in Table 17.4, the balance sheet must balance. So a financial manager must understand that the firm can set an investment budget and a financing plan, but those will then determine what is available to pay out. Alternatively, a firm could decide on an investment budget and payout policy, but those will then determine the firm's financing position—perhaps in unintended ways. The bottom line is that a financial manager must balance all these linked decisions, and a careful forecast allows him or her to see the consequences of decisions.

3. What is the basic idea behind the percent of sales method for forecasting?

4. How does the pro forma balance sheet help the financial manager forecast net new financing?

TABLE 17.5

KXS Forecasted Production Capacity Requirements

1	Year	2011	2012	2013	2014	2015	2016
2	**Production Volume (000s units)**						
3	Market Size	10,000	10,500	11,025	11,576	12,155	12,763
4	Market Share	10.0%	11.0%	12.0%	13.0%	14.0%	15.0%
5	Production Volume (1 $\times$ 2)	1000	1155	1323	1505	1702	1914
6	**Additional Market Information**						
7	Average Sales Price	$ 74.89	$ 76.51	$ 78.04	$ 79.60	$ 81.19	$ 82.82

17.3 Forecasting a Planned Expansion

The percent of sales method is a useful starting point and may even be sufficient for mature companies with relatively stable but slow growth. Its shortcoming is handling the realities of fast growth requiring "lumpy" investments in new capacity. The typical firm cannot smoothly add capacity in line with expected sales. Instead, it must occasionally make a large investment in new capacity that it expects to be sufficient for several years. This kind of capacity expansion also implies that new funding will happen in large, infrequent financing rounds, rather than small increments each year as sales grow. However, we can address these realities in our long-term forecasting by modelling our capacity needs and capital expenditures directly. In this section, we consider a planned expansion by KXS and generate pro forma statements that allow us to decide whether the expansion will increase the value of KXS. First, we identify capacity needs and how to finance that capacity. Next, we construct pro forma income statements and forecast future free cash flows. Finally, we use those forecasted free cash flows to assess the impact of the expansion on firm value.

KXS's managers have constructed a detailed sales forecast by first forecasting the size of the market and what market share KXS can expect to capture. While the size of the market is generally based on demographics and the overall economy, KXS's market share will depend on the appeal of its product and its price, which KXS has forecast as well. KXS currently has the capacity to produce a maximum of 1.1 million units (i.e., 1100 thousand units). However, as detailed in Table 17.5, KXS expects both the total market size and its share of the market to grow to the point at which the company will quickly exceed that capacity. Thus, KXS is considering an expansion that will increase its capacity to 2 million units—enough to handle its projected requirements through 2016.

KXS Design's Expansion: Financing Needs

The first step in our analysis is estimating KXS's financing needs based on the capital expenditures required for the expansion.

Capital Expenditures for the Expansion. The new equipment to increase KXS's capacity will cost $20 million and will need to be purchased in 2012 to meet the company's production needs. Table 17.6 details KXS's forecasted capital expenditures and depreciation over the next five years. Based on the estimates for capital expenditures and depreciation, this spreadsheet tracks the book value of KXS's plant, property, and equipment, starting from the book value's level at the beginning of 2011.[4] The depreciation entries in

---

[4]In Table 17.6, and elsewhere in the chapter, we display rounded numbers. Calculations such as Closing Book Value are based on the actual numbers in the spreadsheet with all significant digits. As a result, there will occasionally be a small discrepancy between the Excel-calculated value shown and the hand-calculated value using the rounded numbers displayed.

TABLE 17.6	KXS Forecasted Capital Expenditures						
1	Year	2011	2012	2013	2014	2015	2016
2	**Fixed Assets and Capital Investment ($000s)**						
3	Opening Book Value	49,919	49,427	66,984	67,486	67,937	68,344
4	Capital Investment	5000	25,000	8000	8000	8000	8000
5	Depreciation	−5492	−7443	−7498	−7549	−7594	−7634
6	Closing Book Value	49,427	66,984	67,486	67,937	68,344	68,709

Table 17.6 are based on the appropriate depreciation schedule for each type of property. Those calculations are quite specific to the nature of the property and are not detailed here. Assume the depreciation shown will be used for tax purposes.[5] KXS has ongoing capital investment requirements to cover the replacement of existing equipment—these were expected to be $5 million per year without the new equipment. The additional $20 million is reflected in 2012, bringing the total to $25 million for 2012 and increasing expected recurring investment to $8 million per year in years 2013 to 2016.

Financing the Expansion. While KXS believes it can fund recurring investment from its operating cash flows, as shown in Table 17.7, it will have to seek external financing for the $20 million in new equipment. KXS plans to finance the new equipment by issuing 10-year coupon bonds with a coupon rate of 6.8%. Thus, KXS will pay only interest on the bonds until the repayment of principal in 10 years. The principal on its outstanding debt of $4500 is also not due before 2016.

Given KXS's outstanding debt, its interest expense each year is computed as follows:[6]

$$\text{Interest in Year } t = \text{Interest Rate} \times \text{Ending Balance in Year } (t-1) \qquad (17.1)$$

As we saw in Chapter 15, the interest on the debt will provide a valuable tax shield to offset KXS's taxable income.

KXS Design's Expansion: Pro Forma Income Statement

The value of any investment opportunity arises from the future cash flows it will generate. To estimate the cash flows resulting from the expansion, we begin by projecting KXS's future earnings. We then consider KXS's working capital and investment needs and estimate its free cash flows. With its free cash flows and projected interest

TABLE 17.7	KXS Planned Debt and Interest Payments							
1	Year		2011	2012	2013	2014	2015	2016
2	**Debt and Interest Table ($000s)**							
3	Outstanding Debt		4500	24,500	24,500	24,500	24,500	24,500
4	Net New Borrowing		—	20,000	—	—	—	—
5	Interest on Debt	6.80%	306	306	1666	1666	1666	1666

[5]Firms often maintain separate books for accounting and tax purposes, and they may use different depreciation assumptions for each. Because depreciation affects cash flows through its tax consequences, tax depreciation, specifically capital cost allowance, is more relevant for valuation.

[6]Equation 17.1 assumes that changes in debt occur at the end of the year. If debt changes during the year, computing interest expenses based on the average level of debt during the year provides a more accurate measure.

tax shields, we can compute the value of KXS with and without the expansion to decide whether the benefit of the new equipment is worth the cost.

Forecasting Earnings. To build the pro forma income statement, we begin with KXS's sales. We calculate sales for each year from the estimates in Table 17.5 as follows:

$$\text{Sales} = \text{Market Size} \times \text{Market Share} \times \text{Average Sales Price} \qquad (17.2)$$

For example, in 2012, KXS has projected sales of 10.5 million units $\times$ 11% market share $\times$ \$76.51 average sales price = \$88.369 million. We will assume that costs except depreciation will continue to be 78% of sales, so that our projected costs, except depreciation in 2012, will be 78% $\times$ \$88,369 = \$68,928. To arrive at forecasted earnings, we take the following steps:

▶ Deducting these operating expenses from KXS's sales, we can project EBITDA over the next five years as shown in Table 17.8.

▶ Subtracting the depreciation expenses we estimated in Table 17.6, we arrive at KXS's earnings before interest and taxes.

▶ We next deduct interest expenses according to the schedule given in Table 17.7.

▶ The final expense is the corporate income tax. KXS pays a 35% tax rate, and the income tax is computed as follows:

$$\text{Income Tax} = \text{Pre-tax Income} \times \text{Tax Rate} \qquad (17.3)$$

After subtracting the income tax from the pre-tax income, we arrive at the forecasted net income, as shown in the bottom line in Table 17.8.

Working Capital Requirements. We have one more step before we are ready to forecast the free cash flows for KXS. Recall that increases in working capital reduce free cash flows. Thus, we still need to forecast KXS's working capital needs. The spreadsheet in Table 17.9 lists KXS's current working capital requirements and forecasts the firm's future working capital needs. (See Chapter 18 for a further discussion of working capital requirements and their determinants.) We have forecast that the minimum required cash will be 16% of sales, accounts receivable will be 19% of sales, inventory will be 20% of sales, and accounts payable will be 16% of sales, all as they were in 2011.

The minimum required cash represents the minimum level of cash needed to keep the business running smoothly, allowing for the daily variations in the timing of income and expenses. Firms generally earn little or no interest on these balances, which are held in cash or in a chequing or short-term savings account. As a consequence, we account

TABLE 17.8   Pro Forma Income Statement for KXS Expansion

1	Year	2011	2012	2013	2014	2015	2016
2	Income Statement ($000s)						
3	Sales	74,889	88,369	103,247	119,793	138,167	158,546
4	Costs Except Depreciation	−58,413	−68,928	−80,533	−93,438	−107,770	−123,666
5	EBITDA	16,476	19,441	22,714	26,354	30,397	34,880
6	Depreciation	−5492	−7443	−7498	−7549	−7594	−7634
7	EBIT	10,984	11,998	15,216	18,806	22,803	27,246
8	Interest Expense (net)	−306	−306	−1666	−1666	−1666	−1666
9	Pre-tax Income	10,678	11,692	13,550	17,140	21,137	25,580
10	Income Tax	−3737	−4092	−4742	−5999	−7398	−8953
11	Net Income	6941	7600	8807	11,141	13,739	16,627

| TABLE 17.9 | KXS Projected Working Capital Needs | | | | | |

1	Year	2011	2012	2013	2014	2015	2016
2	**Working Capital ($000s)**						
3	**Assets**						
4	Cash	11,982	14,139	16,520	19,167	22,107	25,367
5	Accounts Receivable	14,229	16,790	19,617	22,761	26,252	30,124
6	Inventory	14,978	17,674	20,649	23,959	27,633	31,709
7	Total Current Assets	41,189	48,603	56,786	65,886	75,992	87,201
8	**Liabilities**						
9	Accounts Payable	11,982	14,139	16,520	19,167	22,107	25,367
10	Total Current Liabilities	11,982	14,139	16,520	19,167	22,107	25,367
11	**Net Working Capital**						
12	Net Working Capital (7–10)	29,207	34,464	40,266	46,719	53,885	61,833
13	Increase in Net Working Capital		5257	5802	6453	7166	7948

for this opportunity cost by including the cash balance as part of the firm's working capital. We will make the assumption that KXS distributes all cash in excess of the minimum required cash as dividends. If our forecast shows that KXS's cash flows will be insufficient to fund the minimum required cash, then we know that we need to plan to finance those cash needs. Again, identifying these future funding needs is one of the advantages of forecasting.

If KXS instead retained some cash above the amount needed for transactions, the company would probably invest it in some short-term securities that earn interest. Most companies choose to do this to provide funds for future investment so that they do not need to raise as much capital externally. In this case, the excess amount of cash would not be included in working capital. We discuss cash management in Chapter 18.

Forecasting the Balance Sheet

We have enough data now to forecast the balance sheet for our planned expansion. Recall from Section 17.2 that with the percent of sales method that forecasting the balance sheet helps us identify any future funding needs, because the balance sheet must balance. Here, we have explicitly planned for the funding of the expansion in 2012. Nonetheless, we can check to make sure that our debt issue will be enough and then forecast past the expansion to see if we will need any future financing. Table 17.10 shows the balance sheet for 2011 and 2012 filled in with the information we have so far. The only piece of information we are missing is the dividend amount, so we assume for now that we will not pay any dividends in 2012.

As we can see from the column for 2012 in the pro forma balance sheet, KXS's balance sheet does not initially balance: the liabilities and equity are greater than the assets. In Section 17.2, KXS faced the opposite situation—its assets were greater than its liabilities and equity—and this told KXS's managers that they needed external financing. When liabilities and equity are greater than the assets, we have generated more cash than we had planned to consume, and we need to decide what to do with it. KXS has these options:

▶ Build up extra cash reserves (which would increase the cash account to bring assets in line with liabilities and equity).

▶ Pay down (retire) some of its debt.

▶ Distribute the excess as dividends.

▶ Repurchase shares.

TABLE 17.10   Pro Forma Balance Sheet for KXS, 2012

1 Year	2011	2012	Source for 2012 Data	2012 (Revised)
2 Balance Sheet ($000s)				
3 Assets				
4 Cash and Cash Equivalents	11,982	14,139	Table 17.9	14,139
5 Accounts Receivable	14,229	16,790	Table 17.9	16,790
6 Inventories	14,978	17,674	Table 17.9	17,674
7 Total Current Assets	41,189	48,603	Lines 4 + 5 + 6	48,603
8 Property, Plant, and Equipment	49,427	66,984	Table 17.6	66,984
9 Total Assets	90,616	115,587	Lines 7 + 8	115,587
10 Liabilities				
11 Accounts Payable	11,982	14,139	Table 17.9	14,139
12 Debt	4500	24,500	Table 17.7	24,500
13 Total Liabilities	16,482	38,639	Lines 11 + 12	38,639
14 Stockholders' Equity				
15 Starting Stockholders' Equity	69,275	74,134	2011 Line 18	74,134
16 Net Income	6941	7600	Table 17.8	7600
17 Dividends	−2082	0	Assumed	−4786
18 Stockholders' Equity	74,134	81,734	Lines 15 + 16 + 17	76,948
19 Total Liabilities and Equity	90,616	120,373	Lines 13 + 18	115,587

Let's assume that KXS's managers choose to distribute the excess as dividends. The excess is the amount by which liabilities and equity exceeds assets: $120,373 − $115,587 = $4,786. The final column of Table 17.10, labelled "2012 (Revised)," shows the new pro forma balance sheet, including KXS's planned dividend. The balance sheet now balances! We can do this for the full forecast horizon (2012–2016). The completed pro forma balance sheet is shown in the chapter appendix.

The general lesson from the example in Section 17.2, as well as in this section, is summarized in Table 17.11.

Concept Check

5. What is the advantage of forecasting capital expenditures, working capital, and financing events directly?

6. What role does minimum required cash play in working capital?

TABLE 17.11   Pro Forma Balance Sheets and Financing

Liabilities and equity are...	less than assets	greater than assets
	New financing needed—the firm must borrow or issue new equity to fund the shortfall.	Excess cash available—the firm can retain it as extra cash reserves (thus increasing assets), pay dividends, or reduce external financing by retiring debt or repurchasing shares.

Growth and Firm Value

We just analyzed an expansion for KXS that involved an expensive capital investment. For KXS, this forecast would be a starting point for the capital budgeting analysis necessary to decide whether the expansion is a positive-*NPV* project. It is important to remember that not all growth is worth the price. It is possible to pay so much to enable growth that the firm, on net, is worth less. Even if the cost of the growth is not an issue, other aspects of growth can leave the firm less valuable. For example, expansion may strain managers' capacity to monitor and handle the firm's operations, surpass the firm's distribution or quality control capabilities, or even change customers' perceptions of the firm and its brand.

For example, in Starbucks's 2005 annual report, chairman Howard Schultz and CEO Jim Donald wrote to shareholders that Starbucks planned to continue opening new stores—1800 in 2006 alone—and planned revenue growth of approximately 20% for the next five years. Around the time that Starbucks's shareholders were reading this (early 2006), the price of the company's stock was about $36. By the end of 2007, Starbucks's stock price had fallen to $21, Jim Donald had been fired as CEO, and chairman and founder Howard Schultz had written a memo to employees that Starbucks's recent expansion had caused it to "lose its soul," meaning that the Starbucks experience that was the key to its success and the loyalty of its customers had been watered down. To distinguish between growth that adds to or detracts from the value of the firm, we will discuss two growth rates that factor in financing needs and revisit our top decision rule: *NPV* analysis.

Sustainable Growth Rate and External Financing

The Starbucks example makes the point that not all growth is valuable growth. The distinction between value-enhancing and value-destroying growth can be made only through careful *NPV* analysis. However, this distinction is often confused with the concept of a firm's **internal growth rate**—the maximum growth rate a firm can achieve without resorting to external financing. Intuitively, this is the growth the firm can support by reinvesting its earnings. A closely related and more commonly used measure is the firm's **sustainable growth rate**—the maximum growth rate the firm can sustain without issuing new equity or increasing its debt-to-equity ratio. Let's discuss each of these in turn.

internal growth rate The maximum growth rate a firm can achieve without resorting to external financing.

sustainable growth rate The maximum growth rate a firm can achieve without issuing new equity or increasing its debt-to-equity ratio.

Internal Growth Rate Formula. Both of these benchmark growth rates are aimed at identifying how much growth a firm can support based on its existing net income. For a firm that does not pay any dividends, its internal growth rate is its return on assets, because that tells us how fast it could grow its assets using only its net income. If the firm pays some of its net income out as a dividend, then its internal growth rate is reduced to only the growth supported by its retained earnings. This reasoning suggests a more general formula for the internal growth rate:

$$\text{Internal Growth Rate} = \left(\frac{\text{Net Income}}{\text{Beginning Assets}} \right) \times (1 - \text{payout ratio}) \qquad (17.4)$$

$$= ROA \times \text{retention rate}$$

plowback ratio Also called the retention ratio, 1 minus the payout ratio of the firm.

Recall from Chapter 9 that the fraction of net income retained for reinvestment in the firm is called the retention rate. In the context of internal and sustainable growth rates, the retention rate is often called the **plowback ratio**. The internal growth rate is simply the return on assets (*ROA*) multiplied by the retention rate (plowback ratio).

Sustainable Growth Rate Formula. The sustainable growth rate allows for some external financing. It assumes that no new equity will be issued and that the firm's managers want to maintain the same debt-to-equity ratio. Thus, it tells us how fast the firm can grow by reinvesting its retained earnings and issuing only as much new debt as can be supported by those retained earnings. The formula for the sustainable growth rate is as follows:

$$\text{Sustainable Growth Rate} = \left(\frac{\text{Net Income}}{\text{Beginning Equity}}\right) \times (1 - \text{payout ratio}) \qquad (17.5)$$

$$= ROE \times \text{retention rate}$$

Sustainable Growth Rate Versus Internal Growth Rate. Because your return on equity (*ROE*) will be larger than your *ROA* any time you have debt, the sustainable growth rate will be greater than the internal growth rate. While the internal growth rate assumes no external financing, the sustainable growth rate assumes that you will make use of some outside financing equal to the amount of new debt that will keep your debt-equity ratio constant as your equity grows through reinvested net income.

EXAMPLE 17.3

Internal and Sustainable Growth Rates and Payout Policy

Problem

Your firm has $70 million in equity and $30 million in debt and forecasts $14 million in net income for the year. It currently pays dividends equal to 20% of its net income. You are analyzing a potential change in payout policy—an increase in dividends to 30% of net income. How would this change affect your internal and sustainable growth rates?

Solution

Plan

We can use Equations 17.4 and 17.5 to compute your firm's internal and sustainable growth rates under the old and new policy. To do so, we'll need to compute its ROA, ROE, and retention rate (plowback ratio). The company has $100 million (= $70 million in equity + $30 million in debt) in total assets.

$$ROA = \frac{\text{Net Income}}{\text{Beginning Assets}} = \frac{14}{100} = 14\% \quad ROE = \frac{\text{Net Income}}{\text{Beginning Equity}} = \frac{14}{70} = 20\%$$

$$\text{Old Retention Rate} = (1 - \text{payout ratio}) = (1 - 0.20) = 0.80$$

$$\text{New Retention Rate} = (1 - 0.30) = 0.70$$

▶ **Execute**

Using Equation 17.4 to compute the internal growth rate before and after the change, we have the following:

$$\text{Old Internal Growth Rate} = ROA \times \text{retention rate} = 14\% \times 0.80 = 11.2\%$$

$$\text{New Internal Growth Rate} = 14\% \times 0.70 = 9.8\%$$

Similarly, we can use Equation 17.5 to compute the sustainable growth rate before and after:

$$\text{Old Sustainable Growth Rate} = ROE \times \text{retention rate} = 20\% \times 0.80 = 16\%$$

$$\text{New Sustainable Growth Rate} = 20\% \times 0.70 = 14\%$$

▶ **Evaluate**

By reducing the amount of retained earnings available to fund growth, an increase in the payout ratio necessarily reduces your firm's internal and sustainable growth rates.

TABLE 17.12	Summary of Internal Growth Rate Versus Sustainable Growth Rate	

	Internal Growth Rate	**Sustainable Growth Rate**
Formula	*ROA* × retention rate	*ROE* × retention rate
Maximum growth financed only by	retained earnings	retained earnings and new debt that keeps the debt-equity ratio constant
To grow faster, a firm must	reduce payout or raise external capital	reduce payout, or raise new equity, or increase leverage

Whenever you forecast growth greater than the internal growth rate, you will have to either reduce your payout ratio (increase your plowback ratio), plan to raise additional external financing, or both. If your forecasted growth is greater than your sustainable growth rate, you will have to increase your plowback ratio, raise additional equity financing, or increase your leverage (increase your debt faster than keeping your debt-equity ratio constant would allow). Table 17.12 compares internal and sustainable growth rates.

While the internal and sustainable growth rates are useful in alerting you to the need to plan for external financing, they cannot tell you whether your planned growth increases or decreases the firm's value. The growth rates do not evaluate the future costs and benefits of the growth, and the Valuation Principle tells us that the value implications of the growth can be assessed only by doing so. *There is nothing inherently bad or unsustainable about growth greater than the sustainable growth rate as long as that growth is value increasing. The firm will simply need to raise additional capital to finance the growth.*

For example, in the 1990s Starbucks's average revenue growth was above 50%, even though its average *ROE* was 12%. Starbucks has never paid dividends, so its retention rate is 1, making its sustainable growth rate at the time also 12%.

$$SGR = ROE \times \text{retention rate} = 12\% \times 1 = 12\%$$

Despite expanding at 4 times its sustainable growth rate, Starbucks's value increased almost 10 times (1000%), as shown in Figure 17.1.

Conversely, Starbucks's recent experience illustrates that sustainable growth need not be value-increasing growth. We noted at the beginning of this section that, starting in 2006, Starbucks was aiming for annual growth of 20%. How does this compare with its sustainable growth rate at the time? When Schultz and Donald wrote their letter to shareholders, Starbucks's *ROE* was 20% (based on its 2005 annual report). Again, Starbucks has never paid dividends, so its retention rate is 1, making its sustainable growth rate also 20%. Thus, 20% growth was sustainable—it just wasn't value increasing.[7] As we discussed in Chapters 13 and 14, there are costs to seeking external financing—the flotation and issuance costs associated with issuing new equity or new bonds. Thus, the internal growth rate indicates the fastest growth possible without incurring any of these costs. The sustainable growth rate still assumes that some new debt will be sought, so the company reduces, but does not eliminate entirely, its costs of external financing when growing at the sustainable growth rate. Thus, managers, especially those at small firms, concerned with these costs might track these growth rates. However, these costs are generally small relative to the *NPV* of, for example, an expansion plan.

---

[7]This textbook's website contains a spreadsheet with a proposed further expansion of *KXS* Designs that allows you to explore further the differences between sustainable growth, internal growth rate, and value-increasing growth.

FIGURE 17.1   Starbucks's Stock Price During Periods of Growth at, Above, and Below Its *SGR*

The graph shows Starbucks's stock price since 2000. During most of its early years, Starbucks grew at well above its sustainable growth rate (*SGR*) and its value increased substantially. In 2006, it planned growth at its *SGR* but suffered a share decrease in value. The graph demonstrates that there is not necessarily a relationship between a firm's growth relative to its *SGR* and whether that growth is valuable.

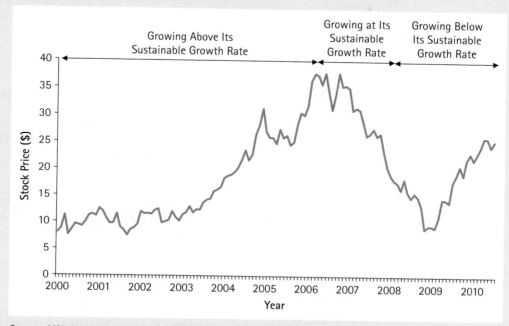

Sources: MSN Money website, http://money.msn.com and authors' calculations.

While these costs are usually small relative to the *NPV* of expanding the business, ignoring them completely would be a mistake. The proper way to incorporate them is to calculate the cash outflow associated with these costs and subtract it from the *NPV* of the expansion. The point remains that growth above a firm's internal or sustainable growth rates is not necessarily bad, but will require external financing and the costs associated with that financing.

7. What is the difference between internal growth rate and sustainable growth rate?

8. If a firm grows faster than its sustainable growth rate, is that growth value decreasing?

17.5 Valuing the Planned Expansion

As the last section made clear, growth can increase or decrease the value of the firm. Planning for and forecasting the impact of growth is just the first step in the analysis of whether the growth will make sense for the shareholders. Our forecasting exercise in Section 17.3 gave us the implications of the planned expansion for the debt, net income, and working capital of KXS. Now we are ready to determine whether the expansion is a good idea. The Valuation Principle guides us here—we need to forecast the cash flows and compute their present value.

Forecasting Free Cash Flows

We now have the data needed to forecast KXS's free cash flows over the next five years. KXS's earnings are available from the income statement (Table 17.8), as are its depreciation and interest expenses. Capital expenditures are available from Table 17.6, and changes in net working capital can be found in Table 17.9. We combine these items to estimate the free cash flows in the spreadsheet shown in Table 17.12.

To compute KXS's free cash flows, which exclude cash flows associated with leverage, we first adjust net income by adding back the after-tax interest payments associated with the net debt in its capital structure:[8]

$$\text{After-Tax Interest Expense} = (1 - \text{Tax Rate})$$
$$\times (\text{Interest on Debt} - \text{Interest on Excess Cash}) \qquad (17.6)$$

Because KXS has no excess cash, its after-tax interest expense in 2012 is $(1 - 35\%) \times$ $306 = 199 (thousand), providing unlevered net income of $7600 + 199 = 7799. We could also compute the unlevered net income in Table 17.13 by starting with *EBIT* and deducting taxes. For example, in 2012 *EBIT* is forecasted as $11.998 million (Table 17.8), which amounts to the following:

$$\$11.998 \times (1 - 35\%) = \$7.799 \text{ million after taxes}$$

To compute KXS's free cash flows from its unlevered net income, we add back depreciation (which is not a cash expense) and deduct KXS's increases in net working capital and capital expenditures. The free cash flows on line 9 of Table 17.13 show the cash the firm will generate for its investors, both debt and equity holders.[9] While KXS will generate substantial free cash flows over the next five years, the level of free cash flows varies substantially from year to year. They are even forecasted to be negative in 2008 (when the expansion takes place).

As we noted, free cash flows are the total cash available to all investors (debt and equity holders). To determine the amount that can be paid out to equity holders, we can

TABLE 17.13   KXS Forecasted Free Cash Flows

	Year	2012	2013	2014	2015	2016
1						
2	Free Cash Flow ($000s)					
3	Net Income	7600	8807	11,141	13,739	16,627
4	Plus: After-Tax Interest Expense	199	1083	1083	1083	1083
5	Unlevered Net Income	7799	9890	12,224	14,822	17,710
6	Plus: Depreciation	7443	7498	7549	7594	7634
7	Less: Increases in *NWC*	−5257	−5802	−6453	−7166	−7948
8	Less: Capital Expenditures	−25,000	−8000	−8000	−8000	−8000
9	Free Cash Flow of Firm	−15,015	3586	5320	7250	9396

---

[8]If KXS had some interest income or expenses from working capital, we would *not* include that interest here. We adjust only for interest that is related to the firm's *financing*—that is, interest associated with debt and excess cash (cash not included as part of working capital).

[9]While we are maintaining the assumption that, after paying the interest on its debt, KXS will distribute any excess funds to shareholders as dividends, this payout decision has no impact on the amount of free cash flows the firm generates in the first place, and hence has no impact on the value we will compute for KXS.

adjust the free cash flows to account for all (after-tax) payments to or from debt holders. For example, in 2012 KXS will pay after-tax interest of $199,000 and receive $20 million by issuing new debt as follows:

($000s)	2012
Free Cash Flows	−15,015
Less: After-tax Interest Expense	−199
Plus: Increase in Debt	20,000
Free Cash Flows to Equity	4786

Note that the free cash flows that are available to equity holders in 2012, $4.786 million, are exactly the amount of dividends we forecasted at the end of Section 17.3. This is no coincidence—we chose in that section to pay out all excess available cash flows as a dividend. This is exactly what the free cash flows to equity tell us—the total amount of excess cash flows that belongs to the equity holders for them to use to pay dividends, repurchase shares, retain in the firm as cash, or retire debt. (See the appendix to this chapter for a forecast of free cash flows to equity and dividends through 2016.)

Common Mistake   Confusing Total and Incremental Net Working Capital

When calculating free cash flows from earnings, students often make the mistake of subtracting the firm's *total* net working capital each year rather than only the incremental change in net working capital. Remember that only a change in net working capital results in a new cash inflow or outflow for the firm. Subtracting the entire *level* of net working capital will reduce the free cash flows, often even making them negative, and lead the student to understate the *NPV* of the decision.

KXS Design's Expansion: Effect on Firm Value

We've accomplished a lot by carefully forecasting the impact of the planned expansion on KXS's net income, capital expenditures, and working capital needs. First, we identified future financing needs, allowing us ample time to plan to secure the necessary funding. Next, in order to construct our pro forma statements, we built an Excel model of the interactions between sales growth, costs, capital investment, working capital needs, and financing choices. This model allows us to study how changes in any of these factors will affect the others and our expansion plans.[10] Remember the lesson from sensitivity and scenario analysis in Chapter 8—these numbers are only forecasts, and therefore you need to see how reasonable deviations from the forecast would affect the value of the expansion. Nonetheless, as a starting point, we use these forecasts to provide our best estimate of whether the expansion plan is a good idea—does it increase the value of KXS? There are two ways of doing this: (1) value the whole company with and without the expansion and compare the values or (2) value only the incremental changes to the company caused by the expansion, as we did in Chapter 8's capital budgeting exercise. We will go the first route to provide an example of how to do whole-company valuation. However, you could arrive at the same answer by following the incremental approach.

As we learned in Chapter 15, absent distress costs, the value of a firm with debt is equal to the value of the firm without debt plus the present value of its interest tax

---

[10]You can download a copy of the forecasting model in Excel from this textbook's website and experiment with changes in these factors yourself.

shields. Our careful forecast of the financing of KXS's expansion allows us to apply the same approach to valuing the expansion: we compute the present value of the *unlevered* free cash flows of KXS and add to it the present value of the tax shields created by our planned interest payments.[11] However, we have forecast cash flows only to 2012, so we will need to account for the remaining value of KXS at that point. We do so using the tools developed in Chapter 9 for valuing common stock.

Multiples Approach to Continuation Value. Practitioners generally estimate a firm's **continuation value** (also called the terminal value) at the end of the forecast horizon using a valuation multiple. Explicitly forecasting cash flows is useful in capturing those specific aspects of a company that distinguish the firm from its competitors in the short run. However, because of competition between firms, the long-term expected growth rates, profitability, and risk of firms in the same industry should move toward one another. As a consequence, long-term expectations of multiples are likely to be relatively homogeneous across firms in a given sector. Thus, a realistic assumption is that a firm's multiple will eventually move toward the industry average. Because distant cash flows are difficult to forecast accurately, estimating the firm's continuation, or terminal, value based on a long-term estimate of the valuation multiple for the industry is a common (and, generally, reasonably reliable) approach.

Of the different valuation multiples available, the *EBITDA* (earnings before interest, taxes, depreciation, and amortization) multiple is most often used in practice. In most settings, the *EBITDA* multiple is more reliable than sales or earnings multiples because it accounts for the firm's operating efficiency and is not affected by leverage differences between firms. We discussed the use of multiples in valuation in Chapter 9. As in that context, here we estimate the continuation value using an *EBITDA* multiple as follows:

$$\text{Continuation Enterprise Value at Forecast Horizon} = \textit{EBITDA} \text{ at Horizon} \times \textit{EBITDA} \text{ Multiple at Horizon} \tag{17.7}$$

From the income statement in Table 17.8, KXS's *EBITDA* in 2016 is forecast to be \$34.880 million. Firms in KXS's industry are valued at an average *EBITDA* multiple of 9. If we assume that the appropriate *EBITDA* multiple in 2016 is unchanged from the current value of 9, then KXS's continuation value in 2016 is \$34.880 × 9 = \$313.920 million. This assumption is important—the *EBITDA* multiple at the horizon will have a large impact on our value calculation. A careful analysis of the prospects for industry growth (which tends to be related to higher multiples) at the horizon is important. Here, we assume that the design and apparel industry is mature and will remain relatively stable, but this assumption can be probed, especially in sensitivity analysis.

KXS Design's Value with the Expansion. Assume that KXS's financial managers have estimated KXS's unlevered cost of capital to be 10% (specifically, 10% is their pre-tax WACC; see the details regarding the estimation of the cost of capital in Chapter 12). Now we have all the inputs we need to value KXS with the expansion. Table 17.14 presents the calculation. First, we compute the present value of the forecasted free cash flows of the firm over the next five years. These are the cash flows available to both bondholders and equity holders, so they are free of any effects of leverage. Because they represent cash flows to both debt and equity holders, and because we will account for the benefits of the interest tax shield

---

[11]This approach is called the adjusted present value because it adjusts the present value of the unlevered free cash flows for the effect of the interest tax shields.

continuation value
The value of a project's remaining free cash flows beyond the forecast horizon.

TABLE 17.14	Calculation of KXS Firm Value with the Expansion

	Year	2011	2012	2013	2014	2015	2016
1							
2	Free Cash Flow of Firm ($000s)		−15,015	3586	5320	7250	9396
3	PV(Free Cash Flow) (at 10%)	4097					
4	Continuation Value						313,920
5	PV(Continuation Value) (at 10%)	194,920					
6	Net Interest Expense		−306	−1666	−1666	−1666	−1666
7	Interest Tax Shield		107	583	583	583	583
8	PV(Interest Tax Shield) (at 6.8%)	1958					
9	Firm Value (3 + 5 + 8)	200,974					

separately, we discount KXS's free cash flows at the firm's pre-tax WACC of 10%. Using the free cash flows we forecasted for 2012–2016 in Table 17.13, we get a present value of $4097:

$$PV(FCF) = \frac{-15{,}015}{(1.10)^1} + \frac{3586}{(1.10)^2} + \frac{5320}{(1.10)^3} + \frac{7250}{(1.10)^4} + \frac{9396}{(1.10)^5} = 4097 \qquad (17.8)$$

Even though the *PV* of the cash flows over the next five years is small, the expansion pays off in the long run by providing higher free cash flows from 2016 onward. This growth results in a higher *EBITDA* in 2016 than would otherwise be possible, and thus a higher continuation value once that *EBIDTA* is multiplied by the continuation multiple of 9. The $313,920 continuation value in 2016 that we calculated is included in Table 17.14. However, because it is a 2016 value, we need to discount it to the present as follows:

$$PV(\text{Continuation Value}) = \frac{313{,}920}{(1.10)^5} = 194{,}920 \qquad (17.9)$$

Finally, because we are financing the expansion with debt, we will have additional interest tax shields. The total net interest expense is included in Table 17.14, and the interest tax shield there is calculated as we did in Chapter 15, by multiplying the interest expense by the tax rate (35% for KXS):

$$\text{Interest Tax Shield} = \text{Net Interest Expense} \times \text{Tax Rate} \qquad (17.10)$$

Also as we did in Chapter 15, we calculate the present value of the interest tax shield using the interest rate on debt as the discount rate, *not* using the WACC. Recall that the reason for doing so is that the tax shield is only as risky as the debt that creates it, so the proper discount rate is the debt's interest rate, here at 6.8%:[12]

$$PV(\text{Interest Tax Shield}) = \frac{107}{(1.068)^1} + \frac{583}{(1.068)^2} + \frac{583}{(1.068)^3} + \frac{583}{(1.068)^4}$$
$$+ \frac{583}{(1.068)^5} = 1958 \qquad (17.11)$$

---

[12]We have not ignored the rest of the interest tax shields from the new debt. The value of those shields is subsumed in the continuation value of the firm. When we say that the firm will be worth 9 times *EBITDA*, we are saying that the total value at that point, including all unused tax shields, will be 9 times *EBITDA*.

TABLE 17.15   KXS's Sales Forecast Without Expansion

1	Year	2011	2012	2013	2014	2015	2016
2	Production Volume	1000	1100	1100	1100	1100	1100
3	Sales Price	$74.89	$76.51	$78.04	$79.60	$81.19	$82.82
4	Sales Revenue	$74,889	$84,161	$85,844	$87,561	$89,312	$91,099

The total value of KXS with the expansion is the sum of the present values of the forecasted unlevered free cash flows, the continuation value of the firm, and the interest tax shields. As shown in Table 17.14, the total firm value is $200.974 million.

KXS Design's Value Without the Expansion. But how do we know if the expansion is a good idea? We can compare KXS's value with the expansion to its value without the expansion. If KXS does not invest in the new equipment, it will be stuck with a maximum capacity of 1100 units. While its sales revenue will grow due to price increases, its main source of growth will be cut off. Table 17.15 shows the sales revenue without the expansion. By 2012, KXS reaches maximum production capacity and can no longer expand. Comparing the sales revenue in Table 17.15 to the sales revenue with the expansion given in Table 17.8, we see how much higher sales are forecasted to be with the expansion.

We can complete the same process for forecasting the free cash flows of the firm without the expansion as we did for the firm with the expansion. In this case, we would find that the 2016 *EBITDA* would be only $20,042, so the continuation value would drop to $20,042 × 9 = $180,378. Also, KXS will not be taking on any additional debt, so the interest expense will remain constant at $306 per year. The final result of the valuation is presented in Table 17.16.

While the *PV* of the free cash flows over the next five years is higher because we don't have to spend $20 million for the new equipment, the lower growth substantially reduces our continuation value, and the reduced debt (because we do not need to borrow to fund the equipment) produces a much lower present value of interest tax shields as well. The resulting firm value is almost $60 million lower without the expansion than it is with the expansion. Thus, the expansion is certainly a good idea for KXS.

Optimal Timing and the Option to Delay

We just showed that if the alternative is not to expand at all, KXS should definitely expand in 2012. However, what if it also has the option to simply delay expansion to 2013 or later, rather than not to expand at all? If we repeat the valuation analysis

TABLE 17.16   KXS's Value Without the Expansion

1	Year	2011	2012	2013	2014	2015	2016
2	Free Cash Flow of Firm ($000s)		5324	8509	8727	8952	9182
3	*PV*(Free Cash Flow) (at 10%)	30,244					
4	Continuation Value						180,378
5	*PV*(Continuation Value) (at 10%)	112,001					
6	Net Interest Expense			−306	−306	−306	−306
7	Interest Tax Shield			107	107	107	107
8	*PV*(Interest Tax Shield) (at 6.8%)	441					
9	Firm Value (3 + 5 + 8)	142,686					

above for expansion in each year from 2012 to 2016, we get the following firm values in 2011:[13]

Expand in...	2012	2013	2014	2015	2016
KXS's Firm Value in 2011 ($000s)	200,974	203,553	204,728	204,604	203,277

KXS's firm value is maximized by delaying the expansion to 2014. The reason is that while delaying expansion means that KXS cannot produce enough units to meet demand, the shortfall is not too great until 2014. The value gained from putting off such a large financial outlay is greater than the value lost from forgone sales.

The timing analysis recalls an important point from Chapter 8: managers often have real options embedded in capital budgeting decisions. In this case, it is important for KXS's managers to realize that the alternative is not expand or do nothing. Rather, it is expand or delay expansion for another year (or more). As we see here, this option is valuable, allowing KXS's managers to add almost $4 million in additional value to the firm.

Concept Check

9. What is the multiples approach to continuation value?

10. How does forecasting help the financial manager decide whether to implement a new business plan?

---

[13]Interested students may perform this analysis for themselves using the spreadsheet that accompanies this chapter on the textbook's website.

MyFinanceLab

Here is what you should know after reading this chapter. MyFinanceLab will help you identify what you know, and where to go when you need to practice.

Key Points and Equations	Key Terms	Online Practice Opportunities
17.1 Goals of Long-term Financial Planning ▶ Building a financial model to forecast the financial statements and free cash flows of a firm allows the financial manager to: • identify important linkages. • analyze the impact of potential business plans. • plan for future funding needs.		MyFinanceLab Study Plan 17.1
17.2 Forecasting Financial Statements: The Percent of Sales Method ▶ One common approach to forecasting is the percent of sales approach in which you assume that costs, working capital, and total assets will remain a fixed percentage of sales as sales grow.	net new financing, p. 583 percent of sales method, p. 581 the plug, p. 585	MyFinanceLab Study Plan 17.2 Spreadsheet Tables 17.1–17.4

▶ A pro forma income statement projects the firm's earnings under a given set of hypothetical assumptions.

▶ A pro forma balance sheet projects the firm's assets, liabilities, and equity under the same assumptions used to construct the pro forma income statement.

▶ Forecasting the balance sheet with the percent of sales method requires two passes.

▶ The first pass reveals by how much equity and liabilities would fall short of the amount needed to finance the expected growth in assets.

▶ The amount by which the financing falls short is called the plug, and indicates the total net new financing needed from external sources.

▶ In the second pass, the pro forma balance sheet shows the necessary financing from the planned sources and is in balance.

17.3 Forecasting a Planned Expansion

▶ An improvement over the percent of sales method is to forecast the firm's working capital and capital investment, along with planned financing of those investments directly.

▶ Such a financial model will have the correct timing of external financing and capital investment so that we can estimate the firm's future free cash flows.

MyFinanceLab
Study Plan 17.3

Spreadsheet
Tables 17.5–17.10

17.4 Growth and Firm Value

▶ Two common concepts are internal growth rate and sustainable growth rate.

▶ The internal growth rate identifies the maximum rate at which the firm can grow without external financing:

internal growth rate, p. 592
plowback ratio, p. 592
sustainable growth rate, p. 592

MyFinanceLab
Study Plan 17.5

$$\text{Internal Growth Rate} = ROA \times \text{retention rate} \qquad (17.4)$$

▶ The sustainable growth rate identifies the maximum rate at which the firm can grow if it wants to keep its D/E ratio constant without any new equity financing:

$$\text{Substainable Growth Rate} = ROE \times \text{retention rate} \qquad (17.5)$$

▶ Neither the internal growth rate nor the sustainable growth rate indicates whether planned growth is good or bad. Only an *NPV* analysis can tell us whether the contemplated growth will increase or decrease the value of the firm.

17.5 Valuing the Planned Expansion

▶ In addition to forecasting cash flows for a few years, we need to estimate the firm's continuation value at the end of the forecast horizon.

▶ We discussed continuation values in depth in Chapter 9. One method is to use a valuation multiple based on comparable firms.

▶ Given the forecasted cash flows and an estimate of the cost of capital, the final step is to combine these inputs to estimate the value of the firm based on the business plan. We can compare this with the value of the firm without the new plan to determine whether to implement the plan.

continuation value, p. 598

MyFinanceLab
Study Plan 17.4

Interactive Financial
Statement Model

Spreadsheet
Tables 17.12–17.15

Review Questions

1. What is the purpose of long-term forecasting?

2. What are the advantages and disadvantages of the percent of sales method?

3. What is gained by forecasting capital expenditures and external financing specifically?

4. How can the financial manager use the long-term forecast to decide on adopting a new business plan?

5. What can the sustainable growth rate tell a financial manager and what can it not tell?

Problems

All problems in this chapter are available in MyFinanceLab.

Forecasting Financial Statements: The Percent of Sales Method

1. Your company has sales of $100,000 this year and cost of goods sold of $72,000. You forecast sales to increase to $110,000 next year. Using the percent of sales method, forecast next year's cost of goods sold.

2. For the next fiscal year, you forecast net income of $50,000 and ending assets of $500,000. Your firm's payout ratio is 10%. Your beginning stockholders' equity is $300,000 and your beginning total liabilities are $120,000. Your non-debt liabilities such as accounts payable are forecasted to increase by $10,000. What is your net new financing needed for next year?

 3. Assume your beginning total liabilities in Problem 2 is $100,000. What amount of equity and what amount of debt would you need to issue to cover the net new financing in order to keep your debt-equity ratio constant?

For Problems 4 to 6, use the following income statement and balance sheet for Jim's Espresso:

Income Statement		Balance Sheet	
Sales	200,000	Assets	
Costs Except Depreciation	(100,000)	Cash and Equivalents	15,000
EBITDA	100,000	Accounts Receivable	2000
Depreciation	(6000)	Inventories	4000
EBIT	94,000	Total Current Assets	21,000
Interest Expense (net)	(400)	Property, Plant, and Equipment	10,000
Pre-tax Income	93,600	Total Assets	31,000
Income Tax	(32,760)		
Net Income	60,840	Liabilities and Equity	
		Accounts Payable	1500
		Debt	4000
		Total Liabilities	5500
		Stockholders' Equity	25,500
		Total Liabilities and Equity	31,000

 4. Jim's Espresso expects sales to grow by 10% next year. Using the percent of sales method, forecast the following:
     a. Costs
     b. Depreciation
     c. Net income
     d. Cash
     e. Accounts receivable
     f. Inventory
     g. Property, plant, and equipment

 5. Assume that Jim's Espresso pays out 90% of its net income. Use the percent of sales method to forecast the following:
     a. Stockholders' equity
     b. Accounts payable

 6. What is the amount of net new financing needed for Jim's Espresso?

7. If Jim's Espresso adjusts its payout policy to 70% of net income, how will the net new financing change?

For Problems 8 to 11, use the following income statement and balance sheet for Global Corp.:

Figures in $ millions

Net Sales	186.7	Assets	23.2
Costs Except Depreciation	−175.1	Cash	
EBITDA	11.6	Accounts Receivable	18.5
Depreciation and Amortization	−1.2	Inventories	15.3
EBIT	10.4	Total Current Assets	57
Interest Income (expense)	−7.7		
Pre-tax Income	2.7	Net Property, Plant, and Equipment	113.1
Taxes	−0.7	Total Assets	170.1
Net Income	2.0	Liabilities and Equity	
		Accounts Payable	34.7
		Long-Term Debt	113.2
		Total Liabilities	147.9
		Total Stockholders' Equity	22.2
		Total Liabilities and Equity	170.1

 8. Global Corp. expects sales to grow by 8% next year. Using the percent of sales method, forecast:

a. Costs

b. Depreciation

c. Net income

d. Cash

e. Accounts receivable

f. Inventory

g. Property, plant, and equipment

h. Accounts payable

 9. Assume that Global pays out 50% of its net income. Use the percent of sales method to forecast stockholders' equity.

 10. What is the amount of net new financing needed for Global?

11. If Global decides that it will limit its net new financing to no more than $9 million, how will this affect its payout policy?

Forecasting a Planned Expansion

For problems in this section, download the KXS spreadsheets available on the text-book's website.

 12. Assume that KXS's market share will increase by 0.25% per year rather than the 1% used in the chapter (see Table 17.5) and that its prices remain as in the chapter. What production capacity will KXS require each year? When will an expansion become necessary (i.e., when will production volume exceed 1100)?

13. Under the assumption that KXS's market share will be 0.25% higher in each subsequent year (for e.g. 2011 will be 10.25%, 2012 will be 10.50%, and so on), you determine that the plant will require an expansion in 2013. The expansion will cost $20 million. Assuming that the financing of the expansion will be delayed accordingly, calculate the projected interest payments and the amount of the projected interest tax shields (assuming that KXS still uses a 10-year bond and interest rates remain the same as in the chapter) through 2016.

 14. Under the assumption that KXS's market share will increase by 0.25% per year (and the investment and financing will be adjusted as described in Problem 13), you project the following depreciation:

Year	2011	2012	2013	2014	2015	2016
Depreciation ($000s)	5492	5443	7398	7459	7513	7561

Using this information, project net income through 2016 (i.e., reproduce Table 17.8 under the new assumptions).

 15. Assuming that KXS's market share will increase by 0.25% per year (implying that the investment, financing, and depreciation will be adjusted as described in Problems 13 and 14), and that the working capital assumptions used in the chapter still hold, calculate KXS's working capital requirements though 2016 (that is, reproduce Table 17.9 under the new assumptions).

Growth and Firm Value

 16. Information for a company is provided in the table below:

Net Income	$50,000
Beginning Total Assets	$400,000
Beginning Stockholders' Equity	$250,000
Payout Ratio	0%

Calculate the following for the company:
a. Internal growth rate
b. Sustainable growth rate
c. Sustainable growth rate if it pays out 40% of its net income as a dividend

 17. Did KXS's expansion plan call for it to grow slower or faster than its sustainable growth rate?

18. Your firm has an *ROE* of 12%, a payout ratio of 25%, $600,000 of stockholders' equity, and $400,000 of debt. If you grow at your sustainable growth rate this year, how much additional debt will you need to issue?

19. IZAX, Co. has the following items on its balance sheet:

Assets		Liabilities and Equity	
Cash	$50,000	Debt	$100,000
PPE	$350,000	Equity	$300,000

Its net income this year is $20,000 and it pays dividends of $5000. If it grows at its internal growth rate, what will its D/E ratio be next year?

20. Using data available on the textbook's website, compute the sustainable and internal growth rates for Boeing, Coca-Cola, and Google at the start of 2007. Next, compute their actual growth rates in 2007 and the change in their stock prices over the same period. Is there a relation between their growth relative to *SGR* or *IGR* and the change in their value?

Valuing the Planned Expansion

 21. Forecast KXS's free cash flows (reproduce Table 17.13), assuming KXS's market share will increase by 0.25% per year; investment, financing, and depreciation will be adjusted accordingly; and working capital will be as you projected in Problem 15.

 22. Calculate the continuation value of KXS using your reproduction of Table 17.8 from Problem 14, and assuming an *EBITDA* multiple of 8.5.

 23. Assuming a cost of capital of 10%, compute the value of KXS under the 0.25% growth scenario.

Chapter 17 APPENDIX   The Balance Sheet and Statement of Cash Flows

The information we have calculated so far can be used to project KXS's balance sheet and statement of cash flows through 2016. While these statements are not critical for our valuation of the expansion, they often prove helpful in providing a more complete picture of how a firm will grow during the forecast period. These statements for KXS are shown in the spreadsheets in Table 17.17 and Table 17.18.

The balance sheet (Table 17.17) continues the work we started in Table 17.10. Current assets and liabilities come from the net working capital spreadsheet (Table 17.9). The inventory entry on the balance sheet includes both raw materials and finished goods. Property, plant, and equipment information comes from the forecasted capital expenditure spreadsheet (Table 17.6), and the debt comes from Table 17.7.

TABLE 17.17   Pro Forma Balance Sheet for KXS, 2011–16

	Year	2011	2012	2013	2014	2015	2016
1							
2	**Balance Sheets ($000s)**						
3	**Assets**						
4	Cash and Cash Equivalents	11,982	14,139	16,520	19,167	22,107	25,367
5	Accounts Receivable	14,229	16,790	19,617	22,761	26,252	30,124
6	Inventories	14,978	17,674	20,649	23,959	27,633	31,709
7	**Total Current Assets**	41,189	48,603	56,786	65,886	75,992	87,201
8	Property, Plant, and Equipment	49,427	66,984	67,486	67,937	68,344	68,709
9	**Total Assets**	90,616	115,587	124,272	133,823	144,335	155,910
10							
11	**Liabilities**						
12	Accounts Payable	11,982	14,139	16,520	19,167	22,107	25,367
13	Debt	4500	24,500	24,500	24,500	24,500	24,500
14	**Total Liabilities**	16,482	38,639	41,020	43,667	46,607	49,867
15							
16	**Stockholders' Equity**						
17	Starting Stockholders' Equity	69,275	74,134	76,948	83,252	90,156	97,729
18	Net Income	6940	7600	8807	11,141	13,739	16,627
19	Dividends	−2082	−4786	−2503	−4237	−6167	−8313
20	Stockholders' Equity	74,134	76,948	83,252	90,156	97,729	106,042
21	**Total Liabilities and Equity**	90,616	115,587	124,272	133,823	144,335	155,910

KXS's book value of equity will steadily grow as the company expands and remains profitable, paying out only a portion of its net income each year. Its debt will jump from $4500 to $24,500 in 2012 when it finances its expansion. KXS's other liabilities—accounts payable—will grow steadily with sales. KXS's book debt-equity ratio will jump from $4500/$74,134 = 6% in 2011 to $24,500/$76,948 = 32% in 2012, and then will steadily decline to 23% by 2016.

The statement of cash flows in Table 17.18 starts with net income. Cash from operating activities includes depreciation as well as *changes* to working capital items (other than cash) from Table 17.9. Cash from investing activities includes the capital expenditures in Table 17.6. Cash from financing activities includes net borrowing from

TABLE 17.18   Pro Forma Statement of Cash Flows for KXS, 2011–16

	Year	2011	2012	2013	2014	2015	2016
2	Statement of Cash Flows ($000s)						
3	Net Income		7600	8807	11,141	13,739	16,627
4	Depreciation		7443	7498	7549	7594	7634
5	Changes in Working Capital						
6	Accounts Receivable		−2561	−2827	−3144	−3491	−3872
7	Inventory		−2696	−2976	−3309	−3675	−4076
8	Accounts Payable		2157	2381	2647	2940	3261
9	Cash from Operating Activities		11,942	12,884	14,884	17,107	19,574
10	Capital Expenditures		−25,000	−8000	−8000	−8000	−8000
11	Other Investment		—	—	—	—	—
12	Cash from Investing Activities		−25,000	−8000	−8000	−8000	−8000
13	Net Borrowing		20,000	—	—	—	—
14	Dividends		−4786	−2503	−4237	−6167	−8313
15	Cash from Financing Activities		15,214	−2503	−4237	−6167	−8313
16							
17	Change in Cash (9 + 12 + 15)		2157	2381	2647	2940	3261

Table 17.7, and dividends are equal to free cash flows to equity because we assume KXS pays out all excess cash. We can compute *FCF* to equity from Table 17.13 using the following equation:

$$FCF \text{ to Equity} = FCF \text{ of the Firm} + \text{Net Borrowing} - \text{After-tax Interest Expense} \tag{17.12}$$

KXS is not planning to raise any additional equity financing, so there are no capital contributions on the cash flow statement. As a final check on the calculations, note the change in the minimum cash balance shown on the balance sheet (Table 17.18). For example, in 2012, the change in cash and cash equivalents is $2.157 million, which is the amount by which 2012 cash exceeds 2011 cash on the balance sheet.

18 Working Capital Management

notation

CCC	cash conversion cycle	*NPV*	net present value
EAR	effective annual rate	*r*	discount rate
g	perpetuity growth rate		

INTERVIEW WITH Jessica Rempel,
TD Commercial Banking

University of Manitoba, 2009

Jessica Rempel works as an analyst for TD Commercial Banking, where she helps manage a portfolio of commercial clients with large borrowing needs. "I monitor a client's risk based on their financial statements to ensure that they can make their payments on existing credit arrangements as well as for any new credit requests."

A 2009 graduate of the University of Manitoba, Jessica keeps an eye on how clients manage their working capital to ensure that they will have no problems repaying their loans. Since default on a loan can occur with just a single missed interest payment, it is important for companies to have enough cash on hand to continue meeting the terms of their credit agreements. "The most common credit facility we provide is an operating line," Jessica says. "I need to look at the quality of their accounts receivable and their inventory management in order to make sure they'll have enough liquidity to handle the size of their financing request."

This requires an in-depth knowledge of accounting and finance, as a lot of Jessica's responsibilities involve sifting through a firm's financial information to find pertinent information. "When we get their financial statements, we'll make sure they are still meeting their debt covenants and that their performance is satisfactory."

In Chapter 2, we defined a firm's net working capital as its current assets minus its current liabilities. Net working capital is the capital required in the short term to run the business. Thus, working capital management involves short-term asset accounts such as cash, inventory, and accounts receivable, as well as short-term liability accounts such as accounts payable. The level of investment in each of these accounts differs from firm to firm and from industry to industry. It also depends on factors such as the type of business and industry standards. Some firms, for example, require heavy inventory investments because of the nature of their business.

Consider Viterra, a grain handling company, and Wyndham Worldwide Corporation, the owner and operator of hotels. Inventory amounted to 20% of Viterra's total assets at the end of 2010, whereas Wyndham's investment in inventory was less than 4%. A grain handler requires a large investment in inventory, but a hotel chain's profitability is generated primarily from its investment in plant, property, and equipment—that is, its hotels and furnishings.

There are opportunity costs associated with investing in inventories and accounts receivable, and from holding cash. Excess funds invested in these accounts could instead be used to pay down debt or be returned to shareholders in the form of a dividend or share repurchase. This chapter focuses on the tools firms use to manage their working capital efficiently and thereby minimize these opportunity costs. We begin by discussing why firms have working capital and how it affects firm value. In a perfect capital market, many of the working capital accounts would be irrelevant. Not surprisingly, the existence of these accounts for real firms can be traced to market frictions. We discuss the costs and benefits of trade credit and evaluate the tradeoffs firms make in managing various working capital accounts. Finally, we discuss the cash balance of a firm and provide an overview of the short-term investments in which a firm may choose to invest its cash.

18.1 Overview of Working Capital

Most projects require the firm to invest in net working capital. The main components of net working capital are cash, inventory, receivables, and payables. Working capital includes the cash that is needed to run the firm on a day-to-day basis. It does not include excess cash, which is cash that is not required to run the business and can be invested at a market rate. As we discussed in Chapter 12, excess cash may be viewed as part of the firm's capital structure, offsetting firm debt. In Chapter 8, we discussed how any increases in net working capital represent an investment that reduces the cash that is available to the firm. The Valuation Principle tells us that the value of the firm is the present value of its free cash flows. Therefore, working capital alters a firm's value by affecting its free cash flows. In this section, we examine the components of net working capital and their effects on the firm's value.

The Cash Cycle

The level of working capital reflects the length of time between when cash goes out of a firm at the beginning of the production process and when it comes back in. Take Intel, for example. Let's trace the path of $1000 worth of inventory and raw materials through Intel's production process.

▶ First, Intel buys $1000 of raw materials and inventory from its suppliers, purchasing them on credit, which means that the firm does not have to pay cash immediately at the time of purchase.

▶ About 53 days later, Intel pays for the materials and inventory, so almost two months have passed between when Intel purchased the materials and when the cash outflow occurred.

▶ After another 20 days, Intel sells the materials (now in the form of finished microprocessors) to a computer manufacturer, but the sale is on credit, meaning that the computer manufacturer does not pay cash immediately. A total of 73 days has passed between when Intel purchased the materials and when it sold them as part of the finished product.

▶ About 37 days later, the computer manufacturer pays for the microprocessors, producing a cash inflow for Intel.

operating cycle The average length of time between when a firm originally receives its inventory and when it receives the cash back from selling its product.

cash cycle The length of time between when a firm pays cash to purchase its initial inventory and when it receives cash from the sale of the output produced from that inventory.

cash conversion cycle (***CCC***) A measure of the cash cycle calculated as the sum of a firm's inventory days and accounts receivable days, less its accounts payable days.

A total of $53 + 20 + 37 = 110$ days have passed from when Intel originally bought the raw materials until it received the cash from selling the finished product. Thus, Intel's *operating cycle* is 110 days: a firm's **operating cycle** is the average length of time between when the firm originally purchases its inventory and when it receives the cash back from selling its product. A firm's **cash cycle** is the length of time between when the firm pays cash to purchase its initial inventory and when it receives cash from the sale of the output produced from that inventory. For Intel, the cash cycle is 57 days: the 20 days it holds the material after paying for it plus the 37 days it waits to receive cash after selling the finished product. Some companies actually have a *negative* cash cycle; they are paid for the product before they have to pay for the cost of producing it! This is generally possible only if companies keep very low inventory and have the size to force their suppliers to wait to be paid. Example 18.1 goes through an example of this for Loblaw Companies Limited. Figure 18.1 illustrates the operating and cash cycle.

Some practitioners measure the cash cycle by calculating the *cash conversion cycle*. The **cash conversion cycle (*CCC*)** is defined as follows:

$$CCC = \text{Inventory Days} + \text{Accounts Receivable Days} - \text{Accounts Payable Days} \quad (18.1)$$

| FIGURE 18.1 | The Cash and Operating Cycle for a Firm |

The cash cycle is the average time between when a firm pays for its inventory and when it receives cash from the sale of its product. If the firm pays cash for its inventory, this period is identical to the firm's cash cycle. However, most firms buy their inventory on credit, which reduces the amount of time between the cash investment and the receipt of cash from that investment.

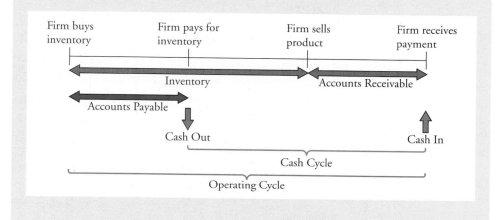

where

$$\text{Inventory Days} = \frac{\text{Inventory}}{\text{Average Daily Cost of Goods Sold}}$$

$$\text{Accounts Receivable Days} = \frac{\text{Accounts Receivable}}{\text{Average Daily Sales}}$$

$$\text{Accounts Payable Days} = \frac{\text{Accounts Payable}}{\text{Average Daily Cost of Goods Sold}}$$

| EXAMPLE 18.1 | **Problem** |
| Computing the Cash Conversion Cycle | The following information is from Loblaws 2010 income statement and balance sheet (numbers are $millions). Use it to compute Loblaws cash conversion cycle. |

Sales	30,997
Cost of Merchandise Inventories Sold	23,393
Accounts Receivable	724
Inventories	2114
Accounts Payable	3416

Solution

▶ Plan

The *CCC* is defined above as Inventory Days + Accounts Receivable Days − Accounts Payable Days. Thus, we need to compute each of the three ratios in the *CCC*. In order to do that, we need to convert Sales and Cost of Goods Sold (*COGS*) into their average daily amounts simply by dividing the total given for the year by 365 days in a year.

▶ Execute

Average Daily Sales = Sales/365 Days = 30,997/365 = 84.92
Average Daily *COGS* = *COGS*/365 Days = 23,393/365 = 64.09

$$\text{Inventory Days} = \frac{\text{Inventory}}{\text{Average Daily Cost of Goods Sold}} = \frac{2114}{64.09} = 32.98$$

$$\text{Accounts Receivable Days} = \frac{\text{Accounts Receivable}}{\text{Average Daily Sales}} = \frac{724}{84.92} = 8.53$$

$$\text{Accounts Payable Days} = \frac{\text{Accounts Payable}}{\text{Average Daily Cost of Goods Sold}} = \frac{3416}{64.09} = 53.30$$

Thus, Loblaws *CCC* = 32.98 + 8.53 − 53.30 = −11.79!

▶ Evaluate

Loblaw actually has a *negative* cash conversion cycle, meaning that it generally receives cash for its goods *before* it pays its suppliers. Loblaw is able to do this because it sells directly to the consumer, so it charges your credit card or receives cash as soon as you make your purchase. This results in a relatively low receivables balance. At the same time, Loblaws suppliers allow it to wait over 53 days before paying them. This more than offsets the number of days capital is tied up in inventory and receivables.

All of these ratios can be computed from the firm's financial statements. We discussed how to compute and use them in Chapter 2. Even though the cash conversion cycle is an important metric on its own, a financial manager needs to keep an eye on each of its components, as they all contain valuable information about how efficiently the firm is managing its working capital. Higher accounts receivable days may signal that the firm is having trouble collecting from its customers, and low accounts payable days might suggest that the firm is not taking full advantage of opportunities to delay payment to suppliers. Finally, high inventory days would focus a manager on why the firm needs to have its inventory on hand so long before it sells the product.

Working Capital Needs by Industry

The longer a firm's cash cycle, the more working capital the firm has, and the more cash it needs to carry to conduct its daily operations. Table 18.1 provides data on the working capital needs for selected firms in a variety of industries.

Because of the characteristics of the different industries, working capital levels vary significantly. As illustrated in the previous example, a retail store typically sells on a cash-only basis, so you would expect accounts receivable to be a very small percentage of its sales.[1] Lululemon and Indigo have very low accounts receivable balances as a

---

[1]When you use your Visa or MasterCard to pay for your groceries, it is a cash sale for the store. The credit card company pays the store cash on receipt of the credit slip, even if you do not pay your credit card bill on time.

TABLE 18.1

Working Capital in Various Industries

Company	Industry	Accounts Receivable Days	Inventory Days	Accounts Payable Days	CCC
Shaw Communications	Communications, media cable, and entertainment	19	10	116	−87
Forzani Group	Merchandising speciality stores	19	30	112	−63
WestJet Airlines	Air transport	2	3	50	−45
Loblaw Companies	Merchandising food stores	9	33	53	−12
Suncor Energy	Oil and gas, integrated oils	56	45	99	2
Indigo Books & Music	Merchandising specialty stores	3	91	73	21
Potash Corp. of Saskatchewan	Industrial products, chemicals, and fertilizers	41	61	62	40
Barrick Gold	Gold and precious metals	12	161	131	42
Lululemon Athletica	Merchandising clothing stores	7	70	18	59
Research In Motion	Industrial products technology—hardware	63	27	27	63
Molson Coors Brewing	Consumer products, breweries, and beverages	86	50	41	95
Bombardier	Industrial products and transportation equipment	36	119	52	103
Viterra	Agricultural industries	62	109	41	130
Cangene	Consumer products biotechnology/pharmaceuticals	43	373	103	313

Source: Latest data available in early 2011 from the SEDAR website, www.sedar.com.

percentage of sales. Similar results hold for WestJet Airlines, because many of its customers pay in advance for airline tickets with cash or credit cards. Inventory represents a large percentage of sales for firms such as Cangene, which have a long development and sales cycle. Note also the wide variation in the firms' cash conversion cycles. For example, WestJet's cash conversion cycle is negative, reflecting the fact that it receives cash from its customers before having to pay its suppliers.

Firm Value and Working Capital

To understand why working capital management can increase firm value, recall that any funds your company has from investors need to earn an opportunity cost of capital for those investors. Working capital ties up funds that could be deployed elsewhere in the firm to earn a return. For example, imagine $50,000 in raw materials sitting in a factory waiting to be used. That $50,000 needs to earn a return, so any delay in converting that material into a product that can be sold reduces its return. If you could improve your production process so that at any one time only $30,000 of raw material was waiting to be used, you would have freed up $20,000 to be invested elsewhere or returned to the shareholders. Similarly, when you allow your customers to pay within 30 days, you are giving them a 30-day interest-free loan. However, your investors and banks have not given you interest-free funds! If you can reduce the time it takes customers to pay without reducing sales, you can improve the return your investors earn on the business.

Any reduction in working capital requirements generates a positive free cash flow that the firm can distribute immediately to shareholders. For example, if a firm is able to reduce its required net working capital by $50,000, it will be able to distribute this $50,000 as a dividend to its shareholders immediately, or use it as a source of funds for other productive projects.

Recall that the Valuation Principle implies that the value of the firm is the present value of its free cash flows. Managing working capital efficiently will increase those free cash flows, allowing a manager to maximize firm value. We now turn our attention to some specific working capital accounts.

EXAMPLE 18.2

The Value of
Working Capital
Management

Problem

The projected net income and free cash flows next year for River City Paints are given in the following table (in $thousands):

Net Income	20,000
+ Depreciation	+5000
− Capital Expenditures	−5000
− Increase in Working Capital	−1000
= Free Cash Flow	19,000

River City expects capital expenditures and depreciation to continue to offset each other, and both net income and increase in working capital to grow at 4% per year. River City's cost of capital is 12%. If River City were able reduce its annual increase in working capital by 20% by managing its working capital more efficiently without adversely affecting any other part of the business, what would be the effect on River City's value?

Solution

▶ **Plan**

A 20% decrease in required working capital from its starting point would reduce the starting point from $1,000,000 per year to $800,000 per year. The working capital increases would still grow at 4% per year, but each increase would then be 20% smaller because of the 20% smaller starting point. We can value River City using the formula for a growing perpetuity from Chapter 4 (Equation 4.7):

$$PV = \frac{\text{Cash Flow}}{r - g}$$

We can calculate River City's free cash flow using the information contained in the table above: Net Income + Depreciation − Capital Expenditures − Increases in Working Capital.

▶ **Execute**

Currently, River City's value is as follows:

$$\frac{20{,}000{,}000 + 5{,}000{,}000 - 5{,}000{,}000 - 1{,}000{,}000}{0.12 - 0.04} = 237{,}500{,}000$$

If the company can manage its working capital more efficiently, the value will be as follows:

$$\frac{20{,}000{,}000 + 5{,}000{,}000 - 5{,}000{,}000 - 800{,}000}{0.12 - 0.04} = 240{,}000{,}000$$

▶ **Evaluate**

Although the change will not affect River City's earnings (net income), it will increase the free cash flow available to shareholders and increase the value of the firm by $2.5 million.

Concept Check

1. What is the difference between a firm's cash cycle and operating cycle?

2. How does working capital affect a firm's value?

18.2 Trade Credit

trade credit The difference between receivables and payables that is the net amount of a firm's capital consumed as a result of those credit transactions; the credit that a firm extends to its customers.

When a firm allows a customer to pay for goods at some date later than the date of purchase, it creates an account receivable for the firm and an account payable for the customer. Accounts receivable represent the credit sales for which a firm has yet to receive payment. The accounts payable balance represents the amount that a firm owes its suppliers for goods that it has received but for which it has not yet paid. The credit that the firm is extending to its customer is known as **trade credit**; the difference between receivables and payables is the net amount of a firm's capital consumed as a result of those credit transactions. A firm would, of course, prefer to be paid in cash at the time of purchase. A "cash-only" policy, however, may cause it to lose its customers to competition. Even after a customer decides to pay a bill, there is a delay before the money is credited to the firm because of processing and mailing the payment. In this section, we demonstrate how managers can compare the costs and benefits of trade credit to determine optimal credit policies.

Trade Credit Terms

To see how the terms of trade credit are quoted, let's consider some examples. If a supplier offers its customers terms of "net 30," payment is not due until 30 days from the date of the invoice. Essentially, the supplier is letting the customer use its money for an extra 30 days. (Note that "30" is not a magic number; the invoice could specify "net 40," "net 15," or any other number of days as the payment due date.)

cash discount The percentage discount offered on a payment if the buyer pays early.

discount period The number of days a buyer has to take advantage of the cash discount.

credit period The total length of time credit is extended to the buyer.

Sometimes the selling firm will offer the buying firm a discount if payment is made early. The terms "2/10, net 30" mean that the buying firm will receive a 2% discount if it pays for the goods within 10 days; otherwise, the full amount is due in 30 days. The **cash discount** is the percentage discount offered if the buyer pays early, in this case 2%. The **discount period** is the number of days the buyer has to take advantage of the cash discount; here it is 10 days. Finally, the **credit period** is the total length of time credit is extended to the buyer—the total amount of time the buyer has to pay. It is 30 days in our example. Firms offer discounts to encourage customers to pay early so that the selling firm gets cash from the sale sooner. However, the amount of the discount also represents a cost to the selling firm, because it does not receive the full selling price for the product. This timeline shows the terms of our 2/10, net 30 example:

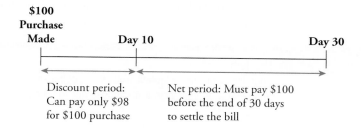

Trade Credit and Market Frictions

In a perfectly competitive market, trade credit is just another form of financing. As we learned in Chapter 15, financing decisions are irrelevant under the assumptions of perfect capital markets. In reality, product markets are rarely perfectly competitive, so firms can maximize their value by using their trade credit options effectively.

Common Mistake   Using *APR* Instead of *EAR* to Compute the Cost of Trade Credit

Some managers fail to fully recognize the cost of trade credit by using the annual percentage rate (*APR*, or simple interest) rather than the effective annual rate (*EAR*) to compute the annual cost for comparison with other financing options. Recall from Chapter 5 that whereas the *EAR* appropriately accounts for the compounding "interest on interest" effect over the year, the *APR* ignores compounding. Thus, in our example below with 2.04% interest over 20 days, the corresponding *APR* would be (365/20) × 2.04 = 37.23%, which is less than the true effective annual cost of this credit: 44.6%.

Cost of Trade Credit. Trade credit is, in essence, a loan from the selling firm to its customer. The price discount represents an interest rate. Often, firms offer favourable interest rates on trade credit as a price discount to their customers. Therefore, financial managers should evaluate the terms of trade credit to decide whether to use it.

How do we compute the interest rate on trade credit? Suppose a firm sells a product for $100 but offers its customer terms of 2/10, net 30. The customer doesn't have to pay anything for the first 10 days, so it effectively has a zero-interest loan for this period. If the customer takes advantage of the discount and pays within the 10-day discount period, the customer pays only $98 for the product. The cost of the discount to the selling firm is equal to the discount percentage times the selling price. In this case, it is 0.02 × $100, or $2.

Rather than pay within 10 days, the customer has the option to use the $98 for an additional 20 days (30 − 10 = 20). The interest rate for the 20-day term of the loan is $2/$98 = 2.04%. To compare this 20-day interest rate with interest rates available from other financing sources, we convert it to an *EAR* using Equation 5.1 from Chapter 5, where *n* is the number of 20-day periods in a year:

$$EAR = (1 + r)^n - 1$$

With a 365-day year, there are 365/20 (18.25) 20-day periods in a year. Thus, this 2.04% rate over 20 days corresponds to the following *EAR*:

$$EAR = (1.0204)^{365/20} - 1 = 44.6\%$$

Therefore, by not taking the discount, the firm is effectively paying 2.04% to borrow the money for 20 days, which translates to an *EAR* of 44.6%! If the firm can obtain a bank loan at a lower interest rate, it would be better off borrowing at the lower rate and using the cash proceeds of the loan to take advantage of the discount offered by the supplier.

EXAMPLE 18.3

Estimating the
Effective Cost of
Trade Credit

Problem

Your firm purchases goods from its supplier on terms of 1/15, net 40. What is the effective annual cost to your firm if it chooses not to take advantage of the trade discount offered?

Solution

▶ **Plan**

Using a $100 purchase as an example, 1/15, net 40 means that you get a 1% discount if you pay within 15 days, or you can pay the full amount within 40 days. One percent of $100 is a $1 discount, so you can either pay $99 in 15 days, or $100 in 40 days. The difference is 25 days, so you need to compute the interest rate over the 25 days and then compute the *EAR* associated with that 25-day interest rate.

> ▶ **Execute**
>
> The implied interest rate is $1/$99 = 0.0101, or 1.01% for 25 days. There are 365/25 = 15.6 periods of 25 days in a year. Thus, your effective annual rate is $(1.0101)^{14.6} - 1 = 0.158$, or 15.8%.

> ▶ **Evaluate**
>
> If you really need to take the full 40 days to produce the cash to pay, you would be better off borrowing the $99 from the bank at a lower rate and taking advantage of the discount.

Benefits of Trade Credit. For a number of reasons, trade credit can be an attractive source of funds. First, trade credit is simple and convenient to use, and it has lower transaction costs than alternative sources of funds. For example, no paperwork must be completed, as would be the case for a loan from a bank. Second, it is a flexible source of funds and can be used as needed. Finally, it is sometimes the only source of funding available to a firm.

Trade Credit Versus Standard Loans. You might wonder why companies would ever provide trade credit. After all, most companies are not banks, so why are they in the business of making loans? Several reasons explain their willingness to offer trade credit. First, providing financing at below-market rates is an indirect way to lower prices for only certain customers. Consider, for example, an automobile manufacturer. Rather than lowering prices on all cars, the financing division may offer specific credit terms that are attractive to customers with bad credit, but unattractive to customers with good credit. In this way, the car manufacturer is able to discount the price only for those customers with bad credit who otherwise might not be able to afford the car.

Second, because a supplier may have an ongoing business relationship with its customer, it may have more information about the credit quality of the customer than a traditional outside lender such as a bank would have. The supplier may also be able to increase the likelihood of payment by threatening to cut off future supplies if payment is not made. Finally, if the buyer defaults, the supplier may be able to seize the inventory as collateral. This inventory is likely to be more valuable to a company within the industry, such as the supplier (which presumably has other customers), than to an outsider.

Managing Float

collection float The amount of time it takes for a firm to be able to use funds after a customer has paid for its goods.

One factor that contributes to the length of a firm's receivables and payables is the delay between the time a bill is paid and the time the cash is actually received. This delay, or processing float, will affect a firm's working capital requirements.

Collection Float. The amount of time it takes for a firm to be able to use funds after a customer has paid for its goods is referred to as **collection float**. Firms can reduce their working capital needs by reducing their collection float. Collection float is determined by three factors, as shown in Figure 18.2:

mail float The time it takes a firm to receive a customer's payment cheque after the customer has mailed it.

> ▶ **Mail float:** How long it takes the firm to receive a payment cheque after the customer has mailed it

FIGURE 18.2

Collection Float

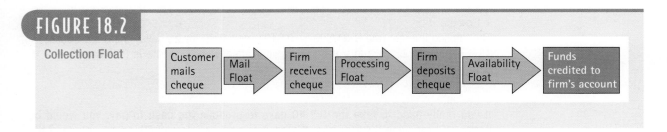

processing float The time it takes a firm to process a customer's payment cheque and deposit it in the bank.

availability float The time it takes a bank to give a firm credit for customer payments the firm has deposited in the bank.

disbursement float The amount of time it takes before a firm's payments to its suppliers actually result in a cash outflow for the firm.

▶ **Processing float:** How long it takes the firm to process a customer's payment cheque and deposit it in the bank

▶ **Availability float:** How long it takes a bank to post the funds from customer payments the firm has deposited in the bank

Disbursement Float. The amount of time it takes before payments to suppliers actually result in a cash outflow for the firm is referred to as **disbursement float**. Similar to the collection float, it is a function of mail time, processing time, and cheque-clearing time. Although a firm may try to extend its disbursement float in order to lengthen its payables and reduce its working capital needs, it risks making late payments to suppliers. In such a case, the firm may be charged an additional fee for paying late or may be required to pay cash before delivery (CBD) or cash on delivery (COD) for future purchases. In some cases, the supplier may refuse to do business in the future with the delinquent firm.

Electronic Cheque Processing. Firms can employ several methods to reduce their collection and disbursement floats. In addition, many countries have streamlined the way cheques are handled. In the 1980s, Singapore began making electronic images of cheques. By 2001, the cheque-clearing systems in Singapore, Spain, the United Kingdom, and Australia allowed for the clearing of cheques through the use of image transmissions rather than physically moving actual paper cheques. In 2004, the United States adopted such a system. In Canada, the Canadian Payments Association had been working on the "Truncation and Electronic Cheque Presentment" system, with a goal of implementation by 2009. The 11-year-old project was scrapped in October of 2008, and banks have developed and implemented their own imaging projects to try to gain efficiencies. These systems allow for cheques to clear more quickly. As the efficiency increases, it may be possible for financial institutions to reduce the hold period that is sometimes applied when a cheque is deposited. If this occurs, then a firm's collection float would be reduced. So far, though, evidence from the United States shows that even though the funds are taken out of the cheque writer's account almost immediately, the cheque recipient's account is not credited as quickly.

There are, however, several ways that a firm *can* reduce its collection float. For example, the firm may streamline its in-house cheque-processing procedures. In addition, with electronic collection, funds are automatically transferred from the customer's bank account to the firm's bank account on the payment date, reducing the collection float to zero. The methods a firm employs to reduce its collection float are not without costs, of course. New cheque processing systems could be expensive and disruptive, and hiring a collection agency to speed up collections generates costs such as fees to the agency, as well as bad will with the firm's customers. Therefore, to decide which method, if any, to employ, the firm must compare the costs and benefits of systems that allow it to use its cash for a longer period.

3. What does the term "2/10, net 30" mean?

4. List three factors that determine collection float.

18.3 Receivables Management

So far, we have discussed the costs and benefits of trade credit in general. Next, we look at some issues that arise specifically from the management of a firm's accounts receivable. In particular, we focus on how a firm adopts a policy for offering credit to its customers and how it monitors its accounts receivable on an ongoing basis.

Determining the Credit Policy

Establishing a credit policy involves three steps that we will discuss in turn:

1. Establishing credit standards
2. Establishing credit terms
3. Establishing a collection policy

Establishing Credit Standards. Management must first decide on its credit standards. Will it extend credit to anyone who applies for it? Or will it be selective and extend credit only to those customers who have very low credit risk? Unless the firm adopts the former policy, it will need to assess the credit risk of each customer before deciding whether to grant credit. Large firms perform this analysis in-house with their own credit departments. Small firms purchase credit reports from credit rating agencies such as Dun & Bradstreet.

Many firms will consider additional factors when deciding whether to grant credit to a particular customer. For example, in order to win sales a firm may be more likely to grant credit if the customer is expected to be a repeat customer. If the cost of the credit is small relative to the purchase price, the firm may also adopt a less restrictive policy. Thus, while credit risk is the starting point, the firm's managers may choose to extend credit strategically when dealing with potentially important customers or high-margin sales.

> ### The 5 C's of Credit
>
> Lenders have coined the phrase "The 5 C's of Credit" to summarize the qualities they look for before granting credit:
>
> **Character:** Is the borrower trustworthy, with a history of meeting its debt obligations?
>
> **Capacity:** Will the borrower have enough cash flow to make its payments?
>
> **Capital:** Does the borrower have enough capital (net worth) to justify the loan?
>
> **Collateral:** Does the borrower have any assets that can secure the loan?
>
> **Conditions:** How are the borrower and the economy performing and how are they expected to perform?

The decision of how much credit risk to assume plays a large role in determining how much money a firm ties up in its receivables. Although a restrictive policy can result in a lower sales volume, the firm will have a smaller investment in receivables. Conversely, a less selective policy will produce higher sales, but the level of receivables will also rise.

Establishing Credit Terms. After a firm decides on its credit standards, it must next establish its credit terms. The firm decides on the length of the period before payment must be made (the "net" period) and chooses whether to offer a discount to encourage early payments. If it offers a discount, it must also determine the discount percentage and the discount period. If the firm is relatively small, it will probably follow the lead of other firms in the industry in establishing these terms.

EXAMPLE 18.4

Evaluating a Change in Credit Policy

Problem

Your company currently sells its product with a 1% discount to customers who pay cash immediately. Otherwise, the full price is due within 30 days. Half of your customers take advantage of the discount. You are considering dropping the discount so that your new terms would just be net 30. If you do that, you expect to lose some customers who were willing to pay only the discounted price, but the rest will simply switch to taking the full 30 days to pay. You estimate that you will sell 20 fewer units per month (compared to 500 units currently). Your variable cost per unit is $60, and your price per unit is $100. If your required return is 1% per month, should you change your policy?

Solution

▶ **Plan**

To decide whether to change your policy, compute the *NPV* of the change. It costs you $30,000 to make the 500 units. You receive payment for half of the units immediately at a price of $99 per unit (1% discount). The other half of the payment comes in 30 days at a price of $100 per unit. At that point, you are starting over again with the next set of product. Thus, you can think of your cash flows in any 30-day period as shown in the table below:

	Now	30 days	
Produce first set of 500 units at $60 apiece	−30,000		
Customers pay for 250 units at $99 apiece	+24,750		
Customers pay for 250 units at $100 apiece		+25,000	. . .
Produce next set of 500 units at $60 apiece		−30,000	. . .
Customers pay for 250 units at $99 apiece		+24,750	. . .
Total	−5250	+25,000 − 5250	. . .

Under the new policy, your cash flows would change to the following:

	Now	30 days	
Produce first set of 480 units at $60 apiece	−28,800		
Customers pay for 480 units at $100 apiece		+48,000	. . .
Produce next set of 480 units at $60 apiece		−28,800	. . .
Total	−28,800	+48,000 − 28,800	

With these cash flows, we are ready to compute the *NPV* of the policy change.

▶ **Execute**

$$NPV_{current} = -5250 + \frac{25,000 - 5250}{0.01} = 1,969,750$$

$$NPV_{new} = -28,800 + \frac{48,000 - 28,800}{0.01} = 1,891,200$$

So the *NPV* of the change will be $1,969,750 - \$1,891,200 = -\$78,550$.

▶ **Evaluate**

You shouldn't make the change, because you will lose too many customers, even though your remaining customers will be paying the full price. The *NPV* helps us weigh this tradeoff—the present value of the costs outweighs the present value of the benefits, so the decision is not a good one.

Establishing a Collection Policy. The last step in the development of a credit policy is to decide on a collection policy. The content of this policy can range from doing nothing if a customer is paying late (generally not a good choice), to sending a polite letter of inquiry, to charging interest on payments extending beyond a specified period, to threatening legal action at the first late payment.

Monitoring Accounts Receivable

After establishing a credit policy, a firm must monitor its accounts receivable to analyze whether its credit policy is working effectively. Two tools that firms use to monitor the accounts receivable are the *accounts receivable days* (or average collection period) and the *aging schedule*.

accounts receivable days
The average number of days that a firm takes to collect on its sales.

Accounts Receivable Days. The **accounts receivable days** is the average number of days that it takes a firm to collect on its sales. A firm can compare this number to the payment policy specified in its credit terms to judge the effectiveness of its credit policy. If the credit terms specify "net 30" and the accounts receivable days outstanding is 50 days, the firm can conclude that its customers are paying 20 days late, on average.

The firm should also look at the trend in the accounts receivable days over time. If the accounts receivable days ratio of a firm has been approximately 35 days for the past few years and it is 43 days this year, the firm may want to reexamine its credit policy. Of course, if the economy is sluggish, the entire industry may be affected. Under these circumstances, the increase might have little to do with the firm itself.

Accounts receivable days can be calculated from the firm's financial statement. Outside investors commonly use this measure to evaluate a firm's credit management policy. A major weakness of the accounts receivable days is that it is merely one number and conceals much useful information. Seasonal sales patterns may cause the number calculated for the accounts receivable days to change depending on when the calculation takes place. The number can also look reasonable even when a substantial percentage of the firm's customers are paying late.

aging schedule
Categorizes a firm's accounts by the number of days they have been on the firm's books. It can be prepared using either the number of accounts or the dollar amount of the accounts receivable outstanding.

Aging Schedule. An **aging schedule** categorizes accounts by the number of days they have been on the firm's books. It can be prepared using either the number of accounts or the dollar amount of the accounts receivable outstanding. For example, assume that a firm selling on terms of 2/15, net 30 has $530,000 in accounts receivable that has been on the books for 15 or fewer days in 220 accounts. The firm has another $450,000 that has been on the books for 16 to 30 days and is made up of 190 accounts, and $350,000 has been on the books for 31 to 45 days and represents 80 accounts. The firm has $200,000 that has been on the books for 46 to 60 days in 60 accounts. Yet another $70,000 has been on the books for more than 60 days and is made up of 20 accounts. Table 18.2 includes aging schedules based on the number of accounts and dollar amounts outstanding.

TABLE 18.2	**(a) Number of Accounts**		

Aging Schedules

(a) Number of Accounts

Days Outstanding	Number of Accounts	Percentage of Accounts (%)
1–15	220	38.6
16–30	190	33.3
31–45	80	14.0
46–60	60	10.5
60+	20	3.5
	570	100.0

(b) Dollar Amounts Outstanding

Days Outstanding	Amount Outstanding ($)	Percentage Outstanding (%)
1–15	530,000	33.1
16–30	450,000	28.1
31–45	350,000	21.9
46–60	200,000	12.5
60+	70,000	4.4
	1,600,000	100.0

In this case, if the firm's average daily sales are $65,000, its accounts receivable days is $1,600,000/$65,000 = 25$ days. But on closer examination, using the aging schedules in Table 18.2, we can see that 28% of the firm's credit customers (and 39% by dollar amounts) are paying late.

EXAMPLE 18.5
Aging Schedules

Problem

Financial Training Systems (FTS) bills its accounts on terms of 3/10, net 30. The firm's accounts receivable include $100,000 that has been outstanding for 10 or fewer days, $300,000 outstanding for 11 to 30 days, $100,000 outstanding for 31 to 40 days, $20,000 outstanding for 41 to 50 days, $10,000 outstanding for 51 to 60 days, and $2000 outstanding for more than 60 days. Prepare an aging schedule for FTS.

Solution

▶ **Plan**

An aging schedule shows the amount and percentage of total accounts receivable outstanding for different lengths outstanding. With the available information, we can calculate the aging schedule based on dollar amounts outstanding.

▶ **Execute**

Days Outstanding	Amount Outstanding ($)	Percentage Outstanding (%)
1–10	100,000	18.8
11–30	300,000	56.4
31–40	100,000	18.8
41–50	20,000	3.8
51–60	10,000	1.9
60+	2000	0.3
	532,000	100.0

▶ **Evaluate**

FTS does not have an excessive percentage outstanding at the long-end of the table (only 6% of the company's accounts receivable are more than 40 days outstanding).

payments pattern The pattern of the percentage of monthly sales for which the firm collects payment in each month after the sale.

If the aging schedule gets "bottom-heavy"—that is, if the percentages in the lower half of the schedule, representing late-paying firms, begin to increase—the firm will probably need to revisit its credit policy. The aging schedule is also sometimes augmented by analysis of the **payments pattern**, which provides information on the percentage of monthly sales for which the firm collects payment in each month after the sale. By examining past data, a firm may observe that 10% of its sales are usually collected in the month of the sale, 40% in the month following the sale, 25% two months after the sale, 20% three months after the sale, and 5% four months after the sale. Management can compare this normal payments pattern to the current payments pattern. Knowledge of the payments pattern is also useful for forecasting the firm's working capital requirements.

Concept
Check

5. Describe three steps in establishing a credit policy.

6. What is the difference between accounts receivable days and an aging schedule?

18.4 Payables Management

A firm should choose to borrow using accounts payable only if trade credit is the cheapest source of funding. The cost of the trade credit depends on the credit terms. The higher the discount percentage offered, the greater the cost of forgoing the discount. The cost of forgoing the discount is also higher with a shorter loan period. When a company has a choice between trade credit from two different suppliers, it should take the least expensive alternative.

In addition, a firm should always pay on the latest day allowed. For example, if the discount period is 10 days and the firm is taking the discount, payment should be made on day 10, not on day 2. If the discount is not taken and the terms are 2/10, net 30, the full payment should be made on day 30, not on day 16. A firm should strive to keep its money working for it as long as possible without developing a bad relationship with its suppliers or engaging in unethical practices. In this section, we examine two techniques that firms use to monitor their accounts payable.

Determining Accounts Payable Days Outstanding

Similar to the situation with its accounts receivable, a firm should monitor its accounts payable to ensure that it is making its payments at an optimal time. One method is to calculate the accounts payable days outstanding and compare it to the credit terms. The accounts payable days outstanding is the accounts payable balance expressed in terms of the number of days of cost of goods sold. If the accounts payable outstanding is 40 days and the terms are 2/10, net 30, the firm can conclude that it generally pays late and may be risking supplier difficulties. Conversely, if the accounts payable days outstanding is 25 days and the firm has not been taking the discount, the firm is paying too early. It could be earning another five days' interest on its money.

EXAMPLE 18.6

Accounts Payable Management

Problem

The Rowd Company has an average accounts payable balance of $250,000. Its average daily cost of goods sold is $14,000, and it receives terms of 2/15, net 40 from its suppliers. Rowd chooses to forgo the discount. Is the firm managing its accounts payable well?

Solution

▶ Plan

Given Rowd's accounts payable balance and its daily *COGS*, we can compute the average number of days Rowd takes to pay its vendors by dividing the average balance by the daily costs. Given the terms from its suppliers, Rowd should either be paying on the 15th day (the last possible day to get the discount) or on the 40th day (the last possible day to pay). There is no benefit to paying at any other time.

▶ Execute

Rowd's accounts payable days outstanding is $250,000/$14,000 = 17.9 days. If Rowd made payment three days earlier, it could take advantage of the 2% discount. If, for some reason, it chose to forgo the discount, it should not be paying the full amount until the 40th day.

▶ Evaluate

The firm is not managing its accounts payable well. The earlier it pays, the sooner the cash leaves Rowd. Thus, the only reason to pay before the 40th day is to receive the discount by paying before the 15th day. Paying on the 18th day not only misses the discount, but also costs the firm 22 days (40 − 18) use of its cash.

Stretching Accounts Payable

stretching the accounts payable A firm's practice of ignoring a payment due period and paying later.

Some firms ignore the payment due period and pay the amount owed later, in a practice referred to as **stretching the accounts payable**. Given terms of 2/10, net 30, for example, a firm may choose not to pay the amount owed until 45 days have passed. Doing so reduces the direct cost of trade credit because it lengthens the time that a firm has use of the funds. Although the interest rate per period remains the same—$2/$98 = 2.04%—the firm is now using the $98 for 35 days beyond the discount period, rather than 20 days as provided by the trade credit terms.

EXAMPLE 18.7

Cost of Trade Credit with Stretched Accounts Payable

Problem

What is the effective annual cost of credit terms of 1/15, net 40 if the firm stretches the accounts payable to 60 days?

Solution

▶ Plan

First, we need to compute the interest rate per period. The 1% discount means that on a $100 purchase, you can either pay $99 in the discount period, or keep the $99 and pay $100 later. Thus, you pay $1 interest on the $99. If you pay on time, then this $1 in interest is over the 25-day period between the 15th day and the 40th day. If you stretch, then this $1 in interest is over the 45-day period between the 15th day and the 60th day.

▶ Execute

The interest rate per period is $1/$99 = 1.01%. If the firm delays payment until the 60th day, it has use of the funds for 45 days beyond the discount period. There are 365/45 = 8.11 45-day periods in one year. Thus, the effective annual cost is $(1.0101)^{8.11} - 1 = 0.0849$, or 8.49%.

▶ Evaluate

Paying on time corresponds to a 25-day credit period, and there are 365/25 = 14.6 periods of 25 days in a year. Thus, if the firm pays on the 40th day, the effective annual cost is $(1.0101)^{14.6} - 1 = 0.1580$, or 15.8%. By stretching its payables, the firm substantially reduces its effective cost of credit.

Firms may also make a payment on the 30th day but pay only the discounted price. Some may pay only the discounted price and pay even later than the 30th day. Although all of these actions will reduce the effective annual rate associated with the trade credit, the firm may incur costs as a result of these actions. Suppliers may react to a firm whose payments are always late by imposing terms of cash on delivery (COD) or cash before delivery (CBD). The delinquent firm then bears the additional costs associated with these terms and may have to negotiate a bank loan to have the cash available to pay. The supplier may also discontinue business with the delinquent customer, leaving the customer to find another source, which may be more expensive or of lower quality. A poor credit rating might also result, making it difficult for the firm to obtain good terms with any other supplier. Moreover, when a firm explicitly agrees to the terms of the sale, violating these terms constitutes unethical business behaviour.

Concept Check

7. What is the optimal time for a firm to pay its accounts payable?

8. What do the terms "COD" and "CBD" mean?

18.5 Inventory Management

As we discussed earlier, in a perfect capital markets setting, firms would not need to have accounts payable or receivable. Interest rates on trade credit would be competitive, and firms could use alternative sources of financing. However, unlike trade credit, inventory represents one of the required factors of production. Therefore, even in a perfect markets setting, firms still need inventory.

Inventory management receives extensive coverage in a course on operations management. Nevertheless, it is the firm's financial manager who must arrange for the financing necessary to support the firm's inventory policy and who is responsible for ensuring the firm's overall profitability. Therefore, the role of the inventory manager is to balance the costs and benefits associated with inventory. Because excessive inventory uses cash, efficient management of inventory increases firm value.

Benefits of Holding Inventory

stock-out The situation in which a firm runs out of inventory.

For several reasons, a firm needs its inventory to operate. First, inventory helps minimize the risk that the firm will not be able to obtain an input it needs for production. If a firm holds too little inventory, a **stock-out**—running out of inventory—may occur and lead to lost sales. Disappointed customers may switch to one of the firm's competitors.

Second, firms may hold inventory because factors such as seasonality in demand mean that customer purchases do not perfectly match the most efficient production cycle. Consider the case of the Snowdrift Toy Company. As is typical for many toy manufacturers, 80% of Snowdrift's annual sales occur between September and December, in anticipation of the holiday gift season. It is more efficient for Snowdrift to manufacture toys at relatively constant levels throughout the year. If Snowdrift produces its toys at a constant rate, its inventory levels will increase to very high levels by August, in anticipation of the increase in sales beginning in September. In contrast, Snowdrift may consider a seasonal manufacturing strategy, producing more toys between September and December when sales are high. Under this strategy, inventory would not accumulate, freeing up cash flow from working capital and reducing the costs of inventory. However, seasonal manufacturing incurs additional costs, such as increased wear and tear on the manufacturing equipment during peak demand and the need to hire and train seasonal workers. Snowdrift must weigh the costs of the inventory buildup under constant production against the benefits of more efficient production. The optimal choice is likely to involve a compromise between the two extremes, so Snowdrift will carry some inventory.

Costs of Holding Inventory

As suggested by the Snowdrift Toy example, tying up capital in inventory is costly for a firm. We can classify the direct costs associated with inventory into three categories:

▶ *Acquisition costs* are the costs of the inventory itself over the period being analyzed (usually one year).

▶ *Order costs* are the total costs of placing an order over the period being analyzed.

▶ *Carrying costs* include storage costs, insurance, taxes, spoilage, obsolescence, and the opportunity cost of the funds tied up in the inventory.

Minimizing these total costs involves some tradeoffs. For example, if we assume no quantity discounts are available, the lower the level of inventory a firm carries, the lower its carrying cost but the higher its annual order costs because it needs to place more orders during the year.

"just-in-time" (JIT) inventory management
The practice of acquiring inventory precisely when the firm needs it so that the firm's inventory balance is always zero, or very close to it.

Some firms seek to reduce their carrying costs as much as possible. With **"just-in-time" (JIT) inventory management,** a firm acquires inventory precisely when needed so that its inventory balance is always zero, or very close to it. This technique requires exceptional coordination with suppliers, as well as a predictable demand for the firm's products. In 2007, Boeing established a global production system for its new 787 "Dreamliner." Very little of the new plane is actually produced at its plant in Everett, Washington. Rather, all of the plane's major systems, including the fuselage and wings, are produced elsewhere and are flown to the final assembly plant using a specially modified 747 cargo plane. The pieces arrive very shortly before they are needed in the final assembly of the airplane, so Boeing does not have to incur the carrying costs of maintaining a large inventory. However, such a plan has risks, as Boeing initially had substantial troubles with its contracted producers finishing their parts on time. Consequently, the firm delayed the delivery of the first planes and faced significant financial penalties from doing so.

Even if your company does not practice JIT inventory management, it may be forced to adopt it if a major customer does so. For example, in 1999, Toys 'R Us instituted JIT, which caused one of its suppliers, toy manufacturer Hasbro, to make changes in its production schedule.[2]

Concept Check

9. What are the direct costs of holding inventory?

10. Describe "just-in-time" inventory management.

---

[2]Hasbro 1999 annual report.

18.6 **Cash Management**

In the perfect markets setting, the level of cash is irrelevant. With perfect capital markets, a firm is able to raise new money instantly at a fair rate, so it can never be short of cash. Similarly, the firm can invest excess cash at a fair rate to earn an *NPV* of zero.

In the real world, of course, markets are not perfect. Liquidity has a cost; for example, holding liquid assets may earn a below-market return, and a firm may incur transaction costs if it needs to raise cash quickly. Similarly, recall from Chapter 15 that holding excess cash has a tax disadvantage. In these cases, the optimal strategy for a firm is to hold cash in anticipation of seasonalities in demand for its products and random shocks that affect its business. Risky firms and firms with high-growth opportunities tend to hold a relatively high percentage of assets as cash. Firms with easy access to capital markets (for which the transaction costs of accessing cash are therefore lower) tend to hold less cash.[3] In this section, we examine the firm's motivation for holding cash, tools for managing cash, and the short-term securities in which firms invest.

Motivation for Holding Cash

A firm holds cash for three reasons:

▶ To meet its day-to-day needs

▶ To compensate for the uncertainty associated with its cash flows

▶ To satisfy bank requirements

We will now examine in detail each of these motivations for holding cash.

transactions balance
The amount of cash a firm needs to be able to pay its bills.

Transactions Balance. Just like you, a firm or business must hold enough cash to pay its bills. The amount of cash a firm needs to be able to pay its bills is sometimes referred to as a **transactions balance**. The amount of cash a firm needs to satisfy the transactions balance requirement depends on both the average size of the transactions made by the firm and the firm's cash cycle, discussed earlier in the chapter.

precautionary balance
The amount of cash a firm holds to counter the uncertainty surrounding its future cash needs.

Precautionary Balance. The amount of cash a firm holds to counter the uncertainty surrounding its future cash needs is known as a **precautionary balance**. The size of this balance depends on the degree of uncertainty surrounding a firm's cash flows. The more uncertain future cash flows are, the harder it is for a firm to predict its transactions need, so the larger the precautionary balance must be.

compensating balance
An amount a firm's bank may require the firm to maintain in an account at the bank as compensation for services the bank may perform.

Compensating Balance. A firm's bank may require it to hold a **compensating balance** in an account at the bank as compensation for services that the bank performs. Compensating balances are typically deposited in accounts that either earn no interest or pay a very low interest rate. This arrangement is similar to a bank offering individuals free chequing as long as their balances do not fall below a certain level—say, $1000. Essentially, the customer has $1000 cash that she cannot use unless she is willing to pay a service charge. Similarly, the cash that a firm has tied up to meet a compensating balance requirement is unavailable for other uses.

---

[3]See T. Opler, L. Pinkowitz, R. Stulz, and R. Williamson, "The Determinants and Implications of Corporate Cash Holdings," *Journal of Financial Economics* 52 (1) (1999): 3–46.

Cash Balances

Corporate liquidity is measured as corporate investments in short-term, marketable securities. In the United States, it rose from $3.6 trillion in 1999 to $5.6 trillion in 2007, an increase of almost 55%. According to a 2004 survey of more than 360 companies conducted by Treasury Strategies, Inc., a Chicago consultant, more than half of those firms consider themselves to be net investors, having more short-term investments than short-term debt outstanding.

Why have companies been accumulating more cash? Factors include a shift away from industries such as manufacturing that spend heavily on plant and equipment, strength in sectors such as financial services that have low capital expenditures and high cash flows, and reluctance by companies to invest heavily after the technology spending spree in the late 1990s. As a result, corporate savings have reached an all-time high.

How are companies investing their cash? A 2007 survey by Treasury Strategies indicated that 20% is invested in money market funds and accounts, 18%

is invested in bonds and notes, and the remainder is invested directly in commercial paper, certificates of deposit, repurchase agreements, and other investments.

During the 2008 financial crisis, short-term credit markets froze, and many businesses that relied on short-term credit found themselves unable to conduct business. You might expect that businesses that held a lot of cash were in good shape. However, during the crisis cash-holding firms did not know what to do with the cash. Before it became clear that governments were going to bail out large banks, firms had to worry about how secure their cash was. In the event of a bank bankruptcy, the firm risked losing access to its cash in the short term and perhaps ultimately losing the cash altogether. For firms that relied on cash balances to conduct business, the impact of the breakdown in financial markets was potentially as big as for firms that relied on credit.

Source: Authors' calculations from Federal Reserve Data and Treasury Strategies 2007 Corporate Liquidity Research Overview.

Alternative Investments

In our discussion of collection and disbursement floats, we assumed that the firm will invest any cash in short-term securities. In fact, the firm may choose from a variety of short-term securities that differ somewhat with regard to their default risk and liquidity risk. The greater the risk, the higher the expected return on the investment. The financial manager must decide how much risk she is willing to accept in return for a higher yield. If her firm expects to need the funds within the next 30 days, the manager will probably avoid the less liquid options. Table 18.3 briefly describes the most frequently used short-term investments; these short-term debt securities are collectively referred to as *money market securities*.

Thus, a financial manager who wants to invest the firm's funds in the least risky security will choose to invest in treasury bills. However, if the financial manager wishes to earn a higher return on the firm's short-term investments, she may opt to invest some or all of the firm's excess cash in a riskier alternative, such as commercial paper.

Concept Check

11. List three reasons why a firm holds cash.

12. What tradeoff does a firm face when choosing how to invest its cash?

TABLE 18.3	Money Market Investment Options			
Investment	**Description**	**Maturity**	**Risk**	**Liquidity**
Cash management bills	Very short-term debt of the Canadian government.	One day up to less than three months when newly issued.	Default risk free.	Very liquid and marketable.
Treasury bills	Short-term debt of the Canadian government. Provincial governments also issue their own treasury bills.	Three, 6, or 12 months when newly issued.	Default risk free.	Very liquid and marketable.
Term deposits, certificates of deposit (CDs), guaranteed investment certificates (GICs)	Short-term debt issued by banks.	Term deposits have maturities up to one year. CD maturities are 30 days to five years. GIC maturities are one to five years.	If the issuing bank is insured by the CDIC, any amount up to $100,000 is free of default risk because it is covered by the insurance. Any amount in excess of $100,000 is not insured and is subject to default risk.	These are generally not liquid. CDs from U.S. banks do have a liquid secondary market.
Repurchase agreements	Essentially a loan arrangement wherein a securities dealer is the "borrower" and the investor is the "lender." The investor buys securities, such as treasury bills, from the securities dealer, with an agreement to sell the securities back to the dealer at a later date for a specified higher price.	Very short term, ranging from overnight to approximately three months.	The security serves as collateral for the loan, and therefore the investor is exposed to very little risk. However, the investor needs to consider the creditworthiness of the securities dealer when assessing the risk.	No secondary market exists.
Banker's acceptances	Drafts written by the borrower and guaranteed by the bank on which the draft is drawn. Typically used in international trade transactions. The borrower is an importer who writes the draft in payment for goods.	Typically one to six months.	Because both the borrower and a bank have guaranteed the draft, there is very little risk.	When the exporter receives the draft, he may hold it until maturity and receive its full value, or he may sell the draft at a discount prior to maturity.
Bearer deposit notes	Short-term discount notes issued by banks.	Up to one year.	Guaranteed by the issuing bank, but not by the CDIC, these notes entail very little risk.	Secondary market exists.
Commercial paper	Short-term, unsecured debt issued by large corporations. The minimum denomination is $25,000, but most commercial paper has a face value of $100,000 or more.	Typically one to six months.	Default risk depends on the creditworthiness of the issuing corporation.	Secondary market exists.

MyFinanceLab

Here is what you should know after reading this chapter. MyFinanceLab will help you identify what you know, and where to go when you need to practice.

Key Points	Key Terms	Online Practice Opportunities
18.1 Overview of Working Capital ▶ Working capital management involves managing a firm's short-term assets and short-term liabilities. ▶ A firm's cash cycle is the length of time between when the firm pays cash to purchase its initial inventory and when it receives cash from the sale of the output produced from that inventory. The operating cycle is the average length of time between when a firm originally purchases its inventory and when it receives the cash back from selling its product.	cash conversion cycle (CCC), p. 612 cash cycle, p. 612 operating cycle, p. 612	MyFinanceLab Study Plan 18.1
18.2 Trade Credit ▶ Trade credit is effectively a loan from the selling firm to its customer. The cost of trade credit depends on the credit terms. The cost of not taking a discount that is offered by a supplier implies an interest rate for the loan. ▶ Firms provide trade credit to their customers for two reasons: (a) as an indirect way to lower prices and (b) because firms may have advantages in making loans to their customers relative to other potential sources of credit. ▶ A firm should compare the cost of trade credit with the cost of alternative sources of financing in deciding whether to use the trade credit offered. ▶ The collection float is the amount of time it takes for a firm to be able to use funds after a customer has paid for its goods. Firms can reduce their working capital needs by reducing their collection float.	availability float, p. 620 cash discount, p. 617 collection float, p. 619 credit period, p. 617 disbursement float, p. 620 discount period, p. 617 mail float, p. 619 processing float, p. 620 trade credit, p. 617	MyFinanceLab Study Plan 18.2
18.3 Receivables Management ▶ Establishing a credit policy involves three steps: establishing credit standards, establishing credit terms, and establishing a collection policy. ▶ The accounts receivables days and aging schedule are two methods used to monitor the effectiveness of a firm's credit policy.	accounts receivable days, p. 623 aging schedule, p. 623 payments pattern, p. 625	MyFinanceLab Study Plan 18.3

18.4 Payables Management

▶ Firms should monitor accounts payable to ensure that they are making payments at an optimal time.

▶ Firms hold inventory to avoid lost sales due to stock-outs and because of factors such as seasonal demand.

stretching the accounts payable, p. 626

MyFinanceLab
Study Plan 18.4

18.5 Inventory Management

▶ Because excessive inventory uses cash, efficient inventory management increases the firm's free cash flow and thus increases firm value.

▶ The costs of inventory include acquisition costs, order costs, and carrying costs.

"just-in-time" (JIT) inventory management, p. 628

stock-out, p. 627

MyFinanceLab
Study Plan 18.5

18.6 Cash Management

▶ If a firm's need to hold cash is reduced, the funds can be invested in a number of different short-term securities, including cash management bills, treasury bills, term deposits, certificates of deposit, guaranteed investment certificates, repurchase agreements, banker's acceptances, bearer deposit notes, and commercial paper.

compensating balance, p. 629

precautionary balance, p. 629

transactions balance, p. 629

MyFinanceLab
Study Plan 18.6

Review Questions

1. What does a firm's cash cycle tell us?

2. Answer the following:
   a. What is the difference between a firm's cash cycle and its operating cycle?
   b. How will a firm's cash cycle be affected if a firm increases its inventory, all else being equal?
   c. How will a firm's cash cycle be affected if the firm begins to take the discounts offered by its suppliers, all else being equal?

3. Does an increase in a firm's cash cycle necessarily mean that the firm is managing its cash poorly?

4. Why is trade credit important?

5. What are the ways that receivables management can affect a firm's value?

6. What are the three steps involved in establishing a credit policy?

7. What factors determine how a firm should manage its payables?

8. What is meant by "stretching the accounts payable"?

9. What are the tradeoffs involved in reducing inventory?

10. What are the different ways you can invest your firm's cash?

11. Which of the following short-term securities would you expect to offer the highest before-tax return: treasury bills, certificates of deposit, short-term tax exempts, or commercial paper? Why?

Problems

All problems in this chapter are available in MyFinanceLab. An asterisk (*) indicates problems with a higher level of difficulty.

Overview of Working Capital

1. Homer Boats has accounts payable days of 20, inventory days of 50, and accounts receivable days of 30. What is its operating cycle?

2. FastChips Semiconductors has inventory days of 75, accounts receivable days of 30, and accounts payable days of 90. What is its cash conversion cycle?

3. The following financial information is for Westerly Industries:

Sales	$ 100,000
Cost of Goods Sold	$ 80,000
Accounts Receivable	$ 30,000
Inventory	$ 15,000
Accounts Payable	$ 40,000

   What is Westerly's cash conversion cycle?

4. Aberdeen Outboard Motors is contemplating building a new plant. The company anticipates that the plant will require an initial investment of $2 million in net working capital today. The plant will last 10 years, at which point the full investment in net working capital will be recovered. Given an annual discount rate of 6%, what is the net present value of this working capital investment?

5. Your firm currently has net working capital of $100,000 that it expects to grow at a rate of 4% per year forever. You are considering some suggestions that could slow that growth to 3% per year. If your discount rate is 12%, how would these changes affect the value of your firm?

 6. The Greek Connection had sales of $32 million in 2011, and a cost of goods sold of $20 million. A simplified balance sheet for the firm appears below:

THE GREEK CONNECTION
Balance Sheet As of December 31, 2011
($thousands)

Assets			Liabilities and Equity		
Cash	$	2000	Accounts payable	$	1500
Accounts receivable		3950	Notes payable		1000
Inventory		1300	Accruals		1220
Total current assets	$	7250	Total current liabilities	$	3720
Net plant, property,			Long-term debt	$	3000
and equipment	$	8500	Total liabilities	$	6720
Total assets	$	15,750	Common equity	$	9030
			Total liabilities and equity	$	15,750

a. Calculate the Greek Connection's net working capital in 2011.

b. Calculate the cash conversion cycle of the Greek Connection in 2011.

c. The industry average accounts receivable days is 30 days. What would the cash conversion cycle for the Greek Connection have been in 2011 had it matched the industry average for accounts receivable days? (See MyFinanceLab for the data in Excel format.)

Trade Credit

 7. Assume the credit terms offered to your firm by your suppliers are 3/5, net 30. Calculate the cost of the trade credit if your firm does not take the discount and pays on day 30.

 8. Your supplier offers terms of 1/10, net 45. What is the effective annual cost of trade credit if you choose to forgo the discount and pay on day 45?

*9. The Fast Reader Company supplies bulletin board services to numerous hotel chains nationwide. The owner of the firm is investigating the desirability of employing a billing firm to do her billing and collections. Because the billing firm specializes in these services, collection float will be reduced by 20 days. Average daily collections are $1200, and the owner can earn 8% annually (expressed as an *APR* with monthly compounding) on her investments. If the billing firm charges $250 per month, should the owner employ the billing firm?

*10. The Saban Corporation is trying to decide whether to switch to a bank that will accommodate electronic funds transfers from Saban's customers. Saban's financial manager believes the new system would decrease its collection float by as much as five days. The new bank would require a compensating balance of $30,000, whereas its present bank has no compensating balance requirement. Saban's average daily collections are $10,000, and it can earn 8% on its short-term investments. Should Saban make the switch? (Assume the compensating balance at the new bank will be deposited in a non–interest-earning account.)

Receivables Management

11. The Manana Corporation had sales of $60 million this year. Its accounts receivable balance averaged $2 million. How long, on average, does it take the firm to collect on its sales?

12. The Mighty Power Tool Company has the following accounts on its books:

Customer	Amount Owed ($)	Age (days)
ABC	50,000	35
DEF	35,000	5
GHI	15,000	10
KLM	75,000	22
NOP	42,000	40
QRS	18,000	12
TUV	82,000	53
WXY	36,000	90

The firm extends credit on terms of 1/15, net 30. Develop an aging schedule using 15-day increments through 60 days, and then indicate any accounts that have been outstanding for more than 60 days.

Payables Management

 13. Simple Simon's Bakery purchases supplies on terms of 1/10, net 25. If Simple Simon's chooses to take the discount offered, it must obtain a bank loan to meet its short-term financing needs. A local bank has quoted Simple Simon's owner an interest rate of 12% on borrowed funds. Should Simple Simon's enter the loan agreement with the bank and begin taking the discount?

 14. Your firm purchases goods from its supplier on terms of 3/15, net 40.
  a. What is the effective annual cost to your firm if it chooses not to take the discount and makes its payment on day 40?
  b. What is the effective annual cost to your firm if it chooses not to take the discount and makes its payment on day 50?

 ***15.** Use the financial statements supplied below for International Motor Corporation (IMC) to answer the following questions. (See MyFinanceLab for the data in Excel format.)
  a. Calculate the cash conversion cycle for IMC for both 2010 and 2011. What change has occurred, if any? All else being equal, how does this change affect IMC's need for cash?
  b. IMC's suppliers offer terms of net 30. Does it appear that IMC is doing a good job of managing its accounts payable?

INTERNATIONAL MOTOR CORPORATION
Income Statement ($ millions)
for the Years Ending December 31

	2010	2011
Sales	$60,000	$75,000
Cost of goods sold	52,000	61,000
Gross profit	$ 8000	$14,000
Selling, general, and administrative expenses	6000	8000
Operating profit	$ 2000	$ 6000
Interest expense	1400	1300
Earnings before tax	$ 600	$ 4700
Taxes	300	2350
Earnings after tax	$ 300	$ 2350

INTERNATIONAL MOTOR CORPORATION
Balance Sheet ($ millions)
As of December 31

Assets	2010	2011	Liabilities	2010	2011
Cash	$ 3080	$ 6100	Accounts payable	$ 3600	$ 4600
Accounts			Notes payable	1180	1250
receivable	2800	6900	Accruals	5600	6211
Inventory	6200	6600	Total current		
Total current assets	$12,080	$19,600	liabilities	$10,380	$12,061
Net plant, property,			Long-term debt	$ 6500	$ 7000
and equipment	$23,087	$20,098	Total liabilities	$16,880	$19,061
Total assets	$35,167	$39,698	Equity		
			Common stock	$ 2735	$ 2735
			Retained earnings	$15,552	$17,902
			Total equity	$18,287	$20,637
			Total liabilities		
			and equity	$35,167	$39,698

Inventory Management

16. Your company had $10 million in sales last year. Its cost of goods sold was $7 million and its average inventory balance was $1,200,000. What was its average days of inventory?

17. Happy Valley Homecare Suppliers, Inc. (HVHS) had $20 million in sales in 2010. Its cost of goods sold was $8 million, and its average inventory balance was $2,000,000.
    a. Calculate the average number of days inventory outstanding ratios for HVHS.
    b. The average days of inventory in the industry is 73 days. By how much would HVHS reduce its investment in inventory if it could improve its inventory days to meet the industry average?

Data Case

You are the CFO of Target. This afternoon you played golf with a member of the company's board of directors. Somewhere on the back nine, the board member enthusiastically described a recent article she had read in a leading management journal. This article noted several companies that had improved their stock price performance through effective working capital management, and the board member was intrigued. She wondered whether Target was managing its working capital effectively and, if not, whether Target could accomplish something similar. How was Target managing its working capital, and how does it compare to its competitor Wal-Mart, a company well known for working capital management?

On returning home, you decide to do a quick preliminary investigation using information freely available on the internet.

1. Obtain Target's financial statements for the past four years from the MSN Money website (http://money.msn.com).
   a. Enter the ticker symbol (TGT) in the box and click on "Get Quote."
   b. Next click on "Financial Results" and then "Statements."
   c. The income statements will come up first. Place the cursor in the statement and right-click. Select "Export to Microsoft Excel" from the menu. If you do not have that option, you can copy and paste the data into Excel.
   d. Go back to the webpage and click on "Balance Sheets" at the top of the page; repeat the download procedure for the balance sheets.
   e. Copy and paste the balance sheet so that it is on the same worksheet as the income statement.

2. Obtain Wal-Mart's ratios for comparison from the Reuters website (www.reuters.com/finance/stocks).
   a. Enter the ticker symbol (WMT) in the box, select "Financials," and click on "Search."
   b. Scroll down to find the efficiency ratios, and copy and paste them into your spreadsheet where Target's financial statements are located.

3. Compute the cash conversion cycle for Target for each of the last four years.
   a. Compute the inventory days using "Cost of Revenue" as cost of goods sold and a 365-day year.
   b. Compute accounts receivable days using a 365-day year.
   c. Compute accounts payable days using a 365-day year.
   d. Compute the cash conversion cycle for each year.

4. How has Target's *CCC* changed over the last few years?

5. Compare Target's inventory and receivables turnover ratios for the most recent year to the industry average.
   a. Compute the inventory turnover ratio as cost of revenue/inventory.
   b. Compute the receivable turnover ratio as Total Revenue/Net Receivables.
   c. How do Target's numbers compare to Wal-Mart's?

6. Determine how Target's free cash flow would change if Target's inventory and accounts receivable balances were adjusted to meet Wal-Mart's ratios.

7. Determine the amount of additional free cash flow that would be available if Target adjusted its Accounts Payable Days to 75 days.

8. Determine the net amount of additional free cash flow and Target's cash conversion cycle if its inventory and receivables turnover ratios were at Wal-Mart's levels and its payable days were 75 days.

9. What are your impressions regarding Target's working capital management based on this preliminary analysis? Discuss any advantages and disadvantages of bringing the cash conversion cycle more in line with Wal-Mart's.

19 Short-Term Financial Planning

LEARNING OBJECTIVES

▶ Forecast cash flows and short-term financing needs

▶ Understand the principle of matching short-term needs to short-term funding sources

▶ Know the different types of bank loans and their tradeoffs

▶ Understand the use of commercial paper as an alternative to bank financing

▶ Use financing secured by accounts receivable or inventory

▶ Know how to create a short-term financial plan

notation

EAR	effective annual rate
APR	annual percentage rate

INTERVIEW WITH Elysse Dalla-Longa,
GE Capital

University of Calgary, 2010

"Calculating discounted cash flows, projecting future cash flows, evaluating a potential borrower's ability to repay—I deal with all of these things on a daily basis."

After graduating from the University of Calgary in 2010, Elysse Dalla-Longa joined the commercial leadership program at GE Capital. The program allows new employees to discover their areas of interest as they rotate through the different divisions, all the while providing them with experience and skills applicable in a variety of situations. As a member of the risk team, Elysse evaluates potential borrowers. "I am currently specializing in asset-based lending, providing debt financing for small-to-midmarket companies."

When extending credit to businesses, it is important to be able to determine the borrower's ability to repay the loan. This usually involves forecasting cashflows, which is difficult given their uncertain nature. Elysse has used her finance background throughout her leadership program. "From a credit and risk perspective, when determining who to lend to, I use a great many of the skills I learned in finance classes," she says. "Calculating discounted cash flows, projecting future cash flows, evaluating a potential borrower's ability to repay—I deal with all of these things on a daily basis."

Hasbro is a multinational corporation, with year-end 2009 assets of $3.9 billion. Hasbro designs
and manufactures toys throughout the world; its major product lines include the Playskool, Tonka, and Transformers brands. Typically, the demand for toys is highly seasonal, with demand peaking during the fall in anticipation of December's holiday retailing season. As a result, Hasbro's revenues vary dramatically throughout the calendar year. For example, revenues during the fourth quarter of the calendar year are typically more than twice as high as revenues in the first quarter.

Hasbro's varying business revenues cause its cash flows to be highly cyclical. The firm generates surplus cash during some months; it has a great demand for capital during other months. These seasonal financing requirements are quite different from its ongoing, long-term demand for permanent capital. How does a company such as Hasbro manage its short-term cash needs within each calendar year?

In this chapter, we analyze short-term financial planning. We begin by showing how companies forecast their cash flows to determine their short-term financing needs, and we explore the reasons why firms use short-term financing. Next, we discuss the financing policies that guide these financing decisions. Finally, we compare alternative ways a company can finance a shortfall during periods when it is not generating enough cash, including short-term financing with bank loans, commercial paper, and secured financing.

19.1 Forecasting Short-Term Financing Needs

The first step in short-term financial planning is to forecast the company's future cash flows. This exercise has two distinct objectives. First, a company forecasts its cash flows to determine whether it will have surplus cash or a cash deficit for each period. Second, management needs to decide whether that surplus or deficit is temporary or permanent. If it is permanent, it may affect the firm's long-term financial decisions. For example, if a company anticipates an ongoing surplus of cash, it may choose to increase its dividend payout. Deficits resulting from investments in long-term projects are often financed using long-term sources of capital, such as equity or long-term bonds.

In this chapter, we focus specifically on short-term financial planning. With this perspective, we are interested in analyzing the types of cash surpluses or deficits that are temporary and, therefore, short-term in nature. When a company analyzes its short-term financing needs, it typically examines cash flows at quarterly intervals.

Application: Whistler Snowboards, Inc.

To illustrate, let's assume that it is currently December 2012 and consider the case of Whistler Snowboards, Inc. Whistler manufactures snowboarding equipment, which it sells primarily to sports retailers. Whistler anticipates that in 2013 its sales will grow by 10% to $20 million and its total net income will be $1,950,000. Assuming that both sales and production will occur uniformly throughout the year, management's forecast of its quarterly net income and statement of cash flows for 2013 is presented in the spreadsheet in Table 19.1.[1] (Also shown, in grey, is the income statement from the fourth quarter of 2012.)[2]

From this forecast, we see that Whistler is a profitable company. Its quarterly net income is almost $500,000. Whistler's capital expenditures are equal to depreciation. While Whistler's working capital requirements increase in the first quarter due to the increase in sales, they remain constant thereafter and so have no further cash flow consequences. Based on these projections, Whistler will be able to fund projected sales growth from its operating profit and, in fact, will accumulate excess cash on a continuing basis. Given similar growth forecasts for next year and beyond, this surplus is likely to be long-term. Whistler could reduce the surplus by paying some of it out as a dividend or by repurchasing shares.

Let's now turn to Whistler's potential short-term financing needs. Firms require short-term financing for three reasons: negative cash flow shocks, positive cash flow shocks, and seasonalities.

Negative Cash Flow Shocks

Occasionally, a company will encounter circumstances in which cash flows are temporarily negative for an unexpected reason. These situations, which we refer to as *negative cash flow shock*, can create short-term financing needs.

---

[1]In this table, and elsewhere in the chapter, we display rounded numbers. Calculations such as net income are based on the actual numbers in the spreadsheet with all significant digits. As a result, there will occasionally be a small discrepancy between the Excel-calculated value shown and the hand-calculated value using the rounded numbers displayed.

[2]Given the coverage we have provided in Chapters 2 and 17 on how to construct pro forma financial statements, we do not discuss those details here. For simplicity, we have assumed that Whistler has no debt and earns no interest on retained cash.

TABLE 19.1	Projected Financial Statements for Whistler Snowboards, 2013, Assuming Level Sales					
1	**Quarter**	**2012Q4**	**2013Q1**	**2013Q2**	**2013Q3**	**2013Q4**
2	**Income Statement ($000s)**					
3	Sales	4545	5000	5000	5000	5000
4	Cost of Goods Sold	−2955	−3250	−3250	−3250	−3250
5	Selling, General, and Administrative	−455	−500	−500	−500	−500
6	*EBITDA*	1136	1250	1250	1250	1250
7	Depreciation	−455	−500	−500	−500	−500
8	*EBIT*	682	750	750	750	750
9	Taxes	−239	−263	−263	−263	−263
10	**Net Income**	443	488	488	488	488
11	**Statement of Cash Flows**					
12	Net Income		488	488	488	488
13	Depreciation		500	500	500	500
14	Changes in Working Capital					
15	Accounts Receivable		−136	—	—	—
16	Inventory		—	—	—	—
17	Accounts Payable		48	—	—	—
18	**Cash from Operating Activities**		899	988	988	988
19	Capital Expenditures		−500	−500	−500	−500
20	Other Investment		—	—	—	—
21	**Cash from Investing Activities**		−500	−500	−500	−500
22	Net Borrowing		—	—	—	—
23	Dividends		—	—	—	—
24	Capital Contributions		—	—	—	—
25	**Cash from Financing Activities**		—	—	—	—
26	**Change in Cash and Equivalents** (18 + 21 + 25)		399	488	488	488

Returning to the Whistler Snowboards example, assume that during April 2013 management learns that some manufacturing equipment has broken unexpectedly. If replacing the equipment is costly enough, Whistler's cash reserves would be insufficient to pay for a replacement. Whistler will have to borrow (or arrange for another financing source) to cover the shortfall. However, once the equipment is replaced, the company will continue to generate positive cash flow in subsequent quarters, and will have generated enough in cumulative cash flow to repay the loan. Therefore, this negative cash flow shock has created the need for short-term financing.

Positive Cash Flow Shocks

We next analyze a case in which a positive cash flow shock affects short-term financing needs. Although this surprise is good news, it still creates demand for short-term financing.

During the first quarter of 2013, a major sporting goods chain agrees to sell Whistler snowboards exclusively. The opportunity to grow comes with large upfront marketing, working capital, and production capacity expenses.

The unexpected event in this case—the opportunity to grow more rapidly—is positive. It results, however, in a negative net cash flow during the first quarter, due primarily to the new marketing expenses and capital expenditures. Because the company will be even more profitable in subsequent quarters, this financing need is temporary.

Seasonalities

For many firms, sales are seasonal. When sales are concentrated during a few months, sources and uses of cash are also likely to be seasonal. Firms in this position may find themselves with a surplus of cash during some months that is sufficient to compensate for a shortfall during other months. However, because of timing differences, such firms often have short-term financing needs.

To illustrate, let's return to the example of Whistler Snowboards. In Table 19.1, management assumed that Whistler's sales occur uniformly throughout the year. In reality, for a snowboard manufacturer, sales are likely to be highly seasonal. Assume that 20% of sales occur during the first quarter, 10% during each of the second and third quarters (largely southern hemisphere sales), and 60% of sales during the fourth quarter, in anticipation of the (northern hemisphere) winter snowboarding season. The spreadsheet in Table 19.2 presents the resulting statement of cash flows. These forecasts continue to assume production occurs uniformly throughout the year.

From Table 19.2, we see that Whistler is still a profitable company, and its annual net income still totals $1,950,000. However, the introduction of seasonal sales creates some dramatic swings in Whistler's short-term cash flows. There are two effects of seasonality on cash flows. First, although the cost of goods sold fluctuates proportionally with sales, other costs (such as administrative overhead and depreciation) do not, leading to large changes in the firm's net income by quarter. Second, net working capital changes are more pronounced. In the first quarter, Whistler receives cash by collecting the receivables from last year's high fourth quarter sales. During the second and third quarters, the company's inventory balance increases. Given capacity constraints in its manufacturing equipment, Whistler produces snowboards throughout the year,

| TABLE 19.2 | Projected Financial Statements for Whistler Snowboards, 2013, Assuming Seasonal Sales |

	Quarter	2012Q4	2013Q1	2013Q2	2013Q3	2013Q4
1						
2	Income Statement ($000s)					
3	Sales	10,909	4000	2000	2000	12,000
4	Cost of Goods Sold	−7091	−2600	−1300	−1300	−7800
5	Selling, General, and Administrative	−773	−450	−350	−350	−850
6	*EBITDA*	3045	950	350	350	3350
7	Depreciation	−455	−500	−500	−500	−500
8	*EBIT*	2591	450	−150	−150	2850
9	Taxes	−907	−158	53	53	−998
10	Net Income	1684	293	−98	−98	1853
11	**Statement of Cash Flows**					
12	Net Income		293	−98	−98	1853
13	Depreciation		500	500	500	500
14	Changes in Working Capital					
15	Accounts Receivable		2073	600	—	−3000
16	Inventory		−650	−1950	−1950	4550
17	Accounts Payable		48	—	—	—
18	**Cash from Operating Activities**		2263	−948	−1548	3903
19	Capital Expenditures		−500	−500	−500	−500
20	Other Investment		—	—	—	—
21	**Cash from Investing Activities**		−500	−500	−500	−500
22	Net Borrowing		—	—	—	—
23	Dividends		—	—	—	—
24	Capital Contributions		—	—	—	—
25	**Cash from Financing Activities**		—	—	—	—
26	**Change in Cash and Equivalents** (18 + 21 + 25)		1763	−1488	−2048	3403

even though sales during the summer are low. Because production occurs uniformly, accounts payable do not vary over the year. Inventory, however, builds up in anticipation of fourth quarter sales—and increases in inventory use cash. As a consequence, Whistler has negative net cash flows during the second and third quarters, primarily to fund its inventory. By the fourth quarter, high sales recover cash for the company.

Seasonal sales create large short-term cash flow deficits and surpluses. During the second and third quarters, the company will need to find additional short-term sources of cash to fund inventory. During the fourth quarter, Whistler will have a large short-term surplus. Given that its seasonal cash flow needs are likely to recur next year, Whistler may choose to invest this cash in one of the short-term investment options discussed in Chapter 18. Management can then use this cash to fund some of its short-term working capital needs during the following year.

The Cash Budget

The statement of cash flows section of Table 19.2 reflects assumptions made by Whistler's managers about the timing of cash receipts and disbursements throughout the year. Once Whistler's managers forecast the sales and production costs for the year, they must also forecast when Whistler will actually receive the cash for those sales and when it will need to pay its suppliers. They do this in a **cash budget**, a forecast of cash inflows and outflows on a quarterly (or sometimes monthly) basis used to identify potential cash shortfalls.

cash budget A forecast of cash inflows and outflows on a quarterly (or sometimes monthly) basis.

For example, based on experience, Whistler assumes that it will receive payment for 70% of its sales in the quarter they are made, with the remaining 30% coming in the following quarter (this corresponds with an accounts receivable payment period of about one month). So each quarter, cash receipts will be 30% of last quarter's sales in receivables plus 70% of the current quarter's sales:

$$\text{Whistler's Quarterly Cash Receipts} = 30\% \times \text{Last Quarter's Sales} + 70\% \times \text{This Quarter's Sales}$$

Using this assumption and the sales forecast from Table 19.2, we can forecast Whistler's cash receipts. Note that sales in 2012Q4 were $10,909, so beginning receivables are 30% × $10,909 = $3273. Table 19.3 presents the projected cash receipts.

The next step is to forecast cash disbursements. As we mentioned earlier, although Whistler's sales are seasonal, it produces a constant amount each quarter and simply builds up inventory. Thus, each quarter it pays its suppliers a level amount for materials. These costs are reflected in the income statement when sales occur, but the cash outflow happens when the firm pays its suppliers.

This can be seen by adding the inventory line to the cost of goods sold line in Table 19.2. In 2013Q1 it is −2600 − 650 = −3250, and it is in for the rest of the quarters in 2013 as well, reflecting the steady production of snowboards. Whistler's managers forecast that of the $3250 of cost of goods sold in each quarter, they will need to pay $2725 in the quarter, carrying $525 in accounts payable into the next quarter. Each quarter, their cash disbursements on materials will be last quarter's accounts payable plus $2725 of the current quarter's costs. Because Whistler's production was lower

TABLE 19.3 Projected Cash Receipts for Whistler Snowboards, Assuming Seasonal Sales

1	Quarter	2013Q1	2013Q2	2013Q3	2013Q4
2	Beginning Receivables ($000s)	3273	1200	600	600
3	Sales	4000	2000	2000	12,000
4	Cash Collections (Line 2 + 70% of Line 3)	6073	2600	2000	9000
5	Ending Receivables (30% of Line 3)	1200	600	600	3600

TABLE 19.4   *Projected Cash Disbursements for Whistler Snowboards, Assuming Seasonal Sales*

Panel (a) Calculating Payments to Suppliers

	1 Quarter	2013Q1	2013Q2	2013Q3	2013Q4
2	**Payment to Suppliers**				
3	Last Quarter's AP	477	525	525	525
4	This Quarter's Payments	2725	2725	2725	2725
5	Total Payments	3202	3250	3250	3250
6					
7	Ending AP (3250 − Line 4)	525	525	525	525

Panel (b) Total Cash Disbursements

	1 Quarter	2013Q1	2013Q2	2013Q3	2013Q4
2	Cash Collections (from Line 4 of Table 19.3)	6073	2600	2000	9000
3					
4	**Disbursements**				
5	Payments to Suppliers (from Line 5 of panel [a])	−3202	−3250	−3250	−3250
6	SG&A + Taxes + Interest (from Lines 5 and 9 of Table 19.2)	−608	−297	−297	−1848
7	Capital Expenditures (from Line 19 of Table 19.2)	−500	−500	−500	−500
8	Total Disbursements	−4310	−4047	−4047	−5598
9					
10	Net Cash Flow (Line 2 + Line 8)	1763	−1447	−2047	3402

in 2012, it had lower costs, so it ended 2012 with lower accounts payable than it will have going forward. Table 19.4 shows that it will have $477 in accounts payable for the first quarter of 2013 only, before it rises to $525 for the rest of the quarters. Using that fact and the assumption we just made, we can forecast their disbursements on materials. The other cash disbursements will be selling, general, and administrative expenses (SG&A), and taxes and interest, as well as any capital expenditures, each of which is forecasted in Table 19.2. The table also shows Whistler's forecasted cash disbursements.

Now that we have the quarterly net cash flow, we can generate Whistler's cash budget. We need two more pieces of information: the amount of cash Whistler will start 2013 with and the minimum amount of cash it needs on hand for transactions purposes. Whistler will start 2013 with $1 million in cash, and its managers have set $500,000 as the minimum acceptable cash balance. Putting it all together, we have Whistler's cash budget, shown in Table 19.5.

Looking at the cash budget, we can immediately see that there will be a substantial cash shortfall in the third quarter. Having identified the shortfall, Whistler's managers can prepare external financing to cover it. We discuss the factors that determine how to cover such a shortfall in the next two sections.

Concept Check

1. How do we forecast the firm's future cash requirements?

2. What is the effect of seasonalities on short-term cash flows?

TABLE 19.5   Cash Budget for Whistler Snowboards, 2013

	1 Quarter	2013Q1	2013Q2	2013Q3	2013Q4
2	Beginning Cash Balance	1000	2763	1316	−731
3	Net Cash Flow	1763	−1447	−2047	3402
4	Ending Cash Balance	2763	1316	−731	2671
5	Minimum Cash Balance	500	500	500	500
6	Surplus (Deficit)	2263	816	−1231	2171

The Matching Principle

In a perfect capital market, the choice of financing is irrelevant; thus, how the firm chooses to finance its short-term cash needs cannot affect the firm's value. In reality, important market frictions exist, including transaction costs. For example, one transaction cost is the opportunity cost of holding cash in accounts that pay little or no interest. Firms also face high transaction costs if they need to negotiate a loan on short notice to cover a cash shortfall. Firms can increase their value by adopting a policy that minimizes these kinds of costs. One such policy is known as the matching principle. The **matching principle** states that short-term cash needs should be financed with short-term debt and long-term cash needs should be financed with long-term sources of funds.

Permanent Working Capital

Permanent working capital is the amount that a firm must keep invested in its short-term assets to support its continuing operations. Because this investment in working capital is required as long as the firm remains in business, it constitutes a long-term investment. The matching principle indicates that the firm should finance this permanent investment in working capital with long-term sources of funds. Such sources have lower transaction costs than short-term sources of funds that have to be replaced more often.

Temporary Working Capital

Another portion of a firm's investment in its accounts receivable and inventory is temporary and results from seasonal fluctuations in the firm's business or unanticipated shocks. This **temporary working capital** is the difference between the firm's actual level of investment in short-term working capital needs and its permanent working capital investment. Because temporary working capital represents a short-term need, the firm should finance this portion of its investment with short-term financing.

Permanent Versus Temporary Working Capital

To illustrate the distinction between permanent and temporary working capital, we return to the Whistler Snowboards example. Table 19.2 presented cash flow forecasts assuming seasonal sales. In the spreadsheet in Table 19.6, we report the underlying levels of working capital that correspond to these forecasts.

In Table 19.6, we see that working capital for Whistler varies from a minimum of $2,125,000 in the first quarter of 2013 to $5,425,000 in the third quarter. The minimum level of working capital, or $2,125,000, can be thought of as the firm's permanent working capital. The difference between this minimum level and the higher levels in subsequent quarters (for example, $5,425,000 − $2,125000 = $3,300,00 in the third quarter) reflects Whistler's temporary working capital requirements.

matching principle The principle that states that a firm's short-term cash needs should be financed with short-term debt and long-term cash needs should be financed with long-term sources of funds.

permanent working capital The amount that a firm must keep invested in its short-term assets to support its continuing operations.

temporary working capital The difference between the firm's actual level of investment in short-term working capital needs and its permanent working capital requirements.

TABLE 19.6

Projected Levels of Working Capital for Whistler Snowboards, 2013, Seasonal Sales

	Quarter	2012Q4	2013Q1	2013Q2	2013Q3	2013Q4
1						
2	Net Working Capital Requirements ($000s)					
3	Minimum Cash Balance	500	500	500	500	500
4	Accounts Receivable	3273	1200	600	600	3600
5	Inventory	300	950	2900	4850	300
6	Accounts Payable	−477	−525	−525	−525	−525
7	Net Working Capital	3596	2125	3475	5425	3875

Financing Policy Choices

Following the matching principle should, in the long run, help minimize a firm's transaction costs.[3] But what if, instead of using the matching principle, a firm financed its permanent working capital needs with short-term debt? When the short-term debt comes due, the firm will have to negotiate a new loan. This new loan will involve additional transaction costs, and it will carry whatever market interest rate exists at the time. As a result, the firm is also exposed to interest rate risk.

aggressive financing policy The financing of part or all of a firm's permanent working capital with short-term debt.

Aggressive Financing Policy. Financing part or all of the permanent working capital with short-term debt is known as an **aggressive financing policy**. An ultra-aggressive policy would involve financing even some of the plant, property, and equipment with short-term sources of funds.

When the yield curve is upward sloping, the interest rate on short-term debt is lower than the rate on long-term debt. In that case, short-term debt may appear cheaper than long-term debt. However, we know that with perfect capital markets, Modigliani and Miller's propositions from Chapter 15 apply: the benefit of the lower rate from short-term debt is offset by the risk that the firm will have to refinance the debt in the future at a higher rate. This risk is borne by the equity holders, and so the firm's equity cost of capital will rise to offset any benefit from the lower borrowing rate.

Why, then, might a firm choose an aggressive financing policy? Such a policy might be beneficial if the market imperfections mentioned in Chapter 16, such as agency costs and asymmetric information, are important. The value of short-term debt is less sensitive to the firm's credit quality than long-term debt is; therefore, the value of short-term debt will be less affected by management's actions or information. As a result, short-term debt can have lower agency and lemons costs than long-term debt does, and an aggressive financing policy can benefit shareholders. On the other hand, by relying on short-term debt the firm exposes itself to **funding risk**, which is the risk of incurring financial distress costs should the firm not be able to refinance its debt in a timely manner or at a reasonable rate.

funding risk The risk of incurring financial distress costs should a firm not be able to refinance its debt in a timely manner or at a reasonable rate.

conservative financing policy The financing of a firm's short-term needs with long-term debt.

Conservative Financing Policy. Alternatively, a firm could finance its short-term needs with long-term debt, a practice known as a **conservative financing policy**. For example, when following such a policy, a firm would use long-term sources of funds to finance its fixed assets, permanent working capital, and some of its seasonal needs. The firm would use short-term debt very sparingly to meet its peak seasonal needs. To implement such a policy effectively, there will necessarily be periods when excess cash is available—those periods when the firm requires little or no investment in temporary working capital. In an imperfect capital market, this cash will earn a below-market interest rate, thereby reducing the firm's value. It also increases the possibility that managers of the firm will use this excess cash unproductively—for example, on perquisites for themselves.

In Figure 19.1, we illustrate aggressive and conservative financial policies for Whistler. With an aggressive policy, Whistler relies entirely on short-term financing to fund its inventory buildup, so its borrowing reaches a peak, along with its inventory, in the third quarter. With a conservative policy, the firm uses long-term borrowing to ensure that it will have enough cash to pay for its peak inventory. In this case, Whistler's

---

[3]Some evidence indicates that most firms appear to follow the matching principle. See W. Beranek, C. Cornwell, and S. Choi, "External Financing, Liquidity, and Capital Expenditures," *Journal of Financial Research* (Summer 1995): 207–222; and M.H. Stohs and D.C. Mauer, "The Determinants of Corporate Debt Maturity Structure," *Journal of Business* 69 (3) (1996): 279–312.

FIGURE 19.1   Financing Policy Choices for Whistler Snowboards

Assuming $25,000 in fixed assets, the figure shows the levels of fixed assets (green), permanent working capital ($2125, yellow), and seasonal inventory (grey) for Whistler Snowboards. In panel (a), each quarter shows the mix of long-term financing (purple) and short-term debt (red) used to finance the assets and working capital. In the aggressive policy illustrated in panel (a), Whistler maintains no excess cash reserves and instead finances its working capital entirely through short-term borrowing. The amount of borrowing must match the amount of working capital.

Panel (b) illustrates a conservative policy, in which Whistler maintains enough cash reserves to cover its peak temporary financing needs. The company does this with $30,425 in long-term financing, which is enough to finance its fixed assets, permanent working capital, and peak inventory. Whistler's total working capital is constant at $5425, but the composition of the working capital varies over the year as the company draws down its cash reserves (blue) to build inventory and then replenishes the cash reserves when it sells the inventory.

Panel (a) Aggressive financing policy: All working capital is financed with short-term debt.

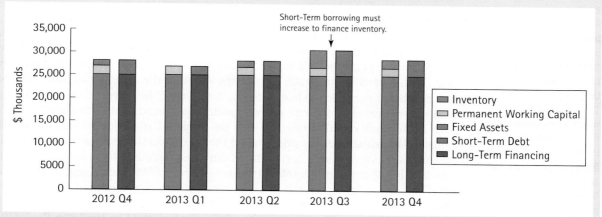

Panel (b) Conservative financing policy: Working capital is financed with long-term debt.

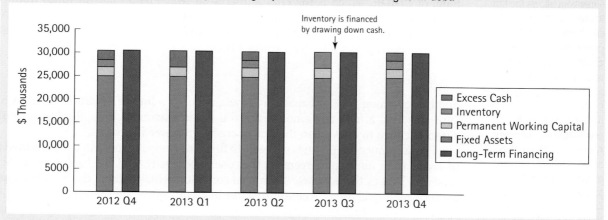

borrowing does not fluctuate at all, but rather it draws down its cash reserves so that they are at a minimum when its inventory is at its peak.

Once a firm determines its short-term financing needs, it must choose which instruments it will use for this purpose. In the rest of this chapter, we survey the specific financing options that are available: bank loans, commercial paper, and secured financing.

3. What is the matching principle?

4. What is the difference between temporary and permanent working capital?

19.3 Short-Term Financing with Bank Loans

One of the primary sources of short-term financing, especially for small businesses, is the commercial bank. Each of Canada's major chartered banks has a commercial banking division. Bank loans are typically initiated with a **promissory note**, which is a written statement that indicates the amount of the loan, the date payment is due, and the interest rate. In this section, we examine three types of bank loans: a single, end-of-period-payment loan; a line of credit; and a bridge loan. In addition, we compare the interest rates of these bank loans and present the common stipulations and fees associated with them.

Single, End-of-Period-Payment Loan

The most straightforward type of bank loan is a single, end-of-period-payment loan. Such a loan agreement requires that the firm pay interest on the loan and pay back the principal in one lump sum at the end of the loan. The interest rate may be fixed or variable. With a fixed interest rate, the specific rate that the commercial bank will charge is stipulated at the time the loan is made. With a variable interest rate, the terms of the loan may indicate that the rate will vary with some spread relative to a benchmark rate, such as the **bank rate** (the rate at which the Bank of Canada lends to financial institutions) or the *prime rate*. The **prime rate** is the rate banks charge their most creditworthy customers. However, large corporations can often negotiate bank loans at an interest rate that is *below* the prime rate. For example, in its 2009 annual report, Hasbro indicated that the weighted average interest rate it paid on average short-term borrowings from domestic institutions was 1.2% in 2009. By comparison, the average prime rate in 2009 was 3.25%.[4] Another common benchmark rate is the **London Inter-Bank Offered Rate**, or **LIBOR**, which is the rate of interest at which banks borrow funds from each other in the London interbank market. It is quoted for maturities of one day to one year for 10 major currencies. As it is a rate paid by banks with the highest credit quality, most firms will borrow at a rate that exceeds LIBOR.

Line of Credit

Another common type of bank loan arrangement is a **line of credit**, in which a bank agrees to lend a firm any amount up to a stated maximum. This flexible agreement allows the firm to draw upon the line of credit whenever it chooses.

Firms frequently use lines of credit to finance seasonal needs. An **uncommitted line of credit** is an informal agreement that does not legally bind the bank to provide the funds. As long as the borrower's financial condition remains good, the bank is happy to advance additional funds. A **committed line of credit** consists of a legally binding written agreement that obligates the bank to provide funds to a firm (up to a stated credit limit) regardless of the financial condition of the firm (unless the firm is bankrupt) as long as the firm satisfies any restrictions in the agreement. These arrangements are typically accompanied by a compensating balance requirement (i.e., a requirement that the firm maintain a minimum level of deposits with the bank) and restrictions regarding the

promissory note
A written statement that indicates the amount of a loan, the date payment is due, and the interest rate.

bank rate The rate at which the Bank of Canada lends to financial institutions.

prime rate The rate banks charge their most creditworthy customers.

London Inter-Bank Offered Rate (LIBOR) The rate of interest at which banks borrow funds from each other in the London interbank market.

line of credit A bank loan arrangement in which a bank agrees to lend a firm any amount up to a stated maximum. This flexible agreement allows the firm to draw upon the line of credit whenever it chooses.

uncommitted line of credit A line of credit that is an informal agreement and does not legally bind a bank to provide the funds a borrower requests.

committed line of credit A legally binding written agreement that obligates a bank to provide funds to a firm (up to a stated credit limit) regardless of the financial condition of the firm (unless the firm is bankrupt) as long as the firm satisfies any restrictions in the agreement.

---

[4]Hasbro 2009 annual report and the Federal Reserve Statistical Release website.

level of the firm's working capital. The firm pays a commitment fee of 0.25% to 0.5% of the unused portion of the line of credit in addition to interest on the amount that the firm borrowed. The line of credit agreement may also stipulate that at some point in time the outstanding balance must be zero. This policy ensures that the firm does not use the short-term financing to finance its long-term obligations.

Banks usually renegotiate the terms of a line of credit annually. A **revolving line of credit** is a committed line of credit, which a company can use as needed, that involves a solid commitment from the bank for a longer period of time, typically two to three years. A revolving line of credit with no fixed maturity is called **evergreen credit**. In its 2009 annual report, Hasbro reported that it relied on a $500 million revolving credit facility as the primary source of financing for its seasonal working capital requirements.

Bridge Loan

A **bridge loan** is another type of short-term bank loan that is often used to "bridge the gap" until a firm can arrange for long-term financing. For example, a real estate developer may use a bridge loan to finance the construction of a shopping mall. After the mall is completed, the developer will obtain long-term financing. Other firms use bridge loans to finance plant and equipment until they receive the proceeds from the sale of a long-term debt or an equity issue. After a natural disaster, lenders may provide businesses with short-term loans to serve as bridges until they receive insurance payments or long-term disaster relief.

Bridge loans are often quoted as discount loans with fixed interest rates. With a **discount loan**, the borrower is required to pay the interest at the *beginning* of the loan period. The lender deducts interest from the loan proceeds when the loan is made.

Common Loan Stipulations and Fees

We now turn to common loan stipulations and fees that affect the effective interest rate on a loan. Specifically, we look at loan commitment fees, loan origination fees, and compensating balance requirements.

Commitment Fees. Various loan fees charged by banks affect the effective interest rate that the borrower pays. For example, the commitment fee associated with a committed line of credit increases the effective cost of the loan to the firm. The "fee" can really be considered an interest charge under another name. Suppose that a firm has negotiated a committed line of credit with a stated maximum of $1 million and an interest rate of 10% (*EAR*) with a bank. The commitment fee is 0.5% (*EAR*). At the beginning of the year, the firm borrows $800,000. It then repays this loan at the end of the year, leaving $200,000 unused for the rest of the year. The total cost of the loan is as follows:

Interest on borrowed funds = 0.10($800,000)	$80,000
Commitment fee paid on unused portion = 0.005($200,000)	$1000
Total cost	$81,000

Loan Origination Fee. Another common type of fee is a **loan origination** fee, which a bank charges to cover credit checks and legal fees. The firm pays the fee when the loan is initiated, which makes the loan similar to a discount loan. The loan origination fee reduces the amount of usable proceeds that the firm receives and, like the commitment fee, is effectively an additional interest charge.

To illustrate, assume that Timmons Towel and Diaper Service is offered a $500,000 loan for three months at an *APR* of 12%. This loan has a loan origination fee of 1%. The loan origination fee is charged on the principal of the loan; thus, the fee in this case

---

revolving line of credit A line of credit, which a company can use as needed, that involves a solid commitment from a bank for a longer time period, typically two to three years.

evergreen credit A revolving line of credit with no fixed maturity.

bridge loan A type of short-term bank loan that is often used to "bridge the gap" until a firm can arrange for long-term financing.

discount loan A type of bridge loan in which the borrower is required to pay the interest at the beginning of the loan period. The lender deducts interest from the loan proceeds when the loan is made.

loan origination fee The fee a bank charges to cover credit checks and legal fees.

amounts to 0.01 × $500,000 = $5000, so the actual amount borrowed is $495,000. The interest payment for three months is $500,000(0.12/4) = $15,000. These cash flows are shown here on a timeline:

Thus actual three-month interest rate paid is as follows:

$$\frac{515,000}{495,000} - 1 = 4.04\%$$

Expressing this rate as an *EAR* gives $1.0404^4 - 1 = 17.17\%$.

Compensating Balance Requirements. Regardless of the loan structure, the bank may include a compensating balance requirement in the loan agreement that reduces the usable loan proceeds. Recall from Chapter 18 that a compensating balance requirement means that the firm must hold a certain percentage of the principal of the loan in an account at the bank. Assume that rather than charging a loan origination fee, Timmons Towel and Diaper Service's bank requires that the firm keep an amount equal to 10% of the loan principal in a non–interest-bearing account with the bank as long as the loan remains outstanding. The loan is for $500,000, so this requirement means that Timmons must hold 0.10 × 500,000 = $50,000 in an account at the bank. Thus, the firm has only $450,000 of the loan proceeds actually available for use, although it must pay interest on the full loan amount. At the end of the loan period, the firm owes $500,000 × (1 + 0.12/4) = $515,000 and so must pay $515,000 − 50,000 = $465,000 after applying its compensating balance to the repayment. These cash flows are shown here on a timeline:

The actual three-month interest rate paid is as follows:

$$\frac{465,000}{450,000} - 1 = 3.33\%$$

Expressing this as an *EAR* gives $1.0333^4 - 1 = 14.01\%$.

We assumed that Timmons's compensating balance is held in a non–interest-bearing account. Sometimes a bank will allow the compensating balance to be held in an account that pays a small amount of interest to offset part of the interest expense of the loan.

EXAMPLE 19.1

Compensating Balance Requirements and the Effective Annual Rate

Problem

Assume that Timmons Towel and Diaper Service's bank pays 1% (*APR* with quarterly compounding) on its compensating balance accounts. What is the *EAR* of Timmons's three-month loan?

Solution

▶ **Plan**

The interest earned on the $50,000 will reduce the net payment Timmons must make to pay off the loan. Once we compute the final payment, we can determine the implied three-month interest rate and then convert it into an *EAR*.

▶ **Execute**

The balance held in the compensating balance account will grow to $50,000(1 + 0.01/4 = $50,125). Thus, the final loan payment will be $500,000 + $15,000 − $50,125 = $464,875.

Notice that the interest on the compensating balance accounts offsets some of the interest that Timmons pays on the loan. The new cash flows are shown here on a timeline:

The actual three-month interest rate paid is as follows:

$$\frac{464{,}875}{450{,}000} - 1 = 3.31\%$$

Expressing this as an *EAR* gives $1.0331^4 - 1 = 13.89\%$.

▸ **Evaluate**

As expected, because the bank allowed Timmons to deposit the compensating balance in an interest-bearing account, the interest earned on the compensating balance reduced the overall interest cost of Timmons for the loan from 14.01% to 13.89%.

Concept Check

5. What is the difference between an uncommitted line of credit and a committed line of credit?

6. Describe common loan stipulations and fees.

19.4 Short-Term Financing with Commercial Paper

commercial paper
Short-term, unsecured debt issued by large corporations that is usually a cheaper source of funds than a short-term bank loan.

direct paper Commercial paper that a firms sells directly to investors.

dealer paper Commercial paper that dealers sell to investors in exchange for a spread (or fee) for their services.

Commercial paper is short-term, unsecured debt used by large corporations that is usually a cheaper source of funds than a short-term bank loan. The minimum face value is $25,000, and most commercial paper has a face value of at least $100,000. Like long-term debt, commercial paper is rated by credit-rating agencies. The interest on commercial paper is typically paid by selling it at an initial discount.

The average maturity of commercial paper is 30 days, and the maximum maturity is one year. Extending the maturity beyond one year triggers a registration requirement with the relevant provincial securities commission, which increases issue costs and creates a time delay in the sale of the issue. Commercial paper is referred to as either *direct paper* or *dealer paper*. With **direct paper**, the firm sells the security directly to investors. With **dealer paper**, dealers sell the commercial paper to investors in exchange for a spread (or fee) for their services. The spread decreases the proceeds that the issuing firm receives, thereby increasing the effective cost of the paper. Like long-term debt, commercial paper is rated by credit-rating agencies.

EXAMPLE 19.2

The Effective Annual Rate of Commercial Paper

Problem

A firm issues three-month commercial paper with a $100,000 face value and receives $98,000. What effective annual rate is the firm paying for its funds?

Solution

▸ **Plan**

First, put the firm's cash flows on a timeline:

The three-month rate can be computed by comparing the present value ($98,000) with the future value ($100,000). From there, we can convert it into an *EAR* using Equation 5.1: EAR = equivalent one-year = $(1 + r)^n - 1$, where *n* is the number of three-month periods in a year.

▶ **Execute**

The actual three-month interest rate paid is as follows:

$$\frac{100,000}{98,000} - 1 = 2.04\%$$

Expressing this as an *EAR* gives $1.0204^4 - 1 = 8.42\%$.

▶ **Evaluate**

The financial manager needs to know the *EAR* of all of the firm's funding sources to be able to make comparisons across them and choose the least costly way to finance the firm's short-term needs.

Concept Check

7. What is commercial paper?

8. What is the maximum maturity of commercial paper?

19.5 Short-Term Financing with Secured Financing

secured loan A type of corporate loan in which specific assets, most typically a firm's accounts receivable or inventory, are pledged as the firm's collateral.

factors Firms that purchase the receivables of other companies.

pledging of accounts receivable agreement An agreement in which a lender reviews the credit sales of the borrowing firm and decides which credit accounts it will accept as collateral for the loan, based on its own credit standards.

factoring of accounts receivable arrangement An arrangement in which a firm sells receivables to the lender (i.e., the factor), and the lender agrees to pay the firm the amount due from its customers at the end of the firm's payment period.

Businesses can also obtain short-term financing by using a **secured loan**, a type of corporate loan in which specific assets, most typically the firm's accounts receivables or inventory, are pledged as a firm's collateral. Commercial banks, finance companies, and **factors**, which are firms that purchase the receivables of other companies, are the most common sources for secured short-term loans.

Accounts Receivable as Collateral

Firms can use accounts receivable as security for a loan by pledging or factoring. We'll examine these uses of accounts receivable to secure loans in the following sections.

Pledging of Accounts Receivable. In a **pledging of accounts receivable agreement**, the lender reviews the invoices that represent the credit sales of the borrowing firm and decides which credit accounts it will accept as collateral for the loan, based on its own credit standards. The lender then typically lends the borrower some percentage of the value of the accepted invoices—say, 75%. If the borrowing firm's customers default on their bills, the firm is still responsible to the lender for the money.

Factoring of Accounts Receivable. In a **factoring of accounts receivable arrangement**, the firm sells receivables to the lender (i.e., the factor), and the lender agrees to pay the firm the amount due from its customers at the end of the firm's payment period. For example, if a firm sells its goods on terms of net 30, then the factor will pay the firm the face value of its receivables, less a factor's fee, at the end of 30 days. The firm's customers are usually instructed to make payments directly to the lender. In many cases, the firm can borrow as much as 80% of the face value of its receivables from the factor, thereby receiving its funds in advance. In such a case, the lender will charge interest on the loan in addition to the factor's fee. The lender charges the factor's fee, which may range from 0.75% to 1.5% of the face value of the accounts receivable, whether or not the firm borrows any of the available funds. Both the interest rate and the factor's fee vary, depending on such issues as the size of the borrowing firm and the dollar volume of its receivables. The dollar amounts involved in factoring agreements may be substantial. As of December 2009, for example, Hasbro had approximately $250 million of its accounts receivable under factoring arrangements.

A 17th-Century Financing Solution

In recent years, it has become more difficult for small businesses to obtain funding so as to purchase inventory. Several factors have contributed to this trend. First, the largest Canadian chartered banks have acquired many small, regional banks that were traditionally important sources of loans to small businesses. Second, large banks have tightened lending requirements for small borrowers. Third, many small businesses rely increasingly on foreign suppliers that demand payment up front, increasing the immediate demand for capital by small businesses.

Some small businesses have started to rely on a 400-year-old solution: venture merchant financing. This type of financing arrangement began in the 17th century, when groups of investors would provide capital for the voyages of Dutch sea captains. The captains would sail the seas, using the capital to purchase exotic merchandise. On their return, the merchant bankers would take about one-third of the captains' profits when the goods were sold as compensation for the financing.

Now consider the Kosher Depot, which sells exotic kosher foods to restaurants and supermarkets in Westbury, New York. It wanted to grow but lacked access to capital to purchase more specialty-foods inventory. Kosher Depot arranged a two-year, $3.3 million venture merchant financing arrangement with Capstone Business Credit. Kosher Depot would prearrange sales and notify Capstone, which would use its capital to buy the goods for Kosher Depot. Capstone would purchase and import the goods, storing them in its own warehouses. The warehouses then filled the orders received by Kosher Depot. For its services, Capstone received about 30% of the profits.

The cost of this arrangement—the 30% margin charged by the venture merchant—may be expensive relative to some of the alternative financing arrangements discussed in this chapter. However, the price may be worthwhile for a small business with no other short-term alternatives.

Source: Marie Leone, "Capital Ideas: A Little Cash'll Do Ya," http://CFO.com, March 3, 2005

---

with recourse A financing arrangement in which the lender can claim all the borrower's assets—not just explicitly pledged collateral—in the event of a default.

A factoring arrangement may be **with recourse**, meaning that the lender can seek payment from the borrower should the borrower's customers default on their bills. Alternatively, the financing arrangement may be **without recourse**, in which case the lender's claim on the borrower's assets in the event of a default is limited to only explicitly pledged collateral. In this latter case, the factor will pay the firm the amount due regardless of whether the factor receives payment from the firm's customers. If the arrangement is with recourse, the lender may not require that it approve the customers' accounts before sales are made. If the factoring agreement is without recourse, the borrowing firm must receive credit approval for a customer from the factor prior to shipping the goods. If the factor gives its approval, the firm ships the goods and the customer is directed to make payment directly to the lender.

without recourse A financing arrangement in which the lender's claim on the borrower's assets in the event of a default is limited to only explicitly pledged collateral.

Inventory as Collateral

Inventory can be used as collateral for a loan in one of three ways: as a floating lien, as a trust receipt, or in a warehouse arrangement. These options are discussed in the following sections.

floating lien (general lien or **blanket lien)** A financial arrangement in which all of a firm's inventory is used to secure a loan.

Floating Lien. In a **floating lien**, **general lien**, or **blanket lien** arrangement, all of the firm's inventory is used to secure the loan. This arrangement is the riskiest setup from the standpoint of the lender, because the value of the collateral used to secure the loan

trust receipts loan (floor planning) A type of loan in which distinguishable inventory items are held in a trust as security for the loan. As these items are sold, the firm remits the proceeds from their sale to the lender in repayment of the loan.

warehouse arrangement An arrangement in which the inventory that serves as collateral for a loan is stored in a warehouse.

public warehouse A business that exists for the sole purpose of storing and tracking the inflow and outflow of inventory, providing the lender tighter control over the inventory.

field warehouse A warehouse arrangement that is operated by a third party but is set up on the borrower's premises in a separate area so that the inventory collateralizing the loan is kept apart from the borrower's main plant.

dwindles as inventory is sold. When a firm becomes financially distressed, management may be tempted to sell the inventory without making payments on the loan. In such a case, the firm may not have enough funds to replenish its inventory. As a result, the loan may become under-collateralized. To counter this risk, this type of loan bears a higher interest rate than the next two arrangements discussed. In addition, lenders will lend a low percentage of the value of the inventory.

Trust Receipt. With a **trust receipts loan**, or **floor planning**, distinguishable inventory items are held in a trust as security for the loan. As these items are sold, the firm remits the proceeds from their sale to the lender in repayment of the loan. The lender will periodically have its agent verify that the borrower has not sold some of the specified inventory and failed to make a repayment on the loan. Car dealerships often use this type of secured financing arrangement to obtain the funds needed to purchase vehicles from the manufacturer.

Warehouse Arrangement. In a **warehouse arrangement**, the inventory that serves as collateral for the loan is stored in a warehouse. A warehouse arrangement is the least risky collateral arrangement from the standpoint of the lender. This type of arrangement can be set up in one of two ways.

The first method is to use a **public warehouse**, which is a business that exists for the sole purpose of storing and tracking the inflow and outflow of the inventory. The lender extends a loan to the borrowing firm, based on the value of the inventory stored. When the borrowing firm needs the inventory to sell, it returns to the warehouse and retrieves it upon receiving permission from the lender. This arrangement provides the lender with the tightest control over the inventory. Public warehouses work well for some types of inventory, such as wine and tobacco products, which must age before they are ready to be sold. It is not practical for items that are subject to spoilage or are bulky and, therefore, difficult to transport to and from the warehouse.

The second option, a **field warehouse**, is operated by a third party but is set up on the borrower's premises in a separate area so that the inventory collateralizing the loan is kept apart from the borrower's main plant. This type of arrangement is convenient for the borrower but gives the lender the added security of having the inventory that serves as collateral controlled by a third party.

Warehouse arrangements are expensive. The business operating the warehouse charges a fee on top of the interest that the borrower must pay the lender for the loan. However, the borrower may also save on the costs of storing the inventory herself. Because the warehouser is a professional at inventory control, little loss due to damaged goods or theft is likely to occur, which in turn lowers insurance costs. Because the control of the inventory remains in the hands of a third party, lenders may be willing to lend a greater percentage of the market value of the inventory than they would under other inventory arrangements.

EXAMPLE 19.3

Calculating the Effective Annual Cost of Warehouse Financing

Problem

The Row Cannery wants to borrow $2 million for one month. Using its inventory as collateral, it can obtain a 12% (*APR*) loan. The lender requires that a warehouse arrangement be used. The warehouse fee is $10,000, payable at the end of the month. Calculate the effective annual rate of this loan for Row Cannery.

Solution

▶ **Plan**

The monthly interest rate is 12%/12 = 1%. We need to compute the total cash flows Row will owe at the end of the month (including interest and the warehouse fee). By scaling those cash flows by the amount of the loan, we will have a total monthly cost for the loan that we can then convert to an *EAR*.

▶ **Execute**

At the end of the month, Row will owe $2,000,000 × 1.01 = $2,020,000 plus the warehouse fee of $10,000. The cash flows are shown here on a timeline:

```
        0                          1
        ├──────────────────────────┤
   $2,000,000              −$2,030,000
```

The actual one-month interest rate paid is as follows:

$$\frac{2,030,000}{2,000,000} - 1 = 1.5\%$$

Expressing this as an *EAR* gives $1.015^{12} - 1 = 0.196$, or 19.6%.

▶ **Evaluate**

The warehouse arrangement is quite costly: the *EAR* on the loan itself is $(1.01)^{12} - 1 = 0.1268$, or 12.68%, but the warehouse arrangement raises it to 19.6%!

The method that a firm adopts when using its inventory to collateralize a loan will affect the ultimate cost of the loan. The blanket lien agreement exposes the lender to the most risk and will, therefore, carry the highest interest rate of the three types of arrangements discussed. Although a warehousing arrangement provides the greatest amount of control over the inventory to the lender, resulting in a lower interest rate on the loan itself, the borrowing firm must pay the additional fees charged by the warehouser and accept the inconvenience associated with the loss of control. Although a trust receipts arrangement may offer a lower interest rate than a blanket lien and allows the firm to avoid the high fees associated with a warehouse arrangement, it can be used only with certain types of inventory.

Concept Check

9. What is factoring of accounts receivable?

10. What is the difference between a floating lien and a trust receipt?

19.6 Putting It All Together: Creating a Short-Term Financial Plan

Let's return to Whistler Snowboards. In Table 19.2, we found that, due to the seasonal nature of the company's sales, there would be wide swings in its forecasted cash flows—with large positive cash flows in the first and fourth quarters and big negative ones in the second and third quarters of the year. A financial manager at Whistler would need to plan for how to deal with those cash flow swings, and in particular how to finance any shortfalls. To do so, she would prepare a spreadsheet tracking Whistler's cash balance and short-term financing, such as the one shown in Table 19.7. Whistler will end the fourth quarter of 2012 with $1 million in cash, and it needs to maintain a minimum cash balance of $500,000 to meet its basic transaction needs. Given the cash flows projected in Table 19.2, it will have a cash deficit by the third quarter of 2013.

TABLE 19.7	Projected Cash Balance and Short-Term Financing at Whistler Snowboards				
1 Quarter		2012Q4	2013Q1	2013Q2	2013Q3	2013Q4
2 Cash Balance and Short-Term Financing ($000s)					
3 Starting Cash Balance			1000	2763	1315	500
4 Change in Cash and Equivalents			1763	−1448	−2048	3403
5 Minimum Cash Balance			500	500	500	500
6 Surplus (Deficit) Relative to Minimum (3 + 4 − 5)			2263	815	−1233	3403
7 Increase (Decrease) in Short-Term Financing			0	0	1233	−1269
8 Existing Short-Term Financing			0	0	0	1269
9 Total Short-Term Financing (7 + 8)			0	0	1233	0
10 Ending Cash Balance (3 + 4 + 7)		1000	2763	1315	500	2633

The analysis identifies two decisions facing the financial manager: what to do with the excess cash generated in the first quarter, and how to finance the third quarter deficit. The analysis currently assumes that the excess cash is held as just that—cash. However, as we discussed in the last chapter, there are many different options for investing excess cash, even over short horizons, which would generate (taxable) interest income. With such investments, the beginning cash in a quarter would be equal to the ending cash in the previous quarter plus the after-tax portion of the interest received.

Turning to the third quarter deficit, we see that cash flows in the fourth quarter will be large enough to pay off any financing of the third quarter deficit. After reviewing their options, Whistler's managers decide to obtain a one-quarter bank loan with a single repayment. Their bank charges them 3% interest per quarter, so they will need to repay $1233(1.03) = $1270 in the fourth quarter, which they will easily be able to do, given their excess cash flow at that time. By creating a short-term financial plan, the managers can anticipate upcoming shortfalls, allowing them enough time to investigate the least costly way to finance those shortfalls.

MyFinanceLab

Here is what you should know after reading this chapter. MyFinanceLab will help you identify what you know, and where to go when you need to practice.

Key Points	Key Terms	Online Practice Opportunities
19.1 Forecasting Short-Term Financing Needs ▶ The first step in short-term financial planning is to forecast future cash flows. The cash flow forecasts allow a company to determine whether it has a cash flow surplus or deficit, and whether the surplus or deficit is short term or long term. ▶ Firms need short-term financing to deal with seasonal working capital requirements, negative cash flow shocks, or positive cash flow shocks.	cash budget, p. 645	MyFinanceLab Study Plan 19.1 Spreadsheet Tables 19.1–19.4

19.2 The Matching Principle

▶ The matching principle specifies that short-term needs for funds should be financed with short-term sources of funds, and long-term needs should be financed with long-term sources of funds.

aggressive financing policy, p. 648
conservative financing policy, p. 648
funding risk, p. 648
matching principle, p. 647
permanent working capital, p. 647
temporary working capital, p. 647

MyFinanceLab Study Plan 19.2

Spreadsheet Table 19.5

19.3 Short-Term Financing with Bank Loans

▶ Bank loans are a primary source of short-term financing, especially for small firms.
▶ The most straightforward type of bank loan is a single, end-of-period-payment loan.
▶ Bank lines of credit allow a firm to borrow any amount up to a stated maximum. The line of credit may be uncommitted, which is a non-binding, informal agreement, or, more typically, may be committed.
▶ A bridge loan is a short-term bank loan that is used to bridge the gap until the firm can arrange for long-term financing.
▶ The number of compounding periods and other loan stipulations, such as commitment fees, loan origination fees, and compensating balance requirements, affect the effective annual rate of a bank loan.

bank rate, p. 650
bridge loan, p. 651
committed line of credit, p. 650
discount loan, p. 651
evergreen credit, p. 651
line of credit, p. 650
loan origination fee, p. 651
London Inter-Bank Offered Rate (LIBOR), p. 650
prime rate, p. 650
promissory note, p. 650
revolving line of credit, p. 651
uncommitted line of credit, p. 650

MyFinanceLab Study Plan 19.3

19.4 Short-Term Financing with Commercial Paper

▶ Commercial paper is a method of short-term financing that is usually available only to large companies with high-quality credit ratings. It is a low-cost alternative to a short-term bank loan for those firms with access to the commercial paper market.

commercial paper, p. 653
dealer paper, p. 653
direct paper, p. 653

MyFinanceLab Study Plan 19.4

19.5 Short-Term Financing with Secured Financing

▶ Short-term loans may also be structured as secured loans. The accounts receivable and inventory of a firm typically serve as collateral in short-term secured financing arrangements.
▶ Accounts receivable may be either pledged as security for a loan or factored. In a factoring

factoring of accounts receivable arrangement, p. 654
factors, p. 654
field warehouse, p. 656
floating lien (general or blanket lien), p. 655

MyFinanceLab Study Plan 19.5

arrangement, the accounts receivable are sold to the lender (or factor), and the firm's customers are usually instructed to make payments directly to the factor.

▶ Inventory can be used as collateral for a loan in several ways: a floating lien (also called a general or blanket lien), a trust receipts loan (or floor planning), or a warehouse arrangement. These arrangements vary in the extent to which specific items of inventory are identified as collateral; consequently, these arrangements vary in the amount of risk the lender faces.

pledging of accounts receivable agreement, p. 654
public warehouse, p. 656
secured loan, p. 654
trust receipts loan (floor planning), p. 656
warehouse arrangement, p. 656
without recourse, p. 655
with recourse, p. 655

19.6 Putting It All Together: Creating a Short-Term Financial Plan

▶ A short-term financial plan tracks a firm's cash balance and new and existing short-term financing. The plan allows managers to forecast shortfalls and plan to fund them in the least costly manner.

MyFinanceLab
Study Plan 19.6

Spreadsheet
Table 19.6

Review Questions

1. What are the objectives of short-term financial planning?

2. What are seasonalities, and what role do they play in short-term financial planning?

3. Which of the following companies are likely to have high short-term financing needs? Why?
   a. A clothing retailer
   b. A professional sports team
   c. An electric utility
   d. A company that operates toll roads
   e. A restaurant chain

4. Why is it important to distinguish between permanent and temporary shortfalls?

5. What is the difference between permanent working capital and temporary working capital?

6. Describe the different approaches a firm could take in preparing for cash flow shortfalls.

7. What are the different bank financing options, and what are their relative advantages?

8. What is the difference between evergreen credit and a revolving line of credit?

9. What is the difference between direct paper and dealer paper?

10. What is the difference between pledging accounts receivable to secure a loan and factoring accounts receivable? What types of short-term secured financing can a firm use to cover shortfalls?

11. What will a short-term financial plan enable a financial manager to do?

Problems

All problems in this chapter are available in MyFinanceLab.

Forecasting Short-Term Financing Needs

 1. Sailboats Etc. is a retail company specializing in sailboats and other sailing-related equipment. The following table contains financial forecasts as well as current (month 0) working capital levels.

($000s)				Month			
	0	1	2	3	4	5	6
Net Income		10	12	15	25	30	18
Depreciation		2	3	3	4	5	4
Capital Expenditures		1	0	0	1	0	0
Levels of Working Capital							
Accounts Receivable	2	3	4	5	7	10	6
Inventory	3	2	4	5	5	4	2
Accounts Payable	2	2	2	2	2	2	2

a. During which month are the firm's seasonal working capital needs the greatest?
b. When does the firm have surplus cash?

2. Emerald City Umbrellas sells umbrellas and rain gear in Seattle, so its sales are fairly level across the year. However, it is branching out to other markets where it expects demand to be much more variable across the year. Its expected sales in its new market are as follows:

Q1	Q2	Q3	Q4
$20,000	$50,000	$10,000	$50,000

It carries inventory equal to 20% of the next quarter's sales, has accounts payable of 10% of the next quarter's sales, and accounts receivable of 20% of this quarter's sales.
a. Assume that the company starts with $4000 in inventory, $2000 in accounts payable, and no accounts receivable for the new market. Forecast its working capital levels and changes over the four quarters.
b. If Emerald City Umbrellas has net income equal to 20% of sales, what will its financing needs be over the next quarter?

The Matching Principle

The following table includes quarterly working capital levels for your firm for the next year. Use it to answer Problems 3 to 7.

($000s)		Quarter		
	1	2	3	4
Cash	100	100	100	100
Accounts Receivable	200	100	100	600
Inventory	200	500	900	50
Accounts Payable	100	100	100	100

 3. What are the permanent working capital needs of your company? What are the temporary needs?

 4. If you choose to use only long-term financing, what total amount of borrowing will you need to have on a permanent basis? Forecast your excess cash levels under this scenario.

 5. If you hold only $100 in cash at any time, what is your maximum short-term borrowing and when?

6. If you choose to enter the year with $400 total in cash, what is your maximum short-term borrowing?

7. If you want to limit your maximum short-term borrowing to $500, how much excess cash must you carry?

Short-Term Financing with Bank Loans

8. The Hand-to-Mouth Company needs a $10,000 loan for the next 30 days. It is trying to decide which of three alternatives to use:

Alternative A:	Forgo the discount on its trade credit agreement that offers terms of 2/10, net 30.
Alternative B:	Borrow the money from Bank A, which has offered to lend the firm $10,000 for 30 days at an *APR* of 12%. The bank will require a (no-interest) compensating balance of 5% of the face value of the loan and will charge a $100 loan origination fee, which means Hand-to-Mouth must borrow even more than the $10,000.
Alternative C:	Borrow the money from Bank B, which has offered to lend the firm $10,000 for 30 days at an *APR* of 15%. The loan has a 1% loan origination fee.

Which alternative is the cheapest source of financing for Hand-to-Mouth?

9. Consider two loans with one-year maturities and identical face values: an 8% loan with a 1% loan origination fee, and an 8% loan with a 5% (no-interest) compensating balance requirement. Which loan would have the higher effective annual rate? Why?

10. Which of the following one-year, $1000 bank loans offers the lowest effective annual rate?
    a. A loan with an *APR* of 6%, compounded monthly
    b. A loan with an *APR* of 6%, compounded annually, with a compensating balance requirement of 10% (on which no interest is paid)
    c. A loan with an *APR* of 6%, compounded annually, with a 1% loan origination fee

11. The Needy Corporation borrowed $10,000 from Bank Ease. According to the terms of the loan, Needy must pay the bank $400 in interest every three months for the three-year life of the loan, with the principal to be repaid at the maturity of the loan. What effective annual rate is Needy paying?

Short-Term Financing with Commercial Paper

12. The Treadwater Bank wants to raise $1 million using three-month commercial paper. The net proceeds to the bank will be $985,000. What is the effective annual rate of this financing for Treadwater?

13. Magna Corporation has an issue of commercial paper with a face value of $1,000,000 and a maturity of six months. Magna received net proceeds of $973,710 when it sold the paper. What is the effective annual rate of the paper to Magna?

14. Assume that the prime rate is 8% *APR*, compounded quarterly. How much dollar savings in interest did Treadwater (Problem 12) and Magna (Problem 13) achieve by accessing the commercial paper market?

15. The Signet Corporation has issued four-month commercial paper with a $6 million face value. The firm netted $5,870,850 on the sale. What effective annual rate is Signet paying for these funds?

Short-Term Financing with Secured Financing

16. The Ontario Steel Corporation has borrowed $5 million for one month at a stated annual rate of 9%, using inventory stored in a field warehouse as collateral. The

warehouser charges a $5000 fee, payable at the end of the month. What is the effective annual rate of this loan?

17. The Rasputin Brewery is considering using a public warehouse loan as part of its short-term financing. The firm will require a loan of $500,000. Interest on the loan will be 10% (*APR*, annual compounding) to be paid at the end of the year. The warehouse charges 1% of the face value of the loan, payable at the beginning of the year. What is the effective annual rate of this warehousing arrangement?

Creating a Short-Term Financial Plan

 18. Construct a short-term financial plan for Whistler Snowboards based on its expansion opportunity described in the "Positive Cash Flow Shocks" part of Section 19.1. Base the plan on the following table, which forecasts additional capital expenditures, marketing (SG&A), and working capital in Q1 and Q2, along with higher sales in Q2 to Q4. Assume that Whistler ends 2012 with $1 million in cash and that its bank will offer it a short-term loan at the rate 2.5% per quarter. (*See MyFinanceLab for the data in Excel format.*)

1	Quarter	2012Q4	2013Q1	2013Q2	2013Q3	2013Q4
2	Income Statement ($000s)					
3	Sales	4545	5000	6000	6000	6000
4	Cost of Goods Sold	−2955	−3250	−3900	−3900	−3900
5	Selling, General, and Administrative	−455	−1000	−600	−600	−600
6	*EBITDA*	1136	750	1500	1500	1500
7	Depreciation	−455	−500	−525	−525	−525
8	*EBIT*	682	250	975	975	975
9	Taxes	−239	−88	−341	−341	−341
10	Net Income	443	162	634	634	634
11	Statement of Cash Flows					
12	Net Income		162	634	634	634
13	Depreciation		500	525	525	525
14	Changes in Working Capital					
15	Accounts Receivable		−136	−300	—	—
16	Inventory		—	—	—	—
17	Accounts Payable		48	105	—	—
18	Cash from Operating Activities		574	964	1159	1159
19	Capital Expenditures		−1500	−525	−525	−525
20	Other Investment		—	—	—	—
21	Cash form Investing Activities		−1500	−525	−525	−525
22	Net Borrowing		—	—	—	—
23	Dividends		—	—	—	—
24	Capital Contributions		—	—	—	—
25	Cash from Finacing Activities		—	—	—	—
26	Change in Cash and Equivalents		−926	439	634	634

Integrative Case

This case draws on material from Chapters 17 to 19.

Idexo Corporation is a privately held designer and manufacturer of licensed college apparel in Ottawa, Ontario. In late 2010, after several years of lacklustre performance by the firm, the firm's owner and founder, Rebecca Ferris, returned from retirement to replace the current CEO, reinvigorate the firm, and plan for its eventual sale or a possible IPO. She has hired you to assist with developing the firm's financial plan for the next five years.

In 2010, Idexo had total assets of about $103 million and annual sales of $100 million (see Table 1). The firm was profitable, with expected 2010 earnings of over $9 million, for a net profit margin of 9.1%.[5] However, revenue growth has slowed dramatically in recent years, and the firm's net profit margin has actually been declining. Ferris is convinced the firm can do better. After only several weeks at the helm, she has already identified a number of potential improvements to drive the firm's future growth.

TABLE 1

Idexo's 2010 Income Statement and Balance Sheet

1	Year	2010
2	**Income Statement ($000s)**	
3	Sales	100,000
4	Cost of Goods Sold	
5	Raw Materials	−21,333
6	Direct Labour Costs	−24,000
7	**Gross Profit**	54,667
8	Sales and Marketing	−15,000
9	Administration	−18,000
10	*EBITDA*	21,667
11	Depreciation	−6667
12	*EBIT*	15,000
13	Interest Expense (net)	−1021
14	**Pre-tax Income**	13,979
15	Income Tax	−4893
16	**Net Income**	9086

1	Year	2010
2	**Balance Sheet ($000s)**	
3	**Assets**	
4	Cash and Cash Equivalents	15,000
5	Accounts Receivable	20,000
6	Inventories	8219
7	**Total Current Assets**	43,219
8	Property, Plant, and Equipment	60,000
9	Goodwill	—
10	**Total Assets**	103,219
11	**Liabilities and Stockholders' Equity**	
12	Accounts Payable	6205
13	Debt	20,000
14	**Total Liabilities**	26,205
15	**Stockholders' Equity**	77,014
16	**Total Liabilities and Equity**	103,219

[5]See Table 1 for further projected income and balance sheet information for 2010.

Operational Improvements. On the operational side, Ferris is quite optimistic regarding the company's prospects. The market is expected to grow by 6% per year, and Idexo produces a superior product. Idexo's market share has not grown in recent years, because prior management devoted insufficient resources to product development, sales, and marketing. At the same time, Idexo has overspent on administrative costs. Indeed, as shown in Table 1, Idexo's current administrative expenses are $18 million/$100 million = 18% of sales, which exceeds its expenditures on sales and marketing (15% of sales). Competitors spend less on administrative overhead than on sales and marketing.

Ferris plans to cut administrative costs immediately to 15% of sales and redirect resources to new product development, sales, and marketing. By doing so, she believes Idexo can increase its market share from 10% to 14% over the next four years. Using the existing production lines, the increased sales demand can be met in the short run by increasing overtime and running some weekend shifts. The resulting increase in labour costs, however, is likely to lead to a decline in the firm's gross margin to 53%. Table 2 shows sales and operating-cost projections for the next five years based on this plan, including the reallocation of resources from administration to sales and marketing over the five-year period, and an increase in Idexo's average selling price at a 2% inflation rate each year.

TABLE 2

Idexo's Sales and Operating-Cost Projections

1	Year		2010	2011	2012	2013	2014	2015
2	Sales Data	Growth/Yr						
3	Market Size (000s units)	6.0%	20,000	21,200	22,472	23,820	25,250	26,765
4	Market Share	*1.0%	10.0%	11.0%	12.0%	13.0%	14.0%	14.0%
5	Average Sales Price ($/unit)	2.00%	50.00	51.00	52.02	53.06	54.12	55.20
6								
7	Operating Expense and Tax Data							
8	Gross Margin		54.7%	53.0%	53.0%	53.0%	53.0%	53.0%
9	Sales and Marketing (% sales)		15.0%	16.5%	18.0%	19.5%	20.0%	20.0%
10	Administration (% sales)		18.0%	15.0%	15.0%	14.0%	13.0%	13.0%
11	Tax Rate		35.0%	35.0%	35.0%	35.0%	35.0%	35.0%

*Market Share growth is expected through 2014 only.

Expansion Plans. Table 3 shows the forecast for Idexo's capital expenditures over the next five years. Based on the estimates for capital expenditures and depreciation, this spreadsheet tracks the book value of Idexo's plant, property, and equipment starting from its level at the end of 2010. Note that investment is expected to remain relatively low over the next two years—slightly below depreciation. Idexo will expand production during this period by using its existing plant more efficiently.

TABLE 3

Idexo's 2010 Capital Expenditure Forecast

1	Year	2010	2011	2012	2013	2014	2015
2	Fixed Assets and Capital Investment ($000s)						
3	Opening Book Value	60,167	60,000	58,500	57,150	73,935	77,341
4	Capital Investment	6500	5000	5000	25,000	12,000	8000
5	Depreciation	−6667	−6500	−6350	−8215	−8594	−8534
6	Closing Book Value	60,000	58,500	57,150	73,935	77,341	76,807

However, once Idexo's volume grows by more than 50% over its current level, the firm will need to undertake a major expansion to increase its manufacturing capacity. Based on the projections in Table 2, sales growth exceeds 50% of current sales in 2011. Therefore, Table 3 budgets for a major expansion of the plant at that time, leading to a large increase in capital expenditures in 2013 and 2014.

Working Capital Management. To compensate for its weak sales and marketing efforts, Idexo has sought to maintain the loyalty of its retailers, in part through a very lax credit policy. This policy affects Idexo's working capital requirements: for every extra day that customers take to pay, another day's sales revenue is added to accounts receivable (rather than received in cash). From Idexo's current income and balance sheet (Table 1), we can estimate the number of days of receivables as follows:

$$\text{Accounts Receivable Days} = \frac{\text{Accounts Receivable (\$)}}{\text{Sales Revenue (\$/yr)}} \times 365 \text{ days/yr}$$

$$= 20 \text{ million}/100 \text{ million} \times 365 = 73 \text{ days}$$

The standard for the industry is 45 days. Ferris believes that Idexo can tighten its credit policy to achieve this goal without sacrificing sales.

Ferris does not foresee any other significant improvements in Idexo's working capital management, and expects inventories and accounts payable to increase proportionately with sales growth. The firm will also need to maintain a minimum cash balance equal to 30 days sales revenue to meet its liquidity needs. It earns no interest on this minimal balance, and Ferris plans to pay out all excess cash each year to the firm's shareholders as dividends.

Capital Structure Changes: Levering Up. Idexo currently has $20 million in debt outstanding with an interest rate of 6.8%, and it will pay interest only on this debt during the next five years. The firm will also obtain additional financing at the end of years 2013 and 2014 associated with the expansion of its manufacturing plant, as shown in Table 4. While Idexo's credit quality will likely improve by that time, interest rates may also increase somewhat. You expect that rates on these future loans will be about 6.8% as well.

TABLE 4	Idexo's Debt and Interest Forecast						
1	Year	2010	2011	2012	2013	2014	2015
2	Debt and Interest Table ($000s)						
3	Outstanding Debt	20,000	20,000	20,000	35,000	40,000	40,000
4	Interest on Term Loan 6.80%		−1360	−1360	−1360	−2380	−2720

Given Idexo's outstanding debt, its interest expense each year is computed as follows:

$$\text{Interest in year } t = \text{Interest Rate} \times \text{Ending Balance in Year } t - 1$$

The interest on the debt will provide a valuable tax shield to offset Idexo's taxable income.

Case Questions

1. Based on the forecasts above, use the spreadsheet below to construct a pro forma income statement for Idexo over the next five years. What is the annual growth rate of the firm's net income over this period?

1 Year	2010	2011	2012	2013	2014	2015
2 Income Statement ($000s)						
3 Sales	100,000					
4 Cost of Goods Sold	−45,333					
5 Gross Profit	54,667					
6 Sales and Marketing	−15,000					
7 Administration	−18,000					
8 *EBITDA*	21,667					
9 Depreciation	−6667					
10 *EBIT*	15,000					
11 Interest Expense (net)	−1021					
12 Pre-tax Income	13,979					
13 Income Tax	−4893					
14 Net Income	9086					

2. Use the spreadsheet below to project Idexo's working capital needs over the next five years. Why is the increase in net working capital negative in 2011? Why does the increase in net working capital decline from 2014 to 2015?

1 Year	2010	2011	2012	2013	2014	2015
2 Working Capital ($000s)						
3 Assets						
4 Accounts Receivable	20,000					
5 Inventories	8219					
6 Minimum Cash Balance	8219					
7 Total Current Assets	36,438					
8 Liabilities						
9 Accounts Payable	6205					
10 Net Working Capital	30,233					
11 Increase in Net Working Capital						

3. Based on the forecasts you have already developed, use the spreadsheet below to project Idexo's free cash flow for 2011 to 2015. Will the firm's free cash flow steadily increase over this period? Why or why not?

1 Year	2010	2011	2012	2013	2014	2015
2 Free Cash Flow ($000s)						
3 Net Income						
4 Plus: After-Tax Interest Expense						
5 Unlevered Net Income						
6 Plus: Depreciation						
7 Less: Increases in *NWC*						
8 Less: Capital Expenditures						
9 Free Cash Flow of Firm						
10 Plus: Net Borrowing						
11 Less: After-Tax Interest Expense						
12 Free Cash Flow to Equity						

4. (Optional) Recall that Idexo plans to maintain only the minimal necessary cash and pay out all excess cash as dividends.

   a. Suppose that, at the very end of 2010, Ferris plans to use all excess cash to pay an immediate dividend. How much cash can the firm pay out at this time? Compute a new 2010 balance sheet reflecting this dividend using the spreadsheet below.

   b. Forecast the cash available to pay dividends in future years—the firm's *free cash flow to equity*—by adding any new borrowing and subtracting *after-tax* interest expenses from free cash flow each year. Will Idexo have sufficient cash to pay dividends in all years? Explain.

   c. Using your forecast of the firm's dividends, construct a pro forma balance sheet for Idexo over the next five years.

1	Year	2010	2011	2012	2013	2014	2015
2	Balance Sheet ($000s)						
3	Assets						
4	Cash and Cash Equivalents						
5	Accounts Receivable						
6	Inventories						
7	Total Current Assets						
8	Property, Plant, and Equipment						
9	Goodwill						
10	Total Assets						
11	Liabilities and Stockholders' Equity						
12	Accounts Payable						
13	Debt						
14	Total Liabilities						
15	Stockholders' Equity						
16	Starting Stockholders' Equity						
17	Net Income						
18	Dividends						
19	Capital Contributions						
20	Stockholders' Equity						
21	Total Liabilities and Equity						

5. In late 2010, soon after Ferris's return as CEO, the firm receives an unsolicited offer of $210 million for its outstanding equity. If Ferris accepts the offer, the deal would close at the end of 2010. Suppose Ferris believes that Idexo can be sold at the end of 2015 for an enterprise value equal to nine times its final *EBITDA*. Idexo's unlevered cost of capital is 10% (specifically, 10% is the pre-tax WACC). Based on your forecast of Idexo's free cash flow in 2011 to 2015 in Question 3, and its final enterprise value in 2015, estimate the following:

   a. Idexo's unlevered value at the end of 2010.

   b. The present value of Idexo's interest tax shields in 2011 to 2015. (Recall that these tax shields are fixed and so have the same risk level as the debt.)

   c. Idexo's enterprise value at the end of 2010. (Add the present value of the interest tax shield in 5b to the unlevered value of the firm in 5a.)

   d. Idexo's equity value today. (Adjust the enterprise value in 5c to reflect the firm's debt and excess cash at the end of 2010.)

   e. Based on your analysis, should Ferris sell the company now?

PART 8

Special Topics

Valuation Principle Connection. In Part 8, the final section of the text, we address special topics in corporate financial management. The Valuation Principle continues to provide a unifying framework as we consider these topics. Chapter 20 discusses options; the key to understanding how to value them comes from the Law of One Price application of the Valuation Principle. In Chapter 21, we focus on corporations' use of options and other methods to manage risk. We use the Valuation Principle to evaluate the costs and benefits of risk management. Chapter 22 introduces the issues a firm faces when making a foreign investment, and addresses the valuation of foreign projects. We will see that the Law of One Price generates several important relations that will drive our valuation of foreign cash flows. Chapter 23 introduces an alternative to long-term debt financing, leasing. By presenting leasing as a financing alternative, we apply the Law of One Price to determine that the benefits of leasing must derive from the tax differences, incentive effects, or other market imperfections. The Law of One Price continues to provide a unifying framework as we consider the topics of Mergers and Acquisitions in Chapter 24 and Corporate Governance in Chapter 25.

Option Applications and Corporate Finance

LEARNING OBJECTIVES

▸ Understand basic option terminology

▸ Explain the difference between calls and puts; determine their payoffs and profits from holding each to expiration

▸ Analyze the factors that affect option prices

▸ Be familiar with the Black-Scholes Option Pricing Formula

▸ Describe the relation that must hold between the prices of similar *calls* and *puts* on the same stock

▸ Demonstrate how options are applied in corporate finance

notation

PV	present value	*NPV*	net present value
Div	dividend		

University of Quebec at Montreal and the Warsaw School of Economics, 2011

"I valued the intellectual property using the Black-Scholes model in conjunction with traditional discounted cash flow techniques because discounted cash flow doesn't take into account the notion of managerial flexibility in terms of management's option to choose to delay the project, or not to undertake it at all."

After receiving a Bachelor of Arts degree in political science from the University of Toronto in 2005, John Lundy went on to obtain a Master of Business Administration degree from the University of Quebec at Montreal and the Warsaw School of Economics in 2011. He currently works as the financial strategy manager for an investment company in Warsaw, Poland. "I have a wide variety of responsibilities that fall under my purview, and the position has exposed me to many different aspects of financial management," John says. "I often need to update the inputs and assumptions regarding initial capital outlays, revenue, and cost structure projections, create sensitivity analyses, and demonstrate the valuations of the project to highlight its *NPV* and *IRR*," he continues. "The MBA program's corporate finance class really helped me to solidify my understanding of financial modelling and the techniques used in business planning."

Some of John's responsibilities are valuing projects undertaken by firms in which his company has a significant investment. One of the ways he goes about these valuations is by using a technique to value options. "I work on valuations on the holding-company level as well, assessing the optimal revenue-stream structure for the project, and I create the best deal terms for joint-venture partnerships on the individual project level," John says. "The most interesting area for me in terms of valuations was the valuation of the company's intellectual property. Many firms have significant intellectual property assets that exist off-book, and ours was no different, so I set out to value the intellectual property as a real option. The real option valuation method values intellectual property through the use of the Black-Scholes Option Pricing Model, where you have project-specific equivalents to the traditional financial stock option in the model inputs, and the output value of the option to undertake the project is equal to the value of the firm's intellectual property, as the project couldn't be undertaken without it," he explains.

"One must be careful to try to properly assess the volatility of the project's cash flows, which is by far the most daunting task, as it heavily influences the final output value," John continues. "If the firm has undertaken similar projects in the past, one could look at the volatility of its previous cash flows as a proxy for the valuation. These concepts and the application of the Black-Scholes model to non-financial assets have been backed both by academic literature and in practice. I valued the intellectual property using the Black-Scholes model in conjunction with traditional discounted cash flow techniques because discounted cash flow doesn't take into account the notion of managerial flexibility in terms of management's option to choose to delay the project, or not to undertake it at all."

Since the introduction of publicly traded options on the Chicago Board Options Exchange (CBOE) in 1973, financial options have become one of the most important and actively traded financial assets. The Montreal Exchange was the first to trade stock options in Canada in 1975. Over time the Montreal Exchange added options on other products: fixed income securities (1991), stock indexes (1999), exchange-traded funds (2000), and the U.S. dollar (2005). In May 2008, the Montreal Exchange merged with the TSX Group to become the TMX Group. Options have become important tools for corporate financial managers. For example, many large corporations have operations in different parts of the world, so they face exposure to exchange rate risk and other types of business risk. To control this risk, they often use options as part of their corporate risk management practices.

In this chapter, we introduce the financial option, a financial contract between two parties. In Chapter 8, we briefly discussed the idea of real options, or the value of flexibility when managing projects. Here, we delve further into understanding what options are and what factors affect their value. To start, we provide an overview of the basic types of financial options, introduce important terminology, and describe the payoffs of various option-based strategies. We next discuss the factors that affect option prices. Finally, we model the equity and debt of the firm as options to gain insight into the conflicts of interest between equity holders and debt holders, as well as the pricing of risky debt.

20.1 Option Basics

financial option A contract that gives its owner the right (but not the obligation) to purchase or sell an asset at a fixed price at some future date.

call option A financial option that gives its owner the right to buy an asset.

put option A financial option that gives its owner the right to sell an asset.

option writer The seller of an option contract that the seller does not currently own.

derivatives Securities whose cash flows depend solely on the prices of other marketed assets.

warrant A call option written by a company itself on new stock.

exercising the option The enforcement, by the holder of an option, of the agreement to buy or sell a share of stock at the agreed-upon price.

strike (exercise) price The price at which an option holder buys or sells a share of stock when the option is exercised.

American option The most common kind of option, which allows the holder to exercise the option on any date up to and including the expiration date.

expiration date The last date on which an option holder has the right to exercise the option.

European option An option that allows the holder to exercise the option only on the expiration date.

A **financial option** contract gives its owner the right (but not the obligation) to purchase or sell an asset at a fixed price at some future date. There are two distinct kinds of option contracts: *call options* and *put options*. A **call option** gives the owner the right to *buy* the asset; a **put option** gives the owner the right to *sell* the asset. An option is a contract between two parties. For every owner of a financial option, there is also an **option writer**, the seller and originator of an option contract, who is the person who takes the other side of the contract. In effect, option writers have sold an option that they did not currently own, so they increased the number of options existing in the market. Options are part of a broader class of securities called **derivatives**, because they derive their value solely from the price of another asset.

The most common option contracts are options on shares of stock. A stock option gives the holder the option to buy or sell a share of stock on or before a given date for a given price. For example, a call option on Telus Corporation stock might give the holder the right to purchase a share of Telus for $75 per share at any time up to, for example, January 17, 2014. Similarly, a put option on Telus stock might give the holder the right to sell a share of Telus stock for $70 per share at any time up to, say, February 21, 2014.

When a company writes a call option on *new* stock to be issued by the company, it is called a **warrant**. A regular call option is written by a third party on existing stock. When a holder of a warrant exercises it and thereby purchases stock, the company delivers this stock by issuing new stock. In all other respects, a warrant is identical to a call option.

Option Contracts

Practitioners use specific words to describe the details of option contracts. When a holder of an option enforces the agreement and buys or sells a share of stock at the agreed-upon price, he is **exercising the option**. The price at which the option holder buys or sells the share of stock when the option is exercised is called the **strike price** or **exercise price**.

There are two kinds of options. **American options**, the most common kind, allow their holders to exercise the option on any date up to and including a final date called the **expiration date**. **European options** allow their holders to exercise the option only on the expiration date—that is, holders cannot exercise the option before the expiration date. The terms "American" and "European" have nothing to do with the location where the options are traded: both types are traded worldwide.

As with other financial assets, options can be bought and sold. Standard stock options are traded on organized exchanges, while more specialized options are sold through dealers. The oldest and largest options exchange is the CBOE. By convention, all traded options expire on the Saturday following the third Friday of the month. The market price of the option is also called the option premium.

The option buyer, also called the option holder, holds the right to exercise the option and has a *long* position in the contract. The option seller, also called the option writer, sells (or writes) the option and has a *short* position in the contract. Because the long side has the option to exercise, the short side has an *obligation* to fulfill the contract. For example, suppose you own a call option on Bombardier stock with an exercise price of $25. Bombardier stock is currently trading for $40, so you decide to exercise the option. The person holding the short position in the contract is obligated to sell you a share of Bombardier stock for $25. Your positive **payoff** of $15—the difference between the price you pay for the share of stock and the price at which you can sell the share in the market—implies the person short in the option has a negative payoff of −$15.

Investors make the decision to exercise options only when they will have a positive payoff; this decision is made by the person who has the long position in the option. Consequently, whenever an option is exercised, the person holding the short position has a negative payoff that funds the positive payoff of the long party. That is, the obligation will be costly. Why, then, do people write options? The answer is that when you sell an option you get paid for it—options always have non-negative prices. This upfront payment compensates the seller for the risk of loss in the event that the option holder chooses to exercise the option. So, for the buyer of an option, the **profit** consists of the payoff minus the upfront amount paid for the option. For the seller of an option, the profit consists of the payoff plus the amount received when the option was originally sold. If all this new terminology is confusing, rest assured that you will become comfortable with it as you proceed through the chapter. We provide a summary of the new terms in Table 20.1.

payoff The amount received or paid at the time the exercise/don't exercise decision is made.

profit The net of the payoff and, if purchased, the amount paid by the buyer, or, if sold, the amount received by the seller.

Stock Option Quotations

Table 20.2 shows near-term options on Bow.com as though they were taken from the CBOE website (www.cboe.com) on November 30, 2012. Call options are listed on the left and put options on the right. Each line corresponds to a particular option. The first two digits in the option name refer to the year of expiration. The option name also includes the month of expiration, the strike or exercise price, and the ticker symbol of the individual option (in parentheses). The first line in the left column of Table 20.2 is a call option with an exercise price of $45 that expires on the Saturday following the third Friday of December 2012 (December 22, 2012). The columns to the right of the name

TABLE 20.1 The Language of Options	Call option	Option to buy the stock at a prespecified price
	Put option	Option to sell the stock at a prespecified price
	Strike (exercise) price	The prespecified price in the option contract
	Write an option	Sell an option that you did not currently own
	Exercise an option	Enforce the option holder's right to buy or sell the stock as specified in the option contract
	American option	An option that can be exercised any time on or before the expiration date
	European option	An option that can be exercised only on the expiration date
	Warrant	A call option written by the firm whereby new stock will be issued if the warrant is exercised
	Payoff	The amount received or paid at the time the exercise/don't exercise decision is made
	Profit	The net of the payoff and, if purchased, the amount paid by the buyer, or, if sold, the amount received by the seller

TABLE 20.2	Option Quotes for Bow.com Stock

Bow
Nov 30, 2012 @ 11:35 ET (Data 15 Minutes Delayed)   Bid 48.35   Ask 48.37

48.35−
Vol 3831766

Calls	Last Sale	Net	Bid	Ask	Vol	Open Int	Puts	Last Sale	Net	Bid	Ask	Vol	Open Int
12 Dec 45.00 (BQW LI-E)	4.00	pc	3.70	3.90	0	16021	12 Dec 45.00 (BQW XI-E)	0.30	−0.05	0.30	0.40	30	20788
12 Dec 47.50 (BQW LW-E)	2.20	−0.25	1.90	2.00	86	18765	12 Dec 47.50 (BQW XW-E)	0.75	−0.15	0.95	1.05	292	13208
12 Dec 50.00 (BQW LJ-E)	0.80	—	0.75	0.85	144	9491	12 Dec 50.00 (BQW XJ-E)	2.30	+0.20	2.30	2.40	177	5318
12 Dec 55.00 (BQW LK-E)	0.15	pc	0.05	0.10	0	2497	12 Dec 55.00 (BQW XK-E)	6.10	pc	6.60	6.80	0	895
13 Jan 45.00 (BQW AI-E)	4.93	pc	4.80	5.00	0	18765	13 Jan 45.00 (BQW MI-E)	1.20	−0.10	1.20	1.30	8	29717
13 Jan 47.50 (BQW AW-E)	3.70	+0.10	3.20	3.30	5	8068	13 Jan 47.50 (BQW MW-E)	1.95	+0.15	2.05	2.15	10	6632
13 Jan 50.00 (BQW AJ-E)	2.15	+0.15	1.95	2.05	208	27416	13 Jan 50.00 (BQW MJ-E)	3.30	+0.20	3.30	3.50	162	6668
13 Jan 55.00 (BQW AK-E)	0.70	+0.10	0.60	0.70	65	8475	13 Jan 55.00 (BQW MK-E)	6.90	−2.50	7.00	7.10	67	5621

Source: Bow.com is a hypothetical stock, but the quotes are based on those from the Chicago Board Options Exchange website, www.cboe.com.

open interest The total number of contracts of a particular option that have been written and not yet closed.

at-the-money A term describing options whose exercise prices are equal to the current stock price.

in-the-money A term describing an option whose value if immediately exercised would be positive.

display market data for the option. The first of these columns shows the last sales price, followed by the net change from the previous day's last reported sales price ("pc" indicates that no trade has occurred on this day, so the last sales price is the previous day's last reported sales price), the current bid and ask prices, and the daily volume. The final column is the **open interest**, the total number of contracts of that particular option that have been written and not yet repurchased by a writer so as to close the short position.

The top line of the option quote displays information about the stock itself. In this case, Bow's stock last traded at a price of $48.35 per share. We also see the current bid and ask prices for the stock, as well as the volume of trade.

When the exercise price of an option is equal to the current price of the stock, the option is said to be **at-the-money**. Notice that much of the trading occurs in options that are closest to being at-the-money—that is, calls and puts with exercise prices of either $47.50 or $50. Notice how the December 50 calls have high volume. They last traded for 80 cents, midway between the current bid price (75 cents) and the ask price (85 cents), which indicates that the trade probably occurred recently, because the last traded price is a current market price.

Stock option contracts are always written on 100 shares of stock. If, for instance, you decided to purchase one December 47.50 call contract, you would be purchasing an option to buy 100 shares at $47.50 per share. Option prices are quoted on a per-share basis, so the ask price of $2.00 implies that you would pay $100 \times \$2 = \$200$ for the contract. Similarly, if you decide to buy a December 45 put contract, you would pay $100 \times \$0.40 = \$40$ for the option to sell 100 shares of Bow.com stock for $45 per share.

Note from Table 20.2 that, for each expiration date, call options with lower strike prices have higher market prices—the right to buy the stock at a lower price is more valuable than the right to buy it for a higher price. Conversely, because the put option gives the holder the right to sell the stock at the strike price, puts with higher strikes are more valuable (for the same expiration date). On the other hand, holding fixed the strike price, both calls and puts are more expensive for a longer time to expiration. Because these options are American-style options that can be exercised at any time, having the right to buy or sell for a longer period is valuable.

If the payoff from exercising an option immediately is positive, the option is said to be **in-the-money**. Call options with strike prices below the current stock price are in-the-money, as are put options with strike prices above the current stock price.

EXAMPLE 20.1

Purchasing Options

Problem

It is midday on November 30, 2012, and you have decided to purchase 10 January call contracts on Bow.com stock with an exercise price of $50. Because you are buying, you must pay the ask price. How much money will this purchase cost you? Is this option in-the-money or out-of-the-money?

Solution

▶ **Plan**

From Table 20.2, the ask price of this option is $2.05. Remember that the price quoted is per share and that each contract is for 100 shares.

▶ **Execute**

You are purchasing 10 contracts and each contract is on 100 shares, so the transaction will cost $10 \times 100 \times \$2.05 = \$2050$ (ignoring any commission fees). Because this is a call option and the exercise price is above the current stock price ($48.35), the option is currently out-of-the-money.

▶ **Evaluate**

Even though the option is currently out-of-the-money, it still has value. During the time left to expiration, the stock could rise above the exercise (strike) price of $50.

---

out-of-the-money
A term describing an option that, if exercised immediately, results in a loss of money.

deep in-the-money
A term describing options that are in-the-money and for which the strike price and the stock price are very far apart.

deep out-of-the-money
A term describing options that are out-of-the-money and for which the strike price and the stock price are very far apart.

hedging The practice of reducing risk by holding contracts or securities whose payoffs are negatively correlated with some risk exposure.

speculating The practice of using securities to place a bet on the direction in which the investor believes the market is likely to move.

Conversely, if the payoff from exercising the option immediately is negative, the option is **out-of-the-money**. Call options with strike prices above the current stock price are out-of-the-money, as are put options with strike prices below the current stock price. Of course, someone long in an option would not choose to exercise an out-of-the-money option, so the actual payoff at the time the exercise/don't exercise decision is made will be zero for out-of-the-money options, as nobody would exercise them. Options for which the strike price and the stock price are very far apart are referred to as **deep in-the-money** or **deep out-of-the-money**.

Options on Other Financial Securities

Although the most commonly traded options are written on stocks, options on other financial assets do exist. Perhaps the most well known are options on stock indexes in the United States such as the S&P 100 index, the S&P 500 index, the Dow Jones Industrial index, and the NYSE index. These options have become very popular because they allow investors to protect the value of their investments from adverse market changes. In Canada, the Montreal Exchange's only broad index option is on the S&P TSX 60. In addition, Montreal offers options on exchange-traded funds (such as iShares) that track the S&P TSX 60, various industry sectors, fixed income products, and selected commodity prices.

As we will see shortly, a stock index put option can be used to offset the losses on an investor's portfolio in a market downturn; this is an example of *hedging*. In general, **hedging** is accomplished by holding contracts or securities whose payoffs are negatively correlated with some risk exposure that already exists. Options also allow investors to **speculate**, or place a bet on the direction in which they believe the market is likely to move. By purchasing a call, for example, investors can bet on a market rise with a much smaller investment than they could by investing in the market index itself.

Options Are for More Than Just Stocks

Although the examples in this chapter are mainly about options on stocks, there are options on a wide variety of other assets. For example, options are also traded on government debt securities and bankers' acceptances. These options allow investors to bet on or hedge interest-rate risk. There are also options on currencies, gold, platinum, and other commodities such as copper and oil. In Montreal, there is an option contract on 10,000 U.S. dollars. On the ICE Futures Canada exchange, headquartered in Winnipeg, options on canola, feed wheat, and western barley are traded. The main markets for options on other agricultural commodities, metals, and energy are either in Chicago or New York. Some of these include options on wheat, soybeans, livestock, cotton, orange juice, and sugar. These options allow both farmers and large agribusinesses to hedge their risks from fluctuations in production and prices.

Concept Check

1. Does the holder of an option have to exercise it?
2. What is the difference between an American option and a European option?

20.2 Option Payoffs and Profits at Expiration

With our new understanding of the basics of puts and calls, we are now prepared to examine their values. From the Valuation Principle, the value of any security is determined by the future cash flows an investor receives from owning it. Therefore, before we can assess what an option is worth, we must determine an option's payoff at the time of expiration.

The Long Position in an Option Contract

Assume you own an option with a strike price of $20. If, on the expiration date, the stock price is greater than the strike price, say $30, you can make money by exercising the call (by paying $20, the strike price for the stock) and immediately selling the stock in the open market for $30. The $10 difference is the option's payoff at expiration and is what it is worth one moment before it expires. Consequently, when the stock price on the expiration date exceeds the strike price, the value of the call is the difference between the stock price and the strike price. When the stock price is less than the strike price at expiration, the holder will not exercise the call, so the option is worth nothing. In other words, the value of an option just as it is about to expire is simply the payoff, assuming the optimal exercise/don't exercise decision is made. These payoffs are plotted in Figure 20.1.

Thus, the value of the call at expiration is as follows:

Call Value at Expiration

$$\text{Call Value} = \text{Stock Price} - \text{Strike Price}, \quad \text{if Stock Price} > \text{Strike}$$
$$= 0, \quad \text{if Stock Price} \le \text{Strike} \qquad (20.1)$$

The holder of a put option will exercise the option if the stock price is below the strike price. Because the holder receives the strike price when the stock is worth less, the holder's payoff is equal to Strike Price − Stock Price. If the stock price is above the exercise price, the optimal exercise/don't exercise decision is to not exercise and receive a $0 payoff. Thus, the value of a put at expiration is as follows:

Put Price at Expiration

$$\text{Put Value} = \text{Strike Price} - \text{Stock Price}, \quad \text{if Stock Price} < \text{Strike}$$
$$= 0, \quad \text{if Stock Price} \ge \text{Strike} \qquad (20.2)$$

FIGURE 20.1

Payoff of a Call Option with a Strike Price of $20 at Expiration

If the stock price is greater than the strike price ($20), the call will be exercised. The holder's payoff is the difference between the stock price and the strike price. If the stock price is less than the strike price, the call will not be exercised and so has no value.

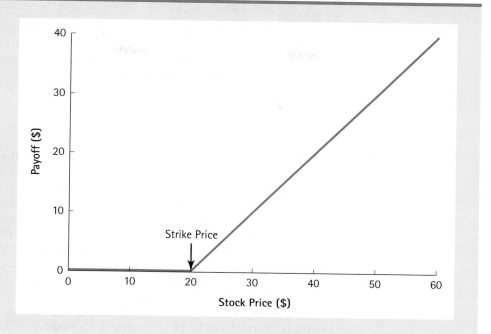

EXAMPLE 20.2

Payoff of a Put Option at Maturity

Problem

You own a put option on Tim Hortons Inc. stock with an exercise price of $20 that expires today. Plot the value of this option as a function of the stock price.

Solution

▶ **Plan**

From Equation 20.2, and the fact that the strike price is $20, we see that the value of the put option is as follows:

Put Value = 20 − Stock Price, if Stock Price < 20; = 0, if Stock Price ≥ 20

▶ **Execute**

Plotting this function gives the following:

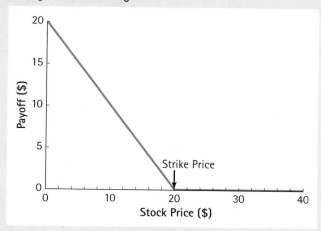

▶ **Evaluate**

Because the put option allows you (the long party) to force the put writer to buy the stock for $20, regardless of the current market price, we can see that the put option payoff increases as Tim Hortons' stock price decreases. For example, if Tim Hortons' price were $10, you could buy a share of Tim Hortons in the market for $10 and then sell it to the put writer for $20, generating a payoff of $10.

The Short Position in an Option Contract

An investor holding a short position in an option has written the option and sold it to the long party; thus the short party has an obligation. This investor takes the opposite side of the contract to the investor who is long; so if the long party exercises, the short party must fulfill the obligations of the option contract. Thus, the short position's cash flows are the negative of the long position's cash flows. Because an investor who is long in an option can receive money only at expiration—that is, the investor will not exercise an option that is out-of-the-money—a short investor can only pay money.

To demonstrate, assume you have a short position in a call option with an exercise price of $20. If the stock price is greater than the strike price of a call—for example, $25—the holder will exercise the option. You then have the obligation to sell the stock for the strike price of $20. Because you must purchase the stock at the market price of $25, you lose the difference between the two prices, or $5. However, if the stock price is less than the strike price at the expiration date, the holder will not exercise the option, so in this case you lose nothing; you have no obligation. These payoffs are plotted in Figure 20.2.

FIGURE 20.2   Short Position in a Call Option at Expiration

If the stock price is greater than the strike price, the call will be exercised. A person on the short side of a call will lose the difference between the stock price and the strike price. If the stock price is less than the strike price, the call will not be exercised, and the seller will have no obligation.

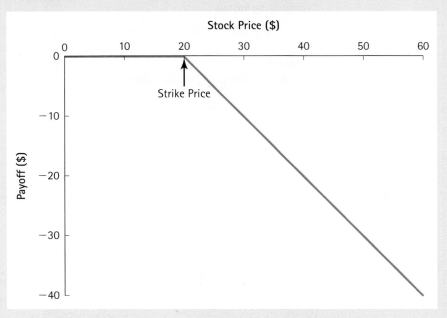

EXAMPLE 20.3

Payoff of a Short
Position in a Put
Option

Problem

You are short in a put option on Tim Hortons stock with an exercise price of $20 that expires today. What is your payoff at expiration as a function of the stock price?

Solution

▶ **Plan**

Again, the strike price is $20 and in this case your cash flows will be opposite of those from Equation 20.2, as depicted in the previous example. Thus, your cash flows will be as follows:

$$-(20 - \text{Stock Price}) = -20 + \text{Stock Price, if Stock Price} < 20$$
$$= 0, \text{ if Stock Price} \geq 20$$

▶ **Execute**

The graph below plots your cash flows:

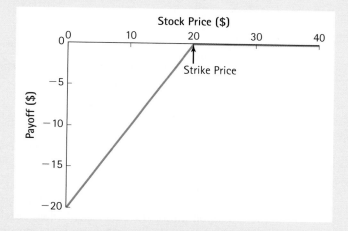

▶ **Evaluate**

Because the put option allows the option owner to force you, the put writer, to buy the stock for $20, regardless of the current market price, we can see that the put option payoff for the writer decreases as Tim Hortons' stock price decreases. For example, if Tim Hortons' price were $10, the option owner could buy a share of Tim Hortons in the market for $10 and then sell it to you, the put writer, for $20, making the writer's payoff equal to −$10 (the writer acquires something worth $10 but pays $20 for it).

Notice that because the stock price cannot fall below zero, the downside for a short position in a put option is limited to the strike price of the option. A short position in a call, however, has no limit on the downside (see Figure 20.2).

Profits for Holding an Option to Expiration

Although payouts on a long position in an option contract are never negative, the *profit* from purchasing an option and holding it to expiration could be negative. That is, the payout at expiration might be less than the initial cost of the option.

To illustrate, let's consider the potential profits from purchasing the 13 January 50.00 call option on Bow.com stock quoted in Table 20.2. The option costs $2.05 and expires in 52 days. It is customary to ignore the time value of money when determining

FIGURE 20.3

Profit from Holding a Call Option to Expiration

The curves show the profit per share from purchasing the January call options in Table 20.2. Note that all of the payoff diagrams are shifted down by the amount of the option's premium. Thus, even if the payoff is positive, if it is not enough to offset the premium you paid to acquire the option, your profit will be negative.

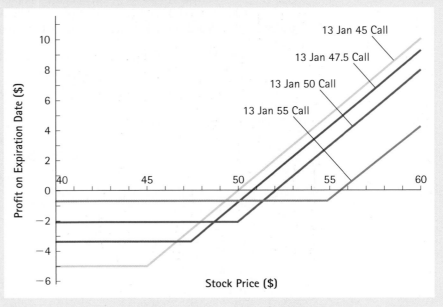

option profits, because the time frame of analysis is usually quite short. The profit is the call payoff minus the $2.05 spent when purchasing the option. Once the cost of the position is taken into account, you make a positive profit only if the stock price exceeds $52.05. As we can see from Table 20.2, the further in-the-money the option is, the higher its initial price and thus the larger your potential loss. An out-of-the-money option has a smaller initial cost and hence a smaller potential loss. The probability of a profit, however, is also smaller because the stock price where profits become positive is higher.

Because a short position in an option is the other side of a long position, the profits from a short position in an option are the negative of the profits of a long position. For example, a short position in an out-of-the-money call like the 13 January 55 Bow.com call in Figure 20.3 produces a small positive profit if Bow.com's stock is below $55.70 but leads to losses if the stock price is above $55.70.

EXAMPLE 20.4

Profit on Holding a Position in a Put Option Until Expiration

Problem

Assume you decided to purchase each of the January put options quoted in Table 20.2. Plot the profit of each position as a function of the stock price on expiration.

Solution

▶ **Plan**

Suppose P is the price of each put option on November 30. Then your cash flows on the expiration date will be as follows:

$$\text{(Strike Price} - \text{Stock Price)} - P, \text{ if Stock Price} < \text{Strike Price,}$$
$$\text{or} \quad 0 - P, \text{ if Stock Price} \geq \text{Strike Price}$$

▶ **Execute**
The graph below plots your cash flows:

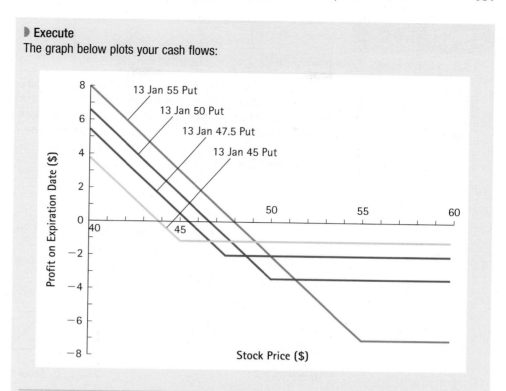

▶ **Evaluate**
The graph illustrates the same tradeoff between the maximum loss and the potential for profit as for the call options. The greatest profit potential comes from the most expensive option, so if that option expires worthless, you have lost the greatest amount.

Returns for Holding an Option to Expiration

We can also compare options based on their potential returns. Figure 20.4 shows the return from purchasing one of the January 2013 options in Table 20.2 on November 30, 2012, and holding it until the expiration date. Let's begin by focusing on call options, shown in panel (a). In all cases, the maximum loss is 100%—the option may expire worthless. Notice how the curves change as a function of the strike price—the distribution of returns for out-of-the-money call options is more extreme than that for in-the-money calls. That is, an out-of-the-money call option is more likely to have a −100% return, but if the stock goes up sufficiently, it will also have a much higher return than an in-the-money call option. Similarly, all call options have more extreme returns than the stock itself (given Bow.com's initial price of $48.35, the range of stock prices shown in the plot represent returns from −17% to +24%). As a consequence, the risk of a call option is amplified relative to the risk of the stock, and the amplification is greater for deeper out-of-the-money calls. Thus, if a stock had a positive beta, call options on the stock would have even higher betas and expected returns than the stock itself.

Now consider the returns for put options. Look carefully at panel (b) in Figure 20.4. The put position has a higher return in states with *low* stock prices; that is, if the stock has a positive beta, the put has a negative beta. Hence, put options on positive beta stocks have lower expected returns than the underlying stocks. The deeper out-of-the-money the put option is, the more negative its beta and the lower its expected return. As a result, put options are generally not held as an investment, but rather as insurance to hedge other risk in a portfolio. We explore the idea of using options for insurance further in Section 20.5.

FIGURE 20.4

Option Returns from Purchasing an Option and Holding It to Expiration

Panel (a) shows the return on the expiration date from purchasing one of the January call options in Table 20.2 on November 30, 2012, and holding the position until the expiration date. Panel (b) shows the same return for the January put options in the table. Notice how the returns are more sensitive to a change in the stock price the further out-of-the-money the option is. For example, in panel (a), the slope of the return line after the strike price is reached is steeper for options that are further out-of-the-money. For the January 55 call, a small change in the stock price can lead to a large change in the return. A similar effect is seen for puts in panel (b).

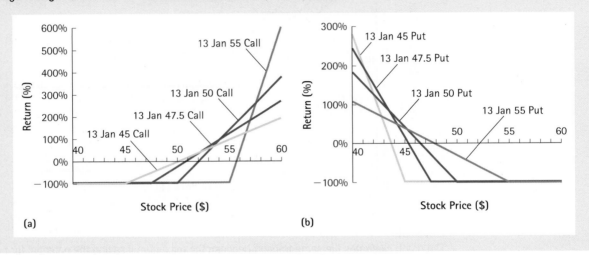

(a)   (b)

At this point, we have discussed the cost (premium) of buying an option, the pay-offs at expiration, and the profits. It is a lot to keep track of, but it is usually helpful to remember that there are only three things being exchanged: (1) the option premium, (2) the strike price, and (3) the share of stock. Further, because an option is a contract between two parties, the losses of one party are the gains of the other. We summarize these relationships in Table 20.3 for the 13 January 50 calls and puts on Bow.com stock from Table 20.2. When reading the table, keep in mind that if you own the option and exercising it would create a negative payoff, you will choose not to exercise, so the payoff will be zero (see Equations 20.1 and 20.2).

TABLE 20.3

Payoffs, Profits, and Returns to Buying or Writing Options in Table 20.2

	At Purchase	At Expiration If Stock Price = 40		At Expiration If Stock Price = 60	
		Payoff	Profit	Payoff	Profit
Buy a "13 January 50" Call	Pay $2.05	$0	0 − 2.05 = −$2.05 −100% return	$10	10 − 2.05 = $7.95 387.8%
Write a "13 January 50" Call	Receive $2.05*	$0	2.05 − 0 = $2.05	−$10	2.05 − 10 = −$7.95
Buy a "13 January 50" Put	Pay $3.50	50 − 40 = $10	10 − 3.50 = $6.50 185.7% return	$0	0 − 3.50 = −$3.50 −100% return
Write a "13 January 50" Put	Receive $3.50*	40 − 50 = −$10	3.50 − 10 = −$6.50	$0	3.50 − 0 = $3.50

Option contracts are for options on 100 shares. Payoffs and profits shown are for *one* option on *one* share.

*Assumes written options were sold at the ask price.

3. How are the profits from buying an option different from the payoff to the option at expiration?

4. How are the payoffs to buying a call option related to the payoffs from writing a call option?

20.3 Factors Affecting Option Prices

When we discussed Table 20.2, we noted some relationships between the option prices and different characteristics of the options. In this section, we identify and explain all the factors that affect the price of an option.

Strike Price and Stock Price

As we noted earlier for the Bow.com option quotes in Table 20.2, the value of an otherwise identical call option is higher if the strike price the holder must pay to buy the stock is lower. Because a put is the right to sell the stock, puts with a lower strike price are less valuable.

For a given strike price, the value of a call option is higher if the current price of the stock is higher, as there is a greater likelihood the option will end up in-the-money. Conversely, put options increase in value as the stock price falls.

Option Prices and the Exercise Date

For American options, the longer the time to the exercise date, the more valuable the option. To see why, let's consider two options: an option with one year until the exercise date and an option with six months until the exercise date. The holder of the one-year option can turn her option into a six-month option by simply exercising it early. That is, the one-year option has all the same rights and privileges as the six-month option, so by the Valuation Principle, it cannot be worth less than the six-month option. That is, *an American option with a later exercise date cannot be worth less than an otherwise identical American option with an earlier exercise date*. Usually the right to delay exercising the option is worth something, so the option with the later exercise date will be more valuable.

What about European options? The same argument will not work for European options, because a one-year European option cannot be exercised early at six months. As a consequence, a European option with a later exercise date may potentially trade for less than an otherwise identical option with an earlier exercise date. For example, think about a European call on a stock that pays a liquidating dividend in six months (a liquidating dividend is paid when a corporation chooses to go out of business, sells off all of its assets, and pays out the proceeds as a dividend). A one-year European call option on this stock would be worthless, but a six-month call would have value.

Option Prices and the Risk-Free Rate

The value of a call option is increasing in the risk-free rate and the value of a put option is decreasing in the risk-free rate. The intuition is that a higher discount rate reduces the present value of the strike price. Because you must pay the strike price to exercise a call option, reducing the present value of your payment increases the value of the option. However, because you *receive* the strike price when you exercise a put, reducing the present value decreases the value of the put option. We note, however, that given normal swings in the risk-free rate, they would be unlikely to change enough over the life of an option to have a substantial impact on the price of the option—that is, option values are not particularly sensitive to changes in the risk-free rate.

Option Prices and Volatility

An important criterion that determines the price of an option is the volatility of the underlying stock. In fact, *the value of an option generally increases with the volatility of the stock.* The reasoning behind this result is that an increase in volatility increases the likelihood of very high and very low returns for the stock. The holder of a call option benefits from a higher payoff when the stock goes up and the option is in-the-money, but earns the same (zero) payoff no matter how far the stock drops once the option is out-of-the-money. *Because of this asymmetry of the option's payoff, an option holder gains from an increase in volatility.* Consider Example 20.5.

Example 20.5 confirms our supposition that the value of a call option is increasing in the volatility of the underlying stock. The same holds for puts. Recall that adding a put option to a portfolio is equivalent to buying insurance against a decline in value. Insurance is more valuable when there is higher volatility—hence, put options on more volatile stocks are also worth more. Table 20.4 summarizes the factors that affect option values and how an increase in each factor affects those values.

EXAMPLE 20.5

Option Value and Volatility

Problem

Three European call options with a strike price of $50 are written on three different stocks. Suppose that tomorrow, the lowest-volatility stock (Stock A) will have a price of $50 for certain. The medium-volatility stock (Stock B) will be worth either $60 or $40, with each price having equal probability. The high-volatility stock (Stock C) will be worth either $80 or $20, with each price having equal probability. If the expiration date of all options is tomorrow, which option will be worth more today?

Solution

▶ **Plan**

The value of the options will depend on the value of the stocks at expiration. The value of the options at expiration will be the stock price tomorrow minus 50 if the stock price is greater than $50, and $0 otherwise.

▶ **Execute**

The lowest-volatility stock, Stock A, will be worth $50 for certain, so its option will be worth $0 for certain. The medium-volatility stock, Stock B, will be worth either $40 or $60, so its option will pay off either $0 or $60 − 50 = $10. The call option on Stock B will have an expected payoff of $\left(\frac{1}{2} \times 0\right) + \left(\frac{1}{2} \times 10\right) = \$5$ and, ignoring the time value of money, its value today would be $5. The high-volatility stock, Stock C, will be worth either $20 or $80, so its option will pay off either $0 or $80 − 50 = $30. The call option on Stock C will have an expected payoff of $\left(\frac{1}{2} \times 0\right) + \left(\frac{1}{2} \times 30\right) = \$15$ and, ignoring the time value of money, its value today would be $15. Because options have no chance of a negative payoff, the one that has a 50% chance of a $30 payoff has to be worth more than the one that has a 50% chance of a $10 payoff, and that has to be worth more than the option on the lowest-volatility stock (with no chance of a positive payoff at all).

▶ **Evaluate**

Because volatility increases the chance that an option will have higher payoffs, the options have very different values even though the expected value of both stocks tomorrow is $50—the lowest-volatility stock will be worth this amount for sure, and the medium-volatility stock, Stock B, also has an expected value of $\left(\frac{1}{2} \times 40\right) + \left(\frac{1}{2} \times 60\right) = \$50$, as does the high-volatility stock, Stock C, with expected value of $\left(\frac{1}{2} \times 20\right) + \left(\frac{1}{2} \times 80\right) = \$50$.

TABLE 20.4		American		European	
		Call	Put	Call	Put
How an Increase in Each Factor Affects Option Values	Stock price	Increases value	Decreases value	Increases value	Decreases value
	Strike price	Decreases value	Increases value	Decreases value	Increases value
	Time to expiration	Increases value	Increases value	Uncertain	Uncertain
	Risk-free rate	Increases value	Decreases value	Increases value	Decreases value
	Volatility of stock price	Increases value	Increases value	Increases value	Increases value

Concept Check

5. Can a European option with a later exercise date be worth less than an identical European option with an earlier exercise date?

6. Why are options more valuable when there is increased uncertainty about the value of the stock?

20.4 The Black-Scholes Option Pricing Formula

In Nobel Prize-winning research, Professors Fischer Black and Myron Scholes derived a formula for the price of a European-style call option for a non–dividend-paying stock. The formula now serves as the basis of pricing for options contracts traded worldwide. Their formula is as follows:

Black-Scholes Price of a Call Option on a Non–Dividend-Paying Stock

$$\text{Call Price} = \text{Stock Price} \times N(d_1) - PV(\text{Strike Price}) \times N(d_2) \qquad (20.3)$$

The present value is calculated using the risk-free rate, and $N(d_1)$ and $N(d_2)$ are probabilities. The expressions for d_1 and d_2 are complicated and explaining them is better left to your later finance courses.[1] However, we note here that they contain only the stock price, strike price, risk-free rate, time to expiration of the option, and volatility of the stock. Thus, Black and Scholes confirmed our discussion from the last section that these five factors are the only ones relevant to the value of an option. What is just as notable is what is not relevant: we do not need to know the expected return of the stock. You might wonder how it is possible to compute the value of a security such as an option that appears to depend critically on the future stock price without knowing the expected return of the stock. In fact, the expected return of the stock is already incorporated into the current stock price, and the value of the option today depends on the stock price today.

---

[1]For the curious student, they are: $d_1 = \frac{\ln[\text{Stock Price}/PV(\text{Strike Price})]}{\sigma\sqrt{T}} + \frac{\sigma\sqrt{T}}{2}$ and $d_2 = d_1 - \sigma\sqrt{T}$, where σ is the annual standard deviation of the stock return and T is the time to expiration of the option (in years). We also note that $N(\cdot)$ in Equation 20.3 refers to the cumulative normal distribution function.

Fortunately, you do not need to know the Black-Scholes formula to use it. There are many online option pricing calculators and even add-ins for Excel based on the formula. In Figure 20.5, we show one such calculator from the Options Industry Council:

So far, we have discussed the factors affecting the prices of individual calls and puts. You may have noticed that in Figure 20.5 the prices of both the put and call for the stock are displayed. In fact, those prices cannot move independently of each other. In the next

FIGURE 20.5

Online Option Pricing Calculator

This option pricing calculator is based on the Black-Scholes option pricing formula. Here, we selected "Black-Scholes (European)" in the "Model/Exercise" box and then entered a stock price of $46, a strike price of $45, expiration in February 2013, a risk-free interest rate of 1%, annual volatility (standard deviation) of the stock return of 25%, and no dividends. The right side of the screen shows that the call value is $8.19 (and the put value is $6.07). The other outputs on the right side of the screen are called "the Greeks" because they are mostly Greek letters (vega is not a real Greek letter). Interested students can go to the website and click on the question mark next to each Greek letter to learn its meaning. Note that the option values will vary depending on how close you are to the expiration date, so you should not expect to get the same values shown when you try the calculator.

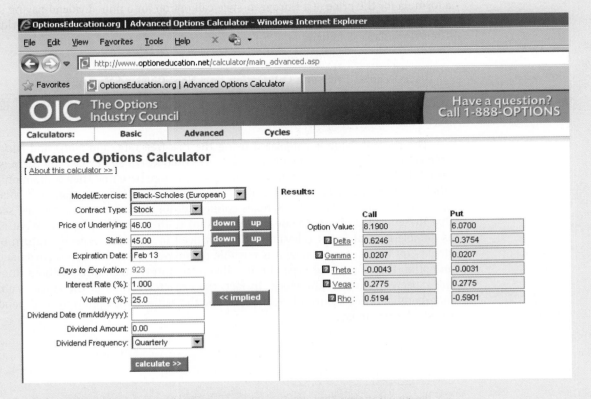

Source: Options Industry Council website, www.optioneducation.net/calculator/main_advanced.asp.

section, we will demonstrate a powerful relationship that links the price of a put to the price of a call on the same stock.

7. What factors are used in the Black-Scholes formula to price a call option?

8. How can the Black-Scholes formula not include the expected return on the stock?

20.5 Put-Call Parity

As we have seen, the payoffs to both puts and calls depend on the price of the underlying stock. The expected payoffs determine the prices of the options, so the prices of puts and calls depend partly on the price of the underlying stock. Because the prices of both a put and a call on a given stock are influenced by the price of that same stock, their prices are related to each other. In this section, we develop that relationship by showing that both puts and calls can be packaged in different ways to achieve the same objective—to provide insurance against a drop in the price of a stock. Then we use the Valuation Principle's Law of One Price to show that if the two packages provide exactly the same payoffs, they must have the same price.

Portfolio Insurance

protective put The purchasing of a put option on a stock you already own.

Let's see how we can use combinations of options to insure a stock against a loss. Assume you currently own Bow.com stock and you would like to insure the stock against the possibility of a price decline. To do so, you could simply sell the stock, but you would also give up the possibility of making money if the stock price increases. How can you insure against a loss without relinquishing the upside? You can purchase a put option while still holding the stock, sometimes known as a **protective put**.

For example, suppose you want to insure against the possibility that the price of Bow's stock will drop below $45. You decide to purchase a January 45 European put option. The orange line in Figure 20.6, panel (a), shows the value of the combined position on the expiration date of the option. If Bow's stock is above $45 in January, you keep the stock. If it is below $45, you exercise your put and sell it for $45. Thus, you get the upside but are insured against a drop in the price of Bow's stock.

portfolio insurance A protective put written on a portfolio rather than a single stock.

You can use the same strategy to insure against a loss on an entire portfolio of stocks by using put options on the portfolio as a whole rather than just a single stock. Consequently, holding stocks and put options in this combination is known as **portfolio insurance**.

Non–Dividend-Paying Stock. You can also achieve portfolio insurance by purchasing a bond and a call option. Let's return to the insurance we purchased on Bow's stock. Bow's stock does not pay dividends, so there are no cash flows before the expiration of the option. Thus, instead of holding a share of Bow's stock and a put, you could get the same payoff by purchasing a risk-free zero-coupon bond with a face value of $45 and a European call option with a strike price of $45. In this case, if Bow is below $45, you receive the payoff from the bond. If Bow is above $45, you can exercise the call and use the payoff from the bond to buy the stock for the strike price of $45. The orange line in Figure 20.6, panel (b), shows the value of the combined position on the expiration date of the option; it achieves exactly the same payoffs as owning the stock itself and a put option.

Consider the two different ways to construct portfolio insurance illustrated in Figure 20.6: (1) purchase the stock and a put or (2) purchase a bond and a call. Because

FIGURE 20.6

Portfolio Insurance

The plots show two different ways to insure against the possibility of the price of Bow.com stock falling below $45. The orange line in panel (a) indicates the value on the expiration date of a position that is long one share of Bow.com stock and one European put option with a strike of $45 (the blue dashed line is the payoff of the stock itself). The orange line in panel (b) shows the value on the expiration date of a position that is long a zero-coupon risk-free bond with a face value of $45 and a European call option on Bow.com with a strike price of $45 (the green dashed line is the bond payoff).

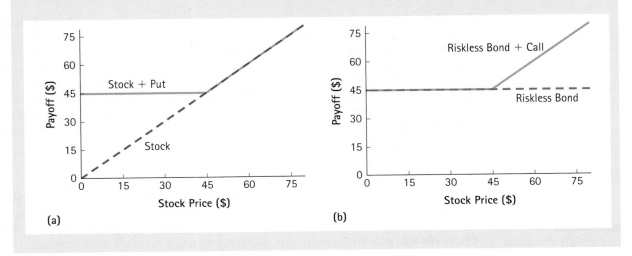

(a)   (b)

both positions provide exactly the same payoff, the Valuation Principle and, in particular, the Law of One Price, require that they must have the same price:

$$\text{Stock Price} + \text{Put Price} = PV(\text{Strike Price}) + \text{Call Price}$$

The left side of this equation is the cost of buying the stock and a put; the right side is the cost of buying a zero-coupon bond with face value equal to the strike price of the put and a call option (with the same strike price as the put). Recall that the price of a zero-coupon bond is the present value of its face value, which we have denoted by PV(Strike Price). Rearranging terms gives an expression for the price of a European call option for a non–dividend-paying stock:

put-call parity
(for non–dividend paying stocks) The relationship that gives the price of a call option in terms of the price of a put option plus the price of the underlying stock minus the present value of the strike price.

$$\text{Call Price} = \text{Put Price} + \text{Stock Price} - PV(\text{Strike Price}) \qquad (20.4)$$

This relationship between the value of the stock, the bond, and the call and put options is known as **put-call parity**. It says that the price of a European call equals the price of the stock plus an otherwise identical put minus the price of a bond with a face value equal to the strike price that matures on the exercise date of the option. In other words, you can think of a call as a combination of a levered position in the stock, Stock Price $- PV$(Strike Price), plus insurance against a drop in the stock price, the put.

EXAMPLE 20.6

Using Put-Call
Parity

Problem

You are an options dealer who deals in non-publicly traded options. One of your clients wants to purchase a one-year European call option on HAL Computer Systems stock with a strike price of $20. Another dealer is willing to write a one-year European put option on HAL stock with a strike price of $20, and sell you the put option for a price of $2.50 per share. If HAL pays no dividends and is currently trading for $18 per share, and if the risk-free interest rate is 6%, what is the lowest price you can charge for the call option and still guarantee yourself a profit?

Solution

▶ **Plan**

We can use put-call parity to determine the price of the option:

$$\text{Call Price} = \text{Put Price} + \text{Stock Price} - PV(\text{Strike Price})$$

In order to price a one-year European call with a strike price of $20, we need to know the price of a one-year European put with the same strike price, the current stock price, and the risk-free interest rate. We have all of that information, so we're ready.

$$\text{Call Price} = \text{Put Price} + \text{Stock Price} - PV(\text{Strike Price})$$
$$= \$2.50 + \$18 - \$20/1.06 = \$1.632$$

▶ **Evaluate**

Put-call parity means that we can replicate the payoff of the one-year call option with a strike price of $20 by holding the following portfolio: buy the one-year put option with a strike price of $20 from the dealer, buy the stock, and sell a one-year, risk-free zero-coupon bond with a face value of $20. With this combination, we have the following final payoff, depending on the final price of HAL stock in one year, S_1:

		Payoff	
		Final HAL Stock Price	
		$S_1 \times \$20$	$S_1 \geq \$20$
	Buy put option	$20 - S_1$	0
+	Buy stock	S_1	S_1
+	Sell bond	-20	-20
=	Portfolio	0	$S_1 - 20$
+	Sell call option	0	$-(S_1 - 20)$
=	Total payoff	0	0

Note that the final payoff of the portfolio of the three securities matches the payoff of a call option. Therefore, we can sell the call option to our client and have future payoff of zero no matter what happens. Doing so is worthwhile as long as we can sell the call option for more than the cost of the portfolio, which we found to be $1.632.

Dividend-Paying Stock. What happens if the stock pays a dividend? In that case, the two different ways to construct portfolio insurance do not have the same payout, because the stock will pay a dividend while the zero-coupon bond will not. Thus, the two strategies will cost the same to implement only if we add the present value of future dividends to the combination of the bond and the call, as follows:

$$\text{Stock Price} + \text{Put Price} = PV(\text{Strike Price}) + PV(\text{Dividends}) + \text{Call Price}$$

The left side of this equation is the value of the stock and a put; the right side is the value of a zero-coupon bond, a call option, and the future dividends paid by the stock during the life of the options. Rearranging terms gives the general put-call parity formula:

Put-Call Parity

$$\text{Call Price} = \text{Put Price} + \text{Stock Price} - PV(\text{Strike Price}) - PV(\text{Dividends}) \qquad (20.5)$$

In this case, the call is equivalent to having a levered position in the stock without dividends plus insurance against a fall in the stock price.

Concept Check

9. Explain put-call parity.

10. If a put option trades at a higher price from the value indicated by the put-call parity equation, what action should you take?

20.6 Options and Corporate Finance

We briefly explored real options in capital budgeting in Chapter 8. We also noted in Chapter 14 that the ability to retire (or call) a bond early was a valuable option for the firm, and that the ability to convert the bond into shares of stock was an option for the bondholders. We can now say more formally that when a firm issues a convertible bond, the firm is essentially issuing a package of a straight bond and warrants on its stock.

One other very important corporate finance application of options is interpreting the capital structure of the firm as options on the firm's assets. Specifically, a share of stock can be thought of as a call option on the assets of the firm with a strike price equal to the value of debt outstanding.[2] To illustrate, consider a single-period world in which at the end of the period the firm is liquidated. If the firm's asset value does not exceed the value of debt outstanding at the end of the period, the firm must declare bankruptcy and the equity holders receive nothing. Conversely, if the asset value exceeds the value of debt outstanding, the equity holders get whatever is left once the debt has been repaid. Figure 20.7 illustrates this payoff. Note how the payoff to equity looks exactly the same as the payoff of a call option.

Viewed this way, a share of equity is a call option on the firm's assets. In fact, debt holders can be thought of as owning the firm, but they have written to equity holders a call option on the firm's assets with a strike price equal to the required debt payment. Recall that the price of an option increases with the volatility level of the underlying

---

[2]This insight has been known at least since Black and Scholes wrote their groundbreaking option valuation paper. See F. Black and M. Scholes, "The Pricing of Options and Corporate Liabilities," *Journal of Political Economy* 81 (3) (1973): 637–654.

FIGURE 20.7

Equity as a Call Option

If the value of the firm's assets exceeds the required debt payment, the equity holders receive the value that remains after the debt is repaid. Otherwise, the firm is bankrupt and its equity is worthless. Thus, the payoff to equity is equivalent to a call option on the firm's assets with a strike price equal to the required debt payment.

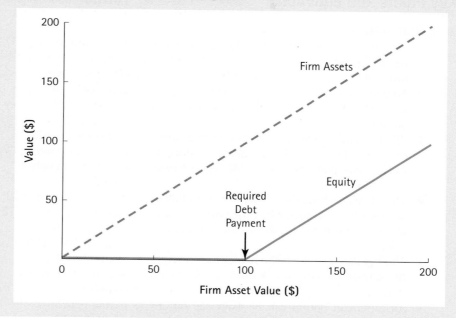

security. That means equity holders benefit from high-volatility investments. Because the price of equity is increasing with the volatility of the firm's assets, equity holders benefit from a zero-*NPV* project that increases the volatility of the firm's assets. However, debt holders, as lenders to the firm, do not benefit from an increase in the risk of the firm's assets. Thus, the project increases the value of equity but decreases the value of the debt claims. In fact, because the project is a zero-*NPV* one, taking it on does not change the value of the firm as a whole. The value of the debt claims decreases by exactly the amount the value of the equity increases. This effect creates a conflict of interest between equity holders and debt holders. Options pricing theory helps us understand why this conflict of interest arises.

The option price is more sensitive to changes in volatility for at-the-money options than it is for in-the-money options. In the context of corporate finance, equity is at-the-money when a firm is close to bankruptcy. In this case, the loss in equity value that results from taking on a negative-*NPV* investment might be outweighed by the gain in equity value from the increase in volatility. Hence, equity holders have an incentive to take on negative-*NPV*, high-volatility investments. As we saw in Chapter 15, this excessive risk-taking problem is of concern to debt holders, who bear its cost.

Concept Check

11. Explain how equity can be viewed as a call option on the firm.

12. Under what circumstances would equity holders have a possible incentive to take on negative-*NPV* investments?

MyFinanceLab

Here is what you should know after reading this chapter. MyFinanceLab will help you identify what you know, and where to go when you need to practice.

Key Points and Equations	Terms	Online Practice Opportunities
20.1 Option Basics	American option, p. 672	MyFinanceLab
▶ An option that gives the holder the right (but not the obligation) to purchase an asset at some future date is known as a call option.	at-the-money, p. 674	Study Plan 20.1
	call option, p. 672	
	deep in-the-money, p. 675	
▶ An option that gives the holder the right to sell an asset at some future date is known as a put option.	deep out-of-the-money, p. 675	
	derivatives, p. 672	
▶ When a holder of an option enforces the agreement and buys or sells the share of stock at the agreed-upon price, the holder is exercising the option.	European option, p. 672	
	exercising an option, p. 672	
	expiration date, p. 672	
▶ The price at which the holder agrees to buy or sell the share of stock when the option is exercised is known as the strike price or exercise price.	financial option, p. 672	
	hedging, p. 675	
	in-the-money, p. 674	
	open interest, p. 674	
▶ The last date on which the holder has the right to exercise the option is known as the expiration date.	option writer, p. 672	
	out-of-the-money, p. 675	
	payoff, p. 673	
▶ An American option can be exercised on any date up to, and including, the exercise date. A European option can be exercised only on the expiration date.	profit, p. 673	
	put option, p. 672	
	speculating, p. 675	
	strike (exercise) price, p. 672	
▶ If you would make money by exercising an option immediately, the option is in-the-money. Conversely, if you would lose money by exercising an option immediately, the option is out-of-the-money.	warrant, p. 672	

20.2 Option Payoffs and Profits at Expiration

▶ The value of a call option at expiration

$$= \text{Stock Price} - \text{Strike Price, if Stock Price} > \text{Strike;}$$
$$= 0, \text{ if Stock Price} \leq \text{Strike} \qquad (20.1)$$

▶ The value of a put option at expiration

$$= \text{Strike Price} - \text{Stock Price, if Stock Price} < \text{Strike;}$$
$$= 0, \text{ if Stock Price} \geq \text{Strike} \qquad (20.2)$$

▶ An investor holding a short position in an option has an obligation; he or she takes the opposite side of the contract to the investor who holds the long position.

MyFinanceLab
Study Plan 20.2

20.3 Factors Affecting Option Prices

▶ Call options with lower strike prices are more valuable than otherwise identical calls with higher strike prices. Conversely, put options are more valuable with higher strike prices.

▶ Call options increase in value, and put options decrease in value, when the stock price rises.

▶ The value of an option generally increases with the volatility of the stock.

MyFinanceLab
Study Plan 20.3

20.4 The Black-Scholes Option Pricing Formula

▶ The Black-Scholes option pricing formula shows that the price of an option on a non–dividend-paying stock is a function of only the current stock price, the strike price, the time to expiration, the volatility of the stock, and the risk-free rate.

MyFinanceLab
Study Plan 20.4

20.5 Put-Call Parity

▶ Put-call parity relates the value of the European call to the value of the European put and the stock:

Call Price = Put Price + Stock Price
$-$ PV(Strike Price) $-$ PV(Dividends)   (20.5)

portfolio insurance, p. 687
protective put, p. 687
put-call parity, p. 688

MyFinanceLab
Study Plan 20.5

20.6 Options and Corporate Finance

▶ Equity can be viewed as a call option on the firm.

▶ The debt holders can be viewed as owning the firm and having sold a call option with a strike price equal to the required debt payment.

MyFinanceLab
Study Plan 20.6

Review Questions

1. Explain what the following financial terms mean:
   a. Option
   b. Expiration date
   c. Strike price
   d. Call
   e. Put

2. What is the difference between a European option and an American option?

3. Explain the difference between a long position in a put and a short position in a call.

4. What position has more downside exposure: a short position in a call or a short position in a put? That is, in the worst case, in which of these two positions would your losses be greater?

5. If you own a call option at expiration and the stock price equals the strike price, is your profit zero?

6. Is an increase in a stock's volatility good for the holder of a call option? Is it good for the holder of a put option?

7. Why are the prices of puts and calls on the same stock related?

8. Explain why an option can be thought of as an insurance contract.

9. Explain why equity can be viewed as a call option on a firm.

Problems

All problems in this chapter are available in MyFinanceLab. An asterisk (*) indicates problems with a higher level of difficulty.

Option Basics

1. Below is an option quote on IBM from the CBOE website:

IBM (INTL BUSINESS MACHINES)   102.22   +1.39
Jul 13, 2009 @ 13:26 ET   Bid 102.2   Ask 102.22   Size 6×6   Vol 5683797

Calls	Last Sale	Net	Bid	Ask	Vol	Open Int	Puts	Last Sale	Net	Bid	Ask	Vol	Open Int
09 Jul 95.00 (IBM GS-E)	7.50	0.95	7.40	7.60	26	8159	09 Jul 95.00 (IBM SS-E)	0.31	−0.24	0.25	0.35	2039	11452
09 Jul 100.00 (IBM GT-E)	3.50	0.72	3.40	3.50	1764	14436	09 Jul 100.00 (IBM ST-E)	1.25	−0.65	1.20	1.25	2262	19401
09 Jul 105.00 (IBM GA-E)	0.91	0.26	0.90	1.00	1945	23210	09 Jul 105.00 (IBM SA-E)	3.79	−1.56	3.60	3.80	379	8000
09 Jul 110.00 (IBM GB-E)	0.15	0.07	0.10	0.15	632	20808	09 Jul 110.00 (IBM SB-E)	7.57	−1.53	7.80	8.00	35	6536
09 Aug 95.00 (IBM HS-E)	8.75	1.35	8.40	8.60	32	1532	09 Aug 95.00 (IBM TS-E)	1.51	−0.49	1.50	1.60	1076	2766
09 Aug 100.00 (IBM HT-E)	5.11	0.91	4.80	5.00	122	2754	09 Aug 100.00 (IBM TT-E)	2.90	−0.86	3.00	3.20	513	5322
09 Aug 105.00 (IBM HA-E)	2.40	0.44	2.35	2.40	456	6091	09 Aug 105.00 (IBM TA-E)	5.99	−0.81	5.50	5.70	52	1586
09 Aug 110.00 (IBM HB-E)	0.95	0.25	0.90	0.95	207	3429	09 Aug 110.00 (IBM TB-E)	10.60	−0.40	9.10	9.30	10	751

a. Which option contract had the most trades today?

b. Which option contract is being held the most overall?

c. Suppose you purchase one option with symbol IBM GA-E. How much will you need to pay your broker for the option (ignoring commissions)?

d. Suppose you sell one option with symbol IBM GA-E. How much will you receive for the option (ignoring commissions)?

e. The calls with which strike prices are currently in-the-money? Which puts are in-the-money?

Option Payoffs and Profits at Expiration

 2. You own a call option on Intuit stock with a strike price of $40. When you purchased the option, it cost you $5. The option will expire in exactly three months' time.

a. If the stock is trading at $55 in three months, what will be the payoff of the call? What will be the profit of the call?

b. If the stock is trading at $35 in three months, what will be the payoff of the call? What will be the profit of the call?

c. Draw a payoff diagram showing the value of the call at expiration as a function of the stock price at expiration.

d. Redo (c), but instead of showing payoffs, show profits.

3. Assume that you have shorted the call option in Problem 2; when you originally sold (wrote) the option, you received $5.

    a. If the stock is trading at $55 in three months, what will your payoff be? What will your profit be?

    b. If the stock is trading at $35 in three months, what will your payoff be? What will your profit be?

    c. Draw a payoff diagram showing the payoff at expiration as a function of the stock price at expiration.

    d. Redo (c), but instead of showing payoffs, show profits.

 4. You own a put option on Ford stock with a strike price of $10. When you bought the put, its cost to you was $2. The option will expire in exactly six months' time.

    a. If the stock is trading at $8 in six months, what will be the payoff of the put? What will be the profit of the put?

    b. If the stock is trading at $23 in six months, what will be the payoff of the put? What will be the profit of the put?

    c. Draw a payoff diagram showing the value of the put at expiration as a function of the stock price at expiration.

    d. Redo (c) but instead of showing payoffs, show profits.

 5. Assume that you have shorted the put option in Problem 4. When you sold (wrote) the put, you received $2.

    a. If the stock is trading at $8 in three months, what will your payoff be? What will your profit be?

    b. If the stock is trading at $23 in three months, what will your payoff be? What will your profit be?

    c. Draw a payoff diagram showing the amount you owe at expiration as a function of the stock price at expiration.

    d. Redo (c), but instead of showing payoffs, show profits.

6. You are long both a call and a put on the same share of stock with the same exercise date. The exercise price of the call is $40 and the exercise price of the put is $45. Plot the value of this combination as a function of the stock price on the exercise date.

7. You are long two calls on the same share of stock with the same exercise date. The exercise price of the first call is $40 and the exercise price of the second call is $60. In addition, you are short two otherwise identical calls, both with an exercise price of $50. Plot the value of this combination as a function of the stock price on the exercise date.

*8. A forward contract is a contract to purchase an asset at a fixed price on a particular date in the future. Both parties are obligated to fulfill the contract. Explain how to construct a forward contract on a share of stock from a position in options.

9. You own a share of Costco stock. You are worried that its price will fall and would like to insure yourself against this possibility. How can you purchase insurance against a fall in the price of the stock?

Factors Affecting Option Prices

10. What is the maximum value that a call option and a put option can have?

11. Why is an American option with a longer time to expiration generally worth more than an otherwise identical option with a shorter time to expiration?

Put-Call Parity

12. Dynamic Energy Systems stock is currently trading for $33 per share. The stock pays no dividends. A one-year European put option on Dynamic with a strike price of $35 is currently trading for $2.10. If the risk-free interest rate is 10% per year, what is the price of a one-year European call option on Dynamic with a strike price of $35?

13. You happen to be checking the newspaper and notice an arbitrage opportunity. The current stock price of Intrawest is $20 per share and the one-year risk-free interest rate is 8%. A one-year put on Intrawest with a strike price of $18 sells for $3.33, while the identical call sells for $7. Explain what you must do to exploit this arbitrage opportunity.

Options and Corporate Finance

*14. Express the position of an equity holder in terms of put options.

15. Express the position of a debt holder in terms of put options.

Data Case

Your uncle owns 10,000 shares of Wal-Mart stock. He is concerned about the short-term outlook for Wal-Mart's stock due to an impending "major announcement." This announcement has received much attention in the press, so he expects the stock price will change significantly in the next month but is unsure whether it will be a profit or a loss. He hopes the price will increase, but he also doesn't want to suffer if the price were to fall in the short term.

His broker recommended he buy a "protective put" on the stock, but your uncle has never traded options before and is not much of a risk taker. He wants you to devise a plan for him to capitalize if the announcement is positive but still be protected if the news causes the price to drop. You realize that a protective put will protect him from the downside risk, but you think a strategy of purchasing a call and a put with the same exercise price (known as a "straddle") may offer similar downside protection, while increasing the upside potential. You decide to show him both strategies and the resulting profits and returns he could obtain from each.

1. Download option quotes on options that expire in approximately one month on Wal-Mart from the Chicago Board Options Exchange website (www.cboe.com) into an Excel spreadsheet. If you choose to download "near-term at-the-money" options you will get a range of options expiring in about a month. You can get active quotes only while the exchange is open; bid or ask prices are not available when it is closed.

2. Determine your uncle's profit and return using the protective put.
   a. Identify the expiring put with an exercise price closest to, but not below, the current stock price. Determine the investment required to protect all 10,000 shares.
   b. Determine the put price at expiration for each stock price at $5 increments from $25 to $65 using Equation 20.2.
   c. Compute the profit (or loss) on the put for each stock price used in part (b).
   d. Compute the profit on the stock from the current price for each stock price used in part (b).
   e. Compute his overall profit (or loss) of the protective put, that is, combining the put and his stock for each price used in parts (c) and (d).
   f. Compute the overall return of the protective put.

3. Determine your uncle's profit and return using the straddle.
   a. Compute the investment your uncle would have to make to purchase the call and put with the same exercise price and expiration as the put option in question 2, to cover all 10,000 of his shares.
   b. Determine the value at expiration of the call and the put options at each $5 increment of stock prices from $25 to $65 using Equations 20.1 and 20.2.
   c. Determine the profit (or loss) on the options at each stock price used in part (b).
   d. Determine the profit (or loss) on the stock from the current price for each stock price used in part (b).
   e. Compute his overall profit (or loss) of the stock plus the straddle, that is, combining the position in both options and his stock for each price used in parts (c) and (d).
   f. Compute the overall return of this position.

4. Was the broker correct that the protective put would prevent your uncle from losing if the announcement caused a large decrease in the stock value? What is your uncle's maximum possible loss using the protective put?

5. What is the maximum possible loss your uncle could experience using the straddle?

6. Which strategy, the protective put or the straddle, provides the maximum upside potential for your uncle? Why does this occur?

Risk Management

21

notation				
	r_f	risk-free interest rate	$Pr(\cdot)$	probability of
	r_L	cost of capital for an insured loss	$\tilde{r}_t$	floating interest rate on date t
	β_L	beta of an insured loss	NPV	net present value

INTERVIEW WITH Ashlea Ochsner,
Scotiabank

Saint Mary's University

"A large part of my job deals with risk management, determining the different risk factors in each business segment."

Ashlea Ochsner, who graduated from Saint Mary's University with a Bachelor of Commerce degree, currently works at Scotiabank, where she specializes in business banking. "I help businesses with short-term and long-term financial planning." Her work requires her to forecast her clients' future cash flows, which, for some businesses, can vary substantially over the course of a year due to various risk factors.

The changes in a company's cash position throughout the year may require the company to have access to different amounts of credit at different times. Ashlea's job is to determine how much credit a firm needs, and how much it can handle. "Knowledge of finance helps me in my position because I deal with the day-to-day finances of businesses in Toronto," she says. "When businesses have needs for debt financing, my knowledge of financial statement analysis helps me determine the company's financial strength, any positive or negative trends, and any risk factors."

Part of the difficulty with forecasting future cash flows is the uncertain nature of a firm's revenues. "A large part of my job deals with risk management, determining the different risk factors in each business segment," Ashlea explains. "Whether it be a business such as a restaurant, or a professional medical corporation, each has different risks associated with the business revenues or costs and thus different risks for the bank when we extend credit."

All firms are subject to risk from a variety of sources: changes in consumers' tastes and cost of raw materials, employee turnover, the entry of new competitors, and countless other uncertainties. Entrepreneurs and corporate managers willingly take on these risks in the pursuit of high returns and accept risk as part of the cost of doing business. But as with any other cost, firms should manage risk to minimize its effect on the value of the firm.

The primary method of risk management is prevention. For example, firms can avoid or at least reduce many potential risks by increasing safety standards in the workplace, by making prudent investment decisions, and by conducting appropriate due diligence when entering into new relationships. But some risks are too costly to prevent and are the inevitable consequences of running a business. As discussed in Part 6 of the text, the firm shares these business risks with its investors through its capital structure. Some of the risk is passed on to debt holders, who bear the risk that the firm will default. Most of the risk is held by equity holders, who are exposed to the volatility of the stock's realized return. Both types of investors can reduce their risk by holding the firm's securities in a well-diversified portfolio.

Not all risks need to be passed on to the firm's debt and equity holders. Insurance and financial markets allow firms to trade risk and shield their debt holders and equity holders from some types of risk. For example, after a fire shut down its processing plant in January 2005, Suncor Energy received more than $200 million in settlements from insurance contracts covering both the damage to the plant and the lost business while the plant was being repaired. Much of the loss from the fire was thus borne by Suncor's insurers rather than by its investors. At the beginning of 2005, Dell held contracts to protect more than $5 billion worth of projected foreign revenues from fluctuations in exchange rates, and General Electric had contracts to prevent a rise in interest rates from increasing its borrowing costs on more than $24 billion of short-term debt. In 2007, Southwest Airlines received $686 million from financial contracts that compensated it for the rise in the cost of jet fuel.

In this chapter, we consider the strategies that firms use to manage and reduce the risk borne by their investors. We begin with the most common form of risk management, insurance. After carefully considering the costs and benefits of insurance, we look at the ways firms can use financial markets to off-load the risks associated with changes in commodity prices, and interest rate movements. (We address exchange rate fluctuations in the following chapter.)

21.1 Insurance

property insurance
A type of insurance companies purchase to compensate them for losses to their assets due to fire, storm damage, vandalism, earthquakes, and other natural and environmental risks.

business liability insurance A type of insurance that covers the costs that result if some aspect of a business causes harm to a third party or someone else's property.

business interruption insurance A type of insurance that protects a firm against the loss of earnings if the business is interrupted due to fire, accident, or some other insured peril.

key personnel insurance
A type of insurance that compensates a firm for the loss or unavoidable absence of crucial employees in the firm.

Insurance is the most common method firms use to reduce risk. Many firms purchase **property insurance** to insure their assets against hazards such as fire, storm damage, vandalism, earthquakes, and other natural and environmental risks. Other common types of insurance include the following:

▶ **Business liability insurance**, which covers the costs that result if some aspect of the business causes harm to a third party or someone else's property

▶ **Business interruption insurance**, which protects the firm against the loss of earnings if the business is interrupted due to fire, accident, or some other insured peril

▶ **Key personnel insurance**, which compensates the firm for the loss or unavoidable absence of crucial employees in the firm

In this section, we illustrate the role of insurance in reducing risk and examine its pricing and potential benefits, as well as its costs for a firm.

The Role of Insurance: A Simplified Example

To understand the role of insurance in reducing risk, consider an oil refinery with a 1-in-5000, or 0.02%, chance of being destroyed by a fire in the next year. If it is destroyed, the firm estimates that it will lose $150 million in rebuilding costs and lost business. We can summarize the risk from fire with a probability distribution:

Event	Probability	Loss ($ millions)
No fire	99.98%	0
Fire	0.02%	150

Given this probability distribution, the firm's expected loss from fire each year is as follows:

$$(99.98\% \times \$0) + (0.02\% \times \$150 \text{ million}) = \$30,000$$

insurance premium
The fee a firm pays to an insurance company for the purchase of an insurance policy.

While the expected loss is relatively small, the firm faces a large downside risk if a fire does occur. If the firm could eliminate completely the chance of fire for less than the present value of $30,000 per year, it would do so; such an investment would have a positive *NPV*. But avoiding *any* chance of a fire is probably not feasible with current technology (or at least would cost far more than $30,000 per year). Consequently, the firm can manage the risk by instead purchasing insurance to compensate its loss of $150 million. In exchange, the firm will pay an annual fee, called an **insurance premium**, to the insurance company. In this way, insurance allows the firm to exchange a random future loss for a certain upfront expense.

Insurance Pricing in a Perfect Market

When a firm buys insurance, it transfers the risk of the loss to an insurance company. The insurance company charges an upfront premium to take on that risk. At what price will the insurance company be willing to bear the risk in a perfect market?

In a perfect market without other frictions, insurance companies should compete until they are just earning a fair return and the *NPV* from selling insurance is zero. The *NPV* is zero if the price of insurance equals the present value of the expected payment; in that case, we say the price is **actuarially fair**. Actuaries are professionals who attempt to figure the likelihood and severity of insurance claims. These are the probability and expected payment in the event of a loss, so when we say a price is actuarially fair, we mean that the price is fair given the present value of the expected claim. If r_L is the appropriate cost of capital given the risk of the loss, we can calculate the actuarially fair premium as follows:[1]

actuarially fair price
A price such that the *NPV* from selling the insurance is zero because the price of the insurance equals the present value of the expected payment.

Actuarially Fair Insurance Premium

$$\text{Insurance Premium} = \frac{Pr(\text{Loss}) \times E[\text{Payment in the Event of Loss}]}{1 + r_L} \qquad (21.1)$$

The cost of capital r_L used in Equation 21.1 depends on the risk that is insured. Consider again the oil refinery. The risk of fire is surely unrelated to the performance of the stock market or the economy. Instead, this risk is specific to this firm and, therefore, diversifiable in a large portfolio. As we discussed in Chapter 10, by pooling together the risks from many uncorrelated policies, insurance companies can create very low-risk portfolios whose annual claims are relatively predictable. In other words, the risk of fire has a beta of zero, so it will not command a risk premium. In this case, $r_L = r_f$, the risk-free interest rate.

Not all insurable risks have a beta of zero. Some risks, such as hurricanes and earthquakes, create losses of tens of billions of dollars and may be difficult to diversify completely.[2] Other types of losses may be correlated across firms. Increases in the cost of health care or more stringent environmental regulations raise the potential claims from health insurance and liability insurance for all firms. Finally, some risks can have a causal effect on the stock market: The September 11, 2001, terrorist attacks in the United States cost insurers $34 billion[3] and also led to a 12% decline in the S&P 500 in the first week of trading following the attacks.

For risks that cannot be fully diversified, the cost of capital r_L will include a risk premium. By its very nature, insurance for nondiversifiable hazards is generally a negative-beta asset (it pays off in bad times); the insurance payment to the firm tends to be *larger* when total losses are high and the market portfolio is low. Thus, the risk-adjusted

---

[1]Equation 21.1 assumes insurance premiums are paid at the start of the year and payments in the event of loss are made at the end of the year. Extending this to alternative timing assumptions is straightforward. An actuarially fair insurance premium will generate a zero *NPV* from selling the insurance as long as there are not other costs associated with managing the insurance contract (e.g., administration costs).

[2]For example, insured losses from hurricanes Katrina, Rita, and Wilma, which pummelled the southeastern United States in 2005, exceeded $40 billion, with total economic losses topping $100 billion. When insuring large risks such as these, many insurance companies buy insurance on their own portfolios from reinsurance companies. Reinsurance firms pool risks globally from different insurance companies worldwide. For natural disasters, typically one-fourth to one-third of the insured losses are passed on to reinsurers.

[3]Including property, life, and liability insurance, as estimated by the Insurance Information Institute, www.iii.org.

rate r_L for losses is *less than* the risk-free rate r_f, leading to a *higher* insurance premium, as shown in Equation 21.1 and demonstrated in Example 21.1. Although firms that purchase insurance earn a return $r_L \leq r_f$ on their investment, because of the negative beta of the insurance payoff, it is still a zero-*NPV* transaction.[4]

EXAMPLE 21.1

Insurance Pricing and the CAPM

Problem

As the owner of the CN Tower in Toronto, you decide to purchase insurance that will pay $1 billion in the event the building is destroyed by terrorists. Suppose the likelihood of such a loss is 0.1%, the risk-free interest rate is 4%, and the expected return of the market is 10%. If the risk has a beta of zero, what is the actuarially fair insurance premium? What is the premium if the beta of terrorism insurance is −2.5?

Solution

▶ **Plan**

The expected loss is 0.1% × $1 billion = $1 million.

Given a risk-free rate of 4% and an expected market return of 10%, we can use the Capital Asset Pricing Model (CAPM) to compute the rate of return we would use to compute the fair insurance premium under the two scenarios of a zero beta and a beta of −2.5. Once we have the rate of return, we will divide the expected loss (the cash flow) by 1 + rate of return, as shown in Equation 21.1.

▶ **Execute**

If the risk has a beta of zero, we compute the insurance premium using the risk-free interest rate:

$$\$1 \text{ million}/1.04 = \$961,538$$

Given a beta for the loss, βL, of −2.5, the required return is as follows:

$$r_L = r_f + \beta_L(r_{mkt} - r_f) = 4\% - 2.5(10\% - 4\%) = -11\%$$

In this case, the actuarially fair premium is $1 million/(1 − 0.11) = $1,123,596.

▶ **Evaluate**

Although this premium exceeds the expected loss when there is a negative beta, it is a fair price given the negative beta of the risk. The insurance pays off exactly when the cash flows from your business operations are likely to be very low.

The Value of Insurance

In a perfect capital market, insurance will be priced so that it has an *NPV* of zero for both the insurer and the insured. But if purchasing insurance has an *NPV* of zero, what benefit does it have for the firm?

Modigliani and Miller have already provided us with the answer to this question: in a perfect capital market, there is no benefit to the firm from any financial transaction, *including insurance*. Insurance is a zero-*NPV* transaction that has no effect on value. Although insurance allows the firm to divide its risk in a new way (e.g., the risk of fire is held by insurers, rather than by debt and equity holders), the firm's total risk—and, therefore, its value—remains unchanged.

---

[4]Not all insurance must have a zero or negative beta; a positive beta is possible if the amount of the insured loss is higher when market returns are also high.

Thus, similar to a firm's capital structure, the value of insurance must come from reducing the cost of market imperfections on the firm. Let's consider the potential benefits of insurance with respect to the market imperfections that we considered in Part 6 of the text.

Bankruptcy and Financial Distress Costs. When a firm borrows, it increases its chances of experiencing financial distress. In Chapter 15, we saw that financial distress may impose significant direct and indirect costs on the firm, including agency costs such as excessive risk taking and underinvestment. By insuring risks that could lead to distress, the firm can reduce the likelihood that it will incur these costs.

For example, for an airline with a large amount of leverage, the losses associated with an accident involving one of its planes may lead to financial distress. While the actual losses from the incident might be $150 million, the costs from distress might be an additional $40 million. The airline can avoid these distress costs by purchasing insurance that will cover the $150 million loss. In this case, the $150 million paid by the insurer is worth $190 million to the firm.

Issuance Costs. When a firm experiences losses, it may need to raise cash from outside investors by issuing securities. Issuing securities is an expensive endeavour. In addition to underwriting fees and transaction costs, there are costs from underpricing due to adverse selection, as well as potential agency costs due to reduced ownership concentration. Because insurance provides cash to the firm to offset losses, it can reduce the firm's need for external capital and thus reduce issuance costs.

EXAMPLE 21.2

Avoiding Distress and Issuance Costs

Problem
Suppose the risk of an airline accident for a major airline is 1% per year, with a beta of zero. If the risk-free rate is 4%, what is the actuarially fair premium for a policy that pays $150 million in the event of a loss? What is the *NPV* of purchasing insurance for an airline that would experience $15 million in financial distress costs and $10 million in issuance costs if it were uninsured in the event of a loss?

Solution

▶ **Plan**
The expected loss is 1% × $150 million = $1.5 million, but the total value to the airline is $150 million plus an additional $25 million in distress and issuance costs that it can avoid if it has insurance. The premium is based solely on the expected loss, as the present value of the expected loss shown in Equation 21.1. Because the beta is zero, the appropriate discount rate is 4%.

▶ **Execute**
The actuarially fair premium is $1.5 million/1.04 = $1.44 million.

The *NPV* of purchasing the insurance is the expected benefit, including avoiding the distress and issuance costs, net of the premium:

$$NPV = -1.44 + 1\% \times (150 + 25)/1.04 = \$0.24 \text{ million}$$

▶ **Evaluate**
The insurance company charges a premium to cover the expected cash flow it must pay, but receiving the insurance payment may be worth more than the amount of the payment. The insurance payment allows the firm to avoid other costs, so it is possible for the premium to be actuarially fair and for the insurance to still be a positive-*NPV* investment.

Tax Rate Fluctuations. When a firm is subject to graduated income tax rates, insurance can produce a tax savings if the firm is in a higher tax bracket when it pays the premium than the tax bracket it is in when it receives the insurance payment in the event of a loss.

Consider a canola farmer with a 10% chance of a weather-related crop failure. If the risk of crop failure has a beta of zero and the risk-free rate is 4%, the actuarially fair premium per $100,000 of insurance is as follows:

$$\frac{1}{1.04} \times 10\% \times \$100,000 = \$9615$$

Suppose the farmer's current tax rate is 35%. In the event of a crop failure, however, the farmer expects to earn much less income and face a lower 15% tax rate. Then the farmer's *NPV* from purchasing insurance is positive:

$$NPV = -\$9615 \times (1 - 0.35) + \underbrace{\frac{1}{1.04} \times 10\% \times \$100,000}_{= \$9615} \times (1 - 0.15)$$

$$= \$1923$$

The benefit arises because the farmer is able to shift income from a period in which he has a high tax rate (by purchasing insurance) to a period in which he has a low rate (when overall income is reduced and the insurance payout is received). This tax benefit of insurance can be large if the potential losses are significant enough to have a substantial impact on a firm's marginal tax rate.

Debt Capacity. Firms limit their leverage to avoid financial distress costs. Because insurance reduces the risk of financial distress, it can relax this tradeoff and allow the firm to increase its use of debt financing. In fact, it is not unusual for creditors to require the firm to carry insurance as part of a covenant. In Chapter 15, we found that debt financing provides several important advantages for the firm, including lower corporate tax payments due to the interest tax shield, lower issuance costs, and lower agency costs (through an increase in equity ownership concentration and a reduction in excess cash flow).

Managerial Incentives. By eliminating the volatility that results from perils outside management's control, insurance turns the firm's earnings and share price into informative indicators of management's performance. The firm can therefore increase its reliance on these measures as part of performance-based compensation schemes, without exposing managers to unnecessary risk. In addition, by lowering the volatility of the stock, insurance can encourage concentrated ownership by an outside director or investor who will monitor the firm and its management.

Risk Assessment. Insurance companies specialize in assessing risk. In many instances, they may be better informed about the extent of certain risks that may affect the firm than the firm's own managers. This knowledge can benefit the firm by improving its investment decisions. Requiring the firm to purchase fire insurance, for example, implies that the firm will consider differences in fire safety, through their effects on the insurance premium, when choosing a warehouse. Otherwise, the managers might overlook such differences. Insurance firms also routinely monitor the firms they insure and can make value-enhancing safety recommendations.

The Costs of Insurance

When insurance premiums are actuarially fair, using insurance to manage the firm's risk can reduce costs and improve investment decisions. But in reality, market imperfections exist that can raise the cost of insurance above the actuarially fair price and offset some of these benefits.

Insurance Market Imperfections. Three main frictions may arise between the firm and its insurer. First, transferring the risk to an insurance company entails administrative and overhead costs. The insurance company must employ sales personnel who seek out clients, underwriters who assess the risks of a given property, appraisers and adjusters who assess the damages in the event of a loss, and lawyers who can resolve potential disputes that arise over the claims from a loss. Insurance companies will include these expenses when setting their premiums. In 2009, expenses for the property and casualty insurance industry amounted to approximately 27% of premiums charged.[5]

A second factor that raises the cost of insurance is adverse selection. Recall that a manager's desire to sell equity may signal that the manager knows the firm is likely to perform poorly. Similarly, a firm's desire to buy insurance may signal that it has above-average risk. If firms have private information about how risky they are, insurance companies must be compensated for this adverse selection with higher premiums.

Agency costs are a third factor that contributes to the price of insurance. Insurance reduces the firm's incentive to avoid risk. This change in behaviour that results from the presence of insurance is referred to as **moral hazard**. For example, after purchasing fire insurance, a firm may decide to cut costs by reducing expenditures on fire prevention. The extreme case of moral hazard is insurance fraud, in which insured parties falsify or deliberately cause losses to collect insurance money. Property and casualty insurance companies estimate that moral hazard costs account for more than 11% of premiums.[6]

Addressing Market Imperfections. Insurance companies try to mitigate adverse selection and moral hazard costs in a number of ways. To prevent adverse selection, they screen applicants to assess their risk as accurately as possible. Just as medical examinations are often required for individuals seeking life insurance, plant inspections and reviews of safety procedures are required to obtain large commercial insurance policies. To deter moral hazard, insurance companies routinely investigate losses to look for evidence of fraud or deliberate intent.

Insurance companies also structure their policies to reduce these costs. For example, most policies include both a **deductible**, which is the initial amount of the loss that is not covered by insurance and must be paid by the insured, and **policy limits**, provisions that limit the amount of the loss that is covered regardless of the extent of the damage. These provisions mean that the firm continues to bear some of the risk of the loss even after it is insured. In this way, the firm retains an incentive to avoid the loss, reducing moral hazard. Also, because a risky firm will prefer lower deductibles and higher limits (because it is more likely to experience a loss), insurers can use the firm's policy choice to help identify its risk and reduce adverse selection.

moral hazard A reduction, due to a firm's purchasing of insurance, of the firm's incentive to avoid risk.

deductible A provision in an insurance policy in which an initial amount of loss is not covered by the policy and must be paid by the insured.

policy limits Provisions in an insurance policy that limit the amount of loss that the policy covers regardless of the extent of the damage.

EXAMPLE 21.3

Adverse Selection and Policy Limits

Problem

Your firm faces a potential $100 million loss that it would like to insure. Because of tax benefits and the avoidance of financial distress and issuance costs, each $1 received in the event of a loss is worth $1.50 to the firm. Two policies are available: one pays $55 million and the other pays $100 million if a loss occurs. The insurance company charges 20% more than the actuarially fair premium to cover administrative expenses. To account for adverse selection, the insurance company estimates a 5% probability of loss for the $55 million policy and a 6% probability of loss for the $100 million policy.

Suppose the beta of the risk is zero and the risk-free rate is 5%. Which policy should the firm choose if its risk of loss is 5%? Which should it choose if its risk of loss is 6%?

---

[5]Robert Hartwig, "2009 Year End Results," Insurance Information Institute.
[6]Insurance Research Council estimate (2002).

Solution

▶ **Plan**

The premium for each policy will be based on the expected loss using the insurance company's estimate of the probability of loss:

$55 million policy: 5% chance of loss $100 million policy: 6% chance of loss

Because it is charging 20% more than the actuarially fair premium, the insurance company will set the premium at 1.20 times the present value of expected losses.

However, the value of the policy to you depends on your estimate of the true probability of loss, which is based on your own assessment and does not depend on the size of the policy. Because each $1 of insured loss benefits your firm by $1.50, you are willing to pay 1.50 times the present value of the expected loss.

Because the beta of the risk is 0, the risk-free rate of 5% is the appropriate discount rate for all calculations.

▶ **Execute**

The premium charged for each policy is as follows:

$$\text{Premium ($55 million policy)} = \frac{5\% \times \$55 \text{ million}}{1.05} \times 1.20 = \$3.14 \text{ million}$$

$$\text{Premium ($100 million policy)} = \frac{6\% \times \$100 \text{ million}}{1.05} \times 1.20 = \$6.86 \text{ million}$$

If the true risk of a loss is 5%, the *NPV* of each policy is as follows:
NPV ($55 million policy):

$$= -\$3.14 \text{ million} + \frac{5\% \times \$55 \text{ million}}{1.05} \times 1.50 = \$0.79 \text{ million}$$

NPV ($100 million policy):

$$= -\$6.86 \text{ million} + \frac{5\% \times \$100 \text{ million}}{1.05} \times 1.50 = \$0.28 \text{ million}$$

Thus, with a 5% risk, the firm should choose the policy with lower coverage. If the risk of a loss is 6%, the policy with higher coverage is superior:
NPV ($55 million policy):

$$= -\$3.14 \text{ million} + \frac{6\% \times \$55 \text{ million}}{1.05} \times 1.50 = \$1.57 \text{ million}$$

NPV ($100 million policy):

$$= -\$6.86 \text{ million} + \frac{6\% \times \$100 \text{ million}}{1.05} \times 1.50 = \$1.71 \text{ million}$$

▶ **Evaluate**

Note that the insurance company's concerns regarding adverse selection are justified: firms that are riskier will choose the higher-coverage policy.

The Insurance Decision

In a perfect capital market, purchasing insurance does not add value to the firm. It can add value in the presence of market imperfections, but market imperfections are also likely to raise the premiums insurers charge. For insurance to be attractive, the benefit to the firm must exceed the additional premium the insurer charges.

For these reasons, insurance is most likely to be attractive to firms that are currently financially healthy, do not need external capital, and are paying high current tax rates. They will benefit most from insuring risks that can lead to cash shortfalls or financial distress, and that insurers can accurately assess and monitor to prevent moral hazard.

Full insurance is unlikely to be attractive for risks about which firms have a great deal of private information or that are subject to severe moral hazard. Also, firms that are already in financial distress have a strong incentive not to purchase insurance—they need cash today and have an incentive to take risk because future losses are likely to be borne by their debt holders.

Concept Check

1. How can insurance add value to a firm?
2. Identify the costs of insurance that arise due to market imperfections.

21.2 Commodity Price Risk

Firms use insurance to protect against the unlikely event that their real assets are damaged or destroyed by hazards such as fire, hurricane, accident, or other catastrophes that are outside their normal course of business. At the same time, many risks that firms face arise naturally as part of their business operations. For many firms, changes in the market prices of the raw materials they use and the goods they produce may be the most important source of risk to their profitability. In the airline industry, for example, the second-largest expense after labour is jet fuel. When oil prices multiplied by over eight times between 1999 and 2008, most major carriers struggled to remain profitable. The determinants of airline revenues are complex, but it is clear that airlines have limited ability to pass on these costs in the form of higher ticket prices. For an airline, the risk from increases in the price of oil is clearly one of the most important risks that it faces.

In this section, we discuss the ways firms can reduce, or *hedge*, their exposure to commodity price movements. Like insurance, hedging involves contracts or transactions that provide the firm with cash flows that offset its losses from price changes.

Hedging with Vertical Integration and Storage

Firms can hedge risk by making real investments in assets with offsetting risk. The most common strategies are *vertical integration* and *storage*.

Vertical Integration. The merger of a firm and its supplier (or a firm and its customer) is referred to as **vertical integration**. Because an increase in the price of the commodity raises the firm's costs and the supplier's revenues, these firms can offset their risks by merging. For example, in 2005, Japanese tire maker Bridgestone purchased a large Indonesian rubber plantation to control its costs. As the price of rubber increases, so will the profits of the rubber plantation, offsetting the higher costs of making tires. Similarly, airlines could offset their oil price risk by merging with an oil company.

While vertical integration can reduce risk, it does not always increase value. Recall the key lesson of Modigliani and Miller: firms add no value by doing something investors can do for themselves. Investors concerned about commodity price risk can diversify by "vertically integrating" their portfolios and buying shares of the firm and its supplier. Because the acquiring firm often pays a substantial premium over the current share price of the firm being acquired, the shareholders of the acquiring firm

vertical integration The merger of two companies in the same industry that make products required at different stages of the production cycle.

would generally find it cheaper to diversify on their own. Vertical integration can add value if combining the firms results in important synergies. For example, Boeing ultimately decided to purchase a number of its suppliers involved in its 787 "Dreamliner" to improve quality control and coordination, and reduce production delays. In many instances, however, diseconomies would be the more likely outcome, as the combined firm would lack a strategic focus (e.g., airlines combined with oil producers). Finally, vertical integration is not a perfect hedge: a firm's supplier is exposed to many other risks besides commodity prices. By integrating vertically, the firm eliminates one risk but acquires others.

Storage. A related strategy is the long-term storage of inventory. An airline concerned about rising fuel costs could purchase a large quantity of fuel today and store the fuel until it is needed. By doing so, the firm locks in its cost for fuel at today's price plus storage costs. But for many commodities, storage costs are much too high for this strategy to be attractive. Such a strategy also requires a substantial cash outlay upfront. If the firm does not have the required cash, it would need to raise external capital—and consequently would suffer issuance and adverse selection costs. Finally, maintaining large amounts of inventory would dramatically increase working capital requirements, a cost for the firm. Storage of inventory also does not work for firms that produce and sell commodities; managers at these firms are concerned about the price at which their commodity is *sold*; storage of inventory would actually be counterproductive as a hedging strategy for commodity sellers, as they would have a greater quantity waiting to be sold and would be subject to the commodity price risk on this greater quantity.

Hedging Strategy Leads to Promotion ... Sometimes

A good example is provided by Southwest Airlines. In early 2000, when oil prices were close to $20 per barrel, CFO Gary Kelly developed a strategy to protect the airline from a surge in oil prices. By the time oil prices soared above $30 per barrel later that year and put the airline industry into a financial crisis, Southwest had already signed contracts guaranteeing a price for its fuel equivalent to $23 per barrel. The savings from its fuel hedge amounted to almost 50% of Southwest's earnings that year, as shown in Figure 21.1. Kelly was promoted to become Southwest's CEO, and Southwest has continued this strategy to hedge fuel costs. Between 1998 and 2008, Southwest saved $3.5 billion over what it would have spent if it had paid the industry's average price for jet fuel, accounting for 83% of the company's profits during that period.

Of course, like insurance, commodity hedging does not always boost a firm's profits. Had oil prices fallen below $23 per barrel in the fall of 2000, Southwest's hedging policy would have reduced the firm's earnings by obligating it to pay $23 per barrel for its oil (and perhaps Kelly might not have gone on to be CEO). Presumably, Southwest felt that it could afford to pay

$23 per barrel for oil even if the price fell. While the long-term contracts would have been costly, they would not have led to financial distress. In other words, the long-term contracts stabilized Southwest's earnings at an acceptable level, no matter what happened to oil prices. Figure 21.1 illustrates how hedging stabilizes earnings.

Air Canada also has a history of fuel hedging. From 1994 to 1996, oil prices had increased by about 33%. In 1997, Air Canada signed contracts locking in about one-half of its anticipated 1998 fuel needs at an oil price of $19 per barrel. Unfortunately, in 1998, oil prices dropped to about $12 per barrel, and Air Canada lost the equivalent of $89 million because of these contracts. Nobody was promoted because of this result.

Southwest increased its fuel hedges in the years that followed, but Air Canada hedged a lower proportion of its fuel costs. At the end of 2007, Air Canada had hedges for its anticipated fuel needs of about 20% for 2008, 3% for 2009, and 2% for 2010. At the beginning of 2007, Southwest had 100% of its fuel costs hedged. At the beginning of 2008, Southwest had its anticipated fuel costs hedged as follows: 70% for 2008 at $51 per barrel, 55% for 2009 at $51 per barrel, 30% for 2010 at $63 per barrel, and 15% for each of 2011 and 2012 at $63 to $64 per barrel. Which strategy will be better depends on oil prices. By early July 2008, oil was over $145 per barrel, so Southwest's strategy looked better.

WestJet followed an alternative strategy; at the end of 2007, WestJet had no outstanding fuel hedges. Certainly, the hedging strategy of Southwest helped its earnings in mid-2008, but as oil prices dropped rapidly with the onset of the world financial crisis and fell below $40 per barrel by the end of 2008, Southwest's hedging strategy hurt its earnings. In 2009, Southwest's hedging actually reduced its earnings by about $245 million. Was WestJet the winner in terms of these hedged or unhedged strategies? Again, time will tell. By early 2011, oil prices were again over $100 per barrel.

Predicting prices for the future is always very difficult. Thus, hedging should not be done because of a feeling as to where prices will go; it should be done on the basis of whether benefits besides price stability, such as reducing financial distress costs, will result from the strategy.

Hedging with Long-Term Contracts

An alternative to vertical integration or storage is a long-term supply contract. Firms routinely enter into long-term lease contracts for real estate, fixing the price at which they will obtain office space many years in advance. Similarly, utility companies sign long-term supply contracts with power generators, and steelmakers sign long-term contracts with mining firms for iron ore. Through these contracts, both parties can achieve price stability for their product or input.

FIGURE 21.1

Commodity Hedging Smoothes Earnings

By locking in its fuel costs through long-term supply contracts, Southwest Airlines has kept its earnings stable in the face of fluctuating fuel prices. The figure corresponds to the Southwest hedge described in the "Hedging Strategy ..." box above. With a long-term contract at a price of $23 per barrel, Southwest would gain by buying at this price if oil prices go above $23 per barrel. If oil prices fall below $23 per barrel, Southwest would lose from its commitment to buy at a higher price. Note that the figure assumes no changes to the firm's revenues or other costs.

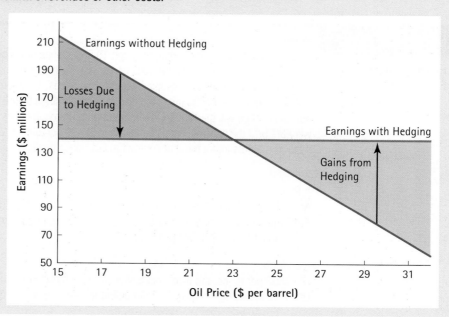

Of course, similar to insurance, commodity hedging does not always boost a firm's profits. Consider a steelmaker and an iron ore producer that lock in the iron ore price for future transactions through long-term contracts. The steelmaker agrees to buy the iron ore and the iron ore producer agrees to sell it; they fix the price today for future transactions. If the market price of iron ore rises, then the steelmaker's profits will be boosted and the iron ore producer's profits will be reduced relative to what would have happened without the long-term contracts. On the other hand, if the market price of iron ore falls, then the steelmaker's profits will be reduced while the iron ore producer's profits will be boosted relative to what would have happened without the long-term contracts. In other words, the long-term contracts can be used to stabilize earnings at an acceptable level, no matter what happens to the iron ore prices. Figure 21.1 illustrates how hedging stabilizes earnings for the purchaser of a commodity.

forward contract
A customized agreement between two parties who are known to each other whereby they agree to trade an asset on some future date at a price that is fixed today.

One form of long-term contact is called a **forward contract**. A forward contract is a customized agreement between two parties who are known to each other whereby they agree to trade a certain quantity of an asset on some future date at a price that is fixed today. Forward contracts and many other types of long-term supply contracts are bilateral contracts negotiated by a buyer and a seller to suit their particular needs. Unfortunately, such contracts have several potential disadvantages:

1. They expose each party to the risk that the other party may default and fail to live up to the terms of the contract. Thus, although long-term contracts insulate the firms from commodity price risk, they expose them to credit (default) risk.

2. Long-term contracts cannot be entered into anonymously; the buyer and seller know each other's identity. This lack of anonymity may have strategic disadvantages, as a party's willingness to enter into the contract reveals information to its rivals about its risk exposures.

3. The market value of the long-term contract at any point in time may not be easy to determine, making it difficult to track gains and losses, and it may be difficult or even impossible to cancel the contract if necessary.

An alternative strategy that avoids these disadvantages is to hedge with futures contracts. In the next section we investigate this strategy.

EXAMPLE 21.4

Hedging with a
Forward Contract

Problem
Consider a chocolate maker that will need 10,000 tonnes of cocoa beans next year. Due to political unrest in Ivory Coast, where 40% of the world's cocoa beans are produced, there is a lot of uncertainty about cocoa beans supply and future prices. The current market price of cocoa beans is $2900 per tonne. At this price, the firm expects earnings before interest and taxes of $44 million next year. What will the firm's *EBIT* be if the price of cocoa beans rises to $3500 per tonne? What will *EBIT* be if the price of cocoa beans falls to $2600 per tonne? What will *EBIT* be in each scenario if the firm enters into a forward contract to buy cocoa beans for a fixed price of $2950 per tonne?

Solution

▶ **Plan**
At $2900 per tonne, the firm's *EBIT* is $44 million. For every dollar above $2900 per tonne, its *EBIT* will decrease by $10,000 (for 10,000 tonnes) and similarly will increase by $10,000 for every dollar below $2900 per tonne.

▶ **Execute**
At $3500 per tonne, the firm's costs will increase by ($3500 − $2900) × 10,000 = $6 million. Other things being equal, *EBIT* will decline to $44 million − $6 million = $38 million.

If the price of cocoa beans falls instead to $2600 per tonne, *EBIT* will rise to $44 million — ($2600 − $2900) × 10,000 = $47 million.

Alternatively, the firm can avoid this risk by entering into the forward contract that fixes the price in either scenario at $2950 per tonne, for an *EBIT* of $44 million — ($2950 − $2900) × 10,000 = $43.5 million.

▶ **Evaluate**

The firm can completely reduce its cocoa-price risk by entering into the forward contract. The cost is accepting lower (by $500,000) profits for certain. Note, though, there are still risks of supply disruption and other risks within the firm that could be important if management is concerned about risk management.

Hedging with Futures Contracts

futures contract

A standardized agreement between two anonymous parties traded on an organized futures exchange that contracts the two parties to trade an asset on some future date at a price that is fixed today.

A commodity *futures contract* is a type of long-term contract designed to avoid the disadvantages cited above. A **futures contract** is a standardized agreement to trade an asset on some future date, at a price that is locked in today. Futures contracts are traded anonymously on a futures exchange at a publicly observed market price and generally are very liquid. The party who has entered into a futures contract to buy a commodity is said to be "long" in the futures contract; the party who has entered into a futures contract to sell a commodity is said to be "short" in the futures contract. Both the buyer and the seller can get out of the contract at any time by finding a third party to take over the contract at the current market price. Given that the futures contract trades on an organized futures exchange and that supply and demand forces determine current market prices, parties will always be standing by to enter into these futures contracts and take over the positions of the original parties. Finally, through a mechanism we will describe shortly, futures contracts are designed to almost completely eliminate credit risk.

Figure 21.2 shows the prices in September 2010 of futures contracts for light, sweet crude oil traded on the New York Mercantile Exchange (NYMEX). Each contract represents a commitment to trade 1000 barrels of oil at the futures price on its delivery date. For example, by trading the March 2011 contract, buyers and sellers agreed in September 2010 to exchange 1000 barrels of oil in March 2011 at a price of $79.96 per barrel. By doing so, they are able to lock in the price they will pay or receive for oil six months in advance.

The futures prices shown in Figure 21.2 are not prices that are paid on the date the contract is entered. Rather, they are prices *agreed* to on the date the contract is entered but to be paid in the future. The futures prices are determined in the market based on supply and demand for each delivery date. They depend on expectations of future oil prices, adjusted by an appropriate risk premium.

After the passage of time, oil rose to over $100 per barrel in March, 2011; those who originally entered into a contract to buy oil for $79.96 per barrel gained over $20 per barrel (having effectively locked in a price to buy at the lower original futures price instead of the new higher market price), while those who originally entered into a contract to sell for $79.96 lost over $20 per barrel (having effectively locked in a price to sell at the original lower futures price instead of the new higher market price).

Mitigating Credit Risk in Futures Contracts. If a buyer commits to purchase crude oil in December 2013 for $130 per barrel, how can the seller be assured that the buyer will honour that commitment? If the actual price of oil in December 2013 is only $100 per barrel, the buyer will have a strong incentive to renege and default on the contract. Similarly, the seller will have an incentive to default if the actual price of oil is more than $130 in December 2013.

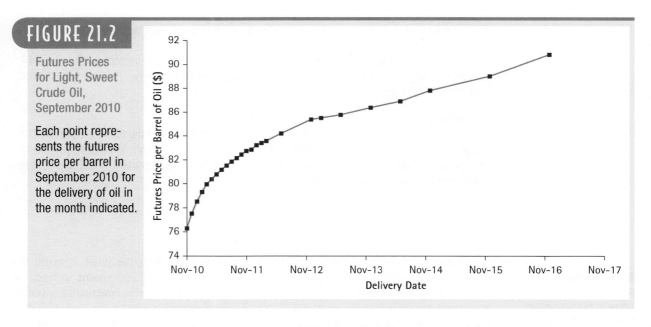

FIGURE 21.2

Futures Prices for Light, Sweet Crude Oil, September 2010

Each point represents the futures price per barrel in September 2010 for the delivery of oil in the month indicated.

margin Collateral that investors are required to deposit into their brokerage account when entering a transaction that could generate losses beyond the initial investment.

marking to market The daily exchange of cash flows based on computing gains and losses due to the daily change in the market price of a futures contract.

margin call A requirement for investors to inject new cash into their brokerage account when their account balance falls below a maintenance margin requirement due to marking to market cash flows.

Default Risk Prevention. Futures exchanges use two mechanisms to prevent buyers or sellers from defaulting. First, investors (both the long and short parties to the futures contract) are required to post collateral, called **margin**, when using futures contracts. This collateral serves as a guarantee that traders will meet their obligations. In addition, cash flows are exchanged on a daily basis, rather than waiting until the end of the contract, through a procedure called **marking to market**. That is, gains and losses are computed each day based on the change in the market price of the futures contract. If, due to the marking to market, an investor's account falls below a required maintenance margin amount, then the investor will be subject to a **margin call** and required to inject new cash into the account. After the marking to market each day, both parties essentially have new futures contracts rewritten with prices based on the new market conditions. The combination of rewritten contracts at the new futures price and the exchange of cash flows through marking to market results in two effects: (1) there is no longer an incentive to default on the futures contract, as it reflects current market conditions and (2) each party's net purchase or sale price for the commodity (based on a combination of the new futures price and the marking to market cash flows exchanged) is kept at the original futures price that existed when the parties entered the futures contract.

Suppose that the price of the December 2013 futures contract varies, as shown in Table 21.1, over the 700 remaining trading days between May 2011 and the delivery date in December 2013. A buyer who enters into the contract on date 0 has committed to pay the futures price of $130 per barrel for oil. If the next day the futures price is only $128 per barrel, the buyer has a loss of $2 per barrel on her position. This loss is settled immediately by deducting $2 from the buyer's margin account. If the price rises to $129 per barrel on day 2, the gain of $1 is added to the buyer's margin account. This process continues until the contract delivery date, with the daily gains and losses shown. The buyer's cumulative loss or gain is the sum of these daily amounts and always equals the difference between the original contract price of $130 per barrel and the current contract price.

In December 2013, delivery takes place at the final futures price, which is equal to the actual price of oil at that time.[7] In the example in Table 21.1, the buyer ultimately

---

[7]At its delivery date, a futures contract is a contract for immediate delivery. Thus, by the Law of One Price, its price must be the actual price of oil in the market.

TABLE 21.1

Example of Marking to Market and Daily Settlement for the December 2013 Light, Sweet Crude Oil Futures Contract ($/bbl)

Trading Day		May 2011						Dec 2013		
	0	1	2	3	4	...	698	699	700
Futures price	130	128	129	127	126	...	105	107	108
Daily marked to market profit/loss		−2	1	−2	−1	...	...	2	1
Cumulative profit/loss		−2	−1	−3	−4	...	−25	−23	−22

pays $108 per barrel for oil and has lost $22 per barrel in her margin account. Thus, her total cost is $108 + $22 = $130 per barrel, the price for oil she originally committed to. Through this daily marking to market, the contracted futures price is rewritten every day to reflect current market conditions, and buyers and sellers pay for any losses or receive any gains as they occur, rather than waiting until the final delivery date. In this way, the parties to the contract avoid the risk of default.[8]

In essence, the December 2013 futures contract is the same as a forward contract with a set price of $130 per barrel of oil. However, with a forward contract that is between two individual parties, there is potential for one party to default if the market price diverges from the forward price. With a futures contract, the buyer and the seller of a futures contract can close their positions at any time (and accept the cumulative losses or gains in their margin accounts), and the contract will then be reassigned to a new buyer or seller, because the contract is continually rewritten to reflect current market conditions. Because of this liquidity and the lack of credit risk, commodity futures contracts are the predominant method by which many firms hedge oil price risk. Similar futures contracts exist for many other commodities, including natural gas, coal, electricity, silver, gold, aluminum, canola, barley, soybeans, corn, wheat, rice, cattle, pork bellies, cocoa, sugar, carbon dioxide emissions, and even frozen concentrated orange juice. In addition, futures contracts exist for many financial products such as currency exchange, fixed income (interest-rate-related) instruments, and stock indices.

Hedging with Options Contracts

In addition to long-term contracts and derivatives such as forward and futures contracts, options are also be very useful for hedging. We described call and put options in detail in Chapter 20; such options exist on a wide variety of commodities.[9] Let's consider how a hedge using futures contracts can be replaced with a hedge using options contracts.

Consider the steel mill and the iron ore companies discussed earlier. They could use futures contracts to hedge against changes in iron ore prices. The steel mill, needing to buy iron ore in the future, would go long in a futures contract on iron ore, and the iron ore producer would go short in a futures contract on iron ore. The steel mill is concerned about iron ore prices increasing and wants to protect itself from that when

---

[8]For this system to work, the buyer's margin account must always have a sufficient balance to cover at least one day's potential loss. If a buyer's remaining margin in the account is too low, below a required maintenance margin amount, then the futures exchange will require the buyer to replenish the account through a margin call. If the buyer fails to do so, the account will be closed and the buyer's contract will be assigned to a new buyer.

[9]In most cases, these options are actually options on futures contracts for the commodity. This distinction is not that important for our purposes, because under the Law of One Price, at the maturity of the options and futures contracts, the futures price becomes a contract for immediate delivery, and thus the futures price will equal the spot price of the commodity.

it comes time to buy the ore. Can the steel mill get protection from increasing iron ore prices using an options contract? The answer is yes. Consider which options contract allows the owner of the contract to buy an asset for a fixed amount even though the price of the asset has risen. Of course, this is a call option contract. So the steel mill company may choose to hedge by buying call options on iron ore rather than hedging through a long futures contract to buy the ore. If iron ore prices rise above the strike price of the call option, the steel mill can exercise the call option and purchase the iron ore at the strike price.

What about the iron ore producer? In the case of a futures contract, the producer would have entered into a short futures contract so as to lock in a price to sell the iron ore in the future. That protects the iron ore producer in case iron ore prices drop. The way to protect against a price drop of iron ore using options is to purchase a put option on iron ore. If the iron ore price drops below the strike price of the put option, the iron ore producer can exercise the put option and sell the iron ore at the strike price. The put option sets a minimum at which the iron ore producer will be able to sell the ore.

To summarize, if a company will need to purchase a commodity in the future, its management can hedge with options by buying a call option on the commodity. If a company will need to sell a commodity in the future, its management can hedge with options by buying a put option on the commodity.

Comparing Futures Hedging with Options Hedging

Table 21.2 shows the alternative ways to hedge using futures or options. These alternatives protect against unfavourable changes in the commodity prices; however, there are important differences between a futures hedging strategy and an options hedging strategy. When an options contract is purchased, the buyer must pay for it (i.e., it is costly). With a futures hedging strategy, there is no cost to enter into the contract. In effect, the party who takes the long futures position does not have to pay the party who takes the short futures position at the time the contract is entered, because both parties are simply signing a contract at a fair market price for a future transaction. (Note that the initial margin requirement is paid by both the long and short parties to a futures contract; the margin is collateral backing up the contract, but it is not a cost of the contract.)

A second difference between hedging with options versus futures is the nature of the final cash flows. With a futures contract, the final price is fixed regardless of whether the market price rises or falls. For example, a firm that has contracted to buy a commodity through a long futures contract is protected against a price rise, but the firm also misses out on the potential savings if the price falls. With an options hedge, the firm is protected against an unfavourable price change, because the option can be exercised; however, if there is a favourable price change, the option can be left to expire unexercised, and the firm can transact at the new favourable price. Example 21.5 shows how the different types of hedges can produce very different net results.

TABLE 21.2   Alternative Ways for a Firm to Hedge: Futures Versus Options Strategies

Firm's Exposure to a Change in the Commodity Price	Hedge to Protect Against an Unfavourable Price Change	
	Futures Strategy	Options Strategy
Firm intends to buy the commodity in the future: concerned about a price increase	Long futures contract	Purchase a call option
Firm intends to sell the commodity in the future: concerned about a price decrease	Short futures contract	Purchase a put option

EXAMPLE 21.5

Hedging: Futures
Versus Options

Problem

It is April, and Magda Nowak is planting her canola crop on her farm near Trembowla, Manitoba. She expects to grow 1000 tonnes of canola over the season and plans to sell it in November after the harvest is done. Also on this April day, Japan Canola Crushers (JCC) is planning on buying 1000 tonnes of canola in November so that the company can export it to Japan as an input into their canola oil plant. Both Magda and JCC are concerned about the price for canola in November and are considering hedging. The following data about current futures and options contracts are available:

- Futures contracts for delivery in November are available with a futures price of $600 per tonne.

- Call options on canola with expiration in November are available with a strike price of $600 per tonne. These call options cost $34 (per option on one tonne).

- Put options on canola with expiration in November are available with a strike price of $600 per tonne. These put options cost $36 (per option on one tonne).

Solution

▶ **Plan**

Since Magda will be growing canola, she is concerned about the price dropping by the time she harvests and sells it. She can either enter into short futures contracts on 1000 tonnes of canola or she can purchase put options on 1000 tonnes of canola. JCC, on the other hand, will be buying canola once it is harvested and is concerned that the price will rise before the purchase. JCC can either enter into long futures contracts on 1000 tonnes of canola or JCC can buy call options on 1000 tonnes of canola.

▶ **Execute**

Consider the futures hedges of the two parties. Entering into futures contracts for 1000 tonnes at $600 per tonne ensures that, after all futures price changes and marking to market, the net result will be that Magda receives $600,000 and JCC pays $600,000 for the canola in November.

Alternatively, consider the options hedges. First, let's consider Magda's situation. To purchase the put options, she had to pay for puts on 1000 tonnes of canola:

$$\$36 \text{ per put option per tonne} \times 1000 \text{ tonnes} = \$36,000$$

If the price of canola in November is less than $600 per tonne, she will exercise her put options and sell her canola at the strike price of $600. In this case, the net amount she receives (after deducting the cost of purchasing the put options) is as follows:

$$\text{Magda's net amount received if puts are exercised} = \$600,000 - \$36,000 = \$564,000$$

On a per tonne basis, Magda's net amount is $564 per tonne whenever the price of canola is $600 or below. If the price of canola is above $600, then Magda will let her put options expire and sell the canola for the more favourable higher market price that exists in November. On a per tonne basis, Magda will net whatever the market price is (over $600) minus the $36 option cost originally paid.

Now consider JCC's situation with the call option hedge. To purchase the call options, JCC had to pay for calls on 1000 tonnes of canola:

$$\$34 \text{ per call option per tonne} \times 1000 \text{ tonnes} = \$34,000$$

If the price of canola in November is greater than $600 per tonne, JCC will exercise the call options and buy the canola at the strike price of $600. In this case, the net amount JCC pays (after including the cost of purchasing the call options) is as follows:

$$\text{JCC's net amount paid if calls are exercised} = \$600,000 + \$34,000 = \$634,000$$

On a per tonne basis, JCC's net amount paid is $634 per tonne whenever the price of canola is $600 or above. If the price of canola is below $600, then JCC will let the call options expire and buy the canola for the more favourable lower market price that exists in November. On a per tonne basis, JCC's net cost of the canola will be whatever the market price is (under $600) plus the $34 option cost originally paid.

Evaluate

Both Magda and JCC can completely eliminate canola price risk by using the futures contracts and locking in a price of $600 per tonne. A benefit of using futures is that there is no additional cost of the hedge, but a drawback is that favourable price changes cannot be exploited.

With options hedges, both Magda and JCC can eliminate their exposure to unfavourable price changes. A drawback of options hedges is that they are costly: Magda must pay $36,000 for the put options, and JCC must pay $34,000 for the call options. A benefit of options hedges, though, is that if there is a favourable price change, the party can benefit from it. The graphs below show the net cash flows from the hedges for Magda and JCC:

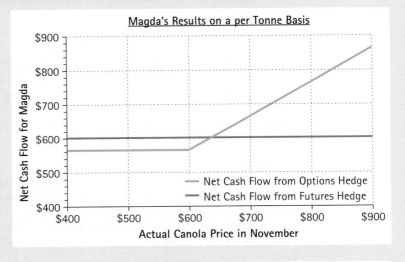

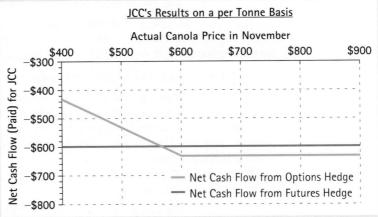

An additional benefit of an options hedge versus a futures hedge arises when there is the possibility that the hedge will not actually be needed. Consider Magda in Example 21.5. She is planting her canola crop and expects to grow 1000 tonnes of canola to sell in November. But what happens if a major hailstorm occurs, resulting in the destruction of her crop and many other farmers' crops, and a canola price that jumps to $800 per tonne? Without any canola to sell, Magda no longer needs to hedge against canola price changes. With the put options hedge, she can simply let her put option expire worthless and lose the original $36,000 she paid for the put options. However, with a short futures position, she does not have the canola available that she contracted to deliver. She will have to close out her futures contract on 1000 tonnes of canola at $800 per tonne. The net effect of the marking to market between when she entered into the short futures contracts at $600 and closes out at $800 is as follows:

$$\text{Magda's loss on short futures position}$$

$$-\$200 \text{ per tonne} \times 1000 \text{ tonnes} = -\$200,000$$

With her valuable crop lost, Magda ends up losing an additional $200,000 due to her futures position. Clearly she would have preferred the put option hedge in this case.

Deciding to Hedge Commodity Price Risk

natural hedge The ability of a firm to pass on cost increases to its customers or revenue decreases to its suppliers.

liquidity risk The risk of being forced to liquidate an investment (at a loss) because the cash is required to satisfy another obligation (most often a margin requirement).

basis risk The risk that arises because the value of a futures contract is not perfectly correlated with a firm's exposure.

In a perfect market, commodity supply contracts, futures contracts, and options contracts are zero-*NPV* investments that do not change the value of the firm. But hedging commodity price risk can benefit the firm by reducing the costs of other frictions. Just as with insurance, the potential benefits include reduced financial distress and issuance costs, tax savings, increased debt capacity, and improved managerial incentives and risk assessment. Commodity futures and options markets, in particular, provide valuable information to commodity producers and users. For example, an oil firm can lock in a future sale price or fix a minimum for the future sale price of oil before it spends millions of dollars on drilling a new well. A canola farmer unsure of future canola prices can lock in the futures price or she can use a put option on canola to ensure her price does not fall below a minimum level. The farmer, knowing her actual costs of seed, fertilizer, and so on, can determine before planting whether she will have a profitable season and can avoid financial distress.

Hedging commodity price risk has potential benefits similar to those of buying insurance, but it does not have the same costs. In comparison with the market for hazard insurance, the commodity markets are less vulnerable to the problems of adverse selection and moral hazard. Firms generally do not possess better information than outside investors do regarding the risk of future commodity price changes, nor can they influence that risk through their actions. Also, futures and options contracts are very liquid and do not entail large administrative costs.

Common Mistake   **Mistakes When Hedging Risk**

There are several common mistakes to avoid when hedging risk.

Not Accounting for Natural Hedges

Even though purchases of a commodity may be a firm's largest expense, they may not be a source of risk if the firm can pass along those costs to its customers. For example,

gas stations do not need to hedge their cost of oil, because the price of gasoline—and thus their revenues—fluctuates with it. When a firm can pass on cost increases to its customers or revenue decreases to its suppliers, it has a **natural hedge** for these risks. A firm should hedge risks to its profits only after such natural hedges are accounted for, lest it over-hedge and increase risk.

Exposing the Firm to Liquidity Risk

When hedging with futures contracts, the firm stabilizes its earnings by offsetting business losses with gains on the futures contracts and by offsetting business gains with losses on the futures contracts. In the latter scenario, the firm runs the risk of receiving margin calls on its futures positions before it realizes the cash flows from the business gains. To hedge effectively, the firm must have, or be able to raise, the cash required to meet these margin calls, or it may be forced to default on its positions. Hence, when hedging with future contracts, the firm is exposed to **liquidity risk**. Such was the case for Metallgesellschaft Refining and Marketing (MGRM), which shut down in 1993 with more than $1 billion in losses in the oil futures market. MGRM had written long-term contracts to supply oil to its customers and hedged its risk that oil prices might rise by buying oil futures.

When oil prices subsequently dropped, MGRM faced a cash flow crisis and could not meet the margin calls on its futures positions. Hedging with options contracts does not create the potential for this problem (although options do entail an upfront cost that does not exist with futures contracts).

Mismatching Contracts and Risk Exposure

Futures and options contracts are available only for a set of standardized commodities, with specific delivery dates and locations. Thus, while a futures contract that promises to deliver canola in Saskatchewan in November is a reasonable hedge for canola purchased at the port of Vancouver in December, it will not be a perfect match. **Basis risk** is the risk that arises because the value of the futures contract will not be perfectly correlated with the firm's exposure.

Firms that hedge commodity price risk must hire expert traders who understand the nature of the contracts and the various markets in which they trade. Often a firm will allow its traders some leeway to do additional trading (beyond that needed for hedging). In effect, the firm also allows its traders to *speculate* by entering into contracts that do not offset actual risks. Traders who **speculate** use securities to bet on the direction in which they believe the market price is likely to move. Speculating increases the firm's risk rather than reducing it. Unless a firm monitors traders carefully, when it authorizes traders to trade contracts to hedge, the firm opens the door to the possibility of speculation. The firm must guard against the potential to speculate which adds risk to the firm through appropriate governance procedures.

speculation The use of securities to place a bet on the direction in which the trader believes the market is likely to move.

Differing Hedging Strategies at U.S. Airlines

In mid-2005, oil prices rose to more than $60 per barrel. As a result of its aggressive hedging policy, Southwest Airlines was paying slightly more than $26 per barrel for 85% of its oil at the time. Many of the major U.S. airlines, however, lacked the cash or creditworthiness necessary to enter into long-term contracts. In 2004, Delta was forced to sell its supply contracts to raise cash so as to avoid defaulting on its debt. United Airlines, which filed for bankruptcy protection in December 2002, had only 30% of its fuel hedged in 2005 at a price of $45 per barrel. By 2008, when oil prices were over $130 per barrel, the prices from 2005 looked like a relative bargain. In keeping with its strategy, Southwest had entered into long-term hedges so that most of its fuel costs in 2008 were locked in at $60 per barrel.

These differences in strategy are somewhat understandable given the airlines' differing financial positions. Southwest is currently profitable and would like to reduce its risk of becoming financially distressed by hedging its fuel costs. Delta and United are already in financial distress, so hedging would not avoid these costs. And for equity holders, taking a risk by not hedging may be the best strategy—a sudden drop in oil prices would lead to a windfall for equity holders, while losses from further increases would likely be borne by debt holders in default.

Source: Eric Roston, "Hedging Their Costs," *Time*, June 20, 2005

Concept Check

3. Discuss risk-management strategies that firms use to hedge commodity price risk.

4. What are the potential risks associated with hedging using futures contracts?

Interest Rate Risk

Firms that borrow must pay interest on their debt. An increase in interest rates raises firms' borrowing costs and can reduce their profitability. In addition, many firms have fixed long-term future liabilities, such as capital leases or pension fund liabilities. A decrease in interest rates raises the present value of these liabilities and can lower the value of the firm. Thus, when interest rates are volatile, interest rate risk is a concern for many firms.

Interest Rate Risk Measurement: Duration

duration The sensitivity to interest rate changes of an asset or a liability.

Financial managers need to know the **duration**—the sensitivity to interest rate changes—of their assets and liabilities. In Chapter 6 on bonds, we saw increased sensitivity of bonds to interest rates for longer maturity bonds. For example, for a 10-year, zero-coupon bond, an increase of one percentage point in the yield to maturity from 5% to 6% causes the bond price per $100 face value to fall as follows:

$$\frac{100}{1.05^{10}} = \$61.39 \text{ to } \frac{100}{1.06^{10}} = \$55.84$$

This represents a price change of $(55.84 - 61.39)/61.39 = -9.0\%$. The price of a five-year bond drops only 4.6% for the same yield change. The interest rate sensitivity of a *single* cash flow is roughly proportional to its maturity. The farther away the cash flow is, the larger the effect of interest rate changes on its present value. The idea can be expanded to a security or asset that produces multiple cash flows. While the specific formula for duration is beyond the scope of this book, the idea is that securities whose value comes mostly from later cash flows have a longer duration (higher interest rate sensitivity) than do securities whose value comes mostly from earlier cash flows.

Duration-Based Hedging

A firm's market capitalization (equity) is determined by the difference in the market value of its assets and its liabilities. If changes in interest rates affect these values, they will affect the firm's equity value. Thus, we can assess a firm's sensitivity to interest rates by examining its balance sheet. Moreover, by restructuring the balance sheet to reduce its duration, we can hedge the firm's interest rate risk.

Banks: An Example. Consider a typical bank. These institutions hold short-term deposits, in the form of chequing and savings accounts, as well as guaranteed investment certificates. They also make long-term loans, such as car loans and home mortgages. Most banks face a problem, because the duration of the loans they make is generally longer than the duration of their deposits. When the durations of a firm's assets and liabilities are significantly different, the firm has a **duration mismatch**. This mismatch puts the bank at risk if interest rates change significantly.

duration mismatch A significant difference between the durations of a firm's assets and liabilities.

How can a bank reduce its sensitivity to interest rates? It must reduce the duration of its assets or increase the duration of its liabilities. Because it can't easily increase the duration of its liabilities (it can't force people to leave their money in the bank longer than they want to), it must focus on its assets (mortgage loans). By selling the mortgages to another mortgage servicer in exchange for cash, the bank can reduce its asset interest rate sensitivity to zero. In fact, many banks sell their mortgage loans to reduce their sensitivity to interest rate risk.

Swap-Based Hedging

A bank can reduce its interest rate sensitivity by selling assets. For most firms, selling assets is not an attractive prospect, as those assets are typically necessary to conduct the firms' normal business operations. Interest rate swaps are an alternative means of modifying the firms' interest rate risk exposure without buying or selling assets. An **interest rate swap** is a contract a firm enters into with a bank in which the firm and the bank agree to exchange the coupons from two different types of loans. In this section, we describe interest rate swaps and explore how they are used to manage interest rate risk.

In a standard interest rate swap, one party agrees to pay coupons based on a fixed interest rate in exchange for receiving coupons based on the prevailing market interest rate during each coupon period. An interest rate that adjusts to current market conditions is called a *floating rate*. Thus, the parties exchange a fixed-rate coupon for a floating-rate coupon, which explains why this swap is also called a "fixed-for-floating interest rate swap."

To demonstrate how an interest swap works, consider a five-year, $100 million interest rate swap with a 7.8% fixed rate. Standard swaps have semi-annual coupons, so the fixed coupon amounts would be $1/2(7.8\% \times \$100$ million$) = \$3.9$ million every six months. The floating-rate coupons are typically based on a six-month market interest rate, such as the six-month treasury bill rate or the six-month London Inter-Bank Offered Rate (LIBOR).[10] This rate varies over the life of the contract. Each coupon is calculated based on the six-month interest rate that prevailed in the market six months prior to the coupon payment date. Table 21.3 calculates the cash flows of the swap under a hypothetical scenario for LIBOR rates over the life of the swap. For example, at the first coupon date in six months, the fixed coupon is $3.9 million and the floating-rate coupon is $1/2(6.8\% \times \$10$ million$) = \$3.4$ million, for a net payment of $0.5 million from the fixed- to the floating-rate payer.

Each payment of the swap is equal to the difference between the fixed- and floating-rate coupons. Unlike an ordinary loan, there is no payment of principal. Because the $100 million swap amount is used only to calculate the coupons but is never actually paid, it is referred to as the **notional principal** of the swap. Finally, there is no initial cash flow associated with the swap. That is, the swap contract—like forward and futures contracts—is typically structured as a "zero-cost" security. The fixed rate of the swap

interest rate swap
A contract in which two parties agree to exchange the coupons from two different types of loans.

notional principal The calculated amount of the coupon payments in an interest rate swap.

| TABLE 21.3 | Cash Flows ($ millions) for a $100 Million Fixed-for-Floating Interest Rate Swap |

Year	Six-Month LIBOR	Fixed Coupon	Floating-Rate Coupon	New Swap Cash Flow: Fixed-for-Floating
0.0	6.8%			0.0
0.5	7.2%	3.9	3.4	0.5
1.0	8.0%	3.9	3.6	0.3
1.5	7.4%	3.9	4.0	−0.1
2.0	7.8%	3.9	3.7	0.2
2.5	8.6%	3.9	3.9	0.0
3.0	9.0%	3.9	4.3	−0.4
3.5	9.2%	3.9	4.5	−0.6
4.0	8.4%	3.9	4.6	−0.7
4.5	7.6%	3.9	4.2	−0.3
5.0		3.9	3.8	0.1

---

[10]The LIBOR is the rate at which major international banks with offices in London stand ready to accept deposits from one another. It is a common benchmark interest rate for swaps and other financial agreements.

contract is set based on current market conditions so that the swap is a fair deal (i.e., it has an *NPV* of zero) for both sides.

Interest rate forward contracts, futures contracts, and options contracts also exist and can be used to manage interest rate risk. Swaps, however, are by far the most common strategy used by corporations.

Combining Swaps with Standard Loans. Corporations routinely use interest rate swaps to alter their exposure to interest rate fluctuations. The interest rate a firm pays on its loans can fluctuate for two reasons. First, the risk-free interest rate in the market may change. Second, the firm's credit quality, which determines the spread the firm must pay over the risk-free interest rate, can vary over time. By combining swaps with loans, firms can choose which of these sources of interest rate risk they will tolerate and which they will eliminate.

EXAMPLE 21.6

Using Interest Rate Swaps

Problem

Bolt Industries is facing increased competition and wants to borrow $10 million in cash to protect against future revenue shortfalls. Currently, long-term AA rates are 10%. Given its credit rating, Bolt can borrow at 10.5%. The company is expecting interest rates to fall over the next few years, so it would prefer to borrow at short-term rates and refinance after rates drop. However, Bolt's management is afraid that its credit rating may deteriorate as competition intensifies, which may greatly increase the spread the firm must pay on a new loan. How can Bolt benefit from declining interest rates without worrying about changes in its credit rating?

Solution

▶ **Plan**

Bolt wants to convert its long-term fixed rate into a floating rate (one that will decline if market interest rates decline). It can do this by entering into a swap in which it will receive a fixed rate (which can then be used to pay its fixed long-term obligation) and pay a floating rate $\tilde{r}_t$. Its net exposure will be the floating rate.

▶ **Execute**

Bolt can borrow at the long-term rate of 10.5% and then enter into a swap in which it receives the long-term AA fixed rate of 10% and pays the short-term rate $\tilde{r}_t$. Its net borrowing cost will then be as follows:

Long-term Loan Rate	+ Floating Rate Due on Swap	− Fixed Rate Received from Swap	= Net Borrowing Cost
10.5%	+ $\tilde{r}_t$	− 10%	= $\tilde{r}_t + 0.5$

▶ **Evaluate**

In this way, Bolt locks in its current credit spread of 0.5% but gets the benefit of lower rates as rates decline. The tradeoff is that if rates increase instead, the firm is worse off.

As a financial manager, hedging interest rate risk can help your firm avoid financial distress costs of the types we described in Chapter 15. If the business is performing fundamentally well, you do not want a sudden shift in borrowing costs to cause a cash flow problem that can lead to distress. As we have seen in this section, there are tools such as duration matching and swaps available to help you avoid such costs.

5. What is the intuition behind the calculation of duration?

6. How do firms manage interest rate risk?

MyFinanceLab

Here is what you should know after reading this chapter. MyFinanceLab will help you identify what you know, and where to go when you need to practice.

Key Points and Equations	Key Terms	Online Practice Opportunities
21.1 Insurance ▶ Insurance is a common method firms use to reduce risk. In a perfect market, the price of insurance is actuarially fair. An actuarially fair insurance premium is equal to the present value of the expected loss: $$\frac{Pr(\text{Loss}) \times E[\text{Payment in the Event of Loss}]}{1 + r_L} \quad (21.1)$$ ▶ Insurance for large risks that cannot be well diversified has a negative beta, which raises its cost. ▶ The value of insurance comes from its ability to reduce the cost of market imperfections for the firm. Insurance may be beneficial to a firm because of its effects on bankruptcy and financial distress costs, issuance costs, taxes, debt capacity, and risk assessment. ▶ The costs of insurance include administrative and overhead costs, adverse selection, and moral hazard.	actuarially fair price, p. 701 business interruption insurance, p. 700 business liability insurance, p. 700 deductible, p. 705 insurance premium, p. 700 key personnel insurance, p. 700 moral hazard, p. 705 policy limits, p. 705 property insurance, p. 700	MyFinanceLab Study Plan 21.1
21.2 Commodity Price Risk ▶ Firms use several risk-management strategies to hedge their exposure to commodity price movements. ▶ Firms can make real investments in assets with offsetting risk using techniques such as vertical integration and storage. ▶ Firms can enter into long-term contracts with suppliers or customers or use forward contacts to acheive price stability. ▶ Firms can hedge risk using futures contracts or option contracts that are available in financial markets.	basis risk, p. 717 forward contract, p. 710 futures contract, p. 711 liquidity risk, p. 717 margin, p. 712 margin call, p. 712 marking to market, p. 712 natural hedge, p. 717 speculation, p. 718 vertical integration, p. 707	MyFinanceLab Study Plan 21.2
21.3 Interest Rate Risk ▶ Firms face interest rate risk when exchange rates are volatile. The interest rate sensitivity of a stream of cash flows is greater if more of the value of the stream comes from later cash flows.	duration, p. 719 duration mismatch, p. 719 interest rate swap, p. 720 notional principal, p. 720	MyFinanceLab Study Plan 21.3

▶ Firms can manage interest rate risk by buying or selling assets to match the interest rate sensitivity of their assets to the interest rate sensitivity of their liabilities.

▶ Interest rate swaps allow firms to separate the risk of interest rate changes from the risk of fluctuations in the firm's credit quality.

▶ By borrowing long term and entering into an interest rate swap in which the firm receives a fixed-rate coupon and pays a floating-rate coupon, the firm will pay a floating interest rate plus a spread that is fixed, based on its initial credit quality.

▶ By borrowing short term and entering into an interest rate swap in which the firm receives a floating-rate coupon and pays a fixed-rate coupon, the firm will pay a fixed interest rate plus a spread that will float with its credit quality.

▶ Firms use interest rate swaps to modify their interest rate risk exposure without buying or selling assets.

Review Questions

1. Why is it possible for a firm to pay an actuarially fair price for insurance and still have the insurance purchase be a positive-*NPV* investment?

2. How can an insurance company mitigate adverse selection and moral hazard?

3. What are some common approaches to hedging commodity price risk?

4. Can hedging lead to losses?

5. How can a firm become exposed to interest rate risk?

6. How can a firm use a swap to manage its interest rate risk?

Problems

All problems in this chapter are available in MyFinanceLab. An asterisk (*) indicates problems with a higher level of difficulty.

Insurance

1.   The William Companies (WMB) owns and operates natural gas pipelines that deliver 12% of the natural gas consumed in the United States. WMB is concerned that a major hurricane could disrupt its Gulfstream pipeline, which runs 691 miles through the Gulf of Mexico. In the event of a disruption, the firm anticipates a loss of profits of $65 million. Suppose the likelihood of a disruption is 3% per year, and the beta associated with such a loss is −0.25. If the risk-free interest rate is 5% and the expected return of the market is 10%, what is the actuarially fair insurance premium?

2. Genentech's main facility is located in south San Francisco. Suppose that Genentech would experience a direct loss of $450 million in the event of a major earthquake that disrupted its operations. The chance of such an earthquake is 2% per year, with a beta of -0.5.

    a. If the risk-free interest rate is 5% and the expected return of the market is 10%, what is the actuarially fair insurance premium required to cover Genentech's loss?

    b. Suppose Genentech's insurance company raises the premium by an additional 15% over the amount calculated in part (a) to cover its administrative and overhead costs. What amount of financial distress or issuance costs would Genentech have to suffer if it were not insured to justify purchasing the insurance?

3. Your firm imports manufactured goods from China. You are worried that Canada-China trade negotiations could break down next year, leading to a moratorium on imports. In the event of a moratorium, your firm expects its operating profits to decline substantially and its marginal tax rate to fall from its current level of 40% to 10%.

    An insurance firm has agreed to write a trade insurance policy that will pay $500,000 in the event of an import moratorium. The chance of a moratorium is estimated to be 10%, with a beta equal to -1.5. Suppose the risk-free interest rate is 5% and the expected return of the market is 10%.

    a. What is the actuarially fair premium for this insurance?

    b. What is the *NPV* of purchasing this insurance for your firm? What is the source of this gain?

4. Your firm faces a 9% chance of a potential loss of $10 million next year. If your firm implements new policies, it can reduce the chance of this loss to 4%, but these new policies have an upfront cost of $100,000. Suppose the beta of the loss is 0, and the risk-free interest rate is 5%.

    a. If the firm is uninsured, what is the *NPV* of implementing the new policies?

    b. If the firm is fully insured, what is the *NPV* of implementing the new policies?

    c. Given your answer to part (b), what is the actuarially fair cost of full insurance?

    d. What is the minimum-size deductible that would leave your firm with an incentive to implement the new policies?

    e. What is the actuarially fair price of an insurance policy with the deductible in part (d)?

Commodity Price Risk

*5. BHP Billiton is the world's largest mining firm. BHP expects to produce 2 billion pounds of copper next year, with a production cost of $0.90 per pound.

    a. What will be BHP's operating profit from copper next year if the price of copper is $1.25, $1.50, or $1.75 per pound, and the firm plans to sell all of its copper next year at the going price?

    b. What will be BHP's operating profit from copper next year if the firm enters into a contract to supply copper to end users at an average price of $1.45 per pound?

    c. What will be BHP's operating profit from copper next year if copper prices are described as in part (a), and the firm enters into supply contracts as in part (b) for only 50% of its total output?

    d. Describe situations for which each of the strategies in parts (a), (b), and (c) might be optimal.

6. Your utility company will need to buy 100,000 barrels of oil in 10 days time, and it is worried about fuel costs. Suppose you go long on 100 oil futures contracts, each for 1000 barrels of oil, at the current futures price of $60 per barrel. Suppose futures prices change each day as follows:

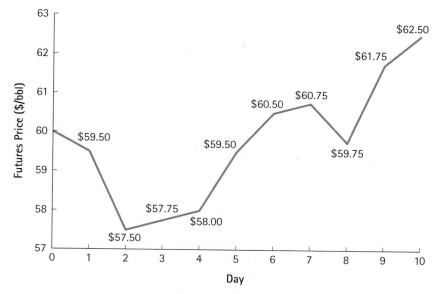

   a. What is the marking-to-market profit or loss (in dollars) that you will have on each date?
   b. What is your total profit or loss after 10 days? Have you been protected against a rise in oil prices?
   c. What is the largest cumulative loss you will experience over the 10-day period? In what case might this be a problem?

7. Suppose Starbucks consumes 100 million pounds of coffee beans per year. As the price of coffee rises, Starbucks expects to pass along 60% of the cost to its customers through higher prices per cup of coffee. To hedge its profits from fluctuations in coffee prices, Starbucks should lock in the price of how many pounds of coffee beans using supply contracts?

*8. It is April, and Hans Anderson is planting his barley crop near Plunkett, Saskatchewan. He is concerned about losing his farm if his operations result in a loss at the end of the season. He expects to harvest 3000 tonnes of barley and sell it in October. Futures contracts are available for October delivery with a futures price of $200 per tonne. Options with strike price of $200 per tonne are also available; puts cost $15 and calls cost $18.
   a. Describe how Hans can fully hedge using futures contracts.
   b. Given the strategy in (a), what will be the total net amount received by Hans (for all 3000 tonnes) if the price of barley in October is as follows:
      i. $150 per tonne
      ii. $200 per tonne
      iii. $250 per tonne
   c. Describe how Hans can fully hedge using options.
   d. Given the strategy in (c), what will be the total net amount received by Hans (for all 3000 tonnes) if the price of barley in October is as follows:
      i. $150 per tonne
      ii. $200 per tonne
      iii. $250 per tonne

e. Hans has asked for your advice regarding hedging. Discuss how the each of the following individually will influence your advice.
  i. Hans does not expect to have much cash available between May and September.
  ii. Hans thinks there is a 25% chance his crop will be destroyed by hail before he has a chance to harvest it.
  iii. Hans's farming business will go bankrupt if his net revenues in October do not cover his costs. He estimates his costs will be $570,000. If his business goes bankrupt, Hans's bank will foreclose and take his house and farm.
  iv. Hans's farming business will go bankrupt if his net revenues in October do not cover his costs. He estimates his costs will be $700,000. If his business goes bankrupt, Hans's bank will foreclose and take his house and farm.

*9. It is March, and Alberta Oil Refinery Ltd (AOR) has enough crude oil in inventory to continue refinery operations until September. AOR expects to need to purchase 500,000 barrels of oil in September. Management at AOR is concerned about oil price volatility. Futures contracts for September delivery are available with a futures price of $110 per barrel. Options contracts with a strike price of $110 and expiration in September are also available; puts cost $25 and calls cost $20.
  a. Describe how AOR can fully hedge using oil futures contracts.
  b. Given the strategy in (a), what will be the total net amount paid by AOR (for all 500,000 barrels) if the price of oil in September is as follows:
    i. $60 per barrel
    ii. $110 per barrel
    iii. $160 per barrel
  c. Describe how AOR can fully hedge using options.
  d. Given the strategy in (c), what will be the total net amount paid by AOR (for all 500,000 barrels) if the price of oil in September is as follows:
    i. $60 per barrel
    ii. $110 per barrel
    iii. $160 per barrel
  e. AOR has asked for your advice regarding hedging. Discuss how the each of the following individually will influence your advice.
    i. AOR does not expect to have much cash available between April and August.
    ii. AOR thinks that a drop in oil prices will occur if the economy goes into recession. There is a 33% chance this will happen. In a recession, demand for AOR's refined oil products will drop by half.
    iii. AOR will experience extreme financial distress costs if its net revenues in August do not cover the net costs of oil purchased then. AOR net revenues are estimated to be $60 million.
    iv. AOR will experience extreme financial distress costs if its net revenues in August do not cover the net costs of oil purchased then. AOR net revenues are estimated to be $50 million.
    v. AOR can pass along any price increases in oil by increasing the prices of its refined products.

Interest Rate Risk

*10. Assume each of the following securities has the same yield to maturity: a five-year zero-coupon bond; a nine-year zero-coupon bond; a five-year annuity; and a nine-year annuity. Rank these securities from lowest to highest duration.

*11. Your firm needs to raise $100 million in funds. You can borrow short term at a spread of 1.00% over LIBOR. Alternatively, you can issue 10-year fixed-rate bonds at a spread of 2.50% over 10-year treasuries, which currently yield 7.60%. Current 10-year interest rate swaps are quoted at LIBOR versus the 8.00% fixed rate.

   Management believes that the firm is currently "underrated" and that its credit rating is likely to improve in the next year or two. Nevertheless, the managers are not comfortable with the interest rate risk associated with using short-term debt.

   a. Suggest a strategy for borrowing the $100 million. What is your effective borrowing rate?

   b. Suppose the firm's credit rating does improve three years later. It can now borrow at a spread of 0.50% over treasuries, which now yield 9.10% for a seven-year maturity. Also, seven-year interest rate swaps are quoted at LIBOR versus 9.50%. How would you lock in your new credit quality for the next seven years? What is your effective borrowing rate now?

International Corporate Finance

notation

C_{FOC}	foreign currency cash flow	r_{wacc}	weighted average cost of capital
S	spot exchange rate	D	market value of debt
F	forward exchange rate	E	market value of equity
r^*_{HOC}	home currency cost of capital	r_E	required return on equity
r_{HOC}	home currency risk-free interest rate	r_D	required return on debt
r^*_{FOC}	foreign currency cost of capital	τ_c	corporate tax rate
r_{FOC}	foreign currency risk-free interest rate		

INTERVIEW WITH Dave Vogt,
Albert's Controls

University of Manitoba, 2011

Dave Vogt graduated from the University of Manitoba with a Bachelor of Commerce degree in 2011. He is now the general manager at Albert's Controls, a heating, ventilation, and air conditioning (HVAC) wholesaling company based in Winnipeg that imports and exports HVAC parts and systems all over the world. The company conducts many large transactions in foreign currencies. Dave is in charge of shipping, receiving, customs brokerage, and currency exchange. "We are an HVAC wholesaler, which requires us to deal with suppliers in many different countries. We have a large number of foreign exchange transactions every week."

Having to deal with different currencies exposes the firm to extra risk that is outside their main line of business, and Dave's finance education has been a big help to this small family firm. "The knowledge I've gained from my finance courses has given me a better understanding of the risks involved in international transactions, and how we can deal with those risks," Dave says.

"Currency fluctuations have a big impact on our input costs, so we need to be careful in hedging our currency risk," he continues. "We keep a close eye, in particular, on the movement of the Canadian dollar/U.S. dollar exchange rate." Dave's experience illustrates the benefit of learning basic finance skills, even for those who end up in non-finance occupations. "Sometimes, as a student, all you're thinking about is what's going to be on the next exam. But you never know what will come in handy when you enter the workforce."

"The knowledge I've gained from my finance courses has given me a better understanding of the risks involved in international transactions, and how we can deal with those risks."

In the 1990s, Starbucks Coffee Company identified Japan as a potentially lucrative new market for the company's coffee products and decided to invest as much as 10 million USD[1] in fiscal year 1996 to begin operations there. Because Starbucks realized it needed specialized knowledge of the Japanese market, it established a joint venture with Sazaby, Inc., a Japanese retailer and restaurateur. This venture, called Starbucks Coffee Japan Ltd., intended to open as many as 12 stores in this initial phase. Although stores opened more slowly than expected, the venture had more than 200 stores and sales of 29 billion JPY (252 million USD) by 2001, and it opened its 500th store in November 2003. To finance this growth, Starbucks Coffee Japan Ltd. used the Japanese capital markets. It held an initial public offering of shares on the Osaka Stock Exchange in October 2001 with a market capitalization of 90.88 billion JPY (756 million USD), raising 18.8 billion JPY (156 million USD) in additional capital for expansion. How did Starbucks' managers decide to undertake this investment opportunity? Why did they decide to use the Japanese domestic market to finance it rather than their home markets in the U.S.?

---

[1]We will use a three-letter currency code to indicate a country's currency; for example: CAD = Canadian dollar, USD = U.S. dollar, JPY = Japanese yen. Using the currency codes avoids the confusion caused by the fact that many countries use the same symbol for their currency (e.g., $ is used in Canada, Australia, the United States, and several other countries). For a list of countries, their three-letter currency codes, and their symbols, see the website maintained by Professor Werner Antweiler at the University of British Columbia's Sauder School of Business: http://fx.sauder.ubc.ca/currencies.html.

This chapter focuses on some of the special factors a firm faces when making a foreign investment. There are three key issues that arise when considering an investment in a foreign project such as Starbucks Coffee Japan Ltd.:

▶ The project will most likely generate foreign-currency cash flows, although the firm cares about the home-currency value of the project.

▶ Interest rates and costs of capital will likely be different in the foreign country as a result of the macroeconomic environment.

▶ The firm will probably face a different tax rate in the foreign country and will be subject to both foreign and domestic tax codes.

We begin this introduction to international finance with an overview of currency exchange rates and markets and the risk that comes from currency exchange rate fluctuations. From there, we extend the discussion of risk management in Chapter 21 to examine how a firm can manage currency exchange rate risk. Next, we discuss how a financial manager should evaluate foreign projects. We begin by examining *internationally integrated capital markets,* which provides a useful benchmark for comparing different methods of valuing a foreign project. We next explain how to value a foreign project and address the three key issues mentioned above. We then value foreign-currency cash flows using two valuation methodologies and consider the implications of foreign and domestic tax codes. Finally, we explore the implications of internationally segmented capital markets.

22.1 Currency Exchange Rates

Currency exchange rate The price of one country's currency in terms of another country's currency.

The price of one country's currency in terms of another country's currency is called a **currency exchange rate**. For example, if a Canadian is planning a trip to the United States and she decides to purchase some U.S. currency, she will have to exchange CAD for USD. Suppose the exchange rate is 0.9645 CAD/USD. That means that the price of 1 USD is 0.9645 CAD. If the Canadian traveller wanted to buy 1000 USD to take on the trip, she would have to pay 1000 USD × 0.9645 CAD/USD = 964.50 CAD. As travellers, we often exchange our currencies in our local bank or at a kiosk at an airport. These retail currency exchange providers make up a small portion what is called the foreign exchange market.

The Foreign Exchange Market

foreign exchange (FX or forex) market A market where currencies are traded that has no central physical location.

Imagine a market that is open 24 hours a day during the week, has no central physical location, and experiences *daily* turnover of over 3 trillion USD worth of currencies. The **foreign exchange (FX** or **forex) market**, where currencies are traded, is such a market. There are many reasons to trade currencies, but we will focus on those of a financial manager in a firm doing business in more than one country (a multinational firm). Consider Brookfield Asset Management Inc., headquartered in Toronto. It owns real estate, renewable-power plants, infrastructure, and other assets in 20 countries around the world. Thus, its revenues come in many different currencies. However, because it is a Canadian company, Brookfield's management will eventually want to exchange their profits in the various currencies back into Canadian dollars. In addition to its revenues, Brookfield has costs that are incurred in many currencies, even beyond the 20 countries where it operates; for example, other currencies may be used when Brookfield purchases power generation equipment from suppliers in countries where Brookfield does not have operations. Because of its multinational operations, Brookfield must regularly transact in the FX market. However, the FX market is not just important for large multinational enterprises. Many businesses import or export some of their products from abroad, and the FX market affects them too. Tourists need access to foreign currencies when they travel, so the value of the home currency in relation to other currencies may affect which vacation destination is chosen. Even purely domestic businesses need to be aware of FX markets, because as the value of the home currency appreciates or depreciates relative to other currencies, it affects potential competition from foreign firms.

The top 10 players in the FX market ranked in Euromoney's 2010 survey are Deutsche Bank, UBS, Barclays Capital, Citibank, Royal Bank of Scotland, JP Morgan, HSBC, Credit Suisse, Goldman Sachs, and Morgan Stanley. These banks' trading accounted for over 77% of FX trades; they trade on their own account and for client multinational firms. The Bank of Montreal was noted for its large jump in market share of FX trading, moving from 43rd place in 2009 to 30th place in 2010. Some large multinational firms trade for themselves. Other players in the market are government central banks, hedge funds and other investment managers, and retail brokers. Even though there are over 150 currencies in the world, just two of them, the U.S. dollar and the euro, account for more than half of all trading volume in the FX market. Figure 22.1 shows the 20 most traded currencies in 2010. Note that the total volume sums to 200%,

FIGURE 22.1   The Most Traded Currencies

Counting 100% of buying currencies and 100% of selling currencies, for a total of 200%, this table lists the top 20 traded currencies in 2010. Note that these 20 currencies accounted for more than 191% of the total of 200%. The USD, EUR, JPY, and GBP accounted for over 155% of the total of 200%.

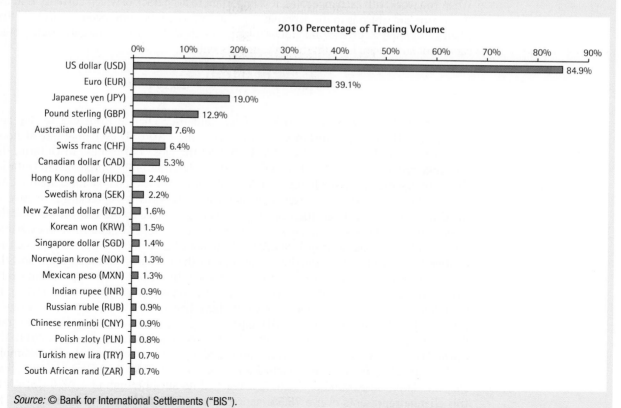

Source: © Bank for International Settlements ("BIS").

not 100%, because there is a currency on the buy and sell side of every transaction. To put these percentages in context, in April 2010, about 3.6 trillion USD of currencies were exchanged in various types of transactions.

Exchange Rates

Table 22.1 shows the foreign currency exchange rates as of noon, April 13, 2011, as reported by the Bank of Canada. These rates are all between a particular foreign currency and the Canadian dollar. For example, the first line indicates that one Argentine peso (ARS) can be purchased for 0.2310 CAD, or equivalently, 4.329 ARS buys 1 CAD. This is determined by calculating the inverse of the ARS/CAD exchange rate as follows:

1 ARS is worth 0.2310 CAD,

So the exchange rate is $\dfrac{0.2310\ \text{CAD}}{\text{ARS}}$

Taking the inverse, this is equivalent to $\dfrac{1\ \text{ARS}}{0.2310\ \text{CAD}} = \dfrac{4.329\ \text{ARS}}{\text{CAD}}$,

so 4.329 ARS buys 1 CAD

Thus, if we want to convert from 100 ARS to CAD, we multiply the number of ARS by the CAD/ARS exchange rate: 100 ARS × 0.2310 CAD/ARS = 23.10 CAD. Conversely, if we want to convert from 23.10 CAD to ARS, we multiply the number of CAD by the ARS/CAD exchange rate: 23.10 CAD × 4.329 ARS/CAD = 100 ARS. (Note that this is the same as dividing the number of CAD by the CAD/ARS exchange rate: 23.10 CAD ÷ 0.2310 CAD/ARS = 100 ARS. When you work with exchange rates, it is important to keep track of which currency is in the numerator and which is in the denominator. You can see in the conversions we just did that when we multiply a currency amount by the appropriate exchange rate, the old currency units cancel out and we are left with the new currency units:

$$100\ \cancel{\text{ARS}} \times \frac{0.2310\ \text{CAD}}{\cancel{\text{ARS}}} = 23.10\ \text{CAD}$$

Most exchange rates are market prices, and they change from day to day and even within the day. For instance, in Table 22.1, the CAD/USD exchange rate at noon on April 13, 2011, was 0.9640 CAD/USD, but by the close of business in Ontario, the exchange rate had dropped to 0.9624 CAD/USD, and as midnight approached in Ontario, the exchange rate had risen to 0.9627 CAD/USD. Since these exchange rates are the CAD price of 1.00 USD, when the exchange rate drops, the USD is depreciating relative to the CAD, and when it rises, the USD is appreciating relative to the CAD. If we took the inverse of each of these exchange rates, we would have USD/CAD, and such an exchange rate would tell us the value of 1.00 CAD in terms of USD. When the USD is depreciating relative to the CAD, as we saw by the change in the CAD/USD between noon and the close of business, the inverse exchange rates show that the CAD is appreciating relative to the USD. Looking at the inverse rates, at noon we would have had 1.0373 USD/CAD, and at the close of business we would have had 1.0391 USD/CAD; this change is consistent with the value of the CAD appreciating relative to the USD. Exchange rate fluctuations are not always so small like the fluctuations of rates on April 13, 2011. The USD/CAD rate has moved over a wide range and sometimes very quickly. For example, on January 21, 2002, the rate touched a record low of 0.6179 USD/CAD and, less than six years later, on November 7, 2007, it reached its all time high of 1.1030 USD/CAD; this change represents over a 78.5% appreciation of the CAD relative to the USD. The continual and sometimes large changes in exchange rates mean that just as it will be

TABLE 22.1	Foreign Currency	Number of Canadian Dollars to Buy One Unit of Foreign Currency
Canadian Dollar Daily Noon Currency Exchange Rates on April 13, 2011	Argentinian peso (floating rate)	0.2310
	Australian dollar	1.0126
	Bahamian dollar	0.9640
	Brazilian real	0.6052
	CFA (African Financial Community) franc	0.002127
	CFP (Pacific Financial Community) franc	0.01169
	Chilean peso	0.00204
	Chinese renminbi	0.1475
	Colombian peso	0.000531
	Croatian kuna	0.1895
	Czech Republic koruna	0.0573
	Danish krone	0.1871
	East Caribbean dollar	0.3610
	European euro	1.3955
	Fijian dollar	0.5419
	Ghanaian cedi (new)	0.6367
	Guatemalan quetzal	0.1232
	Honduran lempira	0.05102
	Hong Kong dollar	0.123974
	Hungarian forint	0.005228
	Icelandic krona	0.008538
	Indian rupee	0.02168
	Indonesian rupiah	0.000111
	Israeli new shekel	0.2824
	Jamaican dollar	0.0113
	Japanese yen	0.01153
	Malaysian ringgit	0.3188
	Mexican peso	0.08164
	Moroccan dirham	0.1231
	Myanmar (Burma) kyat	0.1811
	Netherlands Antilles guilder	0.5509
	New Zealand dollar	0.7614
	Norwegian krone	0.1771
	Pakistan rupee	0.01144
	Panamanian balboa	0.9640
	Peruvian new sol	0.3427
	Philippine peso	0.02229
	Polish zloty	0.3522
	Romanian new leu	0.3398

(Continued)

Foreign Currency	Number of Canadian Dollars to Buy One Unit of Foreign Currency
Russian ruble	0.03422
Serbian dinar	0.01376
Singapore dollar	0.7675
South African rand	0.1423
South Korean won	0.000887
Sri Lanka rupee	0.008732
Swedish krona	0.1542
Swiss franc	1.0782
Taiwanese new dollar	0.0332
Thai baht	0.03197
Trinidad & Tobago dollar	0.1511
Tunisian dinar	0.7045
Turkish new lira	0.6357
United Arab Emirates dirham	0.2625
U.K. pound sterling	1.5698
U.S. dollar	0.9640
Venezuelan bolivar fuerte	0.2245
Vietnamese dong	0.000046

The daily noon exchange rates for major foreign currencies are published every business day at about 12:30 p.m. EST. They are obtained from market or official sources around noon; various currencies in Canadian dollars are converted from U.S. dollar quotes of the exchange rates. The rates are nominal quotations—neither buying nor selling rates—and are intended for statistical or analytical purposes. Rates available from financial institutions will differ.

Source: Bank of Canada.

hard for you to plan your budget for your vacation abroad, companies doing business abroad face considerable risk from changes in exchange rates. We discuss those risks and how to mitigate them in the next section.

1. What is an exchange rate?

2. Why would multinational companies need to exchange currencies?

22.2   Exchange Rate Risk

Multinational firms face the risk of exchange rate fluctuations. In this section, we consider two strategies that firms use to hedge this risk: currency forward contracts and currency options.

Exchange Rate Fluctuations

floating rate An exchange rate that changes constantly depending on the supply and demand for each currency in the market.

Like most currencies, the CAD exchange rate with other currencies is a **floating rate**; this means CAD exchange rates change constantly depending on the quantity supplied and demanded for each currency in the market. The supply and demand for each currency is driven by three factors:

▶ *Firms trading goods:* A Canadian Audi dealer exchanges CAD for EUR to buy cars from the German automaker.

▶ *Investors trading securities:* A U.S. investor exchanges USD for CAD to buy shares in Canadian oil companies operating in the Alberta tar sands.

▶ *The actions of central banks in each country:* The Chinese government exchanges CNY for USD to purchase U.S. bonds to hold in China's official reserves in an effort to slow the appreciation of the CNY.

Because the supply and demand for currencies varies with global economic conditions, exchange rates are volatile. Figure 22.2 shows the CAD price of USD from January 1, 2001, through April 13, 2011. Notice that the price of the USD often varies by as much as 10% over periods as short as a few months. From 2002 to 2007, the value of the USD dropped more than 40% relative to the CAD.

Fluctuating exchanges rates cause a problem known as the *importer-exporter dilemma* for firms doing business in international markets. This is particularly important to Canada-U.S. trade, as our two countries are each other's biggest trading partners. To illustrate, consider the problem faced by Modern Bathrooms, a bathroom renovation company. Modern Bathrooms needs to import steam generators from a U.S. supplier, ThermaSol, so it can install steam rooms in customers' homes. If ThermaSol sets the price of its parts in USD, then Modern Bathrooms faces the risk that the CAD may fall, making the USD, and therefore the steam generators, more expensive. If ThermaSol sets its prices in CAD for its Canadian customers, then ThermaSol faces the risk that the CAD may fall and it will receive fewer USD for the steam generators it sells to Canadians.

FIGURE 22.2　　CAD/USD Noon Exchange Rates from January 1, 2001, to April 13, 2011

The exchange rates show the cost of 1 USD in terms of CAD. Note, on January 21, 2002, it took over 1.6183 CAD to buy 1 USD due to the depressed value of the CAD. On November 7, 2007, the CAD reached its most valuable point relative to the USD and it only took 0.9066 CAD to buy 1 USD.

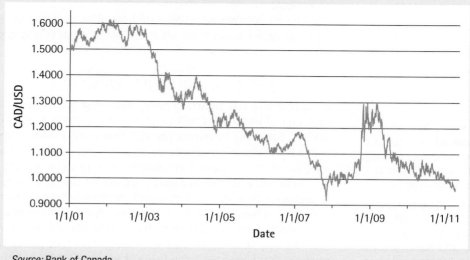

Source: Bank of Canada.

The problem of exchange rate risk is a general problem in any import-export relationship. If neither company will accept the exchange rate risk, the transaction may be difficult or impossible to negotiate. Example 22.1 demonstrates the potential magnitude of the problem.

EXAMPLE 22.1

The Effect of Exchange Rate Risk

Problem

In March 2009, Whole Foods Market in the United States ordered its 2010 shipment of shampoos from Avalon Natural Products' Canadian manufacturing facility when the exchange rate was 1.3000 CAD per USD. They agreed to a price of 520,000 CAD, to be paid when the shampoos were delivered in one year's time. One year later, the exchange rate was 1.0251 CAD per USD. What was the actual cost in USD for Whole Foods Market when the payment was due? If the price had instead been set at 400,000 USD (which had equivalent value at the time of the agreement), how many CAD would Avalon have received?

Solution

▶ **Plan**

The price is set in CAD, 520,000, but the CAD/USD exchange rate will fluctuate over time, and the problem asks us to consider what would happen if it goes to 1.0251 CAD/USD, which means that USD are worth less (it takes more USD to buy one CAD).

We can always convert between CAD and USD at the going exchange rate by multiplying the CAD/USD exchange rate by the number of USD or by dividing the number of CAD by the CAD/USD exchange rate.

▶ **Execute**

With the price set at 520,000 CAD, Whole Foods Market had to pay 520,000 CAD ÷ 1.0251 CAD/USD = 507,267.58 USD. This cost is 107,267.58 USD, or 26.8% higher than it would have been if the price had been set in USD (400,000 USD, given the original exchange rate of 1.3000 CAD/USD).

If the price had been set in USD, Whole Foods Market would not have had any exchange rate risk. However, from Avalon's point of view, given the original exchange rate of 1.3000 CAD/USD, Whole Foods Market would have paid 400,000 USD, which would have been worth only 400,000 USD × (1.0251 CAD/USD) = 410,040 CAD to Avalon at the actual time of payment. This is more than 21% less than if the price was set at 520,000 CAD.

▶ **Evaluate**

Whether the price was set in CAD or USD, one of the parties would have suffered a substantial loss. Because neither knows which will suffer the loss ahead of time, each has an incentive to hedge.

Hedging with Forward Contracts

Exchange rate risk naturally arises whenever transacting parties use different currencies: one of the parties will be at risk if exchange rates fluctuate. The most common method firms use to reduce the risk that results from changes in exchange rates is to hedge the transaction using *currency forward contracts*. These are special cases of forward contracts (discussed in Chapter 21) applied to currency exchange rates.

currency forward contract A contract that sets a currency exchange rate and an amount to exchange in advance.

forward exchange rate The exchange rate set in a currency forward contract that applies to an exchange that will occur in the future.

A **currency forward contract** is a contract that sets the exchange rate and an amount to exchange in advance. It is usually written between a firm and a bank, and it fixes a currency exchange rate for a transaction that will occur at a future date. A currency forward contract specifies (1) an exchange rate, (2) an amount of currency to exchange, and (3) a delivery date on which the exchange will take place. The exchange rate set in the contract is referred to as the **forward exchange rate**, because it applies to an exchange that will occur in the future. By entering into a currency forward contract, a firm can lock in an exchange rate in advance and reduce or eliminate its exposure to fluctuations in a currency's value.

If the forward contract allows the importer to eliminate the risk of a stronger CAD, where does the risk go? At least initially, the risk passes to the bank that has written the forward contract. Because the bank agrees to exchange CAD for USD at a fixed rate, it will experience a loss if the CAD increases in value. In Example 22.2, the bank receives only 393,900 USD in the forward contract but gives up CAD that are worth 507,267.58 USD.

EXAMPLE 22.2

Using a Forward Contract to Lock in an Exchange Rate

Problem

In March 2009, banks were offering one-year currency forward contracts with a forward exchange rate of 0.7575 USD/CAD. Suppose that at that time, Whole Foods Market placed the order with Avalon's Canadian manufacturing facility with a price of 520,000 CAD and simultaneously entered into a forward contract to purchase 520,000 CAD at a forward exchange rate of 0.7575 USD/CAD in one year. What payment would Whole Foods Market be required to make when the shampoo shipment took place in 2010?

Solution

▶ **Plan**

If Whole Foods Market enters into a forward contract locking in an exchange rate of 0.7575 USD/CAD, then it doesn't matter what the actual exchange rate is in March 2010—Whole Foods Market will be able to buy 520,000 CAD for 0.7575 USD/CAD.

▶ **Execute**

Even though the CAD appreciated by March 2010, making the CAD more expensive, Whole Foods Market would obtain the 520,000 CAD using the forward contract at the forward exchange rate of 0.7575 USD/CAD. Thus, in March 2010, Whole Foods must pay

$$520{,}000 \text{ CAD} \times 0.7575 \text{ USD/CAD} = 393{,}900 \text{ USD.}$$

Whole Foods Market would pay this amount to the bank in exchange for 520,000 CAD, which is then paid to Avalon.

▶ **Evaluate**

This forward contract would have been a good deal for Whole Foods Market, because without the hedge, the company would have had to exchange USD for CAD at the prevailing exchange rate. In Example 22.1, we saw that the prevailing exchange rate in March 2010 was 1.0251 CAD/USD (or approximately 0.9755 USD/CAD), and this would have resulted in Whole Foods Market paying 507,267.58 USD for the CAD funds. However, the exchange rate could have moved the other way. If the exchange rate had fallen to 0.7000 USD/CAD, the forward contract still commits Whole Foods to pay 0.7575 USD/CAD. In other words, the forward contract locks in the exchange rate and eliminates the risk—whether the movement of the exchange rate is favourable or unfavourable.

Why is the bank willing to bear this risk? First, the bank is much larger and has more capital than a small importer, so it can bear the risk without being in jeopardy of financial distress. More importantly, in most settings the bank will not even hold the risk. Instead, the bank will find another party willing to trade CAD for USD (such as a Canadian company that imports from the United States). By entering into a second forward contract with offsetting risk, the bank can eliminate its risk altogether.

This situation is illustrated in Figure 22.3. A U.S. importer, who must pay for goods with CAD, purchases CAD from the bank through a forward contract with a forward exchange rate of 0.7575 USD per CAD. This transaction locks in the U.S. importer's cost

FIGURE 22.3

The Use of Currency Forwards to Eliminate Exchange Rate Risk

In this example, the Canadian importer and the U.S. importer both hedge their exchange rate risk by using currency forward contracts at 0.7575 USD/CAD (shown in red). By writing offsetting contracts, the bank bears no exchange rate risk and earns a fee from each transaction.

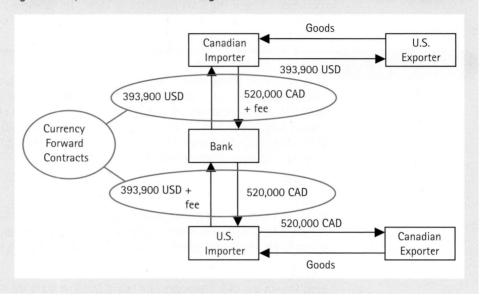

at 393,900 USD. Similarly, a Canadian importer, who must pay for goods in USD, uses a forward contract to sell the CAD to the bank, locking in the Canadian importer's cost at 520,000 CAD. The bank holds both forward contracts—the first to exchange USD for CAD and the second to exchange CAD for USD. The bank bears no exchange rate risk and earns fees from both the U.S. and Canadian importers. Most of the large Canadian banks offer services in both Canada and the United States, so they are able to accommodate clients (such as these importers) in both countries.

Cash-and-Carry and the Pricing of Currency Forwards

An alternative method, the *cash-and-carry strategy*, also enables a firm to eliminate exchange rate risk. Because this strategy provides the same cash flows as the forward contract, we can use it to determine the forward exchange rate using the Law of One Price. Let's begin by considering the different ways investors can exchange foreign currency in the future for dollars in the future.

currency timeline
A diagram that indicates time horizontally by dates (as in a standard timeline) and currencies (as in dollars and euros) vertically.

Currency Timeline. Currency forward contracts allow investors to exchange a foreign currency in the future for dollars in the future at the forward exchange rate. We illustrate such an exchange in the **currency timeline** in Figure 22.4, which indicates time horizontally by dates (as in a standard timeline) and currencies vertically (CAD and USD). Thus "CAD in one year" corresponds to the upper-right point in the timeline, and "USD in one year" corresponds to the lower-right point in the timeline. To convert cash flows between points, we must convert them at an appropriate rate. The forward exchange rate, indicated by $F_{USD/CAD}$, tells us the rate at which we can exchange CAD for USD in one year using a forward contract.

spot exchange rate
The current foreign exchange rate.

Figure 22.4 also illustrates other transactions that we can use to move between dates or currencies in the timeline. We can convert CAD to USD today at the current exchange rate, also referred to as the **spot exchange rate**, $S_{USD/CAD}$. By borrowing or lending at the CAD interest rate r_{CAD}, we can exchange CAD today for CAD in one year. Finally, we can convert USD today for USD in one year at the USD interest rate r_{USD}, which is the rate at which banks will borrow or lend on USD-denominated accounts.

Cash-and-Carry Strategy. As Figure 22.4 shows, combining these other transactions provides an alternative way to convert CAD to USD in one year. The **cash-and-carry strategy** consists of the following three simultaneous trades:

1. Borrow CAD today using a one-year loan with the interest rate r_{CAD}.
2. Exchange the CAD for USD today at the spot exchange rate $S_{USD/CAD}$.
3. Invest the USD today for one year at the interest rate r_{USD}.

In one year's time, we will owe CAD (from the loan in transaction 1) and receive USD (from the investment in transaction 3). That is, we have converted CAD in one year to USD in one year, just as with the forward contract. This method is called a cash-and-carry strategy because we borrow cash that we then carry (invest) in the future.

Covered Interest Parity. Because the forward contract and the cash-and-carry strategy accomplish the same conversion, by the Law of One Price they must do so at the same rate. Equation 22.1 expresses the forward exchange rate in terms of the spot exchange rate and the interest rates in each currency. Note that on both sides of the equation, the ultimate units are USD/CAD in one year.

$$\underbrace{\text{Forward Rate}}_{\substack{\text{USD in one year} \\ \text{CAD in one year}}} = \underbrace{\text{Spot Rate}}_{\substack{\text{USD today} \\ \text{CAD today}}} \times \underbrace{\frac{1 + r_{USD}}{1 + r_{CAD}}}_{\substack{\text{USD in one year/USD today} \\ \text{CAD in one year/CAD today}}} \tag{22.1}$$

Let's evaluate Equation. 22.1 in light of our assumptions in Examples 22.1 and 22.2. In March 2009, the spot exchange rate was 1.3000 CAD/USD (which is about 0.76923 USD/CAD), and let's suppose one-year interest rates were 1.42925% for USD and 3.00%

cash-and-carry strategy
A strategy used to lock in the future cost of an asset by buying the asset for cash today and storing (or "carrying") it until a future date.

FIGURE 22.4　　Currency Timeline Showing Forward Contract and Cash-and-Carry Strategy

The cash-and-carry strategy (three transactions in red) replicates the forward contract (in blue) by borrowing in one currency, converting to the other currency at the spot exchange rate, and investing in the new currency.

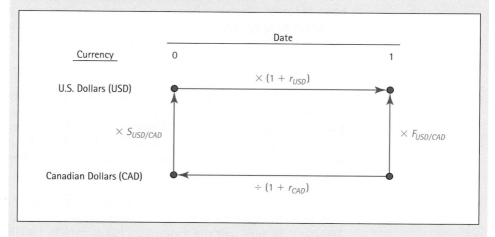

for CAD. From Equation 22.1, the no-arbitrage forward exchange rate in at that time for an exchange to take place one year later was

$$F = S \times \frac{1 + r_{USD}}{1 + r_{CAD}} = \frac{0.76923\ \text{USD}}{\text{CAD}} \times \frac{1.0142925}{1.03} = \frac{0.7575\ \text{USD}}{\text{CAD}}$$

which is the rate offered by the bank in Example 22.2.

Covered interest parity equation The equation stating that the difference between the forward and spot exchange rates is related to the interest rate differential between the currencies.

Equation 22.1 is referred to as the **covered interest parity equation**; it states that the difference between the forward and spot exchange rates is related to the interest rate differential between the currencies. When the interest rate differs across countries, investors have an incentive to borrow in the low-interest rate currency and invest in the high-interest rate currency. Of course, there is always the risk that the high-interest rate currency could depreciate while the investment is held. Suppose you try to avoid this risk by locking in the future exchange rate using a forward contract. Equation 22.1 implies that the forward exchange rate will exactly offset any benefit from the higher interest rate, eliminating any arbitrage opportunity.

Equation 22.1 easily generalizes to a forward contract over any time period. Using the same logic, but investing or borrowing for T years rather than one year, the no-arbitrage forward rate for an exchange that will occur T years in the future is:

$$\underbrace{\text{Forward Rate}_T}_{\displaystyle \frac{\text{USD in } T \text{ years}}{\text{CAD in } T \text{ years}}} = \underbrace{\text{Spot Rate}}_{\displaystyle \frac{\text{USD today}}{\text{CAD today}}} \times \underbrace{\frac{(1 + r_{USD})^T}{(1 + r_{CAD})^T}}_{\displaystyle \frac{\text{USD in } T \text{ years/USD today}}{\text{CAD in } T \text{ years/CAD today}}} \quad (22.2)$$

In this equation, the spot and forward rates are in units of USD/CAD, and the interest rates are the current risk-free T-year rates from the yield curve for each currency. (A useful rule to remember is that the ratio of interest rates must match the units of the exchange rate. Because the exchange rate is USD/CAD, we multiply by the USD interest rate and divide by the CAD interest rate. We could also solve the problem by converting all the rates to CAD/USD.)

Advantages of Forward Contracts. Why do firms use forward contracts rather than the cash-and-carry strategy? First, the forward contract is simpler, requiring one transaction rather than three, so it may have lower transaction fees. Second, many firms are not able to borrow easily in different currencies and may pay a higher interest rate if their credit quality is poor. Generally speaking, cash-and-carry strategies are used primarily by large banks, which can borrow easily and face low transaction costs. Banks use such a strategy to hedge their currency exposures that result from commitments to forward contracts.

Hedging Exchange Rate Risk with Options

Currency options are another method that firms commonly use to manage exchange rate risk. Currency options, as with the stock options introduced in Chapter 20, give the holder the right—but not the obligation—to exchange currency at a given exchange rate. Currency forward contracts allow firms to lock in a future exchange rate; currency options allow firms to insure themselves against the exchange rate moving beyond a certain level.

Forward Contracts Versus Options. To demonstrate the difference between hedging with forward contracts and hedging with options, let's examine a specific situation. Assume it is April and the forward exchange rate is 1.0380 USD/CAD for September

TABLE 22.2 Net Cost of CAD (USD/CAD) When Hedging with a Currency Call Option with a Strike Price of 1.0350 USD/CAD and an Initial Premium of 0.0255 USD/CAD

September Spot Exchange Rate	Exercise Call Option?	Exchange Rate Taken	+	Cost of Option	=	Total
0.9500	No	0.9500		0.0255		0.9755
1.0000	No	1.0000		0.0255		1.0255
1.0500	Yes	1.0350		0.0255		1.0605
1.1000	Yes	1.0350		0.0255		1.0605

delivery. Instead of locking in this exchange rate using a forward contract, a U.S. firm that will need CAD in September can buy a call option on the CAD, giving it the right to buy CAD at a maximum price.[2] Suppose a call option on the CAD with a September expiration and strike price of 1.0350 USD/CAD trades for 0.0255 USD (per call on 1 CAD). That is, for a cost of 0.0255 USD, the firm can buy the right—but not the obligation—to purchase 1 CAD for 1.0350 USD/CAD in September. By doing so, the firm protects itself against a large increase in the value of the CAD but still benefits if the CAD declines.

Table 22.2 shows the outcome from hedging with a call option if the actual exchange rate in September is one of the values listed in the first column. If the spot exchange rate is less than the 1.0350 USD/CAD strike price of the option, then the firm will not exercise the call option and will convert USD to CAD at the spot exchange rate. If the spot exchange rate is more than 1.0350 USD/CAD, the firm will exercise the call option and convert USD to CAD at the rate of 1.0350 USD/CAD (see the second and third columns). We then add the initial cost of the call option (fourth column) to determine the total USD cost per CAD paid by the firm (fifth column).[3]

The data from Table 22.2 is plotted in Figure 22.5, where we compare hedging with options to the alternative of hedging with a forward contract or not hedging at all. If the firm does not hedge at all, its cost for CAD is simply the spot exchange rate. If the firm hedges with a forward contract, it locks in the cost of CAD at the forward exchange rate and the firm's cost is fixed. As Figure 22.5 shows, hedging with options represents a middle ground: the firm puts a *cap* on its potential cost but will benefit if the CAD depreciates in value.

Advantages of Options. Why might a firm choose to hedge with options rather than forward contracts? Many managers want the firm to benefit if the exchange rate moves in its favour, rather than being stuck paying an above-market rate. Firms also prefer options to forward contracts if the transaction they are hedging might not take place. In this case, a forward contract could commit them to making an exchange at an unfavourable rate for currency they do not need, whereas an option allows them to walk away from the exchange. In any case, it is worth noting that an option holder can always sell the position at a gain rather than demanding delivery of the currency, so if the transaction does not take place and the option is in-the-money, the company need not actually demand delivery of the foreign currency.

[2]Currency options can be purchased over the counter from a bank or on an exchange. The CME Group is one exchange offering currency options.

[3]In computing the total cost, we have ignored the small amount of interest that could have been earned on the option premium.

FIGURE 22.5   Comparison of Hedging the Exchange Rate Using a Forward Contract, a Call Option, or No Hedge

The forward hedge locks in an exchange rate and so eliminates all risk. Not hedging leaves the firm fully exposed. Hedging with a call option allows the firm to benefit if the exchange rate falls and protects the firm from a very large increase.

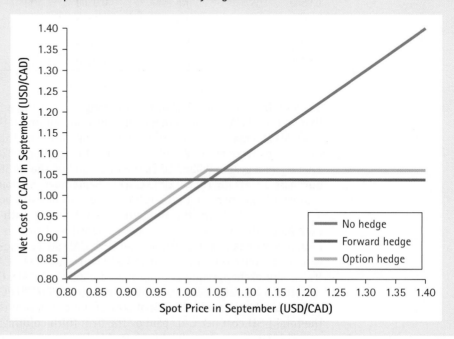

Concept Check

3. How can firms hedge exchange rate risk?
4. Why might a firm prefer to hedge exchange rate risk with options rather than forward contracts?

22.3 Internationally Integrated Capital Markets

Does the value of a foreign investment depend on the currency we use in the analysis? To address this important question, we will develop a conceptual benchmark based on the assumptions that any investor can exchange either currency in any amount at the spot rate or forward rates, and is free to purchase or sell any security in any amount in either country at their current market prices. Under these conditions, which we term **internationally integrated capital markets**, the value of an investment does *not* depend on the currency we use in the analysis.

Consider a risky foreign asset that is expected to pay the cash flow, C_{FOC}, in one period.[4] In a normal market, the price of this asset in a foreign market is the present value of this cash flow using the cost of capital of a investor local to that market:

$$PV_{FOC} = \frac{C_{FOC}}{(1 + r^*_{FOC})} \qquad (22.3)$$

internationally integrated capital markets Markets in which any investor can exchange currencies in any amount at the spot or forward rates and is free to purchase or sell any security in any amount in any country at its current market prices.

---

[4]*FOC* is the hypothetical code for the foreign currency.

A Canadian investor who wants to purchase this asset in CAD will have to pay

$$PV_{CAD} = S \times \frac{C_{FOC}}{(1 + r^*_{FOC})} \tag{22.4}$$

where S is the current spot exchange rate in CAD per FOC (foreign currency). Now any Canadian investor who actually purchased this security would have to convert the future cash flow into CAD, so the payoff to such an investor is the CAD cash flow it produces. To value this cash flow, assume that the Canadian investor contracts today to convert the *expected* cash flow in one period at the forward rate, F, quoted as CAD per FOC. If we assume that spot exchange rates and the foreign currency cash flows of the security are uncorrelated, then this Canadian investor's expected CAD cash flow is $F \times C_{FOC}$.[5] If r^*_{CAD} is the appropriate cost of capital from the standpoint of a Canadian investor, the present value of this expected cash flow is

$$PV_{CAD} = \frac{F \times C_{FOC}}{(1 + r^*_{CAD})} \tag{22.5}$$

By the Law of One Price, this value must be equal to what the Canadian investor paid for the security:

$$S \times \frac{C_{FOC}}{(1 + r^*_{FOC})} = \frac{F \times C_{FOC}}{(1 + r^*_{CAD})}$$

Rearranging terms gives

$$\underset{CAD/FOC}{F} = \underset{CAD/FOC}{S} \times \frac{(1 + r^*_{CAD})}{(1 + r^*_{FOC})} \tag{22.6}$$

This condition ought to look familiar, because Equation 22.6 is simply covered interest parity (Equation 22.1), here derived for risky cash flows rather than riskless cash flows.

EXAMPLE 22.3

Present Values and Internationally Integrated Capital Markets

Problem

You are a Canadian who is trying to calculate the present value of a 10 million JPY cash flow that will occur one year in the future. You know that the spot exchange rate is $S = 110$ JPY/CAD and the one-year forward rate is $F = 105.8095$ JPY/CAD. You also know that the appropriate CAD cost of capital for this cash flow is $r^*_{CAD} = 5\%$ and that the appropriate JPY cost of capital for this cash flow is $r^*_{JPY} = 1\%$. What is the present value of the 10 million JPY cash flow from the standpoint of a Japanese investor, and what is the CAD equivalent of this amount? What is the present value of the 10 million JPY cash flow from the standpoint of a Canadian investor who first converts the 10 million JPY into CAD and then applies the CAD discount rate?

Solution

▶ **Plan**

For the Japanese investor, we can compute the present value of the future JPY cash flow at the JPY discount rate and use the spot exchange rate to convert that amount to CAD.

---

[5] The actual cash flow in foreign currency will be $C_{FOC} + \varepsilon$ where ε is the uncertainty in the cash flow and has an expected value of zero. In CAD terms, this cash flow is $F \times C_{FOC} + S_1 \times \varepsilon$ because the forward contract is only for the amount C_{FOC}; the rest must be converted at the prevailing spot rate in one period, S_1. Taking expectations, $E[S_1 \times \varepsilon] = E[S_1] \times E[\varepsilon] = 0$ because spot rates are uncorrelated with the project cash flows and $E[\varepsilon] = 0$.

For the Canadian investor, we can convert the future JPY cash flow to CAD at the forward rate and compute the present value using the CAD discount rate.

▶ **Execute**

For the Japanese investor, the CAD present value of the JPY cash flow is:

$$10{,}000{,}000 \text{ JPY}/(1.01) = 9{,}900{,}990 \text{ JPY}$$

and the CAD equivalent is

$$9{,}900{,}990/110 = 90{,}009 \text{ CAD}$$

(Note that we adjusted the formula in Equation 22.4 because the exchange rate is expressed as JPY per CAD rather than CAD per JPY.)

The present value from the standpoint of a Canadian investor who first converts the 10 million JPY into CAD using the forward rate and then applies the CAD cost of capital is:

$$(10{,}000{,}000 \text{ JPY}/105.8095)/1.05 = 90{,}009 \text{ CAD}$$

(Again, we have adjusted the formula in Equation 22.5 because the exchange rate is expressed as JPY per CAD.[6])

▶ **Evaluate**

Because the Canadian and Japanese capital markets are internationally integrated, both methods produce the same result.

Concept Check

5. What assumptions are needed to have internationally integrated capital markets?

6. What implication do internationally integrated capital markets have for the value of the same asset in different countries?

22.4 Valuation of Foreign Currency Cash Flows

The most obvious difference between a domestic project and a foreign project is that the foreign project will most likely generate cash flows in a foreign currency. If the foreign project is owned by a domestic corporation, managers and shareholders need to determine the home currency value of the foreign currency cash flows.

In an internationally integrated capital market, two equivalent methods are available for calculating the *NPV* of a foreign project:

1. Calculate the *NPV* in the foreign country and convert it to the home currency at the spot rate.

2. Convert the cash flows of the foreign project into the home currency and then calculate the *NPV* of these cash flows.

---

[6]It is best to always write down the cash flows along with their currency signs so that you can keep track of them. Then by crossing out currency signs as you go, you can be sure that you will be left with an answer in the correct currency.

The first method is essentially what we have done throughout this book (calculating the *NPV* of a project in a single currency) with the added step at the end of converting the *NPV* into the home currency using spot rates. Because this method should be familiar to you at this stage, we will concentrate on the second method. The second valuation method requires converting to the expected CAD value of the foreign currency cash flows and then proceeding to value the project as if it were a domestic project.

Application: Ityesi, Inc.

Ityesi, Inc., a manufacturer of custom packaging products headquartered in Canada, wants to apply the weighted average cost of capital (WACC) technique to value a project in the United Kingdom. Ityesi is considering introducing a new line of packaging in the United Kingdom that will be the company's first foreign project. The project will be completely self-contained in the United Kingdom, such that all revenues are generated and all costs are incurred there.

Engineers expect the technology used in the new products to be obsolete after four years. The marketing group expects annual sales of 37.5 million GBP per year for this product line. Manufacturing costs and operating expenses are expected to total 15.625 million GBP and 5.625 million GBP per year, respectively. Developing the product will require an upfront investment of 15 million GBP in capital equipment that will be obsolete in four years and an initial marketing expense of 4.167 million GBP. Ityesi pays a corporate tax rate of 40% no matter in which country it manufactures its products. The expected GBP free cash flows of the proposed project are projected in Table 22.3.

Ityesi's managers have determined that there is no correlation between the uncertainty in these cash flows and the uncertainty in the spot CAD/GBP exchange rate. As we explained in the last section, under this condition, the expected value of the future cash flows in CAD is the expected value in GBP multiplied by the forward exchange rate. Obtaining forward rate quotes for as long as four years in the future is difficult, so Ityesi's managers have decided to use the covered interest rate parity formula (the generalized version shown in Equation 22.2) to compute the forward rates.

TABLE 22.3	Year	0	1	2	3	4
Expected Foreign Free Cash Flows from Ityesi's U.K. Project	Incremental Earnings Forecast (million GBP)					
	1 Sales	—	37.500	37.500	37.500	37.500
	2 Cost of Goods Sold	—	(15.625)	(15.625)	(15.625)	(15.625)
	3 **Gross Profit**	—	21.875	21.875	21.875	21.875
	4 Operating Expenses	(4.167)	(5.625)	(5.625)	(5.625)	(5.625)
	5 Depreciation	—	(3.750)	(3.750)	(3.750)	(3.750)
	6 *EBIT*	(4.167)	(12.500)	(12.500)	(12.500)	(12.500)
	7 Income tax at 40%	1.667	(5.000)	(5.000)	(5.000)	(5.000)
	8 **Unlevered Net Income**	(2.500)	7.500	7.500	7.500	7.500
	Free Cash Flow					
	9 Plus: Depreciation	—	3.750	3.750	3.750	3.750
	10 Less: Capital Expenditures	(15.000)	—	—	—	—
	11 Less: Increases in *NWC*	—	—	—	—	—
	12 **GBP Free Cash Flow**	(17.500)	11.250	11.250	11.250	11.250

TABLE 22.4		0	1	2	3	4
	CAD Free Cash Flow (million CAD)					
Expected CAD Free Cash Flows from Ityesi's U.K. Project	1 GBP Free Cash Flow (million GBP)	(17.500)	11.250	11.250	11.250	11.250
	2 Forward Exchange Rate (CAD/GBP)	2.0000	1.9439	1.8894	1.8364	1.7850
	3 CAD Value of GBP Free Cash Flow	(35.000)	21.869	21.256	20.660	20.081

Forward Exchange Rates. The current spot exchange rate, S, is 2.00 CAD/GBP. Suppose that the yield curve in both countries is flat: the risk-free rate on CAD, r_{CAD}, is 4%, and the risk-free interest rate on pounds, r_{GBP}, is 7%. Using the covered interest parity condition for a multiyear forward exchange rate (Equation 22.2), we have:

$$F_1 = S \times \frac{(1 + r_{CAD})}{(1 + r_{GBP})} = (2.00 \text{ CAD/GBP})\frac{(1.04)}{(1.07)} = 1.9439 \text{ CAD/GBP}$$

$$F_2 = S \times \frac{(1 + r_{CAD})^2}{(1 + r_{GBP})^2} = (2.00 \text{ CAD/GBP})\frac{(1.04)^2}{(1.07)^2} = 1.8894 \text{ CAD/GBP}$$

$$F_3 = S \times \frac{(1 + r_{CAD})^3}{(1 + r_{GBP})^3} = (2.00 \text{ CAD/GBP})\frac{(1.04)^3}{(1.07)^3} = 1.8364 \text{ CAD/GBP}$$

$$F_4 = S \times \frac{(1 + r_{CAD})^4}{(1 + r_{GBP})^4} = (2.00 \text{ CAD/GBP})\frac{(1.04)^4}{(1.07)^4} = 1.7850 \text{ CAD/GBP}$$

Free Cash Flow Conversion. Using these forward exchange rates, we can now calculate the expected free cash flows in CAD by multiplying the expected cash flows in GBP by the forward exchange rate, as shown in Table 22.4.

The Value of Ityesi's Foreign Project with WACC. With the cash flows of the U.K. project now expressed in CAD, we can value the foreign project as if it were a domestic CAD project. We proceed, as we did in Chapter 12, under the assumption that the market risk of the U.K. project is similar to that of the company as a whole; as a consequence, we can use Ityesi's costs of equity and debt in Canada to calculate the WACC.[7]

Ityesi has built up 20 million CAD in cash for investment needs and has debt of 320 million CAD, so its net debt is $D = 320 - 20 = 300$ million CAD. This amount is equal to the market value of its equity, implying a (net) debt-equity ratio of 1. Ityesi intends to maintain a similar (net) debt-equity ratio for the foreseeable future. The WACC thus assigns equal weights to equity and debt, as shown in Table 22.5.

With Ityesi's cost of equity at 10% and its cost of debt at 6%, we calculate Ityesi's WACC as follows:

$$r_{wacc} = \frac{E}{E + D}r_E + \frac{D}{E + D}r_D(1 - T_C)$$

$$= (0.5)(10.0\%) + (0.5)(6.0\%)(1 - 40\%) = 6.8\%$$

---

[7]The risk of the foreign project is unlikely to be *exactly* the same as the risk of domestic projects (or the firm as a whole), because the foreign project contains residual exchange rate risk that the domestic projects often do not contain (e.g., political or macroeconomic risks specific to the foreign country). In Ityesi's case, managers have determined that the additional risk premium for this risk is small, so for practical purposes they have chosen to ignore it and just use the domestic cost of capital.

| TABLE 22.5 | Ityesi's Current Market Value Balance Sheet (million CAD) and Cost of Capital Without the U.K. Project |

Assets		Liabilities		Cost of Capital	
Cash	20	Debt	320	Debt	6%
Existing	600	Equity	300	Equity	10%
Assets	620		620		

We can now determine the value of the foreign project, including the tax shield from debt, by calculating the present value of the future free cash flows using the WACC:

$$\frac{21.869}{1.068} + \frac{21.256}{1.068^2} + \frac{20.660}{1.068^3} + \frac{20.081}{1.068^4} = 71.506 \text{ million CAD}$$

Because the upfront cost of launching the product line in dollars is only 35 million CAD, the net present value is $71.506 - 35 = 36.506$ million CAD. Thus Ityesi should undertake the U.K. project.

The Law of One Price as a Robustness Check

To arrive at the *NPV* of Ityesi's project required making a number of assumptions—for example, that international markets are integrated, and that the exchange rate and the cash flows of the project are uncorrelated. The managers of Ityesi will naturally worry about whether these assumptions are justified. Luckily, there is a way to check the analysis.

Recall that there are two ways to compute the *NPV* of the foreign project. Ityesi could just as easily have computed the foreign *NPV* by discounting the foreign cash flows at the foreign cost of capital and converting this result to a domestic *NPV* using the spot rate. Except for the last step, this method requires doing the same calculation we have performed throughout this book—that is, calculate the *NPV* of a (domestic) project. Determining the *NPV* requires knowing the cost of capital—in this case, the cost of capital for an investment in the United Kingdom. Recall that to estimate this cost of capital we use return data for publicly traded single-product companies—in this case, U.K. firms. For this method to provide the same answer as the alternative method, the estimate for the foreign cost of capital, r^*_{GBP}, must satisfy the Law of One Price, which from Equation 22.6 implies:

$$(1 + r^*_{GBP}) = \frac{S}{F} \times (1 + r^*_{CAD}) \tag{22.7}$$

If it does not, then Ityesi's managers should be concerned that the simplifying assumptions in their analysis are not valid: market frictions exist so that the market integration assumption is not a good approximation of reality, or perhaps there is a significant correlation between spot exchange rates and cash flows.

We can rewrite Equation 22.7 as follows. Using the covered interest rate parity relationship (Equation 22.1), we have:

$$\frac{S}{F} = \frac{(1 + r_{GBP})}{(1 + r_{CAD})} \tag{22.8}$$

Here, r_{GBP} and r_{CAD} are the foreign and domestic risk-free interest rates, respectively. Combining Equations 22.7 and 22.8, and rearranging terms gives the foreign cost of capital in terms of the domestic cost of capital and interest rates:

$$r^*_{GBP} = \frac{(1 + r_{GBP})}{(1 + r_{CAD})} \times (1 + r^*_{CAD}) - 1 \tag{22.9}$$

If the simplifying assumptions Ityesi made in calculating the *NPV* of its U.K. project are valid, then the cost of capital estimate calculated using Equation 22.9 will be close to the cost of the capital estimate calculated directly using comparable single-product companies in the United Kingdom.

EXAMPLE 22.4

Internationalizing the Cost of Capital

Problem

Use the Law of One Price to infer the GBP WACC from Ityesi's CAD WACC. Verify that the *NPV* of Ityesi's project is the same when its GBP free cash flows are discounted at this GBP WACC and converted at the spot rate.

Solution

▶ **Plan**

We can use Equation 22.9 to compute the GBP WACC. The market data we need is:

$$r_{CAD} = 4\%, \quad r_{GBP} = 7\%, \quad r^*_{CAD} = 6.8\%$$

Finally, we'll need the spot exchange rate (2.00 CAD/GBP) to convert the GBP *NPV* to CAD.

▶ **Execute**

Applying Equation 22.9, we have:

$$r^*_{GBP} = \frac{(1 + r_{GBP})}{(1 + r_{CAD})} \times (1 + r^*_{CAD}) - 1 = \frac{(1.07)}{(1.04)} \times (1.068) - 1 = 0.0988$$

The GBP WACC is 9.88%.

We can now use Ityesi's GBP WACC to calculate the present value of the GBP free cash flows in Table 22.3:

$$\frac{11.250}{1.0988} + \frac{11.250}{1.0988^2} + \frac{11.250}{1.0988^3} + \frac{11.250}{1.0988^4} = 35.754 \text{ million GBP}$$

The *NPV* in GBP of the investment opportunity is $35.754 - 17.5 = 18.254$ million GBP. Converting this amount to CAD at the spot rate gives 18.254 million GBP $\times$ 2.00 CAD/GBP = 36.508 million CAD, which is exactly the *NPV* we calculated before except for a slight difference due to rounding.

▶ **Evaluate**

The Canadian and U.K. markets are integrated, and our simplifying assumptions for the WACC valuation method are valid.

---

7. Explain two methods we use to calculate the *NPV* of a foreign project.

8. When do these two methods give the same *NPV* of the foreign project?

22.5 Valuation and International Taxation

In this chapter, we assume that Ityesi pays a corporate tax rate of 40% no matter where its earnings are generated. In practice, determining the corporate tax rate on foreign income is complicated, because corporate income taxes must be paid to two national governments: the host government (the United Kingdom in this example) and the home government (Canada). If the foreign project is a separately incorporated subsidiary of

repatriated earnings The profits from a foreign project that a firm brings back to its home country.

the parent company, the amount of taxes a firm pays generally depends on the amount of profits repatriated (brought back to the home country)—the **repatriated earnings**. International taxation is a complex subject to which specialized experts devote considerable time. In this introductory setting, we aim only to provide a broad overview and sense of the issues involved.

A Single Foreign Project with Immediate Repatriation of Earnings

We begin by assuming that the firm has a single foreign project and that all foreign profits are repatriated immediately. The general international arrangement prevailing with respect to taxation of corporate profits is that the host country gets the first opportunity to tax income produced within its borders. The home government then gets an opportunity to tax the income to the domestic firm from a foreign project. In particular, the home government must establish a tax policy specifying its treatment of foreign income and foreign taxes paid on that income. In addition, it needs to establish the timing of taxation.

Canadian tax policy requires Canadian corporations to pay taxes on their foreign income at the same rate as profits earned in Canada. However, a full tax credit is given for foreign taxes paid *up to* the amount of the Canadian tax liability. In other words, if the foreign tax rate is less than the Canadian tax rate, the company pays total taxes equal to the Canadian tax rate on its foreign earnings. In this case, all of the company's earnings are taxed at the same rate no matter where they are earned—the working assumption we used for Ityesi.

If the foreign tax rate exceeds the Canadian tax rate, companies must pay this higher rate on foreign earnings. Because the Canadian tax credit exceeds the amount of Canadian taxes owed, no tax is owed in Canada. Note that Canadian tax policy does not allow companies to apply the part of the tax credit that is not used to offset domestic taxes owed, so this extra tax credit is wasted. In this scenario, companies pay a higher tax rate on foreign income and a lower (Canadian) tax rate on income generated in Canada.

Multiple Foreign Projects and Deferral of Earnings Repatriation

Thus far, we have assumed that the firm has only one foreign project and that it repatriates earnings immediately. Neither assumption is realistic. Firms can lower their taxes by pooling multiple foreign projects and deferring the repatriation of earnings. Let's begin by considering the benefits of pooling the income on all foreign projects.

Pooling Multiple Foreign Projects. Under Canadian tax law, Canadian-based multinational corporations may use any excess tax credits generated in high-tax foreign countries to offset their net Canadian tax liabilities on earnings in low-tax foreign countries. Thus, if the Canadian tax rate exceeds the combined tax rate on all foreign income, it is valid to assume that the firm pays the same tax rate on all income no matter where it is earned. Otherwise, the firm must pay a higher tax rate on its foreign income.

Deferring Repatriation of Earnings. Now consider an opportunity to defer repatriation of foreign profits. This consideration is important, because a Canadian tax liability is not incurred until the profits are brought back home if the foreign operation is set up as a separately incorporated subsidiary (rather than as a foreign branch). If a company chooses not to repatriate 12.5 million GBP in pre-tax earnings, for example, it effectively reinvests those earnings abroad and defers its Canadian tax liability. When the foreign tax rates exceed the Canadian tax rates, there are no benefits to deferral, because in such a case there is no additional Canadian tax liability.

When the foreign tax rate is less than the Canadian tax rate, deferral can provide significant benefits. Deferring repatriation of earnings lowers the overall tax burden in much the same way as deferring capital gains lowers the tax burden imposed by the capital gains tax. Other benefits from deferral arise because the firm effectively gains a real option to repatriate income at times when repatriation might be cheaper. For example, we have already noted that by pooling foreign income, the firm effectively pays the combined tax rate on all foreign income. Because the income generated across countries changes, this combined tax rate will vary from year to year. In years in which it exceeds the Canadian tax rate, the repatriation of additional income does not incur an additional Canadian tax liability, so the earnings can be repatriated tax free.

9. What tax rate should we use to value a foreign project?

10. How can a U.S. firm lower its taxes on foreign projects?

Internationally Segmented Capital Markets

To this point, we have worked under the assumption that international capital markets are integrated. Often, however, this assumption is not appropriate. In some countries, especially in the developing world, all investors do not have equal access to financial securities. In this section, we consider why countries' capital markets might not be integrated—a case called **segmented capital markets**.

> **segmented capital markets** Capital markets that are not internationally integrated.

Many of the interesting questions in international corporate finance address the issues that result when capital markets are internationally segmented. In this section, we briefly consider the main reasons for segmentation of the capital markets and the implications for international corporate finance.

Differential Access to Markets

In some cases, a country's risk-free securities are internationally integrated, but markets for a specific firm's securities are not. Firms may face differential access to markets if there is any kind of asymmetry with respect to information about them. For example, Ityesi may be well known in Canada and enjoy easy access to CAD equity and debt markets there, because it regularly provides information to an established community of analysts tracking the firm. It may not be equally well known in the United Kingdom and, therefore, may have difficulty tapping into the GBP capital markets, because it has no track record there. For this reason, investors in the United Kingdom may require a higher rate of return to persuade them to hold GBP stocks and bonds issued by the Canadian firm.

With differential access to national markets, Ityesi would face a higher GBP WACC than the GBP WACC implied by Equation 22.9. Ityesi would then view the foreign project as less valuable if it raises capital in the United Kingdom rather than in Canada. In fact, to maximize shareholder value, the firm should raise capital at home; the method of valuing the foreign project as if it were a domestic project would then provide the correct *NPV*. Differential access to national capital markets is common enough that it provides the best explanation for the existence of **currency swaps**, which are like the interest rate swap contracts we discussed in Chapter 21, but with the holder receiving coupons in one currency and paying coupons denominated in a different currency. Currency swaps generally also have final face value payments, also in different currencies. Using a currency swap, a firm can borrow in the market where it has the best access to capital, and then "swap" the coupon and principal payments to whichever currency it would prefer to make payments in. Thus, swaps allow firms to mitigate their exchange rate risk exposure between assets and liabilities, while still making investments and raising funds in the most attractive locales.

> **currency swaps** A contract in which parties agree to exchange coupon payments and a final face value payment that are in different currencies.

Macro-Level Distortions

Markets for risk-free instruments may also be segmented. Important macroeconomic reasons for segmented capital markets include capital controls and foreign exchange controls that create barriers to international capital flows and thus segment national markets. Many countries regulate or limit capital inflows or outflows, and many do not allow their currencies to be freely converted into dollars, thereby creating capital market segmentation. Similarly, some countries restrict who can hold financial securities.

Political, legal, social, and cultural characteristics that differ across countries may require compensation in the form of a country risk premium. For example, the rate of interest paid on government bonds or other securities in a country with a tradition of weak enforcement of property rights is not likely to truly be a risk-free rate. Instead, interest rates in the country will reflect a risk premium for the possibility of default, so relations such as covered interest rate parity will likely not hold exactly.

EXAMPLE 22.5

Risky Government Bonds

Problem

For July 27, 2009, the spot exchange rate between Russian rubles and U.S. dollars was 30.9845 RUB/USD, and the one-year forward exchange rate was 33.7382 RUB/USD. At the time, the yield on short-term Russian government bonds was about 11%, while the comparable one-year yield on U.S. Treasury securities was 0.5%. Using the covered interest parity relationship, calculate the implied one-year forward rate. Compare this rate to the actual forward rate, and explain why the two rates differ.

Solution

▶ **Plan**

Using the covered interest parity formula, the implied forward rate is:

$$F = S \times \frac{(1 + r_{RUB})}{(1 + r_{USD})}$$

Thus, we need the spot exchange rate, 30.9845 RUB/USD, the USD interest rate, 0.5%, and the RUB interest rate, 11%.

▶ **Execute**

$$F = S \times \frac{(1 + r_{RUB})}{(1 + r_{USD})} = 30.9845 \frac{RUB}{USD} \times \frac{1.110}{1.005} = 34.2217 \frac{RUB}{USD}$$

The implied forward rate is higher than the current spot rate because Russian government bonds have higher yields than U.S. government bonds. The difference between the implied forward rate and the actual forward rate probably reflects the default risk in Russian government bonds (the Russian government defaulted on its debt as recently as 1998). A holder of 100,000 RUB seeking a true risk-free investment could convert the RUB to USD, invest in U.S. Treasury securities, and convert the proceeds back to RUB at a rate locked-in with a forward contract. By doing so, the investor would earn

$$\frac{100{,}000 \text{ RUB}}{30.9845 \frac{RUB}{USD} \text{ today}} \times \frac{1.005 \text{ USD in 1 yr}}{1 \text{ USD today}} \times \left(33.7382 \tfrac{RUB}{USD} \text{ in 1 yr}\right)$$

$$= 109{,}432 \text{ RUB in 1 yr}$$

for an effective RUB risk-free rate of 9.432%.

▶ **Evaluate**

The higher rate of 11% on Russian bonds reflects a credit spread of 11% − 9.432% = 1.568% to compensate bondholders for the additional default risk of the Russian bonds compared to the American bonds.

Implications of Internationally Segmented Capital Markets

A segmented financial market has an important implication for international corporate finance: one country or currency has a higher rate of return than another country or currency, when the two rates are compared in the same currency. If the return difference results from a market friction such as capital controls, corporations can exploit this friction by setting up projects in the high-return country/currency and raising capital in the low-return country/currency. Of course, the extent to which corporations can capitalize on this strategy is naturally limited: if such a strategy was easy to implement, the return difference would quickly disappear as corporations competed to use the strategy. Nevertheless, certain corporations might realize a competitive advantage by implementing such a strategy. For example, as an incentive to invest, a foreign government might strike a deal with a particular corporation that relaxes capital controls for that corporation alone.

As Example 22.6 demonstrates, the existence of segmented capital markets makes many decisions in international corporate finance more complicated but potentially more lucrative for a firm that is well positioned to exploit the market segmentation.

EXAMPLE 22.6

Valuing a Foreign Acquisition in a Segmented Market

Problem

Camacho Enterprises is a U.S. company that is considering expanding by acquiring Xtapa, Inc., a firm in Mexico. The acquisition is expected to increase Camacho's free cash flows by 21 million MXN (Mexican pesos) the first year; this amount is then expected to grow at a rate of 8% per year. The price of the investment is 525 million MXN, which is 52.5 million USD at the current exchange rate of 10 MXN/USD. Based on an analysis in the Mexican market, Camacho has determined that the appropriate after-tax MXN WACC is 12%. If Camacho has also determined that its after-tax USD WACC for this expansion is 7.5%, what is the value of the Mexican acquisition? Assume that the Mexican and U.S. markets for risk-free securities are integrated and that the yield curve in both countries is flat. U.S. risk-free interest rates are 6%, and Mexican risk-free interest rates are 9%.

Solution

▶ **Plan**

We can calculate the *NPV* of the expansion in MXN and convert the result into USD at the spot rate. The free cash flows are:

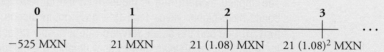

We can also compute the *NPV* in USD by converting the expected cash flows into USD using forward rates. The *N*-year forward rate (Equation 22.2) expressed in MXN/USD is:

$$F_N = S \times \frac{(1 + r_{MXN})^N}{(1 + r_{USD})^N} = 10 \times \left(\frac{1.09}{1.06}\right)^N = 10 \times 1.0283^N = 10.283 \times 1.0283^{N-1}$$

▶ **Execute**

The net present value of the MXN cash flows at the MXN WACC is:

$$NPV = \frac{21}{0.12 - 0.08} - 525 = 0$$

Thus, the purchase is a zero-*NPV* transaction. Presumably, Camacho is competing with other Mexican companies for the purchase.

To compute the *NPV* using the USD WACC, we need to convert the MXN cash flows to USD cash flows. The USD expected cash flows are the MXN cash flows (from the earlier timeline) converted at the appropriate forward rate (we divide by the forward rate because it is in MXN/USD):

$$C_{MXN}^N / F_N = \frac{21(1.08)^{N-1}}{10.283 \times 1.0283^{N-1}} = 2.0422 \times 1.0503^{N-1}$$

The USD expected cash flows are therefore:

0	1	2	3	
−52.5 USD	2.0422 USD	2.0422 (1.0503) USD	2.0422 (1.0503)² USD	...

Thus, the USD cash flows grow at about 5.03% per year. The *NPV* of these cash flows is:

$$NPV = \frac{2.0422}{0.075 - 0.0503} - 52.5 = 30.18 \text{ million USD}$$

▶ **Evaluate**
We calculated two different *NPV*s, but which *NPV* more accurately represents the benefits of the expansion? The answer depends on the source of the difference. To compute the USD expected cash flows by converting the MXN expected cash flows at the forward rate, we must accept the assumption that spot rates and the project cash flows are uncorrelated. The difference might simply reflect that this assumption failed to hold. Another possibility is that the difference reflects estimation error in the respective WACC estimates.

If Camacho is relatively confident in its assumptions about spot rates and its WACC estimates, a third possibility is that Mexican and U.S. capital markets are not integrated. In this case, Camacho, because of its access to U.S. capital markets, might have a competitive advantage. Perhaps other companies with which it is competing for the purchase of Xtapa are all Mexican firms that do not have access to capital markets outside of Mexico. Hence, Camacho can raise capital at a cheaper rate. Of course, this argument also requires that other U.S. companies not be competing for the purchase of Xtapa. Camacho, however, might have special knowledge of Xtapa's markets that other U.S. companies lack. This knowledge would give Camacho a competitive advantage in the product market over other U.S. companies and would put it on an equal footing in the product market with other Mexican companies. Because Camacho would have a competitive advantage in capital markets over other Mexican companies, the *NPV* of the purchase would be positive for Camacho but zero for the other bidders for Xtapa.

Concept Check

11. What are the reasons for segmentation of capital markets?
12. What is the main implication for international corporate finance of a segmented financial market?

22.7 Capital Budgeting with Exchange Rate Risk

The final issue that arises when a firm is considering a foreign project is that the cash flows of the project may be affected by exchange rate risk. The risk is that the cash flows generated by the project will depend on the future level of the exchange rate. A large part of international corporate finance addresses this foreign exchange risk. This section offers an overview with respect to valuation of foreign currency cash flows.

The working assumptions made thus far in this chapter are that the project's free cash flows are uncorrelated with the spot exchange rates. Such an assumption often makes sense if the firm operates as a local firm in the foreign market—it purchases its inputs and sells its outputs in that market, and price changes of the inputs and outputs are uncorrelated with exchange rates. However, many firms use imported inputs in their production processes or export some of their output to foreign countries. These scenarios alter the nature of a project's foreign exchange risk and, in turn, change the valuation of the foreign currency cash flows.

Application: Ityesi, Inc.

As an example, let's reconsider what happens if the Ityesi project in the United Kingdom imports some materials from Canada. In this case, the project's GBP free cash flows will be correlated with exchange rates. Assuming the cost of the material in Canada remains stable, if the value of the CAD appreciates against the GBP, the GBP cost of these materials will increase, thereby reducing the GBP free cash flows. The reverse is also true: if the CAD depreciates, then the GBP free cash flows will increase. Hence, our working assumption that changes in the free cash flows are uncorrelated with changes in the exchange rate is violated, and it is no longer appropriate to calculate the expected CAD free cash flows by converting the expected GBP free cash flows at the forward rate.

Whenever a project has cash flows that depend on the values of multiple currencies, the most convenient approach is to separate the cash flows according to the currency they depend on. For example, a fraction of Ityesi's manufacturing costs may be for inputs whose cost fluctuates with the value of the CAD. Specifically, suppose 5.625 million GBP of the costs are denominated in GBP, and an additional 20 million CAD (or 10 million GBP at the current exchange rate of 2.00 CAD/GBP) is for inputs whose price fluctuates with the value of the dollar. In this case, we would calculate Ityesi's GBP-denominated free cash flows excluding these CAD-based costs, as shown in Table 22.6.

| TABLE 22.6 | Ityesi's GBP-Denominated Free Cash Flows |

Year		0	1	2	3	4
Incremental Earnings Forecast (million GBP)						
1	Sales	—	37.500	37.500	37.500	37.500
2	Cost of Goods Sold	—	(5.625)	(5.625)	(5.625)	(5.625)
3	**Gross Profit**	—	31.875	31.875	31.875	31.875
4	Operating Expenses	(4.167)	(5.625)	(5.625)	(5.625)	(5.625)
5	Depreciation	—	(3.750)	(3.750)	(3.750)	(3.750)
6	*EBIT*	(4.167)	(22.500)	(22.500)	(22.500)	(22.500)
7	Income tax at 40%	1.667	(9.000)	(9.000)	(9.000)	(9.000)
8	**Unlevered Net Income**	(2.500)	13.500	13.500	13.500	13.500
Free Cash Flow						
9	Plus: Depreciation	—	3.750	3.750	3.750	3.750
10	Less: Capital Expenditures	(15.000)	—	—	—	—
11	Less: Increases in *NWC*	—	—	—	—	—
12	**GBP Free Cash Flow**	(17.500)	17.250	17.250	17.250	17.250

TABLE 22.7

Expected CAD Free
Cash Flows from
Ityesi's U.K. Project

CAD Free Cash Flow (million CAD)	0	1	2	3	4
1 GBP Free Cash Flow (million GBP)	(17.500)	17.250	17.250	17.250	17.250
2 Forward Exchange Rate (CAD/GBP)	2.0000	1.9439	1.8894	1.8364	1.7850
3 CAD Value of GBP Free Cash Flow (1 × 2)	(35.000)	33.533	32.593	31.679	30.791
4 CAD Costs	—	(20.000)	(20.000)	(20.000)	(20.000)
5 Income tax at 40%	—	8.000	8.000	8.000	8.000
6 **Free Cash Flow**	(35.000)	21.533	20.593	19.679	18.791

If the revenues and costs in the spreadsheet in Table 22.6 are not affected by changes in the spot exchange rates, it makes sense to assume that changes in the free cash flows are uncorrelated with changes in the spot exchange rates. Hence, we can convert the GBP-denominated free cash flows to equivalent CAD amounts using the forward exchange rate, as we did in Section 22.4. The spreadsheet shown in Table 22.7 performs this calculation, with the CAD value of the GBP-denominated free cash flow shown in line 3.

Next, we add the CAD-based cash flows to determine the project's aggregate free cash flow in CAD terms. This calculation is done in lines 4 through 6 of Table 22.7. Note that we deduct Ityesi's CAD-denominated costs, and then add the tax shield associated with these costs. Even if the taxes will be paid in GBP in the United Kingdom, they will fluctuate with the CAD cost of the inputs and so can be viewed as a CAD-denominated cash flow.

Given the CAD-denominated free cash flow in line 6 of Table 22.7, we can now compute the *NPV* of the investment using Ityesi's CAD WACC:[8]

$$\frac{21.533}{1.068} + \frac{20.593}{1.068^2} + \frac{19.679}{1.068^3} + \frac{18.791}{1.068^4} - 35.000 = 33.814 \text{ million CAD}$$

Conclusion

The Ityesi example was simplified because we could easily isolate the cash flows that would vary perfectly with the CAD/GBP exchange rate from those that would be uncorrelated with the exchange rate. In practice, determining these sensitivities may be difficult. If historical data are available, the tools of regression can be used to identify the exchange rate risk of project cash flows, in much the same way that we used regression to identify the market risk of security returns earlier in the text.

In this chapter, we have endeavoured to provide an introduction to international capital budgeting. This topic is sufficiently complicated that entire textbooks have been devoted to it. Hence, it is difficult to do justice to this issue in a single chapter's treatment. Nonetheless, we have provided a basic framework for approaching the problem.

Concept Check

13. What conditions cause the cash flows of a foreign project to be affected by exchange rate risk?

14. How do we make adjustments when a project has inputs and outputs in different currencies?

---

[8]We again use the domestic WACC to discount the cash flows, because we continue to assume that any additional risk premium for the exchange rate risk is small. If this assumption does not hold, then the CAD costs and the CAD value of the expected GBP free cash flows would have to be discounted at different rates to reflect the additional exchange rate risk in the GBP free cash flows.

MyFinanceLab

Here is what you should know after reading this chapter. MyFinanceLab will help you identify what you know, and where to go when you need to practice.

Key Points and Equations	Key Terms	Online Practice Opportunities
22.1 Currency Exchange Rates ▶ Currencies are traded on the foreign exchange market. ▶ It has very high volume, is dominated by large international banks, and operates 24 hours a day during the week. ▶ A currency exchange rate is a price for one currency denominated in another currency.	currency exchange rate, p. 730 foreign exchange (FX or forex) market, p. 730	MyFinanceLab Study Plan 22.1
22.2 Exchange Rate Risk ▶ Firms can manage exchange rate risk in financial markets using currency forward contracts to lock in an exchange rate in advance, and using currency options contracts to protect against an exchange rate moving beyond a certain level. ▶ The cash-and-carry strategy is an alternative strategy that provides the same cash flows as the currency forward contract. By the Law of One Price, we determine the forward exchange rate by the cost-of-carry formula, called the covered interest parity equation. Using *FOC* to represent any foreign currency, for an exchange that will take place in one year, the corresponding forward exchange rate is $$\underbrace{\text{Forward Rate}}_{\substack{\text{FOC in one year}\\\text{CAD in one year}}} = \underbrace{\text{Spot Rate}}_{\substack{\text{FOC today}\\\text{CAD today}}} \times \underbrace{\frac{1 + r_{FOC}}{1 + r_{CAD}}}_{\substack{\text{FOC in one year/FOC today}\\\text{CAD in one year/CAD today}}} \quad (22.1)$$ ▶ Currency options allow firms to insure themselves against the exchange rate moving beyond a certain level. A firm may choose to use options rather than forward contracts if • it would like to benefit from favourable exchange rate movements but not be obligated to make an exchange at unfavourable rates. • there is some chance that the transaction it is hedging will not take place.	cash-and-carry strategy, p. 739 covered interest parity equation, p. 740 currency forward contract, p. 736 currency timeline, p. 738 floating rate, p. 734 forward exchange rate, p. 736 spot exchange rate, p. 783	MyFinanceLab Study Plan 22.2
22.3 Internationally Integrated Capital Markets ▶ The condition necessary to ensure internationally integrated capital markets is that the value of a foreign investment does not depend on the currency (home or foreign) used in the analysis.	internationally integrated capital markets, p. 742	MyFinanceLab Study Plan 22.3

▶ Two methods are used to value foreign currency cash flows when markets are internationally integrated and uncertainty in spot exchange rates are uncorrelated with the foreign currency cash flows:

- Compute the expected value of the foreign currency cash flows in the home currency by multiplying the expected value in the foreign currency by the forward exchange rates, and then compute the *NPV* of these home currency cash flows using the domestic cost of capital.
- Calculate the foreign currency value of a foreign project as the *NPV* of the expected foreign currency future cash flows discounted at the foreign cost of capital, and then convert the foreign currency *NPV* into the home currency using the current spot exchange rate.

22.4 Valuation of Foreign Currency Cash Flows

▶ When markets are internationally integrated and uncertainty in spot exchange rates is uncorrelated with the foreign currency cash flows, the foreign and domestic WACCs are related as follows (using *FOC* for the foreign currency):

$$r^*_{FOC} = \frac{1 + r_{FOC}}{1 + r_{CAD}} \times (1 + r^*_{CAD}) - 1 \quad (22.9)$$

MyFinanceLab
Study Plan 22.4

Spreadsheet
Table 22.2

22.5 Valuation and International Taxation

▶ A Canadian corporation pays the higher of the foreign or domestic tax rate on its foreign project, so project valuation should use the higher of these two rates as well. The Canadian corporation may be able to reduce its tax liability by undertaking foreign projects in other countries whose earnings can be pooled with those of the new project or by deferring the repatriation of earnings.

repatriated earnings, p. 749

MyFinanceLab
Study Plan 22.5

22.6 Internationally Segmented Capital Markets

▶ Capital markets might be internationally segmented. The implication is that one country or currency has a higher cost of capital than another country or currency, when the two are compared in the same currency.

currency swaps, p. 750
segmented capital markets, p. 750

MyFinanceLab
Study Plan 22.6

22.7 Capital Budgeting with Exchange Rate Risk

▶ When a project has inputs and outputs in different currencies, the foreign-denominated cash flows are likely to be correlated with changes in spot rates. To correctly value such projects, the foreign and domestic cash flows should be valued separately.

MyFinanceLab
Study Plan 22.7

Spreadsheet
Table 22.5

Spreadsheet
Table 22.6

Review Questions

1. How is an exchange rate used?

2. What are some reasons a financial manager would need to access the foreign exchange market?

3. What are the differences between hedging exchange rate risk with options versus forwards?

4. What does it mean to say that international capital markets are integrated?

5. What assumptions are necessary to value foreign cash flows using the domestic WACC method?

6. How are Canadian firms taxed on their foreign earnings?

7. If international markets are segmented, how does that change the way the financial manager approaches valuation problems?

8. How does exchange rate risk affect our approach to valuation?

Problems

All problems in this chapter are available in MyFinanceLab. An asterisk (*) indicates problems with a higher level of difficulty.

Currency Exchange Rates

1. You have just landed in London with 500 CAD in your wallet. Stopping at the foreign exchange booth, you see that pounds are being quoted at 1.95 CAD/GBP. For how many pounds can you exchange your 500 CAD?

2. Your firm needs to pay its French supplier 500,000 EUR. If the exchange rate is 0.65 EUR/CAD, how many dollars will you need to make the exchange?

Exchange Rate Risk

 3. Your start-up company has negotiated a contract to provide a database installation for a manufacturing company in Poland. That firm has agreed to pay you 100,000 CAD in three months time when the installation will occur. However, it insists on paying in Polish zloty (PLN). You don't want to lose the deal (the

company is your first client!) but are worried about the exchange rate risk. In particular, you are worried the PLN could depreciate relative to the CAD. You contact Fortis Bank in Poland to see if you can lock in an exchange rate for the PLN in advance.

a. The current spot exchange rate is 2.3117 PLN per CAD. The three-month forward exchange rate is 2.2595 PLN per CAD. How many PLN should you demand in the contract to receive 100,000 CAD in three months if you hedge the exchange rate risk with a forward contract?

b. Given the bank forward rates in part (a), were short-term interest rates higher or lower in Poland than in Canada? Explain.

 *4. You are a broker for frozen seafood products for Choyce Products. You just signed a deal with a Belgian distributor. Under the terms of the contract, in one year you will deliver 4000 kilograms of frozen king crab for 100,000 EUR. Your cost for obtaining the king crab is 110,000 CAD. All cash flows occur in exactly one year.

a. Plot your profits in one year from the contract as a function of the exchange rate in one year, for exchange rates from 0.75 CAD/EUR to 1.50CAD/EUR. Label this line "Unhedged Profits."

b. Suppose the one-year forward exchange rate is 1.25 CAD/EUR. Suppose you enter into a forward contract to sell the EUR you will receive at this rate. In the figure from part (a), plot your combined profits from the crab contract and the forward contract as a function of the exchange rate in one year. Label this line "Forward Hedge."

c. Suppose that instead of using a forward contract, you consider using options. A one-year call option to buy EUR at a strike price of 1.25 CAD/EUR is trading for 0.10 CAD/EUR. Similarly, a one-year put option to sell EUR at a strike price of 1.25 CAD/EUR is trading for 0.10 CAD/EUR. To hedge the risk of your profits, should you buy or sell the call or the put?

d. In the figure from parts (a) and (b), plot your "all in" profits using the option hedge (combined profits of crab contract, option contract, and option price) as a function of the exchange rate in one year. Label this line "Option Hedge." (*Note:* You can ignore the effect of interest on the option price.)

e. Suppose that by the end of the year, a trade war erupts, leading to a European embargo on North American food products. As a result, your deal is cancelled, and you don't receive the EUR or incur the costs of procuring the crab. However, you still have the profits (or losses) associated with your forward or options contract. In a new figure, plot the profits associated with the forward hedge and the options hedge (label each line). When there is a risk of cancellation, which type of hedge has the least downside risk? Explain briefly.

Internationally Integrated Capital Markets

5. You are a Canadian investor who is trying to calculate the present value of a 5 million EUR cash inflow that will occur one year in the future. The spot exchange rate is $S = 1.25$ CAD/EUR and the forward rate is $F_1 = 1.215$ CAD/EUR. You estimate that the appropriate CAD discount rate for this cash flow is 4% and the appropriate EUR discount rate is 7%.

a. What is the present value of the 5 million EUR cash inflow computed by first discounting the EUR and then converting it into CAD?

b. What is the present value of the 5 million EUR cash inflow computed by first converting the cash flow into CAD and then discounting?

c. What can you conclude about whether these markets are internationally integrated, based on your answers to parts (a) and (b)?

6. Mamma Mia Enterprises, a Canadian manufacturer of children's toys, has made a sale in Poland and is expecting a 4 million PLN cash inflow in one year. The current spot rate is 2.040 PLN/CAD and the one-year forward rate is 2.055 PLN/CAD.

   a. What is the present value of Mamma Mia's 4 million PLN inflow computed by first discounting the cash flow at the appropriate PLN discount rate of 10% and then converting the result into CAD?

   b. What is the present value of Mamma Mia's 4 million PLN inflow computed by first converting the cash flow into CAD and then discounting at the appropriate CAD discount rate of 6%?

   c. What can you conclude about whether these markets are internationally integrated, based on your answers to parts (a) and (b)?

Valuation of Foreign Currency Cash Flows

 7. Etemadi Amalgamated, a U.S. manufacturing firm, is considering a new project in Portugal. You are in Etemadi's corporate finance department and are responsible for deciding whether to undertake the project. The expected free cash flows, in EUR, are shown here:

Year	0	1	2	3	4
Free Cash Flow (EUR million)	−15	9	10	11	12

   You know that the spot exchange rate is $S = 1.15$ USD/EUR. In addition, the risk-free interest rate on USD is 4% and the risk-free interest rate on EUR is 6%.

   Assume that these markets are internationally integrated and the uncertainty in the free cash flows is not correlated with uncertainty in the exchange rate. You determine that the USD WACC for these cash flows is 8.5%. What is the USD present value of the project? Should Etemadi Amalgamated undertake the project?

 8. Etemadi Amalgamated, the U.S. manufacturing company in Problem 7, is still considering a new project in Portugal. All information presented in Problem 7 is still accurate, except the spot rate is now $S = 0.85$ USD/EUR, about 26% lower. What is the new present value of the project in dollars? Should Etemadi Amalgamated undertake the project?

9. You work for a Canadian firm, and your boss has asked you to estimate the cost of capital for countries using the EUR. You know that $S = 1.20$ CAD/EUR and $F_1 = 1.157$ CAD/EUR. Suppose the CAD WACC for your company is known to be 8%. If these markets are internationally integrated, estimate the EUR cost of capital for a project with free cash flows that are uncorrelated with spot exchange rates. Assume the firm pays the same tax rate no matter where the cash flows are earned.

10. Montreal Light, a Canadian light fixtures manufacturer, is considering an investment in Japan. The CAD cost of equity for Montreal Light is 11%. You are in the corporate treasury department, and you need to know the comparable cost of equity in JPY for a project with free cash flows that are uncorrelated with spot exchange rates. The risk-free interest rates on CAD and JPY are $r_{CAD} = 5\%$ and $r_{JPY} = 1\%$, respectively. Montreal Light is willing to assume that capital markets are internationally integrated. What is the JPY cost of equity?

11. The dollar cost of debt for Javelin Consulting, a Canadian research firm, is 7.5%. The firm faces a tax rate of 30% on all income, no matter where it is earned. Managers in the firm need to know its JPY cost of debt because they are considering launching a new bond issue in Tokyo to raise money for a new investment there. The risk-free

interest rates on CAD and JPY are $r_{CAD} = 5\%$ and $r_{JPY} = 1\%$, respectively. Javelin Consulting is willing to assume that capital markets are internationally integrated and that its free cash flows are uncorrelated with the JPY–CAD spot rate. What is Javelin Consulting's after-tax cost of debt in JPY? (*Hint:* Start by finding the after-tax cost of debt in CAD and then find the JPY equivalent.)

12. McCain Foods, a Canadian food processing and distribution company, is considering an investment in Germany. You are in McCain's corporate finance department and are responsible for deciding whether to undertake the project. The expected free cash flows, in EUR, are uncorrelated to the spot exchange rate and are shown here:

Year	0	1	2	3	4
Free Cash Flow (EUR million)	−25	12	14	15	15

The new project has similar dollar risk to McCain's other projects. Management at the company knows that its overall CAD WACC is 9.5% and so is comfortable using this WACC for the project. The risk-free interest rate on CAD is 4.5% and the risk-free interest rate on EUR is 7%.

a. McCain is willing to assume that capital markets in Canada and the European Union are internationally integrated. What is the company's EUR WACC?

b. What is the present value of the project in EUR?

Valuation and International Taxation

13. Tailor Johnson, a U.S. maker of fine menswear, has a subsidiary in Ethiopia. This year, the subsidiary reported and repatriated earnings before interest and taxes (*EBIT*) of 100 million ETB (Ethiopian birrs). The current exchange rate is 8 ETB/USD or 0.125USD/ETB. The Ethiopian tax rate on this activity is 25%. Tax law in the United States requires Tailor Johnson to pay taxes on the Ethiopian earnings at the same rate as profits earned in the United States, which is currently 45%. However, the United States gives a full tax credit for foreign taxes paid up to the amount of the U.S. tax liability. What is Tailor Johnson's U.S. tax liability on its Ethiopian subsidiary?

*14. Tailor Johnson, the menswear company with a subsidiary in Ethiopia described in Problem 13, is considering the tax benefits resulting from deferring repatriation of the earnings from the subsidiary. Under U.S. tax law, the U.S. tax liability is not incurred until the profits are brought back home. Tailor Johnson reasonably expects to defer repatriation for 10 years, at which point the ETB earnings will be converted into USD at the prevailing spot rate, S_{10}, and the tax credit for Ethiopian taxes paid will still be converted at the current exchange rate = 0.125 USD/ETB. Tailor Johnson's after-tax cost of debt is 5%.

a. Suppose the exchange rate in 10 years is identical to this year's exchange rate, so $S_{10} = 0.125$ USD/ETB. What is the present value of deferring the U.S. tax liability on Tailor Johnson's Ethiopian earnings for 10 years?

b. How will the exchange rate in 10 years affect the actual amount of the U.S. tax liability? Write an equation for the U.S. tax liability as a function of the exchange rate S_{10}.

15. Qu'Appelle Enterprises, a Canadian import-export trading firm, is considering its international tax situation. Canadian tax law requires Canadian corporations to pay taxes on their foreign earnings at the same rate as profits earned in Canada; this rate is currently 35%. However, a full tax credit is given for the foreign taxes paid up to the amount of the Canadian tax liability. Qu'Appelle has major operations in Poland,

where the tax rate is 20%, and in Sweden, where the tax rate is 60%. The profits, which are fully and immediately repatriated, and foreign taxes paid for the current year are shown here:

	Poland	Sweden
Earnings before interest and taxes (*EBIT*)	80 million CAD	100 million CAD
Host country taxes paid	16 million CAD	60 million CAD
Earnings before interest and after taxes	64 million CAD	40 million CAD

a. What is the Canadian tax liability on the earnings from the Polish subsidiary assuming the Swedish subsidiary did not exist?

b. What is the Canadian tax liability on the earnings from the Swedish subsidiary assuming the Polish subsidiary did not exist?

c. Under Canadian tax law, Qu'Appelle is able to pool the earnings from its operations in Poland and Sweden when computing its Canadian tax liability on foreign earnings. Total *EBIT* is thus 180 million CAD, and the total host country taxes paid is $76 million CAD. What is the total Canadian tax liability on foreign earnings? Show how this relates to the answers in parts (a) and (b).

Internationally Segmented Capital Markets

*16. Suppose the interest on Russian government bonds is 7.5%, and the current exchange rate is 28 RUB per CAD. If the forward exchange rate is 28.5 RUB per CAD, and the current Canadian risk-free interest rate is 4.5%, what is the implied credit spread for Russian government bonds?

Capital Budgeting with Exchange Rate Risk

 *17. Assume that in the original Ityesi example in Table 22.3, all sales actually occur in Canada and are projected to be 75 million CAD per year for four years. Keeping other costs the same, calculate the *NPV* of the investment opportunity.

Data Case

You are a senior financial analyst with IBM in its capital budgeting division. IBM is considering expanding in Australia due to its positive business atmosphere and cultural similarities to the United States.

The new facility would require an initial investment in fixed assets of 5 billion AUD and an additional capital investment of 3% would be required each year in years 1 to 4. All capital investments would be depreciated straight line over the five years that the facility would operate. First-year revenues from the facility are expected to be 6 billion AUD and grow at 10% per year. Cost of goods sold would be 40% of revenue; the other operating expenses would amount to 12% of revenue. Net working capital requirements would be 11% of sales and would be required the year prior to the actual revenues. All net working capital would be recovered at the end of the fifth year. Assume that the tax rates are the same in the two countries, that the two markets are internationally integrated, and that the cash flow uncertainty of the project is uncorrelated with changes in the exchange rate. Your team manager wants you to determine the *NPV* of the project in U.S. dollars using a cost of capital of 12%.

1. Go to the NASDAQ website (www.nasdaq.com).

   a. Enter the ticker symbol for IBM (IBM) in one of the boxes and click on "Summary Quotes."

b. Click on "Company Financials" in the menu on the left. When the income statement appears, place the cursor inside the statement and right-click. Select "Export to Microsoft Excel" from the menu. If this option does not appear, then copy and paste the information.

2. Obtain exchange rates and comparable interest rates for Australia at the Bloomberg website (www.bloomberg.com).
   a. Place the cursor on "Market Data" and click on "Currencies" in the drop-down menu. Export the currency table to Excel and paste it into the same spreadsheet as the IBM income statement.
   b. Go back to the webpage and click on "Rates & Bonds" in the menu on the left. Next, click on "Australia" to get the interest rates for Australia. Right-click and export the table to Excel; paste it into the spreadsheet.
   c. Go back to the webpage and click on "U.S." Download the Treasury data and paste it into the spreadsheet.

3. You may have noticed that the one-year and four-year rates are not available at Bloomberg.com for the U.S. Treasury. Go to the U.S. Treasury website (www.treas.gov).
   a. To find the one-year rate, type "yield curve" into the search box at the top of the page and select the second link that appears. Be sure it is *not* the link for the "real" rates. Export the yields into Excel into the same spreadsheet as the other data. Add the one-year yield to the other Treasury rates.
   b. To find an estimate of the four-year yield, calculate the average of the three- and five-year yields from the Treasury yield curve.

4. In your Excel spreadsheet, create a new worksheet with a timeline for the project's expected cash flows.
   a. Compute the tax rate as the four-year average of IBM's annual income tax divided by annual earnings before tax.
   b. Determine the expected free cash flows of the project.

5. Note that the free cash flows you calculated in Question 4 are in Australian dollars. Use Equation 22.2 to determine the forward exchange rates for each of the five years of the project. Then use the forward rates to convert the cash flows to U.S. dollars.

6. Compute the *NPV* of the project in U.S. dollars using the 12% required return given by your team manager.

23 Leasing

notation

L	lease payments	τ_c	marginal corporate income tax rate
PV	present value	r_U	unlevered cost of capital
r_D	debt cost of capital	r_{wacc}	weighted average cost of capital

INTERVIEW WITH Rennie Zegalski,
CB Richard Ellis Manitoba

University of Manitoba, 1995

"Time value of money and amortization are the two key principles I use on a daily basis in leasing."

Rennie Zegalski is a Sales Associate at CB Richard Ellis Manitoba, specializing in retail sales and leasing. CBRE is the world's largest full-service commercial real estate brokerage, representing many retailers and landlords. Rennie requires the use of the skills he learned in finance class as part of his responsibilities. "**Time value of money and amortization are the two key principles I use on a daily basis in leasing**. In determining rents, market knowledge is used along with financial analysis of the deal particulars," he says. "If the landlord is required to do work, then this must be factored into a deal and the cost amortized over the lease term."

Rennie, who received a BComm from the University of Manitoba in 1995, explains the landlord's main considerations when entering into a lease agreement: "At the end of the day, the landlord needs to determine if the net effective rent attained will cover his costs (mortgage and capital) and allow a return," he says. "If there is no return to a landlord, then the deal won't make sense and he'll wait for a more attractive deal," Rennie continues. "Sometimes space sits vacant for a while but landlords know there will be vacancy from time to time and this is accounted for in their return calculation."

Rennie gives the following advice to students: "Be proficient in the use of your financial calculator! This is very important and needs to be understood. Also, with respect to finding a job, I think it is very important to use your years in university to establish friendships. The business world is all about relationships, and I have friends from university whom I've connected with and we've assisted each other in business."

To implement an investment project, a firm must acquire the necessary property, plant, and equipment. As an alternative to purchasing these assets outright, the firm can lease them. You are probably familiar with leases if you have leased a car or rented an apartment. These consumer rentals are similar to the leases used by businesses: the owner retains title to the asset, and the firm pays for its use of the asset through regular lease payments. When firms lease property, plant, or equipment, the leases generally exceed one year. This chapter focuses on such long-term leases.

If you can purchase an asset, you can probably lease it. Commercial real estate, computers, trucks, copy machines, airplanes, and even power plants are examples of assets that firms can lease rather than buy. Equipment leasing is a rapidly growing industry, with more than one-half of the world's leasing now being done by companies in Europe and Asia. More than 25% of the world's jet fleet, by dollar value, is leased.[1] One of the biggest aircraft leasing companies by fleet size is GE Capital Aviation Services. As of 2010, GE owns and manages over 1800 aircraft, the world's largest commercial airplane fleet.[2] GE leases these commercial aircraft to some 245 airline customers in 75 countries.

As you will learn, leases are not merely an alternative to purchasing; they also function as an important financing method for tangible assets. In fact, long-term leasing is the most common method of equipment financing. How do companies such as GE Capital Aviation Services set the terms for their leases? How do their customers—the commercial airlines—evaluate and negotiate these leases? In this chapter, we first discuss

[1]Beacon Funding (www.beaconfunding.com/vendor_programs/statistics.aspx).
[2]GE Capital Aviation Services Global Fact Sheet (www.gecas.com/en/docs/GECASFSnov2010.pdf).

the basic types of leases and provide an overview of the accounting and tax treatment of leases. We then show how to evaluate the lease-versus-buy decision. Firms often cite various benefits to leasing as compared to purchasing property and equipment, and we conclude the chapter with an evaluation of their reasoning.

23.1 The Basics of Leasing

A lease is a contract between two parties: the *lessee* and the *lessor*. The **lessee** is liable for periodic payments in exchange for the right to use the asset. The **lessor** is the owner of the asset, who is entitled to the lease payments in exchange for lending the asset.

Most leases involve little or no upfront payment. Instead, the lessee commits to make regular lease (or rental) payments for the term of the contract. At the end of the contract term, the lease specifies who will retain ownership of the asset and at what terms. The lease also specifies any cancellation provisions, the options for renewal and purchase, and the obligations for maintenance and related servicing costs.

Examples of Lease Transactions

Many types of lease transactions are possible based on the relationship between the lessee and the lessor. In a **sales-type lease**, the lessor is the manufacturer (or a primary dealer) of the asset. For example, IBM both manufactures and leases computers. Similarly, Xerox leases its copy machines. Manufacturers generally set the terms of these leases as part of a broader sales and pricing strategy, and they may bundle other services or goods (such as software, maintenance, or product upgrades) as part of the lease.

In a **direct lease**, the lessor is not the manufacturer but is often an independent company that specializes in purchasing assets and leasing them to customers. For example, Ryder Systems, Inc. owns more than 135,000 commercial trucks, tractors, and trailers, which it leases to small businesses and large enterprises throughout Canada, the United States, and the United Kingdom. In many instances of direct leases, the lessee identifies the equipment it needs first and then finds a leasing company to purchase the asset.

If a firm already owns an asset that it would prefer to lease, it can arrange a **sale and leaseback** transaction. In this type of lease, the lessee receives cash from the sale of the asset and then makes lease payments to retain the use of the asset. In 2002, San Francisco Municipal Railway (Muni) used the $35 million in proceeds from the sale and leaseback of 118 of its light-rail vehicles to offset a large operating budget deficit. The purchaser, CIBC World Markets, received a tax benefit from depreciating the rail cars, something Muni could not do as a public transit agency.

With many leases, the lessor provides the initial capital necessary to purchase the asset, and then receives and retains the lease payments. In a **leveraged lease**, however, the lessor borrows from a bank or other lender to obtain the initial capital for the purchase, using the lease payments to pay the interest and principal on the loan. Also, in some circumstances, the lessor is not an independent company but rather a separate business partnership, called a **special-purpose entity (SPE)**, which is created by the lessee for the sole purpose of obtaining the lease. SPEs are commonly used in **synthetic leases**, which are designed to obtain specific accounting and tax treatment (discussed further in Section 23.2).

---

lessee The party in a lease who is liable for periodic payments in exchange for the right to use the asset.

lessor The party in a lease who is the owner of the asset and is entitled to the lease payments.

sales-type lease A lease in which the lessor is the manufacturer (or a primary dealer) of the asset.

direct lease A lease in which the lessor is not the manufacturer of the asset but is often an independent company that specializes in purchasing assets and leasing them to customers.

sale and leaseback A lease in which the lessee receives cash from the sale of the asset and then makes lease payments to retain the use of the asset.

leveraged lease A lease in which the lessor borrows from a bank or other lender to obtain the initial capital for the purchase of an asset, using the lease payments to pay the interest and principal on the loan.

special-purpose entity (SPE) An entity created by the lessee for the sole purpose of obtaining the lease.

synthetic lease A lease that is designed to obtain specific accounting and tax treatment.

Lease Payments and Residual Values

Suppose your business needs a new $20,000 electric forklift for its warehouse operations, and you are considering leasing the forklift for four years. In this case, the lessor will purchase the forklift and allow you to use it for four years. At that point, you will return the forklift to the lessor. How much should you expect to pay for the right to use the forklift for the first four years of its life?

residual value the leased asset's market value at the end of the lease

The cost of the lease will depend on the asset's **residual value**, which is its market value at the end of the lease. Suppose the residual value of the forklift in four years will be $6000. If lease payments of amount L are made monthly, then the lessor's cash flows from the transaction are as follows (note that lease payments are typically made at the beginning of each payment period):

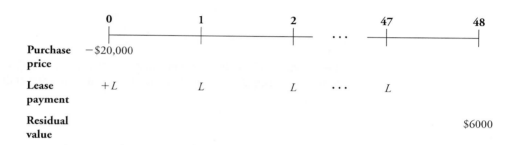

In a perfect capital market (where lessors compete with one another in initiating leases), the lease payment should be set so that the *NPV* of the transaction is zero and the lessor breaks even:

$$PV(\text{Lease Payments}) = \text{Purchase Price} - PV(\text{Residual Value}) \qquad (23.1)$$

In other words, *in a perfect market, the cost of leasing is equivalent to the cost of purchasing and reselling the asset.* In effect, this is just another example of the application of the Law of One Price.

Thus, the amount of the lease payment will depend on the purchase price, the residual value, and the appropriate discount rate for the cash flows.

EXAMPLE 23.1

Lease Terms in a Perfect Market

Problem

Suppose the purchase price of the forklift is $20,000, its residual value in four years is certain to be $6000, and there is no risk that the lessee will default on the lease. If the risk-free interest rate is a 6% APR with monthly compounding, what would be the monthly lease payment for a four-year lease in a perfect capital market?

Solution

▶ **Plan**

Because all cash flows are risk free, we can discount them using the risk-free interest rate of 6%/12 − 0.5% per month using Equation 23.1. Once we know the *PV* of the monthly lease payments, we can solve for the payment as the cash flow in an annuity due.

▶ **Execute**

$$PV(\text{Lease Payments}) = \$20,000 - \$6000/1.005^{48} = \$15,277.41$$

Because the first lease payment starts today, we can view the lease as an initial payment of L plus a 47-month annuity of L. Thus, using the annuity formula, we need to find L so that

$$15,277.41 = L + L \times \frac{1}{0.005}\left(1 - \frac{1}{1.005^{47}}\right) = L \times \left[1 + \frac{1}{0.005}\left(1 - \frac{1}{1.005^{47}}\right)\right]$$

Solving for L, we get

$$L = \frac{15,277.41}{1 + \frac{1}{0.005}\left(1 - \frac{1}{1.005^{47}}\right)} = \$357.01 \text{ per month}$$

▶ **Evaluate**
If the lessee pays $357.01 per month, starting immediately, the PV of the 48 lease payments will equal the price of the forklift less the PV of its residual value at the end of the lease.

Leases Versus Loans

Alternatively, you could obtain a four-year loan for the purchase price and buy the forklift outright. If M is the monthly payment for a fully amortizing loan, the lender's cash flows will be as follows:

Assuming the loan is fairly priced, the loan payments would be such that

$$PV(\text{Loan Payments}) = \text{Purchase Price} \tag{23.2}$$

Comparing Equation 23.2 with Equation 23.1, we see that while with a standard loan we are financing the entire cost of the asset, with a lease we are financing only the cost of the economic depreciation of the asset during the term of the lease. Because we are getting the entire asset when we purchase it with the loan, the loan payments are higher than the lease payments.

EXAMPLE 23.2

Loan Payments in a
Perfect Market

Problem
Suppose you purchase the forklift for $20,000 by borrowing the purchase price using a four-year annuity loan. What would the monthly loan payment be in a perfect capital market where the risk-free interest rate is a 6% APR with monthly compounding, assuming no risk of default? How does this compare with the lease payment of Example 23.1?

Solution

▶ **Plan**

Because all cash flows are risk free, we can discount them using the risk-free interest rate of 6%/12 − 0.5% per month. Because loan payments are made at the end of each month, we can use the annuity formula to value the loan payments.

▶ **Execute**

Equation 23.2 becomes the following:

$$M \times \frac{1}{0.005}\left(1 - \frac{1}{1.005^{48}}\right) = 20{,}000$$

Solving for M gives the loan payments:

$$M = \frac{20{,}000}{\dfrac{1}{0.005}\left(1 - \dfrac{1}{1.005^{48}}\right)} = \$469.70 \text{ per month}$$

▶ **Evaluate**

Of course, while the lease payments are lower, with the lease, we have the use of the forklift for four years only. With the loan, we own the forklift for its entire life.

Calculating Auto Lease Payments

Rather than use the annuity formula to calculate the lease payments, as we did in Example 23.1, in many cases practitioners use the following approximation to calculate the lease payments, where the purchase price includes any fees charged on the lease (and is net of any down payment), the term is the number of payment periods, and the interest rate is for a payment period:

$$L = \underbrace{\frac{\text{Purchase Price} - \text{Residual Value}}{\text{Term}}}_{\text{Average Depreciation}}$$

$$+ \underbrace{\left(\frac{\text{Purchase Price} + \text{Residual Value}}{2}\right) \times \text{Interest Rate}}_{\text{Financing Cost}}$$

The idea behind this approximation is that the first term is the average depreciation over a payment period and the second term is the interest cost associated with the average value of the asset. The sum is what you have to pay to use the asset over one payment period.

Despite its simplicity, this formula is very accurate for lease terms up to five years and interest rates up to 10%. Using it to calculate the lease payments in Example 23.1 gives the following:

$$\frac{20{,}000 - 6000}{48} + \left(\frac{20{,}000 + 6000}{2}\right) \times 0.005$$

$$= \$356.67$$

This is within $1 of the amount calculated in Example 23.1.

This approximation for the lease payment is used to calculate the payment on automobile leases. In that case, the formula is often stated as follows:

$$L = \frac{\text{Purchase Price} - \text{Residual Value}}{\text{Term}}$$

$$+ (\text{Purchase Price} + \text{Residual Value}) \times \text{Money Factor}$$

This leaves many first-time car lessees wondering why they have to pay interest on both the purchase price and the residual value. In reality, all that has happened is that the factor of 2 is subsumed into the money factor; that is, the money factor is half the interest rate.

The monthly loan payments in Example 23.2 exceed the lease payments in Example 23.1. This difference does not mean the lease is superior to the loan. While the lease payments are lower, with the lease, we have use of the forklift for four years only. If we purchase the forklift using the loan, we own it after four years and can sell it for its residual value of $6000. Alternatively, if we lease the forklift and want to keep it after the lease terminates, we can purchase it for its fair market value of $6000. Once we consider the benefit of this residual value, by the Law of One Price, the total cost of purchasing with either the loan or the lease is the same. That is, combining Equation 23.1 and Equation 23.2, we have

$$PV(\text{Lease Payments}) + PV(\text{Residual Value}) = PV(\text{Loan Payments}) \qquad (23.3)$$

In other words, in a perfect market, the cost of leasing and then purchasing the asset is equivalent to the cost of borrowing to purchase the asset.[3] This is another example of the application of the Law of One Price.

End-of-Term Lease Options

In Example 23.1, we assumed that at the end of the lease the forklift would be returned to the lessor, who would then obtain its residual market value of $6000. In reality, other lease terms are possible. In many cases, the lease allows the lessee to obtain ownership of the asset for some price, as in these types of leases:

fair market value (FMV) lease A lease that gives the lessee the option to purchase the asset at its fair market value at the termination of the lease.

▶ A **fair market value (FMV) lease** gives the lessee the option to purchase the asset at its fair market value at the termination of the lease. (Depending on the asset, determining its fair market value may be complicated. The lease will typically stipulate a procedure for doing so and often will require that an independent third party provide estimates of the fair market value.) With perfect capital markets, there is no difference between an FMV lease and a lease in which the assets are retained by the lessor, because acquiring the asset at its fair market value is a zero-*NPV* transaction.

$1.00 out lease (finance lease) A lease in which ownership of the asset transfers to the lessee at the end of the lease for a nominal cost of $1.00.

▶ In a **$1.00 out lease** (also known as a **finance lease**), ownership of the asset transfers to the lessee at the end of the lease for a nominal cost of $1.00. Thus, the lessee will continue to have use of the asset for its entire economic life. The lessee has effectively purchased the asset by making the lease payments. As a result, this type of lease is in many ways equivalent to financing the asset with a standard loan.

fixed price lease A lease in which the lessee has the option to purchase the asset at the end of the lease for a fixed price that is set up front in the lease contract.

▶ In a **fixed price lease**, the lessee has the option to purchase the asset at the end of the lease for a fixed price that is set up front in the lease contract. This type of lease is very common for consumer leases (such as for autos). Notice that this kind of lease gives the lessee an option: at the end of the lease, if the market value of the asset exceeds the fixed price, the lessee can buy the asset at below its market value; if the market value of the asset does not exceed the fixed price, however, the lessee can walk away from the lease and purchase the asset for less money elsewhere. Consequently, the lessor will set a higher lease rate to compensate for the value of this option to the lessee.

fair market value cap lease A lease in which the lessee can purchase the asset at the minimum of its fair market value and a fixed price (the "cap").

▶ In a **fair market value cap lease**, the lessee can purchase the asset at the minimum of its fair market value and a fixed price (the "cap"). The lessee has the same option as in a fixed price lease, although the option in this case is easier to exercise because the lessee does not have to find a similar asset elsewhere to buy when the fixed price exceeds the market value.

---

[3]For a theoretical analysis of competitive lease pricing, see M. Miller and C. Upton, "Leasing, Buying, and the Cost of Capital Services," *Journal of Finance* 31(3) (1976): 761–786; and W. Lewellen, M. Long, and J. McConnell, "Asset Leasing in Competitive Capital Markets," *Journal of Finance* 31(3) (1976): 787–798.

EXAMPLE 23.3

Lease Payments
and End-of-Lease
Options

Problem

Compute the lease payments for the forklift lease of Example 23.1 if the lease is (a) a fair market value lease, (b) a $1.00 out lease, or (c) a fixed price lease that allows the lessee to buy the asset at the end of the lease for $4000.

Solution

▶ **Plan**

With the FMV lease, the lessee can buy the forklift for its fair market value of $6000 at the end of the lease. The lessor obtains a residual value of $6000, either from the forklift itself or from the payment from the lessee. Thus, the lease payments will be unchanged from Example 23.1, or $357 per month.

With the $1.00 out lease, the lessor receives essentially no residual value. Thus, the lease payments themselves will have to compensate the lessor for the full $20,000 purchase price.

With the fixed price lease, because the forklift will be worth $6000 for certain, the lessee will exercise the option to purchase it for $4000. As a result, the lessor will receive only $4000 at the end of the lease.

▶ **Execute**

The lease payments for the $1.00 out lease must have a present value of $20,000, so they are

$$L = \frac{20,000}{1 + \frac{1}{0.005}\left(1 - \frac{1}{1.005^{47}}\right)} = \$467.36 \text{ per month}$$

For the fixed price lease to have an *NPV* of zero, the present value of the lease payments must be $20,000 - \$4000/1.005^{48} = \$16,851.61$. Therefore, the lease payment will be

$$L = \frac{16,851.61}{1 + \frac{1}{0.005}\left(1 - \frac{1}{1.005^{47}}\right)} = \$393.79 \text{ per month}$$

▶ **Evaluate**

The $1.00 out lease payments are slightly less than the loan payments of $470 per month calculated in Example 23.2, because the lease payments occur at the beginning—rather than the end—of the month. The fixed-price lease payment exceeds that of the FMV lease due to the lessee's ability to buy the asset at a discount at the end of the lease.

Other Lease Provisions

Leases are privately negotiated contracts and can contain many more provisions than are described here. For example, they may include early cancellation options that allow the lessee to end the lease early (perhaps for a fee). They may contain buyout options that allow the lessee to purchase the asset before the end of the lease term. Clauses may allow the lessee to trade in and upgrade the equipment to a newer model at certain points in the lease. Each lease agreement can be tailored to fit the precise nature of the asset and the needs of the parties at hand.

These features of leases will be priced as part of the lease payment. Terms that give valuable options to the lessee raise the amount of the lease payments, whereas terms that restrict these options will lower them. Absent market imperfections, leases represent another form of zero-*NPV* financing available to a firm, and the Modigliani & Miller propositions apply: leases neither increase nor decrease firm value, but serve only to divide the firm's cash flows and risks in different ways.[4]

Concept Check

1. In a perfect capital market, how is the amount of a lease payment determined?
2. What types of lease options would raise the amount of the lease payment?

23.2 Accounting, Tax, and Legal Consequences of Leasing

We have seen that with perfect capital markets, leasing represents yet another zero-*NPV* financing alternative for a firm. Thus, the decision to lease is often driven by real-world market imperfections related to leasing's accounting, tax, and legal treatment. In particular, when a firm leases an asset, a number of important questions arise: Should the firm list the asset on its balance sheet and deduct depreciation expenses? Should the firm list the lease as a liability? Can the lease payments be deducted for tax purposes? In the event of bankruptcy, is the leased asset protected from creditors? As we will see in this section, the answers to these questions depend on how the lease is structured.

Lease Accounting

When publicly traded firms disclose leasing transactions in their financial statements, they must follow the recommendations of the Accounting Standards Board (AcSB). As mentioned in Chapter 2, International Financial Reporting Standards (IFRS) will be adopted as Canadian Generally Accepted Accounting Principles (GAAP) for public companies. For lessees, IFRS distinguishes two types of leases based on the lease terms, and this classification determines the lease's accounting treatment:

> **operating lease** A lease that is viewed as a rental for accounting purposes. The lessee reports the entire lease payment as an operating expense.

▷ An **operating lease** is viewed as a rental for accounting purposes. In this case, the lessee reports the entire lease payment as an operating expense. The lessee does not deduct a depreciation expense for the asset and does not report the asset, or the lease payment liability, on its balance sheet. Operating leases are disclosed in the notes of the lessee's financial statements.

> **finance lease** A lease that transfers substantially all the risks and rewards incidental to ownership of an asset. It is viewed as an acquisition for accounting purposes. The asset acquired is listed on the lessee's balance sheet.

▷ A **finance lease** is viewed as an acquisition for accounting purposes. The asset acquired is listed on the lessee's balance sheet, and the lessee incurs depreciation expenses for the asset. In addition, the present value of the future lease payments is listed as a liability, and the interest portion of the lease payment is deducted as an interest expense.[5]

The different accounting treatment for each type of lease will affect the firm's balance sheet as well as its debt-equity ratio, as shown in Example 23.4.

---

[4]For an analysis of options embedded in lease contracts, see J. McConnell and J. Schallheim, "Valuation of Asset Leasing Contracts," *Journal of Financial Economics* 12(2) (1983): 237–261; and S. Grenadier, "Valuing Lease Contracts: A Real-Options Approach," *Journal of Financial Economics* 38(3) (1995): 297–331.

[5]The accounting treatment of leases can be more complex when agreements involve sales and leaseback transactions. Special guidelines, not dealt with in this textbook, also exist that are unique to manufacturers and dealers granting finance leases.

EXAMPLE 23.4

Leasing and the
Balance Sheet

Problem

Maritime Cruise Lines currently has the following balance sheet (in millions of dollars):

Assets		Liabilities	
Cash	100	Debt	900
Property, Plant, and Equipment	1500	Equity	700
Total Assets	1600	Total Debt plus Equity	1600

Maritime is about to add a new fleet of cruise ships. The price of the fleet is $400 million. What will Maritime's balance sheet look like if (a) it purchases the fleet by borrowing the $400 million, (b) it acquires the fleet through a $400 million finance lease, or (c) it acquires the fleet through an operating lease?

Solution

▶ **Plan**

For parts (a) and (b), the balance sheet consequences are the same: the fleet becomes a new asset of the firm, and the $400 million becomes an additional liability. If the fleet is acquired through an operating lease, as described in part (c), there is no change in the original balance sheet.

▶ **Execute**

For (a) and (b):

Assets		Liabilities	
Cash	100	Debt	1300
Property, Plant, and Equipment	1900	Equity	700
Total Assets	2000	Total Debt plus Equity	2000

Note that the firm's debt-equity ratio increases in this case (from $900/700 = 1.29$ to $1300/700 = 1.86$).

For part (c), there is no change to the balance sheet: the fleet is not listed as an asset, and the lease is not viewed as a liability. Thus, the apparent leverage ratio is unchanged.

▶ **Evaluate**

The finance lease has the same effect on the firm's balance sheet and leverage ratio as does buying the asset by borrowing, because the lease provides close to the same benefits as owning the assets. The operating lease, however, does not affect the balance sheet or its leverage.

Because finance leases increase the apparent leverage on the firm's balance sheet, firms sometimes prefer to have a lease categorized as an operating lease to keep it off the balance sheet. IFRS (under International Accounting Standard [IAS] 17) does not provide separate guidance for lessees and lessors when determining the classification of a lease. Instead, examples are provided of situations that individually or in combination would normally lead to a lease being classified as a finance lease.[6]

---

[6]BDO Dunwoody LLP.

These are as follows:

1. The lease transfers ownership of the asset to the lessee by the end of the lease term.

2. The lessee has the option to purchase the asset at a price that is expected to be sufficiently lower than the fair value at the date the option becomes exercisable for it to be reasonably certain, at the inception of the lease, that the option will be exercised.

3. The lease term is for the major part of the economic life of the asset, even if title is not transferred.

4. At the inception of the lease, the present value of the minimum lease payments amounts to at least substantially all of the fair value of the leased asset.

5. The leased assets are of such a specialized nature that only the lessee can use them without major modifications.

Other indicators that individually, or in combination, could also lead to a lease being classified as a finance lease are as follows:

1. If the lessee can cancel the lease, the lessor's losses associated with the cancellation are borne by the lessee

2. Gains or losses from the fluctuation in the fair value of the residual accrue to the lessee (e.g., in the form of a rent rebate equalling most of the sales proceeds at the end of the lease).

3. The lessee has the ability to continue the lease for a secondary period at a rent that is substantially lower than market rent.

These conditions are designed to identify situations in which the lease provides the lessee with use of the asset for a large fraction of its useful life. For example, a $1.00 out lease satisfies the second condition and so would be ruled a finance lease for accounting purposes. Firms that prefer to keep a lease off the balance sheet will often structure lease contracts to avoid these conditions.

EXAMPLE 23.5

Operating Versus Finance Leases

Problem

Consider a seven-year fair market value lease for a $12.5 million Gulfstream jet with a remaining useful life of 10 years. Suppose the monthly lease payments are $175,000 and the appropriate discount rate is a 6% APR with monthly compounding. Would this lease be classified as an operating lease or a finance lease for the lessee? What if the lease contract gave the lessee the option to cancel the contract after five years?

Solution

▶ **Plan**

We compute the present value of the monthly lease payments at the beginning of the lease using the annuity formula with a monthly interest rate of $6\%/12 = 0.5\%$ and $7 \times 12 - 1 = 83$ monthly payments after the initial payment. If the PV of the minimum lease payments is at least substantially all of the fair market value of the jet, it will be classified as a capital lease. If the contract can be cancelled after five years, then the lease will be a finance lease only if the PV of the lease payments over the first five years is at least substantially all of the fair market value of the jet.

> ▶ **Execute**

$$PV(\text{Lease Payments}) = 175{,}000 \times \left[1 + \frac{1}{0.005}\left(1 - \frac{1}{1.005^{83}}\right)\right] = \$12.04 \text{ million}$$

Because the present value of the lease payments is 12.04/12.50 − 96.3% of the value of the jet, the lease satisfies situation 4 above and so is a finance lease.

If the lessee can cancel the contract after five years, then the minimum number of lease payments is 60 under the contract. In this case,

$$PV(\text{Lease Payments}) = 175{,}000 \times \left[1 + \frac{1}{0.005}\left(1 - \frac{1}{1.005^{59}}\right)\right] = \$9.10 \text{ million}$$

This is only 9.10/12.5 = 73% of the value of the jet. As no other situations for a finance lease seem to present in this scenario, the lease would be classified as an operating lease.

> ▶ **Evaluate**
>
> Simply by adding a cancellation option, the lease can be classified as an operating lease such that it would have no impact on the balance sheet of the lessee.

The Tax Treatment of Leases

The categories used to report leases on the financial statements affect the values of assets on the balance sheet, but they have no direct effect on the cash flows that result from a leasing transaction. The Canada Revenue Agency (CRA) had its own classification rules under Interpretation Bulletin IT-233R that effectively ruled that leases that resulted in eventual ownership should be treated as a sale transaction and not a lease. However, on June 14, 2001, the CRA cancelled the interpretation bulletin and announced that the legal form of the contract would be central to determining whether the transaction was a sale or lease. A lease contract would be treated as a lease, and a sale contract would be treated as a sale. However, if the contract were designed strictly to avoid tax, the General Anti-avoidance Rule (GAAR) could be used to reassess the case. In addition, under the Specialized Leasing Property Rules, certain assets held under financial (i.e., finance) leases could be fully treated as a lease for tax purposes. These "exempt assets" allow the lessor to claim the capital cost allowance (CCA) deductions and the lessee to claim rental expense. Exempt assets include rail cars, trucks for hauling freight, office furniture and equipment, personal items such as furniture, appliances, furnaces and hot-water tanks, passenger vehicles, vans, and pickup trucks. Non-exempt items include most other assets.[7]

For the remainder of the discussion, we will refer to operating leases and financial leases of exempt assets as *true tax leases* and other leases as *non-tax leases*. Thus, with a **true tax lease**, the lessor receives the CCA deductions associated with the ownership of the asset. The lessee can deduct the full amount of the lease payments as an operating expense, and these lease payments are treated as revenue for the lessor.

true tax lease A lease in which the lessor receives the depreciation deductions associated with the ownership of the asset. The lessee can deduct the full amount of the lease payments as an operating expense, and these lease payments are treated as revenue for the lessor.

---

[7]*Sources:* Income Tax Act (Canada); Income Tax Regulations (Canada); Interpretation Bulletin IT-233R; *Income Tax Technical News,* No. 21, June 14, 2001, Canada Customs and Revenue Agency. A reference regarding leasing and taxes in Canada is by John Tobin, Jim Hong, and Richard Johnson, "Canada: Asset/Equipment Finance and Leasing," found in the *2007/2008 Lexpert/CCCA Corporate Counsel Directory and Yearbook,* 6th edition.

non-tax lease A lease in which the lessee receives the depreciation deductions for tax purposes, and can also deduct the interest portion of the lease payments as an interest expense. The interest portion of the lease payment is interest income for the lessor.

Although the legal ownership of the asset resides with the lessor, in a **non-tax lease** the lessee receives the CCA deductions. The lessee can also deduct the interest portion of the lease payments as an interest expense. The interest portion of the lease payment is interest income for the lessor.

For example, suppose a piece of industrial equipment costing $2,000,000 had a CCA rate of 20%. It would take 11 years before the firm could claim 90% of the available CCA on the asset. However, by acquiring the asset through a four-year $1.00 out lease, with payments of $500,000 per year, a firm could receive 100% of the $2,000,000 total deduction at a faster rate if the lease were categorized as a true tax lease.[8] The CRA rules prevent this type of transaction by categorizing such a lease as a non-tax lease because it is a non-exempt asset.

Leases and Bankruptcy

When a firm files for bankruptcy under the Companies' Creditors Arrangement Act (CCAA) or the Bankruptcy and Insolvency Act (BIA), the firm's assets are protected from seizure by its creditors while existing management is given the opportunity to propose

---

Synthetic Leases

Synthetic leases are designed to be treated as an operating lease for accounting purposes and as a non-tax lease for tax purposes. With a synthetic lease, the lessee is able to deduct depreciation and interest expenses for tax purposes, just as if it had borrowed to purchase the asset, but does not need to report the asset or the debt on its balance sheet.

To obtain this accounting and tax treatment, synthetic leases have typically been structured by creating a special-purpose entity (SPE) that will act as the lessor and obtain financing, acquire the asset, and lease it to the firm. To ensure that the lease qualifies as an operating lease, the lease is structured so that it (1) provides a fixed purchase price at the end of the lease term based on an initial appraised value (and so is not a bargain price), (2) has a term less than 75% of the economic life of the asset (which is renewable under certain conditions), and (3) has minimum lease payments with a present value less than 90% of the fair value of the property. In addition, to avoid balance sheet consolidation, the owner of record of the SPE must make an initial minimum equity investment of 3% that remains at risk during the entire lease term. The lease can qualify as a non-tax lease by designating some portion of the lease payments as interest.

A major motivation for such leases appears to be that they allow firms to use debt while avoiding the accounting consequences of debt. In particular, by keeping the debt off the balance sheet, the firm's debt-equity ratio is improved, its return on assets is generally raised, and, if the lease payments are less than the interest and depreciation expenses, the firm's reported earnings per share will be higher.

These types of transactions were used and abused by Enron Corporation to boost its earnings and hide its liabilities prior to its downfall. In the wake of the Enron scandal, the Financial Accounting Standards Board has significantly tightened the requirements for SPEs, raising the at-risk equity investment of the SPE to 10% and requiring that ownership truly be independent from the lessor. With the adoption of International Financial Reporting Standards (IFRS) in Canada, consolidation of the SPE with its related company is necessary if the substance of the relationship is for the SPE mainly to benefit its related company. Thus, the debt of the SPE would no longer be hidden off the balance sheet. Investors have also reacted skeptically to such deals, forcing many firms to avoid synthetic leases or unwind structures that were already in place. For example, in 2002, Krispy Kreme Doughnut Corporation reversed its decision to use a synthetic lease to fund a new $35 million plant after an article critical of the transaction was published in *Forbes* magazine.

---

[8]This transaction would have the opposite tax consequence for the lessor: The lease payments would be taxed as revenues, but the cost of the asset would be depreciated at the CCA rate. However, there can be an advantage if the lessor is in a lower tax bracket than the lessee.

a reorganization plan. Even secured lenders are prevented from taking the assets that serve as collateral for their loans during this period, which can last from a few months to several years. Instead, bankruptcy law permits the firm to continue to use the assets in an effort to remain a going concern. When Air Canada filed for protection under the CCAA in 2003, it was still able to use its planes even though most of them were leased.

The treatment of leased property in bankruptcy will depend on whether the lease is classified as a *security interest* or a *true lease* by the bankruptcy judge. If the lease is deemed to be a **security interest**, the firm is assumed to have effective ownership of the asset and the asset is protected against seizure. The lessor is then treated as any other secured creditor and must await the firm's reorganization or ultimate liquidation.

If the lease is classified as a **true lease** in bankruptcy, then the lessor retains ownership rights over the asset. A special provision exists in the case of aircraft. Within 60 days of filing under the CCAA, the lessee must choose whether to continue or repudiate an aircraft lease. If it continues the lease, it must settle all pending claims and continue to make all promised lease payments (including maintenance and insurance). If it repudiates the lease, the asset must be returned to the lessor (with any pending claims of the lessor becoming unsecured claims against the bankrupt firm). Air Canada had 278 aircraft leased at the beginning of 2003. By the time its CCRA proceedings finished, it had repudiated 29 of the leases and an additional 19 leases had ended with either consensual returns or lease expirations.

If a lease contract is characterized as a true lease in bankruptcy, the lessor is in a somewhat superior position than the lender if the firm defaults. By retaining ownership of the asset, the lessor has the right to repossess it if the lease payments are not made, even if the firm seeks bankruptcy protection. While a benefit to the lessor, this right of repossession limits the options for the firm in the event of financial distress.[9]

Whether a transaction is classified as a true lease or a security interest will depend on the facts of each case, but the distinction is very similar to the accounting and tax distinctions made earlier. Operating and true tax leases are generally viewed as true leases by the courts, whereas capital and non-tax leases are more likely to be viewed as a security interest. In particular, leases for which the lessee obtains possession of the asset for its remaining economic life (either within the contract or through an option to renew or purchase at a nominal charge) are generally deemed security interests.[10]

security interest A lease in which the lessee is assumed to have effective ownership of the asset and the asset is protected against seizure.

true lease A lease in which in bankruptcy the lessor retains ownership rights over the asset.

3. How is a $1.00 out lease characterized for accounting and tax purposes?

4. Is it possible for a lease to be treated as an operating lease for accounting purposes and as a non-tax lease for tax purposes?

23.3 The Leasing Decision

How should a firm decide whether to buy or lease an asset? Recall that in a perfect market the decision is irrelevant, so the real-world decision depends on market frictions. In this section, we consider one important market friction—taxes—and evaluate the

---

[9]For an analysis of the consequences of this treatment of leases for a firm's borrowing capacity, see A. Eisfeldt and A. Rampini, "Leasing, Ability to Repossess, and Debt Capacity," *Review of Financial Studies*, 22 (4): 1621–1657.

[10]See Article 1 of the Uniform Commercial Code, Section 1-203 at www.law.upenn.edu/bll/ulc/ulc. htm#ucc1.

financial consequences of the leasing decision from the perspective of the lessee. We show how to determine whether it is more attractive to lease an asset or to buy it and (potentially) finance the purchase with debt. First, we consider a true tax lease, then we turn to non-tax leases at the end of the section.

Cash Flows for a True Tax Lease

If a firm purchases a piece of equipment, the expense is a capital expenditure. Therefore, the purchase price can be depreciated over time, generating a CCA tax shield. If the equipment is leased and the lease is a true tax lease, there is no capital expenditure, but the lease payments are an operating expense.

Let's compare the cash flows arising from a true tax lease with those arising from a purchase using an example. Spafax Canada Inc., a magazine publisher, needs new equipment. It can purchase the equipment for $50,000 in cash. The equipment will last five years and will be subject to a CCA rate of 45%. This means that Spafax can deduct CCA as per Table 23.1. For example, in year 1, Spafax can claim a CCA deduction of $11,250. Given its tax rate of 35%, Spafax will therefore save $3937.50 in taxes due to the CCA tax shield.

Alternatively, Spafax can lease the equipment instead of purchasing it. The equipment qualifies as exempt assets (therefore, a true tax lease), and thus the lessor can claim CCA deductions while Spafax will claim rental expense. A five-year lease contract will cost $12,000 per year. Spafax must make these payments at the beginning of each year. Because the lease is a true tax lease, Spafax deducts each lease payment as an operating expense in the year in which it occurs. Thus, an income tax savings of $4200 occurs at the end of each year. The lease contract does not provide for maintenance or servicing of the equipment, so these costs are identical whether the equipment is leased or purchased.

Table 23.1 shows the free cash flow consequences of buying and leasing. Here we consider only the cash flows that differ as a result of leasing versus buying. We do not need to consider cash flows that would be the same in both situations, such as the

TABLE 23.1	Cash Flows ($) Consequences from Leasing Versus Buying							
Buy	**Year**	**0**	**1**	**2**	**3**	**4**	**5**	**6**
1	Capital Expenditures	(50,000)	—	—	—	—	—	—
2	CCA Deduction*	—	11,250	17,438	9591	5275	2901	3546
3	CCA Tax Shield	—	3938	6103	3357	1846	1015	1241
4	**Free Cash Flow (Buy)**	(50,000)	3938	6103	3357	1846	1015	1241
Lease								
5	Lease Payments	(12,000)	(12,000)	(12,000)	(12,000)	(12,000)	—	—
6	Income Tax Savings†	—	4200	4200	4200	4200	4200	—
7	**Free Cash Flow (Lease)**	(12,000)	(7800)	(7800)	(7800)	(7800)	4200	—

Notes:

*Equations 8.1 and 8.2 are used to determine UCC and CCA. Assuming disposal for $0 at the beginning of year 6, the remaining UCC is claimed as a terminal loss and is shown as the year 6 CCA deduction amount.

†To keep consistency with the assumption that an asset purchased at the beginning of year 1 (thus year 0 on the timeline) results in a series of CCA tax shields starting at the end of year 1, lease payments made at the beginning of a year are assumed to generate an income tax savings at the end of the year too.

sales revenues generated by having the equipment and maintenance expenses. We have also assumed that the equipment will have no residual value after five years: thus, if purchased, it will be disposed of for $0. If any of these differences existed, we would include them in the cash flows. Recall from Equation 8.9 of Chapter 8 that free cash flow can be calculated as *EBITDA* less taxes, capital expenditures, and increases in net working capital, plus the CCA tax shield (i.e., tax rate × CCA deduction). Thus, if Spafax buys, the only change to free cash flow is from capital expenditures and the CCA tax shield, and if Spafax leases, the only change is a reduction in *EBITDA*, and therefore taxes, from the lease payment.

Note that the cash flows of leasing differ from buying. A purchase requires a large initial outlay followed by a series of CCA tax shields. In contrast, the cost of a leased equipment is more evenly spread out over time.

Lease Versus Buy (an Unfair Comparison)

Is it better for Spafax to lease or buy the equipment? To begin to answer this question, let's compare the present value of the cash flows in each transaction (or, equivalently, we can compute the *NPV* of the difference between the cash flows). To compute the present value, we need to determine the cost of capital.

The appropriate cost of capital depends, of course, on the risk of the cash flows. Lease payments are a fixed obligation of the firm. If Spafax fails to make the lease payments, it will default on the lease. The lessor will seek the remaining lease payments and, in addition, will take back the equipment. In that sense, a lease is similar to a loan secured with the leased asset as collateral. Moreover, as discussed in Section 23.2, in a true lease the lessor is in an even better position than a secured creditor if the firm files for bankruptcy. Thus, *the risk of the lease payments is no greater than the risk of secured debt*, so it is reasonable to discount the lease payments at the firm's secured borrowing rate.

The tax savings from the lease payments and from depreciation expenses are also low-risk cash flows, as they are predetermined and will be realized as long as the firm generates positive income.[11] Therefore, a common assumption in practice is to use the firm's borrowing rate for these cash flows as well.

If Spafax's borrowing rate is 8%, the cost of buying the equipment has the following present value:

$$PV(\text{Buy}) = -50{,}000 + \frac{3938}{1.08} + \frac{6103}{1.08^2} + \frac{3357}{1.08^3} + \frac{1846}{1.08^4} + \frac{1015}{1.08^5} - \frac{1241}{1.08^6}$$

$$= -\$35{,}627$$

The cost of leasing the equipment has the following present value:

$$PV(\text{Lease}) = -12{,}000 - \frac{7800}{1.08} - \frac{7800}{1.08^2} - \frac{7800}{1.08^3} - \frac{7800}{1.08^4} + \frac{4200}{1.08^5} = -\$34{,}976$$

Thus, leasing is cheaper than buying, with a net savings of $35,627 − $34,976.

The preceding analysis ignores an important point, however. When a firm enters into a lease, it is committing to lease payments that are a fixed future obligation of

---

[11]Even if income is negative, these tax benefits may still be obtained through carryback or carryforward provisions that allow the firm to apply these credits against income generated in past or future years.

the firm. If the firm is in financial distress and cannot make the lease payments, the lessor can seize the equipment. Moreover, the lease obligations themselves could trigger financial distress. Therefore, when a firm leases an asset, it is effectively adding leverage to its capital structure (whether or not the lease appears on the balance sheet for accounting purposes).

Because leasing is a form of financing, we should compare it to other financing options that Spafax may have. Rather than buy the asset outright, Spafax could borrow funds (or reduce its planned cash balances, and thereby increase its net debt) to finance the purchase of the equipment, thus matching the leverage of the lease. If Spafax does borrow, it will also benefit from the interest tax shield provided by leverage. This tax advantage may make borrowing to buy the equipment more attractive than leasing. Thus, to evaluate a lease correctly, we should compare it to purchasing the asset using an equivalent amount of leverage. In other words, the appropriate comparison is not lease versus buy, but rather lease versus borrow.

Lease Versus Borrow (the Right Comparison)

lease-equivalent loan
The loan that is required on the purchase of the asset that leaves the purchaser with the same obligations as the lessee would have.

To compare leasing to borrowing, we must determine the amount of the loan that leads to the same level of fixed obligations that Spafax would have with the lease. We call this loan the **lease-equivalent loan**. That is, the lease-equivalent loan is the loan that is required on the purchase of the asset that leaves the purchaser with the same obligations as the lessee would have.[12]

The Lease-Equivalent Loan. To compute the lease-equivalent loan in Spafax's case, we first compute the difference between the cash flows from leasing versus buying, which we refer to as the incremental free cash flow of leasing. As Table 23.2 shows, relative to buying, leasing saves cash up front but results in lower future cash flows. The incremental free cash flow in years 1 through 6 represents the effective leverage the firm takes on by leasing.

Alternatively, Spafax could take on this same leverage by purchasing the equipment and taking on a loan with these same after-tax debt payments. How much could Spafax borrow by taking on such a loan? Because the future incremental cash flows are the after-tax payments Spafax will make on the loan, the initial balance on the lease-equivalent loan is the present value of these cash flows using Spafax's after-tax cost of debt:

$$\text{Loan Balance} = PV(\text{Future FCF of Lease Versus Buy at } r_D(1 - T_c)) \qquad (23.4)$$

TABLE 23.2	Incremental Free Cash Flows ($) of Leasing Versus Buying						
	Year	0	1	2	3	4	5	6
1	FCF Lease (Line 7, Table 23.1)	(12,000)	(7800)	(7800)	(7800)	(7800)	4200	—
2	Less: FCF Buy (Line 4, Table 23.1)	50,000	(3938)	(6103)	(3357)	(1846)	(1015)	(1241)
3	Lease − Buy	38,000	(11,738)	(13,903)	(11,157)	(9646)	3185	(1241)

---

[12]For a development of this method, see S. Myers, D. Dill, and A. Bautista, "Valuation of Financial Lease Contracts," *Journal of Finance* 31(3) (1976): 799–819.

Using Spafax's after-tax borrowing cost of 8% $(1 - 35\%) = 5.2\%$, the initial loan balance is

$$\text{Loan Balance} = \frac{11{,}738}{1.052} + \frac{13{,}903}{1.052^2} + \frac{11{,}157}{1.052^3} + \frac{9646}{1.052^4} - \frac{3185}{1.052^5} + \frac{1241}{1.052^6}$$

$$= \$39{,}622 \tag{23.5}$$

Equation 23.5 implies that if Spafax is willing to take on the future obligations implied by leasing, it could instead buy the equipment and borrow $39,622. This exceeds the savings in year 0 from leasing of $38,000 shown in Table 23.2. Thus, by buying and borrowing using the lease-equivalent loan, Spafax saves an additional $39,622 − $38,000 = $1622 initially, and so leasing the equipment is unattractive relative to this alternative.

We verify this result explicitly in the spreadsheet in Table 23.3. There, we compute the cash flows that result from buying the equipment and borrowing using the lease-equivalent loan. Line 1 shows the lease-equivalent loan balance, which we compute at each date by applying Equation 23.4. Line 2 shows the initial borrowing and principal payments of the loan (computed as the change in the loan balance from the prior year). Line 3 shows the interest due each year (8% of the prior loan balance), and line 4 computes the interest tax shield (35% of the interest amount). Line 5 then totals the after-tax cash flows of the loan, which we combine with the free cash flow from buying the equipment, to compute the total cash flow from buying and borrowing on line 7.

Comparing the cash flows from buying the equipment and financing it with the lease-equivalent loan (line 7 of Table 23.3) with the cash flows of the lease (line 1 of Table 23.2), we see that in both cases Spafax has a net future obligation of $7800 per year for four years followed by an inflow of $4200 in year 5. But while the leverage is the same for the two strategies, the initial cash flow is not. With the lease, Spafax will pay $12,000 initially; with the loan, Spafax will pay the purchase price of the equipment minus the amount borrowed, or $50,000 − $39,622 = $10,378. Again, we see that borrowing to buy the equipment is cheaper than the lease, with a savings of $12,000 − $10,378 = $1622. For Spafax, the lease is not attractive. If Spafax is willing to take on that much leverage, it would be better off doing so by borrowing to purchase the equipment, rather than leasing it.

TABLE 23.3	Cash Flows ($) from Buying and Borrowing Using the Lease-Equivalent Loan						
Year	0	1	2	3	4	5	6
Lease-Equivalent Loan							
1 Loan Balance (PV at 5.2%)	39,622	29,945	17,599	7358	(1906)	1180	—
Buy with Lease Equivalent Loan							
2 Net Borrowing (Repayment)	39,622	(9677)	(12,346)	(10,242)	(9264)	3085	(1180)
3 Interest (at 8%)		(3170)	(2396)	(1408)	(589)	152	(94)
4 Interest Tax Shield at 35%		1109	838	493	206	(53)	33
5 Cash Flows of Loan (After-tax)	39,622	(11,738)	(13,903)	(11,157)	(9646)	3185	(1241)
6 FCF Buy		(50,000)	3938	6103	3357	1846	1015
7 Cash Flows of Borrow + Buy	(10,378)	(7800)	(7800)	(7800)	(7800)	4200	—

A Direct Method. Now that we have seen the role of the lease-equivalent loan, we can directly compare leasing with an equivalent debt-financed purchase. Because the incremental cash flows from leasing versus borrowing are relatively affordable, it is appropriate to use the cost of debt, adjusted for taxes, as the discount rate. So $r = r_0(1 - T_c)$. Thus, *we can compare leasing to buying the asset using equivalent leverage by discounting the incremental cash flows of leasing versus buying using the after-tax borrowing rate.*

In Spafax's case, discounting the incremental free cash flow in Table 23.2 at Spafax's after-tax borrowing cost of 8% $\times$ (1 − 35%) = 5.2%, we get

$$NPV(\text{Lease Versus Borrow}) = 38,000 - \frac{11,738}{1.052} - \frac{13,903}{1.052^2} - \frac{11,157}{1.052^3} - \frac{9646}{1.052^4}$$

$$+ \frac{3185}{1.052^5} - \frac{1241}{1.052^6} = -\$1622$$

Note that this is precisely the difference we calculated earlier.

The Effective After-Tax Lease Borrowing Rate. We can also compare leasing and buying in terms of an effective after-tax borrowing rate associated with the lease. This is given by the IRR of the incremental lease cash flows in Table 23.2, which we can calculate as 7%:

$$41,875 - \frac{11,625}{1.07} - \frac{11,625}{1.07^2} - \frac{11,625}{1.07^3} - \frac{11,625}{1.07^4} - \frac{3500}{1.07^5} = 0$$

Thus, the lease is equivalent to borrowing at an after-tax rate of 7%. This option is not attractive compared to the after-tax rate of only 8% $\times$ (1 − 35%) = 5.2% that Spafax pays on its debt. Because we are borrowing (positive followed by negative cash flows), a lower IRR is better. But be careful with this approach—as discussed in Chapter 7, if the cash flows alternate signs more than once, the IRR method cannot be relied upon.

Evaluating a True Tax Lease

In sum, when evaluating a true tax lease, we should compare leasing to a purchase that is financed with equivalent leverage. We suggest the following approach:

1. Compute the *incremental cash flows* for leasing versus buying, as we did in Table 23.2. Include the CCA tax shield (if buying) and the tax deductibility of the lease payments (if leasing).

2. Compute the *NPV* of leasing versus buying using equivalent leverage by discounting the incremental cash flows at the *after-tax borrowing rate*.

If the *NPV* computed in step 2 is negative, then leasing is unattractive compared to traditional debt financing. In this case, the firm should not lease, but rather should acquire the asset using an optimal amount of leverage (based on the trade-offs and techniques discussed in Part 6).

If the *NPV* computed in step 2 is positive, then leasing does provide an advantage over traditional debt financing and should be considered. Management should recognize, however, that while it may not be listed on the balance sheet, the lease increases the firm's effective leverage by the amount of the lease-equivalent loan.[13]

---

[13]If financial distress or other costs of leverage are large, the firm may wish to offset some of this increase in leverage by reducing other debt of the firm.

EXAMPLE 23.6

Evaluating New
Lease Terms

Problem

Suppose Spafax rejects the lease we analyzed, and the lessor agrees to lower the lease rate to $11,400 per year. Does this change make the lease attractive?

Solution

▶ **Plan**

The incremental cash flows with the lower lease rate are shown in the following table:

Buy	Year	0	1	2	3	4	5	6
1	Capital Expenditures	(50,000)	—	—	—	—	—	—
2	CCA Deduction	—	11,250	17,438	9591	5275	2901	3546
3	CCA Tax Shield	—	3938	6103	3357	1846	1015	1241
4	Free Cash Flow (Buy)	(50,000)	3938	6103	3357	1846	1015	1241
Lease								
5	Lease Payments	(11,400)	(11,400)	(11,400)	(11,400)	(11,400)	—	—
6	Income Tax Savings	—	3990	3990	3990	3990	3990	—
7	Free Cash Flow (Lease)	(11,400)	(7410)	(7410)	(7410)	(7410)	3990	—
Lease Vs. Buy								
8	Lease − Buy		38,600	(11,348)	(13,513)	(10,767)	(9256)	2975	(1241)

Note: The following data were used to create this table: asset cost = 50,000; lease payments = 11,400; CCA rate $d = 45\%$; $\tau_c = 35\%$.

We can recompute the *NPV* of leasing versus borrowing using the cash flows from the lower lease rate.

▶ **Execute**

Using Spafax's after-tax borrowing cost of 5.2%, the gain from leasing versus an equivalently leveraged purchase is

$$NPV(\text{Lease Versus Borrow}) = 38,600 - \frac{11,348}{1.052} - \frac{13,513}{1.052^2} - \frac{10,767}{1.052^3}$$

$$- \frac{9256}{1.052^4} + \frac{2975}{1.052^5} - \frac{1241}{1.052^6}$$

$$= 38,600 - 38,409$$

$$= \$191$$

Therefore, the lease is attractive at the new terms.

▶ **Evaluate**

By reducing the lease payments by $600 ($390 after-tax) each, we can make the lease more attractive than borrowing and buying. It is important to re-evaluate the decision when the lease terms change.

Evaluating a Non-tax Lease

Evaluating a non-tax lease is much more straightforward than evaluating a true tax lease. For a non-tax lease, the lessee still receives the CCA deductions (as though the asset were purchased). Only the interest portion of the lease payment is deductible, however. Thus, in terms of cash flows, a non-tax lease is directly comparable to a traditional loan. Therefore, it is attractive if it offers a better interest rate than would be available with a loan. To determine whether it does offer a better rate, we can discount the lease payments at the firm's *pre-tax* borrowing rate and compare it to the purchase price of the asset.

EXAMPLE 23.7

Comparing a Non-tax Lease with a Standard Loan

Problem

Suppose the lease in Example 23.6 is a non-tax lease. Would it be attractive for Spafax in this case?

Solution

▶ **Plan**

Instead of purchasing the equipment for $50,000, Spafax will pay lease payments of $11,400 per year. That is, Spafax is effectively borrowing $50,000 by making payments of $11,400 per year. Given Spafax's 8% borrowing rate, we can calculate how much Spafax could borrow if it made payments of $11,400 per year on a standard loan. If that amount is more than $50,000, then it would be better off borrowing than leasing.

▶ **Execute**

$$PV(\text{Lease Payments}) = 11{,}400 + \frac{11{,}400}{1.08} + \frac{11{,}400}{1.08^2} + \frac{11{,}400}{1.08^3} + \frac{11{,}400}{1.08^4} = \$49{,}158$$

▶ **Evaluate**

By making the same payments on a loan, Spafax could raise less than $50,000. Thus, the lease is attractive at these terms if it is a non-tax lease: Spafax's lease payments are less than the payments that would be required on a $50,000 loan.

For both the true tax lease and the non-tax lease, we have ignored the residual value of the asset, any differences in the maintenance and service arrangements with a lease versus a purchase, and any cancellation or other lease options. If these features are present, they should also be included when comparing leasing versus a debt-financed purchase.

Concept Check

5. What discount rate should be used for the incremental lease cash flows to compare a true tax lease to borrowing?

6. How can we compare a non-tax lease to borrowing?

 23.4 **Reasons for Leasing**

In Section 23.3, we saw how to determine whether a lease is attractive for the potential lessee. A similar but reverse argument can be used from the standpoint of the lessor. The lessor could compare leasing the equipment to lending the money to the firm so that it can purchase the equipment. Under what circumstances would leasing be profitable for both the lessor and the lessee? If a lease is a good deal for one of the parties, is it a bad deal for the other? Or are there underlying economic sources of value in a lease contract?

Valid Arguments for Leasing

For a lease to be attractive to both the lessee and the lessor, the gains must come from some underlying economic benefits that the leasing arrangement provides. Here, we consider some valid reasons for leasing.

Tax Differences. With a true tax lease, the lessee replaces CCA and interest tax deductions with a deduction for the lease payments. Depending on the timing of the payments, one set of deductions will have a larger present value. A tax gain occurs if the lease shifts the more valuable deductions to the party with the higher tax rate. Generally speaking, if the asset's CCA deductions are more rapid than its lease payments, a true tax lease is advantageous if the lessor is in a higher tax bracket than the lessee. In contrast, if the asset's CCA deductions are slower than its lease payments, there are tax gains from a true tax lease if the lessor is in a lower tax bracket than the lessee.

EXAMPLE 23.8

Exploiting Tax Differences Through Leasing

Problem

Suppose Spafax is offered a true tax lease for the equipment at a lease rate of $11,400 per year. Show that this lease is profitable for Spafax as well as for a lessor with a 55% tax rate and an 8% borrowing cost.

Solution

▶ **Plan**

We already evaluated the lease with these terms in Example 23.6. There, we found that the *NPV* of leasing versus borrowing was $191 for Spafax. Now we need to consider the lease from the standpoint of the lessor. The lessor will buy the equipment and then lease it to Spafax. We can calculate the incremental cash flows for the lessor from buying and leasing, evaluate them at the after-tax rate, and compute the *NPV* for the lessor. (Using the after-tax rate for the lessor implies that the lessor will borrow against the future free cash flows of the transaction.)

▶ **Execute**

Buy	Year	0	1	2	3	4	5	6
1	Capital Expenditures	(50,000)	—	—	—	—	—	—
2	CCA Deduction	—	11,250	17,438	9591	5275	2901	3546
3	CCA Tax Shield	—	6188	9591	5275	2901	1596	1950
4	Free Cash Flow (Buy)	(50,000)	6188	9591	5275	2901	1596	1950

Lease								
5	Lease Payments	11,400	11,400	11,400	11,400	11,400	—	—
6	Income Tax	—	(6270)	(6270)	(6270)	(6270)	(6270)	—
7	Free Cash Flow (Lease)	11,400	5130	5130	5130	5130	(6270)	—

Lessor Free Cash Flow								
8	Buy and Lease	(38,600)	11,318	14,721	10,405	8031	(4674)	1950

Note: The following data were used to create this table: asset cost = 50,000; lease payments = 11,400; CCA rate $d = 45\%$; $\tau_c = 55\%$.

Evaluating the cash flows at the after-tax rate of $8\% \times (1 - 55\%) = 3.6\%$, we find the *NPV* = $30.27 > 0 for the lessor.

▶ **Evaluate**

Both sides gain from the transaction due to the difference in tax rates. The gain comes from the fact that for the lessor, his or her asset's CCA deductions provide more accelerated tax deductions than the taxes the lessor pays on the lease payments. Because the lessor is in a higher tax bracket than Spafax, shifting the faster tax deductions to the lessor is advantageous.

Reduced Resale Costs.   Many assets are time consuming and costly to sell. If a firm needs to use the asset for only a short time, leasing it is probably less costly than buying and later reselling the asset. In this case, the lessor is responsible for finding a new user for the asset. Lessors are often specialized in finding new users and so face much lower costs. For example, car dealerships are in a better position to sell a used car at the end of a lease than a consumer is. Some of this advantage can be passed along through a lower lease rate. In addition, while owners of assets are likely to resell them only if the assets are "lemons," a short-term lease can commit the user of an asset to return it regardless of its quality. In this way, leases can help mitigate the adverse selection problem in the used goods market.[14]

Efficiency Gains from Specialization.   Lessors often have efficiency advantages over lessees in maintaining or operating certain types of assets. For example, a lessor of office copy machines can employ expert technicians and maintain an inventory of spare parts required for maintenance. Some types of leases may even come with an operator, such as a truck with a driver (in fact, the term "operating lease" originated from such leases). By offering assets together with these complementary services, lessors can achieve efficiency gains and offer attractive lease rates. In addition, if the value of the asset depends on these additional services, then a firm that purchases the asset would be dependent on the service provider, who could then raise the price for services and exploit the firm.[15] By leasing the asset and the services as a bundle, the firm maintains its bargaining power by retaining its flexibility to switch to a competing equipment lessor.

Reduced Distress Costs and Increased Debt Capacity.   As noted in Section 23.2, assets leased under a true lease are not afforded bankruptcy protection and can be seized in the event of default. In addition, the lessor may be better able to recover the full economic value of the asset (by re-leasing it) than a lender would. Because of the higher recovery value in the event of default, a lessor may be able to offer more attractive financing through the lease than an ordinary lender could. Recent studies suggest that this effect is important for small firms and firms that are capital constrained.[16]

Transferring Risk.   At the beginning of a lease, there may be significant uncertainty about the residual value of the leased asset, and whoever owns the asset bears this risk. Leasing allows the party best able to bear the risk to hold it. For example, small firms with a low tolerance for risk may prefer to lease rather than purchase assets.

Improved Incentives.   When the lessor is the manufacturer, a lease in which the lessor bears the risk of the residual value can improve incentives and lower agency costs. Such a lease provides the manufacturer with an incentive to produce a high-quality, durable product that will retain its value over time. In addition, if the manufacturer is a

---

[14]For evidence of this effect, see T. Gilligan, "Lemons and Leases in the Used Business Aircraft Market," *Journal of Political Economy* 112(5) (2004): 1157–1180.

[15]This concern is often referred to as the *hold-up problem*. The importance of the hold-up problem in determining the optimal ownership of assets was identified by B. Klein, R. Crawford, and A. Alchian, "Vertical Integration, Appropriable Rents, and the Competitive Contracting Process," *Journal of Law and Economics* 21 (1978): 297–326.

[16]See S. Sharpe and H. Nguyen, "Capital Market Imperfections and the Incentive to Lease," *Journal of Financial Economics* 39(2–3) (1995): 271–294; J. Graham, M. Lemmon, and J. Schallheim, "Debt, Leases, Taxes, and the Endogeneity of Corporate Tax Status," *Journal of Finance* 53(1) (1998): 131–162; and A. Eisfeldt and A. Rampini, "Leasing, Ability to Repossess, and Debt Capacity," *Review of Financial Studies,* 22 (4): 1621–1657.

monopolist, leasing the product gives the manufacturer an incentive not to overproduce and lower the product's residual value, as well as an ability to restrict competition from sales of used goods.

Despite these potential benefits, significant agency costs may also be associated with leasing. For leases in which the lessor retains a substantial interest in the asset's residual value, the lessee has less of an incentive to take proper care of an asset that is leased rather than purchased.[17]

Suspect Arguments for Leasing

Some reasons that lessees and lessors cite for preferring leasing to purchasing are difficult to justify economically. While they may be important in some circumstances, they deserve careful scrutiny.

Avoiding Capital Expenditure Controls. One reason some managers will choose to lease equipment rather than purchase it is to avoid the scrutiny from superiors that often accompanies large capital expenditures. For example, some companies may place limits on the dollar amounts a manager can invest over a certain period; lease payments may fall below these limits, whereas the cost of the purchase would not. By leasing, the manager avoids having to make a special request for funds. This reason for leasing is also apparent in the public sector, where large assets are often leased to avoid asking the government or the public to approve the funds necessary to purchase the assets. However, the lease may cost more than the purchase, wasting stockholder or taxpayer dollars in the long run.

Preserving Capital. A common argument made in favour of leasing is that it provides "100% financing" because no down payment is required, so the lessee can save cash to use for other needs. Of course, the firm can also borrow to purchase an asset (possibly using the asset as collateral). For most large corporations, the amount of leverage the firm can obtain through a lease is unlikely to exceed the amount of leverage the firm can obtain through a loan. Thus, this benefit is likely to exist only for small or highly capital-constrained firms.

Reducing Leverage Through Off–Balance-Sheet Financing. By carefully avoiding the four criteria that define a capital lease for accounting purposes, a firm can avoid listing the long-term lease as a liability. Because a lease is equivalent to a loan, the firm can increase its actual leverage without increasing the debt-to-equity ratio on its balance sheet. But whether they appear on the balance sheet or not, lease commitments are liabilities for the firm. As a result, they will have the same effect on the risk and return characteristics of the firm as other forms of leverage do. Most financial analysts and sophisticated investors understand this fact and consider operating leases (which must be listed in the footnotes of the financial statements) to be additional sources of leverage.

Concept Check

7. What are some of the potential gains from leasing if the lessee plans to hold the asset for only a small fraction of its useful life?

8. If a lease is not listed as a liability on the firm's balance sheet, does it mean that a firm that leases rather than borrows is less risky?

---

[17]As an example, auto manufacturers require individuals who lease their cars to provide proper maintenance. Without such requirements, individuals would be tempted to avoid paying for oil changes and other maintenance near the end of the lease term. Of course, there are other ways lessees may abuse their cars (e.g., driving at excessive speeds) that cannot be easily controlled.

Key Points	Key Terms	Online Practice Opportunities
23.1 The Basics of Leasing ▶ A lease is a contract between two parties: the lessee and the lessor. The lessee is liable for periodic payments in exchange for the right to use the asset. The lessor, who is the owner of the asset, is entitled to the lease payments in exchange for lending the asset. ▶ Many types of lease transactions are possible, depending on the relationship between the lessee and the lessor. ▶ In a sales-type lease, the lessor is the manufacturer or primary dealer of the asset. ▶ In a direct lease, the lessor is an independent company that specializes in purchasing assets and leasing them to customers. ▶ If a firm already owns an asset it would prefer to lease, it can arrange a sale and leaseback transaction. ▶ In a perfect market, the cost of leasing is equivalent to the cost of purchasing and reselling the asset. Also, the cost of leasing and then purchasing the asset is equivalent to the cost of borrowing to purchase the asset. ▶ In many cases, the lease provides options for the lessee to obtain ownership of the asset at the end of the lease. Some examples include fair market value leases, $1.00 out leases, fixed price leases, and fair market value cap leases.	$1.00 out lease (finance lease), p. 770 direct lease, p. 766 fair market value cap lease, p. 770 fair market value (FMV) lease, p. 770 fixed price lease, p. 770 lessee, p. 766 lessor, p. 766 leveraged lease, p. 766 residual value, p. 767 sale and leaseback, p. 766 sales-type lease, p. 766 special-purpose entity (SPE), p. 766 synthetic lease, p. 766	MyFinanceLab Study Plan 23.1
23.2 Accounting, Tax, and Legal Consequences of Leasing ▶ Under IFRS, two types of leases are recognized based on the lease terms: operating leases and finance leases. Operating leases are viewed as rentals for accounting purposes. Finance leases are viewed as purchases. ▶ The CRA separates leases into two broad categories: true tax leases and non-tax leases. With a true tax lease, the lessee deducts lease payments as an operating expense. With a non-tax lease, the lessee must depreciate the asset and can expense only the interest portion of the lease payments.	finance lease, p.772 non-tax lease, p. 776 operating lease, p. 772 security interest, p. 777 true lease, p. 777 true tax lease, p. 775	MyFinanceLab Study Plan 23.2

▶ In a true lease, the asset is not protected in the event that the lessee declares bankruptcy, and the lessor can seize the asset if lease payments are not made. If the lease is deemed a security interest by the bankruptcy court, then the asset is protected and the lessor becomes a secured creditor.

23.3 The Leasing Decision

▶ To evaluate the leasing decision for a true tax lease, managers should compare the cost of leasing with the cost of financing using an equivalent amount of leverage.

    ▶ Compute the incremental cash flows for leasing versus buying.

    ▶ Compute the *NPV* by discounting the incremental cash flows at the after-tax borrowing rate.

▶ The cash flows of a non-tax lease are directly comparable to the cash flows of a traditional loan, so a non-tax lease is attractive only if it offers a better interest rate than a loan.

lease-equivalent loan, p. 780

MyFinanceLab
Study Plan 23.3

23.4 Reasons for Leasing

▶ Good reasons for leasing include tax differences, reduced resale costs, efficiency gains from specialization, reduced bankruptcy costs, risk transfer, and improved incentives.

▶ Suspect reasons for leasing include avoiding capital expenditure controls, preserving capital, and reducing leverage through off–balance-sheet financing.

MyFinanceLab
Study Plan 23.4

Review Questions

1. Why would a firm enter into a sale and leaseback transaction?

2. What are the main differences between fair market value, $1 out, fixed price, and fair market value cap leases?

3. How are operating leases different from capital leases?

4. Which classification of a lease is more important for cash flows and valuation: that of the IFRS or Canada Revenue Agency?

5. What is the advantage of a synthetic lease?

6. Why does it matter whether the lease is classified as a security interest or as a true lease?

7. Why is comparing leasing versus buying an unfair comparison?

8. What are the main steps in evaluating a true tax lease?

9. Explain why preserving capital and reducing leverage are suspect reasons for leasing.

Problems

Problems in this chapter are available in MyFinanceLab.

The Basics of Leasing

1. Suppose an H1200 supercomputer has a cost of $200,000 and will have a residual market value of $60,000 in five years. The risk-free interest rate is 5% APR with monthly compounding.
   a. What is the risk-free monthly lease rate for a five-year lease in a perfect market?
   b. What would be the monthly payment for a five-year $200,000 risk-free loan to purchase the H1200?

2. Suppose the risk-free interest rate is 5% APR with monthly compounding. If a $2 million MRI machine can be leased for seven years for $22,000 per month, what residual value must the lessor recover to break even in a perfect market with no risk?

3. Consider a five-year lease for a $400,000 bottling machine, with a residual market value of $150,000 at the end of the five years. If the risk-free interest rate is 6% APR with monthly compounding, compute the monthly lease payment in a perfect market for the following leases:
   a. A fair market value lease
   b. A $1.00 out lease
   c. A fixed price lease with an $80,000 final price

Accounting, Tax, and Legal Consequences of Leasing

 4. Acme Distribution currently has the following items on its balance sheet:

Assets		Liabilities	
Cash	20	Debt	70
Property, Plant, and Equipment	175	Equity	125

How will Acme's balance sheet change if it enters into an $80 million finance lease for new warehouses? What will its book debt-equity ratio be? How will Acme's balance sheet and debt-equity ratio change if the lease is an operating lease?

5. Your firm is considering leasing a $50,000 copier. The copier has an estimated economic life of eight years. Suppose the appropriate discount rate is 9% APR with monthly compounding. Classify each lease below as a finance lease or operating lease:
   a. A four-year fair market value lease with payments of $1150 per month
   b. A six-year fair market value lease with payments of $790 per month
   c. A five-year fair market value lease with payments of $925 per month
   d. A five-year fair market value lease with payments of $1000 per month and an option to cancel after three years with a $9000 cancellation penalty

The Leasing Decision

6. Craxton Engineering will either purchase or lease a new $756,000 fabricator. If purchased, the fabricator will be depreciated for tax purposes on a straight-line basis over seven years. Craxton can lease the fabricator for $130,000 per year for seven years. Craxton's tax rate is 35%. (Assume the fabricator has no residual value at the end of the seven years.)

   a. What are the free cash flow consequences of buying the fabricator?

   b. What are the free cash flow consequences of leasing the fabricator if the lease is a true tax lease?

   c. What are the incremental free cash flows of leasing versus buying?

 7. Riverton Mining plans to purchase or lease $220,000 worth of excavation equipment. If purchased, the equipment will be depreciated for tax purposes on a straight-line basis over five years, after which it will be worthless. If leased, the annual lease payments will be $55,000 per year for five years. Assume Riverton's borrowing cost is 8%, its tax rate is 35%, and the lease qualifies as a true tax lease.

   a. If Riverton purchases the equipment, what is the amount of the lease-equivalent loan?

   b. Is Riverton better off leasing the equipment or financing the purchase using the lease-equivalent loan?

   c. What is the effective after-tax lease borrowing rate? How does this compare to Riverton's actual after-tax borrowing rate?

 8. Suppose Clorox can lease a new computer data processing system for $975,000 per year for five years. Alternatively, it can purchase the system for $4.25 million. Assume Clorox has a borrowing cost of 7% and a tax rate of 35%, and the system will be obsolete at the end of five years.

   a. If Clorox will depreciate (for tax purposes) the computer equipment on a straight-line basis over the next five years, and if the lease qualifies as a true tax lease, is it better to finance the purchase of the equipment or to lease it?

   b. Suppose that if Clorox buys the equipment, it will use accelerated depreciation for tax purposes. Specifically, the CCA rate will be 45% and any undepreciated capital cost in year 6 will be taken as a terminal loss. Compare leasing with purchase in this case.

 9. Suppose Procter and Gamble (P&G) is considering purchasing $15 million in new manufacturing equipment. If it purchases the equipment, P&G will depreciate it for tax purposes on a straight-line basis over five years, after which the equipment will be worthless. P&G will also be responsible for maintenance expenses of $1 million per year. Alternatively, it can lease the equipment for $4.2 million per year for the five years, in which case the lessor will provide necessary maintenance. Assume P&G's tax rate is 35% and its borrowing cost is 7%.

   a. What is the *NPV* associated with leasing the equipment versus financing it with the lease-equivalent loan?

   b. What is the break-even lease rate—that is, what lease amount could P&G pay each year and be indifferent about leasing versus financing a purchase?

Reasons for Leasing

 10. Suppose Netflix is considering the purchase of special software to facilitate its move into video-on-demand services. In total, the firm will purchase $48 million in new software. This software will qualify for CCA deductions at a rate of 100%. However, because of the firm's substantial loss carryforwards, Netflix estimates its marginal tax rate to be 10% over the next five years, so it will get very little tax benefit from

the CCA deductions. Thus Netflix considers leasing the software instead. Suppose Netflix and the lessor face the same 8% borrowing rate, but the lessor has a 40% tax rate. For the purpose of this question, assume the software is worthless after five years, the lease term is five years, and the lease qualifies as a true tax lease.

a. What is the lease rate for which the lessor will break even?
b. What is the gain to Netflix with this lease rate?
c. What is the source of the gain in this transaction?

24

Mergers and Acquisitions

notation

A	pre-merger total value of acquirer	P_T	pre-merger share price of target
EPS	earnings per share	S	value of all synergies
N_A	pre-merger number of shares of acquirer outstanding	T	pre-merger total value of target
N_T	pre-merger number of shares of target outstanding	x	number of new shares issued by acquirer to pay for target
P/E	price-earnings ratio		
P_A	pre-merger share price of acquirer		

George Yao,
Morgan Stanley

University of Toronto, 2009

"The primary driver for a company to merge with, acquire, or be sold to another company is to drive shareholder value."

George Yao graduated from the University of Toronto with a Master of Business Administration in 2009 and is now an investment banker for Morgan Stanley, where he specializes in mergers and acquisitions. "The primary driver for a company to merge with, acquire, or be sold to another company is to drive shareholder value, which, to a large extent, means return on financial investment. Hence, it is important to have the financial expertise in identifying viable and value-added financial transactions and investments, structuring favourable transactions, and measuring return appropriately."

Firms wishing to acquire or merge with other firms face the difficult problem of integrating the operations of the two firms in a way that generates the most value possible. George helps clients identify the benefits from integrating with another firm. "Shareholder value creation can come in various forms, such as streamlining of business segments to focus on core value-added activities, and diversification across geography, products, and services to elevate growth and reduce risks stemming from technology, geopolitics, economic trends, and so on. We often use complex financial methodologies to assess the intrinsic and market-based values of companies to help our clients in identifying such strategic alternatives that can enhance shareholder value."

How a firm pays for an acquisition can also be a decision requiring a thorough analysis. "Value creation often can be enhanced further by the consideration and structure of a transaction. For example, we often have to identify the most cost-effective instrument (or combination of instruments) that can be employed to finance the transaction in order to maximize return among a number of potential options."

George's finance education provided him with the knowledge and skills necessary to help clients reach the right conclusions. "The entire process requires in-depth understanding of various key financial principles and strong familiarity of the interconnectedness of financial markets. Learning about finance provided me with the analytical tools required to navigate through the complex tasks involved in execution of mergers and acquisitions."

On July 14, 2008, St. Louis-based Anheuser-Busch agreed to an acquisition by Belgium-based beer giant InBev for $70 per share in cash. The agreement ended 150 years of independence for the brewer of iconic Budweiser beer. In fact, Anheuser-Busch's board had flatly rejected InBev's initial $65 per share offer, preferring to remain independent. However, the sweetened offer, valuing the company at $60 billion, was too compelling a deal for Anheuser's board to pass up. Next, InBev's managers faced the daunting task of integrating Anheuser's organization and brands into their global company and generating enough value from the transaction to justify the price they paid. Given the complexity and potential sums of money at stake, it is clear that some of the most important decisions financial managers make concern mergers and acquisitions.

In this chapter, we first provide some historical background about the market for mergers and acquisitions. Next, we discuss some of the reasons why a corporate financial manager may decide to pursue an acquisition. We then review the takeover process. Finally, we address the question of who benefits from the value that is added when a takeover occurs.

24.1 Background and Historical Trends

acquirer (or bidder)
A firm that, in a takeover, buys another firm.

target A firm that is acquired by another in a merger or acquisition.

takeover Either a merger or an acquisition, by which ownership and control of a firm can change.

Mergers and acquisitions are part of what is often referred to as "the market for corporate control." When one firm acquires another, there is typically a buyer, the **acquirer** or **bidder**, and a seller, the **target** firm. There are two primary mechanisms by which ownership and control of a public corporation can change: either another corporation or group of individuals can acquire the target firm, or the target firm can merge with another firm. In both cases, the acquiring entity must purchase the stock or existing assets of the target either for cash or for something of equivalent value (such as shares in the acquiring or newly merged corporation). For simplicity, we refer to either mechanism as a **takeover.**

The global takeover market is highly active, averaging more than $1 trillion per year in transaction value. Table 24.1 lists the 20 largest transactions completed during the 10-year period from August 2000 through July 2010. As the table indicates, many takeovers happen between well-known companies, and individual transactions can involve huge sums of money.

TABLE 24.1   Twenty Largest Merger Transactions, August 2000–July 2010

Date Announced	Date Completed	Target Name	Acquirer Name	Value ($ billions)
Apr. 2007	Nov. 2007	ABN-AMRO Holding NV	RFS Holdings BV	98
Mar. 2006	Dec. 2006	BellSouth Corp	AT&T Inc	89
Oct. 2004	Aug. 2005	Shell Transport & Trading Co	Royal Dutch Petroleum Co	80
Feb. 2006	July 2008	Suez SA	Gaz de France SA	75
Jan. 2004	Aug. 2004	Aventis SA	Sanofi-Synthelabo SA	65
Jan. 2009	Oct. 2009	Wyeth	Pfizer Inc	64
July 2002	Apr. 2003	Pharmacia Corp	Pfizer Inc	60
June 2008	Nov. 2008	Anheuser-Busch Cos	InBev NV	60
Jan. 2004	July 2004	Bank One Corp, Chicago, IL	JPMorgan Chase & Co	58
Jan. 2005	Oct. 2005	Gillette Co	Procter & Gamble Co	57
Oct. 2003	Apr. 2004	FleetBoston Financial Corp, MA	Bank of America Corp	49
Sep. 2008	Jan. 2009	Merrill Lynch & Co Inc	Bank of America Corp	48
Feb. 2004	Oct. 2004	AT&T Wireless Services Inc	Cingular Wireless LLC	47
Dec. 2004	Aug. 2005	Nextel Communications Inc	Sprint Corp	46
Mar. 2009	Nov. 2009	Schering-Plough Corp	Merck & Co Inc	45
Feb. 2007	Oct. 2007	TXU Corp	Private equity syndicate	44
Oct. 2000	Oct. 2001	Texaco Inc	Chevron Corp	43
July 2007	Nov. 2007	Alcan Inc	Rio Tinto Canada Holdings Inc	43
Feb. 2005	Oct. 2005	UFJ Holdings Inc	Mitsubishi Tokyo Financial Grp	41
Dec. 2009	June 2010	XTO Energy Inc	Exxon Mobil Corp	40

Source: Thomson Financials' SDC M&A Database.

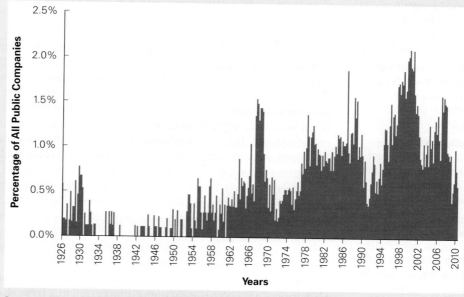

FIGURE 24.1

Percentage of Public Companies Taken Over Each Quarter, 1926–2010

Mergers appear to occur in distinct waves, with the most recent waves occurring in the 1980s, 1990s, and 2000s.

Source: Authors' calculations based on Center for Research in Security Prices data.

Merger Waves

merger waves Peaks of heavy activity followed by quiet troughs of few transactions in the takeover market.

The takeover market is also characterized by **merger waves**—peaks of heavy activity followed by quiet troughs of few transactions. Figure 24.1 displays the time series of takeover activity from 1926 to 2010. Merger activity is greater during economic expansions than during contractions and correlates with bull markets. Many of the same technological and economic conditions that lead to bull markets also motivate managers to reshuffle assets through mergers and acquisitions. Thus, the same economic activities that drive expansions most likely also drive peaks in merger activity.[1]

Figure 24.1 shows that the periods of the greatest takeover activity occurred in the 1960s, 1980s, 1990s, and 2000s. Each merger wave was characterized by a typical type of deal. The increase in activity in the 1960s is known as the "conglomerate wave," because firms typically acquired firms in unrelated businesses. At the time, it was thought that managerial expertise was portable across business lines and that the conglomerate business form offered great financial advantages. This conglomerate fad eventually fell out of favour, and the 1980s were known for hostile, "bust-up" takeovers, in which the acquirer purchased a poorly performing conglomerate and sold off its individual business units for more than the purchase price. The 1990s, in contrast, were known for "strategic" or "global" deals that were more likely to be friendly and to involve companies in related businesses; these mergers often were designed to create strong firms on a scale that would allow them to compete globally. At the end of 2004, takeover activity began to pick up again, starting the next big merger wave, marked by consolidation in

---

[1]See J. Harford, "What Drives Merger Waves," *Journal of Financial Economics* 77 (2005): 529–560, for an analysis of why these waves occur.

horizontal merger
A merger in which the target and acquirer are in the same industry.

vertical merger A merger in which the target's industry buys or sells to the acquirer's industry.

conglomerate merger
A merger in which the target and acquirer operate in unrelated industries.

stock swap A merger deal in which the target shareholders receive stock as payment for target shares.

term sheet A summary of the structure of a merger transaction that includes details such as who will run the new company, the size and composition of the new board, the location of the headquarters, and the name of the new company.

many industries such as telecommunications and software. In this wave, private equity played a larger role than it had in the past, and some private equity groups such as KKR, TPG, Blackrock, and Cerberus took ever-larger firms such as Hertz (see Chapter 14), Chrysler, and Harrah's private. The financial crisis and severe contraction of credit in 2008 brought an abrupt end to the latest merger wave.

Types of Mergers

While we tend to talk about merger waves and mergers in general, the term "merger," as commonly used, encompasses several types of transactions that vary by the relationship between the target and the acquirer and by the method of payment used in the transaction. If the target and acquirer are in the same industry, the merger is typically called a **horizontal merger**, whereas if the target's industry buys or sells to the acquirer's industry, it is called a **vertical merger**. Finally, if the target and acquirer operate in unrelated industries, the deal is a **conglomerate merger**. Conglomerate mergers, while popular in the 1960s, have generally fallen out of favour with shareholders because of the difficulty in creating value when combining two unrelated businesses.

Deals also vary based on whether the target shareholders receive stock or cash as payment for target shares. When they receive stock, the deal is often called a **stock swap**, because target shareholders are swapping their old stock for new stock in either the acquirer or a newly created merged firm. The consideration paid to target shareholders can be very complex, including debt instruments, options, and mixes of any of these with cash and/or stock. Commonly, however, target shareholders receive stock, cash, or a mix of the two.

While news reports understandably focus on the price and method of payment, the structure of a merger transaction, summarized in a **term sheet**, can be simple or incredibly complex. The items to negotiate include, among other things, who will run the new company, the size and composition of the new board, the location of the headquarters, and even the name of the new company.

Concept Check

1. What are merger waves?

2. What is the difference between a horizontal and a vertical merger?

24.2 Market Reaction to a Takeover

In Canada and most U.S. states, the law requires that when existing shareholders of a target firm are forced to sell their shares, they receive a fair value for their shares. Typically this concept is interpreted as the value exclusive of any value that arises because of the merger itself. For practical purposes, this principle translates into the share price prior to the merger. As a consequence, a bidder is unlikely to acquire a target company for less than its current market value. Instead, most acquirers pay a substantial **acquisition premium**, which is the percentage difference between the acquisition price and the pre-merger price of the target firm.

acquisition premium
The percentage difference between the acquisition price and the pre-merger price of a target firm that the acquirer in a takeover pays.

Table 24.2 lists the average historical premium and market reaction to a takeover.[2] As the table shows, acquirers pay an average premium of 43% over the pre-merger price

[2]The original research done in the 1970s and 1980s documented that shareholders experience significant gains (between 20% and 30%) upon successful takeover of their firms. More recent papers have found combined losses on the order of $240 billion in capitalization at the announcement of takeover bids. This finding appears to be driven by spectacular losses from some large takeovers of public targets, especially in the late 1990s.

TABLE 24.2	Average Acquisition Premium and Stock Price Reactions to Mergers

Premium Paid over Pre-merger Price	Announcement Price Reaction	
	Target	Acquirer
43%	15%	1%

Source: Handbook of Corporate Finance: Empirical Corporate Finance, Vol. 2, Chapter 15, pp. 291–430, B.E. Eckbo, ed., Elsevier/North-Holland Handbook of Finance Series, 2008.

of the target. When a bid is announced, the target shareholders enjoy a gain of 15% on average in their stock price. Although acquirer shareholders see an *average* gain of 1%, in half of the transactions the bidder price *decreases* (in effect the median gain is not significantly different from 0%). These facts raise three important questions that we answer in this chapter:

1. Why do acquirers pay a premium over the market value for a target company?
2. Although the price of the target company rises on average on the announcement of the takeover, why does it rise less than the premium offered by the acquirer?
3. If the transaction is a good idea, why does the acquirer not consistently experience a large price increase?

Let's start with the first question—why do acquirers pay a premium over market value? In fact, this question has two parts: (1) Why is the target worth a premium over the current market value? and (2) Even if the target is worth more than its pre-merger value, why do acquirers pay more than the pre-merger market price? In the next section, we answer the first part of this question. We delay the discussion of the second part until the end of the chapter, when we fully understand the mechanics of the takeover process.

3. On average, what happens to the target share price on the announcement of a takeover?
4. On average, what happens to the acquirer share price on the announcement of a takeover?

24.3 Reasons to Acquire

For most investors, an investment in the stock market is a zero-*NPV* investment. How, then, can an acquirer pay a premium for a target and still satisfy the requirement that the investment be a positive-*NPV* investment opportunity? The answer is that an acquirer might be able to add economic value, as a result of the acquisition, that an individual investor cannot add. The basis of the assumption that the value of the combined companies will be worth more than the sum of the two companies' individual values is the assumption that they will create *synergies*. We discuss some examples of synergies below, but for simplicity in this section we refer to any additional value created as **synergies**.

synergies Value obtained from an acquisition that could not be obtained if the target remained an independent firm; i.e., value in excess of the firms' stand-alone value.

Large synergies are by far the most common justification that bidders give for the premium they pay for a target. An extreme example is SBC's acquisition of AT&T in 2005 for more than $15 billion. In interviews immediately after the announcement, SBC's Chairman Ed Whitacre was quick to point out that the projected synergies of $15 billion alone could justify the price SBC agreed to pay for AT&T, let alone AT&T's assets.

Such synergies usually fall into two categories: cost reductions and revenue enhancements. Cost-reduction synergies are more common and easier to achieve, because they generally translate into layoffs of overlapping employees and elimination of redundant resources. This was the case in the SBC/AT&T acquisition, which forecasted 13,000 layoffs in the first year. If the merger will create possibilities to expand into new markets or gain more customers, then the merger partners will predict synergies that enhance their revenue. For example, when Delta and Northwest airlines announced their merger agreement in April 2008, they forecasted $200 to $300 million per year in revenue-enhancement synergies because their expanded network and flight options would bring in more customers and increase customer loyalty.

Let's examine in detail the synergies most often cited by acquirers to justify takeovers.

Economies of Scale and Scope

economies of scale The savings a large company can enjoy from producing goods in high volume. Such savings are not available to a small company.

A large company can enjoy **economies of scale**, or savings from producing goods in high volume, that are not available to a small company. For example, in Stride Rite's acquisition of sports shoemaker Saucony in 2005, one motivation was to reduce Saucony's manufacturing costs because, due to its larger size, Stride Rite could negotiate superior manufacturing contracts in China. Larger firms can also benefit from **economies of scope**, which are savings that come from combining the marketing and distribution of different types of related products (e.g., soft drinks and snack foods).

economies of scope The savings large companies can realize that come from combining the marketing and distribution of different types of related products.

There may also be costs associated with size. Chief among these is that larger firms are more difficult to manage. In a small firm, the CEO is often close to the firm's operations. He or she can keep in touch with the firm's largest customers and most important personnel, thereby keeping abreast of changing market conditions and potential problems. Because they receive information quickly, small firms are often able to react in a timely way to changes in the economic environment.

Vertical Integration

vertical integration The merger of two companies that make products required at different stages of the production cycle for the final good; also, the merger of a firm and its supplier or a firm and its customer.

Vertical integration refers to the merger of two companies that make products required at different stages of the production cycle of the final good. A company might conclude that it can enhance its product if it has direct control of the inputs required to make the product. Similarly, another company might not be happy with how its products are being distributed, so it might decide to take control of its distribution channels.

The principal benefit of vertical integration is coordination. By putting two companies under central control, management can ensure that both companies work toward a common goal. For example, oil companies are often vertically integrated. They generally own all stages of the production process, from the oil fields to the refineries and so on, even down to the gas stations that distribute their primary product—gasoline. Many also have divisions that prospect for new oil.

Vertically integrated companies are large, and as we have already pointed out, large corporations are more difficult to run. Consequently, not all successful corporations are vertically integrated. A good example is Microsoft Corporation. Microsoft has chosen to make the operating system that the vast majority of computers use, but not the computers themselves. Many experts have argued that a key factor in Microsoft's early success over rivals IBM and Apple was its decision not to integrate vertically.

Expertise

Firms often need expertise in particular areas to compete more efficiently. Faced with this situation, a firm can enter the labour market and attempt to hire personnel with the required skills. However, hiring experienced workers with the appropriate talent might be difficult in the case of an unfamiliar, new technology. A more efficient solution may be to purchase the talent as an already functioning unit by acquiring an existing firm. For example, in 2000, Paris-based AXA bought Sanford C. Bernstein, a Wall Street private partnership, to gain expertise and a pre-existing client base in the huge U.S. asset management market. Similarly, U.K. builder Amec bought a large stake in Spie Batignolles, a French contractor, to gain local contacts and expertise in the French building industry. Such mergers are common in high-tech industries. Networking firm Cisco Systems is known for its strategy of buying young start-up firms that have developed promising new networking technologies.

Monopoly Gains

It is often argued that merging with or acquiring a major rival enables a firm to substantially reduce competition within the industry and thereby increase profits. Society as a whole bears the cost of monopoly strategies, so most countries have antitrust laws that limit such activity and protect the free enterprise system.

The extent to which these laws are enforced tends to vary across countries and over time, depending on the policy of current leaders. When General Electric (GE) agreed to buy Honeywell in October 2000, the U.S. Justice Department approved the deal with limited conditions. However, the European Commission (EC) determined that putting GE's aircraft leasing division and Honeywell's extensive avionics product line under the same management would lead to unacceptable anticompetitive effects in the avionics market. Despite substantial concessions by GE and top-level political lobbying by U.S. officials, the EC refused to approve the deal, and it was eventually called off. The GE/Honeywell deal was the first time a merger of two U.S. companies that had been approved by U.S. authorities was blocked by European officials. The EC had no direct jurisdiction over the merger of the companies, but it was in the position to impose crippling restrictions on sales inside the European Union. In 2009, Suncor Energy Inc. and Petro-Canada announced plans to merge. Canada's Competition Bureau indicated that competition would be lessened substantially in some markets—particularly in southern Ontario and the greater Toronto area. Consequently, to receive approval for the merger, the Bureau required Suncor and Petro-Canada to sell over 100 retail gas stations in southern Ontario and commit to sell to other parties for 10 years the following: 98 million litres of gasoline each year, storage and distribution network capacity.

Monopoly power could be very valuable, and we would expect that in the absence of strong antitrust laws, many companies would merge. However, while all companies in an industry benefit when competition is reduced, only the merging company pays the associated costs (e.g., from integrating the target and managing a larger corporation). Perhaps this reason, along with existing antitrust regulations, accounts for the lack of convincing evidence that monopoly gains result from the reduction of competition following takeovers. For example, financial researchers have found that the share prices of other firms in the same industry did not significantly increase following the announcement of a merger within the industry.[3]

Efficiency Gains

Another justification acquirers cite for paying a premium for a target is efficiency gains, which are often achieved through an elimination of duplication—for example, as in the SBC/AT&T merger mentioned earlier. Acquirers also often argue that they can run the target organization more efficiently than existing management could.

---

[3]See B.E. Eckbo, "Horizontal Mergers, Collusion and Stockholder Wealth," *Journal of Financial Economics* 11(1) (1983): 241–273; and R. Stillman, "Examining Antitrust Policy Toward Horizontal Mergers," *Journal of Financial Economics* 11(1) (1983): 225–240.

Although in theory a chief executive of an inefficiently run corporation can be ousted by current shareholders voting to replace the board of directors, very few managers are replaced in this way. Instead, unhappy investors typically sell their stock, so the stock of a corporation with an inept chief executive trades at a discount relative to the price at which it would trade if it had more capable leadership. In such a situation, an acquirer could purchase shares at the discounted price to take control of the corporation and replace the chief executive with a more effective one. Once the benefits of the new management team become obvious to investors, the discount for the old management will likely disappear and the acquirer can resell its shares for a profit.

Although identifying poorly performing corporations is relatively easy, fixing them is another matter entirely. Takeovers relying on the improvement of target management are difficult to complete, and post-takeover resistance to change can be great. Thus, not all inefficiently run organizations necessarily become more efficient following a takeover.

Tax Savings from Operating Losses

When a firm makes a profit, it must pay taxes on the profit. However, when it incurs a loss, the government does not rebate taxes. Thus, it might appear that a conglomerate has a tax advantage over a single-product firm simply because losses in one division can be offset by profits in another division. Let's illustrate this scenario with an example.

Although Example 24.1 is an extreme case, it illustrates a benefit of conglomeration. In Canada and the United States, however, these benefits are mitigated because

---

EXAMPLE 24.1

Taxes for a Merged Corporation

Problem

Consider two firms, Yin Corporation and Yang Corporation. Both corporations will either make $50 million or lose $20 million every year with equal probability. The only difference is that the firms' profits are perfectly negatively correlated. That is, any year Yang Corporation earns $50 million, Yin Corporation loses $20 million, and vice versa. Assume that the corporate tax rate is 34%. What are the total expected after-tax profits of both firms when they are two separate firms? What are the expected after-tax profits if the two firms are combined into one corporation called Yin-Yang Corporation but are run as two independent divisions? (Assume it is not possible to carry back or carry forward any losses.)

Solution

▶ **Plan**

We need to calculate the after-tax profits of each firm in both the profitable and unprofitable states by multiplying profits by (1 − tax rate). We can then compute expected after-tax profits as the weighted average of the after-tax profits in the profitable and unprofitable states. If the firms are combined, their total profits in any year would always be $50 million − $20 million, so the after-tax profit will always be $30 × (1 − tax rate).

▶ **Execute**

Let's start with Yin Corporation. In the profitable state, the firm must pay corporate taxes, so after-tax profits are $50 × (1 − 0.34) = $33 million. No taxes are owed when the firm reports losses, so the after-tax profits in the unprofitable state are −$20 million.

Thus, the expected after-tax profits of Yin Corporation are 33 (0.5) + (−20) (0.5) = $6.5 million. Because Yang Corporation has identical expected profits, its expected profits are also $6.5 million. Thus, the total expected profit of both companies operated separately is $13 million.

The merged corporation, Yin-Yang Corporation, would have after-tax profits of $30 × (1 − 0.34) = $19.8 million.

> ▶ **Evaluate**
> Yin-Yang Corporation has significantly higher after-tax profits than the total stand-alone after-tax profits of Yin Corporation and Yang Corporation. This is because the losses on one division reduce the taxes on the other division's profits.

the tax authorities allow companies to carry losses forward up to 20 years. That is, a company can use losses to offset earnings up to 20 years in the future. Furthermore, companies with current-year losses can also use them to offset earnings for the three prior years in Canada and the two prior years in the United States. These carryback and carryforward provisions deliver most of the tax benefits of conglomeration (except time value differences) to a small firm with volatile earnings. While these rules would reduce the tax benefit in Example 24.1, they also create a motive for profitable firms to acquire targets with large tax loss carryforwards in order to reap the tax savings from them. However, both the CRA in Canada and the IRS in the United States will disallow a tax break if it can show that the principal reason for a takeover is tax avoidance, so it is unlikely that such a tax benefit could, by itself, be a valid reason to acquire another firm.

Diversification

The benefits of diversification are frequently cited as a reason for a conglomerate merger. The justification for these benefits comes in three forms: direct risk reduction, lower cost of debt or increased debt capacity, and liquidity enhancement. We discuss each in turn.

Risk Reduction. Like a large portfolio, large firms bear less idiosyncratic risk, so often mergers are justified on the basis that the combined firm is less risky. The problem with this argument is that it ignores the fact that investors can achieve the benefits of diversification themselves by purchasing shares in the two separate firms. Because most stockholders will already be holding a well-diversified portfolio, they get no further benefit from the firm diversifying through acquisition. Moreover, as we have already pointed out, there are costs associated with merging and with running a large diversified firm. Because it may be harder to measure performance accurately in a conglomerate, agency costs may increase and resources may be inefficiently allocated across divisions. As a result, it is cheaper for investors to diversify their own portfolios than to have the corporation do it through acquisition.

Debt Capacity and Borrowing Costs. All else being equal, larger, more diversified firms have a lower probability of bankruptcy, given the same degree of leverage. Consequently, such firms can increase leverage further and enjoy greater tax savings without incurring significant costs of financial distress. Thus, increased tax benefits and reduction in bankruptcy costs from leverage are potential benefits of diversifying mergers that diversified investors cannot achieve on their own. Of course, to justify a merger, these gains must be large enough to offset any disadvantages of running a larger, less-focused firm.

Liquidity. Shareholders of private companies are often underdiversified: they have a disproportionate share of their wealth invested in the private company. Consequently, when an acquirer buys a private target, it provides the target's owners with a way to reduce their risk exposure by cashing out their investment in the private target and reinvesting in a diversified portfolio. This liquidity that the bidder provides to the owners of a private firm can be valuable and often is an important incentive for the target shareholders to agree to the takeover.

Earnings Growth

It is possible to combine two companies with the result that the earnings per share of the merged company exceed the pre-merger earnings per share of either company, *even when the merger itself creates no economic value*. Let's look at how this can happen.

EXAMPLE 24.2

Mergers and Earnings per Share

Problem

Consider two corporations that both have earnings of $5 per share. The first firm, Upper Canada Enterprises, is a mature company with few growth opportunities. It has 1 million shares that are currently outstanding, priced at $60 per share. The second company, Lower Canada Corporation, is a young company with much more lucrative growth opportunities. Consequently, it has a higher value: although it has the same number of shares outstanding, its stock price is $100 per share. Assume Lower Canada acquires Upper Canada using its own stock, and the takeover adds no value. In a perfect market, what is the value of Lower Canada after the acquisition? At current market prices, how many shares must Lower Canada offer to Upper Canada's shareholders in exchange for their shares? Finally, what are Lower Canada's earnings per share after the acquisition?

Solution

▶ **Plan**

Because the takeover adds no value, the post-takeover value of Lower Canada is just the sum of the values of the two separate companies: 100×1 million $+ 60 \times 1$ million $-$ $160 million. To acquire Upper Canada, Lower Canada must pay $60 million. We need to first calculate how many shares Lower Canada must issue to pay Upper Canada shareholders $60 million. The ratio of Lower Canada shares issued to Upper Canada shares will give us the exchange ratio. Once we know how many new shares will be issued, we can divide the total earnings of the combined company by the new total number of shares outstanding to get the earnings per share.

▶ **Execute**

At its pre-takeover stock price of $100 per share, the deal requires issuing 600,000 shares ($60 million/$100 = 600,000). As a group, Upper Canada's shareholders will then exchange 1 million shares in Upper Canada for 600,000 shares in Lower Canada. The exchange ratio is the ratio of issued shares to exchanged shares: 600,000/1 million = 0.6. Therefore, each Upper Canada shareholder will get 0.6 shares in Lower Canada for each 1 share in Upper Canada. Notice that the price per share of Lower Canada stock is the same after the takeover: the new value of Lower Canada is $160 million, and there are 1.6 million shares outstanding, giving it a stock price of $100 per share.

However, Lower Canada's earnings per share have changed. Prior to the takeover, both companies earned $5/share $\times$ 1 million shares = $5 million. The combined corporation thus earns $10 million. There are 1.6 million shares outstanding after the takeover, so Lower Canada's post-takeover earnings per share are

$$EPS = \frac{\$10 \text{ million}}{1.6 \text{ million shares}} = \$6.25/\text{share}$$

By taking over Upper Canada, Lower Canada has raised its earnings per share by $1.25.

▶ **Evaluate**

Because no value was created, we can think of the combined company as simply a portfolio of Lower Canada and Upper Canada. Although the portfolio has higher total earnings per share, it also has lower growth, because we have combined the low-growth Upper Canada with the high-growth Lower Canada. The higher current earnings per share has come at a price—lower earnings per share growth.

As Example 24.2 demonstrates, by acquiring a company with low growth potential (and thus a low *P/E* multiple), a company with high growth potential (and high *P/E* multiple) can raise its earnings per share. In the past, people have cited this increase as a reason to merge. Of course, a savvy investor will see that the merger *adds no economic value*. All that has happened is that the high-growth company, by combining with a low-growth company, has lowered its overall growth rate. As a result, its *P/E* multiple should fall, which results from its earnings per share rising. Thus, we can draw no conclusion regarding whether a merger was beneficial solely by looking at its impact on the acquirer's earnings per share.

EXAMPLE 24.3

Mergers and the Price-Earnings Ratio

Problem

Calculate Lower Canada's price-earnings ratio before and after the takeover described in Example 24.2.

Solution

▶ **Plan**

The price-earnings ratio is price per share/earnings per share. Lower Canada's price per share is $100 both before and after the takeover, and its earnings per share is $5 before and $6.25 after the takeover.

▶ **Execute**

Before the takeover, Lower Canada's price-earnings ratio is

$$P/E = \frac{\$100/\text{share}}{\$5/\text{share}} = 20$$

After the takeover, Lower Canada's price-earnings ratio is

$$P/E = \frac{\$100/\text{share}}{\$6.25/\text{share}} = 16$$

▶ **Evaluate**

The price-earnings ratio has dropped to reflect the fact that after taking over Upper Canada, Lower Canada derives more of its value from earnings from current projects than from its future growth potential.

Managerial Motives to Merge

Most of the reasons given so far are economically motivated, shareholder-driven incentives to merge. However, managers sometimes have their own reasons to merge. Studies have consistently found that the stock price of large bidders drops on average when a bid is announced, especially when the target is publicly traded. Two possible explanations might be conflicts of interest with their shareholders and overconfidence.

Conflicts of Interest. Managers may prefer to run a larger company due to the additional pay and prestige it brings. Because most CEOs hold only a small fraction of their firm's stock, they may not bear enough of the cost of an otherwise bad merger that increases their personal benefits.[4] For example, a CEO who owns 1% of her firm's stock bears 1% of every dollar lost on a bad acquisition but enjoys 100% of the gains in

[4]M. Jensen highlighted the agency conflict in acquisition decisions in his 1986 paper, "Agency Costs of Free Cash Flow, Corporate Finance and Takeovers," *American Economic Review* 76 (1986): 323–329.

compensation and prestige that come with being the CEO of a larger company. If the acquisition destroys $100 million in shareholder value but increases the present value of her compensation by more than $1 million, she will prefer to execute the merger anyway. Why would the board of directors create these incentives? Either due to poor monitoring of the manager, or belief that the strategy is correct even if the stock market disagrees, boards typically increase the pay of CEOs along with the size of the firm, even if the size comes at the expense of poorly performing acquisitions.[5]

Overconfidence. As explained in Chapter 10, people in general tend to be overconfident about their abilities. Psychological research has shown that it takes repeated failures for people to change their beliefs that they are above-average at some activity. Most CEOs perform at most one large acquisition during their tenure as CEO. In a well-known 1986 paper,[6] Richard Roll proposed the "hubris hypothesis" to explain takeovers, which maintains that overconfident CEOs pursue mergers that have a low chance of creating value because they truly believe that their ability to manage is great enough to succeed. The critical distinction between this hypothesis and the incentive conflict discussed above is that overconfident managers believe they are doing the right thing for their shareholders but irrationally overestimate their own abilities. Under the incentive conflict explanation, managers know they are destroying shareholder value but personally gain from doing so.

5. What are the reasons most often cited for a takeover?

6. Explain why risk-diversification benefits and earnings growth are not good justifications for a takeover intended to increase shareholder wealth.

24.4   The Takeover Process

In this section, we explore how the takeover process works. We begin by establishing how a bidder determines the initial offer. We then review the tax and accounting issues specific to a takeover and explain the regulatory approval process. We end by discussing board approval, including defensive strategies that boards implement to discourage takeovers.

Valuation

In Chapter 9, we demonstrated how to value the stock of a company. Recall that there are two broad categories of valuation approaches, which can be applied here to valuing a target company. The first—and simplest—approach compares the target to other comparable companies. Although this approach is easy to implement, it gives at best a rough estimate of value. Valuing the target using a multiple based on comparable firms does not directly incorporate the operational improvements and other synergistic efficiencies that the acquirer intends to implement. Purchasing a corporation usually constitutes a very large capital investment decision, so it requires a more accurate estimate of value, including careful analysis of both operational aspects of the firm and the ultimate cash

---

[5]J. Harford and K. Li, "Decoupling CEO Wealth and Firm Performance: The Case of Acquiring CEOs," *Journal of Finance* 62 (2007): 917–949, shows that in 75% of mergers where the acquiring shareholders lose money, acquiring CEOs are financially better off.

[6]R. Roll, "The Hubris Hypothesis of Corporate Takeovers," *Journal of Business* 59(2) (1986): 197–216.

flows the deal will generate. Thus, the second approach to valuation requires making a projection of the expected cash flows that will result from the deal, and valuing those cash flows.

A key issue for takeovers is quantifying and discounting the value added as a result of the merger. As demonstrated in Section 24.3, a takeover can generate many different sources of value, which we can characterize as the takeover synergies.

We know that the price paid for a target is equal to the target's pre-bid market capitalization plus the premium paid in the acquisition. If we view the pre-bid market capitalization as the stand-alone value of the target,[7] then from the bidder's perspective, the takeover is a positive-*NPV* project only if the premium it pays does not exceed the synergies created. Although the premium that is offered is a concrete number, the synergies are not—investors might well be skeptical of the acquirer's estimate of their magnitude. The bidder's stock price reaction to the announcement of the merger is one way to gauge investors' assessments of whether the bidder overpaid or underpaid for the target. As Table 24.2 shows, the average stock price reaction is 1%, but as we noted, the median is closer to zero. Thus, the market, on average, believes that the premium is approximately equal to the synergies. Nonetheless, there is large variation in the premium across deals. One recent large-scale study of the value effects of mergers found that positive reactions to bids are concentrated in smaller bidders. In fact, during the 1990s, 87 large public acquirers announced bids that resulted in $1 billion or more in value reduction at announcement.[8] This finding is likely related to some of the managerial motives discussed in the previous section.

The Offer

Once the acquirer has completed the valuation process, it is in the position to make a tender offer—that is, a public announcement of its intention to purchase a large block of shares for a specified price. A bidder can use either of two methods to pay for a target: cash or stock. In a cash transaction, the bidder simply pays for the target, including any premium, in cash. In a stock-swap transaction, the bidder pays for the target by issuing new stock and giving it to the target shareholders. The "price" offered is determined by the **exchange ratio**—the number of bidder shares received in exchange for each target share—multiplied by the market price of the acquirer's stock.

exchange ratio In a takeover, the number of bidder shares received in exchange for each target share.

A stock-swap merger is a positive-*NPV* investment for the acquiring shareholders if the share price of the merged firm (the acquirer's share price after the takeover) exceeds the pre-merger price of the acquiring firm. We can write this condition as follows. Let A be the pre-merger, or stand-alone, value of the acquirer, and T be the pre-merger (stand-alone) value of the target. Let S be the value of the synergies created by the merger. If the acquirer has N_A shares outstanding before the merger, and issues x new shares to pay for the target, then the acquirer's share price should increase post-acquisition if

$$\frac{A + T + S}{N_A + x} > \frac{A}{N_A} \qquad (24.1)$$

The left side of Equation 24.1 is the share price of the merged firm. The numerator indicates the total value of the merged firm: the stand-alone value of the acquirer

---

[7]Rumors about a potential bid for the target will often push its share price up in anticipation of the premium offer. Practitioners refer to the "unaffected" target price, meaning the target's share price before it was affected by rumours of a takeover. This price would be used to compute the stand-alone value of the target.

[8]S. Moeller, R. Stulz, and F. Schlingemann, "Wealth Destruction on a Massive Scale: A Study of Acquiring Firm Returns in the Recent Merger Wave," *Journal of Finance* 60(2) (2005): 757–782.

and target plus the value of the synergies created by the merger. The denominator represents the total number of shares outstanding once the merger is complete. The ratio is the post-merger share price. The right side of Equation 24.1 is the pre-merger share price of the acquirer: the total pre-merger value of the acquirer divided by the pre-merger number of shares outstanding.

Solving Equation 24.1 for x gives the maximum number of new shares the acquirer can offer and still achieve a positive *NPV*:

$$x < \left(\frac{T + S}{A}\right) N_A \tag{24.2}$$

We can express this relationship as an exchange ratio by dividing by the pre-merger number of target shares outstanding, N_T:

$$\text{Exchange Ratio} = \frac{x}{N_T} < \left(\frac{T + S}{A}\right) \frac{N_A}{N_T} \tag{24.3}$$

We can also rewrite Equation 24.3 in terms of the *pre-merger* target and acquirer share prices, $P_T = T/N_T$ and $P_A = A/N_A$:

$$\text{Exchange Ratio} < \frac{P_T}{P_A}\left(1 + \frac{S}{T}\right) \tag{24.4}$$

EXAMPLE 24.4

Maximum Exchange Ratio in a Stock Takeover

Problem
At the time Sprint announced plans to acquire Nextel in December 2004, Sprint stock was trading for $25 per share and Nextel stock was trading for $30 per share. If the projected synergies were $12 billion, and Nextel had 1.033 billion shares outstanding, what is the maximum exchange ratio Sprint could offer in a stock swap and still generate a positive *NPV*? What is the maximum cash offer Sprint could make?

Solution

▶ **Plan**
We can use Equation 24.4 to compute the maximum shares Sprint could offer and still have a positive *NPV*. To compute the maximum cash offer, we can calculate the synergies per share and add that to Nextel's current share price.

▶ **Execute**
Using Equation 24.4,

$$\text{Exchange Ratio} < \frac{P_T}{P_A}\left(1 + \frac{S}{T}\right) = \frac{30}{25}\left(1 + \frac{12}{31}\right) = 1.665$$

That is, Sprint could offer up to 1.665 shares of Sprint stock for each share of Nextel stock and generate a positive *NPV*.

For a cash offer, given synergies of $12 billion/1.033 billion shares = $11.62 per share, Sprint could offer up to $30 + 11.62 = $41.62.

▶ **Evaluate**
Both the cash amount and the exchange offer ($25 × 1.665 = $41.62) have the same value. That value is the most that Nextel is worth to Sprint—if Sprint pays $41.62 for Nextel, it is paying full price plus paying Nextel shareholders for all the synergy gains created, leaving none for Sprint shareholders. Thus, at $41.62, buying Nextel is exactly a zero-*NPV* project.

Merger "Arbitrage"

Once a tender offer is announced, there is no guarantee that, in fact, the takeover will take place at this price. Often acquirers have to raise the price to consummate the deal. Alternatively, the offer may fail. When an acquirer bids for a target, the target firm's board may not accept the bid and may recommend that existing shareholders not tender their shares, even when the acquirer offers a significant premium over the pre-offer share price. Even if the target board supports the deal, there is also the possibility that regulators might not approve the takeover. When the London Stock Exchange and the TMX Group (the owner of the TSX in Canada) agreed to merge in 2011, the price of TMX did not reflect what its value would be if the merger succeeded, because of substantial doubt as to whether the needed approval from the provincial and federal authorities would occur. Because of this uncertainty about whether a takeover will succeed, the market price generally does not rise by the amount of the premium when the takeover is announced.

risk arbitrageurs Traders who, once a takeover offer is announced, speculate on the outcome of the deal.

This uncertainty creates an opportunity for investors to speculate on the outcome of the deal. Traders known as **risk arbitrageurs**, who believe that they can predict the outcome of a deal, take positions based on their beliefs. While the strategies these traders use are sometimes referred to as arbitrage, they are actually quite risky, so they do not represent a true arbitrage opportunity in the sense we have defined in this book. Let's illustrate the strategy using the 2002 stock-swap merger of Hewlett-Packard (HP) and Compaq.

In September 2001, HP announced that it would purchase Compaq by swapping 0.6325 shares of HP stock for each share of Compaq stock. After the announcement, HP traded for $18.87 per share, so the implied value of HP's offer was $18.87 \times 0.6325 = $11.9353. Yet, the price of Compaq was only $11.08 per share after the announcement, $0.8553 below the value of HP's offer. Thus, a risk arbitrageur who simultaneously purchased 10,000 Compaq shares and sold short 6325 HP shares would net $6325 \times $18.87 - 10,000 \times $11.08 = $8553 immediately. Then, if the takeover was successfully completed on the original terms, the 10,000 Compaq shares would convert into 6325 HP shares, allowing the risk arbitrageur to cover the short position in HP and be left with no net exposure. Thus, the arbitrageur would pocket the original $8553 as a profit.[9]

merger-arbitrage spread In a takeover, the difference between a target stock's price and the implied offer price.

The potential profit described above arises from the difference between the target's stock price and the implied offer price, and is referred to as the **merger-arbitrage spread**. However, it is not a true arbitrage opportunity, because there is a risk that the deal will not go through. If the takeover did not ultimately succeed, the risk arbitrageur would eventually have to unwind his position at whatever market prices prevailed. In most cases, these prices would have moved against him (in particular, the price of Compaq would be likely to decline if the takeover did not occur), so he would face losses on the position.

The HP-Compaq takeover was distinctive in that the uncertainty about the success of the deal stemmed largely from acquirer discomfort with the deal rather than from target shareholder discomfort. Although initially supportive of the merger, the Hewlett family got cold feet. About two months after the deal was announced, Walter Hewlett disclosed his family's opposition to it. On the day of Walter Hewlett's announcement, the price of HP stock rose to $19.81, while Compaq's stock price fell to $8.50, causing the merger-arbitrage spread to widen to $19.81 \times 6325 - $8.5 \times 10,000 = $40,298. We plot the merger-arbitrage spread for the HP-Compaq merger in Figure 24.2. The risk-arbitrage strategy outlined above is effectively a short position on this spread,

---

[9]For simplicity, we are ignoring dividend payments made during the period. HP paid $0.24 and Compaq paid $0.075 in dividends prior to the completion of the merger, reducing slightly the profit from the trade by $10,000 \times $0.075 - 6325 \times $0.24 = -$768.

FIGURE 24.2   Merger-Arbitrage Spread for the Merger of HP and Compaq

The plot shows the potential profit, given that the merger was ultimately successfully completed, from purchasing 10,000 Compaq shares and short-selling 6325 HP shares on the indicated date. A risk arbitrageur who expects the deal to go through can profit by opening the position when the spread is large and closing the position after it declines.

which pays off if the spread declines. Thus, an arbitrageur who opened the strategy when the deal was announced and closed it after Walter Hewlett announced his opposition would face a loss of $40,298 − $8553 = $31,745.

Although the Hewlett family members were large shareholders of HP, they were not controlling shareholders; they did not have enough shares to block the deal single-handedly. Hence, a battle for control of HP ensued between the Hewlett family and then-CEO Carly Fiorina, the driving force behind the acquisition of Compaq. This conflict was resolved months later only when HP shareholders, by a slim margin, voted in favour of issuing new shares, thereby effectively approving the merger and netting a profit for any risk arbitrageur who stayed the course. As is clear from Figure 24.2, arbitrageurs who did not have the stomach to hold on would have faced large losses at several points during the roller-coaster ride. And while HP CEO Carly Fiorina survived this early challenge to her authority, the performance of HP following the merger vindicated Hewlett's position. HP's board ultimately fired Fiorina in 2005.

Tax and Accounting Issues

Once the terms of trade have been decided, the tax and accounting implications of a merger can be determined. How the acquirer pays for the target affects the taxes of both the target shareholders and the combined firm. Any cash received in full or partial exchange for shares triggers an immediate tax liability for target shareholders. They will have to pay a capital gains tax on the difference between the price paid for their shares in the takeover and the price they paid when they first bought the shares. If the acquirer pays for the takeover entirely by exchanging bidder stock for target stock, then the tax liability is deferred until the target shareholders actually sell their new shares of bidder stock.

step up Increase the book value of a target's assets to the purchase price when an acquirer purchases those assets directly instead of purchasing the target stock.

If the acquirer purchases the target assets directly (rather than the target stock), then the acquirer can **step up** the book value of the target's assets to the purchase price. This higher depreciable basis reduces future taxes through larger depreciation charges. The same treatment applies to a *forward cash-out merger*, in which the target is merged into the acquirer and target shareholders receive cash in exchange for their shares.

While the method of payment (cash or stock) affects how the value of the target's assets is recorded for tax purposes, it does not affect the combined firm's financial statements for financial reporting. The combined firm must mark up the value assigned to the target's assets on the financial statements by allocating the purchase price to target assets according to their fair market value. If the purchase price exceeds the fair market value of the target's identifiable assets, then the remainder is recorded as goodwill and is examined annually by the firm's accountants to determine whether its value has decreased. For example, in HP's takeover of Compaq, HP recorded more than $10 billion in goodwill. The footnotes to the statements attributed the goodwill to the value of the Compaq brand name, which is assumed to have an indefinite life.

Even when a merger has a positive *NPV*, bidding managers are typically very concerned with the effect of the merger on earnings. This is the other side of the earnings-growth argument as a reason to merge. Just as merging two companies can increase earnings without affecting economic value, it can also decrease earnings without affecting economic value. Nevertheless, acquirers are hesitant to commit to a deal that would be dilutive to earnings per share, even if only in the short run.

Board and Shareholder Approval

For a merger to proceed, both the target and the acquiring board of directors must approve the deal and put the question to a vote of the shareholders of the target (and, in some cases, the shareholders of the acquiring firm as well).

friendly takeover A takeover in which the target's board of directors supports a merger, negotiates with potential acquirers, and agrees on a price that is ultimately put to a shareholder vote.

In a **friendly takeover**, the target board of directors supports the merger, negotiates with potential acquirers, and agrees on a price that is ultimately put to a shareholder vote. Although it is rare for acquiring boards to oppose a merger, target boards sometimes do not support the deal even when the acquirer offers a large premium. In a **hostile takeover**, the board of directors (together with upper-level management) fights the takeover attempt. To succeed, the acquirer must garner enough shares to take control of the target and replace the board of directors. When a takeover is hostile, the acquirer is often called a **corporate raider** (or **raider**).

hostile takeover A takeover in which an individual or organization, sometimes referred to as a corporate raider, purchases a large fraction of a target corporation's stock and in doing so gets enough votes to replace the target's board of directors and its CEO.

If the shareholders of a target company receive a premium over the current market value of their shares, why would a board of directors ever oppose a takeover? There are a number of reasons. The board might legitimately believe that the offer price is too low. In this case, a suitor that is willing to pay more might be found or the original bidder might be convinced to raise its offer. Alternatively, if the offer is a stock-swap, target management may oppose the offer because they feel the acquirer's shares are overvalued, and therefore that the value of the offer is actually less than the stand-alone value of the target. Finally, managers (and the board) might oppose a takeover because of their own self-interests, especially if the primary motivation for the takeover is efficiency gains. In this case, the acquirer probably plans to undertake a complete change of leadership of the corporation. Upper-level managers could view opposing the merger as a way of protecting their jobs (and the jobs of their employees). In fact, this concern is perhaps the single biggest reason for the negative associations that hostile takeovers generate. Bear in mind that if substantial efficiency gains are indeed possible, current management is not doing an effective job. A takeover, or threat thereof, might be the only recourse investors have to fix the problem.

corporate raider (or **raider**) The acquirer in a hostile takeover.

In theory, the duty of the target board of directors is to choose the course of action that is in the best interests "of the corporation" in Canada or in the best interests "of the target shareholders" in the United States. In practice, the courts in the United States and, more recently, in Canada have given target directors wide latitude under what is called the "business judgment rule" to determine the best course for their companies, including spurning a premium offer if the directors can reasonably argue that more value will eventually be realized for their shareholders by remaining independent. The premise of this rule is that absent evidence of misconduct or self-dealing, the court will not substitute its judgment for that of the elected, informed directors.

In merger transactions, however, there is heightened judicial scrutiny under what is commonly referred to as the "Revlon duties" and "Unocal," named after the U.S. cases in which they were established. The Revlon duties state that if a change of control is going to occur, then directors must seek the highest value (they cannot favour one controlling entity over another based on anything other than value to shareholders). In Canada, the Supreme Court rejected the precedent from the Revlon case and required that no one stakeholder (equity holder or debt holder) be given priority by a target's management in their response to a takeover attempt. The Unocal case, in the United States, established that when the board takes actions deemed as defensive (we discuss these in detail in the next section), its actions are subject to extra scrutiny to ensure that they are not coercive or designed simply to preclude a deal. The board must believe that there is a threat to its corporate strategy, and the board's defences must be proportional to the magnitude of the threat. Rulings similar to the Unocal case have emerged in Canada.

Concept Check

7. What are the steps in the takeover process?

8. What do risk arbitrageurs do?

24.5 Takeover Defences

For a hostile takeover to succeed, the acquirer must go around the target board and appeal directly to the target shareholders. The acquirer can do this by making an unsolicited offer to buy target stock directly from the shareholders (a tender offer). The acquirer will usually couple this with a **proxy fight**: the acquirer attempts to convince target shareholders to unseat the target board by using their proxy votes to support the acquirer's candidates for election to the target board. Target companies have a number of strategies available to them to stop this process. These strategies can force a bidder to raise its bid or entrench management more securely, depending on the independence of the target board. We begin with the most effective defensive strategy, the poison pill.

Poison Pills

A **poison pill** is a rights offering that gives existing target shareholders the right to buy shares in the target or the acquirer at a deeply discounted price once certain conditions are met. The acquirer is specifically excluded from this right. Because target shareholders can purchase shares at less than the market price, the rights offering dilutes the value of any shares held by the acquirer. This dilution makes the takeover so expensive for the acquiring shareholders that they choose to pass on the deal.

proxy fight In a hostile takeover, the acquirer's attempts to convince the target's shareholders to unseat the target's board by using their proxy votes to support the acquirer's candidates for election to the target's board.

poison pill A rights offering that gives the target shareholders the right to buy shares in either the target or an acquirer at a deeply discounted price, as a defence against a hostile takeover.

The poison pill was invented in 1982 by a takeover lawyer, Martin Lipton, who successfully warded off a takeover attempt of El Paso Electric by General American Oil.[10] Because the original poison pill goes into effect only in the event of a complete takeover (i.e., a purchase of 100% of the outstanding shares), one way to circumvent it is to not do a complete takeover. The first time this work-around was used was by Sir James Goldsmith, who took control of Crown Zellerbach by purchasing slightly more than 50% of the outstanding stock. Because he did not purchase the rest, Crown Zellerbach's poison pill was ineffective.

In response to the takeover of Crown Zellerbach, corporate lawyers have perfected the original poison pill. Most poison pills now specify that if a raider acquires more than a trigger amount (typically 20%) of the target shares (but chooses not to execute a complete takeover by purchasing all outstanding shares), existing shareholders—with the exception of the acquirer—have the right to buy more shares in the target at a discounted price.

The term *poison pill* comes from the world of espionage. Once caught, a spy is supposed to take his own life by swallowing a poison pill rather than give up important secrets. Poison pills are very effective in stopping takeovers, but where is the suicide analogy? The answer is that by adopting a poison pill, a company effectively entrenches its management by making it much more difficult for shareholders to replace bad managers, thereby potentially destroying value. Financial research has verified this effect. A firm's stock price typically drops when it adopts a poison pill. Furthermore, once firms have adopted poison pills, these same firms have below-average financial performance.[11]

Not surprisingly, companies adopting poison pills are harder to take over, and when a takeover occurs, the premium that existing shareholders receive for their stock is higher. Therefore, because a poison pill increases the cost of a takeover, all else being equal, a target company must be in worse shape (there must be a greater opportunity for profit) to justify the expense of waging a takeover battle.

A poison pill also increases the bargaining power of the target firm when negotiating with the acquirer, because completing the takeover is more difficult without the cooperation of the target board. If used effectively, this bargaining power can allow target shareholders to capture more of the takeover gains by negotiating a higher premium than they would get if no pill existed. Numerous studies on the impact of anti-takeover provisions on takeovers have found that such provisions result in higher premiums accruing to existing shareholders of the target company.[12]

Staggered Boards

A determined bidder that faces a poison pill has another available option: get its own slate of directors for the target board, which it can submit at the next annual shareholders meeting. If the target shareholders elect those candidates, then the new directors can cancel the poison pill and accept the bidder's offer. To prevent such a coup from

---

[10]For a brief history, see Len Costa, "The Perfect Pill," *Legal Affairs* (March 2005), www.legalaffairs.org.

[11]P. Malatesta and R. Walkling, "Poison Pill Securities: Stockholder Wealth, Profitability and Ownership Structure," *Journal of Financial Economics* 20(1) (1988): 347–376; M. Ryngaert, "The Effects of Poison Pills Securities on Stockholder Wealth," *Journal of Financial Economics* 20(1) (1988): 377–417; and D. Stangeland, "Why Are Anti-Takeover Devices Being Used?" *Business Quarterly*, 1995.

[12]R. Comment and G.W. Schwert, "Poison or Placebo: Evidence on the Deterrence and Wealth Effects of Modern Antitakeover Measures," *Journal of Financial Economics* 39(1), (1995): 3–43; N. Varaiya, "Determinants of Premiums in Acquisition Transactions," *Managerial and Decision Economics* 8(3) (1987): 175–184; and R. Heron and E. Lie, "On the Use of Poison Pills and Defensive Payouts by Takeover Targets," *Journal of Business* 79(4) (2006): 1783–1807.

staggered (classified) board In some public companies, a board of directors whose three-year terms are staggered so that only one-third of the directors are up for election each year.

happening, about two-thirds of public companies in the United States have a **staggered** (or **classified**) **board**. These are less typical in Canada. In a typical staggered board, every director serves a three-year term and the terms are staggered so that only one-third of the directors are up for election each year. Thus, even if the bidder's candidates win board seats, the bidder will control only a minority of the target board. A bidder's candidate would have to win a proxy fight two years in a row before the bidder had a majority presence on the target board. The length of time required to execute this manoeuvre can deter a bidder from making a takeover attempt when the target board is staggered. Most experts consider a poison pill combined with a staggered board to be the most effective defence available to a target company.

White Knights

When a hostile takeover appears to be inevitable, a target company will sometimes look for another, friendlier company to acquire it. This company that comes charging to the target's rescue is known as a **white knight**. The white knight will make a more lucrative offer for the target than the hostile bidder did. Incumbent managers of the target maintain control by reaching an agreement with the white knight to retain their positions.

white knight A target company's defence against a hostile takeover attempt, in which the target looks for another, friendlier company to acquire it.

white squire A variant of the white knight defence, in which a large, passive investor or firm agrees to purchase a substantial block of shares in a target with special voting rights.

golden parachute An extremely lucrative severance package that is guaranteed to a firm's senior managers in the event that the firm is taken over and the managers are let go.

One variant on the white knight defence is the **white squire** defence. In this case, a large investor or firm agrees to purchase a substantial block of shares in the target with special voting rights. This action prevents a hostile raider from acquiring control of the target. The idea is that the white squire itself will not choose to exercise its control rights.

Golden Parachutes

A **golden parachute** is an extremely lucrative severance package that is guaranteed to a firm's senior managers in the event that the firm is taken over and the managers are let go. For example, when Ronald Perelman successfully acquired Revlon Corporation, the firm's former chairman, Michael Bergerac, was reported to have received a golden parachute compensation package worth in excess of $35 million.

Golden parachutes have been criticized because they are seen both as excessive and a misuse of shareholder wealth. In fact, the empirical evidence does not support this view.[13] If anything, it supports the view that an adoption of a golden parachute actually creates value. If a golden parachute exists, management will be more likely to be receptive to a takeover. This means the existence of golden parachutes lessens the likelihood of managerial entrenchment. Researchers have found that stock prices rise on average when companies announce that they plan to implement a golden parachute policy, and that the number of firms bidding against one another for the target and the size of the takeover premium are higher if a golden parachute agreement exists.

Recapitalization

Another defence against a takeover is a recapitalization, in which a company changes its capital structure to make itself less attractive as a target. For example, a company with a lot of cash might choose to pay out a large dividend. Companies without a lot of cash might instead choose to issue debt and then use the proceeds to pay a dividend or repurchase stock.

Why does increasing leverage make a firm less attractive as a target? In many cases, a substantial portion of the synergy gains that an acquirer anticipates from a takeover are from tax savings from an increase in leverage as well as other cost reductions. By increasing leverage on its own, the target firm can reap the benefit of the interest

---

[13]M. Narayanan and A. Sundaram, "A Safe Landing? Golden Parachutes and Corporate Behavior," *University of Michigan Business School Working Paper No. 98015* (1998).

tax shields. In addition, the need to generate cash to meet the debt service obligations provides a powerful motivation to managers to run a corporation efficiently. In effect, the restructuring itself can produce efficiency gains, often removing the principal motivation for the takeover in the first place.

Other Defensive Strategies

Corporate managers and defence advisors have devised other mechanisms to forestall a takeover. A corporation's charter can require a supermajority (sometimes as much as 80%) of votes to approve a merger. It can also restrict the voting rights of very large shareholders. Finally, a firm can require that a "fair" price be paid for the company, where the determination of what is "fair" is up to the board of directors or senior management. Beauty is always in the eye of the beholder, so "fair" in this case usually implies an optimistic determination of value.

We might expect the presence of defensive strategies to reduce firm value. However, Gregg Jarrell and Annette Poulsen[14] found that, on average, the public announcement of anti-takeover amendments by 600 firms in the period 1979 to 1985 had an insignificant effect on the value of announcing firms' shares.

Regulatory Approval

All mergers must be approved by regulators. In Section 24.3, we discussed monopoly gains from takeovers and the use of antitrust regulations to limit them and protect the free enterprise system. In Canada, the Competition Bureau monitors potential monopoly combinations. In the United States, antitrust enforcement is governed by three main statutes: the Sherman Act, the Clayton Act, and the Hart-Scott-Rodino Act. The Sherman Act of 1890, which was passed in response to the formation of huge oil trusts such as Standard Oil, prohibits mergers that would create a monopoly or undue market control. The Clayton Act, enacted in 1914, strengthened the government's hand by prohibiting companies from acquiring the stock (or, as later amended, the assets) of another company if it would adversely affect competition. Under both the Sherman and Clayton acts, the government had to sue to block a merger. Often by the time a decision was rendered, the merger had taken place and was difficult to undo. The Hart-Scott-Rodino (HSR) Act of 1976 put the burden of proof on the merging parties. Under the HSR Act, all mergers above a certain size (the formula for determining whether a transaction qualifies is complicated, but it comes out to approximately $60 million) must be approved by the government before the proposed takeovers occur. The government cannot delay the deal indefinitely, however, because it must respond with approval or a request for additional information within 20 days of receiving notification of the proposed merger. The U.S. government has been very active in enforcing competition policy and is rated by the Global Competition Review in the "elite" category for enforcement (the United Kingdom and European Union competition commissions are also rated elite). Some criticisms have been made regarding Canada's Competition Bureau, because it does not appear to act as vigorously. Canada's Competition Bureau was rated in the "good" category by the Global Competition Review.

The European Commission has established a process similar to the process under the HSR Act, which requires merging parties to notify the EC, provide additional information if requested about the proposed merger, and wait for approval before proceeding. As discussed in the Honeywell/GE example, even though the EC technically lacks legal authority to block a merger of foreign companies, it can stop a takeover by imposing

---

[14]G. Jarrell and A. Poulsen, "Shark Repellents and Stock Prices: The Effects of Antitakeover Amendments Since 1980," *Journal of Financial Economics* 19 (1988): 127–168.

Weyerhaeuser's Hostile Bid for Willamette Industries

In November 2000, Weyerhaeuser, a forest products company based in Federal Way, Washington, announced a hostile bid of $48 per share for its smaller neighbour, Willamette Industries, based in Portland, Oregon. Weyerhaeuser had been pursuing Willamette in private since 1998, when Steve Rogel unexpectedly resigned as CEO of Willamette to become CEO of Weyerhaeuser. Each time Rogel approached his old employer in private, he was rebuffed. The response to the hostile tender offer was no different. Despite the fact that the bid represented a substantial premium to the firm's pre-bid stock price, the Willamette board rejected the offer and urged its shareholders not to tender their shares to Weyerhaeuser.

Willamette's defences included a staggered board and a poison pill, so Weyerhaeuser made its tender offer conditional on Willamette's board cancelling the poison pill. Consequently, Weyerhaeuser initiated a proxy fight at the next annual shareholders' meeting in June 2001. One of the directors up for re-election at that time was Duane McDougall, Willamette's CEO. One month before

the meeting, Weyerhaeuser increased its offer to $50 per share, but Willamette's board still believed that the offer was too low and worried that too many of its long-time employees would face layoffs after the merger. Nonetheless, at the annual meeting, Weyerhaeuser's slate received 1.4% more votes than Willamette's, thereby removing Willamette's CEO from its board.

The loss of the board seats did not change Willamette's position. Willamette unsuccessfully searched for a white knight to generate a bidding contest that would force Weyerhaeuser to up its bid. It also entered into talks to buy Georgia-Pacific's building products division. Such a deal would have increased its size and added enough debt to its balance sheet to render the firm unattractive to Weyerhaeuser.

In the end, Weyerhaeuser increased its offer to $55.50 per share in January 2002, and Willamette finally agreed to a deal and called off its negotiations with Georgia-Pacific. Even without the presence of other bidders, Willamette's board was able to get what it considered to be a fair price from Weyerhaeuser.

restrictions on the combined firm's operations and sales in Europe. Although globally a proposed takeover might have to satisfy antitrust rules in more than 80 jurisdictions, practically the most important jurisdictions besides the home jurisdiction of the firm are Europe and the United States.

Another regulatory hurdle may come into play when a merger involves companies in two different countries. Many countries have regulatory authorities that oversee foreign takeovers, and they may prevent foreign takeovers that are not in the best interest of their own country. Canada is one such country. A transaction may require approval under the Investment Canada Act (ICA). When control of a Canadian company with assets of $312 million or more will transfer from Canadian control to foreign control, the transaction will be subject to regulatory review.[15] The proposed takeover of Saskatchewan-based PotashCorp (the world's largest fertilizer company by capacity) was a notable example of the importance of this Canadian regulatory feature. Management at PotashCorp lobbied vigorously in the media and with the provincial and federal governments to block the takeover of PotashCorp by BHP, Billiton because PotashCorp was a strategic resource in Canada and the takeover would not be good for Canadians. Eventually the takeover was cancelled following the ruling by Industry Minister Tony Clement that the takeover did not pass the "net benefit assessment" under the ICA.

Regulatory approval can block mergers of companies that want to merge or it can be used by a target (with appropriate lobbying) as a method to defend against unwanted takeovers.

---

[15]The threshold of $312 million is applied in cases where the acquiring company is a member of the World Trade Organization (WTO). In cases where the acquirer is not a WTO member, thresholds for review are much lower.

Concept
Check

9. What defensive strategies are available to help target companies resist an unwanted takeover?

10. How can a hostile acquirer get around a poison pill?

24.6   Who Gets the Value Added from a Takeover?

Now that we have explained the takeover process, we can return to the remaining questions posed at the beginning of this chapter: why does the price of the acquiring company not rise at the announcement of the takeover, and why is the bidder forced to pay a premium for the target?

You might imagine that the people who do the work of acquiring the corporation and replacing its management will capture the value created by the merger. Based on the average stock price reaction, it does not appear that the acquiring corporation generally captures this value. Instead, the premium the acquirer pays is approximately equal to the value it adds, which means the *target* shareholders ultimately capture the value added by the acquirer. To see why, we need to understand how market forces react to a takeover announcement.

The Free Rider Problem

Assume you are one of the 1 million shareholders of HighLife Corporation, all of whom own one share of stock. HighLife has no debt. Its chief executive is not doing a good job, preferring to spend his time using the company's jets to fly to the corporate condo in Whistler, B.C., rather than running the company in Regina. As such, the shares are trading at a substantial discount. They currently have a price of $45 per share, giving HighLife a market value of $45 million. Under a competent manager, the company would be worth $75 million. HighLife's corporate charter specifies that a simple majority is required to make all decisions, so to take control of HighLife a shareholder must purchase half the outstanding shares.

Suppose Mr. T. Boone Icon decides to fix the situation (and make a profit at the same time) by making a tender offer to buy half the outstanding shares for $60 per share in cash. If fewer than 50% of the shareholders tender their shares, the deal is off.

In principle, this idea could land T. Boone a handsome profit. If 50% of shareholders tender their shares, those shares will cost him $60 × 500,000 = $30 million. Once he has control of the firm, he can replace the managers. When the executive jets and the Whistler condo are sold and the market realizes that the new managers are serious about improving performance, the market value of the firm will rise to $75 million. Hence T. Boone's shares will be worth $75 per share, netting him a profit of $15 × 500,000 = $7.5 million. But will 50% of the shareholders tender their shares?

The offer price of $60 per share exceeds the value of the firm if the takeover does not go through ($45 per share). Hence, the offer is a good deal for shareholders overall. But if all shareholders tender their shares, as an individual shareholder, you could do better by not tendering your share. Then if T. Boone takes control, each of your shares will be worth $75 rather than the $60 you would get by tendering. In this case, it is wiser to not tender. Of course, if all shareholders think this way, no one will tender their shares, and T. Boone's deal will not get off the ground. The only way to persuade shareholders to tender their shares is to offer them at least $75 per share, which removes any profit opportunity for T. Boone. The problem here is that existing shareholders do not have to invest time and effort, but still participate in all the gains from the takeover that

Mr. T. Boone Icon generates—hence the term "free rider problem." By sharing the gains in this way, T. Boone Icon is forced to give up substantial profits and thus will likely choose not to bother at all.

Toeholds

One way for Mr. T. Boone Icon to get around the problem of shareholders' reluctance to tender their shares is to buy the shares in the market anonymously. However, Canadian securities laws and the SEC in the United States make it difficult for investors to buy much more than about 10% of a firm in secret.[16] After T. Boone acquires such an initial stake in the target, called a **toehold**, he would have to make his intentions public by informing investors of his large stake. To successfully gain control of HighLife, he would have to announce a tender offer to buy an additional 40% of the shares for $75 per share. Once in control, he would be able to sell his stake for $75 per share. Assuming he accumulated the first 10% for $50 per share, his profits in this case will be $25 \times 100,000 = $2.5 million. Not bad, but substantially less than the value he is adding.

Why should investors care whether T. Boone's profits are substantially lower than the value he is adding? The answer is that people like T. Boone perform an important service. Because of the threat that such a person might attempt to take over their company and fire them, chief executives are less likely to shirk their duties. Thus, the more profitable we make this activity, the less likely we will have to resort to it. If $2.5 million is not enough to justify T. Boone's time and effort, he will not try to acquire HighLife. Current management will remain entrenched, and T. Boone will think about acquiring the company only if further erosion in the stock price makes the deal lucrative enough for him.

A number of legal mechanisms exist that allow acquirers to avoid the free rider problem and capture more of the gains from the acquisition. We describe the two most common, the leveraged buyout and the freezeout merger, next.

The Leveraged Buyout

The good news for shareholders is that another significantly lower-cost mechanism allows people like T. Boone Icon to take over companies and fire underperforming managers. Recall from Chapter 15 that this mechanism is called the leveraged buyout (LBO). Let's illustrate how it works by returning to HighLife Corporation.

Assume that T. Boone chooses not to buy any shares in the market secretly, but instead announces a tender offer for half the outstanding shares at a price of $50 per share. However, instead of using his own cash to pay for these shares, he borrows the money through a shell corporation (one that is created for the sole purpose of making the acquisition) by *pledging the shares themselves as collateral on the loan*. The only time he will need the money is if the tender offer succeeds, so the banks lending the money can be certain that he will have control of the collateral. Even more important, if the tender offer succeeds, with control of the company, T. Boone can merge the target with the shell corporation, effectively attaching the loans directly to the target—that is, it is as if the target corporation, and not T. Boone, has borrowed the money. At the end of this process, T. Boone still owns half the shares, but the *corporation* is responsible for repaying the loan. T. Boone has effectively acquired half the shares without paying for them!

toehold An initial ownership stake in a firm that a corporate raider can use to initiate a takeover attempt.

---

[16]In Canada, the rules require an investor to issue a press release once the 10% threshold is reached. If a takeover bid is already outstanding, a 5% threshold triggers the requirement for a press release. In the United States, the rules actually require that any shareholder who owns more than 5% of a firm publicly disclose this fact, but the time delays in the disclosure process allow investors to accumulate more than 5% of the firm before this information is made public.

You might imagine that no shareholder would be willing to tender her shares under these circumstances. Surprisingly, this conclusion is wrong. If you tender your shares, you will receive $50 for each of them. If you do not tender your shares, but enough other shareholders do, then T. Boone will take control of the company. After he replaces the managers, the enterprise value of the company will be $75 million. What will your shares be worth if you did not tender them?

For simplicity, assume that there are no frictions or taxes. To gain control of the firm, T. Boone borrowed $25 million to purchase half the outstanding shares ($50 × 500,000). Because this debt is now attached to HighLife, the total value of HighLife's equity is just the total value of the company, minus the value of debt:

$$\text{Total Value of HighLife Equity} = \$75 \text{ million} - \$25 \text{ million} = \$50 \text{ million}$$

The total number of outstanding shares is the same (remember that T. Boone purchased existing shares), so the price per share is $50 million ÷ 1 million = $50/share. If the tender offer succeeds, you will be indifferent. Whether you tender your shares or keep them, each is always worth $50. If you keep your shares and the tender offer fails, the price per share stays at $45. Clearly, it is always in your best interests to tender your shares, so T. Boone's tender offer will succeed. T. Boone also makes substantially more profits than he would if he used a toehold strategy—his profits are the value of his shares upon completion of the takeover: $50 × 500,000 = $25 million.

EXAMPLE 24.5

Leveraged Buyout

Problem

FAT Corporation stock is currently trading at $40 per share. There are 20 million shares outstanding, and the company has no debt. You are a partner in a firm that specializes in leveraged buyouts. Your analysis indicates that the management of this corporation could be improved considerably. If the managers were replaced with more capable ones, you estimate that the value of the company would increase by 50%. You decide to initiate a leveraged buyout and issue a tender offer for at least a controlling interest—50% of the outstanding shares. What is the maximum amount of value you can extract and still complete the deal?

Solution

▶ **Plan**

Currently, the value of the company is $40 × 20 million = $800 million, and you estimate you can add an additional 50%, or $400 million. If you borrow $400 million and the tender offer succeeds, you will take control of the company and install new management. The total value of the company will increase by 50% to $1.2 billion. You will also attach the debt to the company, so the company will now have $400 million in debt. You can then compute the value of the post-takeover equity and your gain. You can repeat this computation assuming you borrow more than $400 million and confirming that your gain does not change.

▶ **Execute**

The value of the equity once the deal is done is the total value minus the debt outstanding:

$$\text{Total Equity} = \$1200 \text{ million} - \$400 \text{ million} = \$800 \text{ million}$$

The value of the equity is the same as the pre-merger value. You own half the shares, which are worth $400 million, and paid nothing for them, so you have captured the value you anticipated adding to FAT.

What if you borrowed more than $400 million? Assume you were able to borrow $450 million. The value of equity after the merger would be as follows:

$$\text{Total Equity} = \$1200 \text{ million} - \$450 \text{ million} = \$750 \text{ million}$$

This is lower than the pre-merger value. Recall, however, that in Canada and the United States, existing shareholders must be offered at least the pre-merger price for their shares. Because existing shareholders anticipate that the share price will be lower once the deal is complete, all shareholders will tender their shares. This implies that you will have to pay $800 million for these shares, and so to complete the deal, you will have to pay $800 million − $450 million = $350 million out of your own pocket. In the end, you will own all the equity, which is worth $750 million. You paid $350 million for it, so your profit is again $400 million.

▶ **Evaluate**
In each case, the most you can gain is the $400 million in value you add by taking over FAT. Thus, you cannot extract more value than the value you add to the company by taking it over.

The examples we have illustrated are extreme in that the acquirer takes over the target without paying any premium and with no initial investment. In practice, premiums in LBO transactions are often quite substantial—while they can avoid the free rider problem, acquirers must still get board approval to overcome other defences such as poison pills, as well as outbid other potential acquirers. Also, lenders typically require that the acquirer have a substantial equity stake as protection for the debt holders, in case the claimed post-acquisition benefits do not materialize. In the $15.2 billion Hertz LBO (at the time, the second largest in history), which we described in Chapter 14, the acquirers contributed $2.3 billion in cash out of a total of $5.6 billion that was paid for Hertz's equity.

From 2003 to 2007, there was a surge in LBO activity, fuelled by a combination of huge flows of capital to buy out (private equity) firms, and increased appetite for risk by lenders willing to allow buyout groups to leverage their equity investment at attractive terms. Buyout firms took many companies private with the stated goal of increasing their performance without concern for perceived pressure from public investors to meet short-term earnings targets. They also employed so-called roll-up strategies whereby they would buy many smaller, already private firms in a particular industry and consolidate them into a larger player. The typical LBO has a planned exit in five years, either by taking the firm public again or selling it to an operating firm or another private equity group. In 2008, the financial crisis and contraction of credit put an almost complete halt to private equity activity. Some highly levered private equity transactions from the peak faltered under their debt load during the recession. For example, Chrysler, which had been purchased and taken private from DaimlerChrysler AG by private equity firm Cerberus Group, declared bankruptcy in 2009, wiping out Cerberus' stake in the firm.

management buyout (MBO) A leveraged buyout in which the buyer group includes the firm's own management.

The Leveraged Buyout of RJR Nabisco by KKR

By the summer of 1988, Ross Johnson, CEO of RJR Nabisco (RJR), and former graduate of the University of Manitoba, was becoming increasingly worried about the poor stock price performance of the conglomerate. Despite a strong earnings record, management had not been able to shake loose its image as a tobacco company, and the stock price was languishing at $55 per share. In October 1988, Johnson and a small team of RJR's executives, backed by the Wall Street firms of Shearson Lehman Hutton and Salomon Brothers, announced a bid of $75 per share for the company. At this price, the deal would have been valued at $17.6 billion, more than twice as large as the largest LBO completed up to that point. Because this deal involved the current management of the company, it falls into a special category of LBO deals called **management buyouts (MBOs)**.

The announcement focused Wall Street's attention on RJR. Even at this substantial premium, the MBO appeared to be a good deal for Johnson and his team, because soon after the offer went public, it became hotly contested. Foremost among the contenders was the firm of Kohlberg, Kravis, and Roberts (KKR). KKR launched its own bid with a cash offer of $90 per share. A bidding war ensued in which the offer price ultimately rose to $109 per share, valuing the deal at more than $25 billion. In the end, both Johnson and KKR offered very similar deals, although management's final bid was slightly higher than KKR's. Eventually, RJR's board accepted KKR's bid of $109 per RJR share. The offer price comprised $81 per share in cash, $18 per share in preferred stock, and $10 per share in debenture securities.

From an economic point of view, this outcome is surprising. One would think that, given their inside knowledge of the company, management would be in the best position not only to value it, but also to run it. Why, then, would an outsider choose to outbid an insider for a company? The answer in RJR's case appeared to point to the managers themselves. As the deal proceeded, it became increasingly obvious to investors that executives (and members of the board of directors) enjoyed perks that were unprecedented. For example, Johnson had the personal use of numerous corporate apartments in different cities and literally a fleet of corporate jets that he, the top executives, and members of the corporate board used for personal travel. In their leveraged buyout proposal, they had obtained a 4% equity stake for top executives that was worth almost $1 billion, $52.5 million in golden parachutes, and assurances that the RJR air force (the fleet of corporate jets) and the flamboyant Atlanta headquarters would not be subject to budget cutting.

The Freezeout Merger

freezeout merger
A situation in which the laws on tender offers allow an acquiring company to freeze existing shareholders out of the gains from merging by forcing non-tendering shareholders to sell their shares for the tender offer price.

Although a leveraged buyout is an effective tool for a group of investors to use to purchase a company, it is less well suited to the case of one company acquiring another. An alternative is the **freezeout merger**: the laws on tender offers allow the acquiring company to freeze existing shareholders out of the gains from merging by forcing non-tendering shareholders to sell their shares for the tender offer price. In Canada, it is a requirement that 90% of the target's shares be acquired by the bidder before a freezeout can be implemented. Let's see how this is accomplished.

An acquiring company makes a tender offer at an amount slightly higher than the current target stock price. If the tender offer succeeds, the acquirer gains control of the target and merges its assets into a new corporation, which is fully owned by the acquirer. In effect, the non-tendering shareholders lose their shares because the target corporation no longer exists. In compensation, non-tendering shareholders get the right to receive the tender offer price for their shares. The bidder, in essence, gets complete ownership of the target for the tender offer price.

Because the value the non-tendering shareholders receive for their shares is equal to the tender price (which is more than the pre-merger stock price), the law generally recognizes it as fair value, and non-tendering shareholders have no legal recourse. Under these circumstances, existing shareholders will tender their stock, reasoning that there is no benefit to holding out: if the tender offer succeeds, they get the tender price anyway; if they hold out, they risk jeopardizing the deal and forgoing the small gain. Hence the acquirer is able to capture almost all the value added from the merger and, as in a leveraged buyout, is able to effectively eliminate the free rider problem.

The freezeout tender offer has a significant advantage over a leveraged buyout because an acquiring corporation need not make an all-cash offer. Instead of paying the target's shareholders in cash, it can use shares of its own stock to pay for the acquisition. In this case, the bidder offers to exchange each shareholder's stock in the target for stock in the acquiring company. As long as the exchange rate is set so that the value in the acquirer's stock exceeds the pre-merger market value of the target stock, the non-tendering shareholders will receive fair value for their shares and will have no legal recourse.

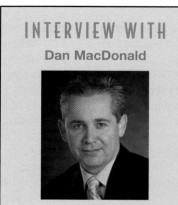

*D*an MacDonald is president and CEO of InNOVAcorp. Based in Halifax, InNOVAcorp is an early-stage venture capital firm, focusing on high-potential venture-grade companies in the areas of information technology, life sciences, and clean technology.

QUESTION: *How did you get to be where you are today in terms of your professional career?*

ANSWER: I have gotten to where I am today by being honest and having high integrity. I have been on a journey of learning as much as I can about the businesses that I have been in. I have changed careers four times: from engineering to marketing to general management and now into investments and mergers and acquisitions. I have been able to do that because I have learned as much as I possibly can about the businesses and business models I have been in.

QUESTION: *Why does a company choose to acquire other companies?*

ANSWER: Companies acquire other companies to grow. The goal may be to gain a particular market share jump—for example, to move from being a tier three player to being tier two or tier one. Another goal is to gain instant access to an installed base of customers. A third goal might be to get a particular piece of strategic technology. In the pharmaceutical industry, one of the most famous acquisitions was Pfizer's acquisition of Warner Lambert, which allowed Pfizer to acquire a blockbuster drug named Lipitor. Companies really decide whether to build or buy, be it technology, a market base, or market share. Public companies are expected to deliver growth at a rate of 10+% per year. Sometimes that is impossible to do organically. Acquisitions make that growth possible.

QUESTION: *Why do mergers and acquisitions fail?*

ANSWER: Often companies are acquired for their culture—perhaps they move quickly, penetrate particular markets, or build particular technologies. Ironically, mergers and acquisitions fail because of culture clash and integration. Acquisition negotiations start quietly, involving a few senior people over a long period of due diligence, discussion, and discovery. When the intent to acquire is actually announced, it catches both cultures by surprise. Efficiencies result from overlap, and the two cultures usually clash over who has highest value in those parts of the business. After the upfront and financial transactions, senior management rarely has the energy to invest enough time on cultural integration. Often some of the best value from the acquired culture gets stamped out. The leadership team of the acquiring company must make it clear to all those people involved that there are particular pieces of the acquired culture that they want to remain, to encourage, and to flourish.

QUESTION: *Are there any common flaws in the negotiations component of an acquisition?*

ANSWER: Flaws usually occur when defining expectations. If one public company acquires another, that is easier because the financial information and data are already public. When acquiring a private company, much less data is available. Often there are things that the acquiring company really never gets to know truly until a year or more after the acquisition, such as the state of quality of the product, the state of satisfaction of the customers, or the satisfaction of the employees.

QUESTION: *Can you comment on the value creation process in an acquisition?*

ANSWER: Value can be added when you find what you really need as a company. This is a little counterintuitive. If you are a company with a very well-known corporate brand, you should not be buying companies to strengthen your brand. You should be buying very specific special technologies or products that you can bring into your portfolio to leverage your brand. If you are a company trying to break into a new market segment where you do not have brand awareness, it might make sense to buy a brand that is already in that market area.

QUESTION: *What do you look out for in an acquisition?*

ANSWER: I have been personally involved in about a dozen acquisitions. Whether I am buying or selling a company, I try to make sure that everyone agrees on the key value and focus on that.

QUESTION: *Can you comment on the typical fate of the acquired company's senior management team?*

ANSWER: The senior leadership team from the acquired company had a lot to do with the reason for the acquisition. They were the visionaries who built the value that is being acquired. The senior management from the acquired company had an agenda and a vision that they were driving every day. In the acquired system, their decision-making power has often been significantly diminished. Very few senior management folks from the acquired company last more than a year or two. But people who are interested in staying with an acquiring company can definitely navigate that professionally.

Competition

The empirical evidence in Table 24.2 suggests that, despite the availability of both the freezeout merger and the leveraged buyout as acquisition strategies, most of the value added still appears to accrue to the target shareholders. That is, on average, acquirers do not have a positive price reaction on the announcement of a takeover. Why do acquirers choose to pay so large a premium that they effectively hand the value they create to the target company's shareholders?

In addition to the presence of the takeover defences we have previously discussed, the most likely explanation is the competition that exists in the takeover market. Once an acquirer starts bidding on a target company and it becomes clear that a significant gain exists, other potential acquirers may submit their own bids. The result is effectively an auction in which the target is sold to the highest bidder. Even when a bidding war does not result, most likely it is because, rather than participate in a bidding war, an acquirer offered a large enough initial premium to forestall the process. In essence, it must give up most of the value added to the target shareholders.

Concept Check

11. What mechanisms allow corporate raiders to get around the free rider problem in takeovers?

12. Based on the empirical evidence, who gets the value added from a takeover? What is the most likely explanation of this fact?

MyFinanceLab

Here is what you should know after reading this chapter. MyFinanceLab will help you identify what you know, and where to go when you need to practice.

Key Points	Terms	Online Practice Opportunities
24.1 Background and Historical Trends ▶ Mergers can be horizontal, vertical, or conglomerate. ▶ The global takeover market is active, averaging more than $1 trillion per year in transaction value. The periods of greatest activity were the 1960s, 1980s, 1990s, and 2000s. ▶ During the 1960s, deals were aimed at building conglomerates. In the 1980s, the trend reversed and conglomerates were split into individual businesses. In the 1990s, there was a rise in "strategic" or "global" deals designed to create firms that could compete globally. From 2004 to 2008, further consolidation and global-scale deals contributed to the most recent merger wave.	acquirer (bidder), p. 796 conglomerate merger, p. 798 horizontal merger, p. 798 merger waves, p. 797 stock swap, p. 798 takeover, p. 796 target, p. 796 term sheet, p. 798 vertical merger, p. 798	MyFinanceLab Study Plan 24.1
24.2 Market Reaction to a Takeover ▶ While on average the shareholders of the acquiring firm obtain small or no gains, shareholders from the acquired firm typically enjoy gains of 15% on the announcement of a takeover bid.	acquisition premium, p. 798	MyFinanceLab Study Plan 24.2

24.3 Reasons to Acquire

▶ The most common justifications given for acquiring a firm are the synergies that can be gained through an acquisition.

▶ The most commonly cited sources of synergies are economies of scale and scope, the control provided by vertical integration, gaining monopolistic power, the expertise gained from the acquired company, improvements in operating efficiency, and benefits related to diversification, such as increased borrowing capacity and tax savings.

▶ Shareholders of a private company that is acquired gain by switching to a more liquid investment.

▶ Some mergers are motivated by incentive conflicts or overconfidence of the acquirer management.

economies of scale, p. 800
economies of scope, p. 800
synergies, p. 799
vertical integration, p. 800

MyFinanceLab
Study Plan 24.3

24.4 The Takeover Process

▶ From the bidder's perspective, a takeover is a positive-*NPV* project only if the premium paid does not exceed the synergies created. The bidder's stock price reaction to the announcement of the merger is one way to gauge investors' assessments of whether the bidder overpaid or underpaid for the target.

▶ A tender offer is a public announcement of an intention to purchase a large block of shares for a specified price. Making a tender offer does not guarantee that a deal will take place.

▶ Bidders use either of two methods to pay for a target: cash or stock. In a cash transaction, the bidder simply pays for the target in cash. In a stock-swap transaction, the bidder pays for the target by issuing new stock and giving it to the target shareholders. The method used by the bidder to pay for the acquired firm has tax and accounting implications.

▶ For a merger to proceed, both the target and the acquiring boards of directors must approve the merger and put the question to a vote of the shareholders of the target (and, in some cases, the shareholders of the acquiring firm as well).

▶ In a friendly takeover, the target board of directors supports the merger and negotiates with the potential acquirers.

▶ If the target board opposes the merger, then the acquirer must go around the target board and appeal directly to the target shareholders, asking them to elect a new board that will support the merger.

corporate raider
  (or raider), p. 811
exchange ratio, p. 807
friendly takeover, p. 811
hostile takeover, p. 811
merger-arbitrage spread,
  p. 809
risk arbitrageurs, p. 809
step up, p. 811

MyFinanceLab
Study Plan 24.4

24.5 Takeover Defences

▶ A target board of directors can defend itself in several ways to prevent a merger. The most effective defence strategy is the poison pill, which gives target shareholders the right to buy shares in either the target or the acquirer at a deeply discounted price. The purchase is effectively subsidized by the existing shareholders of the acquirer, making the takeover very expensive.

▶ Another effective defence strategy is having a staggered board, which prevents a bidder from acquiring control over the board in a short period of time.

▶ Other defences include looking for a friendly bidder (a white knight), making it expensive to replace management, and changing the capital structure of firm.

golden parachute, p. 814
poison pill, p. 812
proxy fight, p. 812
staggered (classified) board, p. 814
white knight, p. 814
white squire, p. 814

MyFinanceLab
Study Plan 24.5

24.6 Who Gets the Value Added from a Takeover?

▶ When a bidder makes an offer for a firm, the target shareholders can benefit by keeping their shares and letting other shareholders sell at a low price. However, because all shareholders have the incentive to keep their shares, no one will sell. This scenario is known as the free rider problem.

▶ To overcome this problem, bidders can acquire a toehold in the target, attempt a leveraged buyout, or, if the acquirer is a corporation, offer a freezeout merger.

freezeout merger, p. 821
management buyout (MBO), p. 820
toehold, p. 818

MyFinanceLab
Study Plan 24.6

Review Questions

1. What are the two primary mechanisms under which ownership and control of a public corporation can change?

2. Why do you think mergers cluster in time, causing merger waves?

3. What are some reasons why a horizontal merger might create value for shareholders?

4. Why do you think shareholders from target companies enjoy an average gain when acquired, while acquiring shareholders on average often do not gain anything?

5. If you are planning an acquisition that is motivated by trying to acquire expertise, you are basically seeking to gain intellectual capital. What concerns would you have in structuring the deal and the post-merger integration that would be different from the concerns you would have when buying physical capital?

6. Do you agree that the European Union should be able to block mergers between two U.S.-based firms? Why or why not?

7. How do the carryforward and carryback provisions of the Canadian or U.S. tax codes affect the benefits of merging to capture operating losses?

8. Diversification is good for shareholders, so why shouldn't managers acquire firms in different industries to diversify a company?

9. How does a toehold help overcome the free rider problem?

Problems

All problems in this chapter are available in MyFinanceLab. An asterisk (*) indicates problems with a higher level of difficulty.

1. Your company has earnings per share of $4. It has 1 million shares outstanding, each of which has a price of $40. You are thinking of buying TargetCo, which has earnings per share of $2, 1 million shares outstanding, and a price per share of $25. You will pay for TargetCo by issuing new shares. There are no expected synergies from the transaction.
   a. If you pay no premium to buy TargetCo, what will your earnings per share be after the merger?
   b. Suppose you offer an exchange ratio such that, at current pre-announcement share prices for both firms, the offer represents a 20% premium to buy TargetCo. What will your earnings per share be after the merger?
   c. What explains the change in earnings per share in part (a)? Are your shareholders any better or worse off?
   d. What will your price-earnings (*P/E*) ratio be after the merger (if you pay no premium)? How does this compare to your (*P/E*) ratio before the merger? How does this compare to TargetCo's pre-merger (*P/E*) ratio?

2. If companies in the same industry as TargetCo (from Problem 1) are trading at multiples of 14 times earnings, what would be one estimate of an appropriate premium for TargetCo?

3. You are invested in GreenFrame, Inc. The CEO owns 3% of GreenFrame and is considering an acquisition. If the acquisition destroys $50 million of GreenFrame's value, but the present value of the CEO's compensation increases by $5 million, will he be better or worse off?

The Takeover Process

4. Loki, Inc. and Thor, Inc. have entered into a stock-swap merger agreement whereby Loki will pay a 40% premium over Thor's pre-merger price. If Thor's pre-merger price per share was $40 and Loki's was $50, what exchange ratio will Loki need to offer?

5. The NFF Corporation has announced plans to acquire LE Corporation. NFF is trading for $35 per share and LE is trading for $25 per share, implying a pre-merger value of LE of $4 billion. If the projected synergies are $1 billion, what is the maximum exchange ratio NFF could offer in a stock swap and still generate a positive *NPV*?

6. Let's reconsider part (b) of Problem 1. The actual premium that your company will pay for TargetCo when it completes the transaction will not be 20%, because on the announcement the target price will go up and your price will go down to reflect the fact that you are willing to pay a premium for TargetCo without any synergies. Assume that the takeover will occur with certainty and all market participants know this on the announcement of the takeover (ignore time value of money).
   a. What is the price per share of the combined corporation immediately after the merger is completed?

    b. What is the price of your company immediately after the announcement?

    c. What is the price of TargetCo immediately after the announcement?

    d. What is the actual premium your company will pay?

*7. ABC has 1 million shares outstanding, each of which has a price of $20. It has made a takeover offer of XYZ Corporation, which has 1 million shares outstanding and a price per share of $2.50. Assume that the takeover will occur with certainty and all market participants know this. Furthermore, there are no synergies to merging the two firms.

    a. Assume ABC made a cash offer to purchase XYZ for $3 million. What happens to the price of ABC and XYZ on the announcement? What premium over the current market price does this offer represent?

    b. Assume ABC makes a stock offer with an exchange ratio of 0.15. What happens to the price of ABC and XYZ this time? What premium over the current market price does this offer represent?

    c. At current market prices, both offers are to purchase XYZ for $3 million. Does that mean that your answers to parts (a) and (b) must be identical? Explain.

Takeover Defences

*8. BAD Company's stock price is $20, and the firm has 2 million shares outstanding. You believe you can increase the company's value if you buy it and replace the management. Assume that BAD has a poison pill with a 20% trigger. If it is triggered, all BAD's shareholders—other than the acquirer—will be able to buy one new share in BAD for each share they own at a 50% discount. Assume that the price remains at $20 while you are acquiring your shares. If BAD's management decides to resist your buyout attempt, and you cross the 20% threshold of ownership,

    a. How many new shares will be issued and at what price?

    b. What will happen to your percentage ownership of BAD?

    c. What will happen to the price of your shares of BAD?

    d. Do you lose or gain from triggering the poison pill? If you lose, where does the loss go (who benefits)? If you gain, from where does the gain come (who loses)?

Who Gets the Value Added from a Takeover?

*9. You work for a leveraged buyout firm and are evaluating a potential buyout of UnderWater Company. UnderWater's stock price is $20, and it has 2 million shares outstanding. You believe that if you buy the company and replace its management, its value will increase by 40%. You are planning on doing a leveraged buyout of UnderWater, and will offer $25 per share for control of the company.

    a. Assuming you get 50% control, what will happen to the price of non-tendered shares?

    b. Given the answer in part (a), will shareholders tender their shares, not tender their shares, or be indifferent?

    c. What will your gain from the transaction be?

Corporate Governance

MyFinanceLab Additional Online Chapter 25, Corporate Governance, can be found on MyFinanceLab at www.myfinancelab.com.

Credits

Index

KEY EQUATIONS